Introduction to

Psychology

7th Edition

Rod Plotnik

PSY 2510
James J. Berry, PhD
Dennis R. Sobol, PhD

THOMSON

WADSWORTH

D1318695

COPYRIGHT © 2004 by Wadsworth Group. Wadsworth is an imprint of the Wadsworth Group, a division of Thomson Learning Inc. Thomson Learning™ is a trademark used herein under license.

Printed in the United States of America

Wadsworth/Thomson Learning
10 Davis Drive
Belmont, CA 94002-3098
USA

For information about our products, contact us:
Thomson Learning Academic Resource Center
1-800-423-0563
http://www.wadsworth.com

International Headquarters
Thomson Learning
International Division
290 Harbor Drive, 2nd Floor
Stamford, CT 06902-7477
USA

UK/Europe/Middle East/South Africa
Thomson Learning
Berkshire House
168-173 High Holborn
London WCIV 7AA

Asia
Thomson Learning
60 Albert Street, #15-01
Albert Complex
Singapore 189969

Canada
Nelson Thomson Learning
1120 Birchmount Road
Toronto, Ontario MIK 5G4
Canada
United Kingdom

ALL RIGHTS RESERVED. No part of this work covered by the copyright hereon may be reproduced or used in any form or by any means—graphic, electronic, or mechanical, including photocopying, recording, taping, Web distribution, or information storage and retrieval systems—without the written permission of the publisher.

ISBN 0-534-27033-6

The Adaptable Courseware Program consists of products and additions to existing Wadsworth Group products that are produced from camera-ready copy. Peer review, class testing, and accuracy are primarily the responsibility of the author(s).

For permission to use material from this text or product, submit a request online at
http://www.thomsonrights.com
Any additional questions about permissions can be submitted by email to thomsonrights@thomson.com

Custom Contents

In revising the 7th edition, I worked with a remarkable group of creative people, each of whom deserves special thanks.

Publisher

For the past 15 years my editor has been Vicki Knight, who is surely one of the best editors in publishing. She has always been very supportive, gives great advice, and, best of all, understands what this book is about and knows all the ins and outs of publishing so she really gets things done.

Monica Sarmiento, editorial assistant to Vicki Knight, had the trying job of making sure that all the modules were sent to reviewers and preparing packets for class testing.

Developmental Editor

Kate Barnes wrote the materials for the Links for Learning feature and descriptions for PowerStudy at the end of each module and in the visual preface.

Cover Designers

As always, Vernon Boes came up with a great cover image. Roger Knox is the creative person who did the wonderful cover design. Choosing a cover is difficult because we all have very strong opinions. I think this is the best cover ever, but Vicki tells me, "that's what you always say." This time it's true.

Concept Illustrators

In every module you'll discover Bill Ogden and Philip Dvorak's creative drawings and figures that help make the book visually exciting. During the revision I was very saddened when Bill Ogden died suddenly. He had a creative talent like no other and was always a delight to work with. Bill's art throughout this text is a fitting tribute to his genius.

Taking his place were two new illustrators, Bill Riesser and Mike Meyer, who created some wonderful new illustrations and figures.

Photo Researcher

Once again, Linda Rill was in charge of photo research and permissions, and there is no one as good at this as Linda.

Manuscript Editor

I had the best manuscript editor ever in Carol Reitz, whose editorial skills really did improve the book.

Production: Part 1

The job of Nancy Shammas at New Leaf Publishing Services was to make sure that every page was perfect and ready for print.

Keeping track of everything at Wadsworth Publishing was Kirk Bomont, Senior Production Editor, who made sure that everything was where it should be.

Production: Part 2

The person who made sure the individual pages were turned into a complete book is "geeze" Louise Gelinas of LaurelTech. She kept track of a record number of photos and artwork (more than 2000 pieces) and kept the book on schedule.

Special thanks goes to Ed Scanlon at LaurelTech who worked at record speed to check and correct all of the QuarkXpress files.

Marketing Communication

When you read the great advertising copy and see the brochures, think of Brian Chaffee and Joy Westberg, who were able to describe the "soul" of the book.

You can also go online to the Wadsworth Web site and see a virtual tour of the 7th edition created by Jean Thompson and Shelley Field.

Sales

Chris Caldeira's job is to make sure that all the sales representatives know what the book is about and how to describe it to potential adopters. She was a bundle of energy and we talked about ideas for marketing the 7th edition for five hours nonstop!

Study Guide

Matthew Enos used his friendly and helpful teaching skills to write the Study Guide, whose previous editions were so highly praised by students. Eric Bohman at William Rainey Harbor College did a great job on the Study Guide's language development section.

Supplements

Jennifer Wilkinson, senior assistant editor, was responsible for organizing and keeping track of all the many supplements.

Gail Knapp and Lynn Thigpen, both at Mott Community College, used their creative talents to revise the Instructor's Resource Manual and make it one of the best ever.

Once again Greg Cutler at Bacy de Noc Community College, MI, used his critical thinking skills to write the Test Bank, which received high marks in previous editions.

John Phelan at Western Oklahoma State University was the multimedia manager who developed the wonderful multimedia tools that accompany this text (PowerPoint Presentation Tool, PsychLink).

Joe Morrissey at SUNY @ Binghamton did the clever self-study assessment questions that help students determine what they know or don't know (but should learn).

Special Colleague and Motivator

While working on the 7th edition I alternated between "It's wonderful," and "I quit." Through it all, my friend and colleague Sandy Mollenauer provided emotional support, encouragement, and understanding.

PowerStudy 2.0

One of the most exciting projects that I have ever been associated with has been PowerStudy, which is a new and revolutionary multimedia presentation for students, developed by Professor Tom Doyle.

Tom is an absolute genius for figuring out how to use Director and to create the best animations and interactive activities that you'll ever see. Printed samples of Tom's wonderful work can be seen on pages xxxv-xxxviii but his true creativity is best appreciated by viewing the three CDs that make up PowerStudy 2.0.

Darin Derstine, senior technology project manager, deserves special mention because he worked with Tom to guide PowerStudy 2.0 through the many potential pitfalls associated with developing a huge multimedia project like PowerStudy 2.0.

CEO, Thomson Higher Education

Last, I must thank my big boss, CEO Susan Badger, who fully supported the nontraditional look of the 7th edition and also the development of the revolutionary learning tool, PowerStudy.

I especially want to thank the many reviewers who put in an amazing amount of time and energy to consider and comment on various aspects of this textbook.

I would like to explain why I was not able to include all your valuable suggestions.

Sometimes your suggestions were great but required inserting material for which there simply was no room.

Other times, one reviewer might suggest changing something that another reviewer really liked, so I tried to work out the best compromise.

Still other times, reviewers forcefully argued for entirely different points so that I felt like the proverbial starving donkey trying to decide which way to turn between two stacks of hay.

For all these reasons, I could not make all your suggested changes but I did give them a great deal of thought and used as many as I possibly could.

I do want each reviewer to know that his or her efforts were invaluable in the process of revising and developing a textbook. If it were within my power, I would triple your honorariums and give you each a year-long sabbatical.

Glen Adams, Harding University

Nelson Adams, Winston-Salem State University

Marlene Adelman, Norwalk Community Technical College

Edward Aronow, Montclair State University

Irwin Badin, Montclair State University

George Bagwell, Colorado Mountain College-Alpine Campus

Roger Bailey, Southwestern College

Susan Barnett, Northwestern State University

Beth Barton, Coastal Carolina Community College

Beth Benoit, University of Massachusetts-Lowell

John B. Benson, Texarcana College

Kristen Biondolillo, Arkansas State University

Angela Blankenship, Halifax Community College

Pamela Braverman Schmidt, Salem State College

Linda Brunton, Columbia State Community College

Lawrence Burns, Grand Valley State University

Ronald Caldwell, Blue Mountain Community College

James Calhoun, University of Georgia

Peter Caprioglio, Middlesex Community-Technical College

Donna M. Casperson, Harrisburg Area Community College

Hank Cetola, Adrian College

Larry Christensen, Salt Lake Community College

Saundra K. Ciccarelli, Gulf Coast Community College

Gerald S. Clack, Loyola University

J. Craig Clarke, Salisbury State University

Jay Coleman, University of South Carolina, Columbia

Richard T. Colgan, Bridgewater State College

Lorry J. Cology, Owens Community College

Laurie Corey, Westchester Community College

Shaunna Crossen, Penn State University, Berk-Lehigh Valley College

Sandy Deabler, North Harris College

Paul H. Del Nero, Towson State University

Bradley Donohue, University of Nevada, Las Vegas

Jean Edwards, Jones County Junior College

Tami Eggleston, McKendree College

Nolen U. Embry, Lexington Community College

Charles H. Evans, LaGrange College

Melissa Faber, Lima Technical College

Mike Fass, Miami-Dade Community College, North Campus

Mary Beth Foster, Purdue University

Jan Francis, Santa Rosa Junior College

Grace Galliano, Kennesaw State College

John T. Garrett, Texas State Technical College

Philip Gray, D'Youville College

Charles M. Greene, Florida Community College at Jacksonville

Lynn Haller, Morehead State University

Verneda Hamm Baugh, Kean University

Sheryl Hartman, Miami Dade Community College

Debra Lee Hollister, Valencia Community College

Donna Holmes, Becker College

Lucinda Hutman, Elgin Community College

Terry Isbell, Northwestern State University

Charles Jeffreys, Seattle Central Community College

Eleanor Jones, Tidewater Community College

Linda V. Jones, Ph.D., Blinn College

Stan Kary, St. Louis Community College at Florissant Valley

Paul Kasenow, Henderson Community College

Don Kates, College of DuPage

Mark Kelland, Lansing Community College

Arthur D. Kemp, Ph.D., Central Missouri State University

Richard Kirk, Texas State Technical College

Dan Klaus, Community College of Beaver City

Gail Knapp, Mott Community College

John C. Koeppel, University of Southern Mississippi

Jan Kottke, California State University-San Bernardino

Joan Krueger, Harold Washington College

Doug Krull, Northern Kentucky University

Diane J. Krumm, College of Lake County

Raymond Launier, Santa Barbara City College

Eamonn J. Lester, St. Philips College

John Lindsay, Georgia College & State University

Alan Lipman, Georgetown University

Karsten Look, Columbus State Community College

Jerry Lundgren, Flathead Valley Community College

Linda V. Jones, Ph.D., Blinn College

Frank MacHovec, Rappahannock Community College

Sandra Madison, Delgado Community College

Mary Lee Meiners, San Diego Miramar College
Diane Mello-Goldner, Pine Manor College
Laurence Miller, Western Washington University
Lesley Annette Miller, Triton College
Alinde Moore, Ashland University
John T. Nixon, SUNY-Canton
Art Olguin, Santa Barbara City College
Carol Pandey, Pierce College
Christine Panyard, University of Detroit-Mercy
Jeff Parsons, Rockefeller University
Ron Payne, San Joaquin Delta College
Bob Pellegrini, San Jose State University
James Previte, Victor Valley College
Joan Rafter, Hudson Community College
Robert R. Rainey, Jr., Florida Community College
    at Jacksonville
Lillian Range, University of Southern Mississippi
S. Peter Resta, Prince George's Community College
Vicki Ritts, St. Louis Community College, Meramac
Bret Roark, Oklahoma Baptist University
Ann E. Garrett Robinson, Gateway Community Technical
    College
Michael Schuller, Fresno City College
Alan Schultz, Prince George's Community College
Robert Schultz, Fulton Montgomery Community College
Debra Schwiesow, Creighton University
Harold Siegel, Rutger's University
N. Clayton Silver, University of Nevada, Las Vegas
Kimberly Eretzian Smirles, Ph.D., Emmanuel College
James Spencer, West Virginia State College
Deborah Steinberg, Jefferson Community College
Kimberly Stoker, MS, Holmes Community College
Julie Stokes, California State University-Fullerton
Ted Sturman, University of Southern Maine
Clayton N. Tatro, Garden City Community College
Annette Taylor, University of San Diego
Andy Thomas, Tennessee Technical University
Larry Till, Cerritos College
Susan Troy, Northeast Iowa Community College
Jane Vecchio, Holyoke Community College
Randy Vinzant, Hinds Community College
Benjamin Wallace, Cleveland State University
James Ward, Western New England College
Mary Scott West, Virginia Intermont College
Fred W. Whitford, Montana State University
John Whittle, Northern Essex Community College
Ellen Williams, Mesa Community College
Matthew J. Zagumny, Tennessee Technological University
Gene Zingarelli, Santa Rosa Community College

Special help on the 7th ed

Marlene Adelman, Norwalk Community College
Joan Bihun, University of Colorado at Denver
Randy Cole, Piedmont Technical College
Lorry Cology, Owens Community College
Michael Durnam, Adams State College
Diane Feibel, Raymond Walters College
Bob Ferguson, Buena Vista University
Michael Firmin, Cedarville University
Rita Flattley, Pima Community College
Robert Gates, Cisco Junior College
Andrew Getzfeld, New Jersey City University
Marjan Ghahramanlou, The Community College of
    Baltimore, Catonsville
Kendra Gilds, Lane Community College
Bill Hardgrave, Aims Community College
Sheryl Hartman, Miami-Dade Community College
Roger Hock, Mendocino College
Quentin Hollis, Bowling Green Community College
Wendy Jefferson-Jackson, Montgomery College
Joanne Karpinen, Hope College
Matthew Krug, Wisconsin Lutheran College
Haig Kouyoumdjian, University of Nebraska, Lincoln
Kristen Lavallee, Penn State University
Frank MacHovec, Rappahannock Community College
Laura Madson, New Mexico State University
Ernest Marquez, Elgin Community College
Peter Matsos, Riverside Community College
Grant McLaren, Edinboro University
Malcolm Miller, Fanshawe College
Gloria Mitchell, De Anza College
Peggy Norwood, Community College of Aurora
Julie Penley, El Paso Community College
Judith Phillips, Palomar College
Melissa Riley, University of Mississippi
Harvey Schiffman, Rutgers University Piscataway Campus
Harold Siegel, Rutgers University Newark Campus
Mark Stewart, American River College
Clayton Teem, Gainesville College
Jeff Wachsmuth, Napa Valley College
Janice Weaver, Ferris State University

Module 1: Discovering Psychology

© Ian Parnell

Growing Up in a Strange World

Why does Donna flap her hands?

When Donna was about 3 years old, she ate lettuce because she liked rabbits and they ate lettuce. She ate jelly because it looked like colored glass and she liked to look at colored glass.

She was told to make friends, but Donna had her own friends. She had a pair of green eyes named Willie, which hid under her bed, and wisps, which were tiny, transparent spots that hung in the air around her.

When people spoke, their words were strange sounds with no meaning, like mumble jumble. Donna did learn the sounds of letters and how they fit together to make words. Although she didn't learn the meanings of words, she loved their sounds when she said them out loud. As a child, she was tested for deafness because she did not use language like other children. She did not learn that words had meaning until she was a teenager.

When people talked to Donna, especially people with loud or excited voices, she heard only "blah, blah, blah." Too much excited talk or overstimulation caused Donna to stare straight ahead and appear to be frozen. Donna later called this state "involuntarily anesthetized."

Donna was in and out of many schools because she failed her exams, refused to take part in class activities, walked out of classes she didn't like, and sometimes threw things.

When Donna did make a friend, she tried to avoid getting a friendly hug, which made her feel as if she were burning up inside and going to faint. Eventually she learned to tolerate being hugged but never liked it (Williams, 1992). Donna Williams had all the symptoms of autism.

Although relatively rare, autism affects 2 to 4 times as many boys as girls, occurs in all parts of the world, and is currently reported to be about 10 times more prevalent now (1 to 2 in 500 births) than it was in the 1970s (1 in 2,500 births) (Kabot et al., 2003). Some parents blamed the increase in autism on childhood vaccinations, but researchers have shown that is not true (Holden, 2003c). Researchers believe that the dramatic increase in autism is due, in part, to better diagnosis in recent years and to some interaction between genes and environmental factors, none of which have yet been identified (Yeargin-Allsop et al., 2003).

Autism is marked by especially abnormal or impaired development in social interactions, such as hiding to avoid people, not making eye contact, not wanting to be touched. Autism is marked by difficulties in communicating, such as grave problems in developing spoken language or in initiating conversations. Autistics are characterized by having very few activities and interests, spending long periods repeating the same behaviors (hand flapping), or following the same rituals. Signs of autism usually appear when a child is 2 or 3 years old (American Psychiatric Association, 1994).

Some autistic children avoid social interactions.

A very small percentage of autistics are called savants because they have incredible artistic or memory skills. For example, one savant has memorized 7,600 books; another can speak only 100 words but can play over 7,000 songs, most heard only once; another can solve calendar puzzles, such as figuring out the day of the week for a date ten years ago (Treffert & Wallace, 2002).

Donna Williams (1992) is an example of a savant who developed exceptional language skills. At age 25, in four almost-nonstop weeks, she wrote a 500-page book that described what it was like to be autistic. In this and her more recent book (D. Williams, 1994), Donna describes how common sights, sounds, and images become strangely distorted, which makes getting through an ordinary day like finding one's way out of a terribly complex maze.

As we describe Donna's experiences, you'll see how psychologists try to answer questions about complex behaviors, such as autism, as well as countless other behaviors that are discussed in the 25 modules of this text. For example, one question that psychologists have studied involves a problem that you may be interested in—test anxiety.

Test Anxiety

Why are your hands sweating?

If you're like many other students, you probably experience some degree of test anxiety.

Test anxiety refers to a combination of physiological, emotional, and cognitive components that are caused by the stress of taking exams and that may interfere with one's ability to think, reason, and plan (Oostdam & Meijer, 2003).

For some students, test anxiety is an unpleasant experience but doesn't necessarily interfere with exam performance. For other students, test anxiety not only is an unpleasant experience but also seriously interferes with doing well on exams. We'll discuss what psychologists have discovered about test anxiety, such as its different components, why students differ in how much test anxiety they feel, and, perhaps most important, how to decrease test anxiety.

There are several ways to decrease test anxiety.

What's Coming

In this module, we'll explore the goals of psychology, the major approaches that psychologists use to understand behavior and answer questions, the historical roots of psychology, current research areas, and possible careers in the broad field of psychology. Let's begin with how psychologists study complex problems, such as Donna's autistic behaviors.

A. Definition & Goals

What do psychologists study?

When you think of psychology, you may think of helping people with mental problems. However, psychologists study a broad range of behaviors, including Donna's autistic behaviors and students' test anxiety, as well as hundreds of other behaviors. For this reason, we need a very broad definition of psychology.

Psychology is the systematic, scientific study of behaviors and mental processes.

What's important about this definition is that each of its terms has a broader meaning. For example, *behaviors* refers to observable actions or responses in both humans and animals. Behaviors might include eating, speaking, laughing, running, reading, and sleeping. *Mental processes,* which are not directly observable, refer to a wide range of complex mental processes, such as thinking, imagining, studying, and dreaming. The current broad definition of psychology grew out of discussions and heated arguments among early psychologists, who defined psychology much more specifically, as we'll discuss later in this module.

Although the current definition of psychology is very broad, psychologists usually have four specific goals in mind when they study some behavior or mental process, such as Donna's autistic experiences.

Goals of Psychology

What are some of Donna's unusual behaviors?

Donna (photo below) knows that she has some unusual behaviors. For example, she says that she doesn't like to be touched, held, or hugged, doesn't like to make eye contact when speaking to people, hates to talk to someone who has a loud voice, and really dislikes meeting strangers. If you were a psychologist studying Donna's unusual behaviors, you would have the following four goals in mind: to describe, explain, predict, and control her behavior.

1 Describe Donna says that when she was a child, she wondered what people were saying to her because words were just lists of meaningless sounds. When people or things bothered her, she would endlessly tap or twirl her fingers to create movements that completely held her attention and helped her escape from a world that often made no sense.

The first goal of psychology is to describe the different ways that organisms behave.

As psychologists begin to describe the behaviors and mental processes of autistic children, such as difficulties in learning language, they begin to understand how autistic children behave. After describing behavior, psychologists try to explain behavior, the second goal.

2 Explain Donna's mother believed that autism was caused by evil spirits. Donna thinks her autism may result from metabolic imbalance.

The second goal of psychology is to explain the causes of behavior.

The explanation of autism has changed as psychologists learn more about this complex problem. In the 1950s, psychologists explained that children became autistic if they were reared by parents who were cold and rejecting (Blakeslee, 2000a). In the 1990s, researchers discovered that autism is caused by genetic and biological factors that result in a maldeveloped brain (Courchesne et al., 2003). Being able to describe and explain behavior helps psychologists reach the third goal, which is to predict behavior.

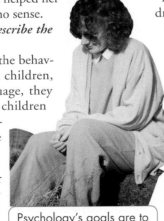

Psychology's goals are to describe, explain, predict, and control Donna's autistic behaviors.

3 Predict Donna says that one of her biggest problems is being so overloaded by visual sensations that she literally freezes in place. She tries to predict when she will freeze up by estimating how many new stimuli she must adjust to.

The third goal of psychology is to predict how organisms will behave in certain situations.

However, psychologists may have difficulty predicting how autistic children will behave in certain situations unless they have already described and explained their behaviors. For example, from the first two goals, psychologists know that autistic children are easily overwhelmed by strange stimuli and have difficulty paying attention. Based on this information, psychologists can predict that autistic children will have difficulty learning in a school environment because there are too many activities and stimuli in the classroom (Gresham et al., 1999). However, if psychologists can predict behavior, then they can often control behavior.

4 Control Donna knows one reason she fears meeting people is that social interactions cause a tremendous sensory overload that makes her freeze up. She controls her social fear by making a rule to meet only one person at a time.

For some psychologists, the fourth goal of psychology is to control an organism's behavior. However, the idea of control has both positive and negative sides. The positive side is that psychologists can help people, such as Donna, learn to control undesirable behaviors by teaching better methods of self-control and ways to deal with situations and relationships (Howlin, 1997). The negative side is the concern that psychologists might control people's behaviors without their knowledge or consent. In Module 2, we'll discuss the strict guidelines that psychologists have established to prevent potential abuse of controlling behavior and to protect the rights and privacy of individuals, patients, and participants in experiments.

Because many behaviors, such as autism, are enormously complex, psychologists use a combination of different approaches to reach the four goals of describing, explaining, predicting, and controlling behavior. To reach these goals, psychologists may use one or a combination of the following six approaches.

How do psychologists answer questions?

Psychologists have many questions about Donna's unusual behaviors. For example, why did Donna believe that objects were alive and made their own sounds? "My bed was my friend; my coat protected me and kept me inside; things that made noise had their own unique voices, which said vroom, ping, or whatever. I told my shoes where they were going so they would take me there" (Blakely, 1994, p. 14).

Why did Donna initially hear words as meaningless sounds that people were constantly saying to her? Why did she develop her own signaling system, such as raising two fingers or scrunching her toes to signal that no one could reach her? Why did she freeze up when staring at soap bubbles in the sink? In trying to answer questions about Donna's strange and intriguing behaviors, psychologists would use a combination of different approaches.

Approaches to understanding behavior include the biological, cognitive, behavioral, psychoanalytic, humanistic, and cross-cultural. Each approach has a different focus or perspective and may use a different research method or technique.

We'll summarize these six commonly used approaches and then discuss them in more detail on the following pages.

Donna would tell her shoes where she was going so they would take her there.

1 As a child, was Donna unable to learn that words had meaning because of some problem with the development of her brain?

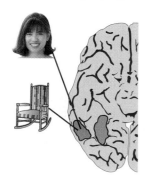

The ***biological approach*** focuses on how our genes, hormones, and nervous system interact with our environments to influence learning, personality, memory, motivation, emotions, and coping techniques.

2 How was Donna able to develop her own signaling system that involved gestures instead of words?

The ***cognitive approach*** examines how we process, store, and use information and how this information influences what we attend to, perceive, learn, remember, believe, and feel.

3 Why did Donna make it a rule to avoid leaving soap bubbles in the sink?

The ***behavioral approach*** studies how organisms learn new behaviors or modify existing ones, depending on whether events in their environments reward or punish these behaviors.

4 Why did Donna develop alternate personalities, such as Willie who had "hateful glaring eyes, a rigid corpselike stance, and clenched fists"?

The ***psychoanalytic approach*** stresses the influence of unconscious fears, desires, and motivations on thoughts, behaviors, and the development of personality traits and psychological problems later in life.

5 How was Donna able to overcome her early language problems and write a book in four weeks?

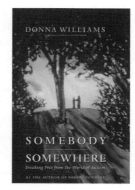

The ***humanistic approach*** emphasizes that each individual has great freedom in directing his or her future, a large capacity for personal growth, a considerable amount of intrinsic worth, and enormous potential for self-fulfillment.

6 Why did her mother believe that autism was caused by evil spirits? What do other peoples and cultures believe causes it?

The ***cross-cultural approach*** examines the influence of cultural and ethnic similarities and differences on psychological and social functioning of a culture's members.

By using one or more of these six different approaches, psychologists can look at autism from different viewpoints and stand a better chance of reaching psychology's four goals: to describe, explain, predict, and control behavior. We'll use the problems of autism and test anxiety to show how each approach examines these problems from a different perspective.

B. Modern Approaches

Biological Approach

Are their brains different?

As Donna explains, autism has a huge effect on all parts of her life. "Autism makes me feel everything at once without knowing what I am feeling. Or it cuts me off from feeling anything at all" (D. Williams, 1994, p. 237). Donna's description of how autism so drastically affects her life raises questions about whether her brain has not developed normally or functions differently. To answer this question, researchers use the biological approach.

The *biological approach* examines how our genes, hormones, and nervous system interact with our environments to influence learning, personality, memory, motivation, emotions, coping techniques, and other traits and abilities.

Researchers using the biological approach, often called psychobiologists, use different research methods, including taking computerized photos of how the living brain functions (p. 70). For example, the top figure (based on computerized photos of living brains) shows that the normal brain uses one area (blue—fusiform gyrus) to process *faces* of people and a different area (red—inferior temporal gyrus) to process inanimate *objects,* such as a chair. In comparison, the bottom figure shows that the autistic brain uses the area that usually processes inanimate objects (red—inferior temporal gyrus) to also process human faces (Schultz et al., 2000). In addition, researchers reported that, based on brain wave activity, 3-year-old autistic children were unable to distinguish their mother's face from that of strangers but could distinguish between favorite and new toys (Dawson et al., 2002). These studies are examples of using the biological approach to look inside the human brain to explain why autistic individuals show little interest in

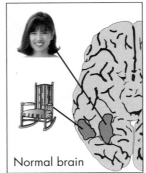

Normal brain

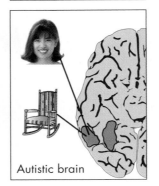

Autistic brain

looking at a person's face during social interactions or in identifying facial emotional expressions.

Psychobiologists have shown that genetic factors influence a wide range of human behaviors, which we'll discuss throughout this text. The genes (p. 68) use a chemical alphabet to write instructions for the development of the brain and body and the manufacture of chemicals that affect mental health, learning, emotions, personality traits, and everything we do (Rutter & Silberg, 2002). For example, it is known that autism runs in families, and this genetic involvement is supported by the finding that if one identical twin has autism, then there is a 60–75% chance that the other twin will have signs of autistic behavior (J. M. Nash, 2002a). This finding is an example of using the biological approach to answer questions by looking for defects in the genes.

Also using the biological approach to examine physiological factors in autism, researchers analyzed blood that had been collected a few days after birth from children who later developed autism. Compared with normal children, those who developed autism had greater amounts of those chemicals that affect brain development (Nelson et al., 2001). This early imbalance in brain chemicals may explain why children develop autistic symptoms at 2 to 3 years of age.

Essentially, psychobiologists study how the brain affects the mind and vice versa, an experience that many students are familiar with and it's called test anxiety.

Biological Approach to Test Anxiety

Why do my hands sweat?

You've probably experienced one component of test anxiety, called the emotional component. This component includes a variety of physiological responses, such as increased heart rate, dry mouth, and sweaty palms. An interesting feature of sweaty palms, called palmar sweating, is that it is caused by stressful feelings and is not related to changes in room temperature (Kohler & Troester, 1991). In fact, palmar sweating is one of the measures used in the lie detection test, which we'll discuss in Module 16.

As you take an exam—or even think about taking one—your stressful thoughts trigger the emotional component, which can interfere with processing information and increase your chances of making mistakes (Cassady & Johnson, 2001).

Sweaty hands often indicate stress.

The figure on the right shows how easily your stressful thoughts can trigger palmar sweating, which is one measure of the emotional component of test anxiety. As subjects did mental arithmetic, which involved counting backward from 2007 in steps of 7, there was a significant increase in this palmar sweating (Kohler & Troester, 1991). If a simple task of counting backward increased palmar sweating, a sign of physiological and emotional arousal, imagine the increased arousal that occurs while taking an exam!

One way to reduce the emotional and physiological component of test anxiety is through stress-reducing activities. For example, students who completed a stress-reduction program that included relaxation exercises and soothing imagining reported less test anxiety than students who were on a waiting list for the program (Zeidner, 1998). In Module 21, we'll describe several methods of reducing stress that will be especially useful in reducing the emotional component of test anxiety.

Cognitive Approach

Was Donna an unusual autistic?

Autistic individuals usually have difficulty developing language skills. For example, Donna writes, "Autism makes me hear other people's words but be unable to know what the words mean. Autism stops me from finding and using my own words when I want to. Or makes me use all the words and silly things I do not want to say" (D. Williams, 1994, p. 237). Although Donna did not understand words until she was an adolescent, she eventually learned to both speak and write, has written two very creative books (Williams, 1992, 1994), and has learned French and German. Because of her remarkable language abilities, Donna is said to be a high-functioning autistic, or savant. To discover why autistic individuals differ in their development of language and social skills, psychologists use the cognitive approach.

The cognitive approach focuses on how we process, store, and use information and how this information influences what we attend to, perceive, learn, remember, believe, and feel.

Unlike Donna Williams who speaks fluently and is considered a high-functioning autistic, the photo on the right shows Tito Mukhopadhyay, a severely autistic teenager who often seems overcome by various movements, whose speech is virtually unintelligible, but who has the unusual ability of being able to answer questions or explain what he's thinking or doing by writing or typing on the keyboard he is holding. For example, when Tito was being tested in a laboratory, he repeatedly stopped and started bursts of activity, such as rocking rhythmically, standing and spinning, making loud smacking noises, or flapping his fingers. When asked why he does this, Tito didn't answer verbally but wrote, "I am calming myself. My senses are so disconnected I lose my body,

Tito is severely autistic but can type answers to questions.

so I flap. If I don't do this, I feel scattered and anxious" (Blakeslee, 2002, p. D1). When asked why he doesn't look at people when he talks, he wrote that he can only concentrate on one sense at a time and most of the time he chooses hearing. Thus, there is a major cognitive difference between normal individuals who can respond simultaneously to more than one sensory input, such as seeing and hearing, and autistics who are limited to concentrating on one sense at a time.

Some cognitive researchers combine the study of cognitive skills with identifying their corresponding areas in the brain. This exciting new approach is called cognitive neuroscience (Rapp, 2000).

Cognitive neuroscience involves taking pictures and identifying the structures and functions of the living brain during performance of a wide variety of mental or cognitive processes, such as thinking, planning, naming, and recognizing objects.

For example, when listening to a conversation, 95% of right-handers use primarily the left sides of their brains and very little of the right sides to process this verbal information. In contrast, researchers found that autistic individuals used primarily the right sides of their brains and very little of the left sides when listening to a conversation (Muller et al., 1999). This reversing of brain sides as well as having difficulties in processing verbal information may help explain why autistic individuals have problems acquiring cognitive, language, and communication skills.

In recent years, the cognitive approach along with its newer relative, cognitive neuroscience, have become very popular because they have proved useful in answering questions about many aspects of cognitive skills, emotions, personality traits, and social behaviors (Cacioppo, 2002; Lane & Nadel, 2000).

For example, the cognitive approach has much to say about test anxiety, especially about worrying too much.

Cognitive Approach to Test Anxiety

Can you worry too much?

Students who experience test anxiety must deal with two components. The first component, which we already described, is increased physiological arousal, which is the emotional component. Cognitive psychologists have identified a second component, the cognitive component, which is excessive worrying, usually about doing poorly on exams.

Excessive worrying about your performance can interfere with your ability to read accurately, understand what you are reading, and identify important concepts (Cassady & Johnson, 2001). For these reasons, it is easy to see how excessive worrying can impair performance on exams. An interesting finding, shown in the right graph, was that female college freshmen reported significantly more

What happens if I worry too much about exams?

worry and anxiety than did males (H. T. Everson et al., 1994). Women may report more worry and anxiety than men because women are generally more sensitive to negative feedback, such as grades and exam scores (Zeidner, 1998).

In related studies, researchers found that the cognitive component could either help or hinder performance. Students who channeled their worry into com-

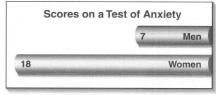

Scores on a Test of Anxiety

| 7 | Men |
| 18 | Women |

plaining rather than studying performed poorly because their worry interfered with their reading the exam material and caused them to make more reading errors (Calvo & Carreiras, 1993). In contrast, students who channeled their worry into studying performed better and achieved higher grades because they were better prepared (Endler et al., 1994).

These studies indicate that the cognitive component of test anxiety—excessive worrying—may either help or hinder cognitive performance, depending on how students channel their worries.

B. Modern Approaches

Behavioral Approach

No leaving soap suds in the sink!

Why have a "no soap suds" rule?

If Donna happened to leave soap suds in the sink, she might see a rainbow of colors reflected in the bubbles. She would become so completely absorbed in looking at the brilliant colors that she could not move; she would be in a state of temporary paralysis. Donna made her "no soap suds" rule to prevent the environment from triggering an autistic behavior—temporary paralysis. Donna and her husband, who is also autistic, have developed many rules to control some of their unwanted behaviors. Here are some of their rules: *No lining feet up with furniture; No making the fruit in the bowl symmetrical; No reading newspaper headlines in gas stations or at newsstands* (Blakely, 1994, p. 43). These rules, which help Donna and her husband avoid performing repetitive and stereotyped behaviors, illustrate the behavioral approach.

The *behavioral approach* analyzes how organisms learn new behaviors or modify existing ones, depending on whether events in their environments reward or punish these behaviors.

Donna and her husband's rules are examples of a basic behavioral principle: Rewards or punishments can modify, change, or control behavior. Psychologists use behavioral principles to teach people to be more assertive or less depressed, to toilet train young children, and to change many other behaviors. Psychologists use behavioral principles to train animals to press levers, to use symbols to communicate, and to perform behaviors on cue in movies and television shows.

> Seeing a dazzling rainbow in soap suds stopped Donna in her tracks.

Largely through the creative work and original ideas of B. F. Skinner (1989), the behavioral approach has grown into a major force in psychology. Skinner's ideas stress the study of observable behaviors, the importance of environmental reinforcers (reward and punishment), and the exclusion of mental processes. His ideas, often referred to as strict behaviorism, continue to have an impact on psychology. In Module 10, we'll explain how Skinner's ideas were integrated into a program that taught autistic children new social behaviors that enabled them to enter and do well in public grade schools.

However, some behaviorists, such as Albert Bandura (2001), disagree with strict behaviorism and have formulated a theory that includes mental or cognitive processes in addition to observable behaviors. According to Bandura's *social cognitive approach,* our behaviors are influenced not only by environmental events and reinforcers but also by observation, imitation, and thought processes. In Module 10, we'll discuss how Bandura's ideas explain why some children develop a fear of bugs.

Behaviorists have developed a number of techniques for changing behaviors. As we mentioned earlier, they used relaxation exercises to reduce the emotional component of test anxiety. Next, you'll see how they have used self-management skills to reduce the cognitive component of test anxiety.

Behavioral Approach to Test Anxiety

Can I redirect my worrying?

We discussed how excessive worrying, which is the cognitive component of test anxiety, can improve test performance if you can channel your worry into studying for exams. One method to redirect worry into studying more is to use a system of *self-management* based on a number of behavioral principles (Kennedy & Doepke, 1999).

Researchers found that the following self-management practices are related to increasing studying time and achieving better grades: (1) select a place that you use exclusively for study; (2) reward yourself for studying; (3) keep a record of your study time; (4) establish priorities among projects; (5) specify a time for each task; (6) complete one task before going on to another. Notice that each of these self-management practices derives from our basic behavioral principle: Events in your environment can modify your behaviors through rewards and punishments. As the graph on the right shows, 53% of freshmen who learned and used self-management practices survived into their sophomore year compared to the survival rate of only 7% of freshmen who did not learn self-management practices (Long et al., 1994).

> I heard that self-management can help me stay in college.

In later modules, we'll give many examples of how behavioral principles can be used to modify a wide range of behaviors and thought patterns.

1. Researchers identified freshmen who had poor study skills and divided them into two groups. One group was given a self-management course to improve their study skills, while a second group was not.

7% 53%

2. 7% of freshmen who did not take the self-management course survived into the second semester of their sophomore year.

3. 53% of freshmen who did take the self-management course survived into the second semester of their sophomore year.

How was Donna's childhood?

When she was about 3 years old, Donna faced a number of personal problems: having an alcoholic mother who hit and verbally abused her, having a father who was often gone, and being sent to a "special needs" school. Apparently in trying to deal with these problems, Donna developed other personalities. One personality was Willie, a child with "hateful glaring eyes, a pinched-up mouth, rigid corpselike stance, and clenched fists," who stamped and spit but also did well in school. The other was Carol, a charming, cooperative little girl who could act normal and make friends (S. Reed & Cook, 1993). Why Donna developed other personalities to deal with difficult childhood experiences would be carefully looked at in the psychoanalytic approach (Lanyado & Horne, 1999).

The *psychoanalytic approach* is based on the belief that childhood experiences greatly influence the development of later personality traits and psychological problems. It also stresses the influence of unconscious fears, desires, and motivations on thoughts and behaviors.

In the late 1800s, Sigmund Freud, a physician, treated a number of patients with psychological problems. On the basis of insights from therapy sessions, Freud proposed some revolutionary ideas about the human mind and personality development. For example,

Donna had an alcoholic and verbally abusive mother and a mostly absent father.

one hallmark of Sigmund Freud's psychoanalytic approach is the idea that the first five years have a profound effect on later personality development. According to the psychoanalytic approach, Donna's first five years with a verbally abusive mother and mostly absent father would profoundly affect her later personality development.

In addition, Freud reasoned that thoughts or feelings that make us feel fearful or guilty, that threaten our self-esteem, or that come from unresolved sexual conflicts are automatically placed deep into our unconscious. In turn, these unconscious, threatening thoughts and feelings give rise to anxiety, fear, or psychological problems. Because Freud's patients could not uncover their unconscious fears, he developed several techniques, such as dream interpretation, to bring hidden fears to the surface. Freud's belief in an unconscious force that influenced human thought and behavior was another of his revolutionary ideas (Hansen, 2000).

Many of Freud's beliefs, such as the existence of unconscious feelings and fears, have survived, while other ideas, such as the all-importance of a person's first five years, have received less support. Many of Freud's terms, such as id, ego, superego, and libido, have become part of our everyday language. We'll discuss Freud's theory of personality in Module 19.

Unlike the biological, cognitive, and behavioral approaches, the psychoanalytic approach would search for hidden or unconscious forces underlying test anxiety.

Psychoanalytic Approach to Test Anxiety

Is test anxiety related to procrastination?

We discussed two components of test anxiety—excessive worrying and increased physiological responses—that can impair a student's performance on exams. Researchers also found that students with high test anxiety are much more likely to procrastinate than students with low test anxiety (N. A. Milgram et al., 1992).

Procrastination refers to the tendency to always put off completing a task to the point of feeling anxious or uncomfortable about one's delay.

Researchers estimate that about 20% of adults are chronic procrastinators and from 30 to 70% of students procrastinate or deliberately delay completing assignments or studying for exams (Ferrari & Tice, 2000). Some of the more obvious reasons students give for procrastinating include being lazy or undisciplined, lacking motivation, and not knowing how to organize their time or set deadlines (Ariely & Wertenbroch, 2002).

However, the psychoanalytic approach would look beneath these obvious reasons and try to identify unconscious personality problems that may underlie procrastination. Because unconscious reasons for procrastination are difficult to uncover, psychologists studied the personality of procrastinators by giving them standard paper-and-pencil personality tests.

Based on personality tests, researchers concluded that students who are regular procrastinators may have low self-esteem, are too dependent on others, or have such a strong fear of failure that they do not start the task

The best thing to do is to put off doing it for a few more days.

(Blunt & Pychyl, 2000). Thus, the psychoanalytic approach would point to underlying personality problems as the probable cause of procrastination.

The psychoanalytic approach would also study how childhood experience may have led to procrastination. For instance, researchers found that procrastinators tend to be raised by authoritarian parents who stress overachievement, set unrealistic goals for their children, or link achievement to giving parental love and approval. A child who is raised by parents like these may feel very anxious when he or she fails at some task and will be tempted to put off such tasks in the future (Pychyl et al., 2002).

Psychologists know that ingrained personality characteristics, such as procrastination, remain relatively stable and persist across time unless a person makes a deliberate effort to change them. In Modules 21, 23, and 24, we'll discuss several effective methods that psychologists have developed to change personality characteristics.

B. Modern Approaches

Humanistic Approach

What was Donna's potential?

Donna says that one reason she wrote her books was to escape her prison of autism. Autism has trapped her in a world where she sometimes blinks compulsively, switches lights on and off for long periods of time, rocks back and forth, freezes up, stares off into space without being able to stop herself, hates to be touched, cannot stand to enter public places, and hates to make eye contact with others (Williams, 1992).

When Donna and her husband were dating, they confided to each other that they didn't feel sexual attraction or sexual feelings like other couples. Something had been left out of their lives and made them asexual (D. Williams, 1994).

Donna's struggle to free herself from autism, develop close personal relationships, and reach her true potential characterizes the humanistic approach.

The *humanistic approach* emphasizes that each individual has great freedom in directing his or her future, a large capacity for achieving personal growth, a considerable amount of intrinsic worth, and enormous potential for self-fulfillment.

Donna echoes the humanistic approach when she writes, "Autism tried to rob me of life, of friendship, of caring, of sharing, of showing interest, of using my intelligence . . . it tries to bury me alive. . . ." The last words in her book are "I CAN

Although the vast majority of autistics have great difficulty with language, Donna had an amazing ability for written and spoken language.

FIGHT AUTISM. . . . I WILL CONTROL IT. . . . IT WILL NOT CONTROL ME" (D. Williams, 1994, p. 238).

Humanists believe that, like Donna, we may have to struggle to reach our potential, but we have control of our fate and are free to become whatever we are capable of being. The humanistic approach emphasizes the positive side of human nature, its creative tendencies, and its inclination to build caring relationships. This concept of human nature—freedom, potential, creativity—is the most distinctive feature of the humanistic approach and sets it far apart from the behavioral and psychoanalytic approaches (Hansen, 2000).

The humanistic approach officially began in the early 1960s with the publication of the *Journal of Humanistic Psychology.* One of the major figures behind establishing the journal and the humanistic approach was Abraham Maslow, who had become dissatisfied with the behavioral and psychoanalytic approaches. To paraphrase Maslow (1968), the humanistic approach was to be a new way of perceiving and thinking about the individual's capacity, freedom, and potential for growth. Many of humanism's ideas have been incorporated into approaches for counseling and psychotherapy.

Because of its free-will concept of human nature and its lack of rigorous experimental methods, many behaviorists regard the humanistic approach as more of a philosophy of life than a science of human behavior.

The humanistic approach also applies to dealing with a student's problems, such as test anxiety and procrastination.

Humanistic Approach to Test Anxiety

How can students reach their potentials?

We've all had the experience of getting exams back and looking at the grades. Researchers wanted to know if you would give different reasons for earning high scores than for earning low scores. For example, researchers asked children to explain why they performed well or poorly on reading and math exams. Children who performed well said that their good performance resulted from their effort and ability. Children who performed poorly said it was primarily because the task was too difficult and they lacked the ability (S. M. Bell et al., 1994). Based on these findings, researchers suggested that teachers be especially encouraging and supportive to children who do poorly, so that they will not give up but rather try to develop their academic potential. This advice to teachers is a good example of applying the humanistic approach to help individuals reach their highest potential.

What are the ways that I can improve?

Psychologists have also studied students whose academic performance ranged from poor to very good in order to develop a profile of a successful student. Studies showed that successful students share a number of similar characteristics: they feel competent about meeting the demands of their classes; they believe they can handle test situations; they are very good at organizing their study time and leisure time; they prepare themselves for tests and do not procrastinate (Kleijn et al., 1994).

Based on studies of students' performances, the humanistic approach would say that just as successful students found ways to reach their academic potential, all students should search for ways to reach their own potentials. The humanistic approach emphasizes that students have the capacity to choose, that each is unique or special, and that students should have faith in their personal or subjective feelings (Hansen, 2000).

Cross-Cultural Approach

How is autism diagnosed in other cultures?

Although autism is now recognized in most countries, there are differences among countries in the age at which the diagnosis is first made.

United States. A psychologist in the United States first described the symptoms of autism 60 years ago (L. Kanner, 1943). At that time, autism was thought to be caused by environmental factors, such as having "cold" parents. However, in the 1960s, the focus changed to searching for biological causes (Rimland, 1964). In the United States, the diagnosis of autism usually occurs very early, between 2 and 3 years of age. At this writing, there is no cure for autism but there are a variety of treatment programs, one of which is described on page 232.

China. The problem of autism was not recognized in China until 1987, when a published article described 15 cases of children with autistic symptoms (Tao, 1987). There are several reasons for this time lag in recognizing autism in China. First, most Chinese could not imagine that any disorder, such as autism, could occur in infancy. Second, many Chinese parents were unaware of an infant's developmental stages, such as when an infant first develops social responses and verbal skills. Third,

Chinese parents generally believed that infants would grow out of any early difficulties. Efforts are under way to alert parents and medical professionals to the importance of making an early diagnosis and beginning early treatment (Tao & Yang, 1997).

Germany. Similar to the United States, the recognition of autism in Germany began in the late 1940s. However, unlike the United States' policy of making an early diagnosis of autism, the diagnosis of autism in Germany is hardly ever made in 3-year-olds and generally not until children are 5 or 6 years of age. Efforts are under way to change this policy and diagnose autism and begin treatment at an earlier age (Schmidt, 1997).

These differences in diagnosing autism show the influence of cultural factors and illustrate one of the newer approaches in psychology, the cross-cultural approach (Kagitcibasi & Poortinga, 2000; Triandis & Suh, 2002).

The *cross-cultural approach* studies the influence of cultural and ethnic similarities and differences on psychological and social functioning.

As you'll see next, there are also cross-cultural differences in how students respond to test anxiety.

Cross-Cultural Approach to Test Anxiety

How do other cultures deal with test anxiety?

Culture plays an important role in determining the intensity and expression of anxiety. For example, the highest test anxiety scores were reported by students in Egypt, Jordan, and Hungary. The lowest test anxiety scores were reported by students in China, Italy, Japan, and the Netherlands. Test anxiety scores of students in the United States were somewhere in the middle (Zeidner, 1998).

Some cultural factors that play a role in determining levels of text anxiety include importance of academic success, career opportunities, parental expectations, perceptions of being

Students' level of test anxiety depends on their cultural values.

evaluated, and students' expectations. Researchers suggest that higher test anxiety may also result from special environmental and educational problems or increased competition because of fewer educational opportunities (Zeidner, 1998).

Researchers also discovered that how students evaluate success depends on their cultural values. For example, students in Chile admired successful students, whether or not they thought the success resulted from expending great effort or having natural ability. In contrast, students in America admired successful students much more if they thought the success resulted from expending great effort rather than having natural ability (Betancourt & Lopez, 1993). This study shows how the cross-cultural approach provides different and interesting answers to the same question (H. Keller & Greenfield, 2000).

Many Approaches, Many Answers

Of the six approaches that we have discussed, the cross-cultural approach is the most recent. This approach began in the early 1970s with the publication of the *Journal of Cross-Cultural Psychology* and has since grown in popularity (Triandis & Suh, 2002). In each module, we will highlight a cross-cultural study, which will be indicated by the symbol of multicultural people shown on the right.

The reason modern psychology uses many different approaches to study the same behavior is that the different viewpoint of each approach serves to provide additional information. By combining information from the biological,

cognitive, behavioral, psychoanalytic, humanistic, and cross-cultural approaches, psychologists stand a better chance of reaching their four goals of describing, explaining, predicting, and controlling behavior.

We have discussed the approaches used by modern psychologists so that you can compare them with the different approaches used by early psychologists. As you compare early and modern approaches, you can appreciate how much psychology has changed in the past 100 years.

This symbol indicates a cultural diversity topic.

C. Historical Approaches

How did psychology begin?

Imagine living in the late 1800s and early 1900s, when the electric light, radio, and airplane were being invented and the average human life span was about 30 years. This was the time when psychology broke away from philosophy and became a separate field of study. As they developed this new area, early psychologists hotly debated its definition, approach, and goals (Benjamin, 2000). We'll highlight those early psychologists whose ideas and criticisms shaped the field. We'll begin with the person considered to be the father of psychology, Wilhelm Wundt.

Structuralism: Elements of the Mind

Who established the first lab?

WILHELM WUNDT 1832–1920

There were no bands or celebrations when Wilhelm Wundt established the first psychology laboratory in 1879, in Leipzig, Germany. In fact, his laboratory was housed in several rooms in a shabby building that contained rather simple equipment, such as platforms, various balls, telegraph keys, and metronomes. The heavily bearded Wundt, now considered the father of psychology, would ask subjects to drop balls from a platform or listen to a metronome (figure below) and report their own sensations. Wundt and his followers were analyzing their sensations, which they thought was the key to analyzing the structure of the mind (R. B. Evans, 1999). For this reason they were called structuralists and their approach was called structuralism.

Structuralism was the study of the most basic elements, primarily sensations and perceptions, that make up our conscious mental experiences.

Just as you might assemble hundreds of pieces of a jigsaw puzzle into a completed picture, structuralists tried to combine hundreds of sensations into a complete conscious experience. Perhaps Wundt's greatest contribution was his method of introspection.

Introspection was a method of exploring conscious mental processes by asking subjects to look inward and report their sensations and perceptions.

For example, after listening to a beating metronome, the subjects would be asked to report whether their sensations were pleasant, unpleasant, exciting, or relaxing. However, introspection was heavily criticized for being an unscientific method because it was solely dependent on subjects' self-reports, which could be biased, rather than on objective measurements. Although Wundt's approach was the first, it had little impact on modern psychology. The modern-day cognitive approach also studies mental processes, but with different scientific methods and much broader interests than those of Wundt.

Can you describe each sensation you hear?

It wasn't long before Wundt's approach was criticized for being too narrow and subjective in primarily studying sensations. These criticisms resulted in another new approach, called functionalism.

Functionalism: Functions of the Mind

Who wrote the first textbook?

WILLIAM JAMES 1842–1910

For twelve years, William James labored over a book called *Principles of Psychology*, which was published in 1890 and included almost every topic that is now part of psychology textbooks: learning, sensation, memory, reasoning, attention, feelings, consciousness, and a revolutionary theory of emotions.

For example, why do you feel fear when running from a raging wolf? You might answer that an angry wolf (figure below) is a terrifying creature that causes fear and makes you run—fear makes you run. Not so, according to James, who reasoned that the act of running causes a specific set of physiological responses that your brain interprets as fear—running makes you afraid. According to James, emotions were caused by physiological changes; thus, running produced fear. You'll find out if James's theory of emotions was correct in Module 16.

Unlike Wundt, who saw mental activities as composed of basic elements, James viewed mental activities as having developed through ages of evolution because of their adaptive functions, such as helping humans survive. James was interested in the goals, purposes, and functions of the mind, an approach called functionalism.

Functionalism, which was the study of the function rather than the structure of consciousness, was interested in how our minds adapt to our changing environment.

Functionalism did not last as a unique approach, but many of James's ideas grew into current areas of study, such as emotions, attention, and memory (M. Hunt, 1993). In addition, James suggested ways to apply psychological principles to teaching,

Does running from an angry wolf cause fear?

which had a great impact on educational psychology. For all these reasons, James is considered the father of modern psychology.

Notice that James disagreed with Wundt's structural approach and pushed psychology toward looking at how the mind functions and adapts to our ever-changing world. About the same time that James was criticizing Wundt's structuralism, another group also found reasons to disagree with Wundt; this group was the Gestalt psychologists.

Gestalt Approach: Sensations Versus Perceptions

Who said, "Wundt is wrong"?

**MAX WERTHEIMER
1883–1943**

When you see a road hazard sign like the one in the photo below, you think the lights forming the arrow are actually moving in one direction. This motion, however, is only an illusion; the lights are stationary and are only flashing on and off.

The illusion that flashing lights appear to move was first studied in 1912 by three psychologists; Max Wertheimer, Wolfgang Köhler, and Kurt Koffka. They reported that they had created the perception of movement by briefly flashing one light and then, a short time later, a second light. Although the two bulbs were fixed, the light actually appeared to move from one to the other. They called this the *phi phenomenon;* today it is known as *apparent motion.*

Wertheimer and his colleagues believed that the perception of apparent motion could not be explained by the structuralists, who said that the movement resulted from simply adding together the sensations from two fixed lights. Instead, Wertheimer argued that perceptual experiences, such as perceiving moving lights, resulted from analyzing a "whole pattern," or, in German, a *Gestalt.*

The *Gestalt approach* emphasized that perception is more than the sum of its parts and studied how sensations are assembled into meaningful perceptual experiences.

In our example, Gestalt psychologists would explain that your experience of perceiving moving traffic lights is much more than and very different from what is actually happening—fixed lights flashing in sequence. These kinds of findings could not be explained by the structuralists and pointed out the limitations of their approach (D. J. Murray et al., 2000).

After all these years, many principles of the Gestalt approach are still used to explain how we perceive objects. We'll discuss many of the Gestalt principles of perception in Module 6.

Why do blinking lights seem to move?

Behaviorism: Observable Behaviors

Who offered a guarantee?

**JOHN B. WATSON
1878–1958**

"Give me a dozen healthy infants, well-formed, and my own special world to bring them up in and I'll guarantee to take any one at random and train him to become any type of specialist I might select—doctor, lawyer, artist . . ." (J. B. Watson, 1924).

These words come from John B. Watson, who published a landmark paper in 1913 titled "Psychology as a Behaviorist Views It." In it, he rejected Wundt's structuralism and its study of mental elements and conscious processes. He rejected introspection as a psychological technique because its results could not be scientifically verified by other psychologists. Instead, John Watson very boldly stated that psychology should be considered an objective, experimental science, whose goal should be the analysis of observable behaviors and the prediction and control of those behaviors (Rilling, 2000). It is a small step from these ideas to Watson's famous boast, "Give me a dozen healthy infants . . . ," which illustrates the behavioral approach.

Can anyone guarantee what I will become?

The *behavioral approach* emphasized the objective, scientific analysis of observable behaviors.

From the 1920s to the 1960s, behaviorism was the dominant force in American psychology. Part of this dominance was due to the work of B. F. Skinner and other behaviorists, who expanded and developed Watson's ideas into the modern-day behavioral approach, which is fully discussed in Module 10. However, beginning in the 1970s and continuing into the present, behaviorism's dominance was challenged by the cognitive approach, whose popularity throughout the 1990s surpassed behaviorism (R. B. Evans, 1999).

Survival of Approaches

Which approaches survived?

The survival of each approach—structuralism, functionalism, Gestalt, and behaviorism—depended on its ability to survive its criticisms. Criticisms of Wundt's structural approach gave rise to the functional approach of James and the Gestalt approach of Wertheimer, Köhler, and Koffka. Criticisms of all three approaches—structural, functional, and Gestalt—gave rise to Watson's behavioral approach. Another approach, Sigmund Freud's psychoanalytic approach (see p. 9), which emphasized the influence of unconscious

processes, disagreed with Watson's strict behavioral approach and developed largely in parallel to these other approaches. These disagreements in approaches resulted in heated debates among early psychologists, but they helped psychology develop into the scientific field it is today (R. B. Evans, 1999).

Although early American psychologists differed in their approaches, they shared one underlying theme that was a sign of their times. They discriminated against women and minorities in both academic and career settings. Such discriminatory practices were widespread in early times, and we'll examine that issue next.

D. Cultural Diversity: Early Discrimination

Because psychologists focus on studying and understanding human behavior, you would expect them to be among the first to recognize the mistreatment of and discrimination against other groups. However, psychologists are human and being human, they knowingly or unknowingly adopted and carried out the discriminatory practices that were operating at the time. This means that, for the first 75 of its more than 100 years of existence, the academic policies and career opportunities of American psychology were determined by White males, who both intentionally and unintentionally discriminated against women and people of color. Here are just a few examples.

Women in Psychology

Why couldn't she enter graduate school?

The reason Mary Calkins (on right) could not enter graduate school was that she was a woman, and many universities (Johns Hopkins, Harvard, Columbia) would not admit women. Since Calkins was a faculty member and had established a laboratory in psychology at Wellesley College in 1891, she petitioned and was allowed to take seminars at Harvard. There, she completed all requirements for a Ph.D. and was recommended for a doctorate by her professors, but the Harvard administration declined to grant it because she was a woman (Furumoto, 1989). It was not until 1908 that a woman, Margaret Washburn, was awarded a Ph.D. in psychology.

Mary Calkins was not given a Ph.D. because she was a woman.

Even after women began obtaining doctorates, the only positions open to them were teaching jobs at women's colleges or normal schools, which trained high school teachers (Furumoto & Scarborough, 1986). During the past 25 years, women have made great progress in the field. However, even though women currently earn more Ph.D.s in psychology than men, in 1991 there were more full-time male psychologists (39,180) than women (20,100). In addition, female psychologists earn less than male psychologists, and fewer women are editors of psychology journals (Rabasca, 2000b). Not only did women face discrimination in psychology, but so did people of color.

Minorities in Psychology

Why so few minority students?

In psychology's early days, only a few northern White universities accepted Black students, while all southern White universities denied admission to Black students.

The first African American woman to receive a Ph.D. in psychology was Ruth Howard (photo below), who graduated from the University of Minnesota in 1934. She had a successful career as a clinical psychologist and school consultant.

Between 1920 and 1966, only 8 Ph.D.s in psychology were awarded to Black students, compared to 3,767 doctorates to Whites (R. V. Guthrie, 1976). In 1996, 168 Ph.D.s were awarded to African Americans, 183 to Hispanics, 23 to Native Americans, 131 to Asians, and 2,939 to Whites (Rabasca, 2000).

During the early 1900s, few degrees were awarded to Hispanics. One early exception was

George Sanchez found that intelligence tests were culturally biased.

George Sanchez (photo below), who conducted pioneering work on the cultural bias of intelligence tests given to minority students. Sanchez criticized the claim that Mexican Americans were mentally inferior, saying that this claim was based solely on intelligence tests. Sanchez showed that intelligence tests contained many questions that were biased against minorities and thus resulted in their lower scores (R. V. Guthrie, 1976).

From the founding of the American Psychological Association in 1892 up until 1990, its cumulative membership was 128,000. Of those members, only 700 were African American, 700 were Latino, and 70 were Native American. This limited minority membership indicates how much further psychology must go to remedy its earlier discriminatory practices (Barinaga, 1996).

Ruth Howard was the first Black woman to get a Ph.D. in 1934.

Righting the Wrongs

How much success?

Today, people of color are still underrepresented in academic departments and in graduate programs in psychology, although their numbers and influence are increasing (R. B. Evans, 1999). For example, the American Psychological Association has recognized the need to recruit minority members and has formed a special group to carry out this goal. An increasing number of journals (*Psychology of Women Quarterly, Hispanic Journal of Behavioral Science,* and *Journal of Black Psychology*) are promoting the causes of women and minorities and are fighting discriminatory practices (DeAngelis, 1966). The American Psychological Association (APA) has an official policy supporting equal opportunities "for persons regardless of race, gender, age, religion, disability, sexual orientation and national origin" (Tomes, 2000).

In the late 1990s, several states banned affirmative action programs, which had helped minority students enter college. As a result, university enrollments of minority students in these states have dropped (Steinberg, 2003). Colleges are searching for other ways to recruit minority students (Marklein, 2002).

✔ Concept Review

1. The systematic, scientific study of behaviors and mental processes is called _____.

2. The four goals of psychology are to (a)_____ what organisms do, to (b)_____ the causes of behavior, to (c)_____ behavior in new situations, and to (d)_____ behavior, which has both positive and negative aspects.

3. The approach that focuses on how one's nervous system, hormones, and genes interact with the environment is called the _____ approach.

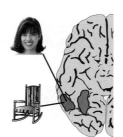

4. The approach that studies how people think, solve problems, and process information is called the _____ approach.

5. The approach that analyzes how environmental rewards and punishments shape, change, or motivate behavior is called the _____ approach.

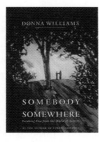

6. The approach that stresses the influence of unconscious feelings, fears, or desires on the development of behavior, personality, and psychological problems is called the (a)_____ approach. This approach also emphasizes the importance of early (b)_____ experiences.

7. The approach that emphasizes freedom of choice, self-fulfillment, and attaining one's potential is called the (a)_____ approach. Many of this approach's concepts have been taken up and used in (b)_____.

8. The newest approach, which focuses on cultural and ethnic influences on behavior, is called the _____ approach.

9. Wundt studied the elements that made up the conscious mind and called this approach (a)_____. Subjects were asked to observe the workings of their minds, a technique that Wundt called (b)_____. Modern-day psychologists who study mental activities with more objective and scientific methods are said to use the (c)_____ approach.

10. William James disagreed with Wundt's structuralism and instead emphasized the functions, goals, and purposes of the mind and its adaptation to the environment; he called this approach (a)_____. James also applied the principles of psychology to teaching, so his approach had a great effect on the field of (b)_____ psychology.

11. Some psychologists disagreed with Wundt's approach of structuralism and instead believed that perceptions are more than the sum of many individual (a)_____. These psychologists called their approach the (b)_____ approach, which studied how sensations were assembled into meaningful (c)_____.

12. John Watson disagreed with Wundt's approach, which was called (a)_____, and disagreed with Wundt's technique of studying the mind, which was called (b)_____. Instead, Watson emphasized the objective, scientific analysis of observable behaviors, which was known as the (c)_____ approach. Later, this approach became a dominant force in psychology through the work of behaviorist (d)_____.

Answers: *1. psychology; 2. (a) describe, (b) explain, (c) predict, (d) control; 3. biological; 4. cognitive; 5. behavioral; 6. (a) psychoanalytic, (b) childhood; 7. (a) humanistic, (b) counseling or psychotherapy; 8. cross-cultural; 9. (a) structuralism, (b) introspection, (c) cognitive; 10. (a) functionalism, (b) educational; 11. (a) sensations, (b) Gestalt, (c) perceptions; 12. (a) structuralism, (b) introspection, (c) behavioral, (d) B. F. Skinner*

Best Strategy for Taking Class Notes?

How good are your class notes?

As you listen to lectures in class, you'll probably be taking notes. But how do you know if you're using the best system or strategy? To research some particular behavior, such as note-taking, psychologists first ask a very specific research question: Which system or strategy for taking notes results in the best performance on tests? One researcher answered this question by using a combination of behavioral and cognitive approaches (A. King, 1992). As we describe this interesting study, notice how it involves the four goals of psychology, beginning with the first goal, describing behavior.

How can I make my notes better?

1st Goal: Describe Behavior

The researcher divided college students into three different groups. Each group was given a different method or strategy for taking notes. As described below, students practiced three different strategies for taking notes: review notes, summarize notes, and answer questions about notes.

A. Review Notes

The strategy that most students use is to try to write down as much as possible of what the professor says. Then, before exams, students review their notes, hoping they took good class notes.

B. Summarize Notes

Students took notes as usual but, after the lecture, used their notes to write a summary of the lecture in their own words.

Students were shown how to identify a main topic and, in their own words, write a sentence about it. Then they identified a subtopic and wrote a sentence that related it to the main topic. When linked together, these sentences created a summary of the lecture, written in the students' own words.

C. Answer Questions about Notes

Students took notes as usual but, after the lecture, used their notes to ask and answer questions about the lecture material. Students were given a set of 13 general questions, such as: **What is the main idea of . . . ? How would you use . . . to . . . ? What is a new example of . . . ? What is the difference between . . . and . . . ?** Students answered each of these questions using their class notes.

After practicing one of these three note-taking strategies, students watched a videotaped lecture and used their particular strategy for taking notes.

2nd Goal: Explain Behavior

A week after each group had watched a videotaped lecture, they were given an exam. The graph on the right shows that the group who used the strategy of taking notes plus answering questions scored significantly higher than the other two groups. The researcher explained that students who took notes and then answered questions about their notes retained more information than students who employed the other two strategies (A. King, 1992).

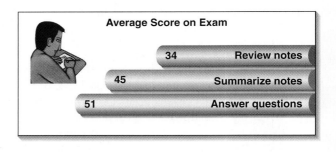

Average Score on Exam

34	Review notes
45	Summarize notes
51	Answer questions

3rd Goal: Predict Behavior

On the basis of these results, the researcher predicts that students who use the strategy that combines note-taking with answering questions are likely to retain more information and perform better on exams than students who use traditional note-taking methods, such as writing as much as they can and then reviewing their notes before exams.

4th Goal: Control Behavior

Students can increase their chances of getting better grades by taking the time to learn a better note-taking strategy. This new strategy involves taking notes and then answering, in their own words, a series of general questions about the lecture material. Although this new note-taking strategy takes a little time to learn, the payoff will be better performance on exams. This and other studies show how students can improve their test-taking performance by using a better strategy of taking notes (Armbruster, 2000).

Purpose of the Research Focus

This study shows how psychologists answered a very practical and important question about how best to take lecture notes. We'll use the Research Focus to show how psychologists use different approaches and research techniques to answer a variety of interesting questions about human behavior.

Each time you see this symbol, it will indicate a Research Focus, which occurs in each module.

Although a large percentage of psychologists engage in research, you'll see next how many others work in a variety of career settings that may or may not involve research.

Psychologist Versus Psychiatrist

What's a psychologist?

Many students think that psychologists are primarily counselors and therapists, even though advanced degrees in psychology are awarded in a dozen different areas. Obtaining an advanced degree in psychology requires that one finish college and spend about two to three years in postgraduate study to obtain a master's degree or four to five years in postgraduate study to obtain a Ph.D. Some careers or work settings require a master's degree, while others require a Ph.D. Many students are confused about the difference between a psychologist, a clinical or counseling psychologist, and a psychiatrist.

A *psychologist* is usually someone who has completed four to five years of postgraduate education and has obtained a Ph.D., PsyD., or Ed.D. in psychology.

Some states permit individuals with master's degrees to call themselves psychologists.

It usually takes about 4 to 5 years after college to become a psychologist.

A *clinical psychologist* has a Ph.D., PsyD., or Ed.D., has specialized in a clinical subarea, and has spent an additional year in a supervised therapy setting to gain experience in diagnosing and treating a wide range of abnormal behaviors.

Similar to clinical psychologists are *counseling psychologists,* who provide many of the same services but usually work with different problems, such as those involving marriage, family, or career counseling. Neither clinical nor counseling psychologists assess the neurological causes of mental problems and do not yet have the authority to prescribe drugs like psychiatrists.

A *psychiatrist* is a medical doctor (M.D.) who has spent several years in clinical training, which includes diagnosing possible physical and neurological causes of abnormal behaviors and treating these behaviors, often with prescription drugs.

After becoming a psychologist, you could choose among the following career settings.

Many Career Settings

Are psychologists usually therapists?

As you can see in the pie chart below, the majority (49%) of psychologists are therapists, while the rest work in four other settings. In the United States and Canada, most psychologists have a Ph.D., PsyD., or Ed.D., which requires four to five years of study after college. In many other countries, most psychologists have a college degree, which requires four to five years of study after high school (Rosenzweig, 1992). Since the 1950s, there has been an increase in psychologists who provide therapy/health services and a decline in those who work in academic/research settings.

The U.S. Department of Labor predicts that employment opportunities for psychologists will grow much faster than the average for other occupations in the coming years (Chamberlin, 2000). Here's a breakdown of where psychologists in the United States currently work (D. Smith, 2002).

49% The largest percentage (49%) of psychologists work as clinical or counseling psychologists in either a *private practice* or *therapy setting,* such as a psychological or psychiatric clinic; a mental health center; a psychiatric, drug, or rehabilitation ward of a hospital; or a private office. The duties of clinical or counseling psychologists might involve doing individual or group therapy; helping patients with problems involving drugs, stress, weight, marriage, family, or career; designing programs for healthier living; or testing patients for psychological problems that developed from some neurological problem.

28% The second largest percentage (28%) of psychologists work in the *academic settings* of universities and colleges. Academic psychologists often engage in some combination of classroom teaching, mentoring or helping students, and doing research in their areas of interest.

13% The third largest percentage (13%) of psychologists work in a variety of other kinds of jobs and career settings.

6% The fourth largest percentage (6%) of psychologists work in *industrial settings,* such as businesses, corporations, and consulting firms. These psychologists, often called industrial/organizational psychologists, may work at selecting personnel, increasing production, or improving job satisfaction and employer–employee relations.

4% The smallest percentage (4%) work in *secondary schools and other settings.* For example, school psychologists conduct academic and career testing and provide counseling for a variety of psychological problems (learning disabilities, attention-deficit/hyperactivity disorder).

If you are thinking of entering the field of psychology today, you have a wide and exciting range of career choices. For those who decide to engage in research, we'll next discuss seven of the more popular research areas that psychologists choose.

G. Research Areas

Which area should I choose?

As you proceed through your introductory psychology course, you'll find that the world of psychology has been divided into at least seven general areas. And, if you go on and enter graduate school in psychology, you'll be expected to specialize in one of these seven areas. Students often find it difficult to choose only one special area of psychology, since they may be interested in two or three. For example, I switched areas three times before deciding upon one of the seven. The reason graduate students are asked to choose one area is that there is such an enormous amount of information that it takes great effort to master even one area. As you read about each research area, think about which one you might prefer. (Percentages given below do not add up to 100% because some miscellaneous areas are not included.)

Social and Personality

How important are first impressions?

How does one develop certain personality traits?

Why do we use stereotypes?

What causes aggression?

These questions come from the two different and sometimes overlapping areas of social psychology and personality psychology.

Social psychology involves the study of social interactions, stereotypes, prejudices, attitudes, conformity, group behaviors, and aggression.

Personality psychology involves the study of personality development, personality change, assessment, and abnormal behaviors.

Many social/personality psychologists work in academic settings, but some work as consultants and personnel managers in business. About 22% of psychologists choose social psychology and 5% choose personality.

Developmental

When does a newborn recognize his or her parents?

What happens to teenagers at puberty?

What happens to memory as a person grows older?

You would be asking these kinds of questions if you were a developmental psychologist.

Developmental psychology examines moral, social, emotional, and cognitive development throughout a person's entire life.

Some developmental psychologists focus on changes in infancy and childhood, while others trace changes through adolescence, adulthood, and old age. They work in academic settings and may consult on day care or programs for the aging. About 25% of psychologists choose this specialty.

Experimental

Why does an animal press a bar to obtain food?

Can learning principles be used to treat a phobia?

Why do we feel fear when we see a snake?

What is taste aversion?

These kinds of questions interest experimental psychologists.

Experimental psychology includes areas of sensation, perception, learning, human performance, motivation, and emotion.

Experimental psychologists conduct much of their research under carefully controlled laboratory conditions, with both animal and human subjects. About 16% of psychologists specialize in experimental psychology. Most work in academic settings, but some also work in business, industry, and government.

Biological

How do brain cells change during Alzheimer's disease?

Do people have predispositions for mental disorders?

Does coffee improve your memory?

Do genes affect your intelligence and personality?

Physiological psychologists or psychobiologists study the biological basis of learning and memory; the effects of brain damage; the causes of sleep and wakefulness; the basis of hunger, thirst, and sex; the effects of stress on the body; and the ways in which drugs influence behavior.

Biological psychology or *psychobiology* involves research on the physical and chemical changes that occur during stress, learning, and emotions, as well as how our genetic makeup, brain, and nervous system interact with our environments and influence our behaviors.

Psychobiologists work in academic settings, hospitals, and private research laboratories. About 8% of psychologists choose this area.

Cognitive

What was unique about Einstein's thought processes?

Can you learn something but not remember it?

Does memory get worse with age?

What are repressed memories?

If these questions interest you, think about being a cognitive psychologist. *Cognitive psychology* involves how we process, store, and retrieve information and how cognitive processes influence our behaviors.

Cognitive research includes memory, thinking, language, creativity, and decision making. Newer areas, such as artificial intelligence, combine knowledge of the brain's functions with computer programming in an attempt to duplicate human thinking and intelligence.

Earlier we discussed a relatively new area that combines cognitive and biological approaches and is called cognitive neuroscience. About 5% of psychologists select this area.

Psychometrics

What do college entrance tests show?

What career best fits my abilities?

How do tests assess abnormal behaviors?

These questions introduce an area called psychometrics, which involves the construction, administration, and interpretation of psychological tests.

Psychometrics focuses on the measurement of people's abilities, skills, intelligence, personality, and abnormal behaviors.

To accomplish their goals, psychologists in this area focus on developing a wide range of psychological tests, which must be continually updated and checked for usefulness and cultural biases. Some of these tests are used to assess people's skills and abilities, as well as to predict their performance in certain careers and situations, such as college or business. About 5% of psychologists select this area.

Making Decisions

What should I do?

If you decide to become a psychologist, you will need to make a series of decisions. The first is whether to obtain a master's degree or a Ph.D. The next decision involves which setting to work in: choosing among private practice, clinic or hospital setting, academic research and/or teaching, industry/business, or counseling and testing in a school setting. You'll also need to specialize in one of the seven areas: social, personality, developmental, experimental, biological, cognitive, or psychometrics. After making all these decisions, you are on your way to having a very interesting and exciting career.

Next, we're going to use research findings from several research areas, including personality, experimental, and cognitive, and give you tips on how to improve your study skills.

H. Application: Study Skills

Improving Study Habits

What problems do over 50% of freshmen report?

In a survey of college freshmen, 57% reported that they had poor study habits, and 54% said that they had problems managing their time (Thombs, 1995). We'll discuss ways to deal with both of these problems, beginning with methods to improve study habits.

Common complaint. The most common student complaint that I hear after exams is, "I read the book and went over my notes three times and still got a C." This complaint points to the most common mistake students make in studying for exams. Because students do read the material and go over their notes several times, they may have a general feeling that they know the material. For example, you have just read about the six modern approaches, the historical approaches, and the differences between a psychologist, clinical psychologist, and psychiatrist. Having read this material, you may generally feel that you know it. However, researchers have discovered a startling fact: There is almost no relationship between how well students think they know material and how well they perform on an exam (Cull & Zechmeister, 1994; Mazzoni & Cornoldi, 1993).

Poor judges. The reason students tend to be poor judges of what they know is that they base their judgments more on what they *generally* know rather than on what they *specifically* remember (Glenberg et al., 1987). For example, you might generally remember the six approaches. However, on an exam you will be asked for specific information, such as names and definitions. One of the best ways to judge how prepared you are for an exam is to test yourself and get feedback from answering specific questions. For instance, can you list the six approaches and

> How do I know when I've studied enough to take a test?

define each one? Because answering specific questions is one way to judge your learning, we have built specific questions and answers into this text. You can test yourself by answering the questions in the Concept Review in each module and by answering the questions in the Summary Test at the end of each module.

Time management. A common problem that students have involves managing their time—specifically, underestimating how long it will take to study all the material. For example, researchers found that about 50% of college students repeatedly anticipated finishing a task earlier than they actually did (Buehler et al., 1994). Part of the problem is that students do not allow enough time for studying more difficult items. Researchers found that students who plan to set aside extra time for studying more difficult items increase their chances of remembering the material (Allgood et al., 2000). One way to achieve better time management involves setting the right kinds of goals.

> *Remember:*
> **To judge how well prepared you are for an exam, ask yourself specific questions about the material. You can do that by taking the tests built into each module—the Concept Review and the Summary Test.**

Setting Goals

What's the best kind of goal to set?

Another way to better manage your study time is to set the right goals, which can vary from studying for a certain period of time to studying until you feel you are well prepared (Flippo & Caverly, 2000). Which of the following goals do you think would make your study time more efficient and improve your test performance?

1 Set a **time goal**, such as studying 10 hours a week or more, and then keep track of your study time during the semester.

> Should my goal be to study 10 hours a week?

2 Set a **general goal**, such as trying to study hard and stay on schedule; then, try to reach this goal during the semester.

3 Set a **specific performance goal**, such as answering at least 80% of the Summary Test questions correctly for each module.

To determine which of these three goals leads to more effective studying, researchers told three different groups of students to set time goals, general goals, or specific performance goals when they studied on their own. The researchers found that students who set specific performance goals did significantly better on the final exam than students who set time or general goals (M. Morgan, 1985). Thus, if you want to improve your study skills, you should think less about the total time you study and concentrate more on reaching a specific performance goal every week. For example, the first week your goal might be to correctly answer 80% of the Summary Test questions. Once you have reached this goal, you could aim to answer 90% of the questions correctly. Setting performance goals rather than time goals is the key to better time management (Barling et al., 1996).

As you'll see next, one way to motivate yourself to reach your performance goals is to reward yourself at the right times.

> *Remember:*
> **One way to make your study time more efficient is to set a specific performance goal and keep track of your progress.**

Rewarding Yourself

What if you reach a goal?

One problem many students have is getting and staying motivated. One reliable solution is to give yourself a reward when you reach a specific goal, such as answering 80% of the questions correctly. The reward may be a special treat (such as a CD, meal, movie, or time with friends) or a positive statement (such as "I'm doing really well" or "I'm going to get a good grade on the test"). Giving yourself a reward (self-reinforcement) is an effective way to improve performance (Allgood et al., 2000).

Motivate yourself with rewards.

Remember:
Immediately after you reach a specific goal, give yourself a reward, which will both maintain and improve your motivation.

Taking Notes

Another way to improve your performance is to take great notes. Students generally make two kinds of mistakes in taking notes. One is to try to write down everything the instructor says, which is impossible and leads to confusing notes. The other is to mechanically copy down terms or concepts that they do not understand but hope to learn by sheer memorization, which is difficult. Researchers have several suggestions for taking good notes (Armbruster, 2000):

1 Write down the information in your own words. This approach will ensure that you understand the material and will increase your chances of remembering it.

2 Use headings or an outline format. This method will help you better organize and remember the material.

3 Try to associate new lecture or text material with material that you already know. It's easier to remember new information if you can relate it to your existing knowledge. That is the reason we have paired terms in the Concept Review section with illustrations, drawings, and photos that you are familiar with from earlier in the text.

4 As we discussed in the Research Focus (p. 16), you can improve your note-taking by asking yourself questions, such as: What is the main idea of . . . ? What is an example of . . . ? How is . . . related to what we studied earlier? Writing the answers in your own words will give you a better chance of remembering the material (A. King, 1992).

Even though you may take great notes and set performance goals, if you procrastinate and put off getting started, as 30 to 70% of students report doing, your best-laid plans will come to nothing (Senécal et al., 1995). We already discussed some of the reasons behind procrastination (p. 9) and here we'll look at ways to overcome it.

Remember:
Go through your lecture notes, ask questions, and write down answers in your own words.

Stopping Procrastination

How do you get started?

Some students find the task of reading assignments, studying for exams, or writing papers so difficult that they cannot bring themselves to start. If you have problems with procrastinating, here are three things you should do to get started (Ariely & Wertenbroch, 2002; Blunt & Pychyl, 2000).

1 *Stop thinking about the final goal*—reading 30 pages or taking two midterm exams—which may seem too overwhelming.

2 Break the final assignment down into a number of *smaller goals* that are less overwhelming and easier to accomplish. Work on the first small goal, and when you finish it, go on to the next small goal. Continue until you have completed all the small goals.

3 Write down a *realistic schedule* for reaching each of your smaller goals. This schedule should indicate the time and place for study and what you will accomplish that day. Use a variety of self-reinforcements to stay on your daily schedule and accomplish your specific goals.

Everyone procrastinates a little, but it becomes a problem if you continually put off starting important projects that have deadlines, such as exams and papers. Take the advice of professionals on stopping procrastination: get organized, set specific goals, and reward yourself (Ariely & Wertenbroch, 2002).

Use three steps to overcome procrastination.

If you adopt these tested methods for improving your study skills, you'll greatly increase your chances of being a successful student (Flippo et al., 2000).

Remember:
One of the most effective ways to start a large assignment is to break it down into a series of smaller goals and work on each goal separately.

Unusual Excuses for Missing Exams

✔ I missed the exam because of my uncle's funeral, and I can't take the make-up tomorrow because I just found out my aunt has a brain tumor.

✔ I can't be at the exam because my cat is having kittens and I'm her coach.

✔ I want to reschedule the final because my grandmother is a nun.

✔ I can't take the exam on Monday because my mom is getting married on Sunday and I'll be too drunk to drive back to school.

✔ I couldn't be at the exam because I had to attend the funeral of my girlfriend's dog.

✔ I can't take the the test Friday because my mother is having a vasectomy. (D. A. Bernstein, 1993, p. 4)

✔ Summary Test

A. DEFINITION & GOALS

1. The broad definition of psychology is the systematic, scientific study of (a)_____ and (b)_____. The term in (a) refers to observable responses of animals and humans, and the term in (b) refers to processes that are not directly observable, such as thoughts, ideas, and dreams.

2. All psychologists agree that the first three goals of psychology are to (a)_____ what organisms do, to (b)_____ how organisms behave as they do, and to (c)_____ how they will respond in the future and in different situations. Some psychologists add a fourth goal, which is to (d)_____ behavior and thus curb or eliminate psychological and social problems.

B. MODERN APPROACHES

3. Because behavior is often so complex, psychologists study it using six different approaches. The approach that focuses on how a person's genetic makeup, hormones, and nervous system interact with the environment to influence a wide range of behaviors is called the _____ approach.

4. The approach that studies how organisms learn new behaviors or change or modify existing ones in response to influences from the environment is called the (a)_____ approach. There are two versions of this approach. One that primarily studies observable behaviors and excludes mental events is called (b)_____ and is best expressed by the ideas of B. F. Skinner; the other, which in-cludes observable behaviors plus cognitive processes, is called the (c)_____ approach and is expressed by the ideas of Albert Bandura and his colleagues.

5. An approach that examines how our unconscious fears, desires, and motivations influence behaviors, thoughts, and personality and cause psychological problems is called the _____ approach. Sigmund Freud developed this approach, as well as the technique of dream interpretation, to bring unconscious ideas to the surface.

6. The approach that investigates how people attend to, store, and process information and how this information affects learning, re-membering, feeling, and believing is called the _____ approach.

7. An approach that emphasizes people's capacity for personal growth, freedom in choosing their future, and potential for self-fulfillment is called the _____ approach. One of the founders of this approach was Abraham Maslow.

8. The approach that studies how cultural and ethnic similarities and differences influence psychological and social functioning is called the _____ approach.

C. HISTORICAL APPROACHES

9. Considered the father of psychology, Wilhelm Wundt developed an approach called (a)_____. This approach studied the elements of the conscious mind by using a self-report technique called (b)_____. Wundt's approach was the beginning of today's cognitive approach.

10. Disagreeing with Wundt's approach, William James said that it was important to study functions rather than elements of the mind. Accordingly, James studied the functions of consciousness as well as how mental process-es continuously flow and adapt to input from the environment. This approach is called _____. James's ideas contributed to the modern area of psychology and have also influenced educational psychology.

11. Also disagreeing with Wundt's approach was a group of psychologists, led by Wertheimer, Köhler, and Koffka, who stated that perceptions cannot be explained by breaking them down into individual elements or sensations. Instead, they believed that perceptions are more than the sum of individual sensations, an idea called the _____ approach.

12. Another psychologist who disagreed with Wundt's approach was John B. Watson. He stated that psychology should use scientific principles to study only observable behaviors and not mental events, an approach called _____. Watson's approach gave rise to the modern behavioral approach.

D. CULTURAL DIVERSITY: EARLY DISCRIMINATION

13. During the first 75 of its more than 100 years of existence, the field of psychology discriminated against (a)_____ and (b)_____, as indicated by the very limited number of these individuals who were granted Ph.D.s or offered positions in major universities. During the past 25 years, the American Psychological Association, minority organizations, and most universities and colleges have been actively recruiting minorities and helping them enter the field of psychology.

E. RESEARCH FOCUS: TAKING CLASS NOTES

14. Three different strategies for note-taking were studied: note-taking plus review, which means writing down almost everything the instructor says; note-taking plus questions, which means asking and answering questions about the lecture material; and note-taking plus summary, which means writing a summary of the lecture in your own words. The note-taking strategy that resulted in the highest exam grades involved (a)_____, and the note-taking strategy that resulted in the lowest exam grades involved (b)_____.

F. CAREERS IN PSYCHOLOGY

15. There are five major settings in which psychologists work and

establish careers. The largest percentage of psychologists work in private practice or (a)_____ settings, where they diagnose and help clients with psychological problems. The second largest group work in (b)_____ settings, doing a combination of teaching and research. The third largest group work in a (c)_____ of settings. The fourth largest group work in (d)_____ settings, where they are involved in selecting personnel, increasing job satisfaction, and improving worker–management relations. The fifth largest group work in other settings, such as (e)_____, where they do academic testing and counseling.

G. RESEARCH AREAS

16. There are six common subareas in which psychologists specialize. Those who are interested in prejudice, attitudes, and group behaviors or in personality development and change specialize in (a)_____ psychology. Those interested in social, emotional, and cognitive changes across the life span specialize in (b)_____ psychology. Those interested in studying sensation, perceptions, learning, and motivation, often under laboratory conditions, specialize in

(c)_____ psychology. Those interested in the interaction among genes, the nervous system, and the environment choose (d)_____. Those interested in how people process, store, and retrieve information choose (e)_____ psychology, and those who are interested in the measurement and testing of skills, abilities, personality, and mental problems specialize in (f)_____.

H. APPLICATION: STUDY SKILLS

17. A common mistake that many students make is that, when they plan their study schedules, they often _____ the time it will take to complete a task.

18. Another common mistake that students make is that they think they know the material after reading the text and reviewing their notes. A better way to judge how prepared you are for an exam is to ask yourself specific (a)_____ rather than to trust your judgment about what you think you know. A good way to make your study time more efficient is to set specific (b)_____ and keep track of your progress. Immediately after you reach a specific performance goal, give yourself a (c)_____, which will both maintain and improve your motivation. To improve your lecture notes, try to associate new lecture material with what you already know, and use your notes to ask and answer (d)_____ in your own words. One of the most effective ways to overcome a strong tendency to delay starting a task, known as (e)_____, is to stop thinking about the final goal. Instead, break down a large assignment into a series of smaller goals and work on each goal separately. Finally, it's best to set a realistic (f)_____ in order to accomplish each of the smaller goals.

Answers: *1. (a) behaviors, (b) mental processes; 2. (a) describe, (b) explain, (c) predict, (d) control; 3. biological; 4. (a) behavioral, (b) strict behaviorism, (c) social learning; 5. psychoanalytic; 6. cognitive; 7. humanistic; 8. cross-cultural; 9. (a) structuralism, (b) introspection; 10. functionalism; 11. Gestalt; 12. behaviorism; 13. (a) women, (b) minorities; 14. (a) answering questions, (b) reviewing notes; 15. (a) therapy or clinical, (b) academic, (c) variety, (d) industrial, (e) schools; 16. (a) social and personality, (b) developmental, (c) experimental, (d) biological or physiological psychology, (e) cognitive, (f) psychometrics; 17. underestimate; 18. (a) questions, (b) performance goals, (c) reward, (d) questions, (e) procrastination, (f) schedule*

Critical Thinking

A New Treatment for Autism?

Questions

Test your thinking power by answering the following questions. If you need help, check the suggested answers at the bottom.

1. What kind of symptoms would doctors use to decide whether or not young Parker Beck was autistic?

2. What did researchers believe was the cause of autism in the past and what do they believe is the cause today?

3. Based on the results from only Parker and three other autistic children, why would parents want their autistic children to be treated with secretin?

Young Parker Beck, who was diagnosed as being autistic, had to see a doctor for his gastrointestinal problems. As part of a regular procedure for diagnosing these problems, Dr. Karoly Horvath, of the University of Maryland Medical Center, gave Parker an injection of a hormone called secretin. In the days following the injection of secretin, Victoria Beck, Parker's mother, noticed a dramatic reduction in Parker's autistic symptoms. Besides seeing an improvement in Parker's digestive problems, Victoria also noticed that Parker was sleeping through the night and even began saying words.

Encouraged by the improvements in Parker's behavior, Victoria persuaded Dr. Horvath to follow up and treat other children with secretin, which was extracted from the small intestine of pigs. Subsequently, Dr. Horvath published a report on three other autistic children who also seemed to have improved after injections of secretin.

After the popular television program "Dateline" reported on Parker's improvement, parents around the country began asking their doctors to treat their autistic children with injections of secretin.

Because of the sudden and widespread use of secretin, the National Institute of Child Health and Human Development quickly organized clinical trials to scientifically evaluate possible benefits of using secretin to reduce autistic symptoms.

Since then, a half-dozen studies have reported that injections of secretin caused no significant improvement in autistic symptoms and any slight improvements were about the same as those observed in children receiving a placebo injection (water). Dr. Adrian Sandler, of Thoms Rehabilitation Hospital in Asheville, said, "We have been unable to show any benefit from the secretin treatment." Another colleague added that, because both secretin and the placebo sometimes resulted in similar improvements, such improvement in symptoms probably resulted from the increased attention and support from both doctors and parents.

However, Dr. Bernard Rimland, of the Autism Research Institute in San Diego, questioned the negative findings because many parents of autistic children had reported improvement in autistic symptoms following injections of secretin. For these reasons, Dr. Rimland remained very optimistic about the value of secretin in reducing autistic symptoms. (Adapted from Thomas H. Maugh II, *Los Angeles Times,* December 9, 1999, p. A1; Owley et al., 2001; Carey et al., 2002; Unis et al., 2002)

4. Why did the National Institute decide to evaluate the effects of secretin on autism?

5. Why might a secretin injection result in the same improvement as taking a placebo?

6. Why did Dr. Rimland downplay the negative results of the reported studies?

Try these InfoTrac search terms: autism; secretin; clinical trials; placebo.

---

1. Autism is marked by especially abnormal or impaired development in social interactions, such as hiding to avoid people, not making eye contact, and not wanting to be touched, and by difficulties in communicating, such as grave problems in developing spoken language or in initiating conversations. Autistics are characterized by having very few activities and interests and spending long periods repeating the same behaviors (hand flapping).
2. In the past, researchers mistakenly believed that autism was caused by having "cold" or withdrawn parents. Today, researchers believe there are genetic and biological causes of autism.
3. At this writing, there is no medical treatment or cure for autism. Lacking medical treatment, many parents are desperate for any treatment that claims to reduce or cure autism.

4. The original finding that secretin helped autistic children was based on limited observations from only four children. The National Institute used a more reliable and scientific approach to determine if secretin really was a useful medical treatment for autism.
5. The parents' belief that their child is being treated for autism (not knowing if it's secretin or a placebo) may result in giving their child more attention, care, and support, which may itself improve an autistic child's behavior.
6. Dr. Rimland, who has an autistic son, puts considerable faith and belief in the observations of those parents who reported that secretin helped their autistic children. However, so far, researchers have not confirmed the parents' positive observations.

Links to Learning

LEARNING ACTIVITIES

- **POWERSTUDY CD-ROM 2.0**
  by Tom Doyle and Rod Plotnik
  Check out the "Discovering Psychology" Module (disk 1) on
  PowerStudy and:
  - Test your knowledge using an interactive version of the Summary Test
    on pages 22 and 23. Also access related quizzes—true/false, multiple
    choice, and matching.
  - Explore an interactive version of the Critical Thinking exercise "A New
    Treatment for Autism?" on page 24.
  - You will also find key terms, a chapter outline including a chapter
    abstract, and a list of hotlinked Web sites that correlate to this module.

- **SELF-STUDY ASSESSMENT**
  Want help studying? For your customized Study Plan go to
  http://psychology.wadsworth.com/plotnik7e/. This program will
  automatically generate pretests and posttests to help you determine
  what concepts you have mastered and what concepts you still need work on.

- **STUDY GUIDE and WEBTUTOR**
  Check the corresponding module in your Study Guide for
  effective student tips and help learning the material presented.

- **INFOTRAC COLLEGE EDITION ONLINE LIBRARY**
  To find interesting and relevant articles go to
  http://www.infotrac-college.com, use your password, and then type
  in search terms such as the ones listed below.

| Behaviorism | Gestalt psychology | Minorities |
| Psychiatry | Study habits | Procrastination |

STUDY QUESTIONS

Use InfoTrac to search for topics mentioned in the following questions (e.g., alcoholism, psychological discrimination, stress management).

*A. Definition & Goals—How would you rank the four goals of psychology in terms of importance? (**Suggested answer page 619**)

B. Modern Approaches—How would psychologists use the six modern approaches to study whether alcoholism runs in families?

C. Historical Approaches—Do any of these historical approaches match your stereotype of what psychology is all about?

*D. Cultural Diversity: Early Discrimination—Why would discriminatory practices exist in psychology, an area devoted to studying human behavior? (**Suggested answer page 619**)

E. Research Focus: Taking Class Notes—What could you do to improve your note-taking skills?

F. Careers in Psychology—If you're thinking about a career in psychology, what setting would you choose?

G. Research Areas—Which of the six subareas of psychology would you study to help people manage stress?

*H. Application: Study Skills—What changes would you make to study most efficiently? (**Suggested answer page 619**)

*These questions are answered in Appendix B.

Module 2: Psychology & Science

The Origin Of MAN

Several Controversies

What is Dusty's problem?

It was 5:00 in the morning when Dusty began throwing a fit. As if driven by an inner motor, all 50 pounds of him was flying around the room, wailing and kicking. This raging activity went on for about 30 minutes; then he headed downstairs for breakfast. While his mother was busy in the kitchen, Dusty grabbed a box of cereal and kicked it around the room, spreading cereal everywhere. When his mother told him to clean up the mess, he got the plastic dustpan but began picking it apart, piece by piece. Next he grabbed three rolls of toilet paper and unraveled them around the house. By then, it was only 7:30. Dusty had not been given his pill because he was seeing his doctor at 4:00 that day (adapted from *Time*, July 18, 1994).

Seven-year-old Dusty has a behavioral problem that has been surrounded with controversy. Dusty was diagnosed as being hyperactive, a problem that is officially called attention-deficit/hyperactivity disorder, or ADHD (American Psychiatric Association, 2000).

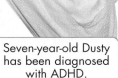

Seven-year-old Dusty has been diagnosed with ADHD.

Attention-deficit/hyperactivity disorder, or *ADHD,* is not diagnosed by any medical tests but on the basis of the occurrence of certain behavioral problems. A child must have six or more symptoms of inattention, such as making careless mistakes in schoolwork, not following instructions, and being easily distracted, and six or more symptoms of hyperactivity, such as fidgeting, leaving classroom seat, running about when should not, and talking excessively. These symptoms should have been present from an early age, persisted for at least six months, and contributed to maladaptive development.

One controversy surrounding ADHD involves diagnosis. Since ADHD is based not on medical tests but rather on the occurrence of certain behavioral problems, how can children with ADHD be distinguished from those who are naturally outgoing and rambunctious (Sciutto et al., 2000)? Because of this difficulty, the American Academy of Pediatrics issued guidelines for diagnosing ADHD (Tanner, 2000). These guidelines stressed that, before the diagnosis of ADHD is made, a number of the symptoms described above should be present for at least six months. The guidelines focused on children aged 6 to 12 because there isn't sufficient evidence for making the diagnosis of ADHD at earlier ages. The goal of these guidelines is to prevent merely rambunctious youngsters from being overmedicated while ensuring that children with ADHD get the help they need (Root & Resnick, 2003).

To help control his ADHD, Dusty is given a popular drug that is a relatively powerful stimulant, called Ritalin (*WRIT-ah-lin*). Ritalin's effects are similar to those of another stimulant, amphetamine. Researchers do not understand why stimulant drugs, such as Ritalin and amphetamine (Adderall), decrease activity in children. Spending on drugs to treat ADHD has reached $1 billion a year, and drug manufacturers spend about $2.5 billion on marketing (Novak, 2001).

Perhaps the major questions surrounding the use of Ritalin concern whether it is being overprescribed, whether it is the most effective treatment, and how long a child with ADHD should remain on the drug (Root & Resnick, 2003). In addition, Ritalin, especially in larger doses, does have side effects that may include loss of appetite and problems with sleeping. A related question is whether children with ADHD should be kept on a diet free of artificial dyes, sweeteners, and sugar, which some parents claim worsen the symptoms. We'll answer these questions in this module.

We're going to use Dusty's problem with ADHD to show how researchers pursue the four goals of psychology that we discussed in Module 1. In Dusty's case, the four goals are (1) to describe Dusty's symptoms, (2) to explain their causes, (3) to predict their occurrence, and (4) to control Dusty's behavior through some behavioral therapy or drug treatment.

Rhino Horn and Magnets

Can beliefs cure like real medicine?

One interesting aspect of trying to control unwanted symptoms with a drug treatment is that sometimes the drug is not really a drug because it has no proven medical effects. For example, in many parts of Asia, people take powdered rhino horn because they believe that it is a medicine for treating hundreds of physical and mental problems. Similarly, in the United States, people are spending $300 million annually on wearing tiny magnets to decrease pain in joints and muscles, even though there is no reliable scientific evidence that magnets work (N. Brody, 2000). The use of rhino horn and tiny magnets, both questionable medical treatments, raises the interesting question of how much one's mind or one's beliefs contribute to the development or treatment of physical symptoms. We'll discuss methods that researchers use to decide whether the effectiveness of a treatment is due to a drug's medical effect or the person's beliefs.

Can rhino horn cure all kinds of problems?

What's Coming

Our main focus in this module is to explore the methods that researchers use to answer questions, such as how to treat ADHD and why placebos work. Specifically, we'll discuss the advantages and disadvantages of three major research methods—surveys, case studies, and experiments. We'll explain which research procedures can identify cause-and-effect relationships and which cannot. We begin with an overview of the three major research methods that psychologists use to answer questions.

A. Answering Questions

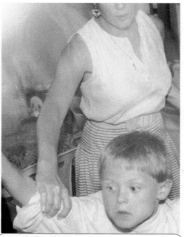

Researchers use three different research methods to study ADHD.

How do researchers study ADHD?

As you look at the photo of Dusty on the right, you see a young boy ready to explode into an uncontrolled burst of activity, a major symptom of ADHD. However, 25 years ago, ADHD was a relatively small problem in the United States, while today it is the most commonly diagnosed behavioral problem in children. ADHD is surrounded with controversy. For example, its name has been changed from hyperactivity to minimal brain damage to attention-deficit disorder and most recently to attention-deficit/hyperactivity disorder (ADHD). The diagnosis of ADHD is not straightforward, since it is based on behavioral symptoms rather than medical tests. The proposed causes of ADHD are many, including various genetic, neurological, cultural, and dietary factors (Root & Resnick, 2003). Finally, the most popular treatment of ADHD involves giving children a stimulant drug.

In the middle of these controversies are parents like Dusty's mother, who, after dealing with a hyperactive and impulsive child from an early age, have little doubt that ADHD exists and that Ritalin decreases hyperactivity and impulsivity. At the same time, critics warn that ADHD may be misdiagnosed or overdiagnosed and that, while Ritalin may reduce activity, it may fail to improve academic performance in grade-school children (Jensen, 1999).

As researchers work to resolve all the controversies surrounding ADHD, they are using three major research methods—survey, case study, and experiment.

Survey

Suppose you wish to know how many children have ADHD, whether it occurs more in boys or girls, which treatment is the most popular, and how many children continue to have problems when they become adults. Researchers obtain this information with surveys.

A *survey* is a way to obtain information by asking many individuals—either person to person, by telephone, or by mail—to answer a fixed set of questions about particular subjects.

The disadvantage of a survey is that such information can contain errors or be biased because people may not remember accurately or answer truthfully. The advantage of a survey is that it is an efficient way to obtain much information from a large number of people.

But if researchers wanted to know more about a particular person, they would use a case study.

Case Study

Suppose you wish to know in greater detail about how a single child, such as Dusty, developed ADHD, performs in school, makes friends, plays team sports, and deals with everyday problems. Or suppose you wish to know about how a family copes with a child who has ADHD. For example, one mother said, "Ritalin doesn't take away the problems at all. It just helps him focus on what he's doing. You can talk to him; he can get his school work done. It still takes him a long time to get things done. He's still behind, emotionally and socially" (*San Diego Tribune,* November 27, 1989). When another mother was told that sugar doesn't increase activity, she replied, "I say, they're nuts! Where were they last Christmas when my sons ate candy canes and green frosting for days and never slept!" (*Los Angeles Times,* February 9, 1994). Researchers gather in-depth data about a particular individual with a case study.

A *case study* is an in-depth analysis of the thoughts, feelings, beliefs, experiences, behaviors, or problems of a single individual.

One disadvantage of a case study is that its detailed information about a particular person, such as Dusty, may not apply to other children with ADHD.

One advantage of a case study is that its detailed information allows greater understanding of a particular person's life.

But if researchers wanted to establish whether sugar really increases activity in children with ADHD, they would use an experiment.

Experiment

Suppose you thought that sugar or artificial dyes caused hyperactivity in your child and you wondered if this were true. For example, based on case studies and parents' reports, one researcher thought that certain artificial dyes, chemicals, and sweeteners increased the activity and impulsive behavior of children diagnosed with ADHD (Feingold, 1975). When researchers want to identify a cause-and-effect relationship, such as whether sugar increases activity, they use an experiment.

An *experiment* is a method for identifying cause-and-effect relationships by following a set of rules and guidelines that minimize the possibility of error, bias, and chance occurrences.

A disadvantage of an experiment is that information obtained in one experimental situation or laboratory setting may not apply to other situations. An experiment's primary advantage is that it has the greatest potential for identifying cause-and-effect relationships with less error and bias than either surveys or case studies.

Which method is best?

Very often, researchers use all three research methods—survey, case study, and experiment—because each provides a different kind of information. Surveys provide information about fixed questions from a large number of people. Case studies give in-depth information about a single person. Experiments point to cause-and-effect relationships. We'll discuss the advantages and disadvantages of each of the three methods, beginning with surveys.

What do surveys tell us?

Almost every day the media report some new survey. Although surveys tell us what others believe or how they behave, survey questions can be written to bias the answers; moreover, people may not always answer truthfully (N. Schwartz, 1999). For example, how many people do you think always wash their hands after going to the bathroom? We'll sample some surveys and then discuss their problems.

Do you wash your hands?

Although 94% of the people surveyed by telephone said that they always washed their hands after going to the bathroom, direct observation of 6,333 people in five major cities found that only 68% really do and that women (74%) washed their hands more often than men (61%) (Manning, 1996).

What's your biggest worry?

A survey of 251,323 college freshmen (class of 2000) reported that 66% are worried about not having the money to finish college (K. R. Weiss, 1997). In a random sample of 1,003 adults in 50 states, 60% agreed that lying is sometimes necessary, especially to protect someone's feelings (Smiley, 2000).

How many children are diagnosed with ADHD?

Recent surveys report that 4–12% of U.S. school-age children are diagnosed with ADHD and that there may be cultural and ethnic differences in the diagnosis of ADHD. The lowest incidence of ADHD is reported in Asian Americans and the highest in African American boys even though their symptoms appear very similar to those of White boys (Allen, 2000; Root & Resnick, 2003).

These examples show that surveys provide a great deal of useful information. However, surveys have potential problems with accuracy (as in the hand-washing survey) and, as you'll see next, with how questions are worded and who asks the questions.

How questions are worded

You may be surprised to learn that surveys may get very different results depending on how questions are worded. Here are two examples:

QUESTION: "Would you say that **industry** contributes more or less to air pollution than **traffic**?"
Traffic contributes more: **24%**
Industry contributes more: 57%

QUESTION: "Would you say that **traffic** contributes more or less to air pollution than **industry**?"
Traffic contributes more: **45%**
Industry contributes more: 32%

These two examples indicate that the way questions are phrased and the way the possible answers are ordered can greatly influence people's responses and, in this case, produce opposite results (reported in *U.S. News & World Report,* Dec. 4, 1995, p. 55).

Who asks the questions

You may also be surprised to learn that the sex or race of the questioner can also affect how people answer the questions.

QUESTION: "The problems faced by Blacks were brought on by Blacks themselves."
When the interviewer was **White, 62%** of Whites who were interviewed agreed.
When the interviewer was **Black, 46%** of Whites who were interviewed agreed.

These two examples indicate that when asked about sensitive or emotional issues, people take into account the race of the interviewer and tend to give socially acceptable rather than honest answers (*U.S. News & World Report,* Dec. 4, 1995, p. 55).

We can conclude that surveys may be biased because people may not answer questions truthfully, may give socially acceptable answers, or may feel pressured to answer in certain ways. Also, surveys can be biased by how questions are worded and by interviewing a group of people who are not representative of the general population (N. Schwartz, 1999). Despite these potential problems, surveys do have advantages.

While guarding against error and bias, surveys can be a useful research tool to quickly and efficiently collect information on behaviors, beliefs, experiences, and attitudes from a large sample of people and can compare answers from various ethnic, age, socioeconomic, and cultural groups.

For example, surveys suggest that ADHD interferes with performance in school settings, decreases the chances of graduating from high school, and may lead to conduct disorder problems in adolescence as well as continued problems in adulthood (Root & Resnick, 2003).

Because surveys indicate that children with ADHD have major problems in school settings, psychologists are developing methods for improving performance. These methods include: teaching ADHD children how to organize their work, giving them constant feedback on reaching their goals, and starting programs that train teachers and families to work together to help ADHD children control their disruptive behaviors (Evans et al., 2001). Thus, another advantage of surveys is their ability to identify problems and evaluate treatment programs.

However, if researchers wish to focus on a particular individual rather than a group, they use a case study.

C. Case Study

What's a case study?

Sometimes researchers answer questions by studying a single individual in great detail, which is called a case study. A *case study* is an in-depth analysis of the thoughts, feelings, beliefs, or behaviors of a single person.

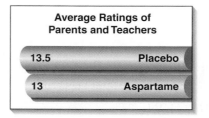

We'll use a different case study, this time focusing on Nick, who is now 11 years old and diagnosed as having ADHD. From the age of 3, Nick has had problems paying attention and completing tasks. Because he was so easily distracted, Nick needed to be called as many as 19 times before he answered, couldn't seem to finish tying his shoes, couldn't pay attention in school, and alternated between bouts of frustration and being an angel. In the first grade, Nick was put on Ritalin, and it made an immediate difference. He called it a "concentrating medicine," and although he still has academic problems, he can better focus on and complete a project (Leavy, 1996). This case study tells us that Ritalin helped Nick concentrate but only partially solved his academic problems. Sometimes case studies help answer questions, but as you'll see next, case studies can also result in wrong or biased answers.

Why did parents make a mistake?

Observations from case studies may be misinterpreted if the observer has preconceived notions of what to look for. For example, beginning in the mid-1970s, parents were told that food with artificial additives, dyes, and preservatives could cause hyperactivity in children (Feingold, 1975). Shortly after, parents reported that, yes indeed, artificial additives caused a sudden increase in restlessness and irritability in their hyperactive children (Feingold, 1975). The parents' reports and beliefs that additives cause hyperactivity are examples of another kind of case study, called a testimonial.

A *testimonial* is a statement in support of a particular viewpoint based on detailed observations of a person's own personal experience.

However, contrary to the parents' testimonials, researchers have generally found that amounts of artificial additives within a normal range did not affect hyperactivity (Kinsbourne, 1994). More recently, there are testimonials from parents that children with attention-deficit disorder who ate foods with an artificial sweetener, aspartame (Nutrasweet), showed noticeable increases in symptoms.

To test the accuracy of these recent testimonials, researchers asked teachers and parents to evaluate the behaviors and cognitive functions of children who were given a capsule containing either ten times their normal daily intake of aspartame or a placebo. Neither parent, child, nor teacher knew if the capsule contained aspartame or the placebo. As the figure on the left shows, there was little or no difference between the effect of aspartame (Nutrasweet) and that of the placebo on the behaviors or cognitive functions of children with attention-deficit disorder (Shaywitz et al., 1994).

Average Ratings of Parents and Teachers	
13.5	Placebo
13	Aspartame

Although testimonials from parents, friends, or peers can be very convincing, we'll point out two problems that make testimonials especially susceptible to error.

What's the problem with testimonials?

One of the major problems with testimonials is that they are based on our personal observations, which have great potential for error and bias. For example, if parents reported that sweeteners increased their son's activity, we would have to rule out personal beliefs and self-fulfilling prophecies.

Personal beliefs. If parents hear that artificial sweeteners may cause physical or psychological problems, they may interpret their child's problems as caused by artificial sweeteners. Because of biased perceptions, parents may overlook other potential causes, such as frustration, anger, or changes in the child's environment, and make the error of focusing only on artificial sweeteners. If we believe strongly in something, it may bias our perception and cause us to credit an unrelated treatment or event as the reason for some change.

Parents mistakenly believed that artificial sweeteners caused ADHD.

Self-fulfilling prophecy. If parents believe that artificial sweeteners cause problems, they may behave in ways—being more strict or less sympathetic—that cause the problems to occur. This phenomenon is called a self-fulfilling prophecy.

A *self-fulfilling prophecy* involves having a strong belief or making a statement (prophecy) about a future behavior and then acting, usually unknowingly, to fulfill or carry out the behavior.

If we strongly believe that something is going to happen, we may unknowingly behave in such a way as to make it happen (R. Rosenthal, 2002). Self-fulfilling prophecies reinforce testimonials and thus keep our biased beliefs alive.

The main disadvantage of testimonials is their high potential for error and bias. But they have the advantage of providing detailed information that may point to potential answers or lead to future studies. We'll discuss how case studies are used in developmental research in Module 18 and clinical research in Module 21.

Next, we'll discuss how testimonials are a popular source of information, especially when we are talking about placebos.

Examples of Mind over Body

Have you taken a placebo?

Psychologists are interested in how the mind influences the body, such as happens when someone takes a pill that happens to be a placebo.

A *placebo* is some intervention, such as taking a pill, receiving an injection, or undergoing an operation, that resembles medical therapy but that, in fact, has no medical effects.

A *placebo effect* is a change in the patient's illness that is attributable to an imagined treatment rather than to a medical treatment.

For example, the results of studies involving 3,000 men showed that a new drug (Uprima) allowed about 56% to have erections and engage in intercourse. However, about 35% of the men reported equally good results from taking another pill that proved to be a placebo (in this case a sugar pill) (Cowley, 2000a). Researchers estimate that between 35 and 75% of

Placebo

Placebos are sugar pills.

patients benefit from taking placebos for a variety of problems (pain, depression, headaches, warts) (Christensen, 2001).

Researchers believe that placebos work by reducing tension and distress and by creating powerful self-fulfilling prophecies so that individuals think and behave as if the drug, actually a placebo, is effective (Christensen, 2001). For example, placebos were compared to real antidepressants or painkillers while pictures (MRIs, p. 70) were taken of the neural responses in the subjects' brains. Individuals who reported that placebos produced relief were found to have activated (with their thoughts) the same brain areas that had been activated by real antidepressants or painkillers, which had also produced relief (Seal, 2002). Thus, placebos may work because individuals' beliefs and thoughts are powerful enough to activate the same brain areas as those activated by real drugs.

As you'll see, testimonials from around the world claim that different kinds of placebos can cure a wide variety of symptoms.

Rhino Horn

Millions of people in China, Thailand, South Korea, and Taiwan claim that rhino horn is an aphrodisiac, will increase their sexual desire and stamina, and is a cure for everything from headaches and nosebleeds to high fevers and typhoid. However, the basic ingredient of rhino horn is compacted hair (keratin), which has no proven medicinal powers (*Sierra,* November/December 1989). A single rhino horn weighing about 4 to 5 pounds will bring from $25,000 to $50,000 on the black market. In the early 1900s, there were about 1 million rhinos. By 1994, poachers had reduced the total number of rhinos to about 10,000, as the desire for rhino horns continued to grow (Berger & Cunningham, 1994).

Bear Gallbladders

In parts of Asia, a very popular "medicine" to treat many kinds of physical problems is a tablet made from bear gallbladders. Some traders are substituting pig gallbladders for bears' and customers are none the wiser, since bear or pig gallbladders are nothing more than placebos (*Time,* November 4, 1991). The price of a single bear gallbladder has risen to an amazing $18,000, and there is now an illegal global trade in animal parts. Poachers threaten some endangered species of bears, such as the grizzly bear in the United States.

Tiger Bones

In the early 1900s, there were 100,000 tigers in Asia, but by 1994 there were fewer than 5,000. The chief reason for this precipitous decline is the use of tiger bones to treat ulcers, typhoid, malaria, dysentery, and burns, to increase longevity, to guard newborn babies from infection, and to cure devil possession (Friend, 1997). In addition, wealthy Taiwanese pay $320 for a bowl of tiger penis soup that is thought to increase flagging libidos (Nagarahole, 1994). Tiger bones and tiger penises function as powerful placebos in traditional Asian medicine.

Magnets

Beginning in the early 1990s, athletes reported a decrease in pain after wearing small magnet pads over their painful injuries. Such testimonials resulted in millions of dollars in sales for magnet pads. Although several earlier studies supported such claims, recent studies that were better designed to eliminate error and bias found no difference in pain reduction between magnets and placebos (J. E. Brody, 2000; Collacott et al., 2000). These researchers concluded that magnet pads do not reduce pain.

Conclusion: Testimonials and Placebos

Why are placebos so popular?

The main reason placebos are used worldwide, even to the point of destroying certain wild animals, is that the placebo's beneficial "medical" effects are supported by countless testimonials. For example, compared to the results of surveys, testimonials are much more convincing because they are based on real-life experiences of friends, peers, and parents, who are honest and believable. However, it is common for people, honest and trustworthy, to unknowingly make a mistake and conclude that a rhino horn, bear gallbladder, tiger bone, or magnet is producing a beneficial "medical" effect when the beneficial effect is actually being caused by the individual's mental thoughts influencing the brain or body's functioning (Christensen, 2001).

As you'll see next, people often make mistakes about the effect of placebos because there is often no way to figure out what causes what.

E. Correlation

Definition

Research suggests that ADHD has a genetic basis.

What's a correlation?

The photo on the left shows Dusty running wild in a supermarket. Researchers would like to know if Dusty's hyperactivity has a genetic basis. One way to identify genetic factors is to study genetic twins because they share 100% of their genes in common. Suppose you were studying the occurrence of ADHD in identical male twins and found that about 70% of the time, if one identical twin had ADHD so did the second twin (Root & Resnick, 2003). This strong relationship between behaviors in identical twins suggests a genetic basis for ADHD. Such a relationship is called a correlation.

A *correlation* is an association or relationship between the occurrence of two or more events.

For example, if one twin has hyperactivity, a correlation will tell us the likelihood that the other twin also has hyperactivity. The likelihood or strength of a relationship between two events is called a correlation coefficient.

A *correlation coefficient* is a number that indicates the strength of a relationship between two or more events: the closer the number is to −1.00 or +1.00, the greater is the strength of the relationship.

We'll explain correlation coefficients in more detail because they can be confusing.

Correlation Coefficients

What are these numbers?

There are two major points to understand about correlations:

First, a correlation means there is an association between two or more events. For example, there is an association, or correlation, between the sex of a child and the occurrence of ADHD; 4 to 5 times more boys are diagnosed with ADHD than girls.

A second point to understand about correlations is that the strength of the relationship or association is measured by a number called a correlation coefficient. Because the correlation coefficient ranges from +1.00 to −1.00, its meaning can be confusing. In the boxes on the right, we'll describe what correlation coefficients mean, beginning at the top of the table with a +1.00.

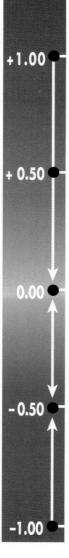

+1.00

+ 0.50

0.00

- 0.50

-1.00

If each of 20 identical pairs showed equal levels of hyperactivity, the correlation coefficient would be positive and perfect and would be indicated by a +1.00 correlation coefficient.

A **perfect positive correlation coefficient** of +1.00 means that an increase in one event is always matched by an equal increase in a second event. For example, if one identical twin has hyperactivity, then the other twin always has hyperactivity. A correlation of +1.00 is virtually never found in applied psychological research (Hemphill, 2003).

If some identical pairs but not all 20 pairs were similar in hyperactivity, the result would be a positive correlation coefficient, which can range from +0.01 to +0.99.

A **positive correlation coefficient** indicates that as one event tends to increase, the second event tends to, but does not always, increase.

As the coefficient increases from +0.01 to +0.99, it indicates a strengthening of the relationship between the occurrence of two events.

If one twin of 20 pairs showed hyperactivity while the other twin sometimes did and sometimes did not show hyperactivity, the result would be no association, or zero correlation (0.00).

A **zero correlation** indicates that there is no relationship between the occurrence of one event and the occurrence of a second event.

If, in some identical pairs, one twin showed an increase while the other showed an equivalent decrease in activity, the result would be a negative correlation coefficient, which can range from −0.01 to −0.99.

A **negative correlation coefficient** indicates that as one event tends to increase, the second event tends to, but does not always, decrease.

As the coefficient increases in absolute magnitude from −0.01 to −0.99, it indicates a strengthening in the relationship of one event increasing and the other decreasing.

If one twin of 20 identical pairs showed hyperactivity and the second twin always showed decreased activity, the correlation coefficient would be negative and perfect and would be indicated by a −1.00 correlation coefficient.

A **perfect negative correlation coefficient** of −1.00 means that an increase in one event is always matched by an equal decrease in a second event. For example, if one identical twin has hyperactivity, then the other twin always has decreased activity. A correlation of −1.00 is virtually never found in applied psychological research (Hemphill, 2003).

Can you recognize a correlation?

The media often headline interesting findings: Thin people live longer than heavier ones; overweight people earn less money than their peers; school uniforms decrease violence. Before you assume that one event causes the other, such as thinness causing one to live longer, you must check to see what researchers did. If researchers

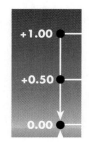

measured only the relationship between two events, such as thinness and length of life, then it's a correlation. In fact, all three findings reported here are correlations. The reason you should check whether some finding is a correlation is that correlations have one very important limitation: They do not identify what causes what. For example, let's look closely at the findings about school uniforms and student behavior problems.

Correlation Versus Causation

The biggest mistake people make in discussing correlations is assuming that they show cause and effect. For instance, many school districts are considering the adoption of mandatory school uniforms because wearing uniforms was related to decreased problems with students' behavior. The graph on the right shows that wearing school uniforms was correlated with a large decrease in carrying weapons, fighting, assaults, and vandalism. Since an increase in wearing uniforms was associated with a drop in problems, this is a negative correlation.

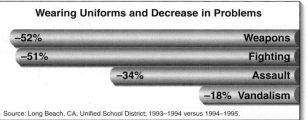

Wearing Uniforms and Decrease in Problems

-52% Weapons
-51% Fighting
-34% Assault
-18% Vandalism

Source: Long Beach, CA, Unified School District; 1993–1994 versus 1994–1995.

Although the correlation between wearing uniforms and decreased problems was impressive, you must keep in mind that

although wearing uniforms may have caused the decrease in school-related problems, correlations themselves cannot demonstrate cause and effect between variables. For example, over the past 26 years, there is a +0.88 correlation between which professional football team (American or National League) wins the Super Bowl and whether the stock market rises or falls. Although +0.88 is a very high positive correlation, it only shows a relationship between two variables because winning a Super Bowl could not possibly cause a rise or fall in the stock market.

Although correlations cannot indicate cause-and-effect relationships, they do serve two very useful purposes: Correlations help predict behavior and also point to where to look for possible causes, as has happened in the case of lung cancer.

Does wearing uniforms decrease school problems?

Correlation as Clues

Although cigarette smoke was positively correlated with lung cancer (right graph), it was unknown whether smoking was the *cause* of cancer. Acting on the clue that some ingredient of cigarette smoke might trigger the development of lung cancer, researchers rubbed tar, an ingredient of cigarette smoke, on the skin of animals. After repeated applications over a period of time, the animals developed cancerous growths. This research proved that tar could cause cancer. More recently, researchers discovered that one particular ingredient of cigarette smoke (benzo[a]pyrene) turns off a gene that normally suppresses tumors. When that particular gene is turned off by cigarette smoke, lung cancer develops (Sozzi et al., 1996). In this case, correlations told researchers where to look for causes of lung cancer. In other cases, correlations help predict behavior.

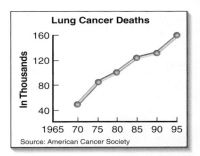

Lung Cancer Deaths

In Thousands

160
120
80
40

1965 70 75 80 85 90 95

Source: American Cancer Society

Correlation and Predictions

Do IQ scores predict academic success?

One way to predict how well students will do in academic settings is by looking at their IQ scores. For example, there is a reasonably high correlation, from +0.60 to +0.70, between IQ scores and performance in academic settings (Anastasi & Urbina, 1997). Thus, we would predict that individuals who score high on IQ tests have the skills to do well in college. However, IQ scores are only relatively good predictors for any single individual because doing well in college involves not only academic skills but also many other motivational, emotional, and personality factors that we'll discuss in Module 13.

So far, we have discussed the advantages and disadvantages of two major research methods—surveys and case studies—that psychologists use to answer questions. We have also explained a statistical procedure—correlation—that shows the strength of relationships and points to possible causes of behaviors. Next, we'll describe the other kinds of research decisions that psychologists make as they try to understand and explain behavior.

F. Decisions about Doing Research

Choosing Research Techniques

What's the best technique for answering a question?

You are constantly asking questions about human behavior, such as "Why did she say that?" or "Why did he behave that way?" Similarly, psychologists are continually asking questions, such as "What percentage of the population is gay?" or "Of what use are SAT scores?" or "How do we diagnose ADHD?"or "Does a specific gene cause obesity?" After asking one of these questions, psychologists must decide which research technique or procedure best answers it. We'll describe four different techniques for finding answers.

Questionnaires and Interviews

What percentage of the population is gay? This question is often answered by doing a survey using interviews or questionnaires.

An *interview* is a technique for obtaining information by asking questions, ranging from open-ended to highly structured, about a subject's behaviors and attitudes, usually in a one-on-one situation.

A *questionnaire* is a technique for obtaining information by asking subjects to read a list of written questions and check off specific answers.

You might think this question about what percentage of the population is gay would be relatively easy to answer. But three different surveys have reported three different answers: 2.3%, 10%, and 22% (Billy et al., 1993; Janus & Janus, 1993; Kinsey et al., 1948). These different answers resulted from surveys using differently worded questions, different groups of people, and different kinds of interview techniques. As we discussed earlier, when it comes to surveys on personal issues—such as Did you vote? Do you wear seat belts? Do you go to church? or What is your sexual preference?—people may give a desirable rather than a honest answer.

Standardized Tests

Of what use are SAT scores? The standardized test that you may be most familiar with is the SAT, which is given to many high school seniors to help predict how they will perform in college. Each year only 0.05% of students who take the SAT score a perfect 1600, a feat accomplished for the first time in 1997 by twins, Courtney and Chris (photo on left).

A *standardized test* is a technique to obtain information by administering a psychological test that has been standardized, which means that the test has been given to hundreds of people and shown to reliably measure thought patterns, personality traits, emotions, or behaviors.

One disadvantage of standardized tests, such as the SAT, is that they may be biased toward a certain group of people. One advantage of standardized tests is that they allow comparisons to be made across schools, states, and groups of people (Anastasi & Urbina, 1997). Another well-known standardized test is the IQ test, which we'll discuss in Module 13.

Courtney and Chris scored perfect 1600s on the SAT.

Laboratory Experiments

How do we diagnose ADHD? As of this writing, the diagnosis of ADHD is based primarily on behavioral symptoms, which are less reliable than medical tests. For this reason, researchers are currently searching for more reliable tests to diagnose ADHD. To identify such tests, researchers are using laboratory experiments.

A *laboratory experiment* is a technique to gather information about the brain, genes, or behavior with the least error and bias by using a controlled environment that allows careful observation and measurement.

Can a laboratory or psychological test be used to diagnose ADHD?

For example, in the photo on the right is an 11-year-old boy who is believed to have ADHD. He is taking a laboratory test that involves pressing a key when he sees a certain star on the screen. In addition, researchers took pictures of his brain (discussed in Module 4) before and after he received Ritalin. By combining these laboratory tests, researchers believe they may be on the track of identifying a more reliable method to diagnose ADHD (Teicher, 2000).

Animal Models

Does a specific gene cause obesity? Over one-third of the adult population in the United States is now overweight, which may lead to serious medical problems, such as heart disease and high blood pressure. To understand the physiological causes of obesity, researchers are using animal models (Foster et al., 1997).

An *animal model* involves examining or manipulating some behavioral, genetic, or physiological factor that closely approximates some human problem, disease, or condition.

For example, researchers have identified a gene in mice that is involved in obesity (Gura, 1997). In the photo, an obese mouse on the left without the gene is compared to a normal mouse on the right. One advantage of the animal model is that it answers questions about physiological factors that cannot be investigated in humans.

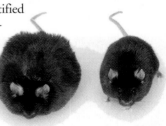

Genetically altered mice are used to study obesity.

Deciding which one or combination of these four research techniques to use depends on the kind of question being asked. As you'll see next, the kind of question also influences which research setting to use.

Choosing Research Settings

Which problems do children with ADHD have?

In trying to understand the kinds of problems faced by children with ADHD, psychologists study these children in different research settings, which may include observing them in the home, in the classroom, on the playground, or at their individual work. In addition, researchers may try to find the causes of ADHD by using different research settings, which may include studying children in the laboratory, hospital, or clinic. All these research settings can be grouped under either laboratory or naturalistic environments. We'll explain each setting and compare their advantages and disadvantages, beginning with more naturalistic environments.

Naturalistic Setting

Parents and teachers want to know if ADHD children have different problems at home (photo below) than in school. Researchers answer this question by studying ADHD children in different naturalistic settings (home versus school) (J. E. Allen, 2000).

Does this ADHD child have different problems in school than at home?

A *naturalistic setting* is a relatively normal environment in which researchers gather information by observing individuals' behaviors without attempting to change or control the situation.

For example, observations of children with ADHD in school settings indicate that they have difficulty remaining in their seats, don't pay attention to the teacher, don't complete their projects, can't sit still, get into trouble, are rude to other students, and get angry when they don't get their way. Parents report that, at home, ADHD children do not respond when called, throw tantrums when frustrated, and have periods of great activity (Hancock, 1996; Henker & Whalen, 1989). Based on these naturalistic observations, researchers and pediatricians developed a list of primary symptoms of ADHD (Tanner, 2000). Similarly, psychologists study how normal people behave in different naturalistic settings, including schools, workplaces, college dormitories, bars, sports arenas, and homeless shelters. One problem with naturalistic observations is that the psychologists' own beliefs or values may bias their observations and cause them to misperceive or misinterpret behaviors. One advantage of naturalistic observations is the opportunity to study behaviors in real-life situations and environments, which cannot or would not be duplicated in the laboratory.

Case studies. As we discussed earlier, a single individual may be studied in his or her natural environment, and this is called a case study. The case study approach is often used in clinical psychology to understand the development of a personality or psychological problem or in developmental psychology to examine a person's behavior across his or her life span.

One ***disadvantage*** of a case study is that the information obtained is unique to an individual and may not apply to, or help us understand, the behaviors of others. One ***advantage*** of a case study is that psychologists can obtain detailed descriptions and insights into aspects of an individual's complex life and behaviors that cannot be obtained in other ways.

As you can see, naturalistic settings are very useful for observing how individuals behave in relatively normal environments. However, since naturalistic settings are uncontrolled and many things happen, researchers find it difficult to identify what causes what. For this reason, researchers may have to answer some questions in a more controlled setting, such as a laboratory or clinic.

Laboratory Setting

Is there something different about the brains of children with ADHD? Questions about the brain are usually answered under very controlled conditions, such as in a laboratory setting.

A *laboratory setting* involves studying individuals under systematic and controlled conditions, with many of the real-world influences eliminated.

For example, researchers used special techniques (MRI brain scans, p. 70) that actually took pictures of the living brains of boys with and without ADHD. Researchers focused on an area called the basal ganglia (shown below in red) because it is involved in paying attention, which is difficult for ADHD children. In boys without ADHD, Ritalin caused decreased activity in the basal ganglia. However, in boys with ADHD, Ritalin caused increased activity in the basal ganglia and increased attention (Gabrieli, 1998). Researchers believe that this is one of the first laboratory tests to clearly distinguish children with and without ADHD.

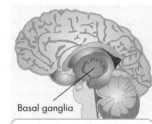

Basal ganglia

Is this part of the brain (basal ganglia) involved in ADHD?

Researchers use laboratory settings to study and identify a wide range of psychological and biological factors involved in motivation, emotion, learning, memory, drug use, sleep, intelligence, and mental disorders.

One disadvantage of laboratory settings is that they may be so controlled or artificial that their results are not always transferable to, or meaningful for, real-life situations. However, one advantage of the laboratory setting is that psychologists can carefully control and manipulate one or more treatments while reducing error or bias from other situational or environmental factors.

Psychologists may use both naturalistic and laboratory settings to obtain a broader understanding of some behavior or problem, such as ADHD (Root & Resnick, 2003).

Researchers may combine the advantages of naturalistic and laboratory settings to identify cause-and-effect relationships. That's what happened when psychologists answered the difficult question: Does Ritalin help children with ADHD?

G. Scientific Method: Experiment

How do researchers reduce error and bias?

There have been many different treatments, including diets, vitamins, drugs, and behavior therapy, that claimed to help children with ADHD, such as Dusty (right photo). To discover which of these claims were valid, researchers followed a general approach called the scientific method.

The *scientific method* is an approach of gathering information and answering questions so that errors and biases are minimized.

Remember that information from surveys, case studies, and testimonials has considerable potential for error and bias. Remember too that information from correlations can suggest, but not pinpoint, cause-and-effect relationships. One way to both reduce error

It takes 7 rules to do an experiment on ADHD.

and bias and identify cause-and-effect relationships is to do an experiment.

An *experiment* is a method of identifying cause-and-effect relationships by following a set of rules and guidelines that minimize the possibility of error, bias, and chance occurrences.

An experiment, which is an example of using the scientific method, is the most powerful method for finding what causes what. We will divide an experiment into seven rules that are intended to reduce error and bias and identify the cause of an effect.

Why seven rules?

Some researchers and parents claimed that diets without sugar, artificial colors, and additives reduced ADHD symptoms, but most of these claims proved false because the rules to reduce error had not been followed (Kinsbourne, 1994). Here are seven rules that reduce error and bias and that researchers follow when conducting an experiment.

Rule 1: **Ask**

Every experiment begins with one or more specific questions that are changed into specific hypotheses.

A *hypothesis* is an educated guess about some phenomenon and is stated in precise, concrete language to rule out any confusion or error in the meaning of its terms.

Hypothesis:

Ritalin will decrease negative classroom behaviors of children diagnosed with ADHD.

Researchers develop different hypotheses based on their own observations or previous research findings. Following this first rule, researchers change the general question—Does Ritalin help children with ADHD?—into a very concrete hypothesis: Ritalin will decrease the negative classroom behaviors of children with ADHD.

Rule 2: **Identify**

After researchers have made their hypothesis, they identify a treatment that will be administered to the subjects. This treatment is called the independent variable.

The *independent variable* is a treatment or something that the researcher controls or manipulates.

The independent variable may be a single treatment, such as a single drug dose, or various levels of the same treatment, such as different doses of the same drug.

In our experiment, the independent variable is administering three different doses of Ritalin and a placebo.

After researchers choose the treatment, they next identify the behavior(s) of the subjects, called the dependent variable, that will be used to measure the effects of the treatment.

Ritalin

Independent Variable:

Drug treatment

Dependent Variable:

Child's negative classroom behaviors

The *dependent variable* is one or more of the subjects' behaviors that are used to measure the potential effects of the treatment or independent variable.

The dependent variable, so called because it is dependent on the treatment, can include a wide range of behaviors, such as observable responses, self-reports of cognitive processes, or recordings of physiological responses from the body or brain. In the present experiment, the dependent variable is the teacher's rating of the child's disruptive classroom behaviors.

Rule 3: **Choose**

After researchers identify the independent and dependent variables, they next choose the subjects for the experiment. Researchers want to choose participants who are representative of the entire group or population, and they do this through a process called random selection.

Random selection means that each participant in a sample population has an equal chance of being selected for the experiment.

Random Selection

Examples of random selection include the way lottery numbers are drawn and selecting people using a random number table.

The reason researchers randomly select participants is to avoid any potential error or bias that may come from their knowingly or unknowingly wanting to choose the "best" subjects for their experiment.

Rule 4: Assign

After randomly choosing the subjects, researchers then randomly assign participants to different groups, either an experimental group or a control group.

Experimental Group

The *experimental group* is composed of those who receive the treatment.

The *control group* is composed of participants who undergo all the same procedures as the experimental participants except that the control participants do not receive the treatment.

Control Group

In this study, some of the children are assigned to the experimental group and receive Ritalin; the other children are assigned to the control group and receive a similar-looking pill that is a placebo.

The reason participants are randomly assigned to either the experimental or control group is to take into account or control for other factors or traits, such as intelligence, social class, economic level, age, personality variables, sex, and genetic differences. Randomly assigning participants reduces the chances that these factors will bias the results.

Rule 5: Manipulate

After assigning participants to experimental and control groups, researchers manipulate the independent variable by administering the treatment (or one level of the treatment) to the experimental group. Researchers give the same conditions to the control group but give them a different level of the treatment, no treatment, or a placebo.

For example, in this study, researchers give the experimental group a pill containing Ritalin, while the control group receives a placebo. Drugs and placebos are given with special care in a double-blind procedure.

A *double-blind procedure* means that neither participants nor researchers know which group is receiving which treatment.

> Double-blind procedure is an important research tool.

A double-blind procedure is essential in drug research to control for self-fulfilling prophecies, placebo effects (see p. 31), or possible influences or biases of the experimenters.

Rule 6: Measure

By manipulating the treatment so that the experimental group receives a different treatment than the control group, researchers are able to measure how the independent variable (treatment) affects those behaviors that have been selected as the dependent variables.

For example, the hypothesis in this study is: Ritalin will decrease negative classroom behaviors of children with ADHD. Researchers observe whether treatment (Ritalin or placebo) changes negative behaviors of ADHD children in the classroom. Negative behaviors, whose frequencies are counted for 30-minute periods, include: getting out of seat, engaging in destructive behavior, disturbing others, swearing, teasing, and not following instructions. As the graph below indicates, ADHD children given placebos show 9.8 negative behaviors per 30-minute period, compared with 4.8 for the children given Ritalin (Pelham et al., 1985). Thus, compared to placebos, Ritalin decreases negative behaviors

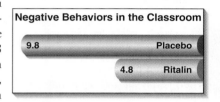

Negative Behaviors in the Classroom

9.8   Placebo

4.8   Ritalin

in ADHD children in the classroom. However, to be absolutely sure, researchers must analyze the results more carefully by using statistical procedures.

Rule 7: Analyze

Although there appears to be a large decrease in negative behaviors, from 9.8 for the placebo control group to 4.8 for the Ritalin experimental group, researchers must analyze the size of these differences with statistical procedures.

Statistical procedures are used to determine whether differences observed in dependent variables (behaviors) are due to independent variables (treatment) or to error or chance occurrence.

Using statistical procedures, which are described in Appendix A, researchers compared the effect of the placebo with that of Ritalin on negative behaviors. They concluded

> Statistical analysis shows if the result occurred by chance.

that, compared with the placebo, Ritalin significantly reduced negative behaviors. In this case, significantly means there was a 95% likelihood that it was Ritalin and not some error or chance occurrence that decreased negative behaviors (Pelham et al., 1985).

These significant findings support the hypothesis that Ritalin decreases negative classroom behaviors of children with ADHD.

Conclusion

What does an experiment tell you?

By following these seven rules for conducting an experiment, researchers reduced the chances that error or bias would distort the major finding, which was that Ritalin reduced negative behaviors of children in the classroom. This example shows that when an experiment is run according to these seven rules, it is a much more powerful method for identifying cause-and-effect relationships than are surveys, testimonials, correlations, or case studies. Even so, researchers usually repeat experiments many times before being confident that the answers they found were correct. That's why a newly reported finding, no matter how significant, is usually regarded as questionable until other researchers have been able to repeat the experiment and replicate the finding.

After the Concept Review, we'll discuss why, after 20 years of research, there are still controversies surrounding ADHD.

✔ Concept Review

1. If psychologists obtain information through an in-depth analysis of the thoughts, beliefs, or behaviors of a single person, this method is called a (a)_____. If a method is used that minimizes error and identifies cause-and-effect relationships, it is called an (b)_____. If individuals are asked a fixed set of questions, it is called a (c)_____. If individuals make statements in support of a particular viewpoint on the basis of personal experience, it is called a (d)_____.

2. Some intervention that is designed to look like a medical treatment but that has no actual medical effect is called a (a)_____. A change in a patient's illness that is due to a supposed treatment and not to any medical therapy is called a (b)_____.

3. Psychologists describe the association, relationship, or linkage among two or more events as a (a)_____. They describe the strength of such a relationship by a number called the (b)_____, which may vary from −1.00 to +1.00. If an increase in one event is associated with an increase in a second event, this relationship is called a (c)_____ correlation. If an increase in one event is associated with a decrease in a second event, this relationship is called a (d)_____ correlation. Finding that two or more events are linked together does not prove that one event (e)_____ the other.

4. Psychologists use at least five common research techniques. They can ask subjects oral or written questions by using (a)_____ and (b)_____. They might ask subjects to answer questions on established tests, which are called (c)_____ tests. They might observe and measure behaviors, brains, or genes with the least error and bias by using a controlled environment, called a (d)_____. They could study some question or problem in animals by developing an (e)_____ that closely approximates the human condition.

5. If psychologists study individuals in their real-life environments, without trying to control the situation, they are using a (a)_____ setting. A variation of this approach is to study a single individual in great depth in his or her own environment, which is called a (b)_____. If psychologists study individuals under carefully controlled conditions, they are using a (c)_____ setting.

Basal ganglia

6. One example of searching for cause-and-effect relationships by following the rules and guidelines of the scientific method is to answer questions by conducting an _____, which has seven rules.

7. If you are conducting an experiment, you should follow 7 rules. Rule 1 is to *ask* specific questions in very concrete terms: these statements are called (a)_____.

Ritalin

Rule 2 is to *identify* the treatment, which is called the (b)_____, and to choose the behaviors or responses that will be observed to judge the effectiveness of the treatment. These behaviors or responses are called the (c)_____.

Rule 3 is to *choose* subjects through a process called (d)_____, which gives everyone in a sample population an equal chance of being selected.

Rule 4 is to *assign* subjects to different groups by random selection. The group that will receive the treatment is called the (e)_____, and the group that undergoes everything but the treatment is called the (f)_____.

Rule 5 is to *manipulate* the (g)_____ by administering it to the experimental group but not the control group.

Placebo

Rule 6 is to *measure* the effects of the independent variable on behaviors that have been selected as the (h)_____.

Rule 7 is to *analyze* the difference between the experimental and control groups by using (i)_____.

8. Researchers usually repeat experiments many times to make sure that their _____ are correct.

Answers: *1. (a) case study, (b) experiment, (c) survey, (d) testimonial; 2. (a) placebo, (b) placebo effect; 3. (a) correlation, (b) correlation coefficient, (c) positive, (d) negative, (e) causes; 4. (a) questionnaires, (b) interviews, (c) standardized, (d) laboratory experiment, (e) animal model; 5. (a) naturalistic, (b) case study, (c) laboratory; 6. experiment; 7. (a) hypotheses, (b) independent variable, (c) dependent variable, (d) random selection, (e) experimental group, (f) control group, (g) independent variable, (h) dependent variables, (i) statistical procedures; 8. answers or results*

Why do controversies still remain?

You might ask why, after 35 years of research, there are still controversies over how best to diagnose and treat ADHD. Although researchers have reached the first goal of psychology, which is to describe ADHD, they have not reached the second goal, which is to explain the causes of ADHD, which will lead to better treatment. Explaining the causes of ADHD means combining biological, psychological, behavioral, and cultural factors, which is a slow process. We'll review the current controversies involving ADHD to show how far researchers have come and how far they have to go.

Controversy: Diagnosis

The first controversy involves the accuracy and reliability of how ADHD is diagnosed. In the United States, about 3 to 5 million school-age children are diagnosed with ADHD, with 4 to 5 times as many boys having ADHD as girls (Root & Resnick, 2003).

The controversy arises from the fact that the current diagnosis of ADHD is based solely on reported and observed behavioral symptoms rather than on medical or laboratory tests. Because the behavioral symptoms vary in severity (more or less), setting (home versus school), and culture (fewer Asian American children than African American), there is the potential for misdiagnosis (Root & Resnick, 2003). For example, parents or teachers may label a child as having ADHD if the child is overwhelmed by the demands of school and

There are three big controversies surrounding ADHD.

acts outgoing, rambunctious, or difficult to discipline (Sinja, 2001). Because of diagnostic difficulties, pediatricians and family doctors were recently given the following guidelines for diagnosing ADHD: Children should be 6–12 years old, show six or more symptoms of inattention and hyperactivity, have symptoms for at least six months, and symptoms should occur in both home and school (J. E. Allen, 2000). The purpose of the guidelines is to prevent the merely rambunctious child from being diagnosed with ADHD and given unnecessary drugs.

The controversy regarding the diagnosis of ADHD will continue until the development of medical tests that confirm the behavioral symptoms, which are not always clear-cut (Root & Resnick, 2003).

Controversy: Treatment

The second controversy involves how best to treat ADHD. As we discussed earlier (p. 30), researchers found that using certain diets that avoid artificial flavors and colors, preservatives, artificial sweeteners, and sugars did little to reduce or stop hyperactive behaviors (Kinsbourne, 1994). More recently, a group of experts in the treatment of ADHD have compared nondrug and drug treatments for ADHD and made the following recommendations.

NONDRUG, BEHAVIORAL TREATMENT

There is a nondrug behavioral treatment program that involves changing or modifying undesirable behaviors by using learning principles (p. 232). Such a behavioral treatment program, which requires considerable efforts by the parents, has been effective in reducing ADHD symptoms (Root & Resnick, 2003).

The group of experts in the treatment of ADHD recommended that a behavioral treatment program be used for preschool-age children with ADHD, for milder forms of ADHD, for children who also have deficits in social skills, and when the family prefers the nondrug, behavioral treatment.

Use of Ritalin 1993–2000 600% Increase

COMBINED DRUG AND BEHAVIORAL TREATMENT

The group of experts recommended a combination of Ritalin (methylphenidate) and behavioral treatment when children have more severe ADHD, when children also have significant aggression or serious problems in school, when ADHD symptoms cause a major disruption in home or school, or when there is need for a rapid response to severe ADHD symptoms (Conners et al., 2001). The use of Ritalin has risen 600% since 1993 (R. Thomas, 2000).

One reason Ritalin has grown 600% in usage since 1993 is that it decreases hyperactivity and increases a child's ability to pay attention. Although Ritalin makes the child easier to manage at home and in school, its side effects include problems with sleeping, eating, and damping of emotional feelings (Sinha, 2001). However, there are numerous cases of children who were diagnosed with ADHD and given Ritalin but showed no improvement because they had been misdiagnosed and actually had other kinds of learning problems (B. Murray, 1997). Thus, the use of Ritalin and/or behavioral treatment for ADHD depends on the severity of the symptoms and concerns of teachers and parents.

Controversy: Long-Term Effects

The third controversy involves the long-term effects of ADHD. Many children diagnosed and treated for ADHD have now reached their early twenties. Researchers found that even when ADHD children are treated with Ritalin, between 30 and 70% continue to have problems as adolescents and adults (Barkley et al., 2002). They are less likely to graduate from high school or attend college (only 1% finish college) and are at risk for showing antisocial behaviors, such as fighting, trouble with the law, or drug abuse (Wilens et al., 1997). Because ADHD

is a continuing problem, researchers encourage parents and teachers to include behavioral programs such as setting goals, establishing rules, and rewarding performance to help those with ADHD deal with adolescence and adulthood (Jensen, 1999). The controversies surrounding ADHD point out the difficulties in understanding, explaining, and treating complex human problems, such as ADHD.

Using Ritalin to treat young children also raises questions about the rights of subjects, both human and animals, in research.

I. Application: Research Concerns

Concerns about Being a Subject

What's it like to be a subject?

Each time you hear about a new research finding—such as a drug to control weight or treat depression, or the discovery of a gene related to happiness, or ways to improve memory—you rarely think about the treatment of subjects, humans and animals, used in these experiments.

For example, if you were asked to volunteer to be a participant, you would certainly be concerned about whether someone has checked to ensure that the experiment is safe, that there are safeguards to protect you from potential psychological or physical harm, and that you won't be unfairly deceived or made to feel foolish. These are all real concerns, and we'll answer each one in turn.

Additionally, a separate and controversial question concerns the use of animals in research. We'll answer this question in some detail since there are many misconceptions about the use and misuse of animals in research.

We'll begin by considering the concerns of human subjects.

Code of Ethics

If you are a college student, there is a good possibility that you will be asked to participate in a psychology experiment. If you are considering becoming a subject, you may wonder what kinds of safeguards are used to protect subjects' rights and privacy.

The American Psychological Association has published a code of ethics and conduct for psychologists to follow when doing research, counseling, teaching, and related activities (American Psychological Association, 1992). This code of ethics spells out the responsibilities of psychologists and the rights of participants.

Besides having to follow a code of ethics, psychologists must submit the details of their research programs, especially those with the potential for causing psychological or physical harm, to university and/or federal research committees (institutional review boards). The job of these research committees is to protect the participants (human or animal) by carefully checking the proposed experiments for any harmful procedures (Azar, 2002).

Are my rights protected?

Experiments are not approved unless any potentially damaging effects can be eliminated or counteracted. Counteracting potentially harmful effects is usually done by thoroughly describing the experiment, a process called debriefing.

Debriefing includes explaining the purpose and method of the experiment, asking the participants their feelings about being participants in the experiment, and helping the participants deal with possible doubts or guilt that arise from their behaviors in the experiment.

During the debriefing sessions, researchers will answer any questions or discuss any problems that participants may have. The purpose of debriefing is to make sure that participants have been treated fairly and have no lingering psychological or physical concerns or worries that come from participating in an experiment (Gurman, 1994).

Role of Deception

When recruiting participants for their experiments, psychologists usually give the experiments titles, such as "Study of eyewitness testimony" or "Effects of alcohol on memory." The reason for using such general titles is that researchers do not want to create specific expectations that may bias how potential participants will behave. It is well known that an experiment's results may be biased by a number of factors: by participants' expectations of how they should behave, by their unknowingly behaving according to self-fulfilling prophecies, or by their efforts to make themselves look good or to please the experimenter.

One way that researchers control for participants' expectations is to use bogus procedures or instructions that prevent participants from learning the experiment's true purpose. However, before researchers can use bogus or deceptive methodology, they must satisfy

Will they try to trick or deceive me?

the American Psychological Association's (1992) code of ethics. For example, researchers must justify the deceptive techniques by the scientific, educational, or applied value of the study and by giving participants a sufficient explanation of the study as soon as possible (Fisher & Fryberg, 1994).

Another way to avoid bias from participants' expectations is to keep both the researcher and participants in the dark about the experiment's true purpose by using a double-blind procedure. As discussed earlier (p. 37), a double-blind procedure means that neither participants nor researchers are aware of the experiment's treatment or purpose.

Thus, researchers must be careful not to reveal too many details about their experiments lest they bias how potential subjects may behave.

How many animals are used in research?

An estimated 18 to 22 million animals are used each year in biomedical research, which includes the fields of psychology, biology, medicine, and pharmaceuticals (Mukerjee, 1997). Although these numbers seem large, they are small in comparison to the 5 billion chickens eaten annually by citizens in the United States. However, it is the use of animals in research that has generated the most concern and debate (Rowan, 1997).

In the field of psychology, about 85% of the nonhuman animals used by researchers are rats and mice, while 10% are cats, dogs, monkeys, and birds (Mukerjee, 1997). We'll examine the justification for using animals in research and how their rights are protected.

Are research animals mistreated?

You may have seen a disturbing photo or heard about a laboratory animal being mistreated (Barnard & Kaufman, 1997). The fact is that, of the millions of animals used in research, only a few cases of animal mistreatment have been confirmed. That is because scientists know that proper care and treatment of their laboratory animals are vital to the success of their research. To abolish the use of all laboratory animals because of one or two isolated cases of mistreatment would be like abolishing all medical practice because of isolated cases of malpractice. Instead, researchers suggest balancing the rights of animals with the needs for advancing the medical, physiological, and psychological health of humans (Holden, 2000).

Is the use of animals justified?

Adrian Morrison, director of the National Institute of Mental Health's Program for Animal Research Issues, recently wrote,

"Because I do experimental surgery, I go through a soul-searching every couple of months, asking myself whether I really want to continue working on cats. The answer is always yes because I know that there is no other way for medicine to progress but through animal experimentation and that basic research ultimately leads to unforeseen benefits" (Morrison, 1993).

According to Frederick King, the former chair of the American Psychological Association's Committee on Animal Research and Experimentation, animal research has resulted in major medical advances, the discovery of treatments for human diseases, and a better understanding of human disorders (F. A. King et al., 1988).

In the field of psychology, animal research and animal models have led to a better understanding of how stress affects one's psychological and physical health, mechanisms underlying learning and memory, and effects of sensory deprivation on development, to mention but a few (Mukerjee, 1997).

Researchers are currently using animals to study epilepsy, Alzheimer's disease, fetal alcohol syndrome, schizophrenia, AIDS, and transplantation of brain tissue, none of which is possible with human subjects.

Who checks on the use of animals in research?

Numerous government and university regulations ensure the proper care and humane treatment of laboratory animals. For example, the U.S. Department of Agriculture conducts periodic inspections of all animal research facilities to ensure proper housing and to oversee experimental procedures that might cause pain or distress. Universities hire veterinarians to regularly monitor the care and treatment of laboratory animals. Finally, universities have animal subject committees with authority to decide whether sufficient justification exists for using animals in specific research projects (Mukerjee, 1997).

How do we strike a balance?

One of the basic issues in animal research is how to strike the right balance between animal rights and research needs (Barnard & Kaufman, 1997). Based on past, present, and potential future benefits of animal research, many experts in the scientific, medical, and mental health communities believe that the conscientious and responsible use of animals in research is justified and should continue. This is especially true in light of recent rules that regulate the safe and humane treatment of animals kept in laboratories or used in research (Botting & Morrison, 1997; Holden, 2000).

The small print in the poster reads, "Without animal research, we couldn't have put an end to polio, smallpox, rubella and diphtheria. Now, some would like to put an end to animal research. Obviously, they don't have cancer, heart disease or AIDS."

Summary Test

A. ANSWERING QUESTIONS

1. Psychologists use at least three methods to answer questions or obtain information. An in-depth analysis of a single person's thoughts and behaviors is called a (a)_____. One advantage of this method is that researchers obtain detailed information about a person, but one disadvantage is that such information may not apply to others. Asking a large number of individuals a fixed set of questions is called a (b)_____. Gathering information in a controlled laboratory setting is called an (c)_____.

B. SURVEYS

2. Measuring the attitudes, beliefs, and behaviors of a large sample of individuals by asking a set of questions is called a _____. One advantage of this method is that psychologists can quickly and efficiently collect information about a large number of people. One disadvantage is that people may answer in a way that they think is more socially acceptable.

C. CASE STUDY

3. A statement that supports a particular viewpoint and is based on a person's own experience is called a (a)_____, which has several potential sources of error and bias. First, strongly held personal beliefs may bias an individual's (b)_____ of events. Second, believing strongly that something will happen and then unknowingly acting in such a way as to make that something occur is a source of error called (c)_____. This source of error is one of the major reasons that people believe that their (d)_____ are true.

D. CULTURAL DIVERSITY: USE OF PLACEBOS

4. Some intervention that resembles a medical therapy but that, in fact, has no medical effects is called a (a)_____. If a person reports an improvement in some medical condition that is due to a supposed treatment rather than some medical therapy, that is called a (b)_____. One reason people around the world believe in placebos is that people give (c)_____ to their effectiveness.

E. CORRELATION

5. If two or more events are associated or linked together, they are said to be (a)_____. The strength of this association is indicated by a number called the (b)_____, which has a range from −1.00 to +1.00.

6. If there were a perfect association between two events—for example, when one increased, the other did also—this would be called a (a)_____. If an increase in one event is usually, but not always, accompanied by an increase in a second event, this would be called a (b)_____. If an increase in one event is always accompanied by a decrease in a second event, this is called a (c)_____. If an increase in one event is usually, but not always, accompanied by a decrease in a second event, this is called a (d)_____.

7. Although a correlation indicates that two or more events are occurring in some pattern, a correlation does not identify which event may (a)_____ the other(s). Although correlations do not identify cause-and-effect relationships, they do provide (b)_____ as to where to look for causes and they help to (c)_____ behavior.

F. DECISIONS ABOUT DOING RESEARCH

8. Psychologists may answer some question by using one or more of five commonly used research techniques. Asking questions about people's attitudes and behaviors, usually in a one-on-one situation, is using an (a)_____. Asking subjects to read a list of questions and indicate a specific answer is using a (b)_____. Asking subjects to complete established tests that measure personality, intelligence, or other behaviors is using (c)_____. If psychologists study subjects' behaviors under carefully controlled conditions that allow manipulation of the treatment, they are conducting a (d)_____. Psychologists can study a problem using animals by developing an (e)_____, which closely approximates the human disease or condition.

Basal ganglia

9. Psychologists conduct research in two common settings. If psychologists obtain information by observing an individual's behaviors in his or her environment, without attempts to control or manipulate the situation, they would be using a _____. The *advantage* of this method is that it gives information that would be difficult to obtain or duplicate in a laboratory. The *disadvantage* of this method is that the psychologists' own beliefs or values may bias their observations and cause them to misinterpret the behaviors under observation.

10. If psychologists study a single individual in considerable depth in his or her own environment, they are using a _____. The *advantage* of this method is that it results in detailed descriptions and insights into many aspects of an individual's life. The *disadvantage* is that the information obtained may be unique and not applicable to others.

11. If psychologists want to study individuals under controlled and systematic conditions, with many of the real-life factors removed, they do the study in a _____. The *advantage* of this setting is that it permits greater control and manipulation of many conditions while ruling out possible contaminating factors. The *disadvantage* of this setting is that it may be too artificial or controlled, so that the results may not necessarily apply to real-life situations.

G. SCIENTIFIC METHOD: EXPERIMENT

12. The scientific method offers a set of rules or guidelines on how to conduct research with a minimum of error or bias. We have divided these guidelines into seven rules. **Rule 1** is to make a statement in precise, concrete terms. Such a statement is called a (a)_____, which researchers often develop based on previous observations or studies. **Rule 2** is to identify the treatment or something the experimenter manipulates, which is called the (b)_____. In addition, the experimenter selects behaviors that are to be used to measure the potential effects of the treatment. These selected behaviors are called the (c)_____, and they may include a wide range of behaviors, such as cognitive processes, observable behaviors, or measurable physiological responses. **Rule 3** is to choose subjects so that each one in a sample has an equal chance of being selected. One procedure for doing so is called (d)_____. **Rule 4** is to assign subjects randomly to one of two groups. The group that will receive the treatment is called the (e)_____, and the group that will undergo everything but the treatment is called the (f)_____. **Rule 5** is to manipulate the (g)_____ by administering it (or one level of it) to the experimental group but not to the control group. The procedure for preventing researchers or subjects from knowing who is getting the

Ritalin

treatment is called the (h)_____. **Rule 6** is to measure the effects of the independent variable on behaviors that have been selected as the (i)_____. **Rule 7** is to analyze differences between behaviors of subjects in the experimental group and those in the control group by using various (j)_____, which determine whether differences were due to the treatment or to chance occurrences. By following these seven rules, researchers reduce the chances that (k)_____ caused their results.

H. RESEARCH FOCUS: ADHD CONTROVERSIES

Use of Ritalin 1993–2000 600% Increase

13. One controversy over ADHD is that, as of this writing, the diagnosis of ADHD is based on (a)_____ observations, which are not always clear-cut, rather than on more reliable (b)_____ tests. Another controversy involves how best to treat ADHD. For more severe ADHD, researchers recommend a combination of (c)_____ and (d)_____ treatment. However, even though Ritalin can decrease hyperactivity in children and increase their ability to pay (e)_____, Ritalin does not necessarily improve reading or social skills and does not necessarily reduce problems occurring during adolescence and adulthood.

I. APPLICATION: RESEARCH CONCERNS

14. One method of counteracting potential harmful effects on experimental subjects is by thoroughly _____ them. This includes explaining the purpose and method of the experiment, asking subjects about their feelings, and helping subjects deal with possible doubts or problems arising from the experiment.

15. The justification for using _____ in research is that it has resulted in major medical advances, treatments for diseases, and understanding of human disorders.

Answers: 1. (a) case study, (b) survey, (c) experiment; 2. survey; 3. (a) testimonial, (b) perceptions, (c) self-fulfilling prophecy, (d) testimonials; 4. (a) placebo, (b) placebo effect, (c) testimonials; 5. (a) correlated, (b) correlation coefficient; 6. (a) perfect positive correlation, (b) positive correlation, (c) perfect negative correlation, (d) negative correlation; 7. (a) cause, (b) clues, (c) predict; 8. (a) interview, (b) questionnaire, (c) standardized tests, (d) laboratory study or experiment, (e) animal model; 9. naturalistic setting; 10. case study; 11. laboratory setting; 12. (a) hypothesis, (b) independent variable, (c) dependent variables, (d) random selection, (e) experimental group, (f) control group, (g) independent variable, (h) double-blind procedure, (i) dependent variables, (j) statistical procedures, (k) error or bias; 13. (a) behavioral, (b) medical or laboratory, (c) Ritalin, (d) behavioral, (e) attention; 14. debriefing; 15. animals

NEWSPAPER ARTICLE

Does Frequent Sex Help Men Live Longer?

by Lawrence K. Altman

Questions

1. Was the original research question to study sex, or was this "sex" finding unexpected?

2. What are the three major methods for answering questions, and which method was used in this study?

3. Does the major finding indicate a cause-and-effect relationship or only a correlation?

4. Why couldn't this study show a cause-and-effect relationship between more sex and living longer?

5. What are the advantage and the disadvantage of this study?

Try these InfoTrac search terms: sex; epidemiology; heart disease; male hormones.

Men who have more orgasms seem to live longer, a statistical study of Welsh villagers in *The British Medical Journal* has found. . . . "Sexual activity seems to have a protective effect on men's health," Dr. George Davey-Smith's team concluded after analyzing death rates of nearly 1,000 men from 45 to 59 in Caerphilly.

Davey-Smith's team assessed the existence of heart disease in the men when they entered the study from 1979 to 1983. After explaining the purpose of their question, they asked the men about the frequency of sexual activity. The answers were put into categories ranging from "never" to "daily." . . . The participants' names were flagged in the British national health service's central registry and the researchers were automatically notified if they died. The death rate was analyzed 10 years after the participants entered the study.

Men who said they had sex twice a week had a risk of dying half that of the less passionate participants who said they had sex once a month, Davey-Smith's team said. . . . Further studies of both sexes are needed to confirm their findings, the authors said.

Two other scientists added a few drops of cold water, cautioning that because of its design (use of surveys), the epidemiological study might not have been able to identify a number of factors that could have inadvertently influenced the findings. One possibility is that the link could be reversed—ill people may be less likely to have sex, according to the critics who commented in the same issue.

The authors said that they had tried to adjust the study's design to account for a factor that might explain the findings—that healthier, fitter men with more healthy life styles engaged in more sex. Even so, they could not explain the differences in risk. Hormonal effects on the body resulting from frequent sex could be among other possible explanations for the findings, Davey-Smith said. (*Source:* New York Times News Service, appeared in *San Diego Union-Tribune,* December 23, 1997)

SUGGESTED ANSWERS

1. The original purpose of this study was to assess heart disease in men. However, in answering the original research question, researchers found another interesting link between sexual activity and length of life, which raised new questions.

2. The three major methods for answering questions are survey, case study, and experiment. In this study, researchers asked men questions about their health and sexual activity, so this study primarily used the survey method.

3. Surveys cannot show cause-and-effect relationships but only associations or correlations between events: men who had sex more often lived longer than men who had sex less often.

4. To show a cause-and-effect relationship, this study must have been designed as an experiment in which an experimental group got one treatment (more sex) while a control group got no or different treatment (less sex). For ethical reasons, such an experiment could not be conducted on humans, so it would be difficult to demonstrate this cause-and-effect relationship.

5. The advantage of this survey study is that it suggests an unexpected cause or explanation of why men live longer (having more sex). One disadvantage of this survey study is that it cannot identify cause-and-effect relationships because many other factors (hormones, different lifestyles) cannot be ruled out.

Links to Learning

LEARNING ACTIVITIES

- **POWERSTUDY CD-ROM 2.0**
  by Tom Doyle and Rod Plotnik
  Check out the "Psychology & Science" SuperModule (disk 1) on PowerStudy. This is a completely self-paced module that is fully narrated. Don't want the narration? It is easy to turn off! This module includes:
  - Videos—Imbedded videos discuss the definition, treatment, behaviors, and possible overdiagnosis of ADHD.
  - Interactive surveys, an entire section on cultural diversity, an explanation of correlation, and an ADHD diagnosis section where you can become the therapist. You will also find numerous drag and drop exercises to help you remember the difference between methods of research and decide which is best for different circumstances.
  - A test of your knowledge using an interactive version of the Summary Test on pages 42 and 43. Also access related quizzes—true/false, multiple choice, and matching.
  - An interactive version of the Critical Thinking exercise "Does Frequent Sex Help Men Live Longer?" on page 44.
  - Key terms, a chapter outline including chapter abstract, and a list of hotlinked Web sites that correlate to this module.

- **SELF-STUDY ASSESSMENT**
  Want help studying? For your customized Study Plan go to **http://psychology.wadsworth.com/plotnik7e/**. This program will automatically generate pretests and posttests to help you determine what concepts you have mastered and what concepts you still need work on.

- **STUDY GUIDE and WEBTUTOR**
  Check the corresponding module in your Study Guide for effective student tips and help learning the material presented.

- **INFOTRAC COLLEGE EDITION ONLINE LIBRARY**
  To find interesting and relevant articles go to **http://www.infotrac-college.com**, use your password, and then type in search terms such as the ones listed below.

  Placebos   Attention-deficit/hyperactivity disorder
  Animal research   Sex and longevity

STUDY QUESTIONS

Use InfoTrac to search for topics mentioned in the following questions (e.g., caffeine, research questions, scientific method).

*A. **Answering Questions**—Which method would you use to find out if caffeine improves memory? (**Suggested answer page 619**)

B. **Surveys**—How believable is a recent survey that reported that people never lie to their best friends?

C. **Case Study**—Why do some people put more faith in testimonials than in proven research?

*D. **Cultural Diversity: Use of Placebos**—Why do Americans think it strange that Asians use rhino horn as medicine? (**Suggested answer page 620**)

E. **Correlation**—How would you explain the positive correlation (0.60) researchers found between drinking coffee and being sexually active after age 60?

*F. **Decisions about Doing Research**—Which research techniques and settings would you use to study mental problems in the homeless? (**Suggested answer page 620**)

G. **Scientific Method: Experiment**—How would you determine whether taking vitamin B reduces stress?

H. **Research Focus: ADHD Controversies**—If you had a child who might have ADHD, what would you do?

I. **Application: Research Concerns**—What concerns might a student have about volunteering to be a subject in an experiment?

*These questions are answered in Appendix B.

Module 3: Brain's Building Blocks

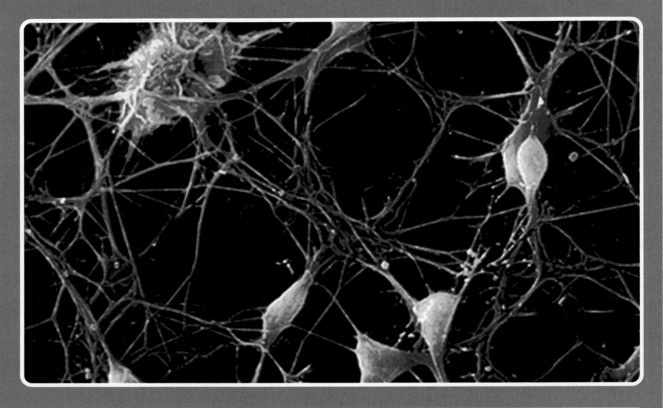

PowerStudy 2.0™
Complete Module

Losing One's Mind

Why does 71-year-old Ina think the baby is hers?

Her children had always called their mother, Ina, "the Rock of Gibraltar." Ina could fix the plumbing, hang wallpaper, and prepare a full dinner from scratch every night, while keeping her six children out of trouble. She could swim faster than anyone, she wanted to be a basketball player, and her late husband called her the most beautiful woman he had ever seen.

But that was before she started to forget things and repeat herself, which could just be part of getting old. But how to explain her mopping the kitchen floor at 2:00 in the morning and refusing to go to bed? Or wearing the same dirty clothes day after day, something she had never done in her entire life? Or being confused at housework? Or thinking that her granddaughter (right photo) is her own child?

Because Ina had always been so healthy, her six grown children thought she must have suffered a stroke or be depressed. When they took Ina in for a checkup, a neurologist confirmed their worst fears. Ina had Alzheimer's (*ALTS-hi-mers*) disease.

In 10% of the cases, *Alzheimer's disease* begins after age 50, but in 90% of the cases, it begins after age 65. Its initial symptoms are problems with memory, such as forgetting and repeating things, getting lost, and being mildly confused. There are also cognitive deficits, such as problems with language, difficulties in recognizing objects, and inability to plan and organize tasks. Over a period of five to ten years, these symptoms worsen and result in profound memory loss, lack of recognition of family and friends, deterioration in personality, and emotional outbursts. There is widespread damage to the brain, especially the hippocampus, which is involved in memory. At present, there is no cure for Alzheimer's, which is always fatal (American Psychiatric Association, 2000).

In the United States, Alzheimer's is the fourth leading cause of death among adults. In 2002, approximately 5 million people—or 5% of adults over age 65—had Alzheimer's disease, and the number of patients is projected to rise dramatically in the coming decades (graph on right) as people are expected to live longer (Cowley, 2002).

Ina's condition worsened through the coming months. She had trouble completing even the simplest tasks, and the day after having a big Thanksgiving celebration with her family, she asked where she had spent the holiday. At times, she recognized her grown children; at other times, she thought they were her cousins. Ina must now be watched almost every minute so that she does not hurt herself or wander off and get lost (adapted from *Newsweek*, December 18, 1989).

She was the family's "Rock of Gibraltar" until she developed Alzheimer's.

For Ina, the worst is yet to come. Her memory will totally disintegrate, she will be completely bedridden, and she will not know who she is or recognize the family she has lovingly raised. When she dies—for Alzheimer's has, at present, no cure—Ina will have lost her memory, her wonderful personality, and all signs of humanity.

Diagnosis and Causes

In Ina's case as well as all cases of individuals with memory and cognitive difficulties, Alzheimer's is diagnosed by identifying a combination of behavioral symptoms and by eliminating other physical problems. Recently, researchers were successful in diagnosing Alzheimer's by injecting chemical markers and identifying brain damage from pictures of living brains (PET scans, p. 71) (Shoghi-Jadid et al., 2002).

Researchers now believe they are very close to figuring out the causes of Alzheimer's disease, which involve genetic, neurological, and possible environmental factors (Bower, 2002b). For example, Alzheimer's incidence is three times higher among individuals who have one parent with Alzheimer's and five times higher if both parents have the disease (Tanzi, 2000). Researchers have also identified several chemicals (proteins and peptides) that occur naturally in all brains but, for some reason, begin to multiply and are believed to cause Alzheimer's. These chemicals seem to act like glue that eventually destroys brain cells (Hardy & Selkoe, 2002). With these new leads, researchers are optimistic about finding the causes of and developing treatments for Alzheimer's. New treatments are needed because current drugs are only moderately effective and short acting in treating early symptoms of Alzheimer's disease (Wilkinson & Muray, 2001).

Dementia on the rise
Alzheimer's patients in the U.S.

Millions: 10.2 (2050), 3.7 (1990)
Years: 1990, 2010, 2030, 2050 (projection)

What's Coming

The reason Alzheimer's disease eventually destroyed Ina's memory, personality, and humanity is that this disease gradually destroys the building blocks that form the brain's informational network. We'll explain the two groups of brain cells—glial cells and neurons—that make up this network. We'll discuss how the cells in one group—neurons—have a remarkable ability to receive and send information. You'll discover how brain cells communicate with chemicals that have the ability to start or stop the flow of information. Finally, we'll explain an experimental treatment of implanting neurons to treat brain diseases. We'll use the story of Ina and Alzheimer's disease to illustrate the brain's building blocks.

A. Overview: Human Brain

As Alzheimer's disease slowly destroys Ina's brain, she is also slowly losing her mind. In Ina's case, Alzheimer's disease has progressed to the point that she can no longer recognize her own children or remember her family gathering on Thanksgiving day.

We'll use Ina's brain and her current problems with Alzheimer's disease to answer four related questions: Why isn't the brain a nose? What's in the brain? Can a brain grow new neurons? Can you take a picture of the mind?

Development of the Brain

Why isn't the brain a nose?

The fact that your brain does not develop into a nose is because of instructions contained in your genes.

Genes are chains of chemicals that are arranged like rungs on a twisting ladder (right figure). There are about 30,000 genes that contain chemical instructions that equal about 300,000 pages of written instructions (N. Wade, 2003a). The chemical instructions in the genes program the development of millions of individual parts into a complex body and brain.

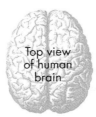

Chemical instructions

An amazing feature of the 30,000 genes is that they are contained in a fertilized egg, which is a single cell about the size of a grain of sand. We'll explain more about the genes and their chemical instructions in the next module (p. 68).

In the brain's early stages of development, it looks nothing like the final product. For example, the figure below looks more like some strange animal than what it really is, a six-week-old human embryo with a developing brain.

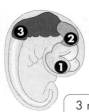

3 major divisions of 6-week-old brain

SIX-WEEK-OLD BRAIN. This drawing represents a greatly enlarged six-week-old human embryo. The 3 labeled areas (in 3 colors) will eventually develop into the 3 major divisions of the mature human brain that is shown below.

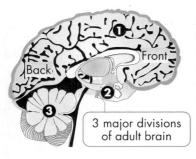

3 major divisions of adult brain

MATURE BRAIN. The 3 labeled areas represent the 3 major divisions of the mature brain that we'll discuss in the next module. The mature human brain (side view) weighs almost 3 pounds and contains about 1 trillion cells (Fischbach, 1992).

In the case of Ina, who developed Alzheimer's disease, researchers think that some of her genetic instructions were faulty. The faulty instructions resulted in an abnormal buildup in the brain of a gluelike substance that gradually destroys brain cells (Cowley, 2000b). Next, we'll explain the two different kinds of brain cells and which ones are destroyed by Alzheimer's disease.

Structure of the Brain

What's in your brain?

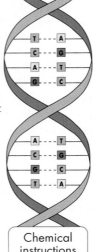

Top view of human brain

On the left is a top view of a human brain. It is shaped like a small wrinkled melon, weighs about 1,350 grams (less than 3 pounds), has a pinkish-white color, and has the consistency of firm Jell-O. Your brain is fueled by sugar (glucose) and has about 1 trillion cells that can be divided into two groups—glial cells and neurons.

GLIAL CELLS. The most numerous brain cells, about 900 billion, are called glial (*GLEE-all*) cells.

Glial cells have at least three functions: providing scaffolding to guide the growth of developing neurons and support mature neurons; wrapping around neurons to form a kind of insulation to prevent interference from other electrical signals; and releasing chemicals that influence a neuron's growth and function (Fields & Stevens-Graham, 2002).

Glial cell

A star-shaped glial cell (astrocyte) is shown above. Glial cells grow throughout one's lifetime. If something causes the uncontrolled growth of glial cells, the result is brain cancer. Alzheimer's disease does not usually destroy glial cells, but it does destroy the second kind of brain cells, which are called neurons.

NEURONS. The second group of brain cells, which number about 100 billion, are called neurons (*NER-ons*); one is shown on the right.

A *neuron* is a brain cell with two specialized extensions. One extension is for receiving electrical signals, and a second, longer extension is for transmitting electrical signals.

Depending upon their size, neurons receive and transmit electrical signals at speeds of up to 200 miles per hour over distances from a fraction of an inch to over 3 feet, such as from your toe to your spinal cord.

Neurons form a vast, miniaturized informational network that allows us to receive sensory information, control muscle movement, regulate digestion, secrete hormones, and engage in complex mental processes such as thinking, imagining, dreaming, and remembering.

Neuron

Ina's brain was constructed from two kinds of building blocks—glial cells and neurons. However, it is the neurons that Alzheimer's disease gradually destroys; the result is that Ina's brain is losing its ability to transmit information, causing memory and cognitive difficulties. Why neurons do not usually repair or replace themselves is our next topic.

Can a brain grow new neurons?

If you had a bird's brain, you could grow new neurons every spring. A male canary learns to sing a breeding song in the spring, but when breeding season is over, the ability to sing the song disappears. However, come next spring, an adult canary's brain begins growing about 20,000 new neurons a day, and, during this short period, the bird relearns the breeding song. These new neurons result in a 50% or more increase in two areas of the canary's brain (left figure) that control singing (G. Miller, 2003). Without a doubt, an adult canary's brain can regularly grow new neurons (Barinaga, 2003a).

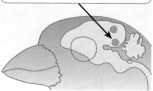

The two red dots show two areas of the mature canary's brain that increase by 50% with the growth of new neurons.

PRIMATE BRAINS. Does the fact that adult canaries as well as adult mice, rats, and other animals can grow new neurons also hold true for adult human brains (Barinaga, 2003a)? Researchers believe that, with few exceptions, the brains of adult primates, such as humans and chimpanzees, develop almost all their neurons at birth and adult brains do not grow new neurons (Kornack & Rakic, 2001).

The few exceptions to the finding that new neurons do not grow in adult brains were found in two areas of the brain—hippocampus (p. 80) and olfactory bulb (p. 107). Researchers concluded that adult monkey and human brains are capable of growing a relatively limited number of new neurons throughout adulthood and that some of these new neurons play an important role in our continuing ability to learn and remember new things (van Praag et al., 2002).

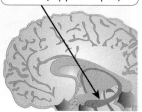

Growth of new neurons is found in this area of mature human brain (hippocampus).

REPAIRING THE BRAIN. Besides having a limited capacity to grow new neurons throughout adulthood, mature human brains also have a limited capacity to replace, rewire, or repair damaged neurons, such as after a stroke, gunshot wound, or blow to the head (Horner & Gage, 2000). For instance, after the brain is accidentally injured, healthy neurons have the ability to send out very short extensions to make some new connections with neurons whose normal connections were damaged. One reason neurons have only a limited capacity to be repaired or rewired after damage is that there is a genetic program that turns off regrowth when neurons become fully grown (McKerracher & Ellezam, 2002). This limited capacity of the adult brain to rewire itself by forming new connections helps explain why people may recover some, but rarely all, of the functions initially lost after brain damage (Gage, 2003).

The reason Alzheimer's disease is so destructive and eventually leads to death is that this disease destroys neurons many times faster than the brain's limited capacity for regrowth, repair, or rewiring. As Alzheimer's destroys Ina's brain, what is happening to her mind?

Can you take a picture of the mind?

As Alzheimer's destroys Ina's brain, she is also losing her mind, which brings us to the mind-body question.

The ***mind-body question*** asks how complex mental activities, such as feeling, thinking, and learning, can be explained by the physical, chemical, and electrical activities of the brain.

Through the centuries, philosophers and scientists have given different answers to the mind-body question, some believing the mind and brain are separate things and others saying the mind and brain are one and the same (Hiltzik, 2002).

For example, Nobel Prize winner and geneticist Francis Crick (2002) believes the mind ***is*** the brain: "You, your joys and your sorrows, your memories and your ambition, your sense of personal identity and free will, are in fact no more than the behavior of a vast assembly of nerve cells and their associated molecules." Although some agree with Crick's answer, that the mind and brain are the same, others reply that mental activities cannot be reduced to the physical activities of the brain (Gold & Stoljar, 1999).

Another answer comes from Nobel Prize winner and neurophysiologist Roger Sperry (1993), who said that the brain is like a coin with two sides. One side consists of physical reactions, such as making chemicals that neurons use for communicating. The other side consists of all of our mental functions, such as thinking, imagining, and deciding. According to Sperry, the brain's chemicals (physical side) influence consciousness and mental activities, which, in turn, influence the production of more or different brain chemicals. There is considerable support for Sperry's idea of continuous interaction between the physical and mental sides (Wakefeld, 2001).

ALZHEIMER'S. In Ina's case, as Alzheimer's disease destroys her brain, she also loses more and more of her mental activities, such as knowing, thinking, and deciding. Researchers can now study a person's mental activities by taking pictures or brain scans of the neural activities going on inside the living brain (brain scans are discussed on pp. 70–71). For example, the top right brain scan shows a great amount of neural activity occurring inside a normal brain (red/yellow indicate most neural activity, blue/green indicate least activity). In comparison, the bottom right brain scan shows relatively little neural activity and thus relatively little mental activity occurring inside an Alzheimer's brain. These kinds of brain scans show that neural activities and mental activities are closely linked, and researchers are studying how these links occur (Gold & Stoljar, 1999).

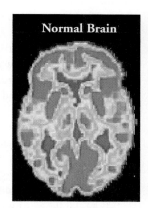

Normal Brain

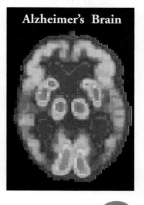

Alzheimer's Brain

Knowing now how important neurons are to your mental and physical functions, we next examine them in more detail.

B. Neurons: Structure & Function

Why could Ina think, move, and talk?

Before Ina developed Alzheimer's disease, she was able to engage in an incredible variety of cognitive and physical behaviors. She was able to think, remember, walk, smile, and speak—all because of the activity of millions of microscopic brain cells called neurons. We'll examine the neuron, which comes in many wondrous shapes and sizes and has only three basic structures—cell body, dendrites, and axon.

> Signals travel away from the cell body, down the axon.

1 The *cell body* (or soma) is a relatively large, egg-shaped structure that provides fuel, manufactures chemicals, and maintains the entire neuron in working order.

In the center of the cell body is a small, oval shape representing the nucleus, which contains genetic instructions (in the form of DNA) for both the manufacture of chemicals and the regulation of the neuron.

2 *Dendrites* (*DEN-drites*) are branchlike extensions that arise from the cell body; they receive signals from other neurons, muscles, or sense organs and pass these signals to the cell body.

At the time of birth, a neuron has few dendrites. After birth, dendrites undergo dramatic growth that accounts for much of the increase in brain size. As dendrites grow, they make connections and form communication networks between neurons and other cells or organs.

3 The *axon* (*AXE-on*) is a single threadlike structure that extends from, and carries signals away from, the cell body to neighboring neurons, organs, or muscles.

Here the axon is indicated by an orange line inside the tube composed of separate gray segments. Axons vary in length from less than a hair's breadth to as long as 3 feet (from your spinal cord to your toes). An axon conducts electrical signals to a neighboring organ (heart), a muscle, or another neuron.

4 The *myelin* (*MY-lin*) *sheath* looks like separate tubelike segments composed of fatty material that wraps around and insulates an axon. The myelin sheath prevents interference from electrical signals generated in adjacent axons.

The axons of most large neurons, including motor neurons, have myelin sheaths. You may have heard the brain described as consisting of gray and white matter. Gray is the color of cell bodies, while white is the color of myelin sheaths.

5 *End bulbs or terminal bulbs* look like tiny bubbles that are located at the extreme ends of the axon's branches. Each end bulb is like a miniature container that stores chemicals called neurotransmitters, which are used to communicate with neighboring cells.

End bulbs reach right up to, but do not physically touch, the surface of a neighboring organ (heart), muscle (head), or another cell body.

6 The *synapse* (*SIN-apse*) is an infinitely small space (20–30 billionths of a meter) that exists between an end bulb and its adjacent body organ (heart), muscles (head), or cell body.

When stimulated by electrical signals from the axon, the end bulbs eject neurotransmitters into the synapse. The neurotransmitters cross the synapse and act like switches to turn adjacent cells on or off. We'll explain this switching process a little later.

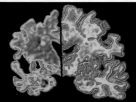

Alzheimer's brain is smaller because it has lost many neurons.

Size of normal brain with all of its neurons intact.

In Alzheimer's disease there is an excessive buildup of gluelike substances, which gradually destroy neurons (Cowley, 2002). In Ina's case, these gluelike substances will destroy more and more of her neurons, causing her brain to actually shrink, as shown by the very deep creases in the Alzheimer's brain (left photo). Researchers are searching for ways to stop the buildup of these gluelike, killer substances.

We have discussed the structure and function of neurons, but it is important not to confuse neurons (in your brain and spinal cord) with nerves (in your body).

Reattaching Limbs

What's unusual about John's arms?

John Thomas was 18 when a farm machine ripped off both of his arms just below his shoulders. Since he was home alone, he had to walk to the farmhouse, kick open the front door, and with a pencil clenched in his teeth, dial the phone for help. When paramedics arrived, he reminded them to get his two arms, which were still stuck in the farm equipment. John was taken to the hospital, where doctors reattached both arms (indicated by red arrows in left photo).

Three months later, John could raise his arms up in the air but could not move them below his elbows. After three years of physical therapy and 15 operations, John could raise both of his reattached arms over his head, make fists, and grip with his hands. Surgeons believe that John will recover additional movement and feelings in his arms, but that may require 2–5 years of physical therapy (*USA Today,* January 12, 1995).

Both his arms were torn off and then reattached.

More recently, doctors have taken a hand from a donor body and reattached the hand to the arm (stump) of a person whose own limb was severed or damaged (Horowitz, 2000). During this operation, nerves, blood vessels, and muscles from a donor's hand (right figure) are reattached to those in the patient's remaining limb. Four years after surgery, patients with reattached donor's hands can feel hot and cold, write, turn a faucet, tie shoe laces, insert coins in vending machines, and put one checker on top of another using their new hands (P. Smith, 2003). The fact that severed nerves in limbs, such as arms, hands, or legs, can be reattached but neurons in a severed spinal cord are very difficult to reattach illustrates a major difference between the peripheral and central nervous systems.

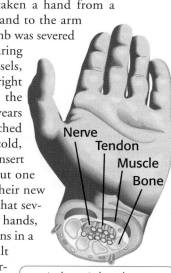

Nerve
Tendon
Muscle
Bone

A donor's hand was attached to a different arm.

Peripheral Nervous System

Why can limbs be reattached?

Severed limbs can be reattached and regain movement and sensation because their nerves are part of the peripheral nervous system.

The *peripheral nervous system* is made up of nerves, which are located throughout the body except in the brain and spinal cord.

Nerves are stringlike bundles of axons and dendrites that come from the spinal cord and are held together by connective tissue (shown in red in right figure). Nerves carry information from the senses, skin, muscles, and the body's organs to and from the spinal cord. Nerves in the peripheral nervous system have the ability to regrow or reattach if severed or damaged.

Peripheral nerves can be reattached.

The fact that nerves can regrow means that severed limbs can be reattached and limb transplants are possible. However, limb transplants are risky because a person must take drugs long-term to suppress his or her own immune system, whose normal job is to destroy "foreign" things, such as a donor's transplanted limb. By suppressing his or her own immune system, a person is at risk for getting serious infectious diseases (J. W. Jones et al., 2000).

The remarkable ability of nerves to regrow and be reattached distinguishes them from neurons.

Central Nervous System

Why wheelchairs?

People may find themselves in wheelchairs after damage to their spinal cords because of what neurons cannot easily do.

The *central nervous system* is made up of neurons located in the brain and spinal cord (shown in blue in left figure). The adult human brain has a limited capacity to grow new neurons and a limited ability to make new connections. Once damaged, neurons usually die and are not replaced.

Because neurons have such a limited capacity for repair or regrowth, people who have an injured or damaged brain or spinal cord experience some loss of sensation and motor movement, depending upon the severity of the damage. For example, Christopher Reeve (right photo) injured his spinal cord in the upper neck and, as a result, has regained only very limited movement and feeling in his hands and feet (Vergano, 2002). Reeve has been confined to a wheelchair because neurons usually have a very limited capacity for regrowth or repair (McKerracher & Ellezam, 2002).

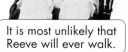

It is most unlikely that Reeve will ever walk.

Currently, one of the most exciting areas of research involves techniques that stimulate the regrowth or repair of damaged neurons. For example, axons, which carry information up and down the spinal cord, normally wither and die after injury, as happened to Reeve. Two methods for promoting the regrowth of axons are providing tubes that guide their growth and injecting growth-producing chemicals (Schwab, 2002). Positive findings in animals offer hope of developing similar methods to treat humans who have suffered brain or spinal cord injury (Seppa, 2000). The newest approach for treating brain damage is to replace damaged neurons by transplanting fetal tissue or stem cells (taken from embyros) into the damaged area. This method has great potential for treating brain diseases, such as Alzheimer's (Begley, 2001c). We'll discuss fetal tissue transplants in the Application section.

Now that you know the structure of the neuron, we'll explain one of its amazing functions: sending information at speeds approaching 200 miles per hour.

D. Sending Information

Sequence: Action Potential

1 Feeling a Sharp Object

When you step on a sharp object, you seem to feel the pain almost immediately because neurons send signals at speeds approaching 200 mph. To feel the pain involves the following series of electrochemical events:

A. Some stimulus, such as a tack, causes a change in physical energy. The tack produces mechanical pressure on the bottom of your foot.

B. Your skin has sensors that pick up the mechanical pressure and transform it into electrical signals. (We'll discuss various kinds of sensors in Module 5.)

C. The sensors' electrical signals are sent by the neuron's axon to various areas in the spinal cord and brain.

D. Finally, your brain interprets these electrical signals as "pain."

We're going to focus on step C and explain how axons send electrical signals by using the analogy of a battery. We'll begin by enlarging the inside of an axon.

2 Axon Membrane: Chemical Gates

Just as a battery has a protective covering, so too does the axon. Think of an axon as a long tube that is not only filled with fluid but also surrounded with fluid. The axon's tube is formed by a thin membrane, similar to a battery's outside covering, which keeps the fluid separate and also has special gates.

The *axon membrane* has chemical gates (shown in red) that can open to allow electrically charged particles to enter or can close to keep out electrically charged particles.

Just as a battery's power comes from its electrically charged chemicals, so does the axon's power to send information. In fact, the axon's electrically charged particles are the key to making it a living battery.

3 Ions: Charged Particles

The fluid inside and outside the axon contains ions.

Ions are chemical particles that have electrical charges. Ions follow two rules: Opposite charges attract (figure below), and like charges repel.

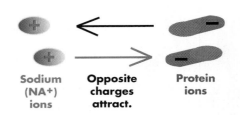

Sodium (NA+) ions — Opposite charges attract. — Protein ions

The fluid contains several different ions, such as sodium, potassium, chloride, and protein. The axon's function is often explained by discussing sodium and potassium ions. However, it is simpler and easier to focus on just sodium ions, which have positive charges and are abbreviated Na^+, and large protein ions, which have negative charges and are labeled protein⁻. Because they have opposite charges, Na^+ ions will be attracted to protein⁻ ions (figure above).

Because the axon's membrane separates the positive sodium ions from the negative protein ions, we have the makings of a living battery, as shown in section 4 on the next page.

Sequence: Nerve Impulse

6 Sending Information

One mistake students make is to think that the axon has ONE action potential, similar to the bang of a gunshot. However, unlike a gunshot, the axon has numerous individual action potentials that move down the axon, segment by segment; this movement is called the nerve impulse.

The *nerve impulse* refers to the series of separate action potentials that take place segment by segment as they move down the length of an axon.

Thus, instead of a single bang, a nerve impulse goes down the length of the axon very much like a lit fuse. Once lit, a fuse doesn't go off in a single bang but rather burns continuously until it reaches the end. This movement of a nerve impulse all the way down to the end of an axon is actually a natural law.

7 All-or-None Law

Why does a nerve impulse travel down the axon's entire length? The answer is the all-or-none law.

The *all-or-none law* says that, if an action potential starts at the beginning of an axon, the action potential will continue at the same speed, segment by segment, to the very end of the axon.

You'll see how the all-or-none law works in the next figure.

8 Nerve Impulse

Notice in this drawing, which continues on the next page, that the nerve impulse is made up of a sequence of six action potentials, with the first action potential occurring at the beginning of the axon.

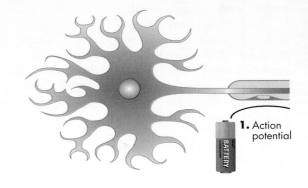

1. Action potential

4 Resting State: Charged Battery

The axon membrane separates positively charged sodium ions on the outside from negatively charged protein ions on the inside. This separation produces a miniature chemical battery that is not yet discharging and, thus, is said to be in its resting state.

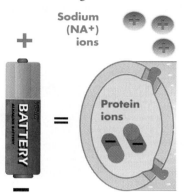

The *resting state* means that the axon has a charge, or potential; it resembles a battery. The charge, or potential, results from the axon membrane separating positive ions on the outside from negative ions on the inside (left figure).

The axon membrane has a charge across it during the resting state because of several factors, the primary one being the sodium pump. (To simplify our explanation of the resting state, we won't discuss other pump or transport systems.)

The *sodium pump* is a transport process that picks up any sodium ions that enter the axon's chemical gates and returns them back outside. Thus, the sodium pump is responsible for keeping the axon charged by returning and keeping sodium ions outside the axon membrane.

In the resting state, the axon is similar to a fully charged battery. Let's see what happens when the resting state is disrupted and the battery discharges.

5 Action Potential: Sending Information

If a stimulus, such as stepping on a tack, is large enough to excite a neuron, two things will happen to its axon. First, the stimulus will eventually open the axon's chemical gates by stopping the sodium pump. Second, when the stoppage of the sodium pump causes the gates to open, thousands of positive sodium ions will rush inside because of their attraction to the negative protein ions. The rush of sodium ions inside the axon is called the action potential.

The *action potential* is a tiny electric current that is generated when the positive sodium ions rush inside the axon. The enormous increase of sodium ions inside the axon causes the inside of the axon to reverse its charge. The inside becomes positive, while the outside becomes negative.

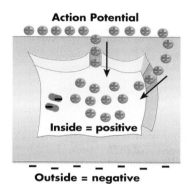

5a Just as a current flows when you connect the poles of a battery, current also flows when sodium ions rush through the opened gates of the axon membrane.

5b During an action potential, the inside of the axon changes to positive and the outside changes to negative. Immediately after the action potential, the sodium pump starts up and returns the axon to the resting state.

At this point, imagine that an action potential has started at the beginning of an axon. How action potentials whiz at race-car speeds down the entire length of an axon is what we'll examine next in the section below, Sequence: Nerve Impulse.

8a According to the all-or-none law, once a nerve impulse begins, it goes to the end of the axon. This means that when action potential 1 occurs, it will be followed in order by potentials 2, 3, 4, 5, and 6. After the occurrence of each action potential, the axon membrane at that point quickly returns to its resting state.

8b Notice that the *myelin sheath* has regular breaks where the axon is bare and uninsulated. It is at these bare points that the axon's gates open and the action potential takes place.

9 End Bulbs and Neurotransmitters

Once the nerve impulse reaches the end of the axon, the very last action potential, 6, affects the end bulbs, which are located at the very end of the axon. This last action potential triggers the end bulbs to release their neurotransmitters. Once released, neurotransmitters cross the synapse and, depending upon the kind, they will either excite or inhibit the function of neighboring organs (heart), muscles (head), or cell bodies.

As you can now see, neurotransmitters are critical for communicating with neighboring organs, muscles, and other neurons. We'll examine transmitters in more detail and show you how they excite or inhibit.

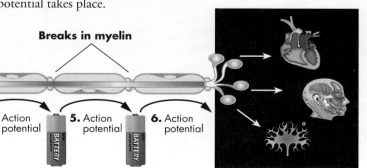

E. Transmitters

What makes your heart pound?

There's no doubt that you have felt your heart pounding when you are afraid, stressed, or angry. One reason for your pounding heart has to do with transmitters.

A *transmitter* is a chemical messenger that transmits information between nerves and body organs, such as muscles and heart.

Why does my heart rate increase when I get angry?

Everything you do, including thinking, deciding, talking, and getting angry, involves transmitters. For example, imagine seeing someone back into your brand new car and then just drive away. You would certainly become angry and your heart would pound. Let's see why getting angry can increase your heart rate from a normal 60 to 70 beats per minute to over 180.

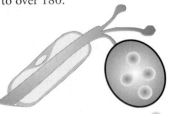

1 In the figure on the left, you see the end of an axon with 3 branches. At the end of the bottom branch is a greatly enlarged *end bulb.* Inside the bulb are 4 colored circles that represent transmitters.

2 When the action potential hits the *end bulb,* it causes a miniature explosion, and the transmitters are ejected outside. Once ejected, transmitters cross a tiny space, or synapse, and, in this case, reach the nearby heart muscle. Think of transmitters as chemical keys that fit into chemical locks on the surface of the heart muscle. End bulbs usually hold either excitatory or inhibitory transmitters, which have opposite effects.

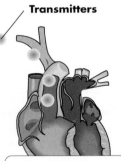

Transmitters

Transmitters can increase or decrease heart rate.

3 Strong emotions cause the release of *excitatory transmitters,* which open chemical locks in the heart muscle and cause it to beat faster (left figure). When you get very angry, excitatory transmitters may cause your heart rate to double or even triple its rate. When you start to calm down, there is a release of *inhibitory transmitters,* which block chemical locks in the heart muscle and decrease its rate (right figure). Think of transmitters acting like chemical messengers that either excite or inhibit nearby body organs (heart), neurons, or muscle fibers. One special class of transmitters that are made in the brain are called neurotransmitters.

Excitatory

Inhibitory

What makes your brain work?

Writing a paper on a computer requires your brain to use millions of neurons that communicate with one another by using chemicals called neurotransmitters. *Neurotransmitters* are about a dozen different chemicals that are made by neurons and then used for communication between neurons during the performance of mental or physical activities.

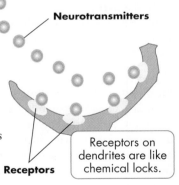

What happens in my brain when I use my computer?

Since billions of neurons that are packed tightly together use different neurotransmitters for eating, sleeping, talking, thinking, and dreaming, why don't neurotransmitters get all mixed up? The answer is that neurotransmitters are similar to chemical keys that fit into specific chemical locks.

1 The figure on the left again shows the end of an axon with 3 branches. We have again enlarged one *end bulb* to show that it contains neurotransmitters (4 colored circles).

2 The action potential causes the end bulbs to eject their neurotransmitters (colored circles), which, in turn, cross the synapse and, in this case, land on the surface of nearby dendrites. The surface of one dendrite is enlarged (right figure) to show its *receptors* (yellow ovals), which are special areas that function like chemical locks.

Neurotransmitters

Receptors on dendrites are like chemical locks.

Receptors

3 Although there are many different neurotransmitters, each one has a unique chemical key that fits and opens only certain chemical locks, or receptors. Thus, billions of neurons use this system of chemical keys that open or close matching locks to communicate and to participate in so many different activities. Also, remember that some neurotransmitters are *excitatory*—they open receptor locks and turn on neurons—while others are *inhibitory*—they close locks and turn off neurons.

Since neurons use neurotransmitters to communicate, any drug that acts like or interferes with neurotransmitters has the potential to change how the brain functions and how we feel, think, and behave. For example, here's what alcohol does.

What does alcohol do?

Drinking alcoholic beverages usually raises the level of alcohol in the blood, which is measured in terms of blood alcohol content (BAC). For example, at low to medium doses (0.01–0.06 BAC), alcohol causes friendliness, loss of inhibitions, decreased self-control, and impaired social judgment; after 3 or 4 drinks, the average person's BAC will range from 0.08 to 0.1, which meets the legal definition of drunkenness in most states. (Alcohol is discussed more fully in Module 8.)

Why do I feel different after drinking?

Alcohol (ethyl alcohol) is a psychoactive drug that is classified as a depressant, which means that it depresses the activity of the central nervous system.

Although alcohol has been around for 3,000 years, it is only recently that researchers have determined its effects on the brain. The effects of alcohol have proved difficult to pin down since it has so many. We'll discuss one of its major effects on the brain.

GABA neurons. Alcohol affects the nervous system in a number of ways, blocking some neural receptors and stimulating others. For example, some neurons are excited by a neurotransmitter called GABA (*GAH-bah*), which the brain normally manufactures. This means that GABA neurons (figure above) have chemical locks that can be opened by chemical keys in the form of the neurotransmitter GABA (Tsai et al., 1995).

GABA keys. Now here's the interesting part. Alcohol molecules so closely resemble those of the GABA neurotransmitter that alcohol can function like GABA keys and open GABA receptors (figure below right). Opening GABA receptors excites GABA neurons.

Although it seems backward, when GABA neurons are *excited*, they *decrease* neural activity and overall produce inhibitory effects, such as reduction in anxiety and tension, loss of inhibitions and self-control, and often an increase in friendliness. Thus, one reason alcohol is such a popular drug is that it reduces tension and anxiety (Stritzke et al., 1996).

One way that alcohol affects the brain is by imitating a naturally occurring neurotransmitter, GABA. Other drugs have different effects on the brain's neurotransmitters, several of which have been recently discovered.

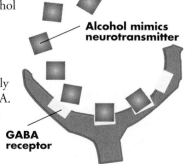

Alcohol mimics neurotransmitter

GABA receptor

What are the latest discoveries?

There are a number of well-known neurotransmitters, such as acetylcholine, GABA, norepinephrine, epinephrine, dopamine, and serotonin. However, researchers continue to discover new ones to add to the list of neurotransmitters.

Endorphins. In the 1970s, researchers discovered that the brain makes its own painkiller, very similar to morphine. They called this neurotransmitter endorphin, which is secreted to decrease the effects of pain during great bodily stress, such as an accident (J. Hughes et al., 1975). We'll discuss the effects of endorphins on page 113.

Anandamide. In the early 1990s, researchers discovered a somewhat surprising neurotransmitter, called anandamide, which is similar in chemical makeup to THC, the active ingredient in marijuana (discussed on p. 186) (Fackelmann, 1993). The figure on the right shows a horizontal section of a rat brain that has been treated with a radioactive version of anandamide. The yellow areas, which were most affected by anandamide, are involved in

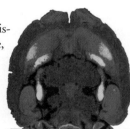

Yellow areas show where marijuana-like anandamide acts.

memory, motor coordination, and emotions (Herkenham, 1996). Researchers speculate that anandamide may help humans deal with stress and pain (Fackelmann, 1993).

Nitric oxide. In the mid-1990s, researchers discovered that a gas, nitric oxide, functions like a neurotransmitter and may be involved in regulation of emotions. For example, mice genetically altered to lack nitric oxide were six times more likely to pick a fight (right figure) compared to normal mice (R. J. Nelson et al., 1995). Based on these results, researchers think that nitric oxide may be involved in turning off aggression in mice and perhaps in humans.

Other chemicals. Currently, researchers have identified over a dozen chemicals that have all the characteristics of neurotransmitters and

Changing neurotransmitter levels in rats causes increased aggression.

up to 100 chemicals that influence communication between neurons but do not have all the characteristics of more traditional neurotransmitters (Synder, 2002). The important point to remember about neurotransmitters is that their system of chemical keys and locks permits very effective communication among billions of neurons, which allow us to move, sense, think, feel, and perform hundreds of other functions.

Now that you are familiar with the structure and function of the neuron and the importance of neurotransmitters, we'll use this knowledge to explain a response that many of you have experienced—what happened when you touched a hot object.

F. Reflex Responses

Can you move without thinking?

If you accidentally touched a hot light bulb, your hand would instantly jerk away, without any conscious thought or effort on your part. This is an example of a reflex.

A *reflex* is an unlearned, involuntary reaction to some stimulus. The neural connections or network underlying a reflex is prewired by genetic instructions.

In some cases, such as when a doctor taps your knee, the knee-jerk reflex is controlled by the spinal cord. In other cases, such as when someone shines a bright light into your eye, the pupillary reflex causes the pupil to constrict. We are all born with a number of programmed reflexes, and all reflexes share the same two or three steps, depending upon how they are wired in the nervous system.

One reason reflexes occur so quickly is that they are genetically programmed and involve relatively few neural connections, which saves time. Here's the sequence for how a reflex occurs:

1 Sensors. The skin of your fingers has specialized sensors, or receptors, that are sensitive to heat. When you touch a hot light bulb, these skin sensors trigger neurons that start the withdrawal reflex.

2 Afferent neuron. From the receptors in your skin, long dendrites carry "pain information" in the form of electrical signals to the spinal cord. These dendrites are part of sensory, or afferent, neurons (red arrows).

Afferent (*AFF-er-ent*), or *sensory, neurons* carry information from the senses to the spinal cord.

Sensory neurons may have dendrites 2 to 3 feet long, to reach from the tips of your fingers to the spinal cord. When the pain information enters the spinal cord, it is transmitted to a second neuron.

3 Interneuron. Once the afferent neuron reaches the spinal cord, it transmits the pain information to a second neuron, called an interneuron.

An *interneuron* is a relatively short neuron whose primary task is making connections between other neurons.

In this example, an interneuron transmits the pain information to a third neuron, called the efferent, or motor, neuron.

4 Efferent neuron. Inside the spinal cord, an interneuron transfers information to a third neuron, called an efferent, or motor, neuron (blue arrows).

Efferent (*EFF-er-ent*), or *motor, neurons* carry information away from the spinal cord to produce responses in various muscles and organs throughout the body.

From the spinal cord, an efferent (motor) neuron sends electrical signals on its 2- to 3-foot-long axon to the muscles in the hand. These electrical signals contain "movement information" and cause the hand to withdraw quickly and without any thought on your part.

In addition, an interneuron will send the pain information to other neurons that speed this information to different parts of the brain. These different parts interpret the electrical signals coming from your hand as being hot and painful. At this point your brain may direct motor neurons to move your facial and vocal muscles so that you look pained and yell "Ouch!" or something much more intense.

Afferent or sensory neuron

Efferent or motor neuron

3. Interneuron makes connections between neurons, which carry message to the brain.

4. Efferent or motor neuron carries neural messages from spinal cord to hand.

2. Afferent or sensory neuron carries neural messages from hand to spinal cord.

The primary reason you automatically withdraw your hand when touching a hot object, turn your head in the direction of a loud noise, or vomit after eating tainted food has to do with survival. Reflexes, which have evolved through millions of years, protect body parts from injury and harm and automatically regulate physiological responses, such as heart rate, respiration, and blood pressure. One primitive reflex that is no longer useful in our modern times is called piloerection, which causes the hair to stand up on your arms when you are cold. Piloerection helped keep heat in by fluffing hair for better insulation, but clothes now do a better job.

After the Concept Review, we'll discuss a very strange neural phenomenon that you may have heard of—phantom limb.

✔ Concept Review

1. The structure that nourishes and maintains the entire neuron is the (a)_____. Branchlike extensions that receive signals from senses and the environment are called (b)_____. A single threadlike extension that speeds signals away from the cell body toward a neighboring cell is the (c)_____. A tubelike structure that insulates the axon from interference by neighboring signals is the (d)_____. Tiny swellings at the very end of the axon are called (e)_____, which store neurotransmitters.

2. Chemicals that have electrical charges are called (a)_____. They obey the rule that opposite charges attract and like charges repel. Although the fluid of the axon contains a number of ions, we have focused on only two, a positively charged (b)_____ ion whose symbol is Na⁺ and a negatively charged (c)_____ ion.

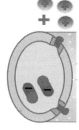

3. If an axon membrane has a potential similar to a charged battery, the axon is in the (a)_____. During this state, the ions outside the membrane are positively charged (b)_____ ions; the ions inside the membrane are negatively charged (c)_____ ions.

4. If an axon membrane is in a state similar to a discharging battery, the axon is generating an (a)_____. During this potential, the chemical gates open and positively charged (b)_____ rush inside, changing the inside of the membrane to a (c)_____ charge, while the outside of the membrane has a (d)_____ charge. As the action potential moves down the axon, it is called an (e)_____. Once it is generated, the impulse travels from the beginning to the end of the axon; this phenomenon is referred to as the (f)_____.

5. The end bulbs of one neuron are separated from the dendrites of a neighboring neuron by an extremely small space called the (a)_____. Into this space, end bulbs release chemicals, called (b)_____, which open/excite or block/inhibit neighboring receptors.

6. From end bulbs, chemical keys or (a)_____ are secreted into the synapse. These chemical keys open matching locks called (b)_____, which are located on the surface of neighboring dendrites, muscles, or organs. Neurotransmitters that open a receptor's lock are called (c)_____; neurotransmitters that block a receptor's lock are called (d)_____.

7. Neurons in the brain and spinal cord make up the (a)_____. If neurons are damaged, they have little ability to (b)_____ and usually die. The mature human brain has a limited ability to regrow (c)_____ throughout adulthood. Information from the body's senses, skin, organs, and muscles is carried to and from the spinal cord by nerves that make up the (d)_____. If this nervous system is damaged, (e)_____ in this system have a remarkable ability to regrow and make new connections. If your finger were accidentally cut off, it could be (f)_____ and there is a good chance that your finger would regain most of its sensory and motor functions.

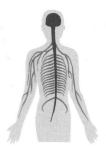

8. If you touch a sharp object, your hand automatically withdraws because of a prewired reflex response. Neurons that carry "pain information" to the spinal cord are called (a)_____ neurons. Inside the spinal cord, there are short neurons, called (b)_____, that make connections between other neurons that carry information to the brain. Neurons that carry information away from the spinal cord to muscles or organs are called (c)_____ neurons.

Answers: 1. (a) cell body or soma, (b) dendrites, (c) axon, (d) myelin sheath, (e) end bulbs; 2. (a) ions, (b) sodium, (c) protein; 3. (a) resting state, (b) sodium, (c) protein; 4. (a) action potential, (b) sodium ions, (c) positive, (d) negative, (e) impulse, or nerve impulse, (f) all-or-none law; 5. (a) synapse, (b) neurotransmitters; 6. (a) neurotransmitters, (b) receptors, (c) excitatory, (d) inhibitory; 7. (a) central nervous system, (b) regrow, repair, or reconnect, (c) neurons, (d) peripheral nervous system, (e) nerves, (f) reattached; 8. (a) sensory, or afferent, (b) interneurons, (c) motor, or efferent

G. Research Focus: What Is a Phantom Limb?

Case Study

Why did Donald cut off his leg?

An interesting and puzzling question for researchers to answer is "How can someone feel a phantom limb?"

This question especially applies to Donald Wyman, who was a bulldozer driver working alone on trees in a remote forest. A giant oak tree accidentally fell and pinned him to the ground. With no one close enough to hear his shouts for help, Donald realized his only hope to get out from under the tree and survive was to cut off his leg, which he did with a 3-inch pocket knife. Although bleeding badly, he dragged himself to his truck and

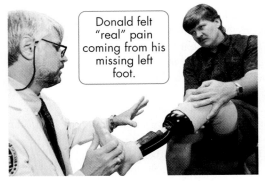

Donald felt "real" pain coming from his missing left foot.

drove a mile and a half to get help. Even though his leg was recovered, it was too damaged to be reattached. Donald is now learning to walk with an artificial leg (left photo) that is fitted to the stump.

Donald is recovering but he says, "The toughest part since the accident is dealing with phantom pain. It feels like somebody's holding an electrical shock to your foot that's not there. It makes you jump around" (*USA Today*, August 31, 1993, p. 2A). Donald's case introduces you to the strange phenomenon of phantom limb.

Definition and Data

What is phantom limb?

Very few symptoms have so surprised doctors as when patients reported feeling strange sensations or movements in arms or legs that had been amputated, a phenomenon called phantom limb.

Phantom limb refers to feeling sensations or movements coming from a limb that has been amputated. The sensations and movements are extremely vivid, as if the limb were still present.

As the figure on the right shows, the vast majority of individuals felt sensations ("pins and needles") or intense pain coming from their removed limbs. Patients insist that the phantom limb pain is real pain and not merely memories of previous pain (A. Hill et al., 1996). In other cases, amputees felt that their removed limbs were not only still present but stuck in certain positions, such as straight out from their bodies, so they felt they had to be very careful not to hit their phantom limbs when going through doorways (Katz, 1992).

From 1866 to the present, there have been at least three answers for what causes the feelings of sensations and movements coming from phantom limbs.

Patients' Reports after Removal of Limbs

80–100%	Report sensations
70–80%	Report pain

Answers: Old and New

1 Sensations come from cut nerves in the stump.

Early researchers thought that the phantom limb sensations come from cut nerves remaining in the stump. However, when these nerves were cut near the spinal cord, phantom limb should have been prevented; but the sensations still remained, so this early answer has been rejected (Melzack, 1997).

2 Sensations come from the spinal cord.

If sensations from phantom limbs do not come from the stump, perhaps they originate in the spinal cord. However, even individuals whose spinal cords have been severed above the stump report phantom limb sensations. Since a severed spinal cord prevents sensations (electrical signals) from reaching the brain, this answer too has been rejected (Melzack, 1997).

3 Sensations come from a body image stored in the brain.

Researchers now have enough data to indicate that the origin of phantom limb sensations must be the brain itself (Melzack, 1997). But having said that, researchers are puzzled about how the brain generates sensations from phantom limbs.

This newest and most creative answer to the origin of phantom limb sensations comes from researcher Ronald Melzack, who has

been studying this problem for about 40 years (Melzack, 1989, 1997). A simplified version of his theory is that each of us has a genetically programmed system of sensations that results in our knowing where our body parts are and in our developing an image of our body. Based on sensations from body parts, the brain pieces together a complete body image. Thus, having a body image, the brain itself can generate sensations as coming from any body part, even if that part is a phantom limb (Melzack, 1997).

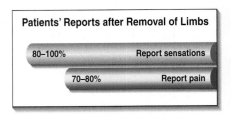

Does pain in the phantom limb come from 1, 2, or 3?

Melzack admits that some of his theory must still be tested, but many researchers agree that it is so far one of the best answers to the 40-year-old question involving phantom limbs (Flor et al., 1995).

The phantom limb phenomenon points out that the brain sometimes functions in mysterious ways. Less mysterious is how certain drugs affect the functioning of the brain and the body.

H. Cultural Diversity: Plants & Drugs

Where did the first drugs come from?

The very first drugs that affected neurotransmitters came from various plants, which people used long before researchers knew what those plants contained. We'll discuss three such drugs—cocaine, curare, and mescaline—which come from plants found in different parts of the world. We'll explain what these plants contain and their actions on the nervous systems.

Cocaine: Blocking Reuptake

For almost 3,500 years, South American Indians have chewed leaves of the coca plant. Following this ancient custom, adult Indians habitually carry bags of toasted coca leaves, which contain cocaine. Throughout the day, they chew small amounts of coca leaves to relieve fatigue and feelings of hunger. Here's how cocaine affects neurotransmitters.

The drawing on the right shows a neuron's end bulb containing the neurotransmitter dopamine (*DOPE-ah-mean*). Once released, dopamine (colored blue circles) reaches the dendrite's receptors, opens their chemical locks, and activates the neuron. However, after a short period of time, the neurotransmitter is normally removed by being transported back into the end bulb through a process called reuptake.

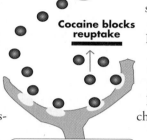

Cocaine blocks reuptake

Cocaine works by blocking reuptake.

Reuptake is a process through which some neurotransmitters, such as dopamine, are removed from the synapse by being transported back into the end bulbs.

If reuptake does not occur, the released neurotransmitter would continually affect the neuron by remaining longer in the synapse. What cocaine does is block reuptake so that dopamine remains longer in the synapse (Stahl, 2000). Because cocaine blocks reuptake, neurons are stimulated longer, resulting in the physiological arousal and feelings of euphoria that are associated with cocaine usage. Researchers now understand why South American Indians chewed coca leaves. The cocaine released from chewing coca leaves blocked the reuptake of dopamine, which in turn caused physiological arousal that relieved fatigue and feelings of hunger.

Curare: Blocking Receptors

When hunting animals, the Indians of Peru and Ecuador coat the ends of blowdarts with the juice of a tropical vine that contains the paralyzing drug curare.

Curare (*cure-RAH-ree*) is a drug that enters the bloodstream, reaches the muscles, and blocks receptors on muscles. As a result, the neurotransmitter that normally activates muscles, which is called acetylcholine, is blocked, and muscles are paralyzed.

Once hit by a curare-tipped blowdart, an animal's limb muscles become paralyzed, followed by paralysis of chest muscles used to breathe.

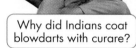

Why did Indians coat blowdarts with curare?

Curare is an example of a drug that stops neural transmission by blocking the muscles' receptors. Today, the purified active ingredient in curare (tubocurarine chloride) is used to induce muscle paralysis in humans, such as when doctors insert a breathing tube down a patient's throat. Curare doesn't easily enter the brain because the body's blood must go through a filtering system before it can enter the brain. This filtering system, called the **blood-brain barrier,** prevents some, but not all, potentially harmful substances in the body's blood supply from reaching the brain.

Mescaline: Mimicking a Neurotransmitter

A golf-ball-sized, gray-green plant (right photo) called peyote cactus grows in Mexico and the southwestern United States. Peyote contains mescaline (Stahl, 2000).

Mescaline (*MESS-ka-lin*) is a drug that causes physiological arousal as well as visual hallucinations. Mescaline's chemical keys are similar to those of the neurotransmitter norepinephrine (*nor-epee-NEFF-rin*).

Because mescaline's chemical keys open the same chemical locks (receptors) as norepinephrine, mescaline produces its effects by mimicking the actions of norepinephrine.

In 1965, an estimated 250,000 members of the Native American Church in the United States and Canada won a Supreme Court case that permits them to be the only group legally authorized to use peyote in their religious services. To enhance meditation, members may

Mescaline comes from peyote cactus.

eat from 4 to 12 peyote buttons, which results in visual sensations, euphoria, and sometimes nausea and vomiting.

Conclusion. These three plants—cocaine, curare, and mescaline—contain potent drugs that illustrate three different ways of affecting the nervous system. Researchers have discovered numerous plants, including the opium poppy, marijuana, and "magic" mushrooms, which contain drugs that in turn affect neurotransmitters (discussed in Module 8).

Neurotransmitters are the keys that turn the brain's functions on or off. For example, Alzheimer's disease interferes with neurons and neurotransmitters and turns off the brain's functions. Such is the case with another terrible disease, called Parkinson's, which we'll discuss next.

I. Application: Experimental Treatments

Parkinson's Disease

Why does Bob's arm shake?

Part of Bob's job was to climb poles and make electrical repairs. He was good at his job until he began to notice that, for no apparent reason, his hands would shake or become rigid. The shakes and tremors in his arms grew worse until he couldn't hold his tools. When his symptoms forced him to stop working, his tremors were so bad that he was too embarrassed to eat out or be seen in public. Many days he had trouble walking because his legs would suddenly become stiff and rigid and he couldn't move. It was like being frozen in space.

Bob had all the symptoms of Parkinson's disease.

Parkinson's disease includes symptoms of tremors and shakes in the limbs, a slowing of voluntary movements, and feelings of depression. As the disease progresses,

patients develop a peculiar shuffling walk and may suddenly freeze in space for minutes or hours at a time. Parkinson's is caused by a destruction of neurons that produce the neurotransmitter dopamine (*DOPE-ah-mean*).

Like most Parkinson's patients, Bob was placed on a medication called L-dopa, which boosts the levels of dopamine in the brain. However, patients must take ever-increasing amounts of L-dopa, until the drug itself causes involuntary jerky movements that may be as bad as those produced by Parkinson's. Thus, L-dopa controls but does not cure the symptoms of Parkinson's, and after prolonged use, L-dopa's beneficial effects may be replaced by unwanted jerky movements.

In spite of taking L-dopa, Bob's symptoms were getting worse. He had heard about an experimental treatment in which fetal brain tissue that contained dopamine-producing neurons was transplanted into an area of the brain called the basal ganglia (*Los Angeles Times,* November 26, 1992).

The *basal ganglia* are a group of structures located in the center of the brain and are involved in regulating movements. To function properly, neurons in the basal ganglia must have a sufficient supply of the neurotransmitter dopamine.

Bob's Parkinson's symptoms had worsened because neurons in his basal ganglia were running out of dopamine. Similarly, when TV actor Michael J. Fox's Parkinson's symptoms worsened, he had to leave his hit sitcom, "Spin City" (Weinraub, 2000). In the United States, about 1.5 million adults, usually over age 50, have Parkinson's disease (Fox was only 34). The causes of Parkinson's disease include genetic and possible environmental factors (Schmid, 2002). To date, Parkinson's has no cure but, as you'll see, several experimental treatments are under study.

Issues Involving Transplants

Why not just use drugs?

Human cells. The majority of patients, like Bob, have found that using L-dopa for 10 years or more to treat Parkinson's disease produces unwanted side effects, such as involuntary movements, as well as the return of some of the original symptoms described above (Troster, 2000).

Because of the disappointing long-term results of using L-dopa to treat Parkinson's disease, researchers are trying alternative treatments, such as fetal brain tissue transplants.

Previously, researchers had shown that when fetal rat brain tissue was transplanted into older rats, the fetal neurons lived, grew, functioned, and allowed brain-damaged older rats to relearn the solutions to mazes (Shetty & Turner, 1996). Following successful fetal transplants in rats and monkeys, researchers have transplanted human fetal brain tissue into patients with Parkinson's disease (Kolata, 2001).

The primary reason for using 6- to 8-week-old fetal tissue for transplants is that this fetal tissue has a unique ability to survive and make connections in a patient's brain or body. Because fetal brain tissue is primed for growth, it has a far greater chance of survival after transplantation than does tissue from mature brains (Barinaga, 2000b). More recently, researchers are exploring the use of stem cells to treat Parkinson's disease and spinal cord injuries.

Stem cells. About four days after a sperm has fertilized an egg, the resulting embryo, which is about the size of the period in this sentence (p. 379), has divided and formed embryonic stem cells (shown on left).

Stem cells, not discovered until 1998, have the amazing capacity to change into and become any one of the 220 cells that make up a human body, including skin, heart, liver, bones, and neurons.

The discovery of stem cells creates new possibilities for treating various body and neurological diseases. For example, when embryonic animal stem cells were transplanted into rats and mice with spinal cord injuries, the stem cells imitated the neighboring neurons and developed into new neurons that, in turn, helped the animals regain their lost functions (N. Wade, 2002).

However, the use of human embryonic stem cells is controversial for ethical and political reasons. That's because these embryos, which are fertilized in laboratories and have the potential to develop into humans, are destroyed when the stem cells are removed. On moral grounds, President George W. Bush limited federal funds for stem cell research. Because stem cell research has such potential, it has received wide support and funding from private and state sources (Perez-Pena, 2003).

The possibility of using stem cells was unknown in the early 1990s, when Bob was thinking about a new treatment for his Parkinson's symptoms. At that time, he chose the newest experimental treatment available, which was having fetal tissue transplanted into his brain.

Embryonic stem cells have the ability to form new brain cells.

Placing tissue in the brain. A neurosurgeon can transplant fetal cells or stem cells into a precise location in either animal or human brains by using the stereotaxic procedure.

The *stereotaxic procedure* (below figure) involves fixing a patient's head in a holder and drilling a small hole through the skull. The holder has a syringe that can be precisely guided to inject cells into a predetermined location in the brain.

As shown below, Bob's head has been fixed in the stereotaxic holder. In this figure, a large part of the skull has been removed to show the brain, but in actual surgery, only a small, pencil-sized hole is drilled in the patient's skull. A long needle from the syringe (lower left in the figure) extends from the holder into the patient's brain area that is involved with regulating movement, the basal ganglia. The surgeon will slowly inject fetal or stem cells into the designated brain area.

The advantages of the stereotaxic procedure are that a thin syringe can be placed in precise locations in the brain and that it causes relatively little damage to the brain. The stereotaxic procedure can be used to either inject solutions or destroy diseased brain tissue.

Results. After surgery, Bob said that he still has his ups and downs but that his symptoms are more controllable. However, because this is a single case study, we do not know whether his improvement is due to the tissue transplants or to the placebo effect—namely, Bob's hopes and expectations.

To control for the placebo effect, a more recent study tested 40 patients with Parkinson's disease. They were randomly assigned to one of two groups: The experimental group had holes drilled in their skulls and fetal tissue was implanted into an area of the brain that controls movement (basal ganglia); the control group (sham operation) had holes drilled in their skulls but nothing was injected into their brains. This procedure, which kept patients from knowing whether or not they had received the transplants, helped prevent the patients' beliefs or expectations from biasing their evaluations and controlled for possible placebo effects.

A year after fetal tissue transplant, researchers asked patients to rate their improvement. There was no significant difference between the ratings of the experimental and control groups, meaning the fetal tissue transplants had not produced any significant improvement compared to the control group (sham operation). In addition, five patients developed serious side effects that involved exaggerated, uncontrollable wiggling and writhing movements, indicating that the fetal tissue transplants were making too much neurotransmitter (dopamine). The only slightly positive finding was that ten patients,

all under the age of 60, showed slightly less rigidity in their movements (Freed et al., 2001).

This experiment was controversial from the beginning because some patients were given sham operations (holes drilled in their skulls but no transplants—these patients were given the option of having the actual transplants a year later) and because of religious and ethical objections to having obtained the fetal tissue from abortions. However, researchers believed that this study was necessary because in previous fetal tissue transplant operations (cost: $40,000 per patient), some Parkinson's patients had reported improvements, which encouraged other patients with this fatal disease, who were desperate for a cure, to seek this experimental treatment (Kolata, 2001). The study suggests that previously reported improvements after fetal tissue transplant, such as reported by Bob, may have, to varying degrees, been due to placebo effects.

From the above study, researchers have learned that fetal tissue does survive and function in adults' brains. But, before more fetal tissue transplants are attempted, critics suggest that researchers need to identify the best location for injecting the tissue into the brain and to prevent the unwanted motor side effects by determining the optimum number of fetal cells to inject.

Another possibility. A more recent study has reported on a new type of cell implant that produced promising results. In the eyeballs (retinas) of cadavers, researchers found cells that make dopamine and can be grown in the laboratory. These dopamine-producing cells were injected into areas of the brain (basal ganglia) that were similar to areas in which fetal tissue was transplanted. Researchers reported that a year after receiving these cell implants, six patients, all of whom had moderate Parkinson's disease, reported a 50% reduction in their symptoms (Maugh, 2002a). However, as you have just learned from the fetal tissue transplant study, even though preliminary studies such as this may seem promising, their promise must be confirmed with better-designed studies using many more patients.

Future. As of this writing, stem cell research is still in its infancy, but already, remarkable success has been reported in using stem cells to treat animals with spinal cord or brain injury (McKay, 2002). Based on animal research, researchers are currently studying how to use stem cells to treat human spinal cord injury and diseases such as Alzheimer's and Parkinson's (Kim et al., 2002).

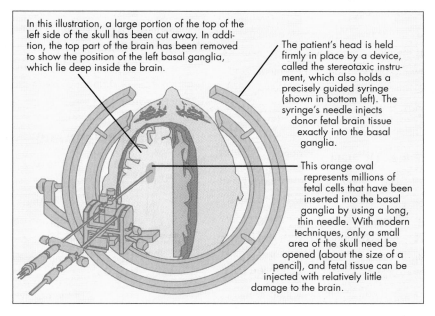

In this illustration, a large portion of the top of the left side of the skull has been cut away. In addition, the top part of the brain has been removed to show the position of the left basal ganglia, which lie deep inside the brain.

The patient's head is held firmly in place by a device, called the stereotaxic instrument, which also holds a precisely guided syringe (shown in bottom left). The syringe's needle injects donor fetal brain tissue exactly into the basal ganglia.

This orange oval represents millions of fetal cells that have been inserted into the basal ganglia by using a long, thin needle. With modern techniques, only a small area of the skull need be opened (about the size of a pencil), and fetal tissue can be injected with relatively little damage to the brain.

Summary Test

A. OVERVIEW: HUMAN BRAIN

1. The brain is composed of a trillion cells that can be divided into two groups. One group of cells has specialized extensions for receiving and transmitting information. These cells, which are called (a)_____, are involved in communicating with other neurons, receiving sensory information, and regulating muscles, glands, and organs. The other group of cells provide the scaffolding to guide and support neurons, insulate neurons, and release chemicals that influence neuron functions. These cells are much more numerous than neurons and are called (b)_____.

2. There is a major difference between the growth of neurons in the brains of humans and in the brains of birds. A mature human brain is normally not capable of developing new (a)_____, which are almost totally present at the time of birth. In contrast, a mature (b)_____ brain has the capacity to develop new neurons.

3. The age-old question of how the brain's membranes, fluids, and chemicals are involved in generating complex mental activities, such as thoughts, images, and feelings, is called the _____ question.

B. NEURONS: STRUCTURE & FUNCTION

4. Although neurons come in wondrous shapes and sizes, they all share three structures. The structure that maintains the entire neuron in working order, manufactures chemicals, and provides fuel is called the (a)_____. The structure with many branchlike extensions that receive signals from other neurons, muscles, or organs and conduct these signals to the cell body is called a (b)_____. The single threadlike extension that leaves the cell body and carries signals to other neurons, muscles, or organs is called the (c)_____. At the very end of this structure are individual swellings called (d)_____, which contain tiny vesicles filled with (e)_____.

5. Surrounding most axons is a fatty material called the (a)_____. This material acts like (b)_____ and diminishes interference from electrical signals traveling in neighboring axons.

6. Neurons do not make physical contact with one another or with other organs. Instead, there is an infinitely small space between a neuron's end bulbs and neighboring dendrites, cell bodies, or other organs. This space is called the (a)_____. When an axon's end bulbs secrete a neurotransmitter, it flows across this space and affects the (b)_____ on the neighboring membrane.

C. NEURONS VERSUS NERVES

7. There are major differences between neurons and nerves. Cells with specialized extensions for conducting electrical signals are called a)_____. These cells, which are located in the brain and spinal cord, make up the (b)_____ nervous system. Stringlike bundles of neurons' axons and dendrites, which are held together by connective tissue, are called (c)_____. These stringlike bundles, which are located throughout the body, make up the (d)_____ nervous system. Nerves carry information back and forth between the body and the spinal cord. If a neuron in the central nervous system is damaged, it normally does not have the capacity to (e)_____. In comparison, a nerve in the (f)_____ nervous system has the capacity to regrow or reattach if cut or damaged. The mature human brain has a limited ability to regrow (g)_____ throughout adulthood.

D. SENDING INFORMATION

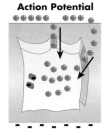

Action Potential

8. The axon membrane has (a)_____ that can be opened or closed. These gates keep some ions inside the membrane and other ions outside. If the axon is ready to conduct but not actually conducting an impulse, the axon is said to be in the (b)_____ state. In this state, most of the positively charged (c)_____ ions are on the outside of the membrane and all the negatively charged (d)_____ ions are trapped inside. In the resting state, the outside of the membrane has a (e)_____ charge compared to the (f)_____ charge on the inside. The process responsible for picking up and transporting sodium ions from the inside to the outside of the axon membrane is called the (g)_____.

9. If a stimulus is strong enough to excite a neuron, two things happen to its axon. First, the stimulus will eventually open the axon's (a)_____. Second, after the gates are opened, the (b)_____ pump is stopped, and all the positive (c)_____ ions rush inside because they are attracted to the negatively charged protein ions. The rush of sodium ions inside generates a tiny electric current that is called the (d)_____. When this current is generated, the inside of the axon membrane changes to a (e)_____ charge and the outside changes to a (f)_____ charge.

10. Once an action potential starts in the axon, it continues, segment by segment, down the entire length of the axon, creating the (a)_____. Once an action potential is triggered in the segment at the beginning of the axon, other action potentials will be triggered in sequence down the entire length of the axon; this phenomenon is called the (b)_____.

E. TRANSMITTERS

11. Once started, the action potential will reach the end bulbs at the end of the axon. The action potential excites the end bulbs and causes them to secrete (a)_____ that were stored in the end bulbs. Neurotransmitters function like chemical keys that unlock chemical locks or (b)_____, which are located on neighboring neurons, muscles, or other organs. If neurotransmitters open the receptors' locks on neighboring cells, they are said to be (c)_____. If neurotransmitters block the receptors' locks, they are said to be (d)_____. Because of these different actions, neurotransmitters can cause different and even opposite responses in neurons, muscles, or organs. There are about a dozen well-known neurotransmitters. One of the newly discovered neurotransmitters that has a chemical makeup similar to THC in marijuana is called (e)_____ and is involved in emotions and motor coordination.

F. REFLEX RESPONSES

12. The movement of automatically withdrawing your hand after touching a hot object is called a (a)_____, which involves several or more neurons. Information is carried to the spinal cord by the (b)_____ neuron. Information is carried from the spinal cord to the muscle by the (c)_____ neuron. Connections between efferent (motor) and afferent (sensory) neurons are made by relatively short (d)_____, which also send signals to the brain. The functions of reflexes include protecting body parts from (e)_____ and automatically regulating the (f)_____ responses of the body.

G. RESEARCH FOCUS: WHAT IS A PHANTOM LIMB?

13. The experience of sensations from a limb that has been amputated is called the (a)_____ phenomenon. About 70–80% of patients report sensations of intense pain coming from limbs that have been amputated. A recent explanation of phantom limb sensations is that they arise from the brain's genetically programmed system of sensations that allows the brain to know the locations of all the body's (b)_____.

H. CULTURAL DIVERSITY: PLANTS & DRUGS

14. One of cocaine's effects on the nervous system is to block the process of (a)_____ so that the neurotransmitter remains longer in the synapse, which causes physiological arousal. A drug that blocks receptors on muscles and causes muscle paralysis is (b)_____. A drug that mimics the naturally occurring neurotransmitter norepinephrine and can produce visual hallucinations is (c)_____.

I. APPLICATION: EXPERIMENTAL TREATMENTS

15. The tremors and rigidity of Parkinson's disease result when a group of structures that regulate movement, called the (a)_____, lose their supply of dopamine. In experimental treatment, fetal brain cells or stem cells can be transplanted into a precise location of a patient's brain by a technique called the (b)_____ procedure. Cells that have the amazing capacity to develop into any of the 220 cells that make up the human body are called (c)_____. These cells can be used to treat spinal cord injuries and diseases like Alzheimer's and Parkinson's because stem cells can develop into (d)_____.

Answers: *1. (a) neurons, (b) glial cells; 2. (a) neurons, (b) bird; 3. mind-body; 4. (a) cell body, or soma, (b) dendrite, (c) axon, (d) end bulbs, (e) neurotransmitters; 5. (a) myelin sheath, (b) insulation; 6. (a) synapse, (b) receptors; 7. (a) neurons, (b) central, (c) nerves, (d) peripheral, (e) regrow, (f) peripheral, (g) neurons; 8. (a) chemical gates, (b) resting, (c) sodium, (d) protein, (e) positive, (f) negative, (g) sodium pump; 9. (a) chemical gates, (b) sodium, (c) sodium, (d) action potential, (e) positive, (f) negative; 10. (a) nerve impulse, (b) all-or-none law; 11. (a) neurotransmitters, (b) receptors, (c) excitatory, (d) inhibitory, (e) anandamide; 12. (a) reflex, or reflex response, (b) sensory, or afferent, (c) motor, or efferent, (d) interneurons, (e) injury or harm, (f) physiological; 13. (a) phantom limb, (b) parts; 14. (a) reuptake, (b) curare, (c) mescaline; 15. (a) basal ganglia, (b) stereotaxic, (c) stem cells, (d) neurons*

Critical Thinking

Would You Want a Head Transplant?

Questions

1. From what you know about the central nervous system, what's the major problem in transplanting a head?

2. Why do researchers first develop new medical procedures in animals before trying them on humans?

3. Why do damaged neurons usually wither and die instead of regrowing?

Everyone knows the story of Dr. Frankenstein, who transplanted a brain into a dead body and brought this creature to life with a jolt from a lightning bolt. As a serious and respected researcher, Dr. Robert J. White, Harvard Medical School graduate and professor of neurosurgery at Case Western Reserve University, believes that a complete head (including brain) transplant is becoming increasingly possible.

Dr. White has been working for the past 40 years on the possibility of transplanting a head. In the 1960s, he succeeded in removing brains from monkeys and keeping the brains alive in special solutions for up to 22 hours. In the 1970s, he successfully removed the complete head from one rhesus monkey and transplanted it onto the body of another monkey. He reports that this "new" monkey with the transplanted head regained consciousness, tried to bite the researchers, moved its eyes, and lived for eight days—dying of lung failure. Although transplanting a head has a number of practical applications, it also raises ethical, religious, and moral questions.

As to practical applications, a head transplant would mean that if quadriplegics' bodies developed life-threatening problems, they could have their healthy heads (and brains) transplanted onto healthy donor bodies and thus keep on living. (Quadriplegics have damaged spinal cords that prevent all movement and sensations from the neck down and

often develop life-threatening lung problems.) Because researchers have not yet solved the problem of how to reconnect spinal cords, the quadriplegic's head could not send or receive information from the donor's body. But if you were a quadriplegic with a diseased and dying body, would you want the choice and chance of living a little longer by having your healthy head transplanted onto a donor's healthy body?

Among the ethical and moral questions are whether someone with a healthy head should be allowed to live on top of a stranger's body. Or, how would a family react to knowing that their dead son's or daughter's body is still alive? Among the religious questions are what happens to a person's mind or soul when the person's head is now transplanted onto a different body. Or, is it right to separate the head from the body for any reason?

Dr. White answers these questions by saying that defining death is a medical and not a religious issue. He believes the body is essentially an "energy pack" and concludes by saying, "If a procedure can help somebody live longer, I think most doctors and patients are willing to do what they can, particularly if the alternative is death." (Adapted from S. LaFee, At hand and ahead, *San Diego Union-Tribune*, March 8, 2000, p. E-1)

4. What advances have been made in getting damaged neurons to regrow and in developing new neurons?

5. How do many neuroscientists view the mind-brain distinction?

6. How does Dr. White answer questions about the mind and soul?

Try these InfoTrac search terms: **organ transplant; neurosurgery; quadriplegia; mind-brain.**

1. Surgeons can transplant many body organs (hearts, lungs, kidneys, even hands) because peripheral nerves regrow. However, the major problem in transplanting a complete head involves reconnecting the head's spinal cord to the spinal cord in the donor's body. That's because damaged or severed neurons that are in the central nervous system do not usually reconnect or regrow.
2. This raises the ethical question of whether animals should be used in research. The major reason researchers first use animals to develop complicated medical procedures, such as heart or future head transplants, is to work out problems and avoid life-threatening risks to humans (see p. 41).
3. Damaged neurons (central nervous system) usually wither and die because of a built-in genetic program that turns off future

regrowth or repair once a neuron is fully grown (see p. 49).
4. Researchers are stimulating damaged neurons to regrow by providing tubes to guide regrowth and by injecting growth-producing chemicals. Experimental treatments include injecting stem cells or fetal tissue into the brain (see pp. 51, 61, and 62).
5. As discussed on page 49, the age-old mind-body (brain) question has several answers. Some philosophers believe that the mind (spirit or soul) and brain are separate things. In contrast, many researchers believe that the mind and the brain are either the same thing or like two sides of a coin.
6. Dr. White seems to believe that the mind (soul, spirit) and brain are one and the same since he defines death as being a medical rather than a spiritual problem.

Links to Learning

KEY TERMS/KEY PEOPLE

action potential, 53

afferent, 56

alcohol, 55

all-or-none law, 52

Alzheimer's disease, 47

anandamide, 55

axon, 50

axon membrane, 52

basal ganglia, 60

bird's brains, 49

cell body, 50

central nervous system, 51

cocaine, 59

curare, 59

dendrites, 50

efferent, 56

end bulbs, 50

endorphins, 55

excitatory
  neurotransmitters, 54

fetal tissue transplants, 60

GABA neurons, 55

gene, 48

glial cell, 48

growth of new neurons, 49

inhibitory neurotransmitters, 54

interneuron, 56

ions, 52

mature brain, 48

mescaline, 59

mind-body question, 49

myelin sheath, 50

nerve, 51

nerve impulse, 52

neuron, 48

neurotransmitter, 54

nitric oxide, 55

Parkinson's disease, 60

peripheral nervous system, 51

phantom limb, 58

primate brains, 49

reattaching limbs, 51

reflex, 56

reflex functions, 56

reflex sequence, 56

repair of neurons, 51

repairing the brain, 49

resting state, 53

reuptake, 59

six-week-old brain, 48

sodium pump, 53

stem cells, 60

stereotaxic procedure, 61

synapse, 50

transmitter, 54

LEARNING ACTIVITIES

- **POWERSTUDY CD-ROM 2.0**
  by Tom Doyle and Rod Plotnik
  Check out the "Brain's Building Blocks" SuperModule (disk 1) on
  PowerStudy. This is a completely self-paced module that is fully narrated.
  Don't want the narration? It is easy to turn off! This module includes:
  - Videos—Ina's daughter discusses the impact of Alzheimer's on her
    mother and the family. Other imbedded videos discuss the apparent
    Alzheimer's boom, Alzheimer's and the brain, as well as Parkinson's
    disease.
  - A multitude of animations designed to help you understand each
    section of your text—for example, an overview of the brain and
    coverage of difficult concepts like the action potential.
  - A test of your knowledge using an interactive version of the Summary
    Test on pages 62 and 63. Also access related quizzes—true/false,
    multiple choice, and matching.
  - An interactive version of the Critical Thinking exercise "Would You
    Want a Head Transplant?" on page 64.
  - Key terms, a chapter outline including chapter abstract, and a list of
    hotlinked Web sites that correlate to this module.

 - **SELF-STUDY ASSESSMENT**
  Want help studying? For your customized Study Plan go to
  http://psychology.wadsworth.com/plotnik7e/. This program will
  automatically generate pretests and posttests to help you determine what
  concepts you have mastered and what concepts you still need work on.

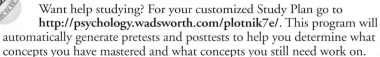 - **STUDY GUIDE and WEBTUTOR**
  Check the corresponding module in your Study Guide for
  effective student tips and help learning the material presented.

- **INFOTRAC COLLEGE EDITION ONLINE LIBRARY**
  To find interesting and relevant articles go to
  http://www.infotrac-college.com, use your password, and then
  type in search terms such as the ones listed below.

Human brain	Neurons	Central nervous system
Cocaine	Reflexes	Nerves

STUDY QUESTIONS

Use InfoTrac to search for topics mentioned in the following questions (e.g., neurotransmitters, phantom limb, fetal tissue transplant).

*A. Overview: Human Brain—Why is it really smart to drive a car
only if it is equipped with driver- and passenger-side airbags?
(**Suggested answer page 620**)

B. Neurons: Structure & Function—How would you decide if a
piece of tissue came from the brain or from a muscle?

C. Neurons Versus Nerves—Headline—"Chimp Brain Transplanted
into Human Skull." Is this possible?

*D. Sending Information—How are the structure and function of
the axon like those of a battery? (**Suggested answer page 620**)

E. Transmitters—What are some of the ways that nerve gas could
cause death?

F. Reflex Responses—How might the reflexes of professional tennis
players differ from those of amateurs?

G. Research Focus: What Is a Phantom Limb?—What problems
might you have after your hand was amputated?

*H. Cultural Diversity: Plants & Drugs—What are the different
ways that drugs can affect neurotransmitters? (**Suggested answer
page 620**)

I. Application: Experimental Treatments—Would you recommend
that a family member with Parkinson's be treated with a fetal transplant?

*These questions are answered in Appendix B.

Module 4: Incredible Nervous System

*PowerStudy 2.0™
Complete Module*

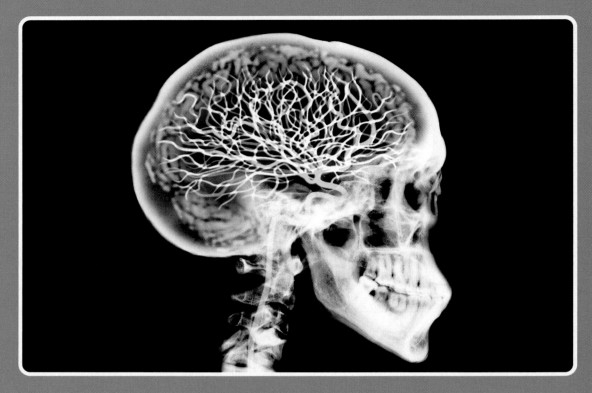

Lucy's Brain: Earliest Ancestor

Although Lucy was fully grown, she was short and slightly built, standing a little under 4 feet tall and weighing about 55 pounds. She had an apelike head, and her face (left drawing)

had a large brow above her eyes and a protruding jaw that held big, uneven front teeth. Lucy had a lot of hair, was very muscular, walked upright on slightly bent legs, and had powerful arms for climbing trees to search for fruits and nuts.

Anthropologists think that Lucy did not make tools, knew nothing of fire, and conversed with hand gestures, waves, and grunts. Lucy's small skull held a brain that was only about the size of a chimpanzee's, which is about

Possible human ancestor lived 3 million years ago.

one-third the size of ours. The males of her species were about a foot taller than Lucy and at least two-thirds heavier.

Anthropologists believe that Lucy's species, formally named *Australopithecus afarensis,* lived about 3 million years ago and may be the earliest ancestor of modern humans (Gibbons, 2002).

We'll use Lucy's brain to illustrate how the human brain is thought to have evolved and increased in size over 3 million years.

Baby Theresa's Brain: Fatal Flaw

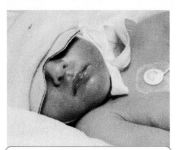

The press called her Baby Theresa. She was one of about 1,000 babies born each year in the United States with a disorder, called anencephaly *(an-in-CEPH-ah-lee),* which is always fatal in the first few years.

Baby Theresa (left photo) was born with almost no brain and therefore would

Theresa was born with almost all of her brain missing.

never develop the functions we associate with being human, such as thinking, talking, reasoning, and planning. She survived for 9 days because a very primitive part of her brain was functioning to keep her alive. This small, primitive brain area lies directly above the spinal cord and regulates vital reflexes, such as breathing, blood pressure, and heart rate. These vital reflexes kept her alive for a short time.

We'll use Baby Theresa's tragic case to illustrate some of the different structures and functions of the brain.

Steve's Brain: Cruel Fate

When Steve walked into the hotel, he felt an incredible pain in his head. He was 28 years old, a successful journalist, and in excellent health, but something terrible was happening.

He could barely talk to the hotel clerk, who said that Steve's room wasn't ready. He slowly walked to a chair and sat down to wait. He glanced at the clock on the wall to

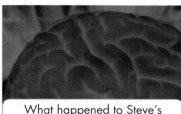

What happened to Steve's brain that prevented him from telling time?

check the time. He could clearly see the hands of the clock, but he could not figure out the time. Like a small child, he said out loud, "The big hand is on twelve and the little hand is on eight." When he heard the words, he knew it was 8 o'clock and wondered why he could tell time by sound but not by sight (S. Fishman, 1988).

We'll use Steve's unsettling experience to show some of the symptoms of brain damage and how neurologists can examine the living brain.

Scott's Brain: Wrong Instructions

"As a very young baby, Scott seemed okay," said his mother, Cindy. "He cooed and smiled at the right times. He babbled at the right times. He seemed normal" (LaFee, 1996, p. E-1). But it was his constant crying that scared her. Scott would walk outside and burst into tears, and no one could comfort him.

As Scott (right photo) got older, other problems developed. He couldn't sit up, he refused to play with other children, and often he was off in a world of his own. An examination of Scott's genetic makeup revealed that he had inherited fragile X syndrome, which is the most common cause of an inherited developmental disorder (Dyer-Friedman et al., 2002).

We'll use Scott's problem to explain how genetic instructions are written and what happens when the instructions have errors.

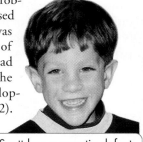

Scott has a genetic defect that affects his functioning.

What's Coming

The brains of Lucy, Baby Theresa, Steve, and Scott raise a number of questions. Lucy's brain brings up the question of evolution, which says that modern brains have been evolving for 3 million years. Baby Theresa's brain raises the question of what it means to be human. Steve's brain brings up the questions of what happens when brains are damaged and whether doctors can look inside living brains. Finally, Scott's brain raises the questions of how brains develop and why things go wrong. We'll answer these questions as well as discuss all the major structures and functions of the human brain.

Let's begin with how genetic instructions are written.

A. Genes & Evolution

What makes brains different?

Your brain and body developed according to complex chemical instructions that were written in a human cell no larger than a grain of sand. The reason brains and bodies have different shapes, colors, and abilities is that they develop from different instructions, which are written at the moment of fertilization.

1 Fertilization. Human life has its beginnings when a father's sperm, which contains 23 chromosomes, penetrates a mother's egg, which contains 23 chromosomes. The result is a fertilized cell called a zygote (shown below).

Sperm + Egg = Zygote

2 Zygote. A zygote (figure above), which is about the size of a grain of sand, is the largest human cell.

A *zygote* is a cell that results when an egg is fertilized. A zygote contains 46 chromosomes arranged in 23 pairs.

A zygote contains the equivalent of 300,000 pages of type-written instructions. For simplicity, the zygote shown above has only 1 pair of chromosomes instead of the usual 23 pairs.

3 Chromosomes. Inside the very tiny zygote are 23 pairs of chromosomes, which contain chemical instructions for development of the brain and body.

A *chromosome* is a short, rodlike, microscopic structure that contains tightly coiled strands of the chemical DNA, which is an abbreviation for deoxyribonucleic (*dee-ox-ee-RYE-bow-new-CLEE-ick*) acid. Each cell of the human body (except for the sperm and egg) contains 46 chromosomes arranged in 23 pairs.

For the sake of simplicity, the cell at the right contains only 4 pairs of chromosomes instead of the usual 23 pairs.

4 Chemical alphabet. Each chromosome contains a long, coiled strand of DNA, which resembles a ladder (left figure) that has been twisted over and over upon itself.

Each rung of the DNA ladder is made up of four chemicals. The order in which the four different chemicals combine to form rungs creates a microscopic chemical alphabet. This chemical alphabet is used to write instructions for the development and assembly of the 100 trillion highly specialized cells that make up the brain and body (Sternberg, 2001).

5 Genes and proteins. On each chromosome are specific segments that contain particular instructions. In the chromosome on the right, each segment is represented by a green band, which represents the location of a gene.

A *gene* is a specific segment on the long strand of DNA that contains instructions for making proteins. Proteins are chemical building blocks from which all the parts of the brain and body are constructed.

For example, genes determine physical traits (eye color, shape of ear lobes) as well as contribute to the development of emotional, cognitive, and behavioral traits (Angier, 2003). When researchers discover a new gene, it means they have identified the exact location of the gene on its chromosome.

6 Genome. The Human Genome Project, which began in 1995 and cost over $2.7 billion, reached its first goal in 2003 of mapping all the human genes (Mestel, 2003a). Unlike earlier estimates of 100,000 human genes, researchers found only about 30,000 human genes (about the same as in a mouse) located on the 23 pairs of chromosomes (Pennisi, 2002). Researchers are now working on the project's other goals: to understand how humans develop physical and psychological traits, to identify sources of genetic diseases, to develop new drugs, and to use gene therapy to treat genetic problems (Kolata, 2003a).

7 Scott's brain: An error in instructions. Earlier, we told you about Scott's unusual physical and behavioral problems. Scott has an inherited genetic disorder called fragile X syndrome.

Fragile X syndrome, an inherited developmental disability, is due to a defect in the X chromosome (shown here as the pinched end of the X chromosome). It can result in physical changes, such as a relatively large head with protruding ears, as well as mild to profound levels of mental retardation.

Fragile X syndrome, which can include changes in both physical features and brain development, illustrates what happens when there is an error in genetic instructions (Loesch et al., 2002). We'll discuss other problems caused by errors in genetic instructions, such as Down syndrome, on page 380.

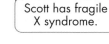

Scott has fragile X syndrome.

Genetic factors. The Human Genome Project and related genetic research are having a tremendous influence on psychology. Researchers are discovering how genetic factors interact with the environment to result in the development of mental retardation, emotional and personality traits, mental disorders, and various cognitive abilities (N. Wade, 2003a).

Next we'll discuss how genetic changes are thought to have affected brain development over millions of years.

What is evolution?

In 1859, Charles Darwin stunned much of the Western world by publishing *Origin of Species,* a revolutionary theory of how species originate, which was the basis for his now famous theory of evolution.

The *theory of evolution* says that different species arose from a common ancestor and that those species that survived were best adapted to meet the demands of their environments.

Although Darwin's theory of evolution is just that—a theory—it has received broad scientific support from both fossil records and more recent examination of genetic similarities and differences among species (Mayr, 2000). The fact that many scientists hold to the theory of evolution clashes with deeply held religious beliefs that place humans on a family tree of their own. According to the theory of evolution, present-day humans descended from a creature that split off from apes millions of years ago. Supporting the theory of evolution is the finding that humans and chimpanzees share at least 98.5% of their DNA or genetic instructions (Balter, 2002).

We will discuss three supposed human ancestors that represent three major milestones in how the human brain is thought to have evolved and developed.

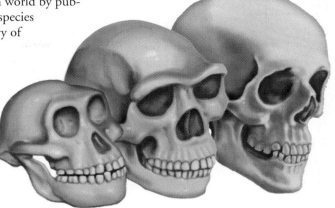

Australopithecus afarensis   *Homo erectus*   *Homo sapiens*

Increasing skull and brain size of proposed ancestors

Perhaps the First Human Brain

Of the three skulls shown above, the smallest one (far left) is thought to have belonged to one of our earliest ancestors, who lived about 3 to 4 million years ago. This proposed ancestor has been given a common name, Lucy, and a scientific name, *Australopithecus afarensis.* Lucy's brain weighed about 500 grams, which is about the size of a chimpanzee's brain and about one-third the size of our brains. Lucy's brain size and skeleton suggest a closer resemblance to apes than to humans. She had long powerful arms and short legs and is thought to have lived mainly on leaves and fruit.

Anthropologists conclude, on the basis of Lucy's rather limited brain size, that her species did not make tools, did not have language, knew nothing of fire, and thus represents the most primitive kind of human (Gibbons, 2002; Lemonick & Dorfman, 1999). Lucy's line died out about a million years ago. Anthropologists believe that another line branched out from Lucy's and gave rise to our genus, which is called *Homo;* this process was accompanied eventually by a threefold increase in brain size.

Brain Doubles in Size

The skull in the middle, which is almost twice as large as Lucy's, belongs to a species named *Homo erectus.* (*Homo* means "man" and *erectus* means "upright.") *Homo erectus,* who lived about one and a half million years ago, is thought to be part of the genus from which modern humans eventually evolved. *Homo erectus* developed a thick-boned skeleton designed for walking upright and was about as tall as modern humans. They are thought to have added meat to their diets.

With a brain size of about 1,000 grams, which was twice as large as Lucy's, *Homo erectus* had increased abilities and made a wide variety of stone tools. The finest was a tear-shaped hand ax, whose production required much more extensive work than any previous tools. There is considerable debate about whether tool-making or the development of language was the main pressure for the doubling in brain size in *Homo erectus* (Gore, 1997; Leonard, 2002). Descendants of *Homo erectus* evolved a still larger brain; these individuals were called *Homo sapiens.*

Brain Triples in Size

The largest skull, on the far right, comes from a modern human, who is called *Homo sapiens* (*sapiens* means "wise"). Our species began about 400,000 years ago and continues to the present day. *Homo sapiens* evolved a brain that weighs about 1,350 grams, or about 3 pounds, which is the average size of our brains today and almost three times the size of Lucy's. With such a significant increase in brain size came four dramatic changes: *Homo sapiens* began growing crops instead of relying on hunting; started to live in social communities instead of roaming the country; developed language, which was a far better way to communicate compared to grunts and gestures; and painted beautiful and colorful representations of animals and humans.

Two forces are thought to be responsible for the evolution of the human brain and its tripling in size: genetic changes or mutations, which are accidental changes in genetic instructions, and natural selection, which means that only those best fitted to their environments will survive (Balter, 2002; Hauser et al., 2002).

Anthropologists believe that it took millions of years for our brains to evolve to their current size. Next, we'll describe how researchers study our modern brains.

B. Studying the Living Brain

Can we look inside the human skull?

We have explained how genetic instructions guide the development and assembly of billions of parts that make up the human brain. We have discussed the anthropologists' belief that the human brain tripled in size through 3 million years of evolution. Now we begin exploring the structure and function of your own brain.

Looking at the skull on the right raises an interesting question: How can researchers look inside the half-inch-thick skull and study the living brain without causing

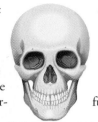

New techniques can take pictures through the skull.

any damage? The answer is that during the past 10 years, researchers have developed several brain scanning techniques that can look through the thick skull and picture the brain with astonishing clarity yet cause no damage to the extremely delicate brain cells. By using these almost science-fiction techniques, researchers are mapping a variety of cognitive functions (reading, listening, doing arithmetic, searching, identifying shapes, faces, and animals) as well as sites of emotional feelings and hunger sensations (Blakeslee, 2000b; Gordon et al., 2000). We'll discuss several brain scanning techniques that take pictures through the skull.

Brain Scans: MRI & fMRI

Why would Steve have an MRI?

At the beginning of this module, we told you about Steve, who was a successful journalist in excellent health. As he walked into his hotel, he felt a sudden searing pain in his head. As he waited for his room, he looked up at the clock and suddenly felt fear because he could clearly see the numbers and the hands but could not figure out the time.

Later, the neurologist told Steve that a blood vessel had burst and blood had flowed into the surrounding area of the brain. The neurologist could identify the exact location and extent of the damaged area by using one of the new brain scanning techniques, called an MRI (photo below).

MRI, or ***magnetic resonance imaging***, involves passing nonharmful radio frequencies through the brain. A computer measures how these signals interact with brain cells and transforms this interaction into an incredibly detailed image of the brain (or body). MRIs are used to study the structure of the brain.

During an MRI procedure, Steve would lie with his head in the center of a giant, donut-shaped machine. Reflections from the radio waves are computer analyzed and developed into very detailed pictures of the living brain, as shown in the photo (below left).

There is also a newer and different version of the MRI, called the fMRI.

The "f" in *fMRI* (functional magnetic resonance imaging) stands for *functional* and measures the activity of specific neurons that are functioning during cognitive tasks, such as thinking, listening, or reading.

For example, the fMRI on the right shows that while the subject was

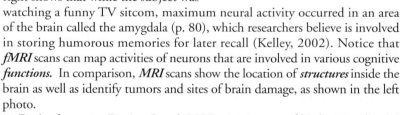

Amygdala is involved in storing humorous bits.

watching a funny TV sitcom, maximum neural activity occurred in an area of the brain called the amygdala (p. 80), which researchers believe is involved in storing humorous memories for later recall (Kelley, 2002). Notice that *fMRI* scans can map activities of neurons that are involved in various cognitive *functions.* In comparison, *MRI* scans show the location of *structures* inside the brain as well as identify tumors and sites of brain damage, as shown in the left photo.

Brain damage. During Steve's MRI scan, images of his brain—slice by slice—appeared on a television screen. Suddenly, standing out from the normal grayish image of a brain slice was an unusual area that indicated dead brain cells (small red area on right of MRI scan). Because the damaged neurons were located in a brain area involved with processing visual information, Steve had experienced visual problems, such as being unable to tell the time by looking at a clock, even though he could see the hands of the clock. However, since only a small part of his visual area was affected, most other functions, such as walking, feeling, speaking, and hearing, were normal. The reason Steve could figure out the time by saying aloud where the big and little hands of the clock were located was that his hearing areas were undamaged.

Advantage. The advantage of the two kinds of MRI scans is that they use nonharmful radio frequencies and give very detailed views of structures and functions inside the living brain (Mayhew, 2003). The use of these two kinds of MRI scans has greatly increased our understanding of the brain.

We'll discuss one other brain scanning technique, called the PET scan, which, similar to the fMRI, is also used to identify cognitive functions.

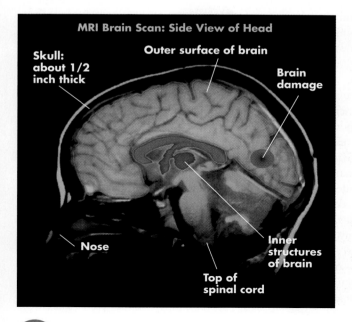

MRI Brain Scan: Side View of Head

Skull: about 1/2 inch thick

Outer surface of brain

Brain damage

Nose

Inner structures of brain

Top of spinal cord

Brain Scans and Cognitive Neuroscience

Are there pictures of thinking?

Currently, one of the most exciting approaches in biological psychology is the area of cognitive neuroscience (p. 7), which involves using imaging techniques to literally light up your thoughts and feelings.

PET scan, or *positron emission tomography,* involves injecting a slightly radioactive

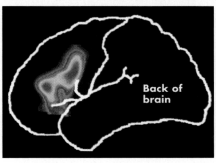

PET scan indicates that when you LOOK at a word, maximum neural activity—areas of red and yellow—occurs in the BACK of your brain.

PET scan indicates that when you SPEAK a word, maximum neural activity—areas of red and yellow—occurs in the FRONT of your brain.

solution into the blood and then measuring the amount of radiation absorbed by brain cells called neurons. Very active neurons absorb more radioactive solution than less active ones. Different levels of absorption are represented by colors—red and yellow indicate maximum activity of neurons, while blue and green indicate minimal activity.

Pictures of thinking and speaking. The PET scan at the top left shows that when the subject was "looking at words" but not speaking them, most neural activity occurred near the back of the brain, which is involved in processing visual information. The PET scan at the bottom left shows that when the subject was "speaking words" instead of just thinking about them, most neural activity occurred near the front part of the brain, which is involved in speaking (Raichle, 1994).

Mapping and understanding. Both PET and fMRI scans are used to identify and map the living brain's neural activity as a person performs complex behavioral and cognitive tasks, such as seeing, moving, thinking, speaking and even remembering humorous bits from TV sitcoms. Currently, PET scans are being replaced by the newer fMRI scans because fMRI scans do not require the injection of slightly radioactive solutions (Canli et al., 2002b).

Next, we'll discuss how brain scans were used to study an interesting puzzle in cognitive neuroscience.

Tools Versus Animals

How do you know if it's a camel or pliers?

An interesting cognitive puzzle is how you can so easily identify thousands of objects. This is a job for PET scans.

Naming animals. As shown at the top right, the thoughts of subjects as they *silently* named animals (camel) activated an area in the back of the brain, which is involved in processing visual information. Researchers think this visual area helps us distinguish sizes, shapes, and colors, such as distinguishing a camel from a horse.

Naming tools. As shown at the bottom right, the thoughts of subjects as they silently named tools (pliers) activated an area in the front of the brain. Researchers think this frontal area helps us think about how we use tools (A. Martin et al., 1996).

Researchers concluded that you are able to identify thousands of objects, in large part, because the brain has two separate built-in systems: one for thoughts about naming animals, which involves distinguishing between sizes, shapes, and colors, and another for thoughts about naming tools, which involves thinking about how tools are used (A. Martin et al., 1996). Other researchers agree that when you see an object, the brain is genetically wired to place different objects, such as tools, animals, faces, and vegetables, into different categories, which are located in different areas of the brain. With this system, you can quickly and easily perceive and make sense of all the objects in your world (Ilmberger et al., 2002).

As we discussed in Module 1 (p. 7), this study is an example of a relatively new area called *cognitive neuroscience,* which identifies and maps differences in neural activity to understand the bases for cognitive functions (Posner & DiGirolamo,

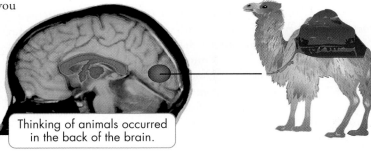

Thinking of animals occurred in the back of the brain.

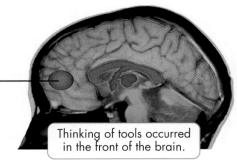

Thinking of tools occurred in the front of the brain.

2000). Later on, we'll discuss a wide range of cognitive processes being studied using brain scans.

Now that you are familiar with ways to study the living brain, we can begin to examine the brain's specific structures and interesting functions.

C. Organization of the Brain

How many nervous systems? Because you have one brain, you may think that means you have one nervous system. In fact, your brain is much more complex: It has two major nervous systems, one of which has four subdivisions. We'll explain the overall organization of the brain's several nervous systems, beginning with its two major divisions, the central and peripheral nervous systems.

A. Major Divisions of the Nervous System

CENTRAL NERVOUS SYSTEM—CNS

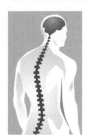

You are capable of many complex cognitive functions—such as thinking, speaking, and reading, as well as moving, feeling, seeing, and hearing—because of your central nervous system.

The *central nervous system* is made up of the brain and spinal cord. From the bottom of the brain emerges the spinal cord, which is made up of neurons and bundles of axons and dendrites that carry information back and forth between the brain and the body.

We'll discuss the major parts of the brain throughout this module.

PERIPHERAL NERVOUS SYSTEM—PNS

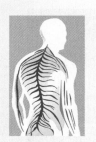

You are able to move your muscles, receive sensations from your body, and perform many other bodily responses because of the peripheral nervous system.

The *peripheral nervous system* includes all the nerves that extend from the spinal cord and carry messages to and from various muscles, glands, and sense organs located throughout the body.

The peripheral nervous system has two subdivisions, the somatic and autonomic nervous systems.

B. Subdivisions of the PNS

SOMATIC NERVOUS SYSTEM

The *somatic nervous system* consists of a network of nerves that connect either to sensory receptors or to muscles that you can move voluntarily, such as muscles in your limbs, back, neck, and chest. Nerves in the somatic nervous system usually contain two kinds of fibers. Afferent, or sensory, fibers carry information from sensory receptors in the skin, muscles, and other organs to the spinal cord and brain. Efferent, or motor, fibers carry information from the brain and spinal cord to the muscles.

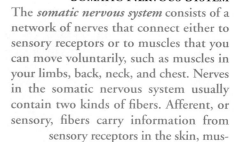

For example, this gymnast controls her muscles, knows where her arms and legs are located in space, and maintains her coordination and balance because the somatic nervous system sends electrical signals back and forth to her brain.

ANS—AUTONOMIC NERVOUS SYSTEM

The *autonomic nervous system* regulates heart rate, breathing, blood pressure, digestion, hormone secretion, and other functions. The autonomic nervous system usually functions without conscious effort, which means that only a few of its responses, such as breathing, can also be controlled voluntarily.

The autonomic nervous system also has two subdivisions, the sympathetic and parasympathetic divisions.

C. Subdivisions of the ANS

SYMPATHETIC DIVISION

The *sympathetic division,* which is triggered by threatening or challenging physical or psychological stimuli, increases physiological arousal and prepares the body for action.

For example, the sight of a frightening snake would trigger the sympathetic division, which, in turn, would arouse the body for action, such as fighting or fleeing.

PARASYMPATHETIC DIVISION

The *parasympathetic division* returns the body to a calmer, relaxed state and is involved in digestion.

For example, when you are feeling calm and relaxed or digesting food, your parasympathetic system is activated.

Now that you know the overall organization of the nervous system, we'll focus on major parts of the brain.

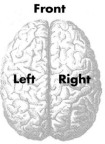

Front

Left | **Right**

Back

Can someone be shot in the head but not die?

A human brain (right figure), which can easily be held in one hand, weighs about 1,350 grams, or 3 pounds, and has the consistency of firm Jell-O. The brain is protected by a thick skull and covered with thin, tough, plasticlike membranes. If shot in the head, a person may or may not die depending on which area was damaged. For example, damage to an area in the forebrain would result in paralysis, damage to an area in the midbrain would result in coma, but damage to an area in the hindbrain would certainly result in death.

We'll begin our exploration of the brain by looking at its three major parts—forebrain, midbrain, and hindbrain—beginning with the forebrain.

1 Forebrain

When you look at the brain, what you are actually seeing is almost all forebrain (figure above). The *forebrain,* which is the largest part of the brain, has right and left sides that are called hemispheres. The hemispheres, which are connected by a wide band of fibers, are responsible for an incredible number of functions, including learning and memory, speaking and language, emotional responses, experiencing sensations, initiating voluntary movements, planning, and making decisions.

The large structure outlined in orange to the left shows only the right hemisphere of the forebrain. The forebrain's right and left hemispheres are both shown in the figure at the top right. The forebrain is very well developed in humans.

Side view of the brain's right hemisphere

2 Midbrain

If a boxer is knocked unconscious, part of the reason lies in the midbrain.

The *midbrain* has a reward or pleasure center, which is stimulated by food, sex, money, music, looking at attractive faces, and some drugs (cocaine); has areas for visual and auditory reflexes, such as automatically turning your head toward a noise; and contains the reticular formation, which arouses the forebrain so that it is ready to process information from the senses (Holroyd & Coles, 2002).

If the reticular formation were seriously damaged—by a blow to the head, for example—a person would be unconscious and might go into a coma because the forebrain could not be aroused (Steriade, 1966).

3c Cerebellum

A person suspected of drunken driving may fail the test of rapidly touching a finger to the nose because of alcohol's effects on the cerebellum.

The *cerebellum,* which is located at the very back and underneath the brain, is involved in coordinating motor movements but not in initiating voluntary movements. The cerebellum is also involved in performing timed motor responses, such as those needed in playing games or sports, and in automatic or reflexive learning, such as blinking the eye to a signal, which is called classical conditioning (discussed in Module 9) (Hazeltine & Ivry, 2002; Spencer et al., 2003).

Because alcohol is a depressant drug and interferes with the functions of the cerebellum, an intoxicated person would experience decreased coordination and have difficulty rapidly touching a finger to the nose, which is one of the tests for being drunk.

Of the brain's three parts, the forebrain is the largest, most evolved, and most responsible for an enormous range of personal, social, emotional, and cognitive behaviors. For those reasons, we'll examine the forebrain in more detail.

3 Hindbrain

The structures and functions of the hindbrain, which are found in very primitive brains, such as the alligator's, have remained constant through millions of years of evolution. The *hindbrain* has three distinct structures: the pons, medulla, and cerebellum.

3a Pons

If someone has a serious sleep disorder, it may involve the pons. In Latin, *pons* means "bridge," which suggests its function.

The *pons* functions as a bridge to interconnect messages between the spinal cord and brain. The pons also makes chemicals involved in sleep (Cirelli et al., 1996).

3b Medulla

If someone dies of a drug overdose, the cause of death probably involved the medulla.

The *medulla,* which is located at the top of the spinal cord, includes a group of cells that control vital reflexes, such as respiration, heart rate, and blood pressure.

Large amounts of alcohol, heroin, or other depressant drugs suppress the functions of cells in the medulla and cause death by stopping breathing.

D. Control Centers: Four Lobes

How do you package 1 trillion cells?

How would you design a brain to hold 1 trillion cells (100 billion neurons and 900 billion glial cells) and be no bigger than a small melon and weigh no more than 3 pounds? You would need to make the cells microscopic in size, which they are, and to organize the billions of cells into different but interconnected areas, which they are. But would you have thought to make the brain's surface very wrinkled? Here's why.

WRINKLED CORTEX

In the photo below you see a computer-enhanced photo of the outside of an adult human brain, which has a very wrinkled surface that is called the cortex (in Latin, *cortex* means "cover").

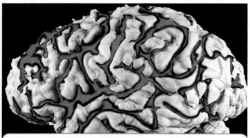

Brain's surface shows its wrinkled cortex.

The *cortex* is a thin layer of cells that essentially covers the entire surface of the forebrain. The vast majority of our neurons are located in the cortex, which folds over on itself so that it forms a large surface area.

To understand the advantage of having a wrinkled cortex, just imagine having to put a large sheet of paper about 18 inches square into a small match box that is 3 inches square. One solution is to crumple (wrinkle) the sheet of paper until it easily fits into the tiny match box. Similarly, imagine many billions of neurons laid on a sheet of paper about 18 inches square. When this large sheet of neurons is wrinkled, the cortex can fit snugly into our much smaller, rounded skulls.

Early researchers divided the wrinkled cortex into four different areas, or lobes, each of which has different functions.

FOUR LOBES

As you look at the brain's cortex, you see a wrinkled surface of peaks and valleys with very few distinguishing features. However, the cortex's appearance is deceiving because its hundreds of different functions are organized into four separate areas called lobes.

The cortex is divided into four separate areas, or *lobes,* each with different functions: the *frontal lobe* is involved with personality, emotions, and motor behaviors; the *parietal* (*puh-RYE-it-all*) *lobe* is involved with perception and sensory experiences; the *occipital* (*ock-SIP-pih-tull*) *lobe* is involved with processing visual information; and the *temporal* (*TEM-purr-all*) *lobe* is involved with hearing and speaking.

Cortex is divided into four different areas, or lobes.

The one brain structure that most clearly distinguishes you from animals is your well-developed cortex, which allows you to read, understand, talk about, and remember the concepts in this text. To understand what life would be like without a cortex, we'll return to the case of Baby Theresa, who was born without any lobes and thus no cortex.

BABY THERESA'S BRAIN: A FATAL DEFECT

At the beginning of this module, we told you about Baby Theresa, who was one of the 1,000 babies born each year in the United States with almost no brain. This rare condition, caused by errors in genetic instructions, is called anencephaly (J. Chen et al., 1996).

Anencephaly (*an-in-CEPH-ah-lee*) refers to the condition of being born with little or no brain. If some brain or nervous tissue is present, it is totally exposed and often damaged because the top of the skull is missing. Survival is usually limited to days; the longest has been two months.

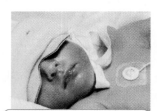

Theresa has anencephaly, meaning little or no brain.

Anencephaly is always fatal because it also includes other serious physical defects, such as damage to the heart (Stumpf et al., 1990). Baby Theresa (photo above), who survived only nine days, had almost no brain tissue and almost no skull (bandaged area above eyes). Lacking most of a brain means that she would be incapable of perceiving, thinking, speaking, planning, or making decisions.

The figure below shows that a baby born with anencephaly has no forebrain. One reason babies with anencephaly may survive for days or weeks is that they may have parts of their hindbrain. As discussed earlier, the hindbrain contains the pons (blue) and medulla (red). The medulla controls vital reflexes, such as breathing, heart rate, and blood pressure, which together can maintain life for a period of time.

This example of anencephaly shows that without the forebrain, a baby may be physiologically alive but show no signs

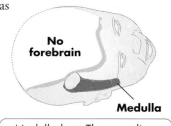

Medulla kept Theresa alive.

of having a mind or possessing cognitive abilities associated with being human. In a real sense, it is the functions of the forebrain's four lobes that define us as human and distinguish us from all other creatures.

Because the four lobes are vital to our existence as humans, we'll discuss each lobe in turn. We'll begin with the frontal lobe and a tragic accident.

What does the biggest lobe do?

The frontal lobe (right figure) is the largest of the brain's four lobes and has a number of important functions (E. Goldberg, 2001; Sylvester et al., 2003).

The *frontal lobe*, which is located in the front part of the brain, includes a huge area of cortex. The frontal lobe is involved in many functions: performing voluntary motor movements, interpreting and performing emotional behaviors, behaving normally in social situations, maintaining a healthy personality, paying attention to things in the environment, making decisions, and executing plans. Because the frontal lobe is involved in making decisions, planning, reasoning, and carrying out behaviors, it is said to have executive functions, much like the duties of a company's executive officer.

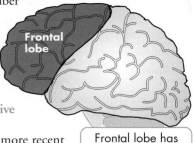

Frontal lobe has executive functions.

Our first clue about the functions of the frontal lobe came from an unusual accident in 1848; our more recent knowledge comes from research using brain scans (fMRI and PET scans). Let's first go back in time and meet Phineas Gage, whose accident led to the discovery of one of the frontal lobe's important functions.

A TERRIBLE ACCIDENT

The accident occurred at about half past four on the afternoon of September 13, 1848, near the small town of Cavendish, Vermont. Railroad crewmen were about to blast a rock that blocked their way. Foreman Phineas Gage filled a deep, narrow hole in the rock with powder and rammed in a long iron rod to tamp down the charge before covering it with sand. But the tamping iron rubbed against the side of the shaft, and a spark ignited the powder. The massive rod—$3\frac{1}{2}$ feet long, $1\frac{1}{4}$ inches in diameter, and weighing 13 pounds—shot from the hole under the force of the explosion. It struck Phineas just beneath his left eye and tore through his skull. It shot out the top of his head and landed some 50 yards away.

Phineas survived, but, following the accident, his personality changed: He went from being a popular, friendly foreman to acting impatient, cursing his workers, and refusing to honor his promises.

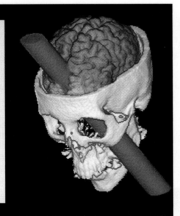

A massive rod (right image) weighing 13 pounds was accidentally driven through the front part of Phineas Gage's frontal lobe. The result, which was similar to having a frontal lobotomy, caused Phineas to have emotional outbursts and problems in making decisions, something he did not experience before this accident.

Researchers recently used Phineas's preserved skull to reconstruct the site and extent of his brain damage. As the figure above shows, the iron rod had passed through and extensively damaged Phineas's frontal lobe. Researchers concluded that Phineas had suffered a crude form of frontal lobotomy, which caused deficits in processing of emotion and decision making that result after damage to the frontal lobe (H. Damasio et al., 1994).

Beginning in the 1930s, doctors performed thousands of lobotomies to treat various mental and behavioral problems.

FRONTAL LOBOTOMY

In 1936, Egas Moniz, a Portuguese neurologist, used an untested surgical treatment, called frontal lobotomy, to treat individuals with severe emotional problems.

A *frontal lobotomy* was a surgical procedure in which about one-third of the front part of the frontal lobe (figure below) was cut away from the rest of the brain.

Moniz first reported that frontal lobotomies did reduce emotional problems in about 35% of severely agitated human patients, although he did no controlled or follow-up studies to check long-term effects (D. R. Weinberger et al., 1995). Based on Moniz's reports of success, about 18,000 frontal lobotomies were performed in the 1940s and 1950s on emotionally disturbed patients who were primarily confined to state mental hospitals that had no other treatments.

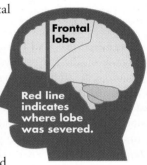

Red line indicates where lobe was severed.

RESULTS OF LOBOTOMIES

Initially, neurologists reported good short-term effects, but better controlled, long-term studies on frontal lobotomies found mixed results: Some patients did become less violent, but others showed no improvement and some became worse (Swayze, 1995). Even those whose social-emotional behaviors improved were often left with serious problems in other areas, such as having difficulty in making and carrying out plans, adjusting to new social demands, or behaving with appropriate emotional responses in social situations (Valenstein, 1986).

Two things happened in the early 1950s that ended the use of frontal lobotomies to treat social-emotional problems. First, follow-up research indicated that lobotomies were no more successful in relieving social-emotional problems than doing nothing. Second, antipsychotic drugs were discovered and showed greater success in treating serious social-emotional problems (Swayze, 1995).

From using frontal lobotomies as treatment, researchers learned two things: (1) careful follow-up work is essential before declaring a treatment successful and (2) the frontal lobe has many different, important functions, which we'll look at next.

D. Control Centers: Four Lobes

How do you move your right hand?

The organization of the frontal lobe is somewhat confusing because it has such a wide range of functions, from motor movements to cognitive processes. We'll first focus on motor movements, which have a very unusual feature.

In the figure on the right, notice that nerves from the right hemisphere (blue) cross over and control the movements of the left hand and left side of the body; nerves from the left hemisphere (red) cross over and control the movements of the right hand and right side of the body. The ability to move your hand or any other part of your body depends on the motor cortex in the right and left frontal lobes.

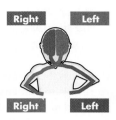

1 Location of Motor Cortex

To move your right hand, you will use the motor cortex in your left frontal lobe.

The ***motor cortex*** is a narrow strip of cortex that is located on the back edge of the frontal lobe and extends down its side. The motor cortex is involved in the initiation of all voluntary movements. The right motor cortex controls muscles on the left side of the body and vice versa.

You can move any individual part of your body at will because of how the motor cortex is organized.

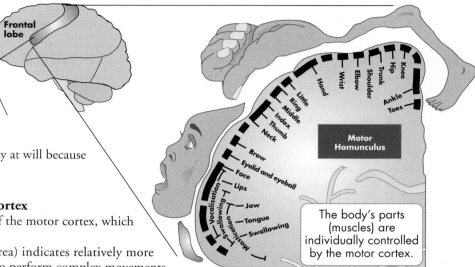

The body's parts (muscles) are individually controlled by the motor cortex.

2 Organization and Function of Motor Cortex

The figure on the right shows an enlarged part of the motor cortex, which is organized in two interesting ways.

First, a larger body part (notice huge hand area) indicates relatively more area on the motor cortex and thus more ability to perform complex movements. A smaller body part (notice small knee area) indicates relatively less area on the motor cortex and thus less ability to perform complex movements. This unusual drawing, which uses sizes of body parts to show the ability to perform complex movements, is called the ***motor homunculus*** (ho-MONK-you-luss). **Second,** each body part has its own area on the motor cortex. This means that damage to one part of the motor cortex could result in paralysis of that part yet spare most other parts. However, recent studies indicate that motor cortex is not as discretely organized as once believed. Instead of each body part having a different, discrete area, there is considerable overlap between body parts in the motor cortex (Helmuth, 2002). Finally, notice that the motor cortex makes up only a relatively small part of the entire frontal lobe.

In a surprising finding, researchers discovered that the motor cortex was involved in remembering the order of events across time, such as the order in which dots appeared on a TV monitor (Georgopoulos, 1999). This means that besides triggering voluntary movements, the motor cortex may also be involved in remembering the order of how stimuli occur across time. Next, we'll explain the frontal lobe's other functions.

3 Other Functions of Frontal Lobe

Brain damage. Much of our knowledge of other frontal lobe functions comes from individuals who had damage to that area. By studying patients like Phineas Gage, researchers found that damage to frontal lobes may result in disruption of personality as well as emotional swings. From studying patients with damage to frontal lobes, researchers found that frontal lobes are involved in paying attention, remembering things, making good decisions, and planning and organizing events (Stuss & Levine, 2002).

Brain scans. Researchers have also identified many cognitive functions of the frontal lobe by taking brain scans while subjects perform various tasks. For example, subjects were shown a noun, such as *hammer*, and asked to think of an appropriate verb, such as *hit*. PET scans, such as the one shown here, indicated that maximum activity (red and yellow areas)

occurred in the frontal lobe. This means that the frontal lobe is involved in our thinking processes (Fiez & Petersen, 1993). Other studies indicate that the frontal lobes are involved in paying attention and learning rules of social and moral behavior (A. Damasio, 1999).

Executive function. Because the frontal lobes are involved in paying attention, organizing, planning, deciding, and carrying out different kinds of cognitive tasks as well as social-emotional behaviors, the frontal lobes are said to have an executive function—that is, act similar to a smart, successful executive of a large organization (E. Goldberg, 2001).

Immediately behind the frontal lobe is the parietal lobe, which, among other things, keeps track of your body's limbs.

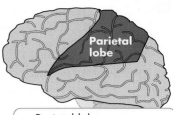

Parietal lobe processes information from body parts.

How do you know where your feet are?

Every second of every minute of every day, your brain must keep track of what's touching your skin, where your feet and hands are, and whether you're walking or running. All this is automatically and efficiently done by your parietal lobe (right figure).

The *parietal lobe* is located directly behind the frontal lobe. The parietal lobe's functions include processing sensory information from body parts, which includes touching, locating positions of limbs, and feeling temperature and pain, and carrying out several cognitive functions, such as attending to and perceiving objects.

For example, the ability to know what you're touching involves the parietal lobe's somatosensory cortex.

1 Location of Somatosensory Cortex

Knowing what you're touching or how hot to make the water for your shower involves the somatosensory cortex.

The *somatosensory cortex* is a narrow strip of cortex that is located on the front edge of the parietal lobe and extends down its side. The somatosensory cortex processes sensory information about touch, location of limbs, pain, and temperature. The right somatosensory cortex receives information from the left side of the body and vice versa.

Your lips are much more sensitive than your elbows because of the way the somatosensory cortex is organized.

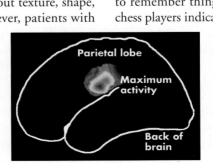

Sensory Homunculus

Information from body parts (skin, muscles, etc.) is individually processed by the somatosensory cortex.

2 Organization of Somatosensory Cortex

The large figure on the right shows an enlarged part of the somatosensory cortex, which is also cleverly organized.

First, notice the different sizes of the body parts drawn on top of the somatosensory cortex. A larger body part (notice large area for lips) indicates relatively more area on the somatosensory cortex and thus more sensitivity to external stimulation. A smaller body part (notice small nose area) indicates relatively less area on the somatosensory cortex and thus less sensitivity to external stimulation. This unusual drawing, which uses sizes of body parts to indicate amount of sensitivity to external stimulation, is called the *sensory homunculus* (*ho-MONK-you-luss*). In Latin, *homunculus* means "little man." Notice that the somatosensory cortex makes up only a small part of the parietal lobe.

Second, notice that each body part has its own area on the somatosensory cortex. This means that damage to one part of the somatosensory cortex could result in loss of feeling to one part of the body yet completely spare all others. Next, we'll explain the parietal lobe's other functions.

3 Other Functions of Parietal Lobe

Brain damage. When you put your hand in your pocket, you can easily tell a key from a nickel from a stick of chewing gum because your parietal lobe digests information about texture, shape, and size and "tells you" what the object is. However, patients with damage to the back of their parietal lobes cannot recognize common objects by touch or feel (Bear et al., 1996). Evidence that the parietal lobes are involved in other cognitive processes comes from studies using PET scans (Banati et al., 2000).

PET scans. Researchers asked subjects to remember letters they saw on a screen by repeating them over and over in their minds. PET scans, such as the one shown here, indicated that

Parietal lobe

Maximum activity

Back of brain

maximum activity during this task occurred in the parietal lobe. Researchers concluded that the parietal lobe is involved when we try to remember things (Paulesu et al., 1993). Other PET studies on chess players indicated that the parietal lobe was involved in perceiving and analyzing the positions of chess pieces on the board (Nichelli et al., 1994).

Thus, case studies and PET scans indicate that the parietal lobe is involved in several cognitive functions, including recognizing objects, remembering items, and perceiving and analyzing objects in space.

Immediately below the parietal lobe is the temporal lobe, which we'll examine next.

D. Control Centers: Four Lobes

Did you hear your name?

You recognize your name when you hear it spoken; because of the way sound is processed in the temporal lobe, you know it's not just some meaningless noise.

The *temporal lobe* is located directly below the parietal lobe and is involved in hearing, speaking coherently, and understanding verbal and written material.

As you'll see, the process of hearing and recognizing your name involves two steps and two different brain areas.

1a Primary Auditory Cortex

The first step in hearing your name occurs when sounds reach specific areas in the temporal lobe called the primary auditory (hearing) cortex—there is one in each lobe.

The *primary auditory cortex* (**shown in red**), which is located on the top edge of each temporal lobe, receives electrical signals from receptors in the ears and transforms these signals into meaningless sound sensations, such as vowels and consonants.

At this point, you would not be able to recognize your name because the primary auditory cortex only changes electrical signals from the ears into basic sensations, such as individual sounds, clicks, or noises. For these meaningless sound sensations to become recognizable words, they must be sent to another area in the temporal lobe, called the auditory association area (Feng & Ratnam, 2000).

Temporal lobe

Temporal lobe processes auditory (hearing) information.

1b Auditory Association Area

The second step in recognizing your name is when the primary auditory cortex sends its electrical signals to the auditory association area; there is one in each lobe.

The *auditory association area* (**shown in blue**), which is located directly below the primary auditory cortex, transforms basic sensory information, such as noises or sounds, into recognizable auditory information, such as words or music.

It is only after auditory information is sent by the primary auditory cortex to the auditory association area that you would recognize sounds as your name, or words, or music (Feng & Ratnam, 2000). So, it is safe to say that you hear with your brain, rather than your ears.

Besides being involved in hearing, the temporal lobe has other areas that are critical for speaking and understanding words and sentences.

2 Broca's Area—Frontal Lobe

Just as hearing your name is a two-step process, so is speaking a sentence. The first step is putting words together, which involves an area in the frontal lobe called Broca's (*BROKE-ahs*) area.

Broca's area, which is usually located in the left frontal lobe, is necessary for combining sounds into words and arranging words into meaningful sentences. Damage to this area results in *Broca's aphasia* (*ah-PHASE-zz-ah*), which means a person cannot speak in fluent sentences but can understand written and spoken words.

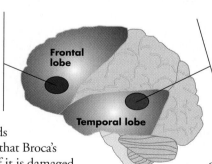

Frontal lobe

Temporal lobe

The reason that saying words and putting words into sentences come naturally to small children is that Broca's area is genetically programmed to do this task. If it is damaged, people with Broca's aphasia have difficulty putting words into sentences. For example, a patient was asked, "What have you been doing in the hospital?" The patient answered, "Yes, sure. Me go, er, uh, P.T. non o'cot, speech . . . two times . . . read . . . wr . . . ripe, er, rike, er, write . . . practice . . . get-ting better" (H. Gardner, 1976, p. 61). The patient was trying to say, "I go to P.T. (physical therapy) at one o'clock to practice speaking, reading, and writing, and I'm getting better."

A patient with Broca's aphasia cannot speak fluently but can still understand words and sentences because of a second area in the temporal lobe—Wernicke's area (Hotz, 2000).

3 Wernicke's Area—Temporal Lobe

The first step in speaking is using Broca's area to combine sounds into words and arrange words into sentences. The second step is to understand sentences, which involves Wernicke's (*VERN-ick-ees*) area.

Wernicke's area, which is usually located in the left temporal lobe, is necessary for speaking in coherent sentences and for understanding speech. Damage to this area results in *Wernicke's aphasia*, which is a difficulty in understanding spoken or written words and a difficulty in putting words into meaningful sentences.

For example, a patient with Wernicke's aphasia said, "You know, once in awhile I get caught up, I mention the tarripoi, a month ago, quite a little, I've done a lot well" (H. Gardner, 1976, p. 68). As this meaningless sentence shows, Wernicke's area is critical for combining words into meaningful sentences and being able to speak coherently (Basso, 2000).

Due to genetic factors, most right-handers (96%) and a majority of left-handers (70–80%) have Broca's and Wernicke's areas in the left hemisphere. In about 20% of left-handers, the language areas are either in the right hemisphere or in both hemispheres (Bower, 2002).

Compared to many other animals, humans rely more heavily on visual information, which is processed in the occipital lobe, our next topic.

Can you see better than dogs?

Dogs have very poor color vision and rely much more on their sense of smell. In comparison, all primates, which include monkeys, apes, and humans, have a relatively poor sense of smell and rely much more on vision for gathering information about their environments.

If you have ever been hit on the back of the head and saw "stars," you already know that vision is located in the occipital lobe.

The *occipital lobe* is located at the very back of the brain and is involved in processing visual information, which includes seeing colors and perceiving and recognizing objects, animals, and people.

Although you see and recognize things with great ease, it is actually a complicated two-step process. Here, we'll give only an overview of that process; we'll go into more detail in Module 5.

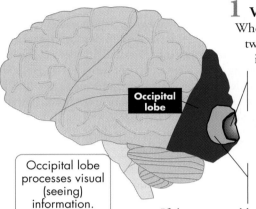

Occipital lobe processes visual (seeing) information.

1 Vision

When you look in the mirror and see your face, you don't realize that seeing your face involves two steps and two different areas in the occipital lobe (Maldonado et al., 1997). The first step in seeing your face involves the primary visual cortex.

The *primary visual cortex*, which is located at the very back of the occipital lobe, receives electrical signals from receptors in the eyes and transforms these signals into meaningless basic visual sensations, such as lights, lines, shadows, colors, and textures.

Since the primary visual cortex produces only meaningless visual sensations (lights, lines, shadows), you do not yet see your face. Transforming meaningless visual sensations into a meaningful visual object occurs in the visual association area (Logothetis, 1999).

The *visual association area*, which is located next to the primary visual cortex, transforms basic sensations, such as lights, lines, colors, and textures, into complete, meaningful visual perceptions, such as persons, objects, or animals.

If there are problems in the second step, such as damage to the visual association area, the person can still see parts of objects but has difficulty combining the parts and seeing or recognizing the whole object (B. Bower, 1996). We'll discuss two unusual visual problems that result from damage to association areas.

2 Visual Agnosia

Since the visual association area is critical for recognizing faces, shapes, and objects, damage to this area results in difficulties of recognition, a condition called visual agnosia (*ag-NO-zee-ah*).

In *visual agnosia*, the individual fails to recognize some object, person, or color, yet has the ability to see and even describe pieces or parts of some visual stimulus.

Here's what happened when a patient with damage to the visual association area was asked to simply copy an object.

A patient who has visual agnosia was asked to make a copy of this horse, something most everyone can do.

The patient drew each part of the horse separately and could not combine individual parts into a meaningful image.

Patients with visual agnosia can see individual parts of an object, such as a horse's leg, but, because of damage to visual association areas, have great difficulty combining parts to perceive or draw a complete and recognizable image, such as a complete horse (Maratsos & Matheny, 1994). Damage to association areas can also result in seeing only half of one's world.

3 Neglect Syndrome

Individuals who have damage to association areas, usually in occipital and parietal lobes, and usually in the right hemisphere, experience a very strange problem called the neglect syndrome.

The *neglect syndrome* refers to the failure of a patient to see objects or parts of the body on the side opposite the brain damage. Patients may dress only one side of their body and deny that opposite body parts are theirs ("that's not my leg").

Here's how a patient with neglect syndrome drew an object.

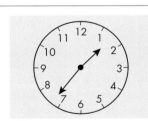 

A patient with neglect syndrome caused by right-sided brain damage was asked to copy this clock.

The patient drew only the right side of the clock because he did not see or recognize things on his left side.

After a stroke or other damage, usually to the occipital and parietal association areas in the right hemisphere, patients may behave as if the left sides of objects or their own bodies no longer exist: they may not shave or dress the left sides of their bodies, which they do not recognize. Neglect syndrome shows the important function of association areas in recognizing things (Springer & Deutsch, 1997).

Now we'll journey beneath the cortex and explore a group of structures that existed in evolutionarily very old, primitive brains.

E. Limbic System: Old Brain

How are you like an alligator?

Your cortex is involved in numerous cognitive functions, such as thinking, deciding, planning, and speaking, as well as other sensory and motor behaviors. But what triggers your wide range of emotional experiences, such as feeling happy, sad, or angry? The answer lies deeper inside the brain, where you'll find a number of interconnected structures that are involved in emotions and are called the limbic system (Dolan, 2002).

The *limbic system* refers to a group of about half a dozen interconnected structures that make up the core of the forebrain. The limbic system's structures are involved with regulating many motivational behaviors such as obtaining food, drink, and sex; with organizing emotional behaviors such as fear, anger, and aggression; and with storing memories.

The limbic system is often referred to as our primitive, or animal, brain because its same structures are found in the brains of animals that are evolutionarily very old, such as alligators. The alligator's limbic system, which essentially makes up its entire forebrain, is primarily involved in smelling out prey, defending territory, hunting, fighting, reproducing, eating, and remembering. The human limbic system, which makes up only a small part of the human forebrain, is involved in similar behaviors.

Alligators and humans have limbic systems.

We'll discuss some of the major structures and functions of the limbic system. The drawing below shows the right hemisphere (left hemisphere cut away). Notice that the limbic structures are surrounded by the forebrain, whose executive functions regulate the limbic system's emotional and motivational behaviors.

Important Parts of Limbic System

1 One limbic structure that is a master control for many emotional responses is the hypothalamus (*high-po-THAL-ah-mus*).

The *hypothalamus* regulates many motivational behaviors, including eating, drinking, and sexual responses; emotional behaviors, such as arousing the body when fighting or fleeing; and the secretion of hormones, such as occurs at puberty.

In addition, the hypothalamus controls the two divisions of the autonomic nervous system discussed on the right-hand page.

The next limbic structure, the amygdala, is also involved in emotions but more so in the forming and remembering of them.

2 The *amygdala* (*ah-MIG-duh-la*), located in the tip of the temporal lobe, receives input from all the senses. It plays a major role in evaluating the emotional significance of stimuli and facial expressions, especially those involving fear, distress, or threat.

When the amygdala is damaged, patients had difficulty recognizing emotional facial expressions and animals did not learn to fear or avoid dangerous situations. Brain scans indicate that the amygdala is involved in identifying emotional facial expressions (Hamann et al., 2002). Researchers report that the amygdala is critical in recognizing emotional facial expressions, including happy faces but especially faces indicating fear, distress, or threat; evaluating emotional situations, especially involving threat or danger; and adding emotional feelings to happy or sad events (going to a funeral, remembering a joke) (Dolan, 2002).

3 This limbic structure, which is like a miniature computer that gathers and processes information from your senses, is called the thalamus (*THAL-ah-mus*).

The *thalamus* is involved in receiving sensory information, doing some initial processing, and then relaying the sensory information to areas of the cortex, including the somatosensory cortex, primary auditory cortex, and primary visual cortex.

For example, if the thalamus malfunctions, you might have difficulty processing sensory information (hearing or seeing).

Our last limbic structure, the hippocampus, is involved in saving your memories.

4 The *hippocampus,* which is a curved structure inside the temporal lobe, is involved in saving many kinds of fleeting memories by putting them into permanent storage in various parts of the brain.

For example, humans with damage to the hippocampus have difficulty remembering new facts, places, faces, or conversations because these new events cannot be placed into permanent storage (Rolls, 2000; Squire & Zola-Morgan, 1991). Think of the hippocampus, which is involved in saving things in long-term storage (see p. 268), as functioning like the "Save" command on your computer.

Limbic system versus frontal lobe. Some of the basic emotional feelings triggered by the limbic system (anger, rage, fear, panic) carry the potential for self-injury or injury to others. Researchers found that our larger and evolutionarily newer frontal lobe, which is involved in thinking, deciding, and planning, plays a critical role in controlling the limbic system's powerful urges (Dolan, 2002).

One particular structure in the limbic system, the hypothalamus, also has an important role in regulating the autonomic nervous system, which we'll examine next.

Why don't you worry about breathing?

You are unaware of what regulates your breathing, heart rate, hormone secretions, or body temperature. You're not concerned about these vital functions because they are usually controlled by a separate nervous system, called the autonomic nervous system, which, in turn, is regulated by a master control center, the hypothalamus (discussed on the previous page).

The autonomic nervous system, which regulates numerous physiological responses, has two divisions, the sympathetic and parasympathetic nervous systems. The sympathetic division is activated when you suddenly see a snake; then the parasympathetic division helps you relax (Cacioppo et al., 2000). We'll explain some of the specific and automatic functions of the sympathetic and parasympathetic divisions.

Sympathetic Nervous System

If you were on a nature hike and suddenly saw a snake, your cortex would activate the hypothalamus, which in turn triggers the sympathetic division of the autonomic nervous system (S. Johnson, 2003).

The *sympathetic division,* which is one part of the autonomic nervous system, is triggered by threatening or challenging physical stimuli, such as a snake, or by psychological stimuli, such as the thought of having to give a public speech. Once triggered, the sympathetic division increases the body's physiological arousal.

All of the physiological responses listed in the left column under *Sympathetic,* such as increased heart rate, increased blood pressure, and dilated pupils, put your body into a state of heightened physiological arousal, which is called the fight-flight response.

The *fight-flight response,* which is a state of increased physiological arousal caused by activation of the sympathetic division, helps the body cope with and survive threatening situations.

You have no doubt experienced the fight-flight response many times, such as when you felt your heart pound and your mouth go dry. Later, we'll discuss the role of the fight-flight response in stressful situations and its role in psychosomatic diseases (pp. 484–489).

Parasympathetic Nervous System

After you have been physiologically aroused by seeing a snake, it is usually some time before your body returns to a calmer state. The process of decreasing physiological arousal and calming down your body is triggered by the hypothalamus, which activates the parasympathetic division.

The *parasympathetic division,* which is the other part of the autonomic nervous system, decreases physiological arousal and helps return the body to a calmer, more relaxed state. It also stimulates digestion during eating.

As shown in the right column under the heading *Parasympathetic,* the parasympathetic division, once activated, decreases physiological arousal by decreasing heart rate, lowering blood pressure, and stimulating digestion. These responses result in the body returning to a more relaxed state.

In dealing with stress, we'll discuss many relaxation techniques (pp. 502–503), such as the relaxation response, various forms of meditation, and biofeedback, which help increase parasympathetic activity, decrease body arousal, and thus help you calm down after stressful experiences.

Sympathetic		Parasympathetic
Pupils dilated, dry; far vision	*Eyes*	Pupils constricted, moist; near vision
Dry	*Mouth*	Salivation
Goose bumps	*Skin*	No goose bumps
Sweaty	*Palms*	Dry
Passages dilated	*Lungs*	Passages constricted
Increased rate	*Heart*	Decreased rate
Supply maximum to muscles	*Blood*	Supply maximum to internal organs
Increased activity	*Adrenal glands*	Decreased activity
Inhibited	*Digestion*	Stimulated
Climax	*Sexual functions*	Arousal

Homeostasis

One problem that some students face is becoming too stressed or upset by life's events. Because it is potentially harmful to your body to stay stressed or aroused, the autonomic nervous system tries to keep the body's arousal at an optimum level, a state called homeostasis.

Homeostasis (*ho-me-oh-STAY-sis*) means that sympathetic and parasympathetic systems work together to keep the body's level of arousal in balance for optimum functioning.

Homeostasis—physiological arousal kept in balance

For instance, your body's balance, or homeostasis, may be upset by the continuous stress of final exams or a difficult relationship. Such stress usually results in continuous physiological arousal and any number of physical problems, including headaches, stomachaches, tight muscles, or fatigue. These physical symptoms, which are called psychosomatic problems, may result in real pain. We'll discuss these problems in Module 21: Health, Stress & Coping (pp. 480–507).

Besides triggering your autonomic nervous system, the hypothalamus is also involved in regulating a complex hormonal system, which we'll examine next.

F. Endocrine System

What is your chemical system?

You have two major systems for sending signals to the body's muscles, glands, and organs. We have already discussed the nervous system, which uses neurons, nerves, and neurotransmitters to send information throughout the body. The second major system for sending information is called the endocrine system.

The *endocrine system* is made up of numerous glands that are located throughout the body. These glands secrete various chemicals, called *hormones,* which affect organs, muscles, and other glands in the body.

The location and function of some of the endocrine system's glands are shown in the figure below.

Control Center

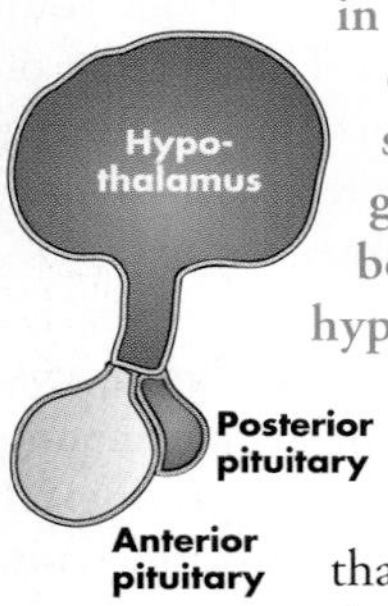

In many ways, the *hypothalamus,* which is located in the lower middle part of the brain, controls much of the endocrine system by regulating the pituitary gland, which is located directly below and outside the brain. The hypothalamus is often called the control center of the endocrine system.

The drawing on the left shows that the hypothalamus is connected to the pituitary gland.

Hypo-thalamus

Posterior pituitary

Anterior pituitary

Endocrine system controls glands located throughout the body.

Other Glands

We'll describe some of the endocrine system's major glands as well as their dysfunctions.

The *pituitary gland,* a key component of the endocrine system, hangs directly below the hypothalamus, to which it is connected by a narrow stalk. The pituitary gland is divided into anterior (front) and posterior (back) sections.

Posterior pituitary. The rear portion of the pituitary regulates water and salt balance.

Dysfunction: Lack of hormones causes a less common form of diabetes.

Anterior pituitary. The front part of the pituitary regulates growth through secretion of growth hormone and produces hormones that control the adrenal cortex, pancreas, thyroid, and gonads.

Dysfunction: Too little growth hormone produces dwarfism; too much causes gigantism. Other problems in the pituitary cause problems in the glands it regulates.

Pancreas. This organ regulates the level of sugar in the bloodstream by secreting insulin.

Dysfunction: Lack of insulin results in the more common form of diabetes, while too much causes hypoglycemia (low blood sugar).

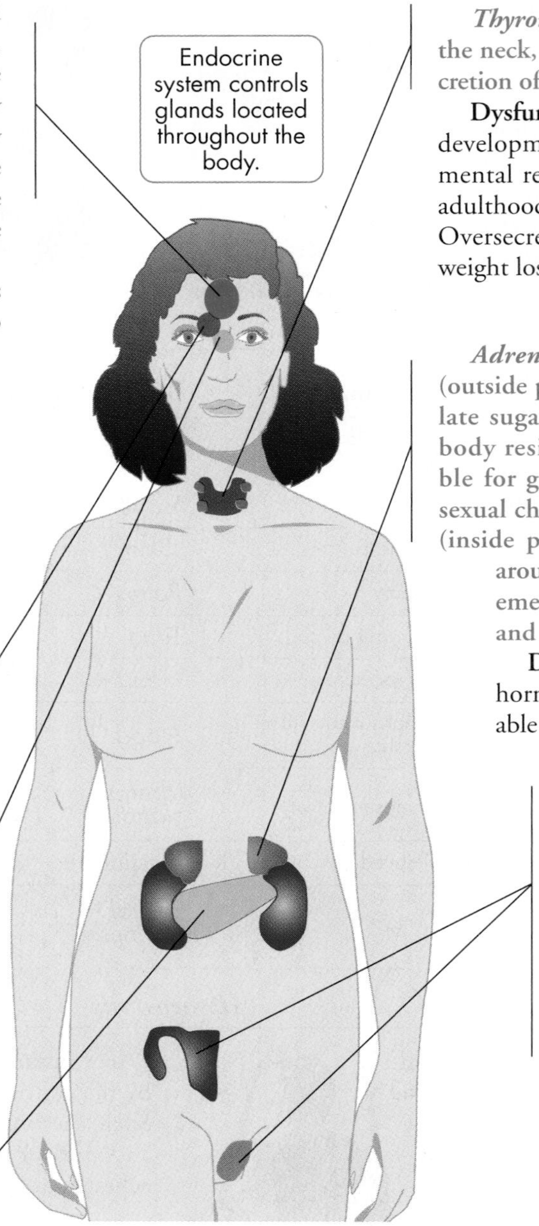

Thyroid. This gland, which is located in the neck, regulates metabolism through secretion of hormones.

Dysfunction: Hormone deficiency during development leads to stunted growth and mental retardation. Undersecretion during adulthood leads to reduction in motivation. Oversecretion results in high metabolism, weight loss, and nervousness.

Adrenal glands. The adrenal cortex (outside part) secretes hormones that regulate sugar and salt balances and help the body resist stress; they are also responsible for growth of pubic hair, a secondary sexual characteristic. The adrenal medulla (inside part) secretes two hormones that arouse the body to deal with stress and emergencies: epinephrine (adrenaline) and norepinephrine (noradrenaline).

Dysfunction: With a lack of cortical hormones, the body's responses are unable to cope with stress.

Gonads. In females, the ovaries produce hormones that regulate sexual development, ovulation, and growth of sex organs. In males, the testes produce hormones that regulate sexual development, production of sperm, and growth of sex organs.

Dysfunction: Lack of sex hormones during puberty results in lack of secondary sexual characteristics (facial and body hair, muscles in males, breasts in females).

Up to this point, we have examined many of the structures and functions that make up the incredible nervous and endocrine systems. After the Concept Review, we'll discuss a question that students often ask: Do the brains of males differ from those of females?

✔ Concept Review

1. A hairlike structure that contains tightly coiled strands of the chemical DNA (deoxyribonucleic acid) is called a (a)_____. A specific segment on the strand of DNA that contains instructions for making proteins is called a (b)_____. A theory that different species arose from a common ancestor and that those species survived that were best adapted to meet the demands of their environments is called the theory of (c)_____.

2. There are several techniques for studying the living brain. One method for identifying structures in the brain involves measuring nonharmful radio frequencies as they pass through the brain; this is called an (a)_____ scan. Another method that is used to study functions of the brain involves measuring the amounts of low-level radioactive substances absorbed by brain cells; this is called a (b)_____ scan.

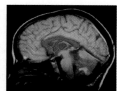

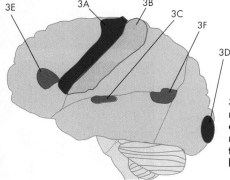

3E 3A 3B 3C 3F 3D

3. The numbers/letters on the drawing match those of the questions below.

3A. The cortical area that controls voluntary movements is called the (a)_____ and is located in the (b)_____ lobe.

3B. The cortical area that receives input from sensory receptors in the skin, muscles, and joints is called the (a)_____ and is located in the (b)_____ lobe.

3C. The cortical area that receives input from sensory receptors in the ears is called the (a)_____ and is located in the (b)_____ lobe.

3D. The cortical area that receives input from sensory receptors in the eyes is called the (a)_____ and is located in the (b)_____ lobe.

3E. The cortical area that is necessary to produce words and arrange them into sentences is called (a)_____ and is located in the (b)_____ lobe.

3F. The cortical area that is necessary for understanding spoken and written words and putting words into meaningful sentences is called (a)_____ and is located in the (b)_____ lobe.

4. The two major divisions of the nervous system are the (a)_____ and the (b)_____. In turn, the peripheral nervous system has two parts: one part is a network of nerves that are connected either to sensory receptors or to muscles that you can move voluntarily and is called the (c)_____; another part regulates heart rate, breathing, blood pressure, digestion, secretion of hormones, and other functions and is called the (d)_____. The brain itself is divided into three major parts: (e)_____, _____, and _____.

5. The old brain that is involved with many motivational and emotional behaviors is called the (a)_____. One structure of the limbic system, the hypothalamus, controls the autonomic nervous system, which has two divisions. The division that responds by increasing the body's physiological arousal is called the (b)_____. This division triggers an increased state of physiological arousal so that the body can cope with threatening situations; this state is called the (c)_____. The other division of the autonomic nervous system that is primarily responsible for returning the body to a calm or relaxed state and is involved in digestion is called the (d)_____. These two divisions work together to keep the body in physiological balance so that it remains or returns to a state of optimal functioning; this state is called (e)_____.

6. A system made up of numerous glands that are located throughout the body and that secrete various hormones is called the (a)_____. The brain area that can be considered the master control for this system is the (b)_____. This brain area is connected to and controls one of the endocrine system's major glands that has an anterior and posterior part and is collectively called the (c)_____.

Answers: 1. (a) chromosome, (b) gene, (c) evolution; 2. (a) MRI, (b) PET; 3A. (a) motor cortex, (b) frontal; 3B. (a) somatosensory cortex, (b) parietal; 3C. (a) primary auditory cortex, (b) temporal; 3D. (a) primary visual cortex, (b) occipital; 3E. (a) Broca's area, (b) frontal; 3F. (a) Wernicke's area, (b) temporal; 4. (a) central nervous system, (b) peripheral nervous system, (c) somatic nervous system, (d) autonomic nervous system, (e) forebrain, midbrain, hindbrain; 5. (a) limbic system, (b) sympathetic nervous system, (c) fight-flight response, (d) parasympathetic nervous system, (e) homeostasis; 6. (a) endocrine system, (b) hypothalamus, (c) pituitary gland

G. Research Focus: Sex Differences in the Brain?

Is this kind of research sexist? Throughout history, politicians have criticized or misused research depending on what was "politically correct" (Lilienfeld, 2003). For example, in the 1920s, U.S. politicians misused research on IQ scores to justify passing discriminatory immigration quotas (p. 296) (S. J. Gould, 1981). In the 1980s, many politicians were critical of homosexuality and denied federal money for AIDS research until the virus became a threat to the heterosexual population (Shilts, 1988). In the 1980s and 1990s, research on sex differences was criticized as "sexist" because it went against the "politically correct" belief that male and female brains are essentially the same (Azar, 1997).

However, using brain scans, researchers have recently reported interesting differences in the structure and function of male and female brains, which are called sex differences (Canli et al., 2002a).

Sex, or *gender, differences* refer to structural or functional differences in cognitive, behavioral, or brain processes that arise from being a male or a female.

Sex differences are neither good nor bad nor sexist but simply ways in which males and females differ. Here are some interesting sex differences.

Differences in Solving Problems

The rotating figure problem is a rather difficult spatial problem, as follows. First, study the target figure on the left. Then, from the three choices at the right, identify the same figure, even though it has been rotated.

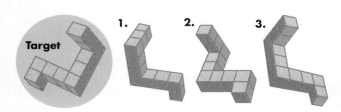

The key to solving this problem is the ability to rotate the target figure in your mind until it matches the rotation of one of the three choices. Researchers consistently report faster or more accurate performance by males than by females in solving rotating figure problems (Kimura, 1992). (Correct answer is 1.)

There are other tasks at which women perform better than men.

For example, look at the house outlined in black (figure above) and find its twin among the three choices. Women are generally faster on these kinds of tests, which measure perceptual speed. In addition, women usually score higher on tests of verbal fluency, in which you must list as many words as you can that begin with the same letter, as in the figure below (Halpern, 2000).

One explanation for these sex differences in skills is that they result from differences in

Limp, Livery, Love, Laser, Liquid, Low, Like, Lag, Live, Lug, Light, Lift, Liver, Lime, Leg, Load, Lap, Lucid, . . .

socialization and learning. Another explanation is that these sex differences have evolved from different skills needed by early humans. Males with good spatial skills had an advantage in hunting, and females with good communication skills had an advantage in child-rearing (Springer & Deutsch, 1997).

Researchers have now begun to look for sex differences in how the brain itself functions.

Differences between Female and Male Brains

To check for sex differences between male and female brains, researchers took brain scans while subjects were solving rotating figure problems.

Problem solving. Brain scans taken during problem solving showed that maximum neural activity in *males* occurred in the right frontal area (upper right figure). In contrast, maximum neural activity in *females* occurred in the right parietal-temporal area (lower right figure). Researchers concluded that solving rotating figure problems showed a significant sex difference in terms of which brain areas were activated, which in turn may be the basis for sex differences in performance on this task (Alivisatos & Petrides, 1997).

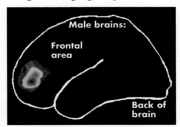

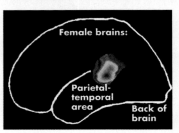

Another interesting PET study found that while escaping from a three-dimensional virtual-reality maze, men were significantly faster (average: 2 min. 22 sec) than women (average: 3 min. 16 sec). Also, men used both sides of their hippocampus, which saves data into permanent storage, while women used only the right hippocampus. Researchers concluded that these brain differences may explain why men are better at finding a specific place in a strange city (Gron et al., 2000).

Emotional memories. How good are you at remembering intense emotional experiences? Brain scans (fMRI) were taken while women and men looked at photos, which they graded from neutral (bookcase) to emotionally intense (dead body). Weeks later, subjects were asked to pick out photos that they had earlier rated as emotionally intense. Women correctly remembered 10–15% more of the intense photos than did men. Equally interesting, brain scans taken while people viewed the emotionally intense photos indicated that more and different brain areas were activated in women than in men. Researchers concluded that, in women, the brain is more effectively wired for coding emotional experiences than in men (Canli et al., 2002a).

In finding sex differences in the brain, researchers warn against using such differences as the basis for promoting discriminatory practices or furthering someone's political agenda (Rogers, 2001).

Skull Size and Intelligence

Which race had the biggest brain?

When he died in 1851, the *New York Times* proudly said that Samuel George Morton, scientist and physician, had one of the best reputations among scholars throughout the world. Morton had spent his lifetime collecting skulls of different races to determine which race had the biggest brain. During Morton's time, it was generally accepted that a bigger brain meant greater intelligence and innate mental ability.

Results in 1839. Morton estimated the size of a brain by pouring tiny lead pellets (the size of present-day BBs) into each skull and then measuring the number of pellets. Using this procedure, he arrived at the following ranking of brain

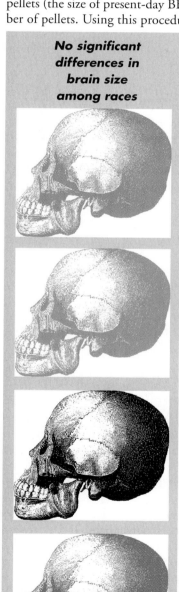

No significant differences in brain size among races

size in different races, from biggest to smallest (see skulls on left): 1, White (Caucasian); 2, yellow (Mongolian); 3, brown (American Indian); and 4, Black (Negro). Along with his racial ranking of decreasing brain size, Morton also believed there was a corresponding decrease in behavioral and cognitive skills (Morton, 1839, cited in S. J. Gould, 1981).

Reanalyzed in 1980. Stephen Jay Gould, a renowned evolutionary biologist, reanalyzed Morton's data on brain size and, unlike Morton's findings, found *no significant difference* in brain size among the four races. Furthermore, Gould concluded that Morton's strong biases that Caucasians should have the biggest brains had unknowingly swayed his scientific judgment to fit his racial prejudices of the 1800s (S. J. Gould, 1981).

Major error. Morton's major error was that he included skulls that matched his personal biased expectations and omitted skulls that did not support his racial beliefs. That is, Morton chose bigger skulls to match his bias of Whites being more intelligent and smaller skulls for other races, whom he considered to be less intelligent (S. J. Gould, 1994).

Although Morton had the reputation for being a respected scholar and although he had asked a legitimate research question—Are there differences in brain size?—he was unable to prevent his strong personal beliefs from biasing his research and finding what he strongly but mistakenly believed.

One way current researchers guard against the problem of biasing their results is by having scientists in other laboratories repeat their studies. If the original findings are repeated in other laboratories, then scientists can be reasonably confident that their original results are valid.

Brain Size and Intelligence

What do brain scans show?

Researchers have studied the relationship between brain size and IQ scores by using brain scans (p. 70), which precisely measure the size of the human brain. For example, researchers found a moderate correlation of about +0.45 between the number of neurons in the frontal lobe, which has an executive function (p. 76), and IQ scores (Thompson et al., 2001). This positive correlation means that, generally, the more neurons in the frontal lobe, the higher the IQ scores.

Female brains. If there is a positive correlation between number of neurons in the frontal lobe and IQ scores, we might expect women generally to have lower IQ scores than men since their brains, as well as their heads, are about 10% smaller than men's (Holden, 1995). Because there is no evidence that women do have lower IQ scores than men, how do we explain this contradiction?

Women's heads and brains are about 10% smaller than men's.

Although women's brains may be smaller, perhaps their brain cells are more tightly packed together. This idea received considerable support when the brains of men and women were examined after death. Researchers reported that, in some areas of women's brains, there were 11–17% more neurons than in corresponding parts of men's larger brains (Witelson et al., 1995). Researchers think that neurons in women's brains are more densely packed.

Correlations. Since studies report a positive correlation between brain size and IQ scores, we'll briefly review what *correlation* means. A correlation indicates only the existence of a relationship between two events but does not identify the cause and effect. For example, being in a stimulating environment may promote brain growth and result in higher IQ scores, or being born with a larger brain may allow one to absorb more from one's environment and score higher on IQ tests.

Thus, at this point in time, a positive correlation between brain size and intelligence may be scientifically interesting but has little practical application.

Before we complete our journey through the brain, we'll take you on one last trip, perhaps the most interesting of all. We'll see what happens when the brain is literally cut in two.

I. Application: Split Brain

Why did Victoria choose a split brain?

Since about the age of 6, Victoria had seizures (also called epileptic seizures). During the seizures, she would lose consciousness, fall to the floor, and although her muscles would jerk uncontrollably, she felt no pain and would remember nothing of the experience. She was given anticonvulsant medicine, which prevented any further seizures until she was 18.

Split-brain operation. When Victoria was 18, for some unknown reason, her seizures returned with greater intensity. And to her dismay, anticonvulsant medication no longer had any effect. The seizures continued for ten years. Finally, when she was 27, she decided that her best chance of reducing her frightening, uncontrollable seizures was to have an operation that had a high probability of producing serious side effects. In this operation, a neurosurgeon would sever the major connection between her right and left hemispheres, leaving her with what is called a split brain (figure below).

Having to choose between a future of uncontrollable seizures and the potential problems of having a split brain, Victoria chose the operation (Sidtis et al., 1981).

In addition to Victoria (identified as V.P. in published reports), dozens of other individuals have also chosen to have a split-brain operation when they found that medicine no longer prevented their severe, uncontrollable seizures.

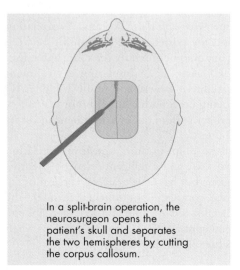

In a split-brain operation, the neurosurgeon opens the patient's skull and separates the two hemispheres by cutting the corpus callosum.

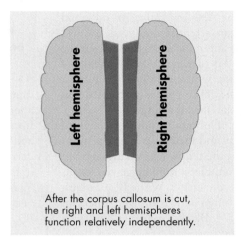

After the corpus callosum is cut, the right and left hemispheres function relatively independently.

A *split-brain operation* involves cutting the wide band of fibers, called the corpus callosum, that connects the right and left hemispheres (figure above). The corpus callosum has 200 million nerve fibers that allow information to pass back and forth between the hemispheres.

A split-brain operation not only disrupts the major pathway between the hemispheres but, to a large extent, leaves each hemisphere functioning independently. In many split-brain patients, severing the corpus callosum prevented the spread of seizures from one hemisphere to the other and thus reduced their frequency and occurrence (Gazzaniga, 1996).

Major breakthrough. It was 1961 when researcher Michael S. Gazzaniga and his colleagues tested the first split-brain patient, known as W.J. in the literature. Researchers first flashed on a screen a number of colors, letters, and pictures of objects. These stimuli were flashed so that they went only to W.J.'s left hemisphere, and he had no difficulty naming them. Then researchers flashed the same stimuli so that they went only to W.J.'s right hemisphere, and W.J. seemed to see nothing, to be blind (Gazzaniga et al., 1962). Gazzaniga calls the discovery that W.J.'s right hemisphere was saying nothing "one of those unforgettable moments in life." Was it true that W.J.'s left hemisphere could talk but not his right?

Testing a patient. To determine what each hemisphere can and cannot do, we can watch as Gazzaniga tests Victoria after her split-brain operation.

Victoria is asked to stare at the black dot between *HE* and *ART* as the word *HEART* is displayed on a screen. Because Victoria's hemispheres are split, information from each side of the black dot will go only to the opposite hemisphere (figure below). This means that Victoria's left hemisphere will see only the word *ART* and her right hemisphere will see only the word *HE*.

When asked, "What did you see?" Victoria says that she saw the word "ART," because it was projected to the left hemisphere, which has the ability to speak.

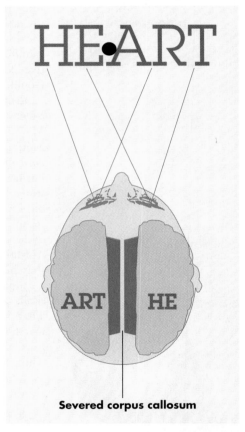

Severed corpus callosum

Although Victoria's right hemisphere saw the word *HE*, the right hemisphere turns out to be mute, meaning that it cannot say what it saw. However, Victoria can point with her left hand to a photo of a man (HE), indicating that the right hemisphere understood the question and saw the word *HE*. (Victoria points with her left hand because her right hemisphere controls the left side of the body.) Although the effects of having a split brain are obvious under special testing, the effects are not so apparent in everyday life.

How does a split brain affect behavior?

Initially after her operation, Victoria reported that when she would choose clothes from her closet, her right hand would grab a blouse but then her left hand would put it back. However, these obvious conflicts between hemispheres are rare and disappear with time.

Four months after her operation, Victoria was alert and talked easily about past and present events. She could read, write, reason, and perform everyday functions such as eating, dressing, and walking, as well as carry on normal conversations. For Victoria with her split brain, as well as for most of us with normal brains, only the left hemisphere can express itself through the spoken word (Springer & Deutsch, 1997). If the speech area is in the left hemisphere, then the right hemisphere is usually mute. (For a small percentage of left-handers, the speech area is in the right hemisphere and the left hemisphere is usually mute.) Thus, one reason a split-brain person appears normal in casual conversation is that only one hemisphere is directing speech. After testing split-brain patients, researchers discovered that each hemisphere is specialized for performing certain tasks.

Different Functions of Hemispheres

Before observing split-brain patients, researchers knew very little about how each hemisphere functioned. But after studying the behaviors of split-brain patients, researchers gained a whole new understanding of what task each hemisphere does best.

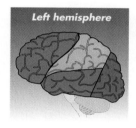

Verbal. Left hemisphere is very good at all language-related abilities: speaking, understanding language, carrying on a conversation, reading, writing, spelling.

Mathematical. Left hemisphere is very good at mathematical skills: adding, subtracting, multiplying, dividing, solving complex problems in calculus and physics, and so on. Generally, the right hemisphere can perform simple addition and subtraction but not more complex mathematics (Sperry, 1974).

Analytic. Left hemisphere appears to process information by analyzing each separate piece that makes up a whole. For example, the left hemisphere would recognize a face by analyzing piece by piece its many separate parts: nose, eyes, lips, cheeks, and so on—a relatively slow process (Levy & Trevarthen, 1976).

Recognizing self. Left hemisphere is primarily involved in identifying one's own face, distinguishing one's face from others, as well as in memories and knowledge of oneself. Thus, the left brain contributes to the conscious understanding of oneself (Turk, 2002).

Nonverbal. Although usually mute, the right hemisphere has a childlike ability to read, write, spell, and understand speech (Gazzaniga, 1998). For example, when spoken to, the right hemisphere can understand simple sentences and read simple words.

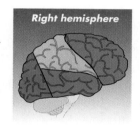

Spatial. Right hemisphere is very good at solving spatial problems, such as arranging blocks to match a geometric design. Because hemispheres control opposite sides of the body, the left hand (right hemisphere) is best at arranging blocks, a spatial task.

Holistic. Right hemisphere appears to process information by combining parts into a meaningful whole. For this reason, the right hemisphere is better at recognizing and identifying whole faces (Levy et al., 1972). The right hemisphere is also good at making and recognizing emotional facial expressions (Springer & Deutsch, 1997).

Recognizing others. Right hemisphere is involved in recognizing familiar faces but not in recognizing one's own face, which primarily involves the left hemisphere (Turk, 2002).

After comparing the left and right hemispheres' functions, you can see that each hemisphere has specialized skills and is better at performing different tasks. These differences raise a popular question: Am I primarily right-brained or left-brained?

The popular press has exaggerated the idea that you are either "right-brained"—creative, intuitive—or "left-brained"—reasonable, logical, and rational.

According to Jerre Levy (1985), who has devoted her career to studying how the brain's hemispheres interact, these distinctions are much too simple. She believes that we are constantly using both hemispheres, since each hemisphere is specialized for processing certain kinds of information. For example, when you read a novel, you are probably using programs in the left hemisphere that allow you to understand language in written form. But at the same time, you are using programs in the right hemisphere to keep track of the overall story, appreciate its humor and emotional content, and interpret any illustrations. Although hemispheres may sometimes work alone, they share much of their information by passing it quickly back and forth through the corpus callosum.

How is my brain organized? Michael Gazzaniga (1998), a cognitive neuroscientist who has studied split-brain patients for over 40 years, believes that each hemisphere of the brain has many different mental programs, such as sensing, thinking, learning, feeling, and speaking, all of which can function simultaneously. For example, when you see someone smile, your brain uses dozens of mental programs from each hemisphere to receive, interpret, and respond to this relatively simple emotional facial expression.

According to Gazzaniga, the brain and mind are built from separate units or modules that are interconnected and work together to carry out specific functions, much as your computer uses many separate programs to perform many different tasks.

Summary Test

A. GENES & EVOLUTION

1. A fertilized egg, which is called a
(a)_____, contains 46 chromo-
somes arranged in 23 pairs. A hairlike structure that contains tightly coiled strands of the
chemical DNA (deoxyribonucleic acid) is
called a (b)_____. A specific seg-
ment on the strand of DNA that contains instructions for making proteins is called a (c)_____.

2. In 1859, Charles Darwin published a revolutionary theory of
(a)_____, which said that different species arose from a
common (b)_____ and that those species survived that
were best adapted to meet the demands of their (c)_____.

B. STUDYING THE LIVING BRAIN

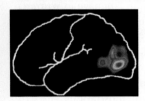

3. There are several recently developed
techniques for studying the living brain. One
technique, which measures nonharmful
radio frequencies as they pass through the
brain, is called an (a)_____
and is used to identify structures in the living brain. Another technique
measures how much of a radioactive substance is taken up by brain
cells and is called a (b)_____. This kind of scan is used
to study brain function and identify the most and least active parts.

C. ORGANIZATION OF THE BRAIN

4. The human nervous system is divided into
two major parts. The brain and spinal cord
make up the (a)_____. The net-
work of nerves outside the brain and spinal
cord makes up the (b)_____.

5. The peripheral nervous system is further divided into two parts.
One part is made up of a network of nerves that either carry messages to muscles and organs throughout the body or carry input
from sensory receptors to the spinal cord; this is called the
(a)_____. The second part of the peripheral nervous system, which regulates heart rate, breathing, digestion, secretion of
hormones, and related responses, is called the (b)_____.

6. The human brain is divided into three major parts. The largest
part is involved in cognitive responses that we characterize as most
human. This part is called the (a)_____, which is divided
into right and left hemispheres. The part that is involved in controlling vital reflexes, sleeping, and coordinating body movements is
called the (b)_____. The part that is involved in visual

and auditory reflexes, as well as alerting the brain to incoming sensations, is called the (c)_____.

7. Beginning in the midbrain and extending downward is a long
column of cells called the _____ that alerts the forebrain
to incoming sensory information.

8. The hindbrain consists of three structures. The structure that serves
as a bridge to connect the brain and body and also manufactures
chemicals involved in sleep is called the (a)_____. The
structure that controls vital reflexes, such as heart rate, blood pressure, and respiration, is called the (b)_____. The structure that was assumed to be involved primarily in coordinating body
movements but has recently been found to have a role in cognitive
functions, such as short-term memory, following rules, and carrying
out plans, is called the (c)_____.

D. CONTROL CENTERS: FOUR LOBES

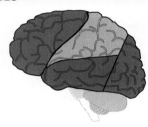

9. The thin outside layer of cells that
has a wrinkled look and covers almost
the entire forebrain is called the
(a)_____. This layer of
cells is divided into four separate areas
or lobes: (b)_____,
_____, _____,
and _____.

10. The lobe that is involved in controlling social-emotional behaviors, maintaining a healthy personality, and making and carrying out
plans is called the _____ lobe.

11. At the back edge of the frontal lobe is a continuous strip called
the _____, which controls the movement of voluntary
muscles. Body parts that have greater capacity for complicated muscle movement have more area on the motor cortex devoted to them.

12. Along the front edge of the parietal lobe is a continuous strip
that receives sensations from the body and is called the
_____. Body parts with greater sensitivity have more
area on the somatosensory cortex devoted to them.

13. An area on the upper edge of the temporal lobe that receives
signals from receptors in the ears and changes them into basic auditory sensations is called the (a)_____. For most individuals, an area in the left temporal lobe is involved in understanding
and speaking coherently; it is called (b)_____ area.
Damage to this area results in inability to understand spoken and
written speech or to speak coherently, a problem called
(c)_____. An area in the frontal lobe, called
(d)_____, is necessary for producing words and

arranging them into fluent sentences. If this area is damaged, the result is a speech problem called (e)_____.

14. An area at the very back of the occipital lobe that receives signals from receptors in the eyes and changes them into basic visual sensations is called the _____.

15. The vast majority of the cortex making up the four lobes is involved in adding meaning, interpretations, and associations to sensory stimuli, as well as in many cognitive functions. Together, these areas are called _____ areas.

E. LIMBIC SYSTEM: OLD BRAIN

16. Inside the forebrain is a central core of interconnected structures known as the primitive, or "animal," brain or, more technically, the (a)_____. Four of the areas that make up the limbic system are the (b)_____, _____, _____, and _____, which are all involved in motivational and emotional behaviors.

17. One structure of the limbic system, the hypothalamus, controls the autonomic nervous system, which has two divisions. The one that arouses the body, increases physiological responses (such as heart rate and blood pressure), and prepares the body for the fight-flight response is called the (a)_____. The division that calms down the body and aids digestion is called the (b)_____. These two divisions work together to keep the body's internal organs in a balanced physiological state, which is called (c)_____.

F. ENDOCRINE SYSTEM

18. Besides the nervous system, a network of glands regulates organs through the secretion of hormones. This chemical system is called the (a)_____. A major gland that controls other glands in this system is the (b)_____ gland, which has an anterior and posterior part.

G. RESEARCH FOCUS: SEX DIFFERENCES IN THE BRAIN?

19. Structural or functional differences in the brain that arise from being male or female are called _____. One example of sex differences in the brain is that males primarily use the frontal area to solve spatial problems, while females use the parietal-temporal area.

H. CULTURAL DIVERSITY: BRAIN SIZE & RACIAL MYTHS

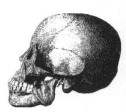

20. In the 1800s, one scientist measured skull size and concluded that a larger brain indicated more intelligence and that the races could be ranked by brain size. However, further analysis of this researcher's data indicated that there was no basis for ranking races by (a)_____. More recent experiments that precisely measured brain size with MRI scans found a modest correlation between brain size and (b)_____. However, we do not know if a stimulating environment causes the brain to grow more or if a larger brain is able to absorb more from the environment.

I. APPLICATION: SPLIT BRAIN

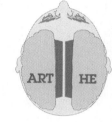

21. The two hemispheres are connected by a major bundle of fibers that is called the _____. Severing this structure produces a condition called a split brain.

22. For most individuals, mental programs for language, speech, and mathematics, as well as for distinguishing one's face from others and for memories and knowledge of oneself are located in the (a)_____; mental programs for solving spatial problems, processing emotional responses, and recognizing familiar faces are located in the (b)_____. In addition, the hemispheres process information in different ways. The left hemisphere processes information in a more piece-by-piece fashion or (c)_____ way. In comparison, the right hemisphere processes information as a meaningful whole; that is, it uses a more (d)_____ approach.

23. One theory of brain organization says that your brain has many separate but interconnected _____ programs that function and work together so that you can perform many cognitive skills.

Answers: *1. (a) zygote, (b) chromosome, (c) gene; 2. (a) evolution, (b) ancestor, (c) environment; 3. (a) MRI scan, (b) PET scan; 4. (a) central nervous system, (b) peripheral nervous system; 5. (a) somatic nervous system, (b) autonomic nervous system; 6. (a) forebrain, (b) hindbrain, (c) midbrain; 7. reticular formation; 8. (a) pons, (b) medulla, (c) cerebellum; 9. (a) cortex, (b) frontal, parietal, temporal, occipital; 10. frontal; 11. motor cortex; 12. somatosensory cortex; 13. (a) primary auditory cortex, (b) Wernicke's, (c) Wernicke's aphasia, (d) Broca's area, (e) Broca's aphasia; 14. primary visual cortex; 15. association; 16. (a) limbic system, (b) hippocampus, hypothalamus, thalamus, amygdala; 17. (a) sympathetic division, (b) parasympathetic division, (c) homeostasis; 18. (a) endocrine system, (b) pituitary; 19. sex differences; 20. (a) brain size, (b) intelligence; 21. corpus callosum; 22. (a) left hemisphere, (b) right hemisphere, (c) analytic, (d) holistic; 23. mental*

Critical Thinking

Can Damaged Brain Learn Morals?

Questions

1. In Module 1, you learned about three major research methods for answering questions about human behavior (p. 28). Which major research method is used in this study?

2. What are the major structures and functions of the limbic system?

3. What does Dr. Damasio expect will happen if the prefrontal cortex is damaged?

When Sheryl (not her real name) was 15 months old, she was run over by a car. The accident damaged an area, called the prefrontal cortex, which is located in the very front part of the frontal lobe, just above the bridge of the nose. Although Sheryl seemed to recover from the injury, by the time she was 3 years old, she didn't respond when her parents told her not to misbehave or physically punished her for doing so.

When Tom (not his real name) was 3 months old, doctors removed a tumor that had damaged his prefrontal cortex. Although Tom recovered from the surgery, by the time he was 9 years old, he showed little motivation, had few friends, and at times would explode with anger.

The effects of early damage to Tom and Sheryl's prefrontal cortexes were studied by Dr. Antonio Damasio and colleagues at the University of Iowa College of Medicine. According to Dr. Damasio, our emotional behaviors are triggered by a primitive brain, called the limbic system, whose urges and emotions are in turn dampened and controlled by the prefrontal cortex, which is involved in making plans and decisions. Dr. Damasio asked what would happen to a person's emotions and urges if one of its major controls, the prefrontal cortex, was damaged in infancy.

As a teenager, Sheryl was disruptive at home and in school, stole from her family, shoplifted, never expressed guilt

or remorse for misdeeds, blamed others for all her problems, and had no plans for her future. Although Tom managed to graduate from high school, he developed a variety of problems, including stealing, getting into fights, and being unable to hold a job.

Dr. Damasio describes Tom and Sheryl as going through life never showing guilt or remorse for bad behaviors, not learning normal social and moral rules. Dr. Damasio believes that Sheryl and Tom never learned the basic moral rules of what's right and wrong because of early brain damage to their prefrontal cortexes.

Some experts believe that Dr. Damasio's findings might be used by criminal lawyers to show that there is a biological basis for bad or antisocial behaviors. However, Dr. Damasio warns that these findings do not show a biological basis for being a psychopath since true psychopaths are very good at deciding, planning, and purposely carrying out a wide range of antisocial behaviors. In comparison, although Tom and Sheryl lacked normal rules of social and moral behavior, they sort of bumbled through life rather than purposely planning their bad behaviors. (Adapted from S. Blakeslee, Brain damage during infancy stunts moral learning, study finds, *Los Angeles Times,* October 19, 1999, p. A-1)

4. Do Tom and Sheryl's behaviors fit with the fact that their prefrontal cortexes were damaged?

5. Do you think these findings will help a lawyer get a client off for committing antisocial behaviors?

6. Why don't these findings provide a biological basis for psychopathic behavior?

Use InfoTrac to search for topics: prefrontal cortex; frontal lobe; antisocial behavior; psychopathology.

1. Three major research methods for answering questions are survey, case study, and experiment. In this article, researchers used the case study approach, which is an in-depth study of individual subjects, in this case, Tom and Sheryl.
2. Hypothalamus regulates many motivational behaviors; amygdala is involved in forming emotional experiences; thalamus receives and relays sensory information; and hippocampus saves certain kinds of memories in long-term storage.
3. Dr. Damasio expects damage to the prefrontal cortex, which is involved in planning and deciding, to cause major problems or deficits in social, emotional, and moral behaviors.

4. Beginning during childhood and continuing through adolescence, Sheryl and Tom show deficits in planning, deciding, and reasoning, which are functions of the prefrontal cortex, which was damaged in infancy.
5. If you were a defense lawyer, why wouldn't you use these findings, that brain damage may decrease moral behavior, to help your client go free instead of going to prison?
6. Psychopaths are individuals who commit antisocial acts but feel little or no guilt, sorrow, or remorse. Dr. Damasio adds that psychopaths purposefully plan their antisocial behaviors, while Sheryl and Tom showed little evidence of such planning.

Links to Learning

LEARNING ACTIVITIES

- **POWERSTUDY CD-ROM 2.0** by Tom Doyle and Rod Plotnik
Check out the "Incredible Nervous System" SuperModule (disk 1) on PowerStudy. This is a completely self-paced module that is fully narrated. Don't want the narration? It is easy to turn off! This module includes:

  - Videos—Imbedded videos cover scans of the nervous system, an exploration of temporal lobe damage, and sex differences in the brain.

  - A multitude of animations—for example, a breakdown of the chromosomal genetic instructions and a virtual discussion of the different types of brain imaging techniques.

  - A test of your knowledge using an interactive version of the Summary Test on pages 88 and 89. Also access related quizzes.

  - An interactive version of the Critical Thinking exercise "Can Damaged Brain Learn Morals?" on page 90.

  - Key terms, a chapter outline including chapter abstract, and a list of hotlinked Web sites that correlate to this module.

- **SELF-STUDY ASSESSMENT**
Want help studying? For your customized Study Plan go to **http://psychology.wadsworth.com/plotnik7e/**. This program will automatically generate pretests and posttests to help you determine what concepts you have mastered and what concepts you still need work on.

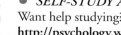

- **STUDY GUIDE and WEBTUTOR**
Check the corresponding module in your Study Guide for effective student tips and help learning the material presented.

- **INFOTRAC COLLEGE EDITION ONLINE LIBRARY**
To find interesting and relevant articles go to **http://www.infotrac-college.com**, use your password, and then type in search terms such as the ones listed below.

Genes	Brain scans	Cortex
Autonomic nervous system	Endocrine system	Brain size

STUDY QUESTIONS

Use InfoTrac to search for topics mentioned in the main heads below (e.g., brain evolution, split brain).

*A. **Genes & Evolution**—If a species of humans with 5-pound brains was discovered, would their behavior differ from ours? (**Suggested answer page 621**)

*B. **Studying the Living Brain**—How would you know if a professional boxer had brain damage? (**Suggested answer page 621**)

C. **Organization of the Brain**—If you had to give up one part of your brain, which one would you sacrifice?

D. **Control Centers: Four Lobes**—Which brain functions would computers be the best and worst at imitating?

E. **Limbic System: Old Brain**—What would happen if your limbic system were replaced with one from an alligator?

F. **Endocrine System**—What is one reason for the different bodies of football players, soccer players, and jockeys?

G. **Research Focus: Sex Differences in the Brain?**—What's the danger of identifying sex differences in the brain?

*H. **Cultural Diversity: Brain Size & Racial Myths**—Why is there a continuing interest in whether a bigger brain is more intelligent? (**Suggested answer page 621**)

I. **Application: Split Brain**—If you were supposed to act like a person with a split brain, what would you do differently?

*These questions are answered in Appendix B.

Module 5: Sensation

Introduction

Electric Billboard in the Brain

Can Katie see without her eyes?

Katie was looking at an electric billboard made up of 36 dots of blue, purple, red, and yellow light. The billboard wasn't on the front of a store or sports stadium; it was in her own head.

When Katie was 22, she lost her eyesight to glaucoma and lived in total darkness for the next 20 years. At the age of 42, she volunteered to have experimental surgery in which 36 tiny gold wires were implanted into the occipital lobe in the back of her brain, which is the area that processes visual information. When researchers pushed a switch, a low-level, nonharmful electrical current passed through these gold wires and activated brain cells. When the brain cells in Katie's visual area were activated, she reported seeing flashes of colored light. By adjusting the electrical current, researchers could vary the brightness and size of the flashes from a tiny dot to the size of a nickel.

Because the implanted gold wires formed a rectangular grid of 36 dots (see figure above), researchers could apply current to particular wires in the grid to form patterns of flashing dots. For example, when the flashing dots formed the pattern shown in the

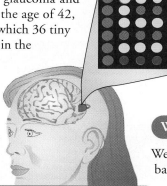

She can "see" the letter "S" when her brain is stimulated.

figure, Katie reported seeing the letter "S" (adapted from *Los Angeles Times,* October 30, 1992).

Although Katie is officially blind because her eyes are not functioning, she can still "see" flashes of colored lights when the visual area of her brain is electrically stimulated. This fact raises an interesting question: How is it possible to see without using one's eyes? As we answer this question, you'll discover that the eye, ear, nose, tongue, and skin are smaller, more complicated, and better recorders than any of the newest, miniaturized, high-tech video cameras, recorders, or digital disks on the market.

What's Coming

We'll discuss six of the major human senses—vision, hearing, balance (vestibular system), taste, olfaction (smell), and touch. We'll also explain how you see color, why some long-playing rock-and-roll musicians have become partially deaf, why you get motion sickness, and why your sense of taste decreases when you have a cold. Although your sense organs—eye, ear, tongue, nose, and skin—look so very different, they all share the three characteristics defined next.

Three Definitions

Your eyes, ears, nose, skin, and tongue are complex, miniaturized, living sense organs that automatically gather information about your environment. We begin with three definitions that will help you understand sensation.

1 Transduction. The first thing each sense organ must do is to change or transform some physical energy, such as molecules of skunk spray, into electrical signals, a process called transduction.

Electrical signal

Transduction refers to the process in which a sense organ changes, or transforms, physical energy into electrical signals that become neural impulses, which may be sent to the brain for processing.

For example, transduction occurs when a skunk's molecules enter your nose, which transforms the molecules into electrical signals, or impulses, that are interpreted by your brain as the very unpleasant odor of a skunk.

2 Adaptation. A short period of time after putting on glasses, jewelry, or clothes, you no longer "feel" them, a process called adaptation.

Adaptation refers to the decreasing response of the sense organs, the more they are exposed to a continuous level of stimulation.

For example, the continuous stimulation of glasses, jewelry, or clothes on your skin results in adaptation so that soon you no longer feel them. Some sense organs adapt very quickly, and some very slowly. However, sense organs do not adapt to intense forms of stimulation, because such stimulation may cause physical damage. Instead, intense stimulation, such as from a very hot shower, may cause pain, which warns us of possible injury.

3 Sensations versus perceptions. Gathering information about the world involves two steps. In the first step, electrical signals reach the brain and are changed into sensations.

Sensations are relatively meaningless bits of information (left figure) that result when the brain processes electrical signals that come from the sense organs.

In the second step, the brain quickly changes sensations, which you're not aware of, into perceptions.

Perceptions are meaningful sensory experiences (right figure) that result after the brain combines hundreds of sensations.

For example, visual sensations would resemble the top figure, showing meaningless lines, colors, and shapes. Visual perceptions would be like the bottom figure, showing a complete "sad-happy" face.

While all sensations begin with step 1, transduction, sense organs use different mechanisms to do it. We'll start with how the visual system does it.

93

A. Eye: Vision

Stimulus: Light Waves

Why can't you see radio waves?

Each sense organ has a different shape and structure; it can receive only a certain kind of stimulus, or physical energy. For instance, the reason you cannot see radio waves is that their waves are not the right length. Although radio waves, along with light waves from the sun, are all forms of electromagnetic energy, they vary in wavelength. For example, the figure below shows that X rays are very short and AM radio waves are very long. Notice that only a small, specific range of wavelengths that come from a light source, called the visible spectrum, is able to excite receptors in your eyes.

Short wavelength   Long wavelength

| Gamma rays | X rays | Ultraviolet rays | | Radar | FM | TV | Shortwave | AM |

10^{-14} 10^{-10} 10^{-8} 10^{-2} 10^{2} 10^{4}

Wavelength in meters (m)

Violet Blue   Green   Yellow   Red

400   500   600   700

Wavelength in nanometers (nm)

Invisible—too short. On this side of the electromagnetic energy spectrum are shorter wavelengths, including gamma rays, X rays, and ultraviolet rays. These waves are invisible to the human eye because their lengths are too short to stimulate our receptors. However, some birds (such as hummingbirds) and insects can see ultraviolet rays to help them find food.

Visible—just right. Near the middle of the electromagnetic spectrum is a small range of waves that make up the visible spectrum.

The *visible spectrum* is one particular segment of electromagnetic energy that we can see because these waves are the right length to stimulate receptors in the eye.

The reason you can see a giraffe is that its body reflects light waves from the visible spectrum back to your eyes. One function of the eyes is to absorb light waves that are reflected back from all the objects in your environment.

Invisible—too long. On this side of the electromagnetic spectrum are longer wavelengths, such as radio and television waves. These waves are invisible to the human eye because their lengths are too long to stimulate the receptors in the eye. Imagine the awful distraction of seeing radio and television waves all day long!

Stimulus. Thus, the most effective stimulus for vision is energy (light waves) from the visible spectrum. However, for you to see anything, reflected light waves must be gathered and changed into electrical signals, and for that process—transduction—we must look inside the eye itself.

Structure and Function

How can you see a giraffe?

For you to see a 16-foot-tall giraffe, your eyes perform two separate processes. First, the eyes gather and focus light waves into a precise area at the back of your eyes. Second, this area absorbs and transforms light waves into impulses, a process known as transduction. We'll follow the path of light waves from the giraffe to the back of your eyes in a series of 7 steps.

1 Image reversed. Notice that, at the back of the eye, the giraffe appears upside down. Even though the giraffe is focused upside down in the eye, somehow the brain turns the giraffe—and all other objects we see—right side up so that we see the world as it really is.

2 Light waves. The problem with light waves is that after they strike an object, such as a giraffe, they are reflected back in a broad beam. You cannot see the giraffe unless your eyes change this broad beam of light waves into a narrow, focused one. Your eye has two structures, the cornea and the lens, that bring an image into focus, much as a camera does.

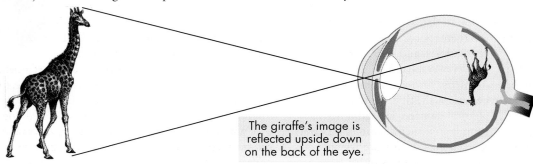

The giraffe's image is reflected upside down on the back of the eye.

3 Cornea. The broad beam of light reflected from the giraffe passes first through the cornea.

The *cornea* is the rounded, transparent covering over the front of your eye. As the light waves pass through the cornea, its curved surface bends, or focuses, the waves into a narrower beam.

4 Pupil. After passing through the cornea, light waves next go through the pupil.

The *pupil* is a round opening at the front of your eye that allows light waves to pass into the eye's interior.

Your pupil grows larger or smaller because of a muscle called the iris.

5 Iris. The opening of the pupil is surrounded by the iris.

The *iris* is a circular muscle that surrounds the pupil and controls the amount of light entering the eye. In dim light, the iris relaxes, allowing more light to enter—the pupil dilates; in bright light, the iris constricts, allowing less light to enter—the pupil constricts. The iris muscle contains the pigment that gives your eye its characteristic color.

If you look in a mirror in bright light, you will see that the iris is constricted and that your pupil—the black dot in the center of your eye—is very small.

6 Lens. After passing through the cornea and pupil, light waves reach the lens.

The *lens* is a transparent, oval structure whose curved surface bends and focuses light waves into an even narrower beam. The lens is attached to muscles that adjust the curve of the lens, which, in turn, adjusts the focusing.

For the eye to see distant objects, light waves need less bending (focusing), so muscles automatically stretch the lens so that its surface is less curved. To see near objects, light waves need more focusing, so muscles relax and allow the surface of the lens to become very curved. Making the lens more or less curved causes light waves to be focused into a very narrow beam that must be projected precisely onto an area at the very back of the eye, called the retina.

7 Retina. Although light waves have been bent and focused, transduction hasn't yet occurred. That is about to change as light waves reach the retina.

The *retina,* located at the very back of the eyeball, is a thin film that contains cells that are extremely sensitive to light. These light-sensitive cells, called photoreceptors, begin the process of transduction by absorbing light waves.

On the following page, we'll describe the two kinds of photoreceptors, how they absorb light waves, and how they carry out the process of transduction. For some people, light waves cannot be focused precisely on the retina because of a problem with the shape of their eyeballs.

Eyeball's Shape and Laser Eye Surgery

Eyeball. Some of us are born with perfectly shaped eyeballs, which contributes to having almost perfect vision. Others, however, are born with eyeballs that are a little too long or too short, resulting in two common visual problems: nearsightedness and farsightedness.

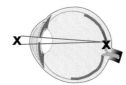 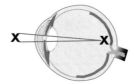  

Normal vision. The shape of your eyeball is primarily determined by genetic instructions. If your eyeball is shaped so that objects are perfectly focused on the back of your retina (**black X**), then both the near and distant objects will appear clear and sharp and you will have very good vision (20/20).

Nearsighted. If you inherit an eyeball that is too long, you are likely nearsighted.

Nearsightedness (myopia) results when the eyeball is too long so that objects are focused at a point in front of the retina (**black X**). In this case, near objects are clear, but distant objects appear blurry.

Common treatments involve corrective lenses or eye surgery.

Farsighted. If you inherit an eyeball that is too short, you are likely farsighted.

Farsightedness (hyperopia) occurs when the eyeball is too short so that objects are focused at a point slightly behind the retina (**black X**). In this case, distant objects are clear, but near objects appear blurry.

Common treatments involve corrective lenses or eye surgery.

Eye surgery. Currently, a popular and successful treatment to correct nearsighted vision is called LASIK. In this procedure, the surface of the eye is folded back and a laser is used to reshape the exposed cornea so that light waves are correctly bent and focused on the retina (Goldstein, 2002).

Next, we'll examine the retina more closely and see exactly how transduction occurs.

A. Eye: Vision

What happens to light waves?

Some miniaturized electronic cameras can record amazingly detailed video pictures. But they are primitive compared to the retina, whose microscopic cells can transform light waves into impulses that carry detailed information to the brain about all kinds of shapes, shadows, sizes, textures, and colors. Think of the retina as a combination of a video camera and a computer whose batteries never run out as it transforms light waves into impulses—the process of transduction. And here's how transduction occurs.

1 You already know that an object, such as a giraffe, reflects light waves that enter the eye and are bent, focused, and projected precisely on the retina, at the very back of the eyeball. The *retina* has three layers of cells. The back layer contains two kinds of photoreceptors that begin the process of transduction, changing light waves into electrical signals. One kind of photoreceptor with a rodlike shape is called a rod and is located primarily in the periphery of the retina. The other photoreceptor with a conelike shape is called a cone and is located primarily in the center of the retina in an area called the *fovea (FOH-vee-ah)*.

We have enlarged a section of retina to show that it has three layers. We'll explain the function of each layer. Start with #2, located below the figure on the far right, and move left to #5.

Retina, located at the back of the eye, contains photoreceptors.

Fovea

Optic nerve sends signals to the brain.

Retina blown up to show its 3 layers.

Light waves pass through spaces between cells to reach rods and cones in back layer of the retina.

Front layer of retina contains **nerve fibers** that carry impulses to the brain.

Middle layer of retina contains **ganglion cells,** in which impulses begin.

Back layer of retina contains photoreceptors, **rods** and **cones,** where transduction occurs.

Nerve fibers

Ganglion cells

Cone

Rod

Rod

Neural impulses move from ganglion cells to nerve fibers and then to the brain.

Rods and **cones** change light waves into electrical signals.

5 *Nerve impulses* generated in ganglion cells exit the back of the eye through the *optic nerve,* which carries impulses toward the brain. The point where the optic nerve exits the eye has no receptors and is called the *blind spot.* You don't notice the blind spot because your eyes are continually moving.

What's surprising about the eye is that it does not "see" but rather is a sophisticated computer for transduction, for changing light waves into impulses. For you to "see something," impulses must reach the visual areas in the brain, our next stop.

4 The process of *transduction* begins when chemicals in the rods and cones break down after absorbing light waves. This chemical breakdown generates a tiny electrical force that, if large enough, triggers *nerve impulses* in neighboring *ganglion cells;* now, transduction is complete.

3 Each eye has about 5 million cones, most located in the retina's fovea (Goldstein, 2002).

Cones are photoreceptors that contain three chemicals called opsins *(OP-sins),* which are activated in bright light and allow us to see color. Unlike rods, cones are wired individually to neighboring cells; this one-on-one system of relaying information allows us to see fine details.

Next, we finally get to transduction, which begins in the rods and cones.

2 Each eye has about 120 million rods, most located in the retina's periphery.

Rods are photoreceptors that contain a single chemical, called rhodopsin *(row-DOP-sin),* which is activated by small amounts of light. Because rods are extremely light sensitive, they allow us to see in dim light, but to see only black, white, and shades of gray.

To see color, we need the cones.

Visual Pathways: Eye to Brain

How do you see rock stars?

There is a lot of truth to the old saying, "Seeing is believing," but most people don't realize that the "seeing" takes place in the brain, not in the eye. So far, we have traced the paths along which light waves enter the eye, are focused on the retina, are changed into impulses, and leave the eye on the optic nerve. Now we will follow the optic nerve as it reaches its final destination in the occipital lobe, at the back of the brain. There, the occipital lobe changes light waves into colorful rock stars.

1 Optic nerve. Nerve impulses flow through the optic nerve as it exits from the back of the eye. This exit point creates a blind spot that we do not normally see because our eyes are constantly moving and cover any areas that might be in the blind spot.

The optic nerves partially cross over and make a major stop in the *thalamus,* which does some initial processing. The thalamus relays the impulses to the back of the occipital lobe in the right and left hemispheres.

2 Primary visual cortex. At the very back of each occipital lobe lies a primary visual cortex, which transforms nerve impulses into simple visual sensations, such as texture, lines, and colors. At this point, you would report seeing only these basic sensations (left figure), not the complete figure of a rock star.

Researchers estimate that about 25% of the entire cortex is devoted to processing visual information, more area than to any other sensory input (Van Essen, 1997). The visual cortex contains many different cells that respond to many different kinds of visual stimulation.

Meaningless stimuli

Specialized cells. From the Nobel Prize–winning research of David Hubel and Torsten Wiesel (1979), we know that different cells in the *primary visual cortex* respond to specific kinds of visual stimuli. For example, some cortical cells respond to lines of a particular width, others to lines at a particular angle, and still others to lines moving in a particular direction. These specialized cortical cells transform different stimuli into simple visual sensations, such as shadows, lines, textures, or angles.

Stimulation or blindness. At the beginning of this module, we told you about Katie, who had 36 tiny wires implanted into her primary visual cortex. When electricity was passed through these wires to stimulate neurons, Katie reported seeing flashes of colored light. She did not see meaningful images, such as a singer, because neurons in the primary visual cortex produce only simple visual sensations.

If part of your primary visual cortex were damaged, you would have a blind spot in the visual field, similar to looking through glasses with tiny black spots painted on the lens. Damage to the entire primary visual cortex in both hemispheres would result in almost total blindness; the ability to tell night from day might remain.

However, to make sense of what you see, such as a rock star, nerve impulses must be sent from the primary visual cortex to neighboring visual association areas.

3 Visual association areas. The primary visual cortex sends simple visual sensations (actually, impulses) to neighboring association areas, which add meaning or *associations* (Van Essen et al., 1992). In our example, the association area receives sensations of texture, line, movement, orientation, and color and assembles them into a meaningful image of a complete rock star (left figure). There are visual association areas in each hemisphere. If part of your visual association area were damaged, you would experience *visual agnosia,* which is difficulty in assembling simple visual sensations into more complex, meaningful images (Zeki, 1993). For instance, a person with visual agnosia could see pieces of things but would have difficulty combining pieces and recognizing them as whole, meaningful objects (see p. 79).

Meaningful rock star

Researchers can use brain scans to show actual neural activity that is occurring in the visual association areas.

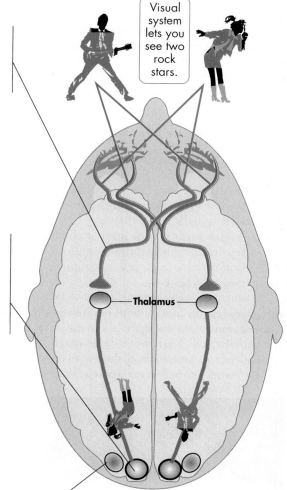

Visual system lets you see two rock stars.

Thalamus

4 This slightly modified brain scan (p. 70) shows that when a subject is silently looking at and reading words, maximum neural activity occurs in the primary visual cortex and nearby visual association areas (red and yellow indicate maximum neural activity; blue and green indicate least) (Posner & Raichle, 1994). These visual areas are located in the occipital lobe (back of the brain). The visual association areas are involved in many visual activities, such as reading, writing, and perceiving objects, animals, people, and colors.

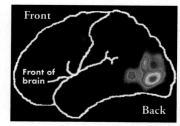

Front

Front of brain

Back

Next we'll explain how the visual system transforms light waves into all the colors of the rainbow.

A. Eye: Vision

What is red?

Debra was born with opaque films over her lenses (cataracts) that made her almost totally blind. For her first 28 years, she could tell night from day but see little else. When a newly developed operation restored much of her vision, she cried with delight as she looked around her hospital room and saw things she had only imagined. "Colors were a real surprise to me," Debra said. "They were so bright. You can't conceive what colors are until you've seen them. I couldn't imagine what a red apple looked like and now I can hold one and actually see red" (*San Diego Tribune*, April 3, 1984).

Red is actually long light waves.

Like Debra, you might assume that a red apple is really red, but you are about to discover otherwise. Objects, such as a red apple, do not have colors. Instead, objects reflect light waves whose different wavelengths are transformed by your visual system into the experience of seeing colors. So, what is red? The answer is that the color red is actually produced by a certain kind of wavelength.

How light waves are turned into millions of colors is a wondrous and interesting process, which begins with a ray of sunlight.

Making Colors from Wavelengths

1. A ray of sunlight is called white light because it contains all the light waves in the visible spectrum, which is what humans can see.

2. As white light passes through a prism, it is separated into light waves that vary in length. Nature creates prisms in the form of raindrops, which separate the passing sunlight into waves of different lengths, creating a spectrum of colors that we call a rainbow.

3. Our visual system transforms light waves of various lengths into millions of different colors. For example, in the figure below, notice that the numbers, which vary from about 400 to 700 (nanometers, or nm), indicate the length of light waves. We see shorter wavelengths as shades of

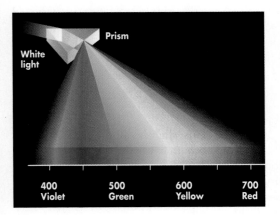

Prism

White light

| 400 Violet | 500 Green | 600 Yellow | 700 Red |

violet, blue, and green, and longer wavelengths as shades of yellow, orange, and red (Abramov & Gordon, 1994).

You see an apple as red because the apple reflects longer light waves, which your brain interprets as red.

Actually, how our visual system transforms light waves into color is explained by two different theories—the trichromatic and opponent-process theories—which we'll examine next.

Trichromatic Theory

The explanation of how you see the many colors in the native face (left photo) began over 200 years ago with the early work of a British physicist, Thomas Young. It was his research that laid the basis for a theory of how you see colors, called the trichromatic *(TRI-crow-MAH-tic)* theory of color.

The *trichromatic theory* says that there are three different kinds of cones in the retina, and each cone contains one of three different light-sensitive chemicals, called opsins. Each of the three opsins is most responsive to wavelengths that correspond to each of the three primary colors, blue, green, and red. All other colors can be mixed from these three primary colors.

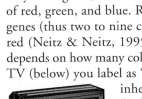

All colors are made from mixing 3 primary colors: red, green, and blue.

According to the recent version of the trichromatic theory, you see the red around the man's eyes because this area reflects light waves of a longer wavelength. You see the green in the feathers because they reflect light waves of medium length. You see the blue in the headband because it reflects light waves of shorter length. The different lengths of light waves are absorbed by three different cones whose chemicals (opsins) are most sensitive to one of the three primary colors—red, green, blue (right figure). Thus, wavelengths of different lengths are changed into one of the three primary colors, which are mixed to produce all colors (Goldstein, 2002).

Red cone   Green cone   Blue cone

Until recently, color vision was believed to involve only three genes, one each to code the three primary colors of red, green, and blue. Researchers discovered that we had as many as two to nine genes (thus two to nine cones) that code the longer wavelengths involved in seeing red (Neitz & Neitz, 1995). This means that seeing a particular color, such as red, depends on how many color genes you have inherited. For example, which bar on the TV (below) you label as "red" depends on which of the genes (two to nine) you've inherited. For example, one person may label deep scarlet as "red" while another sees a pale red. This means that different people may see and label the "same" color, red, very differently (scarlet to pale red), and this difference explains why people may not agree about adjusting the color (red) on their television sets (Lipkin, 1995). Thus, your perception of the color "red" may differ from someone who has different "color genes."

People do NOT all see the same color of red.

To understand how color coding occurs in the brain, we need to examine the second theory of color vision, the opponent-process theory.

Opponent-Process Theory

If you stare at a red square for about 20 seconds and then immediately look at a white piece of paper, you'll see a green square, which is called an afterimage.

An *afterimage* is a visual sensation that continues after the original stimulus is removed.

And if you stare at a blue square, you'll see a yellow afterimage. On the basis of his work with afterimages, physiologist Ewald Hering suggested that the visual system codes color by using two complementary pairs—red-green and blue-yellow. Hering's idea became known as the opponent-process theory.

The *opponent-process theory* says that ganglion cells in the retina and cells in the thalamus of the brain respond to two pairs of colors—red-green and blue-yellow. When these cells are excited, they respond to one color of the pair; when inhibited, they respond to the complementary pair.

 For example, some ganglion and thalamic cells use a *red-green* paired combination: they signal red when excited and green when inhibited.

 Other ganglion and thalamic cells use a *yellow-blue* paired combination: they signal blue when excited and yellow when inhibited.

Thus, different parts of the visual system use different methods to code different colors.

Theories Combined

Because we see colors so automatically and naturally, we don't realize it involves both the opponent-process and trichromatic theories. Here's what happens when we combine the two theories to explain color vision.

First, the trichromatic theory says that there are usually three different kinds of cones (there may be as many as nine) in the retina. Each cone absorbs light waves of different lengths, which correspond to the three primary colors of blue, green, and red. Second, when electrical signals (color information) reach the ganglion cells in the retina and neurons in the thalamus, they use the opponent-process theory, which involves a pair of colors: Activation results in one color of a pair, and inhibition results in the other color. Third, nerve 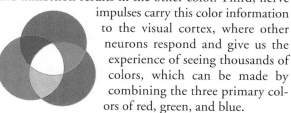 impulses carry this color information to the visual cortex, where other neurons respond and give us the experience of seeing thousands of colors, which can be made by combining the three primary colors of red, green, and blue.

Although most of us have good color vision, some individuals have varying degrees of color blindness.

Color Blindness

This is normal color vision.

The vast majority of us have normal color vision. We see the man on the left with a pinkish face, pale yellow scarf, purple hat, blue coat with orange trim, and brown pipe giving off yellow smoke, all against a two-toned orange background. However, about 1 out of 20 men in the United States see this same man in different shades of greens (photo below right) because they have inherited the most common form of color blindness.

Color blindness is the inability to distinguish two or more shades in the color spectrum. There are several kinds of color blindness.

Monochromats (MOHN-oh-crow-mats) have total color blindness; their worlds look like black-and-white movies. This kind of color blindness is rare and results from individuals having only rods or only one kind of functioning cone (instead of three).

Dichromats (DIE-crow-mats) usually have trouble distinguishing red from green because they have just two kinds of cones. This is an inherited genetic defect, found mostly in males, that results in seeing mostly shades of green (photo right) but differs in severity (Neitz et al., 1996).

This is red-green color blindness.

People don't always realize they have color blindness. For example, a little boy came home complaining about being chased by a green dog. The dog really looked green to the little boy; he did not know he had a form of color blindness.

People in some occupations, such as electrical technicians, are screened for color blindness because they must identify differently colored wires.

Below, you'll see two circles filled with colored dots that are part of a test for color blindness. An individual taking this test is asked to look at each circle and identify what, if any, number is formed by the colored dots.

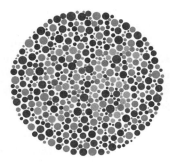

Individuals with normal vision see the number 96, while people with red-green color deficits find this number difficult or impossible to see.

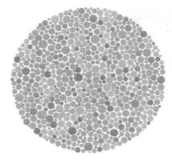

Normal color vision and those with total color blindness should not be able to read any number. The majority of those with red-green deficiencies should read the number 5.

From our discussion of the eye's structure and function, you can see that the eye is an engineering marvel that makes even the most sophisticated video camera seem like an expensive toy.

Next we'll examine an equally astonishing sense organ, the ear.

B. Ear: Audition

What happens when someone yells?

When a cheerleader gives a big yell, she is actually producing the yell by letting out air so that it is alternately compressed and expanded into traveling waves, called sound waves.

Sound waves, which are the stimuli for hearing (audition), resemble ripples of different sizes. Similar to ripples on a pond, sound waves travel through space with varying heights and frequency. Height, which is the distance from the bottom to the top of a sound wave, is called amplitude. Frequency refers to the number of sound waves that occur within 1 second.

We'll demonstrate the concept of amplitude by comparing sound waves of a cheerleader's yell with a child's whisper.

Amplitude and Loudness

Yell. As a cheerleader yells, she lets out an enormous amount of air that is compressed and expanded into very large traveling waves (shown below). Large sound waves are described as having high amplitude, which the brain interprets as loud sounds.

YELL!

Large amplitude means big sound waves and loud sounds.

Whisper. As a child whispers a secret to his friend, he lets out a small amount of air that is compressed and expanded into very small traveling waves. Small sound waves are described as having low amplitude, which the brain interprets as soft sounds.

 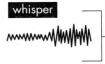

whisper

Small amplitude means small sound waves and soft sounds.

Relationship: amplitude and loudness. You have no difficulty distinguishing between a cheerleader's yell and a child's whisper because your auditory system automatically uses the amplitude of the sound waves to calculate loudness (Zeng & Shannon, 1994).

Loudness is your subjective experience of a sound's intensity. The brain calculates loudness from specific physical energy, in this case the amplitude of sound waves.

A whisper, which results in low-amplitude sound waves, is just above our threshold of hearing. The loudest yell on record, which resulted in high-amplitude sound waves, was about as loud as sound heard near speakers at a rock concert.

If the brain uses amplitude to calculate loudness, what does it use to calculate a sound's low or high pitch?

Frequency and Pitch

Screech or boom. As you listen to someone playing a keyboard, you can tell the difference between high and low notes because your brain is continually discriminating between high and low sounds, which is called pitch.

High frequency means sound waves are close together, resulting in high sounds or pitch.

Low frequency means sound waves are apart, resulting in low sounds or pitch.

High note. Striking the top key on a keyboard produces sound waves that travel rapidly and are described as having high frequency. The brain interprets high frequency as high notes or high pitch.

Low note. Striking the bottom key on a keyboard produces sound waves that travel slowly and are described as having low frequency. The brain interprets slow frequency as low notes or low pitch.

Relationship: frequency and pitch. When you hear a sound, your auditory system automatically uses frequency to calculate pitch.

Pitch is our subjective experience of a sound being high or low, which the brain calculates from specific physical stimuli, in this case the speed or frequency of sound waves. The frequency of sound waves is measured in cycles, which refers to how many sound waves occur within 1 second.

For example, playing the keyboard's highest key produces sound waves with a fast frequency (4,000 cycles per second), which results in high sounds or high pitch; the keyboard's lowest key produces sound waves of slower frequency (27 cycles per second), which results in low sounds or low pitch.

Hearing range. Humans hear sounds only within a certain range of frequencies and this range decreases with age. For example, infants have the widest range of hearing, from frequencies of 20 to 20,000 cycles per second. For college students, it is perhaps 30 to 18,000 cycles per second. With further aging, the hearing range decreases even more so that by age 70, many people have trouble hearing sounds above 6,000 cycles per second.

Next, we'll see how loud a jet plane is compared to a whisper.

MEASURING SOUND WAVES

If the sign on the right were posted in the library, you might not know that it refers to loudness, which is measured in decibels (dB).

A *decibel* is a unit to measure loudness, just as an inch is a measure of length. Our threshold for hearing ranges from 0 decibels, which is absolutely no sound, to 140 decibels, which can produce pain and permanent hearing loss.

The following table contains common sounds with their decibel levels. Notice especially those sound levels that can cause permanent hearing loss.

Please Do Not Talk Above 30 Decibels

Decibel (dB) level	Sounds and their decibel levels	Exposure time and permanent hearing loss
140	Jet engine, gun muzzle blast	Any exposure to sounds this loud is painful and dangerous. That's why aircraft ground personnel should wear ear protectors.
120	Rock concert near speakers, thunderclap, record-setting human yell (115 dB)	Exposure for fifteen minutes or less can produce hearing loss. Rock musicians and fans who do not use ear plugs risk hearing loss.
100	Chain saw, jackhammer, baby screaming, inside of racing car, firecracker	Exposure for 2 hours or more can cause hearing loss. Workers using loud power tools who do not use ear protectors risk hearing loss.
80	Heavy city traffic, alarm clock at 2 feet, subway, personal tape recorders	Constant exposure for 8 hours can produce hearing loss. Music lovers should know that stereo headphones can produce sounds from 80 to 115 dB.
60	Conversation, air conditioner at 20 feet, typewriter	Aging decreases hearing sensitivity, and that's why older adults may ask, "What did you say?" indicating that they may not easily hear normal conversations.
30	Whisper, quiet library, car idling in neutral (45 dB)	Today's cars are engineered for quietness. At idle, many cars are almost as quiet as a library; and at 65 mph (70 dB), they are not much louder than a conversation.
0	Threshold of hearing	If you were boating in the middle of a calm lake, you might say, "Now, this is really quiet." In comparison, most of us are accustomed to relatively noisy city environments.

DECIBELS AND DEAFNESS

It is now well established that continuous exposure to sounds with higher decibel levels for certain periods of time can produce permanent hearing loss. For example, rock musicians, rock fans, hunters, drivers of heavy machinery, airplane workers, and stereo headphone listeners who take no precautions against high decibel levels may suffer significant, permanent hearing losses later (Kulman, 1999).

At the end of this module (p. 115) we'll discuss different causes of deafness and treatment. Now, we'll take you inside the ear and explain how it turns sound waves into wonderful sounds.

B. Ear: Audition

Is that the Rolling Stones or a barking dog?

Most of us think that we hear with our ears and that's how we tell the difference between, for example, the music of the Rolling Stones and the barking of a dog. But nothing is further from the truth. What really happens is that both music and a dog's barks produce only sound waves, which are just the stimulus for hearing (audition). Your ears receive sound waves, but it is your brain that actually does the hearing, distinguishing the difference between the Stones' song, "(I Can't Get No) Satisfaction," and a dog's barks. It's a complicated journey; the first step begins in the outer ear.

1 *Outer Ear*

The only reason your ear has that peculiar shape and sticks out from the side of your head is to gather in sound waves. Thus, sound waves produced by the Rolling Stones are gathered by your outer ear.

The *outer ear* consists of three structures: external ear, auditory canal, and tympanic membrane.

The *external ear* is an oval-shaped structure that protrudes from the side of the head. The function of the external ear is to pick up sound waves and send them down a long, narrow tunnel called the auditory canal.

1a The *auditory canal* is a long tube that funnels sound waves down its length so that the waves strike a thin, taut membrane—the eardrum, or tympanic membrane.

In some cases, the auditory canal may become clogged with ear wax, which interferes with sound waves on their way to the eardrum. Ear wax should be removed by a professional so as not to damage the fragile eardrum.

1b The *tympanic (tim-PAN-ick) membrane* is a taut, thin structure commonly called the eardrum. Sound waves strike the tympanic membrane and cause it to vibrate. The tympanic membrane passes the vibrations on to the first of three small bones to which it is attached.

The tympanic membrane marks the boundary between the outer ear and the middle ear, described below left in #2.

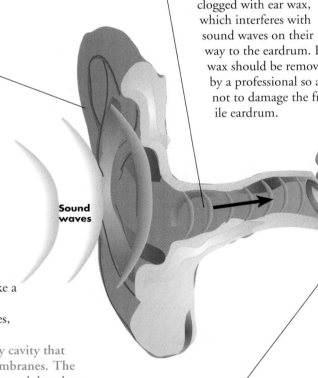

Sound waves

2 *Middle Ear*

The middle ear functions like a radio's amplifier; it picks up and increases, or amplifies, vibrations.

The *middle ear* is a bony cavity that is sealed at each end by membranes. The two membranes are connected by three small bones.

The three tiny bones are collectively called *ossicles (AW-sick-culls)* and, because of their shapes, are referred to as the hammer, anvil, and stirrup. The first ossicle—hammer—is attached to the back of the tympanic membrane. When the tympanic membrane vibrates, so does the hammer. In turn, the hammer sends the vibrations to the attached anvil, which further sends the vibrations to the attached stirrup. The stirrup makes the connection with the end membrane, the oval window. The three ossicles act like levers that greatly amplify the vibrations, which, in turn, cause the attached oval window to vibrate.

Thus, the function of the middle ear is to pick up vibrations produced by the tympanic membrane, amplify these vibrations, and pass them on to the oval window, which marks the end of the middle ear and beginning of the inner ear.

3 *Inner Ear*

The inner ear contains two main structures that are sealed in bony cavities: the cochlea, which is involved in hearing, and the vestibular system, which is involved in balance. We'll discuss the vestibular system on page 105; now, we'll focus on the cochlea.

The *cochlea* (*KOCK-lee-ah*), located in the inner ear, has a bony coiled exterior that resembles a snail's shell. The cochlea contains the receptors for hearing, and its function is transduction—transforming vibrations into nerve impulses that are sent to the brain for processing into auditory information.

Researchers liken the cochlea to an exquisite miniature box that is made of bone and contains precious jewels, which in this case are miniature cells that are the receptors for hearing.

On the next page, we have enlarged and opened the cochlea so you can see the auditory receptors.

3 Inner Ear (continued)

3a If you were to take two drinking straws, hold them side by side, and then wind them around your finger, you would have a huge imitation of a cochlea. The cochlea consists of two long narrow tubes (straws) separated by membranes (basilar and tectorial) but joined together and rolled up, or coiled. The beginning of the coiled compartments is sealed by a membrane, the oval window. So when the ossicles vibrate the oval window, the oval window vibrates the fluid in the cochlea's tubes, where the auditory receptors are located.

3b The auditory receptors, called *hair cells,* are miniature hair-shaped cells that stick up from the cochlea's bottom membrane, called the *basilar (BAZ-ih-lahr) membrane.* Vibration of fluid in the cochlear tubes causes movement of the basilar membrane, which literally bends the hair cells. The mechanical bending of the hair cells generates miniature electrical forces that, if large enough, trigger nerve impulses (transduction). Nerve impulses leave the cochlea as explained above right in #3c.

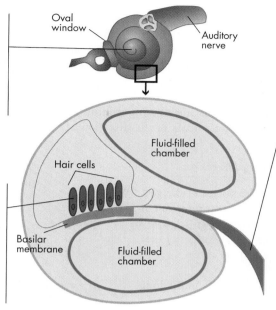

Cochlea changes vibrations into electrical signals.

Oval window
Auditory nerve

Hair cells

Fluid-filled chamber

Basilar membrane

Fluid-filled chamber

Cross Section of Cochlea

3c The *auditory nerve* is a band of fibers that carry nerve impulses (electrical signals) to the auditory cortex of the brain for processing.

Now the cochlea has completed its role of transduction—transforming vibrations into nerve impulses. However, you won't report hearing anything until the impulses reach your brain.

Auditory Brain Areas

How do we tell noise from music?

Just as your eye does not see, your ear does not hear. Rather, sense organs, such as the ear, perform only transduction—transform physical energy into nerve impulses. You don't hear or recognize sound as noise, music, or words until nerve impulses are processed by various auditory areas in the temporal lobes of your brain.

4 Sensations and Perceptions

After nerve impulses reach the brain, a two-step process occurs in which nerve impulses are first transformed into meaningless bits of sounds and then into meaningful sounds. The first step occurs in the primary auditory area, explained in #4a.

4a The *primary auditory cortex*, which is located at the top edge of the temporal lobe, transforms nerve impulses (electrical signals) into basic auditory sensations, such as meaningless sounds and tones of various pitches and loudness.

Next, the primary auditory cortex sends impulses (sensations) to the auditory association area, explained in #4b.

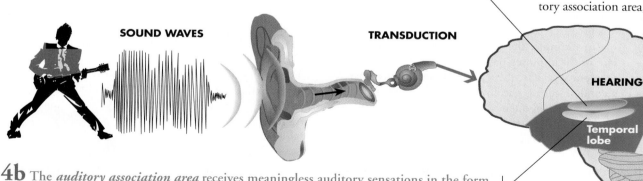

SOUND WAVES

TRANSDUCTION

HEARING

Temporal lobe

4b The *auditory association area* receives meaningless auditory sensations in the form of neural impulses from the neighboring primary auditory area. The auditory association area combines meaningless auditory sensations into perceptions, which are meaningful melodies, songs, words, or sentences.

It takes only a moment from the time sound waves enter your ear until you say, "That's the Stones' song, '(I Can't Get No) Satisfaction.'" But during that amazing moment, sound waves were changed into impulses, impulses into sensations, and finally, sensations into perceptions (Feng & Ratnam, 2000).

Now we'll explain how the brain uses nerve impulses to calculate where a sound is coming from, whether it is a high or low sound, and whether it is a loud or soft sound.

B. Ear: Audition

Where's the sound coming from? If someone yelled, "Watch out!" you would immediately turn your head toward the source of the sound because your brain automatically calculates the source's location. The brain calculates not only the source of the voice but also whether the voice calling your name is high or low or loud or soft. Thus, sound waves contain an amazing amount of information. We'll begin with how your brain calculates the direction of where a sound is coming from.

Calculating Direction

You automatically turn toward the source of the yell, "Watch out!" because your brain instantly calculates the direction or source.

The brain determines the *direction of a sound* by calculating the slight difference in time (see 1 in right figure) that it takes sound waves to reach the two ears, which are about six inches apart (see 2 in right figure) (Goldstein, 1999).

If you have difficulty telling where a sound is coming from, the sound is probably arriving at both ears simultaneously. To locate the direction, you can turn your head from side to side, causing the sound to reach one ear before the other.

The brain uses other cues to calculate a sound's high or low pitch.

WATCH OUT!

1. Source
A sound coming from the right reaches your right ear a split second before it reaches your left ear. The brain automatically interprets this difference in timing as a signal that the source of the sound is to the right. You will automatically turn your head right, to the source of the sound.

Sound waves blocked by head

Right ear   **Left ear**

2. Time difference
Sound waves reach the left ear this much later than they reach the right ear.

Calculating Pitch

Imagine the low, menacing growl of a lion and then the high screech of fingernails on the chalkboard. Your subjective experience of a sound being high or low is referred to as pitch. Exactly how the cochlea codes pitch and the brain interprets the code is rather complicated. We'll focus on two better known theories of pitch, the frequency and place theories.

The *frequency theory*, which applies only to low-pitched sounds, says that the rate at which nerve impulses reach the brain determines how low the pitch of a sound is.

For example, the brain interprets a frequency rate of 50 impulses per second as a lower sound than one with a frequency rate of 200 impulses per second. Hearing the low-pitched roar of a lion involves the frequency theory. Hearing higher-pitched sounds, however, such as the screech of fingernails on a chalkboard, involves another theory, the place theory.

The frequency and place theories explain how we perceive pitch.

The *place theory* says that the brain determines medium- to higher-pitched sounds on the basis of the place on the basilar membrane where maximum vibration occurs.

For example, lower-pitched sounds cause maximum vibrations near the beginning of the cochlea's basilar membrane, while higher-pitched sounds cause maximum vibrations near the end of the membrane. Our auditory system combines the frequency and place theories to transform sound waves into perceptions of low- to high-pitched sounds (Goldstein, 1999).

The brain does one more thing: It calculates how loud a sound is.

Calculating Loudness

You can easily tell the difference between a yell and a whisper because your auditory system transforms the intensity of sound waves into the subjective experiences of a soft whisper or a loud yell. This transformation occurs inside the cochlea.

Compared to a yell, a whisper produces low-amplitude sound waves that set off the following chain of events: fewer vibrations of the tympanic membrane, less movement of fluid in the cochlea, less movement of the basilar membrane, fewer bent hair cells, less electrical force, and finally, fewer nerve impulses sent to the brain, which interprets these signals as a soft sound.

The brain calculates *loudness* primarily from the frequency or rate of how fast or how slowly nerve impulses arrive from the auditory nerve.

For example, the brain interprets a slower rate of impulses as a softer tone (whisper) and a faster rate as a louder tone (yell) (Goldstein, 1999).

Earlier, we said that there are two structures in the inner ear, the cochlea and the vestibular system. If you have ever stood on your head, you have firsthand experience with the vestibular system, our next topic.

The brain calculates loudness from frequency of nerve impulses.

C. Vestibular System: Balance

Position and Balance

What else is in the inner ear?

I guarantee that one question you never ask is, "Where is my head?" Even though your head is in a hundred different positions throughout the day, you rarely forget to duck it as you enter a car or forget whether you're standing on your feet or your hands. That's because the position of your head is automatically tracked by another sense, called your vestibular system.

The *vestibular system*, which is located above the cochlea in the inner ear, includes three *semicircular canals*, resembling bony arches, which are set at different angles (right figure). Each of the semicircular canals is filled with fluid that moves in response to movements of your head. In the canals are sensors (hair cells) that respond to the movement of the fluid. The functions of the vestibular system include sensing the position of the head, keeping the head upright, and maintaining balance.

The vestibular system uses information on the position of your head to indicate whether you're standing on your hands or your feet. A gymnast (left figure) relies heavily on his or her vestibular system to keep balance. Sometimes an inner ear infection affects the vestibular system and results in dizziness, nausea, and the inability to balance. And as you'll see next, the vestibular system is also involved in motion sickness.

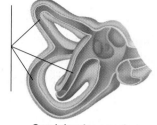
Semicircular canals

Vestibular system says you're upside down.

Motion Sickness

Why am I getting sick?

One of my terrible childhood memories is sitting in the back seat of a moving car and after 30 minutes of curving roads feeling a cold sweat followed by nausea, dizziness, and an extreme desire to lie down anywhere—stationary. Along with about 25% of the U.S. population, I experienced moderate to severe signs of motion sickness. About 55% of people experience only mild symptoms, while the remaining 20% are lucky and rarely experience any. Researchers think that motion sickness results when information provided by the vestibular system doesn't match information coming from other senses (M. Turner & Griffin, 1999).

Motion sickness, which consists of feelings of discomfort, nausea, and dizziness in a moving vehicle, is believed to develop when there is a sensory mismatch between the information from the vestibular system—that your head is physically bouncing around—and the information reported by your eyes—that objects in the distance look fairly steady.

Infants below age 2 rarely have motion sickness, but susceptibility increases from 2 to about 12. After 12, susceptibility decreases in both men and women. Researchers suspect that genetic and not personality factors determine susceptibility to motion sickness (Stern & Koch, 1996).

A number of drugs reduce the symptoms of motion sickness (Attias et al., 1987). As an alternative to drugs, fliers reported a significant reduction in motion sickness after completing a behavioral training program that taught them to perform relaxation responses, think positive thoughts, or use calming images at the first sign of symptoms. Of 53 fliers who had been grounded because of chronic, severe motion sickness, 49 were able to overcome their problem and start flying again after completing the behavioral program (D. R. Jones et al., 1985).

Malfunctioning of the vestibular system can cause terrible symptoms.

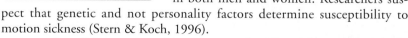
Motion sickness results from mismatch between vestibular and visual systems.

Meniere's Disease and Vertigo

Why is the room spinning?

Imagine suddenly having ringing in your ears like Niagara Falls, walking into the bathroom to find the toilet spinning out of range, or vomiting more than 30 times a day. These are all symptoms of the dreaded Meniere's disease.

Meniere's (main-YERS) *disease* results from a malfunction of the semicircular canals of the vestibular system. The symptoms include sudden attacks of dizziness, nausea, vomiting, spinning, and head-splitting buzzing sounds.

About 7 million Americans suffer from Meniere's disease, which is thought to be caused by a viral infection of the inner ear (Milstein, 1993). The vestibular system is also involved in another problem, called vertigo.

Vertigo, whose symptoms are dizziness and nausea, results from malfunction of the semicircular canals of the vestibular system.

Sophie, 57 years old, was sitting at the dining table. Suddenly she felt dizzy, fell out of her chair, crawled to the bathroom, and vomited. She had to lie in bed to keep from spinning. Sophie was diagnosed as having vertigo and sought help from a "dizzy" clinic (Jauhar, 2001).

Meniere's disease and vertigo share some symptoms and have no known cures. There are "dizzy" clinics that use drug and nondrug methods to decrease symptoms that involve malfunctions of the vestibular system.

If you happen to be reading this book in a car or on a plane and feel a little queasy, relax before reading the next section, which is about tasting and smelling food.

D. Chemical Senses

How does your tongue taste?

You rarely think about the thousands of chemicals you put into your mouth every day, but you do know when something tastes very good or very bad. You also know that if you burn your tongue on hot foods or liquids, your sense of taste can be markedly decreased.

Taste is called a chemical sense because the stimuli are various chemicals. On the surface of the tongue are receptors, called taste buds, for four basic tastes: sweet, salty, sour, and bitter. The function of taste buds is to perform transduction, which means transforming chemical reactions into nerve impulses.

As you imagine biting into and chewing a very bitter slice of lemon, we'll explain how your tongue tastes.

1 Tongue: Five Basic Tastes

You're probably familiar with four basic tastes—*sweet, salty, sour,* and *bitter.* There now appears to be a fifth, called *umami,* a meaty-cheesy taste found in cheese, meat, pizza, and MSG (Travis, 2002). The right figure shows the areas on the tongue that have the most sensors or taste buds.

The reason many of us have a sweet tooth is that, as newborns, we inherited an innate preference for sweet and salty (Netting, 2001). Like most animals, humans avoid bitter-tasting substances, presumably because many poisonous substances taste bitter (Barinaga, 2000a). If you are one of those who like sour lemonade, you know that people can learn to like bitter substances. Tasting begins with what happens in the trenches on the surface of your tongue.

2 Surface of the Tongue

As you chew the lemon, its chemicals, which are the *stimuli* for taste, break down into molecules. In turn, these molecules mix with saliva and run down into narrow trenches on the surface of the tongue. Once inside the trenches, the molecules stimulate the taste buds.

3 Taste Buds

Buried in the trenches on the surface of the tongue are many hundreds of bulblike taste buds.

Taste buds, which are shaped like miniature onions, are the receptors for taste. Chemicals dissolved in the saliva activate the taste buds, which produce nerve impulses that eventually reach areas in the brain's parietal lobe. The brain transforms these nerve impulses into sensations of taste.

Taste buds live in a relatively toxic environment and are continuously exposed to heat, cold, spices, bacteria, and saliva. As a result, taste buds wear out and are replaced about every ten days. The human tongue can have as many as 10,000 taste buds and as few as 500; the number remains constant throughout life (Goldstein, 2002).

Tongue contains sensors (taste buds) for five tastes.

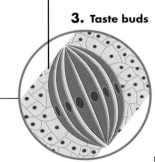

1. Sensors (taste buds) for the five basic tastes are primarily located on back, front, and sides of tongue (blue-shaded areas).

2. Surface of the tongue

Trench contains buried taste buds.

3. Taste buds

Taste buds change dissolved chemicals into electrical signals.

4 All Tongues Are Not the Same

In rare cases, individuals are born without any taste buds and cannot taste anything because they have a genetically determined disorder (Bartoshuk & Beauchamp, 1994). In contrast, about 25% of the population are supertasters, which means they may have two to three times more taste buds than normal, which results in increased sensitivity to sweet, bitter, sour, and salty. For example, supertasters taste sugar to be twice as sweet as most people and get more intense oral burning sensations from the chemical (capsaicin) in chili peppers. Supertasters find grapefruit juice too bitter and don't like broccoli because it also contains a bitter chemical (Drewnowski, 1997).

Researchers found that being a supertaster is an inherited trait and speculate that it may have had some evolutionary advantage. For example, supertasters would be better able to judge whether fruits or berries were poisonous (Bartoshuk, 1997). Today, supertasters may work for food manufacturers and rate the taste of new food products.

But for all of us, our ability to taste is greatly affected by our ability to smell.

5 Flavor: Taste and Smell

If taste receptors are sensitive to only five basic tastes, how can you tell the difference between two sweet tastes, such as a brownie and vanilla ice cream, or between two sour tastes, such as lemon juice and vinegar? The truth is that a considerable percentage of the sensations we attribute to taste are actually contributed by our sense of smell (Stillman, 2002).

We experience *flavor* when we combine the sensations of taste and smell.

You have no doubt experienced the limitations of your taste buds' abilities when you had a cold, which blocks the nasal passages and cuts out the sense of smell. Without smell, foods we usually love now taste very bland.

Since our taste of foods is greatly enhanced by the sense of smell, we'll examine taste or olfaction next.

How does your nose smell?

Every year people in the United States spend about $5 billion on perfumes to make themselves smell better. You may have been impressed that your tongue has up to 10,000 taste buds, but that number pales in comparison to the nose's 6 million receptor cells (Doty, 2001). That's why the sense of smell, more properly called olfaction, is 10,000 times more sensitive than taste (Reyneri, 1984).

Olfaction is called a chemical sense because its stimuli are various chemicals that are carried by the air. The upper part of the nose has a small area that contains receptor cells for olfaction. The function of the olfactory receptors is transduction, to transform chemical reactions into nerve impulses.

We'll explain the steps for olfaction by having you imagine crossing paths with an angry skunk.

1 Stimulus

An angry skunk protects itself by spraying thousands of molecules, which are carried by the air and drawn into your nose as you breathe. The reason you can smell substances such as skunk spray is that these substances are volatile. A volatile substance is one that can release molecules into the air at room temperature. For example, volatile substances include skunk spray, perfumes, and warm brownies, but not glass or steel. We can smell only volatile substances, but first they must reach the olfactory cells in the nose.

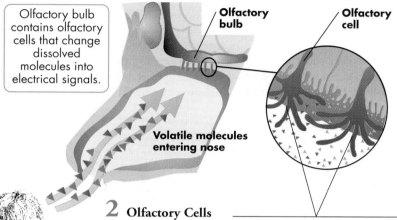

Olfactory bulb contains olfactory cells that change dissolved molecules into electrical signals.

Olfactory bulb

Olfactory cell

Volatile molecules entering nose

2 Olfactory Cells

Olfactory cells are the receptors for smell and are located in two 1-inch-square patches of tissue in the uppermost part of the nasal passages. Olfactory cells are covered with mucus, a gluey film into which volatile molecules dissolve and stimulate the underlying olfactory cells. The olfactory cells trigger nerve impulses that travel to the brain, which interprets the impulses as different smells.

As you breathe, a small percentage of the air entering your nose reaches the upper surface of your nasal passages, where the olfactory receptors are located. People can lose their sense of smell if a virus or inflammation destroys the olfactory receptors, or if a blow to the head damages the neural network that carries impulses to the brain (Bartoshuk & Beauchamp, 1994). About 6%, 17%, and 29% of people in their 50s, 60s, and 70s, lose the ability to detect common odors (Murphy et al., 2002). You don't actually smell anything until neural impulses reach your brain.

3 Sensations and Memories

Nerve impulses from the olfactory cells travel first to the olfactory bulb, which is a tiny, grape-shaped area (green structure in diagram of nose) that lies directly above the olfactory cells at the bottom of the brain. From here, impulses are relayed to the primary olfactory cortex (also called the piriform cortex) located underneath the brain. This cortex transforms nerve impulses into the olfactory sensations of a skunk's spray or a sweet perfume (Doty, 2001).

Although we can identify as many as 10,000 different odors, we soon stop smelling our deodorants or perfumes because of decreased responding, called adaptation, in the olfactory cells (Kurahashi & Menini, 1997).

Smell, in terms of evolution, is a very primitive sense and has important functions.

A nose worth $100,000?

Sophia Grojsman is one of only a dozen master perfumers in the United States who are responsible for creating some of the best-known perfumes (Calvin Klein, Estée Lauder). Known in the trade as a "nose," she earns over $100,000 a year because there is no scientific/computer substitute for her nose and brain's ability to identify, remember, and mix fragrances that elicit pleasant memories and moods. One reason a computerized nose has not yet replaced a human nose is that scientists are only now beginning to understand which combinations of molecular qualities (weight, shape) and olfactory receptors determine which of 10,000 different odors humans can smell (Buck, 1999).

4 Functions of Olfaction

One function of smell is to intensify the taste of food. For example, you could not tell a licorice from an orange jelly bean with your nose held closed. A second function is to warn of potentially dangerous foods; the repulsive odor of spoiled or rotten food does this very effectively. A third and more recently discovered function is to elicit strong memories, often associated with emotional feelings; for example, the smell of pumpkin pie may remind you of a festive family gathering (Hurtley, 2000). For many animals, such as cats and dogs, smell also functions to locate food, mates, and territory.

Next, we examine the sense of touch and explain what happens when you pet a cat.

E. Touch

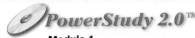

Definition

What happens when fingers feel fur?

If you were to draw your hand across the surface of a cat, you would have the sensations of touching something soft and furry. These sensations are part of the sense of touch.

The sense of *touch* includes pressure, temperature, and pain. Beneath the outer layer of skin are a half-dozen miniature sensors that are receptors for the sense of touch. The function of the touch sensors is to change mechanical pressure or changes in temperature into nerve impulses that are sent to the brain for processing.

We'll examine several miniature mechanical sensors and explain how they function.

Receptors in the Skin

If you were to closely examine the surface of your skin, you would see a relatively smooth membrane covered in some places with hair. Some "touch" sensors are wound around hair follicles (the backs of your arms) and are slightly different from sensors in skin without hair (your palms). However, before we discuss several major touch receptors, we need to examine the different layers of the skin.

1 Skin. The skin, which is the body's largest organ, has three layers. The *outermost layer* of skin is a thin film of dead cells containing no receptors. Immediately below the dead layer are the first receptors, which look like groups of threadlike extensions. In the *middle and fatty layers* of skin are a variety of receptors with different shapes and functions. Some of the major sensors in the middle layer of skin are hair receptors.

2 Hair receptors. In the middle layer are free nerve endings that are wrapped around the base of each hair follicle; these are called *hair receptors.* Hair receptors respond or fire with a burst of activity when hairs are first bent. However, if hairs remain bent for a period of time, the receptors cease firing, an example of *sensory adaptation.* When you first put on a watch, it bends hairs, causing hair receptors to fire; your brain interprets this firing as pressure on your wrist. If you keep the watch on and it remains in place, keeping the hairs bent, the hair receptors adapt or cease firing, and you no longer feel pressure from your watch, even though it is still there. Your skin contains some receptors that adapt rapidly (hair receptors) and others that adapt slowly. Adaptation prevents your sense of touch from being overloaded.

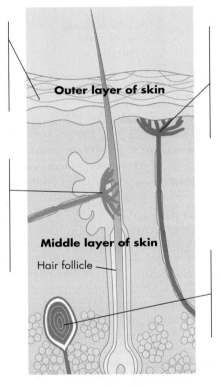

Outer layer of skin

Middle layer of skin

Hair follicle

3 Free nerve endings. Near the bottom of the outer layer of skin is a group of threadlike extensions; these are called *free nerve endings* because they have nothing protecting or surrounding them. One question about free nerve endings is how the same receptor can transmit information about both temperature and pain. Researchers think that different patterns of neural activity may signal different sensations—for example, slow bursts of firing for temperature and fast bursts for pain (Ferster & Spruston, 1995).

4 Pacinian corpuscle. In the fatty layer of skin is the largest touch sensor, called the *Pacinian corpuscle* (*pa-SIN-ee-in CORE-pus-sole*). This receptor, which has distinctive layers like a slice of onion, is highly sensitive to touch, is the only receptor that responds to vibration, and adapts very quickly.

All these receptors send their electrical signals to the brain.

Brain Areas

Did I touch my nose or my toe?

When pressure (touch), temperature, or pain stimulates the skin's receptors, they perform transduction and change these forms of energy into nerve impulses. The impulses go up the spinal cord and eventually reach the brain's somatosensory cortex.

The *somatosensory cortex,* which is located in the parietal lobe, transforms nerve impulses into sensations of touch, temperature, and pain. You know which part is being stimulated because, as we explained earlier (p. 77), different parts of the body are represented on different areas of the somatosensory cortex.

Compared with touch and temperature, the sense of pain is different because it has no specific stimulus and can be suppressed by psychological factors. We'll discuss these interesting aspects of pain, along with acupuncture, later in this module. We'll also discuss later how psychological factors can make foods that we think are truly disgusting become delicacies in other parts of the world. But first, try out your memory on the Concept Review.

Somato-sensory cortex

Parietal lobe

✔ Concept Review

EYE: Numbers on the eye match the numbers of the questions.

1. A transparent, curved structure at the front of the eye, called the _____, focuses or bends light waves into a more narrow beam.

2. A round opening at the front of the eye that allows varying amounts of light to enter the eye is called the _____.

3. A circular, pigmented muscle that dilates or constricts, thus increasing or decreasing the size of the pupil, is called the _____.

4. The function of the transparent, oval structure called the _____ is to bend light waves into a narrower beam of light and focus the beam precisely on a layer of cells in the very back of the eye.

5. Lining the back of the eye is a filmlike layer called the (a)_____, which contains several layers of cells. The back layer of cells has two kinds of photoreceptors, called (b)_____ and (c)_____.

6. This band of nerve fibers, called the (a)_____, exits from the back of the eye and carries impulses to the brain. The point at which this nerve exits is called the (b)_____ because it contains no rods or cones.

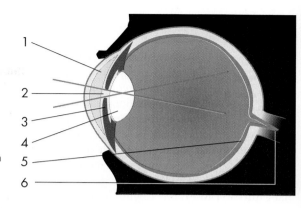

EAR: Numbers on the ear match the numbers of the questions.

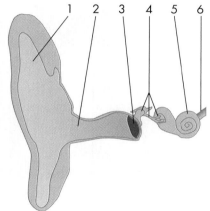

1. The funnel-like structure called the _____ gathers in sound waves from the environment.

2. The short tunnel called the _____ carries sound waves that strike a membrane.

3. The thin, taut membrane at the end of the auditory canal, called the _____, transforms sound waves into vibrations.

4. The three small bones (hammer, anvil, and stirrup) called the (a)_____ are part of the middle ear. They transform vibrations of the tympanic membrane into mechanical movements, which in turn vibrate a second membrane, called the (b)_____.

5. The coiled, fluid-filled structure called the (a)_____ is one part of the inner ear. It contains auditory receptors called (b)_____ that are attached to the basilar membrane.

6. The band of fibers called the _____ carries nerve impulses from the cochlea to the brain.

7. The inner ear contains a group of structures shaped like three tiny arches set at different angles. These structures signal body movement and position and are called the _____ system.

8. Sensors that are located on the surfaces of the tongue respond to five basic tastes, which are (a)_____, _____, _____, _____, and the newly found taste called _____. The sensors or receptors for taste are called (b)_____.

9. Substances give off volatile molecules that are drawn into the nose, dissolve in mucus, and activate the (a)_____. The function of these cells is to produce (b)_____ that are sent to the olfactory bulb and brain for processing.

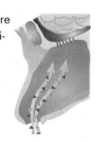

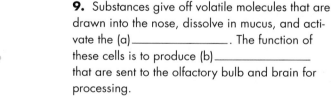

Hair follicle

10. There are several kinds of touch receptors: the (a)_____ is fast adapting; the (b)_____ is also fast adapting; the (c)_____ responds to both touch and vibration.

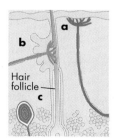

Answers: EYE: 1. cornea; 2. pupil; 3. iris; 4. lens; 5. (a) retina, (b) rods, (c) cones; 6. (a) optic nerve, (b) blind spot; EAR: 1. external ear; 2. auditory canal; 3. tympanic membrane (eardrum); 4. (a) ossicles, (b) oval window; 5. (a) cochlea, (b) hair cells; 6. auditory nerve; 7. vestibular; 8. (a) sweet, salty, sour, bitter, umami, (b) taste buds; 9. (a) olfactory cells, (b) nerve impulses; 10. (a) free nerve ending, (b) hair receptor, (c) Pacinian corpuscle

F. Cultural Diversity: Disgust

Would you eat a worm?

We have discussed how senses transform physical energy into impulses, which eventually become sensations and then perceptions. However, your perceptions are usually influenced by psychological factors, such as learning, emotion, and motivation, so that you never perceive the world exactly like someone else. For example, when offered a fish eye to eat, many of us would react with great disgust. The facial expression to express disgust (right photo) is similar across cultures.

Disgust is triggered by the presence of a variety of contaminated or offensive things, including certain foods, body products, and gore.

We show disgust, which is a universally recognized facial expression, by closing the eyes, narrowing the nostrils, curling the lips downward, and sometimes sticking out the tongue.

Disgust is considered a basic emotion and is specifically related to a particular motivational system (hunger). Children begin to show the facial expression for disgust between the ages of 2 and 4, a time when they are learning which foods in their culture are judged edible and which are considered repugnant (Rozin et al., 2000).

Cultural influence. Your particular culture has a strong influence on which foods you learn to perceive as disgusting and which you think are delicious. We'll describe three foods that are considered delicious in some cultures and disgusting in others.

Plump Grubs

For most U.S. citizens, eating a round, soft, white worm would be totally unthinkable. For the Asmat of New Guinea, however, a favorite delicacy is a plump, white, 2-inch larva—the beetle grub. The natives harvest dozens of the grubs, put them on bamboo slivers, and roast them. A photographer from the United States who did a story on the Asmat tried to eat a roasted grub, but his American tastes would not let him swallow it (Kirk, 1972).

Fish Eyes and Whale Fat

Although some Americans have developed a taste for raw fish (sushi), a common dish in Japan, most would certainly gag at the thought of eating raw fish eyes. Yet for some Inuit (Eskimo) children, raw fish eyes are like candy. Here you see a young girl using the Inuits' all-purpose knife to gouge out the eye of an already-filleted Arctic fish.

Eskimos also hunt a type of whale (the narwhal) that provides much of their protein. They consider the layer of fat under the skin (*mukluk*) a delicacy, and they eat it raw or dried.

Milk and Blood

Several tribes in East Africa supplement their diet with fresh blood that is sometimes mixed with milk. They obtain the blood by puncturing a cow's jugular vein with a sharp arrow. A cow can be bled many times and suffer no ill effects. The blood-milk drink provides a rich source of protein and iron.

CULTURAL INFLUENCES ON DISGUST

The reaction of U.S. college students to eating white, plump grubs (on right, actual size) or cold, glassy fish eyes or having a warm drink of blood mixed with milk is almost always disgust. Researchers believe that showing disgust originally evolved to signal rejection of potentially contaminated or dangerous foods. Today, however, because of cultural and psychological influences, we may show disgust for eating a variety of noncontaminated foods (cat, dog, or horse meat) or situations (touching a dead person) (Rozin et al., 2000). The fact that the same things are viewed as all right in one culture but as disgusting in another graphically shows how much cultural values can influence and bias perceptions.

Just as psychological factors are involved in perceiving taste, they are also involved in experiencing pain.

G. Research Focus: Mind Over Body?

Definitions and Research Methods

Can sugar pills reduce pain?

One of the truly amazing research findings is how sugar pills or placebos can somehow "trick" us into feeling or getting better. For example, because many of us believe that we will be helped by taking pills, about one-third of the population report feeling much better or having less pain after taking a pill, not knowing that it was only a sugar pill—a placebo.

A *placebo* is some intervention, such as taking a pill, receiving an injection, or undergoing an operation, that resembles medical therapy but that, in fact, has no medical effects.

A *placebo effect* is a change in the patient's illness (for better or worse) that is due to the patient's beliefs or expectations rather than the medical treatment.

For example, if people take a pill for headache pain and *believe* or *expect* that the pill will decrease their pain, about 30 to 60% of people will actually feel less pain after taking a placebo (M. Talbot, 2000).

Because the placebo effect can occur after taking any pill (injection or medical procedure), researchers needed to find a method that could separate a person's expectations and beliefs from the actual effects of a new drug or medical treatment. The method that researchers use to separate the effects of a person's expectations (placebo effect) from a pill or medical treatment is called the double-blind design.

In a *double-blind procedure,* neither the researchers ("blind") nor the subjects ("blind") know who is receiving what treatment. Because neither researchers nor subjects know who is receiving which treatment, the researchers' or subjects' expectations have a chance to equally affect both treatments (drug and placebo).

For example, in a double-blind design, headache sufferers would be told that they will be given one of two different kinds of pills to decrease pain. Unknown to the subjects ("blind") and the researchers ("blind"), one of the pills is a drug and one is a placebo. If subjects taking the drug report the same decrease in pain as those taking the placebo, researchers conclude that the drug is no better than a placebo. If subjects taking the drug report less pain than those taking the placebo, researchers conclude that the drug is medically useful because it is better than a placebo.

Over the past 25 years, hundreds of double-blind experiments have found that 30 to 98% of people have reported beneficial effects after taking placebos (M. Talbot, 2000). What follows is a sample of these findings, which demonstrate how people's expectations and beliefs can change placebos into powerful medicine.

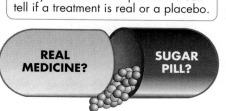

> Only a double-blind procedure can tell if a treatment is real or a placebo.

REAL MEDICINE? SUGAR PILL?

Placebo Results

Here are four convincing examples of pain reduction that involved placebos and double-blind procedures (J. A. Turner et al., 1994).

98% of patients originally reported marked or complete relief of pain from ulcers after medical treatment (gastric freezing). However, in a later double-blind procedure, this treatment was shown to be ineffective.

85% of patients originally reported a reduction in pain from *Herpes simplex* (cold sores and genital sores) after a drug treatment. However, in a later double-blind procedure, this drug was proved to be ineffective.

56% of patients reported a decrease in heart pain (angina pectoris) after being given a medical procedure that, unknown to the patient, involved only a skin incision.

35% of patients who had arthroscopic knee surgery reported decreased pain. About 250,000 patients a year get this surgery ($5,000 each). In a double-blind study, the placebo group (sham surgery) reported a similar decrease (Moseley et al., 2002).

Conclusion: Mind over Body!

Based on findings like those given above, researchers have reached three conclusions (W. A. Brown, 1997; M. Talbot, 2000).

First, potentially very powerful placebo effects, such as reducing pain, getting over colds, or speeding recovery from medical procedures, have been greatly underestimated.

Second, both medication (pills, injections) and fake surgeries can produce significant placebo effects, such as reducing pain, in 15 to 98% of patients.

Third, and of great interest to psychologists, placebos indicate a powerful mind-over-body interaction. This mind-over-body interaction explains why people may really experience and report surprising health benefits from taking a wide variety of placebos on the market, such as unproven herbal remedies.

Researchers suggest that placebos may work by creating positive expectations and beliefs that reduce anxiety and stress. In turn, the reduction of anxiety results in perceiving less pain. And the reduction in stress improves functioning of the immune system so that the body can better fight off toxins and make a quicker recovery from some problem (W. A. Brown, 1997). Thus, there is no question that our minds have powerful effects on our bodies.

Next we'll examine pain in more detail and see how mental factors can affect the perception of pain.

H. Pain

What causes pain?

All of us can relate to pain because at one time or another we have all felt various degrees of pain.

Pain is an unpleasant sensory and emotional experience that may result from tissue damage, one's thoughts or beliefs, or environmental stressors (job, traffic). Pain receptors in the body send nerve impulses to the somatosensory and limbic areas of the brain, where impulses are changed into pain sensations. Pain is essential for survival: it warns us to avoid or escape dangerous situations or stimuli and makes us take time to recover from injury.

This definition of pain differs from the other senses in three ways. First, pain results from many different stimuli (physical injury, loud noises, bright lights, psychological and social stressors), while each of the other senses responds primarily to a single stimulus. Second, the pain's intensity depends not only on the physical stimulus but also on a number of social and psychological factors, including attentional or emotional states. Third, the treatment of pain depends not only on treating any physical injury but also on reducing psychological and emotional distress that may have caused or contributed to the painful sensations (Keefe et al., 2002).

Researchers recognize that pain is a complex process that may or may not include tissue damage and usually involves social, psychological, and emotional factors, which can cause, increase, or decrease painful sensations (Keefe et al., 2002). For example, after men had hot metal plates placed on the backs of their hands, they were given an injection of either a painkiller or a placebo (they did not know which—double-blind procedure). Brain scans were used to identify brain areas that were activated by the painkiller or placebo injections, which had reduced pain. Brain scans showed that the placebo injections that had reduced pain had activated pain-reducing brain circuits that were similar to the circuits activated by real painkillers. This is one of the first studies to show how one's beliefs (in placebos) can activate circuits in the brain, which, in turn, may result in significant changes in perception (decrease in pain) (Petrovic et al., 2002; Ploghaus et al., 2003).

Other psychological factors, such as changes in attention, can also alter perception of pain and answer an interesting question: Why do headaches come and go, depending on what you are doing?

How does the mind stop pain?

Although a headache is painful, the pain may come and go as you shift your attention or become absorbed in some project. This phenomenon is explained by the gate control theory of pain (Melzack & Wall, 1983).

The *gate control theory of pain* says that nonpainful nerve impulses (shifting attention) compete with pain impulses (headache) in trying to reach the brain. This competition creates a bottleneck, or neural gate, that limits the number of impulses that can be transmitted. Thus, shifting one's attention or rubbing an injured area may increase the passage of nonpainful impulses and thereby decrease the passage of painful impulses; as a result, the sensation of pain is dulled. The neural gate isn't a physical structure but rather refers to the competition between nonpainful and painful impulses as they try to reach the brain.

The gate control theory explains that you may not notice pain from a headache or injury while thoroughly involved in some other activity because impulses from that activity close the neural gate and block the passage of painful impulses (right figure above: NO PAIN). However, when you become less involved, there are fewer nonpainful impulses, the neural gate opens (left figure above: PAIN), and you again notice the pain as painful impulses reach the brain (Kugelmann, 1998).

The gate control theory explains how a professional football quarterback was able to play the last six minutes

2. With gate open, we feel pain.

PAIN

Gate **open**

1. Pain signals coming from spinal cord reach the brain.

4. With gate closed, we feel no pain.

NO PAIN

Gate closed

3. Pain signals coming from spinal cord do not reach the brain.

of an important football game with a broken ankle (Associated Press, 2002). The gate control theory says that a football player's intense attentional and emotional involvement in the game caused his brain to send nonpainful impulses that closed neural gates in the spinal cord. The closed neural gates blocked impulses from a painful ankle from reaching his brain and thus prevented feelings of pain. Later, when the game was over, the quarterback's attentional and emotional states calmed down, the neural gates opened, impulses from his broken ankle reached his brain, and he felt considerable pain.

PAIN: PHYSICAL AND PSYCHOLOGICAL

According to the gate control theory, your perception of pain depends not only on a stressful mental state or physical injury but also on a variety of psychological, emotional, and social factors, which can either decrease or increase your perception of pain (Pincus & Morley, 2001).

Your perception of pain from a serious injury can also be reduced by your brain's ability to secrete its own pain-reducing chemicals, called endorphins.

Does the brain make its own painkillers?

Someone who has experienced a serious injury—in football, for example—will usually report that initially the pain was bearable but with time the pain became much worse. One reason pain seems less intense immediately after injury is that the brain produces endorphins.

Endorphins (en-DOOR-fins) are chemicals produced by the brain and secreted in response to injury or severe physical or psychological stress. The pain-reducing properties of endorphins are similar to those of morphine, a powerful painkilling drug.

The brain produces endorphins in situations that evoke great fear, anxiety, stress, or bodily injury, as well as after intense aerobic activity (Tripathi et al., 1993). For example, subjects showed increased levels of endorphins after being stressed by receiving painful electric shocks or by holding their hands in ice water (Millan, 1986). Patients showed increased levels of endorphins after their teeth nerves were touched or their bandages were removed from badly burned areas of the body (Szyfelbein et al., 1985). These studies indicate that the brain produces endorphins to reduce pain during periods of intense physical stress. Endorphins and other painkillers (heroin, morphine, codeine) act mostly to stop receptors from signaling severe, persistent pain but do not stop receptors from signaling quick, sharp pain as from a pinprick (Taddese et al., 1995).

Brain releases endorphins in times of great pain, stress, or fear.

Researchers have identified the genetic code responsible for the development of the endorphin-morphine receptor in the brain. This receptor, which is activated by morphine, heroin, or endorphin, is the key to both reducing pain and causing addiction (Y. Chen et al., 1993). Researchers hope that, as they better understand how this receptor works, they can develop drugs that reduce pain but are not addicting.

ADRENAL CELL TRANSPLANTS

Not only does the brain make endorphins, but so too do the body's adrenal glands (see p. 82), which make an endorphin-like chemical that reduces pain. Researchers removed pain-reducing adrenal gland cells from individuals who were brain-dead and transplanted these cells into the spinal cords of patients suffering from chronic and severe cancer pain. Four of five patients who received transplanted cells reported dramatic decreases in pain (Pappas et al., 1997). Researchers were very encouraged and suggested that transplants of adrenal gland cells that make an endorphin-like chemical represent a promising approach to treating chronic pain.

Endorphins may also be involved in explaining how acupuncture reduces pain.

Can an ancient technique reduce pain?

Initially, scientists trained in the rigorous methods of the West (in particular, the United States) expressed great doubt about an ancient Chinese pain-reducing procedure, traced back to 2500 B.C., called acupuncture.

Acupuncture is a procedure in which a trained practitioner inserts thin needles into various points on the body's surface and then manually twirls or electrically stimulates the needles. After 10–20 minutes of needle stimulation, patients often report a reduction in various kinds of pain.

The mysterious part of this procedure is that the points of insertion—such as those shown in the photograph on the right—were mapped thousands of years ago and, as researchers now know, are often far removed from the sites of painful injury.

Today, modern scientists have explained some of the mystery surrounding acupuncture. First, the points of needle insertion, which seem unrelated to the points of injury, are often close to

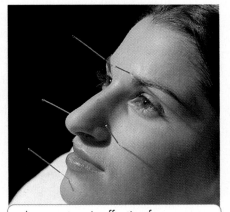

Acupuncture is effective for nausea, headaches, and some kinds of pain.

known pathways that conduct pain. Second, there is some evidence that stimulation of these points causes secretion of endorphins, which we know can reduce pain. For example, if patients are first given a drug (naloxone) that blocks secretion of endorphins, acupuncture does not reduce pain. Third, fMRI brain scans showed that acupuncture decreases neural activity in brain areas involved in pain sensations (Hui et al., 2000; Ulett, 2003).

Studies on the effectiveness of acupuncture in reducing pain of headaches and back pain indicate that 50 to 80% of patients reported short-term improvement but after six months, about 50% of the patients reported a return of their painful symptoms (Ceniceros & Brown, 1998). There is some evidence that acupuncture decreases certain kinds of chronic pain (rotator cuff tendinitis) in athletes (Kleinhenz et al., 1999). The National Institutes of Health concluded that acupuncture is effective for nausea (from chemotherapy or morning sickness) and some kinds of pain (after dental treatment) (Holden, 1997). There is little convincing evidence that acupuncture is effective in treating either heroin, cocaine, or nicotine dependency (Ceniceros & Brown, 1998).

Next we turn to a very practical question: Can a sense be replaced if it is damaged? Of the five major senses—vision, audition, taste, olfaction, and touch—damage to vision and audition is especially disastrous to the quality of life. For that reason, researchers are trying to develop artificial eyes and ears.

I. Application: Artificial Senses

Is an artificial eye possible?

The cause and degree of blindness depend on which part of the visual system is affected. For example, a person would be totally blind if the photoreceptors (rods and cones) in the retina were destroyed (retinitis pigmentosa, an inherited disease) or if the entire retina or optic nerve were damaged. First, we'll look at a microchip that could be implanted into the retina to replace photoreceptors damaged by disease.

Glasses   Microchip implanted in retina

Ganglion cells make impulses.

Microchip

1 Artificial photoreceptors. Some individuals are blind because the front part of the eye is functioning but the photoreceptors (rods and cones) in the retina are damaged by accident or disease. For these individuals, researchers are developing a microchip the size of a match head (black square with white "E") that would be implanted in the back of the retina. This microchip would change light waves into electrical signals that would activate the middle layer of ganglion cells, which are undamaged. The ganglion cells would then make impulses that travel on to the brain for processing. Although this microchip would not restore full vision, it would allow people who are now totally blind to see shades of light. Researchers must still develop a power supply before the microchip can be tested (LaFee, 2000).

For individuals who are blind because their entire eye or optic nerve is damaged, researchers are developing a complete artificial eye that would send impulses directly to the brain.

2 Artificial eye and brain implant. At the beginning of this module, we told you about Katie, who was completely blind because both her eyes were damaged. In Katie's case, 36 tiny wires or electrodes were implanted directly into her visual cortex. When these electrodes were stimulated, Katie saw 36 dots of light, which is far less than needed for something as simple as avoiding objects while walking.

In another attempt to restore some vision (figure below) a blind patient was fitted with a miniature camera that sent electrical signals to 100 electrodes that were implanted directly into the visual cortex, located in the occipital lobe. When activated, the electrodes stimulated neurons in the visual cortex and produced 100 tiny spots of light. This patient could see the letter S when 26 of 100 electrodes were stimulated (LaFee, 2000). Although the 100 electrodes in this patient's visual cortex provided more visual information than did Katie's 36, neither patient was able to see the outlines of objects or walk around with-out using canes.

However, recently, researchers made a significant step forward in developing an artificial visual system.

Camera sent electrical signals directly to brain.

3 Functional vision. The major goal in developing an artificial visual system is to provide enough visual information so that a blind person can function, such as reading letters and distinguishing between and avoiding objects while walking around a room. Researchers are getting closer to reaching this goal (Ritter, 2000).

Recently, Jerry, a 62-year-old man who has been blind since the age of 36, volunteered for having electrodes implanted into his brain's visual cortex (right photo). Jerry also wears a pair of glasses that, on one side, hold a tiny camera and, on the other side, an ultrasonic range finder. The range finder analyzes echoes from high-frequency sounds (beyond our range of hearing) that provide information on location, size, and distance of objects. The tiny camera provides visual information that is like looking through a tunnel opening about 2 inches wide and 8 inches high. Both devices send electrical signals to a small computer that Jerry wears on his hip. In turn, the computer analyzes and relays electrical information to a panel of electrodes that were implanted into and stimulate the visual area in Jerry's occipital lobe (white cords going into skull).

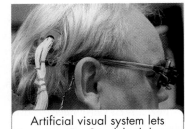

Artificial visual system lets Jerry "see" a 2-inch-high letter.

Using this device, Jerry can recognize a 2-inch letter from 5 feet away and avoid large objects as he moves around a room. This is one of the first examples of using a camera and brain implant to provide useful vision (Dobelle, 2000). Although Jerry's artificial visual system is still relatively primitive, it is a good beginning to providing a blind person with useful and functional visual information (LaFee, 2000).

Researchers are also working on developing an artificial cochlea for the inner ear.

What causes deafness?

There are two major kinds of deafness that have different effects, causes, and treatments. The most severe kind of deafness is caused by damage to the inner ear and is called neural deafness. A less severe kind of deafness is caused by problems in the middle ear and is called conduction deafness.

Conduction Deafness

About 28 million Americans, 10% of the population, have a hearing loss called conduction deafness (Rutherford, 2001).

Conduction deafness can be caused by wax in the auditory canal, injury to the tympanic membrane, or malfunction of the ossicles. All of these conditions interfere with the transmission of vibrations from the tympanic membrane to the fluid of the cochlea, resulting in degrees of hearing loss.

Conduction deafness, occurring in 40% of adults over 70, can often be treated with a hearing aid, which replaces the function of the middle ear. Hearing aids pick up sound waves, change them to vibrations, and send them through the skull to the inner ear.

Neural Deafness

Hellen Keller, who was born deaf and blind, said, "To be deaf is a greater affliction than to be blind." Hellen Keller had neural deafness, which, unlike conduction deafness, is not helped by hearing aids.

Neural deafness can be caused by damage to the auditory receptors (hair cells), which prevents the production of impulses, or by damage to the auditory nerve, which prevents nerve impulses from reaching the brain. Since neither hair cells nor auditory nerve fibers regenerate, neural deafness was generally untreatable until the development of the cochlear implant.

Currently, the only approved treatment for certain kinds of neural deafness is the cochlear implant described below.

Cochlear Implants

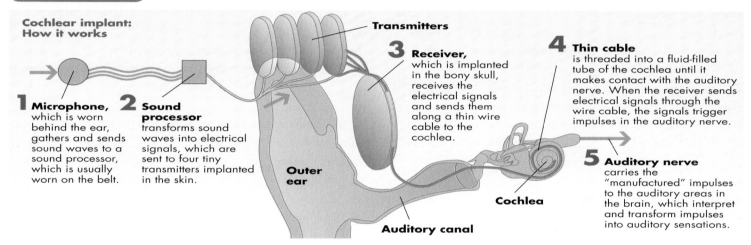

Cochlear implant: How it works

1 Microphone, which is worn behind the ear, gathers and sends sound waves to a sound processor, which is usually worn on the belt.

2 Sound processor transforms sound waves into electrical signals, which are sent to four tiny transmitters implanted in the skin.

Outer ear

Transmitters

3 Receiver, which is implanted in the bony skull, receives the electrical signals and sends them along a thin wire cable to the cochlea.

4 Thin cable is threaded into a fluid-filled tube of the cochlea until it makes contact with the auditory nerve. When the receiver sends electrical signals through the wire cable, the signals trigger impulses in the auditory nerve.

5 Auditory nerve carries the "manufactured" impulses to the auditory areas in the brain, which interpret and transform impulses into auditory sensations.

Cochlea

Auditory canal

Can deaf people hear?

If the auditory nerve is intact, a cochlear implant (figure above) can be used to treat neural deafness that is caused by damaged hair cells, which affects about 90% of those with hearing impairment (Rauschecker & Shannon, 2002).

The *cochlear implant* is a miniature electronic device that is surgically implanted into the cochlea. The cochlear implant changes sound waves into electrical signals that are fed into the auditory nerve, which carries them to the brain for processing.

As you proceed step by step through the figure above, notice that the cochlear implant first changes sound waves into electrical signals (1, 2, and 3) and then sends the electrical signals into the auditory nerve (4), which sends impulses to the brain (5).

Worldwide, about 40,000 adults and children with severe neural deafness have received cochlear implants, and the demand for them grows about 25% a year (Manning, 2000a). The child in the photo at right, deaf from birth, is reacting to hearing his first sounds after receiving a cochlear implant.

Using the newest cochlear implants (costs up to $40,000), adults who had learned to speak before they became deaf were able to understand about 80% of sentences

This child, deaf from birth, reacts after hearing with cochlear implant.

without any facial cues and from 90 to 100% of sentences when watching the speaker's face and lips (speech reading). Many could converse on the telephone (Svirsky et al., 2000; Stone, 2002).

The results are more complicated for children who did not learn to speak before becoming deaf. Researchers reported that when cochlear implants were put in before age $3\frac{1}{2}$, deaf children had the best neurological development, while implants after age 7 resulted in the poorest auditory development (Dorman, 2003). That's because brains of younger children are more flexible or plastic, which means younger brains are better able to develop neurological responses to auditory information and learn to hear and speak (Rauschecker & Shannon, 2002). For example, Julia received an implant when she was $2\frac{1}{2}$, and at age 9 she speaks and reads above her level (Reisler, 2002). However, very young children need intensive speech rehabilitation after cochlear implants (Sharp, 2000). Thus, cochlear implants have proven effective in many adults, adolescents, and children who experienced profound deafness (Dorman, 2003).

As we end this module, notice that we primarily discussed how senses transform energy into electrical impulses. Next, in Module 6, we'll focus on how "meaningless" sensations turn into meaningful perceptions.

A. EYE: VISION

1. Waves in about the middle of the electromagnetic spectrum are visible because they can be absorbed by the human eye. These waves make up the _____ and can be absorbed by receptors at the back of the eye.

2. Upon entering the eye, light waves pass first through a curved, thin, transparent structure called the (a)_____, whose function is to bend or focus light waves into a narrower beam. Next, light waves pass through an opening in the eye called the (b)_____. Around this opening is a circular, pigmented muscle called the (c)_____; its function is to dilate or constrict, thus increasing or decreasing the amount of entering light. Finally, light waves pass through a transparent, oval structure called the (d)_____, whose function is to further focus light waves precisely on the photosensitive back surface of the eye, which is called the (e)_____.

3. The retina has several layers of cells, but only the very back layer contains photoreceptors. The photoreceptors that are used to see in dim light and transmit only black, white, and shades of gray are called (a)_____. Photoreceptors that are used to see in bright light and transmit colors are called (b)_____.

4. When rods absorb light waves, a chemical called (a)_____ breaks down and in turn generates tiny electrical forces that trigger (b)_____ in neighboring cells. Similarly, when cones absorb light waves, chemicals called (c)_____ break down and generate tiny electrical forces.

5. Nerve impulses generated in the eye travel along fibers that combine to form the (a)_____ nerve. This nerve carries nerve impulses to an area in the back of each occipital lobe called the (b)_____, which transforms impulses into simple visual (c)_____, such as lines, shadows, colors, and textures. If the primary visual cortex were totally damaged, the person would be essentially blind. Simple, meaningless sensations are transformed into complete, meaningful images when nerve impulses reach an area of the brain known as (d)_____.

6. We see color because our eyes absorb light waves of different (a)_____, which are transformed by the visual system into our experience of seeing colors. One theory of color applies to how the cones function; this is the (b)_____ theory. A second theory of color applies to how the ganglion and thalamic cells function; this is called the (c)_____ theory of color.

B. EAR: AUDITION

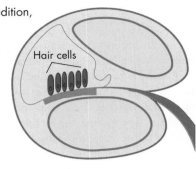

Hair cells

7. The stimuli for hearing, or audition, are sound waves, which have several physical characteristics. The physical characteristic of amplitude or height of sound waves is transformed into the subjective experience of (a)_____, which is measured in units called (b)_____. The frequency of sound waves (cycles per second) is transformed into the subjective experience of (c)_____, which for humans ranges from about 20 to 20,000 cycles per second.

8. The outer ear is composed of a funnel-like shape, called the external ear, whose function is to gather (a)_____. These waves travel down a short tunnel called the (b)_____ and strike a thin, taut membrane called the (c)_____, whose function is to transform sound waves into (d)_____.

9. The middle ear has three tiny bones (hammer, anvil, and stirrup), which together are called (a)_____. Vibrations in the tympanic membrane produce mechanical movements in the ossicles, the third of which is attached to another thin membrane, called the (b)_____, which is made to vibrate.

10. Of several structures in the inner ear, one is a coiled, fluid-filled, tubelike apparatus called the (a)_____, which contains the auditory receptors, called (b)_____. Movement of the fluid in the tube causes movement of the basilar membrane, which in turn causes bending of the hair cells, generating a tiny (c)_____. If this is large enough, it will trigger nerve impulses, which leave the cochlea via the (d)_____ and travel to the brain.

11. Nerve impulses are transformed into rather simple, meaningless auditory sensations when they reach the (a)_____, which is located in the temporal lobe. These sensations are transformed into meaningful and complete melodies, songs, words, or sentences by the auditory (b)_____.

12. To tell the direction of a sound, the brain analyzes the differences in time and intensity between (a)_____ arriving at the left and right ears. The brain determines degrees of loudness by using the (b)_____ of the arriving impulses. The discrimination of different tones or pitches is explained by the (c)_____ and _____ theories.

C. VESTIBULAR SYSTEM: BALANCE

13. Besides the cochlea, the inner ear contains three arch-shaped, fluid-filled structures called _____. The movement of fluid in these organs provides signals that the brain interprets in terms of the movement and position of the head and body. The vestibular system is also involved in motion sickness, Meniere's disease, and vertigo.

D. CHEMICAL SENSES

14. Sensors on the tongue respond to five basic tastes: (a)_____, _____, _____, _____, and _____. The receptors for taste, which are called (b)_____, trigger nerve impulses that travel to the brain, which then transforms them into the sensations of taste.

15. Volatile airborne substances are drawn into the upper part of the nose, where they dissolve in a thin film of mucus. Underneath the mucus are layers of receptors for olfaction (smell), which are called (a)_____. These receptors trigger impulses that travel to an area underneath the brain called the (b)_____. This area transforms impulses into hundreds of different odors.

E. TOUCH

16. The sense of touch actually provides information on three different kinds of stimuli: (a)_____, _____, and _____. The various layers of skin contain different kinds of touch receptors that have different speeds of adaptation. Receptors for the sense of touch trigger nerve impulses that travel to an area in the brain's parietal lobe, called the (b)_____. This area transforms impulses into sensations of pressure, temperature, and pain. The more sensitive the area of the body is to touch, the larger is its area on the cortex.

Hair follicle

F. CULTURAL DIVERSITY: DISGUST

17. A universal facial expression that indicates rejection of food is called (a)_____. Besides our innate preferences for sweet and salty foods and avoidance of bitter substances, most of our tastes are (b)_____ and particular to our culture. The fact that foods considered fine in one culture may seem disgusting to people in another culture indicates how much psychological factors influence taste.

G. RESEARCH FOCUS: MIND OVER BODY?

18. In order to control for the placebo effect, researchers use an experimental design in which neither the researchers nor subjects know who is receiving what treatment. This is the _____ design, which controls for the expectations of both researchers and subjects.

H. PAIN

19. After an injury, you feel two different kinds of pain sensations: at first, there is sharp, localized pain, which is followed by a duller, more generalized pain. The receptors for pain are (a)_____, which send impulses to two areas of the brain, specifically the (b)_____ and _____. If you rub an injured area or become totally absorbed in another activity, you may experience a reduction of pain, which is explained by the (c)_____. Immediately following a serious injury or great physical stress, the brain produces pain-reducing chemicals called (d)_____.

I. APPLICATION: ARTIFICIAL SENSES

20. There are two basic causes of deafness. If the cause is wax in the auditory canal, injury to the tympanic membrane, or malfunction of the ossicles, it is called (a)_____ deafness. If the cause is damage to hair cells in the cochlea or to the auditory nerve, it is called (b)_____ deafness. One treatment for neural deafness is to use a (c)_____, which is more effective if individuals have learned to speak before becoming deaf.

Answers: 1. visible spectrum; 2. (a) cornea, (b) pupil, (c) iris, (d) lens, (e) retina; 3. (a) rods, (b) cones; 4. (a) rhodopsin, (b) impulses, (c) opsins; 5. (a) optic, (b) primary visual cortex, (c) sensations, (d) association areas; 6. (a) lengths, (b) trichromatic, (c) opponent-process; 7. (a) loudness, (b) decibels, (c) pitch; 8. (a) sound waves, (b) auditory canal, (c) eardrum or tympanic membrane, (d) vibrations; 9. (a) ossicles, (b) oval window; 10. (a) cochlea, (b) hair cells, (c) electrical force, (d) auditory nerve; 11. (a) primary auditory cortex, (b) association areas; 12. (a) sound waves, (b) rate, (c) frequency, place; 13. vestibular organs; 14. (a) bitter, sour, salty, sweet, umami, (b) taste buds; 15. (a) olfactory cells, (b) primary olfactory cortex; 16. (a) pressure, temperature, pain, (b) somatosensory cortex; 17. (a) disgust, (b) learned; 18. double-blind; 19. (a) free nerve endings, (b) somatosensory area, limbic system, (c) gate control theory, (d) endorphins; 20. (a) conduction, (b) neural, (c) cochlear implant

Critical Thinking

Can Music Raise a Child's IQ?

Questions

1. The sales clerk supports the Mozart effect by saying that a lot of women are buying the Mozart CD. The sales clerk's statement illustrates what kind of supporting evidence? How good is this kind of evidence?

2. What did the original study say about playing Mozart to children or boosting general intelligence?

3. In what ways did the press and the public change and distort the researchers' original findings?

The young woman, who was 8 months pregnant, asked the sales clerk for the Mozart CD that was supposed to increase a baby's intelligence. The sales clerk said that the Mozart CD was a big seller and that a lot of women were playing Mozart to their unborn children to take full advantage of the Mozart effect.

The "Mozart effect," as it came to be called, began in 1993 with a short study from researchers at the University of Wisconsin–Oshkosh. The researchers played 10 minutes' worth of Mozart's Sonata for Two Pianos in D Major to college students. Then the students took a test that required them to visualize how objects changed over time, such as how a piece of paper that was folded and cut would look when it was unfolded. Subjects who had listened to Mozart showed a slight but temporary rise in scores on this test compared to subjects who sat through 10 minutes of silence. However, the researchers reported that the Mozart effect was not long lasting and had little effect on overall intelligence.

Within no time, the Mozart effect was making headlines around the country: "Mozart Can Boost Intelligence." Advertising for the Mozart CD claimed that listening to Mozart would stimulate young minds, improve intelligence, and raise IQs. Many parents believed the advertising and bought thousands of

"Baby Mozart" video-tapes and CDs. One mother said, "I am six months into my pregnancy and almost immediately upon playing the Mozart CD my baby started actively moving. I can really tell he enjoys it even though I can't see him yet." One governor even wanted to pass a law that would give a free Mozart CD to all pregnant women in his state so that their children would have a boost in intelligence.

However, when researchers looked closely at the Mozart effect they reported a different story. A Harvard neuropsychologist analyzed a dozen studies and reported that listening to classical music had no lasting effect on intelligence. Other researchers at Appalachian State University tried repeating the original Mozart study but were unable to find a "Mozart effect" and concluded that listening to classical music did not affect intelligence scores.

However, one nursery had positive proof of one effect. They had been playing classical music to their young children for the past 30 years. Without a doubt, listening to classical music helps kids relax and take their naps. (Adapted from J. Weiss, So-called Mozart effect may be (yawn) just a dream, *San Diego Union-Tribune*, February, 12, 2000, p. E-5; S. M. Jones & Zigler, 2002)

4. In what ways did the new research differ from the original findings?

5. Is it possible that listening to melodic music, such as Mozart, could improve performance on a test?

Use InfoTrac to search for the term: **Mozart effect.**

1. The sales clerk's statement about other mothers buying the Mozart CD is called a testimonial, which has great potential for error and bias and thus is not very reliable evidence.
2. The original study used college students, not children, did not claim that listening to Mozart boosted general intelligence, and said the effect was not long lasting.
3. Greatly distorting the original findings, the press and general public said that the Mozart effect applied to children, that it boosted IQ scores, and that it would help unborn children.
4. A neuropsychologist reviewed all the previous studies and found

that listening to classical music had no effect on intelligence. Recent attempts by researchers to repeat or replicate the original study's Mozart effect were not successful; that is, listening to classical music had no effect on test scores.

5. Just as listening to melodic classical music, such as Mozart, relaxed and helped children nap, it may have the same relaxing or calming effect on college students. Thus, feeling more relaxed or less anxious and stressed may improve performance on tests since we know that stress and anxiety may interfere with and decrease test performance.

Links to Learning

LEARNING ACTIVITIES

- **POWERSTUDY CD-ROM 2.0**
  by Tom Doyle and Rod Plotnik
  Check out the "Sensation" Module (disk 1) on PowerStudy and:
  - Test your knowledge using an interactive version of the Summary Test on pages 116 and 117. Also access related quizzes—true/false, multiple choice, and matching.
  - Explore an interactive version of the Critical Thinking exercise "Can Music Raise a Child's IQ?" on page 118.
  - You will also find key terms, a chapter outline including a chapter abstract, and a list of hotlinked Web sites that correlate to this module.

- **SELF-STUDY ASSESSMENT**
  Want help studying? For your customized Study Plan go to **http://psychology.wadsworth.com/plotnik7e/**. This program will automatically generate pretests and posttests to help you determine what concepts you have mastered and what concepts you still need work on.

- **STUDY GUIDE and WEBTUTOR**
  Check the corresponding module in your Study Guide for effective student tips and help learning the material presented.

- **INFOTRAC COLLEGE EDITION ONLINE LIBRARY**
  To find interesting and relevant articles go to **http://www.infotrac-college.com**, use your password, and then type in search terms such as the ones listed below.

Human vision	Vestibular system
Ear and hearing	Cochlear implants

STUDY QUESTIONS

Use InfoTrac to search for topics mentioned in the main heads below (e.g., chemical senses, disgust, pain).

*A. Eye: Vision—What kinds of problems in the visual system could result in some form of blindness? (**Suggested answer page 621**)

*B. Ear: Audition—What kinds of problems in the auditory system could result in some form of deafness? (**Suggested answer page 622**)

C. Vestibular System: Balance—How do placebos help about 40–60% of people who suffer from motion sickness?

*D. Chemical Senses—How might a master chef's chemical senses differ from yours? (**Suggested answer page 622**)

E. Touch—What would happen if touch receptors did not show adaptation?

F. Cultural Diversity: Disgust—Why do people often show disgust when offered a new but edible food?

G. Research Focus: Mind over Body?—Why are some drugs initially reported to be effective but later proven to be worthless?

H. Pain—Why can some individuals stand more pain than others?

I. Application: Artificial Senses—Why is it so difficult to build an artificial eye or ear that duplicates the real one?

*These questions are answered in Appendix B.

Module 6: Perception

Silent Messages

How can I be more confident?

Although it seemed like an ordinary week, Maria and her 7-year-old daughter, Gabrielle, would be involved in three relatively normal events that could change their lives forever.

On Tuesday, Maria's new boss unfairly criticized her work and made her feel insecure and unsure of herself. During her lunch hour, she browsed through a bookstore to find something on building confidence. She was intrigued by an audiotape titled "Improve Self-Esteem." The instructions read, "The listener hears only relaxing music, but the unconscious hears and automatically processes subliminal messages that boost self-esteem. In a few short weeks, the listener is guaranteed to have more confidence and self-esteem. If you're not completely satisfied, return the tape for a full refund." Maria had heard about tapes with subliminal persuasion from a friend who claimed that she used a weight-reduction tape that helped her lose 20 pounds. When Maria asked about the effectiveness of subliminal tapes, the salesperson said that he had a friend who increased his motivation to study by listening to one of these tapes. Maria smiled and said, "Well, it's guaranteed, so what have I got to lose?" She bought the tape, put it in her purse, and as she walked out the door, she was already feeling a little more confident.

Can subliminal tapes change a person's behaviors?

Nice Dog, Mean Dog

What's a mean dog?

On Saturday afternoon, Maria took her daughter, Gabrielle, to play at the local park, which had slides, swings, ropes, and even a small trampoline. As Gabrielle was walking toward the trampoline, she saw a beautiful brown dog sitting by its owner. Gabrielle loved animals, and she ran toward the dog. The dog's owner was deep in conversation and did not notice the cute little girl running toward the beautiful Doberman. As Gabrielle came closer, she thrust out her hands to pet the dog's smooth black nose. The movement of Gabrielle's hands startled the dog, who reflexively snarled and then snapped at the hands coming at its nose. Gabrielle felt the pain as the dog's teeth nipped two of her fingers, which immediately started to bleed. The owner turned to see what had happened and quickly pulled the dog away as Maria came running. Maria took Gabrielle in her arms, soothed her, and then examined the small cuts on her fingers. Gabrielle looked at her bleeding fingers and then at the big, ugly, brown dog that had bit her and said in a tearful voice, "I hate that dog. Bad dog." Seeing her daughter's reaction, Maria began to have doubts about her plans to surprise Gabrielle with a cute little puppy for her birthday.

How does a bad experience create a bad perception?

White Spot

Can the doctor be sure?

On Friday, Maria had to take time from work for her annual physical exam, which included a mammogram. In the past, the doctor had simply said that the results of her mammogram were negative. This time, the doctor brought in her mammogram, which looked like an X ray. He pointed to a small white spot and said in a concerned voice, "I'm afraid that this tiny white dot may be a cancerous tumor." The doctor's words took her breath away. Finally, Maria asked in a terrified whisper, "Are you absolutely sure that spot is cancer?" The doctor paused for a minute, looked again at the mammogram, and said, "I can't be absolutely sure the spot is cancerous until we do a biopsy. All I can say is that there is a good possibility that it is." As Maria scheduled her biopsy, she would never forget seeing that white spot on the mammogram.

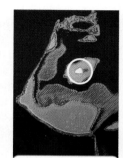

Why should two doctors read each mammogram?

Perceiving Things

What are the three questions?

At first glance, these three events—buying a subliminal tape, being bitten by a dog, and seeing a spot on a mammogram—seem to have nothing in common. In fact, these events raise three basic questions about how we perceive things.

Maria's subliminal tape raises the first question: Are there things that we perceive but are not aware of, and can these things influence our behaviors (Abrams & Greenwald, 2000)?

Maria's mammogram raises the second question: How large or unusual must things be before our senses can detect them? This is a very important question since the answer may have serious health consequences (Swets et al., 2000).

Finally, Gabrielle's painful experience with a dog raises the third question: How much are the things we perceive influenced or biased by our cultural, learning, emotional, and personal experiences (NAMHC, 1996)? These three questions are the key to understanding how we perceive our world.

What's Coming

We'll discuss what perceptual thresholds are, how sensations differ from perceptions, how sensations are combined to form perceptions, how objects can undergo great changes yet appear the same to us, how our senses are fooled by illusions, how cultural experiences change perceptions, whether there is good evidence for ESP (extrasensory perception), and whether the newest kind of perceiving, called virtual reality, can fool our senses into believing we're in a three-dimensional world.

Let's start with the first and most basic perceptual question: At what point do you become aware of seeing, hearing, smelling, tasting, or feeling some stimulus, object, or event?

A. Perceptual Thresholds

When do you know something is happening?

Imagine suddenly becoming deaf or blind, unable to hear what people are saying or to see where you are going. Only then would you realize that your senses provide a continuous stream of information about your world. Your senses tell you that something is out there, and your perceptions tell you what that something is. However, there are some sounds and objects you may not be aware of because the level of stimulation is too low and does not exceed the threshold of a particular sense.

Threshold refers to a point above which a stimulus is perceived and below which it is not perceived. The threshold determines when we first become aware of a stimulus.

Subliminal means that a person has less than a 50% chance of detecting the message.

For example, Maria is not aware of, or does not hear, subliminal messages recorded on tape because these messages are below her absolute threshold for hearing. To understand how the absolute threshold is determined, imagine that Maria is presented with a series of auditory messages that slowly increase in intensity. Maria is asked to press a button when she first hears a message. You may think that there will be a certain level or absolute value of intensity (loudness) at which Maria will first report hearing a tone. The idea that there is an absolute threshold was proposed by Gustav Fechner (1860), an important historical figure in perceptual research. However, as you'll see, Fechner had difficulty identifying the absolute threshold as he defined it.

1 At first, *Gustav Fechner* (*FECK-ner*) defined the absolute threshold as the smallest amount of stimulus energy (such as sound or light) that can be observed or experienced.

According to Fechner's definition, if Maria's hearing could always be measured under exactly the same conditions, her absolute threshold would always remain the same. Although Fechner tried various methods to identify absolute thresholds, he found that an individual's threshold was not absolute and, in fact, differed depending on the subject's alertness and the test situation. Because of this variability in measurement, researchers had to redefine absolute threshold.

2 The graph below shows how the absolute threshold was redefined.

Absolute threshold is the intensity level of a stimulus such that a person will have a 50% chance of detecting it.

According to this updated definition, Maria's absolute threshold is the point on the graph where she has a 50% chance of hearing the message.

Once we have determined Maria's absolute threshold for hearing messages, we can define a subliminal stimulus.

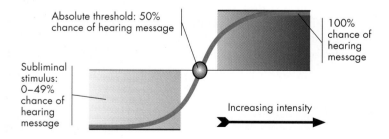

Absolute threshold: 50% chance of hearing message

Subliminal stimulus: 0–49% chance of hearing message

100% chance of hearing message

Increasing intensity

3 The graph above shows that a subliminal stimulus can occur at any point below the absolute threshold (50% chance of hearing).

A *subliminal stimulus* has an intensity that gives a person less than a 50% chance of detecting the stimulus.

Because subliminal messages can occur in a wide range (0–49%), Maria may or may not report hearing them on the tape. For example, Maria would never report hearing messages of very low intensity (0% level) but may sometimes report hearing messages of higher intensity (49%).

We'll discuss whether subliminal messages can change behaviors or attitudes, such as increasing self-esteem, in the Research Focus (p. 135).

4 Although the concept of an absolute threshold may seem abstract, it has very real consequences in detecting breast cancer.

Each year, doctors read about 25 million mammograms (X rays of breasts) to look for white spots that usually stand out on a black background; these white spots indicate tumors (photo right). However, about 40% of women have so much connective breast tissue, which also appears white, that tiny white tumors may go undetected. This problem, combined with doctors' lack of expertise, results in missing 15–30% of tumors on mammograms (Moss, 2002a). After lung cancer, breast cancer is the second most frequently occurring cancer in American women, with approximately 200,000 new cases each year.

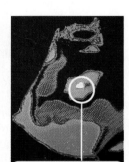

Possible cancerous breast tumor stands out as a white spot.

Accuracy problems. The biggest problem is the lack of expertise among radiologists who read the mammograms. Critics say that standards for reading mammograms are not enforced and this leads to errors (Moss, 2002b). For example, researchers found that if a mammogram is read independently by two doctors, the accuracy of identifying cancerous tumors was improved by 20% (Healy, 2000). Thus, mammogram testing for breast cancer is a practical example of finding ways to lower the threshold for detecting cancerous tumors and thus save patients' lives.

Besides being involved in subliminal messages and mammogram tests, the problem of determining thresholds also applies to the question of how we know a stimulus has decreased or increased in intensity. We'll discuss this next.

Why is that music still too loud?

Suppose people are playing music too loud and you ask them to turn down the volume. Even after they turn it down, it may still seem just as loud as before. The explanation for this phenomenon can be found in the work of another historical figure in perception, E. H. Weber (*VEY-ber*).

Weber worked on the problem of how we judge whether a stimulus, such as loud music, has increased or decreased in intensity. This problem involves measuring the difference in thresholds between two stimuli, such as very loud music and not-quite-so-loud music. To solve this problem, Weber (1834) developed the concept of a just noticeable difference.

A *just noticeable difference*, or *JND*, refers to the smallest increase or decrease in the intensity of a stimulus that a person is able to detect.

Smallest detectable increase or decrease in sound is a JND.

For example, to measure a just noticeable difference in weight, Weber asked people to compare stimuli of varying intensities and indicate when they could detect a difference between them. He discovered that if he presented two stimuli with very low intensities, such as a 2-ounce weight versus a 3-ounce weight, people could easily detect the difference between them. However, if he presented stimuli with high intensities, such as a 40-pound weight versus a 41-pound weight, people could no longer detect the difference. For higher-intensity stimuli, such as heavy weights, a much larger difference in intensity was required for the difference to be noticed (Hellstrom, 2000).

Weber's observations on what it takes to detect just noticeable differences were the basis for what became known as Weber's law.

Weber's law states that the increase in intensity of a stimulus needed to produce a just noticeable difference grows in proportion to the intensity of the initial stimulus.

We'll use Weber's law (please read right figure) to explain how if someone is playing the stereo very loud, it must be turned down a great deal, usually more than the person prefers to turn it down, for you to detect a just noticeable decrease in volume.

Weber's Law Explained

Weber's law explains that, at lower intensities, small changes between two stimuli can be detected as just noticeable differences (JNDs); however, at higher intensities, only larger changes between two stimuli can be detected as JNDs.

Stimulus: Lighter ⟶ Heavier

1 JND. The same height of each step illustrates your ability to detect "one sensory unit" of a *just noticeable difference* between the loudness of two sounds.

3 Higher intensities. The considerable width of this step indicates that, at higher sound intensities, you need a *larger difference* to detect a just noticeable difference between the loudness of two sounds. This statement follows from Weber's law, which says that a larger difference in intensity is required for you to detect a just noticeable difference when judging stimuli of higher intensity.

Besides explaining the problem with loud stereos, Weber's law has many practical applications, such as how to detect a difference in the softness of towels.

2 Lower intensities. The small width of this step indicates that, at lower intensities, you need only a *small difference* in order to detect a just noticeable difference between the loudness of two sounds. This statement follows from Weber's law, which says that only a small difference in intensity is required for you to detect a just noticeable difference when judging stimuli of lower intensity.

Which towel is softer?

Every year, industry and business spend billions of dollars to make sure that consumers can detect just noticeable differences between this year's and last year's cars, shampoos, cereals, and fashions. For example, consumers spend millions of dollars each year on fabric softeners, which are added during washing and are claimed to make clothes feel softer. To test such claims, researchers asked subjects to feel towels washed with and without a fabric softener and rate the softness of the towels on a scale from 1 (hard) to 30 (very soft). Subjects gave an average softness rating of 5 to towels washed repeatedly

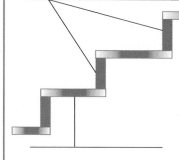

Judging the softness of towels involves noting JND.

without softener and an average rating of 18 to towels washed with softener. Researchers concluded that fabric softeners worked, since subjects could easily detect a just noticeable difference in softness (Ali & Begum, 1994). This is but one practical application of Weber's law and just noticeable difference (JND) in industry.

So far, we've focused on how you become aware of and detect stimuli and distinguish between their intensities. Next, we'll discuss one of the most interesting questions in perception: How do you change meaningless bits of sensations into meaningful and complete perceptions?

B. Sensation Versus Perception

How can I be successful and happy?

Much of your success in being happy and successful depends on your ability to respond intelligently and adapt appropriately to changes in your environment (NAMHC, 1996). The first step in responding and adapting involves gathering millions of meaningless sensations and changing them into useful perceptions. Because your brain changes sensations into perceptions so quickly, automatically, and with very little awareness, you might assume that what you see (sense) is what you perceive. However, the process of changing sensations into perceptions is influenced by whether you are alert, sleepy, worried, emotional, motivated, or affected by the use of a legal or illegal drug. For example, drinking alcohol causes perceptions in social situations to be less rational and more uninhibited, causing people under its influence to act aggressively, make terrible decisions, create problems, or say really dumb things (Carey & Correia, 1997; Ito et al., 1996; Stritzke et al., 1996). As you are about to discover, sensing and perceiving are as different as night and day.

For example, quickly glance at the black-and-white figure below on the left and then look away and describe what you saw.

Sensations

Initially, the left figure appears to be a bunch of meaningless lines, spaces, and blobs, which, for the sake of simplicity, we'll take the liberty of calling visual sensations. In real life, we rarely if ever experience sensations because, as we'll explain on the next page, they are immediately turned into perceptions.

A *sensation* is our first awareness of some outside stimulus. An outside stimulus activates sensory receptors, which in turn produce electrical signals that are transformed by the brain into meaningless bits of information.

Sensations are MEANINGLESS bits of information.

You can approximate how visual sensations may look by placing half of a ping-pong ball over your eye. As you look through this nearly opaque ping-pong ball, you'll see shadows, textures, and dark shapes but nothing meaningful; these are similar to sensations.

Another example that illustrates the difference between sensations and perceptions is the photo below. Your first impression consists of meaningless shapes, textures, and blotches of color, which we'll again take the liberty of calling visual sensations. However, you can turn these meaningless sensations into a meaningful image—a perception—by using the following clues. This photo is an ultrasound image of a fetus in the womb. The fetus is lying on his back with his rounded tummy on the left and his large head on the right. Above his head is the right arm and hand, and you can even count the five tiny fingers. You can also see that the fetus is sucking on his thumb. Once you know what to look for, you automatically change the random blotches of colors and shapes into the perception of a fetus.

Obviously, it would be impossible to respond, adapt, and survive if you had to rely only on sensations. You can now appreciate the importance of changing sensations into perceptions.

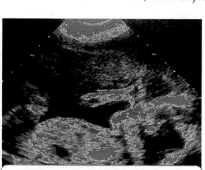

You can turn this sensation into a perception by reading the text (left).

Perceptions

As you look at the right stimulus, your brain is processing many thousands of visual sensations involving lines, curves, textures, shadows, and colors. Then, instantaneously, automatically, and without awareness, your brain combines these thousands of sensations into a perception—an orange tiger's face against a green background.

A *perception* is the experience we have after our brain assembles and combines thousands of individual, meaningless sensations into a meaningful pattern or image. However, our perceptions are rarely exact replicas of the original stimuli. Rather, our perceptions are usually changed, biased, colored, or distorted by our unique set of experiences. Thus, perceptions are our personal interpretations of the real world.

If you now look at the black-and-white drawing on the upper left, your brain will automatically combine the formerly meaningless shapes and blobs into a tiger's face. This is an approximate example of how meaningless sensations are automatically combined to form meaningful perceptions.

One important feature of perceptions is that they are rarely exact copies of the real world. To study how experience can bias our perceptions, researchers asked 20 college students who liked rock music and 20 who disliked it to listen to a 10-second sample of rock music. Then, the subjects in each group were asked to adjust the volume of the rock-music sample to match different levels of intensity, ranging from very soft to extremely loud. Researchers reported that subjects who liked rock music consistently set the volume louder than the reference level, while subjects who disliked rock music consistently set the volume lower (Fucci et al., 1993). This study shows how our experiences can bias our perceptions, usually without our awareness.

To show that no two individuals perceive the world in exactly the same way, we'll explain how your personal experiences change, bias, and even distort your perceptions.

Changing Sensations into Perceptions

How does a "nice" doggie become a "bad" doggie?

It is most unlikely that you have ever experienced a "pure" sensation because your brain automatically and instantaneously changes sensations into perceptions. Despite what you may think, perceptions do not exactly mirror events, people, situations, and objects in your environment. Rather, perceptions are interpretations, which means that your perceptions are changed or biased by your personal experiences, memories, emotions, and motivations. For

There are five steps in forming perceptions.

example, at the beginning of this module we told you how 7-year-old Gabrielle's perception of a dog was changed from "nice" to "bad" by her personal experience of being bitten. The next time Gabrielle sees a dog, she won't see just a four-legged creature with ears, nose, and tail; she will see a "bad" four-legged creature. To understand how sensations become perceptions, we have divided the perceptual process into a series of discrete steps that, in real life, are much more complex and interactive.

1 Stimulus. Since normally we experience only perceptions, we are not aware of many preceding steps. The first step begins with some stimulus, which is any change of energy in the environment, such as light waves, sound waves, mechanical pressure, or chemicals. The stimulus activates sense receptors in the eyes, ears, skin, nose, or mouth. In Gabrielle's case, the stimuli are light waves reflecting off the body of a large, brown dog.

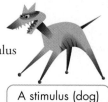

A stimulus (dog) activates receptors in the senses.

2 Transduction. After entering Gabrielle's eyes, light waves are focused on the retina, which contains photoreceptors that are sensitive to light. The light waves are absorbed by photoreceptors, which change physical energy into electrical signals, called transduction. The electrical signals are changed into impulses that travel to the brain. Sense organs do not produce sensations but simply transform energy into electrical signals.

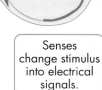

Senses change stimulus into electrical signals.

3 Brain: primary areas. Impulses from sense organs first go to different primary areas of the brain. For example, impulses from the ear go to the temporal lobe, from touch to the parietal lobe, and from the eye to areas in the occipital lobe. When impulses reach primary areas in the occipital lobe, they are first changed into sensations. However, Gabrielle would not report seeing sensations.

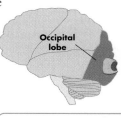

Occipital lobe

Primary areas of brain change electrical signals into sensations.

4 Brain: association areas. Each sense sends its particular impulses to a different primary area of the brain where impulses are changed into sensations, which are meaningless bits of information, such as shapes, colors, and textures (top right). The "sensation" impulses are then sent to the appropriate association area in the brain. The association areas change meaningless bits into meaningful images, called perceptions, such as a dog (bottom right).

In Gabrielle's case, impulses from her eyes would be changed into visual sensations by the primary visual area and into perceptions by the visual association areas. However, Gabrielle's perception of a dog would be changed, biased, and even distorted by many psychological, emotional, and cultural factors.

Sensations are meaningless bits of information.

Association areas change sensations into perceptions—dog.

5 Personalized perceptions. Each of us has a unique set of personal experiences, emotions, and memories that are automatically added to our perceptions by other areas of the brain. As a result, our perceptions are not a mirror but a changed, biased, or even distorted copy of the real world (E. B. Goldstein, 2002). For example, the visual areas of Gabrielle's brain automatically assemble many thousands of sensations into a meaningful pattern, which in this case is a dog. Now, however, Gabrielle doesn't see just an ordinary brown dog because other brain areas add her emotional experience of being bitten. Thus, Gabrielle perceives this brown, four-legged creature to be a "bad dog." For this same reason, two people can look at the same dog and have very different perceptions, such as cute dog, great dog, bad dog, smelly dog, or friendly dog. Thus, your perceptions are personalized interpretations rather than true copies of objects, animals, people, and situations in the real world.

The process of assembling and organizing sensations into perceptions was of great interest to early psychologists, who disagreed on how perceptions were formed. As you'll see next, their debate resulted in a very interesting perceptual controversy.

Perceptions do not mirror reality but rather include our biases, emotions, and memories to reflect reality.

C. Rules of Organization

Structuralists Versus Gestalt Psychologists

What was the great debate?

In the early 1900s, two groups of psychologists engaged in a heated debate over how perceptions are formed. One group, called the structuralists, strongly believed that we added together thousands of sensations to form a perception. Another group, called the Gestalt psychologists, just as strongly believed that sensations were not added but rather combined according to a set of innate rules to form a perception (D. J. Murray et al., 2000). One group won the debate and you might guess which one before you read further.

Structuralists

As you look at the scene in the middle of this page, you perceive a fountain at the bottom with shrubs and palm trees on the sides, all topped by a large dome of glass windows. Is it possible that your brain combined many thousands of individual sensations to produce this complex perception? If you answer yes, you agree with the structuralists.

The *structuralists* believed that you add together hundreds of basic elements to form complex perceptions. They also believed that you can work backward to break down perceptions into smaller and smaller units, or elements.

Structuralists spent hundreds of hours analyzing how perceptions, such as a falling ball, might be broken down into basic units or elements. They believed that once they understood the process of breaking down perceptions, they would know how basic units are recombined to form perceptions. Thus, structuralists believed that you add together basic units to form perceptions, much as you would add a column of numbers to get a total.

For example, structuralists would say that you add together hundreds of basic units, such as colors, bricks, leaves, branches, tiles, pieces of glass, and bits of steel, to form the perception of the scene above. However, the structuralists' explanation of adding bits to form a perception was hotly denied by Gestalt psychologists.

Gestalt Psychologists

The Gestalt psychologists said that perceptions were much too complex to be formed by simply adding sensations together; instead, they believed that perceptions were formed according to a set of rules.

Gestalt psychologists believed that our brains follow a set of rules that specify how individual elements are to be organized into a meaningful pattern, or perception.

Unlike the structuralists, the Gestalt psychologists said that perceptions do not result from adding sensations. Rather, perceptions result from our brain's ability to organize sensations according to a set of rules, much as our brain follows a set of rules for organizing words into meaningful sentences (Palmer, 2002).

So how would Gestalt psychologists explain your perception of the scene on the left? They would say that your perception was not formed by simply adding bits of tile, steel, and foliage into a whole image. Rather, your brain automatically used a set of rules to combine these elements to form a unified whole. To emphasize their point, Gestalt psychologists came up with a catchy phrase, "The whole is more than the sum of its parts," to mean that perceptions are not merely combined sensations. The Gestalt psychologists went one step further; they came up with a list of organizational rules.

Do you add together basic elements to form perceptions or does your brain have rules for forming perceptions?

Evidence for Rules

Who won the debate?

Gestalt psychologists won their debate with the structuralists for two reasons. The first reason comes from our own personal perceptual experiences. For example, as you look again at the beautiful scene above, we must reveal that it is entirely fake. The scene, which looks so realistic and three-dimensional, is actually painted on a flat wall. It seems impossible that we could have such a complex, three-dimensional perceptual experience from simply combining bits and pieces of bricks, branches, leaves, and steel. This fake but truly realistic scene makes the Gestalt motto come to life: "The whole is more than the sum of its parts."

Equally convincing evidence that the whole is greater than the sum of its parts came from a remarkably detailed series of studies in which Gestalt psychologists presented stimuli to subjects and then asked them to describe what they perceived (Rock & Palmer, 1990). On the basis of subjects' reports, researchers discovered that forming perceptions involved more than simply adding and combining individual elements. Modern research has generally supported the early Gestalt conclusion that our brains actually do follow a set of rules for organizing and forming perceptions (Quinn et al., 2002). We'll explain these rules for organizing perceptions next.

How many rules are there?

It is very hard to believe that the scene on the previous page (repeated here on the right) was actually painted on a flat wall. One reason you perceive this scene as complex and 3-dimensional is that the painter followed many of the Gestalt rules of organization (Han & Humphreys, 1999).

Rules of organization, which were identified by Gestalt psychologists, specify how our brains combine and organize individual pieces or elements into a meaningful perception.

As you look at the scene, your brain automatically organizes many hundreds of visual stimuli, including colors, textures, shadows, bricks, steel, glass, leaves, and branches, according to one or more of the six perceptual rules of organization described below. We'll use a relatively simple figure to illustrate each rule.

Figure-Ground

One of the most basic rules in organizing perceptions is picking out the object from its background. As you look at the figure on the left, you will automatically see a white object standing out against a red background, which illustrates the figure-ground principle.

The *figure-ground rule* states that, in organizing stimuli, we tend to automatically distinguish between a figure and a ground: The figure, with more detail, stands out against the background, which has less detail.

There is some evidence that our ability to separate figure from ground is an innate response. For example, individuals who were blind from an early age and had their sight restored as adults were able to distinguish between figure and ground with little or no training (Senden, 1960). The figure-ground rule is one of the first rules that our brain uses to organize stimuli into a perception (Vecera, 2002). This particular image is interesting because, as you continue to stare at it, the figure and ground will suddenly reverse and you'll see profiles of two faces. However, in the real world, the images and objects we usually perceive are not reversible because they have more distinct shapes (Humphreys & Muller, 2000).

Similarity

As you look at this figure filled with light and dark blue dots, you see a dark blue numeral 2.

The *similarity rule* states that, in organizing stimuli, we group together elements that appear similar.

The similarity rule causes us to group the dark blue dots together and prevents us from seeing the figure as a random arrangement of light and dark blue dots.

Closure

Although the lines are incomplete, you can easily perceive this drawing as a cat or dog.

The *closure rule* states that, in organizing stimuli, we tend to fill in any missing parts of a figure and see the figure as complete.

For example, the closure rule explains why you can fill in letters missing on a sign or pieces missing in a jigsaw puzzle.

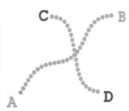

Proximity

Notice that although there are exactly eight circles in each horizontal line, you perceive each line as formed by a different number of groups of circles.

The *proximity rule* states that, in organizing stimuli, we group together objects that are physically close to one another.

You automatically group circles that are close together and thus perceive the first line as composed of three groups (Kubovy & Wagemans, 1995).

Simplicity

Look at figure A and then decide if it is made up of the pieces shown in figure B, C, or D. Almost everyone sees figure A as made up of the pieces in figure B—an oval with an overlapping square.

The *simplicity rule* states that stimuli are organized in the simplest way possible.

For example, almost no one sees figure A as having been formed from the complicated pieces shown in figure C or figure D. This rule says that we tend to perceive complex figures as divided into several simpler figures (Shimaya, 1997).

Continuity

As you scan this figure, keep track of the path that your eyes follow. If you are like most people, your eyes will move from left to right in a continuous line, following the path from A to B or from C to D.

The *continuity rule* states that, in organizing stimuli, we tend to favor smooth or continuous paths when interpreting a series of points or lines.

For example, the rule of continuity predicts that you do not see a line that begins at A and then turns abruptly to C or to D.

Conclusion. These figures demonstrate the Gestalt rules of organizing stimuli into perceptions. Young children slowly learn these perceptual rules and begin to use them as early as 7 months (Quinn et al., 2002). As adults we often use these rules to organize thousands of stimuli into perceptions, especially stimuli in print and advertisements.

Next, we turn to another interesting perceptual question: How can objects change yet appear to remain the same?

D. Perceptual Constancy

Why don't speeding cars shrink?

Perception is full of interesting puzzles, such as how cars, people, and pets can constantly change their 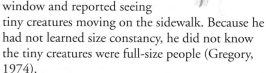 shapes as they move about yet we perceive them as remaining the same size and shape. For example, a car doesn't grow smaller as it speeds away, even though its shape on your retina grows smaller and smaller. A door doesn't become a trapezoid as you walk through it, even though that's what happens to its shape on your retina. These are examples of how perceptions remain constant, a phenomenon called perceptual constancy.

Perceptual constancy refers to our tendency to perceive sizes, shapes, brightness, and colors as remaining the same even though their physical characteristics are constantly changing.

We'll discuss four kinds of perceptual constancy—size, shape, brightness, and color.

Size Constancy

Imagine a world in which you perceived that every car, person, or animal became smaller as it moved away. Fortunately, we are spared from coping with so much stimulus change by perceptual constancy, one type of which is size constancy.

Size constancy refers to our tendency to perceive objects as remaining the same size even when their images on the retina are continually growing or shrinking.

As a car drives away, it projects a smaller and smaller image on your retina (left figure). Although the retinal image grows smaller, you do not perceive the car as shrinking because of size constancy. A similar process happens as a car drives toward you.

As the same car drives closer, notice in the figure below how it projects a larger image on your retina. However, because of size constancy, you do not perceive the car as becoming larger.

Size constancy is something you have learned from experience with moving objects. You have learned that objects do not increase or decrease in size as they move about. For example, an individual who was blind since birth and had his vision restored as an adult looked out a fourth-story window and reported seeing tiny creatures moving on the sidewalk. Because he had not learned size constancy, he did not know the tiny creatures were full-size people (Gregory, 1974).

We also perceive shapes as remaining the same.

Shape Constancy

Each time you move a book, its image on your retina changes from a rectangle to a trapezoid. But you see the book's shape as remaining the same because of shape constancy.

Shape constancy refers to your tendency to perceive an object as retaining its same shape even though when you view it from different angles, its shape is continually changing its image on the retina.

The figure below shows that when you look down at a rectangular book, it projects a rectangular shape on your retina.

However, if you move the book farther away, it projects trapezoidal shapes on your retina (figure below), but you still perceive the book as rectangular because of shape constancy.

Besides size and shape constancy, there is also brightness and color constancy.

Brightness and Color Constancy

If you look into your dimly lit closet, all the brightly colored clothes will appear dull and grayish. However, because of brightness and color constancy, you still perceive brightness and colors and have no trouble selecting a red shirt.

Brightness constancy refers to the tendency to perceive brightness as remaining the same in changing illumination.

Color constancy refers to the tendency to perceive colors as remaining stable despite differences in lighting.

For example, if you looked at this young girl's sweater in bright sunlight, it would be a bright yellow.

If you looked at her same yellow sweater in dim light, you would still perceive the color as a shade of yellow, although it is duller. Because of color constancy, colors seem about the same even when lighting conditions change.

However, if the light is very dim, objects will appear mostly gray because you lose color vision in very dim light.

Perceptual constancy is important because it transforms a potentially ever-changing, chaotic world into one with stability and comforting sameness.

Our next perceptual puzzle is how our eyes can see only two-dimensional images but our brain can transform them into a three-dimensional world.

Binocular (Two Eyes) Depth Cues

How can you see in three dimensions?

Normally, movies are shown in only two dimensions, height and width. But if you have ever seen a movie in 3-D (using special glasses to see three dimensions: height, width, and depth), you know the thrill of watching objects or animals come leaping off the screen so realistically that you duck or turn your head. You may not have realized that your eyes automatically give you a free, no-glasses, 3-D view of the world. And the amazing part of seeing in 3-D is that everything projected on the retina is in only two dimensions, height and width, which means that your brain combines a number of different cues to add a third dimension—depth (Connor, 2002).

Seeing in 3-D means seeing length, width, and DEPTH.

Depth perception refers to the ability of your eye and brain to add a third dimension, depth, to all visual perceptions, even though images projected on the retina are in only two dimensions, height and width.

The object on the left has been given a three-dimensional look by making it seem to have depth. It is impossible for most sighted people to imagine a world without depth, since they rely on depth perception to move and locate objects in space. The cues for depth perception are divided into two major classes: binocular and monocular.

Binocular depth cues depend on the movement of both eyes (*bi* means "two"; *ocular* means "eye").

We'll start with two binocular cues, convergence and retinal disparity.

Convergence

When you have an eye exam, the doctor usually asks you to follow the end of her finger as she holds it a few feet away and then slowly moves it closer until it touches your nose. This is a test for convergence.

Convergence refers to a binocular cue for depth perception based on signals sent from muscles that turn the eyes. To focus on near or approaching objects, these muscles turn the eyes inward, toward the nose. The brain uses the signals sent by these muscles to determine the distance of the object.

The woman in the photo at the right is demonstrating the ultimate in convergence as she looks at

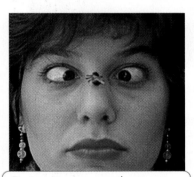

During convergence the eyes turn inward to see objects up close.

the fly on her nose. You can experience convergence by holding a finger in front of your nose and slowly bringing it closer to your nose. Your finger appears to move closer to your nose because the muscles that are turning the eyes inward produce signals corresponding to convergence. The more your eyes turn inward or converge, the nearer the object appears in space. The woman in the photo knows the fly is on her nose because of convergent clues from her turned-in eyes.

The second binocular cue comes from having an eye on each side of your face.

Retinal Disparity

One reason it's an advantage to have an eye on each side of your face is that each eye has a slightly different view of the world, which provides another binocular cue for depth perception called retinal disparity.

Retinal disparity refers to a binocular depth cue that depends on the distance between the eyes. Because of their different positions, each eye receives a slightly different image. The difference between the right and left eyes' images is the retinal disparity. The brain interprets a large retinal disparity to mean a close object and a small retinal disparity to mean a distant object.

The figure at the left shows how retinal disparity occurs: The difference between the image seen by the left eye (1) and the one seen by the right eye (2) results in retinal disparity (3).

1. Left eye sees a slightly different image of the fly.

3. Brain combines the two slightly different images from left and right eyes and gives us a perception of depth.

2. Right eye sees a slightly different image of the fly.

Another example of retinal disparity occurs when viewers wear special glasses to watch a 3-D movie, which has width, height, and depth. Standard 3-D glasses use a red and a green lens, which is a technique to allow the right and left eye to perceive a slightly different view of the same scene. As a result, the brain receives two slightly different images. As the brain automatically combines the slightly different images, we get the feeling of depth—for example, seeing a mad dog jump out of the movie screen into the audience (followed by much screaming).

Individuals who have only one eye still have depth perception because there are a number of one-eyed, or monocular, cues for depth perception, which we'll explain next.

E. Depth Perception

Could a Cyclops land an airplane?

A mythical creature called the Cyclops had only one eye in the middle of his forehead. Although a Cyclops would lack depth perception cues associated with retinal disparity, he would have depth perception cues associated with having one eye, or being monocular (*mon* means "one").

I could land an airplane with one eye!

This means that a Cyclops or an individual with one good eye could land an airplane because of monocular depth cues.

Monocular depth cues are produced by signals from a single eye. Monocular cues most commonly arise from the way objects are arranged in the environment.

We'll show you seven of the most common monocular cues for perceiving depth.

Linear perspective makes you see the road as going on forever.

1 *Linear Perspective*

As you look down a long stretch of highway, the parallel lines formed by the sides of the road appear to come together, or converge, at a distant point. This convergence is a monocular cue for distance and is called linear perspective.

Linear perspective is a monocular depth cue that results as parallel lines come together, or converge, in the distance.

Relative size makes you see the larger man as closer and the smaller men as farther away.

2 *Relative Size*

You expect the runners in the photo above to be the same size. However, since the runner on the right appears larger, you perceive him as closer, while the runner on the left appears smaller and, thus, farther away. The relative size of objects is a monocular cue for distance.

Relative size is a monocular cue for depth that results when we expect two objects to be the same size and they are not. In that case, the larger of the two objects will appear closer and the smaller will appear farther away.

Interposition makes you see the fish in front as closer and those in back as farther away.

3 *Interposition*

As you look at the school of fish in the photo above, you can easily perceive which fish are in front and which are in back, even though all the fish are about the same size. You can identify and point out which fish are closest to you and which are farthest away by using the monocular depth cue of overlap, which is called interposition.

Interposition is a monocular cue for depth perception that comes into play when objects overlap. The overlapping object appears closer and the object that is overlapped appears farther away.

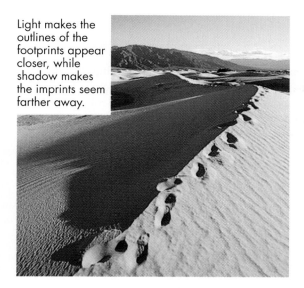

Light makes the outlines of the footprints appear closer, while shadow makes the imprints seem farther away.

4 Light and Shadow

Notice how the brightly lit edges of the footprints appear closer, while the shadowy imprint in the sand appears to recede. Also, the sunny side of the sand dune seems closer, while the back side in shadows appears farther away. The monocular depth cues shown here involve the interplay of light and shadows.

Light and shadow make up monocular cues for depth perception: Brightly lit objects appear closer, while objects in shadows appear farther away.

Texture gradient makes you see the sharply detailed, cracked mud as being closer.

5 Texture Gradient

You can't help but notice how the wide, detailed surface cracks in the mud seem closer, while the less detailed and narrower cracks appear farther away. These sharp changes in surface details are monocular depth cues created by texture gradients.

Texture gradient is a monocular depth cue in which areas with sharp, detailed texture are interpreted as being closer and those with less sharpness and poorer detail are perceived as more distant.

6 Atmospheric Perspective

One of the depth cues you may have overlooked is created by changes in the atmosphere. For example, both the man sitting on the chair and the edge of the cliff appear much closer than the fog-shrouded hills and landscape in the background. These monocular depth cues are created by changes in the atmosphere.

Atmospheric perspective is a monocular depth cue that is created by the presence of dust, smog, clouds, or water vapor. We perceive clearer objects as being nearer, and we perceive hazy or cloudy objects as being farther away.

Atmospheric perspective makes clear objects seem nearer and hazy objects as being farther away.

7 Motion Parallax

In this photo, you can easily tell which riders seem closer to you and which appear farther away. That's because you perceive fast-moving or blurry objects (horsemen on the right) as being closer to you and slower-moving or clearer objects (horsemen on the left) as being farther away. These monocular depth cues come from the way you perceive motion.

Motion parallax makes blurry objects appear closer and clear objects as being farther away.

Motion parallax is a monocular depth cue based on the speed of moving objects. We perceive objects that appear to be moving at high speed as closer to us than those moving more slowly or appearing stationary.

We have just discussed seven monocular cues involved in perceiving depth and distance accurately. Because they are monocular cues—needing only one eye—it means that people with only one eye have depth perception good enough to land a plane, drive a car, or play various sports such as baseball and tennis. If you wish to try some of these monocular cues, just hold your hand over one eye and see if you can avoid objects as you walk around a room.

We turn next to occasions where our perceptual system is fooled, and we see things that are not there. Welcome to the world of illusions.

F. Illusions

What is an illusion?

There are two reasons that much of the time your perceptions of cars, people, food, trees, animals, furniture, and professors are reasonably accurate reflections but, because of emotional, motivational, and cultural influences, never exact copies of reality.

First, we inherit similar sensory systems whose information is processed and interpreted by similar areas of the brain (Franz et al., 2000). However, damage to sensory areas of the brain can result in very distorted perceptions, such as the neglect syndrome (p. 79), in which people do not perceive one side of their body or one side of their environment. The second reason our perceptions are reasonably accurate is that we learn from common experience about the sizes, shapes, and colors of objects. But we've already discussed how perceptions can be biased or distorted by previous emotional and learning experiences, such as perceiving dogs differently after being bitten by one. Now we come to another way that perceptions can be distorted: by changing the actual perceptual cues so you perceive something unlikely, which is called an illusion.

An *illusion* is a perceptual experience in which you perceive an image as being so strangely distorted that, in reality, it cannot and does not exist. An illusion is created by manipulating the perceptual cues so that your brain can no longer correctly interpret space, size, and depth cues.

This impossible figure seems to have two or three prongs!

For example, if you look at the right end of this tuning fork, it appears to have two prongs. But if you look at the left end, it appears to have three prongs. You're looking at a figure that most of us cannot draw because it seems impossible.

An *impossible figure* is a perceptual experience in which a drawing seems to defy basic geometric laws.

One reason the tuning fork appears impossible to figure out and is almost impossible for you to draw has to do with your previous experience with line drawings in books. Because you have seen many three-dimensional objects drawn in books, you tend to perceive the left side of the tuning fork as being three-dimensional (three forks) but you tend to perceive the right side as being two-dimensional (two forks). Later on in the Cultural Diversity feature (p. 137), you'll learn why Africans can easily draw this impossible figure while most college professors cannot (Coren & Ward, 1993).

In this example, we perceive an illusion because the tuning fork is drawn to confuse our previous experiences with two- and three-dimensional objects. One of the oldest illusions that you have often experienced is the moon illusion, which has proven very difficult to explain (L. Kaufman, 2000).

Moon Illusion

Moon appears to be huge when it's near the horizon.

Moon appears 50% smaller when it's high in the sky.

The moon illusion has intrigued people for centuries because it is so impressive. The left photo shows that when a full moon is near the horizon, it appears (or gives the illusion of being) as much as 50% larger than when it is high in the sky (right photo). Here's the interesting part: You perceive this 50% increase in size even though the size of both moons on your retinas is exactly the same.

For the past 50 years, researchers have proposed different explanations for the moon illusion. The most current explanation is based on the theory that your brain automatically estimates how far away an object is and then interprets its size—the farther away the object is, the larger the object is perceived. For example, when look-

ing at a far-off car, your brain automatically estimates the distance as being far away and thus interprets or perceives the car as being a full-sized car and not a small toy car. Similar to you seeing a far-off car and perceiving it as being large or full-sized (not a toy), researchers found that subjects estimated the horizon moon to be much farther away and thus interpreted its size as being larger. In contrast, subjects estimated the elevated moon to be closer and thus perceived it as being smaller (L. Kaufman, 2000).

Besides naturally occurring illusions, there are others that humans have created. One of the most interesting illusions comes from looking inside the Ames room.

Adult woman appears smaller than young boy.

In the Ames room (left photo) you perceive the boy on the right to be twice as tall as the woman on the left. In fact, the boy is smaller than the woman but appears larger because of the design of the Ames room.

The *Ames room*, named after its designer, shows that our perception of size can be distorted by changing depth cues.

The reason the boy appears to be twice as tall as the woman is that the room has a peculiar shape and you are looking in from a fixed peephole. To see how the Ames room changes your depth cues, look at the diagram of the Ames room in the drawing below right. If you view the Ames room from the fixed peephole, the room appears rectangular and matches your previous

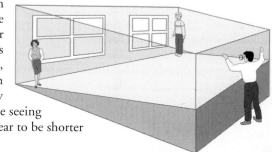

experience with rooms, which are usually rectangular. However, as the right figure shows, the Ames room is actually shaped in an odd way: The left corner is twice as far away from the peephole as the right corner. This means that the woman is actually twice as far away from you as the boy. However, the Ames room's odd shape makes you think that you are seeing the two people from the same distance, and this (illusion) makes the farther woman appear to be shorter than the boy (E. B. Goldstein, 1999).

The next two illusions either change your perceptual cues or rely too much on your previous perceptual experiences.

Ponzo Illusion

Black bars are the same length.

In the figure above, the top black bar appears to be much longer than the bottom black bar. However, if you measure these two bars, you will discover that they are exactly the same size. This is the *Ponzo illusion*. I clearly remember measuring the first time I saw this picture because I couldn't believe the bars were the same size. You perceive the top bar as being farther away, and you have learned from experience that if two objects appear to be the same size but one is farther away, the more distant object must be larger; thus, the top bar appears longer.

Müller-Lyer Illusion

The figures at the left and right illustrate the *Müller-Lyer illusion*. Notice that the left arrow appears noticeably shorter than the right arrow. However, if you measure them, you'll prove that the arrows are of equal length.

One explanation

Left and right arrows are the same length.

for this illusion is that you are relying on size cues learned from your previous experience with corners of rooms. You have learned that if a corner of a room extends outward, it is closer; this experience distorts your perception so that the left arrow appears to be shorter. In contrast, you have learned that if a corner of a room recedes inward, it is farther away, and this experience makes you perceive the right arrow as longer (E. B. Goldstein, 1999). Illusions are fun, but what have we learned?

Learning from Illusions

Most of the time, you perceive the world with reasonable accuracy by using a set of proven perceptual cues for size, shape, and depth. However, illusions teach us that when proven perceptual cues are changed or manipulated, our reliable perceptual processes can be deceived, and we see something unreal or an illusion. Illusions also teach us that perception is a very active process, in which we continually rely on and apply previous experiences with objects when we perceive new situations. For example, you'll discover later (p. 140) how the entertainment industry changes the perceptual rule of closure to create movies, whose motion is a brilliant illusion. After the Concept Review, we'll discuss a form of perception that the U.S. Congress almost outlawed.

✔ Concept Review

1. This figure illustrates the concept of the _____, which is defined as the intensity level of a stimulus such that a person will have a 50% chance of detecting it.

2. The smallest increase or decrease in the intensity of a stimulus that a person can detect is called a (a)_____. The increase in intensity of a stimulus needed to produce a just noticeable difference grows in proportion to the intensity of the initial stimulus; this is called (b)_____ law.

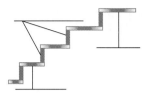

3. Our first awareness of sensory information, in the form of meaningless bits of information, is called a (a)_____. When many bits of sensory information have been assembled into a meaningful image, it is called a (b)_____, which can be biased or distorted by our unique set of experiences.

4. Early psychologists discovered a set of rules or principles that our brains use to automatically group or arrange stimuli into perceptual experiences. These early researchers, who were called _____ psychologists, disagreed with other early psychologists, who were called structuralists.

5. You automatically separate an image into a more dominant, detailed figure and a less detailed background according to the _____ rule.

6. You fill in missing parts to form a complete image as a result of the _____ rule.

7. You see this image as formed by an oval and an overlying square because of the _____ rule.

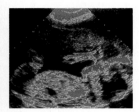

8. You divide each line of this figure into separate groups of objects according to the _____ rule.

9. In this figure, you see a blue numeral 2 instead of light and dark blue circles because of the _____ rule.

10. In this figure, you see a continuous line from A to B, rather than a line from A to C, following the _____ rule.

11. Although physical qualities of stimuli may change, you may perceive them as remaining the same because of (a)_____. For example, as a car drives away from you, its image on your retina becomes smaller but you know that the car does not shrink in size because of (b)_____ constancy. When you close a door, its shape on your retina changes from a rectangle to a trapezoid, but you perceive the door as remaining the same because of (c)_____ constancy. If you had a bright red car, it would appear red in bright light and still appear to be red in dimmer light because of (d)_____ constancy.

12. Cues for depth perception that depend on both eyes are called (a)_____ cues. Cues for depth perception that depend on a single eye are called (b)_____ cues. The binocular cue that occurs when your eyes move inward to track a fly landing on your nose is called (c)_____. The binocular cue that occurs when each eye receives a slightly different image is called (d)_____.

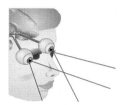

13. Monocular cues for depth perception include: cues from overlapping objects, called (a)_____; cues from two parallel lines converging, called (b)_____; cues from larger and smaller images, called (c)_____; cues from the presence of dust and smog, called (d)_____; and cues from nearer and farther objects moving at different speeds, called (e)_____.

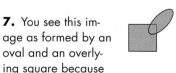

14. If perceptual cues are so changed that our brains can no longer interpret them correctly, we perceive a distorted image of reality, called an (a)_____. Such a distorted perception illustrates that perception is an active process and that we rely on previous (b)_____ when perceiving new situations.

Answers: *1. absolute threshold; 2. (a) just noticeable difference, (b) Weber's; 3. (a) sensation, (b) perception; 4. Gestalt; 5. figure-ground; 6. closure; 7. simplicity; 8. proximity; 9. similarity; 10. continuity; 11. (a) perceptual constancy, (b) size, (c) shape, (d) color; 12. (a) binocular, (b) monocular, (c) convergence, (d) retinal disparity; 13. (a) interposition, (b) linear perspective, (c) relative size, (d) atmospheric perspective, (e) motion parallax; 14. (a) illusion, (b) experiences*

Why did people buy more popcorn?

Sometimes research questions come from unusual places—in this case, a movie theater. In the late 1950s, moviegoers were reported to have bought 50% more popcorn and 18% more Coca-Cola when the words "Eat popcorn" and "Drink Coca-Cola" were projected subliminally (1/3,000 of a second) during the regular movie (McConnell et al., 1958). The concern that advertisers might change consumers' buying habits without their knowledge prompted the U.S. Congress to consider banning any form of subliminal advertising. Congress did not take legislative action because subliminal advertising proved to be ineffective (Pratkanis, 1992). However, history seems to be repeating itself as advertisers now claim that subliminal tapes can change specific behaviors (Epley et al., 1999).

Changing Specific Behaviors

At the beginning of this module, we told you about Maria, who, like millions of other Americans, purchased an audiotape because it claimed to contain subliminal persuasion that would effortlessly change her behavior.

A *subliminal message* is a brief auditory or visual message that is presented below the absolute threshold, which means that there is less than a 50% chance that the message will be perceived.

To answer the research question, Can subliminal messages change specific behaviors? researchers conducted a well-designed experiment that used a double-blind procedure.

Labels did not match subliminal messages.

Method. For several weeks, subjects listened to two different tapes titled either "Improve Self-Esteem" or "Improve Memory." Then they rated any improvement in these behaviors.

Double-blind procedure. Researchers had to control for any possible placebo effects, such as subjects' showing improvement because they believed they were hearing powerful subliminal messages. Therefore, subjects were not told which subliminal messages the tapes contained. For example, some tapes labeled "Improve Memory" contained subliminal messages for improving memory, while others contained subliminal messages for improving self-esteem. Thus, because of the double-blind procedure, subjects were unaware of the fact that the tapes' subliminal messages did not match the tapes' labels.

But, subjects believed what the labels said.

Results. About 50% of the subjects reported improvements in either self-esteem or memory. However, subjects reported improvements in behavior based on what the *tapes' labels promised* rather than on what the subliminal messages were. For example, a subject who listened to a tape labeled "Improve Self-Esteem" reported improvements in self-esteem even though the tape contained subliminal messages for improving memory. These results suggest a self-fulfilling prophecy at work.

Self-fulfilling prophecies involve having strong beliefs about changing some behavior and then acting, unknowingly, to change that behavior.

Researchers concluded that subliminal messages in self-help tapes did not affect the behavior they were designed to change. Instead, any changes in behavior resulted from listeners' beliefs that the tapes would be effective (Epley et al., 1999).

Although subliminal messages are ineffective in changing specific behaviors, there is evidence that your emotional state can unknowingly or subliminally influence perception.

Changing Perceptions

When you're in a happy mood, do you unknowingly or subliminally notice more smiley faces? This is similar to the question that researchers asked: Would subjects who were in a happy mood perceive "happy" words faster than "sad" words, and vice versa (Niedenthal & Setterlund, 1994)?

Method. Subjects were put into happy or sad moods by listening to music that made them feel happy or sad.

After being put into a sad or happy mood, subjects sat in front of a screen that projected strings of words, such as joy, habit, hurt, code, comedy, and weep. As each word appeared, subjects rated it as happy (joy, comedy), sad (hurt, weep), or neutral (habit, code). We have simplified the results by reporting only a sample of their data.

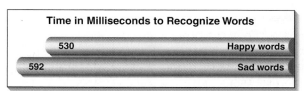

Time in Milliseconds to Recognize Words

530	Happy words
592	Sad words

Results. As shown in the graph above, researchers found that subjects in happy moods perceived happy words significantly faster than sad words. Not shown is that subjects in sad moods perceived sad words faster than subjects who were in happy moods.

Researchers concluded that being in a particular emotional state can affect our perceptions without our awareness. Researchers suggested that these findings may explain what occurs in real life: When we are in a happy state, we are more likely to notice and perceive the things that bring us joy rather than things that make us sad.

These and other studies indicate that subliminal stimuli can influence emotional and cognitive processes, including preferring certain shapes, liking individuals, recognizing words, and being classically conditioned to respond to sad or happy faces, all without any conscious awareness (Abrams & Greenwald, 2000; Epley et al., 1999; Strahan et al., 2002). However, there are yet no well-designed studies to show that subliminal advertising can persuade consumers to choose a specific item or brand (Channouf et al., 2000).

Not only can emotional states unknowingly affect perceptions, but next you'll see how cultural values and experiences can also unknowingly change what you perceive.

H. Cultural Diversity: Influence on Perceptions

What Do Cultural Influences Do?

If you visit ethnic sections of large U.S. cities, such as Chinatown or Little Italy, or visit foreign countries, you become aware of cultural differences and influences. For example, this photo shows two Japanese women in traditional robes and setting, which symbolize the different cultural influences of Japan compared to Western countries.

Cultural influences are persuasive pressures that encourage members of a particular society or ethnic group to conform to shared behaviors, values, and beliefs.

What if you were raised in a different culture?

No one doubts that cultural influences affect the way people eat, dress, talk, and socialize. But you are less likely to notice how cultural influences also affect how you perceive things in your own environment.

For example, cultural anthropologists, who study behaviors in natural settings in other cultures, have reported intriguing examples of how cultural experiences influence perceptual processes. We'll begin with a remarkable finding of why natives were unable to perceive common objects in photos.

Perception of Photos

Could not recognize a dog in a black/white photo

A cultural anthropologist showed African natives black-and-white photos of a cow and a dog, two animals the natives were very familiar with. But when the natives looked at the black-and-white photos, they seemed very puzzled because they did not see any animals. Their expressions suggested that the anthropologist was lying about the black-and-white photos showing a cow and dog. Next, the anthropologist showed the natives color photos of the same two animals. The natives looked at the color photos and smiled and nodded as they now recognized and pointed to the color photos of the cow and dog (Deregowski, 1980).

Because the people of this tribe had never seen black-and-white photos, they had no experience in recognizing

The thing without color is nothing.

The thing with color is a dog.

animals in this format. But when they were shown color photographs, which showed a world more similar to the one they experienced, they immediately recognized the cow and dog. Most likely, the natives drew on their everyday experiences with objects in full color and could recognize what they saw in the photo from what they saw in the real world. This is an example of how cultural experiences can influence perceptual skills, such as the ability to recognize familiar images presented in different photo formats.

How we describe images is another example of how culture influences what we perceive.

Could recognize a dog in a color photo

Perception of Images

Please look at the photo below for a few seconds and then close your eyes and tell what you saw. Dr. Richard Nisbett (2000) and colleagues found that what you see or think about depends, to a large extent, on your culture.

For example, after looking at the underwater scene, Americans tended to begin their descriptions by focusing on the largest fish and making statements like "There was what looked like a trout swimming to the left." Americans are much more likely to zero in on the biggest fish, the brightest object, the fish moving the fastest. "That's where the money is as far as Americans are concerned" (Goode, 2000, p. D4).

Compared to Americans, Japanese subjects were much more likely to begin by setting the scene, saying, for example, "There was a lake or pond" or "The bottom was rocky" or "The water was green." On average, Japanese subjects made 70% more statements about how the background looked than Americans did

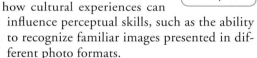
Look at the photo briefly and then close your eyes and describe it.

and twice as many statements about the relationships between the fish and the backgrounds. For instance, compared to Americans, Japanese subjects were more likely to say, "The big fish swam past the gray seaweed." This kind of statement indicates that Japanese focus much more on describing relationships between objects and their backgrounds than do Americans.

Generally, Americans tend to analyze each object separately, which is called analytical thinking—seeing a forest and focusing more on separate trees. In comparison, Easterners (Japanese, Chinese, and Koreans) tend to think more about the relationship between objects and backgrounds, which is called holistic thinking—seeing a forest and thinking about how trees combine to make up a forest. Researchers suggest that these differences in thinking and perceiving (analytical versus holistic) may come from differences in social and religious practices, languages, and even geography (Kitayama et al., 2003; Nisbett, 2000).

Cultures also influence how we see cartoons.

Perception of Motion

For just a moment, look at the cartoon drawing of the dog (below) and notice what its tail is doing. Then look at the female figure (right) and describe what the figure is doing.

Most people in Western cultures immediately perceive what is happening: the dog is wagging its tail and the figure is spinning. Because of our Western cultural experience with cartoon drawings, we have learned to recognize that certain kinds of repeated images (the dog's tail) and certain lines and circles (the dancing figure) indicate movement. We have learned and become so accustomed to seeing these kinds of cartoon drawings indicate motion that the tail and the dancer really do seem to be in motion.

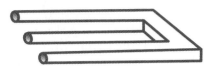

What is the dog's tail doing?

What is this dancer doing?

However, people from non-Western cultures, who have no experience with these cartoon drawings, do not perceive the dog's tail or the figure as moving. Non-Westerners see only an unusual dog that has three tails and a strange figure that is surrounded by circles; they do not perceive any indication of movement in these drawings (S. Friedman & Stevenson, 1980). This is a perfect example of how Western cultural influences shape our perceptions, often without our realizing.

If part of your cultural experience involves seeing 3-dimensional objects in books, you won't be able to draw the next figure.

Perception of 3 Dimensions

Can you draw this impossible figure?

This is the same impossible figure that you saw earlier. As you look at it, it changes almost magically back and forth between a two-pronged and a three-pronged tuning fork. The illusion is that the middle fork is unreal because it seems to come out of nowhere.

When people from industrialized nations try to draw this figure from memory, they almost surely fail. What is interesting is that Africans who have no formal education do not see any illusion but perceive only a two-dimensional pattern of flat lines, which they find easy to draw from memory. In contrast, people with formal education, who have spent years looking at three-dimensional representations in books, perceive this object as having three dimensions, a pattern that is almost impossible to draw (Coren & Ward, 1993).

I can draw that strange thing.

Perception of Beauty

Do you think this woman is attractive?

In the past, when Burmese girls were about 5 years old, they put a brass coil one-third-inch wide around their necks. As they grew older, girls added more brass coils until they had from 19 to 25 wrapped around their necks. The appearance of long necks caused by the brass coils was perceived as being very attractive by Burmese people, who live in southeast Asia. This custom eventually declined as neck coils were no longer considered beautiful, just cruel and uncomfortable. Recently, however, the custom has been revived because now tourists come and pay $12 to see and take photos of women with brass neck coils (Stevens, 1994).

This example illustrates how cultural values influence our perceptions of personal beauty.

Perceptual Sets

Do you think this muscular body is beautiful?

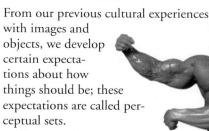

From our previous cultural experiences with images and objects, we develop certain expectations about how things should be; these expectations are called perceptual sets.

Perceptual sets are learned expectations that are based on our personal, social, or cultural experiences. These expectations automatically add information, meaning, or feelings to our perceptions and thus change or bias our perceptions.

For example, as you look at this bodybuilder, you automatically add personal feelings, such as like/dislike and approve/disapprove, as well as impressions of physical characteristics: height, about 6 feet, and weight, about 225 pounds. Because of your perceptual set for bodybuilders, you expect them to be large, and so you will be surprised to learn that this bodybuilder is only 5 feet 2 inches tall and weighs 182 pounds. One function of perceptual sets is to automatically fill in information or add feelings that can greatly modify our perceptions.

These examples show that we rarely perceive the world exactly as it is. Rather, our perceptions can be changed, biased, or distorted by experiences, such as cultural influences and perceptual sets.

Next, we'll discuss a controversial kind of perception that goes by the initials ESP.

I. ESP: Extrasensory Perception

What are psychic powers?

No one doubts your ability to receive information through one or more of your major senses—seeing, hearing, tasting, smelling, and touching—because this ability has been repeatedly demonstrated and reliably measured. In comparison, most research psychologists do not believe that you can receive information outside normal sensory channels, which is called extrasensory perception, because this phenomenon has been neither repeatedly demonstrated nor reliably measured (D. J. Bem & Honorton, 1994).

Extrasensory perception (ESP) is a group of psychic experiences that involve perceiving or sending information (images) outside normal sensory processes or channels. ESP includes four general abilities—telepathy, precognition, clairvoyance, and psychokinesis. Telepathy is the ability to transfer one's thoughts to another or to read the thoughts of others. Precognition is the ability to foretell events. Clairvoyance is the ability to perceive events or objects that are out of sight. Psychokinesis is the ability to exert mind over matter—for example, by moving objects without touching them. Together, these psychic powers or extrasensory perceptions are called psi phenomena.

The term *psi* refers to the processing of information or transfer of energy by methods that have no known physical or biological mechanisms and that seem to stretch the laws of physics.

Believing in ESP. According to Gallup polls, 49% of adult Americans believe in ESP, 36% believe in communication between minds without the use of regular senses, 26% believe in psychics, and 25 to 50% claim to have had one or more extrasensory experiences (Gallup & Newport, 1991; Nisbet, 1998). The reason so many

> Psi refers to getting information by methods that defy the laws of physics.

Americans but so few research psychologists believe in ESP is that researchers demand hard, scientific evidence rather than evidence from testimonials, which are based on personal beliefs or experiences and have a high potential for error and bias.

Testimonials as evidence. In discussing testimonials (p. 30), we pointed out that they seem convincing because they are based on personal experiences. However, there are many examples of testimonials that, when evaluated with scientifically designed experiments, were found to be unproven. For example, researchers found that 35 to 98% of individuals who gave testimonials about becoming ill or getting well after taking a pill, dietary supplement, or herb had unknowingly taken a placebo, a medically useless treatment (Cowley, 2000a). Because many people are so convinced and so willing to provide testimonials that some treatment works (actually a placebo), scientists must seriously question any evidence arising from testimonials. Questioning testimonial evidence applies especially to ESP, which is outside normal senses, defies physical and biological explanations, and stretches the laws of physics (P. Kurtz, 1995; Nisbet, 1998).

Another reason researchers demand reliable and repeatable evidence to prove the existence of ESP is that some demonstrations of psi phenomena have involved trickery or questionable methodology. For example, at least one well-known researcher has used trickery and magic to duplicate many of the better-known demonstrations of ESP, such as mentally bending spoons, starting broken watches, moving objects, and reading messages in sealed envelopes. This researcher's name is the Amazing Randi.

Could you spot a trick?

According to James Randi, known as the Amazing Randi (on the left in the photo), and others acquainted with magic, much of what passes for extrasensory perception is actually done through trickery (Steiner, 1989; Ybarra, 1991). For example, to show how easily people may be fooled, Randi sent two young magicians (also in the photo) to a lab that studied psychic phenomena. Instead of admitting they were magicians, the pair claimed to have psychic powers and to perform psychic feats, such as mentally bending keys and making images on film. After 120 hours of testing, the lab's researchers, who had carefully conducted and supervised the ESP demonstrations, concluded that the two did indeed have genuine psychic abilities. The lab's researchers were not expecting trickery, had not taken steps to prevent it, and were thus totally fooled into believing they were witnessing ESP.

The Amazing Randi (left), professional magician, sent two young magicians to fool researchers into believing that they had psychic powers.

Several years ago, a 2-hour television show under the supervision of James Randi offered $100,000 to anyone who could demonstrate psychic powers. Twelve people claimed to have psychic powers, such as identifying through interviews the astrological signs under which people were born, seeing the auras of people standing behind screens, and correctly reading Zener cards (showing five symbols: square, circle, wavy lines, plus sign, and star). Of the 12 people who claimed psychic powers, none scored above chance on any of these tasks (Steiner, 1989). Although people may claim psychic powers, most cannot demonstrate such powers under controlled conditions, which eliminate trickery, magic, and educated guessing.

James Randi has repeatedly shown that people untrained in recognizing trickery cannot distinguish between psychic feats and skillful tricks. To eliminate any trickery, claims of psychic abilities must withstand the scrutiny of scientific investigation. Let's see how a controlled ESP experiment is designed and conducted.

How do researchers study psychic abilities?

One of the more common demonstrations of psychic ability is to use Zener cards, which show five symbols—circle, waves, square, plus sign, and star (on right). A researcher holds up the back of one card and asks the subject to guess the symbol on the front. If there were 100 trials, the subject could identify 20 symbols correctly simply by guessing (chance level). However, if a subject identifies 25 symbols correctly, which is above chance level, does that mean the subject has psychic powers? This is a simplified example of a very complicated statistical question: How can we determine whether a person has psychic powers or is just guessing correctly? Therefore, to solve one major problem in psi research—how to eliminate guesswork and trickery—researchers use a state-of-the-art method called the Ganzfeld procedure.

The *Ganzfeld procedure* is a controlled method for eliminating trickery, error, and bias while testing telepathic communication between a sender—the person who sends the message—and a receiver—the person who receives the message.

Symbols used to study ESP

In the Ganzfeld procedure, the receiver is placed in a reclining chair in an acoustically isolated room. Translucent ping-pong ball halves are taped over the eyes, and headphones are placed over the ears. The sender, who is isolated in a separate sound-proof room, concentrates for about 30 minutes on a target, which is a randomly selected visual stimulus, such as a photo or art print (right figure). At the end of this period, the receiver is shown four different stimuli and asked which one most closely matches what the receiver was imagining. Because there are four stimuli, the receiver will guess the target correctly 25% of the time. Thus, if the receiver correctly identifies the target more than 25% of the time, it is above chance level and indicates something else is occurring, perhaps extrasensory perception (D. J. Bem & Honorton, 1994).

Ganzfeld procedure involves mentally sending this picture to a person in another room.

We have described the Ganzfeld procedure in detail to illustrate the precautions and scientific methodology that researchers must use to rule out the potential for trickery, error, and bias. The next question is perhaps the most interesting of all: What have researchers learned from recent Ganzfeld experiments?

What is the scientific status of ESP?

The history of psychic research is filled with controversy, especially about replication, which is the ability of other researchers to do similar experiments and obtain similar results. For example, Daryl Bem and Charles Honorton (1994), two respected researchers, reported that the Ganzfeld procedure (described above) provided evidence for mental telepathy; that is, one person mentally transferred information to a person in another room. The biggest question about Bem and Honorton's controversial mental telepathy results was whether their findings could be repeated or replicated by other researchers.

Importance of replication. Science has a powerful weapon for evaluating research findings, called *replication*, that simply says: If other scientists cannot repeat the results, the results probably occurred by chance. More recently, researchers evaluated the results of 30 Ganzfeld experiments conducted by 7 independent researchers. These researchers reported that the original Ganzfeld finding, which supported some kind of mental telepathy, could not be replicated (Milton & Wiseman, 1999). This failure to replicate the Ganzfeld experiments, which represent the best-controlled studies on ESP to date, means that there is currently little or no reliable scientific

The best-known mental telepathy results could not be replicated.

evidence to support the existence of ESP or psi phenomena (Milton & Wiseman, 2001). One of the biggest problems with ESP is that those who claim to have it are rarely subjected to scientific study. Such is the case with so-called psychic hotlines.

Television psychics. Started in the early 1990s was something called psychic hotlines, in which self-claimed "psychics" answered calls from people seeking answers to personal and financial questions. At one time, psychic hotlines took in $100 million a year.

There is no test or training for becoming a psychic, so anyone can claim to be one. Many alleged TV psychics were recruited through want ads and paid $15 to $20 an hour to answer questions from perfect strangers (Nisbet, 1998). For example, well-known TV psychic Miss Cleo, who claimed to be and spoke with a Jamaican accent, was actually born an American citizen and took the Fifth Amendment to avoid self-incrimination when her company was sued for cheating its customers (Christopher, 2003; P. Rogers, 2003). As with other claims for ESP, there is no scientific evidence that self-proclaimed psychics are better at knowing or predicting the future than would occur by chance (Sheaffer, 1997).

TV psychic, Miss Cleo, spoke with a Jamaican accent but was born an American citizen.

Next, we'll discuss several other forms of perceptions that fool our senses into believing that fixed things are moving.

J. Application: Creating Perceptions

Painted 20,000 years ago

Can we create new perceptions? About 20,000 years ago, early humans *(Homo sapiens)* created some of the earliest images by using earth pigments to paint prancing horses on the sides of their caves (right photo) (Fritz, 1995). About 3,000 years ago, Egyptians created some of the most impressive images with their enormous and long-lasting pyramids. Today, computer researchers are using virtual reality techniques to develop new images and perceptions that can put you in the middle of a mind-blowing three-dimensional world. We'll begin our look at how perceptions are created with an old perceptual device that is used in modern billboards.

Creating Movement

The father of the flashing lights used in today's billboards, movie marquees, and traffic arrows was a distinguished Gestalt psychologist named Max Wertheimer. In the early 1900s, Wertheimer spent a considerable amount of time in a darkened room, where he experimented with flashing first one light and then a second light that was positioned some distance away. He discovered that if the time between flashing one light and then the other was adjusted just right, the two flashes were actually perceived as a moving spot of light rather than as two separate flashes. He called this illusion *phi movement.*

Phi movement refers to the illusion that lights that are actually stationary seem to be moving. This illusionary movement, which

Neon billboards use flashing lights to create the illusion of movement.

today is called apparent motion, is created by flashing closely positioned stationary lights at regular intervals.

Each time you pass a traffic arrow composed of flashing lights or perceive a moving string of lights used in an advertising sign, you are seeing a practical application of Wertheimer's phi movement. This phi movement was one of the first examples of how ordinary visual stimuli could be adjusted to create an illusion.

Another example of creating wonderful moving illusions with stationary visual stimuli came from the remarkable genius of Thomas Edison, who invented motion pictures in 1893.

Creating Movies

Movies create the illusion of motion by showing a series of fixed images.

If you attend a track meet and watch a 100-meter race and then, minutes later, watch a videotaped replay of the same race, you perceive motion produced in two very different ways. One kind of motion is real, while the other is an illusion.

Real motion refers to your perception of any stimulus or object that actually moves in space.

As you watch a live 100-meter race, you are perceiving real motion. However, when you watch a replay of that same race, you are seeing apparent motion.

Apparent motion refers to an illusion that a stimulus or object is moving in space when, in fact, the stimulus or object is stationary. The illusion of apparent motion is created by rapidly showing a series of stationary images, each of which has a slightly different position or posture than the one before.

The principle for creating apparent motion is deceptively simple and can be easily discovered by examining the positions of the runner's body in each frame of the time-lapse photo shown above.

Beginning on the left side of the photo, notice that each frame shows only a slight change in the position of the runner's body. However, if these frames were presented rapidly—for example, at the movie standard of 24 frames per second—you would perceive the illusion of an athlete running down the track.

In a series of ingenious experiments, researchers discovered that several complex mechanisms built into our visual system detect cues that produce the illusion of motion (Ramachandran & Anstis, 1986). One such cue is the closure principle, which means that our brains fill in the motion expected to occur between images that vary only slightly in position and are presented in rapid sequence. Without apparent motion, there would be no movies, television, or flip books.

Currently, researchers have developed a procedure that creates a three-dimensional perceptual experience of walking through a house, dissecting a frog, or doing complicated human surgery. This is the brave new world of virtual reality.

What is a surgical robot?

The invention of the movie camera was revolutionary because it created a new perceptual experience: the illusion that still pictures moved. Currently, another perceptual revolution is under way, and it's called virtual reality.

Virtual reality refers to a perceptual experience of being inside an object, moving through an environment, or carrying out some action that is created or simulated by computer.

Remote and robotic surgery. In a medical application of virtual reality, researchers are developing programs that will allow surgeons to practice their skills with surgical simulators on virtual cadavers as well as perform remote surgery using a surgical robot. For example, a surgeon can insert and maneuver a tiny camera and surgical tools in a patient through a pencil-thin incision between the ribs (Cray, 2000). The surgeon operates by maneuvering the robotic arms (left photo), which are steadier and more precise than a human's

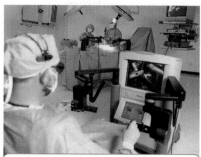

Doctors use virtual reality to guide a robot to perform operations.

arms. Robotic surgery has already been used in heart bypass surgery, without opening the patient's chest (Mackenzie, 2000). Virtual reality technology will soon be used to perform a wide variety of robotic surgical procedures, such as hip replacements and operations on microscopic body tissues or difficult-to-see areas in the brain (Noonan, 2001; Hamilton, 2001).

Psychotherapy. In a psychological application of virtual reality, clients with such fears as spiders, flying, or heights are exposed to the feared stimuli in a three-dimensional environment where everything appears very real.

Therapists use virtual reality to treat phobias (fear of spiders).

In this photo, a client is being treated for fear of spiders. She wears a plastic helmet that contains a computer monitor that puts her inside a virtual reality kitchen in which she sees, touches, and kills spiders. For example, Joanne Cartwright suffered a debilitating fear of spiders. "I washed my truck every night before I went to work in case there were webs," she said. "I put all my clothes in plastic bags and taped duct tape around my doors so spiders couldn't get in. I thought I was going to have a mental breakdown. I wasn't living" (Robbins, 2000, p. D6). Dr. Albert Carlin at the University of Washington gave Joanne 12 virtual reality sessions that decreased her fear. As she said, "I'm amazed because I am doing all this stuff I could never do—camping, hunting and hiking" (Carlin, 2000). Psychotherapists report success in using virtual reality therapy to treat a wide variety of phobias (Bornas et al., 2001; Emmelkamp et al., 2002).

The next topic focuses on how much your first impressions of other people depend on your perceptions of their physical appearances.

Can you name these faces?

Social psychologists have discovered that facial features have a significant effect on our first impressions and perceptions of people. For example, researchers found that we perceive an attractive person as being more interesting, sociable, intelligent, outgoing, and kind (Lemley, 2000). Similarly, first impressions are also influenced by racial stereotypes, both positive and negative, based on physical features such as skin color and hair style. Hollywood hair stylists know that the kind, amount, color, and style of actors' hair can radically change their appearance and our impressions of them. In fact, they use different hair styles to match different roles. For instance, look at the three photos on the right and try to correctly identify each of these famous personalities (answers at the end).

Besides hair color and style, skin color has a considerable impact on first perceptions and impressions. To illustrate how skin color can greatly change your perceptions of people, look at the two photos on the far right and try to correctly identify these two famous people.

Who . . .

. . . am . . .

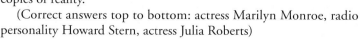

. . . I?

You may have guessed correctly that the two people are the actor-politician Arnold Schwarzenegger of the United States and Queen Elizabeth of England. The editors of *Colors, the Multicultural Magazine* published these computer-colored images to ask their readers: What percentage of your understanding of someone is formed by race? After looking at Queen Elizabeth with the skin color of an Indian and at Arnold Schwarzenegger with the skin color of an African American, you can judge for yourself how much facial coloring influences your impressions and perceptions of others. We'll discuss more on how we perceive people and form impressions in Module 25.

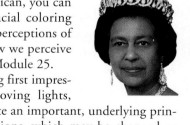

Who are we?

The factors involved in forming first impressions as well as in creating moving lights, movies, and virtual reality illustrate an important, underlying principle of perception: Our perceptions, which may be changed or biased by personal experiences, are interpretations rather than exact copies of reality.

(Correct answers top to bottom: actress Marilyn Monroe, radio personality Howard Stern, actress Julia Roberts)

Summary Test

A. PERCEPTUAL THRESHOLDS

1. We discussed three basic questions that psychologists ask about perception. Our first question—At what point are we aware of a stimulus?— can be answered by measuring the threshold of a stimulus, which is a point above which a stimulus is perceived and below which it is not. The intensity level at which a person has a 50% chance of perceiving the stimulus is called the _____.

2. Our second question—At what point do we know a stimulus intensity has increased or decreased?—can be answered by measuring the smallest increase or decrease in the intensity of a stimulus that a person can detect; this is called a (a)_____. It has been found that the increase in stimulus intensity needed to produce a just noticeable difference increases in proportion to the intensity of the initial stimulus; this is called (b)_____ law.

B. SENSATION VERSUS PERCEPTION

3. Our third question—How are meaningless sensations combined into meaningful perceptions?—can be answered by analyzing our own perceptual experiences. Our first awareness of some outside stimulus is called a (a)_____. This awareness results when some change in energy activates sensory receptors, which produce signals that, in turn, are transformed by the brain into meaningless sensory experiences. When many individual sensations are assembled into a meaningful experience, image, or pattern, it is called a (b)_____. The latter is not an exact replica of the real world but rather a copy that has been changed, biased, or distorted by our unique set of (c)_____. Our brain transforms sensations into perceptions instantaneously, automatically, and without our awareness.

4. The (a)_____ argued that we can explain how perceptions are formed by dividing perceptions into smaller and smaller elements. They believed that we combine basic elements to form a perception. In contrast, the (b)_____ psychologists replied that the formation of perceptions cannot be understood by simply breaking perceptions down into individual components and then studying how we reassemble them. They argued that "the whole is more than the sum of its parts," by which they meant that perceptions are more than a combination of individual elements. The Gestalt psychologists believed that the brain has rules for assembling perceptions, which they called principles of (c)_____.

C. RULES OF ORGANIZATION

5. Many of the rules of perceptual organization involve ways of grouping or arranging stimuli. According to one of these rules, the first thing we do is automatically separate an image into two parts: the more detailed feature of an image becomes the (a)_____ and the less detailed aspects become the (b)_____. According to the (c)_____ rule, stimuli tend to be organized in the most basic, elementary way. According to the (d)_____ rule, stimuli that appear the same tend to be grouped together. According to the (e)_____ rule, stimuli that are near one another tend to be grouped together. According to the (f)_____ rule, stimuli that are arranged in a smooth line or curve tend to be perceived as forming a continuous path. According to the (g)_____ rule, we tend to fill in the missing parts of a figure and perceive it as complete.

D. PERCEPTUAL CONSTANCY

6. Although the size, shape, brightness, and color of objects are constantly changing, we tend to see them as remaining the same, a phenomenon that is called (a)_____. A person walking away does not appear to grow smaller, even though the image on the retina is decreasing in size, because of (b)_____ constancy. Even though the image of a door that is opened and closed changes on the retina from a rectangle to a trapezoid, we see it as retaining its rectangular outline because of (c)_____ constancy. Even though the color and brightness inside a car are altered when we drive from bright into dim light, we tend to see little change because of (d)_____ and _____ constancy.

E. DEPTH PERCEPTION

7. The visual system transforms the two-dimensional image (height and width) of stimuli projected onto the retina into a three-dimensional experience by adding depth. Cues for depth that are dependent on both eyes are called (a)_____; cues for depth that are dependent on only a single eye are called (b)_____. The binocular cue for depth that arises when muscles turn your eyes inward is called (c)_____. The binocular cue for depth that arises because the two eyes send slightly different images to the brain is called (d)_____.

8. There are a number of monocular cues for depth. When an object appears closer because it overlaps another, the cue is called (a)_____. When parallel lines seem to stretch to a point at the horizon and create a sense of distance, the cue is called (b)_____. When two figures are expected to be the same size but one is larger and thus appears closer, the cue is called (c)_____. If dust or smog makes objects appear hazy and thus farther away, the cue is called (d)_____. As texture changes from sharp and detailed to dull and monotonous, it creates the impression of distance; this cue is called (e)_____. The play of light and shadow gives objects a three-dimensional look, a cue that is called (f)_____. As you ride in a car, the impression that near objects are speeding by and far objects are barely moving is called (g)_____.

F. ILLUSIONS

9. For much of the time, our perceptions are relatively accurate reflections of the world (except for anything added by our attentional, motivational, or emotional filters). However, if perceptual cues that we have learned to use and rely on are greatly changed, the result is a distorted image, called an _____. Although illusions are extreme examples, they illustrate that perception is an active, ongoing process in which we use past experiences to interpret current sensory experiences.

G. RESEARCH FOCUS: SUBLIMINAL PERCEPTION

10. Brief auditory or visual messages that are presented below the absolute threshold, which means that their chance of being heard or seen is less than 50%, are called (a)_____. Researchers have concluded that any behavioral changes attributed to subliminal messages actually result because listeners' strong belief that a behavior will change leads them to act, unknowingly, to change that behavior; this is called a (b)_____.

H. CULTURAL DIVERSITY: INFLUENCE ON PERCEPTIONS

11. Experiences that are typical of a society and shared by its members are called _____ influences. These influences have significant effects on the perception of images, constancy, depth, and motion.

12. Because of cultural influences, Americans tend to engage more in (a)_____ thinking, while Easterners (Japanese) engage more in (b)_____ thinking.

I. ESP: EXTRASENSORY PERCEPTION

13. The perception and transmission of thoughts or images by other than normal sensory channels are referred to as psychic experiences or (a)_____ phenomena. ESP, which stands for (b)_____, includes four psychic abilities. The ability to transfer one's thoughts to another or read another's thoughts is called (c)_____. The ability to foretell events is called (d)_____. The ability to perceive events or objects that are out of sight is called (e)_____. The ability to move objects without touching them is called (f)_____. Two reasons many researchers are skeptical of psychic abilities are that some supposedly psychic phenomena were actually accomplished with (g)_____ and some previous studies that supported ESP had questionable (h)_____. Although some studies supported the occurrence of psi phenomena, recent studies showed that the experiments that supported psi phenomena could not be (i)_____.

J. APPLICATION: CREATING PERCEPTIONS

14. When you view objects moving in space, it is called (a)_____ motion. When you view images of stationary objects that are presented in a rapid sequence, it is called (b)_____ motion, which is the basic principle used to create movies. The illusion that stationary lights are moving can be traced to the work of Max Wertheimer, who called this phenomenon (c)_____ movement. A perceptual experience that is created by allowing the viewer to enter and participate in computer-generated images is called (d)_____; it breaks down some of the traditional boundaries between reality and fantasy. Virtual reality has been applied to treat excessive fear of spiders, flying, or heights, which are called (e)_____.

Answers: *1. absolute threshold; 2. (a) just noticeable difference, (b) Weber's; 3. (a) sensation, (b) perception, (c) experiences; 4. (a) structuralists, (b) Gestalt, (c) perceptual organization; 5. (a) figure, (b) ground, (c) simplicity, (d) similarity, (e) proximity, (f) continuity, (g) closure; 6. (a) perceptual constancy, (b) size, (c) shape, (d) color, brightness; 7. (a) binocular, (b) monocular, (c) convergence, (d) retinal disparity; 8. (a) interposition, (b) linear perspective, (c) relative size, (d) atmospheric perspective, (e) texture gradient, (f) light and shadow, (g) motion parallax; 9. illusion; 10. (a) subliminal messages, (b) self-fulfilling prophecy; 11. cultural; 12. (a) analytical, (b) holistic; 13. (a) psi, (b) extrasensory perception, (c) telepathy, (d) precognition, (e) clairvoyance, (f) psychokinesis, (g) trickery, (h) methodology, (i) replicated; 14. (a) real, (b) apparent, (c) phi, (d) virtual reality, (e) phobias*

NEWSPAPER ARTICLE

Can See but Not Recognize His Wife's Face

Questions

1. Why did extensive scarring of the cornea cause total blindness in Mike's right eye?

2. Why did Mike have to wait until 1999 to have the stem cell procedure, and why is there controversy over using these amazing stem cells?

3. Although Mike could see through his right eye, why was his vision so poor?

4. What happened to Mike's brain that prevents him from combining his wife's facial features into a recognizable face?

5. What does Mike's normal ability to track moving objects tell us about his brain?

Use InfoTrac to search for the term: **blindness**

When Mike May was 3 years old, a jar of fuel for a lantern exploded, completely destroying his left eye and so badly scarring the right eye's cornea that his right eye became totally blind. Being totally blind did not stop Mike from playing flag football in elementary school, playing soccer in college, and earning a master's degree.

In 1999, 43 years after Mike was blinded, a surgeon tried to repair Mike's eye by placing stem cells on his right cornea. The stem cells replaced the scarred tissue and literally remade the front of his eye. Next, Mike received a corneal transplant, which allowed light waves to pass into his eye and continue on through a perfectly good lens, retina, optic nerve, and finally the brain's area for processing visual stimuli.

The surgeon believed that Mike would be able to see out of his right eye since everything from the cornea to his brain was in perfect working order. However, when the bandage was removed and Mike looked at the eye chart, instead of recognizing the big **E** from 20 feet away (20/20 vision), he needed to get within 2 feet (20/500 vision). Mike's vision was very poor.

In the first months after surgery, he could see that there were objects on a table, but he could not distinguish between two different objects, such as a ball from a cube, which is a very easy task, even for young sighted children.

Although Mike can see his wife's face and has seen it hundreds of times since surgery, he cannot recognize it. Distinguishing faces and emotional expressions is impossible for Mike and will likely remain so. The reason sighted people can recognize complex objects, such as faces, is that, from birth on, all kinds of visual stimuli were projected to the brain, which had to learn how to combine these stimuli into meaningful perceptions, such as faces, ball, cubes, or animals. Brain scans show that when Mike is looking at faces and objects, that part of his brain that would normally be activated when recognizing objects is silent.

Although Mike has trouble distinguishing between and recognizing objects, he is able to track a moving object and is pretty good at catching a ball thrown to him. Brain scans show that when he is looking at a moving ball, the motion-detection part of his brain is active, similar to a normal brain.

When Mike goes walking, he still depends on his dog or taps his cane on the sidewalk. Even though he can "see," he describes himself as "a blind man with vision." (Adapted from Abrams, 2002)

SUGGESTED ANSWERS

1. As discussed in Module 5 (pp. 94–95), the cornea is the rounded, transparent covering over the front of the eye. The cornea allows light waves to pass into the eye, and its rounded surface bends or focuses light waves onto the lens. Because Mike's cornea was so badly scarred, no light waves could pass into his eye, resulting in total blindness, even though the rest of his optical system (lens, retina, optic nerve, brain's visual areas) was intact.

2. As discussed in Module 4 (p. 60), stem cells, which were not discovered until 1998, have the amazing capacity to change into and become hundreds of other kinds of cells. The use of human embryonic stem cells involves moral and ethical objections because human embryos are destroyed in the process.

3. There is a difference between seeing and perceiving. Mike can see

that something is there, but he cannot easily distinguish or perceive what that "something" is.

4. Because Mike was totally blinded at age 3, his brain was prevented from receiving normal visual stimulation during its development, so his brain was never programmed for perceiving and recognizing visual stimuli, such as a face. Visual stimulation during early childhood is critical and explains why it is now too late for Mike to develop complex visual perceptual skills.

5. When Mike was successfully tracking a moving ball, brain scans showed activity in the motion-detection area of his brain. This means that, unlike developing the ability to distinguish between objects, detecting motion is hard-wired into the brain and does not require years of visual stimulation for normal development.

Links to Learning

LEARNING ACTIVITIES

- *POWERSTUDY CD-ROM 2.0*  by Tom Doyle and Rod Plotnik

Check out the "Perception" Module (disk 1) on PowerStudy and:

- Test your knowledge using an interactive version of the Summary Test on pages 142 and 143. Also access related quizzes—true/false, multiple choice, and matching.
- Explore an interactive version of the Critical Thinking exercise "Can See But Not Recognize His Wife's Face" on page 144.
- You will also find key terms, a chapter outline including chapter abstract, and a list of hotlinked Web sites that correlate to this module.

- *SELF-STUDY ASSESSMENT*

Want help studying? For your customized Study Plan go to **http://psychology.wadsworth.com/plotnik7e/**. This program will automatically generate pretests and posttests to help you determine what concepts you have mastered and what concepts you still need work on.

- *STUDY GUIDE and WEBTUTOR*

Check the corresponding module in your Study Guide for effective student tips and help learning the material presented. Also go to **http://webtutor.thomsonlearning.com** for an interactive version of the Study Guide features.

- *INFOTRAC COLLEGE EDITION ONLINE LIBRARY*

To find interesting and relevant articles go to **http://www.infotrac-college.com**, use your password, and then type in search terms such as the ones listed below.

Color vision

Gestalt psychology

Subliminal messages

Virtual reality

STUDY QUESTIONS

Use InfoTrac to search for topics mentioned in the main heads below (e.g., prenatal influences, cognitive development, child abuse).

*A. Perceptual Thresholds—How does Weber's law apply to how old you perceive someone to be? (**Suggested answer page 622**)

*B. Sensation Versus Perception—What would your life be like if your brain could receive sensations but could not assemble them into perceptions? (**Suggested answer page 622**)

C. Rules of Organization—Why can you still read the message on a faded and torn billboard sign?

D. Perceptual Constancy—If you suddenly lost all perceptual constancy, what specific problems would you have?

E. Depth Perception—Would a one-eyed pitcher have any particular problems playing baseball?

F. Illusions—What has to happen to our perceptual processes before we see an illusion?

G. Research Focus: Subliminal Perception—Could advertisers make any honest claims for subliminal tapes?

*H. Cultural Diversity: Influence on Perceptions—When foreigners visit the United States, what do you think they perceive differently? (**Suggested answer page 622**)

I. ESP: Extrasensory Perception—How could you test your friend's claim of having had a psychic experience?

J. Application: Creating Perceptions—What do illusions add to our perceptions of the world?

*These questions are answered in Appendix B.

Module 9: Classical Conditioning

PowerStudy 2.0™ Complete Module

It's Only Aftershave

What happened to Carla?

"I've got an unusual problem and I thought you might be able to explain what happened." Carla, one of my students, looked troubled.

"I'll help if I can," I replied, and asked her to sit down.

"It all started when my dentist told me that I needed a lot of work on my teeth and gums. I spent many mornings in the dentist's chair, and even though he gave me Novocain, it was painful and very uncomfortable. But here's the strange part that I wish you would explain. I had recently bought my boyfriend a new aftershave, and as the dentist worked on my teeth, I noticed that he was using the same one. You'll think this is silly, but now when I smell my boyfriend's aftershave, I start to feel tense and anxious."

Carla stopped and waited to see if I would tell her that she was just being silly. I didn't, and she continued.

"Finally, I told my boyfriend that he would have to stop using the aftershave I had bought him because it was the same as my dentist's and the smell made me anxious. Well, we got into a big argument because he said that he was nothing like my dentist and I was just being silly. So now my teeth are great, but I feel myself getting anxious each time we get close and I smell his aftershave."

How can smelling aftershave cause anxiety?

I assured Carla that she was not being silly and that many people get conditioned in the dentist's chair. In fact, patients have reported feeling anxious when they enter the dentist's office, smell the antiseptic odor, or hear the sound of the drill (Milgrom et al., 1994). I explained that, without her knowing, she had been conditioned to feel fear each time she smelled her dentist's aftershave and how that conditioning had transferred to her boyfriend. Before I explained how to get "unconditioned," I told her how after only one terrifying experience, I too had been conditioned.

It's Only a Needle

What happened to Rod?

I was about 8 years old when I had to get an injection from my local doctor, whom I really liked. He warned me in a kindly way that the injection might hurt a little. I was feeling OK until I saw the long needle on the syringe. I tried to be brave and think of my fuzzy dog, but as soon as I felt that long needle enter my little butt, everything started to spin. I remember sinking slowly to the floor, and then everything went dark. When I came to, the doctor told me that I had fainted.

How can the sight of a syringe and needle cause terror?

Even after all these years, the sight of a needle can still strike terror into me. To prevent fainting, I always lie down when getting an injection or giving blood. But I'm not alone in my fear of needles and injections; about 10 to 20% of the general population report a similar fear (Page et al., 1997).

Besides learning to fear needles and blood, people can unknowingly learn to feel sick and nauseated, just as Michelle did.

It's Only Dish Soap

What happened to Michelle?

Michelle was nervous and afraid as the nurse put a needle into the vein in her left arm and then opened a valve that allowed chemicals to drip into her bloodstream. Michelle was in the process of receiving chemotherapy to treat her cancer. One serious side effect of chemotherapy is severe nausea, which Michelle experienced after each treatment.

What Michelle wasn't prepared for was how other things could trigger her nausea. In one case, the odor of her dishwashing liquid, which smelled similar to the chemotherapy room, made her feel nauseated. She had to change her brand of detergent because its odor made her salivate, which was the first sign of oncoming nausea (Wittman, 1994). Without her awareness, Michelle had been conditioned to feel nauseated by numerous stimuli involved in her chemotherapy (Montgomery & Bovbjerg, 1997).

The cases of Michelle, Carla, and myself show how we had been conditioned to fear relatively ordinary things, such as aftershave lotion, needles, and the smell of detergent. This conditioning illustrates one kind of learning.

Learning is a relatively enduring or permanent change in behavior that results from previous experience with certain stimuli and responses. The term *behavior* includes both unobservable mental events (thoughts, images) and observable responses (fainting, salivating, vomiting).

In all three cases, conditioning resulted in a relatively enduring change in behavior. In fact, mine has lasted almost 50 years. What happened to each of us involved a particular kind of learning, called classical conditioning, which we'll discuss in this module.

How can smelling dish soap cause nausea?

What's Coming

We'll first discuss three different kinds of learning and then focus on one, classical conditioning. We'll examine how classical conditioning is established and tested, how we respond after being classically conditioned, what we learn during classical conditioning, and how classical conditioning is used in therapy. Let's begin with a look at three different kinds of learning.

A. Three Kinds of Learning

Why is some learning easier?

Some things are difficult to learn, such as all the terms in this module. Other things are easy to learn, such as fear of an injection. To understand why some learning is easy and some hard, we'll visit three different laboratories. You'll see how psychologists identified three different principles that underlie three different kinds of learning: classical conditioning, operant conditioning, and cognitive learning.

Classical Conditioning

Why does the dog salivate?

It is the early 1900s, and you are working as a technician in Russia in the laboratory of Ivan Pavlov. He has already won a Nobel Prize for his studies on the reflexes involved in digestion. For example, he found that when food is placed in a dog's mouth, the food triggers the reflex of salivation (R. B. Evans, 1999).

As a lab technician, your task is to place various kinds of food in a dog's mouth and measure the amount of salivation. But soon you encounter a problem. After you have placed food in a dog's mouth on a number of occasions, the dog begins to salivate merely at the sight of the food.

At first, Pavlov considered this sort of anticipatory salivation to be a bothersome problem. Later, he reasoned that the dog's salivation at the sight of food was also a reflex, but one that the dog had somehow *learned.*

In a well-known experiment, Pavlov rang a bell before putting food in the dog's mouth.

As shown in this graph, after a number of trials of hearing a bell paired with food, the dog salivated at the sound of the bell alone, a phenomenon that Pavlov called a **conditioned reflex** and today is called classical conditioning. Classical conditioning was an important discovery because it allowed researchers to study learning in an observable, or objective, way (Honey, 2000).

Classical conditioning is a kind of learning in which a neutral stimulus acquires the ability to produce a response that was originally produced by a different stimulus.

Next, we'll visit a lab in the United States and observe a different kind of learning.

Operant Conditioning

Why does the cat escape?

It is the late 1800s, and you are now working in the laboratory of the American psychologist E. L. Thorndike. Your task is to place a cat in a box with a door that can be opened from the inside by hitting a simple latch. Outside the box is a fish on a dish. You are to record the length of time it takes the cat to hit the latch, open the door, and get the fish.

Thorndike studied how a cat learned to open a cage to get food nearby.

On the first trial, the cat sniffs around the box, sticks its paw in various places, accidentally hits the latch, opens the door, and gets the fish. You place the cat back into the box for another trial. Again the cat moves around, accidentally strikes the latch, and gets the fish. After many such trials, the cat learns to spend its time around the latch and eventually to hit the latch and get the fish in a very short time.

To explain the cat's goal-directed behavior, Thorndike formulated the law of effect.

The *law of effect* says that if some random actions are followed by a pleasurable consequence or reward, such actions are strengthened and will likely occur in the future.

Thorndike's law of effect was important because it identified a learning process different from Pavlov's conditioned reflex. Today, the law of effect has become part of operant conditioning (R. B. Evans, 1999).

Operant conditioning refers to a kind of learning in which the consequences that follow some behavior increase or decrease the likelihood of that behavior's occurrence in the future.

We will discuss operant conditioning in Module 10. Our next lab has a big plastic doll and a bunch of kids.

Cognitive Learning

Why do they punch the doll?

It is the 1960s, and you are in Albert Bandura's laboratory, where children are watching a film of an adult who is repeatedly hitting and kicking a big plastic doll. Following this film, the children are observed during play.

Bandura found that children who had watched the film of an adult modeling aggressive behavior played more aggressively than children who had not seen the film (Bandura et al., 1963). The children's change in behavior, which was increased aggressive responses, did not seem to be based on Pavlov's conditioned reflexes or Thorndike's law of effect. Instead, the entire learning process appeared to take place in the children's minds, without their performing any observable responses or receiving any noticeable rewards. These mental learning processes are part of cognitive learning, which is a relatively new approach that began in the 1960s (Lieberman, 2000).

Cognitive learning is a kind of learning that involves mental processes, such as attention and memory; may be learned through observation or imitation; and may not involve any external rewards or require the person to perform any observable behaviors.

Bandura's study demonstrated a third principle of learning, which essentially says that we can learn through observation or imitation. *We will discuss cognitive learning in Modules 10, 11, and 12.*

Now, let's return to Pavlov's laboratory and examine his famous discovery in greater detail.

B. Procedure: Classical Conditioning

What's the procedure?

Imagine that you are an assistant in Pavlov's laboratory and your subject is a dog named Sam. You are using a procedure that will result in Sam's salivating when he hears a bell, a response that Pavlov called a ***conditioned reflex***. Today, we call Pavlov's procedure ***classical conditioning***, which involves the following three steps.

Step 1. Choosing Stimulus and Response

Terms. Before you begin the procedure to establish classical conditioning in Sam, you need to identify three critical terms: *neutral stimulus, unconditioned stimulus,* and *unconditioned response.*

Neutral stimulus. You need to choose a neutral stimulus.

A *neutral stimulus* is some stimulus that causes a sensory response, such as being seen, heard, or smelled, but does not produce the reflex being tested.

Your neutral stimulus will be a tone (bell), which Sam the dog hears but which does not normally produce the reflex of salivation.

Unconditioned stimulus. You need to choose an unconditioned stimulus, or UCS.

An *unconditioned stimulus,* or *UCS,* is some stimulus that triggers or elicits a physiological reflex, such as salivation or eye blink.

Your unconditioned stimulus will be food, which when presented to Sam will elicit the salivation reflex, that is, will make Sam salivate.

Unconditioned response. Finally, you need to select and measure an unconditioned response, or UCR.

The *unconditioned response,* or *UCR,* is an unlearned, innate, involuntary physiological reflex that is elicited by the unconditioned stimulus.

For instance, salivation is an unconditioned response that is elicited by food. In this case, the sight of food, which is the unconditioned stimulus, will elicit salivation in Sam, which is the unconditioned response.

Step 2. Establishing Classical Conditioning

Trial. A common procedure to establish classical conditioning is for you first to present the neutral stimulus and then, a short time later, to present the unconditioned stimulus. The presentation of both stimuli is called a *trial.*

Neutral stimulus. In a typical trial, you will pair the neutral stimulus, the tone, with the unconditioned stimulus, the food. Generally, you will first present the neutral stimulus (tone) and then, a short time later, present the unconditioned stimulus (food).

 **+**

Unconditioned stimulus (UCS). Some seconds (but less than a minute) after the tone begins, you present the unconditioned stimulus, a piece of food, which elicits salivation. This trial procedure is the one most frequently used in classical conditioning.

→

Unconditioned response (UCR). The unconditioned stimulus, food, elicits the unconditioned response, salivation, in Sam. Food and salivation are said to be unconditioned because the effect on Sam is inborn and not dependent on some prior training or learning.

Step 3. Testing for Conditioning

Only CS. After you have given Sam 10 to 100 trials, you will test for the occurrence of classical conditioning. You test by presenting the tone (conditioned stimulus) without showing Sam the food (unconditioned stimulus).

Conditioned stimulus. If Sam salivates when you present the tone alone, it means that the tone has become a conditioned stimulus.

A *conditioned stimulus,* or *CS,* is a formerly neutral stimulus that has acquired the ability to elicit a response that was previously elicited by the unconditioned stimulus.

In this example, the tone, an originally neutral stimulus, became the CS.

Conditioned response. When Sam salivates to the tone alone, this response is called the conditioned response.

The *conditioned response,* or *CR,* which is elicited by the conditioned stimulus, is similar to, but not identical in size or amount to, the unconditioned response.

One thing to remember is that the conditioned response is usually similar in appearance but smaller in amount or magnitude than the unconditioned response. This means that Sam's conditioned response will involve less salivation to the tone (conditioned stimulus) than to the food (unconditioned stimulus).

Predict. One question you may ask about classical conditioning is: What exactly did Sam learn during this procedure? One thing Sam learned was that the sound of a bell predicted the very likely occurrence of food (Rescorla, 1988). Classical conditioning helps animals and humans predict what's going to happen and thus provides information that may be useful for their survival (Lieberman, 2000).

Next we'll use the concepts of classical conditioning to explain how Carla was conditioned to her dentist's aftershave.

B. Procedure: Classical Conditioning

Terms in Classical Conditioning

What happened to Carla? After many trips to her dentist, Carla unknowingly experienced classical conditioning, which explains why she now feels anxious and tense when she smells a certain aftershave lotion. As we review the steps involved in classical conditioning, you will see how they apply to Carla's situation.

Step 1. Selecting Stimulus and Response

Terms. To explain how classical conditioning occurs, it's best to start by identifying three terms: *neutral stimulus, unconditioned stimulus,* and *unconditioned response.*

 The *neutral stimulus* in Carla's situation was the odor of the dentist's aftershave lotion, which she smelled while experiencing pain in the dentist's chair. The aftershave is a neutral stimulus because although it affected Carla (she smelled it), it did not initially produce feelings of anxiety. In fact, initially Carla liked the smell.

 The *unconditioned stimulus* for Carla was one or more of several dental procedures, including injections, drillings, and fillings. These dental procedures are unconditioned stimuli (UCS) because they elicited the unconditioned response (UCR), which was feeling anxious and tense.

 The *unconditioned response* was Carla's feeling of anxiety, which is a combination of physiological reflexes, such as increased heart rate and blood pressure and rapid breathing, as well as negative emotional reactions. Carla's unconditioned response (anxiety) was elicited by the unconditioned stimulus (painful dental procedure).

Step 2. Establishing Classical Conditioning

Trial. One procedure to establish classical conditioning is for the neutral stimulus to occur first and be followed by the unconditioned stimulus. Each presentation of both stimuli is called a *trial.*

 In Carla's case, the *neutral stimulus* was smelling the dentist's aftershave while she was experiencing a number of painful dental procedures.

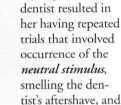 Carla's many trips to the dentist resulted in her having repeated trials that involved occurrence of the *neutral stimulus,* smelling the dentist's aftershave, and occurrence of the *unconditioned stimulus,* having painful dental procedures.

 The painful dental procedures elicited the *unconditioned response* (feelings of anxiety) as well as other physiological responses, such as increases in heart rate, blood pressure, and breathing rate.

Step 3. Testing for Conditioning

Only CS. A test for classical conditioning is to observe whether the neutral stimulus, when presented alone, elicits the conditioned response.

Conditioned stimulus. When Carla smelled her boyfriend's aftershave, which was the same as the dentist's, she felt anxious. The aftershave's smell, formerly a neutral stimulus, had become a *conditioned stimulus* because it elicited anxiety, the conditioned response.

Conditioned response. Whenever Carla smelled the aftershave (conditioned stimulus) used by both her dentist and her boyfriend, it elicited the *conditioned response,* feeling anxious. However, remember that the conditioned response is similar to, but of lesser intensity than, the unconditioned response. Thus, the anxiety elicited by smelling the aftershave was similar to, but not as great as, the anxiety Carla felt during painful dental procedures.

Dental fears. Through classical conditioning, Carla learned that the smell of a certain aftershave predicted the likely occurrence of pain and made her feel anxious. Researchers suggest that children and adults who developed an extreme fear or phobia of dental procedures learned such fears through classical conditioning (Townsend et al., 2000). However, just as classical conditioning can elicit fears, it can also be used to treat them through an "unconditioning" procedure that we'll discuss in the Application section on page 206.

Next, we'll describe several other behaviors that are associated with classical conditioning.

C. Other Conditioning Concepts

What else happened to Carla?

Carla's experience in the dentist's office of being classically conditioned to feel anxious when she smelled a particular aftershave has several other interesting features. Carla found that similar odors also elicited anxious feelings but that other odors did not; her anxiety when smelling her boyfriend's aftershave gradually decreased, but accidentally meeting the dentist and smelling his aftershave triggered some anxiety. Pavlov found that these phenomena were associated with classical conditioning, and he named them generalization, discrimination, extinction, and spontaneous recovery.

1. *Generalization*

Why her shampoo?

During Carla's conditioning trials, the neutral stimulus, which was the odor of the dentist's aftershave, became the conditioned stimulus that elicited the conditioned response, anxiety. However, Carla may also feel anxiety when smelling other similar odors, such as her own hair shampoo; this phenomenon is called generalization.

Generalization is the tendency for a stimulus that is similar to the original conditioned stimulus to elicit a response that is similar to the conditioned response. Usually, the more similar the new stimulus is to the original conditioned stimulus, the larger will be the conditioned response.

Pavlov suggested that generalization had an adaptive value because it allowed us to make an appropriate response to stimuli that are similar to the original one. For example, although you may never see your friend's smiling face in exactly the same situation, generalization ensures that the smiling face will usually elicit positive feelings.

Reacting to similar odors is generalization.

2. *Discrimination*

Why not her nail polish?

Carla discovered that smells very different from that of the aftershave did not elicit anxiety; this phenomenon is called discrimination.

Discrimination occurs during classical conditioning when an organism learns to make a particular response to some stimuli but not to others.

For example, Carla had learned that a particular aftershave's smell predicted the likelihood of a painful dental procedure. In contrast, the smell of her nail polish, which was very different from that of the aftershave, predicted not painful dental procedures but nice-looking fingernails.

Discrimination also has an adaptive value because there are times when it is important to respond differently to related stimuli. For example, you would respond differently to the auditory stimulus of a police siren than to the auditory stimulus of a baby's cries.

Not reacting to a new odor is discrimination.

3. *Extinction*

What about her boyfriend?

If Carla's boyfriend did not change his aftershave and she repeatedly smelled it, she would learn that it was never followed by painful dental procedures, and its smell would gradually stop making her feel anxious; this phenomenon is called extinction.

Extinction refers to a procedure in which a conditioned stimulus is repeatedly presented without the unconditioned stimulus and, as a result, the conditioned stimulus tends to no longer elicit the conditioned response.

The procedure for extinguishing a conditioned response is used in therapeutic settings to reduce fears or phobias. For example, clients who had a conditioned fear of needles and receiving injections were repeatedly shown needles and given injections by qualified nurses. After exposure to the conditioned stimuli during a 3-hour period, 81% of the clients reported a significant reduction in fear of needles and receiving injections (Ost et al., 1992). This kind of exposure therapy is a practical application of Pavlov's work and will be discussed more fully in Module 22.

Not reacting to a previously powerful stimulus is extinction.

4. *Spontaneous Recovery*

Would the anxiety come back?

Suppose Carla's conditioned anxiety to the smell of the aftershave had been extinguished by having her repeatedly smell her boyfriend's lotion without experiencing any painful consequences. Some time later, when Carla happened to accidentally meet her dentist in the local supermarket, she might spontaneously show the conditioned response and feel anxiety when smelling his aftershave; this is called spontaneous recovery (D. C. Brooks, 2000).

Spontaneous recovery is the tendency for the conditioned response to reappear after being extinguished even though there have been no further conditioning trials.

Spontaneous recovery of the conditioned response will not persist for long and will be of lesser magnitude than the original conditioned response. If the conditioned stimulus (smell of aftershave) is not presented again with the unconditioned stimulus (painful dental procedure), the spontaneously recovered conditioned response will again undergo extinction and cease to occur. Thus, once Carla had been classically conditioned, she would have experienced one or more of these four phenomena.

Now that you are familiar with the procedure and concepts of classical conditioning, we'll explore its widespread occurrence in the real world.

Having a reaction come back is spontaneous recovery.

D. Adaptive Value & Uses

How useful is classical conditioning?

Pavlov believed that animals and people evolved the capacity for classical conditioning because it had an adaptive value (Lieberman, 2000).

Adaptive value refers to the usefulness of certain abilities or traits that have evolved in animals and humans and tend to increase their chances of survival, such as finding food, acquiring mates, and avoiding pain and injury.

We'll discuss several examples, such as learning to avoid certain tastes, salivating at the sight of food, and avoiding pain, which support Pavlov's view that classical conditioning is useful because it has an adaptive value.

Taste-Aversion Learning

What do you learn from getting sick?

Rat exterminators have firsthand knowledge of classical conditioning's adaptive value. Exterminators find that while some rats eat enough bait poison to die, others eat only enough to get sick. Once rats get sick on a particular bait poison, they quickly learn to avoid its smell or taste, called *bait shyness*, and never again eat that bait poison. This kind of learning is a form of classical conditioning called taste-aversion learning (Loy & Hall, 2002).

Taste-aversion learning is how rats avoid poison.

Taste-aversion learning refers to associating a particular sensory cue (smell, taste, sound, or sight) with getting sick and thereafter avoiding that particular sensory cue in the future.

The adaptive value of taste-aversion learning for rats is obvious: By quickly learning to avoid the smells or taste associated with getting sick, such as eating poison bait, they are more likely to survive.

Humans. It is likely that in your lifetime, you too will experience taste-aversion learning. For example, if you have eaten something and gotten sick after taking a thrill ride, you may avoid the smell or taste of that particular food. Similarly, people who get sick from drinking too much of a particular alcoholic drink (often a sweet or distinctive-tasting drink) avoid that drink for a long period of time (Lieberman, 2000).

I'm starting to get a sick feeling!!!

Taste-aversion learning may also warn us away from eating poisonous plants that cause illness or even death, such as eating certain varieties of mushrooms. All these examples of taste-aversion learning show the adaptive value of classical conditioning, which is to keep us away from potentially unpleasant or dangerous situations, such as taking thrill rides, overdrinking, or eating poisonous plants.

As many people have learned, taste-aversion learning can develop after a single experience and may last weeks, months, or even as long as 4 to 5 years (Logue et al., 1981; Rozin, 1986).

The study of taste-aversion learning changed two long-held beliefs about classical conditioning.

Explanation

Is only one trial enough?

For a long time, psychologists believed that bait shyness was not due to classical conditioning. They were sure that classical conditioning required many trials (not a single trial of getting sick) and that the neutral stimulus (smell or taste) must be followed within seconds by the unconditioned response (nausea), and certainly not hours later (getting sick). Psychologist John Garcia thought otherwise.

One-trial learning. Garcia showed that taste-aversion learning did occur in one trial and, more surprisingly, did occur even though there was an hour or more delay between the neutral stimulus (smell or taste) and the unconditioned response (sickness or vomiting). Garcia's findings proved that taste-aversion learning is a form of classical conditioning (Loy & Hall, 2002).

Taste-aversion learning occurs in one trial.

Preparedness. An interesting finding was that animals acquired taste aversion differently. For example, rats, which have poor vision but great senses of taste and olfaction (smell), acquired taste aversion easily to smell and taste cues but were rarely conditioned to light cues (Garcia et al., 1966). Similarly, quails, which have poor olfaction but great vision, acquired taste aversion more easily to visual cues (Wilcoxon et al., 1971). Garcia concluded that, depending on the animal, different stimuli or cues have different potentials for becoming conditioned stimuli. These findings challenged the long-standing belief in classical conditioning that all stimuli (smell, taste, visual, auditory) have an equal chance of becoming conditioned stimuli. Garcia's finding that some stimuli were more easily conditioned than others was called preparedness (Seligman, 1970).

Preparedness refers to the phenomenon that animals and humans are biologically prepared to associate some combinations of conditioned and unconditioned stimuli more easily than others.

The idea of preparedness means that different animals are genetically prepared to use different senses to detect stimuli that are important to their survival and adaptation. For example, John Garcia and his colleagues (1974) applied their knowledge of preparedness and taste aversion to the problem of sheep-killing by coyotes. They baited grazing areas with pieces of sheep

Taste-aversion learning is used to stop coyotes from eating sheep.

flesh laced with a chemical that caused coyotes to become nauseated and ill. As a result, coyotes that had acquired a taste aversion showed an estimated 30–60% reduction in sheep-killing (B. Bower, 1997; Gustavson et al., 1976). Taste-aversion learning has applications for sheep ranchers and for people who get sick from overdrinking or eating before going on thrill rides (Loy & Hall, 2002).

Classical Conditioning and Adaptive Value

Why do blue jays avoid monarchs?

Taste-aversion learning helps rats survive by alerting them to the smell and taste of poison, and it also warns blue jays, who feast on butterflies, not to eat monarch butterflies. Monarch butterflies, which have a distinctive coloring pattern, contain a chemical that, when eaten, will make birds sick. Through taste aversion, blue jays learn that the distinctive color pattern of monarch butterflies predicts getting sick, and so blue jays avoid eating monarch butterflies.

Through taste-aversion learning blue jays learn to avoid monarchs.

Like monarch butterflies, many animals have evolved with distinctive markings or colors that, through taste-aversion learning, have become conditioned stimuli that serve as warnings to predators. Thus, classically conditioned taste aversion has survival value for animals. In contrast, things that taste good can produce a classically conditioned response in humans that is also adaptive.

Hot fudge sundaes. The next time you enter a restaurant, read the menu, think about food, and see people eating, notice that you are salivating even though you have no food in your own mouth. Just as Pavlov's dog was conditioned to salivate at the sound of a bell, we have also become conditioned to salivate when only thinking about, imagining, smelling, or seeing food. This is a clear example of how many different kinds of neutral stimuli, such as reading a menu, seeing people eat, or imagining food, can become conditioned stimuli that elicit a conditioned response—salivation.

Salivation serves a very useful purpose: It is a reflex response that normally occurs when you place food in your mouth. One purpose of salivation is to lubricate your mouth and throat to make chewing and swallowing food easier. Thus, being classically conditioned to salivate when reading a menu prepares your mouth for the soon-to-arrive food.

Does thinking about food make you salivate?

Conditioned salivation and taste-aversion learning are examples of how classical conditioning can have an adaptive value (Lieberman, 2000b).

Next, we'll examine how emotional responses can be classically conditioned.

Classical Conditioning and Emotions

Why do people fear needles?

At the beginning of this module, I told a sad but true childhood story of getting an injection that elicited such pain and fear that I fainted. Even 50 years later, I still fear injections and needles and always lie down to avoid fainting. In my case, you can easily identify each element of classical conditioning: The neutral stimulus is the sight of the syringe; the unconditioned stimulus is injection; and the unconditioned response is pain and fear. After a painful injection, the formerly neutral stimulus, the syringe, becomes a conditioned stimulus and elicits the conditioned response, which is fear and even fainting. Because this situation involved the conditioning of an emotional

This situation can condition fear of needles or injections.

response, my fear of injections and needles is called a conditioned emotional response (Rachman, 2002).

A *conditioned emotional response* refers to feeling some positive or negative emotion, such as happiness, fear, or anxiety, when experiencing a stimulus that initially accompanied a pleasant or painful event.

Conditioned emotional responses can have survival value, such as learning to fear and avoid stimuli that signal dangerous situations, like the sound of a rattlesnake or wail of a siren (Forsyth et al., 2000). Conditioned emotional responses can also signal pleasant situations. For example, many couples have a special song that becomes emotionally associated with their relationship. When this song is heard by one in the absence of the other, it can elicit strong emotional and romantic feelings. Thus, different kinds of stimuli can be classically conditioned to elicit strong conditioned emotional responses.

Classical Conditioning in the Brain

Where does it happen?

The young man in the photo is wearing a head gear that delivers a tone (conditioned stimulus) followed by a puff of air (unconditioned stimulus) that elicits his eye blink reflex (unconditioned response). With this classical conditioning procedure, individuals learn to blink about 90% of the time to the tone alone (conditioned response), before the air puff occurs. For both humans and animals, classical conditioning of the eye blink requires the cerebellum (right figure). Lacking the cerebellum, neither humans nor animals can acquire the conditioned eye blink response, which is a highly specific motor response (Clark et al., 2002).

Conditioning eye blink reflex

In contrast to the classically conditioned eye blink reflex, which is a motor response, the young boy on the right is acquiring a classically conditioned emotional response—fear of needles and injections. In both humans and animals, acquiring a conditioned emotional response, especially involving fear, involves a different brain structure called the amygdala (p. 80) (Dolan, 2002). Thus, classically conditioning responses in humans or animals involve different areas of the brain, depending on whether the responses are motor or emotional.

Conditioning emotional response

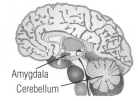

Amygdala
Cerebellum

Next, we'll go to the heart of classical conditioning and examine how and why classical conditioning works.

E. Three Explanations

Do you salivate when thinking of pizza?

Although most of us have had the experience of salivating when thinking about or seeing a favorite food, such as a pizza, researchers have given different explanations of what happens or what is learned during conditioning. We'll discuss three theories—stimulus substitution, contiguity theory, and cognitive perspective—that offer different explanations of why nearly all of us salivate when only thinking about or seeing a delicious pizza.

Stimulus Substitution & Contiguity Theory

Does the bell substitute for food?

The first explanation of classical conditioning came from Pavlov, who said the reason a dog salivated to a tone was that the tone became a substitute for the food, a theory he called stimulus substitution.

Stimulus substitution means that a neural bond or association forms in the brain between the neutral stimulus (tone) and unconditioned stimulus (food). After repeated trials, the neutral stimulus becomes the conditioned stimulus (tone) and acts like a substitute for the unconditioned stimulus (food). Thereafter, the conditioned stimulus (tone) elicits a conditioned response (salivation) that is similar to that of the unconditioned stimulus.

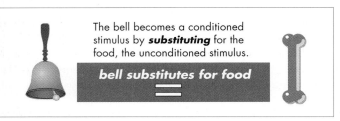

The bell becomes a conditioned stimulus by **substituting** for the food, the unconditioned stimulus.

bell substitutes for food

According to stimulus substitution theory, you salivate when you see a pizza because the act of seeing a pizza (conditioned stimulus) becomes bonded in your nervous system to the pizza itself (unconditioned stimulus). Because of this neural bond or association, the sight of pizza substitutes for the pizza, so that just the sight of a pizza can elicit salivation (conditioned response).

However, researchers discovered that the responses elicited by the unconditioned stimulus were often slightly different from those elicited by the conditioned stimulus. For example, following the unconditioned stimulus, a dog salivated and always chewed, but, following the conditioned stimulus, it salivated but rarely chewed (Zener, 1937). As a result of this and other criticisms of Pavlov's stimulus substitution theory, researchers suggested a different explanation, the contiguity theory.

The *contiguity theory* says that classical conditioning occurs because two stimuli (neutral stimulus and unconditioned stimulus) are paired close together in time (are contiguous). As a result of this contiguous pairing, the neutral stimulus becomes the conditioned stimulus, which elicits the conditioned response.

The contiguity theory says that because seeing a pizza is paired closely in time with eating it, the sight alone begins to elicit salivation. Contiguity theory was the most popular explanation of classical conditioning until the 1960s, when it was challenged by the clever research of psychologist Robert Rescorla (1966).

Cognitive Perspective

Does the bell predict food is coming?

To the surprise of many researchers, Robert Rescorla (1966, 1987, 1988) showed that an association between neutral and unconditioned stimuli did not necessarily occur when the two stimuli were closely paired in time. Instead, he found that classical conditioning occurred when a neutral stimulus contained information about what was coming next; this explanation is called the cognitive perspective.

The *cognitive perspective* says that an organism learns a predictable relationship between two stimuli such that the occurrence of one stimulus (neutral stimulus) predicts the occurrence of another (unconditioned stimulus). In other words, classical conditioning occurs because the organism learns what to expect.

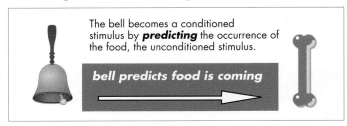

The bell becomes a conditioned stimulus by **predicting** the occurrence of the food, the unconditioned stimulus.

bell predicts food is coming

For example, the cognitive perspective theory would explain that you salivate to the sight of pizza because you have learned a predictable relationship: Seeing a pizza (conditioned stimulus) often leads to eating one (unconditioned stimulus), and your expectation causes salivation (conditioned response).

Support for the cognitive perspective comes from a number of findings. For example, classical conditioning works best if the neutral stimulus (tone) occurs slightly before the unconditioned stimulus (food). In this sequence, the organism learns a relationship between two stimuli: Tone predicts food. However, if the sequence is reversed and the unconditioned stimulus appears before the neutral stimulus, this is called *backward conditioning* and does not usually result in classical conditioning.

The cognitive perspective would explain that backward conditioning makes it impossible to predict a relationship between the neutral and unconditioned stimuli and thus does not usually result in classical conditioning. Currently, there is widespread support for the cognitive perspective, which says that classical conditioning involves learning about predictable relationships, or learning about cause and effect (Pearce & Bouton, 2003).

After the Concept Review, we'll discuss a well-known study of classical conditioning that involves the famous "Little Albert."

✔ Concept Review

 1. In classical conditioning, one of the stimuli that is chosen has two characteristics: The stimulus, such as a tone, must cause some reaction, such as being heard, seen, tasted, or smelled, but it must not elicit the unconditioned response. A stimulus with these two characteristics is called a _____.

 2. In classical conditioning, a second stimulus is chosen that can elicit an unlearned, involuntary physiological reflex, such as salivation. This stimulus is called an _____.

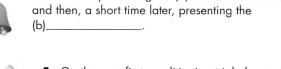 **3.** In classical conditioning, the unconditioned stimulus elicits an unlearned, involuntary physiological reflex, such as salivation, which is called the _____.

 4. A typical trial in classical conditioning involves first presenting the (a)_____ and then, a short time later, presenting the (b)_____.

 **5.** On the very first conditioning trial, the neutral stimulus (tone) did not itself elicit the unconditioned response (salivation). However, on the first trial, the presentation of food, which is called the (a)_____, did elicit salivation, called the (b)_____.

 6. After a dozen trials that paired the tone with the food, you noticed that as soon as the tone was presented, the dog salivated. Because the tone itself elicited a response similar to that elicited by the unconditioned stimulus (food), the tone is called the (a)_____. The salivation elicited by the tone itself is called the (b)_____.

 **7.** During classical conditioning, there is a tendency for a stimulus similar to the original conditioned stimulus to elicit a response similar to the conditioned response. This tendency is called _____.

 **8.** During classical conditioning, an organism learns to make a particular response to some stimuli but not to others; this phenomenon is called _____.

9. If a conditioned stimulus is repeatedly presented *without* the unconditioned stimulus, there is a tendency for the conditioned stimulus to no longer elicit the conditioned response. This phenomenon is called _____.

 10. The tendency for the conditioned response to reappear some time later, even though there are no further conditioning trials, is called _____.

11. The kind of learning in which the cues (smell, taste, auditory, or visual) of a particular stimulus are associated with an unpleasant response, such as nausea or vomiting, is called (a)_____. This kind of learning can even occur after only a single (b)_____.

12. According to Pavlov's original explanation, classical conditioning occurs because of (a)_____, which means that the conditioned stimulus (tone) bonds to the unconditioned stimulus (food). Through this bond, or association, the conditioned stimulus (tone) elicits the conditioned response (salivation) by substituting for the (b)_____ (food). Pavlov's explanation of classical conditioning was criticized, and researchers suggested instead that conditioning occurs because two stimuli are paired close together in time. This explanation, which is called (c)_____ theory, has been challenged, in turn, by more recent explanations.

13. The current and widely accepted explanation of classical conditioning, which is called the (a)_____ perspective, states that animals and humans learn a predictable relationship between stimuli. According to this explanation, a dog learns predictable relationships, such as a tone predicting the occurrence of (b)_____.

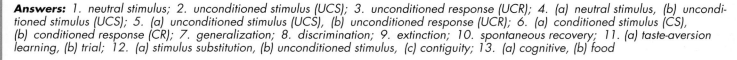
Answers: *1. neutral stimulus; 2. unconditioned stimulus (UCS); 3. unconditioned response (UCR); 4. (a) neutral stimulus, (b) unconditioned stimulus (UCS); 5. (a) unconditioned stimulus (UCS), (b) unconditioned response (UCR); 6. (a) conditioned stimulus (CS), (b) conditioned response (CR); 7. generalization; 8. discrimination; 9. extinction; 10. spontaneous recovery; 11. (a) taste-aversion learning, (b) trial; 12. (a) stimulus substitution, (b) unconditioned stimulus, (c) contiguity; 13. (a) cognitive, (b) food*

Can Emotional Responses Be Conditioned?

Why do people fear spiders?

One of the first attempts to study the development of emotional responses, such as becoming fearful, occurred in the 1920s. At this time, psychologists did not yet know if emotional responses could be conditioned. John Watson realized that he could use Pavlov's conditioning procedure to study the development of emotional behaviors in an objective way. As you may remember from Module 1, John Watson (p. 13) was a strong supporter of behaviorism, which emphasized the study of observable behaviors and the rejection of unobservable mental or cognitive events.

What follows is a first in psychology: an important classic experiment on conditioning emotions that John Watson and his student assistant, Rosalie Rayner, published in 1920.

Method: Identify Terms

Watson questioned the role that conditioning played in the development of emotional responses in children. To answer his question, Watson (photo) tried to classically condition an emotional response in a child.

Subject: Nine-month-old infant.
The subject, known later as Little Albert, was described as healthy, stolid, and unemotional, since "no one had ever seen him in a state of rage and fear. The infant practically never cried" (Watson & Rayner, 1920, p. 3).

Neutral stimulus: White rat.
Watson briefly confronted 9-month-old Albert with a succession of objects, including a white rat, a rabbit, and a dog. "At no time did this infant ever show fear in any situation" (Watson & Rayner, 1920, p. 2).

Rat is neutral stimulus.

Unconditioned stimulus: Noise.
Standing behind Albert, the researchers hit a hammer on a metal bar, which made a loud noise and elicited startle and crying. "This is the first time an emotional situation in the laboratory has produced any fear or crying in Albert" (Watson & Rayner, 1920, p. 3).

BANG !

Bang is UCS.

Unconditioned response: Startle/cry.
Startle and crying were observable and measurable emotional responses that indicated the baby was feeling and expressing fear.

After Watson identified the three elements of classical conditioning, he and his assistant, Rayner, began the procedure for classical conditioning.

Startle is UCR.

Procedure: Establish and Test for Classical Conditioning

Establish. At the age of 11 months, Albert was given repeated trials consisting of a neutral stimulus, a white rat, followed by an unconditioned stimulus, a loud noise. During early trials, he startled at the sight of the rat and on later trials he also cried.

Rat (neutral stimulus) plus loud bang (UCS) elicits startle response (UCR).

Test. When first presented with the rat alone (no noise), Albert startled. Then he was given additional conditioning trials and retested with the rat alone (no noise). "The instant the rat was shown the baby began to cry" (Watson & Rayner, 1920, p. 5). Thus, Watson had succeeded in classically conditioning Albert's emotional response (fear).

Classical conditioning: rat (CS) alone elicits startle response (CR).

Results and Conclusions

Watson and Rayner had shown that Albert developed a conditioned emotional response of startle and crying to the sight of a rat, which lasted about a week and then diminished, or underwent *extinction.*

After Albert was conditioned to fear a white rat, he was shown other objects to test for *generalization.* For example, he crawled away and cried at the sight of a rabbit, and he turned away and cried at the sight of a fur coat. But he showed no fear of blocks, paper, or Watson's hairy head, which indicates *discrimination.*

Watson's conditioning of Albert was more of a demonstration than a rigorously controlled experiment. For example, Watson and Rayner did not use a standardized procedure for presenting stimuli, and they sometimes removed Albert's thumb from his mouth, which may have made him cry. Watson was also criticized for not unconditioning Albert's fears before he left the hospital.

Rabbit elicits startle (CR) is an example of generalization.

Although other researchers failed to replicate Watson and Rayner's results, this was the first demonstration that emotional responses could be classically conditioned in humans (Samelson, 1980). Watson's demonstration laid the groundwork for explaining how people can acquire conditioned emotional responses, such as developing a fear of needles or injections.

We've discussed how emotional responses can be conditioned; next, we'll show how conditioned emotional responses can influence a person's behavior.

In the Dentist's Chair

What goes on at the dentist's?

As you sit in the dentist's chair, two interesting psychological factors are at work: the possibility of being classically conditioned and the possibility of perceiving more or less pain (Johnsen et al., 2003).

Earlier, we discussed the likely possibility of being classically conditioned during dental treatment. For example, in the dentist's chair you'll receive unconditioned stimuli (injection, drilling), which elicit unconditioned responses (pain, fear, and anxiety), which, in turn, can be conditioned to a variety of neutral stimuli

Classical conditioning: smell (CS) plus drilling (UCS) elicits pain (UCR).

(smells, sights, sounds, or images). At the beginning of this module we discussed how Carla's anxiety was conditioned to the smell of the dentist's aftershave lotion (p. 198).

As we also discussed earlier, pain is somewhat unlike other senses in that the intensity of pain can be increased or decreased by a number of psychological factors, such as your ability to relax or refocus your attention on something else (p. 112). Now we'll discuss how cultural factors can influence the conditioning of dental fears, which in turn can increase or decrease the visits to dentists in different countries (Milgrom et al., 1994).

Cultural Practices

Which citizens have most dental fears?

As the graph below indicates, the percentage of children reporting high levels of dental fear is considerably greater in the United States and Asia (Singapore and Japan) than in Scandinavia (Norway and Sweden) (Chellappah et al., 1990; Klingberg & Hwang, 1994; Milgrom et al., 1994; Neverlien & Johnsen, 1991).

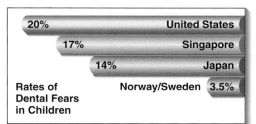

Rates of Dental Fears in Children

- United States 20%
- Singapore 17%
- Japan 14%
- Norway/Sweden 3.5%

One reason behind cultural differences in rates of dental fear is that the countries have different systems of dental care. In Scandinavian countries, dental care is part of a free, universal health care program available to all citizens. Because it is free and easily available, Scandinavian children tend to receive regular dental care rather than be treated only for dental emergencies. These children view dental treatment as unpleasant but necessary.

In contrast, neither America nor Japan provides free, universal dental coverage. Consequently, some children receive treatment only when there is a serious and painful dental problem. As a result, a child's first dental experience is more painful and something to be avoided. This is an example of how cultural practices influence the "painfulness" of dental treatments.

Origins

When did dental fears develop?

American and Asian adults who reported high rates of dental fears were asked when their fears began. About 66% replied that they acquired their dental fears in childhood or adolescence, often after a painful treatment that was necessitated by a dental emergency (Milgrom et al., 1995; Poulton et al., 1997). These fearful adults reported that the more painful their childhood dental experiences had been, the greater was their fear (Milgrom et al., 1992).

Researchers concluded that the majority of dental fears are acquired in childhood or adolescence, often through classical conditioning. In addition, these fears can keep individuals from asking for or receiving dental treatment for future but necessary dental problems (Abrahamsson et al., 2002).

Effects of Fear

Which citizens most avoid dentists?

Once dental fears are established, about 20–40% of these individuals report avoiding regular checkups or routine dental treatment (graph below). Usually, these individuals seek dental treatment only when they have emergency problems,

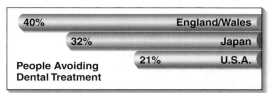

People Avoiding Dental Treatment

- England/Wales 40%
- Japan 32%
- U.S.A. 21%

which tend to involve very painful procedures. As a result, painful emergency dental procedures strengthen their already high level of fears and start a new vicious circle of avoiding dental treatment until the next emergency. From our knowledge of classical conditioning, we know that one way to reduce high levels of dental fear is to receive regular, nonpainful dental checkups and treatment, which will extinguish some of the conditioned emotional responses (Litt et al., 1999).

Based on these data, researchers concluded that cultural differences, such as kind and frequency of dental treatment in childhood and adolescence, affect both a child's perception of pain and the occurrence of conditioned emotional responses—in this case, fear of dentists (Milgrom et al., 1994).

Next, we'll examine another kind of treatment—chemotherapy for cancer—that also involves classical conditioning and results in a terrible problem—conditioned nausea.

H. Application: Conditioned Fear & Nausea

Why do people faint from fear?

At the beginning of this module, I related my childhood experience of receiving an injection and then fainting. This one trial of classical conditioning resulted in my fear of needles, which remains with me to this present day. My

Conditioned emotional response

experience illustrates the powerful effect that conditioned emotional responses can have on our behavior. If you still doubt that relatively nonthreatening stimuli (needle, blood) can be conditioned to elicit such a powerful physiological response as fainting, you'll be convinced by the next study (Page, 2003).

Conditioned Emotional Response

About 5–20% of adults report a fear of needles, injections, or seeing blood that often began before the age of 10 (Vogele et al., 2003). Wondering why some people feel faint at the sight of blood, researchers asked 30 such subjects to watch a movie on open-heart surgery as their heart rates were monitored. During the movie, 4 of the 30 subjects unexpectedly fainted.

For example, the graph shows that after 4 minutes of watching the open-heart surgery movie, one subject

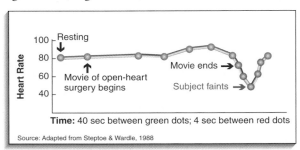

Time: 40 sec between green dots; 4 sec between red dots

Source: Adapted from Steptoe & Wardle, 1988

became so fearful and anxious that his body went into mild shock and he fainted. The reason this subject fainted from simply watching a movie on open-heart surgery was that he had developed a conditioned emotional response, intense fear, to the sight of blood (Steptoe & Wardle, 1988). Intense fear triggers tremendous changes in heart rate and blood pressure that can cause many physiological changes, including fainting.

Classical conditioning can also trigger nausea to a particular odor.

Anticipatory Nausea

At the beginning of this module, we told you about Michelle, who was receiving chemotherapy treatment for breast cancer. One side effect of the powerful anticancer drugs used in chemotherapy is nausea, which may be accompanied by severe vomiting that lasts 6–12 hours.

As Michelle received additional chemotherapy injections, she experienced nausea when she smelled the treatment room or smelled her dish soap, which smelled like the treatment room. Michelle's problem is called anticipatory nausea. *Anticipatory nausea* refers to feelings of nausea that are elicited by stimuli associated with nausea-inducing chemotherapy treatments.

Anticipatory nausea is an example of classical conditioning.

Patients experience nausea after treatment but also before or in anticipation of their treatment. Researchers believe that conditioned nausea occurs through classical conditioning.

For example, by their fourth injection, 60–70% of the patients who receive chemotherapy experience anticipatory nausea when they encounter smells, sounds, sights, or images related to treatment (Montgomery & Bovbjerg, 1997). Even 1–2 years after treatment ends, patients may continue to experience anticipatory nausea if they encounter cues associated with chemotherapy (Fredrickson et al., 1993). What makes conditioned nausea especially troublesome is that current medication does not always control it.

First we'll discuss how conditioned nausea occurs and then how it can be controlled with a nonmedical treatment.

Conditioning Anticipatory Nausea

A few weeks after beginning her chemotherapy, Michelle began to experience anticipatory nausea that was triggered by a number of different stimuli, including the smell of her dish detergent, which smelled similar to the treatment room. Now that you know her situation, perhaps you can identify the terms and explain how classical conditioning occurred.

- **Neutral stimulus** is the smell of the treatment room and her dish detergent, which initially did not cause any nausea.
- **Unconditioned stimulus** is the chemotherapy, which elicits nausea and vomiting.
- **Unconditioned responses** are the nausea and vomiting, which were elicited by chemotherapy, the unconditioned stimulus.

- **Conditioning trials** involve presenting the neutral stimulus, smell of the treatment room (same as her detergent), with the unconditioned stimulus, the chemotherapy.
- **Conditioned stimulus** (smell of the treatment room or detergent), when presented by itself, now elicits the conditioned response (nausea).

Once established, anticipatory nausea can be very difficult to treat and control with drugs (Montgomery & Bovbjerg, 1997). Even after chemotherapy ends, anticipatory nausea may reappear for a while, which is an example of spontaneous recovery.

However, there is a nonmedical treatment for anticipatory nausea, which is also based on classical conditioning. This treatment is called systematic desensitization, which we'll discuss next.

Dish soap is CS.

Can you "uncondition" fearful things?

Because of repeated chemotherapy sessions, Michelle developed anticipatory nausea (right photo), which was not relieved by medication. She is now going to try a nonmedical treatment called systematic desensitization.

Systematic desensitization is a procedure based on classical conditioning, in which a person imagines or visualizes fearful or anxiety-evoking stimuli and then immediately uses deep relaxation to overcome the anxiety. Systematic desensitization is a form of counterconditioning because it replaces, or counters, fear and anxiety with relaxation.

Learning to decrease anxiety through systematic desensitization

Essentially, systematic desensitization is a procedure to "uncondition," or overcome, fearful stimuli by pairing anxiety-provoking thoughts or images with feelings of relaxation. Systematic desensitization was developed by Joseph Wolpe in the early 1950s and has become one of the most frequently used nonmedical therapies for relief of anxiety and fears in both children and adults (M. A. Williams & Gross, 1994). Just as anticipatory nausea is based on Pavlov's classical conditioning, so too is systematic desensitization (Wolpe & Plaud, 1997).

In Michelle's case, she will try to "uncondition," or override, the anxiety-producing cues of chemotherapy, such as smells and sights, with feelings of relaxation. The procedure for systematic desensitization involves the three steps described below (Wolpe & Lazarus, 1966).

Systematic Desensitization Procedure: Three Steps

Step 1. Learning to relax

Michelle is taught to relax by tensing and relaxing sets of muscles, beginning with the muscles in her toes and continuing up

1st step is learning to relax on cue.

to the muscles in her calves, thighs, back, arms, shoulders, neck, and finally face and forehead. She practices doing this intentional relaxation for about 15 to 20 minutes every day for several weeks.

After learning how to relax her body at will, she goes on to Step 2.

Step 2. Making an anxiety hierarchy

Most Stressful
8. Vomiting
7. Feeling nausea
6. Receiving injection
5. In treatment room
4. Smelling chemicals
3. In waiting room
2. Entering clinic
1. Driving to clinic

2nd step is making a list of items that elicit anxiety.

Michelle makes up a list of 7–12 stressful situations associated with chemotherapy treatment. As shown above, she arranges her list of situations in a hierarchy that goes from least to most stressful. For example, the least stressful situations are driving to and entering the clinic, and the most stressful are nausea and vomiting. Now she's ready for Step 3.

Step 3. Imagining and relaxing

Michelle *first* puts herself into a deeply relaxed state and then vividly imagines the least stressful situation, driving to the clinic. She is told to remain in a relaxed state while imagining this situation. If she becomes anxious or stressed, she is told to stop imagining this situation and return instead to a relaxed state. Once she is sufficiently relaxed, she again imagines driving to the clinic. If she can imagine driving to the clinic while remaining in a relaxed state, she goes to the next stressful situation.

She then imagines entering the clinic, while remaining in a relaxed state. She continues up the anxiety hierarchy, imagining in turn each of the eight stressful stimuli while keeping herself in a

Most Stressful
8. Vomiting
7. Feeling nausea
6. Receiving injection
5. In treatment room
4. Smelling chemicals
3. In waiting room
2. Entering clinic
1. Driving to clinic

+

3rd step is combining relaxation with items in anxiety hierarchy.

relaxed state. At the first sign of feeling anxious, she stops and returns to a relaxed state. After returning to a relaxed state, she continues with this procedure until she reaches the most stressful situation in her anxiety hierarchy.

Effectiveness of Systematic Desensitization

As Michelle associates relaxation with each stressful situation in the hierarchy, she overcomes, or counterconditions, each stimulus in her hierarchy. In other words, systematic desensitization can be thought of as using relaxation to get rid of the stressful and anxious feelings that have become associated with a variety of stimuli that are listed in the hierarchy.

Systematic desensitization has been found to be very effective in treating a wide variety of fearful and anxiety-producing behaviors,

including conditioned nausea and fear of blood, injections, snakes, and speaking in public (Hasselt & Hersen, 1994).

We have discussed the many sides of classical conditioning, from salivation to fainting, from taste aversion to little Albert's conditioned emotional responses, from bait shyness in rats to dental fears in humans, from anticipatory nausea to systematic desensitization. It's evident that classical conditioning has a considerable influence on many of our thoughts, emotions, and behaviors.

A. THREE KINDS OF LEARNING

1. A relatively permanent change in behavior that involves specific stimuli and/or responses that change as a result of experience is a definition of _____. The change in behavior includes both unobservable mental events and observable behavioral responses.

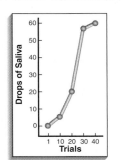

2. Psychologists have identified three different principles that are the basis for three different kinds of learning. One kind of learning can be traced to Pavlov's well-known experiment in which a bell was sounded and then food was placed in a dog's mouth. After a number of trials in which the bell and food were presented, the dog began to salivate to the bell alone. Pavlov called this kind of learning a conditioned reflex, which today is called _____.

3. A second kind of learning grew out of Thorndike's observations of cats learning to escape from a box. To explain a cat's goal-directed behavior of hitting a latch to get food, Thorndike formulated a principle of learning called the (a)_____. This law states that if certain random actions are followed by a pleasurable consequence or reward, such actions are strengthened and will likely occur in the future. Today, the law of effect has become part of the second kind of learning that is called (b)_____.

4. A third kind of learning involves mental processes, such as attention and memory; may be learned through observation or imitation; and may not involve any external rewards or require the person to perform any observable behaviors. This kind of learning is called _____.

B. PROCEDURE: CLASSICAL CONDITIONING

5. Suppose you wanted to classically condition your roommate to salivate at the sight of a psychology textbook. One procedure for establishing classical conditioning would be to present two stimuli close together in time. The presentation of the two stimuli is called a trial. In our example, a typical trial would involve first presenting a psychology textbook, initially called the (a)_____, which does not elicit salivation. A short time later, you would present a piece of brownie, called the (b)_____ stimulus, which elicits salivation. Salivation, an innate, automatic, and involuntary physiological reflex, is called the (c)_____.

6. After giving your roommate about a dozen trials, you observe that, as soon as you show him the psychology text, he begins to salivate. Because the sight of the psychology textbook itself elicits salivation, the psychology text has become a (a)_____. The roommate's salivation at the sight of the psychology book, presented alone, is called the (b)_____. You know that classical conditioning is established when the neutral stimulus becomes the (c)_____ and elicits the (d)_____. Compared to the unconditioned response, the conditioned response is usually similar in appearance but smaller in amount or magnitude.

C. OTHER CONDITIONING CONCEPTS

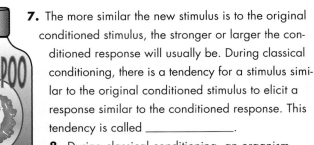

7. The more similar the new stimulus is to the original conditioned stimulus, the stronger or larger the conditioned response will usually be. During classical conditioning, there is a tendency for a stimulus similar to the original conditioned stimulus to elicit a response similar to the conditioned response. This tendency is called _____.

8. During classical conditioning, an organism learns to make a particular response to some stimuli but not to others; this phenomenon is called _____.

9. If a conditioned stimulus is repeatedly presented without the unconditioned stimulus, there is a tendency for the conditioned stimulus to no longer elicit the conditioned response; this phenomenon is called (a)_____. However, if some time later you again presented the psychology text to your roommate without giving him a brownie, he would show salivation, the conditioned response. This recurrence of the conditioned response after it has been extinguished is called (b)_____.

D. ADAPTIVE VALUE & USES

10. After receiving an injection, people may develop fear or anxiety in the presence of stimuli associated with the treatment. If we feel fear or anxiety in the presence of some stimulus that precedes a painful or aversive event, we are experiencing a _____.

11. A powerful form of classical conditioning occurs in real life when a neutral stimulus is paired with an unpleasant response, such as nausea or vomiting. The result of this conditioning is called _____. This form of classical conditioning is unusual in two ways: It may be acquired in a single trial and may last a relatively long period of time; and there may be a considerable lapse of time between the presentations of the two stimuli.

12. We now know that animals and humans are biologically prepared to associate certain combinations of conditioned and unconditioned stimuli more easily than others. This phenomenon is called

_____.

13. Classical conditioning of the eye blink reflex, which is a motor response, requires a brain structure called the (a)_____. Acquiring a classically conditioned emotional response, especially involving fear, involves a different brain structure called the (b)_____.

14. The occurrence of salivation in response to the thought, sight, or smell of food is helpful to digestion and shows that classical conditioning has an _____ role or value.

E. THREE EXPLANATIONS

15. According to Pavlov's explanation, classical conditioning occurs because a neural bond or association forms between the conditioned stimulus and unconditioned stimulus so that the conditioned stimulus eventually substitutes for the unconditioned stimulus. Pavlov's explanation is called _____.

16. The explanation that says that classical conditioning occurs because two stimuli (the neutral and unconditioned stimuli) are paired close together in time is called the _____ theory. However, researchers have shown that contiguity or simply pairing stimuli close together does not necessarily produce classical conditioning.

17. The explanation of classical conditioning that says that an organism learns a relationship between two stimuli such that the occurrence of one stimulus predicts the occurrence of the other is called the (a)_____. This theory is supported by the idea that classical conditioning is not usually learned if the unconditioned stimulus appears before the neutral stimulus, a procedure that is called (b)_____.

F. RESEARCH FOCUS: CONDITIONING LITTLE ALBERT

18. An emotional response, fear, was classically conditioned in Little Albert by presenting a white rat, which was the (a)_____, and then making a loud noise, which was the (b)_____; in turn, the loud noise elicited crying, which was the (c)_____. Albert's conditioned emotional response, crying, also occurred in the presence of stimuli

similar to the white rat, such as a rabbit; this phenomenon is called (d)_____. Albert did not cry at the sight of blocks or papers; this phenomenon is called (e)_____. Watson and Rayner were the first to demonstrate that (f)_____ responses could be classically conditioned in humans.

G. CULTURAL DIVERSITY: CONDITIONING DENTAL FEARS

19. In the United States and Asia, the percentage of children reporting (a)_____ is considerably greater than in Scandinavia. A likely reason for this difference in dental fears is different (b)_____ practices. The majority of people with high levels of dental fears report that these fears originated in childhood, probably through the occurrence of (c)_____.

H. APPLICATION: CONDITIONED FEAR & NAUSEA

20. During chemotherapy, about 60% of the patients develop nausea in anticipation of, or when encountering stimuli associated with, the actual treatment. This type of nausea, which is called _____, cannot always be treated with drugs and may persist long after the chemotherapy ends. Researchers believe that conditioned nausea is learned through classical conditioning.

Most Stressful
8. Vomiting
7. Feeling nausea
6. Receiving injection
5. In treatment room
4. Smelling chemicals
3. In waiting room
2. Entering clinic
1. Driving to clinic

21. A nondrug treatment for conditioned nausea involves a procedure based on classical conditioning in which a person imagines or visualizes fearful or anxiety-evoking stimuli and then immediately uses deep (a)_____ to decrease the anxiety associated with these stimuli. This procedure, which is called (b)_____, is a form of counterconditioning because it uses deep relaxation to replace or decrease the fear or anxiety with particular (c)_____ that are arranged in a hierarchy.

Answers: 1. learning; 2. classical conditioning; 3. (a) law of effect, (b) operant conditioning; 4. cognitive learning; 5. (a) neutral stimulus, (b) unconditioned stimulus, (c) unconditioned response; 6. (a) conditioned stimulus, (b) conditioned response, (c) conditioned stimulus, (d) unconditioned response; 7. generalization; 8. discrimination; 9. (a) extinction, (b) spontaneous recovery; 10. conditioned emotional response; 11. taste-aversion learning; 12. preparedness; 13. (a) cerebellum, (b) amygdala; 14. adaptive, or survival; 15. stimulus substitution; 16. contiguity; 17. (a) cognitive perspective, (b) backward conditioning; 18. (a) neutral stimulus, (b) unconditioned stimulus, (c) unconditioned response, (d) generalization, (e) discrimination, (f) conditioned emotional; 19. (a) dental fears, (b) cultural, (c) classical conditioning; 20. anticipatory nausea; 21. (a) relaxation, (b) systematic desensitization, (c) stimuli or situations

Can Your Beliefs Make You Sick?

The dream of many snackers is to find potato chips that taste great but are also low in calories, which means low in fat. The potato chip eater's dream came true in the late 1990s, when the U.S. Food and Drug Administration (FDA) approved a fat substitute called olestra.

Olestra is not absorbed by the body so it is calorie free and meant that potato chips suddenly lost half their calories. However, one concern with olestra is the possible side effects of nausea, stomach cramps, gas, and loose stools (diarrhea), which had been reported in subjects who had eaten foods containing olestra at every meal for two months. Because of possible side effects, there's a warning label printed on bags containing olestra potato chips: "Olestra may cause abdominal cramping and loose stools." As potato chips and other foods containing olestra became widely available and very popular, there were reports of stomach problems, and critics demanded that olestra be taken off the market.

Researchers studied the side effects of eating potato chips containing olestra by giving each of 1,123 volunteers, ages 13–88, a large bag of potato chips to eat during a movie. Before the movie, volunteers were told that they were taking part in a potato chip test, that they could eat as many chips as they wished, and that there was the possibility of experiencing certain side effects, such as stomach cramps, gas, nausea, or loose stools. But they were not

Olestra may cause abdominal cramping and loose stools.

told that half of them randomly got bags of olestra potato chips while the other half got regular chips. To be extra careful, the researchers who analyzed the data did not know which volunteers got which bags.

When the volunteers were interviewed four days later, 15.8% who had eaten olestra potato chips (ate average of 2.1 ounces) reported having one or more side effects, such as gas, cramping, nausea, or diarrhea. However, 17.6% of those who had eaten regular potato chips (ate average of 2.7 ounces) also reported one or more of these stomach problems. There was no statistical difference between groups, which means that both groups experienced about the same number of stomach-related side effects.

Of those who ate regular potato chips, 17.6% may have reported unpleasant side effects because they were initially told that they might experience stomach problems and their expectations or beliefs somehow produced these side effects.

The olestra warning was lifted in 2003 because the side effects, if they occurred, were mild and rare. (Adapted from Hellmich, 1998; Associated Press, 2003)

Questions

1. Why might people who ate foods containing olestra at every meal for two months be more likely to experience side effects than someone who has a bag of chips once a day?

2. Why wasn't olestra taken off the market when some users reported getting stomach pains or loose stools?

3. What is the name of this research approach in which neither the volunteers nor the researchers knew who received which kinds of potato chips?

4. Don't the numbers prove that those who ate regular chips reported more side effects than those who ate olestra chips?

5. How is it possible for a person's beliefs or expectations to produce physical side effects?

Try InfoTrac to search for terms: olestra, fat substitutes.

1. Those who ate food with olestra 3 times a day for 2 months received a larger dose of olestra than someone who eats only a bag of chips a day. Generally, the higher the dose, the greater the chances of experiencing unwanted side effects.

2. As discussed on pages 30–31, evidence based on personal experiences, which are called testimonials, has a high potential for error and bias and thus is not very reliable. In addition, we know that people's beliefs can greatly influence their responses to placebos and result in real physical benefits or problems (p. 111).

3. In studying effects of chemicals or drugs, researchers use a double-blind procedure (pp. 37, 111), in which neither the subjects nor researchers know who got which treatment. The double-blind procedure greatly reduces error and bias that can come from

beliefs or expectations of either subjects or researchers.

4. The raw numbers (17.6% versus 15.8%) seem to indicate that the group that ate regular potato chips had more side effects. However, researchers used statistical tests (p. 37) and found that this difference (17.6% versus 15.8%) was not due to treatment (eating olestra) but rather to chance (other factors).

5. Most people have experienced stomach problems after eating a variety of foods, and this may result in a kind of classical conditioning called taste-aversion learning (p. 200). Similarly, if people are told and then expect or believe that they may experience stomach problems after eating potato chips (olestra or regular), their beliefs or expectations may somehow trigger or produce these stomach-related side effects (p. 111).

Links to Learning

LEARNING ACTIVITIES

- **POWERSTUDY CD-ROM 2.0**
  by Tom Doyle and Rod Plotnik
  Check out the "Classical Conditioning" SuperModule (disk 1) on PowerStudy. This is a completely self-paced module that is fully narrated. Don't want the narration? It is easy to turn off! This module includes:

  - Videos—Imbedded videos discuss taste aversion in wolves and include a historic 1920 video of Watson's little Albert.
  - A multitude of animations designed to help you understand classical and operant conditioning and cognitive learning.
  - A test of your knowledge using an interactive version of the Summary Test on pages 208 and 209. Also access related quizzes.
  - An interactive version of the Critical Thinking exercise "Can Your Beliefs Make You Sick?" on page 210.
  - Key terms, a chapter outline, and hotlinked Web sites.

- **SELF-STUDY ASSESSMENT**
  Want help studying? For your customized Study Plan go to **http://psychology.wadsworth.com/plotnik7e/**. This program will automatically generate pretests and posttests to help you determine what you have mastered and what needs work.

WebTUTOR

- **STUDY GUIDE and WEBTUTOR**
  Check the corresponding module in your Study Guide for effective student tips and help learning the material presented.

- **INFOTRAC COLLEGE EDITION ONLINE LIBRARY**
  To find interesting and relevant articles go to **http://www.infotrac-college.com**, use your password, and then type in search terms such as the ones listed below.

  Classical conditioning   Operant conditioning
  Emotional conditioning   Phobias

STUDY QUESTIONS

Use InfoTrac to search for topics mentioned in the main heads below (e.g., classical conditioning, conditioned fear).

*A. Three Kinds of Learning—Can you recall situations in which you have experienced each of the three kinds of learning? (**Suggested answer page 624**)

*B. Procedure: Classical Conditioning—How do you explain why your heart pounds when you hear the words "There will be a test next class"? (**Suggested answer page 624**)

C. Other Conditioning Concepts—If a child were bitten by a small brown dog, can you predict what other animals the child would fear?

D. Adaptive Value & Uses—Using the terms and procedures of classical conditioning, can you explain how a person might develop a fear of flying?

E. Three Explanations—How would you explain why your cat runs into the kitchen and salivates each time you open the refrigerator door?

F. Research Focus: Conditioning Little Albert—What happens when you look into your rear-view mirror and see a police car's flashing lights?

G. Cultural Diversity: Conditioning Dental Fears—As a parent, how can you decrease the chances that your child will become fearful of dental treatment?

*H. Application: Conditioned Fear & Nausea—How would systematic desensitization be used to help reduce a student's test anxiety? (**Suggested answer page 624**)

*These questions are answered in Appendix B.

Module 10: Operant & Cognitive Approaches

PowerStudy 2.0™
Complete Module

Learning 45 Commands

How did Bart become a movie star?

It was an unusual movie for two reasons. First, there was almost no dialogue: Human actors spoke only 657 words. Second, the star of the movie was a nonspeaking, nonhuman, 12-year-old, 10-foot-tall, 1,800-pound, enormous brown Kodiak bear named Bart (shown on the left). Bart is one of the world's largest land-dwelling carnivores and can, with one swipe of his massive 12-inch paw, demolish anything in his path. Yet, in the movie, there was big bad Bart, sitting peacefully on his haunches, cradling a small bear cub in his arms. "So what?" you might say, but what you don't know is that, in the wild, a Kodiak bear normally kills and eats any cub it encounters.

Bart the bear learned to perform 45 behaviors on cue through operant conditioning.

Because Bart was found as a cub and raised by a human trainer, Bart grew to act more like an overgrown teddy bear than a natural-born killer. For his role in the movie *The Bear,* Bart learned to perform 45 behaviors on cue, such as sitting, running, standing up, roaring, and, most difficult of all, cradling a teddy bear, which is not what an adult bear does in the wild.

The training procedure seems deceptively simple: Each time Bart performed a behavior on cue, the trainer, Doug Seus, gave Bart an affectionate back scratch, an ear rub, or a juicy apple or pear. For example, when the trainer raised his arms high in the air, it was the signal for Bart to sit and hold the teddy bear. After Bart correctly performed this behavior, Doug would give him a reward. After Bart learned to perform all these behaviors with a stuffed teddy bear, a live bear cub was substituted and the scene was filmed for the movie (Cerone, 1989).

Bart learned to perform 45 behaviors on cue through a kind of learning called operant conditioning.

Operant conditioning, also called instrumental conditioning, is a kind of learning in which an animal or human performs some behavior, and the following consequence (reward or punishment) increases or decreases the chance that an animal or human will again perform that same behavior.

For example, if Bart performed a particular behavior, such as picking up a teddy bear, the consequence that followed—getting a rewarding apple—increased the chance that Bart would again pick up the teddy bear. Because of what Bart learned through operant conditioning, he has starred in 20 movies and is currently the highest paid animal actor, making about $10,000 a day (J. Brennan, 1997). That's a salary that most of us would be very happy to bear!

Operant conditioning seems rather straightforward. You perform an action or operate on your environment, such as studying hard. The consequence of your studying, such as how well you do on exams, increases or decreases the likelihood that you will perform the same behavior—studying hard—in the future.

Besides learning by having your behaviors rewarded or punished, you can also learn in a very different way.

Learning to Golf

What did Jack learn from just watching?

In operant conditioning, the learning process is out in the open: Bart performs an observable response (holds a teddy bear), which is followed by an observable consequence (gets an apple). But there is another kind of learning that involves unobservable mental processes and unobservable rewards that you may give yourself. This kind of learning, called cognitive learning, is partly how Jack learned to golf.

According to his parents, Jack began watching the Golf Channel as a toddler. When he was only 13 months old, Jack was imitating the golfers he had been watching on television. He would take his tiny plastic golf club and hit Wiffle® balls (hollow plastic balls with holes) in the living room, sometimes beaning his dad on the head. Although Jack, now age 3, is much too young to play on a real golf course, he loves to practice on a range and often cries when he has to leave. Three-year-old Jack stands 3 feet 1 inch tall and can drive balls 70 yards and putt from 15 feet (right photo). His father, a casual golfer, was surprised when Jack began taking such a keen interest in golf, something he had only seen on the Golf Channel. On his own initiative and without any special encouragement or guidance from his parents, little Jack had begun imitating what he had seen on television.

The process Jack used to learn golfing is very different from the operant conditioning procedure used to teach Bart new behaviors. During operant conditioning, Bart performed observable behaviors (hold a teddy bear), which were influenced by observable consequences (getting an apple). In comparison, Jack learned how to swing a golf club through observation and imitation, which involved unobservable mental processes and is called cognitive learning. We'll discuss cognitive learning later in this module.

Jack learned to play golf partly from watching the Golf Channel on TV.

What's Coming

In the first half of this module, we'll discuss the history and procedure of operant conditioning, how operant conditioning differs from classical conditioning, how consequences or reinforcers work, and other examples of operant conditioning. In the second half of this module, we'll explain the history of cognitive learning, the theory behind observational learning, and the role of insight learning.

We'll begin with an important study that involved a cat, a puzzle box, and a smelly fish.

A. Operant Conditioning

How did Bart become a movie star?

We told you how a trainer used operant conditioning to teach Bart to perform 45 different behaviors on cue. Operant conditioning has now been applied to many different settings, such as training animals to perform, training children to use the potty, stopping retarded children from injuring themselves, and helping autistic children learn social behaviors. However, the discovery of operant behavior involved two different researchers who worked in two different laboratories on two different kinds of problems. So that you can appreciate the thinking that led to operant conditioning, we'll visit the laboratories of the two important researchers—E. L. Thorndike and B. F. Skinner.

Thorndike's Law of Effect

E. L. THORNDIKE (1874–1949)

It's the late 1800s, and we're in the laboratory of E. L. Thorndike, who is interested in animal intelligence—specifically, in measuring their capacity for reasoning.

Unlike pet owners who assume from anecdotal observations that their animals are intelligent, Thorndike devised a simple but clever way to measure reasoning in a more objective way. He built a series of puzzle boxes from which a cat could escape by learning to make a specific response, such as pulling a string or pressing a bar. Outside the puzzle box was a reward for escaping—a piece of fish.

We watch Thorndike place a cat in the puzzle box and record its escape time. After Thorndike graphs the data (graph below), we see a gradual lessening in the time needed to escape. Notice that on the first trial the cat needed over 240 seconds to hit the escape latch, but by the last trial, the cat hits the escape latch in less than 60 seconds.

Thorndike explains that, with repeated trials, the cat spends more time around the latch, which increases the chances of finding and

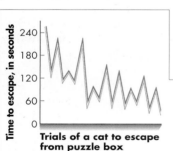

Trials of a cat to escape from puzzle box

Law of effect: In escaping puzzle box, cat's successful responses are strengthened and this results in quicker escape times.

hitting the latch and more quickly escaping to get the fish. To explain why a cat's random trial-and-error behaviors gradually turned into efficient, goal-directed behaviors, Thorndike formulated the law of effect.

The *law of effect* states that behaviors followed by positive consequences are strengthened, while behaviors followed by negative consequences are weakened.

Thorndike's (1898) findings were significant because they suggested that the law of effect was a basic law of learning and provided an objective procedure to study it. Thorndike's emphasis on studying the consequences of goal-directed behavior was further developed and expanded by B. F. Skinner.

Skinner's Operant Conditioning

B. F. SKINNER (1904–1990)

It's the 1930s, and we're in the laboratory of B. F. Skinner, who is interested in analyzing ongoing behaviors of animals. Skinner explains that Thorndike's law of effect is useful since it describes how animals are rewarded for making particular responses. However, in order to analyze ongoing behaviors, you must have an objective way to measure them. Skinner's clever solution is a unit of behavior he calls an operant response (Skinner, 1938).

An *operant response* is a response that can be modified by its consequences and is a meaningful unit of ongoing behavior that can be easily measured.

For example, suppose that out of curiosity Bart picks up a teddy bear. His picking up the teddy bear is an example of an operant response because Bart is acting or operating on the environment. The consequence of his picking up the teddy bear is that he receives an apple, which is a desirable effect. This desirable effect modifies his response by increasing the chances that Bart will repeat the same response.

By measuring or recording operant responses, Skinner can analyze animals' ongoing behaviors during learning. He calls this kind of learning *operant conditioning,* which focuses on how consequences (rewards or punishments) affect behaviors.

A simple example of operant conditioning occurs when a rat in an experimental box accidentally presses a bar. If the bar press is followed by food, this consequence increases the chance that the rat will press the bar again. As the rat presses the bar more times, more food follows, which in turn increases the chances that the rat will continue to press the bar (indicated by the rise of the blue line in the figure below).

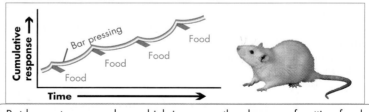

Rat learns to press a bar, which increases the chances of getting food.

Using his newly developed procedure of operant conditioning, B. F. Skinner spent the next 50 years exploring and analyzing learning in rats, pigeons, schoolchildren, and adults.

The 1920s and 1930s gave learning a mighty jolt with the discovery of two general principles—Pavlov's classical conditioning and Skinner's operant conditioning. For the first time, psychologists had two methods to analyze learning processes in an objective way.

Now we'll examine Skinner's ingenious procedure for operant conditioning in more detail.

Why does a rat press a bar?

A rat may initially press a bar out of curiosity, and whether it presses the bar again depends on the consequences. To show how consequences can affect behavior, imagine that you are looking over Skinner's shoulder as he places a rat into a box.

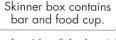
Skinner box contains bar and food cup.

The box is empty except for a bar jutting out from one side and an empty food cup below and to the side of the bar (right figure). This box, called a *Skinner box,* is automated to record the animal's bar presses and deliver food pellets. The Skinner box is an efficient way to study how an animal's ongoing behaviors may be modified by changing the consequences of what happens after a bar press.

As you watch, Skinner explains that the rat is a good subject for operant conditioning because it can use its front paws to manipulate objects, such as a bar, and it has a tendency to explore its environment, which means that it will eventually find the bar, touch it, or even press it.

Skinner goes on to explain the following three factors that are involved in operantly conditioning a rat to press a bar in the Skinner box.

1 The rat has not been fed for some hours so that it will be active and more likely to eat the food reward. A hungry rat tends to roam restlessly about, sniffing at whatever it finds.

2 The goal is to condition the rat to press the bar. By pressing the bar, the rat operates on its environment; thus, this response is called an *operant response.*

3 Skinner explains that a naive rat does not usually waltz over and press the bar. In conditioning a rat to press a bar, Skinner will use a procedure called shaping.

Shaping is a procedure in which an experimenter successively reinforces behaviors that lead up to or approximate the desired behavior.

For example, if the desired behavior is pressing the bar, here's how shaping works.

Shaping: Facing the Bar

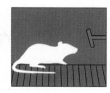

Skinner places a white rat into the (Skinner) box, closes the door, and watches the rat through a one-way mirror. At first, the rat wanders around the back of the box, but when it turns and faces the bar, Skinner releases a food pellet that makes a noise as it drops into the food cup. The rat hears the pellet drop, approaches the food cup, sees, sniffs, and eats the pellet. After eating, the rat moves away to explore the box. But, as soon as the rat turns and faces the bar, Skinner releases another pellet. The rat hears the noise, goes to the food cup, sniffs, and eats the pellet. Shaping is going well.

Shaping: Touching the Bar

As shaping continues, Skinner decides to reinforce the rat only when it actually moves toward the bar. Skinner waits and as soon as the rat faces and then moves toward the bar, Skinner releases another pellet. After eating the pellet, the rat wanders a bit but soon returns to the bar and actually sniffs it. A fourth pellet immediately drops into the cup, and the rat eats it. When the rat places one paw on the bar, a fifth pellet drops into the cup. Notice how Skinner has shaped the rat to spend all its time near the bar.

Shaping: Pressing the Bar

As soon as the rat actually puts its paws on the bar, Skinner releases a pellet. After eating, the rat puts its paws back on the bar and gets a pellet. Now Skinner waits until the rat puts its paws on the bar and actually happens to press down, which releases another pellet. Soon, the rat is pressing the bar over and over to get pellets. Notice how Skinner reinforced the rat's behaviors that led up to or approximated the desired behavior of bar pressing.

Immediate Reinforcement

Depending on the rat and the trainer's experience, it may take from minutes to an hour to shape a rat to press a bar. Skinner explains that in shaping behavior, the food pellet, or *reinforcer,* should follow *immediately* after the desired behavior. By following immediately, the reinforcer is associated with the desired behavior and not with some other behavior that just happens to occur. If the reinforcer is delayed, the animal may be reinforced for some undesired or superstitious behavior.

Superstitious behavior is a behavior that increases in frequency because its occurrence is accidentally paired with the delivery of a reinforcer.

When I was a graduate student, I conditioned my share of superstitious rat behaviors, such as making them turn in circles or stand up instead of pressing the bar. That's because I accidentally but immediately reinforced a rat after it performed the wrong behavior.

Humans, especially professional baseball players, report a variety of superstitious behaviors that were accidentally reinforced after getting a hit. For example, a five-time batting champion (Wade Boggs) eats chicken every day he plays, allows no one else to touch his bats, and believes each bat has a certain number of hits. Once a batter's superstitious behaviors are reinforced, especially after getting a big hit or home run, superstitious behaviors tend to persist and can be very difficult to eliminate. You probably have some of your own!

Next, we'll discuss several interesting examples of operant conditioning in very young humans.

A. Operant Conditioning

Have you been operantly conditioned?

Without realizing it, you may be performing a wide range of behaviors learned through operant conditioning. For example, operant conditioning was involved if you learned to put money into a jukebox to hear music, drive through a yellow traffic light to avoid stopping, study for hours to get good grades, or give flowers to your honey to see him or her smile. And you may continually perform these behaviors

because they are followed by reinforcers that increase the chances that you will perform these same behaviors again. To help you better understand how operant conditioning works, we'll discuss how its procedures and principles have been used by parents to solve two relatively common problems: getting young children to use the toilet and to stop refusing to eat a wide variety of healthy foods.

Toilet Training

Imagine that you are a parent of 3-year-old Sheryl, who is physically mature enough to begin toilet training. Here's how operant conditioning techniques can be applied to teach toilet training.

1. Target behavior. The target behavior or goal is for Sheryl to urinate in the toilet.

4 steps in toilet training

2. Preparation. Before training begins, put all of Sheryl's toys away so that she will not be distracted. Then give her a large glass of apple juice, so that she will have to urinate soon.

3. Reinforcers. Select reinforcers, which can be candy, verbal praise, or a hug. Each time Sheryl performs or emits a desired behavior, you immediately reinforce it. The reinforcer increases the likelihood that the behavior will be repeated.

4. Shaping. Just as Skinner used the shaping procedure in conditioning a rat to press a bar, you can use a similar shaping procedure in conditioning Sheryl to use the toilet. Each time Sheryl performs a behavior that leads to the target behavior (using the toilet), give her a treat, verbal praise, or a hug. For instance, when Sheryl says that she has to go potty, say, "That's great." When Sheryl enters the bathroom, say, "What a good girl." When she lowers her pants by herself, say, "You're doing really good." After Sheryl urinates into the toilet, give her a big hug and perhaps a treat.

Mothers who were supervised as they used this training procedure needed 4–18 hours to toilet train their 2- to 3-year-olds (Berk & Patrick, 1990; Matson & Ollendick, 1977). However children vary in when they are ready to begin toilet training and operant conditioning. Researchers advise that "in most cases there's no clear benefit to starting training before 24 to 27 months and in fact kids who start early often take longer to finish" (Blum, 2003).

Another difficulty parents face is when children eat only one or two favorite foods and refuse all others.

Food Refusal

Some young children with no medical problems may develop a habit of eating only certain foods and refusing all others, which may result in having an unhealthy diet or low weight (Patel et al., 2002). Researchers taught parents how to use the principles of operant conditioning to overcome food refusal in their young children.

1. Target behavior. The target behavior or goal was for the child to taste, chew, and eat a food (usually fruits or vegetables) that she or he has persistently refused to eat.

2. Preparation. Researchers first showed mothers how to shape and reinforce target behaviors. Next, each mother shaped the target behavior in her child in the home setting.

3. Reinforcers. Each time the child performed or emitted a target behavior, the mother immediately reinforced the child with a positive reinforcer, such as praise, attention, or a smile.

4. Shaping. The shaping procedure consisted of having the child notice the food and let it be placed in his or her mouth, letting the child taste the food, and, finally, having the child chew and swallow the food.

The graph below explains and shows the success of using operant conditioning to overcome food refusal in young children (Werle et al., 1993).

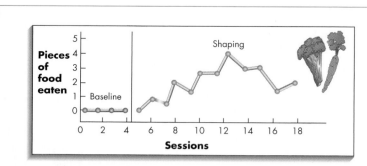

Baseline: During these four sessions, the mother offered nonpreferred food to her child, who refused the food each time.

Shaping: During these sessions, the mother shaped the child to accept nonpreferred food by giving praise, attention, and smiles each time her child made a response that was similar to or approximated the target behavior (chewing and swallowing food). Shaping proved effective in overcoming the child's habit of food refusal. Compare the child's food refusal during baseline to that during shaping sessions.

Notice that the same principles of operant conditioning apply whether the goal is to condition a child to use the potty, to overcome food refusal, or to train Bart the bear to pick up and hold a teddy bear.

Next, we'll compare the principles of operant and classical conditioning.

How are they different?

Earlier in this module, we discussed how Bart the bear was operantly conditioned to hold a teddy bear—something he would never do in the wild. As you may remember from Module 9, we discussed how Sam the dog was classically conditioned to salivate to the sound of a bell—something he would not

Bart—classically or operantly conditioned?

usually do. Although both operant and classical conditioning lead to learning, they have very different procedures and principles, which may be a little confusing. We'll try to clear up any confusion by doing a side-by-side comparison of the principles and procedures of operant and classical conditioning by using the same subject, Bart, one of the world's largest subjects.

Operant Conditioning

1 Goal. The goal of operant conditioning is to *increase or decrease the rate* of some response, which usually involves shaping. In Bart's case, the goal was to increase his rate of holding a teddy bear.

2 Voluntary response. Bart's behavior of holding a teddy bear is a voluntary response because he can perform it at will. Bart must first perform a voluntary response before getting a reward.

3 Emitted response. Bart voluntarily performs or emits some response, which Skinner called the operant response (holding teddy bear). Skinner used the term *emit* to indicate that the organism acts or operates on the environment. In most cases, animals and humans are shaped to emit the desired responses.

4 Contingent on behavior. Bart's performance of the desired response depends on, or is *contingent* on, the consequences, or what happens next. For example, each time Bart holds the teddy bear, the consequence is that he receives an apple. The apple, which is a reward (reinforcer), increases the chances that Bart will perform the desired response in the future.

The reinforcer must occur *immediately after* the desired response. In Bart's case, the reinforcer (apple) would be given immediately after Bart holds the teddy bear. If the reinforcer occurs too late, the result may be the conditioning of unwanted or superstitious responses.

5 Consequences. An animal or human's performance of some behavior is dependent or contingent on its *consequences*— that is, on what happens next. For example, the consequence of Bart's picking up and holding a teddy bear was to get an apple.

Thus, in operant conditioning, an animal or human learns that performing or *emitting* some behavior is followed by a *consequence* (reward or punishment), which, in turn, increases or decreases the chances of performing that behavior again.

Classical Conditioning

1 Goal. The goal of classical conditioning is to create a new response to a *neutral stimulus*. In Bart's case, he will make a new response, salivation, to the sound of a horn, which is the neutral stimulus because it does not usually cause Bart to salivate.

2 Involuntary response. Salivation is an example of a *physiological reflex*. Physiological reflexes (salivation, eye blink) are triggered or elicited by some stimulus and therefore called involuntary responses.

3 Elicited response. As Bart eats an apple, it will trigger the involuntary physiological reflex of salivation. Thus, eating the apple, which is called the *unconditioned stimulus*, triggers or elicits an involuntary reflex response, salivation, which is called the *unconditioned response*.

4 Conditioned response. Bart was given repeated trials during which the neutral stimulus (horn's sound) was

presented and followed by the unconditioned stimulus (apple). After repeated trials, Bart learned a relationship between the two stimuli: The horn's sound is followed by an apple. The horn's sound, or neutral stimulus, becomes the *conditioned stimulus* when its sound alone, before the occurrence of the apple, elicits salivation, which is the *conditioned response*.

For best results, the neutral stimulus is presented slightly before the unconditioned stimulus. If the unconditioned stimulus is presented before the neutral stimulus, this is called *backward conditioning* and produces little if any conditioning.

5 Expectancy. According to the *cognitive perspective* of classical conditioning, an animal or human learns a predictable relationship between, or develops an expectancy about, the neutral and unconditioned stimuli. This means Bart learned to *expect* that the neutral stimulus (horn's sound) is always followed by the unconditioned stimulus (apple). Thus, in classical conditioning, the animal or human learns a *predictable relationship* between stimuli.

One major difference between operant and classical conditioning is that in operant conditioning, the performance of some response depends on its consequence (rewards or punishment). We'll discuss the effects of different kinds of consequences next.

B. Reinforcers

Why are consequences important?

Notice where the man is sitting as he saws off a tree limb. His behavior illustrates a key principle of operant conditioning, which is that *consequences are contingent on behavior.* In this case, the man will fall on his head (consequence) if he cuts off the tree limb (behavior). Furthermore, this consequence will make the tree trimmer think twice before repeating this stupid behavior. Thus, consequences affect behavior, and in operant conditioning, there are two kinds of consequences—reinforcement and punishment.

There are serious consequences to this man's behavior!

Reinforcement is a consequence that occurs after a behavior and increases the chance that the behavior will occur again.

For example, one of the main reasons you study hard for exams is to get good grades (reinforcement). The consequence of getting a good grade increases the chances that you'll study hard for future exams.

Punishment is a consequence that occurs after a behavior and decreases the chance that the behavior will occur again.

For example, one high school used punishment to reduce students' absentee rates. Students who got more than eight unexcused absences lost very desirable privileges (no football games, no prom). In this case, punishing consequences decreased from 15% to 4% the chance of students playing hookey from school (Chavez, 1994).

Sometimes reinforcement and punishment are used together to control some behavior, as was done in treating a serious behavioral disorder called pica.

Pica is a behavioral disorder, often seen in individuals with mental retardation, that involves eating inedible objects or unhealthy substances. This can result in serious physical problems, including lead poisoning, intestinal blockage, and parasites.

Here's an example of how both reinforcement and punishment were used to treat an adolescent who suffered from pica.

CHANGING THE CONSEQUENCES

Walt was 15 years old and suffered from profound retardation. One of Walt's problems was pica, which included eating bits of paper and clothing, metal and plastic objects, and especially paint chips, from which he had gotten lead poisoning.

To control his pica, Walt was given a tray containing nonfood items (fake paint chips made from flour) and food items (crackers). Each time Walt chose a food item, he received a reinforcement—verbal praise. Each time Walt chose a paint chip, he received a mild punishment—having his face washed for 20 seconds. The graph below shows how the consequences (reinforcement or punishment) greatly modified Walt's pica behavior (Johnson et al., 1994).

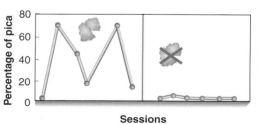

Baseline: During these sessions, Walt chose the non-food items 10—80% of the time. Compare the baseline with training sessions.

Training: During these sessions, Walt was reinforced with praise for choosing food items and punished with face washing for choosing nonfood items. These consequences greatly modified his behaviors so that he chose primarily food items.

Percentage of pica (y-axis: 0, 20, 40, 60, 80); *Sessions* (x-axis)

In this study, reinforcement and punishment proved an effective combination to treat a potentially dangerous problem. Next, we'll discuss two kinds of reinforcements.

How are an apple and an "F" alike?

Although getting an apple and getting a grade of "F" seem very different, they are both consequences that can increase the occurrence of certain behaviors. There are two kinds of reinforcements, or consequences—positive and negative—that increase the occurrence of behaviors.

POSITIVE REINFORCEMENT

Immediately after Bart the bear emitted or performed a behavior (holding a teddy bear), the trainer gave him an apple to increase the likelihood of his repeating that behavior. This situation is an example of positive reinforcement.

Positive reinforcement refers to the presentation of a stimulus that increases the probability that a behavior will occur again.

A *positive reinforcer* is a stimulus that increases the likelihood that a response will occur again.

For example, if you ask a friend for money and get it, the money is a positive reinforcer that will increase the chances of your asking again. There's a second kind of reinforcement, called negative reinforcement.

NEGATIVE REINFORCEMENT

If you have a headache and take an aspirin to get rid of it, your response of taking an aspirin is an example of negative reinforcement.

Negative reinforcement refers to an aversive (unpleasant) stimulus whose removal increases the likelihood that the preceding response will occur again.

If taking an aspirin removes your headache (aversive or unpleasant stimulus), then your response of taking an aspirin is negatively reinforced because it removes the headache and thus increases the chances of your taking an aspirin in the future. Don't be confused by the fact that both positive and negative reinforcers *increase* the frequency of the responses they follow.

Besides positive and negative reinforcers, there are also primary reinforcers, such as food, and secondary reinforcers, such as money and coupons.

How are a hamburger and a coupon alike?

A student might repeat a behavior, such as study, because the consequence is food, a primary reinforcer, or be quiet on the school bus because the consequence is a coupon, a secondary reinforcer.

PRIMARY REINFORCERS

If you made yourself study for 2 hours before rewarding yourself with a hamburger, you would be using a primary reinforcer.

Food: primary reinforcer

A *primary reinforcer* is a stimulus, such as food, water, or sex, that is innately satisfying and requires no learning on the part of the subject to become pleasurable.

Primary reinforcers, such as eating, drinking, or having sex, are unlearned and innately pleasurable. Brain scans (p. 70) showed that these activities activate the brain's built-in or inherited reward/pleasure center (Begley, 2001a). Although brain scans were discovered after Skinner, they have proven him right: Primary reinforcers are innately satisfying and require no training because they automatically activate the brain's built-in reward/pleasure center. In our example, a hamburger is a primary reinforcer for studying. However, many behaviors are aided or maintained by secondary reinforcers.

SECONDARY REINFORCERS

A school bus driver used a secondary reinforcer when he gave each child a coupon good for a pizza if he or she was quiet on the bus. A coupon is an example of a secondary reinforcer.

A *secondary reinforcer* is any stimulus that has acquired its reinforcing power through experience; secondary reinforcers are learned, such as by being paired with primary reinforcers or other secondary reinforcers.

Coupons, or secondary reinforcers, encourage children's good behaviors.

Coupons, money, grades, and praise are examples of secondary reinforcers because their value is learned or acquired through experience (LeBlanc et al., 2000). For example, children learned that coupons were valuable since they could be redeemed for pizza. The coupons became secondary reinforcers that encouraged children to choose a seat quickly and sit quietly so that the driver could get rolling in 5 minutes (K. I. George, 1995). Many of our behaviors are increased or maintained by secondary reinforcers.

Unlike primary and secondary reinforcers, which are consequences that increase behaviors, punishment has a very different effect.

Are there different kinds of punishment?

It is helpful to distinguish between positive and negative punishment.

Positive punishment refers to presenting an aversive (unpleasant) stimulus (such as spanking) after a response. The aversive stimulus decreases the chances that the response will recur.

Negative punishment refers to removing a reinforcing stimulus (a child's allowance) after a response. This removal decreases the chances that the response will recur.

Both positive and negative punishment function as "stop signs"; they stop or decrease the occurrence of a behavior. We'll discuss negative punishment in the Application section. Here, we'll explain how positive punishment was used to treat a serious disorder called self-injurious behavior.

Self-injurious behavior refers to serious and sometimes life-threatening physical damage that a person inflicts on his or her own body; this may include body or head banging, biting, kicking, poking ears or eyes, pulling hair, or intense scratching.

About 8–14% of mentally retarded individuals who live in large residential treatment facilities engage in self-injurious behavior (D. E. Williams et al., 1993). Here's an example of a treatment program that used positive punishment.

POSITIVE PUNISHMENT

Since all other treatments had failed, the State Committee for Behavior Therapy approved a program of using positive punishment to treat Suzanne, who was 24 years old and profoundly mentally retarded. For many years, she engaged in such severe self-biting and eye and ear gouging that she had to continually wear a fencing mask and special gloves to prevent self-injury. Essentially, the program involved giving Suzanne an electric shock each time she bit or harmed herself. As the graph below shows, after a dozen sessions, the use of positive punishment decreased Suzanne's self-injurious behaviors by 99%, to almost zero. After 69 treatment sessions, Suzanne's protective face mask and gloves were removed, and for the first time in 15 years, Suzanne began to feed herself, perform personal care, and refrain from self-injury (D. E. Williams et al., 1993). We'll discuss the pros and cons of using punishment in the Application section on page 233.

She had to wear special gloves so she wouldn't injure herself.

Self-Injurious Behaviors per Minute	
Before treatment	9.3
After punishment	0.07

Before punishment is used, other nonpunishment treatments based on operant conditioning are always tried. For example, some self-injurious behaviors decreased if the therapist gave attention (reinforcement) only when the patient stopped engaging in injurious behaviors or if the therapist reinforced the patient for performing particular noninjurious behaviors, such as playing games or eating candy (Olson & Houlihan, 2000).

Although somewhat confusing, remember that positive and negative punishment *decrease* the likelihood of a behavior occurring again, while positive and negative reinforcement *increase* the likelihood of a behavior occurring again.

C. Schedules of Reinforcement

Why are consequences important? On September 20, 1971, *Time* magazine recognized B. F. Skinner's influence and accomplishments in psychology and education by putting him on its cover (right photo). Just a year earlier, the *American Psychologist* rated B. F. Skinner second, after Freud, in influence on 20th-century psychology.

Skinner is perhaps best known for his discovery of operant conditioning, which is a powerful method for analyzing the individual behaviors of animals and humans. Part of his method was to study how different kinds of consequences or reinforcements affected behavior, and this led to his study of different schedules of reinforcement.

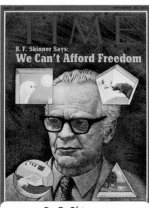

B. F. Skinner
(1904–1990)

A *schedule of reinforcement* refers to a program or rule that determines how and when the occurrence of a response will be followed by a reinforcer.

Skinner pointed out many examples of how schedules of reinforcement both maintained and controlled behaviors. For example, slot machine players don't realize that they are paid off according to a schedule of reinforcement that encourages rapid responding.

Skinner was able to study how different schedules of reinforcement affected behavior because he developed a clever method to record ongoing, individual behaviors. His method included the use of the now-famous "Skinner box" and something called the cumulative record.

Measuring Ongoing Behavior

Skinner showed how different schedules of reinforcement affected an animal's or a human's ongoing behavior with something called a cumulative record.

A *cumulative record* is a continuous written record that shows an animal's or a human's individual responses and reinforcements.

A rat in a Skinner box is shown on the left and a cumulative record is shown below. When the rat is not pressing the bar, a pen draws a straight line on a long roll of paper that unwinds slowly and continuously to the left. When the rat presses the bar, the pen moves up a notch. When the rat makes numerous responses, the pen moves up many notches to draw a line that resembles a stairway going up. If the rat presses the bar slowly, the pen notches up gradually, resulting in a gentler slope. If the rat responds quickly, the pen notches up more quickly, resulting in a steeper slope. A downward blip indicates that the rat received a

Rat in a Skinner box

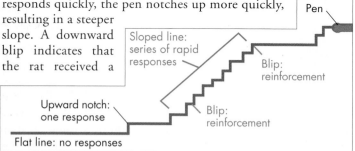

Sloped line: series of rapid responses

Pen

Blip: reinforcement

Upward notch: one response

Blip: reinforcement

Flat line: no responses

food pellet, or reinforcement (only two are shown). The cumulative record shows you an animal's ongoing responses and reinforcements across time.

We'll first look at how two general schedules of reinforcement—continuous and partial reinforcement—can greatly affect ongoing behavior.

Schedules of Reinforcement

When I first began training my dog to "come," I gave him a treat each time he responded to my command by coming to me. Later on, when he had mostly learned to come, I gave him a treat only some of the time. These situations illustrate two general schedules of reinforcement—continuous and partial.

CONTINUOUS REINFORCEMENT

Giving my dog a treat each time he responded to my command by coming to me illustrates the schedule of continuous reinforcement.

Continuous reinforcement means that every occurrence of the operant response results in delivery of the reinforcer.

In the real world, relatively few of our behaviors are on a continuous reinforcement schedule because very few things or people are as reliable as my dog. Continuous reinforcement is often used in the initial stages of operant conditioning because it results in rapid learning of some behavior.

Every response is reinforced.

PARTIAL REINFORCEMENT

After my dog had mostly learned to come on command, I gave him a treat about every fifth time, which illustrates the schedule of partial reinforcement.

Partial reinforcement refers to a situation in which responding is reinforced only some of the time.

In the real world, many of our behaviors are on a partial reinforcement schedule, which is very effective in maintaining behavior over the long run. My dog keeps coming to me on command because some of the time he gets a treat.

Only some responses are reinforced.

We'll discuss the four common schedules of partial reinforcement and show how differently they affect behavior.

Which schedule are you on?

We'll discuss four different schedules of partial reinforcement, each of which has a different effect on controlling and maintaining animal and human behaviors.

Fixed-Ratio Schedule

If factory workers are paid after packing six boxes, they are on a fixed-ratio schedule.

Fixed-ratio schedule means that a reinforcer occurs only after a fixed number of responses are made by the subject.

A fixed-ratio schedule is often used to pay assembly-line workers because it results in fast rates of work.

Fixed-Interval Schedule

If a surfer gets a big wave to ride (the reinforcer) every 30 seconds (waves come in regular sets of big and small), he is on a fixed-interval schedule.

Fixed-interval schedule means that a reinforcer occurs following the first response that occurs after a fixed interval of time.

A fixed-interval schedule has slow responding at first, but as the time for the reinforcer nears, responses increase.

Variable-Ratio Schedule

If a slot machine pays off after an average of 25 pulls, the gambler is on a variable-ratio schedule.

Variable-ratio schedule means that a reinforcer is delivered after an average number of correct responses has occurred.

The variable-ratio schedule produces a high rate of responding because the person (gambler) doesn't know which response will finally produce the payoff.

Variable-Interval Schedule

If a bus arrives (the reinforcer) at your stop an average of 7 minutes late but at variable intervals, the bus rider is on a variable-interval schedule. This reinforces your arriving just a few minutes late for your bus.

Variable-interval schedule means that a reinforcer occurs following the first correct response after an average amount of time has passed.

A variable-interval schedule results in a more regular rate of responding than does a fixed-interval schedule.

In the real world, many of our behaviors are maintained on one or more of these four schedules of partial reinforcement.

Next we'll describe an interesting and unusual application of Skinner's principles of operant conditioning.

How smart are dolphins?

After the Iraqi war, ships carrying food and medicine had to wait outside the ports until the many underwater mines were located. Because the water was dark and murky, human divers could not easily detect the mines, but dolphins had no difficulty since they can "see"

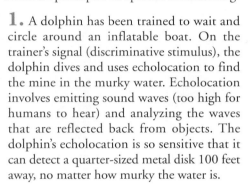

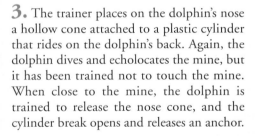

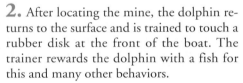

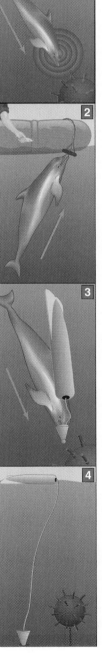

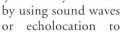

Trainer and dolphin

by using sound waves or echolocation to find objects. Dolphins are trained to detect mines similar to how dogs are trained to detect explosives: Their trainers applied Skinner's principles of operant conditioning.

1. A dolphin has been trained to wait and circle around an inflatable boat. On the trainer's signal (discriminative stimulus), the dolphin dives and uses echolocation to find the mine in the murky water. Echolocation involves emitting sound waves (too high for humans to hear) and analyzing the waves that are reflected back from objects. The dolphin's echolocation is so sensitive that it can detect a quarter-sized metal disk 100 feet away, no matter how murky the water is.

2. After locating the mine, the dolphin returns to the surface and is trained to touch a rubber disk at the front of the boat. The trainer rewards the dolphin with a fish for this and many other behaviors.

3. The trainer places on the dolphin's nose a hollow cone attached to a plastic cylinder that rides on the dolphin's back. Again, the dolphin dives and echolocates the mine, but it has been trained not to touch the mine. When close to the mine, the dolphin is trained to release the nose cone, and the cylinder break opens and releases an anchor.

4. The anchor (sound transmitter) falls to the bottom while the cylinder rises to the surface to mark the location of the mine. Human divers use the cylinder to locate and then detonate the mine. The dolphin is always removed from the area before the mine is detonated. A Navy spokesperson says that the dolphins are well cared for and, for that reason, live in captivity as long as or longer than in the wild (Friend, 2003).

Through operant conditioning, dolphins learned to perform this complex series of behaviors. During operant conditioning, a number of other things are also happening.

D. Other Conditioning Concepts

What else did Bart learn?

During the time that Bart was being operantly conditioned to pick up and hold a teddy bear to a hand signal, he simultaneously learned a number of other things, such as to also hold a bear cub, not to obey commands from a stranger, and to

stop picking up the teddy bear if he was no longer given apples (reinforcers). You may remember these phenomena—generalization, discrimination, extinction, and spontaneous recovery—from our discussion of classical conditioning in Module 9 (p. 199). We'll explain how the same terms also apply to operant conditioning.

Generalization

In the movie, Bart was supposed to pick up and hold a bear cub on command. However, in the wild, adult male Kodiak bears don't pick up and hold cubs; instead, they usually kill them.

Generalization: Bart transfers his response from teddy bear to live cub.

Although Bart was relatively tame, his trainer took no chances of Bart's wilder nature coming out and killing the bear cub. For this reason, the trainer started by conducting the initial conditioning with a stuffed teddy bear. Only after Bart had learned to pick up and hold the teddy bear on cue did the trainer substitute a live bear cub. As the trainer had predicted, Bart transferred his holding the teddy bear to holding the live bear cub, a phenomenon called generalization.

In operant conditioning, *generalization* means that an animal or person emits the same response to similar stimuli.

In classical conditioning, *generalization* is the tendency for a stimulus similar to the original conditioned stimulus to elicit a response similar to the conditioned response.

A common and sometimes embarrassing example of generalization occurs when a young child generalizes the word "Daddy" to other males who appear similar to the child's real father. As quickly as possible, embarrassed parents teach their child to discriminate between the real father and other adult males.

Discrimination

Since Bart had been raised and trained by a particular adult male, he had learned to obey and take cues only from his trainer and not from other males. This is an example of discrimination.

In operant conditioning, *discrimination* means that a response is emitted in the presence of a stimulus that is reinforced and not in the presence of unreinforced stimuli.

In classical conditioning, *discrimination* is the tendency for some stimuli but not others to elicit a conditioned response.

One problem with Bart was that he would repeatedly pick up and hold the teddy bear to receive an apple. To control this problem, the trainer used a cue—raising his arms in the air—to signal that only then would Bart receive an apple for his behavior. This is an example of a discriminative stimulus.

A *discriminative stimulus* is a cue that a behavior will be reinforced.

Discrimination: Bart obeys signals from his trainer but not from a stranger.

If you pay close attention to an animal trainer, you'll notice that discriminative stimuli, such as a hand signal or whistle, are used to signal the animal that the next behavior will be reinforced.

Young children learn to discriminate between stimuli when their parents reinforce their saying "Daddy" in the presence of their real fathers but do not reinforce their children when they call strangers "Daddy."

Extinction and Spontaneous Recovery

Even after filming ended, Bart continued to perform his trained behaviors for a while. However, after a period of time when these behaviors were no longer reinforced, they gradually diminished and ceased. This is an example of extinction.

In operant conditioning, *extinction* refers to the reduction in an operant response when it is no longer followed by the reinforcer.

In classical conditioning, *extinction* refers to the reduction in a response when the conditioned stimulus is no longer followed by the unconditioned stimulus.

After undergoing extinction, Bart may show spontaneous recovery.

Extinction: Bart stops behaviors if reinforcers stop. Spontaneous recovery: After extinction, Bart's behavior returns.

In operant conditioning, *spontaneous recovery* refers to a temporary recovery in the rate of responding.

In classical conditioning, *spontaneous recovery* refers to the temporary occurrence of the conditioned response to the presence of the conditioned stimulus.

Remember that all four phenomena—generalization, discrimination, extinction, and spontaneous recovery—occur in both operant and classical conditioning.

One distinctive characteristic of operant conditioning is that it usually has an observable response and an observable reinforcer. Next, we turn to cognitive learning, which may have neither observable response nor observable reinforcer.

Three Viewpoints of Cognitive Learning

How did Jack learn?

At the beginning of this module, we told you about Jack, who as a toddler loved to watch the Golf Channel. At 13 months, he was imitating what he saw and used a small plastic club to hit Wiffle balls in his family's living room. Jack had learned how to use a golf club not from classical or operant conditioning but from another kind of learning process called cognitive learning.

Cognitive learning, which involves mental processes such as attention and memory, says that learning can occur through observation or imitation and such learn-

He learned by observing.

ing may not involve any external rewards or require a person to perform any observable behaviors.

The roots of cognitive learning extend back to the work of Wundt in the late 1800s (p. 12) and psychologist Edward Tolman in the 1930s. It died in the 1950s, was reborn in the 1960s, and became popular in the 1990s. Currently, cognitive learning is extremely useful in explaining both animal and human behavior and was vital to the development of a new area called cognitive neuroscience (p. 71) (Bandura, 2001). We'll begin by discussing what three famous psychologists had to say about cognitive learning.

Against: B. F. Skinner

Eight days before his death, B. F. Skinner was honored by the American Psychological Association (APA) with the first APA Citation for Outstanding Lifetime Contribution to Psychology. In his acceptance speech to over 1,000 friends and colleagues, Skinner spoke of how psychology was splitting between those who were studying feelings and cognitive processes and those who were studying observable behaviors, such as animals under controlled conditions (figure at right). In a sharp criticism of cognitive learning, Skinner said, "As far as I'm concerned, cognitive science is the creationism [downfall] of psychology" (Vargas, 1991, p. 1).

Skinner's severe criticism of studying cognitive processes caused many in the audience to gasp and only a few to applaud (Vargas, 1991).

In the 1950s and 1960s, Skinner had advocated that psychology's goal should be to study primarily observable behaviors rather than cognitive processes.

However, psychologists gradually discovered that cognitive processes played a major role in human and animal activities and that such activities could not be understood or explained from observable behaviors alone. Today, the study of cognitive processes is a major goal of psychology (Bandura, 2001).

In Favor: Edward Tolman

In the 1930s, about the same time that Skinner was emphasizing observable behaviors, Tolman was exploring hidden mental processes. For example, he would place rats individually in a maze, such as the one shown below, and allow each rat time to explore the maze with no food present. Then, with food present in the maze's food box, he would test the rat to see which path it took. The rat learned very quickly to take the shortest path. Next, Tolman blocked the shortest path to the food box. The first time the rat encountered the blocked shortest path, it selected the next shortest path to the food box. According to Tolman (1948), the rat selected the next shortest path because it had developed a cognitive map of the maze.

A *cognitive map* is a mental representation in the brain of the layout of an environment and its features.

Tolman showed that rats, in addition to forming a cognitive map, learned the layout of a maze without being reinforced, a position very different from Skinner's. Tolman's position is making a comeback as psychologists currently study a variety of cognitive processes in animals (Lieberman, 2000). Tolman's study of cognitive processes in animals laid the groundwork for the study of cognitive processes in humans, which is best shown by the current theory of Albert Bandura (2001).

In Favor: Albert Bandura

Bandura began as a behaviorist in the Skinnerian tradition, which means focusing on observable behaviors and avoiding study of mental events. Since then he has almost entirely shifted to a cognitive approach. In many of his studies, Bandura (1986) has focused on how humans learn through observing things. For example, Bandura says that a child can learn to hate spiders simply by observing the behaviors of someone who shows a great fear of spiders. This is an example of social cognitive learning.

Social cognitive learning results from watching, imitating, and modeling and does not require the observer to perform any observable behavior or receive any observable reward.

Just as Tolman found that learning occurred while rats were exploring, Bandura found that humans learned while observing and that much (most) of human learning takes place through observation. Observational learning, which involves numerous cognitive processes, is a 180-degree change from Skinner's position, which had emphasized observable, noncognitive behaviors.

Following the death of Skinner in 1990, the study of cognitive processes has ballooned in popularity and usefulness. We'll introduce you to cognitive learning by describing one of Bandura's best-known studies, which involved a doll and a considerable amount of kicking and screaming.

E. Cognitive Learning

Do children learn by watching? Perhaps a dozen experiments in psychology have become classics because they were the first to demonstrate some very important principles. One such classic experiment demonstrated the conditioning of emotional responses in "little Albert" (p. 204). Another classic is Albert Bandura (1965) and his colleagues' demonstration that children learned aggressive behaviors by watching an adult's aggressive behaviors. Learning through watching is called observational learning, which is a form of cognitive learning.

Bobo Doll Experiment

Why did children kick the Bobo doll? One reason this Bobo doll study is a classic experiment is that it challenged the earlier idea that learning occurred through either classical or operant conditioning. You'll see that children learned to perform aggressive responses simply from watching.

Procedure. In one part of the room, preschool children were involved in their own art projects. In another part of the room, an adult got up and, for the next 10 minutes, kicked, hit, and yelled ("Hit him! Kick him!") at a large, inflated Bobo doll. Some children watched the model's aggressive behaviors, while other children did not.

After watching, children imitated adults kicking doll.

Sometime later, each child was subjected to a mildly frustrating situation and then placed in a room with toys, including the Bobo doll. Without the child's knowledge, researchers observed the child's behaviors.

Results. Children who had observed the model's aggressive attacks on the Bobo doll also kicked, hit, and yelled ("Hit him! Kick him!") at the doll. Through observational learning alone, these children had learned the model's aggressive behaviors and were now performing them. In comparison, the children who had not observed the model's behaviors did not hit or kick the Bobo doll after they had been mildly frustrated.

Conclusion. Bandura's point is that these children learned to perform specific aggressive behaviors not by practicing or being reinforced but simply by watching a live model perform these behaviors. Observational learning is sometimes called modeling because it involves watching a model and later imitating the behavior.

Another interesting finding of the Bobo doll studies was that children may learn by observing but then not perform the observed behavior. This is an example of the learning-performance distinction.

Learning Versus Performance

Do you learn but not show it? Is it possible that people can learn by observing but not necessarily perform what they have learned? To answer this question, Bandura and colleagues asked a group of children to watch a movie in which someone hit and kicked a Bobo doll. However, after hitting and kicking the doll, the person in the film was punished by being soundly criticized and spanked. Next, each child was left alone in a room filled with toys, including a Bobo doll.

As the experimenters watched each child through a one-way mirror, they found that more boys than girls imitated the model and performed aggressive behaviors on Bobo. But not all the children imitated the model's aggressive behaviors. Next, each child who had not imitated the model's aggressive behaviors on Bobo was offered a reward (a sticker or some fruit juice) to imitate the model's behavior. With the promise of a reward, all of the children imitated the model's aggressive behaviors. We'll examine in more detail the girls' imitated aggressive behaviors, which were similar to the boys' but more dramatic.

As the graph below shows, girls imitated an average of 0.5 aggressive behaviors after watching a film of a model who performed aggressive behaviors on Bobo and then was punished for being aggressive.

In other words, after observing a model being punished for aggressive behaviors, girls imitated almost none of the model's aggressive behaviors. However, when the same girls were promised a reward for imitating the model's aggressive behaviors, these girls imitated an average of 3.0 aggressive behaviors (Bandura, 1965).

Average Number of Aggressive Responses		
0.5	Watched punished model	
3.0	Rewarded for imitating	

So what does this experiment show? It shows that the girls had actually *learned* the model's aggressive behaviors through observation but that some did not *perform* these behaviors until they were rewarded for doing so (Bandura, 1965). This is an example of the learning-performance distinction.

The *learning-performance distinction* means that learning may occur but may not always be measured by, or immediately evident in, performance.

The learning-performance distinction may be demonstrated by young children, often to the embarrassment of their parents. For instance, a young child may overhear a "dirty" word but not repeat the word until out in public. Repeating a "dirty" word shows that the child had learned the word through observation but waited until later to imitate the parent and actually say (perform) the "dirty" word.

Child imitates adult's speech.

Based on the Bobo doll study and others, Bandura developed a theory of cognitive learning that we'll examine next.

Would you hold this spider?

The idea that humans gather information about their environments and the behaviors of others through observation is a key part of Bandura's (2001) social cognitive theory of learning.

Social cognitive theory emphasizes the importance of observation, imitation, and self-reward in the development and learning of social skills, personal interactions, and many other behaviors. Unlike operant and classical conditioning, this theory says that it is not necessary to perform any observable behaviors or receive any external rewards to learn.

Bandura believes that four processes—attention, memory, imitation, and motivation—operate during social cognitive learning. We'll explain how these processes operate in decreasing fear of spiders and snakes.

Social Cognitive Learning: Four Processes

1 Attention

The observer must pay attention to what the model says or does. In the photo at right, a nonfrightened woman (model) holds a huge spider while another woman (observer) looks on in amazement.

2 Memory

The observer must store or remember the information so that it can be retrieved and used later. The observer in the photo will store the image of seeing a nonfrightened woman (model) holding a spider.

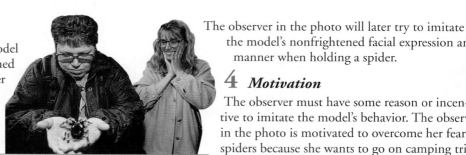

After observing fearless woman, woman in back may learn not to fear spiders.

3 Imitation

The observer must be able to use the remembered information to guide his or her own actions and thus imitate the model's behavior.

The observer in the photo will later try to imitate the model's nonfrightened facial expression and manner when holding a spider.

4 Motivation

The observer must have some reason or incentive to imitate the model's behavior. The observer in the photo is motivated to overcome her fear of spiders because she wants to go on camping trips.

If this observer can successfully imitate the model's calm behavior, then she will overcome her fear of spiders and be able to go camping with her friends. This example shows how Bandura's four mental processes operate during social cognitive learning.

The next study by Bandura shows how social cognitive learning, which usually takes some time and effort, decreased fear of snakes.

Social Cognitive Learning Applied to Fear of Snakes

Background. Although most people are wary of snakes, some develop an intense fear of them. Bandura and colleagues recruited subjects who had developed such an intense fear of snakes that they avoided many normal outdoor activities, such as hiking or gardening (Bandura et al., 1969). The subjects' fear of snakes was objectively measured by noting how many of 29 steps of increasingly frightening actions they would perform. For example, step 1 was approaching a glass cage containing a snake; step 29 was putting the snake in their laps and letting it crawl around while holding their hands at their sides.

Social cognitive learning helped this woman overcome her fear of snakes.

Treatment. One group of subjects watched as a model handled a live, 4-foot, harmless king snake. After watching for 15 minutes, subjects were invited to gradually move closer to the snake. Then the model demonstrated touching the snake and asked the subjects to imitate her actions. As the model held the snake, subjects were encouraged to touch the snake with a gloved hand. Another group of subjects, who also reported an intense fear of snakes, received no treatment (control group).

Results and conclusion. As the graph below shows, subjects who watched a live model handle a snake and who imitated some of the model's behaviors scored an average of 27 on the 29-step approach scale.

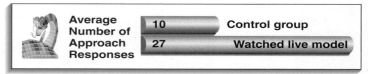

Average Number of Approach Responses		
10	Control group	
27	Watched live model	

In contrast, control subjects scored an average of only 10 approach behaviors on the 29-step scale. This study clearly showed that behavior can be greatly changed through social cognitive learning, which emphasized observation and imitation.

Bandura believes that humans acquire a great amount of information about fears, social roles, discrimination, and personal interactions through social cognitive learning. We'll discuss other aspects of cognitive learning and memory in Modules 11 and 12.

Next, we'll describe another kind of cognitive learning that involves what is often described as the "ah-ha!" feeling.

E. Cognitive Learning

What's the "ah-ha!" feeling?

Earlier we told you that Thorndike studied how cats learned to escape from a puzzle box to get a piece of fish. Thorndike concluded that learning occurred through a process of trial and error as cats gradually formed associations between moving the latch and opening the door. None of the cats showed any evidence of suddenly discovering the solution of how to escape the box.

About the same time that Thorndike in America was studying the trial-and-error learning of cats escaping from a puzzle box, Wolfgang Köhler in Germany was studying how

AH-HA!

Flash of insight

chimpanzees learned to obtain bananas that were out of reach. Köhler challenged Thorndike's conclusion that animals learned only through trial and error. Köhler suggested instead that cats and other animals that were observed under the proper circumstances could solve a problem in a sudden flash, known as insight or "ah-ha!" (Cook, 2002).

Insight is a mental process marked by the sudden and expected solution to a problem: a phenomenon often called the "ah-ha!" experience.

Here's an example of Köhler's chimp, Sultan, who showed insight in getting a banana that was hanging out of reach.

Insight in Animals

How did the chimp get the banana?

This classic experiment in psychology suggested a new kind of learning.

What Köhler (1925) did was to hang a banana from the ceiling in a room that had a box placed off to one side. The banana was too high for Sultan the chimp to grab by reaching or jumping. When Sultan first entered the room, he paced restlessly for about 5 minutes. Then he seized the box, moved it toward the banana, climbed onto the box, jumped up, and seized the banana. On his second try, Sultan quickly moved the box directly beneath the banana and jumped up to get it.

What intrigued Köhler about Sultan's problem-solving behavior was that it seemed to differ greatly from the random trial-and-error behavior of Thorndike's cats. Before Sultan arrived at a solution, he might pace about, sit quietly, or vainly grasp at the out-of-reach banana. Then, all of a sudden, he seemed to hit on the solution and immediately executed a complicated set of behaviors, such as standing on a box, to get the banana. Köhler believed that Sultan's sudden solution to a problem was an example of *insight,* a mental process quite different from what Thorndike had observed in the random trial-and-error learning of cats.

However, critics of Köhler's insight studies pointed out that he did not explain how chimps solved problems; rather, he simply described the process. Critics also noted that chimpanzees that were best at solving Köhler's problems were those that had had the most experience getting or retrieving objects. Thus, the development of insight seems to depend, to a large extent, on previous experience.

Köhler replied that his studies on insight were more a way to study problem solving than an explanation of what was happening in the chimp's head. The significance of Köhler's work was that it represented a method for studying learning that was different from either classical conditioning or random trial-and-error learning (Pierce, 1999). Since the early 1990s, there has been a renewed interest in studying the workings of the animal mind, which is currently called animal cognition (Lieberman, 2000).

Let's look at an example of insight learning in humans.

Chimp stood on a box to be able to reach the banana.

Insight in Humans

Can you solve this puzzle?

Just as Sultan the chimp seemed to suddenly arrive at a solution to a problem, humans also report the experience of suddenly and unexpectedly solving a challenging or difficult problem. We call this phenomenon the "ah-ha!" experience or a flash of insight (G. Cook, 2002). You may have an "ah-ha!" experience if you can figure out what critical piece of information is needed to make the following story make sense.

A man walks into a bar and asks for a glass of water. The bartender points a gun at the man. The man says, "Thank you," and walks out.

If you solved this puzzle, you had an insight!

Obviously, something critical happened between two events: ". . . asks for a glass of water" and "The bartender points a gun at the man." Some subjects solved this problem in a relatively short time, while others could not solve this problem in the 2-hour time limit.

I never solved the problem until I read the hint: The man has hiccups. Think about cures for hiccups and you may have an "ah-ha!" experience (answer at bottom of page). There was a difference between nonsolvers and solvers in the cognitive strategy that they used. The nonsolvers focused on the obvious elements, such as man, bartender, gun, and glass of water, and not on new concepts (hiccups, cure) that would lead to a solution. In comparison, the solvers spent more time on bringing in new information, and when they finally found the missing piece of information (cure for hiccups), the solution arrived suddenly, like the "ah-ha!" experience that Köhler defined as insight (Durso et al., 1994).

We have discussed three examples of cognitive learning: Tolman's idea of cognitive maps, Bandura's theory of social cognitive learning, and Köhler's study of insightful problem solving. In addition, we'll discuss cognitive learning in Modules 11 and 12.

After the Concept Review, we'll explain why biological factors make some things easier and some things harder to learn.

Answer: The man drank the water, but it didn't cure his hiccups. The bartender thought a surprise or fright might do the trick. He points a gun at the man, who is frightened, and so his hiccups stop. The man says, "Thank you," and walks out.

✔ Concept Review

1. The kind of learning in which the consequences that follow some behavior increase or decrease the likelihood that the behavior will occur in the future is called _____.

2. In operant conditioning, the organism voluntarily performs or (a)_____ a behavior. Immediately following an emitted behavior, the occurrence of a (b)_____ increases the likelihood that the behavior will occur again.

3. Because an organism may not immediately emit the desired behavior, a procedure is used to reinforce behaviors that lead to or approximate the final target behavior. This procedure is called _____.

4. In operant conditioning, the term *consequences* refers to either (a)_____, which increases the likelihood that a behavior will occur again, or (b)_____, which decreases the likelihood that a behavior will occur again.

5. If the occurrence of some response is increased because it is followed by a pleasant stimulus, the stimulus is called a (a)_____. An increase in the occurrence of some response because it is followed either by the removal of an unpleasant stimulus or by avoiding the stimulus is called (b)_____.

6. A stimulus, such as food, water, or sex, that is innately satisfying and requires no learning to become pleasurable is a (a)_____. A stimulus, such as grades or praise, that has acquired its reinforcing power through experience and learning is a (b)_____.

7. The various ways that reinforcers occur after a behavior has been emitted are referred to as (a)_____ of reinforcement. For example, if each and every target behavior is reinforced, it is called a (b)_____ schedule of reinforcement. If behaviors are not reinforced each time they occur, it is called a (c)_____ schedule of reinforcement.

8. When an organism emits the same response to similar stimuli, it is called (a)_____. When a response is emitted in the presence of a stimulus that is reinforced and not in the presence of unreinforced stimuli, it is called (b)_____. A decrease in emitting a behavior because it is no longer reinforced is called (c)_____. If an organism performs a behavior without its being reinforced, it is called (d)_____.

9. A kind of learning that involves mental processes, that may be learned through observation and imitation, and that may not require any external rewards or the performance of any observable behaviors is referred to as _____.

10. Tolman studied the behavior of rats that were allowed to explore a maze without any reward given. When food was present, rats quickly learned to select the next shortest path if a previously taken path was blocked. Tolman said that rats had developed a mental representation of the layout, which he called a _____.

11. Although an organism may learn a behavior through observation or exploration, the organism may not immediately demonstrate or perform the newly learned behavior. This phenomenon is known as the _____ distinction.

12. According to Bandura, one form of learning that develops through watching and imitation and that does not require the observer to perform any observable behavior or receive a reinforcer is called (a)_____ learning. Bandura believes that humans gather much information from their (b)_____ through social cognitive learning.

13. Bandura's theory of social cognitive learning involves four mental processes. The observer must pay (a)_____ to what the model says or does. The observer must then code the information and be able to retrieve it from (b)_____ for use at a later time. The observer must be able to use the coded information to guide his or her (c)_____ in performing and imitating the model's behavior. Finally, the observer must be (d)_____ to perform the behavior, which involves some reason, reinforcement, or incentive.

14. In Köhler's study of problem solving in chimps, he identified a mental process marked by the sudden occurrence of a solution, which he termed (a)_____. This phenomenon is another example of (b)_____ learning.

Answers: *1. operant conditioning; 2. (a) emits, (b) reinforcement or reinforcer; 3. shaping; 4. (a) reinforcement, (b) punishment; 5. (a) positive reinforcer, (b) negative reinforcement; 6. (a) primary reinforcer, (b) secondary reinforcer; 7. (a) schedules, (b) continuous, (c) partial; 8. (a) generalization, (b) discrimination, (c) extinction, (d) spontaneous recovery; 9. cognitive learning; 10. cognitive map; 11. learning-performance; 12. (a) social cognitive, (b) environments; 13. (a) attention, (b) memory, (c) motor control, (d) motivated; 14. (a) insight, (b) cognitive*

F. Biological Factors

Why would a monkey make a snowball?

You may remember having difficulty learning to read, write, ride a bike, drive a car, put on makeup, or shave. But do you remember having problems learning to play? For a young child, playing just seems to come naturally. Just as children engage in play behavior with little or no encouragement, reward, or learning, so too do monkeys. For example, young monkeys learn to roll snowballs and carry them around for apparently no other reason than for play (right photo). In fact, most young mammals engage in various play behaviors, which are not easily explained by the three traditional learning procedures—classical conditioning, operant conditioning, and cognitive learning (Brownlee, 1997). Observations of animals and humans indicate that

Animals have innate tendencies, such as playing with objects.

some behaviors, such as play, are easily and effortlessly learned partly because of innate biological factors.

Biological factors refer to innate tendencies or predispositions that may either facilitate or inhibit certain kinds of learning.

Researchers suggest that animals and humans may have evolved biological predispositions to learn play behaviors because they have adaptive functions—for example, developing social relationships among peers and learning behaviors useful for adult roles (S. L. Brown, 1994; Marten et al., 1996). This means that animals and humans have innate biological factors or predispositions that make certain kinds of learning, such as play behavior, very easy and effortless.

Besides play behavior, we'll discuss two other examples of learning—imprinting and preparedness—that are learned early and easily because of biological factors.

Why do young chicks follow their mother?

Soon after they hatch and without any apparent learning, baby chicks follow their mother hen. This following behavior was not explained by any of the principles of learning identified by Pavlov (classical conditioning), Thorndike (trial-and-error learning), or Skinner (operant conditioning). The baby chick's seemingly unlearned behavior of following its mother was a different kind of learning that was first identified by ethologists.

Ethologists are behavioral biologists who observe and study animal behavior in the animal's natural environment or under relatively naturalistic conditions.

For example, an Austrian ethologist, Konrad Lorenz (1952), studied chicks, goslings, and ducks, which can all move around minutes after hatching. He discovered that these baby animals followed the first moving object they saw, which was usually their mother. This following behavior is an example of imprinting.

Baby ducks automatically follow first moving object.

Imprinting refers to inherited tendencies or responses that are displayed by newborn animals when they encounter certain stimuli in their environment.

Imprinting is an unlearned behavior that is based on biological factors and that has great survival value: It increases the chances that newly hatched birds will remain with and follow their parent instead of wandering off into the waiting jaws of predators. Besides being unlearned, Lorenz noted two other major differences between imprinting and other kinds of learning.

Sensitive period. Unlike classical conditioning, operant conditioning, and cognitive learning, which occur throughout an animal's life, imprinting occurs best during the first few hours after hatching. This brief time period is called the critical, or sensitive, period.

The *critical,* or *sensitive, period* refers to a relatively brief time during which learning is most likely to occur.

Normally, the first object that newly hatched ducks see is their parent, upon whom they imprint. Thus, imprinting is a way for newly hatched animals to establish social attachments to members of their species. Although newly hatched birds will imprint on almost any moving object that they first see, including a human, a colored ball, or a glove, they imprint more strongly on moving objects that look or sound like their parent. Only birds that can walk immediately after hatching show imprinting, which promotes their survival (Bateson, 1991).

Irreversible. Unlike classical conditioning, operant conditioning, and cognitive learning, whose effects are usually reversible, imprinting is essentially irreversible. Most likely, imprinting evolved to be irreversible so that a young duck would not imprint on its mother one week and then imprint on a sly fox the next week.

In a program to prevent the California condor from becoming extinct, condor chicks are hatched at the San Diego Zoo and raised by humans. Because imprinting occurs very early and is irreversible, special precautions are taken so that the condor will not imprint on humans.

For example, the young condor chick shown on the right is being fed by a puppet that resembles an adult condor's head rather than a human's hand. The "puppet mother" helps the young condor imprint on real condor characteristics. When this condor grows up and is reintroduced into the wild, it will establish social relationships with, and attempt to mate with, its own species.

"Puppet mother" feeds baby condor.

Another example of how biological factors increase the ease and speed of learning is evident in something called prepared learning.

Prepared Learning

Why was learning to talk so easy?

You easily learned to talk but probably had trouble learning to read because of how your brain is organized, which illustrates the importance of biological factors. We'll discuss how biological factors help humans learn to speak different languages and birds learn to remember thousands of places where they hid food.

Incredible Memory

How do birds remember?

There are small birds, called Clark's nutcrackers, that live in an area where almost no food is available in the winter. During autumn, nutcrackers hide stores of food in underground places in perhaps as many as 2,500 to 6,000 different locations. During winter, nutcrackers survive by finding and digging up their hidden stores of food. How do nutcrackers locate their thousands of hidden stores? One reason is preparedness, which we also discussed earlier (p. 200).

Remembers thousands of hidden food places

Preparedness, or *prepared learning,* refers to the innate or biological tendency of animals to recognize, attend to, and store certain cues over others, as well as to associate some combinations of conditioned and unconditioned stimuli more easily than others.

Under seminatural conditions, researchers observed the amazing ability of nutcrackers to hide and find hundreds of hidden stores of food. Researchers found that nutcrackers use natural landmarks (trees, stones, bushes) to form cognitive maps that help them remember the locations of their hidden stores (Bednekoff et al., 1997).

One reason nutcrackers have such phenomenal memories is that the areas of their brains involved in memory are larger than the same areas in birds that do not store food. Specifically, the hippocampus, which is involved in transferring short-term memories into long-term memories, is larger in nutcrackers than in nonstoring birds (Shettleworth, 1993). Thus, the nutcracker is biologically prepared for

Hippocampus

surviving winters by having a larger hippocampus (right figure), which helps it better remember the locations of thousands of food stores.

Just as some birds are biologically prepared to remember the locations of critical hidden stores, humans are biologically prepared to make sounds and speak at least one of 6,800 different languages.

Incredible Sounds

How do infants make "word" sounds?

In the late 1940s, two psychologists raised a chimp in their home, along with their own child, because they wanted to know if this "speaking" environment would help a chimp learn to speak. However, after 6 years of trying, the chimp had learned to say a grand total of three words, "mama," "papa," and "cup" (Hayes & Hayes, 1951). At that time, these two psychologists did not know that the chimp's vocal apparatus and brain were not biologically prepared to produce sounds and words necessary for human speech (see the discussion of animal language on pp. 322–323).

Chimp does not have vocal structures to speak.

The reason humans but not chimps or other animals learn to speak so easily is that humans' vocal apparatus and brains are biologically prepared, or innately wired, for speaking (Pinker, 1994).

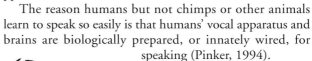

Infant's brain is prewired for speaking.

For example, the brain of a newborn infant is biologically prepared to recognize the difference between human speech sounds. Researchers discovered this ability by playing speech sounds to infants whose rate of sucking on a nipple was being recorded. After newborns heard the sound "ba" over and over, their rate of sucking slowed, indicating that they were paying little attention to the sound. But, as soon as researchers played the sound "pa," the infants' rate of sucking increased, indicating that they had noticed the relatively small change between the sounds "ba" and "pa." This study showed that infants' brains are prewired or biologically prepared (below figure) to recognize and discriminate among sounds that are essential for learning speech (Buonomano & Merzenich, 1995). In fact, infants all around the world make similar babbling sounds, which indicates the influence and importance of biological factors in learning to speak.

Conclusion. The learning principles of Pavlov, Thorndike, and Skinner do not, by themselves, explain how rats form cognitive maps, how infants easily produce and discriminate among human speech sounds, how nutcrackers remember thousands of hiding places for stored food, why monkeys spend time making and rolling snowballs, and why newborn chicks follow the first moving object. All these examples indicate how

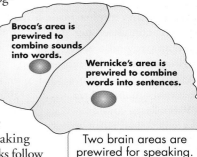

Broca's area is prewired to combine sounds into words.

Wernicke's area is prewired to combine words into sentences.

Two brain areas are prewired for speaking.

innate biological factors, such as differences in size or organization of brain structures, play a major role in preparing and helping animals and humans learn certain kinds of behaviors that are useful for maintenance and survival.

Next, we'll return to operant conditioning and discuss how its learning principles helped parents manage childhood problems.

G. Research Focus: Noncompliance

How Can Parents Deal with "NO"?

Why study a single subject?

When researchers study a group of subjects, information on any single subject may be lost in the group's combined scores. One advantage of operant conditioning is that a researcher can observe, study, and modify the ongoing behavior of a single subject. The ability to focus on a single subject's behavior makes operant conditioning a powerful procedure for changing undesirable behaviors. One kind of undesirable behavior in young children can be the persistent refusal of parental requests. We'll look at 4-year-old Morgan, who is becoming unmanageable because of a problem called noncompliance.

Noncompliance refers to a child refusing to follow directions, carry out a request, or obey a command given by a parent or caregiver.

Child constantly refusing or saying "NO" is a common complaint of many parents.

Noncompliance is a common complaint of parents in general and the most frequent problem of parents who bring their children to clinics for treatment of behavioral problems (Wierson & Forehand, 1994).

When saying "NO!" becomes a big problem, parents can be trained to use operant conditioning to decrease their child's persistent refusal. Parental training may involve different kinds of operant conditioning procedures, such as using verbal praise or giving attention to increase the occurrence of positive behaviors or using negative punishment to decrease undesirable behaviors. We'll focus on one form of negative punishment—time-out.

Time-out is a form of negative punishment in which reinforcing stimuli are removed after an undesirable response. This removal decreases the chances that the undesired response will recur.

Because Morgan persistently said "NO!" to her mother's requests, researchers showed Morgan's mother how to use time-out periods.

Study: Using Time-Out to Reduce Noncompliance

Researchers began by explaining to parents how to use the principles of operant conditioning to overcome a child's persistent "NO!"

Subjects. They were 4-year-old girls who were normal in every way but had a long history of saying "NO!" to parental requests. Their mothers had volunteered for this study because they wanted help with this problem.

Procedure. Researchers first observed mothers making typical requests and noted the children's rate of refusal, which is called the baseline. Then, mothers were shown how to use several procedures, but we'll focus on the most successful, time-outs.

If Morgan's mother made a request and Morgan complied, her mother reinforced Morgan's response with praise. However, if Morgan refused, her mother used the time-out procedure. Morgan was led to the corner of another room and told to do nothing (no TV, books, or toys) but to sit quietly and silently in a chair facing the wall for 1 minute. After 1 minute, Morgan was allowed to leave the corner and rejoin her mother. At that point, the mother made another request of Morgan. If Morgan complied, praise was given; if she showed noncompliance ("NO!"), the time-out procedure was used. All procedures were conducted in the home by the mother.

Results. The changes in Morgan's behavior after her mother began using time-out periods are shown in the graph below (Rortvedt & Miltenberger, 1994).

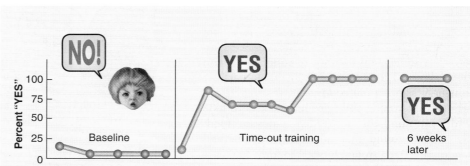

Baseline: Remember that during baseline, the researcher observed only the number of times that Morgan refused or agreed with her mother's request. During baseline, Morgan's mother made 5–8 requests during each session. Notice that during the last five sessions, Morgan showed mostly 0% compliance, despite her mother's scolding, pleading, or reprimanding.

Time-out: During time-out training, each time Morgan refused her mother's request, she was given a time-out period. Notice that Morgan's percentage of compliance started out at 12%, reached 60% on sessions 8–11, and then reached 100%.

Six weeks later, in a follow-up session using time-out, Morgan again showed 100% compliance with her mother's requests.

Conclusion. Studies like this show that the time-out procedure is effective in reducing undesirable behaviors, including noncompliance, temper tantrums, and disruptive activities (J. Taylor & Miller, 1997). The time-out procedure is an example of negative punishment, in which removing some stimulus, freedom to play, decreases the undesirable response, noncompliance. Negative punishment (time-out) is generally preferable to positive punishment (spanking) because positive punishment may cause negative emotional reactions as well as negative feelings toward the punisher (parents). The time-out procedure is an example of how operant conditioning principles may be applied to modify human behavior. We'll discuss the pros and cons of punishment more fully in the Application section on page 233.

Dealing with noncompliance is one example of how learning principles can be applied to human behavior. Another example involves learning how to play the violin.

What's the Suzuki method?

In the 1940s, a violin player and teacher from Japan, Shinichi Suzuki, developed a remarkably successful method for teaching violin playing to very young children (Suzuki, 1998). His method, called the *Suzuki method,* was brought to the United States in the mid-1960s and has generated incredible enthusiasm among children, parents, and music teachers ever since (Lamb, 1990).

It's interesting to learn that the basic principles of the Suzuki method for teaching young children to play the violin

Suzuki's method of teaching young children to play musical instruments has many similarities with Bandura's principles of social cognitive learning.

are very similar to Bandura's four mental processes for social cognitive learning. What's different is that Suzuki developed his learning principles after years of actually teaching young children to play the violin, while Bandura developed his four mental processes of observational learning after years of research with young children. We'll discuss how even though Suzuki the teacher and Bandura the researcher lived in very different cultures thousands of miles apart, their experiences led them to very similar conclusions about how children learn.

Different Cultures but Similar Learning Principles

1 Attention

Bandura states that the observer must pay attention to what the model says and does.

Similarly, Suzuki advises parents to teach violin information only when the child is actually looking at and watching the parent. Parents are told to stop teaching and wait if the child rolls on the floor, jumps up and down, walks backward, or talks about unrelated things.

The recommended age for starting a child with the Suzuki method is 3 for girls and 4 for boys. Parents are cautioned, however, that the attention span of the 3- to 4-year-old child is extremely limited, usually from 30 seconds to at most several minutes at a time.

2 Memory

Bandura says that the observer must code the information in such a way that it can be retrieved and used later.

Similarly, Suzuki tells parents that they should present information in ways that a young child can understand (Bandura would say code). Because a 3- to 4-year-old child does not have fully developed verbal skills or memory, little time is spent giving verbal instructions. Instead, the young child is given violin information through games and exercises. For example, children are taught how to hold the violin, use the bow, and press the strings by first playing games with their hands. Children are taught how to read music (notes) only when they are older and have gained some technical skill at playing the violin.

3 Imitation

Bandura says the observer must be able to use the information to guide his or her own actions and thus imitate the model's behavior.

Similarly, Suzuki suggests that children start at about 3 or 4 years old, the earliest age when they can physically perform the required movements and imitate their parents and teachers. Girls can start earlier than boys because girls physically mature earlier. For other instruments, the starting times are different—piano, 4–5 years; cello, 5 years; flute, 9 years—because these instruments require more physical dexterity. As you have probably guessed, 3- and 4-year-olds start with miniature violins and move up to bigger ones as they develop.

4 Motivation

Bandura says that the observer must have some reason, reinforcement, or incentive to perform the model's behaviors.

Similarly, Suzuki emphasizes that the most important role of the parent is to constantly reward and reinforce the child for observing and "doing what Mommy or Daddy is doing." Suzuki recommends several ways to keep motivation high in young children: Be an active and interested model for the child, play violin games that are fun for the child, avoid games or lessons that involve competition, and *never* push the child beyond the level that he or she is capable of reaching (Slone, 1985).

Social cognitive learning involves attention, memory, imitation, and motivation.

Conclusion. Parents and teachers who have used the Suzuki method report great success (Lamb, 1990). As you can judge, the basic principles of the Suzuki method for teaching violin are quite similar to Bandura's four mental processes for social cognitive learning. Both Suzuki and Bandura recognized the importance of observational learning and how much information children can learn from watching and imitating models. Suzuki's successful method of teaching violin to young children provides support for Bandura's four mental processes that he believes are involved in social cognitive learning.

Next, we'll discuss how operant learning principles were used to develop a method for teaching autistic children.

I. Application: Behavior Modification

What is behavior mod?

In this module, we discussed using operant conditioning principles to decrease food refusal in young children, to toilet train children (p. 216), to prevent eating paint chips (p. 218), to stop a severe form of self-injury (p. 219), and to decrease noncompliance (refusal) in children (p. 230). These are all examples of behavior modification (Kazdin, 2001).

Behavior modification is a treatment or therapy that changes or modifies problems or undesirable behaviors by using principles of learning based on operant conditioning, classical conditioning, and social cognitive learning.

For over 35 years, psychologist and researcher Ivar Lovaas of the University of California at Los Angeles has used behavior modification or, more colloquially, behavior mod to treat autism.

Autism is marked by poor development in social relationships, such as not wanting to be touched, not making eye contact, and

Behavior mod is used to treat autism.

hiding to avoid people (see drawing); great difficulty developing language and communicating; very few activities and interests; and long periods of time spent repeating the same behaviors or motor patterns, or following rituals that interfere with more normal functioning. Symptoms range from mild to severe and usually appear when a child is about 2 to 3 years old (American Psychiatric Association, 2000). (We discussed the symptoms and causes of autism more thoroughly in Module 1.)

The above symptoms, especially deficits in forming relationships and communicating, require early and intensive treatment. Without treatment, many autistics will remain socially unresponsive (Kabot et al., 2003). We'll discuss the behavior mod treatment developed by Dr. Ivar Lovaas, who combined principles of operant conditioning and social cognitive learning (O. I. Lovaas & Buch, 1997).

What kind of training?

Dr. Lovaas's program at UCLA, which is called the Young Autism Project, treats 2- to 3-year-old autistic children with a 40-hour-per-week program that runs for 2 to 3 years. Here's part of the program.

Program. Dr. Lovaas's training program actually consists of hundreds of separate teaching programs, many of them using principles of operant conditioning: Select a specific *target behavior*, *shape the behavior*, and use *positive reinforcers* of praise and food that are given immediately after the child emits the desired behavior. For example, here's a program to increase making eye contact.

Target behavior is getting the child to make eye contact following the command "Look at me."

Shaping the behavior involves two steps.

Step 1. Have the child sit in a chair facing you. Give the command "Look at me" every 5–10 seconds. When the child makes a correct response of looking at you, say "Good looking" and simultaneously reward the child with food.

Step 2. Continue until the child repeatedly obeys the command "Look at me." Then gradually increase the duration of the child's eye contact from 1 second to periods of 2 to 3 seconds.

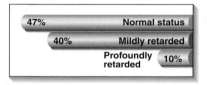

47%   **Normal status**

40%   **Mildly retarded**

Profoundly retarded   10%

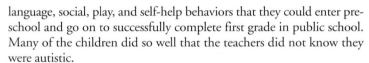

47% improved.

Using this behavior mod program, therapists and parents have had success in teaching autistic children to make eye contact, to stop constant rocking, to respond to verbal requests such as "Wash your hands," to interact with peers, to speak, and to engage in school tasks such as reading and writing (O. I. Lovaas, 1993).

Results. Lovaas and his colleagues did a long-term study of 19 children diagnosed as autistic. Behavior modification training went on for at least 40 hours per week for 2 years or more. The graph above shows that, at the end of training, 47% (9/19) of the autistic children reached normal status (O. I. Lovaas, 1987). These children acquired sufficient

language, social, play, and self-help behaviors that they could enter preschool and go on to successfully complete first grade in public school. Many of the children did so well that the teachers did not know they were autistic.

However, even with intensive training, 40% of autistic children remained mildly retarded, and 10% remained profoundly retarded and were assigned to classes for children with mental retardation. In comparison, in a control group of autistic children who received only minimal treatment, only 2% achieved normal intellectual and educational functioning, while 45% remained mildly retarded and 53% remained severely retarded (Eikeseth, 2001; O. I. Lovaas & Buch, 1997; McEachin et al., 1993). Lovaas and colleagues concluded that without intensive behavior modification treatment, autistic children will continue to show severe behavioral deficits.

Follow-up. A six-year follow-up study of the nine children who had reached normal status found that they had kept their gains and were still functioning normally (O. I. Lovaas, 1999). A recent follow-up study of the same nine children, now 20 to 30 years old, showed that eight appeared normal—that is, did not score differently from other normal adults on a variety of tests—while one had personality problems but would not be classified as autistic (Lovaas, 1999).

However, critics question whether the promising results from these nine individuals can be applied to all autistic children, since these nine may have had less severe symptoms to begin with (Gresham et al., 1999).

Health care specialists concluded that autism therapy can be effective provided it begins early (child 2–3 years old) and includes one-on-one training for a minimum of 25 hours a week, 12 months a year for several years (Tarkan, 2002). However, such therapy is so costly ($33,000 a year) that less than 10% of autistic children are receiving the recommended level of treatment (Lord, 2002).

Biofeedback

How can we reduce tension?

Many people develop a variety of psychosomatic problems, which result from stressful or disturbing thoughts that lead to real aches and pains in the body. For example, psychosomatic problems include back pain, muscle tension, high blood pressure, stomach distress, and headaches. One procedure to reduce psychosomatic problems is based on operant conditioning and is called biofeedback.

Biofeedback is a training procedure through which a person is made aware of his or her physiological responses, such as muscle activity, heart rate, blood pressure, or temperature. After becoming aware of these physiological responses, a person tries to control them to decrease psychosomatic problems.

Stress may cause a buildup of muscle tension.

For example, headaches may be caused or worsened by muscle tension, of which the sufferer may be totally unaware. The left figure shows that the forehead and neck have wide bands of muscles where tension can lead to pain and discomfort. Through video or audio (bio)feedback, a person can be made aware of muscle tension and learn how to reduce the tension.

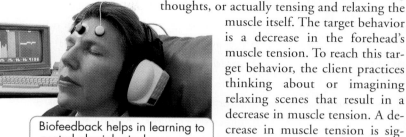
Biofeedback helps in learning to control physiological responses.

As shown in the photo below, small sensors attached to the client's forehead detect activity in the large muscle that stretches across the top front part of the head. The woman is trying to relax her forehead muscle by imagining relaxing scenes, thinking relaxing thoughts, or actually tensing and relaxing the muscle itself. The target behavior is a decrease in the forehead's muscle tension. To reach this target behavior, the client practices thinking about or imagining relaxing scenes that result in a decrease in muscle tension. A decrease in muscle tension is signaled by a decrease in an audio signal, which acts as a reinforcer. After a number of these sessions, the client learns to decrease muscle tension with the goal of staying relaxed the next time she gets upset.

Biofeedback is often used in conjunction with other forms of medical treatment or psychotherapy and can help a person reduce blood pressure, decrease headaches, and reduce anxiety (Pawlow & Jones, 2002; Stetter & Kupper, 2002). We'll discuss other methods of reducing stress and associated psychosomatic problems in Module 21.

Our last example deals with concerns about using punishment to decrease undesirable behaviors.

Pros and Cons of Punishment

Should it be used?

About 74% of parents use spanking as a discipline for children under age 17, and 94% of parents use it to discipline 3- and 4-year olds (Straus & Stewart, 1999). Since spanking may immediately stop undesirable behaviors, it has been and remains a popular form of discipline. But spanking is surrounded with controversy because it is associated with numerous negative side effects and may be a less desirable form of punishment (discipline) than the time-out procedure (Benjet & Kazdin, 2003). We'll discuss the pros and cons of each.

SPANKING: POSITIVE PUNISHMENT

Since spanking involves the presentation of an aversive stimulus (pain), it is an example of positive punishment. Researchers disagree on the use of spanking. Some argue that all spanking is bad because it is associated with numerous short- and long-term negative side effects, such as the child imitating and modeling aggressive behavior and developing other conduct problems (Gershoff, 2002). Others agree that severe spanking administered by harsh parents is always bad but mild to moderate spanking used as one form of discipline by loving parents does not necessarily have undesirable or negative side effects (Baumrind et al., 2002).

Effects of punishment depend on its usage.

Some of the undesirable effects of positive punishment can be reduced if it is given immediately after the behavior, if it is just severe enough to be effective, if it is delivered consistently, if the child is told the reason for the punishment, and, perhaps most important, if

punishment is used in combination with positively reinforcing a desirable behavior (Benjet & Kazdin, 2003). One disadvantage of positive punishment is that it points out only what the child should not do, while positive reinforcers have the advantage of encouraging the child to engage in desirable behaviors.

TIME-OUT: NEGATIVE PUNISHMENT

Another form of discipline is time-out, which was discussed earlier (p. 230). Time-out is an example of negative punishment because it involves the removal of a reinforcing stimulus (desirable reward) so that some undesirable response will not recur. For example, after misbehaving, a child is given a time-out period (stays in a corner without any games, books, or toys). Time-out is most effective when used consistently and combined with teaching the child alternative desired behaviors using positive reinforcers (Taylor & Miller, 1997).

Time-out has fewer undesirable side effects than spanking.

Compared to punishment, time-out has fewer undesirable side effects; it does not provide a model of aggression and does not elicit severe negative emotional reactions. Thus, when it is necessary to discipline a child, care should be taken in choosing between positive punishment (spanking) and negative punishment (time-out). Although both kinds of punishment stop or suppress undesirable behaviors, spanking has more negative side effects than time-out, and time-out has been shown to be effective in eliminating undesirable behaviors. Both kinds of punishment are best used in combination with positive reinforcers so the child also learns to perform desirable behaviors (Rosellini, 1998).

Summary Test

A. OPERANT CONDITIONING

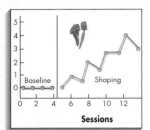

1. A kind of learning in which the consequences that follow some behavior increase or decrease the likelihood that the behavior will occur again is called _____.

2. To explain how random trial-and-error behaviors of cats became goal-directed behaviors, Thorndike formulated the _____, which says that behaviors are strengthened by positive consequences and weakened by negative consequences.

3. Skinner used the term *operant* (a)_____ to describe something that can be modified by its consequences. Operant responses provide one way to separate ongoing behaviors into units that can be observed and measured. Skinner believed that Pavlov's conditioning, which involves physiological (b)_____, was not very useful in understanding other forms of ongoing behaviors.

4. Suppose you wished to operantly condition your dog, Bingo, to sit up. The procedure would be as follows. You would give Bingo a treat, which is called a (a)_____, after he emits a desired behavior. Because it is unlikely that Bingo will initially sit up, you will use a procedure called (b)_____, which is a process of reinforcing those behaviors that lead up to or approximate the final desired behavior—sitting up. Immediately after Bingo emitted a desired behavior, you would give him a (c)_____.

5. Any behavior that increases in frequency because of an accidental pairing of a reinforcer and that behavior is called a _____ behavior.

6. The essence of operant conditioning can be summed up as follows: Consequences or reinforcers are contingent on _____.

7. If you compare classical and operant conditioning, you will find the following differences. In classical conditioning, the response is an involuntary (a)_____ that is elicited by the (b)_____. In operant conditioning, the response is a voluntary (c)_____ that is performed or (d)_____ by the organism. In classical conditioning, the unconditioned stimulus is presented at the beginning of a trial and elicits the (e)_____. In operant conditioning, the organism emits a behavior that is immediately followed by a (f)_____.

B. REINFORCERS

8. In operant conditioning, the term *consequences* refers to what happens after the occurrence of a behavior. If a consequence increases the likelihood that a behavior will occur again, it is called a (a)_____. If a consequence decreases the likelihood that a behavior will occur again, it is called a (b)_____.

9. If a stimulus increases the chances that a response will occur again, that stimulus is called a (a)_____. If the removal of an aversive stimulus increases the chances that a response will occur again, that aversive stimulus is called a (b)_____. Both positive and negative reinforcements (c)_____ the frequency of the response they follow. In contrast, punishment is a consequence that (d)_____ the likelihood that a behavior will occur again.

10. The stimuli of food, water, and sex, which are innately satisfying and require no learning to become pleasurable, are called (a)_____. The stimuli of praise, money, and good grades have acquired their reinforcing properties through experience; these stimuli are called (b)_____.

C. SCHEDULES OF REINFORCEMENT

11. A program or rule that determines how and when the occurrence of a response will be followed by a reinforcer is called a _____.

12. If you received reinforcement every time you performed a good deed, you would be on a (a)_____ schedule. This schedule is often used at the beginning of operant conditioning because it results in a rapid rate of learning. If your good deeds were not reinforced every time, you would be on a (b)_____ schedule. This schedule is more effective in maintaining the target behavior in the long run. There are four kinds of partial reinforcement schedules.

D. OTHER CONDITIONING CONCEPTS

13. The phenomenon in which an organism emits the same response to similar stimuli is called (a)_____. If a response is emitted in the presence of a reinforced stimulus but not in the presence of unreinforced stimuli, the organism is exhibiting (b)_____. If an organism's response is no longer reinforced, it will stop emitting this behavior, which is an example of (c)_____. However, even without reinforcement, an organism may perform the behavior, which is an example of (d)_____.

E. COGNITIVE LEARNING

14. The kind of learning that involves mental processes such as attention and memory, that may be learned through observation and imitation, and that may not involve any external rewards or require the person to perform any observable behaviors is called (a) _____. According to Tolman, rats developed a mental representation of the layout of their environment, which he called a (b)_____.

15. If an observer learns a behavior through observation but does not immediately perform the behavior, this is an example of the _____ distinction.

16. During his studies of problem solving in chimpanzees, Köhler used the term _____ to describe a mental process marked by the sudden occurrence of a solution.

17. Köhler's study of insightful problem solving, Bandura's theory of observational learning, and Tolman's idea of cognitive maps represent three kinds of _____ learning.

F. BIOLOGICAL FACTORS

18. Innate tendencies or predispositions that may either facilitate or inhibit learning are referred to as _____.

19. The innate tendency of newborn birds to follow the first moving object that they encounter soon after birth is called (a)_____. This kind of learning occurs best during a critical or sensitive period and is essentially (b)_____. One function of imprinting is to form social attachments between members of a species.

20. The innate tendency of animals to recognize, attend to, and store certain cues over others and associate some combinations of conditioned and unconditioned stimuli is referred to as _____. An example of this tendency is observed in Clark's nutcrackers, which are preprogrammed to bury and remember thousands of hidden stores of food.

G. RESEARCH FOCUS: NONCOMPLIANCE

21. One of the most common problems faced by parents is dealing with a child who refuses to follow directions or carry out a request or command. This refusal behavior is called _____.

22. An effective way to deal with a child's noncompliance is to use a procedure that involves placing a child in a situation where there is no chance of reinforcers. This mild form of nonphysical punishment is called _____.

H. CULTURAL DIVERSITY: EAST MEETS WEST

23. Suzuki's method and Bandura's theory both emphasize observation, modeling, and imitation. Specifically, both Suzuki and Bandura focus on four concepts: paying (a)_____ to the model, placing the information in (b)_____, using the information to (c)_____ the model's actions, and having (d)_____ to perform the behavior.

I. APPLICATION: BEHAVIOR MODIFICATION

24. Using principles of operant conditioning to change human behavior is referred to as (a)_____. Using these same principles to help individuals learn to control (increase or decrease) some physiological response, such as muscle activity or temperature, is called (b)_____.

25. If an aversive stimulus is presented immediately after a particular response, the response will be suppressed; this procedure is called (a)_____. If a reinforcing stimulus is removed immediately after a particular response, the response will be suppressed; this procedure is called (b)_____. A poorly chosen form of punishment, such as spanking, may have undesirable side effects, such as developing (c)_____ problems and serving as a model for future (d)_____ behaviors.

Answers: *1. operant conditioning; 2. law of effect; 3. (a) response, (b) reflexes; 4. (a) reinforcer, (b) shaping, (c) reinforcer; 5. superstitious; 6. behavior; 7. (a) reflex, (b) unconditioned stimulus, (c) behavior, (d) emitted, (e) unconditioned response, (f) reinforcer; 8. (a) reinforcer, (b) punishment; 9. (a) positive reinforcer, (b) negative reinforcer, (c) increase, (d) decreases; 10. (a) primary reinforcers, (b) secondary reinforcers; 11. schedule of reinforcement; 12. (a) continuous reinforcement, (b) partial reinforcement; 13. (a) generalization, (b) discrimination, (c) extinction, (d) spontaneous recovery; 14. (a) social cognitive learning, (b) cognitive map; 15. learning-performance; 16. insight; 17. cognitive; 18. biological factors; 19. (a) imprinting, (b) irreversible; 20. preparedness, or prepared learning; 21. noncompliance; 22. time-out; 23. (a) attention, (b) memory, (c) imitate, (d) motivation; 24. (a) behavior modification, (b) biofeedback; 25. (a) positive punishment, (b) negative punishment, (c) conduct, (d) aggressive*

Critical Thinking

Is It OK for Parents To Spank Their Kids?

Questions

1. What is your own attitude toward spanking, and how much, if at all, do these findings influence your attitude?

2. Which approach to answering questions did this study use and what are some of the problems with this study?

3. How do Dr. Trumbull's beliefs about spanking differ from those of Straus's study, which shows spanking has damaging effects?

Today, about 64% of American adults approve of spanking. The do-or-don't spanking controversy was sparked by a recent study.

Sociologist Murray Straus reported that the more a parent spanks a child for misbehaving, the worse—over time—that child behaves (*Archives of Pediatrics & Adolescent Medicine*, 1997). Straus says, "We are now able to show that when parents attempt to correct their child's behavior by spanking, it backfires . . . the more they spanked (3 or more times a week), the worse a child behaved two years and four years later" (Schulte, 1997, p. A1).

However, Straus's study has several problems. First, the mothers ranged in age from 14 to 21, not a representative sample of mothers in the United States. Second, the study looked at children ages 6 to 9 but not younger children. Third, the mothers were interviewed twice, two years apart, so there is a question about the reliability and truthfulness of their answers.

Dr. Den Trumbull, a pediatrician and critic of Straus's conclusions, says that spanking is effective and not harmful to development if limited to children between 18 months and 6 years old. On the other hand, spanking may be humiliating and traumatic to children 6–9 years old and may lead to problems down the line. Dr. Trumbull says that he favors spanking (one or two slaps to the buttocks) only as a last resort.

Psychologist Robert Larzelere, director of residential research at Boys Town in Nebraska, which does not allow spanking, reviewed 35 studies and could not find any convincing evidence that nonabusive spanking, as typically used by parents, had damaging effects. Larzelere concluded that whether or not parents spank is less important than how they spank. He says, "If parents use spanking as an occasional backup for say, a time-out, and as part of discipline in the context of a loving relationship, then an occasional spanking can have a beneficial role" (Rosellini, 1998, p. 58). The American Academy of Pediatrics also concluded that in certain circumstances, spanking may be an effective backup to other forms of discipline.

However, psychologist Irwin Hyman concludes, "There's enough evidence to decide we don't need spanking, even if the evidence isn't that strong." (Adapted from M. D. Lemonick, Spare the rod? Maybe, *Time*, August 25, 1997, p. 65; L. Rosellini, When to spank, *U.S. News & World Report*, April 15, 1998, pp. 52–58; B. Schulte, Spanking backfires, the latest study says, Knight-Ridder, appeared in *San Diego Union-Tribune*, August 15, 1997, p. A1)

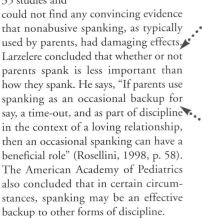

4. What does Dr. Larzelere conclude is important about using spanking?

5. How do spanking and time-out differ?

6. Do you agree with Dr. Hyman that spanking should be banned?

Try InfoTrac to search for terms: spanking; disciplining children.

1. Your attitude toward spanking will be influenced by how you or your brothers and sisters were disciplined by your parents, such as how much they used spanking and any negative effects. If you disapprove of spanking, this study will confirm your belief; if you approve of spanking, this study may cause you to rethink.

2. This study used the survey approach, which is an efficient method to gather data from a large number of people, but they may misremember, forget, or give answers they think the interviewers want to hear. Problems with this study include choosing a very small sample of mothers (ages 14–21) and not including younger children (below the age of 6).

3. Dr. Trumbull believes that spanking is not harmful to younger children—18 months to 6 years—who are the group of children that Straus did not study.

4. Dr. Larzelere believes that how parents spank (doing it in the context of a loving relationship and as a backup to time-out) is MORE important than whether they spank.

5. Spanking is an example of positive punishment—presenting an aversive stimulus (pain); time-out is an example of negative punishment—removing a reinforcer (attention, toys, television).

6. It is almost impossible not to have an emotional reaction when discussing spanking—I feel spanking may be OK as a last resort; I feel it's never all right to hurt a child. This means that your emotional feelings will influence how you respond to research findings. Research findings rarely answer any question absolutely but rather give you some data or facts to think about. For example, if you're against spanking, you'll agree with Dr. Hyman to ban spanking, even if the research doesn't totally support such a ban.

Links to Learning

LEARNING ACTIVITIES

● **POWERSTUDY CD-ROM 2.0**
by Tom Doyle and Rod Plotnik  *PowerStudy 2.0*™

Check out the "Operant & Cognitive Approaches" Super Module (disk 2) on PowerStudy. This is a completely self-paced module that is fully narrated. Don't want the narration? It is easy to turn off! This module includes:

- Videos—Imbedded videos illustrate important discussions like operant conditioning and the Skinner box, how self-injurious behavior is reinforced, and predisposition to play behavior.

- A multitude of animations—for example, a virtual test helps you identify the differences between operant and cognitive learning, and a virtual rat in a Skinner box helps illustrate schedules of reinforcement.

- A test of your knowledge using an interactive version of the Summary Test on pages 234 and 235. Also access related quizzes.

- An interactive version of the Critical Thinking exercise "Is It OK for Parents to Spank Their Kids?" on page 236.

- Key terms, a chapter outline, and hotlinked Web sites.

● **SELF-STUDY ASSESSMENT**
Want help studying? For your customized Study Plan go to **http://psychology.wadsworth.com/plotnik7e/**. This program will automatically generate pretests and posttests to help you determine what you have mastered and what needs work.

WebTUTOR ● **STUDY GUIDE and WEBTUTOR**
Check the corresponding module in your Study Guide for effective student tips and help learning the material presented.

● **INFOTRAC COLLEGE EDITION ONLINE LIBRARY**
To find interesting and relevant articles go to **http://www.infotrac-college.com**, use your password, and then type in search terms such as the ones listed below.

Behavior modification   Biofeedback
Imprinting   Ethologists

STUDY QUESTIONS

Use InfoTrac to search for topics mentioned in the main heads below (e.g., operant conditioning, cognitive learning, behavior modification).

*A. Operant Conditioning—How do you explain why your significant other sulks every time something is wrong even though you've told him or her that it bugs you? (**Suggested answer page 625**)

*B. Reinforcers—How would you use operant conditioning to change a rude friend into a more likable and friendly person? (**Suggested answer page 625**)

C. Schedules of Reinforcement—Which schedules of partial reinforcement best apply to the following behaviors: eating, studying, going to the movies, dating?

D. Other Conditioning Concepts—The first time you visit your 2-year-old niece, she takes one look at you and starts to cry. What happened?

E. Cognitive Learning—Why should parents be especially concerned about what they say and do in the presence of their children?

F. Biological Factors—A 14-year-old boy graduated from college with outstanding grades. How could he learn so much so early?

G. Research Focus: Noncompliance—Why might parents yell, threaten, or spank rather than use a time-out to deal with a child's constant refusals?

*H. Cultural Diversity: East Meets West—Why do the same principles of learning work in very different cultures? (**Suggested answer page 625**)

I. Application: Behavior Modification—How could techniques of behavior modification be used in a computer program to teach children how to do math problems?

*These questions are answered in Appendix B.

Module 11: Types of Memory

PowerStudy 2.0™ Complete Module

Incredible Memory

What's a super memory?

Rajan Mahadevan stood before the packed house of the International Congress on Yoga and Meditation. He recited, from memory, the first 31,811 digits of pi, which is often rounded off to two decimal places, or 3.14. He did not err until the 31,812th digit. This feat took 3 hours and 44 minutes and earned him a place in the *Guinness Book of World Records*.

Rajan memorized 31,811 digits of pi in exact order.

Researcher Charles Thompson discovered that Rajan can quickly recall the digit at any location within the first 10,000 digits of pi. This would be equivalent to memorizing the names of 10,000 people seated in numbered seats and then recalling the name of any single person, such as the one sitting in seat 2,141.

Rajan can repeat a string of 60 numbers after a single hearing, while most of us can repeat about 7–10 random numbers. Rajan is one of a half-dozen people worldwide with such gargantuan memory powers.

Despite Rajan's unbelievable ability to memorize numbers, he seems to be worse than average at recalling faces, and he constantly forgets where he put his keys (C. Thompson et al., 1993). Rajan's pi record has since been broken by Hiroyuki Goto, who correctly repeated 42,195 digits of pi in 9 hours (LaFee, 2001).

No one questions the accuracy of Goto's memories because they can be verified. However, some memories are not so easily verified, as in the case of Holly and her accused father.

Repressed Memory

How true are memories?

The man in the photo at right was accused by his daughter, Holly (photo below), for allegedly molesting her as a child. When Holly was 19, she had gone into therapy for bulimia, which is an eating disorder that involves eating a large amount of food and then often inducing vomiting.

"Holly's supposed memories are the results of drugs and quackery, not anything I did."

Holly's mother had asked a therapist about the causes of bulimia, and the therapist said that one of many causes was sexual molestation. Later, the mother asked Holly if she had ever been sexually molested. "Holly became very red in the face, pushed the chair out, and was crying. She said, 'I don't know. I think so. Maybe,' and then 'Yes'" (Butler, 1994, p. 12). During therapy sessions, Holly reportedly told her therapist about other memories and images of her father molesting her.

Finally, about a year after first entering therapy, Holly accused her father of sexually molesting her. Holly's experience is an example of repressed memories, whose truthfulness and accuracy we'll discuss later in this module.

"I wouldn't be here if there was a question in my mind. I know my father molested me."

Definitions

What are the three processes?

Rajan's amazing ability to recall thousands of digits and Holly's delayed remembering of terrible but difficult-to-verify childhood experiences involve three different memory processes.

Memory is the ability to retain information over time through three processes: encoding (forming), storing, and retrieving. Memories are not copies but representations of the world that vary in accuracy and are subject to error and bias.

We'll briefly define each of the three memory processes because they are the keys to understanding the interesting and complex process of how we remember and thus create the world we live in.

1 Encoding

Rajan developed a method or code to form memories for digits, a process called encoding.

Encoding refers to making mental representations of information so that it can be placed into our memories.

For example, Rajan encoded the number 111 by associating it with Admiral Nelson, who happened to have one eye, one arm, and one leg.

2 Storing

Rajan used associations to encode information because associations are also useful for storing information.

Storing is the process of placing encoded information into relatively permanent mental storage for later recall.

New information that is stored by making associations with old or familiar information is much easier to remember, or retrieve.

3 Retrieving

Rajan was able to recall, or retrieve, 31,811 digits in order.

Retrieving is the process of getting or recalling information that has been placed into short-term or long-term storage.

Only a half-dozen people in the entire world can match Rajan's feat of encoding, storing, and retrieving thousands of digits in order. Most people vary in their accuracy to recall information. For example, adolescents were questioned about dating, their families, and general activities. When asked the same questions 30 years later, they made many errors in recalling the same information (Offer et al., 2000).

We'll discuss three kinds of memory, how memories are encoded, why emotional memories are long-lasting, the issue of repressed memories, and some unusual memory abilities. We'll start with an overview of the three kinds of memory.

A. Three Types of Memory

What are the three types?

We often talk about memory as though it were a single process. In fact, a popular model of memory divides it into three different processes: sensory, short-term, and long-term memory (G. H. Bower, 2000). To illustrate each of these processes, we'll examine what happens as you walk through a big-city mall.

Sensory Memory

As you walk through a busy mall, you are bombarded by hundreds of sights, smells, and sounds, including the music of a lone guitarist playing for spare change. Many of these stimuli reach your sensory memory.

Sensory memory refers to an initial process that receives and holds environmental information in its raw form for a brief period of time, from an instant to several seconds.

For example, after reaching your ears, the guitarist's sounds are held in sensory memory for a second or two. What you do next will determine what happens to the guitarist's sounds that are in your sensory memory.

If you pay no more attention to these sounds in sensory memory, they automatically *disappear* without a trace.

However, if you pay attention to the guitarist's music, the auditory information in sensory memory is transferred into another memory process called short-term memory (Baddeley, 2000).

Short-Term Memory

Because a few notes of the guitarist's song sounded interesting, you shifted your attention to that particular information in sensory memory. Paying attention to information in sensory memory causes it to be automatically transferred into short-term memory.

Short-term memory, also called *working memory,* refers to another process that can hold only a limited amount of information—an average of seven items—for only a short period of time—2 to 30 seconds.

Once a limited amount of information is transferred into short-term, or working, memory, it will remain there for up to 30 seconds. If during this time you become more involved in the information, such as humming to the music, the information will remain in short-term memory for a longer period of time.

However, the music will *disappear* after a short time unless it is transferred into permanent storage, called long-term memory (S. C. Brown & Craik, 2000).

Long-Term Memory

If you become mentally engaged in humming along or wondering why the guitarist's music sounds familiar, there is a good chance that this mental activity will transfer the music from short-term into long-term memory.

Long-term memory refers to the process of storing almost unlimited amounts of information over long periods of time.

For example, you have stored hundreds of songs, terms, faces, and conversations in your long-term memory—information that is potentially available for retrieval. However, from personal experience, you know that you cannot always retrieve things you learned and know you know. In Module 12, we'll discuss reasons for forgetting information stored in long-term memory.

Now that you know what the three memory processes are, we'll explain how they work together.

Memory Processes

1 Sensory memory. We'll explain how the three types of memory described above work and how paying or not paying attention to something determines what is remembered and what is forgotten.

Imagine listening to a lecture. All the information that enters your sensory memory remains for seconds or less. If you *do not pay attention* to information in sensory memory, it is forgotten. If you *do pay attention* to particular information, such as the instructor's words, this information is automatically transferred into short-term memory.

2 Short-term memory. If you *do not pay attention* to information in short-term memory, it is not encoded and is forgotten. If you *do pay attention* by rehearsing the information, such as taking notes, the information will be encoded for storage in long-term memory. That's why it helps to take lecture notes.

3 Long-term memory. Information that is encoded for storage in long-term memory will remain there on a *relatively permanent basis.* Whether or not you can recall the instructor's words from long-term memory depends partly on how they are encoded, which we'll discuss later. This means that poor class notes may result in poor encoding and poor recall on exams. The secret to great encoding and great recall is to associate new information with old, which we'll also discuss later.

Now that we have given you an overview of memory, we'll discuss each of the three types of memory in more detail.

Incoming information → Sensory memory → Selective attention → Short-term memory → REHEARSING → Encoded for storage → Long-term memory

Three types of memory, each with a different function

NO attention → Forgotten

NOT encoded → Forgotten

Do you have a mental video recorder?

Your brain has a mental video-audio recorder that automatically receives and holds incoming sensory information for only seconds or less. This brief period provides just enough time for you to decide whether some particular incoming sensory information is important or interesting and therefore demands your further attention. We'll examine two different kinds of sensory memory: visual sensory memory, called iconic memory, and auditory sensory memory, called echoic memory.

Iconic Memory

What happens when you blink?

About 14,000 times a waking day, your eyes blink and you are totally blind during the blinks (LaFee, 1999). However, the world doesn't disappear during the eye blinks because of a special sensory memory, which is called iconic *(eye-CON-ick)* memory.

Iconic memory is a form of sensory memory that automatically holds visual information for about a quarter of a second or more; as soon as you shift your attention, the information disappears. (The word *icon* means "image.")

You don't "go blind" when both eyes close completely during a blink (about one-third of a second) because the visual scene is briefly held in iconic memory (O'Regan et al., 2000). When your eyes reopen, you don't realize that your eyes were completely closed during the blink because "you kept seeing" the visual information that was briefly stored in iconic memory. Without iconic memory, your world would disappear into darkness during each eye blink.

Iconic memory briefly holds visual information during eye blink.

IDENTIFYING ICONIC MEMORY

Here's the first study that showed the existence and length of iconic memory.

Procedure. Individual subjects sat in front of a screen upon which 12 letters (three rows of four letters) appeared for a very brief period of time (50 milliseconds, or 50/1,000 of a second). After each presentation, subjects were asked to recall a particular row of letters.

Results and conclusion. As shown in the left graph, if subjects responded immediately (0.0-second delay) after seeing the letters, they remembered an average of nine letters. However, a delay of merely 0.5 second reduced memory to an average of six letters, and a delay of 1.0 second reduced memory to an average of only four letters (Sperling, 1960).

Number of Letters Remembered

Delay in Seconds	
0.0	9 letters
0.5	6 letters
1.0	4 letters

Notice that an increased delay in responding resulted in subjects' remembering fewer letters, which indicated the brief duration of iconic memory—seconds or less.

This study demonstrated a sensory memory for visual information, which was called iconic memory. The sensory memory for auditory information is called echoic memory.

Echoic Memory

What did you hear?

Without realizing, you have probably already experienced auditory sensory memory, which is called echoic *(eh-KO-ick)* memory.

Echoic memory is a form of sensory memory that holds auditory information for 1 or 2 seconds.

For instance, suppose you are absorbed in reading a novel and a friend asks you a question. You stop reading and ask, "What did you say?" As soon as those words are out of your mouth, you realize that you can recall, or play back, your friend's exact words. You can play back these words because they are still in echoic memory, which may last as

Echoic memory briefly holds sounds.

long as 2 seconds. In addition to letting you play back things you thought you did not hear, echoic memory also lets you hold speech sounds long enough to know that a sequence of certain sounds forms words (Norman, 1982). Researchers discovered that the length of echoic memory increases as children grow into adults (Gomes et al., 1999).

Here's a quick review of the functions of iconic and echoic memories.

Functions of Sensory Memory

1 Prevents being overwhelmed. Sensory memory keeps you from being overwhelmed by too many incoming stimuli because any sensory informaton you do not attend to will vanish in seconds.

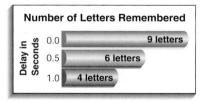

2 Gives decision time. Sensory memory gives you a few seconds to decide whether some incoming sensory information is interesting or important. Information you pay attention to will automatically be transferred to short-term memory.

3 Provides stability, playback, and recognition. Iconic memory makes things in your visual world appear smooth and continuous, such as "seeing" even during blinking. Echoic memory lets you play back auditory information, such as holding separate sounds so that you can recognize them as words.

If you attend to information in sensory memory, it goes into short-term memory, the next topic.

C. Short-Term Memory: Working

What was that phone number?

You have just looked up a telephone number, which you keep repeating as you dial to order a pizza. After giving your order and hanging up, you can't remember the number. This example shows two characteristics of short-term memory.

Short-term memory, more recently called *working memory*, refers to a process that can hold a limited amount of information—an average of seven items—for a limited period of time—2 to 30 seconds. However, the relatively short duration can be lengthened by repeating or rehearsing the information.

For good reason, telephone numbers and postal ZIP codes are seven numbers or fewer because that

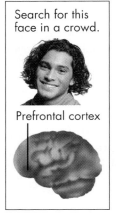

Search for this face in a crowd.

Prefrontal cortex

is about the limit of short-term memory.

Another example of using working memory is when you keep a particular face in mind while searching for that person's face in a crowd (left figure). Brain scans taken during a similar task show that maximum neural activity occurs in an area in the front of the brain called the prefrontal cortex (left figure) (Jiang et al., 2000). Recent studies using brain scans found that when you are paying attention and using working memory to perform a variety of cognitive tasks, maximum neural activity occurs in various areas of the prefrontal cortex (Nyberg et al., 2003).

Although extremely useful, working or short-term memory has the two characteristics of limited duration and limited capacity.

LIMITED DURATION

The new telephone number that you looked up will remain in short-term memory for a brief time, usually from 2 to 30 seconds, and then disappear. However, you can keep information

Short-term memory holds items for 2-30 seconds.

longer in short-term memory by using maintenance rehearsal.

Maintenance rehearsal refers to the practice of intentionally repeating or rehearsing information so that it remains longer in short-term memory.

Researchers studied how long information is remembered without practice or rehearsal by asking participants to remember a series of consonants composed of three meaningless letters, such as

CHJ. Participants were prevented from rehearsing, or repeating, these consonants by having them count backward immediately after seeing the groups of three letters. As the graph below shows, 80% of the participants recalled the groups of three letters after 3 seconds. However, only 10% of participants recalled the groups of three letters after 15

seconds (L. R. Peterson & Peterson, 1950). Since almost all the participants had forgotten the groups of three letters after 15 seconds (if they were prevented from rehearsing), this study clearly showed that information disappears from your short-term memory within seconds unless you continually repeat or rehearse the information.

You can increase the time that information remains in short-term memory by using maintenance rehearsal. However, during maintenance rehearsal, which involves repeating the same thing over and over, new information cannot enter short-term memory.

Not only does short-term or working memory have a limited duration, it also has a limited capacity.

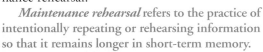

Graph: Percent of Items Correctly Recalled vs. Interval in Seconds. CHJ BDK MXF RTQ. Values at 3, 6, 9, 12, 15 seconds showing decline from 80 to about 10.

LIMITED CAPACITY

In previous modules, we pointed out several studies that are considered classic because they challenged old concepts or identified significant new information. One such classic study is that of George Miller (1956), who was the first to discover that short-term memory can hold only about seven items or bits, plus or minus two. Although this seems like too small a number, researchers have repeatedly confirmed Miller's original finding (Baddeley, 2000). Thus, one reason telephone numbers worldwide are generally limited to seven digits is that seven matches the capacity of short-term memory.

Short-term memory holds about 7 items.

It is easy to confirm Miller's finding with a *memory span test,* which measures the total number of digits that we can repeat back in the correct order after a single hearing. For example, students make few errors when they are asked to repeat seven or eight digits, make some errors with a list of eight or nine digits, and make many errors when they repeat a list that is longer than nine digits. One of the main reasons information disappears from short-term memory is interference (Estevez & Calvo, 2000).

Interference results when new information enters short-term memory and overwrites or pushes out information that is already there.

For example, if you are trying to remember a phone number and someone asks you a question, the question interferes with or wipes away the phone number. One way to prevent interference is through rehearsal. However, once we stop rehearsing, the information in short-term memory may disappear.

Although short-term memory has limited capacity and duration, it is possible to increase both. For example, I use a classroom demonstration in which I guarantee that any student can learn to memorize a list of 23 digits, in exact order, in just 25 seconds. This impressive memory demonstration, which always works, is accomplished by knowing how to use something called chunking.

How does Rajan remember 1113121735 1802?

Although short-term memory briefly holds an average of about seven items, it is possible to increase the length of each item by using a process called chunking (Kimball & Holyoak, 2000).

Chunking is combining separate items of information into a larger unit, or chunk, and then remembering chunks of information rather than individual items.

One of the interesting things about Rajan's prodigious memory for numbers is his ability to chunk. For instance, in about 2 minutes Rajan (right photo) memorized 36 random numbers (in a block of 6 × 6) written on a blackboard. He was able to repeat the numbers forward and backward and to state the numbers in any individual row, column, or diagonal.

When asked about his method for memorizing numbers, he replied that he automatically arranged the numbers into chunks and gave the chunks a name.

For example, here's how he chunked the first 14 numbers: 11131217351802. He chunked 111 and named it "Nelson" because Admiral Nelson had one eye, one arm, and one leg; he chunked 312 and named it the "area code of Chicago"; he chunked 1735 and named it "29" because Ben Franklin was 29 in 1735; and he chunked 1802 as "plus 2" because John Adams occupied the White House in 1800. When Rajan wants to recall the numbers, he does so by remembering a string of associations: Nelson, area code of Chicago, Ben Franklin, and John Adams. As Rajan explains, he doesn't know why he makes particular associations; they just come to him.

Sometimes we use chunking without thinking about it. For example, to remember the 11-digit phone number 16228759211, we break it into four chunks: 1-622-875-9211.

As first suggested by George Miller (1956), chunking is a powerful memory tool that greatly increases the amount of information that you can hold in short-term memory.

Next, we'll review three important functions of short-term memory.

> I have a system for memorizing these 36 numbers in two minutes.

111312
173518
028537
873625
419803
291728

Functions of Short-Term Memory

Why is it also called working memory?

Short-term memory is like having a mental computer screen that stores a limited amount of information that is automatically erased after a brief period of time and replaced by new information, and so the cycle continues. *Short-term memory* is also called *working memory* to indicate that it's an active process. Using brain scans, researchers found that short-term memory involves the front part of the brain, especially the prefrontal area (Nyberg et al., 2003).

There are three important points to remember about short-term memory: 1st—paying attention transfers information into short-term memory; 2nd—after a short time, information disappears unless it is rehearsed; and 3rd—some information is eventually transferred from short-term memory into permanent storage.

1 Attending

Imagine driving along with your radio on while a friend in the passenger seat is talking about the weekend. A tremendous amount of information is entering your sensory memory, but you avoid stimulus overload because incoming information automatically vanishes in seconds unless you pay attention to it.

The moment you pay attention to information in sensory memory, that information enters short-term memory for further processing. For example, while your friend is talking, you don't pay attention to the radio until your favorite song comes on and enters sensory memory. As you pay attention, you hear the radio, even though it has been playing the whole time. One function of short-term memory is that it allows us *to selectively attend to information that is relevant and disregard everything else.*

Once information enters short-term, or working, memory, several things may happen.

2 Rehearsing

Once information enters short-term memory, it usually remains for only seconds unless you rehearse it. For example, the announcer on the car radio gives a phone number to call for free movie tickets. But unless

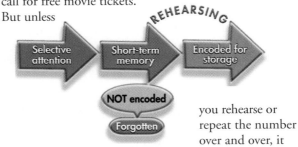

you rehearse or repeat the number over and over, it will probably disappear from your short-term memory because of interference from newly arriving information. Another function of short-term memory is that it allows you *to hold information for a short period of time until you decide what to do with it.*

If you rehearse the information in short-term memory, you increase the chances of storing it.

3 Storing

Rehearsing information not only holds that information in short-term memory but also helps *to store or encode information in long-term memory.* Later, we'll discuss two different kinds of rehearsing (p. 249) and explain why one kind of rehearsing is better than the other for storing or encoding information in long-term memory.

Next, we'll describe the steps in the memory process and why some things are stored in long-term memory.

D. Long-Term Memory: Storing

Is it a thing or a process? Don't think of sensory memory, short-term memory, and long-term memory as *things* or *places* but rather as ongoing and interacting *processes*. To show how these different memory processes interact, we'll describe what happens as you hear a new song on the radio and try to remember the song's title.

1 Sensory memory. As you drive down the highway, you're half listening to the car radio. Among the incoming information, which is held for seconds or less in sensory memory, are the words, "Remember this song, 'Love is like chocolate,' and win two movie tickets."

2 Attention. If you do NOT pay attention to information about winning tickets, it will disappear from sensory memory. If the chance to win tickets gets your attention, information about the song title, "Love is like chocolate," is automatically transferred into short-term memory.

 **3 Short-term memory.** Once the song title is in short-term memory, you have a short time (2–30 seconds) for further processing. If you lose interest in the title or are distracted by traffic, the title will most likely disappear and be forgotten. However, if you rehearse the title or, better yet, form a new association, the title will likely be transferred to and encoded in your long-term memory.

4 Encoding. You place information in long-term memory through a process called encoding. *Encoding is the process of transferring information from short-term to long-term memory by paying attention to it, repeating or rehearsing it, or forming new associations.*

For example, if you simply repeat the title or don't make any new associations, the title may not be encoded at all or may be poorly encoded and thus difficult to recall from long-term memory. However, if you find the title, "Love is like chocolate," to be catchy or unusual, or you form a new association, such as thinking of a chocolate-shaped heart, you will be successful in encoding this title into long-term memory. We'll discuss ways to improve encoding information and thus improve recalling information later in this module.

5 Long-term memory. Once the song title is encoded in long-term memory, it has the potential to remain there for your lifetime.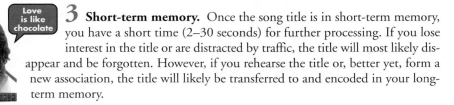

Long-term memory refers to the process of storing almost unlimited amounts of information over long periods of time with the potential of retrieving, or remembering, such information in the future.

For example, later you may try to recall the song title from long-term memory by placing it back into short-term memory. How easily and accurately you can recall or retrieve information depends on many factors (S. C. Brown & Craik, 2000).

6 Retrieving. When people talk about remembering something, they usually mean retrieving or recalling information from long-term memory.

Retrieving is the process of selecting information from long-term memory and transferring it back into short-term memory.

There are several reasons you can't remember or retrieve the song's title. You may not have effectively encoded the title into long-term memory because you got distracted or neglected to form a new association (chocolate heart). The key to successfully retrieving information from long-term memory is to effectively encode information, usually by making associations between new and old information, which we'll soon discuss.

How big and how accurate? **Capacity and permanency.** Researchers estimate that long-term memory has an almost unlimited capacity to store information. Anything stored has the potential to last a lifetime, provided drugs or disease do not damage the brain's memory circuits (Bahrick, 2000).

Chances of retrieval. Although all information in long-term memory has the potential to be retrieved, how much you can actually retrieve depends on a number of factors, including how it was encoded and the amount of interference from related information. The next question is: How accurate are your long-term memories?

Accuracy of long-term memory. Researchers found that the content and accuracy of long-term memories may undergo change and distortion across time and not always be as accurate as people think. For example, college freshmen were asked to recall grades from all four years of high school. As the graph below shows, students accurately recalled 89% of grades of A but

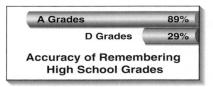

Accuracy of Remembering High School Grades

only 29% of grades of D. Thus, students were much more accurate recalling positive events, grades of A, than they were recalling negative events, grades of D (Bahrick et al., 1996).

This and other studies show that we do not recall all events with the same accuracy, sometimes inflating positive events and eliminating negative ones (Koriat et al., 2000). The reasons we may change, distort, or forget information are discussed in Module 12.

Next, we'll explain how psychologists demonstrated the existence of two separate memory processes: a short-term and a long-term memory process.

What is the evidence?

Most researchers agree that there are two memory systems (A. J. Green et al., 2000). One system involves short-term memory, which stores limited information for a brief period of time and then the information disappears. For example, a stranger tells you his or her name but a few minutes later you have totally forgotten the name because it disappeared from short-term memory. A second system involves long-term memory, which stores large amounts of information for very long periods of time.

For example, you can recall in great detail many childhood memories that years ago were stored in long-term memory. Other evidence for two memory systems comes from findings that brain damage can wipe out long-term memory while completely sparing short-term memory. Still other evidence for two memory systems comes from research on how you remember items in a relatively long list. We'll give you a chance to memorize a list of items, which will show that you have two separate memory systems—short- and long-term memory.

Primacy Versus Recency

Can you remember this list?

Please read the following list only once and try to remember the animals' names:

> bear, giraffe, wolf, fly, deer,
> elk, gorilla, elephant, frog, snail,
> turtle, shark, ant, owl

Immediately after reading this list, write down (in any order) as many of the animals' names as you can remember.

If you examine the list of names that you wrote down, you'll discover a definite pattern to the order of the names that you remembered. For example, here's the order in which names in the above list would most likely be remembered.

First items: Primacy effect. In studies using similar lists, subjects more easily recalled the *first* four or five items (bear, giraffe, wolf, fly) because subjects had more time to rehearse the first words presented. As a result of rehearsing, these first names were transferred to and stored in long-term memory, from which they were recalled. This phenomenon is called the primacy effect.

The *primacy effect* refers to better recall, or improvement in retention, of information presented at the beginning of a task.

Middle items.  Subjects did not recall many items from the *middle* of the list (gorilla, elephant, frog) because they did not have much time to rehearse them. When they tried to remember items from the middle of the list, their attention and time were split between trying to remember the previous terms and trying to rehearse new ones. Less rehearsal meant that fewer middle names were stored in long-term memory; more interference meant that fewer names remained in short-term memory.

Last items: Recency effect. Subjects more easily recalled the *last* four or five items (turtle, shark, ant, owl) because they were still available in short-term memory and could be read off a mental list. This phenomenon is called the recency effect.

The *recency effect* refers to better recall, or improvement in retention, of information presented at the end of a task.

Together, these two effects are called the primacy-recency effect.

The *primacy-recency effect* refers to better recall of information presented at the beginning and end of a task.

As we'll explain next, the primacy-recency effect is evidence that short- and long-term memory are two separate processes.

Short-Term Versus Long-Term Memory

Why didn't you remember "elephant"?

One reason you probably didn't remember the name "elephant" is that it came from the middle of the list. The middle section of a list is usually least remembered because that information may no longer be retained in short-term memory and may not have been encoded in long-term memory. Evidence for the primacy-recency effect is shown in the graph below (Glanzer & Cunitz, 1966).

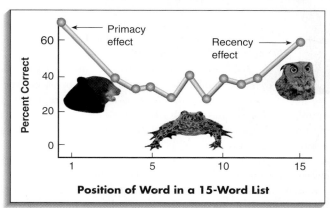

Position of Word in a 15-Word List

For example, subjects showed better recall (70%) for the first items presented, which is the primacy effect. The primacy effect occurs because subjects have more time to rehearse the first items, which increases the chances of transferring these items into long-term memory. Remember that rehearsal has two functions: keeping information longer in short-term memory and promoting encoding—the transfer of information into long-term memory.

In addition, subjects showed better recall (60%) for the last items presented, which is the recency effect. Sometimes subjects say that they can still "hear these words" and usually report these items first. The recency effect occurs because the last items are still in short-term memory, from which they are recalled (Glanzer & Cunitz, 1966).

The occurrence of the primacy-recency effect suggested the existence of two separate kinds of memory processes, which we now call short-term and long-term memory (R. C. Atkinson & Shiffrin, 1968; Neath, 1998).

Next, you'll discover that instead of one, there are several different kinds of long-term memory.

D. Long-Term Memory: Storing

Declarative Versus Procedural or Nondeclarative

Where do I store reading and skiing?

When I ski down a hill, I can't tell you how I am able to control my muscles to keep my balance and make my turns. However, after I read a scientific article, I can tell you much of what I have read. These two activities, skiing and reading, use two different kinds of long-term memory. The discovery that there are two kinds of long-term memory is a relative new finding, and like many discoveries in science, it was found quite by accident.

Researchers were testing a patient, well known in memory circles as H. M., who suffered severe memory loss because of an earlier brain operation to reduce his seizures. H. M.'s task seemed simple: draw a star by guiding your hand while looking into a mirror. However, this mirror-drawing test is relatively difficult because looking into a mirror reverses all hand movements: up is down and down is up. As H. M. did this task each day, his drawing improved, indicating that he was learning and remembering the necessary motor skills. But here's the strange part. Each and every day, H. M. would insist that he had never seen or done mirror-drawing before (N. J. Cohen, 1984).

How could H. M. have no memory of mirror-drawing, yet show a steady improvement in his performance as he practiced it each day? Based on H. M.'s mirror-drawing as well as data from other patients and numerous animal studies, researchers discovered that there are two different kinds of long-term memory, each involving different areas of the brain (Nyberg & Cabeza, 2000; Squire, 1994).

You'll understand why H. M. could improve at mirror-drawing but not remember doing it after you learn about the two kinds of long-term memory—declarative and procedural.

Declarative Memory

Which bird cannot fly?
What did you eat for breakfast?

You would recall or retrieve answers to these questions from one particular kind of long-term memory called declarative memory.

Declarative memory involves memories for facts or events, such as scenes, stories, words, conversations, faces, or daily events. We are aware of and can recall, or retrieve, these kinds of memories.

There are two kinds of declarative memory—semantic and episodic (Eichenbaum, 1997).

Semantic memory
"Which bird cannot fly?" asks you to remember a fact, which involves semantic *(sah-MANT-ic)* memory.

Semantic memory is a type of declarative memory and involves knowledge of facts, concepts, words, definitions, and language rules.

Most of what you *learn* in classes (facts, terms, definitions) goes into semantic memory (Schacter et al., 2000).

Episodic memory
"What did you eat for breakfast?" asks you to remember an event, which involves episodic *(ep-ih-SAW-dik)* memory.

Episodic memory is a type of declarative memory and involves knowledge of specific events, personal experiences (episodes), or activities, such as naming or describing favorite restaurants, movies, songs, habits, or hobbies.

Most of your college activities and experiences go into episodic memory (Tulving, 2002).

Since his brain operation, H. M. cannot remember new facts (semantic memory) or events (episodic memory). Thus, H. M. has lost declarative memory, which explains why he does not remember events, such as doing mirror-drawing (Cohen, 1984).

However, H. M.'s motor skills improved during mirror-drawing, which indicates another kind of long-term memory.

Procedural or Nondeclarative Memory

How did you learn to play tennis?
Why are you afraid of spiders?

Even though you can play tennis and are afraid of spiders, you can't explain how you control your muscles to play tennis or why you're so terrified of such a tiny (usually harmless) bug. That's because motor skills and emotional feelings are stored in procedural memory.

Procedural memory, also called *nondeclarative memory,* involves memories for motor skills (playing tennis), some cognitive skills (learning to read), and emotional behaviors learned through classical conditioning (fear of spiders). We cannot recall or retrieve procedural memories.

Even if you have not played tennis for years, you can pick up a racket and still remember how to serve because that information is stored in procedural memory. But you cannot describe the sequence of movements needed to serve a ball because these skills are stored in procedural memory. Similarly, if you learned to fear spiders through classical conditioning, you cannot explain why you're afraid because the reasons are stored in procedural memory. Although procedural memories greatly influence our behavior, we have neither awareness of nor ability to recall these memories (Mayes, 2000).

Now we can explain H. M.'s strange behavior. He was able to improve at mirror-drawing because it involved learning a motor skill that was stored in procedural memory. But he could not talk about the skill because no one is aware of or can recall procedural memories. Although H. M. gradually improved at mirror-drawing, he could not remember the event of sitting down and drawing because that involves declarative (episodic) memories, which were damaged in his brain surgery (Hilts, 1995). The study of H. M. is a classic study because it first demonstrated the existence of two kinds of long-term memory: declarative memory and procedural memory. We'll discuss the brain systems underlying these types of long-term memory in Module 12.

Hormones and Memories

Do hormones affect memories?

Many of us have vivid memories that involve highly charged emotional situations (Winningham et al., 2000). For example, imagine the emotional excitement Venus Williams (right photo) felt after winning the 2000 Wimbledon tennis championship. Her winning point was followed by giant leaps around the court. Venus said, "I've been working so hard all of my life to be here. This is unbelievable" (Peyser, 2000, p. 46). She will remember this event the rest of her life because something happens during strong emotions that increases the chances of remembering the particular situation, person, or event.

What actually happens to improve memory during an emotional event involves a long-term research program that began in animals. In Module 2 we explained that researchers may use an animal model (p. 34) to answer questions that for safety, moral, or ethical reasons cannot involve human subjects. Because of safety concerns,

Excitatory hormones can "stamp in" memories.

neuropsychologist James McGaugh (1999) began using an animal model to study how hormones produced during emotional states affect memory. He found that certain drugs or hormones associated with emotional experiences could either increase or decrease the recall of long-term memories. For example, if rats were given an injection of a hormone (epinephrine) that is normally produced by the body during emotional or stressful states, rats remembered better what they had just learned (McGaugh, 1990). This was a new and interesting finding and made him wonder why emotional experiences should improve long-term memories for related events.

After McGaugh found that the "emotional" hormones and drugs could be safely used in animals, he began his work with human subjects. His study on animals and humans of why emotional events seemed to "stamp in" memories spanned 40 years of research. Here's one of his interesting studies.

Memories of Emotional Events

Can drugs block emotional memories?

After almost 20 years of research using an animal model, McGaugh found a way to safely study this phenomenon in humans.

Subjects. Those in the experimental group received a drug (propranolol) that decreases or blocks the effects of hormones (epinephrine and norepinephrine) that are normally produced during emotional states. After taking this drug, experimental subjects would still feel emotions, but the drug would block the secretion of those emotionally produced hormones that had been shown to increase memory in animals. Subjects in the control group received a placebo, but because of the double-blind procedure, no subjects knew whether they were given a drug or a placebo.

Procedure. So that the drugs would have time to act, subjects were given either a placebo or the drug 1 hour before seeing a series of slides. To prevent their expectations from biasing the results, subjects did not know whether they got a drug or a placebo.

Each subject watched a series of 12 slides and heard an accompanying story. The beginning of the slide story was emotionally neutral and simply described a mother leaving home with her son to visit her husband's workplace. The middle of the slide story was emotionally charged and described the son having a terrible accident in which his feet were severed and his skull was damaged. The end of the slide story was emotionally neutral and described the mother leaving the hospital to pick up her other child from preschool. Subjects were tested for retention of the slide story a week later.

Hypothesis. Based on their results from the animal model, McGaugh and his colleagues guessed that if a drug blocked the effects of memory-enhancing hormones normally produced during

emotional situations, subjects who took the drug should show poor retention for emotional events.

Results and conclusion. Researchers found that both drug and placebo subjects remembered about the same number of neutral events. However, the graph below shows that, compared to subjects in the placebo group, subjects given a drug that blocked "emotional" hormones remembered significantly fewer emotionally charged events (Cahill et al., 1994). Other studies on humans found that, just as in rats, intense feelings triggered by emotional or stressful situations are encoded, or "carved in stone," by hormones released during emotionally charged situations and that these memories are better remembered (Hamann et al., 1999; McGaugh, 1999). McGaugh's research is a good example of using an animal model to lay the basis for similar studies in humans. But of what use is it to animals or humans for emotional memories to be better remembered?

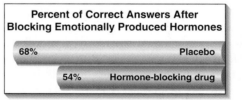

Percent of Correct Answers After Blocking Emotionally Produced Hormones

68%	Placebo
54%	Hormone-blocking drug

Based on years of research, McGaugh believed that one reason emotions seem to "stamp in" memories is to help a species survive. For instance, if emotions stamped in memories of dramatic or life-threatening situations, our early ancestors would better pay attention to and remember to avoid these dangers and thus increase their chances of survival (Dolan, 2002).

An important clinical application of McGaugh's research is that it explains why bad emotional memories, such as those formed after witnessing or being in a terrible accident or suffering physical or sexual abuse, are stamped in and thus become so powerful and so difficult to treat and overcome. McGaugh is now working on this problem.

While McGaugh's research shows that emotional feelings are easily encoded, you'll see next that nonemotional information, such as learning terms and definitions, can be encoded only with hard work.

F. Encoding: Transferring

How do we store memories?

It's very common for someone to say, "Let me tell you about my day," and then proceed to describe in great detail a long list of mostly bad things, including long, word-for-word conversations. You can easily recall these detailed personal experiences, even though you took no notes. That's because many personal experiences are automatically, and with no effort on your part, encoded in your long-term memory.

Encoding refers to acquiring information or storing information in memory by changing this information into neural or memory codes.

Let me tell you about my awful day First . . .

Why is it that detailed personal experiences and conversation seem to be encoded effortlessly and automatically and easily recalled? Why is it that much of book learning, such as memorizing terms or definitions, usually requires deliberate effort and considerable time and may still not be easily recalled when taking exams? The answer is that there are to two different kinds of encoding: automatic and effortful encoding.

Encoded for storage → *Long-term memory*

Automatic Encoding

Why are some things easy to encode?

Just as most of us can easily and in great detail recall all the annoying things that happened today, the person below is recalling a long list of very detailed personal activities that were automatically encoded into his long-term memory. In fact, many personal events (often unpleasant ones), as well as things we're interested in (movies, music, sports) and a wide range of skills (riding a bike) and habits, are automatically encoded (Murnane et al., 1999).

Automatic encoding is the transfer of information from short-term into long-term memory without any effort and usually without any awareness.

I bought this hat at a second-hand store for a quarter, and then I bought these shoes from a guy who said that he makes them from old tires . . .

Personal events. One reason many of your personal experiences and conversations are automatically encoded is that they hold your interest and attention and easily fit together with hundreds of previous associations. Because personal experiences, which are examples of *episodic information,* are encoded automatically into long-term memory, you can easily recall lengthy conversations, facts about movies and sports figures, television shows, clothes you bought, or food you ate.

Interesting facts. You may know avid sports fans or watchers of popular TV programs who remember an amazing number of facts and details, seemingly without effort. Because these kinds of facts (*semantic information)* are personally interesting and fit with previous associations, they are automatically and easily encoded into declarative long-term memory.

Skills and habits. Learning how to perform various motor skills, such as playing tennis or riding a bike, and developing habits, such as brushing your teeth, are examples of *procedural information,* which is also encoded automatically. For example, H. M. learned and remembered how to mirror-draw because mirror-drawing is a motor skill that is automatically encoded into procedural long-term memory.

On the other hand, factual or technical information from textbooks is usually not encoded automatically but rather requires deliberate, or effortful, encoding, which we'll discuss next.

Effortful Encoding

Why are some things hard to encode?

The person below is pulling his hair because learning unfamiliar or complicated material almost always involves *semantic information,* such as complex terms, which is difficult to encode because such information is often uninteresting, complicated, or requires making new or difficult associations. For all these reasons, semantic information, such as terms, can be encoded only with considerable concentration and effort.

Effortful encoding involves the transfer of information from short-term into long-term memory either by working hard to repeat or rehearse the information or, especially, by making associations between new and old information.

I've been studying these terms for hours and I still can't remember their definitions.

You already know that some information, such as learning a skill, habit, or interesting personal event, is often encoded effortlessly and automatically. In contrast, semantic information, such as learning hundreds of new or difficult terms, facts, concepts, or equations, usually requires effortful encoding because you must form hundreds of new associations. Forming new associations is often just plain hard work and is made even more difficult if you are simultaneously taking two or three difficult classes or have limited time because of other responsibilities, such as a part-time job.

Although there are two methods of effortful encoding—rehearsing and forming associations—the most effective method involves forming associations between the new information that you are trying to learn and the old information that you have already stored in long-term memory. The better the effortful encoding, the better the recall on exams. We'll explain the two methods of effortful encoding, rehearsing and forming associations, and why the second method is more effective and results in better recall.

How much do you remember?

Think of encoding information in your brain as similar to saving information on a gigantic computer hard drive. Unless you have a very good system for labeling and filing the hundreds of computer files, you will have great difficulty finding or retrieving a particular file from the hard drive. Similarly, how easily you can remember or retrieve a particular memory from your brain depends on how much effort you used to encode the information. There are two kinds of effortful encoding: maintenance rehearsal and elaborative rehearsal (S. C. Brown & Craik, 2000).

MAINTENANCE REHEARSAL

The easiest way to remember information for only a short period of time, such as a new phone number, for example, 926-4029, is to simply repeat or rehearse it. This kind of effortful encoding is called maintenance rehearsal.

Maintenance rehearsal refers to simply repeating or rehearsing the information rather than forming any new associations.

Maintenance rehearsal works best for maintaining or keeping information longer in *short-term memory*, such as remembering a phone number for a few seconds while dialing it. However, if you want to remember the phone number later, maintenance rehearsal is not a good encoding process because it does not include a system for keeping track of how and where that particular phone number will be stored. If you need to remember a phone number for a long period of time and avoid having to keep looking it up, you'll need to use another form of effortful encoding called elaborative rehearsal.

Maintenance rehearsal is not a very effective encoding process.

ELABORATIVE REHEARSAL

There are some phone numbers and much information from lectures and textbooks that you want to encode so that you remember the information for long periods of time. To have the greatest chance for remembering something, it's best to encode information using elaborative rehearsal.

Elaborative rehearsal involves using effort to actively make meaningful associations between new information that you wish to remember and old or familiar information that is already stored in long-term memory.

Elaborative rehearsal is a very effective encoding process.

For example, using elaborative rehearsal, you could associate this phone number, 926-4029, with age: An old person is "926," I'm not "40," but I wish I were "29." To recall this number, you think of the different age associations and those associations lead to the phone number.

To test the usefulness of elaborative rehearsal, students were asked to remember many groups of three words each, such as *dog, bike,* and *street.* Students who encoded the words with maintenance rehearsal (repeating words) did poorly on recall. In comparison, students who encoded the words using elaborative rehearsal, that is, taking the effort to make associations among the three words (dog rides a bike down the street), had significantly better recall (McDaniel & Einstein, 1986).

Effectiveness. Elaborative rehearsal is such an effective system of encoding because by making associations between new and old information you create cues for locating or retrieving the new information from long-term memory. For example, thinking of the association (dog rides a bike down the street) helps you remember the three words (dog, bike, street).

How important are associations?

The poorest system for encoding information is to simply repeat the information, which is maintenance rehearsal. The best encoding system is to make associations, which is elaborative rehearsal. How much effort and time you put into encoding information is the basis for the levels-of-processing theory (Craik & Lockhart, 1972).

The *levels-of-processing theory* says that remembering depends on how information is encoded. If you encode by paying attention only to basic features (length of phone number), information is encoded at a shallow level and results in poor recall. If you encode by making new associations, this information will be encoded at a deeper level, which results in better recall.

For example, students were shown a series of words and asked a question after each one. The questions were of three types, designed to trigger three different levels of processing.

1. Shallow processing question:
"Is the word printed in capital letters?" Asks about one physical feature of the word.

2. Deeper processing question:
"Does the word rhyme with *rain?*" Asks about sound properties of the word.

3. Deepest processing question:
"Does the word fit into the sentence 'She was late for the _____'?" Asks about the meaning of the word.

After students answered these questions, they were tested to see how many of the original words they recognized.

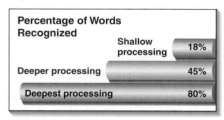

Percentage of Words Recognized

Shallow processing	18%
Deeper processing	45%
Deepest processing	80%

As shown in the graph above, students recognized the smallest percentage of words after shallow processing and the most after the deepest processing (Craik & Tulving, 1975).

This study clearly demonstrates that the system you use to process or encode information has a great effect on how easily you can remember or retrieve the information (Roediger et al., 2002). As we'll discuss in Module 12, a major reason for forgetting is poor encoding (S. C. Brown & Craik, 2000).

Next, we'll discuss a kind of memory that has resulted in great controversy because of the difficulties in determining whether the event ever happened.

G. Repressed Memories

Recovered Memories

Who's to blame?

At the beginning of this module, we discussed the case of Holly (left photo), who had accused her father (right photo) of sexual molestation beginning when she was 6 years old. Holly's memories of sexual abuse first surfaced during therapy sessions 13 years later, when she was 19. The father sued Holly's therapist for implanting false memories. The jury partly agreed with the father in deciding that Holly's memories were probably false and that the therapist had not implanted the memories but had carelessly reinforced them (Butler, 1994). A state appeals court dismissed Holly's case against her father because some of her testimony about sexual abuse was obtained under sodium amytal, the so-called truth serum, which was administered by her

"He abused me."

"I did not."

therapist. Because testimony taken under sodium amytal is often unreliable, it has been barred in California's courts since 1959 (*Los Angeles Times,* August 21, 1997).

Holly's case illustrates one of the more explosive issues in psychology, the problem of repressed and recovered memories.

Psychiatrist Harold Lief, one of the first to question the accuracy of repressed memories, said, "We don't know what percent of these recovered memories are real and what percent are pseudomemories (false). . . . But we do know there are hundreds, maybe thousands of cases of pseudomemories and that many families have been destroyed by them" (J. E. Brody, 2000a, p. D8).

We'll discuss four major issues related to repressed and recovered memories.

Definition of Repressed Memories

What's different about a repressed memory?

The idea of repressed memories is based on Sigmund Freud's theory of repression, which underlies much of his psychoanalytic theory of personality (discussed in Module 19).

Repression is the process by which the mind pushes a memory of some threatening or traumatic event deep into the unconscious. Once in the unconscious, the repressed memory cannot be retrieved at will and may remain there until something releases it and the person remembers it.

Some therapists believe that children who are sexually abused cope with such traumatic situations and their feelings of guilt by repressing the memories. For example, a client may enter therapy with sexual problems or a mood disorder and later in therapy uncover repressed memories, such as being sexually abused as a child, as the cause of her current problems. Clients usually have total amnesia

Repressed memories are difficult to recover.

(loss of memory) for the traumatic experience, their recovery of repressed memories usually occurs in the first 12 months of therapy, and recovered memories usually involve specific incidents (Andrews et al., 2000).

Based on clients' experiences, therapists believe that repressed memories of sexual abuse do occur. However, a prominent memory researcher disagrees: "The idea that forgetting in abuse survivors is caused by a special repression mechanism—something more powerful than conscious suppression—is still without a scientific basis" (Schacter, 1996, p. 264). Thus, the controversy over repressed memories continues.

Researcher Elizabeth Loftus (1997b) partly blamed increased reports of recovered memories on some therapeutic practices.

Therapist's Role in Recovered Memories

How does a therapist know?

Therapists who treat survivors of incest and other traumatic situations maintain that repressed memories are so completely blocked that it may take deliberate suggestion and effort to release them, sometimes using images, hypnosis, or so-called truth serum, sodium amytal.

For example, in one case a client recalls that her therapist insisted that she showed signs of having been sexually abused during childhood and probably had terrible memories buried in her unconscious. The client was dubious at first but, wanting to please her therapist, finally admitted to being raped at the age of 4. However, after leaving the hospital and enlisting help from new therapists, she concluded that the sexual assaults had never happened (Bower, 1993a). Whatever the therapists' good intentions, Loftus (1993; 1997b) wonders

The therapist may have suggested traumatic memories.

if some therapists are suggesting or implanting traumatic memories in their clients rather than releasing repressed ones. Most often, repressed memories and resulting accusations of sexual abuse were reported by women (87%) who were in therapy for depression or eating disorders (Gudjonsson, 1997).

There are also many examples of therapists who have helped clients recover and deal with terrible repressed memories (Gold et al., 1994). Thus, therapists are in the difficult position of trying to distinguish accurate accounts of repressed memories from those that may have been shaped or reinforced by the suggestions or expectations of the therapist (Byrd, 1994).

Questions about whether repressed memories can be influenced by a therapist's suggestions raise the issue of whether false memories can be implanted.

Do people believe "fake" memories?

Because, in some cases, it appears that therapists' suggestions may have contributed to implanting false memories, researchers studied whether fake memories could in fact be implanted and later recalled as being "true."

Researchers gave 24 adults a booklet that contained descriptions of three events that occurred when each adult was 5 years old (Loftus, 1997a). Two of the childhood events had *really happened* because they were obtained from parents or relatives. One childhood event of being lost in a shopping mall, crying, being comforted by an elderly woman, and finally getting reunited with the family had *not happened,* according to parents and relatives. After reading the three events described in the booklet, the adults (aged 18–53) were asked to write what they remembered of the event or, if they did not remember, to write "I do not remember this."

The graph above shows that 68% of subjects remembered some or most of the two *true events* from their childhood. However, about 29% also said that they remembered having experienced the one *false event of* being lost in the mall at age 5. (Loftus, 1997a).

Researchers concluded that although the memory of being lost in a mall is neither as terrible nor as terrifying as the memory of being abused, this study does show that false memories can be implanted through suggestion alone. Even on a follow-up interview, subjects continued to insist that they remembered the false event.

There are now many similar studies reporting that false memories can be implanted in both children and adults (Loftus, 2003; S. M. Smith et al., 2003). However, the fact that false memories can be implanted and later recalled as true does in no way disprove the occurrence of repressed memories. Rather, studies on implanting false memories simply show that a false suggestion can grow into a vivid, detailed, and believable personal memory (Ceci, 2000; Loftus, 2000).

The repeated finding that false memories can be implanted in children and adults and later remembered as "true" raises a question about the accuracy of repressed memories that are later recovered and believed to be true.

Percentage of Subjects Who Remembered True and False Memories

Recalled events after reading booklet	False	29%
	True	68%

About 29% of subjects said that they remembered a childhood event that never happened (false) and 68% remembered childhood events that did happen (true).

How accurate are repressed memories?

Some individuals may initially enter therapy for help with mood disorders or eating problems but during the course of therapy, they recovered memories, apparently repressed, of childhood sexual abuse. Since researchers have shown that "false" memories can be implanted through suggestion and believed to be "true" memories, some question whether a client's recovered memories are accurate or were implanted by the therapist's suggestions.

In a few cases, the accuracy of recovered memories can be established. For example, a client who suffered from obesity entered a hospital weight-reduction program that also included psychotherapy. During therapy, she experienced flashbacks of being sexually abused from about age 5 by her older brother, who had since been killed in the war. When she searched through his things, she found a diary in which he had described sexual experiments with his little sister (B. Bower, 1993a). In this case, the woman's repressed memories of sexual abuse were proved accurate by confirming evidence, her brother's diary.

In many cases, the accuracy of recovered memories cannot be clearly established because there is no collaborating evidence of the client's report that the traumatic event really did occur 20–30 years earlier. Therapists tend to believe their client's report of recovered memories partly because there is little reason for their client to lie and partly because childhood sexual abuse may

Some question the accuracy of repressed memories.

explain their client's current problems (Loftus, 1993).

There is reason to question the accuracy of recovered memories if they were obtained under hypnosis or "truth serum" (sodium amytal). In those situations, people often become more open to suggestion and may later recall events that had been suggested during hypnosis as being true (Lynn et al., 2003).

Another reason to question the accuracy of recovered memories is reports of more than 300 clients who later retracted charges of childhood sexual abuse based on memories that were recovered in therapy (de Rivera, 1997). In about a dozen other cases, clients have successfully sued and won large monetary awards from their therapists for implanting false memories of child abuse (Loftus, 1999). All these examples question the accuracy of some recovered memories.

Conclusions. Memory researcher Elizabeth Loftus (1997a; 2003) states that there are examples of recovered memories that are accurate. However, she questions the accuracy of recovered memories for three reasons: Research has shown that memories that are very detailed but later proven false can be implanted in both children and adults; some clients later retracted their recovered memories; and memories might have been implanted by therapists' suggestions and/or the clients needed and used these memories to explain their current psychological problems. For these reasons, new guidelines have cautioned therapists against using forceful or persuasive suggestions that might elicit memories from their clients (J. E. Brody, 2000a).

The debate over repressed and recovered memories, which reached its peak in the mid-1990s, has recently decreased because some therapists have been sued by their patients over the accuracy of recovered memories and researchers have showed that false memories could be implanted in both children and adults (Lynn et al., 2003).

✔ Concept Review

1. Three processes are involved in memory: the process in which information is placed or stored in memory by making mental representations is called (a)_____; the process of placing encoded information into a permanent mental state is called (b)_____; the process of getting information out of short-term or permanent storage is called (c)_____.

2. The initial step in memory is a process that holds visual and auditory information in its raw form for a very brief period of time, from an instant to several seconds; this process is called _____.

3. Memory that holds raw visual information for up to a quarter of a second is called (a)_____. Memory that holds raw auditory information for up to several seconds is called (b)_____. The process for controlling the transfer of information from sensory memory to the next memory process is (c)_____.

4. The kind of memory that has a limited capacity of about seven items (plus or minus two) and a short duration (2–30 seconds) for unrehearsed information is called either (a)_____ or _____. One way to increase this memory capacity is by combining separate pieces of information into larger units, which is called (b)_____. One way to increase the duration of this memory is by repeating the information, which is called (c)_____.

5. The kind of memory that can store almost unlimited amounts of information over a long period of time is _____, whose accuracy may undergo change and distortion across time.

6. The process for controlling the transfer of information from short-term memory into long-term memory is called _____, which may be automatic or may involve deliberate effort.

7. The process for selecting information from long-term memory and transferring it back into short-term memory is _____.

8. The better recall of items at the beginning of a list is called the (a)_____ effect. The better recall of items at the end of a list is called the (b)_____ effect. Evidence that there are two kinds of memory, short- and long-term, comes from the (c)_____ effect.

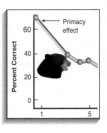

9. There are two kinds of encoding. Simply repeating or rehearsing the information is called (a)_____. Actively making associations between new and old information already stored is called (b)_____.

10. One kind of long-term memory that involves memories for facts or events, such as scenes, stories, words, conversations, faces, or daily events, is called (a)_____ memory. We can retrieve these memories and are conscious of them. One kind of declarative memory that involves events or personal experiences is called (b)_____ memory. A second kind of declarative memory that involves general knowledge, facts, or definitions of words is called (c)_____ memory.

11. A second kind of long-term memory that involves performing motor or perceptual tasks, carrying out habits, and responding to stimuli because of classical conditioning is called _____ memory. We cannot retrieve these memories and are not conscious of them.

12. Something happens that is so threatening, shocking, or traumatic that our mind pushes that memory into the unconscious, from which it cannot be retrieved at will. This phenomenon is called _____.

13. During very emotional or stressful situations, the body secretes chemicals called (a)_____ that act to make encoding very effective, and this results in vivid, long-term memories. Researchers believe that this hormonal encoding system for stressful or emotional events has helped our species (b)_____.

Answers: 1. (a) encoding, (b) storage, (c) retrieval; 2. sensory memory; 3. (a) iconic memory, (b) echoic memory, (c) attention; 4. (a) short-term, or working, memory, (b) chunking, (c) rehearsal, or maintenance rehearsal; 5. long-term memory; 6. encoding; 7. retrieval; 8. (a) primacy, (b) recency, (c) primacy-recency; 9. (a) maintenance rehearsal, (b) elaborative rehearsal; 10. (a) declarative, (b) episodic, (c) semantic; 11. procedural or nondeclarative; 12. repression, or repressed memory; 13. (a) hormones, (b) survive

United States Versus Africa

What do you remember best?

If you went to grade school in the United States, you spent considerable time in your first 8 years learning to read and write. In the U.S. culture, reading and writing skills are viewed as being not only very important for personal growth and development but also necessary for achieving success in one's career. For similar reasons, the schools of many industrialized cultures place heavy emphasis on teaching reading and writing, which allow individuals to encode great amounts of information in long-term memory. In addition, reading and writing skills are necessary for being admitted to and doing well in college.

In contrast, if you went to grade school in the more rural countries of Africa, you would have spent your first 8 or so years learning primarily through the spoken word rather than the written word. In the less industrialized countries of Africa, such as Ghana, there are fewer public

In more rural parts of Africa (Ghana), children must rely more on oral than written information.

or private schools, fewer textbooks and libraries. As a result, these cultures are said to have a strong *oral tradition*, which means that these people have considerable practice in passing on information through speaking and retelling. The Ghana culture emphasizes the oral tradition, which means encoding information after hearing it rather than after reading it.

With Ghana's emphasis on oral tradition, we would expect that African people would better encode and remember information that was spoken. In comparison, with the United States' emphasis on *written tradition*, we would expect that American people would better encode and remember information that was read rather than spoken. Let's see if this hypothesis has been supported.

Remembering Spoken Information

WAR OF THE GHOSTS

One night, two young men from Egulac went down to the river to hunt seals, and while they were there it became foggy and calm. Then they heard war cries, and they thought: "Maybe this is a war party." They escaped to the shore and hid behind a log. Now canoes came up, and they heard the noise of paddles and saw one canoe coming up to them. There were five men in the canoe, and they said:

"What do you think? We wish to take you along. We are going up the river to make war on the people."

One of the young men said: "I have no arrows."

"Arrows are in the canoe," they said.

"I will not go along. I might be killed. My relatives do not know where I have gone. But you," he said, turning to the other, "may go with them."

So one of the young men went, but the other returned home.

And the warriors went up the river to a town on the other side of Kalama. The people came down to the water, and they began to fight, and many were killed (story continues but is too long for full reprint).

Who best remembers what they heard?

On the left is part of a story called "War of the Ghosts," which was read aloud in English to college students at Winneba Training College in Ghana and at New York University. Each group of students heard the story twice and were told to just listen to the story so that they would not take notes on their own. They were not told that they would be tested on its content.

Although English was not the native language of the Ghanaian students, they had learned English in previous schooling, and English was used exclusively in their Training College. Sixteen days after hearing "War of the Ghosts," students were asked to write down as much of the text as they could remember. Researchers scored the amount and accuracy of recalled information by counting the number of ideas or themes and the total number of words (330). The "War of the Ghosts" story has been used frequently in memory research because it can be broken down into 21 themes, or ideas, and easily scored. For example, two of the 21 themes or ideas are (1) two young men went to hunt seals and (2) they heard war cries.

As the graph on the right shows, Ghanaian students remembered a significantly higher percentage of themes and a larger number of words than did American students. The Ghanaian students' superior performance was even more remarkable since they were tested by having to write the themes or ideas in English, which was their second language.

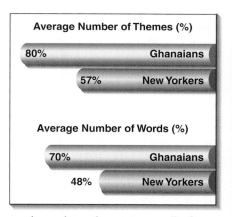

Average Number of Themes (%)

80% Ghanaians

57% New Yorkers

Average Number of Words (%)

70% Ghanaians

48% New Yorkers

These results support the idea that the Ghanaian students showed superior recall of spoken information because of their long oral tradition, which involves practicing encoding information through hearing rather than reading (Ross & Millsom, 1970). This study indicates that a culture's emphasis on how information is presented or taught can influence how information or events are encoded and how easily they can be recalled.

Next, we'll examine some unusual cases of encoding and retrieving information.

I. Application: Unusual Memories

Photographic Memory

Can you recall everything?

One kind of unusual memory that many of us wish we had is the ability to remember everything with little or no difficulty. Such an amazing memory is commonly called a photographic memory.

Photographic memory, which occurs in adults, is the ability to form sharp, detailed visual images after examining a picture or page for a short period of time and to recall the entire image at a later date.

She could perfectly visualize her class notes so didn't have to study for exams.

There are no reports of someone developing a photographic memory and only one or two reports of adults who had a truly photographic memory (Stromeyer, 1970). Sometimes people with exceptional memories are mislabeled as having photographic memories. For example, Rajan, who we described earlier as memorizing 31,811 numbers,

denies that he has a photographic memory.

At a recent national memory contest (U.S. Memoriad), Tatiana Cooley (left photo) came in first by doing incredible memory feats, such as pairing 70 names and faces after studying a stack of 100 faces for just 20 minutes. As a child, Tatiana's mother would read to her, and when Tatiana was $2\frac{1}{2}$ years old, she read one of the books back to her mother. In college, Tatiana says, "I remember visualizing the notes that I had taken in class and being able to recall them verbatim for tests so I didn't have to study" (Rogers & Morehouse, 1999, p. 90). To keep her memory sharp, she spends 45 minutes each day memorizing the order in which cards appear in a freshly shuffled deck. Wow! Tatiana's ability to visually remember her notes during exams comes close to satisfying the definition for having a photographic memory.

Although there are few examples of adults with photographic memories, a very small percentage of children do have photographic memories.

Eidetic Imagery

Can you memorize this picture?

A small number of children have the ability to look at a picture for a few seconds and then describe it in great detail. This kind of remarkable memory is called eidetic *(eye-DET-ick)* imagery.

Eidetic imagery, which is a form of photographic memory that occurs in children, is the ability to examine a picture or page for 10–30 seconds and then for several minutes hold in one's mind a detailed visual image of the material.

For example, an 11-year-old girl was given the following instructions: "Look at this picture from Rudyard Kipling's *The Jungle Book* for a few minutes. Hold the details of this picture in your mind's eye for several minutes. Now, close your eyes and describe what you see."

After the picture (at right) was removed, the young girl closed her eyes and, without hesitation, she described the picture in great detail, as follows: "Ground is dark greenish brown, then there's a mama and a little leopard and there's a native sitting against him. Then there's a pool with a crab coming out . . . with a fish in it, and I think there are turtles walking in front and a porcupine down near the right. There's a tree that separates a cow in half. The cow's brown and white, and there's something up in the tree—I can't see the bottom right-hand corner. There's a sun with a lot of rays on it near the top on the right . . . eight rays . . . the porcupine has a lot of bristles on it . . . the right is disappearing. I can still see that cow that's divided by the tree . . . Oh, there's a crocodile or alligator in the right-hand corner . . . It's very faint . . . It's gone" (Haber, 1980, p. 72).

What is unusual about her description is not only the amount of detail but also the fact that she seems

to be examining a vivid visual image of the actual drawing that seems to be held for a time in her mind's eye.

This girl's description is an example of eidetic imagery, which has been shown to be a real phenomenon that occurs in only about 5–8% of preadolescent children. The small percentage of children with eidetic imagery almost always lose the ability around adolescence (Neath, 1998). Why eidetic imagery drops out in adults is not known, but some suggest it may be because adults learn to use and rely more on words than on pictures (Crowder, 1992). The one or two times eidetic imagery did occur in adults it was usually called photographic memory.

Many of us have experienced a very vivid and detailed memory that is called a "flashbulb memory."

Eidetic imagery: The young girl closed her eyes and, without hesitation, she described the picture in great detail, as follows: "Ground is dark greenish brown, there's a little leopard, and there's a native sitting against him. There's a pool with a crab coming out and fish in it, and a turtle walking, and at the top a sun with lots of rays. . . ."

What makes a memory so vivid?

Although it happened almost 20 years ago, I have a detailed memory of a pickup truck turning over and bouncing as it hit the side of the freeway. I can play back this terrible scene in great detail and vivid color as if I were watching a crash scene in a movie. Many individuals have had a similar experience, and this kind of memory event is called a flashbulb memory (R. Brown & Kulik, 1977).

Flashbulb memories are vivid recollections, usually in great detail, of dramatic or emotionally charged incidents that are of interest to the person. This information is encoded effortlessly and may last for long periods of time.

IMPACT AND ACCURACY

Flashbulb memories usually involve events that are extremely surprising, emotionally arousing, or have very important meaning or consequences for the person. For example, when people were questioned about what they were doing when they heard that President Kennedy or Reagan had been shot, or when the space shuttle *Challenger* exploded, about 80–90% could recall vivid details seven months later (Pillemer, 1984). Researchers concluded that only events that are personally significant and have an emotional impact result in the formation of flashbulb memories (P. S. R. Davidson & Glisky, 2002).

Although flashbulb memories are reported with great confidence and in vivid details, this does not mean the memories are necessarily accurate. That's because people mistake the vividness of flashbulb memories for their accuracy. In fact, researchers report that although flashbulb memories are very vivid, this does not guarantee any special accuracy (Talarico & Rubin, 2003).

MOST-REMEMBERED EVENTS

As you can see in the center table, the top five flashbulb memories of college students involved a car accident, a college roommate, high school graduation and prom, and a romantic experience, all of which are emotionally charged events (D. C. Rubin & Kozin, 1984).

Initially, flashbulb memories were claimed to represent a special kind of memory that was complete, accurate, vivid, and immune to forgetting (R. Brown & Kulik, 1977). Since then, several studies have investigated these claims and reported that flashbulb memories do not seem to be a separate, special kind of memory because flashbulb memories are subject to inaccuracies, change with retelling, and are even forgotten over time (Schooler & Eich, 2000).

Examples of Flashbulb Memories

Cues	Percent*
A car accident you were in or witnessed	85
When you first met your college roommate	82
Night of your high school graduation	81
Night of your senior prom (if you went or not)	78
An early romantic experience	77
A time you had to speak in front of an audience	72
When you got your college admissions letter	65
Your first date—the moment you met him/her	57
Day President Reagan was shot in Washington	52
Night President Nixon resigned	41
First time you flew in an airplane	40
Moment you opened your SAT scores	33
Your 17th birthday	30
Day of the first space shuttle flight	24
The last time you ate a holiday dinner at home	23
Your first college class	21
The first time your parents left you alone for some time	19
Your 13th birthday	12

*Percentage of students in the memory experiment who reported that events on the experimenter's list were of flashbulb quality (Rubin & Kozin, 1984).

MULTINATIONAL STUDY

In a multinational study of flashbulb memory, British and non-British people were asked what they were doing when they heard that the former Prime Minister Margaret Thatcher had resigned. Of the 215 British residents surveyed one year later, 86% reported having flashbulb memories, which occurred spontaneously and proved to be vivid, accurate, and full of detail. In comparison, less than 29% of 154 non-British subjects from North America and Denmark reported flashbulb memories of this event (Conway et al., 1994). These researchers concluded that flashbulb memories represent a special kind of automatic encoding that occurs when events are emotionally and personally interesting. In addition, flashbulb memories have been found to be long-lasting, 50 years or more (Tekcan & Peynircioglu, 2002).

FLASHBULB MEMORIES: BRAINS AND HORMONES

Researchers think the reason flashbulb memories are so detailed and long-lasting is that their emotionally arousing content activates a special brain area and several hormones. For example, researchers believe that flashbulb memories involve a brain structure called the amygdala (p. 80), which plays a key role in processing and encoding strong emotional experiences (P. S. R. Davidson & Glisky, 2002).

Also, in the earlier Research Focus (p. 247), we discussed how emotionally triggered hormones are involved in encoding long-term memories as if "in stone" (McGaugh, 1999). The secretion of these "emotional" hormones is thought to play an important role in encoding emotionally charged personal experiences into long-lasting memories (Schooler & Eich, 2000).

MEMORY: PICTURES VERSUS IMPRESSIONS

Each of us has a remarkable memory system that can encode, store, and retrieve unlimited amounts of information over long periods of time. But it's important to remember that memories are not perfect pictures of objects, people, and events but rather our personal impressions of these things. For example, the things that you remember when you're in a good mood and having a "good day" are very different from the things that you remember when you're in a bad mood and having a "bad day." This means that what you remember and recall may be changed, biased, or distorted by a wide range of emotional feelings, personal experiences, stressful situations, or social influences (Roediger & McDermott, 2000).

✔ Summary Test

A. THREE TYPES OF MEMORY

1. The study of memory, which is the ability to retain information over time, includes three separate processes. The first process—placing information in memory—is called (a)_____. The second process, which is filing information in memory, is called (b)_____. The third process—commonly referred to as remembering—is called (c)_____.

2. Although we think of memory as a single event, it is really a complex sequence that may be separated into three different kinds of memory. The initial memory process that holds raw information for up to several seconds is called _____. During this time, you have the chance to identify or pay attention to new information.

3. If you pay attention to information in sensory memory, this information is automatically transferred into a second kind of memory process, called _____ memory.

4. If you rehearse or think about information in short-term memory, that information will usually be transferred or encoded into the third, more permanent kind of memory process called _____.

B. SENSORY MEMORY: RECORDING

5. Visual sensory memory, known as (a)_____ memory, lasts about a quarter of a second. Auditory memory, known as (b)_____ memory, may last as long as two seconds. Sensory memory has many functions; for example, it prevents you from being overwhelmed by too much incoming information and gives you time to identify the incoming data and pay attention to them.

C. SHORT-TERM MEMORY: WORKING

6. If you pay attention to information in sensory memory, it is automatically transferred to short-term memory, which has two main characteristics. The first is that unrehearsed information will disappear after 2–30 seconds, indicating that short-term memory has a limited (a)_____. The second characteristic is that short-term memory can hold only about seven items (plus or minus two), indicating that short-term memory has a limited (b)_____. You can increase the length of time that

information remains in short-term memory by intentionally repeating the information, which is called (c)_____. You can considerably increase the capacity of short-term memory by combining separate items of information into larger units, which is called (d)_____.

D. LONG-TERM MEMORY: STORING

7. Let's follow the progress of information from the time it enters sensory memory to its storage in long-term memory. For an instant to several seconds, incoming raw information is held in (a)_____. If you do not pay attention to this information, it disappears forever; if you pay attention, that information is automatically transferred to short-term memory. The transfer of information from sensory memory to short-term memory is controlled by the process of (b)_____.

8. If information in short-term memory is not (a)_____, it will disappear in 2–30 seconds. If you rehearse or think about information in short-term memory, it may be transferred into long-term memory. The transfer of information from short-term into long-term memory is controlled by a process called (b)_____. In some cases, information is transferred automatically; in other cases, this transfer process may require deliberate effort.

9. The process of selecting information from long-term memory and transferring it back into short-term memory is called _____. Because information has been encoded into long-term memory does not guarantee that such information can always or easily be remembered or retrieved.

10. One demonstration of the existence of, and difference between, short-term and long-term memory is observed in the order that subjects remember items from a multiple-item list. Subjects tend to have better recall of items at the beginning of a list; this tendency is called the (a)_____ effect and involves long-term memory. Subjects tend to have better recall of items at the end of the list; this tendency is called the (b)_____ effect and involves short-term memory. The order in which subjects recall items from a long list is called the (c)_____ effect.

11. There are two different kinds of long-term memory. One kind involves memories of facts or events, such as scenes, stories, words, conversations, faces, or daily events. We can retrieve these memories and are conscious of them; they constitute (a)_____ memory. There are two kinds of declarative memory. One kind consists of factual knowledge of the world, concepts, word definitions, and language rules; this is called (b)_____ memory. The second kind of declarative memory consists of knowledge about personal experiences (episodes) or activities; this is called (c)_____ memory.

12. A second kind of long-term memory involves memories for performing motor or perceptual tasks, carrying out habits, and responding to stimuli because of classical conditioning; this is called _____ memory. We cannot retrieve these memories and are not conscious of them.

E. RESEARCH FOCUS: DO EMOTIONS AFFECT MEMORIES?

13. There are times when for safety, moral, or ethical reasons researchers cannot use human subjects but instead use an (a)_____ model. Using this model, researchers found that during emotional or stressful situations, the body secretes chemicals called (b)_____, which make encoding so effective that these situations become very vivid long-term memories. One reason for the evolution of this carved-in-stone memory system is to help the species survive by remembering dangerous situations.

F. ENCODING: TRANSFERRING

14. The process of storing information in memory by making mental representations is called (a)_____. There are two processes for encoding information. Most procedural and episodic information is transferred from short-term into long-term memory without any effort, and usually without any awareness, through a process called (b)_____ encoding. Much semantic information is transferred from short-term into long-term memory by deliberate attempts to repeat, rehearse, or make associations. Together, these deliberate attempts are referred to as (c)_____ encoding.

15. There are two kinds of effortful encoding, which differ in their effectiveness. Encoding by simply repeating or rehearsing the information is called (a)_____. This method is not very effective because it involves little thinking about the information or making new associations. Encoding that involves thinking about the information and making new associations is called (b)_____.

16. One theory says that memory depends on how information is encoded in the mind. If we pay attention only to basic features of the information, it is encoded at a shallow level, and poor memory results. If we form new associations, the information is encoded at a deeper level, and good memory results. This theory is called _____.

G. REPRESSED MEMORIES

17. If something happens that is threatening, shocking, or traumatic, our minds may push that information deep into the unconscious, from which it may one day be released and enter consciousness. This phenomenon is called (a)_____ and is the theory behind the formation of (b)_____ memories. Unless there is corroborating evidence, the accuracy of repressed memories is difficult to establish.

H. CULTURAL DIVERSITY: ORAL VERSUS WRITTEN

18. Students from Ghana, Africa, remembered more information when it was read to them than did American students who heard the same information. These results show how Ghana's tradition of passing on information orally, which is an example of _____ influences, improves both encoding and recalling or retrieving information.

I. APPLICATION: UNUSUAL MEMORIES

19. The ability of certain children to examine a picture or page for 10–30 seconds and then retain a detailed visual image of the material for several minutes is called (a)_____ imagery. In adults, the ability to form sharp, detailed visual images after a short period and recall the entire image at a later date is called (b)_____ memory. Memories that are vivid recollections, usually in great detail, of dramatic or emotionally charged incidents are called (c) _____. Although very vivid, these memories are not necessarily completely accurate.

Answers: 1. (a) encoding, (b) storing, (c) retrieving; 2. sensory memory; 3. short-term, or working; 4. long-term memory; 5. (a) iconic, (b) echoic; 6. (a) duration, (b) capacity, (c) maintenance rehearsal, (d) chunking; 7. (a) sensory memory, (b) attention; 8. (a) rehearsed, (b) encoding; 9. retrieval, or retrieving; 10. (a) primacy, (b) recency, (c) primacy-recency; 11. (a) declarative, (b) semantic, (c) episodic; 12. procedural or nondeclarative; 13. (a) animal, (b) hormones; 14. (a) encoding, (b) automatic, (c) effortful; 15. (a) maintenance rehearsal, (b) elaborative rehearsal; 16. levels of processing; 17. (a) repression, (b) repressed; 18. cultural; 19. (a) eidetic, (b) photographic, (c) flashbulb memories

Critical Thinking

Were Preschool Children Implanted with False Memories?

Questions

1. What major problems arise when young children are aked about being sexually abused?

2. What is unusual about this mother's accusations, and why were her accusations taken seriously?

3. Is this an example of repressed and recovered memories in children?

In Manhattan Beach, California, a grand jury accused preschool teachers of committing 115 instances of child abuse. Those accused included Ray Buckey; his mother, Peggy Buckey; his elderly grandmother and founder of the preschool, Virginia McMartin; his sister, Peggy Ann Buckey; and three other teachers. The abusive acts that the teachers allegedly committed against the preschool children (ages 2 to 5) included rape, sodomy, oral copulation, animal sacrifice, and satanic rituals. These accusations resulted in the longest (7 years) and costliest ($16 million) trial in American history.

The mother of one child, who had been at the preschool a total of only 14 times and never been in Ray Buckey's classes, accused Ray Buckey of making her boy ride naked on a horse, of molesting him while Ray was dressed as a fireman, cop, clown, and Santa Claus. The same mother also claimed that other preschool teachers had jabbed scissors into her son's eyes and staples into his ears, nipples, and tongue and that Peggy Buckey had killed a baby and made her son drink the blood.

Nearly 400 children were interviewed by social workers from the Children's Institute, who concluded that 369 of the 400 preschool children had been molested. However, before the children were interviewed, none had hinted or made any claims of being sexually abused.

During the interviews, social workers told the children about how other children had already agreed to being sexually abused. The social workers praised and told the children that they were "smart" if they agreed that sexual abuses had occurred and told them that they were "dumb" if they denied that abuse had occurred.

When the interviews, which were videotaped, were carefully reviewed, it became clear that the children soon learned what to say to please the social workers. Not only did children agree to being abused but added more instances, such as tales of horses being killed with baseball bats, of children digging up bodies at a cemetery, and of children being abused at car washes.

After a 7-year-long trial, the jury found the teachers not guilty of child abuse. The jurors agreed with the defense attorneys, who argued that during the interviews the social workers had used suggestions and persuasions to get the preschool children to agree to being abused.

After the not guilty verdict, one of the mothers said, "There is absolutely no shred of doubt in my mind that my three children were abused. I will always believe that all those teachers had abused all of those kids" (Sauer, p. D2). (Adapted from M. Sauer, Decade of accusations, *San Diego Union-Tribune*, August 29, 1993, p. D1)

4. What kind of effects might the interview techniques used by the social workers have on the young children?

5. Is there any evidence that false memories can be implanted in children?

6. After the not guilty verdict, why do you think this mother still believed that her children were molested?

Try InfoTrac to search for terms: **false memories; interviewing children.**

SUGGESTED ANSWERS

1. Some of the problems are that very young children do not understand what sexual abuse is or may not want to talk about such experiences, or they look to their parents or trustworthy adults for advice and answers.
2. This mother's accusations against Ray Buckey seem well beyond what could have happened in a preschool, which is a fairly public place. One reason this mother's accusations were taken seriously was that she was apparently relating what her young child had told her and her child had no reason to lie.
3. Because there is considerable controversy about the occurrence and accuracy of repressed and recovered memories in adults, there would be even more controversy about these phenomena occurring in very young children.

4. By suggesting that "smart" children would agree that the abuse had occurred while "dumb" children would deny such abuse, the interviewers were pressuring the children into giving answers that the interviewers were looking for and not trying to find out what, if anything, happened to the children.
5. There is considerable research showing that false memories can be implanted and become real in the minds of young children. Even after being told that the implanted memories were false, some children continued to believe that the "false" implanted memories were "true" and that the events "really happened."
6. This mother, through repeated questions and suggestions, may have unknowingly implanted false memories in her children. Once implanted, false memories may become real, detailed, and vivid. As a result, the children believe the "false" events happened and the mother has no reason to doubt her children.

Links to Learning

LEARNING ACTIVITIES

- **POWERSTUDY CD-ROM 2.0**
  by Tom Doyle and Rod Plotnik

Check out the "Types of Memory" **SuperModule** (disk 2) on PowerStudy. This is a completely self-paced module that is fully narrated. Don't want the narration? It is easy to turn off! This module includes:

- Videos—Two videos explore Rajan's phenomenal ability to remember. Other imbedded videos discuss short-term memory and chunking.
- A multitude of animations—for example, a virtual dolphin teaches you about the training procedure for mine detection, and an animated exercise helps you remember the three main types of memory— sensory, short-term, and long-term.
- A test of your knowledge using an interactive version of the Summary Test on pages 256 and 257. Also access related quizzes.
- An interactive version of the Critical Thinking exercise "Were Preschool Children Implanted with False Memories?" on page 258.
- Key terms, a chapter outline, and hotlinked Web sites.

- **SELF-STUDY ASSESSMENT**
  Want help studying? For your customized Study Plan go to **http://psychology.wadsworth.com/plotnik7e/**. This program will automatically generate pretests and posttests to help you determine what you have mastered and what needs work.

WebTUTOR

- **STUDY GUIDE and WEBTUTOR**
  Check the corresponding module in your Study Guide for effective student tips and help learning the material presented.

- **INFOTRAC COLLEGE EDITION ONLINE LIBRARY**
  To find interesting and relevant articles go to **http://www.infotrac-college.com**, use your password, and then type in search terms such as the ones listed below.

| Declarative memory | Eidetic imagery |
| Encoding | Episodic memory |

STUDY QUESTIONS

Use InfoTrac to search for topics mentioned in the following questions (e.g., alcoholism, psychological discrimination, stress management).

*A. Three Types of Memory—Why does seeing an ambulance speed by remind you of your father's heart attack and his trip to the hospital? (**Suggested answer page 625**)

B. Sensory Memory: Recording—Why doesn't the world disappear for the short period of time when your eyes are completely closed during blinking?

C. Short-Term Memory: Working—If you took a drug that blocked short-term memory, what would be different about your life?

D. Long-Term Memory: Storing—What would your life be like if you had declarative memory but no procedural memory?

E. Research Focus: Do Emotions Affect Memories?—Why do people who suffer traumatic situations, such as sexual abuse or job layoffs, have difficulty getting on with their lives?

*F. Encoding: Transferring—Why is it important that teachers make learning interesting and meaningful? (**Suggested answer page 626**)

G. Repressed Memories—What are some of the ways that therapists can guard against clients reporting repressed memories that are false?

*H. Cultural Diversity: Oral Versus Written—How might playing video games affect a child's encoding process? (**Suggested answer page 626**)

I. Application: Unusual Memories—If you could have one unusual memory ability, which would you choose, and how would it make your life different?

*These questions are answered in Appendix B.

Module 12: Remembering & Forgetting

PowerStudy 2.0™
Complete Module

Watching a Crime

How much can you remember? It was about nine at night when you entered the campus building, climbed one flight of stairs, and began walking down the long hallway. You had just finished your psychology paper and were going to slip it under the instructor's door.

Everything happened very quickly.

From about the middle of the dimly lit hallway, a man with reddish hair and wearing a brown leather jacket jumped out from behind a half-open door and ran at you. Instinctively, you threw out your hands and tried to ward off the oncoming threat. With a quick motion, the man grabbed your blue shoulder bag and pushed you down. At that instant, your eyes met. He pointed at you with a menacing gesture and said, "Don't move or make a sound." Then he checked the hallway, stepped around you, and was gone (adapted from Buckout, 1980).

1,800 people identified the wrong mugger.

A 12-second filmed sequence with a storyline similar to this one was shown on television. In the TV film, the assailant's face was on the screen for several seconds. Next, the viewers were asked to watch a lineup of six men and then to call the TV station and identify which was the assailant. Of the more than 2,000 viewers who called in, only 200 identified the correct man; 1,800 selected the wrong one (Buckout, 1980).

Without looking back, try to answer the following questions (answers at bottom):

 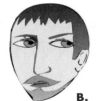    

A. **B.** **C.** **D.** **E.** **F.**

1. What color was the mugger's jacket? _____

2. What color and type was the student's bag? _____

3. Besides the bag, what else was the student carrying? _____

4. The mugger's exact words were "Don't make a sound." True or false?

5. When thrown down, the student yelled out "Stop!" True or false?

6. Of the 2,000 viewers who called in, 1,800 identified the correct assailant. True or false?

Answers: 1. brown; 2. blue, shoulder bag; 3. psychology paper; 4. false; 5. false; 6. false

Recall Versus Recognition

Which is easier? You probably found the first three questions harder because they involve recall.

Recall involves retrieving previously learned information without the aid of or with very few external cues.

For example, in questions 1–3, you were asked to recall colors or objects without having any choices. Students must use recall to answer fill-in-the-blank or essay questions.

You probably thought the last three questions were easier because they involve recognition.

Recognition involves identifying previously learned information with the help of more external cues.

In questions 4–6, you have only to recognize whether the information provided is correct. Students use recognition to decide which of the choices is correct on multiple-choice tests. Since multiple-choice tests involve recognition, they are generally considered easier than fill-in-the-blank and essay questions, which involve recall. Later in this module, we'll discuss why recall is more difficult than recognition.

Eyewitness Testimony

Which face did you see? Question 6 asks about a very curious result. Although the assailant's face was on the television screen for several seconds, 90% of the viewers identified the *wrong* person in a six-man lineup. (For example, from the six faces below, can you identify the correct mugger? Answer below.) How can you clearly see someone's face and not remember it? The answer to this question comes from studies on how eyewitness memories can be affected by suggestions, misleading questions, and false information. Although we generally assume that eyewitness testimony is the most accurate kind of evidence, you'll see that this is not always true. We'll discuss accuracy and problems of eyewitness testimony at the end of this module. (Mugger had reddish hair.)

What's Coming

We'll discuss how you organize thousands of events, faces, and facts and file this information in long-term memory. We'll explain the most common reasons for forgetting, the biological bases for memory, methods to improve memory, the creation of false memories, and the accuracy of eyewitness testimony.

We'll begin with a huge problem that you face every day: How do you file away and organize your many, many thousands of memories?

261

A. Organization of Memories

Filing and Organizing 87,967 Memories

How do you store memories?

One of the great puzzles of memory is how you file and store zillions of things over your lifetime. Suppose this past month you stored 91 faces, 6,340 concepts, 258 songs, 192 names, 97 definitions, 80,987 personal events, 1 dog, and 1 cat. How did you store these 87,967 memories so that you can search and retrieve one particular item from long-term memory?

There are several theories for how we file and organize memories; we'll discuss one of the more popular theories, which is called network theory (J. L. McClelland, 2000).

Network theory says that we store related ideas in separate categories, or files, called nodes. As we make associations among information, we create links among thousands of

Network theory says we store memories by filing them into categories.

nodes, which make up a gigantic interconnected network of files for storing and retrieving information.

Network theory may become clearer if you imagine that the mental files, or nodes, are like thousands of cities on a map and the connections or associations between them are like roads. Just as you follow different roads to go from city to city, you follow different associative pathways to go from idea to idea. Storing new events, faces, and thousands of other things would be similar to erecting new buildings in the cities and also building new roads between the cities (B. Schwartz & Reisberg, 1991). Here's how one cognitive psychologist, Donald Norman, used network theory to explain how he retrieved a particular memory.

Network Theory of Memory Organization

Where do the roads lead?

Just as you might follow a road map (right figure) to reach a particular city, cognitive psychologist Norman followed a cognitive map to remember the name of a particular store in San Diego. Although the mental roads that Norman takes may seem strange, these roads repre-

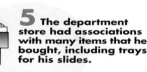

sent personal associations that he created when he filed, or stored, information in long-term memory. As he follows his associations, or mental roads, he travels the cognitive network from node to node or memory to memory in search of a particular name (Norman, 1982). Please begin reading at node 1 and continue to node 6.

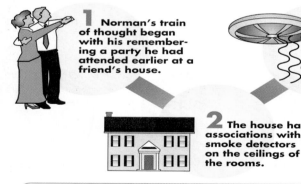

1 Norman's train of thought began with his remembering a party he had attended earlier at a friend's house.

2 The house had associations with smoke detectors on the ceilings of the rooms.

3 The smoke detectors had associations with batteries, which are needed to power the detectors.

4 The batteries had associations with a certain store in San Diego where Norman bought batteries and other items.

5 The department store had associations with many items that he bought, including trays for his slides.

6 As Norman thought of buying slide trays, he remembered the store's name "Nordstrom."

Norman mentally followed a cognitive map, starting with node 1 and following nodes 2, 3, 4, 5, to the name of a store at node 6.

Searching for a Memory

We've all shared Norman's problem of knowing we know something but having difficulty recalling it. This problem relates to how we store memories in long-term memory. According to the network theory of memory, we store memories in nodes that are interconnected after we make new associations. Because the network theory is somewhat complicated, we'll review how it applied to Norman's problem of trying to recall a particular memory.

Nodes. Norman organizes or stores related ideas in separate files, or categories, called nodes. We simplified this process by showing only six nodes, but there may be dozens. Nodes are categories for storing related ideas, such as birds, faces, friends, and store names.

Associations. Norman links the nodes, or categories of ideas, together by making associations or mental roads between new information and old information that was previously stored.

Network. Norman has thousands of interconnected nodes, which form an enormous cognitive network for arranging and storing files. Norman must search through this cognitive network to find a particular node or file, where a specific memory is stored.

Researchers have developed a theory of how we search through thousands of nodes to find a particular one (J. L. McClelland, 2000).

How do you find a specific memory?

How do you find a specific memory to answer these questions: How big is a guppy? Does a rooster have feathers? Does a blue jay have skin? According to network theory, you will search for answers to these questions by using different nodes or memory files.

Nodes are memory files that contain related information organized around a specific topic or category.

According to network theory, the many thousands of nodes or memory files are arranged in a certain kind of order, which is called a network hierarchy (Diesendruck & Shatz, 2001).

A *network hierarchy* refers to the arrangement of nodes or memory files in a certain order or hierarchy. At the bottom of the hierarchy are nodes with very concrete information, which are connected to nodes with somewhat more specific information, which in turn are connected to nodes with general or abstract information.

For example, a partial network hierarchy for nodes or memory files containing information about animals is shown on the right. Depending on whether you're looking for a specific memory (How big is a guppy?) or a more abstract memory (Does a blue jay have skin?), you will search different nodes, as explained next.

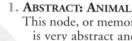
1.ANIMAL

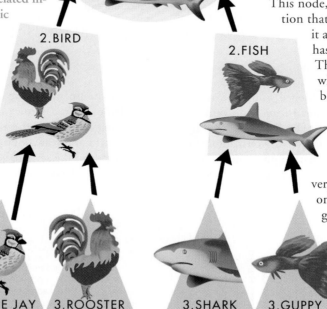
2.BIRD 2.FISH

3.BLUE JAY 3.ROOSTER 3.SHARK 3.GUPPY

Network hierarchy: Arranging memory files (nodes) so that general information is in top file (node #1) and specific information is in bottom files (nodes #3)

1. ABSTRACT: ANIMAL
This node, or memory file, contains information that is very abstract and applies to all animals, such as has skin, can move around, eats, and breathes. This category has answers to very general questions about animals—"Does a blue jay have skin?"

2. MORE SPECIFIC: BIRD OR FISH
This node, or memory file, contains information that is somewhat more specific because it applies to many fish or birds, such as has wings, can fly, and has feathers. This category has answers to somewhat specific questions about fish or birds—"Does a rooster have feathers?"

3. CONCRETE: BLUE JAY, ROOSTER, SHARK, OR GUPPY
This node, or memory file, contains very concrete information that applies only to a specific animal. This category has answers to very specific questions—"How big is a guppy?" "What color is a shark?"

Conclusion. Because network theory doesn't have all the answers to how you file and store information, researchers are developing more complex models, such as neural networks, that try to imitate how the brain organizes and files millions of bits of information (Ratcliff & McKoon, 2000).

Does the brain come with a built-in filing system?

The network theory's idea that information is filed in interconnected nodes or categories is partly supported by recent findings showing that the brain seems to have its own built-in filing system. For example, researchers found that, depending on which area of the brain is damaged, patients lose the ability to identify or process information dealing with a specific category. In some cases, patients could no longer identify faces but had no problems identifying information in other categories, such as those involving tools, animals, furniture, or plants. In other cases, patients could no longer identify plants but could identify information in other categories (tools, animals, etc.) (Schacter et al., 2000). These findings

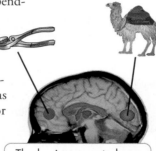
The brain seems to have built-in files or categories.

indicate that the brain has built-in categories for sorting and filing different kinds of information.

By using another research approach involving brain scans (p. 70), researchers found further evidence that the brain uses different areas to process different categories. For example, when subjects were asked to think of objects in a specific category, such as faces, tools, or furniture, researchers found that maximum neural activity occurred in different areas of the brain. As shown in the left figure, when people were thinking of animals, the maximum neural activity occurred in the back of the brain, while thinking of tools produced maximum neural activity in the front of the brain (A. Martin et al., 1996). The finding that the brain comes with prewired categories for processing information helps explain how you can easily sort through a tremendous amount of information and quickly find the answer to a specific question, such as "Does a camel have a hump?" (Low et al., 2003).

B. Forgetting Curves

Early Memories

What's your earliest memory?

The earliest that people in different cultures can recall personal memories averages $3\frac{1}{2}$ years old (Q. Wang, 2003). Researchers did find that children as young as 13 months can recall visual events, such as a sequence of moving toys. However, recalling moving objects is different from recalling personal memories, which is based on having developed a sense of oneself (recognizing the face in mirror as yours), which occurs after age 2 (M. L. Howe, 2003). Another reason we rarely remember personal events before age $3\frac{1}{2}$ is that very young children have little or

Earliest memories at about age $3\frac{1}{2}$

no language skills, so they cannot verbally encode early personal memories and cannot recall them even after they do develop language skills (Simcock & Hayne, 2002). Also, very young children have not yet developed a complete memory circuit in the brain, which occurs after age 2 and is necessary for encoding and retrieving personal memories (Bauer, 2002). But even though you're now an adult with a completely developed memory brain circuit, why do you still forget things, especially when taking exams?

Unfamiliar and Uninteresting

Could you remember LUD, ZIB?

From your experience studying for exams, you know that just because you verbally encode information by listening, reading, or writing doesn't mean that you'll automatically recall this information on exams. The kinds of events that you are more likely to remember or forget can be demonstrated with forgetting curves.

A *forgetting curve* measures the amount of previously learned information that subjects can recall or recognize across time.

We'll examine how two different kinds of information—unfamiliar and familiar—are remembered by using forgetting curves.

One of the earliest psychologists to study memory and forgetting was Hermann Ebbinghaus, who used himself as his only subject. He got around the fact that people have better memories for more familiar events by memorizing only three-letter nonsense syllables, such as **LUD, ZIB, MUC.**

He made up and wrote down hundreds of three-letter nonsense syllables on separate cards and arranged these cards into sets of varying length. To the ticking of a metronome, he turned over each card and read aloud each of the syllables until he had read all the cards in the set. He used only rote memory (made no associations) and needed only one or two readings to memorize a set of seven cards (containing seven nonsense syllables). He needed about 45 readings to memorize a set of 24 cards (Ebbinghaus, 1885/1913).

The forgetting curve on the left shows that Ebbinghaus forgot about half the unfamiliar and uninteresting nonsense syllables within the first hour.

How long do we remember familiar information?

Percent Remembered (y-axis, 0 to 100)

Ebbinghaus forgot the greatest number of nonsense syllables within the first hour.

LUD
ZIB
KON
MUC
SAR

His rate of forgetting leveled off and declined gradually across 31 days.

Time Between Initial Learning and Memory Test

$\frac{1}{3}$ 1   9   24   48

Hours — Days

Familiar and Interesting

Can you remember the names of your high school classmates?

Ebbinghaus's nonsense syllables are certainly uninteresting, which helps explain why he forgot half within the first hour. But what about information that is both familiar and interesting, such as the names and faces of your high school graduating class?

The graph below shows that even after 47 years, subjects correctly matched about 80% of their high school classmates' names with faces; they correctly recalled about 25% after 47 years (Bahrick et al., 1975). Subjects did better on recognition tests (matching names to faces) because they were given clues (names). They did poorer on recall tests (seeing

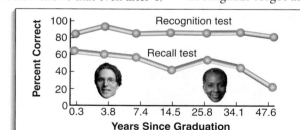

Percent Correct (y-axis, 0 to 100)

Recognition test

Recall test

0.3   3.8   7.4   14.5   25.8   34.1   47.6

Years Since Graduation

faces and asked to recall the names) because they were not given any clues. Similarly, students also show better memory on recognition tests (multiple-choice) than on recall tests (essay or fill-in-the-blank).

Notice that even though names and nonsense syllables were both encoded verbally, subjects correctly recalled about 60% of familiar and interesting information (names and faces) after 7 years, while Ebbinghaus forgot about 80% of the unfamiliar and uninteresting nonsense syllables after about a week. One researcher found that, after 20 years, he best remembered those events that were vivid, rare, and emotionally intense (R. White, 2002).

These studies show that remembering is partly related to how familiar or interesting the information is. However, there are other reasons for forgetting, as you'll see next.

Why do I forget things?

If asked to describe what happened today, you can accurately recall many personal events, conversations, and countless irritations. However, in spite of hours of study, there are many things you seem to have forgotten when you take an exam.

Forgetting refers to the inability to retrieve, recall, or recognize information that was stored or is still stored in long-term memory. We'll summarize a number of reasons people forget things.

Repression

There is a documented case of a man, J.R., who became anxious while watching a movie that featured a main character who struggled with memories of being sexually molested. Later that night, J.R. had a vivid recollection of being sexually abused by a parish priest (Schooler, 1994). J.R.'s case is an example of repression.

Repression, according to Freud, is a mental process that automatically hides emotionally threatening or anxiety-producing information in the unconscious, from which repressed memories cannot be recalled voluntarily, but something may cause them to enter consciousness at a later time.

Earlier we discussed the accuracy of recovered repressed memories involving sexual abuse (pp. 250–251). The J.R. example suggests that a traumatic sexual event can be repressed and recovered later. However, prominent memory researchers have questioned the validity of repressed memories, pointing to the possibility that such memories may have been suggested or implanted during the therapeutic process (Lynn et al., 2003).

Poor Retrieval Cues/Poor Encoding

Studying for exams by cramming or using rote memory may led to forgetting because these techniques result in poor retrieval cues and thus poor encoding or storing.

Retrieval cues are mental reminders that we create by forming vivid mental images or creating associations between new information and information we already know.

What if I study for 2 hours?

Many students don't realize that it's not how long but how well they study. Effective studying is not only memorizing but creating good retrieval cues. The best retrieval cues, which ensure the best encoding, are created by making associations between new information and information already learned. For example, instead of just trying to remember that the hippocampus is involved in memory (pp. 80, 84, 229), try to make a new association, such as a hippo remembered its way around campus.

We'll discuss the importance of and how to form good retrieval cues for effective encoding on page 267.

Interference

If you have to study for several exams and take them on the same day, there is a good chance that you may mix up and forget some of the material because of interference.

What if I have two exams?

Interference, one of the common reasons for forgetting, means that the recall of some particular memory is blocked or prevented by other related memories.

For example, if you are studying for and taking psychology and sociology tests on the same day, you may find that some of the material on social behavior in psychology is similar to but different from material in sociology, and this mix-up will cause interference and forgetting. Because psychologists believe that interference between material is a common cause of forgetting, we'll focus on two different kinds of interference on the next page.

Amnesia

While showing off her new pair of skates, my sister fell down and cracked her head on the hard Minnesota ice. She was knocked unconscious for a short time, and when she woke up the first thing she said was, "What happened?" She couldn't remember what happened because the blow had caused temporary amnesia.

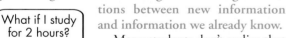

Amnesia, which may be temporary or permanent, is loss of memory that may occur after a blow or damage to the brain or after disease (Alzheimer's, p. 47), general anesthesia, certain drugs, or severe psychological trauma.

Depending on its severity, a blow to the head causes the soft jellylike brain to crash into the hard skull, and this may result in temporary or permanent damage to thousands of neurons (p. 50), which form the communication network of the brain. The reason people who strike their heads during car accidents usually have no memories of the events that occurred immediately before and during the accident is that the brain crashed into the skull, which interferes with the neurons' communication network, disrupts memory, and results in varying degrees of amnesia (Riccio et al., 2003).

Distortion

We may not be aware of the times we misremember something due to memory distortions caused by **bias** or **suggestibility** (Schacter, 2001). For example, bias was operating when college students remembered 89% of their high school A grades but only 29% of D grades or when divorcing couples remembered mostly the bad times, not the good (Bahrick et al., 1996). Suggestibility was operating when victims of crimes wrongly identified persons who were later cleared by DNA evidence (Gorman, 2002). Because of bias and suggestibility, we forget or misremember things, often without our being aware of the memory distortion.

Why did I misremember?

Next, we'll more closely examine two important reasons for forgetting—interference and retrieval cues.

C. Reasons for Forgetting

What if you study for three exams?

Sooner or later, every student faces the problem of having to take exams in several different courses on the same day. This situation can increase the chances of forgetting material because of something called interference.

The theory of *interference* says that we may forget information not because it is no longer in storage or memory but rather because old or newer related information produces confusion and thus blocks retrieval from memory.

Students who take multiple tests on the same day often complain of studying long and hard but forgetting information that they knew they knew. In this case the culprit may be interference. Similarly, if you take two or more classes in succession, you may find that information from one class interferes with learning or remembering information from the others. We'll explain the two kinds of interference—proactive and retroactive—and how each can lead to forgetting.

Proactive Interference

The first thing to remember about interference is that it can act forward, which is called proactive, or act backward, which is called retroactive. The prefix *pro* means "forward," so *proactive* interference "acts forward" to interfere with recalling newly learned information.

Proactive interference occurs when old information (learned earlier) blocks or disrupts the remembering of related new information (learned later).

Here's how proactive interference can work.

1. Psychology information.
For two hours you study for a test in psychology. The more psychology terms you store in memory, the more potential this psychology information has to "act forward" and disrupt any new and related information you study next.

2. Psychology information acts forward.
For the next two hours you study for a test in sociology. You may experience difficulty in learning and remembering this new sociology information because the previously learned psychology terms can "act forward" and interfere with remembering new and related terms from sociology.

3. Proactive interference.
When you take your sociology exam, you may forget some of the sociology terms you studied because of proactive interference: Previously learned psychology terms "act forward" to interfere with or block the recall of the more recently learned and related sociology terms (Jacoby et al., 2001).

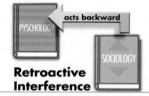

Proactive Interference
Material learned EARLIER (psychology) interferes with learning new information (sociology).

Retroactive Interference

Note that the prefix *retro* means "backward," so *retroactive* interference means "acting backward" to interfere with recalling previously learned information.

Retroactive interference occurs when new information (learned later) blocks or disrupts the retrieval of related old information (learned earlier).

Here's how retroactive interference works.

1. Psychology information.
From 1:00 to 3:00, you study for a test in psychology. Then from 3:00 to 6:00, you study for a test in sociology.

2. Sociology information acts backward.
You may experience difficulty in remembering the psychology terms you learned earlier because the sociology terms recently learned may "act backward" and disrupt earlier learned and related psychology terms.

3. Retroactive interference.
When you take the psychology exam, you may forget some of the psychology terms you studied earlier because of retroactive interference: Recently learned sociology terms "act backward" to interfere with or block the recall of earlier learned and related psychology terms.

Retroactive Interference
Material learned LATER (sociology) disrupts learning new information (psychology).

Interference, both proactive and retroactive, is one of the two common reasons for forgetting (Roediger & McDermott, 2000). Interference may also cause serious mistakes if eyewitnesses identify the wrong person, as happened in the study we discussed at the beginning of this module.

Why Did Viewers Forget the Mugger's Face?

We began this module by asking why only 200 out of 2,000 viewers correctly identified a mugger's face that was shown for several seconds on television. One reason viewers forgot the mugger's face is that one or both kinds of interference were operating.

If *proactive interference* was operating, it means that previously learned faces acted forward to block or disrupt remembering of the newly observed mugger's face.

If *retroactive interference* was operating, it means that new faces learned since seeing the mugger's face acted backward to block or disrupt remembering of the mugger's face.

Thus, we may forget information that we did indeed store in long-term memory because of one or both kinds of interference.

Besides interference, the other most common reason for forgetting involves inadequate retrieval cues, our next topic.

Where did I park it?

Have you ever parked your car in a mall and later roamed around the huge lot trying to find it? In that case, the reason for your forgetting probably involved poor retrieval cues (S. C. Brown & Craik, 2000).

Retrieval cues are mental reminders that you create by forming vivid mental images of information or associating new information with information that you already know.

Poor retrieval cues result in haphazard memory storage.

Retrieval cues are also important in hiding things. Researchers asked students to hide things either in common places, such as drawers or closets, or in unusual places, such as old shoes or cereal boxes. Later, when asked to locate the hidden objects, students remembered objects hidden in common places and forgot those hidden in unusual places (Winograd & Soloway, 1986). Forgetting hiding places (which I have done) and forgetting parking places (which I have done) point to the need for creating good retrieval cues.

Forming Effective Retrieval Cues

One reason we forget things (definitions, names, phone numbers) is that we did not take the time to create effective retrieval cues (discussed on pp. 248–249). You can form effective retrieval cues by creating vivid mental images of the information, making associations between new and old information, or making somewhat bizarre but memorable associations.

For example, researchers wondered which types of sentences students would remember better: common sentences, such as "The sleek new train passes a field of fresh, juicy strawberries," or bizarre sentences, such as "The sleek new train is derailed by the fresh, juicy strawberries." As a computer randomly presented 12 common and 12 bizarre sentences, students were told to form vivid mental images of the scenes. When retested later, subjects recalled significantly more bizarre than common sentences. Researchers concluded that subjects remembered better the bizarre sentences because they formed better mental images or associations, which produced better retrieval cues (Robinson-Riegler & McDaniel, 1994). Poor retrieval cues may also be a problem in eyewitness testimony.

Vivid mental images make great retrieval cues.

Retrieval cues and interference. There have been cases in which eyewitnesses identified assailants who were later proven innocent based on DNA evidence. Even when told that their assailants, who had spent many years in prison, were innocent, the eyewitnesses insisted they had made the correct identifications (Dowling, 2000). One reason eyewitnesses were mistaken is that the emotional and traumatic events prevented them from forming effective *retrieval cues.* Another reason the eyewitnesses made mistakes is *interference;* that is, the faces of the accused assailants somewhat resembled and interfered with their recognizing the real assailants. These examples show that forgetting can result from poor retrieval cues, no associations, or interference (S. C. Brown & Craik, 2000).

Another example of forgetting, which involves retrieval cues and interference, usually begins with someone saying, "It's on the tip of my tongue."

Tip-of-the-Tongue Phenomenon

Most of us have had the frustrating experience of feeling we really do know the name of a movie, person, or song but cannot recall it at this moment. This kind of forgetting is called the tip-of-the-tongue phenomenon.

"It's on the tip of my tongue."

The *tip-of-the-tongue phenomenon* refers to having a strong feeling that a particular word can be recalled, but despite making a great effort, we are temporarily unable to recall this particular information. Later, in a different situation, we may recall the information.

Researchers have found that the tip-of-the-tongue phenomenon is nearly universal, occurs about once a week, and most often involves names of people and objects. Its frequency increases with age, and about half of the time the thing is remembered some minutes later (B. L. Schwartz, 1999).

There are two explanations for the tip-of-the-tongue phenomenon. In some cases, information was encoded with inadequate retrieval cues, and so we must think up other associations (first letter of name, where last seen) for recall. In other cases, information is being blocked by interference from similar-sounding names or objects. Once we think of something else, the interference stops and the information pops into our memory (Schacter, 2001).

An interesting feature of retrieval cues is that such cues can also come from our states of mind.

What happens when you get angry?

When you yell at someone for doing the same annoying thing again, why is it that a long list of related past annoyances quickly comes to mind? One answer involves state-dependent learning.

State-dependent learning means that it is easier to recall information when you are in the same physiological or emotional state or setting as when you originally encoded the information.

For example, getting angry at someone creates an emotional and physiological state that triggers the recall of related past annoyances. Evidence for state-dependent

Being in the same state (emotional) improves recall.

learning comes from a wide range of studies in which subjects (humans, dogs, rats) learned something while they used a certain drug, were in a certain mood, or were in a particular setting and later showed better recall of this information when tested under the original learning conditions (S. C. Brown & Craik, 2000). These state-dependent studies indicate that retrieval cues are created by being in certain physiological or emotional states or in particular settings and that returning to these original states helps recall information that was learned under the same conditions.

Next, we'll look inside the brain to see what happens during remembering and forgetting.

D. Biological Bases of Memory

Where do you put all those memories?

If you learned only 500 new things every day, that adds up to storing 180,000 new memories every year and 3,600,000 memories after twenty years. To figure out how the brain stores and files away 3,600,000 memories (very conservative estimate), researchers have studied formation of memories in sea slugs, which have a relatively simple nervous system,

in brain-damaged individuals, who show deficits in some kinds of memory but not others, and in individuals who are having their brains scanned for neural activity while they are using different kinds of memory (Cabeza & Nyberg, 2003; Zola & Squire, 2000). Based on these studies, researchers have identified the several different areas of the brain that are involved in processing and storing different kinds of thoughts and memories.

1 Cortex: Short-Term Memories

When you look up a new phone number, you can hold it in short-term memory long enough to dial the number. Your ability to hold words, facts, and events in short-term memory depends on activity in the *cortex,* which is a thin layer of brain cells that covers the surface of the forebrain (indicated by thin red line around outside of the brain).

People may have brain damage that prevents them from storing long-term memories, but if their cortex is intact, they may have short-term memory and be able to carry on relatively normal conversations. However, if they cannot store long-term memories, they would not later remember having those conversations.

2 Cortex: Long-Term Memories

If you learn the words to a song, these words are stored in long-term memory. Your ability to remember or recall songs, words, facts, and events for days, months, or years depends on areas widely spread throughout the *cortex.*

People may have brain damage that prevents them from learning or remembering any new songs. However, if they have an intact cortex, they may remember the words from songs they learned before their brain damage because such information would have already been safely stored throughout their cerebral cortex (indicated by thin red line around outside of the brain).

3 Amygdala: Emotional Memories

Suppose that each time you hear a particular song associated with a special person, you have a romantic feeling. The romantic feeling associated with this emotional memory is provided by the *amygdala,* which is located in the tip of the temporal lobe and receives input from all the senses. Humans with damage to the amygdala still have memories but the memories lose their emotional impact, such as no longer finding loud noises unpleasant or no longer recognizing facial expressions as fearful or happy (Hamann et al., 2002). Researchers conclude that the amygdala plays a critical role in recognizing emotional facial expressions, especially fearful or threatening ones, and adding a wide range of emotions (positive and negative) to our memories (Dolan, 2002; Ohman, 2002).

4 Hippocampus: Transferring Memories

Just as the "Save" command on your computer transfers a file into permanent storage on your hard drive, the *hippocampus* transfers words, facts, and personal events from short-term memory into permanent long-term memory. The hippocampus is a curved, finger-sized structure that lies beneath the cortex in the temporal lobe.

Areas of the brain involved in memory

The hippocampus is vital for storing certain kinds of memories. For example, individuals with damage to the hippocampus (and surrounding cortex) cannot save any *declarative memories,* such as new words, facts, or personal events, because the hippocampus is necessary for transferring declarative information from short-term into long-term memory (Zeineh et al., 2003). However, people with hippocampal damage CAN learn and remember *nondeclarative or procedural information,* such as acquiring motor skills or habits (tying one's shoes, walking up the stairs, playing tennis). But, if asked, people with hippocampal damage CANNOT remember actually performing a motor skill (playing tennis) because performing the skill (I played tennis) is a personal event (declarative memory). Thus, the hippocampus is necessary for transferring declarative information (words, facts, and events) from short-term into long-term memory but not for transferring nondeclarative or procedural information (motor skills and habits) (Zola & Squire, 2000).

5 Brain: Memory Model

Recent findings indicate that your *cortex* stores short-term memories as well as long-term memories; your *hippocampus* transfers or saves declarative information in long-term memory but does not transfer nondeclarative or procedural information into long-term memory; and your *amygdala* adds emotional content to positive and negative memories (Tulving & Craik, 2000). Now that you know which areas of the brain store, transfer, or add emotions to memories, we can examine how individual memories are actually formed.

How to make a short-term memory?

Suppose you just looked up the phone number 555-9013 and repeat it as you dial. Researchers believe that your brain may store that number in short-term memory by using interconnected groups of neurons that are called neural assemblies.

Neural assemblies are groups of interconnected neurons whose activation allows information or stimuli to be recognized and held briefly and temporarily in short-term memory.

The figure on the left shows how a very simplified neural assembly might work. Some information, such as repeating a phone number, activates a neural assembly that

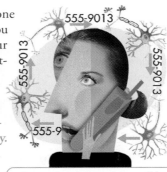

Example of neural assembly

holds the phone number in short-term memory. However, if you switch your attention to something else before encoding the number in long-term memory, this neural assembly stops and the phone number is gone and forgotten. Researchers believe that neural assemblies are one mechanism for holding information in short-term memory (Smith, 2000). However, as you'll see next, permanently storing information in long-term memory involves chemical or structural changes in the neurons themselves.

How to make a long-term memory?

Besides studying memory by genetically altering mice brains, researchers also study memory in sea slugs because their nervous system contains about 20,000 neurons versus billions in the human brain. After the sea slug has learned a simple task, such as tensing its muscular foot in response to a bright light, researchers can dissect the sea slug's nervous system and look for chemical or physical changes associated with learning (Kandel & Abel, 1995). We'll focus on one mechanism—long-term potentiation, or LTP—that researchers believe is involved in forming long-term memories.

LONG-TERM POTENTIATION (LTP)

1 One way to learn the name of the large orange-beaked bird on the left is to

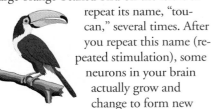

repeat its name, "toucan," several times. After you repeat this name (repeated stimulation), some neurons in your brain actually grow and change to form new connections with other neurons (Goda, 2001). This neural change, which is involved in forming long-term memories, is part of a complicated process called LTP.

Long-term potentiation, or *LTP,* refers to changes in the structure and function of neurons after they have been repeatedly stimulated.

For example, by repeating the name "toucan," you are repeatedly stimulating neurons.

2 We'll use only two neurons (perhaps many hundreds are involved) to make the LTP process easier to understand. In the figure below, repeating the name "toucan" stimulates neuron A, which produces LTP and causes neuron A to grow and form new connections with neuron B.

3 LTP changes the structure and function of neuron A so it becomes associated with the name "toucan." To recall the name of this bird, you activate neuron A, which activates its newly formed connections with neuron B, and this combined neural activation forms the basis for your long-term memory of the name "toucan."

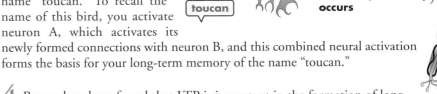

4 Researchers have found that LTP is important in the formation of long-term memory because when the occurrence of LTP was chemically or genetically blocked in sea snails or mice, these animals could not learn a classically conditioned response or learn a water maze (Tonegawa & Wilson, 1997). In other words, blocking the occurrence of LTP also blocked the formation of long-term memories. For this reason, neuroscientists believe that the LTP process, which changes the *structure* and function of neurons, is the most likely basis for learning and memory in animals and humans (Goda, 2001; Tsien, 2000).

How to change memory?

Researchers have changed a mouse's memory by genetically changing its brain. For example, researcher Joe Tsien (2000) inserted a special gene into a fertilized mouse egg that eventually developed into a healthy mouse. The special gene caused changes in a part of the mouse's brain (hippocampus) so that certain brain cells—neurons—could communicate better by making stronger (synaptic) connections with other neurons (see pp. 52–53). The *genetically altered mice*, whose brain cells could better communicate, could also remember which objects they had explored and which objects were new (see right photo) about four

to five times longer than mice with unchanged or normal mice brains. Depending on the genetic changes, mice brains could be given better or worse memories. These results demonstrate that certain genes can change the *structure* of neurons so that they are either better or worse at communicating and better or worse at making memories (Tsien, 2000).

Genes make a mouse smarter.

✔ Concept Review

1. If you retrieve previously learned information without the aid of any external cues, you are using a process of remembering called (a)_____. If you identify or match information that you have previously learned, you are using a process of remembering called (b)_____.

2. Memory files or categories that contain related information organized around a specific topic are called (a)_____. One theory of memory organization says that the separate memory files, or nodes, in which we file related ideas are interconnected in a gigantic system. This idea is called (b)_____.

3. According to network theory, some nodes are arranged so that more concrete information is at the bottom and more abstract information is at the top; this order is called a _____.

4. A diagram of the amount of previously learned information that subjects can recall or recognize across time is called a _____. We tend to remember information that is familiar and interesting and forget information that is unfamiliar and uninteresting.

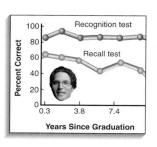

5. According to Sigmund Freud, information that is threatening to our self-concept is automatically driven into our unconscious, from which we cannot retrieve it at will. This process is called _____.

6. One common reason for forgetting is that other related memories already stored in long-term memory may interfere with or block recall of some particular memory; this idea is called _____.

> What if I have two exams?

7. Another reason for forgetting comes from a lack of associations between new information and information we already know; this reason has to do with the quality of the _____.

8. Brain damage, a blow to the head, drug use, or severe psychological stress may cause a form of forgetting called (a)_____, which results when the brain's (b)_____ network is temporarily or permanently disrupted.

9. We may not be aware of times when we misremember something because of distortions in memory. Two common causes of memory distortions are _____ and _____.

> Why did I misremember?

10. If we forget information not because it is lost from storage but rather because other information gets in the way and blocks its retrieval, this process is called (a)_____. If information learned earlier blocks, interferes with, or disrupts the retrieval of information that was learned later, it is called (b)_____. If information learned later blocks, interferes with, or disrupts the retrieval of information learned earlier, it is called (c)_____.

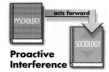

Proactive Interference

11. Mental reminders that we create by making images or associating new information with information that we already know are called (a)_____. If you do not form effective retrieval cues when learning new information, you will likely have a difficult time (b)_____ this information from long-term memory.

12. Sometimes, despite making a great effort, you are temporarily unable to recall information that you absolutely know is in your memory. This is called the _____ phenomenon.

13. According to one memory model of the brain, short-term memories are formed and stored in different parts of the (a)_____. Long-term memories are also stored in different parts of the (b)_____, although these kinds of memories are not formed there. Declarative information is transferred by the (c)_____ into long-term memory, which is stored in different parts of the cortex. However, the hippocampus is not involved in transferring motor skills or habits, which are part of (d)_____ information, into long-term memory. Both positive and negative emotional associations are added to memories by an area in the temporal lobe called the (e)_____.

Answers: *1. (a) recall, (b) recognition; 2. (a) nodes, (b) network theory; 3. hierarchy; 4. forgetting curve; 5. repression; 6. interference; 7. retrieval cues; 8. (a) amnesia, (b) communication; 9. bias, suggestibility; 10. (a) interference, (b) proactive interference, (c) retroactive interference; 11. (a) retrieval cues, (b) recalling or retrieving or remembering; 12. tip-of-the-tongue; 13. (a) cortex, (b) cortex, (c) hippocampus, (d) procedural, (e) amygdala*

Improving Your Memory

Do you complain about forgetting things?

At one time or another, almost everyone complains about forgetting something. Many of my students complain about forgetting information that they really knew but couldn't recall during exams. This kind of forgetting has several causes: There may be *interference (proactive and retroactive)* from information studied for related classes; there may be *poor retrieval cues* that result from trying to learn information by using rote or straight memorization; or students may not use elaborative rehearsal (p. 249), which involves making associations between new and old information.

After about age 40, adults begin to complain about forgetting things that they never forgot before. For example, memory researcher Daniel Schacter, now 50, complains, "Reading a journal article 15 years ago, I would have it at my fingertips. Now, if I don't deliberately try to relate it to what I already know, or repeat it a few times, I'm less likely to remember it" (Schacter, 1997, p. 56). This kind of forgetting is commonly caused by poor retrieval cues, which result from being busy or distracted and not having or taking the time to create meaningful associations.

How can I improve my memory?

If you hear about memory courses that claim to greatly improve your memory, what these courses usually teach are how to use mnemonic methods.

Mnemonic (new-MON-ick) methods are ways to improve encoding and create better retrieval cues by forming vivid associations or images, which improve recall.

We'll discuss two common mnemonic methods—method of loci and peg method—that improve memory (Mason & Kohn, 2001).

Method of Loci

If you need to memorize a list of terms, concepts, or names in a particular order, an efficient way is to use the method of loci.

The *method of loci (LOW-sigh)* is an encoding technique that creates visual associations between already memorized places and new items to be memorized.

We'll use the following three steps of the method of loci to memorize names of early psychologists: Wundt, James, and Watson.

Step 1. Memorize a visual sequence of places (*loci* in Latin means "places"), such as places in your apartment where you can store things. Select easily remembered places such as in your kitchen: sink, cabinet, refrigerator, stove, and closet.

Step 2. Create a vivid association for each item to be memorized. For example, picture Wundt hanging from a bridge and saying, "I wundt jump."

Step 3. Once you have created a list of vivid associations, mentally put each psychologist in one of the selected places: Wundt goes in the sink, James in the cabinet, Watson in the refrigerator.

To recall this list of early psychologists, you take an imaginary stroll through your kitchen and mentally note the image stored in each of your memorized places.

Peg Method

Another useful mnemonic device for memorizing a long list, especially in the exact order, is the peg method.

The *peg method* is an encoding technique that creates associations between number-word rhymes and items to be memorized.

The rhymes act like pegs on which you hang items to be memorized. Let's use the two steps of the peg method to memorize our three early psychologists: Wundt, James, Watson.

Step 1. Memorize the list of peg

one is a bun
two is a shoe
three is a tree
four is a door
five is a hive

words shown on the left, which consists of a number and its rhyming word.

Step 2. Next, associate each of the items you wish to memorize with one of the peg words. For instance, imagine Wundt on a bun, James with two left shoes, and Watson stuck in a tree.

To remember this list of early psychologists, you recall each peg along with its image of an early psychologist that you placed there.

Effectiveness of Methods

A national magazine writer, who was 41 years old and complained about forgetfulness, decided to improve her memory by trying three different methods (Yoffe, 1997).

First, she took a 3-hour memory-enhancement class ($49) that focused on the peg method. The magazine writer concluded that the peg method was impressive and if she were back in college, she would use it to memorize all the new facts.

Second, she listened to an audiocassette program ($79) that promised to release the "perfect photographic memory" that everyone already had. The audio program focused on using the peg method without much application to real life. Contrary to the audiocassette's promise, memory researchers report that photographic memories are as rare as duck's teeth (Schacter, 1996).

Third, she read a memory-improvement book ($10) that described the peg method, how to pay attention, and the importance of creating associations and images.

As this writer's experience illustrates, improving one's memory requires making the effort to use good encoding, such as elaborative rehearsal, which means creating good associations that, in turn, produce good retrieval cues and improve memory.

As the percentage of people over 50 increases, so does interest in *memory-enhancing drugs*, such as the popular herbal supplement ginkgo. However, researchers found that ginkgo did NOT improve memory or concentration in healthy adults (Solomon et al., 2002). Researchers found ways to improve memory in mice, but memory-enhancing drugs for humans are years away (Weed, 2000).

Next, we'll discuss how cultural influences can affect what you remember.

F. Cultural Diversity: Aborigines Versus White Australians

How do you survive in a desert versus an office meeting?

Suppose you lived in the harsh, endless, barren desert world of western Australia, where many of the native Aborigines live (top photo). For about 30,000 years, the Aborigines have survived by using visual landmarks to remember the exact locations of water, food, and game in vast stretches of unmapped country (R. A. Gould, 1969). Because the Aborigines use few, if any, written records, their survival in this barren desert largely depends on their ability to store, or encode, enormous amounts of visual information, such as landmarks for food, water, and game. Lacking reading and writing skills, Aborigines primarily encode information about the desert by using *visual retrieval cues*, which are later used to recall information.

Survival depends on VISUAL cues.

Survival depends on VERBAL cues.

In contrast, most of us live in an industrial urban culture, in which survival largely depends on the ability to read and write and store an enormous amount of verbal, written, and computer-related information (bottom photo). Successfully surviving in an industrial culture is greatly dependent on the ability to store, or encode, enormous amounts of written and verbal information by using *verbal retrieval cues.*

These two examples show that survival in the aboriginal culture depends on encoding and remembering visual information, while surviving in an industrial culture depends on encoding and remembering verbal (written) information. This cultural difference predicts that people would perform differently on tests, depending on whether the tests emphasized visual or verbal retrieval cues.

Visual Versus Verbal Memory

Psychologist Judith Kearins was not surprised to find that Aborigines scored low on Western-style intelligence tests because these tests emphasize verbal retrieval cues and put Aborigines at a disadvantage. Considering their desert culture, she suspected that Aborigines would perform better on tests that took advantage of their ability to encode with visual retrieval cues.

USING VISUAL CUES

To see if Aborigines were better at visual encoding, Kearins developed a test that emphasized visual retrieval cues. This test consisted of looking at 20 objects that were placed on a board divided into 20 squares. Some objects were natural—stone, feather, leaf; others were manufactured—eraser, thimble, ring. Aborigines and white Australian adolescents were told to study the board for 30 seconds (sample section on right). Then all the objects were heaped into a pile in the center of the board and the children were asked to replace the items in their original locations. The 44 Aborigine adolescents had been reared for the most part in desert tribal ways, had learned a nontraditional form of English as a second language, and were now attending school. The 44 white Australian adolescents lived and attended high school in a relatively large urban area (Perth).

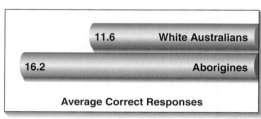
Aborigine students are better at using VISUAL cues than white Australian students.

PERFORMANCE

Kearins tested the adolescents using four different sets of objects—natural, manufactured, or some combination. The graph below shows that the Aborigine adolescents performed significantly better in placing objects back in their original locations than did the white Australian adolescents (Kearins, 1981). Another group of researchers essentially replicated Kearins's results using a younger population (average age of 9) of Aborigines and white Australians (Klich & Davidson, 1983).

11.6	**White Australians**
16.2	**Aborigines**

Average Correct Responses

CULTURE AND RETRIEVAL CUES

Kearins concluded that the Aborigines' survival in the harsh desert landscape encouraged and rewarded their abilities to encode information using visual retrieval cues. In comparison, the urban school setting of the white Australians encouraged and rewarded their ability to encode information using verbal retrieval cues. For example, when questioned about their strategies, many of the Aborigines said that they only remembered the look of the objects on the board. In comparison, white Australians described their strategies in great detail: "I looked at the bottom row and remembered onion, banksia nut, rock, bone, and apple core." These descriptions support the idea that the Aborigines used visual retrieval cues, while the white Australians used verbal retrieval cues. These interesting results suggest that survival needs do shape and reward a particular way of encoding information in memory.

The better performance of Aborigines on visual tasks indicates that culture does influence the encoding and recall of information. Besides culture, other things, such as the age of a child, may also influence encoding and recall, as shown next in studies on implanting false memories in young children.

G. Research Focus: False Memories

Can False Memories Be Implanted?

Is the child telling the truth?

Each year in the United States, over 10,000 children are asked to testify about sexual abuse. In some cases, the children's testimony appears truthful and believable, and the cases are settled. In other cases, especially those involving day-care centers, children may testify about unusual or bizarre sexual practices that raise questions about the reliability of their testimony. For example, in one publicized case, Margaret Kelly Michael, a 26-year-old nursery school teacher, was said to have played the

Researchers implanted false memories in children.

piano while nude, made children drink her urine, raped and assaulted children, and licked peanut butter off children's genitals. Kelly was convicted of 115 counts of sexual abuse committed against 20 children from 3 to 5 years old. After she spent 5 years in prison, her conviction was overturned by a higher court because of concerns that the testimony of 19 child witnesses may have been unreliable due to improper interviewing by therapists (Ceci & Bruck, 1995). Improper interviewing refers to the possibility that the therapists, through repeated suggestions and specific questions, may have implanted false memories in the children. This very serious concern led researchers to study whether false memories could be implanted in young children.

Research Method to Create False Memories

What happens during questioning?

Subjects: Children 3–6 years old

When questioning young children about sexual abuse charges, therapists or officials may repeatedly suggest that certain events happened. Can these repeated suggestions eventually create false memories in young children? To answer this question, psychologist Stephen Ceci and his colleagues (1994) studied 96 children from 3 to 6 years old who came from a wide range of social classes.

Procedure. To obtain a list of true and false events, researchers interviewed the children's parents about events that had occurred within the past 12 months of the children's lives, such as a surprise birthday party, a trip to Disney World, injury, or death of a pet. Each child was then read a list of these events, some of which were fictitious. The children were asked "to think real hard" and identify events that had actually happened to them.

Researchers emphasized that some events on the list had not happened to the children. For example, one fictitious event was "getting one's hand caught in a mousetrap and having to go to the hospital to have it removed." This testing procedure was repeated for each child in seven to ten different interviews, which were spaced about a week apart. In the last session, children were videotaped as they described the events, some true or false.

Results. As shown in the graph below, 91% of the time children correctly identified events that had happened to them, indicating that they had accurate recall. However, 34% of the time children said that they had experienced fictitious events that had only been suggested to them (Ceci et al., 1994). Surprisingly, children remembered fictitious events in great detail.

Here's how one 4-year-old described the fictitious event of getting his hand caught in a mousetrap: "My brother Colin was trying to get Blowtorch [an ac-

Agreeing to false events	34%
Agreeing to true events	91%

tion toy] away from me, and I wouldn't let him take it from me, so he pushed me into the woodpile where the mousetrap was. And then my finger got caught in it. And then we went to the hospital, and my mommy, daddy, and Colin drove me there, to the hospital in our van, because it was far away. And the doctor put a bandage on this finger."

Some believe that children's lies or made-up stories can be detected through facial features (unsure or guilty looks) and speech patterns (stammering, correcting details). To test this belief, the same researchers asked 109 professionals (clinical and developmental psychologists, law enforcement officials, social and psychiatric workers) to judge whether events described by the children were true or fictitious. Professionals who watched videotapes of the children scored no better than chance in distinguishing true from fictitious events. Thus, children were very convincing in describing fictitious events.

Conclusion. When young children were asked repeatedly "to think hard" about true and fictitious events, some children became convinced that some of the fictitious events had actually happened. In addition, children gave such detailed and convincing stories of fictitious events that their stories fooled professional judges. Although this study showed that 91% of the time young children accurately recalled information about past events, it also showed that 34% of the time they turned false memories into true and believable ones.

Because very young children (aged 3 and 4 years) were more open to suggestions than older children (aged 5 and 6 years), researchers emphasize that great care must be taken when questioning young children so that repeated suggestions and interviews do not create and implant false memories (Ceci, 2000; Loftus, 2003).

Children became convinced that false memories were true.

Just as some young children may respond to suggestions and misremember events, some adults may also misremember when giving eyewitness testimony, our next topic.

H. Application: Eyewitness Testimony

How Accurate Is an Eyewitness?

The woman on the witness stand was very emotional as she recalled in vivid detail the hour of terror during which two men had forced her into her car, drove away, and later raped her in the front seat. When she was asked if one of the rapists was present in the courtroom, she pointed directly at the defendant sitting at the table and said, "There is no doubt in my mind."

Eyewitness testimony refers to recalling or recognizing a suspect observed during a potentially very disrupting and distracting emotional situation that may have interfered with accurate remembering.

I have no doubt that he's the one who raped me!

DNA evidence proved he was not the rapist.

For example, the woman's eyewitness testimony was the damning evidence that sent the defendant (an alleged rapist) to prison. After the man spent 10 years in prison, a new defense lawyer asked that the victim's clothes undergo a DNA test, which had not yet been developed at the time of the initial trial. The DNA test proved that the sperm stains on the victim's jeans did not come from the man who was in prison. The man who had been sent to prison because of the victim's eyewitness testimony was found innocent and set free (Dolan, 1995a). This example points to at least three problems with eyewitness testimony.

The first problem is that juries assume that eyewitness testimony is the best kind of evidence because it is so accurate and reliable. However, in the United States (as of this writing), there have been 110 people who were convicted of rape or murder but who have been freed because of DNA evidence. Of the 110 convictions, 83 had been based on (mistaken) eyewitness testimony (Gorman,

2002). Because of apparent problems with eyewitness testimony, the Supreme Court of New York had recently ruled that experts could be called to testify on its reliability and accuracy (McKinley, 2001).

Own-race bias. In the rape case discussed here, the eyewitness was a white female and the accused rapist was a black man. This case brings up another source of eyewitness error: problems in correctly identifying individuals of another race. For example, researchers found that an eyewitness of one race will be less accurate when identifying an accused person of another race. The finding that people better recognize faces of their own race than faces of other races is called *own-race bias,* which can distort and lessen the accuracy of eyewitness testimony (Ferguson et al., 2001).

A second problem with eyewitness testimony is that the police and juries generally assume that the more confident an eyewitness is, the more accurate is the testimony. For example, the witness in this rape case was very confident when she pointed at the accused man and said, "There is no doubt in my mind." However, there is only a moderate association or correlation (+0.37) between how correct the identification of an eyewitness is and how much confidence the eyewitness feels about his or her identification (Wells & Olson, 2003). This means that an eyewitness's confidence is not a good indication of accuracy.

A third problem with eyewitness testimony is that eyewitnesses may make errors if law enforcement officials ask misleading or biased questions or make suggestions about the perpetrator's identification. In these cases, eyewitnesses may unknowingly accept the misinformation as fact and give unreliable testimony (Bower, 2003). For example, consider the following case of an eyewitness's mistaken identity.

Can an Eyewitness Be Misled?

Some years ago a series of armed robberies occurred in the Wilmington, Delaware, area. The police had few leads in the case until a local citizen said that a Roman Catholic priest, Father Bernard Pagano, looked like the sketch of the robber.

At his trial, seven eyewitnesses positively identified Father Pagano (left photo) as the robber. But at the last minute, another man, Ronald Clouser (right photo), stepped forward and confessed to the robberies and Father Pagano was released (Rodgers, 1982).

As you look at these two photos, you will wonder how this case of mistaken identity could possibly have happened. Ronald Clouser is shorter, 14 years younger, and not nearly as bald as Father Pagano; besides, he has different facial features. Why, then, did seven eyewitnesses say with certainty that Father Pagano was the robber they had seen? One reason involves how the witnesses were questioned. Apparently, before the

Seven people identified Father Pagano . . .

. . . but Ronald Clouser confessed to being the robber.

witnesses were questioned and shown photos of the suspects, the police had suggested the possibility that the robber was a priest. After being prompted to look for a priest, the witnesses focused on the few similarities Father Pagano had to the real robber. Because Father Pagano was the only suspect wearing a clerical collar, the witnesses concluded that he must be the robber. This example is but one of many that show how eyewitness testimony may be distorted or biased.

Because of potential problems with eyewitness testimony, the U.S. Department of Justice recently released a guide for collecting and preserving eyewitness evidence (Wells et al., 2000). This guide, based on research findings discussed in this Application section, warns law enforcement agencies about the kinds of errors that eyewitnesses may make. We'll next discuss more of the research findings that show how eyewitness testimony may be changed or biased.

Because of concern about the reliability of eyewitness testimony, Elizabeth Loftus (1979, 2003) studied whether people can be misled and do misremember, especially if they are given false information. We'll describe several of Loftus's experiments that demonstrate how subjects misremembered what they saw or heard.

DID THE CAR PASS THE BARN?

In one experiment, subjects watched a film of an automobile accident and then were questioned about what they saw. One of the questions contained a false piece of information: "How fast was the red sports car going when it passed the barn while traveling along the country road?" Although there was no barn in the film, 17% of the subjects said they had seen a barn, indicating that people may believe misinformation if it fits the overall scene or pattern (Loftus, 1975).

WAS THERE A STOP SIGN?

In a well-known study by Loftus and colleagues, subjects were first shown slides of a traffic accident involving a stop sign and then asked a series of questions about the accident. Some of the questions were not misleading and asked about the presence of a stop sign. Other questions were deliberately misleading and did not mention the stop sign but asked about the presence of a yield sign. Later, when subjects were asked whether they had seen a stop sign or

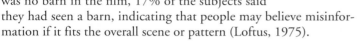

a yield sign, those subjects who had been misled by earlier questions about a yield sign were more likely to report seeing a yield sign than subjects who were not misled (Loftus et al., 1978). These results, which show that subjects can be misled by being given false but related information, have been replicated by many other researchers (Neisser & Libby, 2000).

HOW DOES FALSE INFORMATION ALTER MEMORY?

Based on many such studies, Loftus and Hoffman (1989) concluded that if misleading information is introduced during questioning after an event, people may believe this misinformation and report events that they did not see.

According to Loftus, eyewitnesses believed the false information they were told, rather than what they saw, because the false information altered or overwrote their original, true memory (Loftus & Loftus, 1980). This explanation, which has generated much research and debate, says that people misremember because of a memory impairment: the true memory was erased or overwritten (Payne et al., 1994). However, other researchers argue that the original, true memory is still there but is difficult to retrieve (Zaragoza & Lane, 1994). Whatever the cause, these many studies indicate that people (witnesses) do misremember when given misleading information.

The debate over whether false information overwrites the original memory has not been settled. However, what has been settled is that sometimes people do come to believe that they actually remember seeing things that were merely suggested to them; this phenomenon is called source misattribution.

Source misattribution is a memory error that results when a person has difficulty in deciding which of two or more sources a memory came from: Was the source something the person saw or imagined, or was it a suggestion?

For example, suppose you saw a hit-and-run accident involving a dark red car. During questioning, you are asked the color of the car

Did you see a red or blue car?

that drove off. As you're thinking that the car was dark red, you remember hearing another bystander say, "The car was dark blue."

Source misattribution would occur if you said that the car was dark blue (suggestion you heard) rather than dark red (something you saw). Researchers have found that false suggestions, misleading questions, and misinformation can result in source misattribution and create false memories (Roediger & McDermott, 2000). False memories that can result from source misattribution, such as suggestions or misleading questions, are one reason that court officials may question the accuracy of eyewitness testimony.

Suppose you had witnessed a robbery but had trouble picking the suspect out of a police lineup. To help you provide reliable information about the suspect, you might be questioned using a procedure called the cognitive interview.

The *cognitive interview* is a technique for questioning people, such as eyewitnesses, by having them imagine and reconstruct the details of an event, report everything they remember without holding anything back, and narrate the event from different viewpoints.

The cognitive interview has proved very useful in police interrogation: Detectives trained in cognitive interview techniques obtained 47–60% more information from victims and suspects than detectives using the standard police interrogation method (Gwyer &

A cognitive interview is a more effective method for questioning eyewitnesses.

Clifford, 1997). Researchers concluded that once police officers are trained in cognitive interview procedures, it is a very effective way to increase correct recall and avoid making suggestions or giving misleading information that might create false memories and increase errors of source misattribution (Kebbell et al., 1999).

Psychologists have answered many questions about how eyewitnesses can be misled as well as how to improve the reliability of their testimony, which may result in life or death decisions. Based on this work, England has barred cases when the only evidence is an eyewitness. In the United States, many courts allow experts to testify about the reliability of eyewitnesses so that juries are made aware of the same studies and findings that you have just read (Pezdek, 1995).

A. ORGANIZATION OF MEMORIES

1. If you are asked to retrieve previously learned information without the aid of external cues, you are using a process of remembering called (a)_____, which is generally more difficult. If you are asked to answer multiple-choice questions, you can identify or match information and use a process of remembering called (b)_____, which is generally less difficult.

1.ANIMAL

2. According to one theory of memory organization, we encode or file related ideas in separate categories called _____.

3. We form links between nodes by forming associations. The idea that the interconnected nodes form a gigantic system is called _____ theory.

4. An arrangement in which nodes are organized in a logical manner, with more concrete information at the bottom and more abstract information at the top, is called a _____.

B. FORGETTING CURVES

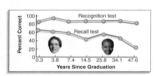

5. If the amount of previously learned information that subjects can recall or recognize across time is plotted, the resulting graph is called a _____. For example, Ebbinghaus demonstrated that the major-ity of nonsense sylla-bles are forgotten relatively quickly—within hours. However, other studies showed that more relevant and interesting information may be remembered for many years.

C. REASONS FOR FORGETTING

6. If you forget because other memories interfere with or prevent re-trieval of some particular memory, it is called (a)_____. If you forget because information that was learned earlier interferes with information learned later, it is called (b)_____ interference. If you forget because information that was learned later inter-feres with information learned earlier, it is called (c)_____ interference.

7. Forgetting information because it was poorly encoded means that you failed to form new associations or re-minders, which results in poor or inadequate _____.

8. Freud said you may forget information that is threatening to your self-concept because it is automatically pushed into your uncon-scious, from which you cannot retrieve it at will. This idea of Freud's is called _____.

9. If a person experiences a blow to the head, has severe psycho-logical trauma, or takes or is given certain drugs, that person may forget things because of having _____.

10. You may not always be aware of when you misremember some-thing or when your memory is distorted because of the influence of _____ and _____.

11. To increase the chances of remembering items from long-term memory, we can create reminders that associate new information with information that we already know; these reminders are called _____.

12. There are times you are absolutely sure that certain information is stored in memory but you are unable to retrieve it. This experience is called the _____ phenomenon.

13. Besides creating retrieval cues, it may also be easier to recall information when you are in the same physiological or emotional state as when you originally learned it; this phenomenon is called _____.

D. BIOLOGICAL BASES OF MEMORY

14. Different areas of the brain are involved in different memory processes. For example, the ability to hold words, facts, or events (de-clarative information) in short-term memory de-pends on activity in the (a)_____. The ability to transfer information about words, facts, and events (declarative information) from short-term into long-term memory depends on activity in the (b)_____. If this structure were damaged, a person could carry on a conversation but would not (c)_____ the con-versation the next day.

15. The ability to recall words, facts, and events (declarative informa-tion) from the past involves activity in the outer covering of the brain, which is called the (a)_____. For example, if patients have an intact cortex, they can remember past events because these events are already stored in the cortex. However, they may have difficulty re-membering any new words, facts, or events (declarative information) because of damage to their (b)_____.

16. The ability to transfer motor skills and habits, which is part of _____ memory, does not involve the hippocampus. Even though a person with damage to the hippocampus can store proce-dural information, that person would have no memory of having en-gaged in that event (declarative information).

17. The area of the brain that adds emotional feelings to memories is called the _____. This area is involved in forming a wide range of happy, sad, or fearful memories.

18. Researchers believe that the brain forms and briefly stores short-term memories by using a circuit of interconnected neurons called _____. When these interconnected neurons stop being activated, the short-term memory vanishes unless it has been encoded in long-term memory.

19. Researchers have evidence that the formation and storage of long-term memories involve the repeated stimulation of neurons, which in turn causes neurons to grow and change to form new connections with other neurons; this phenomenon is called (a)_____. When this process was chemically or genetically blocked, animals were unable to form (b)_____, which points to the importance of LTP in forming long-term memories.

E. MNEMONICS: MEMORIZATION METHODS

20. Although we have the capacity to store great amounts of information, we may not be able to recall some of this information because of forgetting. Techniques that use efficient methods of encoding to improve remembering and prevent forgetting are called (a)_____. The major function of these techniques is to create strong (b)_____ that will serve as effective (c)_____.

21. A method that creates visual associations between memorized places and items to be memorized is called the (a)_____. With another method, one creates associations between number-word rhymes and items to be memorized; this method is called the (b)_____.

F. CULTURAL DIVERSITY: ABORIGINES VERSUS WHITE AUSTRALIANS

22. Data from Aborigine and white Australian children suggest that survival needs may shape and reward a particular way of (a)_____ information in memory. For example, in the industrialized world, people (white Australians) are required to store large amounts of (b)_____. However, Aborigines in the wilds of Australia need to be able to store environmental, or (c)_____, to find their way, locate watering places, and thus increase their chances of survival. Researchers found that Aborigines performed better on tests that required (d)_____ retrieval cues and performed less well on tests that required (e)_____ cues.

G. RESEARCH FOCUS: FALSE MEMORIES

23. During the past 10 years, young children have been called upon to testify in court, particularly in cases of sexual abuse. Because there are records of officials suggesting to young children that certain events have occurred, there is concern that children may come to believe these suggestions. Researchers found that, although young children can accurately recall past events, repeated suggestions may create _____ in young children.

H. APPLICATION: EYEWITNESS TESTIMONY

24. In 83 out of 110 cases, eyewitnesses identified the wrong suspect, which indicates that such eyewitness testimony is not always (a)_____. Another problem is that the accuracy of an eyewitnesses is only moderately related to the how much (b)_____ the eyewitness feels. Eyewitnesses have difficulty identifying a suspect of another race; this is called (c)_____. Eyewitness testimony may not be reliable because witnesses may be influenced by officials who ask (d)_____ questions.

25. When a person has difficulty deciding which of two or more sources is responsible for a memory, it is called (a)_____. Researchers found that misleading questions and false information can cause subjects to (b)_____ events.

26. The recall of eyewitnesses may be improved by having them imagine and reconstruct the details of an event, report everything that they remember, and report things from different viewpoints. This method is called the (a)_____. With this method, eyewitnesses remember much more information about the event than they do when asked standard questions. This questioning procedure also helps to eliminate suggestions or source misattributions, which can result in implanting (b)_____ in witnesses.

Answers: *1. (a) recall, (b) recognition; 2. nodes; 3. network; 4. hierarchy; 5. forgetting curve; 6. (a) interference, (b) proactive, (c) retroactive; 7. retrieval cues; 8. repression; 9. amnesia; 10. bias, suggestibility; 11. retrieval cues; 12. tip-of-the-tongue; 13. state-dependent learning; 14. (a) cortex, (b) hippocampus, (c) remember; 15. (a) cortex, (b) hippocampus; 16. procedural; 17. amygdala; 18. neural assemblies; 19. (a) long-term potentiation, or LTP, (b) long-term memories; 20. (a) mnemonics, (b) associations, (c) retrieval cues; 21. (a) method of loci, (b) peg method; 22. (a) encoding, (b) verbal information, (c) visual information, (d) visual, (e) verbal; 23. false memories; 24. (a) accurate or reliable, (b) confidence, (c) own-race bias, (d) misleading; 25. (a) source misattribution, (b) misremember; 26. (a) cognitive interview, (b) false memories*

Critical Thinking

Why Does Wife Forget, Date, and Remarry Husband?

by Michael Haederle

Questions

1. Of the four reasons for forgetting, which one applies to Krickitt?

2. Krickitt's loss of many long-term memories means that which part of her brain was damaged?

3. How was Krickitt able to remember her parents but not her husband, not their apartment, and not their wedding photos?

LAS VEGAS, N.M.—Shortly after their wedding in 1993, Krickitt suffered a severe head injury in a car crash. When she emerged from a month-long coma, she no longer knew Kim (her husband), having lost all memory of the previous 18 months—including meeting and marrying her husband.

Kim stuck by her as she struggled to heal, and against all odds, they courted and fell in love again. . . .

Emerging from her coma around Christmas, Krickitt was as helpless as a newborn. She needed to be fed, diapered, and bathed. The 5-foot-2 former college gymnast, who'd once performed back flips on a balance beam, had to learn to walk again.

"It was sad to see her in this condition," Kim says. But there was worse news. . . .

When quizzed by a nurse, Krickitt knew she was in Phoenix—although she thought it was 1969 (it was really 1993) and Nixon was the president. She also knew who her parents were. . . . Then the nurse asked "Who's your husband?" Krickitt said, "I'm not married." Kim said, "I was devastated—I was crushed, I was hurt so bad. I hit my hand on the wall." . . .

Krickitt visited their Las Vegas home, hoping the familiar surroundings might jog her memory. She wandered through the apartment she'd shared with Kim, gazing at their wedding photos and fingering her china. Nothing clicked.

"I remember asking, 'How did I do the wife thing? Did I cook for you? Did I bring you lunch?'" she says. Krickitt was unable to drive and couldn't remember directions. Kim worried she'd get lost walking the 100 yards to the grocery store. . . . It was the therapist who suggested that Kim and Krickitt start dating as a way of rebuilding their relationship. On their "date nights," they sampled everything their small town had to offer. "We'd go to Pizza Hut," Kim says. "We'd go to Wal-Mart or go bowling." Sometimes he'd bring her roses. . . . With continued therapy and the passage of time, Krickitt has accepted her new life. . . . It was Krickitt who suggested getting married again.

On Valentine's Day he went to her office with a bunch of red roses and proposed on bended knee. . . . They married (above photo) Sept. 18, 1993, and honeymooned in Maui before settling into their new life together in this small northern New Mexico city. (Source: *Los Angeles Times*, May 23, 1996)

4. Of the two kinds of long-term memory, which involves Krickitt's having to relearn to drive a car?

5. Which part of Krickitt's brain was undamaged and allowed her to store new long-term memories of Kim?

Try InfoTrac to search for terms: amnesia; **long-term memory; short-term memory.**

1. Because of a car accident, Krickitt suffered a severe blow to her head that caused her to go into a coma. In addition, when she came out of her coma, the severe blow to her head caused widespread amnesia, which is forgetting caused by loss of memory.
2. Since long-term memories are stored primarily in the cortex (surface of the brain), this means that areas of Krickitt's cortex were damaged in the accident.
3. Researchers have discovered that different kinds of long-term memories are stored in different parts of the cortex. Krickitt could remember her parents because those memories were stored in a part of her cortex that was undamaged. However, she lost all memory of her husband and being married because those memories were stored in a part of her cortex that was damaged.

4. There are two kinds of long-term memories: declarative and nondeclarative or procedural (p. 246). Learning motor skills and habits involves storing nondeclarative or procedural memories and does not involve the hippocampus.
5. Krickett was able to relearn who Kim was by dating him. Krickett's ability to remember that she was dating and going out with Kim means that she was able to store personal or episodic memories, which are one kind of declarative memories (p. 246). Declarative memories are transferred and stored as long-term memories by the hippocampus, which means that Krickett's hippocampus was undamaged and functioning.

Links to Learning

LEARNING ACTIVITIES

- **POWERSTUDY CD-ROM 2.0**
  by Tom Doyle and Rod Plotnik

Check out the "Remembering & Forgetting" SuperModule (disk 2) on PowerStudy. This is a completely self-paced module that is fully narrated. Don't want the narration? It is easy to turn off! This module includes:

- Videos— An imbedded video in the Reasons for Forgetting section discusses associations.

- A multitude of animations designed to help you understand more about remembering and forgetting. The interactive introduction puts you in the witness stand and asks you to remember; the applications section discusses the problems with eyewitness testimony.

- A test of your knowledge using an interactive version of the Summary Test on pages 276 and 277. Also access related quizzes—true/false, multiple choice, and matching.

- An interactive version of the Critical Thinking exercise "Why Does Wife Forget, Date, and Remarry Husband?" on page 278.

- Key terms, a chapter outline including chapter abstract, and a list of hotlinked Web sites that correlate to this module.

- **SELF-STUDY ASSESSMENT**
  Want help studying? For your customized Study Plan go to **http://psychology.wadsworth.com/plotnik7e/**. This program will automatically generate pretests and posttests to help you determine what concepts you have mastered and what concepts you still need work on.

WebTUTOR
- **STUDY GUIDE and WEBTUTOR**
  Check the corresponding module in your Study Guide for effective student tips and help learning the material presented.

- **INFOTRAC COLLEGE EDITION ONLINE LIBRARY**
  To find interesting and relevant articles go to **http://www.infotrac-college.com**, use your password, and then type in search terms such as the ones listed below.

Amnesia　　　　Retroactive interference
Repression　　　Retrieval cues

STUDY QUESTIONS

Use InfoTrac to search for topics mentioned in the following questions (e.g., forgetting, mnemonics, false memories).

*A. Organization of Memories—How would your memory be affected if you accidentally took a drug that prevented the formation of any new nodes? (**Suggested answer page 626**)

B. Forgetting Curves—Why are you more likely to remember students' names than concepts from high school?

C. Reasons for Forgetting—If you wanted to change your study habits, how would you use information about why we forget?

*D. Biological Bases of Memory—If a virus suddenly destroyed your hippocampus, what effect would it have on your performance in college? (**Suggested answer page 626**)

E. Mnemonics: Memorization Methods—Can you describe a mnemonic method to remember the four reasons for forgetting?

F. Cultural Diversity: Aborigines Versus White Australians—What might be one difference between the ways in which art and English majors encode information?

G. Research Focus: False Memories—When young children are questioned, what precautions should be taken to minimize the creation of false memories?

*H. Application: Eyewitness Testimony—If you were on a jury, what concerns would you have when listening to eyewitness testimony? (**Suggested answer page 626**)

*These questions are answered in Appendix B.

Module 13: Intelligence

Mirror, Mirror, on the Wall, Who Is the Most Intelligent of Them All?

Who is the most intelligent?

For the past 200 years, psychologists have been involved in defining and measuring intelligence, which turns out to be a very complicated business. For example, after reading about the five individuals described below, rank them according to your idea of intelligence. After you have read the module, come back to your ranking and see if you would make any changes.

Based on my idea of intelligence, here's how I have ranked the five individuals: #1____, #2____, #3____, #4____, #5____.

A. Gregg Cox

At age 34, he can speak 64 languages fluently, making him, says the *Guinness Book of World Records,* the planet's greatest linguist. He broke the old record of 58 languages. He began learning languages at age 5, starting with Spanish, Portuguese, Italian, German, and Chinese. Since then, he has been learning about 5 languages a year. He's writing a book—a dictionary.

B. Serena Williams

By age 22, she had won a record-setting three Grand Slam tennis titles in a row for an unheard-of six Grand Slams, which included beating her older sister, Venus, for the 2003 Wimbledon title. She became the first woman tennis player to earn $4 million in a single year. She (and/or her sister Venus) has a chance to become the greatest woman tennis player of all time.

C. Bill Gates

At age 48, he has become the richest man in the U.S.— worth around $61 billion. He began writing computer programs in the eighth grade. As a college sophomore, he dropped out of Harvard and wrote one of the first operating systems to run a computer. In his twenties, he founded Microsoft, whose software operates 90% of the computers in the world.

D. Steve Lu

At age 5, he scored 194 on an IQ test (average is 100). At age 9, he scored 710 on the math part of the SAT (perfect score is 800). He completed 12 years of precollege courses in just 5 years. At age 10, he was a freshman in college. At age 15, he was one of the youngest students ever to be accepted in the graduate computer science program at prestigious Stanford University.

E. Midori

At age 3, she began playing violin. By age 10, she was considered a musical prodigy, another name for a child genius. Also at age 10, she made a big stir in classical music circles by performing professionally with the New York Philharmonic Orchestra. From an early age she was able to memorize and flawlessly perform long and complicated pieces of classical music.

Psychometrics

The problem you faced in trying to rank the intelligence of the above five individuals—Cox, Williams, Gates, Lu, and Midori—is similar to what psychologists faced in having to define and measure intelligence. Since the late 1800s, psychologists have debated the question, What is intelligence? and have developed a number of tests to measure intelligence. Measuring intelligence is part of an area of psychology that is called psychometrics.

Psychometrics, which is a subarea of psychology, is concerned with developing psychological tests that assess an individual's abilities, skills, beliefs, and personality traits in a wide range of settings—school, industry, or clinic.

As you'll discover in this module, the measurement of intelligence and the development of intelligence tests are still being debated (Sternberg et al., 2003b).

What's Coming

We'll discuss the different theories of intelligence, how intelligence is measured, the meaning of IQ scores, the problems with intelligence tests, how genetics and environment influence intelligence, and ways to improve environmental opportunities.

We'll begin with a very old but very basic question: How do we define intelligence?

A. Defining Intelligence

Problem: Definition

What is intelligence?

Gregg Cox: speaks 64 languages

Serena Williams: tennis champ

Bill Gates: head of Microsoft; $61 billion

Steve Lu: 194 IQ; grad school at age15

Midori: child prodigy; violin genius

When college students were asked to estimate IQs, men estimated their own IQs as well as those of their fathers to be higher than their mothers' or sisters', while women underestimated their own and their mothers' IQs (Furnham et al., 2001). In fact, over the past 20 years, men have consistently overestimated and women have consistently underestimated their IQs, even though researchers find no sex differences in IQ scores (Colom et al., 2000).

People generally believe IQ scores measure intelligence. But it's not so simple. For example, how did you rank the intelligence of the five individuals in the left photos, each of whom shows a different yet extraordinary skill or talent? Do these examples point to the existence of different kinds of intelligence (H. Gardner, 2003)?

Many psychologists believe that intelligence is best defined by measuring a variety of cognitive abilities, which is what most intelligence tests measure. For example, Steve Lu received a very high IQ score (194) based on an intelligence test. Others argue that a definition of intelligence based entirely on cognitive abilities is much too narrow. Instead, they believe that there are many kinds of intelligence, such as involving creative dance or motor movements (Serena Williams), musical abilities (Midori), practical skills (Gregg Cox), or solving problems (Bill Gates) (E. Benson, 2003a).

More recently, researchers have pointed to the importance of emotional intelligence, which involves how well people perceive, express, and regulate emotions in themselves and others (Salovey & Pizarro, 2003). We'll discuss emotional intelligence in Module 16 (p. 396).

Here we'll examine three popular definitions of intelligence, beginning with the oldest and perhaps the most widely accepted definition of intelligence, the two-factor theory.

Two-Factor Theory

What is "g"?

In 1904, Charles Spearman reported that he had measured intelligence in an objective way. Spearman was one of the first to use the psychometric approach.

The *psychometric approach* measures or quantifies cognitive abilities or factors that are thought to be involved in intellectual performance.

Spearman (1904) reasoned that by measuring related cognitive factors he would have an objective measure of intelligence. This idea led to his two-factor theory of intelligence.

Spearman's *two-factor theory* says that intelligence has two factors: a general mental ability factor, *g*, which represents what different cognitive tasks have in common, plus many specific factors, *s*, which include specific mental abilities (mathematical, mechanical, or verbal skills).

Spearman believed that factor *g*, or general mental ability, represented a person's mental energy. Today, factor *g* is defined and measured by a person's performance on various and related cognitive abilities. In other words, modern intelligence tests have essentially changed or transformed Spearman's *g* into an objective score, which is commonly known as the IQ score. Today, many psychologists believe that *g*, as represented by IQ scores, is a good measure of a person's general intelligence.

On the basis of Spearman's two-factor theory, which of the five individuals (left photos) is most intelligent?

Many psychologists believe that *g* is the definition of general intelligence, which can be measured by an IQ test and represented by an IQ score. Thus, one way to compare people on intelligence is by using scores from IQ tests. Ranking intelligence by using IQ scores would favor Lu (IQ 194), Bill Gates (one colleague said Gates was "the smartest person he ever knew"), and probably Cox (speaks 64 languages). However, although Williams (world tennis champ)

Steve Lu: 194 IQ; grad school at age 15

and Midori (violin genius) might score high on IQ tests, they would get little or no credit for having exceptional motor, music, or perceptual skills.

ADVANTAGES AND DISADVANTAGES

One advantage of *g* is that it can be objectively defined and measured by an IQ test, which gives a single IQ score that is presumed to reflect a person's general intelligence. Another advantage is that *g* is a good predictor of performance in academic settings and has some success in predicting performance in certain careers (discussed later) (N. Brody, 2000).

One disadvantage of Spearman's *g* is the continuing debate over whether it is the best measure of intelligence. Or as one researcher states, "We know how to measure something called intelligence, but we do not know what has been measured" (N. Brody, 2000, p. 30). A second disadvantage of *g* is that it focuses on cognitive abilities but neglects motor, perceptual, musical, practical, and creative abilities, which some believe indicate other kinds of intelligence (H. Gardner, 2003). A third disadvantage is that *g* and its focus on cognitive abilities is popular in Western cultures but not in many Asian and African cultures, where being intelligent includes other abilities, such as how one relates to and understands others (E. Benson, 2003b). For these reasons, psychologists critical of *g*'s narrow approach to measuring general intelligence have proposed other definitions and ways to measure intelligence. We'll discuss two other definitions of intelligence.

Multiple kinds of intelligence?

Some psychologists reject the idea that intelligence can be reduced to ***g*** and expressed by a single number, an IQ score. Howard Gardner (1999; 2003) argues for broadening the definition of intelligence to include different kinds of abilities, an idea he calls the multiple-intelligence theory.

Gardner's multiple-intelligence theory says that instead of one kind of general intelligence, there are at least seven different kinds, which include verbal intelligence, musical intelligence, logical-mathematical intelligence, spatial intelligence, body movement intelligence, intelligence to understand oneself, and intelligence to understand others.

Gardner states that standard IQ tests measure primarily verbal and logical-mathematical intelligence and neglect other but equally important kinds of intelligence, such as the ones listed above. Gardner (1999; 2003) arrived at his theory of multiple kinds of intelligence after studying which abilities remain following brain damage, how savants and prodigies develop their specialized kinds of intelligence, and how people in different environments develop different abilities in order to adapt and be successful.

Serena Williams: tennis champion

On the basis of Gardner's multiple-intelligence theory, which of the five individuals (previous page) is most intelligent?

According to Gardner's multiple-intelligence theory, there isn't one kind of general intelligence for ranking all individuals. Rather, Gardner views the special abilities of Williams in tennis and Midori in music as representing other kinds of intelligence.

Gardner argues that none of the five is more intelligent but rather that each of the five individuals shows a different kind of ability or intelligence that was developed and adapted to his or her environment.

ADVANTAGES AND DISADVANTAGES

One advantage of Gardner's multiple-intelligence approach is that it does not reduce intelligence to a single IQ score but rather credits people with having different kinds of intelligence.

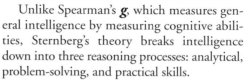

Midori: child prodigy; violin genius

Two disadvantages of this approach are not knowing how many kinds of intelligence there are and not having standard measuring techniques to assess different kinds of intelligence (Callahan, 2000).

Agreeing with Gardner that ***g*** is too narrow a measure of intelligence, Sternberg proposed a triarchic theory.

Three kinds of intelligence?

Criticizing Spearman's ***g*** as too narrow and current IQ tests as limited to measuring only problem-solving skills and cognitive abilities, psychologist Robert Sternberg defined intelligence by ***analyzing*** three kinds of reasoning processes that people use in solving problems. Sternberg (2003a) calls his approach the triarchic theory of intelligence.

Sternberg's triarchic theory says that intelligence can be divided into three different kinds of reasoning processes (***triarchic*** means "three"). The first is using analytical or logical thinking skills that are measured by traditional intelligence tests. The second is using problem-solving skills that require creative thinking and the ability to learn from experience. The third is using practical thinking skills that help a person adjust to, and cope with, his or her sociocultural environment.

Analytical

Problem solving

Practical

Unlike Spearman's ***g***, which measures general intelligence by measuring cognitive abilities, Sternberg's theory breaks intelligence down into three reasoning processes: analytical, problem-solving, and practical skills.

On the basis of Sternberg's triarchic theory of intelligence, which of the five individuals (previous page) is most intelligent?

According to Sternberg's triarchic theory, there isn't one kind of general intelligence for evaluating these five individuals but rather three different reasoning processes (analytical, problem solving, practical) that contribute to and predict the successes of each of the five individuals.

ADVANTAGES AND DISADVANTAGES

One advantage of Sternberg's triarchic theory of intelligence is that it doesn't limit the definition of intelligence to cognitive abilities. Instead, Sternberg's theory evaluates a person's intelligence by measuring three different kinds of reasoning processes and how they contribute to a person's success. For example, a person may be "street smart" or have exceptional practical reasoning skills but may not necessarily score high on traditional intelligence tests.

One disadvantage of the triarchic theory is that Sternberg's research and tests for measuring his proposed three kinds of reasoning processes have so far been criticized as providing little support for his triarchic theory (N. Brody, 2003; Gottfredson, 2003).

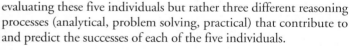

Western psychologists used the psychometric approach to measure cognitive abilities, which led to the development of intelligence tests and IQ scores and the concept of ***g*** as the best measure of intelligence (N. Brody, 2000). Standard intelligence tests remain popular because they have proved useful in predicting performance in academic settings, but they are less predictive for career settings. Newer approaches, such as Gardner's multiple-intelligence approach and Sternberg's triarchic approach, which measure additional abilities

and reasoning skills and represent different kinds of intelligence, hope to replace ***g*** and its IQ score as the best measure of intelligence (H. Gardner, 2003; Sternberg et al., 2003a). Finally, many Asian and African cultures believe that besides cognitive abilities, intelligence should include the ability to relate to and get along with and understand others.

To see how far intelligence testing has come, we'll go back in time and discuss early attempts to define and measure intelligence.

B. Measuring Intelligence

Earlier Attempts to Measure Intelligence

HEAD SIZE AND INTELLIGENCE

Are bigger brains better?

Efforts to measure intelligence began in earnest in the late 1800s. That's when Francis Galton noticed that intelligent people often had intelligent relatives and concluded that intelligence was, to a large extent, biological or inherited. In trying to assess inherited intelligence, Galton measured people's heads and recorded the speed of their reactions to various sensory stimuli. However, his measures proved to be poorly related to intelligence or academic achievement (S. J. Gould, 1996).

Galton switched gears and tried to correlate head size with students' grade point average. For example, he reported that the average head size of Cambridge students who received A's was about 3.3% larger than that of students who received C's (Galton, 1888). However, a review of later studies showed a very low correlation of 0.19 between head size and intelligence (IQ scores) (N. Brody, 1992). Such a low correlation has little practical use in measuring or predicting intelligence. For this reason, using head size as a measure of intelligence was abandoned in favor of using skull or brain size.

BRAIN SIZE AND INTELLIGENCE

Efforts to measure intelligence continued with the work of Paul Broca, a famous neurologist in the late 1800s. Broca claimed that there was a relationship between size of brain and intelligence, with larger brains indicating more intelligence. However, a later re-analysis of Broca's data indicated that measures of brain size proved to be unreliable and poorly correlated with intelligence (S. J. Gould, 1996).

Recently, the sizes of living brains were measured with brain scans (p. 70), which permit more precise measurement. Brain scan studies reported medium-sized positive correlations (+0.32 and +0.39) between brain size and intelligence (IQ scores) (Egan et al., 1994; Wickett et al., 1994). However, such correlations indicate only that a relationship exists; correlations cannot tell us whether bigger brains lead to increased intelligence or whether more cognitive activity leads to bigger brains. These medium-sized correlations indicate a positive relationship between brain size and intelligence (IQ scores) but are too low to have practical value in actually predicting an individual's intelligence.

BRAIN SIZE AND ACHIEVEMENT

Early researchers were reluctant to give up the idea that bigger brains were better. They looked for a relationship between brain size and personal achievement, another measure of intelligence. However, as shown in the center illustration, there is enormous variation in brain size and achievement (S. J. Gould, 1996). Notice that Nobel Prize–winner Einstein's brain (1,230 grams) was slightly below average weight and that two famous authors, poet Walt Whitman (1,200 grams) and novelist Anatole France (1,000 grams), achieved literary fame with brains about half the weight of Jonathan Swift's (2,000 grams), one of the heaviest on record. For comparison, we have included a gorilla brain (500 grams), which is actually quite small considering the size of a gorilla head. It is difficult to test a gorilla's intelligence, but at least one is reported to have learned a vocabulary of 800 hand signs (P. E. Ross, 1991).

BRAIN SIZE, SEX DIFFERENCES, AND INTELLIGENCE

Still believing that bigger brains are better, some researchers claimed that women had lower IQ scores than men because women's brains weigh about 10% less than men's (Holden, 1995). However, a recent study of over 4,000 women and 6,000 men reported that there was little or no difference in intelligence (IQ scores) between men and women. Researchers concluded that the larger size of men's brains does not result in higher IQs (Colom et al., 2000).

MEASURING INTELLIGENCE

As you have seen, there is a long history of scientists trying to measure intelligence. However, all the early attempts to use head, skull, body, or brain size to measure intelligence failed. In fact, a paper presented in 1904 to a German psychological society concluded that there was little hope of developing psychological tests to measure intelligence in an objective way (Wolf, 1973). What's interesting about this paper is that one of the authors was Alfred Binet, who went on to develop the first intelligence test.

We'll explain how Binet succeeded in developing an intelligence test when so many others had failed.

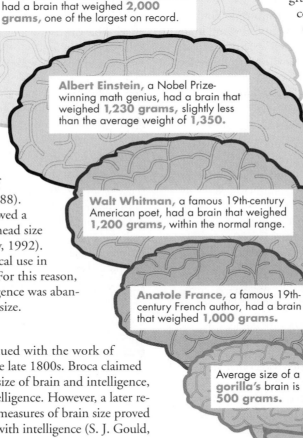

Jonathan Swift, a great 18th-century British writer who wrote *Gulliver's Travels,* had a brain that weighed **2,000 grams,** one of the largest on record.

Albert Einstein, a Nobel Prize-winning math genius, had a brain that weighed **1,230 grams,** slightly less than the average weight of **1,350.**

Walt Whitman, a famous 19th-century American poet, had a brain that weighed **1,200 grams,** within the normal range.

Anatole France, a famous 19th-century French author, had a brain that weighed **1,000 grams.**

Average size of a **gorilla's** brain is **500 grams.**

Brain size doesn't necessarily match performance.

Why did Binet develop an intelligence test?

In the late 1800s, a gifted French psychologist named Alfred Binet realized that Broca and Galton had failed to assess intelligence by measuring brain size. Binet strongly believed that intelligence was a collection of mental abilities and that the best way to assess intelligence was to measure a person's ability to perform cognitive tasks, such as understanding the meanings of words or being able to follow directions.

Binet was very pessimistic about developing an intelligence test. By a strange twist of fate, he was appointed to a commission that was instructed to develop tests capable of differentiating children of normal intelligence from those who needed special help. Binet accepted this challenge with two goals in mind: The test must be easy to administer without requiring any special laboratory equipment, and the test must clearly distinguish between normal and abnormal mental ability (N. Brody, 1992). In 1905, Binet and psychiatrist Theodore Simon succeeded in developing the world's first standardized intelligence test, the Binet-Simon Intelligence Scale (Binet & Simon, 1905).

Alfred Binet
(1857–1911)

The ***Binet-Simon Intelligence Scale*** contained items arranged in order of increasing difficulty. The items measured vocabulary, memory, common knowledge, and other cognitive abilities.

The purpose of this first Binet-Simon Intelligence Scale was to distinguish among mentally defective children in the Paris school system. In Binet's time, intellectually deficient children were divided into three groups: idiots (most severely deficient), imbeciles (moderate), and morons (mildest). These terms are no longer used today because they have taken on very negative meanings. The problems with this first test were that it classified children into only three categories (idiots, imbeciles, and morons) and that it did not have a way to express the results in a single score. However, several years later, Binet corrected both of these problems when he introduced the concept of mental level, or mental age.

MENTAL AGE: MEASURE OF INTELLIGENCE

Binet and Simon revised their intelligence scale to solve several problems in their original scale. In this revised test, they arranged the test items in order of increasing difficulty and designed different items to measure different cognitive abilities. For each test item, Binet determined whether an average child of a certain age could answer the question correctly. For example, a child at age level 3 should be able to point to various parts of the face. A child at age level 9 should be able to recite the days of the week. Because the test items were arranged for each age level (age levels 3 to 13), this new test could identify which average age level the child performed at. If a particular child passed all the items that could be answered by an average 3-year-old but none of the items appropriate for older children, that child would be said to have a mental age of 3.

Thus, if a 6-year-old child could answer only questions appropriate for a 3-year-old child, that child would be given a mental age of 3 and would be considered retarded in intellectual development. Binet's intelligence test became popular because a single score represented mental age.

Which items could an average 3-year-old answer?

Which items could an average 9-year-old answer?

Mental age is a method of estimating a child's intellectual progress by comparing the child's score on an intelligence test to the scores of average children of the same age.

At this point, the Binet-Simon scale gave its results in terms of a mental age but not an IQ score. The idea for computing an IQ score did not occur until some years later, when the scale was revised by L. M. Terman.

What was the big change?

The first big change was when Binet and Simon introduced the concept of mental age. The second big change occurred in 1916, when Lewis Terman and his colleagues at Stanford University in California came up with a new and better method to compute the final score. Improving on the concept of expressing the test results in terms of mental age, Terman devised a formula to calculate an intelligence quotient (IQ) score (Terman, 1916).

Intelligence quotient is computed by dividing a child's mental age (MA), as measured in an intelligence test, by the child's chronological age (CA) and multiplying the result by 100.

Remember that in Binet's test, mental age was calculated by noting how many items a child answered that were appropriate to a certain age. For example, if a 4-year-old girl passed the test items appropriate for a 5-year-old, she was said to have a mental age of 5. A child's chronological (physical) age is his or her age in months and years. To compute her IQ score, we use Terman's formula, shown below.

$$IQ = \frac{MA}{CA} \times 100$$

IQ (Intelligence quotient) = MA (Mental age) / CA (Chronological age) × 100

Formula for calculating IQ score

Thus, for the child in our example, we substitute 5 for MA, 4 for CA, and multiply by 100. We get: 5/4 = 1.25 × 100 = 125. So the child's IQ is 125. An IQ score computed in this traditional way is called a ***ratio IQ*** because the score represents a ratio of mental to chronological age. Today the ratio IQ has been replaced by the ***deviation IQ,*** whose computation is too complex to explain here. The reason for the switch from ratio IQ to deviation IQ is that deviation IQ scores more accurately reflect test performance as children get older.

Since the original Binet-Simon scale in 1905, IQ tests have become very popular and have grown into a large business. We'll look more closely at one of the most widely used IQ tests.

B. Measuring Intelligence

Is IQ the same as intelligence?

We are all curious to learn someone's IQ because we believe that this single score reveals a person's real intelligence. For example, try to match these IQ scores—104, 114, 228—with three famous people—John F. Kennedy, 35th president of the United States; J. D. Salinger, famous novelist *(Catcher in the Rye)*; and Marilyn vos Savant, columnist for *Parade* magazine (answers on right). Knowing the IQ scores of these individuals tells us something of their cognitive abilities, but some psychologists believe that cognitive abilities represent only one kind of intelligence. For example, would you expect Salinger, with his average IQ, to be a very creative novelist, or vos Savant, columnist for *Parade* magazine, to have a high IQ twice that of President Kennedy? The achievements of individuals with average or slightly above average IQs suggest that there are other kinds of intelligence, such as practical, emotional, social, and creative, which may be equally important to one's success in life and career (H. Gardner, 2003; Sternberg et al., 2003b). Now, let's see how IQ scores are measured.

John F. Kennedy: 35th U.S. president

Marilyn vos Savant: columnist for *Parade* magazine

J. D. Salinger: author of *Catcher in the Rye*

Answers: *Salinger, 104; Kennedy, 114; and vos Savant, 228, the highest IQ on record (Cowley, 1994)*

Wechsler Intelligence Scales

The most widely used IQ tests are the Wechsler Adult Intelligence Scale (WAIS-III), for ages 16 and older, and the Wechsler Intelligence Scale for Children (WISC-III), for children of ages 3–16. A trained examiner administers the Wechsler scales on a one-to-one basis.

The *Wechsler Adult Intelligence Scale (WAIS-III)* and *Wechsler Intelligence Scale for Children (WISC-III)* have items that are organized into various subtests. For example, the verbal section contains a subtest of general information, a subtest of vocabulary, and so forth. The performance section contains a subtest that involves arranging pictures in a meaningful order, one that requires assembling objects, and one that involves using codes. The verbal and performance scores are combined to give a single IQ score.

Examples of the subtests for WAIS-III are shown on the right. The Verbal Scale (top right) emphasizes language and verbal skills. Because of this emphasis, a person from a deprived environment or for whom English is a second language might have difficulty on this scale because of lack of verbal knowledge rather than lack of cognitive ability.

In an attempt to measure nonverbal skills and rule out other cultural or educational problems, Wechsler added the Performance Scale (lower right). These performance subtests, which measure problem-solving abilities, require considerable concentration and focused effort, which may be difficult for individuals who are very nervous, are poor test takers, or have emotional problems. Although these IQ tests carefully try to measure verbal and nonverbal abilities, you can see that part of one's success on IQ tests depends on nonintellectual factors, such as cultural, educational, or emotional factors (Kaplan & Saccuzzo, 2001). We'll discuss other problems with IQ tests later in this module.

One reason these IQ tests are widely used is that they have two characteristics of good tests: validity and reliability.

WAIS-III Verbal Scale: Subtests

Subtests for the verbal scale include information, comprehension, arithmetic, similarities, digit span, and vocabulary. These examples resemble the WAIS-III items.

Information
On what continent is France?

Comprehension
Why are children required to go to school?

Arithmetic
How many hours will it take to drive 150 miles at 50 miles per hour?

Similarities
How are a calculator and a typewriter alike?

Digit span
Repeat the following numbers backward: 2, 4, 3, 5, 8, 9, 6.

Vocabulary
What does *audacity* mean?

WAIS-III Performance Scale: Subtests

Subtests for the performance scale include digit symbol, block design, picture completion, picture arrangement, and object assembly. These sample items shown on the right resemble those given for each WAIS-III subtest.

Digit symbol

Shown: 1 2 3 4 — Fill in: 1 4 3 2

Block design
Assemble blocks to match this design.

Picture completion
Tell me what is missing.

Picture arrangement
Put the pictures in the right order.

Object assembly
Assemble the pieces into a complete object.

Can you analyze handwriting?

How truthful are the claims that intelligence and other personality traits can be identified through analyzing handwriting (Searles, 1998)? For example, which one of the four handwriting samples on the right indicates the highest IQ? (Answer at bottom of page.)

Although handwriting analysis may claim to measure intelligence, research shows that its accuracy is usually no better than a good guess (Tripician, 2000).

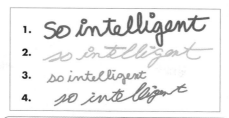

Which handwriting sample, 1, 2, 3, or 4, is from the person with the highest IQ?

The reason handwriting analysis or so-called IQ tests in popular magazines are poor measures of intelligence (IQ) is that they lack at least one of the two important characteristics of a good test. These two characteristics are validity and reliability, which mark the difference between an accurate IQ test (WAIS-III) and an inaccurate test (handwriting analysis).

Validity

Handwriting analysis is fun, but it is a very poor intelligence test because it lacks validity, which is one of the two characteristics of a good test.

Validity means that the test measures what it is supposed to measure.

Although the definition of validity seems simple and short, this characteristic makes or breaks a test. For example, numerous studies have shown that handwriting analysis has little or no validity as an intelligence or personality test (Basil, 1989; Tripician, 2000). Because handwriting analysis lacks the characteristic of validity, it means that this test does not accurately measure what it is supposed to measure. Thus, a test with little or no validity produces results that could be produced by guessing or by chance.

The reason handwriting analysis or tests in popular magazines are not checked for validity is that checking validity is a long, expensive, and complicated process. One way to show a test's validity is to give the new test to hundreds of subjects along with other tests whose validity has already been established. Then the subjects' scores on the new test are correlated with their scores on the tests with proven validity. Another way that the validity of intelligence tests, such as the WAIS-III, was established was to show that IQ scores correlated with another measure of intelligence, such as academic performance (A. S. Kaufman, 2000).

However, if IQ scores are valid measures of cognitive abilities and correlate with academic performance, why do some individuals with high IQs do poorly in college? The developer of the Head Start program, Ed Zigler, believes that academic performance depends on three factors: cognitive abilities; achievement, or the amount of knowledge that a person has accumulated; and motivation (Zigler, 1995). This means that a person may have outstanding cognitive abilities but may lack either the achievement or the motivation to succeed in college.

Besides validity, a good intelligence test should also have reliability.

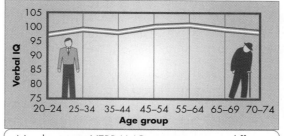

No change in VERBAL IQ scores in seven different age groups indicates that test is reliable.

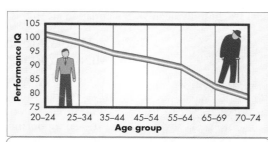

Decrease in OVERALL IQ scores across ages is due to psychological and physiological changes and not reliability problems with IQ test.

Reliability

If your style of handwriting remained constant over time, such as always boldly crossing your *t*'s, then this trait would be reliable.

Reliability refers to consistency: A person's score on a test at one point in time should be similar to the score obtained by the same person on a similar test at a later point in time.

For example, if boldly crossed *t*'s indicated that a person is intelligent, then this measure of intelligence would be reliable. However, there is no evidence that boldly crossed *t*'s indicate that a person is intelligent. So, in this case, handwriting analysis would be a reliable test of intelligence, but since it lacks validity (doesn't measure intelligence) it is a worthless test of intelligence.

Now, suppose you took the WAIS-III as a senior in high school and then retook the test as a junior in college. You would find that your IQ scores would be much the same because each time you would be compared with others of your same age. Because your IQ scores remain similar across time, it would mean that the Wechsler scales, like other standardized IQ tests, have reliability (Berg, 2000).

For example, the top graph shows the results of verbal IQ scores when seven different age groups of subjects were given the WAIS-III. Notice that verbal IQ scores are quite stable from ages 20 to 74, indicating that the Wechsler scales score high in reliability (A. S. Kaufman et al., 1989).

But notice that the lower graph shows that there is an overall decrease in performance IQ scores from ages 20 to 74 (A. S. Kaufman et al., 1989). However, this general decrease in performance scores across one's lifetime reflects changes in psychological and physiological functioning rather than a decrease in the test's reliability.

Researchers have shown that current intelligence tests, which measure primarily cognitive abilities, have relatively good validity and reliability (Kaplan & Saccuzzo, 2001). Even though IQ scores can be measured with good reliability and validity, our next question to answer is: What good or use are IQ scores?

(Handwriting answer: I wrote all four samples so that no matter which one you picked, I would come out a winner.)

C. Distribution & Use of IQ Scores

IQ 50–85

The left photo is of Chris Burke, who starred in the television series "Life Goes On." Burke has Down syndrome, a genetic defect that results in varying degrees of mental retardation and physical symptoms (slanting eyes, flattened nose, visual problems). Although Burke has mild or borderline mental retardation, he acted in a TV series and now sings in a band and gives inspirational talks (Horsburgh et al., 2001). Based on his abilities, Burke's IQ is probably between 50 and 85.

In comparison, the photo on the right is of Marilyn vos Savant, who writes a column for *Parade* magazine and has a reported IQ of 228, the highest on record. To compare the IQs of Burke and vos Savant with those of other people, we need to look at the distribution of IQ scores. IQ scores from established intelligence tests, such as the WAIS-III, are said to have a normal distribution.

A *normal distribution* refers to a statistical arrangement of scores so that they resemble the shape of a bell and, thus, is said to be a bell-shaped curve. A bell-shaped curve means the vast majority of scores fall in the middle range, with fewer scores falling near the two extreme ends of the curve.

IQ 228

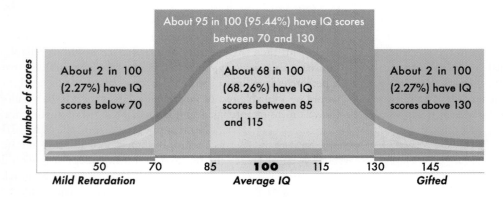

About 95 in 100 (95.44%) have IQ scores between 70 and 130

About 2 in 100 (2.27%) have IQ scores below 70

About 68 in 100 (68.26%) have IQ scores between 85 and 115

About 2 in 100 (2.27%) have IQ scores above 130

Number of scores

50   70   85   **100**   115   130   145
Mild Retardation   **Average IQ**   **Gifted**

For example, a normal distribution of IQ scores is shown at the left and is bell-shaped. The average IQ score is 100, and 95% of IQ scores fall between 70 and 130. An IQ of 70 and below is one sign of mild retardation. An IQ of 145 or higher is one indication of a gifted individual. Thus, one widespread use of IQ tests is to provide general *categories* regarding mental abilities.

Next, we'll examine these guidelines in more detail, beginning with mental retardation.

What is mental retardation?

One use of IQ scores has been to help identify individuals with mental retardation, which was Binet's original goal.

Mental retardation refers to a substantial limitation in present functioning that is characterized by significantly subaverage intellectual functioning, along with related limitations in two of ten areas, including communication, self-care, home living, social skills, and safety (American Association on Mental Retardation, 1993).

Psychologists caution against using IQ scores as the sole test for mental retardation. IQ tests are usually used in combination with observations of adaptive skills, which include social, home living, and communication skills. On the basis of IQ scores and adaptive skills, three levels of retardation have been identified.

1 BORDERLINE MENTALLY RETARDED

These individuals have IQs that range from 50 to 75. With special training and educational opportunities, they can learn to read and write, gain social competency, master simple occupational skills, and become self-supporting members of society. About 70% of individuals with retardation are in this category.

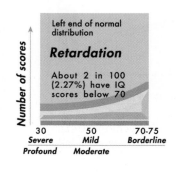

Left end of normal distribution

Retardation

About 2 in 100 (2.27%) have IQ scores below 70

Number of scores

30   50   70-75
Severe   **Mild**   **Borderline**
Profound   **Moderate**

2 MILDLY/MODERATELY MENTALLY RETARDED

These individuals have IQs that range from 35 to 50. With special training and educational opportunities, they can learn to become partially independent in their everyday lives, provided they are in a family or self-help setting.

3 SEVERELY/PROFOUNDLY MENTALLY RETARDED

These individuals have IQs that range from 20 to 40. With special training and educational opportunities, they can acquire limited skills in taking care of their personal needs. However, because of retarded motor and verbal abilities, they require considerable supervision their entire lives.

4 CAUSES

There are two general types of mental retardation—organic and cultural-familial.

Organic retardation results from genetic problems or brain damage.

Chris Burke is an example of someone with organic retardation.

Cultural-familial retardation results from a greatly impoverished environment. There is no evidence of genetic or brain damage.

Approximately 5 million Americans have various degrees of mental retardation.

Next, we move to the middle of IQ's normal distribution.

Since the vast majority of people, about 95%, have IQ scores that fall between 70 and 130, it is interesting to see what IQ scores can tell us.

Do IQ Scores Predict Academic Achievement? Because IQ tests measure cognitive abilities that are similar to those used in academic settings, it is no surprise that there is a medium-strength association, or correlation, between IQ scores and grades (0.50), between IQ scores and reading scores for grade-school children (0.38 to 0.46), and between IQ scores and total years of education that people complete (0.50) (N. Brody, 1997). These medium-strength correlations mean that IQ scores are moderately good at predicting academic performance. However, based on medium-strength correlations alone, it would be difficult to predict a *specific person's academic performance* because performance in academic settings also depends on personal characteristics, such as one's interest in school and willingness to study (Neisser et al., 1996).

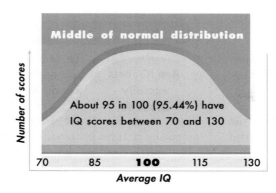

Middle of normal distribution

About 95 in 100 (95.44%) have IQ scores between 70 and 130

Number of scores

70   85   **100**   115   130

Average IQ

IQ scores are useful for predicting academic success.

IQ scores are somewhat useful at predicting job performance.

Do IQ Scores Predict Job Performance? There is a low- to medium-strength correlation (+0.30 to 0.50) between IQ scores and job performance, which means that IQ scores are poor to moderately good at predicting job performance (Neisser et al., 1996). However, such correlations are not very accurate at predicting a *specific person's job performance* because several noncognitive factors that are not measured by IQ tests, such as personality traits (is a can-do person), emotional traits (can deal with stress and get along with co-workers), and practical know-how (figures out how to get job done), play important roles in predicting job performance (Gottfredson, 2002; Sternberg, 2003b). Thus, IQ scores alone are relatively good at predicting performance in academic settings but less successful at predicting job performance in those jobs that demand certain personality traits and/or emotional skills.

Now, we'll examine the right end of the normal distribution—high IQ scores.

Sho Yano (below photo), whose IQ is 200 plus, entered college at age 9, graduated at age 12, plays classical works on the piano, and is the youngest person ever to start a dual M.D.-Ph.D. program at the University of Chicago graduate school. Sho Yano, who says that he liked every class he has taken, is considered a profoundly gifted child.

Although researchers and educators differ in how they define *gifted*, here is one definition that refers to academically gifted children.

A moderately *gifted* child is usually defined by an IQ score between 130 and 150; a profoundly gifted child has an IQ score about 180 or above.

When placed in *regular classrooms,* gifted children face a number of problems: They are bored by the lack of stimulation, they may be viewed as being different, and they may feel lonely or develop social problems because they are labeled nerds or geeks. For these reasons, researchers recommend that gifted children be placed in special academic programs that challenge and help gifted children develop their potentials (Goode, 2002a; Winner, 2000).

How Do Gifted Individuals Turn Out? In the early 1920s, Lewis Terman selected a sample of over 1,500 gifted children with IQs ranging from 130 to 200 (the average was 151). Over the next 65 years, researchers repeatedly tested these individuals to determine what they had achieved and how they had adjusted. Although 10–30% more of the gifted men obtained advanced degrees compared with men in the general population, 30% never finished college, and 2% actually flunked out. Although gifted individuals generally showed better health, adjustment, and

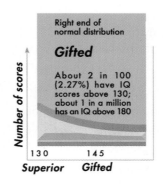

Right end of normal distribution

Gifted

About 2 in 100 (2.27%) have IQ scores above 130; about 1 in a million has an IQ above 180

Number of scores

130   145

Superior   Gifted

IQ of 200+ labels Sho Yano as gifted.

achievement than people with average IQs, about 9% had serious emotional problems, and 7% committed suicide (Holahan & Sears, 1995; Terman & Oden, 1959). As a group, these gifted individuals were generally very successful in life but not at the extraordinary level that might have been expected or predicted from their very high IQ scores (Colangelo, 1997). Contrary to Terman's findings, another researcher followed a group of children with IQs over 180 and found that these extremely smart children often developed social problems, such as being more introverted and lonely than their peers (Hollingworth, 2002). What remains a mystery is why some prodigies or profoundly gifted children do become brilliant adults while others do not and their brilliance seems to fade (Winner, 2002).

Conclusion. IQ scores, the most popular measure of intelligence, have proven moderately useful in predicting academic performance, in helping to define mental retardation, and in identifying the gifted, but they have low to moderate success in predicting job performance. One reason IQ scores are not more predictive is that they do not measure numerous emotional, motivational, and personality factors that also influence behavior.

While IQ tests have proved useful, we'll next examine potential problems in taking and interpreting IQ tests.

D. Potential Problems of IQ Testing

Binet's Two Warnings

What problems did Binet foresee?

You may remember that Binet's original goal was to develop a test that would distinguish between normal and abnormal mental abilities and thus identify children who were mentally retarded and needed special help and education. Although previous attempts to measure intelligence had failed, Binet and Simon succeeded in developing the first scale that identified children with varying degrees of mental retardation. Binet and Simon's scale was the beginning of the modern-day IQ test. However, even in the early 1900s, Binet realized that intelligence tests could be used in two potentially dangerous ways, so he issued the following two warnings:

BINET'S WARNINGS

1 Binet warned that *intelligence tests do not measure innate abilities or natural intelligence;* rather, they measure an individual's cognitive abilities, which result from both heredity and environment.

2 Binet warned that *intelligence tests, by themselves, should not be used to label people* (for example, "moron," "average," "genius"); rather, intelligence tests should be used to assess an individual's abilities and used in combination with other information to make academic or placement decisions about people.

History shows that neither of Binet's warnings were heeded. In the early 1900s it became common practice to treat IQ scores as measures of innate intelligence and to use IQ scores to label people from "moron" to "genius." The U.S. Congress went so far as to pass laws that restricted immigrants based on assumed levels of innate intelligence (S. J. Gould, 1996), an issue we'll discuss in Cultural Diversity.

Along with using IQ scores to label individuals came racial and cultural discrimination, some of which continue to the present. For example, a controversial book, *The Bell Curve* (Herrnstein & Murray, 1994), suggests that racial differences in IQ scores are due primarily to genetic factors, something we'll discuss later in this module. For now, we'll examine three issues surrounding IQ tests: cultural bias, other cultures, and nonintellectual factors.

IQ tests have a history of being used to discriminate.

Racial Discrimination

Are IQ tests racially biased?

There have been a number of court cases regarding the appropriate use of IQ tests. Here is one important case and the judge's ruling.

Larry was an African American child who was assigned to special classes for the educable mentally retarded because he scored below 85 on an IQ test. However, several years later an African American psychologist retested Larry and found that his IQ score was higher than originally thought. Larry was taken out of the special classes, which were considered a dead end, and placed in regular classes that allowed for more advancement. On the basis of Larry's experience, a class action suit was brought against the San Francisco school system on behalf of all African American schoolchildren in the district. The suit was based on the finding that, although African American youngsters made up 27% of all the students enrolled in classes for the mentally retarded, they composed only 4% of the entire school population (Kaplan & Saccuzzo, 2001). African American parents wanted to know why their children were so much more numerous than White children in these special classes. They felt there must be a bias against African American children in the selection process.

Although Larry's case came to trial in the early 1970s, the final decision was given in 1979 by a judge of the federal court of appeals. The judge agreed with the African American parents and found that IQ tests being used in schools (kindergarten through grade 12) to determine mental retardation were biased against people of color. The court ruled that California schools could not place children of color in classes for children with mental retardation on the basis of the IQ test alone. The schools were instructed to come up with an intelligence test that does not favor Whites or else refrain from using a standardized test to identify slow learners.

Definition of mental retardation. In other states, IQ tests are used to define mental retardation, even though these states do not always agree on the definition. For example, in Ohio, a child with an IQ below 80 is considered mentally retarded, while across the border in Kentucky, the same child is placed in a regular classroom and taught along with all the other students. In 39 states, African American students are overrepresented in special education classes, especially when they are students in predominately White school districts. Critics of the special education system argue that African American students are overrepresented not because of their especially high level of disability but because of discriminatory placement procedures, such as the culturally biased IQ tests (J. P. Shapiro et al., 1993).

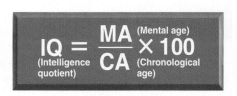

$$IQ = \frac{MA \text{ (Mental age)}}{CA \text{ (Chronological age)}} \times 100$$

(Intelligence quotient)

Educational decisions. Based on the concerns discussed above, psychologists and educators recommend that IQ tests alone not be used as the primary basis for making decisions about a child's educational future. Instead, they suggest that educational decisions, especially about placing a child in a special education class, be made only after considering a wide range of information, which may include IQ scores but also observations and samples of the child's behavior from other different situations (Palomares, 2003).

IQ tests alone should not be used to define mental retardation.

Cultural Bias

What kind of questions? One criticism of IQ tests is that they are culturally biased, especially in favor of industrialized communities, such as the White middle class in the United States (Serpell, 2000).

Cultural bias means that the wording of the questions and the experiences on which the questions are based are more familiar to members of some social groups than to others.

For example, consider this question from an older version of the Wechsler Intelligence Scale for Children: "What would you do if you were sent to buy a loaf of bread and the grocer said he did not have anymore?"

If you think the answer is "Go to another store," you are correct according to the developers of the Wechsler scale. However, when 200 minority children were asked this same question, 61 said they would go home. Asked to explain their answers, they gave reasonable explanations. Some children answered "Go home" because there were no other stores in their neighborhood. Yet the answer "Go home" would be scored

IQ tests are, to some extent, culturally biased.

"incorrect," despite it being correct in the child's experience (Hardy et al., 1976). This example shows that different cultural influences and experiences may penalize some children when taking standardized tests of intelligence. In today's IQ tests, many of the above kinds of biases have been reduced (A. Kaufman, 2003). However, try as they can, researchers believe that it's virtually impossible to develop an intelligence test completely free of cultural bias because tests will reflect, in some part, the concepts and values of their culture (Greenfield, 2003).

In addition, because IQ tests involve being asked and answering questions, children who have had such experiences in their homes or schools will be better able to take these tests. In some cultures, parents do not engage in question-and-answer sessions with their children as parents do in many Western cultures (Greenfield, 1997). This is another example of how cultural influences can affect a child's performance on standard IQ tests.

Other Cultures

Are there different definitions? We have discussed how many Western psychologists believe that the best definition of a person's intelligence is something called **g**, which is primarily measured by assessing cognitive abilities and

Other cultures define intelligence to include more than cognitive abilities.

expressed by IQ scores. However, psychologists studying intelligence in non-Western countries, such as Africa and Asia, find that these cultures have different conceptions and definitions of intelligence.

For example, the Taiwanese conception of intelligence emphasizes how one understands and relates to others, including when and how to show intelligence (Sternberg & Yang, 2003). In Zambia (Africa), parents describe the intelligence of their children as including cognitive abilities as well as showing social responsibility, which is considered equally important (Serpell, 2003). In Micronesia, people demonstrate remarkable navigational skills as they sail long distances using only information from stars and sea currents (Ceci et al., 1997). These navigational abilities certainly indicate a high degree of intelligence that would not be assessed by traditional Western IQ tests.

Thus, the definition of intelligence differs across cultures and challenges the traditional Western concept that intelligence is best measured by something called **g** (Sternberg, 2003b).

Nonintellectual Factors

What if a person is nervous? Maria is 11 years old and has been in the United States for two years. She had a hard time learning English, is not doing well in school, and is terrified about taking tests. Maria comes to take an IQ test, and the psychologist tries to put her at ease. However, Maria is so afraid of failing the IQ test that she just sits and stares at the floor. The psychologist says, "I'm going to give you a word and you tell me what it means." When Maria hears the word, she is now so anxious that she can't concentrate or think of what to say. Maria will probably do poorly on this IQ test because of nonintellectual factors.

Nonintellectual factors refer to noncognitive factors, such as attitude, experience, and emotional functioning, that may help or hinder performance on tests.

For example, nonintellectual factors such as Maria's shyness, fear of strange situations, and anxiety about failing would certainly hinder her test performance (Oostdam & Meijer, 2003). Thus, students with test anxiety or who come from an environment with poor educational opportunities would be handicapped in taking IQ tests.

In comparison, a child who is experienced and confident at taking tests has the kind of nonintellectual factors that would aid

IQ scores are influenced by emotions and experience.

performance. It is well established that numerous nonintellectual factors can have a great influence on how a person performs on IQ tests (Kaplan & Saccuzzo, 2001).

Next, we'll discuss one of the oldest questions about intelligence, the nature-nurture question.

E. Nature-Nurture Question

PowerStudy 2.0™

Definitions

What is the nature-nurture question?

At the beginning of this module, we told you about Midori (right photo), who began playing violin at age 3 and made her professional debut at age 10. Because Midori was a musical genius at such an early age, her exceptional skill was due to nature or heredity, that is, something she was born with. She played professionally until age 23, when she suddenly withdrew for four months. The official reason for her sudden withdrawal was a "digestive disorder," but some reports said that she was actually suffering from an eating disorder. Midori's problem raises questions about the effects of environment (nurture), specifically how to help a child genius adjust to difficult personal and professional pressures at such a young age (Cariaga, 1995). The difficulty Midori faced in balancing

Midori, child prodigy: "If I went back, I would probably do everything differently."

nature or heredity factors (being a child genius) with nurture or environmental factors (facing difficult personal and professional pressures) brings us to the nature-nurture question.

The *nature-nurture question* asks how nature—hereditary or genetic factors—interacts with nurture—environmental factors—in the development of a person's intellectual, emotional, personal, and social abilities.

In the early 1900s, intelligence was believed to be primarily inherited or due to nature (Terman, 1916). In the 1950s, psychology was heavily influenced by behaviorism, which emphasized nurture or environmental factors in the development of intelligence (Skinner, 1953). Today, researchers have found that nature and nurture interact and contribute about equally to the development of intelligence (Pinker, 2002).

Twin Studies

What do genes do?

In exploring how nature and nurture contribute to and interact in the development of intelligence, researchers compared IQ scores in siblings (brothers and sisters) and in fraternal and identical twins.

Fraternal twins, like siblings (brothers and sisters), develop from separate eggs and have 50% of their genes in common. *Identical twins* develop from a single egg and thus have identical genes, which means that they have 100% of their genes in common.

Genetic factors. The graph on the right shows that the correlation in IQ scores between identical twins (0.85), who share 100% of their genes, was higher than the correlation between fraternal twins (0.60), who share 50% of their genes, or between siblings (0.45), who also share 50% of their genes (Plomin & Petrill, 1997). These findings, which come from over 100 studies, indicate that genetic factors contribute about 50% to the development of intelligence, which has a rather specific definition.

Definition of intelligence. As we have discussed, many researchers define intelligence as relating to Spearman's ***g*** factor (see p. 282), which is measured by performance on cognitive tests and results in IQ scores. However, some researchers argue that there are other, equally important kinds of intelligence, such as practical (adjusting to one's environment), social (interacting with others), emotional (perceiving and understanding emotions), as well as creative, musical, and insightful intelligence (Sternberg et al., 2003b). As discussed earlier, these kinds of

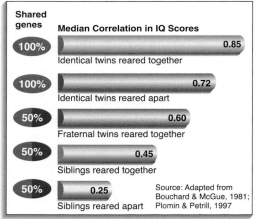

Shared genes	Median Correlation in IQ Scores	
100%	Identical twins reared together	0.85
100%	Identical twins reared apart	0.72
50%	Fraternal twins reared together	0.60
50%	Siblings reared together	0.45
50%	Siblings reared apart	0.25

Source: Adapted from Bouchard & McGue, 1981; Plomin & Petrill, 1997

intelligence are not measured by standard IQ tests, which primarily focus on measuring cognitive abilities.

Interaction of nature and nurture. When researchers report that genetic factors influence intelligence (IQ scores), they mean that genetic factors influence cognitive abilities to varying degrees, depending on the environment (Bishop et al., 2003). For example, what would happen to cognitive skills if a child were rated as being high or low in interacting with his or her environment?

Interaction. An example of how genetic and environmental factors interact in the development of intelligence comes from a study of 3-year-old children who were identified as being either high or low in exploring their environments, which is a personality trait known as stimulation seeking. These children were later given IQ tests at age 11 to determine if being high or low in stimulation seeking affected their IQs. Researchers reported that children who had been rated high in stimulation seeking at age 3 scored significantly higher on IQ tests compared to children who had been rated low in stimulation seeking at age 3. This significant difference in IQ scores (11 points) was not related to the occupation or education of their parents. Researchers concluded that children high in stimulation seeking were more curious and open to learning from their environments, which in turn enhanced the development of their cognitive abilities and resulted in higher scores on IQ tests (Raine et al., 2002).

Thus, genetic factors contribute about 50% to the development of one's intelligence (IQ score), while the other 50% comes from the interaction with environmental factors, which we'll examine next.

How much does environment contribute?

What would happen if children with limited social-educational opportunities and low IQs were adopted by parents who could provide increased social-educational opportunities? Researchers reasoned that if environmental factors influence the development of intelligence, then providing increased environmental opportunities should increase IQ scores.

A group of French researchers studied children who had been abandoned as babies by their lower-class parents and adopted during the first six months of life into upper-middle-class families. The researchers found that the mean IQ of the adopted children was 14 points higher than that of similar children born and raised in lower-class settings by their natural parents. In addition, the adopted children were four times less likely to fail in school. This study suggests that with improved environmental factors— for example, increased social-educational opportunities—intellectual development (as measured by IQ scores) and performance in the classroom can be improved (Schiff et al., 1982).

Children adopted into advantaged homes had higher IQ scores.

In a similar study, African American children from impoverished environments were adopted into middle-class families, some White and some African American; all of the families provided many social-educational opportunities for the adopted children. Researchers found that the IQs of the adopted children were as much as 10 points higher than those of African American children who were raised in disadvantaged homes (Scarr & Weinberg, 1976). In a follow-up study, researchers reported that the adopted children, now adolescents, had higher IQ scores than African American children raised in their own community (Weinberg et al., 1992).

These kinds of studies show that children with poor educational opportunities and low IQ scores can show an increase in IQ scores when they are adopted into families that provide increased educational opportunities. Based on data from adoption studies, researchers concluded that nurture or environmental factors contribute to intellectual development (Duyme, 1999).

What is heritability?

In the last 10 years, researchers have made significant progress in answering the nature-nurture question, and one tool they have used is a number called heritability.

Heritability is a number that indicates the amount or proportion of some ability, characteristic, or trait that can be attributed to genetic factors (nature).

For example, the figure below shows that heritability (nature) for overall intelligence (measured by IQ tests) was about 50%, which means that 50% of general cognitive ability comes from genetic factors. Researchers were also able to calculate the heritability scores for specific cognitive abilities, such as spatial ability (32%), verbal ability (55%), and memory (55%) (McClearn et al., 1997). These studies on heritability show that genetic factors (nature) contribute about half to intelligence.

The next big step in genetic research is the identification of specific genes or groups of genes that contribute to specific cognitive traits used to measure intelligence (Petrill, 2003).

Notice that the heritability numbers in the graph on the left are in the 50% range, which means that genes do not determine or fix these abilities, because the other 50% is coming from environmental

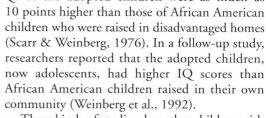

Estimates of Heritability

Nature — genetic factors	Nurture — environmental factors

Intelligence (general abilities)
| 50% | 50% |

Spatial ability
| 32% | 68% |

Verbal ability
| 55% | 45% |

Memory
| 55% | 45% |

factors. You can think of genetic factors as establishing a range of potential abilities or behaviors, which are shaped and molded through interaction with one's environment. This idea of how genetic factors operate is called the reaction range (Bouchard, 1997).

Reaction range indicates the extent to which traits, abilities, or IQ scores may increase or decrease as a result of interaction with environmental factors.

Researchers estimate that the reaction range may vary up or down by as much as 10–15 points in one's IQ score. For example, the figure on the right shows that a person's IQ may vary from 85 to 110, depending on whether he or she has an impoverished or enriched environment (Zigler & Seitz, 1982).

Conclusion. The studies on heritability, twins, and adopted children provide an answer to the nature-nurture question: Nature or heredity contributes about 50% to intelligence (IQ) and environment or nurture contributes about 50%. However, a person's IQ can vary by 10–15 points (IQ reaction range), depending on how heredity interacts with different kinds of environments.

Next, we'll examine the debate over racial differences in IQ scores.

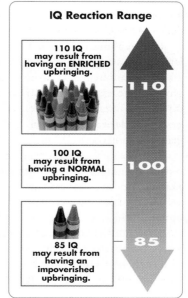

IQ Reaction Range

110 IQ may result from having an **ENRICHED** upbringing.

110

100 IQ may result from having a **NORMAL** upbringing.

100

85 IQ may result from having an **impoverished** upbringing.

85

E. Nature-Nurture Question

Racial Controversy

What is the latest controversy?

In the early 1900s, psychologists believed that intelligence was primarily inherited. This idea reappeared in a relatively recent book, *The Bell Curve,* by psychologist Richard Herrnstein and political scientist Charles Murray (1994). But what brought these authors the greatest publicity was their statement that racial differences in IQ scores were caused primarily by genetic or inherited factors. This and other statements from Herrnstein and Murray's book set off such a heated and often misguided public debate that the American Psychological Association (APA) formed a special task force of prominent researchers. The goal of the APA task force was to summarize what is currently known about intelligence (Neisser et al., 1996). We have already discussed many of the issues raised in the APA report, and we will now focus on the difficult and complex question of racial differences in IQ scores.

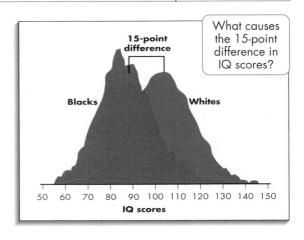

What causes the 15-point difference in IQ scores?

Difference between IQ Scores

Findings. To help you understand the controversy surrounding racial differences in IQ scores, please look at the figure in the upper right. Notice that there are two distributions of IQ scores: The red bell-shaped curve shows the distribution of IQ scores for African Americans (Blacks), and the blue bell-shaped curve shows the distribution of scores for Caucasians (Whites). Although there is much overlap in IQ scores (indicated by overlapping of red and blue areas), researchers generally agree that the average or mean IQ score for African Americans is about 15 points lower than the average IQ score for Caucasians (Bouchard, 1995). This 15-point average difference in IQ scores means that although there are many African Americans with high IQ scores, they are proportionally fewer in number compared to Caucasians.

Two explanations. There are at least two possible explanations for this 15-point difference in average IQ scores. One explanation is that the differences are due to inherited or *genetic factors:* African Americans are genetically inferior to Whites. Another explanation is that the difference is due to a number of *environmental factors:* African Americans have fewer social, economic, and educational opportunities than Whites do.

Although the authors of *The Bell Curve* emphasized the first explanation (genetic factors), you'll see that the APA task force and many other psychologists disagreed.

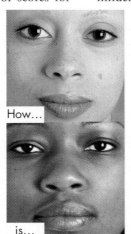

How...

is...

race...

decided?

Cause of IQ Differences

Group differences. In a careful review of *The Bell Curve,* one of the leading researchers in the area of intelligence concluded that the book offered no convincing evidence that genetic factors were primarily responsible for the 15-point IQ difference between African Americans and Caucasians (Sternberg, 1995). This conclusion is based largely on the distinction between whether genetic factors can influence the development of intelligence in an individual and whether they can influence different development of intelligence among races. The APA task force said that there is good evidence that genetic factors play a significant role in the development of an *individual's intelligence.* However, there is no convincing evidence that genetic factors play a primary role in the development of differences in intelligence *among races.* Thus, the APA task force challenged Herrnstein and Murray's statement that IQ *differences among races* are caused primarily by genetic factors (Neisser et al., 1996).

Although no one knows exactly what causes the differences in IQ scores shown in the above graph, the APA task force as well as many other psychologists suggest a number of environmental factors, such as differences in social-economic classes, educational opportunities, family structure, and career possibilities (Loehlin, 2000). Thus, one of *The Bell Curve*'s major conclusions—that racial differences in IQ scores are based primarily on genetic factors—is not supported by the evidence (Neisser et al., 1996). Two prominent researchers concluded that *The Bell Curve*'s argument for racial inferiority appeared to be based on scientific evidence, but closer examination shows that it was not (S. J. Gould, 1996; Sternberg, 1995).

Differences in skin color. Another problem with *The Bell Curve* is its assumption that skin color is a meaningful way to separate races. For example, based on skin color, to which race would you assign the individuals in the four photos on the left? Researchers report that skin color is not reliable in identifying racial makeup because recent studies on DNA (genetic instructions) indicate that people around the world are much more alike than different. In fact, people around the world differ in genetic instructions by only 3–5% (King & Motulsky, 2002). This means that, no matter the color of one's skin, genetic instructions in people around the world vary by about 3–5%. Thus, differences in skin color are only skin deep, and skin color is not a reliable measure to assign people to different races when comparing IQ scores (Venter, 2000).

After the Concept Review, we'll discuss how early racial discrimination was based on IQ scores.

✔ Concept Review

1. One approach to measuring intelligence focuses on quantifying cognitive factors or abilities that are involved in intellectual performance; this is called the (a)_____ approach. Charles Spearman used this approach to develop a two-factor theory of intelligence: one factor is **g**, or (b)_____; the second factor is **s**, or (c)_____.

2. In comparison to Spearman's two-factor approach, Howard Gardner's theory says that there are seven kinds of _____, such as verbal skills, math skills, spatial skills, and movement skills.

3. Another approach to measuring intelligence is by analyzing the kinds of (a)_____ processes that people use to solve problems. An example of this approach is Robert Sternberg's (b)_____ theory of intelligence.

4. Alfred Binet developed an intelligence test that estimated intellectual progress by comparing a child's score on an intelligence test to the scores of average children of the same age. Binet called this concept _____.

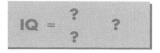

5. Lewis Terman revised Binet's intelligence test, and the most significant change he made was to develop a formula to compute a single score that represents a person's (a)_____. This formula is IQ = (b)_____ age divided by (c)_____ age, times (d)_____.

6. The most widely used series of IQ tests are the (a)_____ Intelligence Scales. These tests organize items into two subtests, which are called (b)_____ and (c)_____ scales. In an attempt to measure nonverbal skills and rule out cultural problems, Wechsler added the (d)_____ scale.

Block design
Assemble blocks to match this design.

Picture completion
Tell me what is missing.

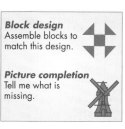

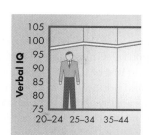

7. A good psychological test has two characteristics. It should give about the same score over time, which is called (a)_____, and it should measure what it is supposed to measure, which is called (b)_____.

8. If IQ scores can be represented by a bell-shaped curve, the pattern is called a _____. The scores have a symmetrical arrangement, so that the vast majority fall in the middle range and fewer fall near the extreme ends of the range.

Middle of normal distribution
About 95 in 100 (95.44%) have IQ scores between 70 and 130
70   85   **100**   115   130
Average IQ

About 2 in 100 (2.27%) have IQ scores below 70
50
Mild Retardation

9. An individual who has a combination of limited mental ability (usually an IQ below 70) and difficulty functioning in everyday life is said to have some degree of (a)_____. If this condition results from genetic problems or brain damage, it is called (b)_____. If this condition results from a greatly impoverished environment, it is called (c)_____. Individuals who have above-average intelligence (usually IQ scores above 130) as well as some superior talent or skill are said to be (d)_____.

Left end of normal distribution
Retardation
About 2 in 100 (2.27%) have IQ scores below 70
30   50   70-75
Severe   Mild   Borderline
Profound   Moderate

10. If the wording of test questions and the experiences on which they are based are more familiar to members of some social groups than to others, the test is said to have a (a)_____. Depending on the culture, (b)_____ can be defined in different ways.

11. When we ask how much genetic factors and how much environmental factors contribute to intelligence, we are asking the (a)_____ question. There is good evidence that genetic factors contribute about (b)_____ and environmental factors contribute about (c)_____ to the development of one's intelligence. The extent to which IQ scores may increase or decrease depending on environmental effects is called the (d)_____.

Intelligence (general abilities)
Spatial ability
Verbal ability
Memory

Answers: 1. (a) psychometric, (b) general intelligence, (c) specific abilities; 2. intelligence; 3. (a) reasoning, (b) triarchic; 4. mental age; 5. (a) intelligence quotient or IQ, (b) mental, (c) chronological, (d) 100; 6. (a) Wechsler, (b) verbal, (c) performance, (d) performance; 7. (a) reliability, (b) validity; 8. normal distribution; 9. (a) mental retardation, (b) organic retardation, (c) cultural-familial retardation, (d) gifted; 10. (a) cultural bias, (b) intelligence; 11. (a) nature-nurture, (b) 50%, (c) 50%, (d) reaction range

F. Cultural Diversity: Races, IQs & Immigration

Misuse of IQ Tests

What were Binet's warnings about using IQ tests?

After Alfred Binet developed the first intelligence tests, he gave two warnings about the potential misuse of IQ tests. He warned that IQ tests do not and should not be used to measure innate intelligence and that IQ tests should not be used to label individuals. However, in the early 1900s the area we know as psychology was just beginning, and American psychologists were very proud of how much they had improved IQ tests. With their improved IQ tests, American psychologists not only used IQ tests to measure what they thought was innate, or inherited, intelligence but also used IQ tests to label people (as morons or imbeciles). As if that weren't bad enough, early psychologists persuaded the U.S. Congress to pass discriminatory immigration laws based on IQ tests. As we look back now, we must conclude that the use and abuse of IQ tests in the early 1900s created one of psychology's sorriest moments. Here's what happened.

In 1924, Congress passed an immigration law to keep out those believed to have low IQs.

Innate Intelligence

One name that we have already mentioned is that of Lewis Terman, who was the guiding force behind revising Binet's intelligence test (which became the Stanford-Binet test) and also developing the formula for computing a single IQ score. Terman, who became head of the Department of Psychology at Stanford University, firmly believed that intelligence was primarily inherited, that intelligence tests measured innate abilities, and that environmental influences were far less important.

One of Terman's goals was to test all children and, on the basis of their IQ scores, to label and sort them into categories of innate abilities. Terman argued that society could use IQ scores (usually of 70 or below) to restrain or eliminate those whose intelligence was too low for an effective moral life (Terman, 1916).

Terman hoped to establish minimum intelligence scores necessary for all leading occupations. For example, he believed that people with IQs below 100 should not be given employment that involves prestige or monetary reward. Those with IQs of 75 or below should be unskilled labor, and those with 75–85 IQs should be semiskilled labor. In Terman's world, class boundaries were to be set by innate intelligence, as measured by his Stanford-Binet IQ test (S. J. Gould, 1996; M. Hunt, 1993).

Terman's belief that IQ tests measured innate intelligence was adopted by another well-known American psychologist, Robert Yerkes.

Classifying Races

Robert Yerkes was a Harvard professor who was asked to develop a test that could be used to classify applicants for the army. Under Yerkes's direction, over 1.75 million World War I army recruits were given IQ tests. From this enormous amount of data, Yerkes (1921) and his colleagues reached three conclusions:

1. They concluded that the average mental age of White American adults was a meager 13 years, slightly above the classification of a moron (a term psychologists used in the early 1900s). The reasons they gave for this low mental age were (using the terminology then current) the unconstrained breeding of the poor and feebleminded and the spread of Negro blood through interracial breeding.

2. They concluded that European immigrants could be ranked on intelligence by their country of origin. The fair peoples of western and northern Europe (Nordics) were most intelligent, while the darker peoples of southern Europe (Mediterraneans) and the Slavs of eastern Europe were less intelligent.

3. They concluded that Negroes were at the bottom of the racial scale in intelligence.

Many of Yerkes's outrageous and discriminatory views resurfaced in the book, *The Bell Curve* (Herrnstein & Murray, 1994), which we discussed earlier. Following Yerkes's lead, IQ scores were next used for racial discrimination.

Immigration Laws

The fact that Yerkes ranked European races by intelligence eventually reached members of the U.S. Congress. Outraged by the "fact" that Europeans of "low intelligence" were being allowed into America, congressmen sought a way to severely limit the immigration of people from southern and eastern Europe. In writing the Immigration Law of 1924, Congress relied, in part, on Yerkes's racial rankings and imposed harsh quotas on those nations they believed to have inferior stock (people from southern and eastern Europe, Alpine and Mediterranean nations).

Stephen Jay Gould (1996), a well-known evolutionary biologist, reviewed Yerkes's data and pointed out a number of problems: poorly administered tests, terrible testing conditions, inconsistent standards for retaking tests, written tests given to illiterate recruits (guaranteeing a low score), and no control for educational level or familiarity with the English language. As a result of these problems, Gould concluded that Yerkes's data were so riddled with errors as to render useless any conclusions about racial differences in intelligence.

Looking back, we see clearly that early psychologists badly misused IQ tests. They forgot that IQ tests are merely one of many tools to assess cognitive abilities, which many consider to be one of many kinds of intelligence (H. Gardner, 1995).

We've discussed how past IQ tests have been misused and how current IQ tests may be biased. Is there a new generation of intelligence tests on the horizon?

G. Research Focus: New Approaches

Can Genius Be Found in the Brain?

There is one question about intelligence that has especially interested researchers: How is the brain of a genius different? For example, how was Albert Einstein able to think of riding through space on a beam of light or create his famous formula ($E = mc^2$), which led to building the atomic bomb?

When Einstein died of heart failure in 1955 at age 76, Dr. Thomas Harvey, who performed the autopsy, removed Einstein's brain and kept it at Princeton University. In 1996, Harvey contacted Dr. Sandra Witelson, a neuroscientist at McMaster University, and asked if she wished to examine Einstein's brain. McMaster University in Ontario, Canada, has a bank of over 100 brains that people have donated for research. Dr. Witelson was able to compare Einstein's 76-year-old brain with brains of similar ages from 35 men and 56 women who were known to have normal intelligence when they died. The results of Dr. Witelson's examination of Einstein's brain are discussed in the figure at the right.

Although the physical differences in Einstein's brain are obvious in the figure,

Normal brain weighs about 1,350 grams. This side view shows the wrinkled cortex, which contains separate areas for different functions (feeling, moving, reading, writing, seeing). Notice the yellow and red areas, which are part of the parietal lobe. The **red area, the inferior parietal lobe,** is especially used for thinking in visual-spatial terms, for mathematical thought, and for imaging how things move in space.

Einstein's brain weighed 1,230 grams, slightly less than normal. Einstein's brain was different in that it lacked the yellow area, which allowed his **red area, the inferior parietal lobe,** to be 15% wider than in normal brains. Researchers believe that Einstein's larger inferior parietal lobe increased his ability to think and imagine such things as space being curved and that time could slow down (Witelson et al., 1999).

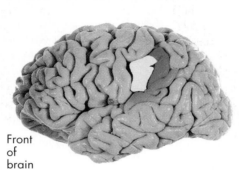

Front of brain

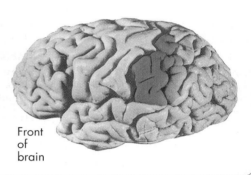

Front of brain

Dr. Witelson cautions that they don't know if every brilliant mathematician also has a larger inferior parietal lobe, which is something only further research can answer. Other researchers wonder if genius can ever be measured or located in the brain, since genius involves a mixture of creative insights, culture, and life experiences that may be unique to that person (Wang, 2000).

Can Spearman's *g* Be Found in the Brain?

What do brain scans show?

Hypothesis. As you may remember, many psychologists believe that Spearman's *g* is a measure of a person's general level of intelligence or of a general mental factor shared by everyone and expressed by an IQ score. Researchers guessed that if Spearman's idea of a general mental factor of *g* was accurate, then a single brain area should be activated when people solve different kinds of cognitive problems, similar to those used in IQ tests. On the other hand, if there was no general factor, but rather multiple kinds of intelligence, then many different parts of the brain should be activated when people solve different kinds of cognitive problems.

Method. To look inside the living brain, researchers took PET scans of the brains of 13 men and women as they solved a series of difficult cognitive tasks (verbal and spatial), similar to those used in IQ tests. PET scans work by measuring the flow of blood to neurons, so that a larger blood flow indicates more neural activity and a smaller blood flow indicates less neural activity (p. 71). PET scans give researchers a picture of neural activity inside the living brain.

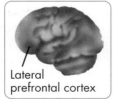

Lateral prefrontal cortex

Results. Researchers found that whether subjects were solving verbal or spatial problems, the same general area in the brain, the lateral prefrontal cortex, was activated (Duncan et al., 2000). Researchers concluded that because one brain area (rather than many) was activated during both spatial and verbal cognitive tasks, this single brain area (lateral prefrontal cortex) may be the neural basis for general intelligence, or Spearman's *g* (left figure).

However, researcher Robert Sternberg (2000) points out that these results show only a correlation or association between activity in a brain area (lateral prefrontal cortex) and performance on cognitive tasks, but correlations cannot point to what causes what. In addition, the prefrontal cortex may not be the neural site for Spearman's *g* because this area also becomes active when we pay attention or use working memory. Finally, Sternberg points out that the researchers did not show whether the lateral prefrontal cortex was activated during creative or practical thought, or during thought required for people to be intelligent in their everyday lives. Thus, there is still some question about whether the lateral prefrontal cortex is the real neural basis for general intelligence or simply associated with paying attention and doing different tasks.

H. Application: Intervention Programs

Definition of Intervention Programs

Why might a child need a head start?

For a moment, imagine what will happen to Nancy's child. Nancy, who is in her mid-twenties, is a single mother with a 3-year-old child. Nancy lives in a lower-class neighborhood and earns less than $5,000 a year doing part-time work. She has completed only two years of high school, has no family and few friends. What effects do you think Nancy's background, educational level, and current impoverished environment will have on her child? Psychologists would predict that Nancy's 3-year-old child will not likely acquire the social, emotional, and cognitive skills and abilities needed to do well in school or society. Her child may need outside help, which may come from an intervention program (Arnold & Doctoroff, 2003).

An *intervention program* helps disadvantaged children from low socioeconomic classes to achieve better intellectual,

Intervention programs create a stimulating environment.

social, and personal-emotional development, as well as physical health.

Intervention programs can give Nancy training in how to be a good parent and provide her child with educational and social opportunities. Perhaps the best-known intervention program in the United States is Head Start, which began in 1965 as a six-to-eight-week program. Researchers later discovered that was too brief to be effective. As a result, Head Start was lengthened to two years, and in 2003, the program enrolled over one million 3- to 5-year-olds across the United States (Schemo, 2003).

We'll focus on some successful intervention programs for disadvantaged children.

Abecedarian Project

This project's goal was to teach youngsters from disadvantaged environments the cognitive and social skills needed for future success in school. Psychologists identified babies who were at high risk of failing in school because they lived in disadvantaged settings. Most of the mothers had low IQ scores, were African American, young, without a high school education, and single. With the mothers' permission, 2- to 3-month-old infants were assigned either to a control group that did not receive any special treatment or to an experimental group. Children in the experimental group spent 6 or more hours daily, five days a week, in a carefully supervised day-care center that continued for four years until the children entered public school at the age of 5.

After four years of this intense intervention program, children in the Abecedarian Project had IQ scores 12 points higher than control children from disadvantaged environments. Once children left the program, some of their IQ gains decreased. However, when the children were retested at ages 12, 15, and 21, researchers found that the children had shown substantial gains in cognitive and academic abilities as a result of early intervention (F. A. Campbell et al., 2001).

Head Start results in long-term personal and social gains.

Head Start

Head Start, which is a day-care program for disadvantaged children, usually lasts for two years, from ages 3 to 5, and has six goals: preschool education, health screening, mental health services, hot meals, social services for the child and family, and involvement and participation of parents in the program (Zigler & Styfco, 1994). More recently, Head Start has emphasized teaching basic academic skills, such as reading, in order to prepare disadvantaged children to do well in kindergarten (Cooper, 1999).

Head Start was initially viewed as something of a failure because two to three years after children left Head Start, few if any differences in IQ or other academic scores were found between those children and control groups (Clarke & Clarke, 1989). However, Head Start showed other important long-term beneficial effects (Zigler & Styfco, 1994):

■ Adolescents who had been in the Head Start program were more likely to be in classes appropriate for their ages rather than to have had to repeat a class, were less likely to show antisocial or delinquent behavior, and were more likely to hold jobs.

■ Mothers whose children had been in the Head Start program reported fewer psychological symptoms, greater feelings of mastery, and greater current life satisfaction.

■ Children who had two years of Head Start and an additional two to seven years of educational help were much more successful in graduating from high school (69%) than a control group (49%).

Another program similar to Head Start, called the Chicago Child Parent Center Program, enrolled children 3–4 years old and lasted for 18 months. Over 1,500 children in this program were tracked from ages 5 to 20 and were found to be more likely to graduate from high school and less likely to be arrested than poor children not in the program (Reynolds et al., 2001).

From studies like these we can draw two conclusions. First, often early and rather large increases (up to 10 points) in IQ scores do not last after the child leaves the intervention program. Second, programs like Head Start result in a number of long-term benefits, such as better social and personal well-being and increased chances of graduating from high school and avoiding crime (Zigler, 1995; Zigler & Styfco, 2001). These encouraging long-term effects indicate that programs like Head Start should not be evaluated solely on IQ scores but also on other personality, motivational, and psychological benefits.

In the early days of Head Start, psychologists were very encouraged to find that the program initially increased disadvantaged children's IQ scores by about 10 points, a very significant amount. One reason IQ scores can be raised in young children from disadvantaged homes is that these children have not been exposed to and have not acquired the kinds of skills and cultural experiences assessed by IQ tests. However, when disadvantaged children are exposed to the enriched environment of Head Start, these children quickly acquire all kinds of new skills and abilities that help them score higher on IQ tests (Spitz, 1997).

For example, researchers compared two groups of disadvantaged children, all of whom had IQ scores below 80 (100 is considered the average IQ). Some of these children, called the experimental group, were placed in a special educational intervention program from ages 3 to 5. Other children, called the control group, were given no additional training and remained in their home environments.

The figure below shows that, after only one year, children in the experimental group (intervention program) showed a significant increase in IQ scores (about 10 points) compared to the children in the control group who remained in disadvantaged home environments (Schweinhart & Weikart, 1980). However, after the children left the intervention program at the age of 5 and entered public school, their IQ scores began a slow but consistent decline. At the same time, the IQ scores of control children began a gradual increase as they benefited from attending public school. By the age of 11, there was no longer any difference in IQ scores.

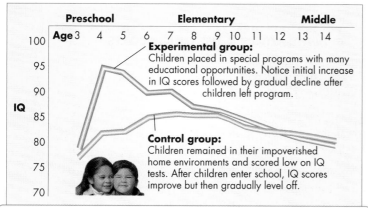

Preschool — Elementary — Middle

Age 3 4 5 6 7 8 9 10 11 12 13 14

IQ: 100 95 90 85 80 75 70

Experimental group: Children placed in special programs with many educational opportunities. Notice initial increase in IQ scores followed by gradual decline after children left program.

Control group: Children remained in their impoverished home environments and scored low on IQ tests. After children enter school, IQ scores improve but then gradually level off.

Initial increase in IQ scores (age 4) gradually disappears after children leave Head Start program and return to less stimulating environments.

One reason for this decline in IQ scores is that after children leave the support of an intervention program, they usually return to less stimulating environments, which offer less educational, social, and motivational support. For this reason, researchers make two strong recommendations: First, programs like Head Start should be lengthened from three to at least five or more years so children have more time to learn and practice their newly acquired social, emotional, and academic skills; and second, parents must become involved in helping their children develop cognitive skills, such as reading to their children (Zigler & Styfco, 2001).

Finally, as we discussed earlier, intervention programs should not be evaluated solely on IQ scores but rather on other social, emotional, and psychological gains that are found to be long-lasting.

The most successful intervention programs have a strong educational emphasis, well-trained teachers, and a low ratio of children to trained teachers.

Researchers make three important points about usefulness of intervention programs and the need for day-care centers:

1 Currently, about 14.5 million children in the United States are living in poverty, which is known to have a devastating negative influence on a young child developing important social-emotional skills and cognitive abilities. In addition, living in poverty is known to lower academic achievement and goals, decrease motivation, and contribute to school failure and drop outs (Arnold & Doctoroff, 2003). Intervention programs help reduce the devastating effects that continuing poverty can have on families and give children a much needed head start (Zigler & Styfco, 2001).

2 About 25 to 30% of children live in single-parent families that are below the poverty line (Kassebaum, 1994). In some cases, impoverished family environments lead to neglect or abuse, which has very negative effects on a child's social, emotional, and intellectual development. Intensive intervention programs during the first years of life are effective in reducing and preventing the significant intellectual dysfunction that may result from continuing poverty and lack of environmental support (Zigler & Styfco, 2001).

3 Currently, over 60% of married mothers with infants below the age of 2 are employed outside the home and need to place their young children in day care. A recent study of 1,300 children in day-care centers in the United States reported that quality day care contributed to a child's well-being and cognitive development. Of the 1,300 children, 83% did just fine in social-emotional adjustment, while 17% experienced some behavior problems, such as being aggressive (NICHD, 2001, 2003). But it is not known if the aggressive behavior was caused by being in day care or by factors in the child's home (Stolberg, 2001).

If day care is needed, researchers emphasize the importance of choosing quality day care, which is one with specially trained teachers and a low ratio of children to teachers.

A. DEFINING INTELLIGENCE

1. A subarea of psychology that is concerned with developing psychological tests to assess an individual's abilities, skills, beliefs, and personality traits in a wide range of settings—school, industry, or clinic—is called _____.

2. Spearman's two-factor theory of intelligence says there is a general factor, called (a)_____, that represents a person's ability to perform complex mental work, such as abstract reasoning and problem solving. The general factor underlies a person's performance across tests. In addition, there is a second factor, called (b)_____, that represents a person's specific mental abilities, such as mathematical or verbal skills. These specific mental abilities may differ across tests.

3. Gardner says that there are seven kinds of intelligence: verbal intelligence, musical intelligence, logical-mathematical intelligence, spatial intelligence, body movement intelligence, intelligence to understand oneself, and intelligence to understand others. This is called the _____ theory.

4. Sternberg's triarchic theory says that intelligence can be divided into three ways of gathering and processing information (*triarchic* means "three"). The first is using (a)_____ skills, which are measured by traditional intelligence tests. The second is using (b)_____ skills that require creative thinking, the ability to deal with novel situations, and the ability to learn from experience. The third is using (c)_____ skills that help a person adjust to, and cope with, his or her sociocultural environment.

B. MEASURING INTELLIGENCE

Block design
Assemble blocks to match this design.

Picture completion
Tell me what is missing.

5. In trying to measure intelligence, researchers through the years have learned that neither skull size nor brain weight is an accurate predictor of _____.

6. The first intelligence test, which was developed by (a)_____, measured vocabulary, memory, common knowledge, and other cognitive abilities. By comparing a child's score with the scores of average children at the same age, Binet was able to estimate a child's (b)_____. Thus, the Binet-Simon Intelligence Scale gave its results in terms of mental age, while the IQ score was later developed by (c)_____, who devised a formula to calculate an individual's intelligence quotient. The formula can be written as IQ = (d)_____.

7. The Wechsler Adult Intelligence Scale (WAIS-III) and Wechsler Intelligence Scale for Children (WISC-III) have items that are organized into various subtests. Subtests for general information, vocabulary, and verbal comprehension are some of those in the (a)_____ section. Subtests that involve arranging pictures in a meaningful order, assembling objects, and using codes are examples of subtests in the (b)_____ section. An individual receives a separate score for each of the subtests; these scores are then combined to yield overall scores for verbal and performance abilities, which, in turn, are combined into a single score, called an (c)_____ score.

8. A good psychological test must have two qualities. One quality ensures that a person's score on a test at one point in time is similar to a score by the same person on a similar test at a later date; this is called (a)_____. The other quality ensures that a test measures what it is supposed to measure; this is called (b)_____. Although the results from analyzing handwriting may be consistent from time to time, this is a poor test of personality or intelligence because handwriting analysis lacks the quality of (c)_____.

C. DISTRIBUTION & USE OF IQ SCORES

9. Suppose IQ scores are in a statistical arrangement that resembles the shape of a bell, with the vast majority of scores falling in the middle range and fewer scores falling near the two extreme ends of the curve. This arrangement is called a _____.

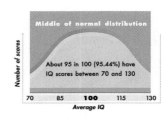

Middle of normal distribution

About 95 in 100 (95.44%) have IQ scores between 70 and 130

Number of scores

70 85 **100** 115 130
Average IQ

10. Substantial limitation in present functioning that is characterized by significantly below average intellectual functioning, along with related limitations in two of ten areas, including communication, self-care, home living, social skills, and safety, is called _____.

11. There are two general causes of mental retardation: genetic problems or brain damage give rise to (a)_____ retardation, and in the absence of apparent genetic or brain damage, greatly impoverished environments can give rise to (b)_____ retardation. Mental retardation is reflected in IQ scores at one end of the normal distribution. At the other end of the normal distribution of IQ scores are those who are considered (c)_____; such people have above average intelligence (usually IQs above 130) as well as some superior talent or skill.

D. POTENTIAL PROBLEMS OF IQ TESTING

12. Binet warned that intelligence tests should not be used to measure (a)_____ mental abilities because intelligence tests measure cognitive abilities, which are influenced by both heredity and environment. Binet also warned that intelligence tests, by themselves, should not be used to (b)_____ people—for example, a moron or a genius. Current IQ tests have been criticized for including wording or experiences that are more familiar to a particular culture, which is called (c)_____. The definition of intelligence differs across (d)_____ and may differ from the Western idea of **g.** One reason individuals may do poorly on IQ tests is noncognitive factors, such as attitude, experience, and emotional functioning, which are called (e)_____.

E. NATURE–NURTURE QUESTION

13. The (a)_____ question refers to the relative contributions that genetic and environmental factors make to the development of intelligence. On the basis of twin studies, researchers generally conclude that about

| Intelligence (general abilities) |
| Spatial ability |
| Verbal ability |
| Memory |

(b)_____ of the contribution to intelligence (IQ scores) comes from genetic factors and about (c)_____ comes from environmental factors. Adoption studies support the idea that environmental factors contribute to intellectual development (as measured by IQ scores). The idea that about half of one's intellectual development is dependent on environmental factors has resulted in (d)_____ programs that give impoverished children increased social-educational opportunities. There is little or no cause-and-effect evidence that the average difference in IQ scores between African Americans and Whites is caused primarily by (e)_____ factors.

F. CULTURAL DIVERSITY: RACES, IQs & IMMIGRATION

14. Early psychologists ignored Binet's warning about misusing IQ tests. For example, in the early 1900s, Terman believed that IQ tests did measure (a)_____ intelligence, and he wanted to use IQ tests to sort people into categories. Terman's view was adopted by Robert Yerkes, who wanted to use IQ tests to rank the intelligence of

(b)_____ entering the United States. In the 1920s, (c)_____ were written to exclude citizens from certain countries because Yerkes had ranked these individuals low in intelligence.

G. RESEARCH FOCUS: NEW APPROACHES

15. In looking for physical differences in Einstein's brain, researchers found that he had a 15% wider (a)_____, which is involved in visual–spatial and mathematical thinking. In using PET scans to identify neural activity in the living brain, researchers found that when subjects solved verbal and spatial problems, the greatest neural activity occurred in the (b)_____. Researchers suggested that this brain area is the neural basis for (c)_____. However, the finding of a relationship between neural activity and solving cognitive problems is a (d)_____, which cannot show what causes what.

H. APPLICATION: INTERVENTION PROGRAMS

16. A program that creates an environment with increased opportunities for intellectual, social, and personality-emotional development is called an (a)_____ program. Although data indicate that IQ increases resulting from intervention programs may be short-lived, there are other long-term positive benefits, such as being more likely to graduate from high school and less likely to be involved in (b)_____ activities. A recent study of 1,300 children in day-care centers in the United States reported that quality day care contributed to a child's (c)_____ and _____. Researchers emphasize the importance of choosing quality day care, which is one with specially trained (d)_____ and a low ratio of (e)_____ to teachers.

Answers: *1. psychometrics; 2. (a) **g**, (b) **s**; 3. multiple-intelligence; 4. (a) analytical, cognitive, or logical, (b) problem-solving, (c) practical; 5. intelligence; 6. (a) Binet and Simon, (b) mental age, (c) Terman, (d) MA/CA × 100; 7. (a) verbal, (b) performance, (c) IQ; 8. (a) reliability, (b) validity, (c) validity; 9. normal distribution; 10. mental retardation; 11. (a) organic, (b) cultural-familial, (c) gifted; 12. (a) innate, (b) label or classify, (c) cultural bias, (d) cultures, (e) nonintellectual factors; 13. (a) nature–nurture, (b) 50%, (c) 50%, (d) intervention, (e) inherited, or genetic; 14. (a) innate, (b) immigrants, (c) immigration laws, or quotas; 15. (a) inferior parietal lobe, (b) lateral prefrontal cortex, (c) general intelligence or Spearman's **g**, (d) correlation; 16. (a) intervention, (b) antisocial, delinquent or criminal, (c) well-being, cognitive development; (d) teachers, (e) children*

Critical Thinking

Can a Successful Bookie Have an IQ of 55?

Questions

1. How smart is Max Weisberg, who as a bookie made $700,000 but doesn't hide his illegal activities and keeps being arrested by police?

2. What is different about the terms used in the past to describe individuals with IQ scores at the lower end?

3. What are three theories of intelligence, and what would each say about Max's intelligence?

Max Weisberg, who is now in his 70s, has been a very successful bookie (person who takes illegal gambling bets). But what's unusual about Max is that even after police in repeated raids have seized nearly $700,000 in cash from his rundown house, even after he's been arrested more times than he can remember, he still takes no precautions to hide his bookmaking activities. He leaves gambling slips all over his house, never hides his cash earnings, and openly takes bets on the telephone even though he's had hours of conversations recorded by the FBI. So, how smart is Max, who as a bookie made $700,000 but takes no precautions to hide his illegal activities?

Determining how smart Max is is not that easy. In 1939, when Max was 15 years old, he was committed to a state school because of "mental deficiency." Later, he was judged to be "feebleminded," and still later a probation report on Max read: "mentally deficient: moron, causes undiagnosed." Later on, when Max scored about 55 on an IQ test, he was judged to be in the mentally retarded category.

A psychologist tested Max to find out how someone who was mentally retarded could be a successful bookie. For example, Max has no idea which direction the sun set (west), who wrote "Hamlet" (Shakespeare), who Louis Armstrong was (jazz singer and trumpet player), or why being a bookie was bad

(it's against the law in most states). However, when Max was asked to repeat 8 numbers in correct sequence, his face lit up and he repeated the numbers without an error. When something involves using numbers, Max is as good as a calculator.

Although an IQ of 55 puts Max in the range of borderline mentally retarded, Max has no trouble remembering and calculating hundreds of complex and difficult numbers related to gambling. For example, if you wanted to make an illegal bet on a professional football team, Max could give you the odds, such as Vikings to win by $10\frac{1}{2}$ points. This means that you win your bet only if the Vikings win by 11 points. If you decided to bet on two or more teams, called "parleys," or bet "over/under," which uses the total scores of games instead of a single game, Max calculates these very complicated odds without using anything more than the head on his shoulders. A person having this unusual combination of a low IQ score but excelling at some skill, such as numbers, is called a savant, which occurs in about 1 in 2,000 of mentally retarded individuals.

After every arrest, Max tells the police that he needs to get out as soon as possible so he can get to a phone and start taking bets. (Adapted from S. Braun, Max the bookie won't stop and that's a sure thing, *Los Angeles Times*, August 7, 1999, p. A1)

4. Based on the normal distribution, where would Max rank in intelligence and what would he be capable of doing?

5. Why doesn't Max understand that bookmaking is illegal and that he must stop or he will keep being arrested?

Try InfoTrac to search for terms: mental retardation; multiple intelligence.

1. As a bookie, Max has to be pretty smart to have made $700,000, but he has to be pretty dumb to leave all his gambling slips and cash lying around the house so the police have an easy time finding evidence to arrest him over and over.
2. Notice that the terms used in the past to describe individuals with lower IQs, such as "mentally deficient," "feebleminded," and "moron," were very unfavorable or derogatory and put the individual in a bad light.
3. According to Spearman's *g*, Max would be rated low in intelligence because his IQ is 55 (normal is 100) and Max is given no credit for his practical abilities (being a very successful bookie). According to Gardner's idea of multiple intelligence, Max certainly has exceptional skills in calculating numbers and is intelligent in that sense. According to Sternberg's triarchic theory, Max

certainly shows considerable practical intelligence in his ability to adapt to his environment (being a very successful bookie).
4. Based on the normal distribution of IQ scores, Max's IQ score of 55 falls in the range for borderline mentally retarded (50–75). In this range, Max should be able to read and write, master a simple occupational skill, and be self-supporting. As it turns out, Max is a very successful, self-supporting bookie.
5. Being mentally retarded means that Max has some limited cognitive capacities (not knowing which direction the sun sets). The reason Max believes that being a bookie is OK is that he says that's what he does and has been doing for 40 years. The idea that being a bookie is illegal or immoral is a concept too complex or abstract for Max to understand, no matter how many times it is explained or he is arrested.

Links to Learning

LEARNING ACTIVITIES

- **POWERSTUDY CD-ROM 2.0** by Tom Doyle and Rod Plotnik
  Check out the "Intelligence" Module (disk 2) on PowerStudy and:
  - Test your knowledge using an interactive version of the Summary Test on pages 300 and 301. Also access related quizzes—true/false, multiple choice, and matching..
  - Explore an interactive version of the Critical Thinking exercise "Can a Successful Bookie Have an IQ of 55?" on page 302.
  - You will also find key terms, a chapter outline including chapter abstract, and a list of hotlinked Web sites that correlate to this module.

- **SELF-STUDY ASSESSMENT**
  Want help studying? For your customized Study Plan go to **http://psychology.wadsworth.com/plotnik7e/**. This program will automatically generate pretests and posttests to help you determine what concepts you have mastered and what concepts you still need work on.

- **STUDY GUIDE and WEBTUTOR**
  Check the corresponding module in your Study Guide for effective student tips and help learning the material presented.

- **INFOTRAC COLLEGE EDITION ONLINE LIBRARY**
  To find interesting and relevant articles go to **http://www.infotrac-college.com**, use your password, and then type in search terms such as the ones listed below.

  Mental Retardation   Intelligence tests   Psychometrics

STUDY QUESTIONS

Use InfoTrac to search for topics mentioned in the main heads below (e.g., intelligence tests, nature–nurture).

*A. **Defining Intelligence**—How intelligent was Ray Kroc, who never finished high school but started the world-famous McDonald's hamburger chain? (**Suggested answer page 627**)

B. **Measuring Intelligence**—Would a new test based on a very accurate count of all the cells in your brain be a good test of intelligence?

C. **Distribution & Use of IQ Scores**—If you were hiring for a large department store, would it help to know the applicants' IQ scores?

*D. **Potential Problems of IQ Testing**—Should we use IQ scores to assign the growing number of students from different cultures to grade levels? (**Suggested answer page 627**)

E. **Nature-Nurture Question**—If parents wanted to adopt a child, how important would it be to know the child's genetic makeup?

F. **Cultural Diversity: Races, IQs & Immigration**—What convinced members of the United States Congress to use IQ scores as the basis for immigration laws?

G. **Research Focus: New Approaches**—Would brain scans provide a less biased, more culture-free measure of intelligence than standard IQ tests?

*H. **Application: Intervention Programs**—Since Head Start fails to raise IQ scores over the long run, should its financial support be reduced? (**Suggested answer page 627**)

*These questions are answered in Appendix B.

Module 14: Thought & Language

BUTTERFLYALPHABET
KJELL B. SANDVED
www.butterflyalphabet.com

©butterflyalphabet.com

Concepts

What is that four-legged thing?

Jeff, who is only 14 months old, walks up to his mother and says, in a somewhat demanding voice, "Juice." Jeff's one-word sentence, "Juice," is shorthand for "Can I please have a glass of orange juice?" Even as a toddler, Jeff already knows a considerable number of words that represent a whole range of objects, such as cookie, car, bottle, bunny, baby, juice, ball, apple, and the most hated words of all for a young child, "wash up." So when Jeff points at an object and says, "Ball," his one-word sentence is short for "That is my ball." Jeff's use of these single-word "sentences" indicates that he is on his way to learning a very complex system of communicating by using language.

Jeff learned that this four-legged animal is a rabbit and not a cat or dog.

Jeff also uses one-word "sentences" to ask questions. For instance, he'll point to a picture in his animal book and ask, "Name?" This means "What is the name of that animal?" Jeff has already learned that a four-legged, fuzzy-tailed, large-eared animal is a bunny; a four-legged, long-nosed animal that barks is a dog; and a four-legged, short-eared animal with a long tail that says "meow" is a cat. Perhaps when Jeff sees an animal, such as a dog, cat, or rabbit, he takes a "mental photo" that he uses for future identifications. But that would mean storing an overwhelming number of "mental photos" of all the animals, objects, and people in his environment. We'll explain a more efficient system that Jeff probably uses to identify animals, objects, and people.

Creativity

How does one become creative?

One of Jeff's favorite things to do is paint the animals in his picture books. Although Jeff makes a terribly wonderful mess, his parents encourage him because they hope that Jeff's early interest in painting may indicate that he has a creative talent for painting or art. How one becomes a creative person is quite a mystery; take the case of Gordon Parks, for example.

No one thought Gordon Parks would amount to much. He was out on the streets at age 15 and never had time to finish high school, where he and his classmates were told, "Don't worry about graduating—it doesn't matter because you're gonna be porters and maids." Parks is African American and grew up in the 1920s, surrounded by segregation, discrimination, and, worst of all, lynchings.

Parks was a teenager when his mother died. He was sent to live with his brother-in-law, but, Parks remembers, "That man didn't like children and didn't want to take me on, and I sensed that the minute I walked into his house." Parks was soon out on the street. He drifted from city to city, lived in flophouses, and worked at odd jobs. What would become of Parks (McKenna, 1994)?

With little formal schooling, Parks became a very creative person.

Parks (right photo) is now in his nineties and looks back on what he has accomplished. With little formal schooling and little professional help, he has written five volumes of poetry and a best-selling autobiography, *The Learning Tree.* He worked as a professional photographer for *Vogue* and *Life* magazines and directed several films (*Shaft* and *The Learning Tree*). He has written 12 books, held an exhibition of his photographs, and published a book of his incredible photos (Parks, 1997). Parks's early years showed no signs of his creativity. We'll discuss what creativity is and what makes creative people different.

Cognitive Approach

How does your mind work?

How do toddlers like Jeff learn to speak a complex language and to recognize hundreds of objects? How did Gordon Parks, with little formal schooling, develop the ability to write and express his creativity in so many ways? The answers to these kinds of questions involve figuring out how our minds work. One way to study mental processes is to use the cognitive approach.

The *cognitive approach* is one method of studying how we process, store, and use information and how this information, in turn, influences what we notice, perceive, learn, remember, believe, and feel.

Of all animals, humans have the greatest language ability.

We have already discussed several aspects of the cognitive approach: learning in Modules 9 and 10, and memory and forgetting in Modules 11 and 12. Here we'll explore two other cognitive processes, thinking and laguage.

Thinking, which is sometimes referred to as reasoning, involves mental processes that are used to form concepts, solve problems, and engage in creative activities.

Language is a special form of communication in which we learn and use complex rules to form and manipulate symbols (words or gestures) that are used to generate an endless number of meaningful sentences.

In fact, thinking and using language are two things we do much better than animals (Kosslyn, 1995).

What's Coming

We'll discuss how we form concepts, solve problems, think creatively, acquire language, and reason. We'll also examine why people have difficulty recognizing words (dyslexia) and how language used by animals is different from the language used by humans.

We'll begin with the interesting question of how Jeff learned to distinguish a rabbit from a dog, and a dog from a cat.

A. Forming Concepts

Is it a dog, cat, or rabbit?

During your childhood, there was a time when every animal you saw was called a "dog." As a child, you gradually learned to tell the difference between a dog, a cat, and a rabbit by forming a different concept for each animal.

A *concept* is a way to group or classify objects, events, animals, or people based on some features, traits, or characteristics that they all share in common.

How you formed the concept of a dog or cat or rabbit has two different explanations: the exemplar model and the prototype theory (Nosofsky & Zaki, 2002).

#1

Exemplar Model

You easily recognize the animals on the left, but the question is How did you know which animal was which? Is it because your mind contains definitions of hundreds of animals?

The *exemplar model* says that you form a concept of an object, event, animal, or person by defining or making a mental list of the essential characteristics of a particular thing.

According to the exemplar model, you formed a concept of a dog, cat, or rabbit by learning its essential characteristics. The essential characteristics of a dog might include that it barks and has a long nose, two ears, two eyes, four legs, some hair, and usually a tail. Similarly, you made mental definitions for all animals. Then, when you looked at the three animals on the left, you automatically sorted through hundreds of animal definitions until you found one that included the essential properties of a dog, cat, or rabbit. Once you found the definition, you knew what the animal was. Although the exemplar model seems like a reasonable method of forming concepts, it has two serious problems.

> One way to form concepts is to make definitions.

PROBLEMS WITH THE EXEMPLAR MODEL

Too many features. In real life, it is very difficult to list all the features that define any object (Rey, 1983). For example, if your list of features to define a dog wasn't complete, the list might also apply to wolves, jackals, coyotes, and skunks. If your list of features to define a dog included every possible feature, such a mental list would be complete but take so long to go through that it would be very slow to use. And worse, you would need a long list of defining features for each and every animal, person, and object. Such a great number of mental lists would tax the best of memories.

Too many exceptions. After making a list of defining features, you would also need to list all the

> **dog** (dog, dag) n.; pl. **dogs, dog.**
> 1. any of a large and varied group of domesticated animals (*Canis familiaris*) that have four legs, a tail, two ears, prominent nose, a hairy coat, and a bark.

exceptions that do not fit into the dictionary definition of dog. For example, some dogs rarely bark, some are very tiny, some are very large, some are hairless, and some are very fuzzy.

Because of these two problems, you would need to check two mental lists—a long list that contained all the defining features and another that contained all the exceptions—before finding the concept that correctly identified the animal, person, or object.

For these reasons, the exemplar model has generally been replaced by a different theory of how we form concepts: the prototype theory.

Prototype Theory

Please look at the three animals on the right, #1, #2, and #3. Despite the great differences in size, color, and facial features of these animals, prototype theory explains why you can easily and quickly recognize each one as a dog.

Prototype theory says that you form a concept by creating a mental image that is based on the average characteristics of an object. This "average" looking object is called a prototype. To identify a new object, you match it to one of your already formed prototypes of objects, people, or animals.

Based on many experiences, you develop prototypes of many different objects, persons, and animals (Rosch, 1978). For example, your prototype of a dog would be a mental image of any particular animal that has *average features* (nose, tail, ears, height, weight). By using your prototype of a dog, you can easily and quickly identify all three animals on the right—the large brown mutt (#1), the tiny Chihuahua (#2), and the colorful Dalmatian (#3)—as being dogs.

#2

#3

ADVANTAGES OF THE PROTOTYPE THEORY

Average features. One advantage of the prototype theory over the exemplar model is that you do not have to make a mental list of all the defining features of an object, which is often impossible. Instead, you form a prototype by creating a mental picture or image of the object, animal, or person that has only average features.

> Another way to form concepts is to form prototypes.

Quick recognition. Another advantage of prototype theory is that it can result in quick recognition, as happened when you identified these different-looking animals (#1, #2, and #3) as dogs. The more a new object resembles a prototype, the more quickly you can identify it; the less it matches your prototype, the longer it takes to identity it.

For example, what is the strange animal on the right, #4, and where is its head? Because this animal's features are not close to your dog prototype, it will take you some time to figure out that it has hair like "dreadlocks," its head is on the right, and it's an unusual dog (called a Puli).

#4

Prototype theory, which explains that you form concepts by creating and using prototypes, is widely accepted and has generally replaced the exemplar model (Minda & Smith, 2001).

Next, we'll discuss when children begin forming concepts.

Early Formation

At the beginning of this module, we described how 14-month-old Jeff had already learned a number of concepts, such as juice, cookie, car, ball, apple, cat, dog, and bunny. Many children 10 to 16 months old can form concepts; that is, they can correctly identify different

BLOCKS

By 10 to 16 months, infants learn a number of concepts.

living things (cat, dog, rabbit) as animals and then place each living thing in the correct category (Quinn, 2002).

Recent studies have reported that children develop many concepts or categories (animal, vegetable, face) by experiencing or interacting with objects and things in their environments, and children show their grasp of concepts even before they have developed much language ability (Mareschal & Quinn, 2001). For example, as 14-month-old Jeff (above photo) plays with different objects in his environment, he will learn that one kind of object is a nonliving thing called a block. Initially, a child's categories may be very broad, such as objects, people, animals, and events.

However, as children gain more experience with objects, animals, people, and things in their environments as well as develop increased language skills, which happens around age 5 (p. 315), they learn to form more complex concepts, such as the qualities of objects—*heavy, shiny, colorful, sweet, bitter*—and the position and placement of objects—*up, down, high, low.* The chances of a child interacting with a wide variety of objects and thus developing many concepts and categories are greatly increased by being raised in a stimulating environment, but chances are hindered in an impoverished one (Quinn, 2002).

Thus, the development and formation of concepts depend, in large part, on the child's opportunity to interact with the environment and, as you'll see next, in part on how the brain is neatly organized to process information into categories.

Categories in the Brain

A child's ability to form and develop concepts is helped not only by having a stimulating environment but also by how the brain is organized. Brain scans and brain stimulation of normal subjects as well as tests on brain-damaged individuals showed that different concepts, such as animals, faces, vegetables/fruits, and nonliving things, are processed and stored in different parts of the brain (Ilmberger et al., 2002). Thus, as children interact with and learn to identify different objects, they can easily place different objects into different categories because the brain is already set up to store different categories in different areas (Ilmberger et al., 2002).

This process of placing things into categories occurs very quickly. For example, you quickly and easily recognize the three objects on the right as turtle, apple, and clown, and you easily place them into three different categories: animal, fruit, and person. Researchers explain that you were able to recognize these three things by matching each to your already formed prototypes of a turtle, apple, and clown (Squire & Knowlton, 1995).

One reason you are not aware of forming prototypes or classifying things into categories is that these cognitive processes occur at an unconscious level, which means that you are unaware of and cannot recall what is happening (p. 246). Evidence that forming prototypes and matching things to prototypes occur at an unconscious (implicit) level comes from studies on patients who had suffered various forms of amnesia or memory loss due to brain damage. Although amnesic patients were able to form prototypes and correctly match things to prototypes, they could not explain how they did it. Researchers concluded that using prototypes involves implicit processes, which we are not aware of and cannot voluntarily recall (Squire & Knowlton, 1995).

As you'll see, not being able to form concepts would make every day a very bad day.

animal

fruit

face

Brain is prewired to make categories.

Functions of Concepts

If you woke up one day to find that you had lost all your concepts, you would indeed have a very bad day. That's because concepts perform two important functions: They organize information and help us avoid relearning (Humphreys & Forde, 2001).

1 **Organize information.** Concepts allow you to group things into categories and thus better organize and store information in memory. For example, instead of having to store hundreds of mental images of many different kinds of dogs, you can store a single prototype of the average dog.

2 **Avoid relearning.** By having concepts that can be used to classify and categorize things, you can easily classify new things without having to relearn what that thing is. For example, once you have a concept for a dog, rabbit, cat, or cookie, you do not have to relearn what that thing is on each new encounter.

Without concepts, our cognitive worlds would consist of unconnected pieces of information. In fact, some forms of brain damage destroy a person's ability to form concepts, so that the person is unable to name or categorize what he or she sees (visual agnosia; see page 79). By using concepts, you can identify, categorize, and store information very efficiently.

What if you had to always relearn that this is a dog?

There is no doubt that concepts are useful for identifying objects and helping us make sense of our world. Next, you'll see that concepts are valuable for solving problems and thinking creatively.

B. Solving Problems

How do experts solve problems?

In 1997, world chess champion, Gary Kasparov (right photo), lost a chess match for the first time to a powerful computer. He played another computer in 2003 and tied (3 games each) (Byrne, 2003). This human-versus-computer chess match was all about thinking and problem solving.

A computer that was unemotional, unconcerned, and uncaring beat me at chess!

Problem solving involves searching for some rule, plan, or strategy that results in our reaching a certain goal that is currently out of reach.

In previous matches, Kasparov had always beat the computer because he was the better thinker and problem solver. For Kasparov, as well as for most of us, problem solving involves three states: (1) the *initial state,* which is thinking about the unsolved problem; (2) the *operations state,* which involves trying various rules or strategies to solve the problem; and (3) the *goal state,* which is reaching the solution. One plan used by expert problem solvers, such as Kasparov, is to think in broader terms of how to solve the problem, while less successful novices become too focused on specifics (Abernethy et al., 1994). For example, expert computer programmers start with the final goal (to write a new chess program) and work their way down to specific solutions. In comparison, novices become bogged down in working on specific steps of the program and never reach the final goal of writing a complete program. Being a successful problem solver involves using different kinds of thinking, some of which can be progammed into a computer.

Different Ways of Thinking

Can a computer think?

In this man-machine chess match, Kasparov's thinking involved a combination of intuition (clever guesses based on years of experience) and creative mental shortcuts, called heuristics. The computer's "thinking" was more fixed because it has been programmed to use a set of rules that lead to specific outcomes, called algorithms. Solving problems by using algorithms or heuristics illustrates two very different ways of thinking (Lohman, 2000).

Algorithms

If you wanted to win at a variety of games, such as chess, checkers, or bridge, you would follow a fixed set of rules that are called algorithms *(AL-go-rhythms).*

Algorithms are a fixed set of rules that, if followed correctly, will eventually lead to a solution.

For example, learning to play chess involves following algorithms that define how pieces move and the results of those moves. The reason relatively few chess players become grand masters like Kasparov is that people vary in their ability to learn and use algorithms.

Initially, Deep Blue was given little chance to beat world chess champion Kasparov because playing chess by using algorithms is a slow process. Instead of using algorithms, chess champion Kasparov was playing with a potentially more powerful set of rules called heuristics.

Heuristics

Kasparov's unique brain, together with his years of experience, allowed him to play chess using heuristics *(hyur-RIS-ticks).*

Heuristics are rules of thumb, or clever and creative mental shortcuts, that reduce the number of operations and allow one to solve problems more easily and quickly.

In the late 1990s, Kasparov's clever and creative shortcuts, or heuristics, had given him the advantage over the fixed and not so creative algorithms of computer programs. However, computers now have been programmed with new algorithms that increase their speed of "thinking" from analyzing 100,000 chess moves per second to 2.5 million. As a result of this increased speed, human chess grand masters, whose thinking focuses on using clever heuristics, no longer have a clear advantage over a computer's "thinking" ability (Boyce, 2002).

Besides being used to solve chess problems, heuristics are often used in daily life to make decisions or draw conclusions (Bailenson et al., 2000). A commonly used heuristic is called the availability heuristic.

The *availability heuristic* says that we rely on information that is more prominent or easily recalled and overlook other information that is available but less prominent or notable.

For example, the murder rate in the United States actually decreased in the late 1990s. However, during this time, network coverage of homicides increased 473%, which made news of murders more available and, according to the availability heuristic, led people to conclude that murder rates had become epidemic (Comarow, 2001).

Using the availability heuristic to make a decision means taking a mental shortcut. Although heuristics allow us to make quick decisions, they may result in bad decisions since we make them using shortcuts, which limits the amount of information we use (F. Bower, 1997).

Artificial Intelligence

It took 50 years of effort before scientists learned how to program a computer that could beat Kasparov at chess. One goal of computer science is to develop *artificial intelligence*, which means programming machines (computers, robots) to imitate human thinking and problem-solving abilities.

For example, scientists recently developed a "thinking" program modeled on how the brain thinks (neural network). Scientists programmed a computer with this "thinking" program and the basic rules of checkers. In no time, the computer taught itself to play checkers at the expert level (Fogel, 2000). Can you imagine a computer teaching itself to play expert checkers? This represents a major breakthrough in artificial intelligence—teaching machines to think like humans.

What if you get stuck?

Most of us have had the experience of getting stuck while trying to solve a problem and wondering what to do next. By studying people who are good at problem solving, such as chess players, engineers, and computer programmers, psychologists have identified a number of useful strategies for solving problems. We'll discuss three problem-solving strategies—changing a mental set, using analogies, and forming subgoals. (Solutions to the first two problems appear on page 317.)

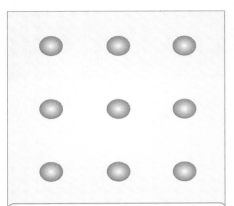

It takes new thinking to connect all dots with 4 straight lines without lifting pencil.

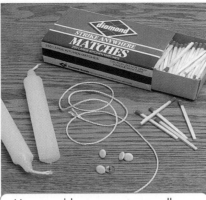

How would you mount a candle on the wall using what you see here?

The best strategy for writing a term paper is to break the task into subgoals.

Changing One's Mental Set

Problem. Connect all nine dots shown above by drawing four straight lines without lifting your pencil from the paper or retracing any lines. If, like most people, you have difficulty solving this problem, it may be because of functional fixedness.

Functional fixedness refers to a mental set that is characterized by the inability to see an object as having a function different from its usual one.

For instance, you probably have a mental set that a straight line must begin and end on a dot. To solve the nine-dot problem, you need to break out of functional fixedness, which involves thinking of a line as continuing past a dot (MacGregor et al., 2001).

The nine-dot puzzle is a good example of the kind of problem that is often solved in a sudden flash, known as insight, which we discussed earlier (p. 226).

Insight is the sudden grasp of a solution after many incorrect attempts.

You can increase your chances of solving a problem by insight if you consider the problem from many different viewpoints and unusual angles and if you decrease your anxiety and concern, which will in turn help you to overcome functional fixedness.

Using Analogies

Problem. Imagine that you have a box of matches, two candles, a piece of string, and several tacks, as shown in the photo above. How would you mount a candle on the wall so that it could be used as a light?

You may solve the candle problem in a flash of insight. However, most of us have to develop a strategy to solve the problem, and a good strategy may involve using an analogy.

An *analogy* is a strategy for finding a similarity between the new situation and an old, familiar situation.

If you adopt an analogy to solve the candle problem, here's how your thinking might proceed: "I'm familiar with using a shelf to hold a candle on the wall. Which of the objects—candle, string, or box—could serve as a shelf? If I remove the matches, I can tack the box to the wall."

As you gain more experience and knowledge, you become better at using analogies to solve problems. This is one reason that businesses prefer employees with experience: These employees are more likely to use analogies to solve problems.

What about the problem every student must face—writing a paper?

Forming Subgoals

Problem. Suppose your assignment is to write a term paper titled "Creativity and Madness." A useful strategy for writing this paper is to divide the assignment or general problem into a number of subgoals.

Using *subgoals* is a strategy that involves breaking down the overall problem into separate parts that, when completed in order, will result in a solution.

As shown in the figure above, the first subgoal is doing library research and finding a number of articles on creativity and madness. The second subgoal is reading the articles and taking notes. The third subgoal is making a detailed outline of the whole paper. A fourth subgoal is using your outline to write the paper. The strategy of working on and completing each specific subgoal makes the overall project more manageable and reduces unproductive worrying and complaining that can interfere with starting and completing your paper.

The strategy of setting specific goals to solve a problem has some advantages: Goals direct and focus your attention, help get you energized and motivated, and increase your persistence and lessen procrastination (Locke & Latham, 2002).

Another problem-solving strategy is to use creative thinking, our next topic.

C. Thinking Creatively

At the beginning of this module, we told you about Gordon Parks (left photo). Parks grew up in the 1920s, a time of segregation, discrimination, and lynchings. As a result of the way Blacks were treated in the 1920s, Parks received little formal schooling or professional help and was told that he should be happy just to look forward to a job as a porter. Despite overwhelming odds, Parks succeeded in writing two novels and five volumes of poetry, directing two movies, and, now in his nineties, having an exhibition of his photographs (right photo) and publishing some in a book (Parks, 1997).

This intriguing story of Gordon Parks raises four interesting questions about creativity: How is creativity defined? Is IQ related to creativity? How do creative people think and behave? Is creativity related to psychological problems? Although there are more than 60 definitions of creativity, we'll begin with the one most commonly used (Boden, 1994).

Gordon Parks had an HBO TV special on his 88th birthday.

With little formal schooling, Gordon Parks became a very creative movie director and photographer.

How Is Creativity Defined?

The definition of creative thinking is somewhat different from that of a creative individual.

Creative thinking is a combination of flexibility in thinking and reorganization of understanding to produce innovative ideas and new or novel solutions (Sternberg, 2001).

A *creative individual* is someone who regularly solves problems, fashions products, or defines new questions that make an impact on his or her society (H. Gardner, 1993).

People can show evidence of creative thinking in many different ways. For example, recognized creative individuals include Albert Einstein, who formulated the theory of relativity; Michelangelo, who painted the Sistine Chapel; Sigmund Freud, who developed psychoanalysis; Dr. Seuss, who wrote rhyming books for children (and adults); the Rolling Stones, a well-known, 40-year-old rock-and-roll band; Ray Kroc, who founded McDonald's worldwide hamburger chain; and Gordon Parks, who is a writer, director, and photographer.

Because there are so many different examples (and kinds) of creativity, psychologists have used three different approaches to measure creativity: the psychometric, case study, and cognitive approaches (Sternberg & O'Hara, 2000).

Psychometric Approach

This approach, which uses objective problem-solving tasks to measure creativity, focuses on the distinction between two kinds of thinking—convergent and divergent (Guilford, 1967; Kitto et al., 1994).

Convergent thinking means beginning with a problem and coming up with a single correct solution.

Examples of convergent thinking include answering multiple-choice questions and solving math problems. The opposite of convergent thinking is divergent thinking.

Divergent thinking means beginning with a problem and coming up with many different solutions.

For example, the two problem-solving tasks on page 309 (nine-dot and candle-match puzzles) are used to assess divergent thinking, which is a popular psychometric measure for creativity (Amabile, 1985; Camp, 1994).

Tests of divergent thinking have good reliability, which means that people achieve the same scores across time (Domino, 1994). However, tests of divergent thinking have low validity, which means that creative persons, such as Gordon Parks, may not necessarily score high on psychometric tests of creativity (H. Gardner, 1993).

Case Study Approach

Because the psychometric approach is limited to using objective tests, it provides little insight into creative minds. In comparison, the case study approach analyzes creative persons in great depth and thus provides insight into their development, personality, motivation, and problems.

For example, Howard Gardner (1993) used the case study approach to analyze seven creative people, including Sigmund Freud. Gardner found that creative people are creative in certain areas but poor in others: Freud was very creative in linguistic and personal areas but very poor in spatial and musical areas. Although case studies provide rich insight into creative minds, their findings may be difficult to generalize: Freud's kind of creativity may or may not apply to Gordon Parks's remarkable achievements (Freyd, 1994).

Cognitive Approach

Although case studies provide detailed portraits of creative people, the findings are very personal or subjective and not easily applied to others. In comparison, the cognitive approach tries to build a bridge between the objective measures of the psychometric approach and the subjective descriptions provided by case studies. The cognitive approach, which is also the newest, identifies and measures cognitive mechanisms that are used during creative thinking (Freyd, 1994).

For example, many individuals have reported that one cognitive mechanism vital to creative thinking is the use of mental imagery, which involves thinking in images, without words or mathematical symbols (Finke, 1993). Thus, the cognitive approach involves analyzing the workings of mental imagery and its relationship to creative thinking.

Now, let's see what these three approaches say about creativity.

Is IQ Related to Creativity?

In some cases, such as Michelangelo, Sigmund Freud, and Albert Einstein, creativity seems to be linked to genius. However, creativity is not the same as intelligence, as best illustrated by savants.

Savants refer to about 10% of autistic individuals who show some incredible memory, music, or drawing talent.

Despite their creativity, many savants score below 70 on IQ tests (the average score is 100). For instance, the detailed drawing of a famous Russian church (right photo) was done by Chris, a 16-year-old savant who has little knowledge or use of language and whose IQ is 52 (Sacks, 1995). Studies show that savants lack verbal intelligence but excell in visual intelligence and that their right hemispheres are more active than their left during creative activities (Treffert & Wallace, 2002).

Drawn by a 16-year-old savant with an IQ of 52.

Instead of linking creativity to genius, some psychologists believe that creativity involves relatively ordinary cognitive processes that result in extraordinary products (Weisberg, 1993). These creative products include inventions (Post-its, genetic crops), new drugs (Viagra), and computer software (video games).

Compared with the general population, creative scientists, writers, and artists generally score above average, with IQs of 120 and higher. However, when IQs of creative individuals are compared among themselves, there is little correlation between creativity and IQ. In other words, those who are generally recognized as creative do tend to have above-average IQ scores, but those with the highest IQs are not necessarily those who are the most creative (Sternberg & O'Hara, 2000).

How Do Creative People Think and Behave?

Researchers have studied creative individuals to identify what is unusual about their work habits and psychological traits (Helson, 1996; Simonton, 2000). Here are some of their findings.

Focus. Creative people tend to be superior in one particular area, such as dance, music, art, science, or writing, rather than many areas. For example, Einstein (drawing at right) was superior in the logical-spatial area—the theory of relativity ($E = mc^2$)—but poor in the personal area—developing close relationships.

Cognition. Creative individuals have the ability to change mental directions, consider problems from many angles, and make use of mental images. They are also interested in solving unusual problems.

$E = mc^2$

Creative people can consider problems from different viewpoints and are driven by strong internal goals.

Personality. On the positive side, creative people tend to be independent, self-confident, unconventional, risk-taking, hard-working, and obsessively committed to their work. On the negative side, they tend to have large egos that make them insensitive to the needs of others. They may pursue their goals at the expense of others, and they may be so absorbed in their work that they exclude others.

Motivation. They are driven by internal values or personal goals; this is called intrinsic motivation. They are less concerned about external rewards such as money or recognition, which is called extrinsic motivation. They are motivated by the challenge of solving problems; their reward is the satisfaction of accomplishment. On average, creative people work on a project for about ten years before reaching their creative peaks.

One question often asked about creative people is whether their creative fires are fueled by psychological or mental problems, such as mood disorders.

Is Creativity Related to Mental Disorders?

There are numerous historical reports of a link between creativity and madness or insanity, more correctly called mental disorders. For example, Mark Twain (Samuel Clemens), Tennessee Williams, Ernest Hemingway, Charles Mingus, Cole Porter, Edgar Allan Poe, and Herman Hesse were all reported to suffer from either depression or manic-depression (swings between euphoria and depression) (Jamison, 1995).

A more formal study of 291 creative writers, artists, composers, thinkers, and scientists indicated that 17–46% suffered from severe mental disorders, especially mood disorders. As the graph on the right shows, writers had the highest percentage of mental disorders, especially alcoholism and depression (Post, 1994).

A number of studies indicate that highly creative people experience major mood disorders more often than other groups in the general population (Jamison, 1995). But does the mood disorder

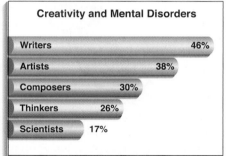

Creativity and Mental Disorders

Writers	46%
Artists	38%
Composers	30%
Thinkers	26%
Scientists	17%

contribute to creativity? One researcher suggested that severe mood change could contribute to creativity by sharpening thoughts and broadening the person's emotional, intellectual, and perceptual views of the world (Jamison, 1995). One interesting finding is that those creative individuals who reported emotional problems said that such problems often began when they were teenagers (Ludwig, 1995).

Although mental disorders may provide a sense of discomfort that may motivate creative activity, there are creative individuals, such as many scientists, who have achieved creative breakthroughs without having severe emotional problems (Waddell, 1998).

Next, we turn to an important component of creative activities, the development of language.

D. Language: Basic Rules

How many languages are there?

Our ability to use language is one of the most remarkable features of our species (McIntosh & Lobaugh, 2003). Currently, people are believed to speak about 6,800 different languages, and about 10 languages die out each year (UNESCO, 2001).

Language is a special form of communication that involves learning complex rules to make and combine symbols (words or gestures) into an endless number of meaningful sentences.

The reason language is such a successful form of communication arises from two amazingly simple principles—words and grammar.

A *word* is an arbitrary pairing between a sound or symbol and a meaning.

For example, the word "*parrot*" does not look like, sound like, or fly like a parrot, but it refers to a certain bird that we call a parrot because all of us memorized this pairing as children. Young adults are estimated to have about 60,000 such pairings or words in their mental dictionaries (Pinker, 1995). However, these 60,000 symbols or words would be rather

Why is this called a parrot?

useless unless the users followed similar rules of grammar.

Grammar refers to a set of rules for combining words into phrases and sentences to express an infinite number of thoughts that can be understood by others.

For instance, our mental rules of grammar immediately tell us that the headline "Parrot Bites Man's Nose" means something very different from "Man Bites Parrot's Nose." It may seem surprising, but speakers of all 6,800 languages learned the same four rules.

Four Rules of Language

As children, each of us learned, without much trouble, the four rules of language. Now, as adults, we use these rules without being aware of how or when we use them. To illustrate the four rules of language, we'll use the word *caterpillar*. As a child, you may have watched its strange crawling motion, or perhaps you were even brave enough to pick it up.

1 The first language rule governs phonology.

Phonology (FOE-nawl-uh-gee) specifies how we make the meaningful sounds that are used by a particular language. Any English word can be broken down into phonemes.

Phonemes (FOE-neems) are the basic sounds of consonants and vowels.

For example, the various sounds of *c* and *p* represent different phonemes, which are some of the sounds in the word *caterpillar*. At about 6 months old, babies begin to babble and make basic sounds, or phonemes. We combine phonemes to form words by learning the second rule.

2 The second language rule governs morphology.

Morphology (mor-FAWL-uh-gee) is the system that we use to group phonemes into meaningful combinations of sounds and words.

A *morpheme (MOR-feem)* is the smallest meaningful combination of sounds in a language.

For example, a morpheme may be
- a word, such as cat,
- a letter, such as the s in cats,
- a prefix, such as the un- in unbreakable,
- or a suffix, such as the -ed in walked.

The word caterpillar is actually one morpheme, and the word caterpillars is two (caterpillar-s). After we learn to combine morphemes to form words, we learn to combine words into meaningful sentences by using the third rule.

Learning and using the word *caterpillar* involve four basic rules.

3 The third language rule governs syntax, or grammar.

Syntax, or *grammar,* is a set of rules that specifies how we combine words to form meaningful phrases and sentences.

For example, why doesn't the following sentence make sense?

Caterpillars green long and are.

You instantly realize that this sentence is nonsensical or ungrammatical because it doesn't follow the English grammar rules regarding where we place verbs and conjunctions. If you apply the rules of English grammar, you would rearrange the combination of words to read: "Caterpillars are long and green." Although you may not be able to list all the rules of grammar, you automatically follow them when you speak. One way you know whether the word *bear* is a noun or a verb is by using the fourth rule.

4 The fourth language rule governs semantics.

Semantics (si-MANT-iks) specifies the meaning of words or phrases when they appear in various sentences or contexts.

For instance, as you read "Did Pat pat a caterpillar's back?" how do you know what the word pat means, since it appears twice in succession. From your knowledge of semantics, you know that the first Pat is a noun and the name of a person, while the second pat is a verb, which signals some action.

Somehow you knew that the same word, pat, had very different meanings depending on the context. How you know what words mean in different contexts is a very intriguing question.

Understanding Language

One of the great mysteries of using and understanding language can be demonstrated by the following two simple but very different sentences.

You picked up a caterpillar.

A caterpillar was picked up by you.

Despite a different word order, you know that these two sentences mean exactly the same thing. How you know that these different sentences mean exactly the same thing was explained by linguist Noam Chomsky (1957). We'll discuss two of Chomsky's revolutionary principles—mental grammar and innate brain program—that allow us to use and understand spoken language with relative ease (Bever & Montalbetti, 2002).

Mental grammar. Almost every sentence we speak or understand is formed from a brand-new combination of words. Chomsky pointed out that the brain does not have the capacity to contain a list of all the sentences we will ever use. Instead, Chomsky argued that the brain contains a program or *mental grammar* that allows us to combine nouns, verbs, and objects in an endless variety of meaningful sentences. Chomsky's principle of mental grammar answers the question of how we can so easily create so many different sentences. The second question that Chomsky answered was: How do we acquire this mental grammar?

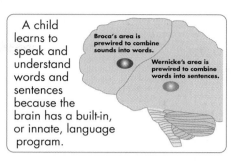

A child learns to speak and understand words and sentences because the brain has a built-in, or innate, language program.

Broca's area is prewired to combine sounds into words.

Wernicke's area is prewired to combine words into sentences.

Innate brain program. How is it possible that 4-year-old children, with no formal schooling and relatively limited instruction from their parents, can speak and understand an endless variety of sentences? For example, the average 4-year-old child can already determine that the sentence "The caterpillar crept slowly across the leaf" is correct but that the sentence "The crept leaf caterpillar slowly the across" is meaningless. Chomsky's answer is that young children can learn these complex and difficult rules of grammar because our brains come with a built-in, or *innate, program* that makes learning the general rules of grammar relatively easy (p. 229). The brain's innate program for learning rules of grammar explains how a child learns most of the complex and difficult rules of grammar by the age of 4 or 5. However, it is the interaction between the gradual development of the brain's innate program and a child's range of environmental experiences that results in learning the complicated rules of grammar (Schlaggar et al., 2002).

But how does an innate grammar program, which could be used by any child in any culture, specify the rules for forming and understanding an endless number of meaningful sentences? Chomsky's answer is perhaps his cleverest contribution.

Different Structure, Same Meaning

One of the most difficult questions that Chomsky had to answer was how an idea can be expressed in several different ways, with different grammatical structures, yet mean the same thing.

He answered this question by making a distinction between two different structures of a sentence: surface structure and deep structure.

Surface structure refers to the actual wording of a sentence, as it is spoken.

Deep structure refers to an underlying meaning that is not spoken but is present in the mind of the listener.

We can illustrate the difference between surface and deep structures with our same two sentences.

You picked up a caterpillar.

A caterpillar was picked up by you.

Notice that these two sentences have different *surface structures,* which means they are worded differently. However, according to Chomsky, you are able to look underneath the different surface structures of the two sentences and recognize that they have the same *deep structure,* which is why you know they have the same meaning.

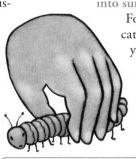

You know that the sentence "You picked up a caterpillar" means the same as "A caterpillar was picked up by you" because you recognize that both have the same deep structure.

Chomsky argues that we learn to shift back and forth between surface and deep structure by applying transformational rules.

Transformational rules are procedures by which we convert our ideas from surface structures into deep structures and from deep structures back into surface ones.

For example, when you hear the two sentences about picking up the caterpillar, you transform the words into their deep structure, which you store in memory. Later, when someone asks what the person did, you use transformational rules to convert the deep structure in your memory back into a surface structure, which can be expressed in differently worded sentences. The distinction between surface and deep structure is part of Chomsky's theory of language.

Chomsky's theory of language says that all languages share a common universal grammar and that children inherit a mental program to learn this universal grammar.

Chomsky's theory of language, which is widely accepted today, was considered a major breakthrough in explaining how we acquire and understand language (Baker, 2002). However, one criticism of Chomsky's theory is that he downplays the importance of different environmental opportunities for hearing and practicing sounds, which have been shown to interact with and influence language development (Schlaggar et al., 2002).

Chomsky's idea of an innate mental grammar would predict that children around the world should go through the same stages of language development. Can this be true for all 6,800 languages?

E. Acquiring Language

What do children's brains do?

If Chomsky is correct that all children inherit the same innate program for learning grammar, then we would expect children from around the world to go through similar stages in developing language and acquiring the rules for using language. And in fact, all children, no matter the culture or the language, do go through the same stages (Pinker, 1994).

Language stages refer to all infants going through four different periods or stages—babbling, single words, two-word combinations, and sentences. All children go through these four stages in the same order, and in each stage, children show new and more complex language skills.

The occurrence of each of the four stages is associated with further development of the brain. At birth, an infant's brain has almost all of its neurons but they have not yet made all their connections (adult brains can grow some new neurons; p. 49).

For example, a 6-month-old infant's brain (left figure) has few neural interconnections, which are associated with performing relatively

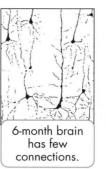

6-month brain has few connections.

simple behaviors, such as babbling. In comparison, a 24-month-old infant's brain (right figure) has hundreds of neural interconnections, which are associated with more complex behaviors, such as using two-word combinations (Bruer, 1999).

Here are the four stages that each of us went through in learning to speak and understand the language of our parents or caregivers.

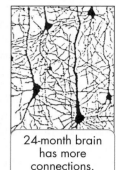

24-month brain has more connections.

Four Stages in Acquiring Language

1 Babbling

One of the key features in human development is that infants begin to make sounds long before they can say real words. Infants repeat the same sounds over and over, and these sounds are commonly called babbling.

Babbling, which begins at about 6 months, is the first stage in acquiring language. Babbling refers to making one-syllable sounds, such as "deedeedee" or "bababa," which are most common across all languages.

Bababa

Babbling is an example of an innate "sound" program in the brain that is involved in making and processing sounds that will eventually be used to form words. Researchers have discovered that by 6 months of age, infants have already learned to discriminate between sounds, such as *ba* from *pa,* and to distinguish sounds in their native language from those used in a foreign language (F. Bower, 2000). These findings indicate that, at an early age, infants have already become accustomed to making and hearing sounds that make up their native languages. At about 9 months, babbling sounds begin to resemble more the vowels and consonants that children will actually use in speaking their native languages.

A 6-month-old brain has limited capacity for language.

In children who can hear, babbling is oral. In deaf children who have been exposed only to the sign language of their deaf parents, babbling is manual and not oral. That is, these babies babble by repeating the same hand sign over and over (Petitto & Marentette, 1991). This means that the brain has an innate program for acquiring language, whether spoken or sign language.

Through endless babbling, infants learn to control their vocal apparatus so that they can make, change, and repeat sounds and imitate the sounds of their parents or caregivers (F. Bower, 2000). After babbling, infants begin to say their first words.

2 Single Word

Shortly before 1 year of age, an infant usually performs a behavior that every parent has been eagerly waiting for: to hear the child's first word. At about 1 year of age, infants not only begin to understand words but also to say single words.

Single words mark the second stage in acquiring language, which occurs at about 1 year of age. Infants say single words that usually refer to what they can see, hear, or feel.

An infant's ability to form sounds into words begins at about 8 months and results from an interaction between the brain's innate language program and the infant's experience with hearing sounds (Jusczyk & Hohne, 1997). About half the infant's single words refer to objects (juice, cookie, doll, dada), and the other half refer to actions, routines, or motions (up, eat, hot, more) (Pinker, 1994). The infant's single words, such as "Milk" or "Go," often stand for longer thoughts such as "I want milk" or "I want to go out."

Milk. Go.

As the infant learns to say words, parents usually respond by speaking in a specific way called parentese (motherese).

Parentese (motherese) is a way of speaking to young children in which the adult speaks in a slower and higher than normal voice, emphasizes and stretches out each word, uses very simple sentences, and repeats words and phrases.

In a study of mothers in the United States, Russia, and Sweden, researchers found that when talking to their infants, these mothers exaggerated certain sounds (vowel sounds), which they did not do when speaking to their husbands (Kuhl et al., 1997). Another researcher, who spent ten years traveling around the world to record child–parent interactions, concludes that parentese has several functions: getting an infant's attention and stimulating infants to make sounds they will need to speak themselves (Fernald, 1992).

Next, the young child begins to combine words.

1-year-old brain has more connections and more capacity for language.

3 Two-Word Combinations

Starting around age 2, children begin using single words that they have learned to form two-word combinations.

Two-word combinations, which represent the third stage in acquiring language, occur at about 2 years of age. Two-word combinations are strings of two words that express various actions ("Me play," "See boy") or relationships ("Hit ball," "Milk gone").

Each of the two words provides a hint about what the child is saying. In addition, the relationship between the two words gives hints about what the child is communicating. For example, "See boy" tells us to look at a specific object; "Daddy shirt" tells us that something belongs to Daddy. The child's new ability to communicate by combining two words and changing their order marks the beginning of learning the rules of grammar. From about 2 years of age through adolescence, a child learns an average of a new word every 2 hours (Pinker, 1994).

A child's language development is partly dependent on how responsive the parent or caretaker is. A more responsive parent is one who shows more contact, awareness, and warmth during the child's verbal interactions. For example, infants whose mothers were more responsive to their speech at 13 months had significantly larger vocabularies at 21 months compared to less responsive mothers (Tamis-LeMonda et al., 1996).

By the age of 2, a child may have a vocabulary of more than 50 words, many of which will be used in two-word combinations. Although children usually go through a stage of forming single words and then two-word combinations, there is no three-word stage. Instead, at a certain point the child will begin to form sentences, which gradually increase in length through the fourth year.

> Hit ball. Me play.

A 2-year-old brain has many connections and more capacity for language.

4 Sentences

Children make a rather large language leap when they progress from relatively simple two-word combinations to using longer and more complex sentences.

Sentences, which represent the fourth stage of acquiring language, occur at about 4 years of age. Sentences range from three to eight words in length and indicate a growing knowledge of the rules of grammar.

However, a child's first sentences differ from adults' in that the child may omit the "small words" and speak in a pattern that is called telegraphic speech.

Telegraphic speech is a distinctive pattern of speaking in which the child omits articles (the), prepositions (in, out), and parts of verbs.

For example, an adult may say, "I'm going to the store." A 3- to 4-year-old child may use telegraphic speech (omit article) and say, "I go to store." However, by the time children are 4 or 5 years old, the structure of their sentences improves and indicates that they have learned the basic rules of grammar.

Basic rules of grammar are the rules for combining nouns, verbs, adjectives, and other parts of speech to form meaningful sentences.

However, as children learn the rules of grammar, they often make errors of overgeneralization.

Overgeneralization means applying a grammatical rule to cases where it should not be used.

For example, after a child learns the rule of forming the past tense of many verbs by adding a *d* sound to the end, he or she may overgeneralize this rule and add a *d* to the past tense of irregular verbs (and say, for instance, "I goed to store"). By the time children enter school, they usually have a good grasp of the general rules of their language.

> I goed to store. I want blue toy.

4- to 5-year-old brain has significantly more connections so that a child can learn the basic rules of complex grammar.

Going Through the Stages

How fast does a child go through the stages?

Parents or caregivers sometimes worry about whether their child is late in developing language. In the real world, normal children pass through the four stages of language at a pace that can vary by a year or more. However, as Chomsky's theory predicts and research has shown, all normal children pass through the four stages, even though some of the stages may begin later or last for shorter or longer periods of time (Pinker, 1994).

As children proceed through the stages, there is a continuous interaction between environmental stimuli and brain development. For example, researchers used brain scans to identify maximum neural activity in 3-month-old infants who were listening to recordings of

1. Babbling   2. Single word   3. Two words   4. Sentences

human speech. The infants showed increased neural activity in brain areas that were similar to those used by adults in speaking and understanding language (Dehaene-Lambertz et al., 2002). This study shows how environmental stimulation—hearing language sounds—activated the "language areas" of infants' brains long before infants actually begin speaking. This study is a good example of how the brain and environment interact in the development of spoken language and points out the importance of caregivers regularly talking to (verbally stimulating) their infants.

Next, we'll discuss a number of innate (genetic) and environmental interactions that are important in the development of language.

E. Acquiring Language

How does a child learn a particular language?

It is quite amazing how children from different countries around the world, such as Africa, Bali, China, Sweden, Japan, United States, Mexico, France, Spain, Russia, and Thailand (right photo), *How did he learn to speak Thai?* can acquire the sounds, words, and rules of their particular native language. Each child learns his or her own native language because of an interaction between innate (genetic) and environmental (learning) factors.

What Are Innate Factors?

All children go through the same four language stages because of innate language factors (Albert et al., 2000).

Innate language factors are genetically programmed physiological and neurological features that facilitate our making speech sounds and acquiring language skills.

We'll examine three innate language features that work together so that we can learn to speak and use language.

Innate physiological features. We have a specially adapted vocal apparatus (larynx and pharynx) that allows us to make sounds and form words. In comparison, the structures of gorillas' and chimpanzees' vocal apparatus prevent them from making the wide variety of sounds necessary to form words (Pinker, 1994). Without our specialized vocal apparatus, we humans would be limited to making "animal" sounds.

Innate neurological features. When people speak or use sign language, certain brain areas are activated. The PET scan above shows a side view of the brain: red and yellow indicate most neural activity (Petitto, 1997). These findings indicate that the left hemisphere of the

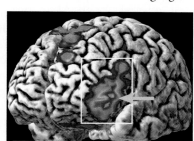
The brain is genetically programmed to speak and understand.

brain is prewired to acquire and use language, whether spoken or signed. In Module 4, we explained how damage to these same language areas (Broca's and Wernicke's areas) disrupts the use and understanding of language (p. 78). Although your brain is prewired for language, there is a best, or critical, time for learning a language.

Innate developmental factors. Researchers have discovered that there is a critical period when acquiring language is the easiest (Stromswold, 1995).

The *critical language period* is the time from infancy to adolescence when language is easiest to learn. Language is usually more difficult to learn anytime after adolescence.

For example, immigrant children do very well learning English as a second language, while immigrant adults, who are past the critical period, have more difficulty and do less well (Jackendoff, 1994). The critical period for learning language also explains why learning your native language was very easy as a child but, as an adult, learning a foreign language is many times more difficult.

Innate biological factors provide the programming so a child can acquire any one of 6,800 languages. Which particular language the child learns depends on his or her environment (parents).

What Are Environmental Factors?

Social interactions. How each child learns a particular language depends on social interactions, one of the environmental factors.

Environmental language factors refer to interactions children have with parents, peers, teachers, and others who provide feedback that rewards and encourages language development, as well as provides opportunities for children to observe, imitate, and practice language skills.

What would happen if a child was deprived of almost all social interactions from ages 1 to 13? Such was the case with Genie, whose mentally disturbed father strapped her to a potty chair in a back room, punished her for making any sounds, and forbid the mother or brother to talk to her. When discovered at age 13 by a social worker, Genie could not speak a single word (Curtiss, 1977). Genie's case illustrates that even though children are prewired by heredity to speak a language, they need certain environmental stimuli, such as listening, speaking, and interacting with others, in order to learn to speak and use language. Genie's case also illustrates the importance of social cognitive learning.

Parentese provides needed stimulation and feedback.

Social cognitive learning emphasizes the acquisition of language skills through social interactions, which give children a chance to observe, imitate, and practice the sounds, words, and sentences they hear from their parents or caregivers.

For example, within eight months of training, Genie had acquired a vocabulary of about 200 words. However, Genie's long period of social deprivation left its mark, and even after years of continued social interactions, her language ability did not develop much beyond that of a 2- or 3-year-old child (J. C. Harris, 1995).

Parentese. Researchers found that 2- and 3-year-old children who had the biggest vocabularies and performed best on developmental language tests were those whose parents were the most talkative during the child's first two years (Hart & Risley, 1996). These studies show the importance of environmental factors, such as parents and caregivers stimulating and encouraging language development by speaking in parentese and by being very responsive to what their child says (Monnot, 1999). All these studies show how environmental and innate factors interact and influence a child's ability to acquire the language skills of a particular culture.

When children master language, they have a powerful tool for thinking, as we'll discuss after the Concept Review.

✔ Concept Review

dog (dog, dag) *n.; pl.* **dogs, dog.**
1. any of a large and varied group of domesticated animals (*Canis familiaris*) that have four legs, a tail, two ears, prominent nose, a hairy coat, and a bark.

1. If you form a concept of an object, event, or characteristic by making a list of the properties that define it, you are forming a concept according to the _____ model.

2. If you form a concept by putting together the average characteristics of an object and then seeing whether a new object matches your average object, you are forming a concept according to (a)_____ theory. If you develop an idea of a dog of average age, height, weight, and color, you have formed a (b)_____ of a dog.

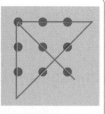

3. If you search for some rule, plan, or strategy that results in your reaching a certain goal that is currently out of reach, you are engaging in an activity called (a)_____. During this activity, you go through three states: contemplating the unsolved problem, which is the (b)_____ state; trying out various operations, rules, or strategies to solve the problem, which is the (c)_____ state; and reaching the solution, which is the (d)_____ state.

Answers to problems on page 309

4. Some problems can be solved by following certain rules. If you correctly follow rules that lead to a certain solution, you are using (a)_____. If you follow rules that reduce the number of operations or allow you to take shortcuts in solving problems, you are using (b)_____.

5. When you use a combination of flexibility in thinking and reorganization of understanding to produce innovative ideas and solutions, you are engaging in (a)_____. If you begin with a problem and come up with many different solutions, you are using (b)_____ thinking, which is one definition of creative thinking. The opposite of this type of thinking is beginning with a problem and coming up with the one correct solution; this is called (c)_____ thinking.

6. A system of symbols that we use in thinking, solving problems, and communicating with others is called (a)_____. There are four rules for learning and using language. How we make the meaningful sounds used by a particular language is covered by the rules of (b)_____. Any English word can be broken down into basic sounds of consonants and vowels, which are called (c)_____. How we group phonemes into meaningful combinations of sounds and words is covered by the rules of (d)_____. The smallest meaningful combination of sounds in a language is called a (e)_____. How we combine words to form meaningful phrases and sentences is specified by the rules of (f)_____. How we know the meanings of words in various contexts is covered by the rules of (g)_____.

7. Chomsky explained that a sentence can be stated in different ways and yet have the same meaning. The actual wording of a sentence is called its (a)_____ structure. The underlying meaning of the sentence that is not spoken but is present in the mind of the listener is called the (b)_____ structure. To convert our ideas from surface structures into deep structures and from deep structures back into surface ones, we use (c)_____ rules.

8. In acquiring language, all children go through the same four stages but at different rates. Beginning at about the age of 6 months, a baby begins making one-syllable sounds, such as "bababa," which is called (a)_____. By about 1 year of age, a child forms (b)_____ words, which usually refer to what the child can see, hear, or feel. At about 2 years of age, a child makes (c)_____, which are strings of two words that express various actions ("Me play") or relationships ("Hit ball," "Milk gone"). At about 4 years of age, a child begins forming sentences, which range from three to eight words in length and indicate a growing knowledge of the rules of (d)_____.

9. One reason all children acquire a language in the same order is that there are genetically programmed physiological and neurological features in the brain and vocal apparatus. These are known as (a)_____ factors. Social interactions between the child and others, which offer opportunities for observation, imitation, and practice, are called (b)_____ factors.

Answers: *1. exemplar model; 2. (a) prototype, (b) prototype; 3. (a) problem solving, (b) initial, (c) operations, (d) goal; 4. (a) algorithms, (b) heuristics; 5. (a) creative thinking, (b) divergent, (c) convergent; 6. (a) language, (b) phonology, (c) phonemes, (d) morphology, (e) morpheme, (f) syntax or grammar, (g) semantics; 7. (a) surface, (b) deep, (c) transformational; 8. (a) babbling, (b) single, (c) two-word combinations, (d) grammar or syntax; 9. (a) innate, (b) environmental*

F. Reason, Thought & Language

Why is this fully dressed man standing in the ocean?

If you saw a nicely dressed older man standing in the ocean, you would naturally wonder what he was doing. To figure out this man's unusual behavior, you could use the personal computer inside your brain, which has a very powerful software program called reasoning (Sloman, 1996).

Reasoning, which often means thinking, is a mental process that involves using and applying knowledge to solve problems, make plans or decisions, and achieve goals.

To figure out why this normal-looking, fully dressed but shoeless man is standing in the ocean, you could use two different kinds of reasoning—deductive or inductive.

Deductive Reasoning

Since you rarely see a nicely dressed older man standing in the ocean, you might assume that he is drunk. The kind of reasoning that begins with a big assumption is called deductive reasoning.

Deductive reasoning begins with making a general assumption that you know or believe to be true and then drawing specific conclusions based on this assumption; in other words, reasoning from a general assumption to particulars.

Your general assumption is that only a drunk person would gleefully walk into the ocean dressed in a suit. This man is doing so. Therefore, he must be drunk. In its simplest form, deductive reasoning follows this formula: If you are given an assumption or statement as true, then there is only one correct conclusion to draw. This formula is often referred to as "If p (given statements), then q (conclusion)." For example:

Statements ("If p"): Only people who are over 21 years of age drink alcohol. That man is drinking alcohol. Conclusion ("Then q"): That man must be over 21 years of age.

One mistake people make in deductive reasoning is that they assume but do not always know if the basic statement or assumption (p) is true. If the basic statement is false—that is, drunkenness is not the only explanation for the man's behavior—then so are the conclusions. Another way to figure out why the man is standing in the ocean is to use inductive reasoning.

You can use either deductive or inductive reasoning to explain what this man is doing.

Inductive Reasoning

Instead of just assuming that this man is standing in the ocean because he's drunk, you walk over and ask some specific questions. After listening to this man's answers, you reach a different explanation for why he's standing in the ocean. The kind of reasoning that starts with specific facts or observations is called inductive reasoning.

Inductive reasoning begins with making particular observations that you then use to draw a broader conclusion; in other words, reasoning from particulars to a general conclusion.

For example, when questioned, the man answers "No" to all the following questions: Did you drink alcohol today? Do you have a job? Are you married? Do you do this often? Have you eaten today? Are you ill? Would you like me to take you home? After considering all these particulars, you reach a general conclusion: Either this man is suffering from Alzheimer's disease or he is lying.

Researchers use inductive reasoning when they use past experiences or observations to form a general hypothesis (Evans, 1993). For instance, researchers observed that when some students take exams they have rapid heart rate, sweaty palms, muscle tension, and increased blood pressure. Based on these particulars, researchers reached the general conclusion that these students have test anxiety.

One big mistake people make in inductive reasoning is jumping to a conclusion before knowing all the facts (Levy, 1997).

Depending on the situation, deductive and inductive reasoning are powerful mental tools provided you're aware of their pitfalls.

Many students found it very difficult to solve the problem given below.

Problem	Reasoning	Solution
If you drop one bullet off a table 3 feet high and fire another one straight across an empty football field, which hits the ground first?	Based on experience, it seems the dropped bullet will land first because it has only 3 feet to travel.	Based on physics, both bullets hit at the same time because downward velocity is independent of horizontal velocity.

On the basis of their experiences, students believed that a dropped bullet would surely hit the ground before one fired parallel to the ground. However, physics principles say that both bullets would hit the ground at the same time, which is completely opposite of students' experiences.

According to Alan Cromer (1993), who taught introductory science classes for 32 years, the formal reasoning needed to solve science problems is very difficult to teach because it often runs counter to our experiences or intuitions. Researchers suggest that our brains are equipped or prewired for reasoning to meet real-world challenges, such as surviving, finding food, and finding mates, rather than solving physics problems, which requires a special kind of abstract reasoning (Cosmides & Tooby, 1994). One reason students may have difficulty in science classes is that their personal experiences interfere with using abstract reasoning.

Because words are so much a part of our reasoning process, we need to know if and how much words can influence or bias our thinking.

Does language influence thinking?

Almost everyone has heard it said that the Inuit (Eskimos) are supposed to have dozens of words for snow because their survival depends on knowing how to travel and hunt in different kinds of snow. This particular observation was first made by amateur linguist Benjamin Whorf (1956), who noticed that languages differed in their vocabularies depending on how much emphasis they gave to different objects and events in their environment. For example, Whorf reasoned that because the Inuit (Eskimos) have many names for snow, they must be able to perceive many more kinds of snow than Americans, for whom snow conditions are less important. On the basis of these kinds of observations, Whorf formulated the theory of linguistic relativity.

The *theory of linguistic relativity* states that the differences among languages result in similar differences in how people think and perceive the world.

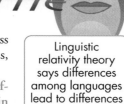

Linguistic relativity theory says differences among languages lead to differences in thinking.

For example, according to the theory of linguistic relativity, people whose language divides colors into only two categories (dark or black and bright or white) should perceive fewer colors. In comparison, people whose language divides colors into eleven categories (black, white, red, yellow, green, blue, brown, purple, pink, orange, gray) should perceive many more colors in their environment. However, researchers discovered that although languages differ in their number of color categories, all languages divide colors into the same basic categories. According to Whorf's theory of linguistic relativity, we would have expected people to perceive colors differently, depending on whether their culture has two or eleven names, but this is not what researchers found (Davies & Corbett, 1997). Thus, people in different cultures seem to perceive colors in similar ways even if they do not have names for different colors (Pinker, 1994).

Now, let's examine Whorf's famous claim that Inuits have more words for snow than do Americans.

Inuit Versus American Words for Snow

In his original article, Whorf (1940) estimated that Inuit (Eskimos) have about seven words for snow: *falling snow, snow on the ground, snow packed hard like ice, slushy snow, drifting snow, snow drift,* and *wind-driven flying snow,* while most Americans use a single word, *snow.* Whorf reasoned that the Inuit's larger vocabulary of snow-related words should make them think and perceive snow very differently than most Americans. Since Whorf's time, the number of snow words attributed to Inuit has ranged from two dozen to about 400 (Pullum, 1991).

We have about the same number of words for snow as you do!

Another linguist did a closer examination and found that Inuit and Americans both have about eight words for snow (English words for snow include *blizzard, sleet, hail, hardpack, powder, avalanche, flurry,* and *dusting*) (L. Martin, 1986). So, as it turns out, Whorf was wrong about how many words Inuit and Americans have for snow. One reason Whorf's story about differences in snow words lives on is that it's a great (but untrue) story (Pullum, 1991).

Although Whorf's story about snow words was untrue, the basic question still remains: Do differences in language mean that people think and perceive the world in different ways? One way to answer this question is to examine how individuals who are bilingual—that is, fluent in two languages—think about and perceive their world.

Thinking in Two Languages

Suppose your native language is Chinese but you are also fluent in English. You are asked to read descriptions of two different people in either Chinese or English and then to write impressions of these individuals. You read a Chinese and an English description of a type of person easily labeled in Chinese—*shi gu,* a person with strong family ties and much worldly experience—but not easily labeled in English. You read an English and a Chinese description of a type of person easily labeled in English—an *artistic* character, a person with artistic abilities who is very temperamental—but not easily labeled in Chinese. Researchers found that when subjects were reading and thinking in Chinese, they formed a clearer impression of the *shi gu* person; when reading and thinking in English, they formed a clearer impression of the artistic character (C. Hoffman et al., 1986). This is one of the few studies that supports the linguistic relativity theory and the idea that language influences thinking (Hardin & Banaji, 1993).

My native language is Chinese but I also speak English, so which do I think in?

Other prominent linguists argue that thoughts or ideas are not the same thing as words (Pinker, 1994, 1995). For example, sometimes we find it difficult to put a thought or idea into words, which would not be the case if every thought had a matching word. Also, how would new words be formed if thoughts depended on words that did not yet exist? For all these reasons, psychologists have generally found little or only weak support for Whorf's theory of linguistic relativity (Davies & Corbett, 1997; Pinker, 1994).

We know that words are important tools for reasoning, so what happens to an individual's thinking if he or she has great difficulty recognizing printed words? Our next topic is dyslexia.

G. Research Focus: Dyslexia

What Kind of Problem Is Dyslexia?

Was that word "bark" or "dark"?

This Research Focus deals with a real-world problem called dyslexia. *Dyslexia* refers to an unexpected difficulty learning to read despite intelligence, motivation, and education. Causes of dyslexia include genetic factors (defects in neural circuitry) and environmental factors (disadvantaged schooling) (Shaywitz et al., 2003).

An example of a dyslexic is 16-year-old Steve Goldberg (right photo), who is motivated and intelligent and has won numerous medals for science projects. However, he cannot read or spell

Why can't I spell the name of my high school?

the name of his high school, read phone numbers, or tell the difference between the words *dark* and *bark*. Dyslexia, which affects boys and girls equally, accounts for 80% of students identified as having learning disabilities.

Although dyslexics struggle with a wide range of long-lasting reading difficulties, many have normal or above-average IQ scores and some have very successful and creative careers: Tom Cruise, movie actor; Jay Leno, TV talk-show host; Agatha Christie, author of 100 mystery books; and Walt Disney, creator of animations (Gorman, 2003).

In studying dyslexia, researchers combined the cognitive approach —what happens when we read (not what you think)—with the physiological approach—what happens inside the brain.

What's Involved in Reading?

Earlier, we explained that children usually have no difficulty learning to speak because their brains come with innate or prewired areas for speaking (p. 316). Learning to read is entirely different from learning to speak because our brains have no innate areas dedicated specifically to reading. Instead, we must spend many years practicing how to read by learning to use three different brain areas that were originally designed to do something else. That's why reading is so difficult to learn (Eden, 2003).

Reading: 3 steps. Learning to read involves using 3 different brain areas, each with a different function (Gorman, 2003; Shaywitz et al., 2003).

1 Phoneme (sound) producer. The first step in reading is to vocalize the word, either silently or out loud. Vocalizing involves changing the letters of each word into their basic sounds, called phonemes. For example, reading the word CAT involves vocalizing or changing the letters C-A-T into the sounds KUH-A-TUH. The phoneme producer is located in brain area #1 (left inferior frontal gyrus) (below figure).

2 Word analyzer. After we vocalize or change a word's letters into sounds, the next step is to make a more complete analysis of a written word, such as pulling the word apart into syllables and linking syllables to their appropriate sounds. The word analyzer is located in brain area #2 (left parieto-temporal area). When first learning how to read, children rely heavily on using the phoneme producer and word analyzer.

CAT

3 Automatic detector. With practice, brain area #3 (left occipito-temporal area), called the automatic detector, becomes more active. The automatic detector takes on a bigger role by developing a permanent file of words so the reader can recognize words on sight, which makes reading a quick, automatic, and effortless process. Normally, these three processes work together almost simultaneously, like members of a team.

Why Can't Dyslexics Read?

One problem dyslexics have is that their phoneme producer is faulty so they cannot easily or quickly distinguish between phonemes *(ba, pa, la)*, and this results in problems distinguishing between like-sounding words *(bark, park, lark)*, which makes reading difficult (Tallal, 1995). Another problem is that dyslexics have defective neural wiring between the phoneme producer (#1) and the word analyzer (#2) and automatic detector (#3). As a result, they cannot easily or quickly recognize words or their meanings, which makes reading a slow and difficult process (Gorman, 2003; Shaywitz et al., 2003).

ba
pa
la

Can Training Help?

Because dyslexic children have deficits in the phoneme analyzer, researchers developed computer games to increase phoneme or sound processing, which is the first step in learning to read. After they played computer reading games, brain scans showed that dyslexic children actually had increased neural activity in brain area #1, phoneme producer, and brain area #2, word analyzer, and had also developed better reading skills (Temple et al., 2003). This study is one of the first to show that remedial reading games helped repair some of the faulty neural circuitry, which in turn resulted in dyslexic children developing better reading skills.

Reading problems should be identified early, ideally between the ages of 5 and 7, when brain circuitry and reading skills are being developed and can be most easily influenced (Lyon, 1999). Parents are advised to encourage their dyslexic children to play rhyming games as well as to have their children read aloud while gently correcting their children's mistakes. Rhyming and reading activities help dyslexic children develop correct associations between sounds and words (Gorman, 2003). According to Dr. Sally Shaywitz (2003), the most successful programs to help dyslexic children use the same core elements: practice with distinguishing between phonemes (playing computer games), building vocabularies, and increasing comprehension.

Differences in Thinking

How does your culture influence your thinking?

If you spend most of your time in one culture, you probably don't realize how much your culture influences your thinking (Hong et al., 2000). For example, look at the underwater scene (top right) and then look away and describe what you saw.

Differences. When American students looked at this underwater scene (top right) and then thought about what they saw, they usually began by describing the biggest, brightest, or most outstanding feature—in this case, focusing on the large fish and what it was doing (swimming to the right). In contrast, when Japanese students looked at the same underwater scene and then thought about what they saw, they usually began by describing the background and saying that the bottom was rocky (Had you noticed?) and the water was green (Had you noticed?). They usually discussed how the fish interact with the background, such as the big fish was swimming toward the seaweed. On average, Japanese subjects made 70% more statements about how the background looked than Americans and 100% more statements about the way the objects (fish) interact with the background.

Based on these kinds of findings, researchers concluded that Americans usually analyze each object separately, which is called

American students' descriptions of these drawings differed from Japanese students'.

analytical thinking, such as seeing a forest and focusing on the biggest or strangest trees. In comparison, Asian people (Japanese, Chinese, and Koreans) think more about the relationship between objects and backgrounds, which is called holistic thinking, such as seeing a forest and thinking about how the many different trees make up a beautiful forest (Norenzayan & Nisbett, 2000). Researchers suggest that differences in thinking between Americans and Asians—analytical versus holistic—come from differences in social and religious practices and languages (Nisbett, 2000).

Other cultural differences in thinking were revealed when American and Asian (Japanese, Chinese, and Korean) students were asked to watch an animated film that showed one fish swimming in front of other fish (bottom right). As you look at this figure, what do you think is happening? American students more often thought that the fish in front was a leader for the other fish. In comparison, Asian students more often thought that the fish in front was being chased by the other fish (Hong et al., 2000). Researchers concluded that cultural factors influence how you think much more than you realize.

Male–Female Differences

Do men and women think differently?

Just as culture influences how we think, so do gender differences. For about 20 years, linguist Deborah Tannen (1990, 1994) has been recording and analyzing the conversations of men and women. She found that men and women think and use language differently.

MEN AND WOMEN USE LANGUAGE DIFFERENTLY

■ Men more frequently use language to express ideas and solve problems. Women more frequently use language to share concerns, daily experiences, and ordinary thoughts.

■ Men use language to maintain their independence and position in their group. Women use language to create connections and develop feelings of intimacy.

■ Men prefer to attack problems, while women prefer to listen, give support, or be sympathetic.

Tannen concluded that neither the female nor the male use of language, which strongly reflects how they think, is necessarily better; the two styles are just different. She added, however, that men and women need to be aware of basic differences in thinking and using language so they can reduce hurt feelings, avoid misunderstandings, and work to improve communication between the sexes.

BRAINS PROCESS WORDS DIFFERENTLY

Not only do men and women use language differently, but their brains process language differently. Researchers used brain scans, in this case MRIs (pp. 70–71), to identify which areas of the brain were most active while men and women performed different language tasks. The MRI scan below left shows that, in women, activity during certain word-processing tasks occurred almost equally in both the right and left hemispheres (red and yellow areas indicate maximum activity). In contrast, the right MRI scan shows that, in men, activity during the same word-processing tasks occurred only in the left hemisphere (Shaywitz et al., 1995). This is the first study to report evidence that men's brains process language differently than do women's brains.

Researchers concluded that the significant neurological differences shown in the MRIs may be the basis for behavioral differences between how men and women process words, which reflects their

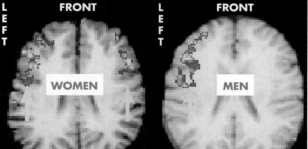

MRI scans showed that women use right and left hemispheres to process language; men use only left.

thinking (Rugg, 1995). However, differences in brain functioning between men and women do not indicate that one brain is better than another; only that they function differently (Halpern, 2003).

Next, we'll discuss the interesting question of whether animals have language and if my dog really understands what I say.

I. Application: Do Animals Have Language?

What does my dog understand?

Like most pet owners, I talk to my dog and he usually behaves as if he understands what I say. For example, my dog Bear (photo below) behaves as if he understands "get your toy," "go for walk," "time to eat," and "watch television." The obvious question is: Has Bear learned a language? The answer to this question hinges on the difference between communication and language. As do many animals, Bear has the ability to communicate.

Communication is the ability to use sounds, smells, or gestures to exchange information.

But language is much more than just communication.

Language is a special form of communication in which an individual learns complex rules for using words or gestures to generate and understand an endless number of meaningful sentences.

Although Bear can communicate—that is, understand my commands and act accordingly—he, like most animals, shows no evidence of meeting the four criteria for having real language.

Dogs communicate but don't have a language.

1 Language, which is a special form of communication, involves *learning a set of abstract symbols* (whether words for spoken language or hand signs for sign language).

2 Language involves *using abstract symbols* (words or signs) to express thoughts or indicate objects and events that may or may not be present.

3 Language involves *learning complex rules of grammar* for forming words into meaningful phrases and sentences.

4 Language involves using the rules of grammar to *generate an endless number of meaningful sentences*.

Because some animals, such as dolphins and pygmy chimps, show an amazing ability to communicate, researchers are debating whether animals can satisfy all four criteria for language (Begley, 1998a; Savage-Rumbaugh & Lewin, 1994). We'll examine how close several animals come to satisfying the four criteria.

Do dolphins use language?

Dolphins are considered very intelligent, not only because of their ability to learn but also because in proportion to the size of their bodies, dolphins' brains are the largest of nonhuman mammals (smaller than human brains but larger than that of great apes) (Tyack, 2000). Because dolphins have relatively large brains, researchers are interested in how well they communicate.

In the wild, dolphins use two kinds of sounds for communication: clicks, which they use to probe the sea and "see" their environment, and whistles, which they use in dolphin-to-dolphin communication, probably to express emotional states and identify the animal to the group (L. Herman, 1999).

In testing the ability of dolphins to communicate, psychologist Louis Herman (1999) has been training dolphins to respond to hand signals or whistles. He has taught two dolphins to respond to approximately 50 such signals.

For example, in the top right photo, Herman is raising his hands, which is part of a signal for "person over," which means "jump over the person in the pool." The bottom right photo shows the dolphin carrying out the command by jumping over the person and not the surfboard.

Herman found that dolphins can understand a variety of hand signals and perform behaviors in sequence. For example, the hand signal combination "basket, right, Frisbee, fetch" means "Go to the Frisbee on the right and take it to the basket."

Hand signals in top photo tell dolphin to "jump over person," which it does in bottom photo.

More recently, Herman combined "words" by using gestures or whistles in basic "sentences," such as "ball fetch surface hoop." The two dolphins responded correctly to both familiar and novel "sentences" about 85% of the time. Herman concluded that the ability of these two dolphins to pass tests of language comprehension (understanding "sentences"), which indicates an understanding of grammar or syntax, means that dolphins have a relatively sophisticated ability to use language (Herman, 1999). Herman's next step is to determine if dolphins use sounds to communicate information to each other.

However, despite Herman's impressive findings, some scientists remain skeptical. For example, David Kastak, a researcher of animal cognition, said, "What dolphins do may turn out to be a lot more complex than what we thought originally, but do they have what we would call language? No. They are not animals using nouns and verbs" (Mastro, 1999, p. E4).

Although dolphins understand a variety of signals, perform behaviors in sequence, form concepts, and even understand "sentences," they show little evidence of using abstract symbols and applying rules of grammar to generate meaningful sentences to communicate information to other dolphins. It is these criteria that distinguish the ability to use language from the ability to communicate with signs, sounds, or gestures.

Next, let's turn to the greater apes, which in terms of evolution are the animals closest to humans.

Gorilla and Chimpanzee

What does a gorilla know?

Gorillas and chimpanzees have relatively large and well-developed brains. A gorilla's brain weighs about 500 grams, a chimpanzee's about 400 grams, and a human's about 1,350 grams. However, because gorillas and chimpanzees lack the vocal apparatus necessary for making speech sounds, researchers have taught them other forms of language, such as American Sign Language (P. E. Ross, 1991).

Shown on the right is researcher Francine Patterson using sign language to communicate with Koko the gorilla, who has a vocabulary of about 800 signs. Similarly, Beatrice and Allen Gardner (1975) taught sign language to a chimpanzee named Washoe, who after four years of training had learned about 160 signs. The finding that gorillas and chimps can learn sign language raised the question of whether they use language in the same way as humans.

Francine Patterson taught Koko the gorilla a vocabulary of about 800 hand signs.

Psychologist Herbert Terrace (1981) analyzed videotapes of chimps using sign language with their trainers. He was particularly interested in the videotapes of a chimp named Nim, who has learned more than 125 signs, such as "give orange me." After observing over 20,000 of Nim's signs on videotape, Terrace concluded that Nim was using signs more as tools to obtain things than as abstract symbols or words and that Nim never learned to form combinations of more than a few words. Perhaps the most devastating criticism was that Nim had primarily learned to imitate or respond to cues from human teachers rather than learning and using rules of grammar to initiate or produce new sentences.

As a result of criticisms by Terrace and others, research monies to study language in animals mostly disappeared in the 1980s (Savage-Rumbaugh & Lewin, 1994). However, in the late 1980s, new findings on bonobos again raised the question of language in animals.

Bonobo Chimp: Star Pupil

Is this the first real sign of language?

The best evidence for language in animals comes from the work of psychologist Sue Savage-Rumbaugh. She reported that Kanzi, a bonobo (commonly called a pygmy chimp), has remarkable language skills that surpass previous accomplishments of common chimps (Savage-Rumbaugh, 1991; Savage-Rumbaugh & Lewin, 1994).

Instead of using sign language, Kanzi "speaks" by touching one of 256 symbols on a board (top right photo), each of which stands for a word. For example, Kanzi (bottom right photo) might signal "Want a drink" by touching the symbol for "drink" or signal "Want to play" by touching in sequence two symbols for "hiding" and "play biting."

By the time Kanzi was 6 years old, he had a vocabulary of 90 symbols; at age 12, he knew about 190 symbols but used about 128 regularly. Even more surprising, Kanzi understands about 200 spoken English words, something that common chimps have failed to master.

Perhaps Kanzi's greatest accomplishment is his knowledge of word order. Psychologists tested the ability of Kanzi to respond to 600 spoken English commands that he had not previously encountered, such as "Put the melon in the potty." Savage-Rumbaugh suggests that Kanzi, now 17 years old, has an ability to use abstract symbols (keyboard) and a kind of primitive grammar (word order) for combining symbols that equals the language ability of a 2-year-old child (Savage-Rumbaugh, 1998). Although chimps can learn more than 400 symbols and even string several symbols together, their language ability is nowhere near that of a high school student who has a vocabulary of 60,000 words and can string these words together into an endless number of meaningful sentences, often about abstract concepts (love, patriotism, courage, honor) (Hauser, 2003).

Why did humans develop a complex language while chimps did not? Researchers now believe that the development of human language was triggered by a major genetic change (R. Klein, 2002). This conclusion is based on a new finding: the discovery of the first human gene (FOXP2) involved specifically in language. Individuals without this "language" gene are normal in other ways but not in communication; they have specific difficulties pronouncing words and speaking grammatically (N. Wade, 2003b). Although ancient humans shared this gene with other animals, researchers discovered that there was an important change in this gene's structure at about the same time that humans and chimps parted evolutionary company.

Some researchers point to a change in the structure of this "language" gene (FOXP2) as the reason that early humans were able to gradually develop their primitive sounds and clicks into the complex, fluent language that we speak today (Paabo, 2003).

BLACKBERRIES	BUTTER	VELVET PLANT
SHOT	STRING	PINE CONE

Examples of symbols and their meanings

Kanzi has an amazing ability to use and respond to either symbols or English words.

Summary Test

A. FORMING CONCEPTS

1. There are two theories of how you have formed your concept of a dog and how you form concepts generally. If you form a concept of an object, event, or characteristic by making a list of the properties that define it, you are using the (a)_____ model. If you form a concept by constructing an idea of the ideal object and then seeing whether a new object matches that idea, you are using (b)_____ theory.

2. A concept is a way to group objects, events, or characteristics on the basis of some common property they all share. Concepts perform two important functions: They allow us to (a)_____ objects, and thus better organize and store information in memory, and to identify things without (b) _____.

B. SOLVING PROBLEMS

3. The process of searching for some rule, plan, or strategy that results in reaching a certain goal that is currently out of reach is called (a)_____. We usually go through three states in solving problems: (b)_____, _____, and _____.

4. We win at games by following rules. If we correctly follow a set of rules that lead to a solution, these rules are called (a)_____. As you gain experience with solving problems, you may use rules of thumb that reduce the number of operations or allow you to take shortcuts in solving problems; these shortcuts are called (b)_____. In making everyday decisions, you rely on information that is more prominent or easily recalled and overlook other information that is available but less prominent or notable; this is an example of using the (c)_____ heuristic.

5. By studying how people eventually solve problems, psychologists have discovered a number of useful strategies, including changing our (a)_____. This often involves breaking out of a pattern called (b)_____, in which we cannot see an object as having a function different from its usual one.

6. The sudden grasp of a solution after many incorrect attempts is called (a)_____. Another kind of thinking that is useful in solving problems is to find (b)_____, which are similarities between new situations and familiar situations. Still another useful strategy for solving problems is to break the problem down into a number of (c)_____, which, when completed in order, will result in a solution.

C. THINKING CREATIVELY

7. A combination of flexibility in thinking and reorganization of understanding to produce innovative ideas and solutions is referred to as (a)_____. Psychologists distinguish between two different kinds of thinking. If you begin with a problem and come up with the one correct solution, it is called (b)_____. If you begin with a problem and come up with many different solutions, it is called (c)_____, which is another definition of creative thinking.

D. LANGUAGE: BASIC RULES

8. Our most impressive skill is thought to be a special form of communication in which an individual learns complex rules to manipulate symbols (words or gestures) and so generates an endless number of meaningful sentences; this form of communication is called _____.

9. All of the 6,800 known languages share four basic language rules, which are normally learned during childhood. The first language rule governs (a)_____, which specifies how we make meaningful sounds that are used by a particular language. The second language rule governs (b)_____, which specifies how we group phonemes into meaningful combinations of sounds and words. The third language rule governs (c)_____, which specifies how we combine words to form meaningful phrases and sentences. The fourth language rule governs (d)_____, which specifies the meanings of words in various contexts.

10. The linguist Noam Chomsky distinguished between how a sentence is worded, which he called the (a)_____ structure, and the meaning of the sentence, which he called the (b)_____ structure. Procedures for converting our ideas from surface structures into deep structures and from deep structures back into surface ones are called (c)_____.

E. ACQUIRING LANGUAGE

11. Children around the world acquire language in the same four stages that are associated with growth and development of the (a)_____. In the first stage, generally at about the age of 6 months, the infant makes one-syllable sounds; this is called (b)_____. By about 1 year of age, a child forms (c)_____, which usually refer to what the child can see, hear, or feel. At about 2 years of age, a child makes (d)_____ to express various actions or relationships. At about 4 years of age, a child is forming sentences, which range from three to eight words in length and indicate a growing knowledge of the (e)_____.

12. A child's beginning sentences differ from adult sentences. A child's speech is called (a)_____ because it omits articles, prepositions, and parts of verbs. In learning the rules for combining nouns, verbs, and adjectives into meaningful sentences, children often apply a grammatical rule to cases where it should not be used. This type of error is called (b)_____. Although all children pass through these stages in the same order, they may go through them at different ages and speeds.

13. Children are able to acquire a language with so little formal training because of genetically programmed physiological and neurological features in the brain and vocal apparatus; these features are called (a)_____ factors. One innate factor is the period of time from infancy to adolescence when language is easier to learn, called the (b)_____. Children acquire the sounds and rules of a particular language because of their interactions with their surroundings; these interactions are called (c)_____ factors. The approach that emphasizes observation, exploration, and imitation in language acquisition is (d)_____.

F. REASON, THOUGHT & LANGUAGE

14. The process by which we use and apply knowledge to achieve certain goals that involve solving problems or making decisions is called (a)_____. This process has two different forms: If you begin with a general assumption and draw specific conclusions, you are using (b)_____ reasoning; if you begin with specific observations and then draw a general conclusion, you are using (c)_____ reasoning.

15. Whorf has suggested that language determines or influences the way people think and that people with different languages think and perceive their world differently. This is called the theory of _____. There is only weak support for Whorf's theory.

G. RESEARCH FOCUS: DYSLEXIA

16. About 80% of learning disabilities is accounted for by (a)_____, which is an unexpected difficulty in reading despite intelligence, motivation, and education. The three steps in reading involve three different brain areas, each with a different function: Brain area #1 is called the (b)_____, brain area #2 is called the (c)_____, and brain area #3 is called the (d)_____. Individuals with dyslexia have a problem with changing letters into sounds or (e)_____ and have faulty (f)_____ connections between brain area #1 and brain areas #2 and #3.

H. CULTURAL DIVERSITY: INFLUENCES ON THINKING

17. Men tend to use language to express ideas, maintain their position in the group, and solve (a)_____, while women use language more to share concerns and daily experiences and develop feelings of (b)_____.

18. MRI scans of the brain have shown that women process some words equally in both (a)_____, while men process words only in the (b)_____ hemisphere.

I. APPLICATION: DO ANIMALS HAVE LANGUAGE?

19. Many animals have the ability to use sounds, smells, or gestures to exchange information; this is the ability to (a)_____. Another question is whether animals can communicate with abstract symbols; this is called (b)_____. To decide that an animal truly uses language, researchers must show that the animal has learned complex rules of (c)_____ to manipulate symbols (words or gestures) and so generate an endless number of meaningful sentences. The best evidence for language in animals is the (d)_____, who has matched the language ability of a 2-year-old child.

Answers: 1. (a) exemplar, (b) prototype; 2. (a) categorize, (b) relearning; 3. (a) problem solving, (b) initial state, operations state, goal state; 4. (a) algorithms, (b) heuristics, (c) availability; 5. (a) mental set, (b) functional fixedness; 6. (a) insight, (b) analogies, (c) subgoals; 7. (a) creative thinking, (b) convergent thinking, (c) divergent thinking; 8. language; 9. (a) phonology, (b) morphology, (c) syntax or grammar, (d) semantics; 10. (a) surface, (b) deep, (c) transformational rules; 11. (a) brain, (b) babbling, (c) single words, (d) two-word combinations, (e) rules of grammar; 12. (a) telegraphic, (b) overgeneralization; 13. (a) innate, (b) critical language period, (c) environmental, (d) social cognitive learning; 14. (a) reasoning, (b) deductive, (c) inductive; 15. linguistic relativity; 16. (a) dyslexia, (b) phoneme producer, (c) word analyzer, (d) automatic detector, (e) phonemes, (f) neural or brain; 17. (a) problems, (b) intimacy; 18. (a) hemispheres, (b) left; 19. (a) communicate, (b) language, (c) grammar, (d) bonobo (pygmy chimp)

Critical Thinking

WHY DO PARENTS SPEAK LOUDLY AND SLOWLY?

by Robert Lee Hotz

Questions

1. What is the term for and what is the purpose of the "baby talk" that parents or caregivers use with their infants?

2. What would happen if parents or caregivers never spoke to their children?

3. Why did the researchers study English, Russian, and Swedish?

The singsong crooning that every adult instinctively adopts for conversation with a newborn baby is more than patronizing gibberish passing between the generations. It is a universal teaching mechanism rooted in the biology of language and the developing human brain, say neuroscientists Patricia Kuhl and her colleagues at the University of Washington in Seattle, who studied how native speakers of English, Swedish, and Russian talk to infants.

Linguists call the special tone adults reserve for speech with infants "parentese," and the new research indicates it is the same in every culture around the world.

To examine the role of parentese, Kuhl and her colleagues in Russia and Sweden investigated differences in how American, Swedish, and Russian mothers speak to their infants and to other adults. The three languages were chosen because each has a significantly different number of vowel sounds. Russian has five vowel sounds, English nine, and Swedish 16.

The researchers recorded 10 women from each of the three countries talking for 20 minutes to their babies, who

ranged in age from 2 to 5 months. Then they recorded the same women talking to other adults. The mothers were told to talk naturally, but were given a list of words containing three common vowel sounds and instructed to work them into their conversations.

For those speaking English, the target words were "bead" for its "ee" vowel sound, "pot" for its "ah" sound, and "boot" for its "oo" sound. Similar words were chosen from Russian and Swedish.

The researchers then used a spectrograph to analyze more than 2,300 instances of how the target words were used in the conversations and discovered that, in all three language groups, the speech directed at infants was stretched out to emphasize the vowel sounds, in contrast to the more normal tone used with adults.

The researchers concluded that the exaggerated speech allowed the mothers to expand the sounds of the vowels so they would be more distinct from each other. It also appears to allow the mothers to produce a greater variety of vowel pronunciations without overlapping other vowel sounds. (Source: *Los Angeles Times,* September 18, 1997)

4. Why did researchers compare how mothers talked to infants and to other adults?

5. What might happen if mothers or caregivers spoke to infants the same way they spoke to adults?

6. How does the mothers speaking parentese fit in with the critical period for language?

Try InfoTrac to search for terms: baby talk; language acquisition.

SUGGESTED ANSWERS

1. "Baby talk" is called parentese (motherese). The purpose of parentese is to teach infants the particular sounds or phonetic building blocks that will be used to form and speak words.
2. For her first 13 years, Genie was punished for making sounds and was never spoken to by her parents. As a result, Genie could not speak a single word and, even with training, developed language skills of only a 2- to 3-year-old child. (Discussion is on page 316.)
3. Researchers chose three different languages because each of these languages had a different number of vowel sounds and researchers wanted to know if mothers would exaggerate the vowel sounds particular to their different languages.
4. Researchers compared how mothers spoke to infants versus adults to see if they used parentese only with infants. It turned out that

mothers exaggerated vowel sounds when speaking to their babies but did not when speaking to other adults.
5. If mothers spoke the same to infants and adults, then infants would not hear the slow, exaggerated vowel sounds (parentese) and would have difficulty learning the particular sounds that make up the particular language of their parents.
6. The critical period says that language is easiest to learn between infancy and adolescence. The use of parentese at the beginning of the critical period gives the infant a great start in developing language and successfully going through the four stages of language (babbling, one word, two-word combinations, sentences).

Links to Learning

LEARNING ACTIVITIES

- *POWERSTUDY CD-ROM 2.0*
  by Tom Doyle and Rod Plotnik
  Check out the "Thought & Language" Module (disk 2) on PowerStudy and:

  - Test your knowledge using an interactive version of the Summary Test on pages 324 and 325. Also access related quizzes—true/false, multiple choice, and matching.
  - Explore an interactive version of the Critical Thinking exercise "Why Do Parents Speak Loudly and Slowly?" on page 326.
  - You will also find key terms, a chapter outline including a chapter abstract, and a list of hotlinked Web sites that correlate to this module.

- *SELF-STUDY ASSESSMENT*
  Want help studying? For your customized Study Plan go to **http://psychology.wadsworth.com/plotnik7e/**. This program will automatically generate pretests and posttests to help you determine what concepts you have mastered and what concepts you still need work on.

WebTUTOR
- *STUDY GUIDE and WEBTUTOR*
  Check the corresponding module in your Study Guide for effective student tips and help learning the material presented.

- *INFOTRAC COLLEGE EDITION ONLINE LIBRARY*
  To find interesting and relevant articles go to **http://www.infotrac-college.com**, use your password, and then type in search terms such as the ones listed below.

  Dyslexia   Inductive reasoning
  Morphology   Savants

STUDY QUESTIONS

Use InfoTrac to search for topics mentioned in the main heads below (e.g., problem solving, creative thinking, language acquisition).

*A. **Forming Concepts**—Why is it difficult to explain to your younger sister or brother that a whale is a mammal and not a fish? (**Suggested answer page 628**)

B. **Solving Problems**—Why is it easier to win at checkers the longer you have been playing?

C. **Thinking Creatively**—How would you teach people to think more creatively?

D. **Language: Basic Rules**—To develop a secret code for sending computer messages across a network, which language rule should you break?

E. **Acquiring Language**—Why might students in college have more difficulty learning a foreign language than students in grade school?

*F. **Reason, Thought & Language**—What problems might result when heads of government speak through translators? (**Suggested answer page 628**)

G. **Research Focus: Dyslexia**—Why does dyslexia cause difficulties with reading but not with engineering and inventive abilities?

*H. **Cultural Diversity: Influences on Thinking**—What kinds of social problems can arise from finding differences between male and female brains? (**Suggested answer page 628**)

I. **Application: Do Animals Have Language?**—When a parrot speaks perfect English and understands dozens of commands, can we conclude it is using language?

*These questions are answered in Appendix B.

Module 15: Motivation

Introduction

Motivation

Why would a paraplegic climb a mountain?

On a cool September morning, two men began to climb a nearly vertical slope rising over 2,200 feet from the floor of Yosemite National Park. Because of the slope's crumbly granite, fewer than 30 people had completed this particular route up Half Dome, Yosemite's well-known landmark. What made this particular climb very difficult and dangerous was that one of the men, Mark Wellman, is a paraplegic.

Some years ago, on a different climb, Mark fell 50 feet into a crevice, hurt his back, and was paralyzed from the waist down. Mark now climbs with his friend Mike Corbett, who takes the lead and sets the supports. Because Mark's legs are paralyzed, he climbs by using the supports to pull himself up inch by inch.

Mark figured that by doing the equivalent of 5,000 pull-ups, each of which would raise him about 6 inches, he could climb the 2,200 feet in seven days. By the end of day seven, however, Mark and Mike were only a little more than halfway up the slope and had to sleep by hanging in sleeping bags anchored to the sheer granite wall.

By day ten, Mark was becoming exhausted as his arms strained to raise his body's weight up the vertical face (left photo). By day 12, the men were almost out of food and water. Finally, on day 13, six days later than planned, Mark pulled himself up the last 6 inches and over the top of Half Dome. When Mark was asked later why he still climbed and risked further injury, he said, "Everyone has their own goals. . . . Never underestimate a person with a disability" (adapted from the *Los Angeles Times*, September 19, 1991, p. A-3).

Reporters who questioned Mark about why he risked his life to climb were really asking about his motivation.

Motivation refers to the various physiological and psychological factors that cause us to act in a specific way at a particular time.

When you are motivated, you usually show three characteristics:

1. You are *energized* to do or engage in some activity.
2. You *direct* your energies toward reaching a specific goal.
3. You have differing *intensities* of feelings about reaching that goal.

We can observe these three characteristics in Mark's behavior:

1. He was energized to perform the equivalent of 5,000 pull-ups during his 13-day climb.
2. He directed his energy toward climbing a particular slope that fewer than 30 other climbers had completed.
3. He felt so intensely about reaching that goal that even when totally exhausted, he still persisted in reaching his goal, the top of Half Dome.

We'll discuss several kinds of motivating forces, including those involved in eating and drinking, sexual behavior, achievement, underachievement, failure, and, of course, climbing mountains.

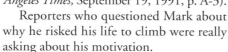

Mark Wellman, a paraplegic, did the equivalent of 5,000 pull-ups to climb the face of Half Dome.

Achievement

Why did friends call him a "White boy"?

Victor remembers being in the seventh grade when some of his Black buddies called him a "White boy" because they thought he was studying too hard. "You can't be cool if you're smart," says Victor, who was Mission Bay High's student body president, had a 3.7 (A–) grade point average, and planned to attend the University of Southern California in the fall (adapted from the *San Diego Union-Tribune,* June 17, 1994).

Victor (photo below) grew up with an obstacle that goes largely unnoticed and is rarely discussed in public: pressure from students in the same racial or ethnic group not to succeed in the classroom. Faced with this negative peer pressure, some minority students (principally Latino, African American, and Native American teenage boys) stop studying, don't do homework, avoid answering questions in class, join gangs, and even drop out of school.

Educators believe that the high dropout rates for some minorities along with peer pressure not to succeed in school result, in part, from a cultural bias against appearing to be too smart or intellectual (McWhorter, 2000). How Victor overcame this negative peer pressure and did succeed will be discussed later in this module.

Victor was proud of his A– average, but some of his peers believed that being smart wasn't cool.

What's Coming

We'll look at four general theories that psychologists use to explain motivation, discuss the differences between social and biological needs, and then focus on specific examples, such as hunger, sexual behavior, and achievement. We'll examine why some people are achievers and others are underachievers. We'll discuss why people become overweight and why dieting is so difficult. We'll look at two serious eating disorders that result more from psychological than from biological factors.

We'll begin with four general theories that psychologists use to explain motivation.

A. Theories of Motivation

Why does Mark climb?

For 13 days, sightseers on the Yosemite valley floor watched Mark pull himself up the granite face of Half Dome. Many asked, "Why is he doing that?" The same can be asked of you: Why are you willing to work hard for four to six years to get a college degree? These are questions about motivation. We'll discuss four general theories of motivation—the instinct, incentive, and cognitive theories, and the newest, the brain's reward/pleasure center theory.

Instinct

Is he driven by instincts?

In the early 1900s, William McDougall (1908) claimed that humans were motivated by a variety of instincts.

Instincts are innate tendencies or biological forces that determine behavior.

McDougall listed about half a dozen instincts, such as combat, curiosity, sympathy, and self-assertion. He might have explained Mark's motivation to climb as arising from instincts involving curiosity and self-assertion. But attributing mountain climbing to an instinct is more like labeling than explaining the underlying motivation. At one point, psychologists had proposed over 6,000 instincts to explain every kind of human motivation. Although instincts proved useless in explaining human motivation, they proved useful in explaining animal behaviors because animal researchers redefined instincts as fixed action patterns (FitzGerald, 1993).

A *fixed action pattern* is an innate biological force that predisposes an organism to behave in a fixed way in the presence of a specific environmental condition.

Animals have innate biological tendencies called instincts.

For example, the above photo shows how a baboon is innately predisposed to behave in a fixed aggressive pattern—opens mouth, stares, rises on hind feet—in the face of a specific stimulus, a threatening cheetah. Ethologists, researchers who study animal behaviors, reported that fixed action patterns help animals adapt to their natural environments. For example, in Module 10 (p. 228) we explained how birds that can walk immediately after birth become attached to, or imprinted on, the first moving object (animal, human, or basketball) that the baby bird encounters. Once imprinted, the bird continues to interact with that bird or object as if it were its parent. Imprinting is an example of a fixed action pattern that is extremely useful in helping young animals survive (Lorenz, 1952).

Instincts represented an early but failed attempt to explain human motivation. We'll jump from the early 1900s to the early 2000s and examine current research that sheds a new light on human motivation.

Brain: Reward/Pleasure Center

What's his reward for climbing?

During his 13 days climbing Half Dome, Mark was motivated to satisfy various biological needs, such as eating and drinking. The human body is set up genetically to send biological signals to the brain, which is genetically wired to interpret the body's biological signals and thus motivate the person to eat or drink by causing feelings of hunger or thirst (Kalat, 2004). Later we'll describe the body's biological signals and how the brain interprets these signals to produce feelings of hunger or fullness.

One reason you are motivated to eat is that chewing on a favorite food can be so pleasurable. Only recently have researchers discovered that this "eating" pleasure comes from the brain's reward/pleasure center (Dackis & O'Brien, 2001; Holroyd & Coles, 2002).

Food triggers reward center.

The *reward/pleasure center* includes several areas of the brain, such as the nucleus accumbens and the ventral tegmental area, and involves several neurotransmitters, especially dopamine. These components make up a neural circuit that produces rewarding and pleasurable feelings.

Researchers discovered the brain's reward/pleasure center (figure below) by using newly developed brain scans (fMRI; p. 70) that can identify neural activity in the living brain. For example, researchers found that cocaine produced its pleasurable feelings by activating two brain areas, nucleus accumbens and ventral tegmental area, that are involved in the brain's reward/pleasure center (Dackis & O'Brien, 2001). Using this same technique, researchers found that a number of other activities also triggered the brain's reward/pleasure center. Thus, animals are motivated to continually press a lever to obtain brain stimulation and people are motivated to eat, develop romantic attachments, engage in sex, gamble, use recreational drugs, look at photos of attractive individuals, and listen to "spine-chilling" music because, as brain scans (fMRIs) have shown, all these behaviors activate the brain's reward/pleasure center (Aharon et al., 2001; Bartels, 2002;

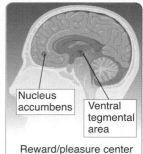

Nucleus accumbens

Ventral tegmental area

Reward/pleasure center

Begley, 2001; Blood & Zatorre, 2001; Breiter et al., 2001; Shizgal & Arvanitogiannis, 2003). This means that many behaviors, such as eating, developing romantic attachments, engaging in sex, gambling, using recreational drugs, and listening to great music, are rewarded and encouraged because they activate the brain's reward/pleasure center.

Why does Mark climb? He may climb because this behavior activates the brain's reward/pleasure center. He may also be motivated to climb by a variety of psychological factors, such as gaining various incentives or fulfilling his expectations, which we'll examine next.

Incentives

Why do you study? The issue of motivation becomes very personal when we ask you to explain why you sacrificed so much and worked so hard to get into college. Now that you're in college, what is motivating you to study for all those exams and write all those papers? One answer is that you are motivated to get a college degree because it is a very big incentive (Petri & Govern, 2004).

The degree was worth the hard work!

*Incentive*s are goals that can be either objects or thoughts that we learn to value and that we are motivated to obtain.

Incentives have two common features. First, they can be either thoughts ("I want to get a degree") or objects (money, clothes) that we LEARN to value. For example, when you were 5 years old, you had not yet learned the value of a good education. Second, the value of incentives can change over time. A pizza is not an incentive at 7 A.M., but it may be an important incentive at 7 P.M. Many of our behaviors are motivated by a variety of incentives, including grades, praise, money, clothes, or academic degrees. You can think of incentives as *pulling* us or motivating us to obtain them.

Would you like a dessert? Incentives explain why there's always room for dessert when we say we are full or why we continue to buy more clothes even when our closets are full. Even though our immediate needs seem to be met ("I'm full" or "I have enough clothes"), highly valued incentives, such as desired foods or great clothes, have the power to motivate or pull us toward obtaining them. Incentives also explain why people often buy things on impulse.

Why does Mark climb? Another reason Mark is motivated to climb probably involves obtaining incentives, such as recognition by national media, speaking invitations, and money ($100,000) from corporate sponsors that he donates to help others with disabilities. However, other equally powerful reasons for Mark's climbing probably involve cognitive factors (Little, 1999).

Cognitive Factors

Why do people run marathons? Thousands of people train for months to run grueling 26-mile-long marathons, in which only the top two or three receive any prize money and the rest receive only T-shirts. What motivates people to endure such agony? The answer can be traced to the early 1960s, when psychologists began applying cognitive concepts to explain human motivation (Bandura, 1986; deCharms, 1980; Deci & Ryan, 1985; Weiner, 1991). These cognitive researchers said that one reason people run marathons, usually for no reward other than a T-shirt, has to do with the difference between extrinsic and intrinsic motivation.

Extrinsic motivation involves engaging in certain activities or behaviors that either reduce biological needs or help us obtain incentives or external rewards.

Intrinsic motivation involves engaging in certain activities or behaviors because the behaviors themselves are personally rewarding or because engaging in these activities fulfills our beliefs or expectations.

Intrinsic motivation explains that people volunteer their services, spend hours on hobbies, run marathons, or work on personal projects because these activities are personally rewarding, fulfilling, or challenging. Intrinsic motivation emphasizes that we are motivated to engage in many behaviors because of our own personal beliefs, expectations, or goals, rather than external incentives (Petri & Govern, 2004).

Why does Mark climb? According to cognitive theory's concept of intrinsic motivation, another reason Mark is motivated to engage in a dangerous and almost impossible climb is that climbing itself is very rewarding to Mark. Mark was an avid climber before he lost the use of his legs, so he continues to climb because it helps him meet his own personal goals and expectations, which are powerful motivators. As Mark said, "Everyone has their own goals."

I need to prove to myself that I can do it!

Explaining Human Motivation

Why did they do that? Why did you pay $65 for a concert ticket? Why did you run a marathon? Why did you study so much for that test? How could you eat a whole pizza? Why did you drink so much last night?

The answers to these questions about human behaviors involve three different factors. You may be motivated because certain behaviors trigger the brain's reward/pleasure center. You may be motivated to obtain incentives, which you have learned to value. You may be motivated by cognitive or intrinsic factors, such as wanting to satisfy your personal beliefs, reach certain goals, or fulfill your expectations. Human motivation is so difficult to explain because it may involve all three of these factors. In addition, you can be motivated by emotional factors (anger, fear, happiness) or personality factors (outgoing, shy, uninhibited), which we'll discuss in Modules 16, 19, and 20.

One of the main functions of emotions is to satisfy a number of biological and social needs, which we'll examine next.

B. Biological & Social Needs

How many needs do you have?

The most popular daytime television programs are the soap operas, which dramatize a whole range of human needs—the good, the bad, the ugly, and the dumb. As the soap opera characters try to satisfy their needs, they get into endless difficulties. We'll discuss some of the more common biological and social needs.

Biological Needs

What are they doing?

It's pretty obvious that the man and his pet pig are about to satisfy their hunger, a basic biological need. *Biological needs* are physiological requirements that are critical to our survival and physical well-being.

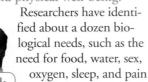
Satisfying biological needs

Researchers have identified about a dozen biological needs, such as the need for food, water, sex, oxygen, sleep, and pain avoidance, all of which help to keep our bodies functioning at their best and thus help us survive (Petri & Govern, 2004).

When genes are defective. Perhaps because biological drives are critical for survival, their automatic regulation is built into a newborn's brain. In rare cases, individuals are born with defective genes that cause biological needs to run amok. For example, some children are born with defective "eating" genes that result in never feeling full but being constantly hungry and obsessed with food and eating (Ledbetter, 2002). Children with this genetic problem (the Prader-Willi syndrome affects the hypothalamus) can never be left alone with food because they will eat everything in sight.

Another kind of rare genetic problem destroys the ability to sleep. As individuals with this genetic defect (fatal familial insomnia) reach their 50s, they find that one day they cannot sleep through the night and from then on they never sleep again. Over a period of several months, these individuals lose the ability to walk, speak, and think. Finally, their sleepless body begins to shut down its functions, resulting in coma and death (Max, 2001). These two examples show that the proper regulation of biological needs is critical for healthy physiological functioning and survival.

When psychological factors interfere. Besides genetic defects, psychological factors can also interfere with the regulation of biological needs. For example, some individuals develop the rare eating disorder anorexia nervosa, which involves self-starvation. Without professional help, these individuals may starve themselves to death. Eating disorders, such as anorexia nervosa, show how psychological factors can override basic biological needs. We'll discuss several eating disorders in the Application section.

Although there are a relatively limited number of biological needs, there are many more social needs.

Social Needs

Why did they get married?

One reason that about 90% of adults in the United States get married is that being married satisfies a number of social needs.

Social needs are needs that are acquired through learning and experience.

Depending on your learning and experiences, you may acquire dozens of social needs, such as the need for achievement, affiliation (forming social bonds), fun (play), relaxation, being helpful, independence, and to nourish (nurturance) (Petri & Govern, 2004).

Getting married satisfies social needs.

One reason marriage is so popular is that it satisfies a number of social needs, including affiliation, nurturance, and achievement. The need for affiliation, or forming lasting, positive attachments, is one of our stronger social needs and is important to maintaining physical health and psychological well-being (Baumeister & Leary, 1995).

In some cases, the distinction between biological and social needs is blurred. For example, we may eat or drink not only to satisfy biological needs but to make social contact or deal with stress. Similarly, we may engage in sex for reproduction, which is a biological need, or to express love and affection, which are social needs. Because we have only so much time and energy to satisfy a relatively large number of biological and social needs, how do we decide which needs to satisfy first? The answer may be found in Maslow's hierarchy.

Satisfying Needs

Which need gets satisfied?

You may remember from Module 1 that one of the founders of the humanistic approach in psychology was Abraham Maslow. Maslow was particularly interested in human motivation, especially in how we choose which biological or social need to satisfy. For example, should you study late for an exam and satisfy your social need to achieve, or go to bed at your regular time and satisfy your biological need for sleep? Maslow (1970) proposed that we satisfy our needs in a certain order or according to a set hierarchy (figure on opposite page).

Maslow's hierarchy of needs is an ascending order, or hierarchy, in which biological needs are placed at the bottom and social needs at the top. According to Maslow's hierarchy, we satisfy our biological needs (bottom of hierarchy) before we satisfy our social needs (top of hierarchy).

Maslow hypothesized that, after we satisfy needs at the bottom level of the hierarchy, we advance up the hierarchy to satisfy the needs at the next level. However, if we are at a higher level and our basic needs are not satisfied, we may come back down the hierarchy. We'll examine Maslow's hierarchy of needs in more detail.

Do you satisfy biological needs first?

Which needs do you satisfy first?

If you were very hungry and very lonely at the same time, which need would you satisfy first, your biological need (hunger) or your social need (affiliation)? One answer to this question can be found in Maslow's hierarchy of needs, which says that you satisfy your biological needs before you can turn your attention and energy to fulfilling your personal and social needs. According to Maslow, when it comes to satisfying your needs, you begin at the bottom of the needs hierarchy, with physiological needs, and then work your way toward the top. After you meet the needs at one level, you

advance to the next level. For example, if your physiological needs at Level 1 are satisfied, you advance to Level 2 and work on satisfying your safety needs. Once your safety needs are satisfied, you advance to Level 3, and so forth, up the needs hierarchy.

Maslow's hierarchy of needs is represented by a pyramid and shows the order in which you satisfy your biological and social needs. The first needs you satisfy are physiological or biological ones, so please go to the bottom of the pyramid and begin reading Level 1. Then continue reading Levels 2, 3, 4, and 5, which takes you up the pyramid.

Level 5 Self-actualization: Fulfillment of one's unique potential. If we face roadblocks in reaching our true potential, we will feel frustrated. For example, if you are majoring in business and your real interest and talent is music, your need for self-actualization may be unsatisfied. According to Maslow, the highest need is self-actualization, which involves developing and reaching our full potential as unique human beings. However, Maslow cautioned that very few individuals reach the level of self-actualization because it is so difficult and challenging. Examples of individuals who might be said to have reached the level of self-actualization are Abraham Lincoln, Albert Einstein, Eleanor Roosevelt, and Martin Luther King, Jr.

Level 4 Esteem needs: Achievement, competency, gaining approval and recognition. During early and middle adulthood, people are especially concerned with achieving their goals and establishing their careers. As we develop skills to gain personal achievement and social recognition, we turn our energies to Level 5.

Level 3 Love and belonging needs: Affiliation with others and acceptance by others. Adolescents and young adults, who are beginning to form serious relationships, would be especially interested in fulfilling their needs for love and belonging. After we find love and affection, we advance to Level 4.

Level 2 Safety needs: Protection from harm. People who live in high-crime or dangerous areas of the city would be very concerned about satisfying their safety needs. After we find a way to live in a safe and secure environment, we advance to Level 3.

Level 1 Physiological needs: Food, water, sex, and sleep. People who are homeless or jobless would be especially concerned with satisfying their physiological needs above all other needs. We must satisfy these basic needs before we advance to Level 2.

Maslow's hierarchy of needs suggests the order in which we satisfy our needs.

Conclusion. One advantage of Maslow's hierarchy is that it integrates biological and social needs into a single framework and proposes a list of priorities for the order in which we satisfy various biological and social needs (Frick, 2000).

One problem with Maslow's hierarchy is that researchers have found it difficult to verify whether his particular order of needs is accurate or to know how to assess some of his needs, especially self-actualization, which very few individuals are able to reach (Geller, 1982). Another problem is that people give different priorities to needs: Some may value love over self-esteem,

or vice versa (Neher, 1991). We'll discuss Maslow's hierarchy of needs later on when we explain humanistic theories of personality (p. 443). Despite criticisms of Maslow's hierarchy, it remains a useful reminder of the number and complexity of human needs.

To give you a sample of how psychologists study human motivation, we have selected two biological needs—hunger and sex—from Maslow's Level 1 and one social need—achievement—from Maslow's Level 4. We consider these needs in the following sections.

C. Hunger

Optimal Weight

Why don't you see fat wolves?

The reason you never see fat wolves is that they, like all animals, have an inherited biological system that carefully regulates their eating so that they maintain their optimal, or ideal, weights (Kolata, 2000b).

Optimal or *ideal weight* results from an almost perfect balance between how much food an organism eats and how much it needs to meet its body's energy needs.

In the wild, animals usually eat only to replace fuel used by their bodies, and thus they rarely get fat. In addition, most wild animals use up a tremendous amount of energy in finding food. In comparison, home pets may become fat because their owners,

Animals rely on a biological system to regulate weight.

having the best of intentions, give the pets too much food or food so tasty that their pets eat too much. And unlike wild animals, home-bound pets may have few opportunities to run around and burn off the extra food or surplus calories.

A *calorie* is simply a measure of how much energy food contains. For example, food high in fats (pizza, cheeseburger, french fries, donuts) usually have twice the calories of foods high in protein (fish, chicken, eggs) or high in carbohydrates (vegetables, fruits, grains). The same factors that make pets overweight also make humans overweight.

Overweight

Why the huge increase?

Like animals, we humans have an inherited biological system that regulates hunger to keep us at our ideal weights. However, there is currently a worldwide problem of overweight and obesity.

Overweight means that a person is 20% over the ideal body weight.

Obesity means that a person is 30% or more above the ideal body weight.

The numbers on the right show that, over the years, the percentage of adult Americans who are overweight or obese has increased dramatically, from 26% in 1976 to 65% in 2003 (J. O. Hill et al., 2003). Overweight and obesity are primarily caused by two factors: eating more than is required

1976	26%
2000	55%
2003	65%

Percent of adult Americans who are overweight or obese

to fuel the body's current energy needs and not getting enough exercise to burn off any extra food (surplus calories) (Pi-Sunyer, 2003). For example, it is well known that during their freshman year, some students gain 15 pounds, primarily because of all-you-can eat dining halls and late-night junk food snacks (J. E. Brody, 2003; Levitsky, 2003).

Being overweight or obese, which has become a worldwide health problem, significantly increases the risk for heart disease, stroke, high blood pressure, clogged arteries, and adult-onset diabetes (J. O. Hill et al., 2003). Most recently, 14% of cancer deaths in men and 20% in women have been attributed to obesity (Calle et al., 2003). In the United States, weight-related costs are estimated to add about $12 billion to the expenses paid by employers (Freudenheim, 2003).

However, you'll see that solving the problem of being overweight or obese is complicated because eating is influenced by three different hunger factors.

Three Hunger Factors

What controls your eating?

Hunger is considered a biological drive because eating is essential to our survival. However, the way in which you satisfy your hunger drive—when, where, and how much you eat—is influenced by three different factors: biological, psychosocial, and genetic (J. O. Hill et al., 2003).

Biological hunger factors come from physiological changes in blood chemistry and signals from digestive organs that provide feedback to the brain, which, in turn, triggers us to eat or stop eating.

If your eating was regulated primarily by biological factors, as in most animals, you would keep your weight at optimal levels. The fact that 65% of adults are overweight or obese and that some individuals suffer from serious eating problems indicates the influence of both psychosocial and genetic factors.

Psychosocial hunger factors come from learned associations between food and other stimuli, such as snacking while

Psychosocial hunger factors can override other factors.

watching television; sociocultural influences, such as pressures to be thin; and various personality problems, such as depression, dislike of body image, or low self-esteem.

Genetic hunger factors come from inherited instructions found in our genes. These instructions determine the number of fat cells or metabolic rates of burning off the body's fuel, which push us toward being normal, overweight, or underweight.

These three hunger factors interact to influence your weight. For example, because of psychosocial factors, some of us eat when we should not, such as during stress. Because of biological factors, some of us may respond too much or too little to feedback from our digestive organs. Because of genetic factors, some of us can eat more calories and still maintain optimal weight. We'll discuss these three hunger factors, beginning with biological factors.

Biological Hunger Factors

Why do you start eating? The Japanese sumo wrestler on the right is Konishiki, nicknamed Meat Bomb. He is 6 feet 1 inch tall and weighs 580 pounds, which is considered normal by sumo standards but obese by Western medical charts. He maintains his huge body by consuming about 10,000 calories daily, which is 3–5 times the amount required by an average-sized man.

Konishiki's eating is partly regulated by biological hunger factors, which come from peripheral and central cues (Woods et al., 2000).

Peripheral cues come from changes in blood chemistry or signals from digestive organs, which secrete various hormones.

Central cues result from activity in different brain areas, which in turn results in increasing or decreasing appetite.

Peripheral and central cues make up a complex biological system that evolved over millions of years to help humans and animals maintain their best weights for survival.

Peripheral Cues

Signals for feeling hungry or full come from a number of body organs that are involved in digestion and regulation of blood sugar (glucose) levels, which is the primary source of fuel for the body and brain.

1 When empty, the *stomach* secretes a newly discovered hormone, ghrelin, which carries "hunger signals" to the brain's hypothalamus, the master control for hunger regulation. When the stomach is full, stretch receptors in its walls send "full signals" to the brain's hypothalamus, which decreases appetite (Grady, 2002).

2 The *liver* monitors the level of glucose (sugar) in the blood. When the level of glucose (blood sugar) falls, the liver sends "hunger signals" to the brain's hypothalamus; when the level of glucose rises, the liver sends "full signals" to the hypothalamus (Woods et al., 2000).

3 The *intestines* also secrete ghrelin, which carries "hunger signals" to the hypothalamus, which increases appetite. The intestines also secrete a newly discovered hormone, PYY, which carries "full signals" to the hypothalamus, which decreases appetite. Finally, the intestines secrete a hormone called CCK (cholecystokinin), which signals the hypothalamus to inhibit eating (Nash, 2002).

4 *Fat cells* secrete a hormone, called leptin, which acts on the brain's hypothalamus. If levels of leptin are falling, the hypothalamus increases appetite; if levels are rising, the hypothalamus decreases appetite. The secretion of leptin helps maintain a constant level of body fat and defend against starving the body to death (Leibel, 2003).

Summary. The stomach and intestines secrete a number of "hunger" or "full" hormone signals that act on the hypothalamus, which is the master control for regulating eating and produces central cues for increasing or decreasing appetite.

Central Cues

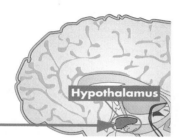
Hypothalamus

1 The brain has an area with different groups of cells that are collectively called the *hypothalamus* (left figure). Each group of cells is involved in a different kind of motivation, including regulation of thirst, sexual behavior, sleep, intensity of emotional reactions, and regulation of hunger. We'll focus on two particular groups of cells, the lateral and ventromedial hypothalamus, that affect hunger in opposite ways, either increasing or decreasing your appetite.

2 The *lateral hypothalamus* refers to a group of brain cells that receives "hunger signals" from digestive organs—increase in ghrelin, fall in level of blood glucose, and fall in levels of leptin. The lateral hypothalamus interprets these "hunger signals" and increases your appetite (Woods et al., 2000).

For example, electrical stimulation of the lateral hypothalamus causes rats to start eating, while destruction of the lateral hypothalamus causes rats to stop eating and even starve without special feeding.

3 The *ventromedial hypothalamus* refers to a group of brain cells that receives "full signals" from digestive organs—full stomach activates stretch receptors, rise in level of blood glucose, rise in levels of leptin, and increase in the hormones, PYY and CCK. The ventromedial hypothalamus interprets these "full signals" and decreases appetite.

For example, electrical stimulation of the ventromedial hypothalamus causes rats to stop eating, while destruction of the ventromedial hypothalamus causes rats to overeat and become obese. In addition, various chemicals affect other cells of the hypothalamus and regulate our appetites for specific foods.

Summary. The hypothalamus is involved in regulating many different kinds of motivated behaviors; in this case, we focused on hunger. The hypothalamus has one group of cells, called the lateral hypothalamus, that responds to "hunger signals" by increasing your appetite so you start eating. The hypothalamus has another group of cells, called the ventromedial hypothalamus, that responds to "full signals" by decreasing your appetite so you stop eating. This wonderfully complex biological system for regulating hunger is hard-wired and present in a newborn's brain. Although this system is designed to keep us at our ideal weights, we'll discuss a number of genetic and psychological factors that can interfere with this system and cause overeating and even starvation.

C. Hunger

Are identical twins always the same weight?

Researchers generally find that identical twins (photo on right), even when separated soon after birth and reared in adopted families, are much more alike in weight than fraternal twins reared apart (Bouchard et al., 1990). This similarity in weight is due to genetic hunger factors.

Genetic hunger factors come from inherited instructions found in our genes. These instructions determine the number of fat cells or metabolic rates of burning off the body's fuel, which push us toward being normal, overweight, or underweight.

Identical twins share the same genes and thus are similar in weight.

On the basis of twin studies, researchers concluded that inherited factors contribute about 70–80% to the maintenance of a particular body size and weight, while environmental factors contribute the other 20–30% (Bulik et al., 2003).

The finding that genetic hunger factors contribute about 70–80% to having a certain body size and weight explains why identical twins have similar body types. The finding that environmental factors contribute about 20–30% to body size explains why one twin may weigh a little more or less than the other. So far, psychologists have identified four genetic hunger factors: fat cells, metabolic rate, set point, and weight-regulating genes.

1 We inherit different numbers of fat cells.

Fat cells, whose number is primarily determined by heredity, do not normally multiply except when people become obese. Fat cells shrink if we are giving up fat and losing weight (left) and greatly enlarge if we are storing fat and gaining weight (right) (N. R. Carlson, 1998).

People who inherit a larger number of fat cells have the ability to store more fat and are more likely to be fatter than average.

2 We inherit different rates of metabolism.

Metabolic rate refers to how efficiently our bodies break food down into energy and how quickly our bodies burn off that fuel.

For example, if you had a low metabolic rate, you would burn less fuel, be more likely to store excess fuel as fat, and thus may have a fatter body. In comparison, if you had a high metabolic rate, you would burn off more fuel, be less likely to store fat, and thus may have a thinner body (left figure). This means that people can consume the same number of calories but, because of different metabolic rates, may maintain, lose, or gain weight. There are only two known activities that can raise metabolic rate: exercise and smoking cigarettes. Researchers found that exercise raises metabolic rate 10–20% and that nicotine raises it 4–10%. That's the reason exercise helps dieters lose weight and smokers generally gain weight when they stop smoking (Audrain et al., 1995).

3 We inherit a set point to maintain a certain amount of body fat.

The *set point* refers to a certain level of body fat (adipose tissue) that our bodies strive to maintain constant throughout our lives.

For example, a person whose body (right figure) has a higher set point will try to maintain a higher level of fat stores and thus have a fatter body. In comparison, a person whose body has a lower set point will maintain a lower level of fat stores and thus have a thinner body (Woods et al., 2000). If a person diets to reduce the level of fat stores, the body compensates to maintain and build back fat stores by automatically lowering metabolic rate and thus consuming less fuel. That's the reason dieters may lose weight for the first two or three weeks and then stop losing; the body has lowered its metabolic rate. Researchers concluded that because the body protects its fat stores, long-term dieting will be unsuccessful in treating overweight people unless they also exercise (Leibel et al., 1995).

4 The most recent findings indicate that we inherit weight-regulating genes.

Weight-regulating genes play a role in influencing appetite, body metabolism, and secretion of hormones (leptin) that regulate fat stores.

For example, the mouse on the left has a gene that increases a brain chemical (neuropeptide Y) that increased eating so that it weighs three times as much as the normal-weight mouse on the right (Gura, 1997). Researchers have also found a gene that can jack up metabolism so that calories are burned off as heat rather than stored as fat (Warden, 1997). This latter finding may explain why about 10% of the population can stay trim on a diet that would make others fat.

You have seen how genetic hunger factors are involved in the regulation of body fat and weight.

Next, we'll explore several psychological factors involved in the regulation of eating and weight.

Always room for dessert?

Many of us have a weakness for certain foods, and mine is for desserts. Even though my biological and genetic hunger factors may tell me (my brain) when to start and stop eating, I can use my large forebrain to override my innately programmed biological and genetic factors. My forebrain allows me to rationalize that one dessert can do no harm. This kind of rationalizing comes under the heading of psychosocial factors.

Psychosocial hunger factors come from learned associations between food and other stimuli, such as snacking while watching television; sociocultural influences, such as pressures to be thin; and various personality traits, such as depression, dislike of body image, or low self-esteem.

Psychosocial hunger factors can have an enormous effect on our eating habits and weight and contribute to many problems associated with eating, such as becoming overweight, eating when stressed or depressed, and bingeing (Ward et al., 2000). We'll discuss three psychosocial hunger factors—learned associations, social-cultural influences, and personality traits.

Learned Associations

The best examples of how *learned associations* influence eating are when we eat not because we're hungry but because it's "lunchtime," because foods smell good, because our friends are eating, or because we can't

Extra large box of popcorn has same calories as a meal!

resist large portions. For example, an extra large box of popcorn is equivalent in calories (900) to a major meal. Health professionals warn that many Americans prefer large portions and tasty junk foods high in calories, and this has resulted in an increasing rate of overweight and obesity in both children and adults (Hellmich, 2002; Rozin et al., 2003).

Researchers are especially concerned about the continued rise in obesity in children, from 7% in 1980 to 15% in 2003 (Horovitz, 2003). Childhood obesity is very difficult to treat, and an obese child has a high probability of becoming an obese adult with the associated health risks we discussed earlier (Manning, 2000b).

Health professionals advise us to unlearn many of our learned food associations. We should eat only when hungry and eat smaller portions and healthier foods (Pi-Sunyer, 2003).

Social-Cultural Influences

Examples of how *social-cultural influences* affect food preferences and body weight may be cited from around the world.

Czech Republic. In the 1970s, the Czech Republic government subsidized cheap fatty sausage and dairy products. The result was that 45% of Czech women and a smaller percentage of men are obese. The Czech Republic has the world's highest death rates from heart disease and has instituted programs to encourage healthier eating habits (Elliott, 1995).

China. In parts of China, fatty fast foods have become very popular along with a more sedentary lifestyle. This has resulted in an increase in obesity and associated diseases of the heart and blood circulation that were previously uncommon in China. In addition, there has been an alarming increase in obesity among children, who are pampered by a culture that prizes well-nourished children as indicating affluence and well-being. With childhood obesity come a severe form of diabetes and a long-term health risk (Mydans, 2003).

In Chinese "xiao pangzi" means "little fatties."

United States. In the United States, there are many cultural pressures on women to be thin. For example, the mass media advertise that the ideal woman is one with a slender body. As a result, many American women report being dissatisfied with their weight and see themselves as overweight even when they are not. An additional problem for women is that their desire to have the ideal slim advertised body may lead to eating disorders (Groesz et al., 2002). In comparison, American men are less concerned with and usually *underestimate* their weights and develop fewer eating problems (Stanford & McCabe, 2002).

Personality Traits

If a person has certain *personality traits,* he or she may be at greater risk for overeating as well as developing serious eating disorders, such as overeating when stressed or depressed, going on food binges (bulimia nervosa), or starving oneself (anorexia nervosa). We'll discuss serious eating problems in the Application section.

The particular personality traits that have been associated with eating problems include depression, anxiety, markedly low self-esteem, heightened sensitivity to rejection, excessive concern with approval from others, high personal standards for achievement, a history of physical or sexual abuse, and the need to have control (over oneself or one's body) (Polivy & Herman, 2002). Someone with these kinds of personality traits, which are often accompanied by stress, anxiety, and emotional upset, may find it very difficult and sometimes almost impossible to control his or her eating (J. E. Brody, 2003). As we'll discuss in the Application section, individuals with serious eating problems may need to seek professional help and counseling.

Although hunger is considered a biological need, you have seen how numerous psychosocial hunger factors can greatly influence where, when, and how the hunger drive is satisfied. And, as we'll discuss in the Application section, there are extreme cases in which psychosocial factors can completely override the hunger drive.

Next, we'll discuss another very important biological need, sexual behavior.

I look too fat!

Personality traits influence eating habits.

D. Sexual Behavior

Why do lions know how to do it?

Although we don't look, sound, or behave the same as lions do, we share similar biological and genetic factors that regulate sexual behavior. The sexual behavior of lions and most animals is controlled chiefly by genetic and biological factors, which means that most animals engage in sex primarily for reproduction.

Genetic sex factors include inherited instructions for the development of sexual organs, the secretion of sex hormones, and the wiring of the neural circuits that control sexual reflexes.

Biological sex factors include the action of sex hormones, which are involved in secondary sexual characteristics (facial hair, breasts), sexual motivation (more so in animals than in humans), and the development of ova and sperm.

Lions, like most animals, generally avoid sexual interactions unless the female is in heat, which means she is ovulating and can be

In most animals, sexual behavior is regulated by genetic and biological factors.

impregnated. In comparison, humans engage in sexual behavior for many reasons, which point to psychological sex factors.

Psychological sex factors play a role in developing a sexual or gender identity, gender role, and sexual orientation. In addition, psychological factors can result in difficulties in the performance or enjoyment of sexual activities.

For example, otherwise healthy men and women may report difficulties in sexual activities arising from stress, anxiety, or guilt, which can interfere with the functioning of genetic and biological sex factors. One reason psychological factors play such an important role in human sexual behavior is that our large forebrains have the capacity to think, reason, and change our minds and thus increase, interfere with, or completely block sexual motivation, performance, or enjoyment.

As we did for the hunger drive, we'll discuss, in order, the influences of genetic, biological, and psychological factors on sexual behavior.

Genetic Influences on Sexual Behavior

Which sex organ?

How we develop a particular sex organ, male or female, is determined primarily by a genetic program that is cotained in a single human cell about the size of a grain of sand (Bancroft, 2002).

SEX CHROMOSOME

Unlike the other cells of our body, which contain 46 chromosomes (23 pairs), the sperm and egg each contain half that number and are called sex chromosomes (figure below).

The *sex chromosome,* which is in the sperm or the egg, contains 23 chromosomes, which in

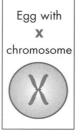

turn have genes that contain instructions for determining the sex of the child.

As we discussed earlier (p. 68), each chromosome is made up of a long strand of DNA (deoxyribonucleic acid). On this long strand of DNA are hundreds of genes, which contain the chemically coded instructions for the development and maintenance of our bodies. In the figure above, notice that some sperm have an **X** chromosome and some have a **Y,** which contain different genetic instructions and, as you'll see, result in the development of different sex organs (penis or vagina).

1 The human egg contains one of the sex chromosomes, which is always an **X** chromosome. Thus, each human egg has a single **X** chromosome.

Egg with **X** chromosome

2 A human sperm also contains one of the sex chromosomes. However, the sperm's chromosome can be either an **X** chromosome, which has instructions for development of *female sex organs* and body, or a **Y** chromosome, which has instructions for *male sex organs* and body. Thus, the sperm (**X** or **Y**) determines the sex of the infant.

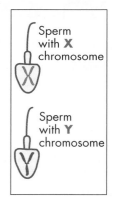

Sperm with **X** chromosome

Sperm with **Y** chromosome

3 During fertilization, a single sperm penetrates an egg and results in a fertilized egg with 23 pairs of chromosomes. If the last pair has the combination **XY,** it means the egg contains the genetic instructions for developing a male's sex organs (top right figure). If the last pair has the combination **XX,** it means the egg contains the genetic instructions for developing a female's sex organs (bottom right figure).

Male instructions

Female instructions

Following fertilization, the human cell, which is called a *zygote,* will divide over and over many thousands of times during the following weeks and months and eventually develop into a female body with female sex organs or a male body with male sex organs.

How an unborn infant actually develops male or female sex organs is an interesting story, especially since everyone begins as a female.

Genetic Influences (continued)

DIFFERENTIATION

Although it would seem that at fertilization you are destined to be either a male or a female, there is actually no physical difference between a male and a female embryo for the first four weeks of development in the womb. During this time period, the embryos are identical and have the potential to develop into either a male or a female. At about the fifth week, the embryo begins to differentiate into either a male or a female because of the presence or absence of certain sex hormones (Bancroft, 2002).

MALE SEX ORGAN AND MALE BRAIN

XY = Testosterone

Presence of testosterone results in a male brain.

In an embryo that began from an **XY** fertilized egg, the **Y** sex chromosome has instructions for the development of male testes. At about the fifth week, the testes begin to grow and produce tiny amounts of male hormones or *androgens*, one of which most people know as *testosterone*. The presence of testosterone does two things: It triggers the development of the male sexual organ (penis), and it programs a particular area of the brain, called the hypothalamus, so that at puberty it triggers the pituitary gland to secrete hormones on a continuous basis, which results in the continuous production of sperm.

FEMALE SEX ORGANS AND FEMALE BRAIN

XX = No Testosterone

Absence of testosterone results in a female brain.

In an embryo that began from an **XX** fertilized egg, the second **X** sex chromosome contains instructions for the development of ovaries, which do not secrete testosterone.

The absence of testosterone in the developing embryo means two things: It leads to the automatic development of female sexual organs (clitoris and vagina), and the hypothalamus, which is normally programmed for female hormonal functions, keeps its female program. Thus, at puberty, this female-programmed hypothalamus triggers the pituitary gland to secrete hormones on a cyclic basis, which results in the menstrual cycle.

IMPORTANCE OF TESTOSTERONE

The *presence* of testosterone, which is secreted by fetal testes, results in male sexual organs and a male hypothalamus; the *absence* of testosterone results in female sexual organs and a female hypothalamus (Kalat, 2004).

When the infant is born, the doctor identifies the infant's sex organs and says those famous words, "It's a boy" or "It's a girl." At that point a hormonal clock begins ticking and its alarm will set off biological factors at puberty.

Biological Influences

You have seen how genetic sex factors influence the development and growth of the body's sex organs. The next big event to affect a person's sex organs and sexual motivation occurs at puberty as a result of biological sex factors.

Sex hormones secreted during puberty both directly and indirectly affect our bodies, brains, minds, personalities, self-concepts, and mental health. We'll focus on how sex hormones affect our bodies.

Sex hormones. At puberty, some yet unknown signal activates cells in the hypothalamus, which triggers a 10- to 20-fold increase in the secretion of sex hormones.

*Sex hormone*s, which are chemicals secreted by glands, circulate in the bloodstream to influence the brain, body organs, and behaviors. The major male sex hormones secreted by the testes are *androgens,* such as testosterone; the major female sex hormones secreted by the ovaries are *estrogens.*

Testosterone

Male hypothalamus triggers release of **testosterone.**

Male–female differences. The presence or absence of testosterone in the womb causes different neural programming so that the male hypothalamus functions differently from the female hypothalamus.

The *male hypothalamus* triggers a continuous release of androgens, such as testosterone, from the testes. The increased level of androgens causes the development of male secondary sexual characteristics, such as facial and pubic hair, muscle growth, and lowered voice.

The *female hypothalamus* triggers a cyclical release of estrogens from the ovaries. The increased level of estrogens causes the development of female secondary sexual characteristics, such as pubic hair, breast development, and widening of the hips. The cyclical release of hormones (estrogen and progesterone) also regulates the menstrual cycle.

Estrogen

Female hypothalamus triggers release of **estrogen.**

SEXUAL MOTIVATION

In humans, normal sexual development and motivation depend upon levels of sex hormones being within the normal range. In rare cases, males are born with an extra **X** chromosome, XXY or Klinefelter's syndrome, which results in undersized testes and penis, decreased secretion of testosterone, infertility, no development of secondary sexual characteristics at puberty, and little or no interest in sexual activity. However, when given testosterone replacement at puberty, they regain sexual interest and drive (Swerdloff, 1998). Thus, the absence of sex hormones interferes with normal sexual development and motivation. But, if a person has a normal level of sex hormones, any increase or decrease in sexual interest and motivation are more dependent on psychological factors, such as feelings, desires, and expectations (Crooks & Baur, 2002). For example, some men and women with normal levels of sex hormones report low sex drives. In these cases, giving additional sex hormones causes little or no increase in the sexual drive, presumably because the causes are psychological (Bancroft, 2002).

At the same time that genetic and biological factors are guiding our bodies toward physical sexual maturity, numerous psychological factors are preparing our minds for psychological sexual maturity. Next, we'll examine these psychological sex factors.

D. Sexual Behavior

How do boys and girls become men and women?

As boys and girls go through puberty, various genetic and biological factors prepare their bodies for sexual maturity (Coleman & Coleman, 2002). At the same time their bodies are developing, boys and girls are observing, imitating, and learning behaviors of their mothers, fathers, older siblings, and other adults in their environments. At this point, psychological sex factors come into play.

Psychological sex factors play a role in developing a sexual or gender identity, gender role, and sexual

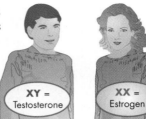

Sex hormones activate many physical and psychological changes.

XY = Testosterone

XX = Estrogen

orientation. In addition, psychological factors can result in difficulties in the performance or enjoyment of sexual activities.

Genetic, biological, and psychological sex factors combine and interact to result in boys and girls developing into sexually mature men and women.

Three psychological sex factors are especially important—gender identity, gender role, and sexual orientation. We'll discuss each in turn, beginning with gender identity.

1st Step: Gender Identity

Between the ages of 2 and 3, a child can correctly answer the question, "Are you a boy or a girl?" The correct answer indicates that the child has already acquired the beginnings of a gender identity (Blakemore, 2003).

Gender identity, which was formerly called sexual identity, refers to the individual's subjective experience and feelings of being either a male or a female.

The doctor's words, "It's a girl" or "It's a boy," set in motion the process for acquiring a gender identity. From that point on, parents, siblings, grandparents, and others behave toward male and female infants differently, so that they learn and acquire their proper gender identity (C. L. Martin et al., 2002). For example, the little girl in the right photo is checking out a pretty dress in the mirror, a behavior that she has observed her mother doing and that she is now imitating.

By age 3, children know if they **are** boys or girls.

Gender identity is a psychological sex factor that exerts a powerful influence on future sexual thoughts and behavior, as clearly illustrated in the case of someone with a gender identity disorder, who is commonly referred to as a transsexual.

Gender identity disorder is commonly referred to as transsexualism. A transsexual is a person who has a strong and persistent desire to be the other sex, is uncomfortable about being one's assigned sex, and may wish to live as a member of the other sex (American Psychiatric Association, 2000).

Transsexuals usually have normal genetic and biological (hormonal) factors, but for some reason, they feel and insist that they are trapped in the body of the wrong sex and may adopt the behaviors, dress, and mannerisms of the other sex. There is no clear understanding of why transsexuals reject their biological sex. Current data indicate that the incidence of transsexualism is about the same for males and females (Bradley & Zucker, 1997). Infrequently, adults with gender identity disorder may seek surgery to change the sex organs that they were born with to the other sex. Because transsexuals acquire gender identities that do not match their external sex organs, they experience problems in thinking and acting and may not easily fit into or be accepted by society (Bradley & Zucker, 1997). However, the vast majority of people do acquire gender identities that match their external sex organs.

As you acquire a male or female gender identity, you are also acquiring a matching gender role.

2nd Step: Gender Roles

After the first step in becoming psychologically sexually mature, which is acquiring a male or female gender identity—"I'm a boy" or "I'm a girl"—comes the second step, which is acquiring a gender role.

Gender roles, which were formerly called sex roles, refer to the traditional or stereotypic behaviors, attitudes, and personality traits that society designates as masculine or feminine. Gender roles greatly influence how we think and behave.

Between the ages of 3 and 4, American children learn the stereotypic or traditional expectations regarding the kinds of toys, clothes, and occupations for men and women. By the age of 5, children have acquired many of the complex thoughts, expectations, and behaviors that accompany their particular gender role of male or female (Eckes & Trautner, 2000).

By age 5, a child knows how a boy or girl **behaves.**

For example, young boys learn stereotypic male behaviors, such as playing sports, competing in games, engaging in rough-and-tumble play, and acquiring status in his group. In comparison, girls learn stereotypic female behaviors, such as providing and seeking emotional support, emphasizing physical appearance and clothes, and learning to cooperate and share personal experiences (Eagly et al., 2000).

As children, we all learned early on to adopt a male or female gender role, often without being aware of how subtly we were rewarded for imitating and performing appropriate sex-typed behaviors. Learning and adopting a gender role continue through adolescence and into adulthood and result in very different gender roles. For instance, adult American women tend to show stereotypic gender roles that can be described as socially sensitive, nurturing, and concerned with others' welfare. In comparison, adult American men tend to show gender roles that can be described as dominant, controlling, and independent (Eagly et al., 2000).

Dominant Controlling Independent

Sensitive Nurturing Concerned

Function. A major function of gender roles is to influence how we think and behave. Notice that male gender roles—dominant, controlling, and independent—can lead to different kinds of sexual thoughts and behaviors than female gender roles—socially sensitive, nurturing, and concerned. Thus, some of the confusion, conflict, and misunderstanding over sexual behavior come from underlying differences in gender roles. A major task a couple will have in establishing a healthy, loving relationship is to work out the many differences in thoughts, beliefs, and expectations that come from combining two different gender roles.

After we acquire a gender role, the next step involves knowing one's sexual orientation.

3rd Step: Sexual Orientation

In answering the question "Do you find males or females sexually arousing?" you are expressing your sexual orientation, which is the third step in reaching psychological sexual maturity.

Sexual orientation, also called sexual preference, refers to whether a person is sexually aroused primarily by members of his or her own sex, the opposite sex, or both sexes.

Homosexual orientation refers to a pattern of sexual arousal by persons of the same sex.

Bisexual orientation refers to a pattern of sexual arousal by persons of both sexes.

Heterosexual orientation refers to a pattern of sexual arousal by persons of the opposite sex.

The vast majority of the American population, about 96–97%, have a heterosexual orientation. The remaining 3–4% have a homosexual orientation, and a very small percentage of these individuals have a bisexual orientation (Laumann et al., 1994).

Of several models that explain how we develop a particular sexual orientation, the interactive model is perhaps the most popular (Money, 1987; Zucker, 1990).

The *interactive model of sexual orientation* says that genetic and biological factors, such as genetic instructions and prenatal hormones, interact with psychological factors, such as the individual's attitudes, personality traits, and behaviors, to influence the development of sexual orientation.

Genetic and biological factors. There is considerable debate over how much genetic and biological factors influence sexual orientation. Some researchers prefer the term *sexual preference* because it suggests that we have considerable freedom in choosing a particular sexual orientation and that genetic and biological factors do not play a major role (Baumrind, 1995; Byne, 1997). Other researchers prefer the term *sexual orientation* because they believe that genetic and biological factors play a major role (Diamond & Sigmundson, 1997). This debate was intensified by a case that involved changing a person's gender identity.

Changing gender identity. In the 1960s, genetic and biological factors were thought to play minor roles in developing gender identity. That's because some babies who were born with inconclusive sex organs (tiny penis, no testicles) were said to be girls and were raised as girls; others were said to be boys and were raised as boys. Later, when these children reached puberty, doctors discovered that some of these "girls" actually had the chromosomes of males and some of the "boys" had the chromosomes of females. However, some of those raised as "girls" decided to remain female and received corrective surgery (a vagina) and hormones (developed breasts). Others raised as "boys" decided to remain male and also received corrective surgery and hormones. In these cases, children chose the gender identity and orientation that matched their upbringing, not their genetic makeup. Based on such cases, researchers believed that gender identity and gender orientation could be changed if, before the age of 2, infants were assigned a gender identity and raised accordingly (Money, 1987). However, another case has questioned this belief.

1st Step: Gender identity

2nd Step: Gender role

3rd Step: Sexual orientation

Tragic case. While doctors were doing a routine medical procedure to repair an 8-month-old male's foreskin, they accidentally destroyed the infant's penis. As a result, doctors advised the parents to raise the boy (John) as a girl (Joan). However, since about the age of 8, Joan had been unhappy being and acting like a female and began to suspect that she was really a boy. By the time Joan was 14, she had received corrective surgery (a vagina) and hormonal treatment to physically look like a girl (developed breasts) but was so unhappy she threatened suicide and told doctors she thought she was a boy. After much discussion, doctors agreed to help Joan change back to John. Now in his 30s, John is married and reports that he never liked being a female and is very happy being a male.

Based on Joan-John's experience, researchers believe that individuals are genetically and biologically predisposed for having a male or female gender identity, which is not easily changed by being raised a certain way (boy or girl) (Diamond & Sigmundson, 1997). This case suggests that, unlike previously believed, humans may have a genetic predisposition to develop a male or female gender identity and gender orientation.

D. Sexual Behavior

Male–Female Sex Differences

How are men different from women?

After we have acquired a gender identity, gender role, and sexual orientation, there remain the sometimes difficult and complex decisions about when, where, and with whom sexual behavior is appropriate. Virtually every sex survey during the past 30 years reports that men think about sex more, have more sexual partners, reach orgasm more, and masturbate more than women (right graph). Why men consistently report more sexual activity and are allowed more sexual freedom than women has come to be known as the double standard (Crawford & Popp, 2003).

The *double standard for sexual behavior* refers to a set of beliefs, values, and expectations that subtly encourages sexual activity in men but discourages the same behavior in women.

The existence of a double standard allowing more freedom in sexual behavior for men than for women is well established (Peplau, 2003). How these male–female differences in sexual behavior came about is explained by two different theories—the biosocial theory and the evolutionary theory.

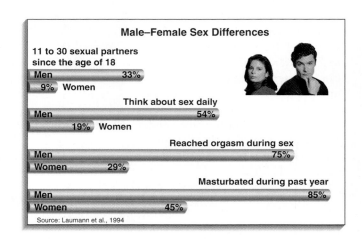

Male–Female Sex Differences

11 to 30 sexual partners since the age of 18
Men 33%
9% Women

Think about sex daily
Men 54%
19% Women

Reached orgasm during sex
Men 75%
Women 29%

Masturbated during past year
Men 85%
Women 45%

Source: Laumann et al., 1994

Because of their importance, we'll discuss how each theory explains the male–female differences in sexual behaviors.

Biosocial Theory

There are two major questions about male–female sexual behavior that need answering. First, why do men consistently report greater interest in sex as shown by increased frequency of sexual activities, greater percentage of extramarital affairs, and desire for more sex partners (about 18 partners) than women (about 4–5 partners) (Buss & Schmitt, 1993)? Second, in an international study of 37 cultures, 10,000 individuals were asked to state their top priorities in choosing a mate. Across all cultures and all racial, political, and religious groups, why do men generally value physical attractiveness more than women, while women value the financial resources of prospective mates twice as much as men do (Buss et al., 1990)? One answer to these questions comes from the biosocial theory of sexual differences.

Biosocial theory, which emphasizes social and cultural forces, says that differences in sexual activities and in values for selecting mates developed from traditional cultural divisions of labor: Women were primarily childbearers and homemakers, while men were primarily providers and protectors.

According to the biosocial theory, the double standard arose from men's roles as protectors and providers, which allowed them greater control of and access to women and in turn allowed and encouraged greater sexual freedom. In comparison, women's roles restricted and discouraged sexual activities and protected against potential problems with jealousy, which could disrupt or interfere with being successful childbearers and homemakers (right photo) (Wood & Eagly, 2002).

Biosocial theory focuses on the importance of different social and cultural pressures that resulted in men and women developing different social roles, which in turn led to men and women developing differences in sexual behavior, which today we call the double standard.

Evolutionary Theory

A different explanation for the differences in sexual behavior between men and women comes from evolutionary theory.

Evolutionary theory, which emphasizes genetic and biological forces, says that our current male–female differences in sexual behavior, which we call the double standard, arise from genetic and biological forces, which in turn grew out of an ancient set of successful mating patterns that helped the species survive.

According to evolutionary theory, men developed a greater interest in sex and desire for many attractive sex partners because it maximized their chances for reproduction. In comparison, women would not benefit from indiscriminate and frequent mating because it would place them at risk for having offspring of low quality and create an unstable environment for raising their children. Instead, women placed a high priority on finding a man who was a good protector and provider, so she and her children would have a better chance for survival, especially during her childbearing years (Gangestad & Simpson, 2000). This evolutionary theory is a relatively new approach to explain the occurrence and development of current male–female differences in sexual behavior (deWaal, 2002).

Provider & protector

Childbearer & homemaker

Although there is considerable debate between supporters of the evolutionary and biosocial theories, some researchers suggest that the best and most complete explanation of male–female sex differences may come from combining the biosocial theory, which emphasizes social-cultural forces, with the evolutionary theory, which emphasizes genetic and biological forces (Baldwin & Baldwin, 1997).

Next, we'll return to a controversial question in sexual behavior: Why does an individual develop a homosexual orientation?

Were the brothers born gay?

Although four major professional health organizations—American Psychological Association, American Psychiatric Association, American Medical Association, American Psychoanalytic Association—have concluded that homosexuality is a normal form of sexual expression, national surveys usually find that only a slight majority (56%) of adult Americans approve of homosexuality, while about half disapprove for a variety of reasons (Goldberg, 1998). According to current national surveys, about 1–3% of the American male population are homosexual (gay) and about 1.4% of the female population are homosexual (lesbian). These recent surveys are considered more accurate than earlier estimates of 10% of the population being homosexual (Kinsey et al., 1948).

Both brothers are gay and share similar genetic factors.

Many people say that they would be more accepting of homosexuality if it were shown to be a genetic predisposition, since it would be similar to inheriting other preferences, such as being left-handed (Leland, 1994). We'll discuss recent genetic/biological and psychological factors that bear on the question of whether brothers Rick and Randy (left photo) were genetically predisposed to be gay or chose to be gay.

Genetic/Biological Factors

During the past 15 years, there has been an increasing search for genetic and hormonal influences that contribute to the development of homosexuality (Rahman & Wilson, 2003). Some of this evidence comes from the study of sexual orientation in twins. For example, a number of studies on identical male and female twins have found that, if one male or female twin of an identical pair was gay, about 48–65% of the time so was the second twin; this compared to 26–30% for fraternal twins and 6–11% for adopted brothers or sisters (Bailey & Zucker, 1995). However, one criticism of these studies is that some of the twins were not reared separately so it is impossible to determine the effects of similar environments on sexual orientation. Another kind of evidence comes from studies on genetic similarities among brothers.

Researchers studied 40 families, each of which had two gay brothers (including Rick and Randy in the photo above). Researchers identified an area at the end of the

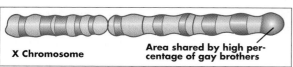

X Chromosome — Area shared by high percentage of gay brothers

X chromosome that was shared by 33 out of 40 pairs of gay brothers (left figure).

Thus, although they are not twins, Rick and Randy, who are gay, share the same section of genetic material (D. Hammer, 1995). Researchers cautioned that they have not found a "homosexual gene" but only identified shared genetic material that may contribute to sexual orientation. This study is the best evidence to date that homosexual orientation is strongly influenced by genetic factors. There is some question about the results, though, since not all researchers have been able to replicate these findings (Rice et al., 1999).

If there were a genetic/biological predisposition to homosexuality, we might expect that a person would become aware of his or her homosexual orientation before learning about or actually engaging in homosexual behavior and despite considerable pressure from parents, siblings, or peers to develop a heterosexual orientation. Researchers report that most gays report becoming aware of their orientation around puberty, usually before actually knowing much about or engaging in homosexual behavior and despite being almost totally surrounded by heterosexual role models (Pillard & Bailey, 1995).

All the above findings suggest that, to a certain extent, Rick and Randy were born with genetic or biological predispositions or tendencies that played a role in the development of a homosexual orientation (Bailey et al., 2000). However, if genetic predisposition was decisive, then we would expect 100% of the pairs of identical twins to have exactly the same sexual orientation, but only about 50% do (Lalumiere et al., 2000). This means that besides genetic/biological factors influencing the development of a homosexual orientation, there may also be psychological factors.

Psychological Factors

In studying psychological factors, researchers ask whether young children who later develop a heterosexual orientation differ from children who develop a homosexual orientation. In answering this question, researchers observed the behaviors of young children and consistently found that young boys who preferred girl playmates and girls' toys, avoided rough-and-tumble play, and engaged in wearing girls' clothing had a tendency to develop a homosexual orientation (Dawood et al., 2000). In addition, adult gay men and lesbian women recalled engaging in more behaviors of the opposite sex as children than did heterosexual adults (Bailey & Zucker, 1995). Although these studies are correlational and cannot show cause and effect, they do suggest that certain psychological factors (kinds of play behaviors and preferences) are associated with developing a homosexual orientation (Dawood et al., 2000).

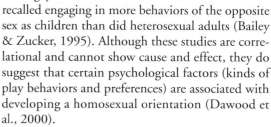

I knew I was gay before I did anything.

One psychological factor that influenced attitudes on homosexuality was that, until the 1970s, virtually all professional health organizations considered homosexuality to be an abnormal condition that often required psychotherapy to change. However, over the past 30 years, countless studies found that homosexuals scored about the same as heterosexuals on a wide variety of mental health tests, meaning that homosexuals are as mentally healthy as heterosexuals (K. P. Rosenberg, 1994). For these reasons, most professional health organizations now consider homosexuality a normal form or expression of sexual behavior and discourage all discriminatory practices toward homosexuals.

Next, we'll discuss several of the more common sexual problems and their treatments.

D. Sexual Behavior

What are some of the problems? Various surveys report that 10–52% of men and 25–63% of women, aged 18 to 59, married and unmarried, experience a variety of sexual problems (Heiman, 2002). Some seek help for their problem, while others are ashamed or embarrassed and suffer in silence. There are two categories of sexual problems—paraphilias and sexual dysfunctions.

Paraphilias, commonly called sexual deviations, are characterized by repetitive or preferred sexual fantasies involving nonhuman objects, such as sexual attractions to particular articles of clothing (shoes, underclothes).

Sexual dysfunctions refer to problems of sexual arousal or orgasm that interfere with adequate functioning during sexual behavior.

When a person seeks help for a sexual problem, the clinician will check whether the causes are organic or psychological.

Organic factors refer to medical conditions or drug or medication problems that lead to sexual difficulties.

For example, certain medical conditions (such as diabetes mellitus), medications (such as antidepressants), and drugs (such as alcohol abuse) can interfere with sexual functioning.

Psychological factors refer to performance anxiety, sexual trauma, guilt, or failure to communicate, all of which may lead to sexual problems.

Four-stage model. To understand how psychological factors cause sexual problems, it helps to know Masters and Johnson's (1966) four-stage model of the sexual response.

Masters and Johnson proposed four stages of the human sexual response.

1st stage: Excitement. The body becomes physiologically and sexually aroused, resulting in erection in the male and vaginal lubrication in the female.

2nd stage: Plateau. Sexual and physiological arousal continues in males and females.

3rd stage: Orgasm. Men have rhythmic muscle contractions that cause ejaculation of sperm. Women experience similar rhythmic muscle contractions of the pelvic area. During orgasm, women and men report very pleasurable feelings.

4th stage: Resolution. Physiological responses return to normal.

Problems. Sexual problems can occur at different stages. For example, some individuals cannot reach stage 1, excitement, while others can reach stages 1 and 2 but not stage 3, orgasm.

There were few successful treatments for sexual problems until Masters and Johnson (1970) published their treatment program, which has several stages. First, the therapist provides basic information about the sexual response and helps the couple communicate their feelings. Then the therapist gives the couple "homework," which is designed to reduce performance anxiety. Homework involves learning to pleasure one's partner without genital touching or making sexual demands. This nongenital pleasuring is called *sensate focus.* After using sensate focus, the couple moves on to genital touching and intercourse. Sex therapists have expanded and modified Masters and Johnson's program and report considerable success with treating many sexual problems (Wincze & Carey, 1991).

We'll discuss two common sexual problems and their treatments.

Premature or Rapid Ejaculation

John and Susan had been married for three years and were both 28 years old. When the clinician asked about their problem, Susan said that sex was over in about 30 seconds because that's how long it took for John to have an orgasm. John replied that he had always reached orgasm very quickly and didn't realize it was a problem. Susan said that it was a problem for her (Althof, 1995). John's problem is called premature ejaculation.

Premature or *rapid ejaculation* refers to persistent or recurrent absence of voluntary control over ejaculation, in which the male ejaculates with minimal sexual stimulation before, upon, or shortly after penetration and before he wishes to.

Premature or rapid ejaculation is the most common male sexual problem and is reported by about 30% of adult men (Byers & Grenier, 2003). A common treatment for it is called the squeeze technique. First, the partner stimulates the man's penis to nearly full erection. Then, the partner squeezes the head of the penis, which reduces arousal and erection. This squeeze procedure is repeated until the male develops a sense of control over arousal and ejaculation (Metz & Pryor, 2000). This procedure has proved successful in treating premature ejaculation.

Inhibited Female Orgasm

Greta and Bill had been married for five years and were in their late twenties. When asked about their problem, Greta said that she didn't think she had ever had an orgasm. She added that she loved Bill very much but that she was becoming less interested in sex (Durand & Barlow, 2003). Greta's problem has a name; it is called inhibited female orgasm.

Inhibited female orgasm refers to a persistent delay or absence of orgasm after becoming aroused and excited.

About 5–10% of women never or almost never reach orgasm, and about 30% do not have orgasms during intercourse. Difficulty in reaching orgasm is the most common complaint of women seeking help for sexual problems (Sarwer & Durlak, 1997).

Psychological treatment begins with sensate focus, during which the couple learns to pleasure each other and the woman learns to relax and enjoy her body's sensations. The man is told how to help a woman reach orgasm—for example, by using his hand or, in Greta's case, using a vibrator (Durand & Barlow, 2003). This program has proved successful in treating inhibited female orgasm.

Next, we'll discuss a sexual problem that involves a potentially deadly transmitted disease—AIDS.

What is AIDS?

On June 5, 1981, the United States Centers for Disease Control issued a report describing five gay men in Los Angeles who had a rare form of pneumonia. Later, this rare pneumonia was determined to be one symptom of the HIV virus.

HIV positive refers to the presence of HIV antibodies, which means that the individual has been infected by the human immunodeficiency virus (HIV), which is believed to cause AIDS.

AIDS (Acquired Immune Deficiency Syndrome) is a life-threatening condition that is present when the individual is HIV positive and has a level of T-cells (CD4 immune cells) no more than 200 per cubic milliliter of blood or has developed one or more of 26 specified illnesses (pneumonia, skin cancer). It may take years or even decades for HIV to develop into AIDS.

HIV Infections Worldwide

North America 942,000

Latin America and Caribbean 1.9 million

Eastern Europe & Central Asia 620,000

Southeast Asia 10 million

North Africa & Middle East 220,000

East Asia 530,000

Sub-Saharan Africa 26 million

The criterion of T-cell levels below 200 became a part of the definition of AIDS in 1993. T-cells are a critical part of the body's immune system, which fights against toxic agents (viruses and bacteria). Because of this change, some people who were previously defined as being HIV positive are now defined as having AIDS, even if no obvious symptoms have developed. Researchers report that the HIV virus originated in African monkeys, then spread to chimpanzees and, in the 1950s, to humans (Bailes et al., 2003).

In 2002, about 42 million people worldwide were infected with HIV/AIDS, and for the first time, women now make up half of the HIV/AIDs cases (Sternberg, 2002). As shown in the map on the left, the AIDS virus is widespread and has reached dangerous and epidemic levels in Sub-Saharan Africa (26 million). It kills 11 people worldwide every minute (Forsyth, 2000). In the United States, AIDS cases rose 2.2% in 2002, the first such rise in a decade (Heinrichs, 2003). We'll discuss three major issues involving AIDS.

Risk for AIDS

The HIV virus cannot survive in air, in water, or on things that people touch. There are no reports of getting AIDS through casual contact, such as through touch. The HIV virus survives best in blood tissues and some bodily fluids (semen and vaginal fluids). Thus, people who come in physical contact with blood or bodily fluids (semen or vaginal fluids) from someone who has the HIV virus are at risk for getting AIDS.

The graph on the right shows that in the United States, those at greatest risk for AIDS are gay men and heterosexual intravenous drug users. However, the risk of AIDS among women in the United States increased from 7% in the early 1980s to 23% in 1998. In the rest of the world, about 75% of AIDS is spread through heterosexual intercourse (Sternberg, 2002).

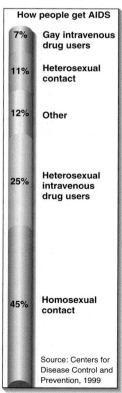

How people get AIDS

7% **Gay intravenous drug users**

11% **Heterosexual contact**

12% **Other**

25% **Heterosexual intravenous drug users**

45% **Homosexual contact**

Source: Centers for Disease Control and Prevention, 1999

Progression of Disease

After infection, the AIDS virus replicates rapidly and intensively. As a result, newly infected individuals are 100–1,000 times more infectious than they are throughout the remainder of the disease (Koopman, 1995). In addition, newly infected individuals have no symptoms and the presence of antibodies to the HIV virus cannot be confirmed biochemically for at least 60 days. Thus, the newly infected person is regarded as a walking time bomb.

HIV destroys T-cells (CD4 cells), which are immune cells that fight off toxic agents (viruses and bacteria). It takes an average of 7 years for a person infected with HIV to develop AIDS (T count below 200) and another 2–3 years after that to develop diseases that result in death. The reason a person with AIDS is especially susceptible to infections and diseases is that the HIV virus slowly destroys a person's immune system's defenses, which means the body loses its ability to fight off toxic agents (infections or diseases).

Because of yet unknown qualities of their immune systems, about 10 to 17% of HIV-infected individuals will be AIDS-free 20 years after infection. Researchers are studying these AIDS-free individuals to find out how their immune systems can fight off AIDS (Kolata, 2000a).

Treatment

In 1996, the number of AIDS-related deaths in the United States fell 23%; in 1997, it fell 45%; and in 1998, it fell 11%. This decrease in AIDS-related deaths was primarily due to several new breakthroughs in drugs that were introduced in 1995. The new drug treatment program has patients taking a drug "cocktail" of many pills daily, which include several new drugs (protease inhibitors and HIV-inhibiting drugs). In many cases, these new  drugs reduce the HIV virus to undetectable levels, but the drugs still do not wipe out the virus. Instead, the virus "hides out" in the body and returns if patients stop taking the drugs, which means these drugs must be taken for life. Because the anti-HIV drugs reduce life-threatening symptoms, these drugs have given AIDS patients a longer and better life (J. Cohen, 2002).

The dramatic decreases in deaths from AIDS because of the drug cocktails used in the early 1990s have slowed greatly since 1999. That's because the HIV virus has become resistant to some of the "new" drugs and some patients have stopped taking the drugs because of bad side effects (nausea, anemia, brittle bones). Researchers are currently searching for new drugs and vaccines to treat HIV/AIDS (Maugh, 2002b; 2003).

Now, we'll discuss a cruel cultural influence on female sexual behavior.

E. Cultural Diversity: Genital Cutting

Good Tradition or Cruel Mutilation?

What is genital cutting?

Men have a long history of trying to control the sexual motivation of women. In many countries, men want to marry virgins and insist that women remain so until marriage, although the men do not hold themselves to the same standards. One extreme example of men controlling the sexual motivation and behavior of women is found in parts of Africa and the Arabian Peninsula, where young girls undergo genital cutting before they become sexually mature (Caldwell et al., 1997).

Genital cutting involves cutting away the female's external genitalia, usually including her clitoris and surrounding skin (labia minora). The remaining edges are sewn together, which leaves only a small opening for urination and menstruation.

Soraya Mire (above photo) remembers the day that her mother said, "I'm going to buy you some gifts." Soraya, who was

At age 13, Soraya Mire underwent genital cutting.

13, obediently got into the car with her mother and driver. They didn't go shopping but stopped at a doctor's house. Once inside, they went into an operating room where a doctor asked Soraya to lie on the operating table. He tied her feet down with a rope so she could not move. Her mother said that it was time for Soraya to become a woman and undergo genital cutting.

Like her mother and her mother's mother, Soraya underwent this ancient rite of passage. But unlike them, Soraya has decided to break the silence and fight this cruel mutilation. Now 36, Soraya has made a documentary film called *Fire Eyes* to protest the current practice of genital cutting (Tawa, 1995).

Researchers estimate that about 2 million women a year and a total of about 100 million women have undergone genital cutting (formerly called female circumcision). Genital cutting is currently practiced in about 28 African countries by peoples of all different socioeconomic classes and ethnic and cultural groups (Lacey, 2002; Nour, 2000).

What Is Its Purpose?

In many of the poorer societies of Africa and Ethiopia, genital cutting is a common ritual to physically mark young girls and increase their chances for future marriage. Recently, conservative Muslim clerics in Egypt overturned a government ban on genital cutting, which serves no hygienic or medically useful purpose (Daniszewski, 1997).

Girls commonly undergo genital cutting before they reach puberty, usually between the ages of 4 and 10. The primary reason for genital cutting is the men's belief that if women are surgically deprived of receiving sexual pleasure, they will remain clean and virginal until marriage. Men in these societies often refuse to marry a woman who has not undergone genital cutting because they believe that she is unclean and not a virgin (A. Walker & Parmar, 1993).

The male equivalent of genital cutting would be amputation of the male's penis.

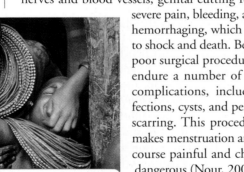

Young girl is being held while undergoing genital cutting.

Are There Complications?

Because of the high social status of Soraya's father, who was a general, her genital cutting was performed by a doctor. However, in the majority of cases, it is done by someone with no medical training who uses a razor blade and less than sterile procedures.

Because the genital area has a high percentage of nerves and blood vessels, genital cutting results in severe pain, bleeding, and even hemorrhaging, which can lead to shock and death. Because of poor surgical procedures, girls endure a number of medical complications, including infections, cysts, and permanent scarring. This procedure also makes menstruation and intercourse painful and childbirth dangerous (Nour, 2000).

Girls submit to the fear, pain, and trauma of genital cutting for varied and complex reasons. Genital cutting is done in the belief that it is for the good of their daughters, that their religion requires it, that it will make their daughters marriageable, and that it is necessary to maintain female chastity (Nour, 2000). However, after genital cutting many women suffer chronic anxiety and depression from worry about their disfigured genitals, difficulties with menstruation, and fear of infertility (Caldwell et al., 1997).

Is There a Solution?

The United Nations health organizations have endorsed laws against genital cutting, but such laws cannot eliminate this strong sociocultural tradition. As one supporter of genital cutting said, "This procedure helps to keep women's sexual drives at acceptable and reasonable levels" (Daniszewski, 1997). Although Westerners are horrified by this barbaric practice, many African societies consider this practice part of their culture and do it out of love for their daughters. For example, when a newspaper in Ghana, Africa, published articles in favor of banning genital cutting, local women had great success in getting support to keep this ancient practice and reject values from the outside world.

In 2002, the Kenyan president banned genital cutting, but it is still being practiced in some regions. Feminists in Africa and Egypt who are fighting this cruel tradition have run into considerable resistance from both men and women who approve of it (Lacey, 2002, 2003). Genital cutting is an extreme example of how far human societies (men) will go to control the sexual behavior of women.

We have discussed two biological drives, hunger and sex. After the Concept Review, we'll examine an important social need—achievement.

✔ Concept Review

1. Physiological or psychological factors that cause us to act in a specific way at a particular time are included in the definition of _____.

2. Innate biological forces predispose an animal to behave in a particular way in the presence of a specific environmental condition. These ways of behaving are called _____.

3. There are several areas in the brain, including the nucleus accumbens and ventral tegmental area, that make up a neural circuit called the (a)_____ center. This center especially uses the neurotransmitter (b)_____. Many behaviors (eating, engaging in sex, gambling) that activate this center are (c)_____ with pleasurable feelings.

4. External stimuli, reinforcers, goals, or rewards that may be positive or negative and that motivate one's behavior are called _____.

5. When we perform behaviors to reduce biological needs or obtain various incentives, we are acting under the influence of (a)_____ motivation. When we perform behaviors because they are personally rewarding or because we are following our personal goals, beliefs, or expectations, we are acting under the influence of (b)_____ motivation.

6. Needs that are not critical to your survival but that are acquired through learning and socialization, such as the needs for achievement and affiliation, are called (a)_____ needs. Needs that are critical to your survival and physical well-being, such as food, water, and sex, are called (b)_____ needs.

7. The ascending order or hierarchy with biological needs at the bottom and social needs at the top is _____. This idea assumes that we satisfy our biological needs before we satisfy our social needs.

8. There are three major factors that influence eating. Cues that come from physiological changes are called (a)_____ factors. Cues that come from inherited instructions are called (b)_____ factors. Cues that come from learning and personality traits are called (c)_____ factors.

9. Biological cues for hunger that come from the stomach, liver, intestines, and fat cells are called (a)_____ cues. Biological cues that come from the brain are called (b)_____ cues.

10. The part of the hypothalamus that is involved in feelings of being hungry is called the (a)_____; the part that is involved in feelings of being full is called the (b)_____.

11. We inherit the following genetic factors involved in weight regulation: a certain number of (a)_____ cells that store fat; a certain (b)_____ rate that regulates how fast we burn off fuel; a certain (c)_____ point that maintains a stable amount of body fat; and weight-regulating (d)_____ that influence appetite, metabolism, and hormone secretion.

12. Psychological factors that influence eating include (a)_____ associations, (b)_____ influences, and (c)_____ variables.

13. Genetic sex factors involve the 23rd chromosome, called the (a)_____, which determines the sex of the child. Biological sex factors include sex hormones, which for the male are called (b)_____ and for the female are called (c)_____. Psychological sex factors include the subjective feeling of being male or female, which is called (d)_____; adopting behaviors and traits that society identifies as male or female, which is called (e)_____; and being more sexually aroused by members of the same or opposite sex, which is called (f)_____.

14. Evidence from the sexual orientation of identical twins and the shared genetic material from gay brothers are examples of (a)_____ factors in the development of a homosexual orientation. Young boys who prefer girls' toys and girl playmates and engage in opposite-sex behaviors show a tendency to develop a homosexual orientation, which shows the effects of (b)_____ factors on sexual orientation.

15. A person who has been infected by the human immunodeficiency virus but has not yet developed any illnesses is said to be (a)_____. A person whose level of T-cells has dropped to 200 per cubic milliliter of blood but who may or may not have developed an illness is defined as having (b)_____.

Answers: 1. motivation; 2. fixed action patterns; 3. (a) reward/pleasure, (b) dopamine, (c) rewarded or encouraged; 4. incentives; 5. (a) extrinsic, (b) intrinsic; 6. (a) social, (b) biological; 7. Maslow's hierarchy of needs; 8. (a) biological, (b) genetic, (c) psychosocial; 9. (a) peripheral, (b) central; 10. (a) lateral hypothalamus, (b) ventromedial hypothalamus; 11. (a) fat, (b) metabolic, (c) set, (d) genes; 12. (a) learned, (b) social-cultural, (c) personality; 13. (a) sex chromosome, (b) androgens, (c) estrogens, (d) gender identity, (e) gender role, (f) sexual orientation; 14. (a) genetic, (b) psychological; 15. (a) HIV positive, (b) AIDS

F. Achievement

Why did Victor succeed? At the beginning of the module, we told you about Victor, an African American high school student whose buddies called him a "White boy" because they thought he was studying too hard. "You can't be cool if you're smart," says Victor, who was Mission Bay High's student body president, had a 3.7 (A–) grade point average, and planned to attend the University of Southern California in the fall (adapted from the *San Diego Union-Tribune,* June 17, 1994).

> It doesn't look cool if you work hard for grades.

Victor (right photo) grew up with an obstacle that goes largely unnoticed and is rarely discussed in public: pressure from students in the same racial or ethnic group not to succeed in the classroom (Steele, 1995). Educators believe that the high dropout rates for minorities result, in part, from peer pressure not to succeed in school or show

academic achievement (McWhorter, 2000). For Victor, academic achievement was one of his many social needs.

Social needs, such as the desire for affiliation or close social bonds, nurturance or need to help and protect others, dominance or need to influence or control others, and achievement or need to excel, are acquired through learning and experience.

If you are working hard to achieve academic success, you are demonstrating your social need for achievement.

The *achievement need* refers to the desire to set challenging goals and to persist in pursuing those goals in the face of obstacles, frustrations, and setbacks.

The achievement need not only is a major concern of college students but also ranks high (Level 4 out of 5) in Maslow's hierarchy of needs. We'll discuss four questions related to the achievement need: How is the need for achievement measured? What is high need for achievement? What is fear of failure? What is underachievement?

How Is the Need for Achievement Measured?

Do you have a strong need to achieve? Researchers David McClelland and John Atkinson tried to answer this question with a test called the Thematic Apperception Test, or TAT.

The *Thematic Apperception Test,* commonly called the *TAT,* is a personality test in which subjects are asked to look

What do you think is going on in this TAT card?

at pictures of people in ambiguous situations and to make up stories about what the characters are thinking and feeling and what the outcome will be.

For example, the sample TAT card on the left shows a young man with a sad expression and a bright sun and fruit tree in the background. If you were taking the TAT, you would be asked to describe what is happening in this card. To measure the level of achievement, your stories would be scored in terms of achievement themes, such as setting goals, competing, or overcoming obstacles (Atkinson, 1958; McClelland et al., 1953). The TAT assumes that the strength of your need to achieve will be reflected in the kinds of thoughts and feelings you use to describe the TAT cards. However, TAT stories are difficult to score reliably because there is no objective way to identify which thoughts and feelings indicate level of achievement (Keiser & Prather, 1990). More recently, objective **paper-and-pencil tests** (p. 474) have been developed to measure achievement motivation because these tests are easier to administer and score and have somewhat better reliability and validity than does the TAT (Kaplan & Saccuzzo, 2001).

However, measuring the need for achievement has proved difficult because it relates to intrinsic motivational factors that include beliefs and expectations, which have proved difficult to quantify (Petri & Govern, 2004).

What Is High Need for Achievement?

There is perhaps no better example of individuals with high need for achievement than Olympic athletes. One example is swimmer Natalie Coughlin, who is two-time NCAA swimmer of the year, has set two world records and 22 American records, is on track to become the first woman to go under one minute in the 100-meter backstroke, and one of five finalists for best amateur athlete. She is training four to five hours a day, six days a week, to compete in the Olympics while maintaining a 3.5 grade point average at the University of California, Berkeley (Lieber, 2002). Natalie has all the marks of someone with a high need for achievement (Atkinson & Raynor, 1974; McClelland, 1985).

Natalie Coughlin trains 4–5 hours a day, 6 days a week.

High need for achievement is shown by those who persist longer at tasks; perform better on tasks, activities, or exams; set challenging but realistic goals; compete with others to win; and are attracted to careers that require initiative.

Although the vast majority of us will not make the Olympics or achieve an A average in college, most of us will show varying degrees of the need to achieve by doing our best, striving for social recognition, and working to achieve material rewards (Hareli & Weiner, 2002).

The idea that there is a need for achievement and that it motivates many of our behaviors has generated a great deal of research. However, measuring a person's need for achievement and making predictions about an individual's level of achievement have proved difficult for two reasons: The TAT and paper-and-pencil tests have limited reliability and validity (p. 287), and achievement motivation is difficult to quantify because it involves intrinsic motivation (pp. 331, 359), which includes one's personal beliefs and expectations (Petri & Govern, 2004).

If we consider one side of a coin to be a need for achievement, then the other side is fear of failure and making excuses for failing.

Fear of Failure

Why do some fail? Just as some individuals may be motivated by a need for achievement, others may be motivated by a fear of failure. Atkinson (1964) believed that, in order to understand fully why a person succeeds or fails in reaching a goal, we must examine not only a person's need for achievement but also the fear of failure.

Fear of failure is shown by people who are motivated to avoid failure by choosing easy, nonchallenging tasks where failure is more unlikely to occur.

For example, fear of failure may motivate a student to study just enough to avoid failing an exam but not enough to get a good grade or set higher academic goals. In fact, the fear of failure is a good predictor of poor grades: The greater a student's fear of failure, the poorer his or her grades (W. E. Herman, 1990). Atkinson said that individuals who are motivated primarily by a fear of failure will never do as well, work as hard, or set goals as high as those who are motivated by a need for achievement. Also, the greater one's fear of failure, the greater the chances of trying to look good by engaging in self-handicapping (Elliot & Church, 2003).

Self-handicapping. If a person is motivated primarily by the fear of failure, how does this individual explain his or her poor performances yet keep a good self-image? One solution is to use self-handicapping (E. Jones & Berglas, 1978).

Self-handicapping refers to doing things that contribute to failure and then using these very things, knowingly or unknowingly, as excuses for failing to achieve some goal.

For example, instead of studying for an exam, a student goes to a movie and then does poorly on the test. He excuses his bad grade by saying he didn't study, which is an example of self-handicapping. Researchers found that individuals with low self-esteem are most likely to engage in self-handicapping because it is one way to look good to their peers and thus protect their already low self-esteem (Elliot & Church, 2003). Self-handicapping excuses may involve health (missed sleep, have a cold), drug usage (have a hangover), unrealistically high goals (how could I possibly do that), or procrastination (I didn't have enough time). In the short term, self-handicapping helps preserve our positive self-image and self-esteem, but in the long term, it interferes with taking personal responsibility to achieve our goals (Covington, 2000).

One example of how fear of failure affects motivation is seen in individuals who are underachievers.

Underachievement

Why do some underachieve? One of my friends described his 14-year-old son, Rich, as having all the brains in the world but doing nothing with them. Although Rich is a computer wizard, he gets terrible grades in school, never does his homework, and doesn't seem to have any ambition. Rich might be called an underachiever.

Underachievers are individuals who score relatively high on tests of ability or intelligence but perform more poorly than their scores would predict.

The most common examples of underachievers are students who score relatively high on ability or intelligence tests but perform poorly in school or academic settings (Lupart & Pyryt, 1996). Researchers found that underachievement is not related to socioeconomic class, that there are two or three male underachievers for every female, and that about 15% of students are underachievers (McCall, 1994).

Characteristics. The psychological characteristics of underachievers include having a poor self-concept, low self-esteem, and poor peer relationships and being shy or depressed. The cognitive characteristics of underachievers include fear of failure, poor perceptions of their abilities, and lack of persistence. This means that underachievers are less likely to persist in getting their college degrees, holding on to jobs, or maintaining their marriages (McCall, 1994). Thus, underachievement reduces performance in academic, job, and marital settings, and its effects may last through adulthood.

The paradox of underachievement is that underachievers have the abilities but are not motivated to use them. Clinicians, counselors, and researchers are developing treatment programs to help underachievers change their beliefs and expectations so they will develop the motivation to use their considerable abilities (McCall, 1994).

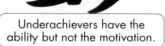

Underachievers have the ability but not the motivation.

Three Components of Success

Why is a person successful? Explaining why some students are more successful than others involves the interaction of three components that we have just discussed: need for achievement, fear of failure, and psychological factors (self-concept, self-esteem, and confidence in one's abilities). For example, researchers wondered why some minority children from low-income homes were successful in school while others were not. Those minority students who succeeded had higher self-esteem, had more confidence in their abilities, and received more support and encouragement from a parent or caregiver (Finn & Rock, 1997). Researchers also found that students who were more successful in school had come from more stimulating home environments (parents spoke more to children, children had more books and watched less television) (Cleveland et al., 2000). Thus, having a stimulating home environment leads to a higher need for achievement, which in turn leads to more success in life. Finally, successful students not only worked harder but also liked what they were doing. This "enjoyment of work" is an important cognitive factor that greatly influences motivation and is our next topic.

Need for Achievement — Fear of Failure — Psychological Factors

BEING SUCCESSFUL

F. Achievement

Do you work for love or money?

Each year, over 1,600 seniors compete in the Westinghouse Science Talent Search to win the most prestigious high school science award in the United States. One winner was Ann Chen (photo below), a high school senior from California. Chen's project involved studying how genes function in the spread of cancer. When interviewed after receiving her award, Chen said that science has been a lifelong interest for her (Balint, 1995). Chen's love of science translates into a motivating force that comes from various cognitive factors.

Cognitive factors in motivation refer to how people evaluate or perceive a situation and how these evaluations and perceptions influence their willingness to work.

Ann Chen perceives science projects as interesting and enjoyable and works hard to complete them. She plans to go to Harvard and get a doctorate in chemistry. Compared to Chen's love of science, other students find science projects hard and boring and take science courses only because they are required. The difference between taking science courses because of a love of science and because of course requirements illustrates the difference between two kinds of motivation—intrinsic motivation and extrinsic motivation.

Intrinsic motivation involves engaging in certain activities or behaviors without receiving any external rewards because the behaviors themselves are personally rewarding or because engaging in these activities fulfills our beliefs or expectations.

Chen's dedication to science is in large part fueled by intrinsic motivation, which is related to feeling competent, curious and interested, having self-determination, and enjoying the task, whether it's a science project, work you like, a hobby, or volunteer work. In comparison, extrinsic motivation involves different factors.

Extrinsic motivation involves engaging in certain activities or behaviors that either reduce biological needs or help us obtain incentives and external rewards.

INTRINSIC MOTIVATION
Competent
Determined
Personally rewarding
Enjoyable

If you do a job, task, or assigned work because it is required, your motivation is often extrinsic, which may involve being evaluated or some competition, seeking recognition, money, or other incentives, such as acquiring a car or home. Another major difference between intrinsic and extrinsic motivation is that working because of intrinsic motivation (loving what you're doing) makes you feel powerfully motivated. Without intrinsic motivation there would be less charitable work and donations and fewer people would volunteer their time or donate their blood (Deci et al., 1999).

So, here's an interesting question: What would happen to intrinsic motivation if you got paid for doing something that you love doing?

EXTRINSIC MOTIVATION
Competitive
Get recognition
Obtain incentives
Make money

What happens if volunteers get paid?

Would receiving money for volunteering to give blood "turn off" or decrease the intrinsic motivation of donors to the point that they might give less blood or none at all?

Researchers generally believed that if people were given external rewards (money, awards, prizes, or tokens) for doing tasks (donating blood) from intrinsic motivation, their performance of and interest in these tasks would decrease (Deci et al., 1999). Because of the widely held belief that external rewards decreased intrinsic motivation, many books advised that rewards should not be used in educational settings, hospitals, or volunteer organizations because such rewards would do more harm than good. Recent reviews of this issue indicate that the effects of external rewards on intrinsic motivation are more complex than originally thought.

Researchers have reached three general conclusions about the influence of external rewards on intrinsic motivation (Deci et al., 1999; Eisenberger et al., 1999; Lepper et al., 1999). First, giving unexpected external rewards does not decrease intrinsic motivation, but people may come to expect such rewards. Second, giving positive verbal feedback for doing work that was better than others may actually increase intrinsic motivation. Third, giving external rewards for doing minimal work or completing a specific project may decrease intrinsic motivation.

Recent studies indicate that, unlike previously thought, external rewards that are unexpected or involve positive verbal feedback may increase intrinsic motivation. External rewards that are tied to doing minimal work or completing a specific project may decrease intrinsic motivation. For example, when parents or teachers praise children, the praise is likely to increase intrinsic motivation if the praise is sincere and promotes the child's feelings of being competent and independent. In contrast, insincere praise, praise for very small accomplishments, or praise that is controlling rather than rewarding may decrease intrinsic motivation (Henderlong & Lepper, 2002).

People who donate blood are usually intrinsically motivated.

For a long time it was also thought that external rewards automatically decreased creative work and interest. But researchers have found that the effects of giving children a reward for completing a creative task depend on how children perceive the reward. If they perceive the reward as a treat, it will increase their intrinsic interest, but if they see the reward as external pressure to be creative, it will decrease their intrinsic interest (Eisenberger & Armeli, 1997). All these studies show that external rewards influence cognitive factors, which in turn may increase or decrease intrinsic motivation.

Next, we'll examine how cognitive factors influence children's motivation and achievement in school.

G. Research Focus: Immigrant Students

Why were researchers surprised?

One goal of research is to solve puzzles about human behavior. We're about to describe a situation that was very puzzling because what psychologists guessed should happen, did not and what should not happen, did. Here's the situation.

Why did immigrant children who first had to learn English do well in school?

Psychologists visited a junior high school and the teacher explained that some of the students only recently immigrated to the United States and had to learn English and adjust to all the cultural differences. All the other students were born in the United States. The psychologists were asked to guess which students—those born in the United States or those who had recently immigrated—were doing better in school and getting better grades.

The psychologists guessed that children who had been born in the United States would be doing better and getting higher grades because they knew the language and the customs. They guessed that the newly arrived immigrant children would not be doing as well because the immigrant students would be seriously handicapped by not knowing the language or the customs. To answer this question, researchers began a large study, which ended in a puzzle.

Procedure and Results

To find out which students were doing better in school, researchers analyzed data from a representative sample of 24,599 eighth-grade students who came from 1,052 randomly selected schools in the United States. Researchers focused on two groups of students, who were Latino, Asian, Black (mostly from the Caribbean), and White (Kao & Tienda, 1995). One group of students was called first generation because both the student and his or her mother were foreign born and had difficulties with the language and customs. The other group was called third generation because both the student and his or her mother were native born (born in the United States) and knew the language and were familiar with the customs.

Researchers compared how first- and third-generation students performed on well-known tests for math and reading. At the end of the test, students were asked about their future academic plans, such as whether they planned to go to college.

In the graph on the right, notice that there are three pairs of bars, and each pair compares the math scores of first- and third-generation Asian, Latino, and Black *immigrant* students. Notice that in each case, the first-generation immigrant students, who faced the most difficulties in language and social adjustment, performed better on math tests (and other tests not shown) than did the third-generation students who were born in the United States.

There were two puzzling findings: Why did first-generation students perform better, and why did more first-generation students plan to go to college?

Conclusions

The puzzle is why and how immigrant students, who are handicapped by language problems, consistently score higher on tests than native-born students. Perhaps this difference in scores between first- and third-generation students was due to different socioeconomic conditions. However, after controlling (by using statistics) for socioeconomic class differences, researchers found that the major reason for the better performance of first-generation minority students was that they had adopted their parents' *hopeful values* about education.

Parental values. The first-generation immigrant mothers and fathers believed that their children would achieve social and economic advantages by obtaining a good education. The parents' hopeful values about educational opportunities translated into encouraging their children to work together, help one another, and spend a significant amount of time doing homework (three hours nightly).

In comparison, third-generation parents who have lived for some years in the United States have become less hopeful about making advances through education. Because they are less hopeful about educational opportunities, they pass along a negative attitude about doing well in school. In turn, negative parental attitudes translate into their children having less motivation, spending less time doing homework, performing poorer on tests, and having less desire to go on to college (Kao & Tienda, 1995).

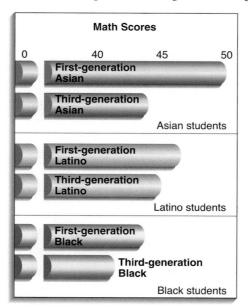

Math Scores

| 0 | 40 | 45 | 50 |

First-generation Asian

Third-generation Asian

Asian students

First-generation Latino

Third-generation Latino

Latino students

First-generation Black

Third-generation Black

Black students

Implications. There is much discussion of how to improve public schools, such as by decreasing class size or making teachers more accountable for their students. This study points to another factor in improving schools, which is to encourage parents to become more involved in their children's education. As this study found, parents' positive or negative attitudes toward education translate into encouraging or discouraging their children, which in turn increases or decreases their children's motivation, performance, and academic achievement.

We have discussed how cognitive factors can influence social needs, such as achievement. Next, we'll discuss how cognitive factors can also influence a biological need, hunger, and result in serious eating disorders.

H. Application: Eating Problems & Treatments

Dieting: Problems, Concerns, and Benefits

Why is dieting so difficult?

Some of us have learned to eat at certain times (learned associations) or eat when stressed (personality variables), or we come from families that encourage eating to show appreciation (cultural influences). Any of these psychosocial factors—learned associations, personality variables, or cultural influences—can override our genetic and biological factors and result in becoming overweight. The percentage of adult Americans who are overweight or obese has increased dramatically, from 26% in 1976 to 65% in 2003 (J. O. Hill et al., 2003). Losing weight is very difficult because the body is genetically designed to store extra calories as fat and because our large forebrains are very good at rationalizing why we need to eat another piece of pizza and have a late-night snack.

We'll use the dieting experiences of television talk-show host Oprah Winfrey to illustrate the difficulties of dieting and how best to maintain an optimal weight.

Overweight and Dieting

In the 1970s, when Oprah Winfrey was in her twenties, she weighed about 140 pounds. By the mid-1980s, Oprah weighed about 190 pounds (left photo), which is considered overweight for her height and frame. She described getting home from work and being overwhelmed by a compulsion to eat. When her weight reached 211, she decided it was time for a diet program (B. Greene & Winfrey, 1996).

190 pounds

In the 1980s, Oprah went on a well-publicized diet in which she lost 67 pounds to weigh 142 pounds. She showed off her slim figure on television (right photo) and said she was finally cured of overeating. She was wrong.

In the 1990s, Oprah did not make the necessary changes in her lifestyle and she regained all her lost weight and then some, reaching about 237 pounds (left photo). Like all bodies, Oprah's body has two physiological factors that make it difficult to keep off lost weight.

142 pounds

Physiological factors. One physiological factor is that Oprah's body, which is set up to store a certain amount of fat, automatically adjusts to any decrease in fat stores by lowering its *rate of metabolism* by 25% (J. M. Friedman, 2003). This results in her body more efficiently burning fuel so she must eat even less or exercise more to avoid regaining lost weight. Another physiological factor is that Oprah's body has a *genetically fixed set point,* which maintains her fat stores at a stable level. If the level of fat stores drops below her set point, her body compensates by increasing her appetite so that her fat stores will return to their former level (Friedman, 2003). This means that the body fights a reduced food intake with two physiological actions: reducing the rate of metabolism and trying to increase fat stores. These factors explain why 90–95% of dieters regain their lost weight within 1–2 years and almost certainly after 5 years (Vogel, 1999).

237 pounds

Like most dieters who have regained their lost weight, Oprah admitted, "I didn't do whatever the maintenance program was. I thought I was cured. And that's just not true. You have to find a way to live in the world with food" (*People,* January 14, 1991, p. 84). After dieting, people like Oprah need to develop a *maintenance program* that involves eating less and exercising more.

Psychological factors. Oprah also realized that food had become more than nutrition. "For me, food was comfort, pleasure, love, a friend, everything. Now I consciously work every day at not letting food be a substitute for emotions" (Tresniowski & Bell, 1996, p. 81). Thus, some dieters need a change in lifestyle so that they don't eat when stressed or depressed. In trying to regulate and maintain her weight at a reasonable level (right photo), Oprah has tried a number of diets. Which diet program should one choose?

170 pounds

Diet Program/Life Style

In the early 2000s, Oprah's weight climbed again and she went on another diet and lost 33 pounds (Oldenburg, 2002). Oprah's difficulties in controlling her weight confirm the experiences of many dieters who found it not only difficult to lose weight but even more difficult to keep the weight off. Researchers agree that the best way to reduce and keep weight off is not by going on one diet after another but rather by committing to a long-term program or lifestyle of exercise and careful eating (W. Evans, 2000). Researchers found that a program of exercise and diet involves four factors: (1) changing one's attitudes toward food (making it less important); (2) changing one's eating patterns (consuming fewer calories); (3) developing a regular exercise program (a critical part of a weight program); and (4) perhaps the most important, sticking to this weight program over the long term, often for a lifetime (J. E. Brody, 2000b).

Low-fat or low-carbohydrate diet? There has been a big debate over which of these diets is more effective. Dieters report that a low-fat diet works better for some, while a low-carbohydrate diet works better for others. However, researchers report that whichever diet you choose, the ONLY reason you lose weight is because you're consuming fewer calories (Christensen, 2003). And, don't forget the exercise.

New hormone. As discussed previously (p. 335), the intestines secrete a newly found hormone, PYY, that decreases appetite and has been found to have lower levels in overweight people. Researchers injected PYY into both overweight and lean people and then gave them an all-you-can-eat buffet. Whether overweight or lean, all ate 30% less, a remarkable finding. Researchers caution that the use of this hormone is still experimental, but it may prove helpful in combating obesity (Batterham et al., 2003).

Next, we'll discuss the causes and treatments of two serious eating disorders.

Must you be thin?

On the beautiful tropical island of Fiji, a bulky body had always been viewed as a beautiful body and women complimented each other on gaining weight. But then TV arrived in 1995 and began showing programs like *Melrose Place* (full

TV programs changed their body image.

of young, slender females) and commercials with slim models. After watching these programs, young girls began to develop a different body image, that of being slim. By 1998, the incidence of an eating disorder (bulimia nervosa) had almost doubled to 29% of young girls. Girls said that they wanted to be thin because everyone on TV who has everything is slim (A. Becker et al., 2002). This is an example of how cultural factors can encourage eating disorders. We'll discuss two serious eating disorders, anorexia nervosa and bulimia nervosa, their causes and treatments.

Anorexia Nervosa

Bonnie (center photo) had developed anorexia nervosa at age 19, when she was in college. She went from 120 to 70 pounds in six months and was hospitalized for treatment (Sohn, 2002). Bonnie, now 35, has the brittle bones of a very old woman because of her eating disorder, anorexia nervosa *(an-uh-REX-see-ah ner-VOH-sah).*

Anorexia nervosa is a serious eating disorder characterized by refusing to eat and not maintaining weight at 85% of what is expected, having an intense fear of gaining weight or becoming fat, and missing at least three consecutive menstrual cycles. Anorexics also have a disturbed body image: They see themselves as fat even though they are very thin (American Psychiatric Association, 2000).

Anorexia nervosa, as defined by these symptoms, is a relatively rare disorder that affects about 1.0% of young women and a much smaller number of men aged 12 to 25.

Risk factors. One risk factor for anorexia nervosa is a dysfunctional family. In Bonnie's case, it was her mom who constantly told her that she was fat and even put padlocks on the kitchen cabinets so she could not have access to food (Sohn, 2002). Another risk involves personality factors, such as being very anxious, compulsive, rigid, and a perfectionist. Recent studies on anorexic identical twins and genetic mapping pointed to genes on chromosome 1 as being factors in developing a severe form of anorexia nervosa (Kaye, 2002; T. Wade, 2002). Thus, there may be multiple risk factors for developing anorexia nervosa.

Treatment. Previous psychological treatments for anorexics had limited success, and drugs have not proved very useful. A relatively new treatment program has reported success by using a form of family therapy. Parents are asked to become involved in helping their anorexic daughter to start eating and then gradually letting her control her eating. Parents are coached in how to help their daughter overcome personality problems (discussed above) that may be worsened by adolescent difficulties (LeGrange, 2002). Generally, recovery is difficult: About 20% of anorexics die prematurely, 30% have recurrent symptoms, and 50% recover enough to maintain a healthy weight and positive self-image (Sohn, 2002).

Anorexics do not see themselves as skinny.

Bulimia Nervosa

Carol's life seemed perfect when she was growing up, but all the time something was terribly wrong. "It was like I had to live in this fantasy world where everything was sweet and good and I got straight A's," Carol explains. "I started work when I was really young and I would do anything for anyone there and everyone thought I was so nice and so sweet. And I was just dying inside, literally." Carol, who began binge eating at the age of 15, was not overweight to begin with. She would eat a huge amount of food in one brief period and then force herself to vomit as a way of avoiding any weight gain (adapted from the *Daily Aztec,* March 22, 1984). Carol's disorder, which is called bulimia nervosa *(boo-LEE-me-ah ner-VOH-sah),* affects about 2% of the general population and about 8% of people who are overweight or obese (DeAngelis, 2002).

Bulimia nervosa is characterized by a minimum of two binge-eating episodes per week for at least three months; fear of not being able to stop eating; regularly engaging in vomiting, use of laxatives, or rigorous dieting and fasting; and excessive concern about body shape and weight (American Psychiatric Association, 2000).

Risk factors. One risk factor involves cultural pressures to develop a slim body, as seen in the increase in bulimia nervosa among Fijian girls. Another risk factor involves personality characteristics, such as being excessively concerned about appearance, being too sensitive, and having low self-esteem and high personal standards for achievement. For some, bouts of depression, anxiety, mood swings, and problems with social relationships may trigger episodes of bulimia nervosa, which may lead to obesity (Stice, 2002).

Treatment. The psychological treatment for bulimia nervosa may involve ways to control weight as well as one of two kinds of psychotherapy: cognitive-behavior therapy, which focuses on substituting positive thoughts for negative ones, or interpersonal therapy, which focuses on improving a person's social functioning (G. T. Wilson et al., 2002). The drug treatment for bulimia nervosa, which involves the use of antidepressant drugs and possible unwanted side effects, was shown to be less effective than psychotherapy and offered no advantage when combined with psychotherapy (Ricca et al., 2001). Follow-up studies report that 52% of bulimics recovered fully, 39% had some symptoms, and 9% had serious symptoms (Collings & King, 1994; DeAngelis, 2002).

The eating disorders of anorexia and bulimia nervosa clearly illustrate how various personality and psychosocial factors can not only influence but even override the normal functioning of one of our basic biological needs, hunger.

Summary Test

A. THEORIES OF MOTIVATION

1. The combined physiological and psychological factors that cause you to act in specific ways at particular times are referred to as (a)_____. When motivated, you usually exhibit three characteristics: you are (b)_____ to do something; you (c)_____ your energies toward a specific goal; and you have different (d)_____ of feelings about reaching that goal.

2. There are four general theories that together help explain human motivation. The theory that applies primarily to animal motivation involves innate biological forces that determine behavior. This is called the (a)_____ theory. The reward/pleasure center theory says there are several areas in the brain, including the (b)_____ and _____ , that especially use the neurotransmitter (c)_____. Many behaviors (eating, engaging in sex, gambling) that activate this center are (d)_____ with pleasurable feelings. The theory that says we are motivated by external rewards is called the (e)_____ theory. The theory that distinguishes between extrinsic and intrinsic motivations is called the (f)_____ theory. If we are motivated because we find the activities personally rewarding or because they fulfill our beliefs or expectations, our motivation is said to be due to (e)_____ motivation.

B. BIOLOGICAL & SOCIAL NEEDS

3. Food, water, and sleep are examples of (a)_____ needs. In comparison, needs that are acquired through learning and socialization are called (b)_____ needs. The theory that we satisfy our needs in ascending order, with physiological needs first and social needs later, is called (c)_____.
According to this theory, needs are divided into five levels: biological, safety, love and belongingness, esteem, and self-actualization.

C. HUNGER

4. If there is an almost perfect balance between how much food an organism needs to maintain the body's energy needs and how much the organism actually eats, the organism's weight is said to be (a)_____. Three different factors influence the hunger drive. Factors that come from physiological changes in blood chemistry and signals from digestive organs that provide feedback to the brain, which, in turn, triggers us to eat or stop eating, are called (b)_____ factors. Factors that come from learned associations between food and other stimuli, sociocultural influences, and various personality problems are called (c)_____ factors. Factors that come from inherited instructions contained in our genes are called (d)_____ factors.

5. Biological factors that influence eating come from two different sources. Cues arising from physiological changes in your blood chemistry and signals from your body organs are called (a)_____; cues from your brain are called (b)_____.

6. Genetic factors that influence hunger come from four different sources: the number of cells that store fat, which are called (a)_____; your rate of burning the body's fuel, which is called your (b)_____; the body's tendency to keep a stable amount of fat deposits, which is called the (c)_____; and a number of (d)_____ genes that influence appetite, metabolism, and secretion of hormones regulating fat stores.

D. SEXUAL BEHAVIOR

7. Human sexual behavior is influenced by three different factors. Inherited instructions for the development of sexual organs, hormonal changes at puberty, and neural circuits that control sexual reflexes are called (a)_____ factors. The fact that humans engage in sexual behavior for many reasons besides reproduction and the fact that humans experience sexual difficulties that have no physical or medical basis indicate the influence of (b)_____ factors on sexual behavior. Factors that regulate the secretion of sex hormones, which play a role in the development of secondary sexual characteristics, influence sexual motivation (more so in animals than in humans), regulate the development of ova and sperm, and control the female menstrual cycle, are called (c)_____ factors.

8. Biological sex factors include the secretion of sex hormones, which is controlled by an area of the brain called the (a)_____. The major male sex hormones secreted by the testes are called (b)_____, and the major female sex hormones secreted by the ovaries are (c)_____. When hormone levels are within the normal range, there is little (d)_____ between levels of sex hormones and sexual motivation in humans.

9. Three psychological sex factors include the individual's subjective experience and feelings of being a male or a female, which is called (a)_____; traditional or stereotypic behaviors, attitudes, and personality traits that society designates as masculine or feminine, which are called (b)_____; and whether a person is sexually aroused primarily by members of his or her own sex, the opposite sex, or both sexes, which is called (c)_____.

10. The findings that identical twins are often alike in their sexual orientation and that homosexual brothers shared similar inherited material indicate the influence of (a)_____ factors on homosexual orientation. The finding that genetic factors do not necessarily determine sexual orientation indicates the influence of (b)_____ factors on sexual orientation.

11. There are two kinds of sexual problems. Problems that are characterized by repetitive or preferred sexual fantasies involving nonhuman objects (articles of clothing) are called (a)_____. Problems of sexual arousal or orgasm that interfere with adequate functioning during sexual behavior are called (b)_____. When a person seeks help for a sexual problem, the clinician will check whether the causes are (c)_____ or _____.

12. If a person has been infected by the human immunodeficiency virus (HIV) but has not yet developed one or more of 26 illnesses, that person is said to be (a)_____. A person whose level of T-cells (CD4 immune cells) has dropped to below 200 per cubic milliliter of blood (one-fifth the level of a healthy person) and who may or may not have any other symptoms is said to have (b)_____.

E. CULTURAL DIVERSITY: GENITAL CUTTING

13. In some cultures the female's external genitalia, usually including her clitoris and surrounding skin (labia minora), are cut away; this practice is called _____. Girls often submit to the fear, pain, and trauma of this procedure so as to gain social status, please their parents, and comply with peer pressure. A number of feminists in Africa have formed a society to fight the sexual mutilation of females.

F. ACHIEVEMENT

14. High in Maslow's needs hierarchy is a desire to set challenging goals and persist in pursuing those goals in the face of obstacles, frustrations, and setbacks. This social need is

called the (a)_____. Someone who persists longer at tasks, shows better performance on tasks, activities, or exams, sets challenging but realistic goals, competes with others to win, and is attracted to careers that require initiative is said to have a high (b)_____. Individuals who score relatively high on tests of

ability or intelligence but perform more poorly than their scores would predict are called (c)_____. Individuals who choose either easy, nonchallenging tasks or challenging tasks where failure is probable and expected are said to be motivated by (d)_____.

15. If you engage in behaviors without receiving any external reward but because the behaviors themselves are personally rewarding, you are said to be (a)_____ motivated. If you engage in behaviors to reduce biological needs or obtain external rewards, you are said to be (b)_____ motivated.

G. RESEARCH FOCUS: IMMIGRANT STUDENTS

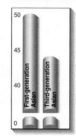

16. Researchers found that the major reason for the greater success of first-generation immigrant students was that they had taken on their (a)_____ hopeful outlook toward advancement through education. This study shows that parents' optimistic or pessimistic attitudes toward education, which are examples of (b)_____ factors, influence their children's academic achievement.

H. APPLICATION: EATING PROBLEMS & TREATMENTS

17. A healthy weight-maintenance program, which can reduce the risk of serious medical problems of
(a)_____ people, involves changing
(b)_____ toward food, changing
(c)_____ patterns, developing an
(d)_____ program, and sticking to a long-term (e)_____ program. Two serious eating disorders are a pattern characterized by bingeing, fear of not being able to stop eating, and regularly purging the body, which is called (f)_____; and another pattern in which a person starves to remain thin, has a fear of being fat, and has a disturbed body image, which is called (g)_____.

Answers: *1. (a) motivation, (b) energized, (c) direct, (d) intensities; 2. (a) instinct, (b) nucleus accumbens, ventral tegmental area, (c) dopamine, (d) rewarded or encouraged, (e) incentive, (f) cognitive, (e) intrinsic; 3. (a) biological, (b) social, (c) Maslow's hierarchy of needs; 4. (a) ideal or optimal, (b) biological, (c) psychosocial, (d) genetic; 5. (a) peripheral cues, (b) central cues; 6. (a) fat cells, (b) metabolic rate, (c) set point, (d) weight-regulating; 7. (a) genetic, (b) psychological, (c) biological; 8. (a) hypothalamus, (b) androgens, (c) estrogens, (d) correlation or association; 9. (a) gender identity, (b) gender roles, (c) sexual orientation; 10. (a) genetic, (b) psychological; 11. (a) paraphilias, (b) sexual dysfunctions, (c) psychological, physiological; 12. (a) HIV positive, (b) AIDS; 13. genital cutting; 14. (a) achievement motive, (b) need for achievement, (c) underachievers, (d) fear of failure; 15. (a) intrinsically, (b) extrinsically; 16. (a) parents', (b) cognitive or psychological; 17. (a) overweight, (b) attitudes, (c) eating, (d) exercise, (e) maintenance, (f) bulimia nervosa, (g) anorexia nervosa*

Critical Thinking

How Effective Is Viagra?

Questions

1. What are the two different causes of sexual problems (dysfunctions), and which one applies to Eric?

2. Why do you think that Viagra was discovered by accident?

3. How is the transmitter involved in producing an erection (a gas called nitric oxide) different from most other transmitters discussed earlier (p. 54)?

Eric (not his real name), who was 64 and happily married, was diagnosed with prostate cancer. He chose to have his prostate gland removed, knowing there was a 50–50 chance of becoming impotent, which is the inability to have an erection (also called erectile dysfunction). After surgery, Eric did become impotent and developed a terrible fear that his wife would leave him. Eric volunteered for a study on a brand new drug to treat impotence. For Eric, the new drug worked so well that he called it a "wonder drug" because it gave him back a normal married life. This drug later became known as Viagra (sildenafil).

What's unusual about Viagra is that it was discovered by accident. Scientists were looking for drugs to treat heart disease and found that, while one drug didn't work on heart disease, it did cause erections. Scientists changed goals and began testing the particular drug on men who were impotent.

It was not until the early 1980s that scientists figured out the plumbing behind erections. They discovered that when a man feels aroused, his penis releases a gas, nitric oxide, which activates an enzyme (cyclic GMP), which triggers the blood vessels in the penis to relax, which allows blood to rush in and cause stiffness (erection). Scientists found that Viagra worked by keeping the enzyme around longer so that blood vessels stayed relaxed longer, which allowed blood to flow in and cause an erection.

Estimates are that between 10 and 20 million American men suffer some degree of impotence. For many of these men, the idea of having an erection 20 to 40 minutes after taking Viagra was very appealing. In the first 3 months, sales of Viagra hit $411 million, making it the most successful prescription drug ever. However, after 7 months, sales had fallen 66% to $141 million for a number of reasons.

One reason was that Viagra did not work in 30–40% of men who tried it. Some men experienced unwanted side effects, such as one man who stopped taking Viagra because "your face gets very hot, you feel like your heart is beating faster than it should, there's anxiety" (Leland, 1998, p. 68). Also, although Viagra can cause erections, it may not resolve the underlying sexual difficulties in unhappy relationships. Finally, 61 deaths have been associated with Viagra, which resulted in a new warning label about not prescribing Viagra for men with certain heart problems.

In women with decreased sexual desire, Viagra has not proved effective, since the percentage of women (21%) who reported improved sexual functioning after Viagra was about the same as for those who took placebos.

For about 70% of men who suffer some degree of impotency, especially after prostate surgery, Viagra appears to be a very good deal. (Adapted from Horowitz, 1999; Leland, 1998; Mestel, 1999; Roan, 1998)

4. Why might men who were not impotent want to try Viagra?

5. What is one reason that Viagra did not work in 30–40% of those who tried it?

6. What is one reason that Viagra did not improve sexual functioning in women?

Try InfoTrac to search for terms: prostate cancer; impotence; Viagra.

---

1. There are two general causes of sexual dysfunctions. One cause involves organic factors, such as medical problems or problems caused by drugs. The other cause involves psychological factors, such as anxiety, sexual trauma, guilt, or communication difficulties, all of which lead to sexual problems. In Eric's case, the cause was organic, since he had no problems with having an erection until his prostate gland was removed.

2. Although finding a pill to treat impotence was a high priority, scientists did not yet understand how erections occurred and so did not know where to look for a drug to treat impotence. It was by accident that scientists, who were initially studying a drug to treat heart disease, found a drug that produced erections.

3. All the transmitters discovered earlier were chemicals (pp. 54–55). That's why finding that the transmitter involved in erections was a gas (nitric oxide) was completely unexpected.

4. Men with no erectile problems may want to try Viagra because they incorrectly believed that Viagra would increase not only erections but also sexual desire and motivation, which it doesn't.

5. The reasons Viagra did not work in 30–40% of men with erectile problems may be serious organic (medical) problems or psychological problems (low sexual motivation, fear or anxiety about performing), which Viagra doesn't necessarily help.

6. One reason Viagra was no more effective than a placebo in improving female sexual functioning was that Viagra essentially deals with the flow of blood into and out of sexual organs and doesn't seem to improve sexual desire. Thus, women's low sexual desire or motivation, which may be a psychological problem, is a difficulty that Viagra doesn't seem to help.

Links to Learning

LEARNING ACTIVITIES

● *POWERSTUDY CD-ROM 2.0*
by Tom Doyle and Rod Plotnik

Check out the "Motivation" Module (disk 2) on PowerStudy and:

- Test your knowledge using an interactive version of the Summary Test on pages 354 and 355. Also access related quizzes—true/false, multiple choice, and matching.
- Explore an interactive version of the Critical Thinking exercise "How Effective Is Viagra?" on page 356.
- You will also find key terms, a chapter outline including chapter abstract, and a list of hotlinked Web sites that correlate to this module.

● *SELF-STUDY ASSESSMENT*
Want help studying? For your customized Study Plan go to **http://psychology.wadsworth.com/plotnik7e/**. This program will automatically generate pretests and posttests to help you determine what concepts you have mastered and what concepts you still need work on.

WebTUTOR ● *STUDY GUIDE and WEBTUTOR*
Check the corresponding module in your Study Guide for effective student tips and help learning the material presented.

● *INFOTRAC COLLEGE EDITION ONLINE LIBRARY*
To find interesting and relevant articles go to **http://www.infotrac-college.com**, use your password, and then type in search terms such as the ones listed below.

Motivation   Gender roles

STUDY QUESTIONS

Use InfoTrac to search for topics mentioned in the main heads below (e.g., motivation, genital cutting, achievement).

*A. Theories of Motivation—Which theory best explains why students work hard to get good grades? (**Suggested answer page 628**)

*B. Biological & Social Needs—How would your needs change if you won a $20-million lottery? (**Suggested answer page 629**)

C. Hunger—As a parent, what would you do to keep you and your children from becoming overweight?

D. Sexual Behavior—What would happen to someone's sexual behavior if, at puberty, no sex hormones were secreted?

E. Cultural Diversity: Genital Cutting—Are there any American cultural traditions that are detrimental to the sexual behavior of men or women?

F. Achievement—Why might some students get the "sophomore blues" and feel less motivated about doing well in college?

G. Research Focus: Immigrant Students—What is one key to unlocking the potential of students from different cultures?

*H. Application: Eating Problems & Treatments—Would you believe an ad that promised you could "lose weight easily and quickly without dieting or exercise by practicing self-hypnosis"? (**Suggested answer page 629**)

*These questions are answered in Appendix B.

Module 16: Emotion

Introduction

Emotional Experience

What did Rick feel during a shark attack?

What happened to Rick at 7:30 in the morning on a warm Thursday was something he would never forget. He had paddled his surfboard about 150 feet from shore to catch the best waves. As he waited, he saw a large green sea turtle swim by and disappear under the deep blue surface. Moments later he felt the water under him start to move. He saw some colors and swirls but thought it must be the turtle swimming around. It wasn't a turtle but a 14-foot tiger shark, a very dangerous killing machine. With one quick motion of its head, the shark tossed Rick and his surfboard into the air. When the board landed, Rick was hanging on to the back while the shark was sinking its rows of jagged teeth into the front of the board. As Rick hung on, he felt his heart pounding like a hammer and heard a snapping sound as the shark broke off a piece of Rick's surfboard. When Rick looked down, he saw one of the shark's big eyes staring right at him, which made his adrenaline flow like a fire hose. Finally, the shark turned and swam away with a big piece of Rick's surfboard stuck in its mouth.

Rick pulled himself on to what was left of his surfboard and paddled toward shore. When he reached the shallows, he stood up on still-shaking knees and walked to the beach, where a

Rick was attacked by a shark, which bit off a large piece of his surfboard!

crowd had gathered. Rick showed them his board with the big piece missing (left photo) and was thankful he wasn't missing a leg or an arm. It was almost a month before Rick was able to go surfing again. As he paddled out, this time with about 20 others, he began to have a weird, terrible feeling that something bad was going to happen again (adapted from the *Los Angeles Times,* February 8, 1993).

Rick experienced a variety of different emotions during and after his shark attack. During the attack, he felt intense anxiety and fear for his life. When he reached shore safely, he felt relief and happiness for having survived with all his limbs intact. Sometime later, he felt some fright and apprehension about surfing again. Although Rick experienced a half-dozen different emotions, they all shared the same four components (N. S. Frijda, 2000).

An *emotion* is defined in terms of four components. First, you interpret or appraise some stimulus (event, object, or thought) in terms of your well-being. Second, you experience a subjective feeling, such as fear or happiness. Third, you have physiological responses, such as changes in heart rate or breathing. Fourth, you may show observable behaviors, such as smiling or crying.

Rick's experience with the shark illustrates the four components of an emotion:

First, he *interpreted* or *appraised* the stimulus, a shark attack, as a very serious threat to his well-being and survival.

Second, he had the *subjective experience* or *feeling* of fear and terror.

Third, he had a variety of *physiological responses,* such as heart pounding and adrenaline pumping, which cause arousal and prepare the body for action, such as swimming away fast.

Fourth, he showed *overt* or *observable behaviors,* such as fearful facial expressions and frantic swimming to escape the shark. In some cases, such as playing poker, a person may experience a wide range of emotions but try to hide his or her overt behaviors by showing no facial expression, commonly known as a "poker face." In other cases, cultural factors influence overt behaviors, such as allowing American women but not usually American men to cry in public.

Although there is general agreement that emotions have four components, there is much discussion of the order in which these four components occur (N. S. Frijda, 2000). For instance, did Rick have to think about the shark before he felt fear, or did he feel fear immediately and then think about how terrified he was? We'll discuss this as well as many other questions about emotions, such as why people can identify a fearful face quicker than a happy one.

Staying Happy

How long do emotions last?

Being attacked by a shark results in a very different emotional experience than winning big bucks in a lottery. Since lotteries began in the late 1970s, about 4,000 people have become instant millionaires. Immediately after winning, the new millionaires reported feeling intense pleasure, being ecstatic, being unbelievably happy, and living in a dream world (Angelo, 1991). But what happens when a winner finally realizes that for the next 20 years he or she will receive a large monthly check? Will the emotional high continue, or will being a millionaire become a taken-for-granted experience?

Ten years after winning a $20-million lottery, would you still be very happy?

Researchers have studied lottery winners to find out what effect such an enormous windfall has had on their lives (L. Gould, 1995). Later in this module, we'll tell you what the researchers discovered about happiness and how it applies to lottery winners and you.

What's Coming

To realize the importance of emotions, just imagine going through one day without them. We'll discuss how emotions occur; how much our physiological responses, facial expressions, and interpretations contribute to emotions; whether feeling or thinking comes first in experiencing an emotion; whether there is a set of basic or universal facial expressions that occur across all cultures; what the functions of emotions are; how specific emotions work; and how emotions are used in lie detection.

We'll begin our discussion of emotions with how a swimmer's sight of a shark causes him or her to feel fear.

A. Peripheral Theories

Why do you feel fear? Seeing a shark swimming nearby causes instant fear. Explaining how this fear arises has taken several different approaches.

The *peripheral theory of emotions* emphasizes how physiological changes in the body give rise to emotional feelings.

The *cognitive appraisal theory of emotions* emphasizes how interpretations or appraisals of situations result in emotional feelings.

The *affective neuroscience approach* studies the underlying neural bases of mood and emotion by focusing on the brain's neural circuits that evaluate stimuli and produce or contribute to experiencing and expressing different emotional states.

We'll begin with one of the peripheral approaches to understanding emotions, the historic James-Lange theory, which says that if you see a bear, you are frightened because you run. Is it true?

James-Lange Theory

This theory, proposed independently in the late 1800s by two psychologists, William James and Carl Lange, emphasizes specific physiological patterns as causing emotional feelings.

The *James-Lange theory* says that our brains interpret specific physiological changes as feelings or emotions and that there is a different physiological pattern underlying each emotion.

James (1884/1969) illustrated his theory with the example of seeing a bear: If you see a bear, "you are frightened because you run" rather than run because you are frightened. According to the James-Lange theory, the order for the occurrence of the four components of an emotion is shown in the right figure.

Criticisms. There are three major criticisms of the James-Lange theory. First, different emotions are not necessarily associated with different patterns of physiological responses. For instance, anger, fear, and sadness share similar physiological patterns of arousal (Cacioppo et al., 2000). Thus, James's bear example was backward: Instead of the act of running making you feel fear, you feel fear and then run.

Second, people whose spinal cords have been severed at the neck are deprived of most of the feedback from their physiological responses (autonomic nervous system), yet they experience emotions with little or no change in intensity. These data are the opposite of what the James-Lange theory would predict, which is that these people should experience little or no emotion (Chwalisz et al., 1988).

Third, some emotions, such as feeling guilty or jealous, may require a considerable amount of interpretation or appraisal of the situation. The sequence involved in feeling a complex emotion like guilt or jealousy points to the influence of cognitive factors on emotional feelings (Ellsworth & Scherer, 2003).

Intensity. Although researchers showed that physiological changes are not the primary cause of emotions, physiological changes (heart pounding, sweaty palms) may increase the intensity of emotional experiences (Cacioppo et al., 2000).

Next, we turn to the second peripheral theory, the facial feedback theory, which offers a different explanation of how emotions occur.

1. Stimulus (shark) triggers different physiological changes in your body.

2. Your brain interprets different patterns of physiological changes.

3. Different physiological changes produce different emotions (fear).

4. You may or may not show observable responses (scream).

Facial Feedback Theory

The idea that feedback from facial muscles causes emotional feelings originated with Charles Darwin (1872/1965) and evolved into today's facial feedback theory (Keltner & Ekman, 2000).

The *facial feedback theory* says that the sensations or feedback from the movement of your facial muscles and skin are interpreted by your brain as different emotions.

According to facial feedback theory, the four components of emotions occur in the order shown in the figure below.

1. Stimulus (shark) triggers changes in facial muscles and skin.

2. Your brain interprets feedback from facial muscles and skin.

3. Different facial feedback results in feeling different emotions (fear).

4. You may or may not show various observable responses (scream).

Criticisms. While it is true that facial expressions of fear, happiness, sadness, and disgust involve different muscle-skin patterns, there is little evidence that it's the feedback from these different muscle groups that actually causes the emotion. For example, if feedback from facial muscles caused emotions, then individuals whose facial muscles are completely paralyzed should not be able to experience emotions, yet they do report feeling emotions (Heilman, 2000).

Although researchers have not confirmed Darwin's original theory that feedback from facial muscles *alone* is sufficient to produce emotions, they have found that feedback from facial muscles, such as those involved in smiling or crying, may influence your mood and overall emotional feeling and increase the intensity of your subjective emotional experience (Kolb & Taylor, 2000).

The peripheral theories of emotions show that physiological changes in the body and feedback from facial muscles contribute to but do not themselves cause different emotions. What can cause an emotion are the thoughts that go on inside your brain (mind).

B. Cognitive Appraisal Theory

Thoughts and Emotions

Can thoughts cause emotions?

Suppose you won a lottery and felt very happy. Weeks later, the thought of winning still makes you feel very happy. The fact that your thoughts alone can give rise to emotions illustrates the importance of cognitive factors. Current cognitive theories of emotions can be traced back to the

original research of Stanley Schachter and Jerome Singer (1962), whose classic experiment was the first to show the importance of cognitive interpretation, or appraisal, in contributing to emotional states.

Schachter-Singer Experiment

As shown in the figure below, Schachter and Singer first injected their subjects with a hormone, epinephrine (adrenaline), that caused physiological arousal, such as increased heart rate and blood pressure. However, subjects were told that the injections were vitamins and were not told that they would experience physiological arousal. After the injections, subjects were placed in different situations—a happy one or an angry one. Those subjects in the happy situation often

reported feeling happy, and their observable behaviors were smiles. However, those in the angry situation often reported feeling angry, and their observable behaviors were angry facial expressions. Schachter and Singer explained that subjects did not know that their physiological arousal was caused by hormone injections and they looked around for other causes in their environment. Subjects interpreted environmental cues, such as being in a happy or angry

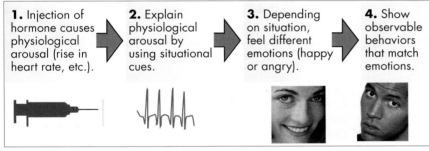

1. Injection of hormone causes physiological arousal (rise in heart rate, etc.).

2. Explain physiological arousal by using situational cues.

3. Depending on situation, feel different emotions (happy or angry).

4. Show observable behaviors that match emotions.

situation, as the cause of their arousal and thus reported feeling happy or angry. The Schachter-Singer cognitive theory was the first to show that cognitive factors, such as your interpretation of events, could influence emotional feelings.

The Schachter-Singer finding that your cognitive processes, such as thoughts, interpretations, and appraisals of situations, can trigger emotions became the basis for today's cognitive appraisal theory of emotions.

Cognitive Appraisal Theory

The cognitive appraisal theory began with the experiment of Schachter and Singer and developed into its present form because of many researchers (Lazarus, 1999; Ellsworth & Scherer, 2003).

The *cognitive appraisal theory* says that your interpretation or appraisal or thought or memory of a situation, object, or event can contribute to, or result in, your experiencing different emotional states.

Suppose you're thinking about having won the lottery last week and planning what to do with all that money. According to the cognitive appraisal theory, the sequence for how thinking results in feeling happy is shown in the figure on the right.

Thought then emotion. Thinking of your first serious kiss can make you feel happy, while thinking of times you were jealous can make you sad or angry. In these cases, as well as in feeling pride, envy, or compassion, the thinking or appraisal occurs before the emotion (Lazarus, 1999).

Emotion without conscious thought. Imagine being on a nature walk, turning a corner, and seeing a huge snake on the path. In this case, the feeling of fear is instant, without conscious thought or appraisal; you don't have to think "that's a dangerous snake and I better be careful." On the next page, we'll discuss how seeing a snake can elicit fear instantaneously,

before awareness or conscious thoughts can occur (Helmuth, 2003b; Zajonc, 1984). Thus, in some situations, such as those that involve personal relationships, problems at work, fond family memories, or terrible tragedies, thoughts precede and result in emotional feelings. In other situations, such as those involving attack or threat to one's personal survival, emotions can occur instantly, without conscious thought or awareness.

1. The stimulus could be an event, object, or thought: "I won $55 million last week."

2. You appraise or think of what you can do: "I can go on a trip around the world."

3. Appraising or thinking about what you can do brings feelings of happiness and joy.

4. You also have physiological responses and observable behaviors (smiling).

The relatively new finding that certain emotions, especially fear, can occur without conscious thought or awareness brings us to the most recent approach to the study of emotions, called affective neuroscience, which we'll discuss next.

C. Affective Neuroscience Approach

What emotion do you feel?

Seeing this ferocious wolf suddenly appear on your nature walk would cause instant fear. The ability of humans to sense and evaluate stimuli as being more or less desirable to their well-being is an important function of emotions, which have four unique qualities (Dolan, 2002a).

How quickly would you react?

1st. Unlike most psychological states, emotions are felt and *expressed in stereotypic facial expressions*, such as showing a fearful expression (open mouth, raised eyebrows), and accompanied by *distinctive physiological responses* (fear is accompanied by a fast heart rate, quick shallow breathing, and sweaty palms).

2nd. Emotions are *less controllable* than we might like and may *not respond to reason*. For example, advising someone to "calm down" or "control your temper" may have little effect. In fact, some people may need to attend anger management programs to help them gain some rational self-control over their hot tempers.

3rd. Emotions have an enormous *influence on many cognitive processes*, such as making decisions, developing personal relationships, and selecting goals. One reason for this is that you essentially have two brains: an older primitive or animal brain, called the limbic system (p. 80), which regulates emotions, and a newer developed forebrain, which influences but doesn't completely control the limbic system. For example, well-known politicians, who intellectually know better, have gotten into trouble by engaging in illicit sexual activities, and some students, who intellectually know better, admit to doing badly in their freshman year and explain that they were emotionally immature.

4th. Some emotions are *hard-wired in the brain*. That's why babies don't have to learn how to cry to gain attention or express basic needs or learn how to smile to show happiness and form social bonds with their parents or caretakers.

Study of emotions. Recently, the study of emotions has become one of the hottest topics in neuroscience, which studies patients who have discrete brain lesions and psychiatric and neurological disorders. Neuroscientists use brain scanning or imaging techniques to identify structures and neural activities in the living brain. These studies contribute to the new affective neuroscience approach to understand mood and emotions (K. J. Davidson et al., 2003).

The *affective neuroscience approach* studies the underlying neural bases of mood and emotion by focusing on the brain's neural circuits that evaluate stimuli and produce or contribute to experiencing and expressing different emotional states.

The word *affective* suggests affect or emotion. The word *neuroscience* suggests research methods that involve studying patients with neurological disorders and using methods that involve brain scans or imaging to identify neural activity in the living brain.

Can you detect a snake quicker than a flower?

Detecting stimuli. If you were shown a number of stimuli, would you detect a snake quicker than a flower? For example, researchers found that, compared to detecting unemotional neutral targets (flowers, mushrooms), we are faster at detecting targets with emotional meaning, such as faces with positive (smiling) or negative (fearful) expressions, and threatening things, such as snakes or spiders. However, we are fastest at identifying emotional stimuli that may pose a threat—fearful faces, snakes (Ohman et al., 2001). These findings support the idea that our brains have evolved the ability to quickly recognize dangerous things in our environment and thus increase our chances for survival. Further support for this idea comes from scanning or imaging studies (p. 70) that point to an emotional detector in the brain.

Emotional detector. Your physical survival depends in part on a brain structure about the size and shape of an almond—the amygdala (R. B. Adams et al., 2003).

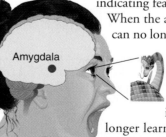

Threat to your survival

The *amygdala* (*ah-MIG-duh-la*) is located in the tip of the brain's temporal lobe and receives input from all the senses. Using all this sensory input, the amygdala monitors and evaluates whether stimuli have positive (happy) or negative (fearful, threatening) emotional significance for our well-being and survival. It is also involved in storing memories that have emotional content.

One researcher said that the amygdala (figure below) is like a guard dog that is constantly sniffing for threats and this gives us an evolutionary advantage in terms of survival (LeDoux, 2003). For example, brain scans indicate that the amygdala is especially activated when we view emotional facial expressions indicating fear or distress (Helmuth, 2003). When the amygdala is damaged, patients can no longer distinguish between fearful and happy facial expressions and no longer perceive loud noises as being unpleasant. Similarly, when the amygdala is damaged in animals, they no longer learn to fear and avoid dangerous situations (Hamann et al., 2002).

Amygdala

Amygdala is an emotional detector and memorizer.

Emotional memorizer. Besides being involved in evaluating positive and negative emotional stimuli, the amygdala is also involved in *storing memories with emotional content* (Kelley, 2002). The amygdala is the reason you can remember that a joke is funny or a face is happy or threatening. This means that the amygdala is involved in both detecting emotional stimuli and remembering emotional content. How the amygdala detects a snake almost instantaneously is a neat trick.

What happens when you feel fear?

Researchers have used brain scanning or imaging techniques (fMRI; p. 70) to measure neural activity and trace neural pathways or circuits throughout the living brain. We'll focus on the neural activity that occurs when a person is confronted with a fearful stimulus, such as seeing a ferocious wolf. This neural circuit is important for our survival and has received considerable attention (Dolan, 2002a; Helmuth, 2003b).

1. Thalamus We'll give a simplified version of the neural activity in the brain that would occur after you see a ferocious wolf. As you look at the right figure, notice that the **#1 blue circuit** begins with the eyes gathering information about the wolf's shape and color. This neural information is sent to a major structure called the *thalamus* (*THAL-ah-mus*), which functions as a major relay station for all the senses (except smell). In turn, the thalamus relays the neural information to the visual cortex, which transforms the neural signals into the image of a ferocious wolf. The visual cortex then relays the "wolf" information to the amygdala, which interprets the neural information and signals the presence of a threat, which results in feelings of fear, an associated fearful facial expression, and probably a lot of yelling and running to escape the threat. And all this happens in about 0.12 second.

2. Amygdala Although 0.12 second is a fast response to a threat, researchers have evidence of an even faster circuit for identifying threatening stimuli. In the left figure, notice the **#2 red circuit**, which goes directly from the thalamus to the amygdala, saving time because it's shorter than the #1 blue circuit. The activation of this #2 red circuit means that the amygdala recognizes the threatening wolf and triggers a fearful response almost instantaneously after seeing the wolf. This is an example of an emotion occurring without any awareness or conscious thought.

Researchers believe that the #2 red circuit evolved because its amazingly quick warning of a threatening stimulus greatly improves our well-being and increases our chances of survival.

3. Prefrontal Cortex The part of your brain that is involved in complex cognitive functions, such as making decisions, planning, and reasoning, is called the prefrontal cortex, indicated in the left figure by the **#3 green oval**. The prefrontal cortex has several functions: It is involved in remembering and experiencing emotions even when the fear object is not present, such as when you tell a friend about your wolf encounter and again feel fear or recall a joke and laugh; it is also involved in anticipating and analyzing the potential rewards, punishments, and emotional consequences of performing or not performing certain behaviors (J. R. Gray et al., 2002). For example, the prefrontal cortex is involved in analyzing the emotional consequences, rewards, and punishments of deciding whether to go to a party instead of studying for an exam. Because reason often has less effect on emotions than you would like, you may decide to go and enjoy the party and live with the potential disappointment and unhappiness of doing poorly on the exam.

In some cases, faulty functioning of the prefrontal cortex, perhaps due to undeveloped neural connections or circuits, may result in less rational control of emotions, which in turn increases the risk for committing impulsive acts of violence or aggression. Researchers warn that this finding points to the need for developing new treatments, both behavioral and drug, to help people suppress impulsive and violent emotions (R. J. Davidson et al., 2000).

The kinds of studies that we have just discussed illustrate the affective neuroscience approach to understanding emotions as well as emotional disorders.

Thalamus
1
Visual cortex
2
Amygdala
3
1
Prefrontal cortex

Fear and the Amygdala

Why do some have more fears?

Some individuals suffer from social phobias, which means they avoid going out in public because they have an enormous fear of being scrutinized, which would surely result in being humiliated or embarrassed. Researchers wondered if these fears might be reflected in the activity of the amygdala, which evaluates and signals threats from the environment.

Individuals with social phobias and healthy individuals were shown color photos and asked to identify only the sex of the individual while researchers used brain scans (fMRIs) to record the neural activity of the amygdala. The photos included happy, fearful, angry, and contemptuous faces, although the subjects were not asked to

notice or comment on the facial differences. Researchers found that when individuals with social phobias were looking at photos of angry and contemptuous faces, there was increased neural activity in the left amygdala compared to the activity of healthy individuals. Researchers concluded that the amygdala of social phobics is particularly active when processing angry and contemptuous faces (M. B. Stein et al., 2002). This study, which is an example of the affective neuroscience approach, identified neurological factors that may be useful in evaluating and treating emotional disorders.

Social fears result in an overactive amygdala.

D. Universal Facial Expressions

Definition

When did you first smile?

When you were about 4–6 weeks old, you began to smile, which greatly pleased your parents. Smiling is considered one of the universal emotional expressions (Ekman, 2003).

Universal emotional expressions are a number of specific inherited facial patterns or expressions that signal specific feelings or emotional states, such as a smile signaling a happy state.

For example, notice that although the four individuals in the photos come from four different countries, they display similar facial expressions—smiles—which you would interpret as showing happiness.

Why do people from different cultures smile the same way?

Cross-Cultural Evidence

How do individuals from relatively isolated cultures in New Guinea, Burma, Thailand, and Borneo (photos top to bottom) know how to smile or what a smile means? One answer is that a smile is one of the unlearned, inherited universal emotional expressions. For example, researchers showed photos of different facial expressions to individuals in 20 different Western cultures and 11 different primitive (illiterate and isolated) cultures. As the graph below indicates, researchers found that individuals in both Western and primitive cultures showed significant agreement on which facial expressions signaled which emotions. Most individuals in Western and primitive cultures agreed that a smile indicated happiness. However, the fewest individuals in Western and primitive cultures agreed that an open-mouth and raised-eyebrows expression indicated surprise.

Based on the cross-cultural findings shown in the right graph, researchers concluded that there are innately or biologically determined universal facial expressions for emotions. Universal emotional signals most likely include facial expressions for happiness, surprise, fear, anger, contempt, disgust, and sadness (Ekman, 2003). Universal emotional expressions are thought to have evolved because they served adaptive and survival functions for our ancestors.

Support for universal emotional expressions also comes from observing the emotional development of infants.

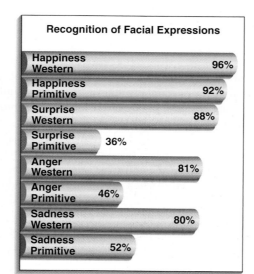

Recognition of Facial Expressions

Happiness Western	96%
Happiness Primitive	92%
Surprise Western	88%
Surprise Primitive	36%
Anger Western	81%
Anger Primitive	46%
Sadness Western	80%
Sadness Primitive	52%

Number of expressions. Researchers generally agree that seven facial expressions for emotions are universal, which means they are recognized across cultures: anger, happiness, fear, surprise, disgust, sadness, and contempt (Ekman, 2003). Other emotions, such as pride, jealousy, and compassion, do not have particular facial expressions.

The existence of universal emotions was scientifically formulated by Charles Darwin (1872/1965), and his ideas have inspired modern-day researchers to study universal emotional expressions (Ekman, 2003). We'll review two kinds of evidence—cross-cultural and genetic—that support the idea of universal emotional expressions.

Genetic Evidence

How does an infant who is born blind learn to smile? Is it possible that the programming of specific facial expressions, such as smiling, is in the DNA, which is a chemically coded alphabet that contains and writes out genetic instructions for the development of the body and brain? One answer to this question comes from observing the development of emotional expressions in infants.

Researchers found that at 4–6 weeks of age, infants begin to smile, which encourages social bonding with parents. The question is whether an infant's smiling is biologically programmed or whether the infant has learned to smile by observing and imitating the parents' facial expressions. The answer is that even infants born blind, who never observe their parents smiling, begin to smile at 4–6 weeks. This observation supports the idea that some facial expressions, such as smiling, are biologically programmed (Eibl-Eibesfeldt, 1973).

Additional evidence for universal emotions comes from reports that all infants develop facial expressions in a predictable order. For instance, newborns show facial expressions signaling disgust or distress in response to foul tastes or odors, infants 4–6 weeks old begin to smile, infants 3–4 months old show angry and sad facial expressions, and infants 5–7 months old show fear. Because infants in all cultures develop these emotional expressions at about the same age and in the same order, we have further evidence for the existence of universal emotions (Izard, 1993; Kopp & Neufeld, 2003).

Researchers conclude that evidence from cross-cultural studies on facial expressions and on the development of emotional expressions in infants indicates strong biological (genetic) influences on the development of emotional expressions (Dunn, 2003). But why should humans have an innate genetic program for the development of facial emotional expressions? There are several interesting answers to this question.

What good are emotions?

To appreciate the value and worth of emotions, try living a single day without feeling or expressing any emotions. It would be one of the worst days of your life because emotions have three important functions. Emotions send powerful *social signals* about how you feel; emotions help you *adapt and survive* in your world; and emotions *arouse and motivate* many of your behaviors. We'll examine each emotional function in turn.

Social Signals

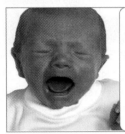

This baby's facial expression is a signal to show others that she is _____.

You would probably fill in the above blank with "distressed, unhappy, in need of something (food, dry diaper)." Thus, one function of emotions is to **send social signals** about one's feelings or needs. Because the baby's facial expression signals distress, she is likely to elicit help, sympathy, or compassion from her parents or caregiver. This is one example of how we may send signals through a variety of facial expressions (Keltner et al., 2003).

Facial expressions that accompany emotions may send social signals about how we feel as well as provide social signals about what we are going to do.

For example, if you smiled at a classmate you did not know, it may signal that you are feeling friendly and perhaps that you wish to talk to and meet this person.

In some cases, facial expressions may not match one's emotions, such as when people adopt a poker face to conceal their emotions or when people cry not because they're sad but because they are so very happy. However, facial expressions generally provide reasonably good information about an individual's emotional state (Keltner et al., 2003).

A lack of facial expressions may be a symptom of serious emotional disorders, which are discussed in Modules 22 and 23.

Survival, Attention & Memory

If you're walking through a strange neighborhood late at night, you may feel fear. Your sense of fear is a signal that all is not well, so you should be careful. Emotions help us evaluate situations (Dolan, 2002a).

The *evolutionary theory of emotions* says that one function of emotions is to help us evaluate objects, people, and situations in terms of how good or bad they are for our well-being and survival (Rozin, 2003).

There are many examples of emotions having survival value: showing anger (below photo) to escape or survive a dangerous or threatening situation, showing disgust to signal the presence of poisonous or rotten food, crying to indicate the need for help or attention, or feeling fear and becoming very watchful when walking home late at night.

This man's facial expression is a signal to show that he is _____, which may help him survive _____ situations.

Besides helping us evaluate situations in terms of our well-being, emotions also affect our attention and memory.

Attention. Feeling very happy when you see your honey means that he or she will get your full attention. Feeling very angry when you are threatened means that you're totally focused on getting out of this situation. These are examples of another function of emotions, which is to **focus one's attention** and thus better detect and respond to emotional situations (Dolan, 2002a).

Memory. Earlier we discussed how strong emotions trigger the secretion of hormones that cause memories to be "written in stone" (p. 247). This illustrates that another function of emotions is to **increase memory and recall** of emotionally charged situations. This results in better remembering situations that are beneficial or dangerous to our well-being.

Arousal and Motivation

Earlier we discussed how Rick's emotional reaction to seeing a shark included a variety of physiological responses, such as heart pounding and adrenaline pumping, that cause arousal. One major function of emotions is to **produce general arousal**, which prepares the body for some action (Hamm et al., 2003). In Rick's case, maximum arousal helped him escape, but in other cases, such as taking a test, maximum arousal may interfere with performance.

In fact, there is a relationship between emotional arousal and performance on a task. That relationship is called the Yerkes-Dodson law.

The *Yerkes-Dodson law* says that performance on a task is an interaction between the level of physiological arousal and the difficulty of the task. For difficult tasks, low arousal results in better performance; for most tasks, moderate arousal helps performance; and for easy tasks, high arousal may facilitate performance.

If we apply the Yerkes-Dodson law to taking difficult exams, we would predict that a person with high test anxiety (high arousal) would do more poorly than someone with comparable ability but low test anxiety. Researchers confirmed their predictions by finding that students who were highly aroused because of either high test anxiety or much coffee (caffeine) scored more poorly on difficult tests than students who had low test anxiety or were less aroused (less caffeine) (K. J. Anderson, 1994). The graph below shows how the optimum level of arousal for best performance depends on the complexity of the task.

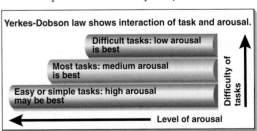

Yerkes-Dobson law shows interaction of task and arousal.

Difficult tasks: low arousal is best
Most tasks: medium arousal is best
Easy or simple tasks: high arousal may be best
Difficulty of tasks
Level of arousal

Besides affecting performance on various tasks, the fact that emotions increase physiological arousal also forms the basis for lie detector tests, discussed in the Application (pp. 370–371).

Next we turn to a positive emotion and the question, Why doesn't happiness last longer?

F. Happiness

What makes you happy?

Pam was unmarried, eight months pregnant, and holding down two jobs when she stopped in at Jackson's Food Store for her morning orange juice and one lottery ticket. She remembers praying, "Please, God, let something happen so I can afford a small studio apartment" (Reed & Free, 1995, p. 63). The next day she was ecstatic when she discovered that her single lottery ticket was worth $87 million (left photo).

Happiness, usually indicated by smiling and laughing, can result from momentary pleasures, such as a funny commercial; short-term joys, such as a great date; and long-term satisfaction, such as an enjoyable relationship.

Inside the brain, the amygdala is involved in recognizing happy facial expressions as well as remembering happy occurrences (laughing at jokes) (Berridge, 2003; Kelley, 2002). In addition, the brain has a special reward/pleasure center that's involved in happiness.

The *reward/pleasure center* includes several areas, such as the nucleus accumbens and ventral tegmental area, and several neurotransmitters, especially dopamine. These and other brain areas make up a neural circuit that produces rewarding and pleasurable feelings, such as happiness.

I won $87 million dollars!

Researchers found that many behaviors—eating, developing romantic attachments, engaging in sex, gambling, using recreational drugs (cocaine), looking at photos of attractive people, and listening to great music—activate the brain's reward/pleasure center (right figure) and result in happy and pleasurable feelings (Berridge, 2003).

For example, the $87-million check that Pam received activated her brain's reward/pleasure center to trigger much happiness, and this occurrence was stored as a happy memory by her amygdala.

Although winning a lottery triggered instant happiness, as did Pam's buying sprees, some months later, she said, "I thought I'd drop everything and travel the world. But my idea of a good time is still to hang out at my brother's house, have dinner, or have a friend over for videos" (Reed & Free, 1995, p. 64). Like most other lottery winners, Pam discovered that money helps and makes life easier but it doesn't buy long-term happiness. Why not?

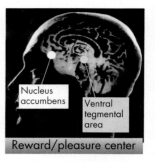

Nucleus accumbens

Ventral tegmental area

Reward/pleasure center

How much happiness can money buy?

When researchers interviewed lottery winners 1 to 12 months after they had won large sums of money, the majority reported positive changes, such as financial security, new possessions, more leisure time, and earlier retirement. However, when asked to rate their happiness one year after winning, lottery winners were no happier than before (Diener & Diener, 1996). Why the happy feeling of winning a lottery doesn't last is explained by the adaptation level theory.

The *adaptation level theory* says that we quickly become accustomed to receiving some good fortune (money, job, car, degree); we take the good fortune for granted within a short period of time; and as a result, the initial impact of our good fortune fades and contributes less to our long-term level of happiness.

According to the adaptation level theory, the immediate emotional high of obtaining good fortune—such as graduating from college, getting married, buying a new car, getting a much-wanted job, or winning a lottery—will fade with time and contributes less and less to our long-term happiness (Brickman et al., 1978; Seligman, 2002). For example, three weeks after winning $87 million, Pam gave birth to Nicholas, and she said, "Winning the lottery was pretty exciting, but it can't compare to Nicholas. I want him to grow up caring about people and knowing the value of work" (Reed & Free, 1995, p. 64).

Long-term happiness. Researchers find that happiness is not a fixed state and does not

Pam said, "Wining the lottery was great, but it can't compare to my baby."

result from getting more money, cars, clothes, or promotions because these achievements gradually lose their emotional appeal, as predicted by the adaptation level theory. Rather, being happy is a continuous process that is associated with making an effort to enjoy simple, daily pleasurable events, people, or situations. It includes a daily diet of little highs as well as pursuing your own personal goals, developing a sense of meaningfulness, having intimate relationships, and not judging yourself against what others do but by your own yardstick (Lykken, 2003; Seligman, 2002). These findings explain Pam's comment that winning the lottery was great but doesn't compare to the joys and meaningfulness she experiences with her child.

Genetic differences in happiness. One reason that some people are just generally happier than others is one's individual *happiness set point*. Each person has a set point for experiencing a certain level of happiness—some more and some less. Although happiness can go up or down, it generally returns to the person's set point. For example, identical twins showed significantly higher correlations in their happiness ratings (0.44 to 0.52) than did fraternal twins (0.08 to −0.02). Researchers estimate that one's personal level for being happy is set half by inherited or genetic influences, which affect the development of helpful or hurtful cognitive and personality traits, and half by various environmental factors, such as one's career, relationships, and finances (Lykken, 2003).

Riches don't guarantee happiness.

Although emotional feelings are common to all people, you'll see next that displays of emotional expressions differ across cultures.

G. Cultural Diversity: Emotions Across Cultures

Showing Emotions

Do you cover your mouth when you laugh?

When I visited Japan, I noticed that the Japanese covered their mouths when laughing, something we Americans never do. This Japanese-American cultural difference in expressing laughter comes from differences in emotional display rules (Ekman, 2003).

Display rules are specific cultural norms or rules that regulate how, when, and where a person expresses emotions and how much emotional expression is appropriate.

Here are examples of how different cultures have developed different display rules for emotional expressions.

Greetings. In some European cultures, the display rule for greeting someone is for the individuals, both men and women, to kiss each other on the cheeks or lips. For Americans, especially straight men, the display rule for greeting is a handshake (maybe a friendly hug), but it is taboo to greet another straight man with a kiss on the cheeks or lips.

Americans don't cover their mouths when they laugh.

Laughing and crying. American display rules generally encourage public displays of emotions, such as open-mouth laughing. In contrast, Japanese display rules for laughing include covering one's open mouth because showing much emotion in public is discouraged (Matsumoto et al., 2002).

Anger. Among the Inuit (Eskimos), feelings of anger are strongly condemned, but among certain Arab groups, a man's failure to respond with anger is seen as dishonorable (Abu-Lughod, 1986; Briggs, 1970).

These examples show how different cultures have developed different display rules for emotional expressions. One may be unaware of such display rules until visiting another culture (Marsh et al., 2003).

Smiling and interpreting. Display rules can also differ within a culture. For example, American adolescent girls and women smile more than boys and men do, and women are better than men at interpreting nonverbal cues (facial expressions and body gestures) (LaFrance et al., 2003).

Potential problems. Because of different display rules for expressing emotions, people from one culture may run into problems when traveling or conducting business in another culture. For example, Westerners often make direct eye contact and may show emotions during business meetings, while Asians avoid direct eye contact and outward expressions of emotions. Because of increased international travel and business, there are now companies devoted to giving advice and training on dealing with the display rules of other cultures (www.communicad.com).

UK & USA = OK
Japan = MONEY
Brazil = INSULT
France = ZERO

Gestures. Similar to how emotional display rules differ, gestures may also have different emotional meanings in different cultures. For example, the common hand gesture of forming a circle (left figure) has four different meaning—OK, MONEY, INSULT, ZERO—depending on the culture (Bibikova & Koteinikov).

These examples show how culture influences the meaning of gestures as well as the expression of emotional display rules.

Depending on your culture, you also rate different emotions as being more or less intense.

Perceiving Emotions

What's the most intense emotion?

Of these five emotions—surprise, anger, happiness, disgust, and sadness—which one do you rate as the most intense? _____

It turns out that your rating depends very much on your culture. For example, because the Japanese have a long history of discouraging any show of emotional intensity in public, researchers guessed that their ratings of emotional intensity would be different from those of Americans, who have a history of showing emotions of all intensities in public (Reitman, 1999).

Researchers asked a group of Japanese and a group of Americans to look at photos of five emotional expressions—anger, surprise, happiness, disgust, and sadness—and rate the intensity of each. Both groups looked at two sets of photos: One depicted a Japanese showing five facial emotional expressions, and the other depicted a Caucasian showing the same five expressions (similar to the photos shown on right).

As predicted, the Japanese gave significantly lower ratings of *emotional intensity* to all five emotional expressions than did the Americans. The Japanese rated disgust as the most intense emotion of the five emotions, while the Americans rated happiness as the most intense (Matsumoto & Ekman, 1989).

This study illustrates how cultures affect the display of emotional expressions and also our perception of an emotion's intensity (Rozin, 2003).

Next, we'll discuss the interesting new area of emotional intelligence.

Japanese rated *disgust* as the most intense of five emotions.

Disgust

Americans rated *happiness* as the most intense of five emotions.

Happiness

Concept Review

1. An emotion is defined in terms of four components: You interpret or (a)_____ some stimulus, thought, or event in terms of your well-being; you have a subjective (b)_____, such as being happy or fearful; you experience bodily responses, such as increased heart rate and breathing, which are called (c)_____ responses; and you often show (d)_____ behaviors, such as crying or smiling.

2. A peripheral theory says that emotions result from specific physiological changes in our bodies and that each emotion has a different physiological pattern. This theory, which says that we feel fear because we run, is called the _____ theory.

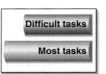

3. Another peripheral theory says that feedback from the movement of facial muscles and skin is interpreted by your brain as an emotion; this theory is called the (a)_____ theory. Although emotions can occur without feedback from facial muscles, facial feedback can influence your mood and contribute to the (b)_____ of an emotion.

4. A theory of emotions that grew out of the work of Schachter and Singer says that your interpretation, appraisal, thought, or memory of a situation, object, or event can contribute to, or result in, your experiencing different emotional states. This is called the _____ theory.

5. The most recent approach to understanding emotions studies the neural bases of mood and emotion by focusing on the brain's neural circuits that evaluate stimuli and produce or contribute to our experiencing and expressing different emotional states. This is called the _____ approach.

6. Emotions have four qualities: They are expressed in stereotypic (a)_____ expressions and have distinctive (b)_____ responses; they are less controllable and may not respond to (c)_____; they influence many (d)_____ functions; and some emotions, such as smiling, are (e)_____ in the brain. The brain area that functions to detect and evaluate stimuli, especially threatening ones, and to store memories with emotional content is called the (f)_____. Because this brain structure receives sensory information so quickly, it triggers a fearful reaction without (g)_____. The brain structure involved in producing emotions from thoughts alone and in analyzing the emotional consequences of actions is called the (h)_____.

7. Specific inherited facial patterns or expressions that signal specific feelings or emotional states across cultures, such as a smile signaling a happy state, are called (a)_____. These emotional expressions, which include anger, happiness, fear, surprise, disgust, sadness, and contempt, are thought to have evolved because they had important (b)_____ and _____ functions for our ancestors.

8. According to one theory, we inherit the neural structure and physiology to express and experience emotions, and we evolved basic emotional patterns to adapt to and solve problems important for our survival; this is called the (a)_____ theory. Facial expressions that accompany emotions send signals about how one (b)_____ and what one intends to do. Emotions focus one's (c)_____ so one can better respond to emotional situations and also increases (d)_____ of situations that may be either beneficial or dangerous to one's well-being.

9. Your performance on a task depends on the amount of physiological arousal and the difficulty of the task. For many tasks, moderate arousal helps performance; for new or difficult tasks, low arousal is better; and for easy or well-learned tasks, high arousal may facilitate performance. This relationship between arousal and performance is known as the _____.

10. According to one theory, you soon become accustomed to big happy events, such as getting a car; this theory is called the (a)_____. Long-term happiness is less dependent on wealth and more dependent on pursuing your own personal (b)_____ and developing meaningful (c)_____. Some people are just generally happier and some are generally less happy because of their happiness (d)_____.

11. Specific cultural norms that regulate when, where, and how much emotion we should or should not express in different situations are called _____. These rules explain why emotional expressions and intensity of emotions differ across cultures.

Answers: *1. (a) appraise, (b) feeling, (c) physiological, (d) observable; 2. James-Lange; 3. (a) facial feedback, (b) intensity; 4. cognitive appraisal; 5. affective neuroscience; 6. (a) facial, (b) physiological, (c) reason, (d) cognitive, (e) hard-wired, (f) amygdala, (g) awareness or conscious thought, (h) prefrontal cortex; 7. (a) universal facial expressions, (b) adaptive, survival; 8. (a) evolutionary, (b) feels, (c) attention, (d) memory, recall; 9. Yerkes-Dodson law; 10. (a) adaptation level theory, (b) goals, (c) relationships, (d) set point; 11. display rules*

What is it and who has it?

One of the exciting things about being a researcher is the chance to come up with new ideas. This happened in the early 1990s, when researchers came up with the idea of emotional intelligence, which they suggested made people more effective in social situations (Salovey & Mayer, 1990). By the mid-1990s, popular magazines, such as *Time,* declared that emotional intelligence may redefine what it means to be smart and may be the best predictor of success in life (Gibbs, 1995).

Emotional intelligence is the ability to perceive emotions accurately, to take feelings into account when reasoning, to understand emotions, and to regulate or manage emotions in oneself and others (Salovey & Pizarro, 2003).

Is emotional intelligence the key to Oprah's success?

Unlike the traditional idea of intelligence involving performance on cognitive tests (IQ scores; p. 282), emotional intelligence involves how well people perceive, express, and regulate emotions in themselves and others. The author of the book *Emotional Intelligence* (Goleman, 1995), said in an interview, "Oprah Winfrey's ability to read people and identify with them is at the heart of her success" (S. A. Brown, 1996, p. 85). In other words, the reason for Oprah's incredible success as a talk-show host is that she rates very high in emotional intelligence. For the past decade, researchers have been working to answer the question: How does one measure emotional intelligence?

How Do We Measure Emotional Intelligence?

In the mid-1990s, there was a best-selling book titled *Emotional Intelligence* (Goleman, 1995). The author, a Harvard-educated psychologist, claimed that emotional intelligence was involved in some of the most important things in our lives, such as managing bad moods, maintaining hope after setbacks, getting along with people, and making critical decisions. This book sparked tremendous interest in educators, businesspeople, parents, and many others, who asked, "Could I teach others how to acquire emotional intelligence as well as improve my own?" However, it would be difficult if not impossible to teach or increase emotional intelligence unless there were some way to accurately measure it. What was needed was a valid and reliable way to measure emotional intelligence (validity and reliability; p. 287).

Emotional intelligence has proved difficult to measure.

Measuring complex behaviors. We have already discussed problems in measuring complex behaviors, such as autism (p. 3), ADHD (p. 39), Alzheimer's disease (p. 47), alcoholism (p. 185), and intelligence (p. 282). In some cases, researchers use a set of behavioral symptoms to measure behaviors, such as autism, ADHD, Alzheimer's disease, and alcoholism. In other cases, researchers use paper-and-pencil tests to measure behavior, such as intelligence.

Similarly, for the past decade, psychologists have been working to develop a paper-and-pencil test to measure the many complex abilities believed to underlie emotional intelligence, such as the ability to express, label, regulate, and understand emotions. A paper-and-pencil test to measure emotional intelligence did not become available until 2001. For that reason, there are only preliminary results, which seem promising and which we'll discuss next (Salovey & Pizarro, 2003).

Is Emotional Intelligence Important?

Here are some common remarks that show how emotions can influence our behaviors.

- "I was so angry, I couldn't think straight."
- "I get worse when people tell me to calm down."
- "When we argue, I often get mad and say the wrong thing."
- "You never try to understand how I feel."
- "Sometimes I act on my feelings, right or wrong."

These kinds of self-reports point to the influence that emotions can have on what we say and do and on our success in life. According to supporters of emotional intelligence, the better our understanding of how emotions work, the more likely we are to find a compromise between our often strong emotional feelings ("I felt like doing that") and our equally strong rational thoughts ("I knew I should not have done that") (Mayer et al., 2000). However, these kinds of self-reports need to be confirmed by a more scientific technique, such as using a valid and reliable emotional intelligence test.

Preliminary findings. Here are some findings reported from recent tests to measure emotional intelligence: Youths who scored higher on emotional intelligence tests were less likely to have smoked cigarettes; school children who scored higher were rated as less aggressive by their peers and as more helpful by their teachers; higher scores on emotional intelligence were related to being more empathetic and satisfied with one's life (Salovey & Pizarro, 2003). These findings are considered preliminary until they are replicated and supported by the findings of other researchers.

However, critics of emotional intelligence point out that in business settings and schools where programs try to teach or improve emotional intelligence, the results have been more hype than substance (Matthews et al., 2003). Although there is still considerable debate about the usefulness of emotional intelligence, no one denies that emotions can exert powerful influences on many of our behaviors.

All agree that emotions play important roles in our lives.

I. Application: Lie Detection

How did a spy pass a lie detector test twice?

For nine years, the Russians paid or promised $4.6 million to Aldrich Ames (photo on right), who was a high-level Central Intelligence Agency official. Later, Ames pleaded guilty to espionage, which involved selling secrets to the Russians. Ames is currently serving a life sentence in prison. The Ames case brings up the issue of lie detection because he reportedly passed at least

> I lied, but I passed two lie detector tests.

two lie detector (polygraph) tests during the time that he was selling U.S. secrets to Russia (R. L. Jackson, 1994). The publicity surrounding this case made people ask, "How could Ames be selling secrets and pass two lie detector tests?" The Ames case raises three questions: What is the theory behind lie detection? How is a lie detector test given? How accurate are lie detector tests?

What Is the Theory?

Does the test measure lying?

The lie detector test is based on the four components of an emotion that we discussed earlier. The first component of an emotion is interpreting or appraising a stimulus. In this case, Ames will need to interpret questions such as "Have you ever sold secrets to Russia?" The second component of an emotion is a subjective feeling, such as whether Ames will feel any guilt or fear when he answers "Yes" or "No" to the question "Have you ever sold secrets to Russia?" The third component of an emotion is the occurrence of various physiological responses (figure below). If Mr. Ames feels guilty about selling secrets, then his guilt feeling will be accompanied by physiological arousal, which includes increases in heart rate, blood pressure, breathing, and sweating of the hands. These physiological responses occur automatically and are usually involuntary because they are controlled by the autonomic nervous system (discussed in Module 4). The fourth component of an emotion is the occurrence of some overt behavior, such as a facial expression. Mr. Ames may be able to control his facial expressions and put on a nonemotional poker face. However, neither the presence nor the absence of expressions is critical to the theory behind lie detector tests.

Lie detector (polygraph) tests are based on the theory that, if a person tells a lie, he or she will feel some emotion, such as guilt or fear. Feeling guilty or fearful will be accompanied by involuntary physiological responses, which are difficult to suppress or control and can be measured with a machine called a polygraph.

A polygraph (lie detector) is about the size of a laptop computer (right figure) and measures chest and abdominal muscle movement during respiration, heart rate, blood pressure, and skin conductance or galvanic skin response.

The *galvanic skin response* refers to changes in sweating of the fingers (or palms) that accompany emotional experiences and are independent of perspiration under normal temperatures (Cacioppo et al., 1993).

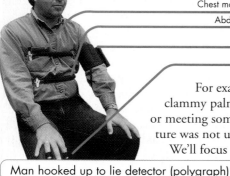

Chest movement during respiration
Abdominal movement during respiration
Heart rate and blood pressure
Skin conductance

For example, you may remember having sweaty or clammy palms when taking exams, giving a public talk, or meeting someone important, even though the temperature was not unduly hot.

We'll focus on the galvanic skin response because its changes are often the most obvious.

Man hooked up to lie detector (polygraph)

What Is a Lie Detector Test?

Is the suspect lying?

Very few details have been released about how Mr. Ames, who apparently lied, passed two lie detector tests. Instead, we'll use a more detailed report of a man named Floyd, who told the truth but failed two lie detector tests.

Floyd was very surprised when two police officers came to his home. They had a warrant and arrested him for the armed robbery of a liquor store. However, the case against Floyd was weak, since none of the witnesses could positively identify him as the robber. Soon after his arrest, the prosecutor offered to drop all charges if Floyd agreed to take, and pass, a lie detector test. Floyd jumped at the chance to prove his innocence and took the test. He failed the lie detector test but insisted that he had not lied and that he be allowed to take a second one, which he also failed. Eventually Floyd was tried, found guilty, and sent to prison. He served several years behind bars before his lawyer tracked down the real robbers, which proved Floyd's innocence (*Los Angeles Times*, December 22, 1980).

Floyd was given the most commonly used procedure for lie detection in criminal investigations, which is called the Control Question Technique (Bashore & Rapp, 1993; Saxe, 1994).

The *Control Question Technique* refers to a lie detection procedure in which the examiner asks two kinds of questions: neutral questions that elicit little emotional response, and critical questions that are designed to elicit large emotional responses. The person answers only "Yes" or "No" to the questions and, if guilty, is expected to show a greater emotional response to the critical questions than to the neutral questions.

NEUTRAL QUESTIONS

These are general questions, such as "Is your name Floyd?" or "Do you live at a particular place?" These questions are designed to elicit few if any emotional responses and are used to establish a baseline for normal physiological responding.

CRITICAL QUESTIONS

These are specific questions about some particular crime or misconduct that only a person who committed the crime would know, such as "Did you rob the liquor store on 5th and Vine?" Critical questions are designed to elicit emotional responses, such as guilt or fear, if the person tells a lie.

As shown in the figure below, Floyd showed very little physiological arousal—as measured by the galvanic skin response—when asked a neutral question, "Is your name Floyd?" However, he showed great physiological arousal when asked a critical question, "Did you rob the liquor store?"

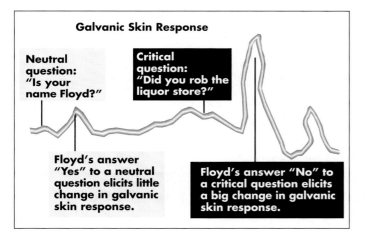

Galvanic Skin Response

Neutral question: "Is your name Floyd?"

Critical question: "Did you rob the liquor store?"

Floyd's answer "Yes" to a neutral question elicits little change in galvanic skin response.

Floyd's answer "No" to a critical question elicits a big change in galvanic skin response.

The examiner decides whether the client is lying or telling the truth by looking at the differences in physiological responses between neutral and critical questions. In Floyd's case, he answered "No" to a number of critical questions, such as "Did you rob the liquor store?" But his "No" answers were accompanied by large increases in galvanic skin response (as well as other responses). For those reasons, the examiner decided that Floyd had lied and thus failed the polygraph test. However, when the real robbers were eventually caught, tried, and sentenced, it proved that Floyd had not lied even though he failed the lie detector test twice. Floyd's case, as well as the Ames case, questions the accuracy of lie detector tests.

Why aren't tests allowed in most courts?

If Floyd was innocent, why did he fail two lie detector exams? If Ames was lying, why did he pass two lie detector tests?

The basic problem with lie detector tests is that researchers have been unable to identify a pattern of physiological responses specific to lying. This means that a number of different emotions—such as guilt, fear, nervousness, or worry—can trigger physiological responses that make a person appear to be lying when he or she may be telling the truth (Fiedler et al., 2002). Because of this serious problem, researchers estimate that lie detector tests are wrong about 25–75% of the time (graph below) (Saxe, 1994; Broad, 2002).

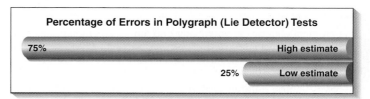

Percentage of Errors in Polygraph (Lie Detector) Tests

75% High estimate

25% Low estimate

Although low error scores (5–10%) for some lie detector tests have been reported, these data come from less realistic laboratory settings that use simple tasks, such as identifying an object about which the subject—often a college student—has been told to lie (Ben-Shakar & Elaad, 2003). The higher error scores reported in the graph come from field studies that simulate more realistic conditions, in which subjects actually steal objects that they are told will be replaced after the test (Bashore & Rapp, 1993; Honts, 1994).

Innocent or faking. Besides high error scores, lie detector tests have two other problems: In one field study, about 40% of subjects were judged to be lying or maybe lying when they were telling the truth (Honts, 1994); and in another field study, about 50% of guilty people who were told to both press their toes to the ground and bite their tongues during control questions passed lie detector tests (Honts et al., 1994).

Restrictions. Because of the above problems, federal law now prohibits most employers from using polygraph tests to screen employees and most state and federal courts prohibit the use of polygraph evidence (Frazier, 2003). In 1998, the United States Supreme Court ruled that polygraph evidence cannot be used in most courts. However, 62% of local law enforcement agencies use lie detectors to screen new employees, and 75% of police believe that polygraph tests are between 86 and 100% effective (K. Johnson, 1999).

New tests. Recent concerns about terrorists and security have increased the need for more reliable methods to detect lies. One of the newest methods involves using brain scans to detect changes in thinking and associated neural activity that occur when lying. Researchers reported distinct patterns of neural activity (prefrontal area) when subjects told lies (Lee et al., 2002). Although these data are preliminary, they suggest that using brain scans may prove to be a more accurate and reliable way to detect lying (Loviglio, 2003).

One curious and little-known fact about lie detector tests is that they are used primarily in the United States. Lie detector (polygraph) tests are almost unknown and are not used in the rest of the industrialized world (Shenour, 1990).

Summary Test

A. PERIPHERAL THEORIES

1. We can define an emotion in terms of four components: We interpret or appraise a (a)_____ in terms of our well-being; we have a subjective (b)_____; we experience various (c)_____ responses, such as changes in heart rate and respiration; and we often show (d)_____ behaviors, such as crying or smiling.

2. Several theories explain what causes emotions. Theories that emphasize changes in the body are called (a)_____ theories. One such theory states that emotions result from specific physiological changes in your body and that each emotion has a different physiological basis; this is called the (b)_____ theory. The major criticism of this theory is that different emotions do not always cause different patterns of physiological arousal. However, feedback from physiological changes may increase the (c)_____ of emotional feelings.

3. According to another peripheral theory, sensations or feedback from the movement of facial muscles and skin are interpreted by your brain and result in an emotion; this is called the (a)_____ theory. However, people with paralyzed facial muscles still experience emotions. Facial feedback may influence your (b)_____ as well as increase the (c)_____ of emotional feelings.

B. COGNITIVE APPRAISAL THEORY

4. A theory of emotions that grew out of the work of Schachter and Singer says that your interpretation, appraisal, thought, or memory of a situation, object, or event can contribute to, or result in, your experiencing different emotional states. This is called the _____ theory.

C. AFFECTIVE NEUROSCIENCE APPROACH

5. The most recent approach to understanding emotions studies the neural bases of mood and emotion by focusing on the brain's neural circuits that evaluate stimuli and produce or contribute to our experiencing and expressing different emotional states. This is called the _____ approach.

6. Emotions have four qualities: They are expressed in stereotypic (a)_____ expressions and have distinctive (b)_____ responses; they are less controllable and may not respond to (c)_____; they influence many (d)_____ functions; and some emotions, such as smiling, are (e)_____ in the brain. The brain area that functions to detect and evaluate stimuli, especially threatening ones, and to store

memories with emotional content is called the (f)_____. Because this brain structure receives sensory information so quickly, it triggers a fearful reaction without (g)_____. The brain structure involved in producing emotions from thoughts alone and in analyzing the emotional consequences of actions is called the (h)_____.

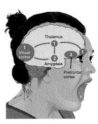

D. UNIVERSAL FACIAL EXPRESSIONS

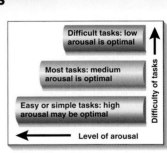

7. Specific inherited facial patterns or expressions that signal specific feelings or emotional states across cultures, such as a smile signaling a happy state, are called (a)_____. These emotional expressions, which are said to include happiness, surprise, fear, anger, contempt, disgust, and sadness, are thought to have evolved because they had important (b)_____ functions for our ancestors. Evidence for universal emotions includes that people in different cultures recognize the same (c)_____ expressions, that infants in different cultures show a predictable (d)_____ in developing facial expressions, and that even blind children, who cannot observe their parents' faces, develop smiling at the same time as sighted children.

E. FUNCTIONS OF EMOTIONS

8. Facial expressions that accompany emotions send signals about how one (a)_____ and what one intends to do. Emotions focus one's (b)_____ so one can better respond to emotional situations and also increases the (c)_____ of situations that may be either beneficial or dangerous to one's well-being.

Difficult tasks: low arousal is optimal
Most tasks: medium arousal is optimal
Easy or simple tasks: high arousal may be optimal

Level of arousal — Difficulty of tasks

9. According to one theory of emotions, we have inherited the neural structure and physiology to express and experience emotions and we evolved basic emotional patterns to adapt to and solve problems important for our survival; this is called the _____ theory.

10. There is a relationship between emotional arousal and your performance on a task; this relationship is called the (a)_____ law. According to this law, low arousal results in better performance on (b)_____ tasks; for most tasks, (c)_____ arousal helps performance; and for easy tasks, (d)_____ arousal may facilitate performance.

F. HAPPINESS

11. Momentary pleasures, short-term joys, or long-term satisfaction can result in an emotional feeling called (a)_____. This emotion also stimulates the brain's reward/pleasure center, which includes several areas, such as the (b)_____ and

_____. The finding that identical twins (share 100% of genes) are significantly more similar in happiness ratings than fraternal twins (share 50% of genes) shows that (c)_____ factors influence our level of happiness.

12. One theory explains that we quickly become accustomed to receiving some good fortune (money, job, car, degree) and, within a relatively short period of time, take the good fortune for granted. As a result, this good fortune contributes little to our long-term level of happiness; this is called the (a)_____ theory. Research shows that long-term happiness is less dependent upon (b)_____ because we soon adapt to our good fortunes. Instead, long-term happiness is more dependent upon pursuing our own personal (c)_____ and developing meaningful (d)_____. One reason some people are generally more happy and some are generally less happy is that each of us seems to have a happiness (e)_____, which is about half set or influenced by environmental factors and about half set or influenced by inherited or genetic factors.

G. CULTURAL DIVERSITY: EMOTIONS ACROSS CULTURES

13. Although many emotional expressions are shared and recognized across cultures, it is also true that cultures have unique rules that regulate how, when, and where we should express emotion and how much emotion is appropriate; these rules are called _____. For example, among the Inuit (Eskimos), feelings of anger are strongly condemned, but among certain Arab groups, a man's failure to respond with anger is seen as dishonorable.

14. Another example of display rules is from a study in which Americans and Japanese rated the intensity of five emotions—surprise, anger, happiness, disgust, and sadness—on a scale from 1 to 10. The emotion rated most intense by the Japanese was (a)_____, while the Americans rated (b)_____ as the most intense of the five emotions. This study illustrates how cultural display rules may differently influence how people perceive the (c)_____ of emotions.

H. RESEARCH FOCUS: EMOTIONAL INTELLIGENCE

15. The ability to perceive and express emotion, understand and reason with emotion, and regulate emotion in oneself and others is called (a)_____. The major problem in studying emotional intelligence is that researchers have not yet developed a reliable and valid method or test to (b)_____ it. One reason researchers believe that emotional intelligence is important is that the better we understand how emotions operate, the better are our chances of finding a way to work out compromises between our strong (c)_____ feelings and our equally strong rational (d)_____.

I. APPLICATION: LIE DETECTION

16. The instrument that is sometimes referred to as a lie detector is correctly called a (a)_____; it measures a person's heart rate, blood pressure, respiration, and emotionally induced hand sweating, which is called the (b)_____ response. To determine whether a person is telling the truth or a lie, the examiner compares the person's physiological responses to (c)_____ and

_____ questions. The basic problem with lie detector tests is that no pattern of physiological responses has been specifically associated with lying. This means that many emotions can cause increased physiological responses that make the person appear to be lying. Because of the relatively high (d)_____ rate, evidence from lie detector tests is not admitted in most courts of law. The newest method to detect lies involves using brain scans to detect changes in thinking and associated (e)_____ that occur when subjects lie.

Answers: *1. (a) stimulus, (b) feeling, (c) physiological, (d) overt; 2. (a) peripheral, (b) James-Lange, (c) intensity; 3. (a) facial feedback, (b) mood, overall feeling, (c) intensity; 4. cognitive appraisal; 5. affective neuroscience; 6. (a) facial, (b) physiological, (c) reason, (d) cognitive, (e) hardwired, (f) amygdala, (g) awareness or conscious thought, (h) prefrontal cortex; 7. (a) universal emotions, (b) adaptive, survival, (c) facial, (d) order; 8. (a) feels, (b) attention, (c) memory, recall; 9. evolutionary; 10. (a) Yerkes-Dodson, (b) difficult, (c) medium, (d) high; 11. (a) happiness, (b) nucleus accumbens, ventral tegmental area, (c) genetic; 12. (a) adaptation level, (b) wealth or material things, (c) goals, (d) relationships or friends, (e) set point; 13. display rules; 14. (a) disgust, (b) happiness, (c) intensity; 15. (a) emotional intelligence, (b) measure, (c) emotional, (d) thoughts; 16. (a) polygraph, (b) galvanic skin, (c) neutral, critical, (d) error, (e) neural activity*

Critical Thinking

Why Do They Have to Learn to Smile?

Questions

1. In the United States, why is smiling in social situations considered an acceptable and even desirable way to behave in public?

2. When having to make money is bucking cultural traditions, what do you think will happen?

3. Even though emotional expressions, such as smiling, are considered universal facial expressions, why don't the Japanese smile more?

In the United States it's very common to see people smiling in public because it's a friendly way to interact socially. In fact, many businesses insist that their salespeople smile at customers because smiling makes the customers feel more comfortable and more likely to buy something. But in Japan, people are very reluctant to show emotions in public and that's become a problem.

Japan is currently going through a recession or downturn in business, so there is increased competition to get new customers and keep current customers happy. Said one gas station attendant who is trying to learn to smile more, "In this recession, customers are getting choosy about their gas stations, so you have to think positively. Laughter and a smile are representative of this positive thinking" (Reitman, 1999, p. A1).

But getting salespeople to smile is a radical change in Japan, whose cultural tradition has long emphasized suppressing any public display of emotions, be it happy, sad, or angry. For example, women never smile at their husbands and members of families rarely touch in public and never hug, even when greeting after a long separation. It's still common for women to place a hand over their mouths when they laugh, and men believe that the correct and proper behavior is to show no emotions in public. Unlike American salespeople who

often smile and make eye contact with their customers, Japanese salespeople are very reserved and greet customers with a simple "welcome"; smiling, up until now, was totally frowned upon.

Because getting salespeople to smile is going against a strong tradition, learning how to smile has grown into a big business in Japan. Employees are now being sent to "smile school," which uses various techniques to teach reluctant and bashful students to smile. For example, one technique in learning how to smile is biting on a chop stick (left photo) and then lifting the edges of the mouth higher than the chopstick. Another technique is to follow "smile" instructions: "Relax the muscle under your nose, loosen up your tongue. Put your hands on your stomach and laugh out loud, feeling the 'poisons' escape" (Reitman, 1999, p. A1).

What is driving all this smiling in Japan is sales and morale. As is well known by American businesses, happy, friendly salespeople are usually the most successful and are great at building company morale. The same is holding true in Japan, where smiley clerks are racking up the most sales and creating a friendly morale. In fact, some foreign firms in Japan, such as McDonald's, put such a high premium on smiling that they turn down applicants with poker faces. (Adapted from Reitman, 1999)

4. Why is it so difficult for many highly motivated Japanese to learn to smile?

5. Why do you think that smiley, friendly salespeople are more successful and better at building morale?

Try InfoTrac to search for terms: smile; **Japanese and smiling.**

1. Smiling is one of the universal facial expressions, which means it occurs and is recognized as a friendly social signal worldwide. However, different countries have different display rules, which regulate how, when, and where its citizens can express emotions. The display rules for the United States encourage the public display of emotional expressions, such as smiling.
2. Cultural display rules have a strong influence on people's behavior (in the United States, women can cry but men should not). It takes a strong motivating force, such as money, to change the cultural display rules, such as making it OK to smile in Japan.
3. Unlike the United States, whose cultural display rules encourage public display of smiling, Japan has had a long tradition of cultural display rules that ban most public display of emotions.

4. Even though many businesses in Japan are now sending their employees to "smile school," employees are finding it difficult to learn to smile because they must first overcome a lifetime habit of being told not to show emotions. Imagine how men in the United States would feel if they were now encouraged to cry in public and were sent to "cry school" to learn how!
5. One reason smiley salespersons are usually more successful is that all their customers come with a built-in or inherited detector for facial expressions, such as smiling. When seeing a salesperson smile (universal facial expression), customers immediately detect that it's a friendly social signal and that the salesperson is acting friendly. As a result, customers feel more friendly and more motivated to agree with the salesperson's suggestions and buy.

Links to Learning

LEARNING ACTIVITIES

- **POWERSTUDY CD-ROM 2.0** by Tom Doyle and Rod Plotnik

  Check out the "Emotion" Module (disk 2) on PowerStudy and:

  - Test your knowledge using an interactive version of the Summary Test on pages 372 and 373. Also access related quizzes—true/false, multiple choice, and matching.
  - Explore an interactive version of the Critical Thinking exercise "Why Do They Have to Learn to Smile?" on page 374.
  - You will also find key terms, a chapter outline including chapter abstract, and a list of hotlinked Web sites that correlate to this module.

- **SELF-STUDY ASSESSMENT**

  Want help studying? For your customized Study Plan go to **http://psychology.wadsworth.com/plotnik7e/**. This program will automatically generate pretests and posttests to help you determine what concepts you have mastered and what concepts you still need work on.

- **STUDY GUIDE and WEBTUTOR**

  Check the corresponding module in your Study Guide for effective student tips and help learning the material presented.

- **INFOTRAC COLLEGE EDITION ONLINE LIBRARY**

  To find interesting and relevant articles go to **http://www.infotrac-college.com**, use your password, and then type in search terms such as the ones listed below.

  Anger   Galvanic skin response
  Happiness   Polygraph

STUDY QUESTIONS

Use InfoTrac to search for topics mentioned in the main heads below (e.g., emotions, facial expressions, brain and emotions).

*A. **Peripheral Theories**—Does someone with many facial expressions experience more emotions than someone with few facial expressions? (**Suggested answer page 630**)

B. **Cognitive Appraisal Theory**—Why would you get very angry if someone backed into your car but calm down as soon as you discovered your mother had done it?

C. **Affective Neuroscience Approach**—What would happen if you took a drug that decreased the activity of your amygdala?

D. **Universal Facial Expressions**—Do animals express emotions with facial expressions that are similar to humans'?

*E. **Function of Emotions**—Why might people who are madly in love have difficulty making the right decisions? (**Suggested answer page 630**)

F. **Happiness**—How might your level of happiness change after you reach a big goal in your life, such as getting a college degree, new job, or relationship?

G. **Cultural Diversity: Emotions Across Cultures**—Is there any truth to the stereotypes that Italians are emotional, British hide their feelings, Germans are serious, and Americans are impulsive?

H. **Research Focus: Emotional Intelligence**—If PET scans could identify emotions, would our criminal justice system benefit from knowing whether violent criminals felt guilt for their crimes?

*I. **Application: Lie Detection**—Would it be fair to use lie detector tests to identify students who are suspected of cheating on exams? (**Suggested answer page 630**)

*These questions are answered in Appendix B.

Module 19: Freudian & Humanistic Theories

Personality

When he had it all, why did he end it all?

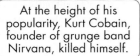

At the height of his popularity, Kurt Cobain, founder of grunge band Nirvana, killed himself.

In the early 1990s, the top grunge band was Nirvana, and their hit song "Smells Like Teen Spirit" was number one in the charts and in the hearts of millions of fans. Nirvana's founder, songwriter, and lead guitar player was Kurt Cobain, whose troubled life was beginning to unravel. Just as his band and career had finally reached the top in the United States and his music was getting international acclaim, he wrote a very revealing one-page note, part of which reads as follows:

"I haven't felt the excitement of listening to as well as creating music, along with really writing for too many years now. I feel guilty beyond words about these things. For example, when we're backstage and the lights go out and manic roar of the crowd goes up, it doesn't affect me the way in which it did for Freddie Mercury, who seemed to love and relish in the love and admiration from the crowd, which is something I totally admire and envy. The fact is, I can't fool you, any one of you. It simply isn't fair to you or to me. The worst crime I can think of would be pull people off by faking it and pretending as if I'm having a hundred percent fun. . . . I've tried everything that's in my power to appreciate it, and I do. God, believe me, I do. But it's not enough . . ." (N. Strauss, 1994, p. 40).

After writing this note, Kurt Cobain, 27 years old, who had a wife and daughter, a hit record, great fame and popularity, opened his wallet to his Washington driver's license, tossed it on the floor, pulled a chair to the window, sat down, took some drugs, pressed the barrel of a 20-gauge shotgun to his head, and pulled the trigger (N. Strauss, 1994).

As Cobain wrote in his diary, "When you wake up this morning, please read my diary. Look through my things and figure me out" (Cobain, 2002). Figuring someone out involves looking into the puzzling, fascinating, and complex issues that make up our innermost selves, our personalities.

Personality refers to a combination of long-lasting and distinctive behaviors, thoughts, motives, and emotions that typify how we react and adapt to other people and situations.

Cobain's rocket to stardom and tragic ending raise a number of questions about personality: How does personality develop? Why do personalities differ? How well do we know ourselves? These kinds of questions are answered by theories of personality.

A *theory of personality* is an organized attempt to describe and explain how personalities develop and why personalities differ.

On the one hand, personality theories try to explain why Cobain's personality put him at risk for suicide. On the other hand, personality theories also try to explain why some individuals have personalities that help them overcome horrendous problems and achieve personal success. One such individual is Charles Dutton.

Changing Personality

How did he change from a criminal to an actor?

Charles Dutton had been in and out of reform schools since he was 12 years old and was finally sent to prison for manslaughter and illegal possession of a firearm. While in prison, he got into trouble for being a ringleader of a riot and was punished with solitary confinement. To pass his time, he took along a friend's book of plays by black authors. Dutton was so moved by the plays' messages that for the first time he thought about channeling his rage and anger into acting.

At one point he spent more than 60 painful days in the prison hospital after a fellow inmate had plunged an ice pick through his neck. During those long days in the hospital, he decided that it was time to put his life in order and accomplish something worthwhile during his remaining time in prison. He obtained a high school equivalency certificate and then a two-year college degree, read dozens of plays, and even started a prison theater. After his parole, he attended college and got his B.A. in drama. His high point came when he was accepted into Yale drama school.

By the early 1990s, ex-problem boy, ex-con, ex-prison terrorist Charles Dutton (right photo) had turned into a very successful actor and starred in his own television series. He has since gone on to star in and direct movies (S. King, 1991; *San Diego Union-Tribune*, 2003). Dutton's story is an emotionally painful search for identity, culminating in the discovery and development of his acting potential. We'll discuss a theory of personality that emphasizes the development of our full potential.

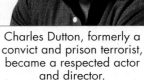

Charles Dutton, formerly a convict and prison terrorist, became a respected actor and director.

What's Coming

We'll discuss two very different theories of personality: Sigmund Freud's psychodynamic theory emphasizes unconscious forces, irrational thoughts, and the lasting impressions of childhood experiences, whereas humanistic theories emphasize our rational processes and our natural striving to reach our true potentials.

We'll begin with a look at Kurt Cobain's problems and where his inner demons came from.

A. Freud's Psychodynamic Theory

Why suicide at age 27?

Freud's theory of personality begins with a controversial assumption that is an important key to unlocking the secrets of personality. To understand how Freud found this key idea, we'll journey back in time to the late 1800s.

At that time, Freud was wondering why several of his women patients had developed very noticeable physical symptoms, such as losing all sensation in their hands or being unable to control the movements of their legs. What most puzzled Freud, who was a medical doctor, was that despite these obvious physical complaints, he could not identify a single physical cause for these symptoms. Somehow, Freud's brilliant mind solved this problem and, in so doing, found an important key to unlocking the secrets of personality. Freud reasoned that since there were no observable physical or neurological causes of the women's physical symptoms, the causes must come from unconscious psychological forces (Westen & Gabbard, 1999).

In the 1800s, Freud's belief that human behavior was influenced by unconscious psychological forces was revolutionary, and it led to his equally revolutionary theory of personality.

Freud's psychodynamic theory of personality emphasizes the importance of early childhood experiences, unconscious or repressed thoughts that we cannot voluntarily access, and the conflicts between conscious and unconscious forces that influence our feelings, thoughts, and behaviors.

Freud believed not only that unconscious psychological forces had

Freud would say that childhood experiences and unconscious forces played a role in Cobain's suicide.

a powerful influence on personality but that these forces originated in early childhood. This means that if Freud were alive today, he would look for reasons behind Kurt Cobain's suicide at age 27 by searching through Kurt's childhood. Here's what Freud would find.

Childhood. When Kurt was 8 years old, his mother filed for divorce, and his parents began their endless fighting. Now Kurt, who had been an outgoing, happy child, became sullen and withdrawn. Because he was skinny and frail, the local town bullies gave him a bad time. Kurt lived sporadically with his father, grandparents, and three sets of aunts and uncles, never finding a real home or anyone to give him love and support. Kurt developed some behavioral problems, such as trouble paying attention, and was given Ritalin (a drug similar in effect to amphetamine) because he was thought to be hyperactive. As if his own problems weren't difficult enough for him to deal with, two of his uncles committed suicide. Friends could see the sadness and loneliness in Kurt's face (Mundy, 1994).

According to Freud, Kurt's childhood, which was full of hurt, pain, and rejection, greatly affected his personality development and caused problems that eventually overwhelmed him. To explain the complex development of someone's personality, such as Kurt Cobain's, is such a difficult task that only a dozen or so psychologists have tried. One of the best-known attempts to explain personality is included in Sigmund Freud's (1901/1960, 1924, 1940) overall theory of psychoanalysis, which includes two related theories: a method of psychotherapy, which we'll discuss in Module 24, and a theory of personality development, which we'll focus on here.

We'll begin with Freud's controversial and revolutionary assumption that unconscious psychological forces influence behavior.

Conscious Versus Unconscious Forces

Was Kurt Cobain aware of all his feelings?

Cobain's life was full of inconsistencies. The closer he got to the top, the less happy he became. "Sometime during the months leading up to the recording sessions for Nirvana's last album, Kurt Cobain wrote a song called 'I Hate Myself and Want To Die.' It was a phrase he used a lot at the time—ever since the band's Australian tour—as a backhanded response to people who kept asking him how he was doing. Cobain thought it was so funny he wanted it to be the title of the album" (Fricke, 1994, p. 63).

Kurt indicated that the title of his song was a joke. In doing so, he was expressing a conscious thought.

Conscious thoughts are wishes, desires, or thoughts that we are aware of, or can recall, at any given moment.

However, Freud theorized that our conscious thoughts are only a small part of our total mental activity, much of which involves unconscious thoughts or forces (Westen & Gabbard, 1999).

Unconscious forces represent wishes, desires, or thoughts that, because of their disturbing or threatening content, we

automatically repress and cannot voluntarily access.

Did Cobain write the song "I Hate Myself and Want To Die" because of some unconscious forces that he was unaware of and had repressed? According to Freud, although repressed thoughts are unconscious, they may influence our behaviors through unconscious motivation.

Unconscious motivation is a Freudian concept that refers to the influence of repressed thoughts, desires, or impulses on our conscious thoughts and behaviors.

Freud used the concept of unconscious forces and motivation to explain why we say or do things that we cannot explain or understand. Once he assumed that there were unconscious forces and motivations, Freud needed to find ways to explore the unconscious.

Freud would say that unconscious thoughts, desires, and feelings influence behaviors.

What was in Kurt's unconscious?

It was one thing for Freud to propose the existence of powerful unconscious psychological forces and motivations, but it was quite another thing for him to show that such unconscious forces actually existed. For example, were there any signs that unconscious psychological forces were making Cobain more and more unhappy as he became more and more successful and popular?

Looking back at Kurt Cobain's suicide, we see there was more truth than jest to the title of his song, "I Hate Myself and Want To Die." One music critic wrote that Cobain was very clever at hiding the true meanings of his lyrics under a layer of the funny or bizarre (Fricke, 1994). The fact that he committed suicide at the height of his career puts a different and tragic light on many of his verses. For example, did Cobain hide some of his unconscious feelings in the following lyrics?

"Everything is my fault / I'll take all the blame" ("All Apologies")

"Monkey see monkey do / I don't know why I'd rather be dead than cool" ("Stay Away")

"One more special message to go / And then I'm done, then I can go home" ("On a Plain")

Freud proposed ways to unlock unconscious wishes and feelings.

Unconscious. If Freud were to examine these lyrics, he might say that they reflected some of Cobain's repressed and unconscious thoughts, desires, and wishes about death and dying. Because neither Cobain nor any of us can easily or voluntarily reveal or talk about our unconscious thoughts and desires, Freud needed to find ways for his patients to reveal their unconscious thoughts and desires, some of which may be psychologically threatening or disturbing. From observing his patients during therapy, Freud believed that he had found three techniques that uncovered, revealed, or hinted at a person's unconscious wishes and desires.

Three techniques. Freud's three techniques to uncover the unconscious were free association, dream interpretation, and analysis of slips of the tongue (commonly known as Freudian slips) (Macmillan, 1997).

Free Association

One of Freud's techniques for revealing the unconscious was to encourage his patients to relax and to sit back or lie down on his now-famous couch and talk freely about anything. He called this process free association.

Free association is a Freudian technique in which clients are encouraged to talk about any thoughts or images that enter their head; the assumption is that this kind of free-flowing, uncensored talking will provide clues to unconscious material.

Free association, which is one of Freud's important discoveries, continues to be used today by some therapists (Macmillan, 1997). However, not all therapists agree that free associations actually reveal a client's unconscious thoughts, desires, and wishes (Grunbaum, 1993).

Dream Interpretation

Freud listened to and interpreted his patients' dreams because he believed that dreams represent the purest form of free association and a path to the unconscious.

Exploring the unconscious with free association, dreams, and slips of the tongue

Dream interpretation, a Freudian technique of analyzing dreams, is based on the assumption that dreams contain underlying, hidden meanings and symbols that provide clues to unconscious thoughts and desires. Freud distinguished between the dream's obvious story or plot, called manifest content, and the dream's hidden or disguised meanings or symbols, called latent content.

For example, Freud interpreted the hidden meaning of dreams' objects, such as sticks and knives, as being symbols for male sexual organs and interpreted other objects (such as boxes and ovens) as symbols for female sexual organs. The therapist's task is to look behind the dream's manifest content (bizarre stories and symbols) and interpret the symbols' hidden or latent content, which provides clues to a person's unconscious wishes, feelings, and thoughts (R. Greenberg & Perlman, 1999).

Freudian Slips

At one time or another, most of us, according to Freud, unintentionally reveal some unconscious thought or desire by making what is now called a Freudian slip (Macmillan, 1997).

Freudian slips are mistakes or slips of the tongue that we make in everyday speech; such mistakes, which are often embarrassing, are thought to reflect unconscious thoughts or wishes.

For example, one of my colleagues was lecturing on the importance of regular health care. She said, "It is important to visit a veterinarian for regular checkups." According to Freud, mistakes like substituting *veterinarian* for *physician* are not accidental but rather "intentional" ways of expressing unconscious desires. As it turns out, my colleague, who is in very good health, was having serious doubts about her relationship with a person who happened to be a veterinarian.

Freud assumed that free association, dream interpretation, and slips of the tongue share one thing in common: They are all mental processes that are the least controlled by our conscious, rational, and logical minds. As a result, he believed that these three techniques allowed uncensored clues to slip out and reveal our deeper unconscious wishes and desires (Macmillan, 1997).

According to Freud's theory, there is a continuing battle going on in our minds between conscious thoughts and unconscious forces. How our minds fight these battles is perhaps one of Freud's best-known theories, and you'll easily recognize many of the terms, including id, ego, and superego.

B. Divisions of the Mind

Id, Ego, and Superego

What was in his suicide note?

Kurt Cobain's suicide note revealed some of his problems and internal struggle. Here are some excerpts from his suicide note (N. Strauss, 1994, p. 40):

"I'm too sensitive. I must be one of those narcissists who only appreciate things when they're alone. Thank you all from the pit of my burning nauseous stomach. It's better to burn out than to fade away."

Cobain's final thoughts suggest that he was fighting a number of psychological and emotional battles. Sometimes his problems became public when, for no apparent reason, he would violently throw or smash his guitar during concerts. According to Freud's theory, some of Cobain's driving forces were arising from unconscious

Freud might say that Cobain's aggressive acts result from inner conflicts between his id and superego.

battles among three separate mental processes, which you know as the id, ego, and superego.

Iceberg example. To understand how the id, ego, and superego interact, imagine an iceberg floating in the sea. The part of the iceberg that is above water represents conscious forces of which we are aware, while parts below the water indicate unconscious forces of which we are not aware.

Freud divided the mind into three separate processes, each with a different function. Because of their different functions, Freud believed that interactions among the id, ego, and superego would result in conflicts (O'Shaughnessy, 1999).

Please begin at the top left with number 1, the id.

1 Id: Pleasure Seeker

Freud believed that mental processes must have a source of energy, which he called the id.

The *id*, which is Freud's first division of the mind to develop, contains two biological drives—sex and aggression—that are the source of all psychic or mental energy; the id's goal is to pursue pleasure and satisfy the biological drives.

Freud assumed that the id operated at a totally unconscious level, which is analogous to an iceberg's massive underwater bulk. The id operates according to the pleasure principle.

The *pleasure principle* operates to satisfy drives and avoid pain, without concern for moral restrictions or society's regulations.

You can think of the id as a spoiled child who operates in a totally selfish, pleasure-seeking way without regard for reason, logic, or morality. Simply following the pleasure principle leads to conflict with others (parents), and this conflict results in the development of the ego.

2 Ego: Executive Negotiator Between Id and Superego

As infants discover that parents put restrictions on satisfying their wishes, infants learn to control their wishes through the development of an ego.

The *ego*, which is Freud's second division of the mind, develops from the id during infancy; the ego's goal is to find safe and socially acceptable ways of satisfying the id's desires and to negotiate between the id's wants and the superego's prohibitions.

Freud said that a relatively large part of the ego's material is conscious (iceberg above water), such as information that we have gathered in adapting to our environments. Smaller parts of the ego's material are unconscious (below water), such as threatening wishes that have been repressed. In contrast to the id's pleasure principle, the ego follows the reality principle.

The *reality principle* has a policy of satisfying a wish or desire only if there is a socially acceptable outlet available.

You can think of the ego as an executive negotiator that operates in a reasonable, logical, and socially acceptable way in finding outlets for satisfaction. The ego works to resolve conflicts that may arise because of different goals of the id and superego.

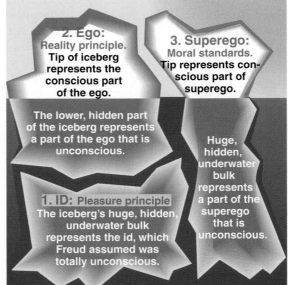

2. Ego: Reality principle. Tip of iceberg represents the conscious part of the ego.

3. Superego: Moral standards. Tip represents conscious part of superego.

The lower, hidden part of the iceberg represents a part of the ego that is unconscious.

1. ID: Pleasure principle. The iceberg's huge, hidden, underwater bulk represents the id, which Freud assumed was totally unconscious.

Huge, hidden, underwater bulk represents a part of the superego that is unconscious.

3 Superego: Regulator

As children learn that they must follow rules and regulations in satisfying their wishes, they develop a superego.

The *superego,* which is Freud's third division of the mind, develops from the ego during early childhood; the superego's goal is to apply the moral values and standards of one's parents or caregivers and society in satisfying one's wishes.

Think of the iceberg's visible tip as representing that part of the superego's moral standards of which we are conscious or aware and the huge underwater bulk as representing the part of the superego's moral standards that are unconscious or outside our awareness.

A child develops a superego through interactions with the parents or caregivers and by taking on or incorporating the parents' or caregivers' standards, values, and rules. The superego's power is in making the person feel guilty if the rules are disobeyed. Because the pleasure-seeking id wants to avoid feeling guilty, it is motivated to listen to the superego. You can think of a superego as a moral guardian or conscience that is trying to regulate or control the id's wishes and impulses.

Disagreements. Freud believed that in some situations there is little or no disagreement between the goals of the id and superego, which means a person experiences little if any conflict. However, in other situations, there could be disagreements between the goals of the id and superego, which result in the ego (executive negotiator) trying to mediate this conflict. Freud describes a number of mental processes that the ego uses to mediate conflicts between the id and superego. We'll next discuss these mental processes, called defense mechanisms.

Why do you feel anxious?

Suppose you know that you should study for tomorrow's exam but at the same time you want to go to a friend's party. Freud explained that in this kind of situation there is a conflict between the desires of the pleasure-seeking id and the goals of the conscience-regulating superego, and this conflict causes anxiety.

Anxiety, in Freudian theory, is an uncomfortable feeling that results from inner conflicts between the primitive desires of the id and the moral goals of the superego.

For example, the study-or-party situation sets up a conflict between the pleasure-seeking goal of the id, which is to go to the party, and the conscience-keeping goal of the superego, which is to stay home and

> What happens if you want to party but know you should study?

study. Caught in the middle of this id-superego conflict is the ego, which like any good executive, tries to negotiate an acceptable solution. However, this id-superego conflict along with the ego's continuing negotiations to resolve this conflict causes anxious feelings. Freud suggested that the ego, as executive negotiator, tries to reduce the anxious feelings by using a number of mental processes, which he called defense mechanisms (Cramer, 2000).

Defense Mechanisms

Have you ever rationalized?

In trying to decide whether to go to a friend's party or stay home and study for an important exam, a student would experience increasing levels of anxiety. Freud reasoned that anxiety is a sure sign of the id-superego inner conflict and that in order to reduce levels of anxiety, the ego may use defense mechanisms (Cramer, 2000, 2003).

Defense mechanisms are Freudian processes that operate at unconscious levels and that use self-deception or untrue explanations to protect the ego from being overwhelmed by anxiety.

According to Freud, a student's ego has two ways to reduce anxiety over deciding to party or study. The student's ego can take realistic steps to reduce anxiety, such as motivating or convincing the student to stay home and study. Or the student's ego can use a number of defense mechanisms, which reduce anxiety by deceiving the student to think it's OK to party and study tomorrow. Here is a brief summary of some of Freud's more popular defense mechanisms (Durand & Barlow, 2003).

Rationalization involves covering up the true reasons for actions, thoughts, or feelings by making up excuses and incorrect explanations.

A student may rationalize that by going to a party tonight he or she will feel more motivated to study for the exam tomorrow, even if he or she will be very tired and in no mood or condition to study tomorrow.

Denial is refusing to recognize some anxiety-provoking event or piece of information that is clear to others.

> Defense mechanisms function like a mental traffic cop trying to reduce conflict and anxiety.

Heavy smokers would be using denial if they disregarded the scientific evidence that smoking increases the risk of lung cancer and cardiovascular disease and in addition would be using rationalization if they say they can quit any time they want.

Repression involves blocking and pushing unacceptable or threatening feelings, wishes, or experiences into the unconscious.

Having feelings of jealousy about your best friend's academic success might be threatening to your self-concept, so you unknowingly block these unwanted feelings by also unknowingly pushing them into your unconscious.

Projection falsely and unconsciously attributes your own unacceptable feelings, traits, or thoughts to individuals or objects.

A student who refuses to accept responsibility for cheating during exams may look at other students and decide that they are cheating.

Reaction formation involves substituting behaviors, thoughts, or feelings that are the direct opposite of unacceptable ones.

A person who feels guilty about engaging in sexual activity may use reaction formation by joining a religious group that bans sex.

Displacement involves transferring feelings about, or response to, an object that causes anxiety to another person or object that is less threatening.

If you were anxious about getting angry at your best friend, you might unknowingly displace your anger by picking an argument with a safer individual, such as a salesclerk, waiter, or stranger.

Sublimation, which is a type of displacement, involves redirecting a threatening or forbidden desire, usually sexual, into a socially acceptable one.

For instance, a person might sublimate strong sexual desires by channeling that energy into physical activities.

Conclusions. Freud believed that defense mechanisms are totally unconscious, which means that, if a best friend or spouse points out that you are being defensive, you will absolutely deny it. We all use defense mechanisms at some time and they can be helpful or harmful. For example, the occasional use of defense mechanisms is normal and helps reduce conflict and anxiety so that we can continue to function as we work on the real cause of our anxiety. However, the overuse of defense mechanisms may prevent us from recognizing or working on the real causes of our anxiety. There is growing scientific evidence that we do indeed use unconscious defense mechanisms much as Freud theorized, which is to reduce anxiety and conflict. In fact, many of us have a dominant or most-often-used defense mechanism, which may be effective in reducing short-term but not necessarily long-term anxiety (Cramer, 2000, 2003).

We have discussed the three divisions of the mind—id, ego, and superego—and how the ego may use defense mechanisms to reduce anxiety. Now we'll turn to how one's ego and personality develop.

C. Developmental Stages

What shaped Kurt's personality?

Imagine a theory so broad that it is able to describe almost exactly how and why your personality developed the way it did and why you did or did not develop certain personality problems along the way. Such is Sigmund Freud's personality theory, which can give a complex description of how each of us develops a different personality.

Case study. For example, let's return to the case of Kurt Cobain, especially his childhood. When Kurt was 5 years old, he was described as an artistic, inquisitive, and energetic child, who was the center of attention, especially at family gatherings. To the delight of all the relatives, Kurt sang, drew pictures, and acted out imaginative skits. Just three years later, when he was 8, Kurt's mother filed for divorce, which triggered years of parental fighting with Kurt caught in the middle. During this time, Kurt changed from being happy, outgoing, and energetic to becoming sullen, shy, and withdrawn (Mundy, 1994).

Psychosexual stages. According to Freud, the development of Kurt's personality, such as becoming outgoing and energetic and then changing to shy and withdrawn, was primarily influenced by how he dealt with the five different kinds of conflicts that occurred at five different times or stages. According to Freud (1940), our personality develops as we pass through and deal with potential conflicts at five psychosexual stages.

According to Freud, Cobain's personality developed as he passed through five psychosexual stages.

Psychosexual stages are five developmental periods—oral, anal, phallic, latency, and genital stages—each marked by potential conflict between parent and child. The conflicts arise as a child seeks pleasure from different body areas that are associated with sexual feelings (different *erogenous zones*). Freud emphasized that the child's first five years were most important in personality development.

You can think of each psychosexual stage as being a source of potential *conflict* between the child's id, which seeks immediate gratification, and the parents, who place restrictions on when, where, and how the gratification can take place. For example, the child may want to be fed immediately, while the parent may wish to delay the feeding to a more convenient time. The kind of interactions that occur between parent and child in satisfying these psychosexual needs and the way a child learns to deal with psychosexual conflicts, especially during breast feeding or toilet training, will greatly influence the personality development as well as future problems and social interactions.

One of Freud's controversial ideas is the relationship between early psychosexual stages and development of later personality, social, and emotional problems. Here is Freud's explanation of how different problems may arise.

Why did Kurt develop problems?

Freud explained that the way a person deals with early psychosexual conflicts lays the groundwork for personality growth and future problems. This means that, to a large extent, Kurt's later personality problems grew out of early childhood experiences. Freud would say that Kurt's problems in finding his identity and dealing with fame and fortune began in childhood, which included being caught in the middle of parents fighting over a divorce, becoming shy and withdrawn, being sent to live with various relatives, and finally hearing about the suicides of two uncles (DeCurtis, 1994).

Fixation. As an adult, there were times when Kurt was happy and smiley (right photo), but at other times he was eerily moody and withdrawn (photo below). The problem for any theory of personality is to explain how problems and contradictions in personality occur. For example, why did Kurt continue to play on center stage and go on world tours yet complain of not enjoying it and having to pretend to be happy? Freud would explain that the development of Kurt's personality depended, to a large extent, on the way he dealt with early psychosexual conflicts. One way a child can deal with or resolve these conflicts—wanting to satisfy all desires but not being allowed to by the parents—is to become fixated at a certain stage.

Healthy personality involves resolving conflicts during psychosexual stages.

Fixation, which can occur during any of the first three stages—oral, anal, or phallic—refers to a Freudian process through which an individual may be locked into a particular psychosexual stage because his or her wishes were either overgratified or undergratified.

For example, if a person were fixated at the oral stage because of *too little* gratification, he might go through life trying to obtain oral satisfaction through eating too much, boasting too much, or focusing on other oral behaviors. If fixation had occurred at the oral stage because of *too much* gratification, he might focus on seeking oral gratification while neglecting to develop other aspects of his personality.

Next, we'll summarize Freud's psychosexual stages, focusing on possible parent–child conflicts, problems from fixation, and implications for future personality and social development.

Fixation at one psychosexual stage could cause intense loneliness.

What happens during the stages?

According to Freud, every child goes through certain situations, such as nursing, bottle feeding, and toilet training, that contain potential conflicts between the child's desire for instant satisfaction or gratification and the parents' wishes, which may involve delaying the child's satisfaction. How these conflicts are resolved and whether a child becomes fixated at one stage because of too much or too little satisfaction greatly influence development of personality and onset of future problems.

1 Oral Stage

Time. Early infancy: first 18 months of life.
Potential conflict. The *oral stage* lasts for the first 18 months of life and is a time when the infant's pleasure seeking is centered on the mouth.

Pleasure-seeking activities include sucking, chewing, and biting. If we were locked into or fixated at this stage because our oral wishes were gratified too much or too little, we would continue to seek oral gratification as adults. *Fixation* at this stage results in adults who continue to engage in oral activities, such as overeating, gum chewing, or smoking; oral activities can be symbolic as well, such as being overly demanding or "mouthing off."

2 Anal Stage

Time. Late infancy: $1\frac{1}{2}$ to 3 years.
Potential conflict. The *anal stage* lasts from the age of about $1\frac{1}{2}$ to 3 and is a time when the infant's pleasure seeking is centered on the anus and its functions of elimination.

Fixation at this stage results in adults who continue to engage in activities of retention or elimination. Retention may take the form of being very neat, stingy, or behaviorally rigid (thus the term *anal retentive*). Elimination may take the form of being generous, messy, or behaving very loose or carefree.

3 Phallic Stage

Time. Early childhood: 3 to 6 years.
Potential conflict. The *phallic* (*FAL-ik*) *stage* lasts from the age of about 3 to 6 and is a time when the infant's pleasure seeking is centered on the genitals.

Freud theorized that the phallic stage is particularly important for personality development because of the occurrence of the Oedipus complex (named for Oedipus, the character in Greek mythology who unknowingly killed his father and married his mother).

The *Oedipus* (*ED-ah-pus*) *complex* is a process in which a child competes with the parent of the same sex for the affections and pleasures of the parent of the opposite sex.

According to Freud, the Oedipus complex causes different problems for boys and girls.

Boys. When a boy discovers that his penis is a source of pleasure, he develops a sexual attraction to his mother. As a result, the boy feels hatred, jealousy, and competition toward his father and has fears of castration. The boy resolves his Oedipus complex by identifying with his father. If he does not resolve the complex, fixation occurs and he may go through life trying to prove his toughness.

Girls. When a girl discovers that she does not have a penis, she feels a loss that Freud called *penis envy*. Her loss makes her turn against her mother and develop sexual desires for her father. A girl resolves her Oedipus complex, sometimes called the Electra complex (for Electra, a woman in Greek mythology who killed her mother), by identifying with her mother. If this complex is not resolved, fixation occurs and the woman may go through life feeling inferior to men.

Over the years, the idea of the Oedipus complex has waned in popularity and credibility, both within psychoanalysis and within the culture at large. That's because there's almost no way to scientifically test this idea. Also, Freud's assertion that the Oedipus complex occurs universally is not supported by data from other cultures (Crews, 1996).

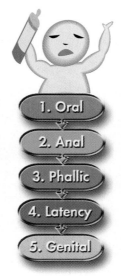

1. Oral
2. Anal
3. Phallic
4. Latency
5. Genital

Freud would say that Kurt's personality depended to a large extent on what happened during five psychosexual stages.

4 Latency Stage

Time. Middle and late childhood: 6 to puberty.
Potential conflict. The *latency stage*, which lasts from about age 6 to puberty, is a time when the child represses sexual thoughts and engages in nonsexual activities, such as developing social and intellectual skills.

At puberty, sexuality reappears and marks the beginning of a new stage, called the genital stage.

5 Genital Stage

Time. Puberty through adulthood.
Potential conflict. The *genital stage* lasts from puberty through adulthood and is a time when the individual has renewed sexual desires that he or she seeks to fulfill through relationships with other people.

How a person meets the conflicts of the genital stage depends on how conflicts in the first three stages were resolved. If the individual is fixated at an earlier stage, less energy will be available to resolve conflicts at the genital stage. If the individual successfully resolved conflicts in the first three stages, he or she will have the energy to develop loving relationships and a healthy and mature personality.

Summary. Freud's psychodynamic theory of personality development made a number of assumptions that, at the time, were revolutionary. His assumptions included the influence of unconscious forces; the division of the mind into the id, ego, and superego; the importance of resolving conflicts at five psychosexual stages; the importance of fixation; and the importance of the first five years to personality development.

Next, we'll discuss what Freud's critics have had to say about his theory and assumptions.

D. Freud's Followers & Critics

What did they argue about?

Because Freud's theory was so creative and revolutionary for its time, it attracted many followers, who formed a famous group called the Vienna Psychoanalytic Society. However, it was not long before members of the society began to disagree over some of Freud's theories and assumptions, such as whether Freud placed too much emphasis on biological urges (sex and aggression), psychosexual stages, and importance of early childhood experience in personality development (Horgan, 1996). We'll focus on three influential followers who eventually broke with Freud's theory.

Carl Jung

Jung disagreed on the importance of the sex drive.

Why did Freud's "crown prince" stop talking to him?

In 1910 Carl Jung, with the whole-hearted support of Sigmund Freud, became the first president of the Vienna Psychoanalytic Society. Freud said that Jung was to be his "crown prince" and personal successor. However, just four years later, Jung and Freud ended their personal and professional relationship and never again spoke to each other.

The main reason for the split was that Jung disagreed with Freud's emphasis on the sex drive. Jung believed the collective unconscious—and not sex—to be the basic force in the development of personality.

The *collective unconscious,* according to Jung, consists of ancient memory traces and symbols that are passed on by birth and are shared by all peoples in all cultures.

Jung's theory of collective unconscious and his elaborate theory of personality, called *analytical psychology,* had more influence on the areas of art, literature, philosophy, and counseling/therapy than on current areas of psychology.

Alfred Adler

Adler disagreed on the importance of biological urges.

Why did one of the society's presidents resign?

Alfred Adler was another contemporary of Freud's who later became president of the Vienna Psychoanalytic Society. However, after Adler voiced his disagreement with Freud at one of the society's meetings, he was so badly criticized by the other members that he resigned as president.

Like Jung, Adler disagreed with Freud's theory that humans are governed by biological and sexual urges. Adler believed that the main factors influencing a child's development were sibling influences and child-rearing practices.

In contrast to Freud's biological drives, Adler proposed that humans are motivated by *social urges* and that each person is a social being with a unique personality. Adler formed his own group, whose philosophy became known as *individual psychology.* In contrast to Freud's emphasis on unconscious forces that influence our behaviors, Adler suggested that we are aware of our motives and goals and have the capacity to guide and plan our futures.

Karen Horney

Horney disagreed on the importance of penis envy.

What would a woman say about penis envy?

Karen Horney was trained as a psychoanalyst; her career reached its peak shortly after Freud's death in 1939. For many years, Horney was dean of the American Institute of Psychoanalysis in New York.

Horney strongly objected to Freud's view that women were dependent, vain, and submissive because of biological forces and childhood sexual experiences. She especially took issue with Freud's idea that penis envy affects girls' development.

In contrast to Freud's psychosexual conflicts, Horney insisted that the major influence on personality development, whether in women or men, can be found in child–parent *social interactions.* Unlike Freud, who believed that every child must experience child–parent conflicts, Horney theorized that such conflicts are avoidable if the child is raised in a loving, trusting, and secure environment. Karen Horney would now be called a feminist and is credited with founding the psychology of women.

Karen Horney is sometimes referred to as a *neo-Freudian* because she changed and renovated Freud's original theory. One of the best-known neo-Freudians was Erik Erikson, who formulated his own theory of personality development, which we discussed in Modules 17 and 18. Erikson proposed that everyone goes through a series of *psychosocial* stages, rather than the *psychosexual* stages proposed by Freud.

Neo-Freudians generally agreed with Freud's basic ideas, such as the importance of the unconscious; the

Neo-Freudians focused on social and cultural factors.

division of the mind into the id, ego, and superego; and the use of defense mechanisms to protect the ego. However, they mostly disagreed with Freud's placing so much emphasis on biological forces, sexual drives, and psychosexual stages. The neo-Freudians turned the emphasis of Freud's psychodynamic theory away from biological drives toward psychosocial and cultural influences (Westen & Gabbard, 1999).

From early on, followers of Freud criticized his theory and, as you'll see, criticisms continue to the present day.

Freudian Theory Today

What is the current status of Freud's theory?

In 1993, *Time* magazine's cover featured a picture of Sigmund Freud with the question "Is Freud Dead?" Answering this question with a loud "Yes" are four scholarly books that seriously question Freud's theory and all its assumptions (Crews, 1996). Answering this question with a loud "No" are 400 members of the American Psychological Association's psychoanalysis division, who meet the attacks on Freud with equally strong defenses (Horgan, 1996). To give you an idea of where Freud's theory stands today, we'll focus on four questions: How valid is Freud's theory? How important are the first five years? Are there unconscious forces? What was the impact of Freud's theory?

1 How Valid Is Freud's Theory?

Too comprehensive. Freud's psychodynamic theory, which includes how the mind develops (id, ego, and superego), how personality develops (psychosexual stages), and how to do therapy (psychoanalysis), is so comprehensive that it can explain almost any behavior. For example, Freud's theory predicts that fixation at the anal stage may result in a person being at one extreme very messy and at the other extreme very neat. Critics argue that Freud's theory is too comprehensive to be useful in explaining or predicting behaviors of specific individuals (Horgan, 1996).

Difficult to test. Current followers agree that some of Freud's concepts, such as the id being the source of energy, the importance of the Oedipus complex in personality development, and basic drives limited to sex and aggression, have proved difficult to test or verify and are now out of date. The same followers add that other Freudian concepts, such as the influence of unconscious forces, long-term effects of early childhood patterns, and existence of defense mechanisms and conflicting cognitive processes, have been experimentally tested and received support (Westen & Gabbard, 1999).

Must be updated. However, even supporters suggest that if psychoanalysis or psychodynamic theory is to survive in the 2000s, Freud's theory must continue to be tested experimentally as well as updated with findings from other areas of psychology. For example, psychodynamic theory needs to include how *genetic factors* account for 20 to 50% of a wide range of behaviors and take into account how *brain development*, which is not complete until early adulthood, is associated with and necessary for the development of related behaviors, thoughts, and feelings (Westen, 1998a).

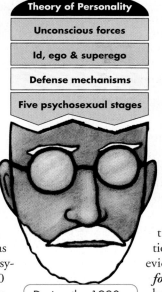

Theory of Personality

Unconscious forces

Id, ego & superego

Defense mechanisms

Five psychosexual stages

During the 1990s, Freud's theory had several major revisions.

3 Are There Unconscious Forces?

One of Freud's major assumptions was that unconscious or repressed forces influence our conscious thoughts and behaviors. In contrast to Freud's theory of the repressed unconscious forces, cognitive neuroscientists have developed a different concept, called implicit or nondeclarative memory (Frensch & Runger, 2003).

Implicit or *nondeclarative memory* means learning without awareness, such as occurs in experiencing emotional situations or acquiring motor habits. Although we are unaware of such learning, it can influence our conscious feelings, thoughts, and behaviors.

Examples of what goes into implicit memory include procedural memories (p. 246), such as motor skills and habits (typing), and classical or conditioned emotional responses, such as irrational fears or phobia. Thus, there is strong evidence for the *influence of unconscious forces* on conscious thoughts, feelings, and behaviors, but these forces are part of a cognitive-emotional system rather than Freud's battleground for conflicts among the id, ego, and superego (Guterl, 2002).

2 How Important Are the First Five Years?

Based on observations of his patients, Freud concluded that personality development is essentially complete after the first five years. However, Freud never did systematic research or collected longitudinal observations to support his hypothesis that personality development is fixed during a child's first five years (Bruer, 1999). In fact, there are two lines of research showing the opposite. First, our earlier discussion of *resilient children* (p. 394) indicated that the occurrence of serious psychological and physical problems during the first five years does not necessarily stunt or inhibit personality development, as Freud predicted. Many children who had experienced poverty, the death of or separation from their parents, or a poor home life developed into healthy, mature adults provided the children had a loving caregiver (E. E. Werner & Smith, 2001).

Second, a number of *longitudinal studies* that followed children into adulthood indicate that personality development is not complete in the first five years but rather continues well into middle adulthood (Caspi & Roberts, 1999). For these reasons, current psychologists question Freud's idea that personality development is complete in the first five years.

4 What Was Freud's Impact?

Freud's theory has had an enormous impact on society, as can be seen in the widespread use of Freudian terms (ego, id, rationalization) in literature, art, and our everyday conversations. Freud's theory also has had a great impact on psychology: Many of his concepts have been incorporated into the fields of personality, development, abnormal psychology, and psychotherapy. However, as we have discussed, some of Freud's terms are out of date (Oedipus complex) and Freud's psychoanalytic theory was modified in the 1990s (Guterl, 2002; Westen & Gabbard, 1999).

Unlike Freud's psychodynamic theory, which paints a picture of humans filled with irrational and unconscious forces with little free choice, we next discuss a family of theories—humanistic theory—that is almost the direct opposite of Freud's theory.

D. *FREUD'S FOLLOWERS & CRITICS*　**441**

E. Humanistic Theories

How did he develop his real potential?

At the beginning of this module, we told you about two very different people. One was rock musician Kurt Cobain, who struggled with numerous personal and drug-related problems. At age 27, when his band, Nirvana, had reached the peak of its fame and popularity, he committed suicide.

The other person was Charles Dutton, who had been in and out of reform schools since he was 12 years old, was sent to prison on charges of manslaughter, and spent time in solitary confinement for his ringleader role in a prison riot. Just when most people would have given up on reforming Dutton, he began to reform himself. Inspired by reading a book of plays, he began to channel his rage against society into becoming a student and then an actor. After leaving prison, Charles Dutton (right photo) worked hard to change his life and became a very successful theater, television, and movie actor and director (Brantley, 2003).

What Dutton and Cobain shared in common as young

When most would have given up, Charles Dutton turned his life around.

men was that neither showed particular evidence of having special talents or great potentials. Few people would have predicted that skinny, frail Cobain would discover the raw power of punk rock and take it further than anyone had before with his band, Nirvana. No one would have predicted that angry, tough, mean Charles Dutton would discover, of all things, acting and would channel his anger into becoming a very successful professional actor. The lives of these two men demonstrate the difficulty in predicting someone's potential and whether he or she will develop it. Developing our potential is at the heart of humanistic theory.

Humanistic theories emphasize our capacity for personal growth, development of our potential, and freedom to choose our destiny.

Humanistic theories reject the biological determinism and the irrational, unconscious forces of Freud's psychodynamic theory. Humanistic theories emphasize freely choosing to go after one's dream and to change one's destiny, as Kristi Yamaguchi did.

Three Characteristics of Humanistic Theories

What was her goal?

Kristi Yamaguchi's goal was to win a gold medal in the Winter Olympics. From early childhood on, she spent thousands of hours practicing, entering grueling competitions, struggling with disappointments, and making personal sacrifices to reach her dream: a gold medal in figure skating at the Winter Olympics (photo below).

Kristi Yamaguchi's life illustrates the humanist's emphasis on developing fully one's potential to lead a rich and meaningful life and becoming the best person one can become (Rabasca, 2000a). Kristi's drive to reach her lifelong dream exemplifies the three characteristics that distinguish humanistic theory from other theories of personality. We'll describe each of the three characteristics unique to humanistic theory: a phenomenological perspective, a holistic view, and a goal of self-actualization (Clay, 2002).

1 Humanistic theories stress learning about the world through personal experiences, which illustrates the phenomenological *(feh-nom-in-no-LODGE-uh-cal)* perspective.

The *phenomenological perspective* means that your perception or view of the world, whether or not it is accurate, becomes your reality.

For instance, Kristi's phenomenological perspective of how she perceived her skating abilities may or may not have been accurate. However, because she believed so strongly that she had the abilities, this perception became her reality. Other examples of phenomenological perspectives are long-held beliefs that women could not perform certain jobs—for example, police officer, doctor, plumber, truck driver, or lawyer. Since women have demonstrated that they can perform these jobs, this particular perception has been proven false. As a result, people (especially men) have developed a new perspective and accepted the reality of what women can accomplish.

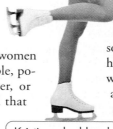

Kristi worked hard to reach her dream—an Olympic gold medal.

2 Humanistic theories emphasize looking at the whole situation or person, which illustrates the holistic *(hole-LIS-tick)* view.

The *holistic view* means that a person's personality is more than the sum of its individual parts; instead, the individual parts form a unique and total entity that functions as a unit.

For example, the holistic view would explain that Kristi outperformed her competitors because of her unique combination of many traits—discipline, ability, motivation, persistence, desire—rather than any single trait.

3 Humanistic theories highlight the idea of developing one's true potential, which is called self-actualization.

Self-actualization refers to our inherent tendency to develop and reach our true potentials.

By winning an Olympic gold medal, Kristi is a wonderful example of someone who developed and reached her true potential and thus achieved a high level of self-actualization. According to humanistic theories, no matter what our skills or abilities, each of us has the capacity for self-actualization and for reaching our own potential. Humanists believe that one's self-esteem, self-expression, belonging, creativity, and love are just as important to human life as the biological needs of food and water (Rabasca, 2000a).

The beginning of humanistic theory in the 1960s can be traced to two psychologists—Abraham Maslow and Carl Rogers. They had surprisingly different backgrounds but arrived at the same uplifting ideas.

Why did a behaviorist become a humanist?

We can trace the official beginning of the humanistic movement to the early 1960s and the publication of the *Journal of Humanistic Psychology*. One of the major figures behind establishing this journal was Abraham Maslow. Interestingly enough, Maslow was trained as a behaviorist, but along the way he felt there was too much emphasis on rewards and punishments and observable behaviors and too little emphasis on other important

aspects of human nature, such as feelings, emotions, and beliefs. For these reasons, Maslow (1968) broke away from the reward/punishment/observable behavior mentality of behaviorism and developed his humanistic theory, which emphasized two things: our capacity for growth, or self-actualization, and our desire to satisfy a variety of needs, which he arranged in a hierarchy.

Maslow's Hierarchy of Needs

Maslow's Hierarchy of Needs

Level 5
Self-actualization: fulfillment of one's unique potential

Level 4
Esteem needs: achievement, competency, gaining approval and recognition

Level 3
Love and belonging needs: affiliation with others and acceptance by others

Level 2
Safety needs: protection from harm and concern about safety and survival

Level 1
Physiological needs: hunger, thirst, sex, and sleep

For just a moment, think of all the needs that you try to meet each day: eating, having a safe place to live, talking to your friends, perhaps working at a part-time job, caring for loved ones, and studying for exams. Maslow believed that you satisfy these needs in a certain order. As you may remember from Module 15 (p. 333), Maslow arranged all human needs into a hierarchy of five major needs.

Maslow's hierarchy of needs arranges needs in ascending order (figure on left), with biological needs at the bottom and social and personal needs at the top. Only when needs at a lower level are met can we advance to the next level.

According to Maslow's hierarchy, you must satisfy your biological and safety needs before using energy to fulfill your personal and social needs. Finally, you can devote time and energy to reaching your true potential, which is called self-actualization, your highest need.

Maslow divided our needs into two general categories: deficiency and growth needs.

Deficiency needs are physiological needs (food, sleep) and psychological needs (safety, love, esteem) that we try to fulfill if they are not met.

Growth needs are those at the higher levels and include the desire for truth, goodness, beauty, and justice.

According to Maslow, we must satisfy our deficiency needs before having the time and energy to satisfy our growth needs and move toward self-actualization.

Self-Actualization

One of the major characteristics of the humanistic movement is the emphasis on a process called self-actualization.

Self-actualization refers to the development and fulfillment of one's unique human potential.

Maslow (1971) developed the concept of self-actualization after studying the lives of highly productive and exceptional people, such as Abraham Lincoln, Albert Einstein, and Eleanor Roosevelt. Maslow believed that these individuals had been able to reach the goal of self-actualization because they had developed the following personality characteristics.

Characteristics of Self-Actualized Individuals

- They perceive reality accurately.
- They are independent and autonomous.
- They prefer to have a deep, loving relationship with only a few people.
- They focus on accomplishing their goals.
- They report peak experiences, which are moments of great joy and satisfaction.

Maslow believed that, although very few individuals reach the level of self-actualization, everyone has a self-actualizing tendency. This tendency motivates us to become the best kind of person we are capable of becoming.

Civil rights leader Martin Luther King, Jr., is an example of a self-actualized person.

There is no doubt that Maslow would also have considered Martin Luther King, Jr., an example of a self-actualized person. Martin Luther King, Jr., devoted his life to achieving civil rights for all people. Here he delivers his famous "I Have a Dream" speech at a civil rights rally in Washington, D.C. He was awarded the Nobel Prize for peace at age 35. He was gunned down by an assassin's bullet at age 39. King's achievements exemplify the humanistic idea of self-actualization.

About the same time that Maslow was making this journey from behaviorism to humanism and developing the concept of self-actualization, another psychologist by the name of Carl Rogers was developing a different but related humanistic theory.

E. Humanistic Theories

What are the two most important concepts?

Carl Rogers was initially trained in the psychodynamic approach, which he used in his practice as a clinical psychologist. However, Rogers began to feel that Freud placed too much emphasis on unconscious, irrational forces and on biological urges, and too little emphasis on human potential for psychological growth. As a result, Rogers gradually abandoned the psychodynamic approach in favor of a new theory of personality that he developed in the 1960s. Rogers's new humanistic theory is often called self theory because of his emphasis on the self or self-concept.

Self theory, also called *self-actualization theory,* is based on two major assumptions: that personality development is guided by each person's unique self-actualization tendency, and that each of us has a personal need for positive regard.

Rogers's first major assumption about self-actualization is similar but slightly different from Maslow's use of the term.

Rogers's self-actualizing tendency refers to an inborn tendency for us to develop all of our capacities in ways that best maintain and benefit our lives.

The self-actualizing tendency relates to *biological functions*, such as meeting our basic need for food, water, and oxygen, as well as *psychological functions*, such as expanding our experiences, encouraging personal growth, and becoming self-sufficient. The self-

actualizing tendency guides us toward positive or healthful behaviors rather than negative or harmful ones. For example, one of the two girls in the photo below has lost the use of her legs and must use a wheelchair. Part of her self-actualizing process will include learning to deal with her disability, engaging in positive healthful behaviors, and getting to know herself.

Because of different experiences, the girl in the wheelchair will likely develop a different concept of self than the other girl.

Self or *self-concept* refers to how we see or describe ourselves. The self is made up of many self-perceptions, abilities, personality characteristics, and behaviors that are organized and consistent with one another.

Because of very different experiences, the girl in the wheelchair will develop a self-concept different from that of her friend who has normal use of her legs. According to Rogers (1980), self-concept plays an important role in personality because it influences our behaviors, feelings, and thoughts. For example, if you have a *positive self-concept*, you will tend to act, feel, and think optimistically and constructively; if you have a *negative self-concept*, you will tend to act, feel, and think pessimistically and destructively.

Sometimes a person may be undecided about his or her real self. As we discover our real self, we may undergo a number of changes in personality.

Real Self Versus Ideal Self

Who is the real David Bowie?

We all change how we see ourselves but probably not as much as rock star David Bowie, who, through the years, has radically changed his looks, clothes, and personal values. For example, Bowie's earlier looks (top photo) and behaviors might be described as having pushed society's limits. Now, however, Bowie is in his 50s and appears quite conventional in hairstyle and clothes (bottom photo), and he has adopted many of society's values, such as getting married. The question is, Which is Bowie's real self?

Carl Rogers said that his clients often asked questions related to their selves: "How do I find myself?" "Why do I sometimes feel that I don't know myself?" "Why do I say or do things that aren't really me?" Rogers developed a clever answer to these relatively common and perplexing questions. He said that there are two kinds of selves: a real self and an ideal self.

The *real self,* according to Rogers, is based on our actual experiences and represents how we really see ourselves.

The *ideal self,* according to Rogers, is based on our hopes and wishes and reflects how we would like to see ourselves.

> My ideal self is based on my hopes and wishes.

> My real self is based on my actual experience.

In some cases, the hopes and wishes of one's ideal self may contradict the abilities and experiences of the real self. For example, a student's ideal self may be someone who is very responsible and studies hard, but the real self may be someone who puts things off and studies less than is required.

Contradiction between ideal and real self. According to Rogers, a glaring contradiction between the ideal and real self can result in personality problems. Rogers suggested that we can resolve contradictions between the ideal and real self by paying more attention to our actual experiences, working to have more positive experiences, and paying less attention to the expectations of others. In working out discrepancies between our ideal and real selves, we may undergo a variety of changes in looks, clothes, and behaviors, such as David Bowie experienced.

Now that you know what the self is, here's how Rogers says that it develops.

Why are there millions of dog owners?

One reason I'm one of the millions of dog owners is that my dog Bear shows great happiness at seeing me, no matter how grouchy, distracted, or sad I may feel or act. In fact, researchers find that because people perceive their pets as showing appreciation, being supportive, and giving pleasure, pets are helpful in reducing stressful feelings and lowering blood pressure (K. Allen, 2003; Stich, 2003).

The need to feel appreciated is so important that in the United States we have a number of days throughout the year that are officially designated for appreciation, such as Mother's, Father's, Grandparent's, and Secretary's days, as well as birthdays and the heartfelt Valentine's Day.

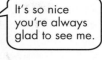

It's so nice you're always glad to see me.

The creation of national appreciation days and the popularity of pets illustrate the second assumption of Carl Rogers's self theory, which is that we humans have a real need for receiving something called positive regard.

Positive regard includes love, sympathy, warmth, acceptance, and respect, which we crave from family, friends, and people important to us.

Rogers believed that positive regard was essential for the healthy development of one's self as well as for successful interpersonal relationships (Liebert & Spiegler, 1994). When we are children, positive regard comes mainly from our parents, siblings, or grandparents. But as we become adults, we learn to provide some of our own positive regard.

Conditional and Unconditional Positive Regard

What's a big problem for teenagers?

Unlike friends and family, pets never pass judgment; they provide endless amounts of positive regard no matter how their owners look, feel, dress, or talk. In contrast, friends and family can be very judgmental and may give only conditional positive regard.

Conditional positive regard refers to the positive regard we receive if we behave in certain acceptable ways, such as living up to or meeting the standards of others.

For instance, one way teenagers display their newly developed independence is by choosing different (radical, awful, outrageous) hairstyles and fashions. In this case, if the teenagers receive only conditional positive regard based on conforming to the more traditional fashion standards of their parents, they may develop a negative self-concept or feel bad or worthless because they displeased or disappointed their parents. Rogers believed that the development of a healthy and positive self-concept depends on

No matter how she dresses, she hopes to get unconditional positive regard.

receiving as much unconditional positive regard as possible.

Unconditional positive regard refers to the warmth, acceptance, and love that others show you because you are valued as a human being even though you may disappoint people by behaving in ways that are different from their standards or values or the way they think.

Parents who provide love and respect, even if a teenager does not always abide by their fashion standards, are showing unconditional positive regard, which will foster the development of a healthy self-concept. However, in real life, receiving unconditional positive regard appears to be more the exception, while receiving conditional positive regard appears to be more the rule (Culp et al., 1991).

Importance of Self-Actualization

What does it take to reach your potential?

In 1945, the Russian ruler, Joseph Stalin, exiled writer Aleksandr Solzhenitsyn (right photo) to Siberia for publishing essays critical of Stalin's abuse of power. In 1976, Solzhenitsyn received the Nobel Prize for his novels, such as *One Day in the Life of Ivan Denisovich,* and was allowed to come to the United States, where, he said, "you can be free."

The life of Solzhenitsyn is a case study in self-actualization. He persisted in developing his potential as a thinker and writer, despite being

I survived Siberia and prison so I could keep writing.

persecuted for years, exiled to the terrible living conditions of Siberia, and forbidden to publish his works. Rogers would explain that Solzhenitsyn persisted in writing because of the tendency for self-actualization, which provides direction and motivation to develop one's potential.

Rogers recognized that our tendency for self-actualization may be hindered, tested, or blocked by a variety of situational hurdles or personal difficulties, as happened to Solzhenitsyn. But like Solzhenitsyn, Rogers believed that we will experience the greatest self-actualization if we work hard and diligently to remove situational problems, resolve our personal problems, and, hopefully, receive tons of unconditional positive regard.

Humanistic theories contain powerful positive messages, but how do these uplifting messages work in real life?

E. Humanistic Theories

What problems do young African Americans face?

Unlike almost every other theory of personality, humanism holds that people are basically good and can achieve their true potentials if the roadblocks placed by society, poverty, drugs, or other evil influences are removed (Megargee, 1997). Based on this belief, one of the primary goals of the humanistic approach is to find ways of removing blocking influences so that people can grow and self-actualize. In the United States, psychologists have identified African American boys as one group of individuals whose paths are often filled with roadblocks. Some of the roadblocks that prevent African American boys from reaching their potentials include peer pressure to act out, to "take nothing from nobody," to turn down educational opportunities and to not "act White" by excelling in school, to hang out on the streets, to join gangs, and to take part in a variety of antisocial and illicit activities (Franklin, 1995; McWhorter, 2000).

I try to show these young boys that someone really cares.

To help remove these roadblocks to healthy personality development in African American boys, counselors are using humanistic ideas, such as providing positive regard and role models for self-actualization. For example, for the past dozen years, counselor Roland Gilbert in San Francisco has been conducting a mentoring program for African American boys who are at high risk for developing personality problems. These boys live in neighborhoods with daily occurrences of violence and drugs; their fathers are often absent; and they have few adult male role models to help them through adolescence's difficult times. At the heart of Gilbert's program are twice-weekly meetings between young African American boys and adult men from the community. During these meetings, the African American men discuss the importance of getting regular jobs, demonstrate how to deal with anger by talking rather than hitting, and provide positive regard by showing that someone really cares (L. Smith, 1993).

In the United States, there are now numerous mentoring programs, such as Big Brothers/Big Sisters of America, which instill a sense of pride and self-worth and give children the motivation to achieve success (P. Hill, 1995). For example, children who participated in mentoring programs reported significantly higher self-concepts than children without mentors (Turner & Scherman, 1996). Thus, applying humanistic principles helped improve the self-concept of children who came from problem families or neighborhoods.

Next, we'll review the important humanistic concepts and discuss what critics have to say about humanistic theories.

How popular is humanism?

Perhaps the main reason humanistic theories, such as those of Maslow and Rogers, continue to be popular is that they view people as basically good and believe that people can develop their true potentials (Clay, 2002). However, these optimistic views of human nature have triggered a number of criticisms.

Impact

In the African American mentoring programs described above, the self-worth of boys at risk is increased when mentors are successful role models who also provide positive regard. These programs illustrate the humanistic theories' emphasis on building self-worth through positive regard. In a real sense, the mentors are removing roadblocks so that each boy can find a path to his true potential through a process called self-actualization (Sapienza & Bugental, 2000).

Humanistic theories have had their greatest impact in counseling, clinical settings, and personal growth programs, where ideas like self-concept, self-actualization, and self-fulfillment have proven useful in developing healthy personalities and interpersonal relationships (Rabasca, 2000a). Compared to Freud's idea that we are driven by unconscious irrational forces, humanism says that we are driven by positive forces that point us toward realizing our good and true selves.

Criticisms

Humanistic theories have come under considerable criticism because Rogers and Maslow provide little or no scientific evidence that an inherent (biological) tendency to self-actualization really exists. Because the major assumption of self-actualization and other humanistic concepts, such as positive regard and self-worth, are difficult to demonstrate experimentally, critics argue that humanistic theories primarily describe how people behave rather than explain the causes of their behaviors. For these reasons, critics regard humanistic theories more as a wonderfully positive view of human nature or a very hopeful philosophy of life rather than as a scientific explanation of personality development (Burger, 2004). Critics note that because humanistic concepts are too descriptive and limited in scope, humanistic theories have had less impact on mainstream psychology and more on humanities. Another major problem is that humanistic theories generally ignore research showing that 20 to 60% of the development of intellectual, emotional, social, and personality traits comes from genetic factors (McClearn et al., 1997). This means that genetic factors must be considered when discussing a person's true potential or a person's ability to achieve self-actualization.

Maslow hoped that humanistic theories would become a third major force in psychology, along with behavioral and psychoanalytic theories. Although it appears that the humanistic approach has not achieved Maslow's goal, many of humanism's ideas gave birth to the human potential movements in the 1960s and 1970s and have been incorporated into approaches for counseling and psychotherapy (Clay, 2002).

✔ Concept Review

1. The combination of long-lasting and distinctive behaviors, thoughts, and emotions that are typical of how we react and adapt to other people and situations forms our _____.

2. Freud's theory of personality, which emphasizes the importance of early childhood experiences and of conflicts between conscious thoughts and unconscious forces, is called a _____ theory.

3. Freud developed three techniques for probing the unconscious. A technique that encourages clients to talk about any thoughts or images that enter their head is called (a)_____. A technique to interpret the hidden meanings and symbols in dreams is called (b)_____. With a third technique, the therapist analyzes the mistakes or (c)_____ that the client makes in everyday speech.

4. Freud considered the mind to have three major divisions. The division that contains the biological drives and is the source of all psychic or mental energy is called the (a)_____. This division operates according to the (b)_____ principle, which demands immediate satisfaction. The division that develops from the id during infancy and whose goal is finding safe and socially acceptable ways of satisfying the id's desires is called the (c)_____. This division operates according to the (d)_____ principle, which involves satisfying a wish only if there is a socially acceptable outlet. The division that develops from the id during early childhood and whose goal is applying the moral values and standards of one's parents and society is called the (e)_____.

5. Conflicts between the id and the superego over satisfaction of desires may cause the ego to feel threatened. When threatened, the ego generates an unpleasant state that is associated with feelings of uneasiness, apprehension, and heightened physiological arousal; this unpleasant state is called (a)_____. Freud suggested that the ego may reduce anxiety by using unconscious mechanisms that produce self-deception; these are called (b)_____.

6. Freud proposed that the major influence on personality development occurs as we pass through five developmental periods that he called the (a)_____ stages, each of which results in conflicts between the child's wishes and parents' restrictions. The result of a person's wishes being overgratified or undergratified at any one of the first three stages is called (b)_____.

7. Personality theories that emphasize our capacity for personal growth, the development of our potential, and freedom to choose our destinies are referred to as _____ theories.

8. Humanistic theories have three characteristics in common. They take the perspective that our perception of the world, whether or not it is accurate, becomes our reality; this is called the (a)_____ perspective. Humanistic theories see personality as more than the sum of individual parts and consider personality as a unique and total entity that functions as a unit; this is the (b)_____ view of personality. Humanistic theories point to an inherent tendency that each of us has to reach our true potential; this tendency is called (c)_____.

9. The idea that our needs occur in ascending order, with biological needs at the bottom and social and personal needs toward the top, and that we must meet our lower-level needs before we can satisfy higher ones is called (a)_____. Our physiological needs (food, sleep) and psychological needs (safety, belongingness, esteem) are called (b)_____ needs because we try to fulfill them if they are not met. The highest need of self-actualization, which includes the desire for truth, goodness, beauty, and justice, is called a (c)_____ need.

10. Carl Rogers's self theory of personality makes two basic assumptions. The first is that personality development is guided by an inborn tendency to develop our potential; this idea is called (a)_____. The second assumption is that each of us has a personal need for acceptance and love, which Rogers called (b)_____. According to Rogers, it is important that we receive love and acceptance despite the fact that we sometimes behave in ways that are different from what others think or value; this type of acceptance is called (c)_____.

11. Rogers proposes that we have two kinds of selves: the self that is based on real-life experiences is called the (a)_____ self; the self that is based on how we would like to see ourselves is called the (b)_____ self.

Answers: *1. personality; 2. psychodynamic; 3. (a) free association, (b) dream interpretation, (c) Freudian slips or slips of the tongue; 4. (a) id, (b) pleasure, (c) ego, (d) reality, (e) superego; 5. (a) anxiety, (b) defense mechanisms; 6. (a) psychosexual, (b) fixation; 7. humanistic; 8. (a) phenomenological, (b) holistic, (c) self-actualization; 9. (a) Maslow's hierarchy of needs, (b) deficiency, (c) growth; 10. (a) self-actualization, (b) positive regard, (c) unconditional positive regard; 11. (a) real, (b) ideal*

F. Cultural Diversity: Unexpected High Achievement

Boat People: Remarkable Achievement

What was different about these children?

I have always been puzzled by why students with similar academic skills perform so differently: some do well on my exams, while others do poorly. A humanist would look at the same differences and ask, "Why are some students developing their potential, while others are not?" One answer comes from studying thousands of Indo-Chinese refugees, known as the boat people, who were allowed to resettle in the United States in the 1970s and 1980s.

On their arrival in America, the boat people's only possessions were the clothes they wore. They knew virtually no English, had almost no knowledge of Western culture, and had no one to turn to for social or financial support. In spite of horrendous difficulties, refugee children achieved such remarkable academic success that American educators were scratching their heads and asking why.

Background. Researchers set out to discover why these refugee children had achieved astonishing scholastic success against overwhelming odds (N. Caplan et al., 1992). The researchers selected a random sample of 200 Indo-Chinese refugee families with a total of 536 school-age children. The children had been in the United States

Refugee boat people's children, who first had to learn English, went on to achieve remarkable academic success.

© Jason Goltz

for an average of $3\frac{1}{2}$ years. They had generally lived in low-income metropolitan areas with troublesome neighborhoods and run-down schools that were plagued with problems and not known for their high academic standards. Despite all these problems, the children of the boat people performed remarkably well in school. Here's what researchers found.

Amazing success. The researchers computed the mean grade point average for the 536 children, who were fairly evenly distributed among grades 1 to 12. They found that 27% of the children had a grade point average (GPA) in the A range, 52% had a GPA in the B range, 17% in the C range, and only 4% had a GPA below C. Equally noteworthy was the children's overall performance in math: almost 50% of the children earned A's, while another 33% earned B's. On national math tests, the Indo-Chinese children's average scores were almost three times higher than the national norm.

After analyzing all these data, researchers were able to identify several reasons why immigrant Indo-Chinese students achieved such high grades.

Values and Motivation

What were their values?

Although Indo-Chinese refugee children had been in the United States for an average of only $3\frac{1}{2}$ years, they were doing better in math than 90% of their peers. It could not be the quality of their schools, which were average, undistinguished low-income schools in metropolitan areas. But clearly there were powerful factors helping these children overcome the problems of learning a second language and adapting to a new culture. Researchers located these powerful factors in the values of the Asian family.

The *primary values* held by the Indo-Chinese families were that parents and children have mutual respect, cooperate freely, and are committed to accomplishment and achievement. A clear example of commitment to accomplishment is the amount of time Indo-Chinese children spend doing homework: They average about 3 hours a day, while American students average about $1\frac{1}{2}$ hours. Thus, among refugee families, doing homework, not watching television, is the main activity; the older children help the younger children.

Another primary value is that parents were very involved in their children's education: Over 50% of parents read aloud and helped with homework. When children were asked, "What accounts for your academic success?" the children most often checked the category, "having a love of learning." Love of learning was one of the values nourished and passed on from parent to child. When children were asked, "How much do you choose your own destiny?" the children answered that they did not trust luck or fate but were the masters of their own destinies.

Parental Values

⬇

Children

Parental values on the importance of education motivated the children.

Parental Attitudes

How did parents help?

One reason Indo-Chinese children earned great academic success was the personal and cultural values transmitted by their parents, who were committed to help their children succeed through educational performance. After studying the immigrant parents' values and how they instilled these values in their children, researchers concluded that for American schools to succeed, parents must become more committed to the education of their children. In this case, Americans can truly learn from the values of these refugees.

In explaining the immigrant children's wonderful academic achievement, humanists would emphasize how parental values served to remove mental roadblocks that otherwise might have hindered their children from developing their true potentials and reaching self-fulfillment.

Next, we turn to a relatively common personality problem, shyness, and discuss how different theories of personality explain its causes.

G. Research Focus: Shyness

What Is Shyness and What Causes It?

What's it like to be shy?

It's one thing to discuss Freud's psychodynamic theory of personality but it's another to see it in action, in this case, to treat shyness.

At some time and in some situations, we have all felt a little shy. However, there are degrees of shyness, and a high degree of shyness can interfere with enjoying personal and social interactions. For example, when Alan was a child, he would walk home from school through alleys to avoid meeting any of his classmates. Although he received a perfect math score on his SAT, he dropped out of the University of Texas because he always felt like a stranger and was continually frustrated by not being able to reach out and make contact with people. He was so shy that he could not even use the Internet. Finally, feeling so lonely, Alan sought help at the Shyness Clinic, which was founded in the 1970s by well-known shyness researcher, Philip Zimbardo of Stanford University (Noriyuki, 1996).

Shyness is a feeling of distress that comes from being tense, stressed, or awkward in social situations and from worrying about and fearing rejection.

Surveys indicate that about 40% of adults report mild but chronic shyness and, although they are good at hiding their shyness, internally they feel distress. About 20% report more severe shyness and are unable to hide their pain and distress (Chavira et al., 2002). The cause and treatment for shyness depend partly on which theory of personality guides our thinking. We'll contrast answers from two different theories: Freud's psychodynamic theory and social cognitive theory.

20–40% are shy.

Psychodynamic Approach

Is shyness due to unresolved conflicts?

As a practicing psychoanalyst, Donald Kaplan (1972) uses his clinical experience and psychodynamic concepts to answer the question, What causes shyness? Kaplan traces the causes of shyness back to *unresolved conflicts* at one or more of Freud's psychosexual stages. For example, one very shy client reported that his mother constantly fed him so that he would never cry or whimper. As a result, Kaplan suggests that this client's unresolved conflict during the oral stage resulted in his feelings of inadequacy and shyness in later social interactions.

According to Kaplan, the symptoms of shyness include both conscious fears, such as having nothing to say, and unconscious fears of being rejected. Shy people may deal with these anxieties by using *defense mechanisms*; for example, one client reduced his anxiety through displacement, by changing his fears of being rejected into opposite feelings of self-righteousness and contempt.

One *advantage* of the psychodynamic approach is that it suggests that a number of causes, such as conscious and unconscious fears, as well as unresolved psychosexual conflicts are involved in shyness.

One *disadvantage* of the psychodynamic approach is that Freudian concepts (unconscious fears, unresolved psychosexual stages) are difficult to verify by experimental methods (Macmillan, 1997). For example, saying that being fixated at the oral stage may result in a person becoming a shy adult is mostly a descriptive guess rather than a testable hypothesis.

A very different account of what causes shyness comes from the social cognitive theory of personality.

The cause and treatment for shyness depend partly on which theory of personality the therapist follows.

Social Cognitive Theory

What are the three factors?

Unlike the Freudian approach, which relies primarily on therapists' personal observations, social cognitive theory uses primarily experimental studies to answer questions about personality. Social cognitive theory breaks shyness down into three measurable or observable components—cognitive, behavioral, and environmental—which can be studied using the experimental method described in Module 2 (Chavira et al., 2002). For example, in a series of longitudinal studies, researchers found that about 10–15% of the population have a shy personality that, to a large extent, comes from *genetic factors*—for example, inheriting a nervous system that is easily aroused by novel stimuli (Kagan, 2003a). By observing the social interactions (the behavioral component) of shy people, researchers found that shy people have too few social and communication skills and, as a consequence, they are continually punished during social interactions (Jackson et al., 1997). By giving personality tests (the cognitive component), researchers found that shy people are overly self-conscious, which leads to worrisome thoughts and irrational beliefs that interfere with social functioning (Romney & Bynner, 1997). Therapies based on social cognitive theory (Module 20) have proved successful in helping shy individuals decrease their anxiety in social situations, develop better social and communication skills, and decrease levels of shyness (Greco & Morris, 2001).

One *advantage* of social cognitive theory is that it breaks shyness down into three measurable or observable components, which can be experimentally studied and appropriate treatments developed.

One *disadvantage* of this approach is that researchers may overlook certain influences that we are neither conscious nor aware of, such as conditioned emotional responses, that can also trigger shy behaviors (Westen, 1998a).

Our discussion of shyness raises the interesting question of how psychologists measure or assess personality traits, such as shyness.

H. Application: Assessment—Projective Tests

How did friends describe Kurt's personality?

At the beginning of this module, we discussed Kurt Cobain, the 27-year-old singer and songwriter, who committed suicide at the height of his fame and fortune. When friends, school-teachers, and writers described Cobain's personality, some said that he was a nice young man, very quiet, a kind, sweet man, and a sincere listener (top photo). Other friends said that he was very moody, extremely intimidating, unhappy, filled with anger, and never close to anyone (bottom photo) (DeCurtis, 1994). When friends were describing Kurt's personality, they were making a kind of psychological assessment.

Psychological assessment refers to the use of various tools, such as psychological tests and/or interviews, to measure various characteristics, traits, or abilities in order to understand behaviors and predict future performances or behaviors.

Psychological tests are usually divided into ability tests and personality tests, which differ considerably. For

Was Cobain generally a kind, sweet man or an angry, moody one?

example, when Kurt entered a drug treatment program, he was most likely given personality tests to identify his personal problems.

Personality tests are used to measure observable or overt traits and behaviors as well as unobservable or covert characteristics. Personality tests are used to identify personality problems and psychological disorders as well as to predict how a person might behave in the future.

Although you may not have taken a personality test, you certainly have taken many ability tests, such as exams. *Ability tests* include achievement tests, which measure what we have learned; aptitude tests, which measure our potential for learning or acquiring a specific skill; and intelligence tests, which measure our general potential to solve problems, think abstractly, and profit from experience (R. M. Kaplan & Saccuzzo, 2001).

The primary tools of assessment are tests of ability and personality. There are two kinds of personality tests. We'll now focus on one kind, projective personality tests, and later (p. 474) discuss objective personality tests. Personality assessment is a $400-million-a-year industry (Talbot, 1999).

In describing Cobain's personality, some listed observable behaviors, such as quiet, kind, and nice, while others hinted at unobservable behaviors, such as filled with anger, not close to anybody. In Freud's psychodynamic theory, observable behaviors reflect conscious wishes, desires, and thoughts, while unobservable behaviors may reflect unconscious forces. Freud developed three techniques for revealing unconscious forces—free association, dream interpretation, and interpretation of slips of the tongue. We now add a fourth technique to reveal hidden or unconscious forces: projective tests.

Projective tests require individuals to look at some meaningless object or ambiguous photo and describe what they see. In describing or making up a story about the ambiguous object, individuals are assumed to project both their conscious and unconscious feelings, needs, and motives.

Although projective tests were not developed by Freud, they are assumed to reveal unconscious thoughts (Masling, 1997). We'll examine the two most widely used projective tests—Rorschach (*ROAR-shock*) inkblot test and Thematic Apperception Test (TAT).

Rorschach Inkblot Test

What do you see in this inkblot?

The Rorschach inkblot test, which was published in the early 1920s by a Swiss psychiatrist, Hermann Rorschach (1921/1942), contains five inkblots printed in black and white and five that have color (the inkblot shown on the left is similar to but is not an actual Rorschach inkblot).

What might this be?

The *Rorschach inkblot test* is used to assess personality by showing a person a series of ten inkblots and then asking the person to describe what he or she thinks an image is.

This test is used primarily in the therapeutic setting to assess personality traits and identify potential problems of adolescents and adult clients (Mestel, 2003b).

Thematic Apperception Test (TAT)

What's happening in this picture?

A person would be shown a picture like the one on the right and asked to make up a plot or story about what the young man is thinking, feeling, or doing. This is an example but not a real TAT card.

The *Thematic Apperception Test,* or *TAT,* involves showing a person a series of 20 pictures of people in ambiguous situations and asking the person to make up a story about what the people are doing or thinking in each situation.

What's happening in this picture?

The TAT, which was developed by Henry Murray (1943), is used to assess the motivation and personality characteristics of normal individuals as well as clients with personality problems (R. M. Kaplan & Saccuzzo, 2001).

Before we discuss how well the Rorschach inkblot test and the TAT assess personality traits and identify potential problems, we'll look at another personality test that you have probably heard of: handwriting analysis. How much can someone learn from just your handwriting?

What does handwriting show?

Handwriting analysts (graphologists) charge about $75 an hour to do personality assessments that they claim reveal a person's strengths and weaknesses, which are important in selecting job applicants and identifying people who may not be trusted (Scanlon & Mauro, 1992).

However, researchers report that handwriting analysis is no better than chance at assessing personality characteristics, rating the success of job applicants, or identifying one's profession (Basil,

Which handwriting reveals an honest and sincere person?

1989; Tripician, 2000). In order for handwriting analysis or any personality assessment test to be an effective personality assessment tool, it must have two characteristics, validity and reliability. Handwriting analysis is no better than chance in assessing personality because it lacks validity.

Validity

Handwriting analysis is fun but no better than chance as a personality test because it lacks validity.

Validity means that the test measures what it says it measures or what it is supposed to measure.

For example, for a personality test to be valid, it must measure personality traits specific to the person rather than general traits that apply to almost everyone. Handwriting analysis does not measure, identify, or predict traits specific to an individual, so it has no validity as a personality test (Basil, 1989; Tripician, 2000).

In addition to validity, a good personality test must also have a second characteristic, reliability.

Reliability

In judging the usefulness of any personality test, the major question is always the same: How good are the test's validity and reliability?

Reliability refers to having a consistent score at different times. A person who takes a test at one point in time should receive the same score on a similar test taken at a later time.

For example, handwriting analysis may have good reliability provided your handwriting remains about the same across time. But, even if handwriting analysis has good reliability, it is still no better than chance at assessing or predicting an individual's personality traits because graphology lacks the important characteristic of validity.

This means that the usefulness of projective personality tests, such as the Rorschach test and TAT, depends on their validity and reliability.

Are they valid and reliable?

Projective tests, such as the Rorschach inkblot test, have been used for over 75 years. However, there is still a debate between therapists, who report that projective tests are useful in assessing personality traits and problems, and researchers, who continue to question the reliability and validity of projective tests (Mestel, 2003b; J. M. Wood et al., 2003). This debate involves the advantages and disadvantages of projective tests.

Advantages

Individuals who take projective tests do not know which are the best, correct, or socially desirable answers to give because the stimuli—the inkblot or the TAT picture—are ambiguous and have no right or wrong answers. Thus, one advantage of projective tests such as the Rorschach and the TAT is that they are difficult to fake or bias, since there are no correct or socially desirable answers.

When clients respond to Rorschach's meaningless inkblots or make up stories about what is happening in TAT's ambiguous pictures, clinicians assume that clients will project their hidden feelings, thoughts, or emotions onto these ambiguous stimuli. Based on this assumption, some clinicians believe that a second advantage of projective tests is that they are another method for assessing a client's hidden and unconscious thoughts and desires of which he or she is normally unaware (Viglione & Hilsenroth, 2001). Other researchers suggest that the Rorschach test is useful as an interview technique in eliciting unique information about the person (Aronow et al., 1995). Thus, the Rorschach test's advantage is obtaining information about the person in a setting where there are no right or wrong answers.

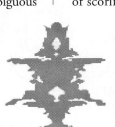

Clinician's experience affects reliability and validity of projective tests.

Disadvantages

One disadvantage of projective tests comes from their use of ambiguous stimuli to which there are no right or wrong answers. The current method of scoring the Rorschach is based on analyzing and making judgments about so many different variables (such as content, theme, color, and detail of the cards) that disagreements often arise over interpretations and classifications (Mestel, 2003b). For example, there are several studies using the Rorschach in which clinicians scored and interpreted the results as indicating that perfectly normal individuals were classified as psychologically disordered (Wood et al., 2003). Although the Rorschach is one of the more popular personality assessment tests, there are numerous studies that point to serious problems in scoring and interpreting responses and making assessments based on the Rorschach test (Wood et al., 2003).

Because of potential problems in scoring and interpreting, projective tests tend to have relatively low reliability and validity, their major disadvantages (R. M. Kaplan & Saccuzzo, 2001).

In spite of these criticisms, some experienced clinicians report that projective tests can provide reliable and valid information about a client's personality and problems, especially when combined with other assessment techniques (Mestel, 2003b). Thus, a clinician's training and experience play a major role in the accuracy of assessing a client's personality and problems using projective tests (R. M. Kaplan & Saccuzzo, 2001).

Summary Test

A. FREUD'S PSYCHODYNAMIC THEORY

1. The lasting behaviors, thoughts, and emotions that typify how we react and adapt to other people and situations make up our (a)_____. An organized attempt to explain how personalities develop and why they differ is called a (b)_____ of personality.

2. Freud's approach, which emphasizes the importance of early childhood experiences and conflicts between conscious and unconscious forces, is called a (a)_____ theory of personality. According to Freud, those wishes, desires, or thoughts of which we are aware or that we can readily recall are (b)_____; those that we automatically repress because of their disturbing or threatening content are (c)_____.

3. Freud's technique of encouraging clients to talk about any thoughts or images that enter their heads is called (a)_____. His assumption that dreams provide clues to unconscious thoughts and desires gave rise to his technique of (b)_____. Mistakes that we make in everyday speech that are thought to reflect unconscious thoughts or wishes are called (c)_____.

B. DIVISIONS OF THE MIND

4. According to Freud, the biological drives of sex and aggression are the source of all psychic or mental energy and give rise to the development of the (a)_____. Because this division of the mind strives to satisfy drives and avoid pain without concern for moral or social restrictions, it is said to be operating according to the (b)_____. During infancy, the second division of the mind develops from the id; it is called the (c)_____. The goal of this second division is to find safe and socially acceptable ways of satisfying the id's desires. The ego follows a policy of satisfying a wish or desire only if a socially acceptable outlet is available; thus it is said to operate according to the (d)_____. During early childhood, the third division of the mind develops from the id; it is called the (e)_____. The goal of this division is to apply the moral values and standards of one's parents and society in satisfying one's wishes.

5. When the id, ego, and superego are in conflict, an unpleasant state of uneasiness, apprehension, and heightened physiological arousal may occur; this is known as (a)_____. The Freudian processes that operate at unconscious levels to help the ego reduce anxiety through self-deception are called (b)_____; they can be helpful or harmful, depending on how much we rely on them.

C. DEVELOPMENTAL STAGES

6. The essence of Freud's theory of personality development is a series of five developmental stages, called (a)_____, during which the individual seeks pleasure from different parts of the body. The stage that lasts for the first 18 months of life is called the (b)_____ stage. It is followed by the (c)_____ stage, which lasts until about the age of 3. The next stage, until about the age of 6, is called the (d)_____ stage. The stage that lasts from about 6 to puberty is called the (e)_____ stage; it is followed by the (f)_____ stage, which lasts through adulthood.

7. The resolution of the potential conflict at each stage has important implications for personality. A Freudian process through which individuals may be locked into earlier psychosexual stages because their wishes were overgratified or undergratified is called _____; it can occur at any of the first three stages.

D. FREUD'S FOLLOWERS & CRITICS

8. Jung believed that the basic force is not the sex drive, as Freud believed, but ancient memory traces and symbols shared by all peoples in all cultures, called the (a)_____. According to Adler's philosophy, each person is a social being with a unique personality and is motivated by (b)_____. Karen Horney disagreed with Freud's emphasis on biological urges and insisted that the major influence on personality development was (c)_____ between parents and child.

9. Those who generally agreed with Freud's basic ideas but disagreed with his emphasis on biological forces, sexual drives, and psychosexual stages are referred to as _____; they turned the emphasis of psychodynamic theory to psychosocial and cultural influences.

10. Criticisms of Freud's psychodynamic theory include that it is so comprehensive that it is not very useful for explaining or predicting behaviors of a specific (a)_____; that some Freudian terms (Oedipal complex) are out of date because they could not be (b)_____; that psychodynamic theory must be updated with findings about (c)_____ factors and the association between (d)_____ development and related behaviors.

E. HUMANISTIC THEORIES

11. Humanistic theories emphasize our capacity for personal growth, development of our potential, and freedom to choose our (a)_____. They stress that our perception of the world becomes our reality; this is called the (b)_____ perspective. These theories emphasize that one's personality is unique, functions as a unit, and is more than the sum of individual parts; together these ideas make up the (c)_____ view. These theories also highlight the idea of an inherent tendency to reach our true potentials, which is called (d)_____.

12. According to Maslow, our needs are arranged in a hierarchy with (a)_____ at the bottom and (b)_____ toward the top.

13. How we see or describe ourselves, including how we perceive our abilities, personality characteristics, and behaviors, is referred to as our (a)_____. According to Carl Rogers, the development of self-concept depends on our interactions with others. If we receive (b)_____ positive regard even when our behavior is disappointing, we will develop a positive self-concept and tend to act, feel, and think optimistically and constructively.

F. CULTURAL DIVERSITY: UNEXPECTED HIGH ACHIEVEMENT

14. Indo-Chinese children overcame problems of language and culture and excelled in American schools in part because of the _____ held by their families, including mutual respect, cooperation, parental involvement, and the belief that they, not fate, controlled their destinies.

© Jason Goltz

G. RESEARCH FOCUS: SHYNESS

15. As a practicing psychoanalyst, Donald Kaplan traces the causes of shyness back to unresolved conflicts at one or more of Freud's

(a)_____. The Freudian approach primarily uses therapists' (b)_____ to answer questions about personality. In comparison, social cognitive theory breaks shyness down into three measurable or observable components that can be investigated using (c)_____.

H. APPLICATION: ASSESSMENT—PROJECTIVE TESTS

16. Tests that are used to measure observable traits and behaviors as well as unobservable characteristics of a person and to identify personality problems and psychological disorders are called _____ tests.

17. Achievement tests measure what we have learned; aptitude tests measure our potential for learning or acquiring a specific skill; and intelligence tests measure our general potential to solve problems, think abstractly, and profit from experience. Collectively, these are called _____ tests.

18. For a test to be useful, it must have two characteristics. First, a test must measure what it is supposed to measure; this is called (a)_____. Second, a person's score on a test at one point in time should be similar to the score obtained by the same person on a similar test at a later point in time; this is called (b)_____.

19. Typically, a combination of tests is used to assess personality. Tests that involve presenting an ambiguous stimulus and asking the person to describe it are called (a)_____ tests. A test used to assess personality in terms of how the subject interprets a series of inkblots is called the (b)_____ test. A test in which the subject is to make up a story about people shown in ambiguous situations is called the (c)_____.

Answers: *1. (a) personalities, (b) theory; 2. (a) psychodynamic, (b) conscious thoughts, (c) unconscious forces or thoughts; 3. (a) free association, (b) dream interpretation, (c) slips of the tongue or Freudian slips; 4. (a) id, (b) pleasure principle, (c) ego, (d) reality principle, (e) superego; 5. (a) anxiety, (b) defense mechanisms; 6. (a) psychosexual stages, (b) oral, (c) anal, (d) phallic, (e) latency, (f) genital; 7. fixation; 8. (a) collective unconscious, (b) social urges, (c) social interactions; 9. neo-Freudians; 10. (a) individual or person, (b) tested or verified, (c) genetic, (d) brain; 11. (a) destinies, (b) phenomenological, (c) holistic, (d) self-actualization; 12. (a) biological needs, (b) social and personal needs; 13. (a) self or self-concept, (b) unconditional; 14. primary values; 15. (a) psychosexual stages, (b) personal observations, (c) experimental studies; 16. personality; 17. ability; 18. (a) validity, (b) reliability; 19. (a) projective, (b) Rorschach inkblot, (c) Thematic Apperception Test (TAT)*

Critical Thinking

NEWSPAPER ARTICLE

Friends, Others Offer Complex View of Rathbun

by Robert J. Lopez and Eric Slater

Questions

1. Which part of Freud's psychodynamic theory might explain why Charles Rathbun murdered a woman?

2. What roles might the Freudian concepts of the id, ego, and superego have had in Rathbun's earlier charge of raping a woman?

3. Following Freud's psychodynamic theory, what kinds of questions might you ask or what techniques might you use to understand Rathbun's behavior?

Charles E. Rathbun is a skilled automobile photographer who was on his way to the top in his highly specialized field.

Yet, as Rathbun sits in Men's Central Jail downtown—charged with murdering model Linda Sobek—a more complex portrait of the 38-year-old is beginning to emerge, one of a man who seemed to have different facets of his personality that he showed to different people— friendly and easygoing to some, a loner who had difficulties with women to others, and an aggressive hothead in some eyes. Problems with women are not new since as a young college student in Ohio, court records show, he was charged and then acquitted of raping a female friend in 1979.

Moving to California eight years ago, Rathbun had no run-ins with the law until he was arrested in Sobek's death and led investigators to her shallow grave. "There is nothing about this guy that would ever suggest that he is in any way capable of this," said Steve Spence, managing editor of *Car and Driver* magazine.

The son of a management consultant, Rathbun was born on Oct. 2, 1957, and was raised in a quiet, middle-class neighborhood in Worthington, a suburb of Columbus. He was the youngest of four children, and has two sisters and a brother. At Worthington High School in the early 1970s, Rathbun developed an interest in photography, taking photos for the school's biweekly newspaper, the *Chronicle*.

After several years of college in Ohio, Rathbun made his way to the car-manufacturing center of Detroit, an ideal place for an ambitious automobile photographer to leave his mark. Jim Haefner hired Rathbun as an assistant in 1985. "He was a nice enough guy— there was just something a little bit different about him," Haefner recalled. "It was just an anger that would come out from time to time. If something frustrated him, he might pick up [a piece of photo equipment] and throw it across the studio. I don't know what was bothering him."

But others in Michigan did not see Rathbun that way. Pamela Powell, who has been a friend of Rathbun's for 10 years, said he was a well-adjusted man who liked old rock 'n' roll and adventure movies. Contrary to some reports, Powell insisted that Rathbun was comfortable around men and women alike, and dated frequently. (Source: *Los Angeles Times,* December 11, 1995)

4. Can you explain why different people offer such different descriptions of Rathbun?

5. How might humanistic theories explain Rathbun's actions?

Try InfoTrac to search for terms: **personality development; self-actualization; rape.**

SUGGESTED ANSWERS

1. The part of Freud's psychodynamic theory that focuses on the development of personality involves how a person goes through the five psychosexual stages and whether fixation occurs. For example, Rathbun may have become fixated at the phallic stage and found it necessary to prove his toughness with women.
2. Rathbun's id, which follows the pleasure principle, wanted to have sex with women. Rathbun's superego, which contains moral standards, would argue against forcing women to have sex. Rathbun's ego, which follows the reality principle, tried to find a socially acceptable outlet for the id's desires. In Rathbun's case, the id's desires apparently won out.
3. Since Freud believed that most personality development and seeds of problems occurred during the first five years, you would ask questions about his early childhood, especially his relationship with his parents. To reveal Rathbun's unconscious forces, you might use free association and dream interpretation.
4. People might have very different impressions of Rathbun because he might have behaved very differently depending on how much he was influenced by different unconscious feelings and thoughts, repressed wishes or desires, or defense mechanisms.
5. Humanistic theories are better at describing positive human growth than criminal behavior. However, a humanist might say that because Rathbun had not received enough love or unconditional positive regard, he developed a poor or negative self-concept, which interfered with his self-actualization and instead led him to commit destructive actions.

Links to Learning

LEARNING ACTIVITIES

- **POWERSTUDY CD-ROM 2.0**
  by Tom Doyle and Rod Plotnik
  Check out the "Freudian & Humanistic Theories" Module (disk 2)
  on PowerStudy and:
  - Test your knowledge using an interactive version of the
    Summary Test on pages 452 and 453. Also access related
    quizzes—true/false, multiple choice, and matching.
  - Explore an interactive version of the Critical Thinking exercise
    "Friends, Others Offer Complex View of Rathbun" on page 454.
  - You will also find key terms, a chapter outline including chapter
    abstract, and a list of hotlinked Web sites that correlate to this
    module.

- **SELF-STUDY ASSESSMENT**
  Want help studying? For your customized Study Plan go to
  http://psychology.wadsworth.com/plotnik7e/. This program
  will automatically generate pretests and posttests to help you
  determine what concepts you have mastered and what concepts you
  still need work on.

WebTUTOR ● **STUDY GUIDE and WEBTUTOR**
  Check the corresponding module in your Study
  Guide for effective student tips and help learning the material
  presented.

- **INFOTRAC COLLEGE EDITION ONLINE LIBRARY**
  To find interesting and relevant articles go to
  http://www.infotrac-college.com, use your password, and
  then type in search terms such as the ones listed below.

  Psychological tests   Abraham Maslow   Sigmund Freud

STUDY QUESTIONS

Use InfoTrac to search for topics mentioned in the main heads below (e.g., shyness, projective tests).

*A. Freud's Psychodynamic Theory—According to Freud, why do
some students plan to study on the weekend but end up partying?
(**Suggested answer p. 632**)

B. Divisions of the Mind—Sheryl wears sexy clothes but claims to
be a feminist. How would Freud explain that?

C. Developmental Stages—How would Freud's theory explain why
you are neat and outspoken while your sister is messy and demanding and feels inferior?

D. Freud's Followers & Critics—Which factors in the development of your personality support Freud's theory and which do not?

E. Humanistic Theories—How would humanistic theories explain
why many students change their majors three to five times during
their college careers?

*F. Cultural Diversity: Unexpected High Achievement—If you
were the principal of a grade school, what might you do to improve
overall student performance? (**Suggested answer p. 632**)

G. Research Focus: Shyness—Carl says that he's always been shy
and it can't be helped. Would a Freudian respond to Carl's problem
in the same way as a cognitive behaviorist?

*H. Application: Assessment—Projective Tests—How useful would
projective tests be for identifying students who are most likely to cheat
on exams? (**Suggested answer p. 632**)

*These questions are answered in Appendix B.

Module 20: Social Cognitive & Trait Theories

Courtesy of Sony Electronics, Inc.

Power of Beliefs

Why did he suffer in prison for 27 years?

He chose to remain in prison rather than change his major beliefs.

Nelson Mandela had been born into a royal tribal African family, but he lost his father at an early age and was raised by a guardian in the tribe. According to tradition, Mandela became a man at 16, when he went through an elaborate public circumcision ceremony. When he was 21, he ran away to the big city. In Johannesburg, he entered college, received his law degree, and began his lifetime struggle to free the black people of South Africa (Ransdell & Eddings, 1994).

In 1964, Nelson Mandela (left photo) was found guilty of plotting against the all-white South African government and sentenced to prison for life. In his defense he said: "During my lifetime I have dedicated myself to this struggle of the African people. I have fought against white domination, and I have fought about black domination. I have cherished the ideal of a democratic and free society in which all persons live together in harmony and with equal opportunities. It is an ideal which I hope to live for and to achieve. But, if need be, it is an ideal for which I am prepared to die" (P. W. Bernstein, 1994, p. 11).

While in prison, he slept on a narrow bed in a barren cubicle, 7 feet wide and 9 feet long. He ate corn porridge, with a piece of meat every other day. He was allowed to write one letter and have one visitor every six months. Mandela endured these long, terrible years because he believed that one day he would be free to continue his fight against oppression. Many times he was offered his release from prison provided that he make no public speeches and cease his freedom-fighting activities. Mandela refused these conditional releases and remained in prison.

Finally, in 1990, at the age of 71, he was released from prison. His time had indeed come, and he repeated the moving speech that he had spoken 27 years earlier (quoted above). Mandela lost no time in resuming his fight against White domination and for equal opportunities for Blacks. For these efforts, Mandela was awarded the Nobel Peace Prize in 1993.

The fulfillment of his life's dream finally came in 1994. At the age of 76, Mandela was elected the first Black president of South Africa. His election marked the end to the horrible and discriminatory practice of apartheid, which had been in effect for almost 300 years and had permitted the White minority to dominate and suppress the Black majority.

What were the forces that shaped Mandela's personality and gave him the strength and motivation to persist in the face of overwhelming adversity? In this module, we'll discuss three forces that shape and mold our personalities.

In a different nation, an ocean away, Beverly Harvard was waging her own personal struggle against forces that said no African American woman should be doing what she wanted to do.

Determination

What's unusual about this woman?

In the 1970s, Beverly Harvard, an African American woman in a southern city (Atlanta, Georgia), was trying to become a police officer. In those days, female police recruits, Black or White, faced rejection, discrimination, and harassment by their male peers, who believed strongly that women had neither the physical strength nor the mental toughness to be police officers (C. Fletcher, 1995). From the 1970s through the 1980s, there were intense legal and political battles in the United States, in which women had to prove that they have what it takes to be good cops. Their struggle is slowly paying off: By the early 1990s, about 10% of this country's police officers were women.

With incredible determination, Beverly Harvard (photo below) worked her way up through the Atlanta police ranks. She put up with the male officers' sarcastic, hurtful, and discriminatory comments and concentrated on doing the best possible job. Finally, after struggling for almost 20 years, she was appointed head of the Atlanta police department. Her appointment in 1994 marked the first time an African American woman had headed a police department in a major city. She had 1,700 police officers under her command, and her motto is "You can talk about what's wrong with the world or help fix it" (Eddings, 1994, p. 87).

For her beliefs, Beverly Harvard fought against sex discrimination for 20 years.

Beverly Harvard, like thousands of female police officers around the country, has shown that women make good cops, partly because of their particular personality traits: women are less authoritarian, more open, better listeners, and less likely to trigger showdowns than are their male counterparts (C. Fletcher, 1995; Munoz, 2003). Apparently, what women may lack in sheer muscle power, they make up for in a winning combination of personality traits.

In this module, we'll discuss personality traits, which are powerful motivating forces that we all have, cannot live without, like to talk about, may be critical of, and are often asked to change but find it difficult to do so.

What's Coming

We'll discuss two theories of personality, each with a different emphasis. The first is social cognitive theory (previously called social learning theory), which stresses the influences of cognitive, learning, and social processes on personality development. The second is trait theory, which focuses on measuring traits and describing how traits make up our different personalities and influence our behaviors.

We'll begin with three social cognitive forces that helped shape Nelson Mandela's personality.

A. Social Cognitive Theory

Review and Definition

What shaped his personality?

How many of us would have stayed in prison for 27 years, as Mandela did, if the only condition for our release was that we not speak in public against the government? What were the forces that shaped Mandela's personality and gave him such courage, self-confidence, and perseverance? In Module 19, we discussed two answers to this question: Freud's psychodynamic theory and humanistic theories.

Freud's psychodynamic theory said that our personality is shaped primarily by our inborn biological urges, especially sex and aggression, and by how we resolve conflicts during the psychosexual stages, especially during the first five years.

Humanistic theories, such as those of Abraham Maslow and Carl Rogers, assume that we are basically good and that our personality is shaped

What gave him the courage to fight for the presidency?

primarily by our inborn tendency for self-actualization, or self-fulfillment, which includes both biological and psychological factors.

Now we discuss two more answers: first, social cognitive theory and, later, trait theory.

Social cognitive theory says that personality development is shaped primarily by three forces: environmental conditions (learning), cognitive-personal factors, and behavior, which all interact to influence how we evaluate, interpret, organize, and apply information.

Social cognitive theory grew out of the research of a number of psychologists, especially Albert Bandura (1986, 2001). According to social cognitive theory, we are neither good nor bad but shaped primarily by three influential factors.

Interaction of Three Factors

For almost his entire life, Nelson Mandela has been fighting the White domination of Blacks in South Africa. During this time, he suffered tremendous personal hardships, including 27 years in prison. You can't help wondering what shaped his personality and gave him the strength,

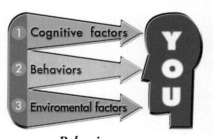

1 Cognitive factors
2 Behaviors
3 Environmental factors
YOU

determination, and character to sacrifice so much to reach his goal of freedom for his people. According to social cognitive theory, Mandela's personality was influenced and shaped by the interactions among three significant forces—namely, cognitive-personal, behavioral, and environmental factors.

Cognitive-Personal Factors

Mandela was born to an African tribal royal family, and he was expected and trained to be a leader someday (photo below). Mandela's family encouraged him to be self-confident, have dignity, and, if needed, be ruthless and determined to achieve his goal (Mathews et al., 1990). Being born into a royal family and being taught to view himself as a leader are examples of cognitive-personal factors that helped shape Mandela's personality.

Cognitive factors include our beliefs, expectations, values, intentions, and social roles. *Personal factors* include our emotional makeup and our biological and genetic influences.

Cognitive factors guide personality development by influencing the way we view and interpret information. For example, Mandela viewed the world from the standpoint of someone trained to lead and help his people. These kinds of beliefs (cognitions) gave Mandela the strength and determination to fight for freedom. Thus, cognitive-personal factors influence our personalities by affecting what we think, believe, and feel, which in turn affect how we act and behave.

Born to a royal family but . . .

Behaviors

All his life Mandela spoke forcefully against oppression (photo top of page), organized political groups, and led marches against unfair domination of his people. These are examples of the kinds of behaviors that also shaped his personality.

Behaviors include a variety of personal actions, such as the things we do and say.

In Mandela's case, the political and social behaviors that he engaged in to help his people achieve freedom in turn strengthened his belief that apartheid (discriminatory practices against Blacks) was morally and politically wrong.

Just as behavior influences our beliefs, so too does our environment influence both.

Environmental Factors

Mandela lived in a society based on apartheid, which meant strict separation of the races, limited opportunities for non-Whites, and the fostering of intense racial hatred (bottom photo). These environmental factors certainly affected Mandela's personality development.

Environmental factors include our social, political, and cultural influences, as well as our particular learning experiences.

Just as our cognitive factors influence how we perceive and interpret our environment, our environment in turn affects our beliefs, values, and social roles.

We can assume that living in such an oppressive environment strengthened Mandela's determination to get a law degree and to devote his life to obtaining freedom for all.

According to Bandura (2001), personality development is influenced by the interactions among these three factors. He especially focused on cognitive-personal factors.

. . . Mandela grew up amid racial hatred.

Cognitive factors—beliefs, values, and goals—influence their personalities.

Why are beliefs important?

Albert Bandura (1986, 2001) originally called his theory of personality development the social learning theory. However, to emphasize the importance of cognitive factors in personality development, he has recently changed the name to the social cognitive theory.

Bandura's social cognitive theory assumes that personality development, growth, and change are influenced by four distinctively human cognitive processes: highly developed language ability, observational learning, purposeful behavior, and self-analysis.

Bandura believes that these four cognitive processes reach their highest level of functioning in humans and that much of human

personality and behavior is shaped by our own thoughts and beliefs.

For example, the young Black men in the photo on the left are wearing T-shirts that say "ANC LIVES." Nelson Mandela helped found a social-political organization whose initials, ANC, stand for African National Congress. For many years Mandela was the head of ANC, whose goal is freedom and equal opportunities for Black Africans. According to Bandura's social cognitive theory, these young men's personalities will, to a large extent, be molded by cognitive factors such as the beliefs, values, and goals of the African National Congress. We'll briefly explain each of Bandura's cognitive factors.

Four Cognitive Factors

At the heart of Bandura's social cognitive theory is the idea that much of personality development is shaped and molded by cognitive processes that influence how we view and interpret the world. And, in turn, how we view and interpret the world influences how we behave. Here's how Bandura's cognitive processes apply to the young Black men who have joined the ANC.

1 Language ability. This is a powerful tool for processing and understanding information that influences personality development. We turn this information into ideas, beliefs, values, and goals, which shape, guide, and motivate our behaviors. For example, the ANC talks about, teaches, and values fighting for freedom. This information motivates its members to become assertive, self-confident, and determined.

2 Observational learning. Almost all of us "people watch"; we observe parents, brothers, sisters, peers, friends, and teachers; by doing so, we learn a great deal. Observational learning involves watching, imitating, and modeling. Most of the time, the observer provides his or her own reward for developing some belief or performing some behavior. For example, observational learning allows the young Black men to imitate and model the personality characteristics of adult role models in the ANC.

3 Purposeful behavior. Our capacity to anticipate events, plan ahead, and set goals influences our personality development, growth, and change. For instance, in fighting for freedom, the young Black men will organize, plan marches, and develop political strategies, which will encourage them to become responsible, confident, and energetic.

4 Self-analysis. This is a powerful internal process that allows us to monitor our own thoughts and actions. By deciding to change our goals or values, we can significantly affect our personality development. For instance, the young Black men use self-analysis to check their personality progress as well as to reward themselves for meeting goals of the ANC.

According to Bandura's social cognitive theory, these four cognitive processes influence our personality development, growth, and change.

To make the relationship between cognitive factors and personality more concrete, we'll focus on three specific beliefs: locus of control (this page), delay of gratification, and self-efficacy (next page).

Locus of Control

Can you control when you'll graduate?

This is the kind of question that intrigued Julian Rotter (1990), who was interested in how social cognitive theory applied to human behavior. Rotter developed a well-known scale to measure a person's expectancies about how much control he or she has over situations, which Rotter called the locus of control.

Can you control when you will graduate?

Locus of control refers to our beliefs about how much control we have over situations or rewards. We are said to have an *internal locus of control* if we believe that we have control over situations and rewards. We are said to have an *external locus of control* if we believe that we do not have control over situations and rewards and that events outside ourselves (fate) determine what happens. People fall on a continuum between internal and external locus of control.

For example, if you believe that when you graduate depends primarily on your motivation and determination, then you have more of an internal locus of control. If you believe that when you graduate depends mostly on chance or things outside your control, then you have more of an external locus of control. Having more of an internal locus of control is an advantage because hundreds of studies report a positive correlation (0.20 to 0.30) between internal locus of control and mental health and psychological functioning (Burger, 2004). For example, people with an internal locus of control are generally higher achievers, are more likely to take preventive health measures, report less stress, and are less depressed than those with an external locus of control (Burger, 2004; Spector et al., 2001).

These findings indicate that a specific belief, such as how much control you believe you have, influences how you perceive your world; and this, in turn, affects how you behave. Next, we'll examine two other beliefs that influence behavior.

A. Social Cognitive Theory

Delay of Gratification

Get it now or wait for better things?

Many young children have a difficult time not grabbing their favorite candy from the low-lying shelves at checkouts in spite of parents promising they'll get candy when they get home. Likewise, adults may see something they didn't intend to buy but do so on impulse, not always getting the best product or deal. These are common examples of a cognitive concept or belief called delay of gratification.

Delay of gratification refers to not taking an immediate but less desirable reward and instead waiting and pursuing an object or completing a task that promises a better reward in the future.

Although related to the ideas of self-control, impulsiveness, and will power, delay of gratification is defined so that it can easily be studied in the laboratory (Mischel et al., 1989). One technique to measure delay of gratification was to show children two objects, one less preferred (a single marshmallow) and one more preferred (two marshmallows). The children were told that to obtain the more preferred reward they had to wait until the experimenter, who had to leave the room, returned after some delay (about 15 minutes). Children were free to end the waiting period by ringing a bell, but then they would get only the less preferred reward. Thus, the child had a real conflict: Accept immediate gratification and take the less preferred reward, or delay gratification and obtain the more preferred reward. How long children could wait depended upon what they attended to. If they pictured the marshmallows in their minds, they could wait about 15 minutes, but if the marshmallows were right in front of them, they waited only 6 minutes (Mischel et al., 1989).

Should I take one marshmallow now or wait and get two later?

Important to delay gratification? Researchers found that the ability to delay gratification influenced many behaviors. For example, 4-year-old children good at delaying gratification tended to be more intelligent, to have greater social responsibility, and to strive for higher achievement. When these very same 4-year-old children were later retested at age 14, they were rated by parents as more competent, more intelligent, and better able to concentrate than those children who were not good at delaying gratification. NOT being able to delay gratification has been linked to a variety of self-regulatory problems, including impulsive violence, eating disorders, abusing drugs, having unprotected sex, and unwanted pregnancies (Peake et al., 2002). All of these studies make an important point: Developing the beliefs and cognitive processes involved in the ability to delay gratification can influence a variety of personal behaviors and social interactions in either positive or negative ways (Peake et al., 2002).

Another cognitive process that affects personality and behavior is how much we believe in our own capabilities.

Self-Efficacy

Can I get better grades?

Students often ask about how to improve their grades. According to Albert Bandura (1999), one reason students differ in whether they receive high or low grades is related to self-efficacy.

Self-efficacy refers to the confidence in your ability to organize and execute a given course of action to solve a problem or accomplish a task.

For example, saying "I think that I am capable of getting a high grade in this course" is a sign of strong self-efficacy. You judge your self-efficacy by combining four sources of information (Bandura, 1999; Zimmerman, 2000):

1. You *use previous experiences* of success or failure on similar tasks to estimate how you will do on a new, related task.
2. You *compare* your capabilities with those of others.
3. You *listen* to what others say about your capabilities.
4. You *use feedback* from your body to assess your strength, vulnerability, and capability.

Why do my friends say that I should be getting better grades?

You would rate yourself as having strong self-efficacy for getting good grades if you had previous success with getting high grades, if you believe you are as academically capable as others, if your friends say you are smart, and if you do not become too stressed during exams. Twenty years of research show that students' levels of self-efficacy are good predictors of their motivation and learning during college (Zimmerman, 2000).

Influence of self-efficacy. According to Bandura's self-efficacy theory, your motivation to achieve, perform, and do well in a variety of tasks and situations is largely influenced by how strongly you believe in your own capabilities. Some people have a strong sense of self-efficacy that applies to many situations (academic settings, sports, and social interactions), others have a strong sense that applies to only a few situations (computers but not social interactions), while still others have a weak sense of self-efficacy, which predicts having less success in many of life's tasks (Eccles & Wigfield, 2002). For example, people with higher self-efficacy had greater success at stopping smoking, losing weight, overcoming a phobia, performing well in school, adjusting to new situations, coping with job stress, playing video games, and tolerating pain (Bandura, 2000; Joseph et al., 2003). These findings indicate that having either high or low self-efficacy can increase or decrease your performance and success in a variety of tasks and personal behaviors.

Conclusion. So far we have discussed three important beliefs: whether you have an internal or external locus of control, how much you can delay gratification, and whether you have high or low self-efficacy. Research on these three beliefs supports the basic assumption of social cognitive theory, which is that cognitive factors influence personality development, which in turn affects performance and success in a variety of tasks and situations.

Where does he get his courage?

Sometimes a person's experience better illustrates the power and importance of beliefs than all the research in the world. Such an experience is that of Christopher Reeve, who once played the role of Superman in movies. In 1995, he severed his spinal cord in a tragic horse-riding accident and lost the ability to move or feel any part of his body below his neck. Although he knows his head is attached to his body, he cannot so much as raise his head to look down at his body. Someone else must move, clothe, and feed him and take care of all his bodily needs. For example, when Reeve accidentally fell and broke his arm, he felt no pain because neural signals from his arm could not reach his perfectly functioning brain. When he goes to sleep, he experiences being whole again through his vivid dreams of riding, acting, and being

I believe that someday I will be able to walk again.

with his family. Strapped to his electric wheelchair, which he controls by breathing, Reeve is able to move about and appear on numerous talk shows. He says, "I'm not trying to be a hero. I'm just trying to cope the best I can" (*People*, May 5, 1998, p. 216). After seven years of persistent and difficult rehabilitation therapy, he has regained some movement and sensations in his hands and can leave his respirator and breathe on his own for several hours—all behaviors that were believed to be forever impossible seven years ago (Kluger, 2002).

One reason for Reeve's hope and determined rehabilitation efforts in the face of hopeless odds is summed up in the title of his recent book, *Nothing is impossible: Reflections on a new life* (2002). Reeve's story illustrates a major assumption of social cognitive theory: Beliefs have a great influence on personality, motivation, and behavior.

We'll evaluate social cognitive theory's approach to personality development and compare it with other theories.

1 Comprehensive Approach

Social cognitive theory focuses on the interaction of three primary forces in the development of personality: cognitive-personal factors, which include beliefs, expectations, social roles, and genetic influences; behaviors, which include actions, conversations, and emotional expressions; and environmental influences, such as social, political, and cultural forces.

Bandura (2001) points out that other theories of personality tend to focus on one or two of these factors but neglect the interaction among all three factors. For example, Freudian and humanistic theories emphasize the effects of personal and cognitive forces on personality development but neglect the significant behavioral, learning, and environmental influences. Thus, one advantage of social cognitive theory is that its approach to personality development is more comprehensive and includes more influential factors than other theories.

2 Experimentally Based

Many of the concepts used in social cognitive theory have been developed from, and based on, objective measurement, laboratory research, and experimental studies. Because social cognitive theory's concepts—such as locus of control, delay of gratification, and self-efficacy—are experimentally based, they can be manipulated, controlled, and tested and are less subject to error and bias.

In comparison, many concepts from Freudian and humanistic theories of personality were developed from clinical interviews and practice and, for that reason, these concepts (oral stage, Oedipal complex, self-actualization, positive regard) are more difficult to test and validate and more open to error and bias.

3 Programs for Change

Because many of the concepts of social cognitive theory are experimentally based and objectively defined (observational learning, self-reward, modeling behavior, self-analysis, and planning), these concepts have been used to develop very successful programs for changing behavior and personality. For example, we earlier discussed two behavioral change programs that were based on social cognitive theory. In one study, individuals who had developed an intense fear of snakes showed decreased fear after observing a fearless model touching and handling a snake (p. 225); in another study, children who had observed an adult's aggressive behaviors imitated and performed similar aggressive behaviors when given an opportunity (p. 224). These are just two examples of behavioral changes that occurred after applying concepts based on social cognitive theory (Bandura, 2001).

4 Criticisms and Conclusions

Critics say that because social cognitive concepts focus on narrowly defined behaviors, such as self-efficacy, locus of control, and delay of gratification, social cognitive theory is a somewhat piecemeal explanation of personality development. They add that social cognitive theory needs to combine these objectively but narrowly defined concepts into a more integrated theory of personality. Finally, critics contend that social cognitive theory pays too little attention to the influence of genetic factors, emotional influences, and childhood experiences on personality development (Bouchard & Loehlin, 2001; Loehlin et al., 2003).

Despite these criticisms, social cognitive theory has had a profound impact on personality theory by emphasizing the objective measurement of concepts, the influence of cognitive processes, and the application of concepts to programs for behavioral change.

Next, we'll discuss an interesting theory of personality that emphasizes describing and assessing differences between individuals and explaining why we do not always act in a consistent way.

B. Trait Theory

Do women make better cops?

At the beginning of this module, we told you about Beverly Harvard (photo below), who in 1994 became the first African American woman appointed to head a police department in a major city (Atlanta, Georgia). In 1992, Elizabeth Watson was the first Caucasian woman to head a major metropolitan police force (Houston, Texas).

Throughout the 1970s, 1980s, and 1990s, women had to fight discrimination and harassment from male police officers who believed that women did not have the physical or mental stuff to be police officers (Copeland, 1999). However, a number of studies have shown that women do make good police officers and, in situations involving domestic abuse, they are more successful than policemen because policewomen have better interpersonal skills than men (K. Johnson, 1998).

Which traits of policewomen make them better at keeping the peace?

Peacekeeper. For example, police officer Kelly, who is female, patrols an area known for problems with street thugs. Although we may think that the best way to control thugs is with threat or force, Kelly rarely uses either. Kelly readily admits that her physical strength cannot always match that of some of the macho males she encounters. "Coming across aggressively doesn't work with gang members," Kelly explains. "If that first encounter is direct, knowledgeable, and made with authority, they respond. It takes a few more words but it works" (McDowell, 1992, p. 70). As another woman police officer said, "We've been learning our whole lives how to deal with things without having to resort to physical strength and physical violence" (Munoz, 2003, p. B2). These examples suggest that, in some situations, women make better and more effective cops than men because they have different personality traits (figure below).

Men. Traits of male officers include being assertive, aggressive, and direct, which help them act as enforcers.

Women. Traits of female officers include being compassionate, sympathetic, and diplomatic, which help them act as peacekeepers.

The reason female police officers act more as peacekeepers and male police officers act more as enforcers may be explained by trait theory.

Trait theory is an approach for analyzing the structure of personality by measuring, identifying, and classifying similarities and differences in personality characteristics or traits.

The basic unit for measuring personality characteristics is the trait.

A *trait* is a relatively stable and enduring tendency to behave in a particular way.

For example, traits of female police officers include being compassionate, sympathetic, and diplomatic, which help them function as peacekeepers, while those of male police officers include being assertive, aggressive, and direct, which help them function as enforcers. Determining exactly how many traits are needed to describe someone's personality took psychologists almost 60 years.

How to describe these five persons?

How would you describe the personalities of a criminal, clown, graduate, nun, and beauty queen? This seemingly impossible task was the major goal of personality researchers. They were determined to find a list of traits whose two characteristics seemed mutually exclusive: The list had to contain very few traits but at the same time be able to describe differences among anyone's and everyone's personality, from avocado grower to zookeeper. The search for this elusive list began in the 1930s with, of all things, a dictionary.

Which . . .

How many traits can there be?

In the 1930s, Gordon Allport and an associate went through the dictionary and selected every term that could distinguish differences among personalities (Allport & Odbert, 1936). They found about 18,000 terms that dealt with all kinds of personality differences; of these, about 4,500 were considered to fit their definition of personality traits. Allport defined *traits* as stable and consistent tendencies in how an individual adjusts to his or her environment. The advantage of Allport's list was that it was comprehensive enough to describe anyone's and everyone's personality. The disadvantage was that it was incredibly long and thus impractical to use in research.

. . . five . . .

Allport's search for a list of defining traits set the stage for future research. However, his list of thousands of traits needed to be organized into far fewer basic traits. This task fell to Raymond Cattell.

Aren't some traits related?

In the 1940s, Raymond Cattell (1943) took Allport's list of 4,500 traits and used factor analysis to reduce the list to the most basic traits.

Factor analysis is a complicated statistical method that finds relationships among many different or diverse items and allows them to be grouped together.

. . . traits . . .

Cattell used factor analysis to search for *relationships* among hundreds of traits on Allport's list so that the original list could be reduced to 35 basic traits, which Cattell called *source traits.* He claimed that these 35 basic traits could describe all differences among personalities. Although Cattell's achievement was remarkable, his list of 35 traits—and even his further reduction of the list to 16 traits—still proved too long to be practical for research and only moderately useful in assessing personality differences. Obviously, Cattell's list needed more reducing, but that was to take another 30 years.

. . . describe . . .

. . . each of these five different personalities?

Can it be done with just five?

From the 1960s to the early 1990s, about a dozen researchers in several countries were using factor analysis to find relationships among lists of adjectives that described personality differences. Doing the impossible, researchers reduced the list of 35 traits to only 5, which make up the five-factor model of personality (Burger, 2004).

The *five-factor model* organizes personality traits and describes differences in personality using five categories, which are *openness, conscientiousness, extraversion, agreeableness,* and *neuroticism.*

These five factors became known as the **Big Five** and are easy to remember if you note that their first letters make the acronym OCEAN. Each of the five factors actually represents a continuum of behavior, as briefly described in the figure below.

Openness

Is open to novel experiences. / Has narrow interests.

Conscientiousness

Is responsible and dependable. / Is impulsive and careless.

Extraversion

Is outgoing and decisive. / Is retiring and withdrawn.

Agreeableness

Is warm and good-natured. / Is unfriendly and cold.

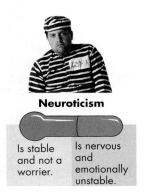

Neuroticism

Is stable and not a worrier. / Is nervous and emotionally unstable.

Hot and cold. You can think of each Big Five factor as a *supertrait* because each factor's thermometer includes dozens of related traits at the hot and cold ends. For example, conscientiousness, at the hot end, includes the traits of being dependable, responsible, deliberate, hardworking, and precise; at the cold end are the traits of being impulsive, careless, late, lazy, and aimless. Although it took 30 years of research, coming up with the Big Five means that trait theory finally achieved its major goal, which was to describe and organize personality characteristics using the fewest number of traits (John & Srivastava, 1999).

Importance of the Big Five

Unlike earlier attempts to identify traits, there is now convincing evidence that the Big Five or five-factor theory can indeed describe personality differences among many thousands of individuals by using only five categories or traits. For example, the personalities of children and adults in the United States as well as in six other very different cultures or countries (Germany, Portugal, Israel, South Korea, Japan, and Philippines) were described by using the Big Five traits (Katigbak et al., 2002).

Big question. Since the five-factor model has been replicated in many different countries, researchers asked if the structure of personality was shaped primarily by different *cultural factors* (child-rearing practices, religious and moral values, language similarities) or primarily by differences in the *basic human ways* of acting and experiencing that are universal, or similar across all peoples and countries.

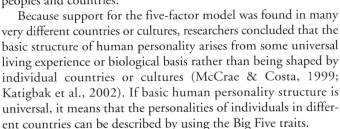

Each letter in the word OCEAN is the first letter of one of the Big Five traits.

Because support for the five-factor model was found in many very different countries or cultures, researchers concluded that the basic structure of human personality arises from some universal living experience or biological basis rather than being shaped by individual countries or cultures (McCrae & Costa, 1999; Katigbak et al., 2002). If basic human personality structure is universal, it means that the personalities of individuals in different countries can be described by using the Big Five traits.

Big Five in the Real World

When you describe a friend's personality, what you are doing (usually without knowing) is using the five supertraits described in the Big Five or five-factor theory. Because personality similarities and differences can be described by five categories, questionnaires based on the five-factor theory can more accurately assess personality and personality problems, which is one of the major tasks of therapists, clinicians, and psychologists.

Although the five-factor theory has proven very useful in describing and organizing personality traits, this theory does not explain how these traits develop across one's lifetime or account for people's behavior in unusual situations, such as risking one's life to climb Mount Everest (McCrae & Costa, 1999).

For instance, the Big Five traits can be used to describe differences between male and female police officers. Compared with policemen, policewomen are generally more agreeable (sympathetic, friendly, helpful), more open (insightful, intelligent), and more extraverted (sociable, talkative). These kinds of traits result in policewomen being less authoritarian, more diplomatic, and better at defusing potentially dangerous situations (Spillar & Harrington, 2000).

Researchers generally agree that the five-factor theory is a giant leap forward in trait theory and is a useful tool for defining personality structures and differences, predicting behaviors, and identifying personality problems (Burger, 2004; McCrae & Costa, 1999).

Although each of us possesses at least five relatively enduring supertraits that push us to behave in a stable way, why do we sometimes contradict ourselves and behave differently in different situations?

B. Trait Theory

How does private life compare to public life?

The best-known right-wing talk-radio host is Rush Limbaugh, who broadcasts his conservative law-and-order views to 20 million fans five days a week. For example, when Grateful Dead guitarist Jerry Garcia died in 1995, Limbaugh said, "When you strip it all away, Jerry Garcia destroyed his life on drugs. And yet he's being honored, like some godlike figure. Our priorities are out of whack, folks" (Laurence, 2003, F7). Talking about drug users, Limbaugh said, ". . . too many whites are getting away with drug use . . . The answer is to go out and find the ones who are getting away with it, convict them and send them up the river, too" (Laurence, 2003, F7).

Then, on October, 16, 2003, the *National Enquirer* headline read, "Rush Limbaugh caught in a drug ring." According to several other respected news accounts, Limbaugh had become a narcotic

Limbaugh preached law and order in public but in private he was a drug addict.

addict (pain pills). His maid claimed that for three years she had bought enough "baby blues" (OxyContin pills) to "kill an elephant." Limbaugh admitted to being a drug addict and went into a drug rehab program (E. Thomas, 2003).

The observation that, like Rush Limbaugh, individuals often behave differently in different situations questions one of the basic assumptions of trait theory, which is that traits create tendencies to behave in certain consistent ways. Psychologist Walter Mischel (1968) was one of the first to conduct a series of classic experiments on why traits fail to predict the behavior of people across different situations.

Experiment: Person-Situation

To test trait theory's basic assumption that people behave consistently across situations, Walter Mischel and Philip Peake (1982) asked college students, "How conscientious are you?" If students answer that they are "very conscientious," trait theory predicts that they will behave conscientiously in many different situations. Mischel then observed how conscientious college students behaved across 19 very different situations, such as attending classes, going to study sessions, getting homework in on time, and keeping their rooms neat.

Students who rated themselves as very conscientious behaved that way day after day in similar situations. However, these same students did not behave conscientiously across all 19 conditions. For example, very conscientious students might clean their rooms daily but not get their homework in on time, or they might attend all their classes but not clean their rooms. Researchers concluded that, as trait theory predicted, students behaved with great consistency in the *same* situation, but contrary to trait theory's prediction, students behaved *differently* or with low consistency across different situations. This finding led to what is now called the person-situation interaction.

The *person-situation interaction* means that a person's behavior results from an interaction between his or her traits and the effects of being in or responding to cues from a particular situation.

The person-situation interaction explains that even if you were an extravert, you would behave differently at a wedding than at a funeral because each of these situations creates different cues to which you respond (Mischel & Shoda, 1995). Similarly, the person-situation interaction describes how Rush Limbaugh could be righteous in criticizing Jerry Garcia's drug use while being a drug addict himself.

The person-situation interaction says that to understand or predict a person's behavior across situations, we must consider both the person's traits and the powerful cues that come from being in each different situation (Malle et al., 2000).

If you are open to new experiences, would you try this? Do you see the dog?

Conclusions

There is no question that humans have stable and consistent parts of their personalities, which are called traits. There is no question that personality differences can be accurately described by using the Big Five traits. However, people may act or behave inconsistently or contradictorily because traits interact with and are partly dependent upon situational cues. This means that even though you consider yourself open to new experiences and often try new things, you might very well draw the line and say "NO!" to potentially dangerous rock climbing (below left photo). Although researchers have found that traits are not consistent across all situations, the concept of traits is still very useful for two reasons (Wiggins, 1997).

Descriptions. First, traits are useful because they provide a kind of shorthand method for describing someone's personality. In fact, if I asked you to describe your best friend, you would essentially list this person's traits.

Predictions. Second, traits are useful because they help predict someone's behavior in future situations. However, you must keep in mind the person-situation interaction, which means you must take into account how the person's traits will interact with the situation's cues. For example, my friends would predict that I generally try to watch my weight but they also know that when placed in front of a dessert counter, I can easily consume my weight in chocolate. However, researchers found it is possible to significantly increase the accuracy of predicting a person's behaviors across situations if that person is actually observed in a number of different settings (Wiggins, 1997).

Conclusion. Most personality researchers agree that traits, such as the Big Five, are useful in describing our stable and consistent behavioral tendencies, yet they warn that traits may not predict behaviors across different situations (Malle et al., 2000).

Does saying that traits are stable and consistent mean that one's personality gradually becomes fixed?

How changeable are your traits?

If you are now 16, 18, 20, 25, or 30, what will your personality be like when you're 40, 50, 60, 70, or 80? The question of how much your personality traits remain the same and how much they change is answered by using a research approach called the longitudinal method.

Longitudinal method means that the same group of individuals is studied repeatedly at many different points in time.

For example, if you asked your parents to list your personality traits at age 3, would these traits match your traits at age 21? In other words, how changeable or fixed are your personality traits?

3 to 18 Years Old

To answer the question of how much personality traits change or remain the same, researchers did a longitudinal study on 1,000 children, whose traits were assessed at age 3 and then reassessed when the same children were 21 years old. Based on their assessment, the personality traits of 3-year-old children were divided into five different personality groups that were labeled undercontrolled, inhibited, confident, reserved, and well-adjusted (Caspi, 2000).

Will this 3-year-old child's personality traits . . .

. . . be similar to those he has at 18 years old?

Consistency. Researchers found significant consistencies between traits assessed at 3 years and at 21 years old. For example, traits of 3-year-old children in the *undercontrolled group* included being impulsive, restless, and distractible. When these 3-year-old children were retested at age 21, their traits were similar and included being reckless, careless, and favoring dangerous and exciting activities. In comparison, traits of 3-year-old children in the *well-adjusted group* included being confident, having self-control, and easily adjusting to new or stressful situations. When these 3-year-old children were retested at age 18, their traits were similar and included being in control, self-confident, and all-around well-adjusted and normal adults. Researchers concluded that the origin or development of a person's more stable personality traits begins around age 3. This means that traits observed at age 3 predict personality traits observed later in the same young adults (Caspi, 2000).

Change. Although there were remarkable consistencies in personality traits between age 3 and age 18, researchers point out that there are often major changes in emotional traits during adolescence. During adolescence, individuals may become less responsible, less cautious, and more moody or impulsive (Caspi & Roberts, 1999).

What happens to personality development after age 18, and does personality ever stop changing?

20 to 80 Years Old

If you are 18, 20, 25, or 30 now, what will your personality be like at 50, 60, 70, or 80? Answers come from a series of longitudinal studies, which reached the following conclusions (McCrae & Costa, 1999; McCrae et al., 2000; Roberts et al., 2002; Trzesniewski et al., 2003).

1 Major changes in personality occur during childhood, adolescence, and young adulthood. Between 20 and 30, both men and women become less emotional, less likely to be thrill seekers, and somewhat more likely to be cooperative and self-disciplined. These personality changes are often associated with becoming more mature.

Before age 30, personality may go through major changes, but . . .

2 In fact, longitudinal studies find that most changes in personality occur before the age of 30 because adolescents and young adults are more willing to adopt new values and attitudes or revise old ones.

3 Personality traits are relatively fixed by age 30, after which changes in personality are few and small. However, after 30, adults continue to grow in their ideas, beliefs, and attitudes as they respond to changing situations and environments. For example, an eager tennis player may, with age, become an eager gardener, but an eager liberal is unlikely to become an eager conservative.

4 Men and women, healthy and sick people, and Blacks and Whites all show the same stable personality pattern after age 30. Because personality is stable, it is somewhat predictable. However, individuals may struggle to overcome or change certain traits (become less shy, more confident), which brings up the question of how much personality changes during adulthood.

5 When middle-aged and older adults were asked to describe the course of their personality development, they all described increases in desirable traits (energetic, realistic, intelligent) as they grew older. But on objective tests, these same individuals showed little or no change in these same traits. These findings indicate that as people grow older, they tend to report more socially desirable or stereotypic responses rather than what actually has occurred.

. . . after age 30, personality is relatively fixed and difficult to change.

Conclusions. Your personality is more likely to change the younger you are, but after age 30, personality traits are relatively stable and fixed. However, depending upon situations, stressors, and challenges, some change can occur. Thus, personality has the interesting distinction of being both stable and changeable (up to a point). One reason personality traits remain relatively stable across time is that they are influenced by genetic factors, which we'll discuss next.

C. Genetic Influences on Traits

Behavioral Genetics

Why are twins so similar?

Jim Lewis (left photo) and Jim Springer (right photo) drove the same model blue Chevrolet, chain-smoked the same brand of cigarettes, owned dogs named Toy, held jobs as deputy sheriff, enjoyed the same woodworking hobby, and had vacationed on the same beach in Florida. When they were given personality tests, they scored almost alike on traits of flexibility, self-control, and sociability. The two Jims are identical twins who were separated four weeks after birth and reared separately. When reunited at age 39, they were flabbergasted at how many things they had in common (Leo, 1987).

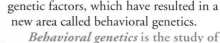

Why did they drive the same kind of car, smoke the same cigarettes, hold the same kind of job, and both name their dogs Toy?

These surprising coincidences come from an ongoing University of Minnesota project on genetic factors (Bouchard, 1994; Bouchard & Loehlin, 2001). One of the project's major questions is whether the similarities between the two Jims are simply coincidence or reflect the influence of genetic factors on personality traits.

Most of us grew up hearing one or both of these phrases: "You're acting just like your father" or "You're behaving just like your mother." What these phrases suggest is that genetic factors that we inherited from our parents are influencing our behaviors. Psychologists have only recently recognized the importance and influence of

genetic factors, which have resulted in a new area called behavioral genetics.

Behavioral genetics is the study of how inherited or genetic factors influence and interact with psychological factors to shape our personality, intelligence, emotions, and motivation and also how we behave, adapt, and adjust to our environments.

Many of us have a difficult time accepting the idea of genetic influences because we equate genetic with *fixed*. However, genetic factors do not fix behaviors but establish a range for a behavior, which environmental factors foster or impede. For example, genetic factors set a range for our height and weight. But our actual height and weight will also depend on how genetic factors interact with environmental influences, such as whether we have a good diet and exercise program.

As we discuss studies showing that genetic factors influence and set a range for development of various personality traits, please remember that our actual traits result from the interaction between genetic factors and environmental influences.

Studying Genetic Influences

What's in the genes?

Few studies have made as great an impact on beliefs about what shapes personality and behavior as the twin study at the University of Minnesota. Until the early 1990s, most psychologists recognized the existence of genetic factors in shaping personality but believed that genetic factors had much less impact than environmental factors. Then in 1990, Thomas Bouchard and his colleagues (1990) published the first study to simultaneously compare four different groups of twins: identical twins reared together, identical twins reared apart, fraternal twins reared together, and fraternal twins reared apart. Remember that identical twins share 100% of their genes, while fraternal twins share only 50% of their genes and thus are no more genetically alike than ordinary brothers and sisters. This study allowed researchers to separate genetic factors (identical versus fraternal twins) and environmental factors (reared together versus reared apart).

We're identical twins, and we share 100% of our genes.

This is a piece of the genetic code, which uses a chemical alphabet (A, C, G, T) to write instructions that influence the development of personality traits.

More than 100 sets of twins in the United States, Great Britain, and many other countries participated in this initial study. Each participant was given over 50 hours of medical and psychological assessment, including four different tests to measure personality

traits. Those identical and fraternal twins who were reared apart were adopted shortly after birth and had not met their twin until this study brought them together for testing. The measure that researchers use to estimate genetic influences is called heritability.

Heritability is a statistical measure that estimates how much of some cognitive, personality, or behavioral trait is influenced by genetic factors.

Heritability is expressed on an increasing scale of influence from 0.0 to 1.0. That is, if genetic factors have no influence, the heritability is 0.0, having half the influence is indicated by 0.5, and having total control over behavior is indicated by 1.0. For example, heritability of IQ is in the range of 50–70% (p. 292), which means that about 50–70% of an individual's IQ score is explained by genetic factors; heritability of mental disorders is about 40–70% (pp. 533–539); and, as we'll discuss next, heritability estimates for personality traits are about 40–50%. However, keep in mind that genetic factors interact with environmental factors, which explain about 40–60% of the development of IQs, mental disorders, and personality traits.

We're fraternal twins, and we share only 50% of our genes.

Do genes influence the Big Five?

Identical twins Jim Lewis and Jim Springer (photos opposite page) were subjects in the now famous Minnesota twin study. Their scores were similar on personality tests that measured the Big Five traits—openness, conscientiousness, extraversion, agreeableness, and neuroticism. (Note that by taking the first letter of each Big Five trait, you make the word OCEAN.) One reason the two Jims' scores on personality tests were so similar was that their genetic factors were identical.

There are now many studies on thousands of twins, both identical and fraternal, who were reared together and apart, and whose data were analyzed by different groups of researchers. Results from earlier studies and two large and recent studies are shown in the graph below (Bouchard & Loehlin, 2001). Researchers estimate that the heritability of personality traits ranges from 0.41 to about 0.51, which means that genetic factors contribute about 40 to 50% to the development of an individual's personality traits.

Even though genetic factors are responsible for about half of each of the Big Five personality traits we develop, that still leaves about half coming from environmental factors. We'll describe two kinds of environmental factors—shared and nonshared—that influence personality development.

Heritability of Big Five Personality Traits	
Earlier twin studies	0.51
Loehlin twin studies	0.42
Minnesota twin studies	0.41

What shapes personality?

As I was growing up, I remember hearing my parents talking (when they thought I wasn't listening) about how different I was from my older brother and sister. My parents questioned how my brother and sister and I could be so (very) different even though we had the same parents, lived in the same house, in the same town, and even went to the same school and church. One reason that brothers and sisters develop such different personalities is that 50% of their genes are different (and 50% are shared). And another important reason that brothers and sisters develop different personalities is that each brother's or sister's unique set of genetic factors interacts differently with his or her environment. Researchers have broken down the contributions to personality development into the following four factors.

40% Genetic Factors

The fingerprints of the two Jims were almost identical because they shared 100% of their genes, and genetic factors contribute 97% to the development of ridges on finger tips (Bouchard et al., 1990). In comparison, the two Jims' scores were similar but not identical on personality traits of self-control, flexibility, and sociability because, although they share 100% of their genes, genetic factors contribute about 40 to 50% to the kind of personality traits they developed. Thus, while genetic factors contribute about half to the development of certain personality traits, the next biggest factor is something of a surprise.

27% Nonshared Environmental Factors

Although we know that the two Jims show remarkable similarities in personality, they also display unique differences. Jim Lewis (left photo) says that he is more easygoing and less of a worrier than his identical twin, Jim Springer (right photo). When the twins get on a plane, Jim Springer worries about the plane being late, while Jim Lewis says that there is no use worrying (*San Diego Tribune,* November 12, 1987). One of the reasons that the two Jims developed different personality traits is that about 27% of the influence on personality development comes from how each individual's genetic factors react and adjust to his or her own environment. These factors are called *nonshared environmental factors* because they involve how each individual's genetic factors react and adjust to his or her particular environment.

26% Error

About 26% of the influence on personality development cannot as yet be identified and is attributed to errors in testing and measurement procedures. As methodology improves, this error percentage will decrease and other factors will increase.

7% Shared Environmental Factors

About 7% of the influence on personality development comes from environmental factors that involve parental patterns and shared family experiences. These factors are called *shared environmental factors* because they involve how family members interact and share experiences. One of the major surprises to come out of the twin studies was how little impact parental practices and shared family experiences have on personality development. Researchers concluded that being raised in the same family contributes little (about 7%) to personality development. Far more

important for personality development are nonshared environmental factors (27%), which refer to how each child's unique genetic factors react and adjust to being in that family (Bouchard & Loehlin, 2001; Plomin & Caspi, 1999). You can think of genetic factors as pushing and pulling personality development in certain directions, while environmental factors join in to push and pull it in the same or different directions.

Next, we'll take a last look at the impact of trait theory.

D. Evaluation of Trait Theory

Could we live without traits?

It would be very difficult to live without traits because you use them constantly, usually without knowing it. For example, whenever you describe someone, or predict how he or she will behave, your descriptions of personality and predictions of behaviors are based almost entirely on knowing the person's

Personal Want Ad

Personal ads are based on traits.

traits. Newspapers are full of personal ads, which are essentially a list of most-desired traits.

Although traits are very useful as a shorthand to describe a person's personality and predict a person's behaviors, critics raise three major questions about traits: How good is the list? Can traits predict? What influences traits? We'll discuss each issue in turn.

How Good Is the List?

The Big Five or five-factor trait theory assumes that all similarities and differences among personalities can be described by an amazingly short but comprehensive list of five traits—openness, conscientiousness, extraversion, agreeableness, and neuroticism (OCEAN). Each of the *Big Five traits* has two poles or two dimensions, which include dozens of related traits. The Big Five traits' ability to describe personality has now been verified in many different countries, with different populations and age groups (John, 1990; McCrae & Costa, 1997).

OCEAN

The Big Five traits have the ability to describe personalities of children and adults in many different countries.

Critics of the five-factor model point out that the data for the model came from questionnaires that may be too structured to give real and complete portraits of personalities. As a result, data from questionnaires may paint too simplistic a picture of human personality and may not reflect its depth and complexity (Block, 1995b). Critics also point out that traits primarily describe a person's personality rather than explain or point out its causes (Digman, 1997).

In defense of the five-factor theory, researchers have shown that the Big Five traits provide a valid and reliable way to describe personality differences and consistencies in our own lives and in our social interactions with others (McCrae & Costa, 1999).

Can Traits Predict?

One of the more serious problems faced by early trait theory involved the assumption that, since traits are consistent and stable influences on our behaviors, traits should be very useful in predicting behaviors.

Rush Limbaugh preached law and order on his talk-radio show but was a drug addict in private.

But how does trait theory explain why Rush Limbaugh behaved so inconsistently? He preached law and order and right-wing conservative moral standards on his radio talk show, but in his private life he had become a drug addict and was allegedly having his maid buy drugs on the black market.

One explanation is that Limbaugh did behave in a consistent moral way in public situations (radio talk shows). However, in other situations, such as his private life, he had become a drug addict. This problem of predicting behavior across situations is known as the *person-situation interaction.* Researchers found that situations may have as much influence on behavior as traits do, so situational influences must be taken into account when predicting someone's behavior (Wiggins, 1997). Researchers found that traits could better predict behaviors if traits were measured under different conditions and situations.

Currently, the Big Five traits are considered useful concepts for describing consistent and stable behavioral tendencies in similar situations, but traits do not necessarily predict behaviors across different situations.

What Influences Traits?

One major surprise coming from twin studies was how relatively little effect parental practices or shared family experiences have on personality development (graph below). Researchers concluded that parental practices or *shared factors* contributed only about 7% to personality development. In contrast, how each child personally reacts or adjusts to parental or family practices, called *nonshared factors*, contributed about 27% to personality development (Bouchard & Loehlin, 2001; Plomin & Crabbe, 2000). This finding questioned a major belief of developmental psychologists, who hold that sharing parental or family environment greatly influences personality development among the siblings (brothers and sisters). Instead, twin research suggests that psychologists need to look more closely at each child's reactions to his or her family environment as a major influence on personality development.

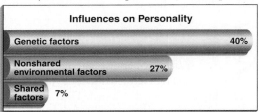

Influences on Personality

Genetic factors	40%
Nonshared environmental factors	27%
Shared factors	7%

Personality development depends more on genetic and nonshared factors (child's individual reactions) than on shared parental influences.

According to behavioral geneticists, the idea of genes influencing complex human behaviors was unthinkable as recently as 15 years ago. Today, however, there is convincing evidence that genetic factors exert a considerable influence on many complex human behaviors, including intelligence, mental health, and personality traits (Plomin & Crabbe, 2000). Yet these same researchers warn that *genetic influences* on human behavior should not be blown out of proportion. Because heritability scores generally do not exceed 50%, this means the remaining 50% or more involves *environmental influences,* especially nonshared environmental influences.

✔ Concept Review

1. Social cognitive theory says that personality development is primarily shaped by three interacting forces: _____, _____, and _____.

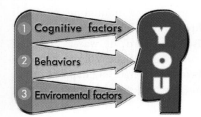

2. The above three forces all interact to influence how we evaluate, interpret, and organize _____ and apply such knowledge to ourselves and others.

3. An example of the social cognitive approach is Bandura's social cognitive theory, which says that personality development, growth, and change are influenced by four distinctively human cognitive processes: highly developed (a)_____ ability, (b)_____ learning, (c)_____ behavior, and (d)_____.

4. Three different beliefs based on social cognitive theory have been shown to influence personality development and behavior. Rotter referred to beliefs concerning how much control we have over situations or rewards. If we believe that we have control over situations and rewards, we are said to have an (a)_____. If we believe that we do not have control over situations and rewards and that events outside ourselves (fate) determine what happens, we are said to have an (b)_____.

Should I take one marshmallow now or wait and get two?

5. According to Bandura, our personal beliefs regarding how capable we are of exercising control over events in our lives—for example, carrying out certain tasks and behaviors—is called (a)_____, which, in turn, affects our performance on a wide variety of behaviors. Mischel devised ways of measuring our ability to voluntarily postpone an immediate reward and persist in completing a task for the promise of a future reward, which is called (b)_____.

6. The approach to describe the structure of personality that is based on identifying and analyzing ways in which personalities differ is known as _____ theory.

7. A relatively stable and enduring tendency to behave in a particular way is called a (a)_____. A statistical procedure that may be used to find relationships among many different or diverse items, such as traits, and form them into selected groups is called (b)_____.

OCEAN

8. The model that organizes all personality traits into five categories that can be used to describe differences in personality is called the (a)_____ model. This model uses the Big Five traits, which are (b)_____, _____, _____, _____, and _____.

9. Research supports the five-factor model and the Big Five traits. Each of the Big Five traits has two poles or dimensions and represents a wide range of _____.

10. Walter Mischel said that to predict a person's behavior we must take into account not only the person's traits but also the effects of the situation; this became known as the (a)_____. According to this idea, a person's behavior results from an (b)_____ between his or her traits and the effects of being in a particular situation.

11. To investigate whether personality changes as people grow older, psychologists study the same individuals at different times; this is called a (a)_____ study. In general, studies have shown that personality is more likely to change if a person is under (b)_____ years old. After that, changes usually involve variations on the same behavioral theme or accompany changes in social roles.

12. The field that focuses on how inherited or genetic factors influence and interact with psychological factors is called (a)_____. A statistical measure that estimates how much of some behavior is due to genetic influences is called (b)_____.

13. Studies have found that about 40% of the influence on personality development comes from (a)_____; about 27% comes from how each person adjusts to his or her own environment, which is called (b)_____; and about 7% comes from parental patterns and family experiences, which are called (c)_____.

Answers: *1. cognitive-personal factors, behavior, environmental influences; 2. information; 3. (a) language, (b) observational, (c) purposeful, (d) self-analysis; 4. (a) internal locus of control, (b) external locus of control; 5. (a) self-efficacy, (b) delay of gratification; 6. trait; 7. (a) trait, (b) factor analysis; 8. (a) five-factor, (b) openness, conscientiousness, extraversion, agreeableness, neuroticism; 9. behaviors; 10. (a) person-situation interaction, (b) interaction; 11. (a) longitudinal, (b) 30; 12. (a) behavioral genetics, (b) heritability; 13. (a) genetic factors, (b) nonshared environmental factors, (c) shared environmental factors*

Total Change in One Day?

What triggers a major change?

Sometimes researchers study unusual behaviors that seem to contradict what is known. For example, anyone who has ever tried to change some behavior finds it difficult because traits are relatively stable and enduring. For this reason, it's difficult to believe people who claim to have totally changed their personalities in minutes, hours, or a single day. Researchers call these sudden and dramatic changes quantum personality changes (Miller & C'deBaca, 1994).

A *quantum personality change* refers to making a very radical or dramatic shift in one's personality, beliefs, or values in minutes, hours, or a day.

For example, here's the quantum personality change of Bill Wilson, who cofounded

How much could you change in one day?

Alcoholics Anonymous (AA). He was in the depths of alcoholic despair and depression when he suddenly saw his room lit with a bright light. In his mind's eye, he saw himself on a mountaintop and felt that spirit winds were blowing through him. Then, suddenly, a simple but powerful thought burst upon him: he was a free man (Kurtz, 1979). This dramatic experience changed Wilson's personality 180 degrees as he went from being a desperate and hopeless drunk to being a sober and dedicated worker who devoted his life to helping others overcome alcoholism.

Reports of sudden and major changes in personality challenge two well-established findings: first, personality traits are stable and enduring tendencies that may change gradually but rarely undergo sudden and dramatic changes; and second, even when people want to change their personalities, as in therapy, it doesn't happen overnight but takes considerable time and effort. Then how can quantum personality changes occur, often in a single day? To answer this question, researchers first had to develop a method to study quantum changes.

Method

Researchers found people who had experienced a quantum personality change through a feature story in the local paper (Albuquerque, New Mexico). Researchers asked for volunteers who, in a relatively short period of time, had experienced a transformation in their basic values, feelings, attitudes, or actions. Out of a total of 89 people who responded, 55 were found acceptable. These 55 subjects were given a series of personality tests and structured interviews (average length 107 minutes).

*Structured interview*s involve asking each individual the same set of relatively narrow and focused questions so that the same information is obtained from everyone.

During structured interviews, all subjects were asked the same detailed questions about the what, when, and where of the unusual experiences that had apparently transformed their personalities so completely.

Structured interviews use the subjects' self-reports to provide information about subjective thoughts, feelings, and experiences, which are most often unobservable cognitive and emotional processes.

Results

Researchers used a variety of personality tests to make sure the subjects (31 women and 24 men) performed within the normal range on personality tests, had no strange problems, and showed no striking or unusual things in common. In fact, based on the battery of personality tests and interviews, all the subjects seemed to be normal, ordinary individuals who had had extraordinary experiences (Miller & C'deBaca, 1994). Here are some of the study's major findings:

■ A majority of subjects (58%) could specify the date and time of day when the quantum experience occurred even though the experience had occurred, on average, 11 years earlier.

As if struck by light or hearing a voice → Quantum personality change

■ A majority of subjects (75%) reported that the quantum experience began suddenly and took them by surprise. For some the experience lasted only minutes (13%), and for most it was over within 24 hours (64%). The actual experiences included being struck by an intense thought, making a total commitment, hearing a voice, and hearing God's voice.

■ A majority of subjects (56%) reported a high level of emotional distress and a relatively high level of negative life experiences in the year before the quantum experience.

■ Most (96%) reported that the quantum experience had made their lives better, and most (80%) stated that the changes had lasted.

■ Most (87%) said that, during the quantum experience, an important truth was revealed to them; 78% said that they were relieved of a mental burden; and 60% said that they felt completely loved.

All of these 55 individuals reported that they had, in a single day or less, experienced a 180-degree change in personality. For the vast majority, the quantum change in personality seems to have resulted from or been triggered by a period of bad times. After the quantum change, subjects reported that their lives had improved.

Conclusions

Researchers concluded that the quantum personality changes reported by the subjects were dramatically larger than are ordinarily observed, occurred in a quicker period of time than is normally reported, and lasted for years (Miller & C'deBaca, 1994).

For most of the subjects, the changes represented an increased sense of meaning, happiness, and satisfaction; some reported a sense of closeness to God. This study suggests that quantum changes in personality do occur and may be one way a person solves some long-standing and stressful personal problem.

In many cases, people who experienced quantum personality changes also reported subsequent changes in behavior.

As you'll see next, how much personality influences behavior is partly dependent on one's culture.

Why was Arien the exception?

One of the most difficult and tragic issues for Westerners to understand is the reasons behind suicide bombers. Recently, a young woman agreed to tell her story of how she became a suicide bomber (Bennet, 2002).

Arien Ahmed (right photo) was a 20-year-old Palestinian student of business administration at Bethlehem University. Five days after she had volunteered to become a suicide bomber, she was pulled out of a marketing

> I believe Israeli forces killed my fiancé and I want to avenge his death.

lecture and shown how to trigger a bomb inside a backpack. She got into a old car with another would-be killer and went on her mission dressed as an Israeli woman. As she walked through an Israeli town carrying a heavy backpack containing a bomb surrounded with nails, she began to have second thoughts. She described a kind of awakening and remembered a childhood belief "that nobody has the right to stop anybody's life." At that moment she decided not to go through with the bombing. She was later arrested by Israeli police (Bennet, 2002). Arien was a rare exception, since suicide bombers almost never fail to complete their deadly missions.

Cultural & Personal Reasons

After Arien was arrested, she said that she agreed to tell her story to discourage other Palestinians from becoming suicide bombers and to gain sympathy for herself. The Israeli Security Agency, which allowed Arien to be interviewed by newspaper reporters, appeared eager to show how easily militants manipulate susceptible people and send them to kill and die (Bennet, 2002).

What conditions lead to suicide attacks? In the mid-1990s, there were more than 20 suicide attacks throughout Turkey. The attacks have since stopped because the Turkish government undertook steps to satisfy the rebel forces' demands. Before 1990, there were no suicide attacks in Chechnya. Since then suicide attacks have begun as Chechnyans fight to win their independence from Russia. For example, in 2003, there were at least seven suicide attacks in Chechnya that killed 165 people. All but one of the Chechnyan suicide bombers were women (Zakaria, 2003). From 1993 to 2003, there were almost 200 Palestinian suicide bomb attacks in Israel, which killed and wounded many hundreds of citizens.

What motivates a suicide bomber? Arien appeared to have been motivated by both personal and cultural reasons. As she told Israeli security agents, her strong *personal reason* was that she wanted to avenge the death of her fiancé, whom she believed had been killed by Israeli forces (who said that her fiancé accidentally blew himself up). After his death, she said, "So I lost all my future." Arien's recruiters told her that dying as a suicide attacker would earn her the reward of rejoining her slain fiancé in paradise. Even though Arien now calls her attempt to be a suicide bomber a mistake, she said she understood it. "It's a result of the situation we live in. There are also innocent people killed on both sides" (Bennet, 2002, A1).

Palestinian psychiatrist Dr. Jyad Sarraj points to strong Muslim *cultural influences* that encourage suicide bombers. For example, Dr. Sarraj says that young adults have grown up in a culture that equates suicide attacks with having power and that suicide attacks make up for the powerlessness of their parents and the frequent humiliations that Palestinians face from Israeli occupation

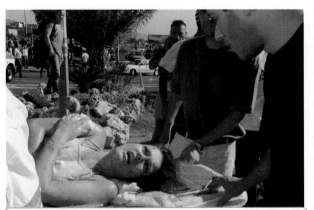

There have been almost 200 suicide bombings in Israel.

(Sarraj, 2002). Dr. Sarraj adds that, like many Palestinians, he condemns killing civilians. However, even he cannot criticize the suicide bombers themselves because their culture considers them to be martyrs and martyrs are considered prophets, who are revered.

Do suicide bombers share certain traits? Almost all of the suicide bombers have been Muslim, relatively young, single (one was the mother of a 3-year-old), varying in education, with some knowledge of political causes and terror tactics (Bennet, 2002; Zakaria, 2003). These traits tend to be general, however, and apply to many Palestinians who do not become suicide bombers. Israel's national security force has studied suicide bombers, and their results are puzzling. Unlike what they believed, they didn't find any specific personality profile or traits that differentiated suicide bombers from nonbombers. However, as in Arien's case, some powerful, tragic emotional event, such as the death of her fiancé, may be the final hurt that, combined with cultural forces, led to becoming a suicide bomber.

What does the future hold? Because of strong Muslim cultural influences, such as suicide bombers being considered martyrs, some Palestinians hope their own children will be suicide bombers and thus become martyrs. There are others who oppose suicide attacks, such as the group of 55 Palestinian intellectuals who recently issued a public plea to halt the suicide bombing attacks on innocent Israeli civilians. Based on what has happened in other countries, government officials believe that suicide attacks will continue until there is a peace settlement in the Middle East. Until then, violent Muslim groups will continue to use suicide bombers because they have widespread cultural approval and are an effective method of killing, instilling fear, and spreading their political message (Bennet, 2002).

Next, we'll briefly review the four major theories of personality to help you understand their major points.

G. Four Theories of Personality

Psychodynamic Theory

Freud's psychodynamic theory, which was developed in the early 1900s, grew out of his work with patients.

Freud's *psychodynamic theory of personality* emphasizes the importance of early childhood experiences, the importance of repressed thoughts that we cannot voluntarily access, and the conflicts between conscious and unconscious forces that influence our thoughts and behaviors. (Freud used the term *dynamic* to refer to mental energy force.)

Conscious thoughts are wishes, desires, or thoughts that we are aware of or can recall at any given moment.

Unconscious forces represent wishes, desires, or thoughts that, because of their disturbing or threatening content, we automatically repress and cannot voluntarily access.

Freud believed that a large part of our behavior was guided or motivated by unconscious forces.

Unconscious motivation is a Freudian concept that refers to the influence of repressed thoughts, desires, or impulses on our conscious thoughts and behaviors.

Freud developed three methods to uncover unconscious processes: *free association, dream interpretation,* and *slips of the tongue* (Freudian slips).

Divisions of the Mind

Freud divided the mind into three divisions: id, ego, and superego.

The first division is the *id*, which contains two biological drives—sex and aggression—that are the source of all mental energy. The id follows the pleasure principle, which is to satisfy the biological drives.

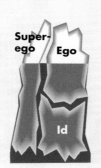

The second division is the *ego*, whose goal is to find socially acceptable ways of satisfying the id's desires within the range of the superego's prohibitions. The ego follows the reality principle, which is to satisfy a wish or desire only if there is a socially acceptable outlet available.

The third division is the *superego*, whose goal is to apply the moral values and standards of one's parents or caregivers and society in satisfying one's wishes.

Psychosexual Stages

Freud assumed that our personality develops as we pass through a series of *five psychosexual stages*.

During these developmental periods—the *oral, anal, phallic, latency,* and *genital stages*—the individual seeks pleasure from different areas of the body associated with sexual feelings. Freud emphasized that the child's first five years were the most important in personality development.

Humanistic Theories

Humanistic theories emphasize our capacity for personal growth, development of our potential, and freedom to choose our destiny. *Humanistic theories* stress three major points—phenomenological perspective, holistic view, and self-actualization.

The *phenomenological perspective* means that our perception of the world, whether or not it is accurate, becomes our reality.

The *holistic view* means that a person's personality is more than the sum of its individual parts; instead, the individual parts form a unique and total entity that functions as a unit.

Self-actualization refers to our inherent tendency to reach our true potentials.

Humanistic theories reject the biological determinism and the irrational, unconscious forces of Freud's psychodynamic theory. Humanistic theories emphasize freely choosing to go after one's dream and change one's destiny.

The beginning of humanistic theory can be traced to two psychologists: Abraham Maslow, who rejected behaviorism's system of rewards and punishment, and Carl Rogers, who rejected Freud's psychodynamic theory with its emphasis on unconscious forces.

Abraham Maslow

Maslow (1968) broke away from the reward/punishment/observable behavior mentality of behaviorism and developed his humanistic theory. *Maslow's humanistic theory* emphasized two things: our capacity for growth or self-actualization and our desire to satisfy a variety of needs.

Maslow's hierarchy of needs arranges needs in ascending order, with biological needs at the bottom and social and personal needs toward the top; as needs at one level are met, we advance to the next level.

Carl Rogers's Self Theory

Carl Rogers rejected the psychodynamic approach because it placed too much emphasis on unconscious, irrational forces. Instead, Rogers developed a new humanistic theory, which is called self theory. *Rogers's self theory*, also called self-actualization theory, has two primary assumptions: Personality development is guided by each person's unique self-actualization tendency, and each of us has a personal need for positive regard.

Rogers said that the *self* is made up of many self-perceptions, abilities, personality characteristics, and behaviors that are organized and consistent with one another.

Social Cognitive Theory

Freud's *psychodynamic theory*, developed in the early 1900s, grew out of his work with patients. Humanistic theories were developed in the 1960s by an ex-Freudian (Carl Rogers) and an ex-behaviorist (Abraham Maslow), who believed that previous theories had neglected the positive side of human potential, growth, and self-fulfillment.

In comparison, *social cognitive theory*, which was developed in the 1960s and 1970s, grew out of a strong research background, unlike the way humanistic and Freudian psychodynamic theories were developed. Social cognitive theory emphasized a more rigorous experimental approach to develop and test concepts that could be used to understand and explain personality development.

Social cognitive theory says that personality development is primarily shaped by three factors: environmental conditions (learning), cognitive-personal factors, and behavior. *Behavior* includes a variety of actions, such as what we do and say. *Environmental influences* include our social, political, and cultural influences as well as our particular learning experiences. Just as our cognitive factors influence how we perceive and interpret our environment, our environment in turn affects our beliefs, values, and social roles. *Cognitive-personal factors* include our beliefs, expectations, values, intentions, and social roles as well as our biological and genetic influences. Thus, what we think, believe, and feel affects how we act and behave.

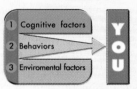

Bandura's Social Cognitive Theory

Perhaps the best example of the social cognitive approach is Bandura's social cognitive theory, which he developed in the 1970s. *Bandura's social cognitive theory* says that personality development, growth, and change are influenced by four distinctively human cognitive processes: highly developed language ability, observational learning, purposeful behavior, and self-analysis.

Bandura's theory emphasizes *cognitive factors*, such as personal values, goals, and beliefs. Three particular beliefs have been shown to influence personality development: *locus of control*, which refers to how much control we think we have over our environment; *delay of gratification*, which involves our voluntarily postponing an immediate reward for the promise of a future reward; and *self-efficacy*, which refers to our personal beliefs of how capable we are in performing specific tasks and behaviors.

One of the *basic assumptions* of social cognitive theory is that our beliefs, values, and goals influence the development of our personalities, which, in turn, affects how we behave.

Should I take one marshmallow now or wait and get two?

Trait Theory

For over 50 years, a *major goal* of personality researchers was to find a way to define the structure of personality with the fewest possible traits. The search for a list of traits that could describe personality differences among everyone, including criminals and nuns, began in the 1930s with a list of about 4,500 traits and ended in the 1990s with a list of only 5 traits.

In the 1990s, trait theory developed the five-factor model, which is based on laboratory research, especially questionnaires and statistical procedures. *Trait theory* refers to an approach for analyzing the structure of personality by measuring, identifying, and classifying similarities and differences in personality characteristics or traits. The basic unit for measuring personality characteristics is the trait. *Traits* are relatively stable and enduring tendencies to behave in particular ways, but behavior is not always the same across different situations.

Trait theory says relatively little about the development or growth of personality but instead emphasizes measuring and identifying differences among personalities.

Five-Factor Model

The *five-factor model* organizes all personality traits into five categories—openness, conscientiousness, extraversion, agreeableness, and neuroticism (OCEAN). These traits, which are referred to as the *Big Five traits*, raise three major issues.

First, although traits are stable tendencies to behave in certain ways, this stability does not necessarily apply across situations. According to the *person-situation interaction*, you may behave differently in different situations because of the effects of a particular situation.

Second, personality traits are both *changeable and stable:* most change occurs before age 30 because adolescents and young adults are more willing to adopt new values and attitudes or revise old ones; most stability occurs after age 30, but adults do continue to grow in their ideas, beliefs, and attitudes.

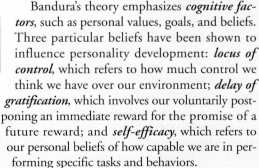

Third, *genetic factors* have a considerable influence on personality traits and behaviors. Genetic factors push and pull the development of certain traits, whose development may be helped or hindered by environmental factors.

Traits are useful in that they provide shorthand descriptions of people and predict certain behaviors.

H. Application: Assessment—Objective Tests

Why are traits big business?

The study of traits has become big business because traits are used in constructing personality tests. For example, if you're applying for a fast-food job, you may be asked to fill out a written questionnaire, which is really a honesty test. The employer knows that about 62% of fast-food workers steal money or give away food to friends and hopes this honesty test will help select a honest employee (K. R. Murphy, 1993). To help employers make hiring decisions, about 5,000 companies administer honesty tests to almost 5 million people each year. Honesty tests, which are the most frequently administered psychological tests in the United States, are examples of objective personality tests (Mumford et al., 2001).

Objective personality tests, also called *self-report questionnaires,* consist of specific written statements that require individuals to indicate, for example, by checking "true" or "false," whether the statements do or do not apply to them.

> I would never give free drinks to my friends—it's against the rules.

Because objective personality tests or self-report questionnaires use very specific questions and require very specific answers, they are considered to be highly *structured,* or *objective.* In comparison, projective tests (pp. 450–451) use ambiguous stimuli (inkblots or photos), have widely varying responses, and are considered to be *unstructured,* or *projective,* personality tests.

It is most likely that, as part of a job interview, you will be asked to take a variety of self-report questionnaires. That's because employers, clinicians, researchers, and government and law enforcement agencies use self-report questionnaires to identify and differentiate personality traits.

The basic assumption behind self-report questionnaires brings us back to the definition of traits. We defined traits as stable and enduring tendencies to behave in certain ways. Self-report questionnaires identify traits, which employers use to predict how prospective employees will behave in their particular jobs or situations (Ozer, 1999).

Before we discuss how valid and reliable self-report questionnaires are in predicting behavior, we'll examine two of the more popular self-report questionnaires.

How honest are most employees?

Objective personality tests are used in both business and clinical settings. In business settings, self-report questionnaires are often used in selecting employees for certain traits, such as being honest and trustworthy, which is why integrity tests are often used (Alliger & Title, 2000).

INTEGRITY TESTS

Integrity or honesty tests are supposed to assess whether individuals have high levels of the trait of honesty. Questions asked on honesty tests are similar to the following (Lilienfeld, 1993).

1. Have you ever stolen merchandise from your place of work?

2. Have you ever been tempted to steal a piece of jewelry from a store?

3. Do you think most people steal money from their workplace every now and then?

4. A person has been a loyal and honest employee at a firm for 20 years. One day, after realizing that she has neglected to bring lunch money, she takes $10 from her workplace but returns it the next day. Should she be fired?

> Would you buy a gold watch from this man?

People strong in the trait of honesty answer: (1) no, (2) no, (3) no, (4) yes.

Notice that some self-report questionnaires, such as the integrity test, focus on measuring a single personality trait, in this case honesty. The next self-report questionnaire, called the MMPI-2, is used primarily in clinical settings and measures a number of traits and personality problems.

MINNESOTA MULTIPHASIC PERSONALITY INVENTORY-2

Suppose a parole board needed to decide if a convicted murderer had changed enough in prison to be let out on parole. To help make this decision, they might use a test that identifies the range of normal and abnormal personality traits, such as the well-known Minnesota Multiphasic Personality Inventory-2 (MMPI-2).

The *Minnesota Multiphasic Personality Inventory (MMPI-2)* is a true-false self-report questionnaire that consists of 567 statements describing a wide range of normal and abnormal behaviors. The purpose of the MMPI-2 is to measure the personality style and emotional adjustment in individuals with mental illness.

The MMPI-2 asks about and identifies a variety of specific personality traits, including depression, hostility, high energy, and shyness, and plots whether these traits are in the normal or abnormal range. A few of the 567 statements used in the MMPI are given below:

- I do not tire quickly.
- I am worried about sex.
- When I get bored, I like to stir up some excitement.
- I believe I am being plotted against.

> Could a test show if a person were ready for parole?

One advantage of this test is that it contains three kinds of scales: *validity scales,* which assess whether the client was faking good or bad answers; *clinical scales,* which identify psychological disorders, such as depression, paranoia, or schizophrenia; and *content scales,* which identify specific areas, such as the anger scale, whose content includes references to being irritable and hotheaded and to difficulties controlling anger (Kaplan & Saccuzzo, 2001).

The MMPI-2 is commonly used to assess a wide range of personality traits, numerous behaviors, health and psychosomatic symptoms, and many well-known psychotic symptoms (Greene & Clopton, 1994). The MMPI-2 and the integrity questionnaire are examples of objective tests used to identify personality traits.

Another method that claims to identify your particular traits involves astrology.

How do horoscopes work?

About 78% of women and 70% of men read horoscopes, and many believe that they are so correct that they were written especially for them (Halpern, 1998). As you read the horoscope on the right, note how many traits apply to you. Because horoscopes contain general traits, people believe horoscopes were written especially for them, a phenomenon called the Barnum principle (Snyder et al., 1977).

The *Barnum principle* (named after the famous circus owner P. T. Barnum) refers to the method of listing many general traits so that almost everyone who reads the horoscope thinks that these traits apply specifically to him or her. But, in fact, these traits are so general that they apply to almost everyone.

Astrologers claim they can identify your personality traits by knowing the sign under which you were born. However, researchers found that horoscopes do not assess personality traits for a particular individual, which means horoscopes lack one of the two characteristics of a good test—validity.

SCORPIO
Oct. 24th to Nov. 21st

You are bright, sincere, and likable but can be too hard on yourself.

VALIDITY

Students claim that the Scorpio horoscope, which I wrote, is accurate for them. The reason I can write "accurate" horoscopes is that I use the *Barnum principle*, which means that I state personality traits in a general way so that they apply to everyone.

I read my horoscope every day, and it's always right on the mark.

Validity means that the test measures what it claims or is supposed to measure.

A personality test that has no validity is no better than chance at describing or predicting a particular individual's traits. For example, researchers found that the 12 zodiac signs were no better than chance at identifying traits for a particular individual (Svensen & White, 1994). Because horoscopes cannot identify or predict traits for a particular person, horoscopes lack validity. The reason horoscopes remain popular and seem to be "accurate" is that astrologers essentially use the Barnum principle, which means their horoscopes are "accurate" for almost everyone. In comparison, integrity tests generally have low validity, while the MMPI-2 has good validity, which means it can describe and predict behaviors for particular individuals (Kaplan & Saccuzzo, 2001). In addition to validity, a good personality test must also have reliability.

RELIABILITY

Even though horoscopes lack validity, they may actually have the second characteristic of a good personality test, reliability.

Reliability refers to consistency: A person's score on a test at one point in time should be similar to the score obtained by the same person on a similar test at a later point in time.

Horoscopes may be reliable if the astrologer remains the same. In comparison, integrity tests and the MMPI-2 have good reliability. However, the MMPI-2 is better than integrity tests because the MMPI-2 has both good validity and reliability, while the integrity test has good reliability but low validity (Kaplan & Saccuzzo, 2001).

Is a monk or a devil more honest?

Self-report questionnaires and objective personality tests are popular and widely used because they assess information about traits in a structured way so that such information can be compared with others who have taken the same tests. For example, employers and government and law enforcement agencies use objective personality tests, such as integrity tests, to compare and select certain traits in job applicants. Researchers use objective personality tests to differentiate between people's traits. Counselors and clinicians use objective personality tests, such as the MMPI-2, to identify personality traits and potential psychological problems (Meyer et al., 2001). We'll discuss the disadvantages and advantages of objective personality tests.

DISADVANTAGES

One disadvantage of objective personality tests is that their questions and answers are very structured, and critics from the psychodynamic approach point out that such structured tests may not assess deeper or unconscious personality factors. A second disadvantage comes from the straightforward questions, which often allow people to figure out what answers are most socially desirable or acceptable and thus bias the test results. For example, one problem with integrity tests is that the answers can be faked so that the person appears more trustworthy (compare the devil's and monk's responses on the right) (Wanek, 1999). Third, many self-report questionnaires measure specific traits, which we know may predict behavior in the same situations but not across situations. This means a person may behave honestly with his or her family but not necessarily with his or her employer.

Of course I'm a very, very honest person.

ADVANTAGES

One advantage of objective personality tests is that they are easily administered and can be taken individually or in groups. A second advantage is that, since the questions are structured and require either a true-false or yes-no answer, the scoring is relatively straightforward. Third, many of the self-report questionnaires have good reliability. For example, the reliability of the MMPI-2 ranges from 0.68 to 0.92 (1.0 is perfect reliability) (Kaplan & Saccuzzo, 2001).

I'm not as honest as I should be.

Which of these two would you trust?

Fourth, the validity of self-report questionnaires varies with the test; it ranges from poor to good. For example, the validity of integrity tests appears to be poor: In one study, a group of monks and nuns scored "more dishonest" than a group of prisoners in jail (Rieke & Guastello, 1995). In comparison, many studies on the MMPI-2 indicate its validity to be good (Kaplan & Saccuzzo, 2001).

Because objective personality tests and projective personality tests (pp. 450–451) have different advantages and disadvantages, counselors and clinical psychologists may use a combination of both to assess a client's personality traits and problems.

✔ Summary Test

A. SOCIAL COGNITIVE THEORY

1. One theory says that personality development is shaped primarily by environmental conditions (learning), cognitive-personal factors, and behavior, which all interact to influence how we evaluate, interpret, and organize information and apply that information to ourselves and others; this is called the _____ theory.

2. Albert Bandura called the version of his original social learning theory the (a)_____ theory. Bandura's theory assumes that four distinctly human cognitive processes—highly developed language ability, observational learning, purposeful behavior, and self-analysis—influence the growth, development, and change in (b)_____.

3. Our highly developed (a)_____ ability provides us with a tool for processing and understanding information, which is critical to personality development. Our capacity for (b)_____ learning allows us to learn through watching, without observable behavior or a reinforcer. Our capacity for forethought enables us to plan ahead and set goals—to perform (c)_____ behavior. Finally, the fact that we can monitor our thoughts and actions as well as set and change goals and values gives us the capacity for (d)_____.

4. The power of beliefs and ideas to change the way that we interpret situations and events is one of the basic assumptions of social cognitive theories. Rotter developed a scale to measure our belief about how much control we have over situations or rewards; he called this belief (a)_____. If we believe that we have control over situations and rewards, we are said to have an (b)_____ locus of control. In contrast, if we believe that we do not have control over situations and rewards and that events outside ourselves determine what happens, we are said to have an (c)_____ locus of control.

5. According to Bandura, our personal belief regarding how capable we are of exercising control over events in our lives is called (a)_____. According to Mischel, our voluntary postponement of an immediate reward and persistence in completing a task for the promise of a future reward is called delay of (b)_____.

B. TRAIT THEORY

6. A relatively stable and enduring tendency to behave in a particular way is called a (a)_____. An approach to understanding the structure of personality by measuring, identifying, and analyzing differences in personality is called (b)_____ theory. In attempting to pare down a list of traits by finding relationships among them, researchers have used a statistical method called (c)_____.

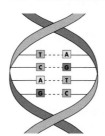

7. The model that organizes all personality traits into five categories is called the (a)_____. These five categories, known as the Big Five, are (b)_____, _____, _____, _____, and _____; their initial letters spell out the word OCEAN.

8. Mischel questioned the basic assumption of trait theory, saying that, if traits represent consistent behavioral tendencies, they should predict behaviors across many different (a)_____. Instead, he found that people behaved with great consistency in the same situation but behaved with low consistency across different situations. Mischel pointed out that predicting a person's behavior must take into account not only the person's traits but also the effects of the situation; this idea became known as the (b)_____ interaction.

C. GENETIC INFLUENCES ON TRAITS

9. How inherited or genetic factors influence and interact with psychological factors—for example, the ways we behave, adapt, and adjust to our environments—is the focus of the field of behavioral (a)_____. Current thinking about genetic factors is that they do not fix behaviors but rather set a range for behaviors. Researchers estimate genetic influences with a measure that estimates how much of some behavior is due to genetic influences; this measure is referred to as (b)_____.

10. Considering the various influences on personality development, researchers estimated that about 40% of the influence comes from (a)_____, which are inherited. About 27% of the influence on personality development comes from environmental factors that involve how each individual reacts and adjusts to his or her own environment; these are called (b)_____ factors. About 7% of the influence on personality development comes from environmental factors that involve parental patterns and shared family experiences; these are called (c)_____ factors. The remaining 26% of the influence on personality development cannot as yet be identified and is attributed to errors in testing and measurement procedures.

D. EVALUATION OF TRAIT THEORY

11. Trait theory assumes that differences among personalities can be described by a short but comprehensive list of traits. Critics of the current list, known as the

OCEAN

(a)_____, point out that the data for the model may paint too simplistic a picture of human personality and may not reflect its depth and complexity. Trait theory assumes that traits are consistent and stable influences on our (b)_____, but critics argue that when traits are measured in one situation, they do not necessarily predict behaviors in other situations.

12. The biggest changes in personality occur during childhood, adolescence, and young adulthood because young men and women are somewhat more likely to be open to new ideas. Personality is less likely to change after age (a)_____. Observations from over 10,000 pairs of twins indicate that (b)_____ factors significantly influence personality traits. Critics warn that inherited factors should not be exaggerated because 50% or more of the influence on traits comes from (c)_____ influences.

E. RESEARCH FOCUS: 180-DEGREE CHANGE

13. If you were to experience a sudden and radical or dramatic shift in personality, beliefs, or values, you would be said to have experienced a (a)_____ in personality. One way researchers studied these changes in personality was to ask each individual the same set of relatively narrow and focused questions so that the same information was obtained from everyone; this method is called the (b)_____.

F. CULTURAL DIVERSITY: SUICIDE BOMBERS

14. Individuals who volunteer to become suicide bombers do so for both strong (a)_____ and _____ reasons. Personal reasons may include such things as wanting to avenge the death of a loved one. Almost all suicide bombers are raised in the Muslim culture, whose beliefs hold that individuals who die as suicide bombers are considered (b)_____, who are revered in this culture as prophets.

15. In pursuing their goals, violent Muslim groups will continue to use suicide bombers because they have widespread (a)_____ approval and are an effective method of killing, instilling (b)_____, and spreading their political (c)_____.

G. FOUR THEORIES OF PERSONALITY

16. How does personality grow and develop? We discussed four different answers. The theory that emphasizes the importance of early childhood, unconscious factors, the three divisions of the mind, and psychosexual stages is called

(a)_____. The theories that focus on the phenomenological perspective, a holistic view, and self-actualization are called (b)_____ theories. The theory that says that personality development is shaped by the interaction among three factors—environmental conditions, cognitive-personal factors, and behavior—is called (c)_____ theory. The theory that emphasizes measuring and identifying differences among personalities is called (d)_____ theory.

H. APPLICATION: ASSESSMENT—OBJECTIVE TESTS

17. Self-report questionnaires, which consist of specific written statements that require structured responses—for example, checking "true" or "false"—are examples of _____ personality tests.

18. A true-false self-report questionnaire containing hundreds of statements that describe a wide range of normal and abnormal behaviors is called the (a)_____. The purpose of this test is to distinguish normal from (b)_____ groups.

19. The method of listing a number of traits in such a general way that almost everyone who reads a horoscope thinks that many of the traits apply specifically to him or her is called the _____ principle.

Answers: 1. social cognitive; 2. (a) social cognitive, (b) personality; 3. (a) language, (b) observational, (c) purposeful, (d) self-analysis; 4. (a) locus of control, (b) internal, (c) external; 5. (a) self-efficacy, (b) gratification; 6. (a) trait, (b) trait, (c) factor analysis; 7. (a) five-factor model, Big Five, (b) openness, conscientiousness, extraversion, agreeableness, neuroticism; 8. (a) situations, (b) person-situation; 9. (a) genetics, (b) heritability; 10. (a) genetic factors, (b) nonshared environmental, (c) shared environmental; 11. (a) Big Five, (b) behaviors; 12. (a) 30, (b) genetic, (c) environmental; 13. (a) quantum change, (b) structured interview; 14. (a) personal, cultural, (b) martyrs; 15. (a) cultural, (b) fear, (c) message; 16. (a) Freud's psychodynamic theory, (b) humanistic, (c) social learning, (d) trait; 17. objective; 18. (a) Minnesota Multiphasic Personality Inventory-2, or MMPI-2, (b) abnormal; 19. Barnum

Critical Thinking

NEWSPAPER ARTICLE

Companies Using Personality Tests for Making Hires That Fit

Questions

1. Why do some employers use both interviews and objective personality tests in deciding whom to hire?

2. Why do companies look for certain traits in selecting employees, and why would Freud question the importance of selecting for traits?

3. If you were using the Big Five traits to design a test for salespeople who work as a team, which traits would you look for?

by Carol Smith

Like a growing number of white-collar workers, Stacy McCollough discovered that an interview and a resume review are no longer the only hurdles to landing a job in today's competitive marketplace. Today, workers going for mid- and upper-level management or sales positions are increasingly likely to have to take hard-to-fool psychological exams as well.

When McCollough applied to work at a medical malpractice insurance brokerage firm, she took a 2-hour test to determine how psychologically fit she was for the job. The test revealed she didn't have the aggressive traits needed to excel as a broker, but it helped the company steer her into a job that made the most of her skills.

Increasingly, companies are finding that an individual's past performance may not be the best predictor of success, because work requirements are changing so rapidly. Instead, companies are looking for new ways to assess intangible skills, such as how people work on teams, how organized they are, or how strategic they are in their thinking.

Although many employers like the tests, applicants aren't always as comfortable. "Some people say they think it's kind of weird—they've already made it to upper management and suddenly they're being given a test," said Barry Lawrence of the Society for

Human Resource Management. "Their attitude is, 'My experience should speak for itself.'"

Most candidates, however, accept testing as part of the hiring process. And test advocates point out that sometimes testing can help a candidate overcome a lack of experience by showing he or she has the right potential for the job.

The tests range from standard psychological profiles, or "personality tests," such as the 60-year-old Minnesota Multiphasic Personality Inventory, to specialized tests such as the Caliper Profile, which has been developed specifically for use in hiring.

While people can sometimes act their way through an interview, it's hard to fool the tests, which have built-in safeguards against cheating.

They are a good reality check on how someone appears in the interview, said human resources specialist Philip Barquer. "You can't fake your character." (Source: *Los Angeles Times*, February 9, 1997)

4. What are some objections to or disadvantages of objective personality tests?

5. When might the MMPI-2 be used in assessing job applicants?

6. Which objective personality test has a scale to detect lying? Can objective personality tests prevent a person from "faking his or her character"?

Try InfoTrac to search for terms: personality tests; Big Five personality traits.

SUGGESTED ANSWERS

1. Some employers believe that applicants may not always be truthful in interviews and that objective personality tests may be more difficult to fool.

2. Employers are looking for certain traits because, according to trait theory, traits are relatively stable and enduring tendencies to behave in certain ways and traits predict how people will behave in similar situations. Freud would point out that traits are important but that behaviors and feelings may be influenced by unconscious forces, of which applicants would not be aware and which are not easily measured by objective personality tests.

3. Salespeople who work as a team might be selected for being high in openness (open to new experiences), extraversion (outgoing and decisive), agreeableness (warm and good-natured), and

conscientiousness (responsible and dependable) but low in neuroticism (stable and not a worrier).

4. Since objective personality tests use very structured questions, simplified yes-no answers, and objective scoring, an applicant can sometimes figure out and give socially acceptable answers and thus bias the test in his or her favor.

5. The MMPI-2 was designed to distinguish normal people from abnormal groups, so it is sometimes used to check for potential personality problems in applicants for sensitive or stressful jobs, such as law enforcement or air-traffic controllers.

6. The MMPI-2 has a scale to detect lying. To some degree, people can "fake their character" on objective personality tests provided they can figure out the socially acceptable or desirable answers.

Links to Learning

LEARNING ACTIVITIES

● *POWERSTUDY CD-ROM 2.0* by Rod Plotnik and Tom Doyle — *PowerStudy 2.0*™
Check out the "Social Cognitive & Trait Theories" Module (disk 3) on PowerStudy and:

- Test your knowledge using an interactive version of the Summary Test on pages 476 and 477. Also access related quizzes—true/false, multiple choice, and matching.
- Explore an interactive version of the Critical Thinking exercise "Companies Using Personality Tests for Making Hires That Fit" on page 478.
- You will also find key terms, a chapter outline including chapter abstract, and a list of hotlinked Web sites that correlate to this module.

● *SELF-STUDY ASSESSMENT*
Want help studying? For your customized Study Plan go to **http://psychology.wadsworth.com/plotnik7e/**. This program will automatically generate pretests and posttests to help you determine what concepts you have mastered and what concepts you still need work on.

WebTUTOR ● *STUDY GUIDE and WEBTUTOR*
Check the corresponding module in your study guide for effective student tips and help learning the material presented.

● *INFOTRAC COLLEGE EDITION ONLINE LIBRARY*
To find interesting and relevent articles go to **http://www.infotrac-college.com**, use your password, and then type in search terms such as the ones listed below.

Behavioral genetics   Trait theory   Albert Bandura
Minnesota Multiphasic Personality Inventory-2

STUDY QUESTIONS

Use Info Trac to search for topics mentioned in the main heads below (e.g., social cognitive theory, trait theory).

*A. Social Cognitive Theory—Why do students invest thousands of dollars and 4 to 6 years of hard work to obtain a college degree? **(Suggested answer p. 632)**

*B. Trait Theory—Would knowing about the Big Five traits help you write an ad to find the perfect roommate or life mate? **(Suggested answer p. 633)**

C. Genetic Influences on Traits—How is it possible that, in the same family, one child may be lively and outgoing and another may be shy and withdrawn?

D. Evaluation of Trait Theory—Why might newlyweds discover that the person they married is not the person they thought they knew?

E. Research Focus: 180-Degree Change—What are some of the reasons that we should be cautious in believing self-reports of dramatic behavioral changes?

F. Cultural Diversity: Suicide Bombers—Being familiar with Muslim cultural beliefs, what can the Israeli government do to stop suicide bombing in the Middle East?

G. Four Theories of Personality—Do you think that all four theories of personality could be or should be reduced to just one?

H. Application: Assessment—Objective Tests—A psychological test in a magazine promises to tell you what kind of mate is perfect for you. Can you believe it?

*These questions are answered in Appendix B.

Glossary

ability tests Achievement tests, which measure what we have learned; aptitude tests, which measure our potential for learning or acquiring a specific skill; and intelligence tests, which measure our general potential to solve problems, think abstractly, and profit from experience.

absolute threshold The intensity level of a stimulus such that a person has a 50% chance of detecting it.

accommodation The process by which a person changes old methods to deal with or adjust to new situations.

achievement need The desire to set challenging goals and to persist in pursuing those goals in the face of obstacles, frustrations, and setbacks.

Acquired Immune Deficiency Syndrome *See* AIDS.

action potential A tiny electric current that is generated when the positive sodium ions rush inside the axon. The enormous increase of sodium ions inside the axon causes the inside of the axon to reverse its charge: The inside becomes positive, while the outside becomes negative.

activation-synthesis theory of dreams The idea that dreaming represents the random and meaningless activity of nerve cells in the brain. According to this theory, the pons, an area in the brain, sends millions of random nerve impulses to the cortex; in turn, the cortex tries to make sense of these signals by creating the feelings, imagined movements, perceptions, changing scenes, and meaningless images that we define as dreams.

actor-observer effect Our tendency, when we are behaving (or acting), to attribute our own behavior to situational factors but, when we are observing, to attribute another person's behavior to his or her personality traits or disposition.

acupuncture An ancient Chinese procedure for the relief of pain, in which a trained practitioner inserts thin needles into various points on the body's surface, often far from the site of the pain, and then manually twirls or electrically stimulates the needles.

adaptation The decreasing response of the sensory organs as they are exposed to a continuous level of stimulation.

adaptation level theory The idea that we quickly become accustomed to receiving some good fortune (money, job, car, degree). We take the good fortune for granted within a short period of time and, as a result, the initial impact of our good fortune fades and contributes less to our long-term level of happiness.

adaptive theory A theory suggesting that sleep evolved as a survival mechanism, since it prevented early humans and animals from wasting energy and exposing themselves to the dangers of nocturnal predators.

adaptive value The usefulness of certain abilities or traits that have evolved in animals or humans that tend to increase their chances of survival, such as the ability to find food, acquire mates, and avoid illness and injury.

addiction A behavioral pattern of drug abuse that is marked by an overwhelming and compulsive desire to obtain and use the drug. Even after stopping, the addict has a tendency to relapse and begin using the drug again.

adolescence A developmental period, lasting from about the ages of 12 to 18, that marks the end of childhood and the beginning of adulthood; it is a transitional period of considerable biological, cognitive, social, and personality changes.

adrenal glands Structures in the endocrine system. The adrenal cortex (outer part) secretes hormones that regulate sugar and salt balances and help the body resist stress; they are also responsible for the growth of pubic hair, a secondary sexual characteristic. The adrenal medulla (inner part) secretes two hormones that arouse the body to deal with stress and emergencies: epinephrine (adrenaline) and norepinephrine (noradrenaline).

affective neuroscience approach The study of the underlying neural bases of mood and emotion by focusing on the brain's neural circuits that evaluate stimuli and produce or contribute to experiencing and expressing different emotional states.

afferent neurons Neurons that carry information from the senses to the spinal cord; also called sensory neurons.

afterimage A visual image that continues after the original stimulus is removed.

age regression In hypnosis, the suggestion that subjects regress, or return, to an earlier time in their lives—for example, to early childhood.

aggression Any behavior directed toward another that is intended to cause harm.

aging process Changes caused by a combination of certain genes and proteins that interfere with organ functioning and by the natural production of toxic molecules (free radicals) that, in turn, cause random damage to body organs and to DNA (the building blocks of life). Such damage eventually exceeds the body's ability to repair itself and results in greater susceptibility to diseases and death.

agoraphobia An anxiety about being in places or situations from which escape might be difficult or embarrassing if a panic attack or paniclike symptoms (sudden dizziness or onset of diarrhea) were to occur.

AIDS (Acquired Immune Deficiency Syndrome) A life-threatening condition that, by the latest definition, is present when the individual is HIV positive and has a level of T-cells (CD4 immune cells) of no more than 200 per cubic milliliter of blood (one-fifth of the level of a healthy person) or has developed one or more of 26 specified illnesses (including recurrent pneumonia and skin cancer).

alarm stage In the general adaptation syndrome, our initial reaction to stress, marked by activation of the fight-flight response, which causes physiological arousal.

alcohol (ethyl alcohol) A psychoactive drug classified as a depressant; it depresses activity of the central nervous system. Alcohol causes friendliness and loss of inhibitions at low doses, impairs drinkers' social judgment and understanding at medium doses, and seriously impairs motor coordination, cognitive abilities, decision making, and speech at higher doses. Very high doses may result in coma and death.

alcoholism A problem involving addiction to alcohol. An alcoholic is a person who has drunk heavily for a long period of time, is addicted to and has an intense craving for alcohol, and, as a result, has problems in two or three major life areas (social, personal, and financial areas, for example).

algorithms Rules that, if followed correctly, will eventually lead to the solution of a problem.

all-or-none law The fact that, once a nerve impulse starts in a small segment at the very beginning of the axon, it will continue at the same speed, segment by segment, to the very end of the axon.

alpha stage In sleep, a stage marked by feelings of being relaxed and drowsy, usually with the eyes closed. Alpha waves have low amplitude and high frequency (8–12 cycles per second).

altered state of consciousness An awareness that differs from normal consciousness; such awareness may be produced by using any number of procedures, such as meditation, psychoactive drugs, hypnosis, or sleep deprivation.

altered state theory of hypnosis The idea that hypnosis is not a trancelike state but rather an altered state of consciousness, during which a person experiences different sensations and feelings. No physiological measures have been found to indicate that a person is in a trance. For another view of hypnosis, see the sociocognitive theory of hypnosis.

altruism Helping or doing something, often at a cost or risk, for reasons other than the expectation of a material or social reward.

Alzheimer's disease A disorder that usually begins after people reach age 50 and is always fatal; it results from widespread damage to the brain, including the hippocampus, and produces deterioration in personality, emotions, cognitive processes, and memory.

Ames room A viewing environment, designed by Albert Ames, that demonstrates how our perception of size may be distorted by manipulating our depth cues.

amnesia Memory loss that may occur after damage to the brain (temporary or permanent), following drug use, or after severe psychological stress.

amniocentesis A medical test performed between weeks 14 and 20 of pregnancy. A long needle is inserted through the mother's abdominal muscles into the amniotic fluid surrounding the fetus. By withdrawing and analyzing fetal cells in the fluid, doctors can identify a number of genetic problems.

amygdala A structure in the limbic system that is located in the tip of the temporal lobe and is involved in forming, recognizing, and remembering emotional experiences and facial expressions.

anal stage Freud's second psychosexual stage, lasting from the age of about $1\frac{1}{2}$ to 3. In this stage, the infant's pleasure seeking is centered on the anus and its functions of elimination.

analogy A strategy for finding a similarity between a new situation and an old, familiar situation.

androgens Male sex hormones.

anencephaly The condition of being born with little or no brain. If some brain or nervous tissue is present, it is totally exposed and often damaged because the top of the skull is missing. Survival is usually limited to days; the longest has been 2 months.

animal model An approach to studying some human problem, situation, or disease by observing, testing, and measuring animals' behavioral, physiological, or neurological changes under conditions that closely approximate it.

anorexia nervosa A serious eating disorder characterized by refusing to eat and not maintaining weight at 85% of what is expected, having an intense fear of gaining weight or becoming fat, and missing at least three consecutive menstrual cycles. Anorexics also have a disturbed body image: They see themselves as fat even though they are very thin.

anterior pituitary The front part of the pituitary gland, a key component of the endocrine system. It regulates growth through the secretion of growth hormone and produces hormones that control the adrenal cortex, pancreas, thyroid, and gonads.

anticipatory nausea Feelings of nausea that are elicited by stimuli associated with nausea-inducing chemotherapy treatments. Patients experience nausea after treatment but also in anticipation of their treatment. Researchers believe that anticipatory nausea occurs through classical conditioning.

antidepressant drugs Drugs used to combat depression. They act by increasing levels of a specific group of neurotransmitters (monoamines, such as serotonin) that is believed to be involved in the regulation of emotions and moods.

antipsychotic drugs *See* neuroleptic drugs.

antisocial personality disorder A pattern of disregarding or violating the rights of others without feeling guilt or remorse. It is found in 3% of the population, predominantly in males.

anxiety An unpleasant state that is associated with feelings of uneasiness, apprehension, and heightened physiological arousal, such as increased heart rate and blood pressure. According to Freud, it arises when there is an unconscious conflict between the id's and superego's desires regarding how to satisfy a need; the ego, caught in the middle, reacts by creating a feeling of anxiety. More modern theories of anxiety are based on conditioned emotional responses and observational learning.

apparent motion An illusion that a stimulus or object is moving in space when, in fact, it is stationary. This illusion is created by rapidly showing a series of stationary images, each of which has a slightly different position or posture than the one before.

approach-approach conflict Having to choose between two situations that both have pleasurable consequences.

approach-avoidance conflict The conflict that arises in a single situation that has both pleasurable and disagreeable aspects.

approaches to understanding behavior Distinctive psychological viewpoints that may involve different methods or techniques—for example, the psychobiological, cognitive, behavioral, psychoanalytic, humanistic, and cross-cultural approaches.

arousal-cost-reward model of helping The idea that we make decisions to help by calculating the costs and rewards of helping.

assimilation The process by which a child uses old methods or experiences to deal with new situations and then incorporates the new information into his or her existing knowledge.

atmospheric perspective In three-dimensional vision, a monocular depth cue that comes into play in the presence of dust, smog, or water vapor. Hazy objects are interpreted as being farther away.

attachment A close fundamental emotional bond that develops between the infant and his or her parent or caregiver.

attention-deficit/hyperactivity disorder (ADHD) A condition diagnosed on the basis of the occurrence of certain behavioral problems, rather than medical tests. A child must have six or more symptoms of inattention (such as making careless mistakes in schoolwork) and six or more symptoms of hyperactivity (such as fidgeting or talking excessively). These symptoms should have been present from an early age, persisted for at least six months, and contributed to maladaptive development.

attitude Any belief or opinion that includes a positive or negative evaluation of some object, person, or event and that predisposes us to act in a certain way toward that object, person, or event.

attributions Our explanations of the causes of events, other people's behaviors, and our own behaviors.

atypical neuroleptic drugs Neuroleptics that somewhat lower levels of dopamine but, more importantly, reduce levels of other neurotransmitters, especially serotonin. One group of these drugs is the benzamides, such as clozapine. These drugs primarily reduce positive symptoms and may slightly improve negative symptoms.

auditory association area An area directly below the primary auditory cortex that receives and transforms meaningless auditory sensations into perceptions or meaningful sounds, such as melodies or words.

auditory canal A long tube in the ear that funnels sound waves down its length so that the waves strike a thin, taut membrane—the eardrum, or tympanic membrane.

auditory nerve A band of fibers that carries impulses (electrical signals) from the cochlea to the brain, resulting in the perception of sounds.

authoritarian parents Parents who attempt to shape, control, and evaluate the behavior and attitudes of their children in accordance with a set standard of conduct, usually an absolute standard that comes from religious or respected authorities.

authoritative parents Parents who attempt to direct their children's activities in a rational and intelligent way. They are supporting, loving, and committed, encourage verbal give-and-take, and discuss their rules and policies with their children.

autism A condition marked by especially abnormal or impaired development in social interactions, spoken language, and sensory-motor systems. Autistics characteristically have few activities or interests and spend long periods repeating the same ritualistic physical behaviors. Signs of autism begin in a child's first three years.

automatic encoding The transfer of information from short-term into long-term memory without any effort and usually without any awareness.

automatic processes Activities that require little awareness, take minimal attention, and do not interfere with other ongoing activities.

autonomic nervous system That portion of the peripheral nervous system that regulates heart rate, breathing, blood pressure, digestion, hormone secretion, and other functions, as well as maintains the body in a state of optimal balance, or homeostasis. It usually functions without conscious effort, which means that only a few of its responses, such as breathing, can also be controlled voluntarily. Its two subdivisions are the sympathetic division and the parasympathetic division.

availability heuristic A rule of thumb by which we rely on information that is more prominent or easily recalled and overlook other information that is available but less prominent or notable.

avoidance-avoidance conflict Having to choose between two situations that both have disagreeable consequences.

axon A single threadlike structure within the neuron. It extends from, and carries signals away from, the cell body to neighboring neurons, organs, or muscles.

Glossary

axon membrane The axon wall, which contains chemical gates that may be opened or closed to control the inward and outward flow of electrically charged particles called ions.

babbling The first stage in acquiring language, in which infants, at an age of about 6 months, begin to make one-syllable sounds such as "deedeedee" or "bababa." Many of these sounds are common across languages.

Bandura's social cognitive theory A personality theory that assumes that personality development, growth, and change are influenced by four distinctively human cognitive processes: highly developed language ability, observational learning, purposeful behavior, and self-analysis. Bandura emphasizes the importance of learning through observation, imitation, and self-reward in the development of social skills, interactions, and behaviors. He contends that we can learn new social skills without performing any observable behaviors or receiving any external rewards. *See also* social cognitive theory.

Barnum principle A technique used in horoscopes and elsewhere, in which a number of traits are listed in such a general way that almost everyone who reads them thinks that these traits apply specifically to him or her. This technique was named after circus owner P. T. Barnum.

basal ganglia A group of structures in the center of the brain that are involved in regulating movements. To function properly, neurons in the basal ganglia must have a sufficient supply of the neurotransmitter dopamine.

basic rules of grammar Rules for combining nouns, verbs, and other parts of speech into meaningful sentences.

basilar membrane A membrane within the cochlea that contains the auditory receptors, or hair cells.

Beck's cognitive theory of depression The idea that when we are depressed, automatic negative thoughts that we rarely notice occur continually throughout the day. These negative thoughts distort how we perceive and interpret the world and thus influence our behaviors and feelings, which in turn contribute to our feeling depressed.

Beck's cognitive therapy *See* cognitive therapy.

behavior modification A treatment or therapy that changes or modifies problems or undesirable behaviors by using learning principles based on operant conditioning, classical conditioning, and social cognitive learning.

behavior therapy A form of psychotherapy in which disruptive behaviors are changed and human functioning is improved on the basis of principles of classical and operant conditioning. It focuses on changing particular behaviors rather than on the underlying mental events or possible unconscious factors. Sometimes called behavior modification or cognitive-behavior therapy.

behavioral approach A psychological viewpoint that analyzes how organisms learn new behaviors or modify existing ones, depending on whether events in their environments reward or punish these behaviors. Historically, as founded by John B. Watson, the behavioral approach emphasized the objective, scientific analysis of observable behaviors.

behavioral genetics The study of how inherited or genetic factors influence and interact with psychological factors to shape our personality, intelligence, emotions, and motivation and also how we behave, adapt, and adjust to our environment.

benzodiazepines Minor tranquilizers (Librium, Valium, Xanax, Dalmane, Halcion) that reduce anxiety and stress. They are frequently prescribed for the short-term (3–4 weeks) treatment of insomnia. Side effects associated with high doses or prolonged usage include daytime drowsiness, loss of memory, tolerance, and dependency.

Binet-Simon Intelligence Scale The world's first standardized intelligence test, containing items arranged in order of increasing difficulty. The items measured vocabulary, memory, common knowledge, and other cognitive abilities.

binocular depth cues In three-dimensional vision, depth cues that depend upon the movement of both eyes (*bi* means "two"; *ocular* means "eye").

biofeedback A training procedure through which a person is made aware of his or her physiological responses, such as muscle activity, heart rate, blood pressure, or temperature, and then tries to increase or decrease these physiological responses.

biological approach A psychological viewpoint that examines how our genes, hormones, and nervous systems interact with our environments to influence learning, personality, memory, motivation, emotions, coping techniques, and other traits and abilities.

biological clocks The body's internal timing devices that are genetically set to regulate various physiological responses for certain periods of time.

biological factors Innate tendencies or predispositions that may either facilitate or inhibit certain kinds of learning.

biological hunger factors Physiological changes in blood chemistry and signals from digestive organs that provide feedback to the brain, which, in turn, triggers us to eat or stop eating.

biological needs Physiological requirements that are critical to our survival and physical well-being.

biological psychology *See* psychobiology.

biological sex factors The action of sex hormones, which is involved in secondary sexual characteristics (facial hair, breasts), sexual motivation (more so in animals than in humans), and the development of ova and sperm.

BioPsychoSocial model The representation of adolescent development as a process that occurs simultaneously on many levels and includes sexual, cognitive, social, and personality changes that interact and influence each other.

biosocial theory A theory that emphasizes social and cultural forces; it says that differences in sexual activities and values for selecting mates developed from traditional cultural divisions of labor: Women were primarily childbearers and homemakers, while men were primarily providers and protectors.

bipolar I disorder A mood disorder characterized by fluctuations between episodes of depression and mania. A manic episode goes on for at least a week, during which a person is unusually euphoric, cheerful, and high and has at least three of the following symptoms: has great self-esteem, has little need of sleep, speaks rapidly and frequently, has racing thoughts, is easily distracted, and pursues pleasurable activities. Formerly called manic-depressive illness.

bisexual orientation A pattern of sexual arousal by persons of either sex.

brightness constancy Our tendency to perceive brightness as remaining the same in changing illumination.

Broca's aphasia An inability to speak in fluent sentences while retaining the ability to understand written or spoken words. It is caused by damage to Broca's area.

Broca's area An area usually located in the left frontal lobe that is necessary for combining sounds into words and arranging words into meaningful sentences. *See* Broca's aphasia.

bulimia nervosa An eating disorder characterized by a minimum of two binge-eating episodes per week for at least three months; fear of not being able to stop eating; regularly engaging in vomiting, use of laxatives, or rigorous dieting and fasting; and excessive concern about body shape and weight.

burnout Feelings of doing poorly at one's job, physically wearing out, and becoming emotionally exhausted due to intense involvement with people who demand too much of one's time and energy and provide too little reward or satisfaction.

bystander effect The phenomenon in which an individual feels inhibited from taking some action because of the presence of others.

caffeine A mild stimulant that produces dilation of blood vessels, increased secretion of stomach acid, and moderate physiological arousal. Psychological effects include a feeling of alertness, decreased fatigue and drowsiness, and improved reaction times. Caffeine, which is present in coffee, tea, chocolate, and other foods, can be addictive, especially in higher doses.

case study An in-depth analysis of the thoughts, feelings, beliefs, experiences, behaviors, or problems of an individual. This research method offers little opportunity to control or manipulate situations or variables.

CAT scan *See* computerized axial tomography.

catatonic schizophrenia A subcategory of schizophrenia characterized by periods of wild excitement or periods of rigid, prolonged immobility; sometimes the person assumes the same frozen posture for hours on end.

catharsis A psychological process through which anger or aggressive energy is released by expressing or letting out powerful negative emotions. Freud's view that catharsis can be helpful in reducing aggression is not supported by most research.

cell body For neurons, a relatively large, egg-shaped structure that provides fuel, manufactures chemicals, and maintains the entire neuron in working order; also called the soma.

central cues Hunger cues associated with the activity of chemicals and neurotransmitters in different areas of the brain.

central nervous system Neurons located in the brain and spinal cord. From the bottom of the brain emerges the spinal cord, which is made up of neurons and bundles of axons and dendrites that carry information back and forth between the brain and the body. Neurons in the central nervous system normally have almost no capacity to regrow or regenerate if damaged or diseased.

central route for persuasion Presenting information with strong arguments, analyses, facts, and logic.

cephalocaudal principle The rule that parts of the body closer to the infant's head develop before parts closer to the feet.

cerebellum A region of the hindbrain that is involved in coordinating movements but not in initiating voluntary movements. It is also involved in cognitive functions, such as short-term memory, following rules, and carrying out plans. Surprising new evidence suggests that the cerebellum is also involved in learning to perform timed motor responses, such as those required in playing games or sports.

challenge appraisal Our conclusion that we have the potential for gain or personal growth in a particular situation but that we also need to mobilize our physical energy and psychological resources to meet the challenging situation.

chi-square A test of statistical significance that compares the actual observed distribution of people (or events) among various categories with the distribution expected purely on the basis of chance.

child abuse and neglect Inadequate care or acts by the parent(s) (physical or emotional abuse) that put a child in danger, cause physical harm or injury, or involve sexual molestation.

Chomsky's theory of language The idea that all languages share a common universal grammar and that children inherit a mental program to learn this universal grammar. This theory includes the concepts of deep structure and surface structure and of transformational rules to convert from one to the other.

chromosome A hairlike structure that contains tightly coiled strands of deoxyribonucleic acid (DNA). Each cell of the human body (except for the sperm and egg) contains 46 chromosomes, arranged in 23 pairs.

chunking Combining separate items of information into a larger unit, or chunk, and then remembering chunks of information rather than individual items. A technique of memory enhancement.

circadian rhythm A biological clock that is genetically programmed to regulate physiological responses within a time period of 24 or 25 hours (about a day); one example is the sleep-wake cycle.

clairvoyance The ability to perceive events or objects that are out of sight.

classical conditioning A kind of learning in which a neutral stimulus acquires the ability to produce a response that was originally produced by a different stimulus.

client-centered therapy An approach developed by Carl Rogers that assumes that each person has an actualizing tendency—that is, a tendency to develop his or her own potential; the therapist's task is to show compassion and positive regard in helping the client reach his or her potential. Also called person-centered therapy.

clinical assessment A systematic evaluation of an individual's various psychological, biological, and social factors, as well as the identification of past and present problems, stressors, and other cognitive and behavioral symptoms.

clinical diagnosis A process of determining how closely an individual's specific symptoms match those that define a particular mental disorder.

clinical interview In assessment, a method of gathering information about relevant aspects of a person's past as well as current behaviors, attitudes, emotions, and details of present difficulties or problems. Some clinical interviews are unstructured, which means that they have no set questions; others are structured, which means that they follow a standard format of asking the same questions.

clinical psychologist An individual who has a Ph.D, has specialized in the clinical subarea, and has spent an additional year in a supervised therapy setting to gain experience in diagnosing and treating a wide range of abnormal behaviors. To train as a clinical psychologist usually requires 4–6 years of work after obtaining a college degree.

closure rule A perceptual rule stating that, in organizing stimuli, we tend to fill in any missing parts of a figure and see the figure as complete.

cocaine A stimulant produced from the leaves of the coca plant. Its physiological and behavioral effects are very similar to those of amphetamine: It produces increased heart rate and blood pressure, enhanced mood, alertness, increased activity, decreased appetite, and diminished fatigue. At higher doses, it can produce anxiety, emotional instability, and suspiciousness.

cochlea A coiled, fluid-filled structure in the inner ear that contains the receptors for hearing. Its function is transduction—transforming vibrations into nerve impulses that are sent to the brain for processing into auditory information.

cochlear implant A miniature electronic device that is surgically implanted into the cochlea to restore hearing in those with neural deafness. It converts sound waves to electrical signals, which are fed into the auditory nerve and hence reach the brain for processing.

cognitive appraisal theory The idea that our interpretation or appraisal of a situation is often the primary cause of emotions.

cognitive approach *See* cognitive psychology.

cognitive-behavior therapy A treatment for phobias and other mental disorders based on a combination of two methods: changing negative, unhealthy, or distorted thoughts and beliefs by substituting positive, healthy, and realistic ones; and changing limiting or disruptive behaviors by learning and practicing new skills to improve functioning. Sometimes called behavior therapy.

cognitive development How a person perceives, thinks, and gains an understanding of his or her world through the interaction and influence of genetic and learned factors.

cognitive developmental theory The idea that, as they develop mental skills and interact with their environments, children learn one set of rules for male behavior and another set of rules for female behavior.

cognitive dissonance A state of unpleasant psychological tension that motivates us to reduce our cognitive inconsistencies by making our beliefs more consistent with one another.

cognitive-emotional-behavioral and environmental factors The factors that contribute to the development of mental disorders, including deficits in cognitive processes, such as having unusual thoughts and beliefs; deficits in processing emotional stimuli, such as under- or overreacting to emotional situations; behavioral problems, such as lacking social skills; and environmental challenges, such as dealing with stressful situations.

cognitive factors According to social cognitive theory, factors that include our beliefs, expectations, values, intentions, and social roles—all of which help to shape our personalities.

cognitive factors in motivation The influence of individuals' evaluations or perceptions of a situation on their willingness to work.

cognitive interview A technique for questioning eyewitnesses and others by having them imagine and reconstruct the details of an event, report everything they remember without holding anything back, and narrate the event from different viewpoints.

cognitive learning A kind of learning that involves mental processes, such as attention and memory; may proceed through observation or imitation; and may not involve any external rewards or require the person to perform any observable behaviors.

cognitive map A mental representation of the layout of an environment and its features.

Glossary

cognitive miser model The idea that, in making attributions, people feel they must conserve time and effort by taking cognitive shortcuts.

cognitive neuroscience An approach to studying cognitive processes that involves taking pictures of the structures and functions of the living brain during the performance of a wide variety of mental or cognitive processes, such as thinking, planning, naming, and recognizing objects.

cognitive perspective The theory that an organism learns a predictable relationship between two stimuli such that the occurrence of one stimulus (neutral stimulus) predicts the occurrence of another (unconditioned stimulus). In other words, classical conditioning occurs because the organism learns what to expect. Formerly called information theory.

cognitive psychology The study of how we process, store, retrieve, and use information and how cognitive processes influence what we attend to, perceive, learn, remember, believe, feel, and do.

cognitive social psychology A subarea of social psychology that focuses on how cognitive processes, such as perceiving, retrieving, and interpreting information about social interactions and events, affect emotions and behaviors and how emotions and behaviors affect cognitions.

cognitive therapy An approach to therapy that focuses on the role of thoughts in our emotions and actions. The widely used version developed by Aaron Beck assumes that we have automatic negative thoughts that we typically say to ourselves without much notice. By continuously repeating these automatic negative thoughts, we color and distort how we perceive and interpret the world and influence how we behave and feel. The goal of the therapy is to change these automatic negative thoughts.

cognitive unconscious Mental structures and processes that, although we are unaware of them, automatically and effortlessly influence our conscious thoughts and behaviors.

collective unconscious According to Jung, ancient memory traces and symbols that are passed on by birth and are shared by all people in all cultures.

color blindness Inability to distinguish between two or more shades in the color spectrum. There are several kinds of color blindness. *See* monochromats and dichromats.

color constancy Our tendency to perceive colors as remaining stable despite differences in lighting.

commitment In Sternberg's triangular theory of love, the component of love associated with making a pledge to nourish the feelings of love and to actively maintain the relationship.

common factors A basic set of procedures and experiences shared by different therapies that account for those therapies' comparable effectiveness despite their different fundamental principles and techniques. Common factors include the growth of a supportive and trusting relationship between therapist and client

and the accompanying development of an accepting atmosphere in which the client feels willing to admit problems and is motivated to work on changing.

communication The ability to use sounds, smells, or gestures to exchange information.

community mental health centers Government-sponsored centers that offer low-cost or free mental health care to members of the surrounding community, especially the underprivileged. The services may include psychotherapy, support groups, or telephone crisis counseling.

companionate love A condition associated with trusting and tender feelings for someone whose life is closely bound up with one's own.

compliance A kind of conformity in which we give in to social pressure in our public responses but do not change our private beliefs.

concept A way to group objects, events, or characteristics on the basis of some common property they all share.

conception The process in which one of the millions of sperm penetrates the ovum's outside membrane; also called fertilization. After penetration, the outside membrane changes and becomes impenetrable to the millions of remaining sperm.

concrete operations stage The third of Piaget's cognitive stages, lasting from about the age of 7 to 11 years. During this stage, children can perform a number of logical mental operations on concrete objects that are physically present.

conditional positive regard Positive regard that depends on our behaving in certain ways—for example, living up to or meeting others' standards.

conditioned emotional response The feeling of some positive or negative emotion, such as happiness, fear, or anxiety, when experiencing a stimulus that previously accompanied a pleasant or painful event. This is an example of classical conditioning.

conditioned response (CR) A response elicited by the conditioned stimulus; it is similar to the unconditioned response but not identical in magnitude or amount.

conditioned stimulus (CS) A formerly neutral stimulus that has acquired the ability to elicit a response previously elicited by the unconditioned stimulus.

conduct disorder A repetitive and persistent pattern of aggressive behavior that has been going on for at least a year and that violates the established social rules or the rights of others. Problems may include threatening to harm people, abusing or killing animals, destroying property, being deceitful, or stealing.

conduction deafness Deafness caused by wax in the auditory canal, injury to the tympanic membrane, or malfunction of the ossicles.

cones Photoreceptors that contain three chemicals called opsins, which are activated in bright light and allow us to see color. Unlike rods, cones are wired individually to neighboring cells; this

one-on-one system of relaying information allows us to see fine details.

conflict The feeling we experience when we must decide between two or more incompatible choices.

conformity Any behavior you perform because of group pressure, even though that pressure might not involve direct requests.

conscious thoughts Wishes, desires, or thoughts that we are aware of, or can recall, at any given moment.

consciousness An individual's different levels of awareness of his or her thoughts and feelings. Creating images in the mind, following thought processes, and having unique emotional experiences are all part of consciousness.

consensus In making attributions, determining whether other people engage in the same behavior in the same situation.

conservation The idea that even though the shape of some object of substance is changed, the total amount remains the same.

consistency In making attributions, determining whether an individual engages in a certain behavior every time he or she is in a particular situation.

contiguity theory The view that classical conditioning occurs because two stimuli (the neutral stimulus and the unconditioned stimulus) are paired close together in time (are contiguous). Eventually, as a result of this contiguous pairing, the neutral stimulus becomes the conditioned stimulus, which elicits the conditioned response.

continuity rule A perceptual rule stating that, in organizing stimuli, we tend to favor smooth or continuous paths when interpreting a series of points or lines.

continuous reinforcement The simplest reinforcement schedule, in which every occurrence of the operant response results in delivery of the reinforcer.

continuum of consciousness The wide range of human experiences, from being acutely aware and alert to being totally unaware and unresponsive.

control group In an experiment, subjects who undergo all the same procedures as the experimental subjects do, except that the control subjects do not receive the treatment.

Control Question Technique A lie-detection procedure in which the examiner asks two kinds of questions: neutral questions that elicit little emotional response and critical questions that are designed to elicit greater emotional responses. The person answers only "Yes" or "No" to the questions and, if guilty, is expected to show a greater emotional response to the critical questions than to the neutral questions.

controlled processes Activities that require full awareness, alertness, and concentration to reach some goal. Because of the strongly focused attention they require, controlled processes often interfere with other ongoing activities.

conventional level Kohlberg's intermediate level of moral reasoning. It consists of two stages: At stage 3, moral decisions are guided most by conforming to the standards of others we value; at stage 4, moral reasoning is determined most by conforming to the laws of society.

convergence In three-dimensional vision, a binocular cue for depth perception based on signals sent from the muscles that turn the eyes. To focus on near or approaching objects, these muscles turn the eyes inward, toward the nose. The brain uses the signals sent by these muscles to determine the distance of the object.

convergent thinking Beginning with a problem and coming up with a single correct solution.

conversion disorder A type of somatoform disorder characterized by unexplained and significant physical symptoms—headaches, nausea, dizziness, loss of sensation, paralysis—that suggest a real neurological or medical problem but for which no physical or organic cause can be identified. Anxiety or emotional distress is apparently converted to symptoms that disrupt physical functioning.

cornea The rounded, transparent covering over the front of the eye. As the light waves pass through the cornea, its curved surface bends, or focuses, the waves into a narrower beam.

correlation An association or relationship between the occurrence of two or more events.

correlation coefficient A number that indicates the strength of a relationship between two or more events. The closer the number is to −1.00 or +1.00, the greater is the strength of the relationship.

cortex A thin layer of cells that essentially covers the entire surface of the forebrain. The cortex consists of the frontal, parietal, occipital, and temporal lobes, whose control centers allow us to carry out hundreds of cognitive, emotional, sensory, and motor functions.

counseling psychologist An individual who has a Ph.D in psychology or education and whose training included work in a counseling setting. Counseling psychologists generally have a less extensive research background than clinical psychologists and work in real-world settings, such as schools, industry, and private practice. Whereas clinical psychologists treat mental disorders, counseling psychologists deal largely with problems of living. To train as a counseling psychologist generally takes 4–6 years after obtaining a bachelor's degree.

counterattitudinal behavior Taking a public position that runs counter to your private attitude.

covariation model A model developed by Harold Kelley that may be used in deciding between internal and external attributions. The model says that, in determining attributions, we should look for factors that are present when the behavior occurs and factors that are absent when the behavior does not occur.

creative individual Someone who regularly solves problems, fashions products, or defines new questions that make an impact on his or her society.

creative thinking A combination of flexibility in thinking and reorganization of understanding to produce innovative ideas and new solutions.

critical language period A period of time from infancy to adolescence when language is easiest to learn; in the period after adolescence through adulthood, language is more difficult to learn.

critical period In imprinting, a relatively brief time during which learning is most likely to occur. Also called the sensitive period.

cross-cultural approach A psychological viewpoint that studies the influence of cultural and ethnic similarities and differences on psychological and social functioning.

cross-sectional method A research design in which several groups of different-aged individuals are studied at the same time.

crowd A large group of persons, most of whom are unacquainted.

cultural bias In testing, the situation in which the wording of the questions and the experiences on which they are based are more familiar to members of some social groups than to others.

cultural-familial retardation Mental retardation that results from greatly impoverished environments, with no evidence of genetic or brain damage.

cultural influences Pervasive pressures that encourage members of a particular society or ethnic group to conform to shared behaviors, values, and beliefs.

cumulative record A continuous written record that shows an organism's responses and reinforcements.

curare A drug that enters the bloodstream, reaches the muscles, and blocks receptors on the muscles. As a result, acetylcholine, the neurotransmitter that normally activates muscles, is blocked, and the muscles are paralyzed.

DARE (Drug Abuse Resistance Program) A drug awareness program taught in the classroom by trained, uniformed police officers. It is based on the idea of using social influence and role-playing to discourage adolescents from starting drug use and to encourage them to refuse drugs in the future.

daydreaming An activity that requires a low level of awareness, often occurs during automatic processes, and involves fantasizing or dreaming while awake.

debriefing A procedure administered to subjects after an experiment to minimize any potential negative effects. It includes explaining the purpose and method of the experiment, asking the subjects their feelings about having been in the experiment, and helping the subjects deal with possible doubts or guilt that arises from their behaviors in the experiments.

decibel A unit to measure loudness. Our threshold for hearing ranges from 0 decibels, which is absolutely no sound, to 140 decibels, which can produce pain and permanent hearing loss.

decision-stage model of helping The idea that we go through five stages in deciding to help: (1) we notice the situation; (2) we interpret it as one in which help is needed; (3) we assume personal responsibility; (4) we choose a form of assistance; and (5) we carry out that assistance.

declarative memory Memories of facts or events, such as scenes, stories, words, conversations, faces, or daily events. We are aware of these kinds of memories and can retrieve them.

deductive reasoning Reasoning from the general to the particular: deriving a conclusion about particulars that is based on a general assumption that one knows or believes to be true.

deep structure According to Chomsky, a sentence's underlying meaning that is not spoken but is present in the mind of the listener.

defense mechanisms Freudian processes that operate at unconscious levels to help the ego reduce anxiety through self-deception.

deficiency needs Physiological needs (food, sleep) and psychological needs (safety, belongingness, and esteem) that we try to fulfill if they are not met.

deindividuation The increased tendency for subjects to behave irrationally or perform antisocial behaviors when there is less chance of being personally identified.

deinstitutionalization The release of mental patients from mental hospitals and their return to the community to develop more independent and fulfilling lives.

delay of gratification Voluntarily postponing an immediate reward to persist in completing a task for the promise of a future reward.

dendrites Branchlike extensions that arise from the cell body; they receive signals from other neurons, muscles, or sense organs and pass them to the cell body.

denial Refusal to recognize some anxiety-provoking event or piece of information.

dependency A change in the nervous system such that a person addicted to a drug now needs to take it to prevent the occurrence of painful symptoms.

dependent personality disorder A pattern of being submissive and clingy because of an excessive need to be taken care of. It is found in 2% of the population.

dependent variable In an experiment, one or more of the subjects' behaviors that are used to measure the potential effects of the treatment or independent variable.

depth perception In visual perception, the ability of the eye and brain to add a third dimension, depth, to visual perceptions, even though the images projected on our retina have only two dimensions, height and width.

descriptive statistics Numbers used to present a collection of data in a brief yet meaningful form.

Glossary

designer drugs Manufactured or synthetic drugs designed to resemble already existing illegal psychoactive drugs and to produce or mimic their psychoactive effects.

developmental norms The average ages at which children perform various skills or exhibit particular abilities or behaviors.

developmental psychologists Psychologists who study a person's biological, emotional, cognitive, personal, and social development across the life span, from infancy through late adulthood.

developmental psychology The study of moral, social, emotional, and cognitive development throughout a person's entire life.

***Diagnostic and Statistical Manual of Mental Disorders*-IV-TR (DSM-IV-TR)** The 2000 edition of the American Psychiatric Association's uniform diagnostic system for assessing specific symptoms and matching them to almost 300 different mental disorders. The DSM-IV-TR has five major dimensions, or axes.

diathesis stress theory of schizophrenia The idea that some people have a genetic predisposition (a diathesis) that interacts with life stressors to result in the onset and development of schizophrenia.

dichromats People who have trouble distinguishing red from green because their eyes have just two kinds of cones. This is an inherited condition, found mostly in males, that results in seeing mostly shades of green, but it differs in severity.

diffusion of responsibility theory The idea that, in the presence of others, individuals feel less personal responsibility and are less likely to take action in a situation where help is required.

direction of a sound The brain determines the direction of a sound by calculating the slight difference in time that it takes sound waves to reach the two ears, which are about 6 inches apart.

discrimination In classical conditioning, the tendency for some stimuli but not others to elicit a conditioned response. In operant conditioning, the tendency for a response to be emitted in the presence of a stimulus that is reinforced but not in the presence of unreinforced stimuli. In social psychology, specific unfair behaviors exhibited toward members of a group.

discriminative stimulus In conditioning, a cue that behavior will be enforced.

disgust A universal facial expression—closing the eyes, narrowing the nostrils, curling the lips downward, and sometimes sticking out the tongue—that indicates the rejection of an item of food.

disorganized schizophrenia A subcategory of schizophrenia marked by bizarre ideas, often about one's body (bones melting), confused speech, childish behavior (giggling for no apparent reason, making faces at people), great emotional swings (fits of laughing or crying), and often extreme neglect of personal appearance and hygiene.

displacement Transferring feelings from their true source to another source that is safer and more socially acceptable.

display rules Specific cultural norms that regulate when, where, and how much emotion we should or should not express in different situations.

dispositional attributions *See* internal attributions.

dissociative amnesia A dissociative disorder characterized by the inability to recall important personal information or events and usually associated with stressful or traumatic events. The importance of the information forgotten or the duration of the memory lapse is too great to be explained by normal forgetfulness.

dissociative disorder A disorder characterized by a disruption, split, or breakdown in a person's normally integrated and functioning consciousness, memory, sense of identity, or perception.

dissociative fugue A disturbance in which an individual suddenly and unexpectedly travels away from home or place of work and is unable to recall his or her past. The person may not remember his or her identity or may be confused about his or her new, assumed identity.

dissociative identity disorder The presence in a single individual of two or more distinct identities or personality states, each with its own pattern of perceiving, thinking about, and relating to the world. Different personality states may take control of the individual's thoughts and behaviors at different times. Formerly called multiple personality disorder.

distinctiveness In making attributions, determining how differently the person behaves in one situation in comparison with other situations.

divergent thinking Beginning with a problem and coming up with many different solutions.

dopamine theory The idea that, in schizophrenia, the dopamine neurotransmitter system is somehow overactive and gives rise to a wide range of symptoms.

double-blind procedure An experimental design in which neither the researchers nor the subjects know which group is receiving which treatment. This design makes it possible to separate the effects of medical treatment from the participants' beliefs or expectations about the treatment.

double standard for sexual behavior A set of beliefs, values, and expectations that subtly encourages sexual activity in men but discourages the same behavior in women.

Down syndrome A genetic disorder that results from an extra 21st chromosome and causes abnormal physical traits (a fold of skin at the corner of each eye, a wide tongue, heart defects) and abnormal brain development, resulting in degrees of mental retardation.

dream interpretation A Freudian technique of dream analysis, based on the assumption that dreams contain underlying, hidden meanings and symbols that provide clues to unconscious thoughts and desires. Freud distinguished between a dream's manifest content—the plot of the dream at the surface level—and its latent content—the hidden or disguised meaning of the plot's events.

dreaming A unique state of consciousness in which we are asleep but we experience a variety of images, often in color. People blind from birth have only auditory or tactile dreams, while sighted people have dreams with astonishing visual, auditory, and tactile images.

Drug Abuse Resistance Program *See* DARE.

DSM-IV-TR *See Diagnostic and Statistical Manual of Mental Disorders*-IV-TR.

dyslexia Reading, spelling, and writing difficulties that may include reversing or skipping letters and numbers. This condition affects 1–2% of children and is now regarded as a neurological disorder rather than a reading problem.

dysthymic disorder A mood disorder characterized by feeling chronically but not continuously depressed for a period of two years. While depressed, a person experiences at least two of the following symptoms: poor appetite, insomnia, fatigue, low self-esteem, poor concentration, and feelings of hopelessness.

eardrum *See* tympanic membrane.

echoic memory A form of sensory memory that holds auditory information for 1 or 2 seconds.

eclectic approach An approach to therapy in which the psychotherapist combines techniques and ideas from many different schools of thought.

ECT *See* electroconvulsive therapy.

efferent neurons Neurons that carry information away from the spinal cord to produce responses in various muscles and organs throughout the body. Also called motor neurons.

effortful encoding The transfer of information from short-term into long-term memory either by working hard to repeat or rehearse the information or by making associations between new and old information.

ego Freud's second division of the mind, which develops from the id during infancy; its goal is to find safe and socially acceptable ways of satisfying the id's desires and to negotiate between the id's wants and the superego's prohibitions.

egocentric thinking Seeing and thinking of the world only from your own viewpoint and having difficulty appreciating someone else's viewpoint.

eidetic imagery The ability to examine a picture or page for 10–30 seconds and then retain a detailed visual image of the material for several minutes. Eidetic memory is found in a small percentage of children and almost always disappears around adolescence.

elaborative rehearsal Making meaningful associations between information to be learned and information already learned. An effective strategy for encoding information into long-term memory.

Electra complex *See* Oedipus complex.

electroconvulsive therapy (ECT) A treatment for depression in which electrodes are placed on the skull and a mild electric current is administered.

As it passes through the brain, the current causes a seizure. Usual treatment consists of 10–12 ECT sessions, at the rate of about three per week.

embryonic stage The second stage of the prenatal period, spanning the 2–8 weeks that follow conception; during this stage, cells divide and begin to differentiate into bone, muscle, and body organs.

EMDR *See* Eye Movement Desensitization and Reprocessing.

emotion A response consisting of four components: interpreting or appraising a stimulus (event, object, or thought) in terms of one's well-being; having a subjective feeling, such as happiness or sadness; experiencing physio-logical responses, such as changes in heart rate or breathing; and possibly showing overt behaviors, such as smiling or crying.

emotion-focused coping Making some effort to deal with the emotional distress caused by a harm/loss or threat appraisal. These efforts include seeking support and sympathy, avoiding or denying the situation, and redirecting our attention.

emotional development The process in which genetic factors, brain changes, cognitive factors, coping abilities, and cultural factors influence and interact in the development of emotional behaviors, expressions, thoughts, and feelings.

emotional intelligence The ability to perceive and express emotion, understand and reason with emotion, and regulate emotion in oneself and others.

encoding Placing or storing information—such as images, events, or sounds (music, noise, speech)—in memory by making mental representations.

end bulbs Bulblike swellings at the extreme ends of axons' branches that store chemicals called neurotransmitters, which are used to communicate with neighboring cells.

endocrine system Numerous glands, located throughout the body, that secrete various chemicals called hormones, which affect organs, muscles, and other glands in the body.

endorphins Chemicals produced by the brain and secreted in response to injury or severe physical or psychological stress. Their powerful pain-reducing properties are similar to those of morphine.

environmental factors Our social, political, and cultural influences as well as our particular learning experiences.

environmental language factors Interactions that children have with parents, peers, teachers, and others whose feedback rewards and encourages language development; these interactions also provide opportunities for children to observe, imitate, and practice language skills.

episodic memory A type of declarative memory, consisting of knowledge about one's personal experiences (episodes) or activities, such as naming or describing favorite restaurants, movies, songs, habits, or hobbies.

ESP *See* extrasensory perception.

estrogen One of the major female hormones. At puberty, estrogen levels increase eightfold and stimulate the development of both primary and secondary sexual characteristics.

ethologists Behavioral biologists who observe and study animal behavior in the animal's natural environment or under relatively naturalistic conditions.

evaluative function The role of our attitudes in helping us to stand up for those beliefs and values that we consider very important to ourselves.

evening persons People who prefer to get up late, go to bed late, and engage in afternoon or evening activities. *See* morning persons.

event schemas Social schemas containing behaviors that we associate with familiar activities, events, or procedures. Also called scripts.

evolution *See* theory of evolution.

evolutionary theory of emotions The theory that says one function of emotions is to help a person evaluate objects, people, and situations in terms of how good or bad they are for the individual's well-being and survival.

evolutionary theory (of gender differences) The idea in sociobiology, which emphasizes genetic and biological forces, that current behavioral and cognitive differences between men and women can be traced back to different survival problems faced by early women and men and the different behaviors they adapted to survive.

exemplar model The idea that a person forms a concept of an object, event, animal, or person by defining or making a mental list of the essential characteristics of that particular thing.

exhaustion stage The third stage in the general adaptation syndrome. In reaction to long-term, continuous stress, there is actual breakdown in internal organs or weakening of the infection-fighting immune system.

experiment A method for identifying cause-and-effect relationships by following a set of rules and guidelines that minimize the possibility of error, bias, and chance occurrences. *See also* laboratory experiment.

experimental group In an experiment, the subjects who receive the treatment.

experimental psychology The study of sensation, perception, learning, human performance, motivation, and emotion in carefully controlled laboratory conditions, with both animal and human subjects.

exposure therapy A treatment for anxiety in which the person is gradually exposed to the real anxiety-producing situations or objects that he or she is attempting to avoid; exposure treatment is continued until the anxiety decreases.

external attributions Explanations of behavior based on the external circumstances or situations. Also called situational attributions.

external ear An oval-shaped structure that protrudes from the side of the head. Its function is to pick up sound waves and send them along the auditory canal.

extinction In classical conditioning, the reduction in a response when the conditioned stimulus is no longer followed by the unconditioned stimulus. As a result, the conditioned stimulus tends to no longer elicit the conditioned response. In operant conditioning, the reduction in the operant response when it is no longer followed by the reinforcer.

extrasensory perception (ESP) A group of psychic experiences that involve perceiving or sending information (images) outside normal sensory processes or channels. ESP includes four general abilities—telepathy, precognition, clairvoyance, and psychokinesis.

extrinsic motivation Engaging in certain activities or behaviors that either reduce our biological needs or help us to obtain incentives or external rewards.

Eye Movement Desensitization and Reprocessing (EMDR) A new technique in which the client focuses on a traumatic memory while visually following the back-and-forth movement of a therapist's hand or pen. The process usually continues for several 90-minute sessions, after which the traumatic memories are greatly reduced or eliminated.

eyewitness testimony Recollection or recognition of a suspect observed during a possibly disruptive emotional situation that may have interfered with accurate remembering.

facial expressions Social signals that accompany emotions and express the state of our personal feelings; they provide social signals that elicit a variety of responses from those around us.

facial feedback theory The idea that sensations or feedback from the movement of facial muscles and skin are interpreted by your brain as emotional feelings.

factor analysis A complicated statistical method that finds relationships among different or diverse items and allows them to be grouped together.

farsightedness A visual acuity problem that may result when the eyeball is too short, so that objects are focused at a point slightly behind the retina. The result is that distant objects are clear, but near objects are blurry.

FAS *See* fetal alcohol syndrome.

fat cells Cells that store body fat. The number of fat cells in the body is primarily determined by heredity. They do not normally multiply except when we become obese. Fat cells shrink as we give up fat and lose weight and greatly enlarge as we store fat and gain weight.

fear of failure A tendency to avoid failure by choosing easy, nonchallenging tasks where failure is unlikely or difficult.

female hypothalamus Because of neural programming in the womb, the hypothalamus, a structure in the brain that controls the endocrine

Glossary

system, functions differently in the male and female. The female hypothalamus triggers a cyclical release of estrogens from the ovaries. The increased estrogen level is responsible for female secondary sexual characteristics, such as pubic hair, breast development, and widening of the hips. The cyclic release of hormones (estrogen and progesterone) also regulates the menstrual cycle.

female secondary sexual characteristics Sexual characteristics whose development in the female is triggered by the increased secretion of estrogen during puberty; they include the growth of pubic hair, development of breasts, and widening of hips.

fertilization *See* conception.

fetal alcohol syndrome (FAS) A condition caused by heavy maternal drinking during pregnancy. It results in a combination of physical changes, such as short stature, flattened nose, and short eye openings, and psychological defects, such as degrees of mental retardation and hyperactivity.

fetal stage The third stage in prenatal development, beginning two months after conception and lasting until birth.

fight-flight response A state of increased physiological arousal that (a) directs great resources of energy to the muscles and brain, (b) can be triggered by either physical stimuli that threaten our survival or psychological situations that are novel, threatening, or challenging, and (c) involves numerous physiological responses that arouse and prepare the body for action—fight or flight. Caused by the activation of the sympathetic nervous system, it helps us to cope with, and survive, threatening situations.

figure-ground rule A perceptual rule stating that, in organizing stimuli, we tend to automatically distinguish between a figure and a ground: The figure, with more detail, stands out against the background, which has less detail.

five-factor model An approach to personality in which all traits are organized under five categories—openness, conscientiousness, extraversion, agreeableness, and neuroticism—that are used to describe differences in personality.

fixation A Freudian process through which an individual may be locked into any one of the three psychosexual stages—oral, anal, or phallic—because his or her wishes were either overgratified or undergratified in that stage.

fixed action pattern An innate biological force that predisposes an organism to behave in a fixed way in the presence of a specific environmental condition. Previously called instinct.

fixed-interval schedule In conditioning, a schedule in which a reinforcer occurs following a subject's first response after a fixed interval of time.

fixed ratio schedule In conditioning, a schedule in which a reinforcer occurd only after a fixed number of responses by the subject.

flash bulb memories Vivid recollections, usually in great deal, of dramatic or emotionally charged incidents, which are encoded effortlessly and may last for long periods of time.

flavor What we experience when we combine the sensations of taste and smell.

fMRI *See* functional magnetic resonance imaging.

foot-in-the-door technique A method of persuasion that relies on the increased probability of compliance to a second request if a person complies with a small first request.

forebrain The largest part of the brain, consisting of left and right hemispheres, which are connected by a wide band of fibers, the corpus callosum. The hemispheres are responsible for a vast array of responses, including learning and memory, speaking and language, emotional responses, experiencing sensations, initiating voluntary movements, planning, and making decisions.

forgetting Inability to retrieve, recall, or recognize information that was stored or is still stored in long-term memory.

forgetting curve A graph measuring the amount of previously learned information that subjects can recall or recognize across time.

formal operations stage Piaget's fourth cognitive stage, lasting from about 12 years of age through adulthood. During this stage, adolescents and adults develop the ability to think about abstract or hypothetical concepts, to consider an issue from another person's viewpoint, and to solve cognitive problems in a logical manner.

fragile X syndrome A defect in the X chromosome that can result in physical changes such as a relatively large head with protruding ears, as well as mild to profound levels of mental retardation.

fraternal twins Twins who develop from separate eggs and share 50% of their genes.

free association A Freudian technique in which clients are encouraged to talk about any thoughts or images that enter their heads; the assumption is that this kind of free-flowing, uncensored talking will provide clues to unconscious material.

frequency distribution The range of scores we get and the frequency of each one, when we measure a sample of people (or objects) regarding some trait.

frequency theory In pitch perception, the idea that, for low-frequency sound waves (1,000 cycles or less), the rate at which nerve impulses reach the brain determines how low a sound is. A rate of 50 impulses per second is interpreted as a lower sound than a rate of 200 impulses per second.

Freud's psychodynamic theory of personality A personality theory that emphasizes the importance of early childhood experiences; repressed thoughts that we cannot voluntarily access; and the conflicts between conscious and unconscious forces that influence our thoughts and behaviors. *See also* psychoanalytic approach.

Freud's theory of dreams A theory that says we have a "censor" that protects us from realizing threatening and unconscious desires or wishes, especially those involving sex or aggression, by transforming them into harmless symbols that appear in our dreams and do not disturb our sleep or conscious thoughts.

Freud's theory of the unconscious The idea that, when faced with very threatening—especially sexual or aggressive—wishes or desires, we automatically defend our self-esteem by placing these psychologically dangerous thoughts into a mental place, the unconscious, that is sealed off from voluntary recall.

Freudian slips Mistakes or slips of the tongue that we make in everyday speech; such mistakes are thought to reflect unconscious thoughts or wishes.

frontal lobe An area in the front part of the brain that includes a huge area of cortex. The frontal lobe is involved in many functions: performing voluntary motor movements, interpreting and performing emotional behaviors, behaving normally in social situations, maintaining a healthy personality, paying attention to things in the environment, making decisions, and carrying out plans.

frontal lobotomy A surgical procedure in which about one-third of the front part of the frontal lobe is separated from the rest of the brain.

frustration The feeling that results when our attempts to reach some goal are blocked.

frustration-aggression hypothesis The idea that, when our goals are blocked, we become frustrated and respond with anger and aggression. *See also* modified frustration-aggression hypothesis.

functional fixedness A mental set characterized by the inability to see an object as having a function different from its usual one.

functional magnetic resonance imaging (fMRI) A brain scan that measures the activity of specific neurons that are functioning during cognitive tasks such as thinking, listening, or reading.

functionalism An early school of psychological thought that emphasized the function rather than the structure of consciousness and was interested in how our minds adapt to our changing environment.

fundamental attribution error Our tendency, when we look for causes of a person's behavior, to focus on the person's disposition or personality traits and overlook how the situation influenced the person's behavior.

galvanic skin response Changes in sweating of the fingers (or palms) that accompany emotional experiences and are independent of perspiration under normal temperatures.

Ganzfeld procedure A controlled method for eliminating trickery, error, and bias while testing telepathic communication between two people.

Gardner's multiple-intelligence theory The idea that, instead of one kind of general intelligence, there are at least seven different kinds: verbal intelligence, musical intelligence, logical-mathematical intelligence, spatial intelligence, body movement intelligence, intelligence to understand oneself, and intelligence to understand others.

GAS *See* general adaptation syndrome.

gate control theory The idea that nonpainful nerve impulses compete with pain impulses as they enter the spinal cord, creating a neural gate through which only the nonpainful impulses pass; the pain impulses do not reach the brain. Thus, feelings of pain may be reduced by rubbing an injured area or becoming absorbed in other activities.

gender identity The individual's subjective experience and feelings of being either a male or a female; formerly called sexual identity.

gender identity disorder Commonly referred to as transsexualism, it is an individual's strong desire or feeling of wanting to be the opposite sex, discomfort with being one's assigned sex, and the wish to live as a member of the other sex.

gender roles Traditional or stereotypic behaviors, attitudes, and personality traits that parents, peers, and society designate as masculine or feminine. Gender roles affect how we think and behave; formerly called sex roles.

gender schemas Sets of information and rules organized around how either a male or a female should think and behave.

gene A specific segment on the strand of DNA (the chromosome) that contains instructions for making proteins, the chemical building blocks from which all the parts of the brain and body are constructed.

general adaptation syndrome (GAS) According to Selye, a series of three stages—alarm, resistance, and exhaustion—that correspond to the three different reactions of the body to stressful situations and that gradually increase the chances of developing psychosomatic symptoms.

generalization In classical conditioning, the tendency for a stimulus that is similar to the original conditioned stimulus to elicit a response that is similar to the conditioned response. Usually, the more similar the new stimulus is to the original conditioned stimulus, the larger will be the conditioned response. In operant conditioning, the situation in which an animal or a person emits the same response to similar stimuli.

generalized anxiety disorder A psychological disorder primarily characterized by excessive and/or unrealistic worry or feelings of general apprehension about events or activities. These anxious feelings occur on a majority of days for a period of at least six months.

genetic factors (in mental disorders) Unlearned or inherited tendencies that influence how a person thinks, behaves, and feels.

genetic hunger factors Inherited instructions found in our genes that influence our hunger; these instructions may determine our number of fat cells or our metabolic rate of burning off

the body's fuel, for example, and push us toward being normal, overweight, or underweight.

genetic marker An identifiable gene or number of genes or a specific segment of a chromosome that is directly linked to some behavioral, physiological, or neurological trait or disease.

genetic sex factors Inherited instructions for the development of sexual organs, the secretion of sex hormones, and the wiring of the neural circuits that control sexual reflexes.

genital cutting The practice of cutting away the female's external genitalia, usually including her clitoris and surrounding skin (labia minora). The remaining edges are sewn together, which leaves only a small opening for urination and menstruation.

genital stage Freud's fifth, and final, psychosexual stage, lasting from puberty through adulthood. In this stage, the individual has renewed sexual desires that he or she seeks to fulfill through relationships with other people.

germinal stage The first stage of prenatal development, lasting two weeks from the moment of conception.

Gestalt approach An older theoretical approach that emphasized the idea that perception is more than the sum of its parts. In contrast to the structuralists, the Gestalt psychologists believed that perceptions are formed by the brain on the basis of a set of rules that specify how individual elements may be organized to form a meaningful pattern—that is, a perception.

gifted A term applied to an individual (usually to a child) who has above-average intelligence as well as some superior talent or skill. A moderately gifted child is usually defined by an IQ score between 130 and 150; a profoundly gifted child has an IQ score of 180 or above.

glial cells Cells in the nervous system that have at least three functions: They provide scaffolding to guide the growth of developing neurons and support mature neurons; they wrap themselves around neurons and form a kind of insulation to prevent interference from other electrical signals; and they release chemicals that influence a neuron's growth and function.

gonads Glands—the ovaries in females and the testes in males—that produce hormones to regulate sexual development, ovulation or sperm production, and the growth of sex organs. They are part of the endocrine system.

grammar A set of rules for combining words into phrases and sentences to express an infinite number of thoughts that can be understood by others.

group A collection of two or more people who interact and share some common attribute or purpose. A group also influences how its members think and behave.

group cohesion Group togetherness, which is determined by how much group members perceive that they share common attributes.

group norms Formal or informal rules about how group members should behave.

group polarization The phenomenon in which group discussion reinforces the majority's point of view and shifts that view to a more extreme position.

groupthink Poor group decision making that occurs when group discussions emphasize cohesion and agreement rather than critical thinking and the best possible outcome.

growth needs According to Maslow, higher-level needs that are not essential to existence, such as the desire for truth, goodness, beauty, and justice.

hair cells The auditory receptors. These miniature hair-shaped cells rise from the basilar membrane in the cochlea.

hallucinations Sensory experiences without any stimulation from the environment. Common symptoms of schizophrenia, hallucinations may be auditory, such as hearing voices, or they may include distorted perceptions, such as feeling that parts of one's body are too small or too large.

hallucinogens Psychoactive drugs that can produce hallucinations—strange perceptual, sensory, and cognitive experiences that the person sees or hears but knows are not occurring in reality. Such unreal experiences are called hallucinations.

happiness A mental state that includes three components: feeling positive emotions, being satisfied with one's life, and not experiencing negative emotions.

hardiness A combination of three personality traits—control, commitment, and challenge—that protect or buffer us from the potentially harmful effects of stressful situations and reduce our chances of developing psychosomatic illness.

harm/loss appraisal Our conclusion that we have already sustained some damage or injury in a particular situation.

hassles Small, irritating, frustrating events that we face daily and that we usually appraise as stressful experiences.

helping *See* prosocial behavior.

heritability A statistical measure that estimates the amount or proportion of some ability, characteristic, or trait that can be attributed to genetic factors.

heterosexual orientation A pattern of sexual arousal by persons of the opposite sex.

heuristics Rules of thumb that reduce the number of operations or allow us to take shortcuts in solving problems.

hierarchy of needs *See* Maslow's hierarchy of needs.

high need for achievement A tendency to persist longer at tasks; show better performance on tasks, activities, or exams; set challenging but realistic goals; compete with others to win; and be attracted to careers that require initiative.

hindbrain An area at the base of the brain that is involved in sleeping, waking, coordinating body

Glossary

movements, and regulating vital reflexes (heart rate, blood pressure, and respiration).

hippocampus A curved structure within the temporal lobe that is involved in transforming many kinds of fleeting memories into permanent storage. It forms part of the limbic system.

histrionic personality disorder A disorder characterized by excessive emotionality and attention seeking. It is found in 2% of the population.

HIV positive Having HIV antibodies, which implies infection by the human immunodeficiency virus (HIV).

holistic view The idea, emphasized in humanistic theories, that a person's personality is more than the sum of its individual parts; instead, the individual parts form a unique and total entity that functions as a unit.

homeostasis The tendency of the sympathetic and parasympathetic divisions of the autonomic nervous system to work together to maintain the body's level of arousal in balance for optimum functioning.

homosexual orientation A pattern of sexual arousal by persons of the same sex.

humanistic approach A psychological viewpoint emphasizing that each individual has great freedom in directing his or her future, considerable capacity for achieving personal growth, intrinsic worth, and enormous potential for self-fulfillment.

humanistic theories *See* humanistic approach.

hypnosis A situation or set of procedures in which a researcher, clinician, or hypnotist suggests to another person that he or she will experience various changes in sensation, perception, cognition, or control over motor behaviors.

hypnotic analgesia Reduction in pain reported by clients after undergoing hypnosis and receiving suggestions that reduced anxiety and promoted relaxation.

hypnotic induction Various methods of inducing hypnosis, such as asking subjects to close their eyes and go to sleep, having them fix their attention on an object (for example, a watch), and instructing them to go into deep relaxation.

hypothalamus A structure of the limbic system that is located near the bottom middle of the brain and regulates many motivational and emotional behaviors. It controls much of the endocrine system by regulating the pituitary gland.

hypothesis An educated guess about some phenomenon, stated in precise, concrete language so as to rule out any confusion or error in the meaning of its terms.

iconic memory A form of sensory memory that holds visual information for about a quarter of a second or more. (The word *icon* means "image.")

id Freud's first division of the mind, which contains two biological drives—sex and aggression—that are the source of all psychic or mental energy. The id's goal is to pursue pleasure and satisfy the biological drives.

ideal self According to Rogers, the self that is based on our hopes and wishes and reflects how we would like to see ourselves; its complement is the real self.

ideal weight *See* optimal weight.

identical twins Twins who develop from a single egg and thus have exactly the same genes.

identity How we describe ourselves, including our values, goals, traits, interests, and motivations.

illusion Perception of an image so distorted that, in reality, it cannot and does not exist. An illusion is created when space, size, and depth cues are manipulated so that our brains can no longer correctly interpret them.

imagined perception In hypnosis, the subject's willingness, at the hypnotist's suggestion, to respond to nonexistent stimuli and imaginary perceptions. It can also include bizarre behaviors, such as imitating Elvis Presley in public.

immune system The body's defense and surveillance network of cells and chemicals that fight off bacteria, viruses, and other foreign or toxic substances.

implicit or nondeclarative memory Mental and emotional processes that we are unaware of but that bias and influence our conscious feelings, thoughts, and behaviors. *See* procedural memory.

impossible figure A perceptual experience in which a drawing seems to defy basic geometric laws.

imprinting Inherited tendencies or responses that are displayed by newborn animals when they encounter certain stimuli in their environment.

incentives Environmental factors, such as external stimuli, reinforcers, or rewards, that motivate our behavior.

independent variable In an experiment, a treatment or something else that the researcher controls or manipulates.

inductive reasoning Reasoning from particulars to the general; using particular experiences or observations to draw a broader conclusion.

inferential statistics A set of procedures for determining what conclusions can be legitimately inferred from a set of data.

informational influence theory The theory that we use the reactions of others to judge the seriousness of the situation.

inhibited/fearful children Kagan's term for children who show reluctance, anxiety, or fear (measured by motor activity, fretting, or crying) when approaching a strange child, exploring novel objects, playing with a peer, or talking to an unfamiliar adult. In addition, inhibited children show increased physiological arousal to novel or strange situations.

inhibited female orgasm A persistent delay or absence of orgasm after becoming aroused and excited.

innate language factors Genetically programmed physiological and neurological features of the brain and vocal apparatus that facilitate our making speech sounds and learning language skills.

insanity According to the legal definition, not knowing the difference between right and wrong.

insecure attachment An emotional bond characteristic of infants who avoid, or show ambivalence toward, their parents.

insight A mental process marked by the sudden and unexpected solution to a problem: a phenomenon often called the "ah-ha!" experience.

insight therapy An approach in which the therapist and client talk about the client's symptoms and problems, with the goal of identifying the cause of the problem. Once the client has an insight into the cause of the problem, possible solutions can be discussed with the therapist.

insomnia Difficulties in going to sleep or in staying asleep through the night. Associated daytime complaints include fatigue, impairment of concentration, memory difficulty, and lack of well-being. About 20–40% of adult Americans report bouts of insomnia.

instincts According to McDougal (1908), innate tendencies or biological forces that determine behavior; now used as a synonym for fixed action pattern.

intelligence quotient (IQ) A measure of intelligence computed by dividing a child's mental age, as measured in an intelligence test, by the child's chronological age and multiplying the result by 100.

interactive model of sexual orientation The theory that genetic and biological factors, such as genetic instructions and prenatal hormones, interact with psychological factors, such as the individual's attitudes, personality traits, and behaviors, to influence the development of sexual orientation.

interference The forgetting process in which the recall of some particular memory is blocked or prevented by new information that overwrites or interferes with it. *See also* proactive interference and retroactive interference.

internal attributions Explanations of behavior on the basis of the internal characteristics (or dispositions) of the person performing the behavior. Also referred to as dispositional attributions.

interneuron A relatively short neuron whose primary task is to make connections between other neurons.

interposition In three-dimensional vision, a monocular depth cue that comes into play when objects overlap. The overlapping object appears closer, and the object that is overlapped appears to be farther away.

interpreting function The role played by our attitudes in providing convenient guidelines by means of which we can interpret and categorize objects and events and decide whether to approach or avoid them.

interval timing clock A sort of timing device, located in the basal ganglia of the brain, that gauges the passage of seconds, minutes, or hours and helps creatures know when to start or stop doing some activity.

intervention program A program for disadvantaged children that creates an environment offering increased opportunities for intellectual, social, and personality-emotional development while ensuring good physical health.

interview A technique for obtaining information by asking questions, ranging from open-ended to highly structured, about a subject's behaviors and attitudes, usually in a one-on-one situation.

intestines The body organ that responds to the presence of food, especially fats, by secreting a hormone called CCK (cholecystokinin), which inhibits eating.

intimacy In Sternberg's triangular theory of love, the component of love associated with feeling close and connected to someone; it develops through sharing and communicating.

intrinsic motivation Engaging in certain activities or behaviors because they are personally rewarding or because we are fulfilling our beliefs or expectations.

introspection A method of exploring conscious mental processes adopted by the structuralists; subjects were asked to look inward and report their sensations and perceptions.

intrusive thoughts Thoughts that we repeatedly experience, that are usually unwanted or disruptive, and that are very difficult to stop or eliminate.

Inuit beliefs about dreams The Inuit, or Eskimo people, like other isolated indigenous people, believe that dreams are ways to enter the spiritual world, where the souls of departed animals, supernaturals, and relatives are made known.

ions Electrically charged chemical particles, which obey the rule that opposite charges attract and like charges repel.

IQ *See* intelligence quotient.

iris A circular muscle that surrounds the pupil and controls the amount of light that enters the eye. In dim light, the iris relaxes, allowing more light to enter—the pupil dilates; in bright light, the iris constricts, allowing less light to enter—the pupil constricts. The iris muscle contains the pigment that gives the eye its characteristic color.

James-Lange theory The idea that our brains interpret specific physiological changes as feelings or emotions and that there is a different physiological pattern underlying each emotion.

jet lag A condition in which travelers' internal circadian rhythm is out of step, or synchrony, with the external clock time at their new location. They experience fatigue, disorientation, lack of concentration, and reduced cognitive skills. It takes about one day to reset the circadian clock for each hour of time change.

just noticeable difference (JND) The smallest increase or decrease in the intensity of a stimulus that a person can manage to detect.

labeling A process of identifying differences among individuals and placing them into specific categories, which may have either positive or negative associations.

laboratory experiment A technique to gather information by studying behavior in a controlled environment that permits the careful manipulation of some treatment and the measurement of the treatment's effects on behavior.

laboratory setting An environment in which individuals may be studied under systematic and controlled conditions, thus eliminating many of the real-world influences.

language A form of communication in which we learn and use complex rules to form and manipulate symbols (words or gestures) that are used to generate an endless number of meaningful sentences.

language stages Four different periods in a child's acquisition of language and grammar—babbling, single words, two-word combinations, and sentences. In each subsequent stage, a child displays new and more complex language skills.

latency stage The fourth of Freud's psychosexual stages, lasting from the age of about 6 to puberty. In this stage, the child represses sexual thoughts and engages in nonsexual activities, such as developing social and intellectual skills.

lateral hypothalamus A group of brain cells that regulates hunger by creating feelings of being hungry.

law of effect The principle that behaviors followed by positive (pleasurable) consequences are strengthened (and thus will likely occur in the future), while behaviors followed by negative consequences are weakened.

learning A relatively permanent change in behavior (both unobservable mental events and observable responses) associated with specific stimuli and/or responses that change as a result of experience.

learning-performance distinction The idea that learning may occur but may not always be measured by, or immediately evident in, performance.

lens A transparent, oval structure in the eye whose curved surface functions to bend and focus light waves into an even narrower beam. The lens is attached to muscles that adjust the curve of the lens, which, in turn, adjusts the focusing.

levels-of-processing theory The theory that memory depends on how well information is encoded in the mind. Information is encoded at a shallow level if we simply pay attention to its basic features but is encoded at a deep level if we form new associations with existing information. According to the theory, poor memory corresponds to information encoded at a shallow level, and good memory to information encoded at deep levels.

lie detector tests *See* polygraph tests.

light and shadow A monocular depth cue; brightly lit objects appear closer, while objects in shadows appear farther away.

light therapy The use of bright, artificial light to reset circadian rhythms and so combat the insomnia and drowsiness that plague shift workers and jet-lag sufferers; it is also used to help people with sleeping disorders in which the body fails to stay in time with the external environment.

limbic system A group of about half a dozen interconnected structures in the core of the forebrain that are involved in many motivational behaviors, such as obtaining food, drink, and sex; organizing emotional behaviors such as fear, anger, and aggression; and storing memories. It is sometimes referred to as our primitive, or animal, brain because the same structures are found in the brains of animals that are evolutionarily very old.

linear perspective In three-dimensional vision, a monocular depth cue associated with the convergence of parallel lines in the far distance.

linguistic relativity *See* theory of linguistic relativity.

liver The body organ that monitors nutrients, especially the level of glucose (sugar) in the blood. When the level of glucose falls, the liver signals hunger; when the level of glucose rises, the liver signals fullness.

lobes The four areas into which the brain's cortex is divided.

locus of control Our beliefs concerning how much control we have over situations or rewards. For each of us, these beliefs lie somewhere on a continuum between internal and external locus of control. We have an internal locus of control if we believe that we have control over situations and rewards and an external locus of control if we believe that we do not have control over situations and rewards and that events outside ourselves (fate) determine what happens.

long-term memory The process that can store almost unlimited amounts of information over long periods of time.

long-term potentiation (LTP) The increased sensitivity of a neuron to stimulation after it has been repeatedly stimulated. Neuroscientists believe that the LTP process may be the basis for learning and memory in animals and humans.

longitudinal method A research design in which the same group of individuals is studied repeatedly at many different points in time.

loudness Our subjective experience of a sound's intensity, which is determined by the height (amplitude) of the sound wave. The brain calculates loudness from the rate of nerve impulses that arrive in the auditory nerve.

LSD (*d*-lysergic acid diethylamide) A very potent hallucinogen. Very small doses can produce experiences such as visual hallucinations, perceptual distortions, increased sensory awareness, and emotional responses that may last 8–10 hours.

LTP *See* long-term potentiation.

magnetic resonance imaging (MRI scan) A technique for studying the structure of the living brain. Nonharmful radio frequencies are passed through the brain, and a computer measures

Glossary

their interaction with brain cells and transforms this interaction into an incredibly detailed image of the brain (or body).

maintenance rehearsal The practice of intentionally repeating or rehearsing information (rather than forming any new associations) so that it remains longer in short-term memory.

major depressive disorder A mood disorder marked by at least two weeks of continually being in a bad mood, having no interest in anything, and getting no pleasure from activities. In addition, a person must have at least four of the following symptoms: problems with eating, sleeping, thinking, concentrating, or making decisions; lacking energy, thinking about suicide, and feeling worthless or guilty. Also called unipolar depression.

major life events Potentially disturbing, troubling, or disruptive situations, both positive and negative, that we appraise as having a significant impact on our lives.

maladaptive behavior approach In defining abnormality, the idea that a behavior is psychologically damaging or abnormal if it interferes with the individual's ability to function in one's personal life or in society.

male hypothalamus Because of neural programming in the womb, the hypothalamus, a structure in the brain that controls the endocrine system, functions differently in the male and female. The male hypothalamus triggers a continuous release of androgens, such as testosterone, from the testes. The increased androgen level is responsible for male secondary sexual characteristics, such as facial and pubic hair, muscle growth, and lowered voice.

male secondary sexual characteristics Sexual characteristics whose development in the male is triggered by the increased secretion of testosterone during puberty; they include the growth of pubic hair, muscle development, and a change (deepening) of the voice.

marijuana A psychoactive drug whose primary active ingredient is THC (tetrahydrocannabinol), which is found in the leaves of the cannabis plant. Low doses produce mild euphoria; moderate doses produce perceptual and time distortions; and high doses may produce hallucinations, delusions, and distortions of body image.

Maslow's hierarchy of needs An ascending order, or hierarchy, in which biological needs are placed at the bottom and social needs at the top. As needs at lower levels are met, we advance to the next higher level. This hierarchy indicates that we satisfy our biological needs before we satisfy our social needs.

mass hysteria A condition experienced by a group of people who, through suggestion, observation, or other psychological processes, develop similar fears, delusions, abnormal behaviors, and in some cases, similar physical symptoms.

maturation The succession of developmental changes that are genetically or biologically programmed rather than acquired through learning or life experiences.

MDMA Also called ecstasy, this drug resembles both mescaline (a hallucinogen) and amphetamine (a stimulant). It heightens sensations, gives a euphoric rush, raises body temperature, and creates feelings of warmth and empathy.

mean The arithmetic average of all the individual measurements in a distribution.

measure of variability An indication of how much scores in a distribution vary from one another.

median The score above and below which half the scores in the distribution fall.

medical therapy Any approach that uses psychoactive drugs, such as tranquilizers and neuroleptics, to treat mental disorders by changing biological factors, such as the levels of neurotransmitters in the brain.

medulla An area in the hindbrain, located at the top of the spinal cord, that includes a group of cells that control vital reflexes, such as respiration, heart rate, and blood pressure.

melatonin A hormone secreted by the pineal gland, an oval group of cells in the center of the human brain. Melatonin secretion, controlled by the suprachiasmatic nucleus, increases with darkness and decreases with light; thus, it plays a role in the regulation of circadian rhythms and in promoting sleep.

memory The ability to retain information over time through the processes of encoding, storing, and retrieving. Memories are not copies but representations of the world that vary in accuracy and are subject to error and bias.

menarche The first menstrual period; it is a signal that ovulation may have occurred and that the girl may have the potential to conceive and bear a child.

Meniere's disease Sudden attacks of dizziness, nausea, vomiting, and head-splitting buzzing sounds that result from a malfunction of the semicircular canals in the vestibular system.

menopause A gradual stoppage in the secretion of the major female hormone (estrogen). This process, which occurs in women at about age 50 (range 35–60), results in the cessation of ovulation and the menstrual cycle.

mental age The estimation of a child's intellectual progress, which is calculated by comparing the child's score on an intelligence test to the scores of average children of the same age.

mental disorder A prolonged or recurring problem that seriously interferes with an individual's ability to live a satisfying personal life and function adequately in society.

mental retardation Substantial limitation in present functioning, characterized by significantly subaverage intellectual functioning along with related limitations in two of ten areas, including communication, self-care, home living, social skills, and safety.

mescaline The active ingredient in the peyote cactus. At high doses, mescaline produces physiological arousal and very clear, colorful, and vivid visual hallucinations. It primarily increases the activity of the neurotransmitters norepinephrine and dopamine. Mescaline does not impair the intellect or cloud consciousness.

meta-analysis A powerful statistical procedure that compares the results of dozens or hundreds of studies to determine the effectiveness of some variable or treatment examined in those studies (for example, a type of therapy).

metabolic rate The efficiency with which the body breaks food down into energy and the speed with which the body burns off that fuel. An inherited trait, it can be raised by exercise or smoking.

methamphetamine (D-methamphetamine) A stimulant similar to amphetamine in both its chemical makeup and its physical and psychological effects. It causes marked increases in blood pressure and heart rate and feelings of enhanced mood, alertness, and energy. Methamphetamine, whose street names are crystal and ice, produces an almost instantaneous high when smoked and is highly addictive.

method of loci A mnemonic device, or encoding technique, that improves encoding by creating visual associations between memorized places and new items to be memorized.

midbrain The part of the brain that contains the reward/pleasure center, which is stimulated by food, sex, money, music, attractive faces, and some drugs (cocaine); contains areas for visual and auditory reflexes, such as automatically turning your head toward a noise; and holds the reticular formation, which arouses the forebrain so that it is ready to process information from the senses.

middle ear A bony cavity that is sealed at each end by a membrane. The two membranes are connected by three small bones, collectively called ossicles. Because of their shapes, these bones are referred to as the hammer, anvil, and stirrup. The ossicles act like levers that greatly amplify vibrations from the eardrum and transmit them to the oval window and inner ear.

mind-body connection The ability of our thoughts, beliefs, and emotions to produce physiological changes that may be either beneficial or detrimental to our health and well-being.

mind-body question The debate about how complex mental activities, such as feeling, thinking, learning, imagining, and dreaming, can be generated by the brain's physical membranes, fluids, and chemicals.

mind-body therapy An approach to healing based on the finding that thoughts and emotions can change physiological and immune responses. It attempts to increase physical and mental well-being by means of mental strategies, such as relaxation, meditation, and biofeedback, as well as social support groups.

Minnesota Multiphasic Personality Inventory-2 (MMPI-2) A true-false self-report questionnaire that consists of 567 statements describing a wide range of normal and abnormal behaviors. The purpose of MMPI-2 is to help distinguish normal from abnormal groups.

mnemonic methods Very effective ways to improve encoding and create better retrieval cues by forming vivid associations or images, which facilitate recall and decrease forgetting.

mode The most frequent measurement in a distribution.

modified frustration-aggression hypothesis The idea that although frustration may lead to aggression, a number of situational and cognitive factors may override the aggressive response.

monochromats Individuals who have total color blindness; their world looks like a black-and-white movie. This kind of color blindness is rare and results from individuals having only rods or only one kind of functioning cone instead of three.

monocular depth cues In three-dimensional vision, depth cues produced by signals from a single eye. They are most commonly determined by the way objects are arranged in the environment.

mood disorder A prolonged and disturbed emotional state that affects almost all of a person's thoughts and behaviors.

moral therapy The belief that mental patients could be helped to function better by providing humane treatment in a relaxed and decent environment. This approach was fundamental to the reform movement of the early 1800s.

morning persons People who prefer to get up early, go to bed early, and engage in morning activities. *See* evening persons.

morphemes The smallest meaningful combination of sounds in a language.

morphology A system that we use to group phonemes—consonants and vowels—into meaningful combinations of sounds and words.

motion parallax In three-dimensional vision, a monocular depth cue based on the speed of moving objects: Objects that appear to be moving at high speed are interpreted as closer to us than those moving more slowly.

motion sickness Feelings of nausea and dizziness experienced in a moving vehicle when information from the vestibular system (that your head is bouncing around) conflicts with that reported by your eyes (that objects in the distance look fairly steady).

motivation Various physiological and psychological factors that cause us to act in a specific way at a particular time.

motor cortex A narrow strip of cortex that is located on the back edge of the frontal lobe and extends down its side. It is involved in the initiation of all voluntary movements. The right motor cortex controls muscles on the left side of the body and vice versa.

motor development The stages of motor skills that all infants pass through as they acquire the muscular control necessary for making coordinated movements.

motor neurons *See* efferent neurons.

MRI scan *See* magnetic resonance imaging.

multiple-intelligence theory *See* Gardner's multiple-intelligence theory.

myelin sheath A tubelike structure of fatty material that wraps around and insulates an axon, preventing interference from electrical signals generated in adjacent axons.

narcolepsy A relatively rare, chronic disorder marked by excessive sleepiness, usually in the form of sleep attacks or short periods of sleep throughout the day. The sleep attacks are accompanied by brief periods of REM sleep and loss of muscle control (cataplexy), which may be triggered by big emotional changes.

naturalistic setting A relatively normal environment in which researchers gather information by observing individuals' behaviors without attempting to change or control the situation.

nature-nurture question The debate concerning the relative contribution of genetic factors (nature) and environmental factors (nurture) to a person's intelligence as well as to his or her biological, emotional, cognitive, personal, and social development.

nearsightedness A visual acuity problem that may result when the eyeball is too long, so that objects are focused at a point slightly in front of the retina. The result is that near objects are clear, but distant objects appear blurry.

negative punishment Removal of a reinforcing stimulus (for example, taking away a child's allowance) after a response. This removal decreases the chances that the response will recur.

negative reinforcement The occurrence of an operant response that either stops or removes an aversive stimulus. Removal of the aversive stimulus increases the likelihood that the response will occur again.

negative symptoms of schizophrenia Symptoms that reflect a decrease in or loss of normal functions: decreased range and intensity of emotions, decreased ability to express thoughts, and decreased initiative to engage in goal-directed behaviors.

neglect syndrome The failure of a patient to see objects or parts of the body on the side opposite the brain damage when the damage is to an association area, usually in occipital and parietal lobes, and usually in the right hemisphere.

nerve impulse A series of separate action potentials that take place, segment by segment, as they move down the length of an axon.

nerves Stringlike bundles of axons and dendrites that are held together by connective tissue. Nerves in the peripheral nervous system have the ability to regrow, regenerate, or reattach if severed or damaged. They carry information from the senses, skin, muscles, and the body's organs to and from the spinal cord.

network hierarchy In the network theory of memory, the arrangement of nodes or categories so that concrete ideas are at the bottom of the hierarchy and are connected to more abstract ideas located above them. The most abstract ideas are at the top of the hierarchy.

network theory The theory that we store related ideas in separate memory categories, or files, called nodes. As we make associations between information, we create links among thousands of nodes, which make up a gigantic interconnected network for storing and retrieving information.

neural assemblies Groups of interconnected neurons whose activation allows information or stimuli to be recognized and held briefly and temporarily in short-term memory.

neural deafness Deafness caused by damage to the auditory receptors (hair cells), which prevents the triggering of impulses, or by damage to the auditory nerve, which prevents impulses from reaching the brain. *See also* cochlear implant.

neuroleptic drugs Drugs that change the levels of neurotransmitters in the brain. They are used to treat serious mental disorders, such as schizophrenia. Also called antipsychotic drugs.

neurons Cells that have specialized extensions for the reception and transmission of electrical signals.

neuroses According to Freud, maladaptive thoughts and actions that arise from some unconscious thought or conflict and indicate feelings of anxiety.

neurotransmitters About a dozen different chemicals that are made by neurons and then used for communication between neurons during the performance of mental or physical activities.

neutral stimulus A stimulus that causes a sensory response, such as being seen, heard, or smelled, but does not produce the reflex being tested.

nicotine A stimulant; it first produces arousal but then produces calming. Present in cigarettes, nicotine increases both heart rate and blood pressure. It improves attention and concentration, may improve short-term memory, but may interfere with complex processing. Regular use of nicotine causes addiction, and stopping leads to withdrawal symptoms.

night terrors Sleep disruptions in children that occur during stage 3 or stage 4 (delta) sleep. They usually start with a piercing scream, after which the child wakes suddenly in a fearful state, with rapid breathing and increased heart rate. The next morning, the child has no memory of the frightening experience.

nightmares Dreams that contain frightening and anxiety-producing images. They usually involve great danger—being attacked, injured, or pursued. Upon awakening, the dreamer can usually describe the nightmare in considerable detail. Nightmares occur during REM sleep.

nodes Memory files that contain related information organized around a specific topic or category.

Glossary

nonbenzodiazepines Drugs, such as Ambien and Sonata, that are becoming popular sleeping pills because they are rapid acting, are of short duration, and have few cognitive side effects.

noncompliance In children, refusal to follow directions, carry out a request, or obey a command given by a parent or caregiver. Noncompliance is one of the most common complaints of parents in general and the most frequent problem of parents who bring their children to clinics for treatment of behavioral problems.

nonintellectual factors Factors such as attitude, experience, and emotional functions that may help or hinder an individual's performance on intelligence tests.

non-REM sleep Stages 1–4 of sleep, in which rapid eye movement does not occur; it makes up about 80% of sleep time.

normal aging A gradual and natural slowing of our physical and psychological processes from middle through late adulthood.

normal curve A graph of a frequency distribution in which the curve tapers off equally on either side of a central high point—in other words, a graph of a normal distribution.

normal distribution A bell-shaped frequency distribution curve. The scores are arranged symmetrically so that the vast majority fall in the middle range, with fewer scores near the two extreme ends of the curve.

obedience Behavior performed in response to an order given by someone in a position of authority.

obesity A body weight 30% or more above the ideal value.

object permanence The understanding that objects or events continue to exist even if they can no longer be heard, touched, or seen.

objective personality tests Tests consisting of specific written statements that require individuals to indicate—for example, by checking "true" or "false"—whether the statements do or do not apply to them; also called self-report questionnaires.

observational learning *See* social cognitive learning.

obsessive-compulsive disorder An anxiety disorder consisting of obsessions, which are persistent, recurring, irrational thoughts, impulses, or images that a person is unable to control and that interfere with normal functioning; and compulsions, which are irresistible impulses to perform over and over some senseless behavior or ritual (hand washing, checking things, counting, putting things in order).

obsessive-compulsive personality disorder A personality disorder characterized by an intense interest in being orderly, achieving perfection, and having control. It is found in 4% of the population.

occipital lobe A region at the very back of the brain that is involved in processing visual information, which includes seeing colors and perceiving and recognizing objects, animals, and people.

Oedipus complex According to Freud, a process in which a child competes with the parent of the same sex for the affections and pleasures of the parent of the opposite sex; called the Electra complex in girls.

olfaction The sense of smell. Its stimuli are various chemicals that are carried by the air.

olfactory cells The receptors for smell, located in the uppermost part of the nasal passages. As volatile molecules dissolve in the mucus covering the cells, they stimulate the receptors, which send nerve impulses to the brain.

operant conditioning A kind of learning in which the consequences—reward or punishment—that follow some behavior increase or decrease the likelihood of that behavior's occurrence in the future. Also called instrumental conditioning.

operant response A response that can be modified by its consequences. Operant responses offer a way of dividing ongoing behavior into meaningful and measurable units.

opiates Drugs derived from the opium poppy, including opium and morphine, which is chemically altered to make heroin. All opiates have three primary effects: analgesia (pain reduction); opiate euphoria, which is often described as a pleasurable state between waking and sleeping; and constipation. Continued use of opiates results in tolerance, physical addiction, and an intense craving for the drug.

opponent-process theory A theory of color vision suggesting that ganglion cells in the retina and cells in the thalamus respond to two pairs of colors: red-green and blue-yellow. When these cells are excited, they respond to one color of the pair; when inhibited, they respond to the complementary pair.

optimal weight The body weight resulting from an almost perfect balance between how much food an organism eats and how much it needs to meet its body's energy needs; also called ideal weight.

optimism A relatively stable personality trait that leads one to believe and expect that good things will happen. It is one of the personality factors associated with lower stress levels and fewer chances of developing psychosomatic symptoms. *See* pessimism.

oral stage Freud's first psychosexual stage, which lasts for the first 18 months of life. In this stage, the infant's pleasure seeking is centered on the mouth.

organic factors Medical conditions or drug or medication problems that lead to sexual difficulties.

organic retardation Mental retardation that results from genetic problems or brain damage.

ossicles *See* middle ear.

outer ear Three structures important to the hearing process: the external ear, auditory canal, and tympanic membrane (eardrum).

overgeneralization A common error during language acquisition, in which children apply a grammatical rule to cases where it should not be used.

overweight A body weight 20% over the ideal value.

ovulation The release of an ovum or egg cell from a woman's ovaries.

pain Sensations caused by various stimuli that activate the pain receptors, free nerve endings. Nerve impulses from these pain receptors travel to the somatosensory and limbic areas of the brain, where they are transformed into pain sensations. Pain is essential for survival: It warns us to avoid or escape dangerous situations or stimuli and makes us take time to recover from injury.

pancreas An organ that regulates the level of sugar in the bloodstream by secreting insulin. It forms part of the endocrine system.

panic attack A period of intense fear or discomfort in which four or more of the following symptoms are present: pounding heart, sweating, trembling, shortness of breath, feelings of choking, chest pain, nausea, feeling dizzy, and fear of losing control or dying.

panic disorder A mental disorder characterized primarily by recurrent and unexpected panic attacks, plus continued worry about having another attack; such worry interferes with psychological functioning.

paranoid personality disorder A pattern of distrust and suspiciousness and perceiving others as having evil motives. It is found in 0.5–2.5% of the population.

paranoid schizophrenia A subcategory of schizophrenia characterized by auditory hallucinations or delusions, such as thoughts of being persecuted by others or delusions of grandeur.

paraphilias Repetitive or preferred sexual fantasies involving nonhuman objects, such as sexual attractions to particular articles of clothing (shoes, underwear); commonly called sexual deviations.

parasympathetic division The subdivision of the autonomic nervous system that decreases physiological arousal and helps return the body to a calmer, more relaxed state. It also stimulates digestion during eating.

parentese A way of speaking to young children in which the adult speaks in a voice that is slower and higher than normal, emphasizes and stretches out each word, uses very simple sentences, and repeats words and phrases. Formerly known as motherese.

parietal lobe An area of the cortex located directly behind the frontal lobe. Its functions include: processing sensory information from body parts, which includes touching, locating positions of limbs, and feeling temperature and pain; and carrying out several cognitive functions, such as attending to and perceiving objects.

Parkinson's disease A condition caused by the destruction of neurons that produce the neurotransmitter dopamine. Symptoms include tremors and shakes in the limbs, a slowing of voluntary movements, and feelings of depression. As the disease progresses, patients develop a peculiar shuffling walk and may suddenly freeze in space for minutes or hours at a time.

partial reinforcement A schedule of reinforcement in which the response is reinforced only some of the time.

passion In Sternberg's triangular theory of love, the component of love associated with feeling physically aroused and attracted to someone.

passionate love A condition that is associated with continuously thinking about the loved one and is accompanied by warm sexual feelings and powerful emotional reactions.

pathological aging Acceleration of the aging process, which may be caused by genetic defects, physiological problems, or diseases.

peg method A mnemonic device, or encoding technique, that creates associations between number-word rhymes and items to be memorized.

perception The experience of a meaningful pattern or image that the brain assembles from thousands of individual, meaningless sensations; a perception is normally changed, biased, colored, or distorted by a person's unique set of experiences.

perceptual constancy Our tendency to perceive sizes, colors, brightness, and shapes as remaining the same even though their physical characteristics are constantly changing.

perceptual sets Learned expectations that are based on our personal, social, or cultural experiences. These expectations automatically add information, meaning, or feelings to our perceptions and thus change or bias our perceptions.

perceptual speed The rate at which we can identify a particular sensory stimulus; this rate slows down noticeably after age 60.

peripheral cues Hunger cues associated with changes in blood chemistry or signals from digestive organs.

peripheral nervous system All the nerves that extend from the spinal cord and carry messages to and from various muscles, glands, and sense organs located throughout the body. It has two divisions: the somatic nervous system and the autonomic nervous system.

peripheral route for persuasion Approaches to persuasion that emphasize emotional appeal, focus on personal traits, and generate positive feelings.

peripheral theories of emotions Theories that attribute our subjective feelings primarily to our body's physiological changes.

permissive parents Parents who are less controlling and behave with a nonpunishing and accepting attitude toward their children's impulses, desires, and actions. They consult with their children about policy decisions, make few demands, and tend to use reason rather than direct power.

person perception The process by which we form impressions of, and make judgments about, the traits and characteristics of others.

person schemas Social schemas including our judgments about the traits that we and others possess.

person-situation interaction The interaction between a person's traits and the effects of being in a particular situation, which, according to Mischel, determines the person's behavior.

personal factors According to social cognitive theory, factors that include our emotional makeup and our biological and genetic influences and that help to shape our personalities.

personal identity *See* identity.

personality A combination of long-lasting and distinctive behaviors, thoughts, motives, and emotions that typify how we react and adapt to other people and situations. *See also* theory of personality.

personality development *See* social development.

personality disorder Any psychological disorder characterized by inflexible, long-standing, maladaptive traits that cause significantly impaired functioning or great distress in one's personal and social life.

personality psychology The study of personality development, personality change, assessment, and abnormal behaviors.

personality tests Tests used to measure a person's observable traits and behaviors and unobservable characteristics. In addition, some are used to identify personality problems and psychological disorders, as well as to predict how a person might behave in the future. Objective personality tests (self-report questionnaires), such as the MMPI, consist of specific statements or questions to which the person responds with specific answers; projective tests, such as the Rorschach inkblot test, have no set answers but consist of ambiguous stimuli that a person interprets or makes up stories about.

pessimism A relatively stable personality trait that leads one to believe and expect that bad things will happen. It is one of the personality factors associated with increased stress levels and chances of developing psychosomatic symptoms. *See* optimism.

PET scan *See* positron emission tomography.

phallic stage Freud's third psychosexual stage, lasting from the ages of about 3 to 6. In this stage, the infant's pleasure seeking is centered on the genitals.

phantom limb The experience of sensations and feelings coming from a limb that has been amputated. The sensations and feelings are extremely vivid, as if the amputated limb were still present.

phenomenological perspective The idea that our perspective of the world, whether or not it is accurate, becomes our reality. This idea is stressed in humanistic theories.

phenothiazines The first group of drugs to reduce schizophrenic symptoms, such as delusions and hallucinations. Discovered in the early 1950s, the phenothiazines operate by blocking or reducing the effects of the neurotransmitter dopamine.

phi movement The illusion that stationary lights are moving. The illusion of movement—today called apparent motion—is created by flashing closely positioned stationary lights at regular intervals.

phobia An anxiety disorder characterized by an intense and irrational fear that is out of all proportion to the danger elicited by the object or situation. In comparison, fear is a realistic response to a threatening situation.

phonemes The basic sounds of consonants and vowels.

phonology Rules specifying how we make the meaningful sounds used by a particular language.

photographic memory The ability to form sharp, detailed visual images after examining a picture or page for a short period of time and to recall the entire image at a later date. Photographic memory is similar to eidetic imagery but occurs in adults.

physiological psychology *See* psychobiology.

Piaget's cognitive stages Four different stages—the sensorimotor, preoperational, concrete operations, and formal operations stages—each of which is more advanced than the preceding stage because it involves new reasoning and thinking abilities.

pica A behavioral disorder in which individuals eat inedible objects or nonnutritive substances. Pica can lead to serious physical problems, including lead poisoning, intestinal blockage, and parasites, and is more often seen in individuals with mental retardation.

pitch Our subjective experience of how low or high a sound is. The brain calculates pitch from the speed (frequency) of the sound waves. The frequency of sound waves is measured in cycles, which refers to how many sound waves occur in 1 second.

pituitary gland A key component of the endocrine system, which hangs directly below the hypothalamus, to which it is connected by a narrow stalk. Its anterior section regulates growth and controls much of the endocrine system, while its posterior section regulates water and salt balance.

place theory The theory that the brain perceives the pitch of a sound by receiving information about where on the basilar membrane a given sound vibrates the most; it applies to medium and higher pitches.

placebo An intervention—taking a pill, receiving an injection, or undergoing an operation—that resembles medical therapy but that, in fact, has no medical effects.

placebo effect A change in the patient's illness that is attributable to an imagined treatment rather than to a medical treatment.

placenta An organ that connects the blood supply of the mother to that of the fetus. The placenta acts like a filter, allowing oxygen and nutrients

Glossary

to pass through while keeping out certain toxic or harmful substances.

pleasure principle The satisfaction of drives and avoidance of pain, without concern for moral restrictions or society's regulations. According to Freud, this is the id's operating principle.

polygraph tests Tests based on the theory that, if a person tells a lie, he or she will feel some emotion, such as guilt or fear. Feeling guilty or fearful will usually be accompanied by involuntary physiological responses, which are difficult to suppress or control and can be measured with a machine called a polygraph.

pons A bridge that connects the spinal cord with the brain and parts of the brain with one another. Cells in the pons manufacture chemicals involved in sleep.

positive punishment The presentation of an aversive stimulus (for example, spanking) after a response. The aversive stimulus decreases the chances that the response will recur.

positive regard Love, sympathy, warmth, acceptance, and respect, which we crave from family, friends, and people important to us.

positive reinforcement The presentation of a stimulus that increases the probability of a behavior's recurrence.

positive reinforcer A stimulus that increases the likelihood that a response will occur again.

positive symptoms of schizophrenia Symptoms that reflect a distortion of normal functions. Distorted thinking results in delusions; distorted perceptions result in hallucinations; distorted language results in disorganized speech.

positron emission tomography (PET scan) A technique to measure the function of the living brain. A slightly radioactive solution is injected into the blood and the amount of radiation absorbed by the brain cells is measured. Very active brain cells—neurons—absorb more radioactive solution than less active ones. A computer transforms the different levels of absorption into colors that indicate the activity of neurons. The colors red and yellow indicate maximum activity of neurons; blue and green indicate minimal activity.

postconventional level Kohlberg's highest level of moral reasoning, at which moral decisions are made after carefully thinking about all the alternatives and striking a balance between human rights and laws of society.

posterior pituitary The rear part of the pituitary gland, a key component of the endocrine system. It regulates water and salt balance.

posthypnotic amnesia Inability to remember what happened during hypnosis, prompted by a specific suggestion from the hypnotist.

posthypnotic suggestion A suggestion given to the subject during hypnosis about performing a particular behavior, in response to a predetermined cue, when the subject comes out of hypnosis.

posttraumatic stress disorder (PTSD) A disabling condition that results from direct personal experience of an event that involves actual or threatened death or serious injury or from witnessing such an event or hearing that such an event has happened to a family member or close friend.

precognition The ability to foretell events.

preconventional level Kohlberg's lowest level of moral reasoning. It consists of two stages: At stage 1, moral decisions are based primarily on fear of punishment or the need to be obedient; at stage 2, moral reasoning is guided most by satisfaction of one's self-interest, which may involve making bargains.

predisposing function The role of our attitudes in guiding or influencing us to behave in specific ways.

prejudice An unfair, biased, or intolerant attitude toward another group of people.

premature ejaculation Persistent or recurrent absence of voluntary control over ejaculation, in that the male ejaculates with minimal sexual stimulation before, upon, or shortly after penetration and before he wishes to; also called rapid ejaculation.

prenatal period The period from conception to birth, which lasts about 266 days (about nine months). It is divided into three phases: the germinal, embryonic, and fetal periods. During the prenatal period, a single cell will divide and grow to form 200 billion cells.

preoperational stage The second of Piaget's cognitive stages, lasting from the ages of about 2 to 7. During this stage, children learn to use symbols (such as words or mental images) to think about things that are not present and to help them solve simple problems.

preparedness The innate or biological tendency of animals and humans to recognize, attend to, and store certain cues over others, as well as to associate some combinations of conditioned and unconditioned stimuli more easily than others. Also called prepared learning.

primacy effect Better recall, or improvement in retention, of information presented at the beginning of a task.

primacy-recency effect Better recall of information presented at the beginning and end of a task.

primary appraisal Our initial, subjective evaluation of a situation, in which we balance the demands of a potentially stressful situation against our ability to meet them.

primary auditory cortex An area at the top edge of the temporal lobe that transforms nerve impulses (electrical signals) into basic auditory sensations, such as meaningless sounds and tones of varying pitch and loudness. Next, it sends impulses (sensations) to the auditory association areas.

primary reinforcer A stimulus, such as food, water, or sex, that is innately satisfying and requires no learning on the part of the subject to become pleasurable.

primary visual cortex A small area, located at the back of each occipital lobe, that receives electrical signals from receptors in the eyes and transforms these signals into meaningless, basic visual sensations, such as lights, lines, shadows, colors, and textures.

principle of bidirectionality The idea that a child's behaviors influence how his or her parents respond and, in turn, the parents' behaviors influence how the child responds.

proactive interference A forgetting process in which information that we learned earlier blocks or disrupts the retrieval of related information that was learned later.

problem-focused coping Solving a problem by seeking information, changing our own behavior, or taking whatever action is necessary.

problem solving Searching for some rule, plan, or strategy in order to reach a certain goal that is currently out of reach.

procedural memory Memories of performing motor or perceptual tasks (playing sports), carrying out habitual behaviors (brushing teeth), and responding to stimuli because of classical conditioning (fearing spiders). We cannot retrieve these memories and are not conscious of them.

processing speed The rate at which we encode information into long-term memory or recall or retrieve information from long-term memory; this rate slows down after age 60.

procrastination The tendency to always put off completing a task to the point of feeling anxious or uncomfortable about one's delay.

prodigy A child who shows unusual talent, ability, or genius at a very early age and does not have mental retardation. A small percentage of autistic children, who have some degree of mental retardation, may also show unusual artistic or mathematical abilities; they are called savants.

progressive relaxation An exercise in which the major muscle groups of the body are tensed and relaxed repeatedly until the individual can relax any group of muscles at will.

projection Unconsciously transferring unacceptable traits to others.

projective tests Tests in which the subject is presented with some type of ambiguous stimulus—such as a meaningless object or ambiguous photo—and then asked to make up a story about the stimulus. The assumption is that the person will project conscious or unconscious feelings, needs, and motives in his or her responses.

prosocial behavior Any behavior that benefits others or has positive social consequences. Also called helping.

prototype theory The idea that we form a concept by first constructing a prototype of an object—that is, a mental image based on its average characteristics. Once we have formed a set of prototypes, we identify new objects by matching them against our prototypes.

proximity rule A perceptual rule stating that, in organizing stimuli, objects that are physically close to one another will be grouped together.

proximodistal principle The rule that parts closer

to the center of the infant's body develop before parts that are farther away.

psi The processing of information or transfer of energy by methods that have no known physical or biological mechanisms and that seem to stretch the laws of physics.

psilocybin A hallucinogen, the active ingredient in magic mushrooms. Low doses produce pleasant and relaxed feelings; medium doses produce distortions in the perception of time and space; and high doses produce distortions in perceptions and body image and sometimes hallucinations.

psychiatrist A medical doctor (M.D.) who has taken a psychiatric residency, which involves additional training in pharmacology, neurology, psychopathology, and therapeutic techniques. In diagnosing the possible causes of abnormal behaviors, psychiatrists focus on biological factors; they tend to view mental disorders as diseases and to treat them with drugs. Psychiatrists who receive additional training in psychoanalytic institutes are called psychoanalysts.

psychoactive drugs Chemicals that affect the nervous system and, as a result, may alter consciousness and awareness, influence sensations and perceptions, and modify moods and cognitive processes. Some are legal (coffee, alcohol, and tobacco) and some are illegal (marijuana, heroin, cocaine, and LSD).

psychoanalysis A form of psychotherapy based on the idea that each of us has an unconscious part that contains ideas, memories, desires, or thoughts that have been hidden or repressed because they are psychologically dangerous or threatening to our self-concept. To protect our self-concept, we automatically build a mental barrier that we cannot voluntarily remove. But the presence of these thoughts and desires gives rise to unconscious conflicts, which, in turn, can result in psychological and physical symptoms and mental disorders.

psychoanalyst *See* psychiatrist.

psychoanalytic approach A psychological viewpoint that stresses the influence of unconscious fears, desires, and motivations on thoughts and behaviors and also the impact of childhood experiences on the development of later personality traits and psychological problems. As applied to mental disorders, this approach traces their origin to unconscious conflicts or problems with unresolved conflicts at one or more of Freud's psychosexual stages. Treatment of mental disorders, in this approach, centers on the therapist's helping the patient to identify and resolve his or her unconscious conflicts.

psychobiological approach *See* biological approach.

psychobiology The scientific study of the physical and chemical changes that occur during stress, learning, and emotions, as well as how our genetic makeup and nervous system interact with our environments and influence our behaviors.

psychodynamic theory of personality *See* Freud's psychodynamic theory of personality.

psychokinesis The ability to exert mind over matter—for example, by moving objects without touching them.

psychological assessment The use of various tools—including psychological tests and interviews—to measure characteristics, traits, or abilities in order to understand behavior and predict future performance or behavior.

psychological factors Performance anxiety, sexual trauma, guilt, or failure to communicate, all of which may lead to sexual problems.

psychological sex factors Factors involved in the development of a gender identity, gender role, and sexual orientation, as well as in difficulties in sexual performance or enjoyment.

psychologist An individual who has completed four to five years of postgraduate education and has obtained a Ph.D in psychology; in some states, an individual with a master's degree.

psychology The systematic, scientific study of behaviors and mental processes.

psychometric approach An approach to the assessment of intelligence that measures or quantifies cognitive abilities or factors that are thought to be involved in intellectual performance.

psychometrics A subarea of psychology concerned with the development of tests to assess an individual's abilities, skills, intelligence, personality traits, and abnormal behaviors in a wide range of settings—school, the workplace, or a clinic.

psychoneuroimmunology The study of the relationship among the central nervous system, the endocrine system, and psychosocial factors such as cognitive reactions to stressful events, the individual's personality traits, and social influences.

psychosexual stages According to Freud, five developmental periods—the oral, anal, phallic, latency, and genital stages—each marked by potential conflict between parent and child. The conflicts arise as the child seeks pleasure from different bodily areas associated with sexual feelings (different erogenous zones). Freud emphasized that the child's first five years were most important in social and personality development.

psychosocial factors Underlying personality traits, amount of social support, and ability to deal with stressful life events—these factors are believed to combine and interact with predisposing biological factors to either increase or decrease a person's vulnerability to the development and maintenance of a mood disorder.

psychosocial hunger factors Learned associations between food and other stimuli, such as snacking while watching television; sociocultural influences, such as pressures to be thin; and various personality problems, such as depression, dislike of body image, or low self-esteem.

psychosocial stages According to Erikson, eight developmental periods during which an individual's primary goal is to satisfy desires associated with social needs: the eight periods are associated, respectively, with issues of trust, autonomy, initiative, industry, identity, intimacy, generativity, and ego integrity.

psychosomatic symptoms Real, physical, and often painful symptoms, such as headaches, muscle pain, and stomach problems, that are caused by psychological factors, such as worry, tension, and anxiety.

psychotherapy Approaches to treating psychological problems that share three characteristics: verbal interaction between therapist and client(s); the development of a supportive relationship during which a client can bring up and discuss traumatic or bothersome experiences that may have led to current problems; and analysis of the client's experiences and/or suggested ways for the client to deal with or overcome his or her problems.

puberty A developmental period, corresponding to the ages of 9–17, when the individual experiences significant biological changes and, as a result, develops secondary sexual characteristics and reaches sexual maturity.

punishment A consequence that occurs after behavior and decreases the likelihood that that behavior will recur.

pupil The round opening at the front of the eye that allows light waves to pass through into the eye's interior.

quantum personality change A sudden and radical or dramatic shift in personality, belief, or values.

questionnaire A method for obtaining information by asking subjects to read a list of written questions and to check off, or rate their preference for, specific answers.

random selection A research design such that each subject in a sample population has an equal chance of being selected to participate in the experiment.

range The two most extreme scores at either end of a distribution.

rape myths Misinformed false beliefs about women that are frequently held by rapists as well as by other men.

rationalization Inventing acceptable excuses for behaviors that make us feel anxious.

reaction formation Turning unacceptable wishes into acceptable behaviors.

reaction range The extent to which traits, abilities, or IQ scores may increase or decrease as a result of interaction with environmental factors.

reaction time The rate at which we respond (see, hear, move) to some stimulus; this rate slows down noticeably after age 60.

real motion Our perception of any stimulus or object that actually moves in space; the opposite of apparent motion.

real self According to Rogers, the self that is based on our actual experiences and represents how we really see ourselves; its complement is the ideal self.

reality principle A policy of satisfying a wish or desire only if a socially acceptable outlet is available. According to Freud, this is the ego's operating principle.

Glossary

reasoning A mental process by which we apply knowledge to achieve goals that involve solving problems or making plans and decisions.

recall Retrieval of previously learned information without the aid of or with very few external cues.

recency effect Better recall, or improvement in retention, of information presented at the end of a task.

recognition The identification of previously learned information with the help of external cues.

reflex An unlearned, involuntary reaction to some stimulus. The neural connections of the network underlying a reflex are prewired by genetic instructions.

reinforcement A consequence that occurs after behavior and increases the likelihood that that behavior will recur.

relative size In three-dimensional vision, a monocular depth cue that results when we expect two objects to be the same size and they are not. In that case, the larger of the objects will appear closer, and the smaller will appear to be farther away.

relaxation response A physiological response induced by sitting or lying in a comfortable position while repeating a meaningless sound over and over to drive out anxious thoughts.

reliability The extent to which a test is consistent: A person's score on a test at one point in time should be similar to the score obtained by the same person on a similar test at a later point in time.

REM (rapid eye movement) sleep The stage of sleep in which our eyes move rapidly back and forth behind closed eyelids. This stage makes up 20% of our sleep time; in a normal night, we experience five or six periods of REM sleep, each one lasting 15–45 minutes. REM brain waves, which have a high frequency and a low amplitude, look very similar to the beta waves that are recorded when we are wide awake and alert; the body's voluntary muscles, however, are paralyzed. Dreams usually occur during REM sleep.

REM behavior disorder A disorder, usually found in older people, in which the voluntary muscles are not paralyzed during REM sleep; sleepers can and do act out their dreams.

REM rebound The tendency of individuals to spend proportionately longer in the REM stage after they have been deprived of REM sleep on previous nights.

repair theory A theory of sleep suggesting that activities during the day deplete key factors in the brain or body that are replenished or repaired by sleep.

repression According to Freud, a mental process that automatically hides emotionally threatening or anxiety-producing information in the unconscious. Repressed information cannot be retrieved voluntarily, but something may cause it to be released and to reenter the person's consciousness at a later time.

resiliency Various personal, family, or environmental factors that compensate for increased life stresses so that expected problems do not develop.

resistance In psychotherapy, especially psychoanalysis, the client's reluctance to work through or deal with feelings or to recognize unconscious conflicts and repressed thoughts.

resistance stage The second stage in the general adaptation syndrome. In reaction to continued stress, most physiological responses return to normal levels, but the body uses up great stores of energy.

resting state A condition in which the axon, like a battery, has a charge, or potential, because the axon membrane separates positive ions on the outside from negative ions on the inside.

reticular formation A column of brain cells that arouses and alerts the forebrain and prepares it to receive information from all the senses. It plays an important role in keeping the forebrain alert and producing a state of wakefulness. Animals or humans whose reticular formation is seriously damaged lapse into permanent unconsciousness or coma.

retina A thin film, located at the very back of the eyeball, that contains cells, called photoreceptors, that are extremely sensitive to light. The retina consists of three layers, the third and deepest of which contains two kinds of photoreceptors, rods and cones, that perform transduction—that is, they change light waves into nerve impulses.

retinal disparity A binocular depth cue that depends on the distance between the two eyes. Because of their different positions, the two eyes receive slightly different images. The difference between these images is the retinal disparity. The brain interprets large retinal disparity to mean a close object and small retinal disparity to mean a distant object.

retrieval cues Mental reminders that we create by forming vivid mental images of information or associating new information with information that we already know. Forgetting can result from not taking the time to create effective retrieval cues.

retrieving The process of getting or recalling information that has been placed into short-term or long-term storage.

retroactive interference A forgetting process in which information that we learned later blocks or disrupts the retrieval of related information that was learned earlier.

reuptake The process by which some neurotransmitters, such as dopamine, are removed from the synapse by being transported back into the end bulbs.

reward/pleasure center The part of the brain that includes the nucleus accumbens and ventral tegmental area and involves several neurotransmitters, especially dopamine. Combined with other brain areas, it forms a neural circuit that produces rewarding and pleasurable feelings.

rods Photoreceptors containing the chemical rhodopsin, which is activated by small amounts of light. Because rods are extremely light sensitive, they allow us to see in dim light but to see only black, white, and shades of gray.

Rogers's self-actualizing tendency An inborn tendency for us to develop all of our capacities in ways that best maintain and benefit our lives.

role schemas Social schemas based on the jobs people perform or the social positions they hold.

Rorschach inkblot test A projective test used to assess personality in which a person is shown a series of ten inkblots and then asked to describe what he or she sees in each.

rules of organization Rules identified by Gestalt psychologists that specify how our brains combine and organize individual pieces or elements into a meaningful whole—that is, a perception.

SAD *See* seasonal affective disorder.

savants Autistic individuals who show some incredible memory, music, or drawing talent. They represent about 10% of the total number of autistics.

schedule of reinforcement In conditioning, a program or rule that determines how and when a response will be followed by a reinforcer.

schemas Mental categories that, like computer files, contain knowledge about people, events, and concepts. Because schemas influence which stimuli we attend to, how we interpret stimuli, and how we respond to stimuli, they can bias and distort our thoughts, perceptions, and behaviors. *See also:* event schemas; gender schemas; person schemas; role schemas; and self schemas.

schizophrenia A serious mental disturbance that lasts at least six months and includes at least two of the following symptoms: delusions, hallucinations, disorganized speech, grossly disorganized behavior, and decreased emotional expression. These symptoms interfere with personal or social functioning. *See also* Type I and Type II schizophrenia.

schizotypical personality disorder A disorder characterized by acute discomfort in close relationships, distortions in thinking, and eccentric behavior. It is found in 3–5% of the population.

scientific method A general approach to gathering information and answering questions so that errors and biases are minimized.

scripts *See* event schemas.

seasonal affective disorder (SAD) A pattern of depressive symptoms that cycle with the seasons, typically beginning in fall or winter. The depression is accompanied by feelings of lethargy, excessive sleepiness, overeating, weight gain, and craving for carbohydrates.

secondary appraisal Deciding what we can do to deal with a potentially stressful situation. We can choose some combination of problem-focused coping, which means doing something about the problem, and emotion-focused coping, which means dealing with our emotions.

secondary reinforcer Any stimulus that has

acquired its reinforcing power through experience; secondary reinforcers are learned, for example, by being paired with primary reinforcers or other secondary reinforcers.

secure attachment An emotional bond characteristic of infants who use their parent as a safe home base from which they can wander off and explore their environments.

self How we see or describe ourselves; also called self concept. The self is made up of many self-perceptions, abilities, personality characteristics, and behaviors that are organized so as to be consistent with one another.

self-actualization Our inherent tendency to reach our true potentials. The concept of self-actualization, developed by Maslow, is central to humanistic theories. *See also* Rogers's self-actualizing tendency.

self-actualization theory *See* self theory.

self-concept *See* self.

self-efficacy Our personal beliefs regarding how capable we are of exercising control over events in our lives, such as completing specific tasks and behaviors.

self-esteem How much an individual likes himself or herself; it includes feelings of self-worth, attractiveness, and social competence.

self-fulfilling prophecy A situation in which a person has a strong belief or makes a statement (prophecy) about a future behavior and then acts, usually unknowingly, to fulfill or carry out that behavior.

self-handicapping A tendency to adopt tactics that are prone to failure and then to use those tactics as excuses for failures in performance, activities, or achieving goals.

self-identity *See* identity.

self-injurious behavior A behavior pattern in which an individual inflicts serious and sometimes life-threatening physical damage on his or her own body; this may take the form of body or head banging, biting, kicking, poking ears or eyes, pulling hair, or intense scratching.

self-perception theory The idea, developed by Daryl Bem, that we first observe or perceive our own behavior and then, as a result, change our attitudes.

self-report questionnaires *See* objective personality tests.

self schemas Social schemas containing personal information about ourselves. They can influence how we behave as well as what we perceive and remember.

self-serving bias Attributing our successes to our dispositions or personality traits and our failures to the situations.

self theory Rogers's humanistic theory, based on two major assumptions: that personality development is guided by each person's unique self-actualization tendency; and that each of us has a personal need for positive regard.

semantic memory A type of declarative memory consisting of factual knowledge about the world, concepts, word definitions, and language rules.

semantics A set of rules that specify the meaning of words or phrases when they appear in various sentences or contexts.

sensation Our first awareness of some outside stimulus; relatively meaningless bits of information that result when the brain processes electrical signals that come from the sense organs.

sensitive period *See* critical period.

sensorimotor stage The first of Piaget's cognitive stages, lasting from birth to about age 2. During this stage, infants interact with and learn about their environments by relating their sensory experiences (such as hearing and seeing) to their motor actions (mouthing and grasping).

sensory homunculus A drawing of the somatosensory cortex that shows the relationship between the size of each body part and the degree of its sensitivity to external stimulation. *Homunculus* means "little man."

sensory memory An initial memory process that receives and holds environmental information in its raw form for a brief period of time, from an instant to several seconds.

sensory neurons *See* afferent neurons.

sentence stage The fourth stage in acquiring language, which begins at about 4 years of age. Sentences range from three to eight words in length and indicate a growing knowledge of the rules of grammar.

separation anxiety An infant's distress—as indicated by loud protests, crying, and agitation—whenever his or her parents temporarily leave.

set point A certain level of body fat (adipose tissue) that our body strives to maintain constant throughout our lives; the set point is an inherited characteristic.

sex chromosome The sperm or the egg. Each contains only 23 chromosomes, on which are the genes bearing the instructions that determine the sex of the child.

sex (gender) differences in the brain Structural or functional differences in cognitive, behavioral, or brain processes that arise from being male or female.

sex hormones Chemicals, secreted by glands, that circulate in the bloodstream and influence the brain, other body organs, and behaviors. The major male sex hormones secreted by the testes are androgens, such as testosterone; the major female sex hormones secreted by the ovaries are estrogens.

sexual dysfunctions Problems of sexual arousal or orgasm that interfere with adequate functioning during sexual behavior.

sexual orientation A person's pattern of primary sexual arousal: by members of his or her own sex, the opposite sex, or both sexes; also called sexual preference.

shape constancy Our tendency to see an object as remaining the same shape when viewed at different angles—that is, despite considerable change in the shape of its image on the retina.

shaping In operant conditioning, a procedure in which an experimenter successively reinforces behaviors that lead up to or approximate the desired behavior.

short-term dynamic psychotherapy A shortened version of psychoanalysis. It emphasizes a limited time for treatment (20–30 sessions) and focuses on limited goals, such as solving a relatively well-defined problem. Therapists take an active and directive role by identifying and discussing the client's problems, resolving issues of transference, interpreting the patient's behaviors, and offering an opportunity for the patient to foster changes in behavior and thinking that will result in more active coping and an improved self-image.

short-term memory A process that can hold a limited amount of information—an average of seven items—for a short time (2–30 seconds), which can be lengthened if you rehearse the information. Sometimes called working memory.

shyness The tendency to feel tense, worried, or awkward in social situations.

similarity rule A perceptual rule stating that, in organizing stimuli, elements that appear similar are grouped together.

simplicity rule A perceptual rule stating that stimuli are organized in the simplest way possible.

single-word stage The second stage in acquiring language, which begins when the child is about 1 year old. Infants say single words that usually refer to what they can see, hear, or feel.

situational attributions *See* external attributions.

size constancy Our tendency to perceive objects as remaining the same size even when their images on the retina are continually growing or shrinking.

skewed distributions Distributions in which more data fall toward one side of the scale than toward the other.

sleep A condition in which we pass through five different stages, each with its own level of consciousness, awareness, responsiveness, and physiological arousal. In the deepest stage of sleep, we enter a state that borders on unconsciousness.

sleep apnea A condition characterized by a cycle in which a sleeper stops breathing for intervals of 10 seconds or longer, wakes up briefly, resumes breathing, and returns to sleep. This cycle can leave apnea sufferers exhausted during the day but oblivious to the cause of their tiredness. It is more common among habitual snorers.

sleepwalking Walking or carrying out behaviors while still asleep. Sleepwalkers generally are clumsy and have poor coordination but can avoid objects; they can engage in very limited conversations. Sleepwalking behaviors can include dressing, eating, performing bathroom functions, and even driving a car. Sleepwalking usually occurs in stage 3 or stage 4 (delta) sleep.

social cognitive learning A form of learning that

Glossary

results from watching, imitating, and modeling and does not require the observer to perform any observable behavior or receive any observable reward. Formerly called observational learning.

social cognitive theory The theory that grew out of the research of a number of psychologists—Rotter, Bandura, and Mischel—that says that personality development is primarily shaped by three forces: environmental conditions, cognitive-personal factors, and behavior, which all interact to influence how we evaluate, interpret, organize, and apply information. *See also* Bandura's social cognitive theory.

social comparison theory The idea that we are driven to compare ourselves to others who are similar to us, so that we can measure the correctness of our attitudes and beliefs. According to Festinger, this drive motivates us to join groups.

social development How a person develops a sense of self or self-identity, develops relationships with others, and develops the skills useful in social interactions.

social facilitation An increase in performance in the presence of a crowd.

social inhibition A decrease in performance in the presence of a crowd.

social needs Needs that are acquired through learning and experience.

social norms approach Relating to abnormality, the idea that a behavior is considered abnormal if it deviates greatly from accepted social standards, values, or norms.

social phobias Irrational, marked, and continuous fear of performing in social situations. The individuals fear that they will humiliate or embarrass themselves.

social psychology A broad field whose goals are to understand and explain how our thoughts, feelings, perceptions, and behaviors are influenced by interactions with others. It includes the study of stereotypes, prejudices, attitudes, conformity, group behaviors, and aggression.

social role theory The theory that emphasizes the importance of social and cultural influences on gender roles and states that gender differences between males and females arise from different divisions of labor.

social support A stress-reducing factor that includes three components: having a group or network of family or friends who provide strong social attachments; being able to exchange helpful resources among family or friends; and feeling, or making appraisals, that we have supportive relationships or behaviors.

socially oriented group A group in which members are primarily concerned about fostering and maintaining social relationships among the members of the group.

sociobiology theory *See* evolutionary theory.

sociocognitive theory of hypnosis The idea that the impressive effects of hypnosis are due to social influences and pressures as well as the subject's personal abilities. For another view, *see* altered state theory of hypnosis.

sodium pump A chemical transport process that picks up any sodium ions that enter the axon's chemical gates and returns them back outside. In this way, the sodium pump is responsible for keeping the axon charged by returning and keeping sodium ions outside the axon membrane.

somatic nervous system A network of nerves that are connected either to sensory receptors or to muscles that you can move voluntarily, such as muscles in your limbs, back, neck, and chest. Nerves in the somatic nervous system usually contain two kinds of fibers: afferent, or sensory, fibers that carry information from sensory receptors in the skin, muscles, and other organs to the spinal cord and brain; and efferent, or motor, fibers that carry information from the brain and spinal cord to the muscles.

somatization disorder A somatoform disorder that begins before age 30, lasts several years, and is characterized by multiple symptoms—including pain, gastrointestinal, sexual, and neurological symptoms—that have no physical causes but are triggered by psychological problems or distress.

somatoform disorder A pattern of recurring, multiple, and significant bodily (somatic) complaints that extend over several years. The physical symptoms (pain, vomiting, paralysis, blindness) are not under voluntary control, have no known physical causes, and are believed to be caused by psychological factors.

somatosensory cortex A narrow strip of the cortex that is located at the front edge of the parietal lobe and extends down its side. It processes sensory information about touch, location of limbs, pain, and temperature. The right somatosensory cortex receives information from the left side of the body and vice versa.

sound waves The stimuli for hearing, or audition. Similar to ripples on a pond, sound waves travel through space with varying heights and speeds. Height, or amplitude, is the distance from the bottom to the top of a sound wave; speed, or frequency, is the number of sound waves that occur within 1 second.

source misattribution A memory error that results when a person has difficulty in deciding which of two or more sources a memory came from: Was the source something the person saw or imagined, or was it a suggestion?

Spearman's *g* *See* two-factor theory.

specific phobias Unreasonable, marked, and persistent fears triggered by anticipation of, or exposure to, a specific object or situation (flying, heights, spiders, seeing blood); formerly called simple phobias.

split-brain operation A procedure for moderating severe, uncontrollable seizures by cutting the corpus callosum, a wide band of nerve fibers that connects the right and left hemispheres.

spontaneous recovery In classical conditioning, the temporary occurrence of the conditioned response to the presence of the conditioned

stimulus In operant conditioning, a temporary recovery in the rate of responding.

stage 1 In sleep, a stage lasting 1–7 minutes in which the individual gradually loses responsiveness to stimuli and experiences drifting thoughts and images. This stage marks the transition from wakefulness to sleep and is characterized by the presence of theta waves, which are lower in amplitude and lower in frequency (3–7 cycles per second) than alpha waves.

stage 2 In sleep, the stage that marks the beginning of what we know as sleep; subjects awakened in stage 2 report having been asleep. EEG tracings show high-frequency bursts of brain activity called sleep spindles.

stages 3 and 4 About 30–45 minutes after drifting off to sleep, we pass rapidly through stage 3 and enter stage 4 sleep, a stage characterized by delta waves, which are of very high amplitude and very low frequency (less than 4 cycles per second). Stage 4 is often considered the deepest stage of sleep because it is the most difficult from which to be awakened. During stage 4, heart rate, respiration, temperature, and blood flow to the brain are reduced, and there is a marked secretion of growth hormone, which controls many aspects of metabolism, physical growth, and brain development. This stage is also called slow-wave or delta sleep.

stages of sleep Distinctive changes in the electrical activity of the brain and accompanying physiological responses of the body that occur as we pass through different stages of sleep. *See also* stage 1, stage 2, stages 3 and 4.

standard deviation A statistic indicating how widely all the scores in a distribution are scattered above and below the mean.

standardized test A technique to obtain information by administering a psychological test that has been standardized, which means that the test has been given to hundreds of people and shown to reliably measure thought patterns, personality traits, emotions, or behaviors.

state-dependent learning The idea that we recall information more easily when we are in the same physiological or emotional state or setting as when we originally encoded the information.

statistical frequency approach In defining abnormality, the idea that a behavior may be considered abnormal if it occurs rarely or infrequently in relation to the behaviors of the general population.

statistical procedures In experiments, procedures to determine whether differences observed in dependent variables (behaviors) are due to independent variables (treatment) or to error or chance occurrence.

statistics Tools researchers use to analyze and summarize large amounts of data.

stereotaxic procedure A method used for the

introduction of material at a precise location within the brain. The patient's head is fixed in a holder, and a small hole is drilled through the skull. The holder has a syringe that can be precisely guided to a predetermined location in the brain.

stereotypes Widely held beliefs that people have certain traits because they belong to a particular group. Stereotypes are often inaccurate and frequently portray the members of less powerful, less controlling groups more negatively than members of more powerful or more controlling groups.

Sternberg's triangular theory of love The idea that love has three components: passion, intimacy, and commitment. Passion is feeling physically aroused and attracted to someone; intimacy is feeling close and connected to someone, through sharing and communicating; and commitment is pledging to nourish the feelings of love and actively maintain the relationship.

Sternberg's triarchic theory The idea that intelligence can be divided into three ways of gathering and processing information (*triarchic* means "three"): using analytical or logical thinking skills that are measured by traditional intelligence tests; using problem-solving skills that require creative thinking, the ability to deal with novel situations, and the ability to learn from experience; and using practical thinking skills that help a person adjust to, and cope with, his or her sociocultural environment.

stimulants Drugs, such as cocaine, amphetamines, caffeine, and nicotine, that increase activity in the nervous system and result in heightened alertness, arousal, and euphoria and decreased appetite and fatigue.

stimulus substitution The theory that, in classical conditioning, a neural bond or association is formed between the neutral stimulus and unconditioned stimulus. After repeated trials, the neutral stimulus becomes the conditioned stimulus, which, in turn, substitutes for the unconditioned stimulus. Thereafter, the conditioned stimulus elicits a response similar to that of the unconditioned stimulus.

stomach The body organ that monitors the amount and kinds of nutrients our body needs to restore our depleted stores of fuel. In addition, after we eat a meal, the stomach's walls are distended and their stretch receptors signal fullness or time to stop eating.

storing The process of placing encoded information into relatively permanent mental storage for later recall.

stress The anxious or threatening feeling that comes when we interpret or appraise a situation as being more than our psychological resources can adequately handle.

stress management program A program to reduce anxiety, fear, and stressful experiences by using a variety of strategies to change three different

aspects of our lives: thoughts (appraisals), behaviors, and physiological responses.

structuralism An early school of psychological thought that emphasized the study of the basic elements—primarily sensations and perceptions—that make up conscious mental experiences. Structuralists argued that we can understand how perceptions are formed by breaking them down into smaller and smaller elements. Then we can analyze how these basic elements are recombined to form a perception. They believed that a perception is simply the sum of its parts.

structured interviews A research technique in which each individual is asked the same set of relatively narrow and focused questions, so that the same information is obtained from everyone.

subgoals In problem solving, a strategy by which the overall problem is broken into separate parts that, when completed in order, will result in a solution.

sublimation A type of displacement in which threatening or forbidden desire, usually sexual, is redirected into socially acceptable forms.

subliminal messages Brief auditory or visual messages that are presented below the absolute threshold, so that their chance of perception is less than 50%.

subliminal stimulus A stimulus whose intensity is such that a person has a less than 50% chance of detecting it.

substance abuse A maladaptive pattern of frequent and continued usage of a substance—a drug or medicine—that results in significant problems, such as failing to meet major obligations and having multiple legal, social, family, health, work, or interpersonal difficulties. These problems must occur repeatedly during a single 12-month period to be classified as substance abuse.

superego Freud's third division of the mind, which develops from the ego during early childhood; its goal is to apply the moral values and standards of one's parents or caregivers and society in satisfying one's wishes.

superstitious behavior In operant conditioning, any behavior that increases in frequency because its occurrence is accidentally paired with the delivery of a reinforcer.

suprachiasmatic nucleus A sophisticated biological clock, located in the hypothalamus, that regulates a number of circadian rhythms, including the sleep-wake cycle. Suprachiasmatic cells are highly responsive to changes in light.

surface structure According to Chomsky, the actual wording of a sentence, as it is spoken.

survey A way to obtain information by asking many individuals—person to person, by telephone, or by mail—to answer a fixed set of questions about particular subjects.

sympathetic division The subdivision of the autonomic nervous system that is triggered by threatening or challenging physical or

psychological stimuli, increasing the body's physiological arousal and preparing the body for action.

synapse An infinitely small space (20–30 billionths of a meter) between an end bulb and its adjacent body organ, muscle, or cell body; it is a space over which chemical messages are transmitted.

syntax *See* grammar.

systematic desensitization A technique of behavior therapy, based on classical conditioning, in which a person is gradually and progressively exposed to fearful or anxiety-evoking stimuli while practicing deep relaxation. Systematic desensitization is a form of counterconditioning because it replaces, or counters, fear and anxiety with relaxation.

***t* test** An estimate of reliability that takes into account both the size of the mean difference and the variability in distributions.

taijin kyofusho (TKS) A mental disorder found only in Asian cultures, particularly Japan. This social phobia is characterized by a morbid fear of offending others through awkward social or physical behavior, such as making eye-to-eye contact, blushing, giving off an offensive odor, having an unpleasant or tense facial expression, or having trembling hands.

tardive dyskinesia A condition characterized by the appearance of slow, involuntary, and uncontrollable rhythmic movements and rapid twitching of the mouth and lips, as well as unusual movements of the limbs. This condition is a side effect of the continued use of typical neuroleptics.

task-oriented group A group in which members have specific duties to complete.

taste A chemical sense that makes use of various chemicals or stimuli.

taste-aversion learning The association of a particular sensory cue (smell, taste, sound, or sight) with an unpleasant response, such as nausea or vomiting, resulting in future avoidance of that particular sensory cue.

taste buds Onion-shaped structures on the tongue that contain the receptors for taste.

TAT *See* Thematic Apperception Test.

telegraphic speech A distinctive speech pattern observed during language acquisition in which the child omits articles, prepositions, and parts of verbs.

telepathy The ability to transfer thoughts to another person or to read the thoughts of others.

temperament An individual's distinctive pattern of attention, arousal, and reactivity to new or novel situations. This pattern appears early, is relatively stable and long-lasting, and is influenced in large part by genetic factors.

temporal lobe A segment of the brain located directly below the parietal lobe that is involved in hearing, speaking coherently, and understanding verbal and written material.

teratogen Any agent that can harm a developing

Glossary

fetus (causing deformities or brain damage). It might be a disease (such as genital herpes), a drug (such as alcohol), or another environmental agent (such as chemicals).

test anxiety A combination of physiological, emotional, and cognitive components that are caused by the stress of taking exams and that may interfere with a student's ability to think, reason, and plan.

testimonial A statement in support of a particular viewpoint based on personal experience.

testosterone The major male hormone, which stimulates the growth of genital organs and the development of secondary sexual characteristics.

texture gradient In three-dimensional vision, a monocular depth cue: Areas with sharp, detailed texture are interpreted as being closer, and those with less sharpness and detail as more distant.

thalamus A structure of the limbic system that is located in the middle of the forebrain and is involved in receiving sensory information, doing some initial processing, and then relaying the sensory information to appropriate areas of the cortex, including the somatosensory cortex, primary auditory cortex, and primary visual cortex.

Thematic Apperception Test (TAT) A personality test in which subjects are asked to look at pictures of people in ambiguous situations and to make up stories about what the characters are thinking and feeling and what the outcome will be.

theory of evolution Darwin's theory that different species arose from a common ancestor and that those species survived that were best adapted to meet the demands of their environments.

theory of linguistic relativity Whorf's theory that the differences among languages result in differences in the ways people think and perceive the world.

theory of personality An organized attempt to describe and explain how personalities develop and why personalities differ.

thinking Mental processes by which we form concepts, solve problems, and engage in creative activities. Sometimes referred to as reasoning.

threat appraisal Our conclusion that harm or loss has not yet taken place in a particular situation but we anticipate it in the near future.

threshold A point above which a stimulus is perceived and below which it is not perceived. *See also* absolute threshold.

thyroid A gland located in the neck that regulates metabolism through secretion of hormones. It forms part of the endocrine system.

time-out In training children, a form of negative punishment in which reinforcing stimuli are removed after an undesirable response. This removal decreases the chances that the response will recur. In time-out, the child is told to sit quietly in the corner of a room or put in some other situation where there is no chance

to obtain reinforcers or engage in pleasurable behaviors.

tip-of-the-tongue phenomenon The situation in which, despite making a great effort, we are temporarily unable to recall information that we absolutely know is in our memory.

TKS *See* taijin kyofusho.

tolerance The reaction of the body and brain to regular drug use, whereby the person has to take larger doses of the drug to achieve the same behavioral effect.

touch The skin senses, which include temperature, pressure, and pain. Touch sensors change mechanical pressure or changes in temperature into nerve impulses that are sent to the brain for processing.

trait A relatively stable and enduring tendency to behave in a particular way.

trait theory An approach for analyzing the structure of personality by measuring, identifying, and classifying similarities and differences in personality characteristics or traits.

transcendental meditation (TM) A meditation exercise in which individuals assume a comfortable position, close their eyes, and repeat and concentrate on a sound to clear their head of all thoughts (worrisome and otherwise).

transduction The process by which a sense organ changes, or transforms, physical energy into electrical signals that become neural impulses, which may be sent to the brain for processing.

transference In psychotherapy, the process by which a client expresses strong emotions toward the therapist because the therapist substitutes for someone important in the client's life, such as the client's mother or father. Freud first developed this concept.

transformational rules According to Chomsky, procedures by which we convert our ideas from surface structures into deep structures and from deep structures back into surface structures.

transmitter A chemical messenger that transmits information between nerves and body organs, such as muscles and heart. *See also* neurotransmitters.

transsexualism *See* gender identity disorder.

triangular theory of love *See* Sternberg's triangular theory of love.

triarchic theory *See* Sternberg's triarchic theory.

trichromatic theory The idea that there are three different kinds of cones in the retina, and each cone contains one of three different light-sensitive chemicals, called opsins. Each opsin is most responsive to wavelengths that correspond to each of the three primary colors—blue, green, and red—from which all other colors can be mixed.

two-factor theory A theory of intelligence proposed by Spearman, according to which a general mental ability factor, g, represents a person's

ability to perform complex mental work, such as abstract reasoning and problem solving, while many specific factors, s, represent a person's specific mental abilities, such as mathematical, mechanical, or verbal skills. Thus, g is constant across tests, while s may vary across tests.

two-word combinations The third stage in acquiring language, which begins at about 2 years of age. The infant says strings of two words that express various actions ("Me play," "See boy") or relationships ("Hit ball," "Milk gone").

tympanic membrane The thin, taut membrane, commonly called the eardrum, that is the boundary between the outer ear and middle ear. Struck by sound waves, it vibrates and passes the vibrations to the ossicles.

Type A behavior A combination of personality traits that may be a risk factor for coronary heart disease. According to the original (1970s) definition, these traits included an overly competitive and aggressive drive to achieve, a hostile attitude when frustrated, a habitual sense of time urgency, a rapid and explosive pattern of speaking, and workaholic tendencies; in contrast, type B behavior was easygoing, calm, relaxed, and patient. In the 1980s, the list of traits was reduced to being depressed, aggressively competitive, easily frustrated, anxious, and angry. In the 1990s, the list was reduced again, to frequent feelings of anger and hostility, which may or may not be publicly expressed. Currently, researchers conclude that individuals who either always show their anger and hostility or always suppress it have large increases in physiological arousal, which can have damaging effects on one's heart and health.

Type I schizophrenia A type of schizophrenia characterized by positive symptoms, such as hallucinations and delusions, which are distortions of normal functions. Individuals diagnosed with Type I schizophrenia have no intellectual impairment, good reaction to medication, and thus a good chance of recovery.

Type II schizophrenia A type of schizophrenia characterized by negative symptoms, such as dulled emotions and little inclination to speak, which are a loss of normal functions. Individuals diagnosed with Type II schizophrenia have intellectual impairment, poor reaction to medication, and thus a poor chance of recovery.

typical neuroleptic drugs Neuroleptics that primarily reduce the levels of the neurotransmitter dopamine. Two of the more common are phenothiazines (for example, Thorazine) and butrophenones (for example, haloperidol). These drugs primarily reduce positive symptoms but have little or no effects on negative symptoms.

unconditional positive regard The warmth, acceptance, and love that others show us because we are valued human beings even though we may behave in ways that disappoint them because they differ from their standards and values or the way they think.

unconditioned response (UCR) An unlearned, innate, involuntary physiological reflex that is elicited by the unconditioned stimulus.

unconditioned stimulus (UCS) A stimulus that triggers or elicits some physiological response, such as salivation or eye blink.

unconscious *See* Freud's theory of the unconscious; cognitive unconscious.

unconscious forces Wishes, desires, or thoughts that, because of their disturbing or threatening content, we automatically repress and cannot voluntarily access.

unconscious motivation A Freudian concept that refers to the influence of repressed thoughts, desires, or impulses on our conscious thoughts and behaviors.

unconsciousness Total loss of awareness and responsiveness to the environment. It may be due to disease, trauma, a blow to the head, or general medical anesthesia.

underachievers Individuals who score relatively high on tests of ability or intelligence but perform more poorly than their scores would predict.

unipolar depression *See* major depressive disorder.

universal emotional expressions A number of specific inherited facial patterns or expressions that signal specific feelings or emotional states, such as a smile signaling a happy state.

uplifts Small, pleasurable, happy, and satisfying experiences that we have in our daily lives.

validity The extent to which a test measures what it is supposed to measure.

variable-interval schedule A conditioning schedule such that the time between the response and the subsequent reinforcer is variable.

variable-ratio schedule A conditioning schedule in which the subject must make a different number of responses for the delivery of each reinforcer.

variance A measure of the variability within two distributions.

ventrolateral preoptic nucleus (VPN) A group of cells in the hypothalamus that acts like a master switch for sleep. Turned on, the VPN secretes a neurotransmitter (GABA) that turns off areas that keep the brain awake; turned off, the VPN causes certain brain areas to become active and we wake up.

ventromedial hypothalamus A group of brain cells that regulates hunger by creating feelings of satiety (*say-TIE-ah-tea*) or fullness.

vertigo Feelings of dizziness and nausea resulting from malfunction of the semicircular canals in the vestibular system.

vestibular system Three semicircular canals in the inner ear that sense the position of the head, keep the head upright, and maintain balance. Fluid in the semicircular canals moves in response to movements of the head, and sensors (hair cells) in the canals respond to the movement of the fluid.

virtual reality A perceptual experience—of being inside an object, moving through an environment, or carrying out some action—that is, in fact, entirely simulated by a computer.

visible spectrum The one particular segment of electromagnetic energy that we can see because these waves are the right length to stimulate receptors in the eye.

visual acuity The ability to see fine details.

visual agnosia A condition caused by damage to the visual association area. An individual with visual agnosia is unable to recognize some object, person, or color and yet is able to see and even describe parts of some visual stimulus.

visual association area An area of the brain, located next to the primary visual cortex, that transforms basic sensations, such as lights, lines, colors, and textures, into complete, meaningful visual perceptions, such as persons, objects, or animals.

visual cliff A glass tabletop with a checkerboard pattern over part of its surface; the remaining surface consists of clear glass with a checkerboard pattern several feet below, creating the illusion of a clifflike drop to the floor.

VPN *See* ventrolateral preoptic nucleus.

vulnerability Psychological or environmental difficulties that make children more at risk for developing later personality, behavioral, or social problems.

Weber's law A psychophysics law stating that the increase in intensity of a stimulus needed to produce a just noticeable difference grows in proportion to the intensity of the initial stimulus.

Wechsler Adult Intelligence Scale (WAIS-III) and Wechsler Intelligence Scale for Children (WISC-III) Intelligence tests that are divided into various subtests. The verbal section contains a subtest of general information, a vocabulary subtest, and so forth. The performance section contains a subtest that involves arranging pictures in a meaningful order, one that requires assembling objects, and one that involves using codes. The verbal and performance scores are combined to give a single IQ score.

weight-regulating genes Genes that play a role in influencing appetite, body metabolism, and secretion of hormones (such as leptin) that regulate fat stores.

Wernicke's aphasia Difficulty in understanding spoken or written words and in putting words into meaningful sentences, as a result of injury to Wernicke's area in the brain.

Wernicke's area An area usually located in the left temporal lobe that plays a role in understanding speech and speaking in coherent sentences. *See* Wernicke's aphasia.

withdrawal symptoms Painful physical and psychological symptoms that occur when a drug-dependent person stops using a drug.

word An arbitrary pairing between a sound or symbol and a meaning.

working memory *See* short-term memory.

Yerkes-Dodson law The principle that performance on a task is an interaction between the level of physiological arousal and the difficulty of the task. For difficult tasks, low arousal results in better performance; for most tasks, moderate arousal helps performance; and for easy tasks, high arousal may facilitate performance.

zygote The cell that results when an egg is fertilized. It contains 46 chromosomes, arranged in 23 pairs.

References

Abelson, R. (2002, June 14). Limits on residents' hours worry teaching hospitals. *New York Times*, A16.

Abernethy, B., Neal, R. J., & Koning, P. (1994). Visual-perceptual and cognitive differences between expert, intermediate, and novice snooker players. *Applied Cognitive Psychology, 8,* 185–211.

Abrahamsson, K. H., Berggren, U., Hallberg, L. R. M., & Carlsson, S. G. (2002). Ambivalence in coping with dental fear and avoidance: A qualitative study. *Journal of Health Psychology, 7,* 653–665.

Abramov, I., & Gordon, J. (1994). Color appearance: On seeing red—or yellow, or green, or blue. *Annual Review of Psychology, 45,* 451–485.

Abramowitz, J. S. (1997). Effectiveness of psychological and pharmacological treatments for obsessive-compulsive disorder: A quantitative review. *Journal of Consulting and Clinical Psychology, 65,* 44–52.

Abrams, M. (2002, June). Sight / Unseen. *Discover,* 54–59.

Abrams, R. L., & Greenwald, A. G. (2000). Parts outweigh the whole (word) in unconscious analysis of meaning. *Psychological Science, 11,* 118–124.

Abu-Lughod, L. (1986). *Veiled sentiments.* Berkeley: University of California Press.

Ackerman, S. J., & Hilsenroth, M. J. (2003). A review of therapist characteristics and techniques positively impacting the therapeutic alliance. *Clinical Psychology Review, 23,* 1–33.

Adams, R. B., Jr., Gordon, H. L., Baird, A. A., Ambady, N., & Kleck, R. E. (2003). Effects of gaze on amygdala sensitivity to anger and fear faces. *Science, 300,* 1536.

Adan, A. (1992). The influence of age, work schedule and personality on morningness dimensions. *International Journal of Psychophysiology, 12,* 95–99.

Ader, F. (1999, June). Cited in B. Azar, Father of PNI reflects on the field growth. *Monitor: American Psychological Association,* 18.

Ader, R. (2001). Psychoneuroimmunology. *Current Directions of Psychological Science, 10,* 94–97.

Ader, R., & Cohen, N. (1975). Behaviorally conditioned immunosuppression. *Psychosomatic Medicine, 37,* 333–340.

Aharon, I., Etcoff, N., Ariely, D., Chabris, C. F., O'Connor, E., & Breiter, H. C. (2001). Beautiful faces have variable reward value: fMRI and behavioral evidence. *Neuron, 30,* 537–551.

Ainsworth, M. D. S. (1979). Infant-mother attachment. *American Psychologist, 34,* 932–937.

Ainsworth, M. D. S. (1989). Attachments beyond infancy. *American Psychologist, 44,* 709–716.

Ajzen, I. (2001). Nature and operation of attitudes. *Annual Review of Psychology, 52,* 27–58.

Albert, M. L., Connor, L. T., & Obler, L. K. (2000). Brain, language, and environment. *Brain and Language, 71,* 4–6.

Ali, L., & Scelfo, J. (2002, December 9). Choosing virginity. *Newsweek,* 61–64.

Ali, S. I., & Begum, S. (1994). Fabric softeners and softness perception. *Ergonomics, 37,* 801–806.

Alivisatos, B., & Petrides, M. (1997). Functional activation of the human brain during mental rotation. *Neuropsychologia, 35,* 111–118.

Allen, J. E. (2000, May 8). How do you know if it's attention deficit/hyperactivity disorder? *Los Angeles Times,* S3.

Allen, K. (2003). Are pets a healthy pleasure? The influence of pets on blood pressure. *Current Directions in Psychology, 12,* 236–239.

Allgood, W. P., Risko, V. J., Alvarez, M. C., & Fairbanks, M. M. (2000). Factors that influence study. In R. F. Flippo & D. C. Caverly (Eds.), *Handbook of college reading and study strategy research.* Mahwah, NJ: Lawrence Erlbaum.

Alliger, G. M., & Title, S. A. (2000). A meta-analytic investigation of the susceptibility of integrity tests to faking and coaching. *Educational & Psychological Measurement, 60,* 59–72.

Allport, G. W. (1935). Attitudes. In C. Murchison (Ed.), *Handbook of social psychology* (Vol. 2). Worcester, MA: Clark University Press.

Allport, G. W., & Odbert, H. S. (1936). Trait-names: A psycho-lexical study. *Psychological Monographs, 47* (Whole No. 211).

Almeida, D. M., Wethingon, E., & Kessler, R. C. (2002). The daily inventory of stressful events. *Assessment, 9,* 41–55.

Alonso-Zaldivar, R. (2002, December). Cell phones and driving: A lethal mix. *Los Angeles Times,* A1.

Althof, S. E. (1995). Pharmacologic treatment of rapid ejaculation. *The Psychiatric Clinics of North America, 18,* 85–94.

Amabile, T. M. (1985). Motivation and creativity: Effects of motivational orientation on creative writers. *Journal of Personality and Social Psychology, 48,* 393–399.

Amass, L. (2003, June). Cited in E. Benson, A new treatment for addiction. *Monitor on Psychology,* 18–20.

American Association on Mental Retardation. (1993). *Mental retardation* (9th ed.). Annapolis Junction, MD: AAMR Publications.

American Psychiatric Association. (2000). *Diagnostic and statistical manual of mental disorders* (4th ed., Text revision). Washington, DC: Author.

American Psychological Association, Division of Psychological Hypnosis. (1993). Hypnosis. *Psychological Hypnosis, 2*(3).

American Psychological Association. (1992). Ethical principles of psychologists and code of conduct. *American Psychologist, 47,* 1597–1611.

American Psychological Association. (1995). *How to choose a psychologist.* Washington, DC: Author.

Anastasi, A., & Urbina, S. (1997). *Psychological testing.* Upper Saddle River, NJ: Prentice-Hall.

Anderson, C. A., & Bushman, B. J. (2002). Human aggression. *Annual Review of Psychology, 53,* 27–51.

Anderson, C. P. (2003, June 23). Cited in D. P. Lange, Couples on the same emotional wavelengths are likelier to succeed. *Los Angeles Times,* F2.

Anderson, K. J. (1994). Impulsivity, caffeine, and task difficulty: A within-subjects test of the Yerkes-Dodson law. *Personality and Individual Differences, 16,* 813–819.

Andreasen, N. C., Nopoulos, P., Schultz, S., Miller, D., Gupta, S., Swayze, V., & Flaum, M. (1994). Positive and negative symptoms of schizophrenia: Past, present, and future. *Acta Psychiatrica Scandinavica, 90,* 510–519.

Andrews, B., Brewin, C. R., Ochera, J., Morton, J., Bekerian, D. A., Davies, G. M., & Mollon, P. (2000). The timing, triggers and qualities of recovered memories in therapy. *British Journal of Clinical Psychology, 39,* 11–26.

Angelo, B. (1991, November 4). Life at the end of the rainbow. *Time.*

Angier, N. (2003, February 25). Not just genes: Moving beyond nature vs. nurture. *New York Times,* D1.

Arantes-Oliveria, N., Berman, J. R., & Kenyon, C. (2003). Healthy animals with extreme longevity. *Science, 302,* 611.

Ariely, D., & Wertenbroch, K. (2002). Procrastination, deadlines, and performance: Self-control by precommitment. *Psychological Science, 13,* 219–224.

Armbruster, B. B. (2000). Taking notes from lectures. In R. F. Flippo & D. C. Caverly (Eds.), *Handbook of college reading and study strategy research.* Mahwah, NJ: Lawrence Erlbaum.

Arnett, J. J. (2000a). Adolescent storm and stress, reconsidered. *American Psychologist, 54,* 317–326.

Arnett, J. J. (2000b). Emerging adulthood. *American Psychologist, 55,* 469–480.

Arnold, D. H., & Doctoroff, G. L. (2003). The early education of socioeconomically disadvantaged children. *Annual Review of Psychology, 54,* 517–545.

Arntz, A. (2003). Cognitive therapy versus applied relaxation as treatment for generalized anxiety disorder. *Behaviour Research and Therapy, 41,* 633–646.

Aronow, E., Reznikoff, M., & Moreland, K. L. (1995). The Rorschach: Projective technique or psychometric test? *Journal of Personality Assessment, 64,* 213–218.

Aronson, E. (1997). Back to future: Retrospective review of Leon Festinger's A theory of cognitive dissonance. *American Journal of Psychology, 110,* 127–157.

Asch, S. E. (1958). Effects of group pressure upon modification and distortion of judgments. In E. E. Maccoby, T. M. Newcomb & E. L. Hartley (Eds.), *Readings in social psychology* (3rd ed.). New York: Holt, Rinehart & Winston.

Aserinsky, E., & Kleitman, N. (1953). Regularly occurring periods of eye motility, and concomitant phenomena during sleep. *Science, 118,* 273–274.

Assanangkornchai, S., Noi-pha, K., Saunders, J. G., & Ralanachaiyavong, S. (2003). Aldehyde dehydrogenase 2 genotypes, alcohol flushing, symptoms and drinking patterns in Thai men. *Psychiatry Research, 118,* 9–17.

Associated Press. (2002, November 18). Loss of McNabb overshadows win. *Los Angeles Times,* D8.

Associated Press. (2003, August 2). Warning on olestra snacks lifted. *Los Angeles Times,* A23.

Atkinson, J. W. (1964). *An introduction to motivation.* Princeton, NJ: Van Nostrand Reinhold.

Atkinson, J. W. (Ed.). (1958). *Motives in fantasy, action and society.* Princeton, NJ: Van Nostrand Reinhold.

Atkinson, J. W., & Raynor, J. O. (Eds.). (1974). *Motivation and achievement.* Washington, DC: V. H. Winston.

Atkinson, R. C., & Shiffrin, R. M. (1968). Human memory: A proposed system and its control processes. In K. W. Spence & J. T. Spence (Eds.), *The psychology of learning and motivation: Advances in research and theory* (Vol. 2). New York: Academic Press.

Attias, J., Gordon, C., Ribak, J., Binah, O., & Arnon, R. (1987). Efficacy of transdermal scopolamine against seasickness: A 3-day study at sea. *Aviation, Space and Environmental Medicine, 58,* 60–62.

Audrain, J. E., Klesges, R. C., & Klesges, L. M. (1995). Relationship between obesity and the metabolic effects of smoking in women. *Health Psychology, 14,* 116–123.

Azar, B. (1997, August). When research is swept under the rug. *APA Monitor.*

Azar, B. (2002, February). Ethics at the cost or research? *Monitor on Psychology,* 38–39.

Azar, B., & Sleek, S. (1994, October). Do roots of violence grow from nature or nurture? *APA Monitor.*

Baars, B. J. (2002). The conscious access hypothesis: Origins and recent evidence. *Trends in Cognitive Sciences, 6,* 47–52.

Babyak, M., Blumenthal, J. A., Herman, S., Khatri, P., Doraiswamy, M., Moore, K., Craighead, W. E., Baldewizc, T. T., & Krishnan, K. R. (2000). Exercise treatment for major depression: Maintenance of therapeutic benefit at 10 months. *Psychosomatic Medicine, 62,* 633–638.

Baddeley, A. (2000). Short-term and working memory. In E. Tulving & F. M. Craik (Eds.), *The Oxford handbook of memory.* New York: Oxford University Press.

Baer, J. S., Sampson, P. D., Barr, H. M., Connor, P. D., & Streissguth, A. P. (2003). A 21-year longitudinal analysis of the effects of prenatal alcohol exposure on young adult drinking. *Archives of General Psychiatry, 60,* 377–385.

Bahrick, H. P. (2000). Long-term maintenance of knowledge. In E. Tulving & F. M. Craik (Eds.), *The Oxford handbook of memory.* New York: Oxford University Press.

Bahrick, H. P., Bahrick, P. O., & Wittlinger, R. P. (1975). Fifty years of memory for names and faces. *Journal of Experimental Psychology: General, 104,* 54–75.

Bahrick, H. P., Hall, L. K., & Berger, S. A. (1996). Accuracy and distortion in memory for high school girls. *Psychological Science, 7,* 265–271.

Bailenson, J. N., Shum, M. S., & Uttal, D. H. (2000). The initial segment strategy: A heuristic for route selection. *Memory & Cognition, 28,* 306–318.

Bailes, E., Gao, F., Bibollet-Ruche, F., Courgnaud, V., Peeters, M., Marx, P. A., Hahn, B. H., & Sharp, P. M. (2003). Hybrid origin of SIV in chimpanzees. *Science, 200,* 1713.

Bailey, J. M., & Zucker, H. J. (1995). Childhood sex-typed behavior and sexual orientation: A conceptual analysis and quantitative review. *Developmental Psychology, 31,* 43–55.

Bailey, J. M., Dunne, M. P., & Martin, N. G. (2000). Genetic and environmental influences on sexual orientation and its correlates in an Australian twin sample. *Journal of Personality and Social Psychology, 78,* 524–536.

Bain, J. (2002, April 30). New treatments may help control sleep apnea. *New York Times,* D6.

Baker, M. C. (2002, January 15). Cited in B. Fowler, Expert says he discerns "hard-wired" grammar rules. *New York Times,* D5.

Baldwin, J. D., & Baldwin, J. I. (1997). Gender differences in sexual interest. *Archives of Sexual Behavior, 26,* 181–210.

Balint, K. (1995, March 4). La Jolla senior, 17, wins top U.S. science prize. *San Diego Union-Tribune.*

Ballenger, J. C. (2001). Overview of different pharmacotherapies for attaining remission in generalized anxiety disorder. *Journal of Clinical Psychiatry, 62 (supplement 19),* 11–19.

Balter, M. (2002). What made humans modern? *Science, 295,* 1219–1225.

Balzar, J. (1997, March 8). A passion for canines, cold winds. *Los Angeles Times.*

Banati, R. B., Goerres, B. W., Tjoa, C., Aggleton, J. P., & Grasby, P. (2000). The functional anatomy of visual-tactile integration in man: A study using positron emission tomography. *Neuropsychologia, 38,* 115–124.

Bancroft, J. (2002). Biological factors in human sexuality. *The Journal of Sex Research, 39,* 15–21.

Bandura, A. (1965). Influence of models' reinforcement contingencies on the acquisition of imitative responses. *Journal of Personality and Social Psychology, 1,* 589–596.

Bandura, A. (1986). *Social foundations of thought and action: A social cognitive theory.* Englewood Cliffs, NJ: Prentice-Hall.

Bandura, A. (1999). Social cognitive theory of personality. In L. A. Pervin & O. P. John (Eds.), *Handbook of personality: Theory and research* (2nd ed.). New York: Guilford.

Bandura, A. (2000). Exercise of human agency through collective efficacy. *Current Directions in Psychological Science, 9,* 75–78.

Bandura, A. (2001). Social cognitive theory: An agentic perspective. *Annual Review of Psychology, 52,* 1–26.

Bandura, A., Blanchard, E. B., & Ritter, B. (1969). Relative efficacy of desensitization and modeling approaches for inducing behavioral, affective and attitudinal changes. *Journal of Personality and Social Psychology, 13,* 173–179.

Bandura, A., Ross, D., & Ross, S. A. (1963). Imitation of film-mediated aggressive models. *Journal of Abnormal and Social Psychology, 66,* 3–11.

Barinaga, M. (1996). Backlash strikes at affirmative action programs. *Science, 271,* 1908–1910.

Barinaga, M. (2000a). Family of bitter taste receptors found. *Science, 287,* 2133–2135.

Barinaga, M. (2000b). Fetal neuron grafts pave the way for stem cell therapies. *Science, 287,* 1421–1422.

Barinaga, M. (2002). How the brain's clock gets daily enlightenment. *Science, 295,* 955–957.

Barinaga, M. (2003a). Newborn neurons search for meaning. *Science, 299,* 32–34.

Barinaga, M. (2003b). Studying the well-trained mind. *Science, 302,* 44–46.

Barkley, R. A., Fischer, M., Smallish, L., & Fletcher, K. (2002). The persistence of attention-deficit/hyperactivity disorder into young adulthood as a function of reporting source and definition of disorder. *Journal of Abnormal Psychology, 111,* 279–289.

Barling, J., Kelloway, E. K., & Cheung, D. (1996). Time management and achievement striving to predict car sales performance. *Journal of Applied Psychology, 81,* 821–826.

Barlow, D. H., & Durand, V. M. (1995). *Abnormal psychology: An integrative approach.* Pacific Grove, CA: Brooks/Cole.

Barlow, D. H., & Durand, V. M. (2001). *Abnormal psychology* (2nd ed.). Belmont, CA: Wadsworth/Thomson.

Barnard, N. D., & Kaufman, S. R. (1997, February). Animal research is wasteful and misleading. *Scientific American,* 80–82.

Bartels, A. (2002, December 16). Cited in C. Carey, The brain in love. *Los Angeles Times,* F1.

Bartoshuk, L. M. (1997). Cited in K. Fackelmann, The bitter truth. *Science News, 152,* 24–25.

Bartoshuk, L. M., & Beauchamp, G. K. (1994). Chemical senses. *Annual Review of Psychology, 45,* 419–449.

Barzilai, N. (2003). Cited in N. Seppa, Centenarian advantage. *Science News, 164,* 243.

Bashore, T. R., & Rapp, P. E. (1993). Are there alternatives to traditional polygraph procedures? *Psychological Bulletin, 113,* 3–22.

Bashore, T. R., & Ridderinkhof, K. R. (2002). Older age, traumatic brain injury, and cognitive slowing: Some convergent and divergent findings. *Psychological Bulletin, 128,* 151–198.

Basil, R. (1989). Graphology and personality: Let the buyer beware. *Skeptical Inquirer, 13,* 241–248.

Basso, A. (2000). The aphasias: Fall and renaissance of the neurological model. *Brain and Language, 71,* 15–17.

Bateman, A. W., & Fonagy, P. (2000). Effectiveness of psychotherapeutic treatment of personality disorder. *British Journal of Psychiatry, 177,* 138–143.

Bates, B. L. (1994). Individual differences in response to hypnosis. In J. W. Rhue, S. J. Lynn & I. Kirsch (Eds.), *Handbook of clinical hypnosis.* Washington, DC: American Psychological Association.

Bates, J. (2000). Temperament as an emotion construct: Theoretical and practical issues. In M. Lewis & J. M. Haviland-Jones (Eds.), *Handbook of emotions* (2nd ed.). New York: Guilford.

Bateson, P. (1991). Is imprinting such a special case? In J. R. Krebs & G. Horn (Eds.), *Behavioural and neural aspects of learning and memory.* Oxford: Oxford University Press.

Batson, C. D. (1998). Who cares? When? Where? Why? How? *Contemporary Psychology, 43,* 108–109.

Batterham, R. L., Cohen, M. A., Ellis, S. M., Le Roux, C. W., Withers, D. J., Frost, G. S., Ghatei, M. R., & Bloom, S. R. (2003). Inhibition of food intake in obese subjects by peptide YY3–36. *New England Journal of Medicine, 349,* 941–948.

Bauer, P. J. (2002). Long-term recall memory: Behavioral and neuro-developmental changes in the first 2 years of life. *Current Directions in Psychological Science, 11,* 139–140.

Baum, D. (1996). *Smoke and mirrors: The war on drugs and the politics of failure.* New York: Little, Brown.

Baum, G. (1994, February 13). Storming the Citadel. *Los Angeles Times.*

Baumeister, R. F. (1995). Disputing the effects of championship pressures and home audiences. *Journal of Personality and Social Psychology, 68,* 644–648.

Baumeister, R. F., & Leary, M. R. (1995). The need to belong: Desire for interpersonal attachments as a fundamental human motivation. *Psychological Bulletin, 117,* 497–529.

Baumeister, R. F., Campbell, J. D., Krueger, J. I., & Vohs, K. D. (2003). Does self-esteem cause better performance, interpersonal success, happiness, or healthier lifestyles? *Psychological Science in the Public Interest, 4,* 1–44.

Baumrind, D. (1991). Effective parenting during the early adolescent transition. In P. A. Cowan & E. M. Hetherington (Eds.), *Advances in family research.* Hillsdale, NJ: Erlbaum.

Baumrind, D. (1993). The average expectable environment is not good enough: A response to Scarr. *Child Development, 64,* 1299–1317.

Baumrind, D. (1995). Commentary on sexual orientation: Research and social policy implications. *Developmental Psychology, 31,* 130–136.

Baumrind, D., Larzelere, R. E், & Cowan, P. A. (2002). Ordinary physical punishment: Is it harmful? Comment on Gershoff (2002). *Psychological Bulletin, 128,* 580–589.

Bear, M. F., Connors, B. W., & Paradiso, M. A. (1996). *Neuroscience: Exploring the brain.* Baltimore, MD: Williams & Wilkins.

Beasley, M., Thompson, T., & Davidson, J. (2003). Resilience in response to life stress: The effects of coping style and cognitive hardiness. *Personality and Individual Differences, 34,* 77–95.

Beck, A. T. (1976). *Cognitive therapy and the emotional disorders.* New York: International Universities Press.

Beck, A. T. (1991). Cognitive therapy: A 30-year retrospective. *American Psychologist, 46,* 368–375.

Beck, A. T., Rush, A. J., Shaw, B. F., & Emery, G. (1979). *Cognitive therapy of depression.* New York: Guilford.

Beck, R., & Fernandez, E. (1998). Cognitive-behavioral therapy in the treatment of anger: A meta-analysis. *Cognitive Therapy and Research, 22,* 63–74.

Becker, A., Burwell, R. A., Gilman, S. E., Herzog, D. B. & Hamburg, P. (2002). Eating behaviours and attitudes following prolonged exposure to television among ethnic Fijian adolescent girls. *British Journal of Psychiatry, 10,* 509–514.

Bednekoff, P. A., Kamil, A. C., & Balda, R. P. (1997). Clark's nutcracker (Aves: Corvidae) spatial memory; Interference effects on cache recovery performance? *Ethology, 103,* 554–565.

Begley, S. (1998a, January 19). Aping language. *Newsweek.*

Begley, S. (1998b, January 26). Is everybody crazy? *Newsweek,* 51–55.

Begley, S. (2001a, February 12). How it all starts inside your brain. *Newsweek,* 40–43.

Begley, S. (2001b, May 21). Roots of evil. *Newsweek,* 36–38.

References

Begley, S. (2001c, July 9). Cellular divide. *Newsweek*, 22–27.

Behrman, A. (1999, January 27). Electroboy. *New York Times Magazine*, 67.

Bell, S. M., McCallum, R. S., Bryles, J., Driesler, K., McDonald, J., Park, S. H., & Williams, A. (1994). Attributions for academic success and failure: An individual difference investigation of academic achievement and gender. *Journal of Psychoeducational Assessment, 13*, 4–13.

Belsky, J. (1993). Etiology of child maltreatment: A developmental-ecological analysis. *Psychological Bulletin, 114*, 413–434.

Bem, D. (1967). Self-perception: An alternative interpretation of cognitive dissonance phenomena. *Psychological Review, 74*, 183–200.

Bem, D. J., & Honorton, C. (1994). Does psi exist? Replicable evidence for an anomalous process of information transfer. *Psychological Bulletin, 115*, 4–18.

Bem, S. L. (1981). Gender schema theory: A cognitive account of sex-typing. *Psychological Review, 88*, 354–364.

Bem, S. L. (1985). Androgyny and gender schema theory: Conceptual and empirical integration. In T. B. Sonderegger (Ed.), *Nebraska symposium on motivation*. Lincoln: University of Nebraska Press.

Bendersky, M., & Lewis, M. (1999). Prenatal cocaine exposure and neonatal condition. *Infant Behavior & Development, 22*, 353–366.

Benes, F. M. (1997). The role of stress and dopamine—GABA interactions in the vulnerability for schizophrenia. *Journal of Psychiatric Research, 31*, 257–275.

Benin, M. H., & Robinson, L. B. (1997, August 25). Marital happiness across the family life cycle: A longitudinal analysis. Cited in *Time*, 24.

Benjamin, L. T., Jr. (2000). The psychology laboratory at the turn of the 20th century. *American Psychologist, 55*, 318–321.

Benjet, C., & Kazdin, A. E. (2003). Spanking children: The controversies, findings, and new directions. *Clinical Psychology Review, 23*, 197–224.

Bennet, J. (2002, June 21). Rash of new suicide bombers showing no pattern or ties. *New York Times*, A1.

Ben-Shakhar, G., & Elaad, E. (2003). The validity of psychophysiological detection of information with the guilty knowledge test: A meta-analysis review. *Journal of Applied Psychology, 88*, 131–151.

Benson, E. (2003a, February). Intelligent intelligence testing. *Monitor on Psychology*, 48–51.

Benson, E. (2003b, February). Intelligence across cultures. *Monitor on Psychology*, 56–58.

Benson, H. (1975). *The relaxation response*. New York: Morrow.

Benson, H. (1997). Cited in W. Roush & Herbert Benson, Mind-body maverick pushes the envelope. *Science, 276*, 357–359.

Benson, H., Lehmann, J. W., Malhotra, M. S., Goldman, R. F., Hopkins, P. J., & Epstein, M. D. (1982). Body temperature changes during the practice of g Tum-mo yoga. *Nature, 295*, 234–235.

Benson, H., Malhotra, M. S., Goldman, R. F., Jacobs, G. D., & Hopkins, P. J. (1990). Three case reports of the metabolic and electroencephalographic changes during advanced Buddhist meditation techniques. *Behavioral Medicine, 16*, 90–95.

Berg, C. A. (2000). Intellectual development in adulthood. In R. J. Sternberg (Ed.), *Handbook of intelligence*. New York: Cambridge University Press.

Berger, J., & Cunningham, C. (1994). Active intervention and conservation: Africa's pachyderm problem. *Science, 263*, 1241–1242.

Berk, L. B., & Patrick, C. F. (1990). Epidemiologic aspects of toilet training. *Clinical Pediatrics, 29*, 278–282.

Berkowitz, L. (1989). Frustration-aggression hypothesis: Examination and reformulation. *Psychological Bulletin, 106*, 59–73.

Berkowitz, L. (1993). *Aggression: Its causes, consequences, and control*. New York: McGraw-Hill.

Bernstein, D. A. (1993, March). Excuses, excuses. *APS Observer*.

Bernstein, P. W. (1994, May 9). The words Nelson Mandela lives by. *U.S. News & World Report*.

Berridge, K. C. (2003). Comparing the emotional brains of human and other animals. In R. J. Davidson, K. R. Scherer & H. H. Goldsmith (Eds.), *Handbook of affective sciences*. New York: Oxford University Press.

Berson, D. M., Dunn, F. A., & Takao, M. (2002). Phototransduction by retinal ganglion cells that set the circadian clock. *Science, 295*, 1070–1073.

Betancourt, H., & Lopez, S. R. (1993). The study of culture, ethnicity, and race in American psychology. *American Psychologist, 48*, 629–637.

Bever, T., & Montalbetti, M. (2002). Noam's ark. *Science, 298*, 1565.

Bibikova, A., & Koteinikov, V. Managing cross-cultural differences. www.1000ventures.com/business_guide/crosscuttings/cross-cultural_differences.html

Biernat, M. (2003). Toward a broader view of social stereotyping. *American Psychologist, 12*, 1019–1027.

Billy, J. O. G., Tanfer, K., Grady, W. R., & Klepinger, D. H. (1993). The sexual behavior of females in the United States. *Family Planning Perspectives, 25*, 52–60.

Binet, A., & Simon, T. (1905). Methodes nouvelles pour le diagnostic du niveau intellectual des anormaux. *L'Annee Psychologique, 11*, 191–244.

Bishop, E. G., Cherny, S. S., Corley, R., Plomin, R., DeFries, J. C., & Hewitt, J. K. (2003). Development genetic analysis of general cognitive ability from 1 to 12 years in a sample of adoptees, biological siblings, and twins. *Intelligence, 31*, 31–49.

Black, D. W., Baumgard, C. H., & Bell, S. E. (1995). A 16- to 45-year follow-up of 71 men with antisocial personality disorder. *Comprehensive Psychiatry, 36*, 130–140.

Black, L., & Flynn, C. (2003, May 7). Glenbrook North, cops investigate brawl at hazing; 5 girls are hurt during "initiation." *Chicago Tribune*, 1.

Blakely, M. R. (1994, May 15). A place of belonging. *Los Angeles Times Magazine*.

Blakemore, J. E. O. (2003). Children's beliefs about violating gender norms: Boys shouldn't look like girls, and girls shouldn't act like boys. *Sex Roles, 48*, 411–419.

Blakeslee, S. (2000a, January 12). Researchers developing bold new theories to explain autism. *San Diego Union-Tribune*.

Blakeslee, S. (2000b, March 14). Just what's going on inside that head of yours? *New York Times*, D6.

Blakeslee, S. (2001, September 25). Watching how the brain works as it weighs a moral decision. *New York Times*, D3.

Blakeslee, S. (2002, November, 11). A boy, a mother and a rare map of autism's world. *New York Times*, D1.

Blass, E. M., & Camp, C. A. (2001). The ontogeny of face recognition: Eye contact and sweet taste induce face preference in 9- and 12-week-old human infants. *Developmental Psychology, 37*, 762–774.

Blass, T. (Ed.). (2000). *Obedience to authority*. Mahwah, NJ: Lawrence Erlbaum.

Bliwise, D. L. (1997). Sleep and aging. In M. R. Pressman & W. C. Orr (Eds.), *Understanding sleep: The evaluation and treatment of sleep disorders*. Washington, DC: American Psychological Association.

Block, J. (1995). Going beyond the five factors given: Rejoinder to Costa & McCrae (1995) and Goldberg & Saucier (1995). *Psychological Bulletin, 117*, 226–229.

Block, J., & Robins, R. W. (1993). Longitudinal study of consistency and change in self-esteem from early adolescence to early adulthood. *Child Development, 64*, 909–923.

Blomberg, J., Lazar, A., & Sandell, R. (2001). Long-term outcome of long-term psychoanalytically oriented therapies: First findings of the Stockholm outcome of psychotherapy and psychoanalysis study. *Psychotherapy Research, 11*, 361–382.

Blood, A. J., & Zatorre, R. J. (2001). Intensely pleasurable responses to music correlate with activity in brain regions implicated in reward and emotion. *Proceedings of the National Academy of Sciences, 98*, 11818–11823.

Blum, N. (2003, April 14). Cited in B. Carey, Ready or not. *Los Angeles Times*, F2.

Blum, N. (2002, September 5). Cited in D. J. Schemo, Mothers of sex-active youths often think they're virgins. *New York Times*, A14.

Blunt, A. K., & Pychyl, T. A. (2000). Task aversiveness and procrastination: A multi-dimensional approach to task aversiveness across stages of personal projects. *Personality and Individual Differences, 28*, 153–167.

Boddy, J. (1988). Spirits and selves in northern Sudan: The cultural therapeutics of possession and trance. *American Ethnologist, 15*, 4–27.

Boden, M. A. (1994). Précis of the creative mind: Myths and mechanisms. *Behavioral and Brain Sciences, 17*, 519–570.

Bond, R., & Smith, P. B. (1996). Culture and conformity: A meta-analysis of studies using Asch's (1952b, 1956) line judgment task. *Psychological Bulletin, 119*, 11–137.

Bondurant, B., & Donat, P. L. N. (1999). Perceptions of women's sexual interest and acquaintance rape. *Psychology of Women Quarterly, 23*, 691–705.

Booth-Kewley, S., & Friedman, H. S. (1987). Psychological predictions of heart disease: A quantitative review. *Psychological Bulletin, 101*, 343–362.

Bootzin, R. R., & Rider, S. P. (1997). Behavioral techniques and biofeedback for insomnia. In M. R. Pressman & W. C. Roo (Eds.), *Understanding sleep: The evaluation and treatment of sleep disorders*. Washington, DC: American Psychological Association.

Borella, P., Bargellini, A., Rovesti, S., Pinelli, M., Vivoli, R., Solfrini, V., & Vivoli, G. (1999). Emotional stability, anxiety, and natural killer activity under examination stress. *Psychoneuroendocrinology, 224*, 613–627.

Born, J., Lange, T., Hansen, K., Molle, M., & Fehm, H. L. (1997). Effects of sleep and circadian rhythm on human circulating immune cells. *Journal of Immunology, 158*, 4454–4464.

Bornas, X., Fullana, M. A., Tortella-Feliu, M., Llabres, J., Garcia de la Banda, G. (2001). Computer-assisted therapy in the treatment of flight phobia: A case report. *Cognitive and Behavioral Practice, 8*, 234–240.

Bornas, X., Tortella-Feliu, M., Llabres, J., & Fullana, M. A. (2001). Computer-assisted exposure treatment for flight phobia: A controlled study. *Psychotherapy Research, 11*, 259–273.

Bornstein, R. F. (2001). The impending death of psychoanalysis. *Psychoanalytic Psychology, 18*, 3–20.

Borton, J. L. D. (2002). The suppression of negative self-referent thoughts. *Anxiety, Stress, and Coping, 15*, 31–46.

Botting, J. H., & Morrison, A. R. (1997, February). Animal research vital to medicine. *Scientific American*, 83–85.

Bouchard, T. J., & McGue, M. (1981). Familial studies of intelligence: A review. *Science, 212*, 1055–1059.

Bouchard, T. J., Jr. (1994). Genes, environment, and personality. *Science, 264*, 1700–1701.

Bouchard, T. J., Jr. (1995). Breaking the last taboo. *Contemporary Psychology, 40*, 415–418.

Bouchard, T. J., Jr. (1997). IQ similarity in twins reared apart: Findings and responses to critics. In R. J. Sternberg & E. Grigorenko (Eds.), *Intelligence, heredity, and environment*. New York: Cambridge University Press.

Bouchard, T. J., Jr., & Loehlin, J. C. (2001). Genes, evolution, and personality. *Behavior Genetics, 31*, 243–273.

Bouchard, T. J., Jr., Lykken, D. T., McGue, M., Segal, N. L., & Tellegen, A. (1990). Sources of human psychological differences: The Minnesota study of twins reared apart. *Science, 250*, 223–228.

Bourgon, L. N., & Kellner, C. H. (2000). Relapse of depression after ECT: A review. *Journal of ECT, 16*, 19–31.

Bower, B. (1993a). Sudden recall. *Science News, 144*, 184–186.

Bower, B. (1993b). Flashbulb memories: Confident blunders. *Science News, 143*, 166–167.

Bower, B. (1996). Creatures in the brain. *Science News, 149*, 234–235.

Bower, B. (1997). Forbidden flavors. *Science News, 151*, 198–199.

Bower, B. (2001). Brains in dreamland. *Science News, 160*, 90–92.

Bower, B. (2002a). Baby facial. *Science News, 161*, 307.

Bower, B. (2002b). Chromosome study homes in on Alzheimer's disease. *Science News, 161*, 116–117.

Bower, B. (2003). Words get in the way. *Science News, 163*, 250–251.

Bower, F. (1997). The power of limited thinking. *Science News, 152*, 334–335.

Bower, F. (2000). Building blocks of talk. *Science News, 157*, 344–346.

Bower, G. H. (2000). A brief history of memory research. In E. Tulving & F. M. Craik (Eds.), *The Oxford handbook of memory*. New York: Oxford University Press.

Bowlby, J. (1969). *Attachment and loss: Vol. 1. Attachment*. New York: Basic Books.

Boyce, N. (2002, October 7). Chips vs. the chess masters. *U.S. News & World Report*, 70–71.

Bradley, C. L. (1997). Generativity-stagnation: Development of a status model. *Developmental Review, 17*, 262–290.

Bradley, S. J., & Zucker, K. J. (1997). Gender identity disorder: A review of the past 10 years. *Journal of the American Academy of Child and Adolescent Psychiatry, 36*, 880–887.

Bragg, R. (1995, July 16). In South Carolina, a mother's defense, and life, could hinge on 2 choices. *New York Times*.

Brantley, B. (2003, February 7). Old Blues, new riffs. *New York Times*, B1.

Braun, A. R., Balkin, T. J., Wesensten, N. J., Gwadry, F., Carson, R. E., Varga, M., Baldwin, P., Belenky, G., & Herscovitch, P. (1998). Dissociated pattern of activity in visual cortices and their projections during human rapid eye movement sleep. *Science, 279*, 91–95.

Brecher, E. M. (1972). *Licit and illicit drugs*. Boston: Little, Brown.

Breiter, H. C., Aharon, I., Kahneman, D., Dale, A., & Shizgal, P. (2001). Functional imaging of neural responses to expectancy and experience of monetary gains and losses. *Neuron, 30*, 619–639.

Brennan, J. (1997, September 28). This 1,800-pound bear is no 800-pound gorilla. *Los Angeles Times/Calendar*.

Brennan, P. A., & Raine, A. (1997). Biosocial bases of antisocial behavior: Psychophysiological, neurological, and cognitive factors. *Clinical Psychology Review, 17*, 589–604.

Breuer, J., & Freud, S. (1895; reprinted 1955). Studies on hysteria. In J. Strachey (Ed. and Trans.), *The standard edition of the complete psychological works of Sigmund Freud*. London: Hogarth.

Brewster, W., DiSaia, P., & Grosen, E. (1999). An experience with estrogen replacement therapy in breast cancer survivors. *International Journal of Fertility, 44*, 186–192.

Brickman, P., Coates, D., & Janoff-Bulman, R. (1978). Lottery winners and accident victims: Is happiness relative? *Journal of Personality and Social Psychology, 36*, 917–927.

Briggs, J. L. (1970). *Never in anger: Portrait of an Eskimo family*. Cambridge, MA: Harvard University Press.

Bright, J. (2003, May 20). Cited in E. Goode, Leading drugs for psychosis come under new scrutiny. *New York Times*, A1.

Broad, W. J. (2002, October 9). Lie-detector tests found too flawed to discover spies. *New York Times*, A1.

Brody, A. L., Saxena, S., Stoessel, P., Gillies, L. A., Fairbanks, L. A., Alborzian, S., Phelps, M. E., Huang, S. C., Wu, H. M., Ho, M. L., Ho, M. K., Scott, C., Maidment, K., & Baxter, L. R., Jr. (2001). Regional brain metabolic changes in patients with major depression treated with either paroxetine or interpersonal therapy. *Archives of General Psychiatry, 58*, 631–640.

Brody, J. E. (1998, January 6). Depression: 2 famous men tell their stories. *San Diego Union-Tribune*.

Brody, J. E. (2000a, April 25). Memories of things that never were. *New York Times*, D8.

Brody, J. E. (2000b, October 17). One-two punch for losing pounds: Exercise and careful diet. *New York Times*, D6.

Brody, J. E. (2002, September 17). Sleep apnea, a noisy but often invisible threat. *New York Times*, D7.

Brody, J. E. (2003, August 18). Skipping a college course: Weight gain 101. *New York Times*, D7.

Brody, J. E. (November 28, 2000). Less pain: Is it the magnets or the mind? *New York Times*, D6.

Brody, N. (1992). *Intelligence*. New York: Academic Press.

Brody, N. (1997). Intelligence, schooling, and society. *American Psychologist, 52*, 1046–1050.

Brody, N. (2000). Theories and measurements of intelligence. In R. J. Sternberg (Ed.), *Handbook of intelligence*. New York: Cambridge University Press.

Brody, N. (2003). What Sternberg should have concluded. *Intelligence, 31*, 339–342.

Broidy, L. M., Nagin, D. S., Tremblay, R. E., Bates, J. E., Brame, B., Dodge, K. A., Fergusson, D., Horwood, J. K., Loeber, R., Laird, R., Lynam, D. R., Moffitt, T. E., Pettit, G. S., & Vitaro, F. (2003). Developmental trajectories of childhood disruptive behaviors and adolescent delinquency: A six-site cross-national study. *Developmental Psychology, 39*, 222–245.

Brooks, C. (1994, February 27). Breakdown into the shadows of mental illness. Special report. *San Diego Union-Tribune*.

Brooks, C. (1995a, February 27). Shadowlands: Three profiled in mental illness series are striving to improve their conditions. *San Diego Union-Tribune*.

Brooks, C. (1995b, June 5). Rod Steiger is powerful voice for mentally ill. *San Diego Union-Tribune*.

Brooks, D. C. (2000). Recent and remote extinction cues reduce spontaneous recovery. *Quarterly Journal of Experimental Psychology, 53B*, 25–58.

Brooks, R., & Goldstein, S. (2002). *Raising resilient children*. New York: McGraw-Hill/Contemporary Books.

Brown, R., & Kulik, J. (1977). Flashbulb memories. *Cognition, 5*, 73–99.

Brown, S. A. (1996, May 13). Talent for living. *People*, 85–86.

Brown, S. C., & Craik, F. I. M. (2000). Encoding and retrieval of information. In E. Tulving & F. M. Craik (Eds.), *The Oxford handbook of memory*. New York: Oxford University Press.

Brown, S. L. (1994, December). Animals at play. *National Geographic*.

Brown, W. A. (1997, January). The placebo effect. *Scientific American*, 90–95.

Brownlee, S. (1997, February 3). The case for frivolity. *U.S. News & World Report*.

Bruer, J. T. (1999). *The myth of the first three years*. New York: Free Press.

Bruner, J. (1997). Celebrating divergence: Piaget and Vygotsky. *Human Development, 40*, 63–73.

Brzezinski, A. (1997). Melatonin in humans. *New England Journal of Medicine, 336*, 186–195.

Buck, L. (1999). Cited in J. Travis, Making sense of scents. *Science News, 155*, 236–238.

Buckley, P. (1989). Fifty years after Freud: Dora, the Rat Man, and the Wolf-Man. *American Journal of Psychiatry, 146*, 1394–1403.

Buckout, R. (1980). Nearly 2,000 witnesses can be wrong. *Bulletin of the Psychonomic Society, 16*, 307–310.

Buddie, A. M., & Miller, A. G. (2002). Beyond rape myths: A more complex view of perceptions of rape myths. *Sex Roles, 45*, 139–160.

Buehler, R., Griffin, D., & Ross, M. (1994). Exploring the "planning fallacy": Why people underestimate their task completion times. *Journal of Personality and Social Psychology, 67*, 366–381.

Bugental, B. B., & Goodnow, J. J. (1998). Socialization processes. In W. Damon & N. Eisenberg (Eds.), *Handbook of child psychology* (5th ed.). New York: John Wiley & Sons.

Bulik, C. M., Sullivan, P. F., & Kendler, K. S. (2003). Genetic and environmental contributions to obesity and eating. *International Journal of Eating Disorders, 33*, 293–298.

Buonomano, D. V., & Merzenich, M. M. (1995). Temporal information transformed into a spatial code by a neural network with realistic properties. *Science, 267*, 1028–1030.

Burge, D., Hammen, C., Davila, J., Daley, S. E., Paley, B., Herzberg, D., & Lindberg, N. (1997). Attachment cognitions and college and work functioning two years later in late adolescent women. *Journal of Youth and Adolescence, 26*, 285–301.

Burger, J. M. (2004). *Personality* (6th ed.). Belmont, CA: Wadsworth.

Burger, J. M., & Guadagno, R. E. (2003). Self-concept clarity and the foot-in-the-door procedure. *Basic and Applied Social Psychology, 25*, 79–86.

Burn, S. M. (2004). *Groups: Theory and practice*. Belmont, CA: Wadsworth/Thomson.

Bushman, B. J. (2002). Does venting anger feed or extinguish the flame? Catharsis, rumination, distraction, anger, and aggressive responding. *Personality and Social Psychology Bulletin, 28*, 724–731.

Buss, D. M. (1994a). *The evolution of desire*. New York: Basic Books.

Buss, D. M. (1994b). Mate preferences in 37 cultures. In W. J. Lonner & R. Malpass (Eds.), *Psychology and culture*. Boston: Allyn & Bacon.

Buss, D. M. (1995). Psychological sex differences. *American Psychologist, 50*, 164–168.

Buss, D. M. (1999). Human nature and individual differences: The evolution of human personality. In L. A. Pervin & O. P. John (Eds.), *Handbook of personality* (2nd ed.). New York: Guilford.

Buss, D. M., & Schmitt, D. P. (1993). Sexual strategies theory: An evolutionary perspective on human mating. *Psychological Review, 100*, 204–232.

Buss, D. M., Abbott, M., Angleitner, A., Asherian, A., Biaggio, A., Blanco-VillaSenor, A., Bruchon-Schweitzer, M., Ch'u, H. Y., Czapinski, J., DeRaad, B., Ekehammar, B., Fioravanti, M., Georgas, J., Gjerde, P., Guttman, R., Hazan, F., Iwawaki, S., Janakiramaiah, H., Khosroshani, F., Kreitler, S.,

References

Lachenicht, L., Lee, M., Liik, K., Little, B., Lohamy, N., Makun, S., Mika, S., Moadel-Shahid, M., Moane, G., Montero, M., Mundy-Casde, A. C., Niit, T., Nsenduluka, E., Peltzer, K., Pienkowski, R., Pirttila-Backman, A., Ponce De Leon, J., Rousseau, J., Runco, M. A., Safir, M. P., Samuels, C., Sanitioso, R., Schweitzer, B., Serpell, R., Smid, N., Spencer, C., Tadinac, M., Todorova, E. N., Troland, K., Van den Brande, L., Van Heck, G., Van Langenhove, L., & Yang, K. S. (1990). International preferences in selecting mates. *Journal of Cross-Cultural Psychology, 21,* 5–47.

Bustillo, J. R., Lauriello, J., Horan, W. P., & Keith, S. J. (2001). The psychosocial treatment of schizophrenia: An update. *American Journal of Psychiatry, 158,* 163–175.

Butler, K. (1994, June 26). A house divided. *Los Angeles Times Magazine.*

Byers, E. S., & Grenier, G. (2003). Premature or rapid ejaculation: Heterosexual couples' perceptions of men's ejaculatory behavior. *Archives of Sexual Behavior, 32,* 261–270.

Byne, W. (1997). Why we cannot conclude that sexual orientation is primarily a biological phenomenon. *Journal of Homosexuality, 34,* 73–80.

Byrd, K. R. (1994). The narrative reconstructions of incest survivors. *American Psychologist, 49,* 439–440.

Byrne, R. (2003, March 2). When man pulled ahead of machine, albeit briefly. *New York Times,* 12.

Cabeza, R., & Nyberg, L. (2003). Special issue of functional neuroimaging of memory. *Neuropsychologia, 41,* 241–244.

Cacioppo, J. T. (2002). Social neuroscience: Understanding the pieces fosters understanding the whole and vice versa. *American Psychologist, 57,* 819–831.

Cacioppo, J. T., & Petty, R. E. (1982). The need for cognition. *Journal of Personality and Social Psychology, 42,* 116–131.

Cacioppo, J. T., Berntson, G. G., Larsen, J. R., Poehlmann, K. M., & Ito, T. A. (2000). The psychophysiology of emotion. In M. Lewis & J. M. Haviland-Jones (Eds.), *Handbook of emotions* (2nd ed., pp. 173–191). New York: Guilford.

Cacioppo, J. T., Klein, D. J., Berntson, G. G., & Hatfield, E. (1993). The psychophysiology of emotion. In M. Lewis & J. M. Haviland (Eds.), *Handbook of emotions.* New York: Guilford.

Cadoret, R. J., Leve, L. D., & Devor, E. (1997). Genetics of aggressive and violent behavior. *Psychiatric Clinics of North America, 20,* 301–322.

Cahill, L., Prins, B., Weber, M., & McGaugh, J. L. (1994). B-adrenergic activation and memory for emotional events. *Nature, 371,* 702–704.

Caldwell, J. C., Orubuloye, I. O., & Caldwell, P. (1997). Male and female circumcision in Africa from a regional to a specific Nigerian examination. *Social Science & Medicine, 44,* 1181–1193.

Callahan, C. M. (2000). Intelligence and giftedness. In R. J. Sternberg (Ed.), *Handbook of intelligence.* New York: Cambridge University Press.

Calle, E. E., Rodriguez, C., Walker-Thurmond, K., & Thun, M. J. (2003). Overweight, obesity, and mortality from cancer in a prospectively studied cohort of U.S. adults. *New England Journal of Medicine, 348,* 1625–1638.

Calvo, M. G., & Carreiras, M. (1993). Selective influence of test anxiety on reading processes. *British Journal of Psychology, 84,* 375–388.

Cam, J., & Farr, M. (2003). 1. Mechanisms of disease: Drug addiction. *New England Journal of Medicine, 349,* 975–986.

Camp, G. C. (1994). A longitudinal study of correlates of creativity. *Creativity Research Journal, 7,* 125–144.

Campbell, F. A., Pungello, E. P., Miller-Johnson, S., Burchinal, M., & Ramey, C. T. (2001). The development of cognitive and academic abilities: Growth curves from an early childhood educational experiment. *Developmental Psychology, 37,* 231–242.

Canfield, R.L. (2003, August 5). Cited in J. E. Brody, Even low lead levels pose perils for children. *New York Times,* D7.

Canli, T., Desmond, J. E., Zhao, Z., & Gabrieli, J. D. E. (2002a). Sex differences in the neural basis of emotional memories. *Proceedings of the National Academy of Sciences, 99,* 10789–10794.

Canli, T., Sivers, H., Whitfield, S. L., Gotlib, I. H., & Gabrieli, J. E. D. (2002b). Amygdala response to happy faces as a function of extraversion. *Science, 296,* 2191.

Caplan, N., Choy, M. H., & Whitmore, J. K. (1992). Indochinese refugee families and academic achievement. *Scientific American, 266,* 36–42.

Caplan, P. (1994, June 5). Cited in A. Japenga, DMS. *Los Angeles Times Magazine.*

Caporael, L. R. (2001). Evolutionary psychology: Toward a unifying theory and a hybrid science. *Annual Review of Psychology, 52,* 607–628.

Carducci, B. J. (1998). *The psychology of personality.* Pacific Grove, CA: Brooks/Cole.

Carey, B. (2002, December 16). The brain in love. *Los Angeles Times,* F1.

Carey, K. B., & Correia, C. J. (1997). Drinking motives predict alcohol-related problems in college students. *Journal of Studies on Alcohol, 58,* 100–185.

Carey, T., Ratliff-Schaub, K., Funk, J., Weinle, C., Myers, M., & Jenks, J. (2002). Double-blind placebo-controlled trial of secretin: Effects on aberrant behavior in children with autism. *Journal of Autism and Developmental Disorders, 32,* 161–167.

Cariaga, D. (1995, April 9). The return of the prodigy. *Los Angeles Times/Calendar,* 54–55.

Carlin, A. (2000, July 4). Cited in J. Robbins, Virtual reality finds a real place as a medical aid. *New York Times,* D6.

Carlson, J. M. (1990). Subjective ideological similarity between candidates and supporters: A study of party elites. *Political Psychology, 11,* 485–492.

Carlson, N. R. (1998). *Physiology of behavior* (6th ed.). Boston: Allyn & Bacon.

Caroff, S. N., Mann, S. C., Campbell, E. C., & Sullivan, K. A. (2002). Movement disorders associated with atypical antipsychotic drugs. *Journal of Clinical Psychiatry, 63* (supplement 4), 12–19.

Carpenter, W. (2003, May 20). Cited in E. Goode, Leading drugs for psychosis come under new scrutiny. *New York Times,* A1.

Carskadon, M. (2000, March 28). Cited in N. Hellmich, Teen's thing: Losing sleep. *USA Today,* 1A.

Carskadon, M. A., & Taylor, J. F. (1997). Public policy and sleep disorders. In M. R. Pressman & W. C. Orr (Eds.), *Understanding sleep: The evaluation and treatment of sleep disorders.* Washington, DC: American Psychological Association.

Cart, J. (2002, February 20). Study finds Utah leads nation in antidepressant use. *Los Angeles Times,* A6.

Cartwright, R. (1988, July–August). Cited in *Psychology Today.*

Cartwright, R. (2002, July 15). Cited in M. H. Gossard, Taking control. *Newsweek,* 47.

Casey, D. E. (2000). Antipsychotic standard of care: Redefining the definition of atypical antipsychotics. *Journal of Clinical Psychiatry, 61* (supplement 3), 3.

Caspi, A. (2000). The child is father of the man: Personality continuities from childhood to adulthood. *Journal of Personality and Social Psychology, 78,* 158–172.

Caspi, A., & Roberts, B. W. (1999). Personality continuity and change across the life course. In L. A. Pervin & O. P. John (Eds.), *Handbook of personality* (2nd ed.). New York: Guilford.

Cassady, J. C., & Johnson, R. E. (2001). Cognitive test anxiety and academic performance. *Contemporary Educational Psychology, 27,* 270–295.

Cattell, R. B. (1943). The description of personality: Basic traits resolved into clusters. *Journal of Abnormal and Social Psychology, 38,* 476–506.

Cavanagh, J. T. O., Carson, A. J., Sharpe, M., & Lawrie, S. M. (2003). Psychological autopsy studies of suicide: A systematic review. *Psychological Medicine, 33,* 395–405.

Ceci, S. J. (2000, April 25). Cited in J. E. Brody, Memories of things that never were. *New York Times,* D8.

Ceci, S. J., & Bruck, M. (1995). *Jeopardy in the courtroom: A scientific analysis of children's testimony.* Washington, DC: American Psychological Association.

Ceci, S. J., Huffman, M. L. C., Smith, E., & Loftus, E. (1994). Repeatedly thinking about a non-event: Source misattributions among preschoolers. *Consciousness and Cognition, 3,* 388–407.

Ceci, S. J., Rosenblum, T., de Bruyn, E., & Lee, D. Y. (1997). A bio-ecological model of intellectual development: Moving beyond h2. In R. J. Sternberg & E. Grigorenko (Eds.), *Intelligence, heredity, and environment.* New York: Cambridge University Press.

Ceniceros, S., & Brown, G. R. (1998). Acupuncture: A review of its history, theories, and indications. *Southern Medical Journal, 91,* 1121–1125.

Cerone, D. (1989, October 22). How to train an 1,800-pound star. *Los Angeles Times/Calendar.*

Chaiken, S., & Eagly, A. H. (1976). Communication modality as a determinant of message persuasiveness and message comprehensibility. *Journal of Personality and Social Psychology, 34,* 605–614.

Chamberlin, J. (2000, February). Where are all these students coming from? *Monitor on Psychology.*

Chambers, R. A., Taylor, J. R., & Potenza, M. N. (2003). Developmental neurocircuitry of motivation in adolescence: A critical period of addiction vulnerability. *American Journal of Psychiatry, 160,* 1041–1052.

Chambless, D. L., & Ollendick, T. H. (2001). Empirically supported psychological interventions: Controversies and evidence. *Annual Review of Psychology, 52,* 685–716.

Channouf, A., Canac, D., & Gosset, O. (2000). Nonspecific effects of subliminal advertising. *European Review of Applied Psychology, 49,* 20–21.

Charney, D. (2003). Cited in C. Holden, Future brightening for depression treatment. *Science, 302,* 810–813.

Charney, D. A., & Russell, R. C. (1994). An overview of sexual harassment. *American Journal of Psychiatry, 151,* 10–17.

Chasnoff, I. (1997, December). Cited in B. Azar, Researchers debunk myth of the "crack baby." *APA Monitor.*

Chavez, S. (1994, January 3). Tough stand on attendance pays off at South Gate High. *Los Angeles Times.*

Chavira, D. A., Stein, M. B., & Malcarne, V. L. (2002). Scrutinizing the relationship between shyness and social phobia. *Anxiety Disorders, 16,* 585–598.

Chellappah, N. K., Viegnehas, H., Milgrom, P., & Lo, B. L. (1990). Prevalence of dental anxiety and fear in children in Singapore. *Community Dentistry Oral Epidemiology, 18,* 269–271.

Chen, J., Chang, S., Duncan, S. A., Okano, H. J., Fishell, G., & Aderem, A. (1996). Disruption of the MacMARCKS gene prevents cranial neural tube closure and results in anencephaly. *Proceedings of the National Academy of Sciences, 93,* 6275–6279.

Chen, S. (2001). The role of theories in mental representations and their use in social perception: A theory-based approach to significant-other representations and transference. In G.B. Moskowitz (Ed.), *Cognitive social psychology*. Mahwah, NJ: Lawrence Erlbaum.

Chen, Y., Mestek, A., Liu, J., Hurley, J. A., & Yu, L. (1993). Molecular cloning and functional expression of a u-opioid receptor from rat brain. *Molecular Pharmacology, 44,* 8–12.

Chin, P. (1994, March 28). Sins of the son. *People,* 38–41.

Chokroverty, S. (2000). *Sleep disorders medicine* (2nd ed.). Boston: Butterworth-Heinemann.

Chomsky, N. (1957). *Syntactic structures.* The Hague: Mouton.

Christensen, D. (2000). Sobering work: Unraveling alcohol's effects on the developing brain. *Science News, 138,* 28–29.

Christensen, D. (2001). Medicinal mimicry. *Science News, 159,* 74–75.

Christensen, D. (2003). Dietary dilemmas. *Science News, 163,* 88–90.

Christopher, K. (2003, March/April). "Miss Cleo" settles with the Federal Trade Commission. *Skeptical Inquirer,* 8.

Chwalisz, K., Diener, E., & Gallagher, D. (1988). Autonomic arousal feedback and emotional experience: Evidence from the spinal cord injury. *Journal of Personality and Social Psychology, 54,* 820–828.

Cialdini, R. B. (2001). *Influence: Science and practice* (4th ed.). New York: Allyn & Bacon.

Cialdini, R. B. (2003, February). The science of persuasion. *Scientific American,* 76–81.

Cirelli, C., Pompeiano, M., & Tononi, G. (1996). Neuronal gene expression in the waking state: A role for locus coeruleus. *Science, 274,* 1211–1215.

Clark, L. A., Watson, D., & Reynolds, S. (1995). Diagnosis and classification of psychopathology: Challenges to the current system and future directions. *Annual Review of Psychology, 46,* 121–153.

Clark, R.E., Manns, J. R., & Squire, L. R. (2002). Classical conditioning, awareness, and brain systems. *Trends in Cognitive Sciences, 6,* 524–531.

Clarke, A. M., & Clarke, A. D. B. (1989). The later cognitive effects on early intervention. *Intelligence, 13,* 289–297.

Clay, R. A. (1997, April). Is assisted suicide ever a rational choice? *APA Monitor.*

Clay, R. A. (2002, September). A renaissance for humanistic psychology. *Monitor on Psychology,* 42–43.

Cleveland, H. H., Jacobson, K. C., Lipinski, J. J., & Rose, D. C. (2000). Genetic and shared environmental contributions to the relationship between the home environment and child and adolescent achievement. *Intelligence, 28,* 69–86.

Clines, F. X. (2001, February 28). Fighting Appalachia's top cash crop, marijuana. *New York Times,* A10.

Cloud, J. (2002, November 4). Is pot good for you? *Time,* 62–66.

Cobain, K. (2002). *Journals.* New York: Riverside Books.

Coccaro, E. F., & Kavoussi, R. J. (1997). Fluoxetine and impulsive aggressive behavior in personality-disordered subjects. *Archives of General Psychiatry, 54,* 1081–1088.

Cohen, A. (1997, September 8). Battle of the binge. *Time.*

Cohen, D. (2002). Cited in B. Bower, Psychotic biology, *Science News, 162,* 195–196.

Cohen, D. B. (1979). *Sleep and dreaming: Origins, nature and functions.* New York: Pergamon Press.

Cohen, J. (2002). Confronting the limits of success. *Science, 296,* 2320–2324.

Cohen, N. J. (1984). Preserved learning capacity in amnesia: Evidence for multiple memory systems. In L. R. Squire & N. Butters (Eds.), *Neuropsychology of memory.* New York: Guilford.

Cohen, S. (2003). Social stress, social support, and the susceptibility to the common cold. *American Psychological Society, 16,* 13.

Cohen, S. L. (2000, March 22). Hi, I'm your doctor. I haven't slept in 36 hours. *USA Today,* 29A.

Cohen, S., Tyrrell, D. A. J., & Smith, A. P. (1997). Psychological stress in humans and susceptibility to the common cold. In T. W. Miller (Ed.), *Clinical disorders and stressful life events.* Madison, CT: International Universities Press.

Coie, J. D., & Dodge, K. A. (1998). Aggression and antisocial behavior. In W. Damon & R. M. Lerner (Eds.), *Handbook of child psychology* (Vol. 1). New York: John Wiley & Sons.

Colangelo, N. (1997). The "termites" grow up and grow old. *Contemporary Psychology, 42,* 208–209.

Colapinto, J. (1996, May 30). Rock & roll heroin. *Rolling Stone.*

Coleman, L., & Coleman, J. (2002). The measurement of puberty: A review. *Journal of Adolescence, 25,* 535–550.

Collacott, E. A., Zimmerman, J. T., White, D. W., & Rindone, J. P. (2000). Bipolar permanent magnets for the treatment of chronic low back pain. *Journal of the American Medical Association, 283,* 1322–1325.

Collings, S., & King, M. (1994). Ten-year follow-up of 50 patients with bulimia nervosa. *British Journal of Psychiatry, 164,* 80–87.

Collins, W. A., Maccoby, E. E., Steinberg, L., Hetherington, E. M., & Bornstein, M. H. (2000). Contemporary research on parenting. *American Psychologist, 55,* 218–232.

Colom, R., Juan-Espinosa, M., Abad, F., & Garcia, L. F. (2000). Negligible sex differences in general intelligence. *Intelligence, 28,* 57–68.

Comarow, A. (2001, April 23). Scary news, soothing numbers. *U.S. News & World Report,* 74.

Compas, B. E., Hinden, B. R., & Gerhardt, C. A. (1995). Adolescent development: Pathways and processes of risk and resilience. *Annual Review of Psychology, 46,* 265–293.

Conner, A. (2000, March). Classic experiments in social psychology. *APS Observer,* 9.

Conners, C. K., March, J. S., Frances, A., Wells, K. C., & Ross, R. (2001). Treatment of attention deficit-hyperactivity disorder: Expert consensus guidelines. *Journal of Attention Disorders, 4,* 7–128.

Connor, C. E. (2002). Reconstructing a 3D world. *Science, 290,* 376–377.

Connor, L. (1982). In A. J. Marsella & G. M. White (Eds.), *Cultural conceptions of mental health and therapy.* Boston: D. Reidel.

Conway, M. A., Anderson, S. J., Larsen, S. F., Donnelly, C. M., McDaniel, M. A., McClelland, A. G. R., Rawles, R. E., & Logie, R. H. (1994). The formation of flashbulb memories. *Memory and Cognition, 22,* 326–343.

Cook, G. (2002, January 2). Aha! Eureka moments start with confusion and end with discovery. *San Diego Union Tribune,* F1.

Cooper, P. J., Zheng, Y., Richard, C., Vavrik, J., Heinrichs, B., & Siegmund, G. J. (2003). The impact of hands-free message reception response on driving task performance. *Accident Analysis and Prevention, 35,* 23–35.

Cooper, R. T. (1999, April 14). Head Start's fresh start. *Los Angeles Times,* B2.

Copeland, L. (1999, December 16). Meet South's new sheriffs. *USA Today,* A1.

Coren, S., & Ward, L. M. (1993). *Sensation and perception* (4th ed.). San Diego: Harcourt Brace Jovanovich.

Corrigan, P. W. (2000). Mental health stigma as social attribution: Implications for research methods and attitude change. *Clinical Psychology: Science and Practice, 7,* 48–67.

Cosmides, L., & Tooby, J. (1994). Cited in B. Bower, Roots of reason. *Science News, 145,* 72–75.

Cottraux, J., Note, I., Albuisson, E., Yao, S. N., Note, B., Mollard, E., Bonasse, F., Jalenaques, I., Guerin, J., & Coudert, A. J. (2000). Cognitive behavior therapy versus supportive therapy in social phobia: A randomized controlled trial. *Psychotherapy and Psychosomatics, 69,* 137–146.

Courchesne, E., Carper, R., & Akshoomoff, N. (2003). Evidence of brain overgrowth in the first year of life in autism. *Journal of the American Medical Association, 290,* 337–344.

Covington, M. V. (2000). Goal theory, motivation, and school achievement: An integrative review. *Annual Review of Psychology, 51,* 171–200.

Cowley, G. (1994, October 24). Testing the science of intelligence. *Newsweek.*

Cowley, G. (2000a, April 24). Looking beyond Viagra. *Newsweek,* 77–78.

Cowley, G. (2000b, July 31). Understanding autism. *Newsweek,* 46–55.

Cowley, G. (2001, February 12). New ways to stay clean. *Newsweek,* 43–47.

Cowley, G. (2002, June 24). The disappearing mind. *Newsweek,* 42–50.

Cowley, G. (2003, February 24). Our bodies our fears. *Newsweek,* 42–49.

Coyne, J. C. (1994). Self-reported distress: Analog or ersatz depression? *Psychological Bulletin, 116,* 29–45.

Coyne, J. C., & Whiffen, V. E. (1995). Issues in personality as diathesis for depression: The case of sociotropy—dependency and autonomy—self-criticism. *Psychological Bulletin, 118,* 358–378.

Craik, F. I. M., & Lockhart, R. S. (1972). Levels of processing: A framework for memory research. *Journal of Verbal Learning and Verbal Behavior, 11,* 671–684.

Craik, F. I. M., & Tulving, E. (1975). Depth of processing and the retention of words in episodic memory. *Journal of Experimental Psychology: General, 104,* 268–294.

Cramer, P. (2000). Defense mechanisms in psychology today. *American Psychologist, 55,* 637–646.

Cramer, P. (2003). Defense mechanisms and physiological reactivity to stress. *Journal of Personality, 71,* 221–244.

Crawford, H. J., Gur, R. C., Skolnick, B., Gur, R. E., & Benson, D. M. (1993). Effects of hypnosis on regional cerebral blood flow during ischemic pain with and without suggested hypnotic analgesia. *International Journal of Psychophysiology, 15,* 181–195.

Crawford, M., & Popp, D. (2002). Sexual double standards: A review and methodological critique of two decades of research. *The Journal of Sex Research, 40,* 13–26.

Cray, D. (2000, July). Incredible shrinking doctors. *Popular Science,* 63–65.

Creed, F. (1993). Stress and psychosomatic disorders. In L. Goldberger & S. Breznitz (Eds.), *Handbook of stress: Theoretical and clinical aspects* (2nd ed.). New York: Free Press.

Crews, F. (1996). The verdict on Freud. *Psychological Science, 7,* 63–68.

Crews, F. (2001, January 2). Cited in M. Crenson, Brain growth gets blame for turbulent teen years. *USA Today,* 6D.

References

Crick, F. (2002, November 17). Cited in M. A. Hiltzik, Nobel Laureate Francis H.C. Crick discovered DNA. Now he's hunting for the very essence of our being—the course of conscious thought. *Los Angeles Times Magazine*, 12–15.

Cromer, A. (1993). *Uncommon sense: The heretical nature of science*. New York: Oxford University Press.

Crooks, R., & Baur, K. (2002). *Our sexuality* (8th ed.). Pacific Grove, CA: Wadsworth.

Crow, T. J. (1985). The two syndrome concept: Origins and current status. *Schizophrenia Bulletin, 11,* 471–486.

Crowder, R. G. (1992). Eidetic imagery. In L. R. Squire (Ed.), *Encyclopedia of learning and memory.* New York: Macmillan.

Cuijpers, P. (2003). Three decades of drug prevention research. *Drugs: Education, Prevention and Policy, 10,* 7–20.

Cull, W. L., & Zechmeister, E. B. (1994). The learning ability paradox in adult metamemory research: Where are the metamemory differences between good and poor learners? *Memory & Cognition, 22,* 249–257.

Culp, R. E., Culp, A. M., Osofsky, J. D., & Osofsky, H. J. (1991). Adolescent and older mothers' interaction patterns with their six-month-old infants. *Journal of Adolescence, 14,* 195–200.

Curtiss, S. (1977). *Genie: A psycholinguistic study of a modern-day "wild child."* New York: Academic Press.

Czeisler, C. A. (1994). Cited in R. Nowak, Chronobiologists out of sync over light therapy patents. *Science, 263,* 1217–1218.

Czeisler, C. A., Duffy, J. F., Shanahan, T. L., Brown, E. N., Mitchell, J. F., Rimmer, D. W., Ronda, J. M., Siva, E. J., Allan, J. S., Emens, J. S., Dijk, K., & Kronauer, R. E. (1999). Stability, precision, and near-24-hour period of the human circadian pacemaker. *Science, 284,* 2177–2181.

Czeisler, C. A., Shanahan, T. L., Klerman, E. B., Martens, H., Brotman, D. J., Emens, J. S., Klein, T., & Rizzo, J. F. (1995). Suppression of melatonin secretion in some blind patients by exposure to bright light. *New England Journal of Medicine, 332,* 6–11.

Dackis, C. A., & O'Brien, C. P. (2001). Cocaine dependence: A disease of the brain's reward center. *Journal of Substance Abuse Treatment, 21,* 111–117.

Dalgard, O. S., Bjork, S., & Tambs, K. (1995). Social support, negative life events and mental health. *British Journal of Psychiatry, 166,* 29–34.

Dalto, C. A., Ossoff, E. P., & Pollack, R. B. (1994). Processes underlying reactions to a campaign speech: Cognition, affect, and voter concern. *Journal of Social Behavior and Personality, 9,* 701–713.

Damasio, A. (1999, October 19). Cited in S. Blakeslee, Brain damage during infancy stunts moral learning, study finds. *Los Angeles Times,* A1.

Damasio, A. R. (1999, December). How the brain creates the mind. *Scientific American,* 112–117.

Damasio, H., Brabowski, T., Frank, R., Galaburda, A. M., & Damasio, A. R. (1994). The return of Phineas Gage: Clues about the brain from the skull of a famous patient. *Science, 264,* 1102–1105.

Damon, W. (1999, August). The moral development of children. *Scientific American,* 73–78.

Dandoy, A. C., & Goldstein, A. G. (1990). The use of cognitive appraisal to reduce stress reactions: A replication. *Journal of Social Behavior and Personality, 5,* 275–285.

Daniszewski, J. (1997, June 25). Female circumcision ban nullified. *Los Angeles Times,* A4.

Darwin, C. (1859). *The origin of species by means of natural selection or the preservation of favored races in the struggle for life.* London: John Murray.

Darwin, C. (1872; reprinted 1965). *The expression of the emotions in man and animals.* Chicago: University of Chicago Press.

Davidson, J. R. T. (1994). International advances in the treatment of social phobia. *Journal of Clinical Psychiatry, 55,* 123–129.

Davidson, P. S. R., & Glisky, E. L. (2002). Is flashbulb memory a special instance of source memory? Evidence from older adults. *Memory, 10,* 99–111.

Davidson, R. J., Putnam, K. M., & Larson, C. L. (2000). Dysfunction in the neural circuitry of emotion regulation—A possible prelude to violence. *Science, 289,* 591–594.

Davidson, R. J., Scherer, K. R., & Goldsmith, H. H. (2003). Chapter 1: Introduction: Neuroscience. In R. J. Davidson, K. R. Scherer & H. H. Goldsmith (Eds.), *Handbook of affective sciences.* New York: Oxford University Press.

Davies, I. R. L., & Corbett, G. G. (1997). A cross-cultural study of colour grouping: Evidence for weak linguistic relativity. *British Journal of Psychology, 88,* 493–517.

Davis, J. (2003, May 23). Cited in K. S. Peterson, Sexually active teens also are often clueless. *USA Today,* 8D.

Davis, J. L., & Petretic-Jackson, P. A. (2000). The impact of child sexual abuse on adult interpersonal functioning: A review and synthesis of the empirical literature. *Aggression and Violent Behavior, 5,* 291–328.

Davis, J. M., Chen, N., & Glick, I. D. (2003). A meta-analysis of the efficacy of second-generation antipsychotics. *Archives of General Psychiatry, 60,* 553–564.

Davis, K. (2003). Cited in C. Holden, Deconstructing schizophrenia. *Science, 299,* 333–335.

Davis, M. C., Matthews, K. A., & Twamley, E. W. (1999). Is life more difficult on Mars or Venus? A meta-analytic review of sex differences in major and minor life events. *Annals of Behavioral Medicine, 21,* 83–97.

Davison, G. C., & Neale, J. M. (1990). *Abnormal psychology* (3rd ed.). New York: Wiley.

Davison, G. C., & Neale, J. M. (1994). *Abnormal psychology* (6th ed.). New York: Wiley.

Dawood, K., Pillard, R. C., Horvath, C., Revelle, W., & Bailey, J. M. (2000). Familial aspects of male homosexuality. *Archives of Sexual Behavior, 29,* 155–163.

Dawson, G., Carver, L., Meltzoff, A. N., Panagiotides, H., McPartland, J., & Webb, S. J. (2002). Neural correlates of face and object recognition in young children with autism spectrum disorders, developmental delay, and typical development. *Child Development, 73,* 700–717.

de Grott, J. M. (2002). The complexity of the role of social support in relation to the psychological distress associated with cancer. *Journal of Psychosomatic Research, 52,* 277–278.

De Gucht, V., & Fischler, B. (2002). Somatization: A critical review of conceptual and methodological issues. *Psychosomatics, 43,* 1–9.

de Rivera, J. (1997). The construction of false memory syndrome: The experience of retractors. *Psychological Inquiry, 8,* 271–292.

de Waal, F. B. M. (2002). Evolutionary psychology: The wheat and the chaff. *Current Directions in Psychological Science, 11,* 187–190.

DeAngelis, T. (1966, March). Women's contributions large; recognition isn't. *Monitor American Psychological Association.*

DeAngelis, T. (1994, February). People's drug of choice offers potent side effects. *APA Monitor.*

DeAngelis, T. (2002, March). Binge-eating disorder: What's the best treatment? *Monitor on Psychology,* 30–32.

deCharms, R. (1980). The origins of competence and achievement motivation in personal causation. In L. J. Fyans, Jr. (Ed.), *Achievement motivation.* New York: Plenum Press.

Deci, E. L., & Ryan, R. M. (1985). *Intrinsic motivation and self-determination in human behavior.* New York: Plenum Press.

Deci, E. L., Koestner, R., & Ryan, R. M. (1999). A meta-analytic review of experiments examining the effects of extrinsic rewards on intrinsic motivation. *Psychological Bulletin, 125,* 627–668.

Deckro, G. R. (2002, September 11). Cited in M. Duenwald, Students find another staple of campus life: Stress. *New York Times,* D5.

DeCurtis, A. (1994, June 2). Kurt Cobain, 1967–1994. *Rolling Stone.*

Deffenbacher, J. (2003, March). Cited in J. D. Holloway, Advances in anger management. *Monitor on Psychology,* 54–55.

Deffenbacher, J. L., Dahlen, E. R., Lynch, R. S., Morris, C. D., & Gowensmith, W. N. (2000). An application of Beck's cognitive therapy to general anger reduction. *Cognitive Therapy and Research, 24,* 689–697.

Dehaene-Lambertz, G., Dehaene, S., & Hertz-Pannier, L. (2002). Functional neuroimaging of speech perception in infants. *Science, 298,* 2013–2015.

Dement, W. C. (1999). *The promise of sleep.* New York: Random House.

Dement, W. C., & Kleitman, N. (1957). The relation of eye movements during sleep to dream activity: An objective method for the study of dreaming. *Journal of Experimental Psychology, 53,* 339–346.

Dennerstein, L., Dudley, E., & Burger, H. (1997). Well-being and the menopausal transition. *Journal of Psychosomatic Obstetrics and Gynecology, 18,* 95–101.

DePetrillo, P. (2003, September 8). Cited in J. Ewers, Drinking in your genes. *U.S. News & World Report,* 44.

Deregowski, J. B. (1980). *Illusions, patterns and pictures: A crosscultural perspective.* Orlando, FL: Academic Press.

Devine, P. G., Hamilton, D. L., & Ostrom, T. M. (Eds.). (1994). *Social cognition: Impact on social psychology.* New York: Academic Press.

Diamond, M., & Sigmundson, H. K. (1997). Sex reassignment at birth. *Archives of Pediatric Adolescent Medicine, 151,* 298–304.

Diener, E., & Diener, C. (1996). Most people are happy. *Psychological Science, 7,* 181–185.

Diesendruck, G., & Shatz, M. (2001). Two-year-olds' recognition of hierarchies: Evidence from their interpretation of the semantic relation between object labels. *Cognitive Development, 16,* 577–594.

Dietrich, K. (2003, August 5). Cited in J. E. Brody, Even low lead levels pose perils for children. *New York Times,* D7.

Digman, J. M. (1997). Higher-order factors of the Big Five. *Journal of Personality and Social Psychology, 73,* 1246–1256.

DiLalla, L. F. (2002). Behavior genetics of aggression in children: Review and future directions. *Developmental Review, 22,* 593–622.

Dinnel, D. L., Kleinknecht, R. A., & Tanaka-Matsumi, J. (2002). A cross-cultural comparison of social phobia symptoms. *Journal of Psychopathology and Behavioral Assessment, 24,* 75–84.

Dion, K. K., Berscheid, E., & Walster, E. (1972). What is beautiful is good. *Journal of Personality and Social Psychology, 24,* 285–290.

Dittmann, M. (2003, February). Psychology's first prescribers. *Monitor on Psychology,* 36–39.

Dixon, W. A., & Reid, J. K. (2000). Positive life events as a moderator of stress-related depressive symptoms. *Journal of Counseling & Development, 78,* 343–347.

Dobelle, W. (2000, January 17). Cited in M. Ritter, Camera wired to brain provides some useful vision for blind man. *San Diego Union-Tribune*, A-6.

Dobson, K. S., & Khatri, N. (2000). Cognitive therapy: Looking backward, looking forward. *Journal of Clinical Psychology, 56*, 907–923.

Dolan, M. (1995a, February 11). When the mind's eye blinks. *Los Angeles Times*.

Dolan, M. (1995b, August 1). Justices rule for adoptive parents of San Diego boy. *Los Angeles Times*.

Dolan, M. (2002, June 7). Fatherhood transcends biology, high court says. *Los Angeles Times*, A1.

Dolan, R. J. (2002). Emotion, cognition, and behavior. *Science, 298*, 1191–1194.

Domhoff, G. W. (2003). *The scientific study of dreams*. Washington, DC: American Psychological Association.

Domino, G. (1994). Assessment of creativity with the ACL: An empirical comparison of four scales. *Creativity Research Journal, 7*, 21–33.

Dorman, M. F. (2003, January 14). Cited in E. Nagourney, Experts urge early ear implants. *New York Times*, D6.

Dorn, L. D., Susman, E. J., & Ponirakis, A. (2003). Pubertal timing and adolescent adjustment and behavior: Conclusions vary by rater. *Journal of Youth and Adolescence, 32*, 157–167.

Doty, R. L. (2001). Olfaction. *Annual Review of Psychology, 52*, 423–452.

Dowling, C. G. (2000, August, 14). Mistaken identity. *People*, 50–55.

Drevets, W. C., Price, J. L., Simpson, J. R., Jr., Todd, R. D., Reich, T., Vannier, M., & Raiche, M. E. (1997). Subgenual prefrontal cortex abnormalities in mood disorders. *Nature, 386*, 824–827.

Drewnowski, A. (1997). Cited in K. Fackelmann, The bitter truth. *Science News, 152*, 24–25.

Drummond, S. P. A. (2000). Cited in B. Bower, Sleepyheads' brains veer from restful path. *Science News, 157*, 103.

DuBois, D. L., Tevendale, H. D., Burk-Braxton, C., Swenson, L. P., & Hardesty, J. L. (2000). Self-system influences during early adolescence: Investigation of an integrative model. *Journal of Early Adolescence, 20*, 12–43.

Duenwald, M. (2003, June 17). More Americans seeking help for depression. *New York Times*, A1.

Duffy, J. (2002, April). Cited in M. Weinstock, Night owls vs. early birds. *Discover*, 11.

Duncan, J., Seitz, R. J., Kolodny, J., Bor, D., Herzog, H., Ahmed, A., Newell, F. N., & Emslie, H. (2000). A neural basis for general intelligence. *Science, 289*, 457–460.

Dunn, J. (2003). Emotional development in early childhood: A social relationship perspective. In R. J. Davidson, K. R. Scherer & H. H. Goldsmith (Eds.), *Handbook of affective sciences*. New York: Oxford University Press.

Dunn, M., & Cutler, N. (2000). Sexual issues in older adults. *AIDS Patient Care and STDs, 14*, 67–69.

Durand, V. M., & Barlow, D. H. (2003). *Essential of abnormal psychology* (3rd ed.). Monterey, CA: Wadsworth/Thomson.

Durso, F. T., Rea, C. B., & Dayton, T. (1994). Graph-theoretic confirmation of restructuring during insight. *Psychological Science, 5*, 94–98.

Duyme, M. (1999). Cited in B. Bower, Kids adopted late reap IQ increases. *Science News, 156*, 54–55.

Dyer-Friedman, J., Glaser, B., Hessl, D., Johnston, C., Huffman, L. C., Taylor, A., Wisbeck, J., & Reiss, A. I. (2002). Genetic and environmental influences on the cognitive outcomes of children with fragile X syndrome. *Journal of the American Academy of Child and Adolescence Psychiatry, 41*, 237–244.

Eagle, M. N. (2000). A critical evaluation of current conceptions of transference and countertransference. *Psychoanalytic Psychology, 17*, 24–37.

Eagly, A. H., Wood, W., & Diekman, A. B. (2000). Social role theory of sex differences and similarities: A current appraisal. In T. Eckes & H. M. Trautner (Eds.), *The developmental social psychology of gender*. Mahwah, NJ: Lawrence Erlbaum.

Earleywine, M. (2002). *Understanding marijuana*. New York: Oxford University Press.

Ebbinghaus, H. (1885; reprinted 1913). *Memory: A contribution to experimental psychology* (H. A. Ruger & C. E. Bussenius, Trans.). New York: Teachers College Press.

Eccles, J. S., & Wigfield, A. (2002). Motivational beliefs, values and goals. *Annual Review of Psychology, 53*, 109–132.

Eckes, T., & Trautner, H. M. (2000). *The developmental social psychology of gender*. Mahwah, NJ: Lawrence Erlbaum.

Eddings, J. (1994, December 26). Atlanta's new top cop makes her mark. *U.S. News & World Report*.

Eden, G. (2003, July 28). Cited in C. Gorman, The new science of dyslexia. *Time*, 52–59.

Edinger, J. D., Wohlgemuth, W. K., Radtke, R. A., Marsh, G. F., & Quillian, R. E. (2001). Cognitive behavioral therapy for treatment of chronic primary insomnia. *Journal of the American Medical Association, 285*, 1856–1864.

Egan, T. (1999, February 28). The war on crack retreats, still taking prisoners. *New York Times*, 1.

Egan, V., Chiswick, A., Santosh, C., Naidu, K., Rimmington, J. E., & Best, J. K. (1994). Size isn't everything: A study of brain volume, intelligence and auditory evoked potentials. *Personality and Individual Differences, 17*, 357–367.

Eibl-Eibesfeldt, I. (1973). The expressive behavior of the deaf-and-blind-born. In M. von Cranach & I. Vine (Eds.), *Social communication and movement*. San Diego, CA: Academic Press.

Eich, E., Macaulay, D., Loewenstein, R. J., & Dihle, P. H. (1997). Memory, amnesia, and dissociative identity disorder. *Psychological Science, 8*, 417–422.

Eichenbaum, H. (1997). Declarative memory: Insights from cognitive neurobiology. *Annual Review of Psychology, 48*, 547–572.

Eikeseth, S. (2001). Recent critiques of the UCLA Young Autism Project. *Behavioral Interventions, 16*, 249–264.

Eisen, M. R. (1994). Psychoanalytic and psychodynamic models of hypnoanalysis. In J. W. Rhue, S. J. Lynn & I. Kirsch (Eds.), *Handbook of clinical hypnosis*. Washington, DC: American Psychological Association.

Eisenberger, R., & Armeli, S. (1997). Can salient reward increase creative performance without reducing intrinsic creative interest? *Journal of Personality and Social Psychology, 72*, 652–663.

Eisenberger, R., Pierce, W. D., & Cameron, J. (1999). Effects of reward on intrinsic motivation—negative, neutral, and positive: Comment on Deci, Koestner, and Ryan (1999). *Psychological Bulletin, 125*, 677–691.

Ekman, P. (2003). *Emotions revealed: Recognizing faces and feelings to improve communication and emotional life*. New York: Times Books.

Elias, M. (1989, August 9). With guidance, a child can control negative traits. *USA Today*.

Elias, M. (2002, July 8). Study: Antidepressant barely better than placebo. *USA Today*, 6D.

Ellason, J. W., & Ross, C. A. (1997). Two-year follow-up of inpatients with dissociative identity disorder. *American Journal of Psychiatry, 154*, 832–839.

Elliot, A. J., & Church, M. A. (2003). A motivational analysis of defensive pessimism and self-handicapping. *Journal of Personality, 71*, 370–396.

Elliott, D. (1995, March 20). The fat of the land. *Newsweek*.

Ellison, P. A., Govern, J. M., Petri, H. L., & Figler, M. H. (1995). Anonymity and aggressive driving behavior. *Journal of Social Behavior and Personality, 10*, 265–272.

Ellsworth, P. C., & Scherer, K. R. (2003). Appraisal processes in emotion. In R. J. Davidson, K. R. Scherer & H. H. Goldsmith (Eds.), *Handbook of affective sciences*. New York: Oxford University Press.

Emery, R. E., & Laumann-Billings, L. (1998). An overview of the nature, causes, and consequences of abusive family relationships. *American Psychologist, 53*, 121–135.

Emmelkamp, P. M. G., Krijn, A., Hulsbosch, A. M., de Vries, S., Schuemie, M. J., & van der Mast, C. A. P. G. (2002). Virtual reality treatment versus exposure in vivo: A comparative evaluation in acrophobia. *Behaviour Research and Therapy, 40*, 509–516.

Ende, G., Braus, D. F., Walter, S., Weber-Fahr, W., & Henn, R. A. (2000). The hippocampus in patients treated with electroconvulsive therapy. *Archives of General Psychiatry, 57*, 937–943.

Endler, N. S., Kantor, L., & Parker, J. D. A. (1994). State-trait coping, state-trait anxiety and academic performance. *Personality and Individual Differences, 16*, 663–670.

Ennett, S. T., Rosenbaum, D. P., Flewelling, R. L., Bieler, G. S., Ringwalt, C. L., & Bailey, S. L. (1994). Long-term evaluation of drug abuse resistance education. *Addictive Behaviors, 19*, 113–125.

Epley, N., Savitsky, K., & Kachelski, R. A. (1999, September/October). What every skeptic should know about subliminal persuasion. *Skeptical Inquirer*, 40–45.

Erickson, M. H. (1980/1941). Hypnosis: A general review. In E. L. Rossie (Ed.), *The collected papers of Milton H. Erickson on hypnosis* (Vol. 30). New York: Irvington.

Erikson, E. H. (1963). *Childhood and society*. New York: Norton.

Erikson, E. H. (1982). *The life cycle completed: Review*. New York: Norton.

Eron, L. D. (1990). Understanding aggression. *Bulletin of the International Society for Research on Aggression, 12*, 5–9.

Eron, L. D., Huesmann, L. R., Dubow, E., Romanoff, R., & Yarmel, P. W. (1987). Aggression and its correlates over 22 years. In D. H. Crowell, I. M. Evans & C. R. O'Donnell (Eds.), *Childhood aggression and violence: Sources of influence, prevention, and control*. New York: Plenum Press.

Estevez, A., & Calvo, M. G. (2000). Working memory capacity and time course of predictive inferences. *Memory, 8*, 51–61.

Evans, J. (1993). The cognitive psychology of reasoning: An introduction. *Quarterly Journal of Experimental Psychology, 46A*, 561–567.

Evans, R. B. (1999, December). A century of psychology. *Monitor on Psychology*.

Evans, S. W., Smith, B. H., Gnagy, E. M., Pelham, W. E., Bukstein, O., Greiner, A. R., Altenderfer, L., & Baron-Myak, C. (2001). Dose-response effects of methylphenidate on ecologically valid measures of academic performance and classroom behavior in adolescents with ADHD. *Experimental and Clinical Psychopharmacology, 9*, 163–175.

Evans, W. (2000, October 17). Cited in J. E. Brody, One-two punch for losing pounds: Exercise and careful diet. *New York Times*, D6.

Everson, H. T., Smodlaka, I., & Tobias, S. (1994). Exploring the relationship of test anxiety and meta-cognition on reading test performance: A cognitive analysis. *Anxiety, Stress, and Coping, 7*, 85–96.

References

Eysenck, H. J. (1994). The outcome problem in psychotherapy: What have we learned? *Behaviour Research and Therapy, 32,* 477–495.

Ezzell, C. (2003, February). Why? The neuroscience of suicide. *Scientific American,* 45–51.

Fackelmann, K. A. (1993). Marijuana and the brain. *Science News, 143,* 88–94.

Faravelli, C., Cosci, F., Ciampelli, M., Scarpareo, M. A., Spiti, R., & Ricca, V. (2003). A self-controlled, naturalistic study of selective serotonin reuptake inhibitors versus tricyclic antidepressants. *Psychotherapy and Psychosomatics, 72,* 95–101.

Farber, B. A. (2000a). Introduction: Understanding and treating burnout in a changing culture. *Journal of Clinical Psychology/In Session, 56,* 589–594.

Farber, B. A. (2000b). Treatment strategies for different types of teacher burnout. *Journal of Clinical Psychology/In Session, 56,* 675–689.

Farley, C. J. (2000, June 5). Rave new world. *Time.*

Fauerbach, J. A., Heinberg, L. J., Lawrence, J. W., Bryant, A. G., & Richter, L. (2002). Coping with body image changes following a disfiguring burn injury. *Health Psychology, 21,* 115–121.

Fechner, G. T. (1860). *Elemente der Psychophysik* (Vol. 1). Leipzig: Brietkopf and Marterl (H. E. Alder, D. H. Howes & E. G. Boring, Trans.). New York: Holt, Rinehart & Winston.

Feingold, B. R. (1975). Hyperkinesis and learning disabilities linked to artificial food flavors and colors. *American Journal of Nursing, 75,* 797–803.

Feng, A. S., & Ratnam, R. (2000). Neural basis of hearing in real-world situations. *Annual Review of Psychology, 51,* 699–725.

Ferguson, D. P., Rhodes, G., Lee, K., & Sriram, N. (2001). "They all look alike to me"; Prejudice and cross-race face recognition. *British Journal of Psychology, 92,* 567–577.

Fernald, A. (1992). Human maternal vocalizations to infants as biologically relevant signals: An evolutionary perspective. In J. H. Barkow, L. Cosmides & J. Tooby (Eds.), *The adapted mind: Evolutionary psychology and the generation of culture.* New York: Oxford University Press.

Ferrari, J. R., & Tice, D. M. (2000). Procrastination as a self-handicap for men and women: A task-avoidance strategy in a laboratory setting. *Journal of Research in Personality, 34,* 73–83.

Ferster, D., & Spruston, N. (1995). Cracking the neuronal code. *Science, 270,* 756–757.

Festinger, L. (1954). A theory of social comparison processes. *Human Relations, 7,* 117–140.

Festinger, L. (1957). *A theory of cognitive dissonance.* Palo Alto, CA: Stanford University Press.

Festinger, L., & Carlsmith, J. M. (1959). Cognitive consequences of forced compliance. *Journal of Abnormal and Social Psychology, 58,* 203–210.

Fiedler, K., Schmid, J., & Stahl, T. (2002). What is the current truth about polygraph lie detection? *Basic and Applied Social Psychology, 24,* 313–324.

Fields, R. D., & Stevens-Graham, B. (2002). New insights into neuron-glial communication. *Science, 298,* 556–562.

Fiez, J. A., & Petersen, S. E. (1993). PET as part of an interdisciplinary approach to understanding processes involved in reading. *Psychological Science, 4,* 287–293.

Fillmore, M. T., Roach, E. L., & Rice, J. T. (2002). Does caffeine counteract alcohol-induced impairment? The ironic effects of expectancy. *Journal of Studies on Alcohol, 63,* 745–754.

Fink, B., & Penton-Voak, I. (2002). Evolutionary psychology of facial attractiveness. *Current Directions in Psychological Science, 11,* 154–158.

Finke, R. A. (1993). Mental imagery and creative discovery. In B. Roskos-Ewoldsen, M. J. Intons-Peterson & R. E. Anderson (Eds.), *Imagery, creativity, and discovery: A cognitive perspective.* Amsterdam: North Holland.

Finkelhor, D. (2002, December 3). Cited in L. Villarosa, To prevent sexual abuse, abusers step forward. *New York Times,* D5.

Finn, J. D., & Rock, D. A. (1997). Academic success among students at risk for school failure. *Journal of Applied Psychology, 82,* 221–234.

Finney, M. L. (2003, March). Cited in D. Smith, Angry thoughts, at-risk hearts. *Monitor on Psychology,* 46–47.

Fischbach, G. D. (1992). Mind and brain. *Scientific American, 267,* 48–57.

Fischer, J. S. (2000, January 24). Taking the shock out of electroshock. *U.S. News & World Report,* 46.

Fisher, C. B., & Fryberg, D. (1994). Participant partners. *American Psychologist, 49,* 417–427.

Fisher, H. (2002, December 16). Cited in B. Carey, The brain in love. *Los Angeles Times,* F1.

Fisher, H. (2003). Cited in L. Helmuth, Caudate-over-heels in love. *Science, 302,* 1320.

Fisher, L. (1995, October 16). Tested by fire. *People.*

Fisher, S. (2002, November 11). Cited in J. M. Nash, Inside the womb. *Time,* 68–78.

Fishman, S. (1988). *A bomb in the brain.* New York: Scribner's.

FitzGerald, G. J. (1993). The reproductive behavior of the stickleback. *Scientific American, 268,* 80–85.

Fletcher, C. (1995). *Breaking and entering: Women cops talk about life in the ultimate men's club.* New York: HarperCollins.

Fletcher, G. J. O., & Simpson, J. A. (2000). Ideal standards in close relationships: Their structure and functions. *Directions in Psychological Science, 9,* 102–105.

Flett, G. L., Vredenburg, K., & Krames, L. (1997). The continuity of depression in clinical and nonclinical samples. *Psychological Bulletin, 121,* 395–416.

Flippo, R. F., & Caverly, D. C. (Eds.). (2000). *Handbook of college reading and study strategy research.* Mahwah, NJ: Lawrence Erlbaum.

Flippo, R. F., Becker, M. J., & Wark, D. M. (2000). Preparing for and taking tests. In R. F. Flippo & D. C. Caverly (Eds.), *Handbook of college reading and study strategy research.* Mahwah, NJ: Lawrence Erlbaum.

Flor, H., Elbert, T., Knecht, S., Wienbruch, C., Pantev, C., Birbaumer, N., Larbig, W., & Taub, E. (1995). Phantom-limb pain as a perceptual correlate of cortical reorganization following arm amputation. *Nature, 375,* 482–483.

Flores, S. A. (1999). Attributional biases in sexually coercive males. *Journal of Applied Social Psychology, 29,* 2425–2442.

Fogel, D. B. (2000, July 25). Cited in J. Glanz, It's only checkers, but the computer taught itself. *New York Times,* D1.

Folkman, S., & Moskowitz, J. T. (2000). Stress, positive emotion, and coping. *Current Directions in Psychological Science, 9,* 115–118.

Forsyth, B. W. C. (2000). The AIDS epidemic: Past and future. *Child and Adolescent Psychiatric Clinics of North America, 9,* 267–277.

Forsyth, J. P., Daleiden, E. L., & Chorpita, B. F. (2000). *Psychological Record, 50,* 17–33.

Foster, G. D., Wadden, T. A., Vogt, R. A., & Brewer, G. (1997). What is reasonable weight loss? Patients' expectations and evaluations of obesity treatment outcomes. *Journal of Consulting and Clinical Psychology, 65,* 79–85.

Foulkes, D. (2003). Cited in C. W. Domhoff, Making sense of dreaming. *Science, 299,* 1987–1988.

Foulks, E. G. (1992). Reflections on dream material from arctic native people. *Journal of the American Academy of Psychoanalysis, 20,* 193–203.

Foxhall, K. (2000, July/August). APA is key to anti-stigma campaign. *APA Monitor on Psychology,* 48–49.

Foxhall, K. (2001, June). Preventing relapse. *Monitor on Psychology,* 46–47.

Frank, D. A., Augustyn, M., Knight, W. G., Pell, T., & Zuckerman, B. (2001). Growth, development, and behavior in early childhood following prenatal cocaine exposure. *Journal of the American Medical Association, 285,* 1613–1625.

Franklin, A. (1995, June). Cited in E. Burnette, Black males retrieve a noble heritage. *APA Monitor.*

Franklin, M. E., Abramowitz, J. S., Bux, D. A., Jr., Zoellner, L. A., & Feeny, N. C. (2002). Cognitive-behavioral therapy with and without medication in the treatment of obsessive-compulsive disorder. *Professional Psychology: Research and Practice, 33,* 162–168.

Franks, C. M. (1994). Behavioral model. In V. B. Van Hasselt & M. Hersen (Eds.), *Advanced abnormal psychology.* New York: Plenum Press.

Franz, V. H., Gegenfurtner, K. R., Bulthoff, H. H., & Fahle, M. (2000). Grasping visual illusions: No evidence for a dissociation between perception and action. *Psychological Science, 11,* 20–25.

Frazier, K. (2003, January/February). National Academy of Science report says polygraph testing too flawed for security screening. *Skeptical Inquirer,* 5–6.

Fredrickson, M., Hursti, T., Salmi, P., Borjeson, S., Furst, C. J., Peterson, C., & Steineck, G. (1993). Conditioned nausea after cancer chemotherapy and autonomic nervous system conditionability. *Scandinavian Journal of Psychology, 34,* 318–317.

Freed, C. R., Greene, P. E., Breeze, R. E., Tsai, W. Y., DuMouchel, W., Kao, R., Dillon, S., Winfield, H., Culver, S., Trojanowski, J. Q., Eidelberg, D., & Fahn, S. (2001). Transplantation of embryonic dopamine neurons for severe Parkinson's disease. *New England Journal of Medicine, 344,* 710–719.

Freedman, R. R. (1991). Physiological mechanisms of temperature biofeedback. *Biofeedback and Self-Regulation, 16,* 95–115.

French, H. W. (2002, August 20). Depression simmers in Japan's culture of stoicism. *New York Times,* A3.

Frensch, P. A., & Runger, D. (2003). Implicit learning. *Current Directions in Psychological Science, 12,* 13–18.

Freud, S. (1900; reprinted 1980). *The interpretation of dreams* (J. Strachey, Ed. and Trans.). New York: Avon.

Freud, S. (1901; reprinted 1960). The psychopathology of everyday life. In J. Strachey (Ed. and Trans.), *The standard edition of the complete psychological works of Sigmund Freud* (Vol. 6). London: Hogarth.

Freud, S. (1909; reprinted 1949). Notes upon a case of obsessional neurosis. In *Collected papers* (Vol. 3), (Alix and James Strachey, Trans.). London: Hogarth.

Freud, S. (1924). *A general introduction to psychoanalysis.* New York: Boni & Liveright.

Freud, S. (1940; reprinted 1961). An outline of psychoanalysis. In J. Strachey (Ed. and Trans.), *The standard edition of the complete psychological works of Sigmund Freud* (Vol. 23). London: Hogarth.

Freudenheim, M. (2003, June 18). Employers plan obesity fight, citing $12-billion-a-year cost. *New York Times,* C2.

Freyd, J. J. (1994). Circling creativity. *Psychological Science, 5,* 122–126.

Frick, W. B. (2000). Remembering Maslow: Reflections on a 1968 interview. *Journal of Humanistic Psychology, 40,* 128–147.

Fricke, D. (1994, June 2). Heart-shaped noise: The music and the legacy. *Rolling Stone.*

Friedman, J. M. (2003). A war on obesity, not the obese. *Science, 299,* 856–858.

Friedman, M., & Rosenman, R. (1974). *Type A behavior and your heart.* New York: Knopf.

Friedman, R. A. (2002, August 27). Like drugs, talk therapy can change brain chemistry. *New York Times,* F4.

Friedman, S., & Stevenson, M. (1980). Perception of movements in pictures. In M. Hagen (Ed.), *Perception of pictures, Vol. 1: Alberti's window: The projective model of pictorial information.* Orlando, FL: Academic Press.

Friend, T. (1994, July 19). Monday just got worse: It's a coronary day. *USA Today,* D1.

Friend, T. (1997, December 9). The race to save the wild tiger from extinction. *USA Today.*

Friend, T. (2003, March 27). A wartime first: Dolphins called to clear mines. *USA Today,* 8D.

Frijda, N. S. (2000). The psychologists' point of view. In M. Lewis & J. M. Haviland-Jones (Eds.), *Handbook of emotions* (2nd ed.). New York: Guilford.

Fristad, M. A., & Shaver, A. E. (2001). Psychosocial interventions for suicidal children and adolescents. *Depression and Anxiety, 14,* 192–197.

Fritz, S. (1995, June). Found: Wonders in a secret cave. *Popular Science.*

Fucci, D., Harris, D., Petrosino, L., & Banks, M. (1993). Effects of preference for rock music on magnitude-production scaling behavior in young adults: A validation. *Perceptual and Motor Skills, 77,* 811–815.

Fuller, R. K., & Hiller-Sturmhofel, S. (1999). Alcoholism treatment in the United States. *Alcohol Research and Health, 23,* 69–77.

Furnham, A., Hosoe, T., & Tang, T. L. (2001). Male hubris and female humility? A cross-cultural study of ratings of self, parental and siblings multiple intelligence in America, Britain, and Japan. *Intelligence, 30,* 101–115.

Furumoto, L. (1989). The new history of psychology. In I. S. Cohen (Ed.), *The G. Stanley Hall lecture series* (Vol. 9). Washington, DC: American Psychological Association.

Furumoto, L., & Scarborough, E. (1986). Placing women in the history of psychology. *American Psychologist, 41,* 35–42.

Gabbard, G. O. (2000). American psychoanalysis in the new millennium. *Journal of the American Psychoanalytic Association, 48,* 293–295.

Gabrieli, J. (1998, December 7). Cited in A. Rogers, Thinking differently. *Newsweek,* 60.

Gage, F. H. (2003, September). Brain, repair yourself. *Scientific American,* 47–53.

Gallagher, R. P. (2002, September 11). Cited in M. Duenwald, Students find another staple of campus life: Stress. *New York Times,* D5.

Galliano, G. (2003). *Gender crossing boundaries.* Belmont, CA: Wadsworth/Thomson Learning.

Gallopin, T. (2000, May 2). Cited in J. O'Neil, The brain cells that make you sleepy. *New York Times,* D7.

Gallup, G. H., Jr., & Newport, F. (1991). Belief in paranormal phenomena among adult Americans. *Skeptical Inquirer, 15,* 137–146.

Galton, F. (1888). Head growth in students at the University of Cambridge. *Nature, 38,* 14–15.

Gangestad, S. W., & Simpson, J. A. (2000). Trade-offs, the allocation of reproductive effort, and the evolutionary psychology of human mating. *Behavioral and Brain Sciences, 23,* 624–644.

Garcia, J., Ervin, F. R., & Koelling, R. A. (1966). Learning with prolonged delay of reinforcement. *Psychonomic Science, 5,* 121–122.

Garcia, J., Hankins, W. G., & Rusinak, K. W. (1974). Behavioral regulation of the milieu interne in man and rat. *Science, 185,* 824–831.

Gardner, B. T., & Gardner, R. A. (1975). Evidence for sentence constituents in the early utterances of child and chimpanzee. *Journal of Experimental Psychology: General, 104,* 244–267.

Gardner, H. (1976). *The shattered mind.* New York: Vintage Books.

Gardner, H. (1993). *Creating minds.* New York: Basic Books.

Gardner, H. (1995, November). Reflections on multiple intelligences. *Phi Delta Kappan.*

Gardner, H. (1999). *Intelligence reframed.* New York: Basic Books.

Gardner, H. (2003). Three distinct meanings of intelligence. In R. J. Sternberg, J. Lautrey & T. I. Lubart (Eds.), *Models of intelligence.* Washington, DC: American Psychological Association.

Garfield, S. L., & Bergin, A. E. (1994). Introduction and historical overview. In A. E. Bergin & S. L. Garfield (Eds.), *Handbook of psychotherapy and behavior change* (4th ed.). New York: Wiley.

Garland, A. R., & Zigler, E. (1993). Adolescent suicide prevention. *American Psychologist, 48,* 169–182.

Garland, J. (2003, August 23). Viagra rivals about to test U.S. market. *San Diego Union-Tribune,* C3.

Gazzaniga, M. S. (1996). Cited in B. Bower, Whole-brain interpreter. *Science News, 149,* 124–125.

Gazzaniga, M. S. (1998, July). The split brain revisited. *Scientific American,* 50–55.

Gazzaniga, M. S., Bogen, J. E., & Sperry, R. W. (1962). Some functional effects of sectioning the cerebral commissures in man. *Proceedings of the National Academy of Science, 48,* 1765–1769.

Geary, D. C., & Huffman, K. J. (2002). Brain and cognitive evolution: Forms of modularity and functions of the mind. *Psychological Bulletin, 128,* 667–698.

Geiger, D. (2002). Cited in K. Cobb, Sleepy heads. *Science News, 162,* 38.

Geller, L. (1982). The failure of self-actualization theory: A critique of Carl Rogers and Abraham Maslow. *Journal of Humanistic Psychology, 22,* 56–73.

Gelman, D. (1991, August 5). The secrets of apt. 213. *Newsweek,* 40–42.

George, K. I. (1995, December 6). Driver gets children to mind pizzas and Qs. *USA Today.*

Georgopoulos, A. (1999). Cited in I. Wickelgren, Memory for order found in the motor cortex, *Science, 283,* 1617–1618.

Gershoff, E. T. (2002). Corporal punishment by parents and associated child behaviors and experiences: A meta-analytic and theoretical review. *Psychological Bulletin, 128,* 539–579.

Giacopassi, D. J., & Dull, R. T. (1986). Gender and racial differences in the acceptance of rape myths within a college population. *Sex Roles, 15,* 63–75.

Gibbons, A. (2002). In search of the first hominids. *Science, 295,* 1214–1219.

Gibbons, F. X., Eggleston, T. J., & Benthin, A. C. (1997). Cognitive reactions to smoking relapse: The reciprocal relation between dissonance and self-esteem. *Journal of Personality and Social Psychology, 72,* 184–195.

Gibbs, N. (1993, July 19). In whose best interest? *Time.*

Gibbs, N. (1995, October 2). The EQ factor. *Time,* 60–68.

Gibson, E. J., & Walk, R. (1960). The visual "cliff." *Scientific American, 202,* 64–71.

Gieddes, J. (1999, August 9). Cited in S. Brownlee, Inside the teen brain. *U.S. News & World Report,* 45–54.

Gigone, D., & Hastie, R. (1997). Proper analysis of the accuracy of group judgments. *Psychological Bulletin, 121,* 149–167.

Gilbert, P. L., Harris, J. H., McAdams, L. A., & Jeste, D. V. (1995). Neuroleptic withdrawal in schizophrenic patients. *Archives of General Psychiatry, 52,* 173–188.

Gilligan, C. (1982). *In a different voice: Psychological theory and women's development.* Cambridge, MA: Harvard University Press.

Gitlin, M. J. (2002). Pharmacological treatment of depression. In I. H. Gotlib & C. L. Hammen (Eds.), *Handbook of depression.* New York: Guilford Press.

Glantz, M. D., & Hartel, C. R. (1999). *Drug abuse: Origins & interventions.* Washington, DC: American Psychological Association.

Glanzer, M., & Cunitz, A. R. (1966). Two storage mechanisms in free recall. *Journal of Verbal Learning and Verbal Behavior, 5,* 351–360.

Glass, R. M. (2001). Electroconvulsive therapy. *Journal of the American Medical Association, 285,* 1346–1348.

Glass, S. (1998, March 5). Truth & D.A.R.E. *Rolling Stone,* 42–43.

Gleick, E. (1997, January 27). And then there were two. . . . *Time,* 38–39.

Gleick, E., Alexander, B., Eskin, L., Pick, G., Skolnik, S., Dodd, J., & Sugden, J. (1994, December 12). The final victim. *People.*

Glenberg, A. M., Sanocki, T., Epstein, W., & Morris, C. (1987). Enhancing calibration of comprehension. *Journal of Experimental Psychology: General, 116,* 119–136.

Goda, Y. (2001, November 30). Cited in J. Ristine, UCSD researchers show how brain circuits change. *San Diego Union-Tribune,* B1.

Gold, I., & Stoljar, D. (1999). A neuron doctrine in the philosophy of neuroscience. *Behavioral and Brain Sciences, 22,* 809–869.

Gold, S. N., Hughes, D., & Hohnecker, L. (1994). Degrees of repression of sexual abuse memories. *American Psychologist, 49,* 441–442.

Goldberg, C. (1998, May 31). Acceptance of gay men and lesbians is growing, study says. *New York Times,* 15.

Goldberg, E. (2001). *The executive brain: Frontal lobes and the civilized mind.* New York: Oxford University Press.

Goldberger, L., & Breznitz, S. (Eds.). (1993). *Handbook of stress: Theoretical and clinical aspects.* New York: Free Press.

Goldfried, M. R., & Davison, G. C. (1976). *Clinical behavior therapy.* New York: Holt, Rinehart & Winston.

Goldsmith, H. H. (2003). Introduction: Genetics and development. In R. J. Davidson, K. B. Scherer & H. H. Goldsmith (Eds.), *Handbook of affective sciences.* New York: Oxford University Press.

Goldstein, E. B. (1999). *Sensation and perception* (5th ed.). Pacific Grove, CA: Brooks/Cole.

Goldstein, E. B. (2002). *Sensation and perception* (6th ed.). Pacific Grove, CA: Wadsworth.

Goleman, D. (1995). *Emotional intelligence: Why it can matter more than IQ.* New York: Bantam Books.

Goleman, D., & Gurin, J. (1993). *Mind/body medicine: How to use your mind for better health.* New York: Consumer Reports.

Gomes, H., Sussman, E., Ritter, W., Kurtzberg, D., Cowan, N., & Vaughan, H. G., Jr. (1999). Electrophysiological evidence of developmental changes in the duration of auditory sensory memory. *Developmental Psychology, 35,* 299–302.

Goode, E. (2000, August 8). How culture molds habits of thought. *New York Times,* D1.

Goode, E. (2002a, March 12). The uneasy fit of the precocious and the average. *New York Times,* D1.

Goode, E. (2002b, March 26). Psychologists get prescription pads and furor erupts. *New York Times,* D1.

Goode, E. (2003a, May 14). Trying to silence the voices of illness. *San Diego Union-Tribune,* F10.

References

Goode, E. (2003b, May 20). Leading drugs for psychosis come under new scrutiny. *New York Times*, A1.

Goodwin, F. K. (2003). Rationale for long-term treatment of bipolar disorder and evidence for long-term lithium treatment. *Journal of Clinical Psychiatry, 64* (supplement 6), 5–12.

Goodwin, I. (2003). The relevance of attachment theory to the philosophy, organization, and practice of adult mental health care. *Clinical Psychology Review, 23,* 35–36.

Gordon, C. M., Dougherty, D. D., Rauch, S. L., Emans, S. J., Grace, E., Lamm, R., Alpert, N. M., Majzoub, J. A., & Fischman, A. J. (2000). Neuroanatomy of human appetitive function: A positron emission tomography investigation. *International Journal of Eating Disorders, 27,* 163–171.

Gore, R. (1997, February). The first steps. *National Geographic,* 72–99.

Gorman, A. (2002, September 2). Witness mistakes costly for accused. *Los Angeles Times,* B1.

Gorman, C. (2003, July 28). The new science of dyslexia. *Time,* 52–59.

Gotlib, I. H., & Hammen, C. L. (Eds.). (2002). *Handbook of depression.* New York: Guilford Press.

Gottesman, I. I. (2001). Psychopathology through a lifespan-genetic prism. *American Psychologist, 56,* 867–877.

Gottfredson, L. S. (2002). Where and why *g* matters: Not a mystery. *Human Performance, 15,* 24–46.

Gottfredson, L. S. (2003). Dissecting practical intelligence theory: Its claims and evidence. *Intelligence, 31,* 342–397.

Gottman, J. (2003, May 1). Cited in B. Carey, For better or worse: Marriage by the numbers. *Los Angeles Times,* F1.

Gottman, J. M. (1999). *Seven principles for making marriage work.* New York: Three Rivers Press.

Gottman, J. M. (2000. September 14). Cited in K. S. Peterson, "Hot" and "cool" phases could predict divorce. *USA Today,* 9D.

Gould, L. (1995, April 23). Ticket to trouble. *New York Times Magazine.*

Gould, R. A. (1969). Subsistence behaviour among the Western Desert Aborigines of Australia. *Oceania, 39,* 253–274.

Gould, S. J. (1981). *The mismeasure of man.* New York: Norton.

Gould, S. J. (1994, November). The geometer of race. *Discover.*

Gould, S. J. (1996). *The mismeasure of man* (revised and expanded). New York: Norton.

Grady, D. (2002, November 26). Why we eat (and eat and eat). *New York Times,* D1.

Graham, L. O. (1995). *Member of the club.* New York: HarperCollins.

Granvold, D. K. (Ed.). (1994). *Cognitive and behavioral treatment.* Pacific Grove, CA: Brooks/Cole.

Gray, J. R., Braver, T. S., & Raichle, M. E. (2002). Integration of emotion and cognition in the lateral prefrontal cortex. *Proceeding of the National Academy of Sciences, 99,* 4115–4120.

Greco, L. A., & Morris, T. L. (2001). Treating childhood shyness and related behavior: Empirically evaluated approaches to promote positive social interactions. *Clinical Child and Family Psychology Review, 4,* 299–318.

Green, A. J., Prepscius, C., & Levy, W. B. (2000). Primacy versus recency in a quantitative model: Activity is the critical distinction. *Learning & Memory, 7,* 48–57.

Green, J. P. & Lynn, S. J. (2000). Hypnosis and suggestion-based approaches to smoking cessation: An examination of the evidence. *International Journal of Clinical and Experimental Hypnosis, 48,* 195–224.

Greenberg, J. (1978). The americanization of Roseto. *Science News, 113,* 378–382.

Greenberg, L. S., & Rice, L. N. (1997). Humanistic approaches to psychotherapy. In P. L. Wachtel & S. B. Messer (Eds.), *Theories of psychotherapy: Origins and evolution.* Washington, DC: American Psychological Association.

Greenberg, R., & Perlman, C. A. (1999). The interpretation of dreams: A classic revisited. *Psychoanalytic Dialogues, 9,* 749–765.

Greene, B., & Winfrey, O. (1996). *Make the connection.* New York: Hyperion.

Greene, R. L., & Clopton, J. R. (1994). Minnesota Multiphasic Personality Inventory–2. In M. E. Maruish (Ed.), *The use of psychological testing for treatment planning and outcome assessment: Introduction.* Hillsdale, NJ: Lawrence Erlbaum.

Greenfield, P. (2003, February). Cited in E. Benson, Intelligence across cultures. *Monitor on Psychology,* 56–58.

Greenfield, P. M. (1997). You can't take it with you. *American Psychologist, 52,* 1115–1124.

Gregory, R. L. (1974). Recovery from blindness: A case study. In R. L. Gregory (Ed.), *Concepts and mechanisms of perception.* London: Gerald Duckworth.

Gresham, F. M., Beebe-Frankenberger, M. E., & MacMillan, D. L. (1999). A selective review of treatments for children with autism: Description and methodological considerations. *School Psychology Review, 28,* 559–575.

Grimaldi, J. V. (1986, April 16). "The mole" evicted from sewer. *San Diego Tribune.*

Groesz, L. M., Levine, M. P., & Murnen, S. K. (2002). The effect of experimental presentation of thin media images on body satisfaction: A meta-analytic review. *International Journal of Eating Disorders, 31,* 1–16.

Grogan, B., Shaw, B., Ridenhour, R., Fine, A., & Eftimiades, M. (1993, May). Their brothers' keepers? *People.*

Gron, G., Wunderlich, A. P., Spitzer, M., Tomczak, R., & Riepe, M. W. (2000). Brain activation during human navigation: Gender-different neural networks as substrate of performance. *Nature Neuroscience, 3,* 404–408.

Grunbaum, A. (1993). *Validation in the clinical theory of psychoanalysis.* Madison, CT: International Universities Press.

Gudjonsson, G. H. (1997). Accusations by adults of childhood sexual abuse: A survey of the members of the British False Memory Society (BFMS). *Applied Cognitive Psychology, 11,* 3–18.

Guilford, J. P. (1967). *The nature of human intelligence.* New York: McGraw-Hill.

Guinness book of records, The. (1995). New York: Bantam.

Gupta, S. (2002, March 11). Is your doctor too drowsy? *Time,* 85.

Gura, T. (1997). Obesity sheds its secrets. *Science, 275,* 751–753.

Gureje, O., Simon, G. E., Ustun, T. B., & Goldberg, D. P. (1997). Somatization in cross-cultural perspective: A World Health Organization study in primary care. *American Journal of Psychiatry, 154,* 989–995.

Gurman, E. B. (1994). Debriefing for all concerned: Ethical treatment of human subjects. *Psychological Science, 5,* 139.

Gustavson, C. R., Kelly, D. J., Sweeney, M., & Garcia, J. (1976). Prey-lithium aversion I: Coyotes and wolves. *Behavioral Biology, 17,* 61–72.

Guterl, F. (2002, November 11). What Freud got right. *Newsweek,* 50–51.

Guthrie, J. P., Ash, R. A., & Bendapudi, V. (1995). Additional validity evidence for a measure of morningness. *Journal of Applied Psychology, 80,* 186–190.

Guthrie, R. V. (1976). *Even the rat was white.* New York: Harper & Row.

Gwyer, P., & Clifford, B. R. (1997). The effects of the cognitive interview on recall, identification, confidence, and the confidence/accuracy relationship. *Applied Cognitive Psychology, 11,* 121–145.

Haber, N. R. (1980, November). Eidetic images are not just imaginary. *Psychology Today.*

Hackmann, A., Clark, D. M., & McManus, F. (2000). Recurrent images and early memories in social phobia. *Behaviour Research and Therapy, 38,* 601–610.

Hadders-Algra, M. (2002). Variability in infant motor behavior: A hallmark of the healthy nervous system. *Infant Behavior & Development, 2,* 433–451.

Halbreich, U. (2003). Anxiety disorders in women: A developmental and lifecycle perspective. *Depression and Anxiety, 17,* 107–110.

Haliburn, J. (2000). Reasons for adolescent suicide attempts. *Journal of the American Academy of Child and Adolescent Psychiatry, 29,* 13.

Halliday, J. (2001, February 28). Red-light scofflaws run but can't hide. *USA Today,* 13A.

Halpern, D. (2003, May). Cited in K. Kersting, Cognitive sex differences: A "political minefield." *Monitor on Psychology,* 54–55.

Halpern, D. F. (1998). Teaching critical thinking for transfer across domains. *American Psychologist, 53,* 449–455.

Halpern, D. F. (2000). *Sex differences in cognitive abilities* (3rd ed.). Hillsdale, NJ: Lawrence Erlbaum.

Hamann, S. B., Ely, T. D., Grafton, S. T., & Kilts, C. D. (1999). Amygdala activity related to enhanced memory for pleasant and aversive stimuli. *Nature Neuroscience, 2,* 289–294.

Hamann, S. B., Ely, T. D., Hoffman, J. M., & Kilts, C. D. (2002). Ecstasy and agony: Activation of the human amygdala in positive and negative emotions. *Psychological Science, 13,* 135–141.

Hamer, D. (2002). Rethinking behavior genetics. *Science, 298,* 71–72.

Hamilton, A. (2001, June 4). Forceps! Scalpel! Robot! *Time,* 64–65.

Hamm, A. O., Schupp, H. T., & Weike, A. I. (2003). Motivational organization of emotions: Autonomic changes, cortical responses, and reflex modulation. In R. D. Lane & L. Nadel (Eds.), *Cognitive neuroscience of emotion.* New York: Oxford University Press.

Hammer, D. (1995). Cited in C. Holden, More on genes and homosexuality. *Science, 268,* 1571.

Han, S., & Humphreys, G. W. (1999). Interactions between perceptual organization based on Gestalt laws and those based on hierarchical processing. *Perception & Psychophysics, 61,* 1287–1298.

Hancock, L. (1996, March 18). Mother's little helper. *Newsweek.*

Hancock, L., Rosenberg, D., Springen, K., King, P., Rogers, P., Brant, M., Kalb, C., & Gegax, T. T. (1995, March 6). Breaking point. *Newsweek.*

Hansen, J. T. (2000). Psychoanalysis and humanism: A review and critical examination of integrationist efforts with some proposed resolutions. *Journal of Counseling and Development, 78,* 21–28.

Hanson, G. R., Venturelli, P. J., & Fleckenstein, A. E. (2002). *Drugs and society* (7th ed.). Boston: Jones and Bartlett.

Hanson, G., & Venturelli, P. J. (1998). *Drugs and society* (5th ed.). Boston: Jones and Bartlett.

Hardin, C., & Banaji, M. R. (1993). The influence of language on thought. *Social Cognition, 11,* 277–308.

Hardy, J. B., Welcher, D. W., Mellits, E. D., & Kagan, J. (1976). Pitfalls in the measurement of intelligence: Are standardized intelligence tests valid for measuring the intellectual potential of urban children? *Journal of Psychology, 94,* 43–51.

Hardy, J., & Selkoe, D. J. (2002). The amyloid hypothesis of Alzheimer's disease: Progress and problems on the road to therapeutics. *Science, 297,* 333–356.

Hareli, S., & Weiner, B. (2002). Social emotions and personality inferences: A scaffold for a new direction in the study of achievement motivation. *Educational Psychologist, 37,* 183–193.

Harmon-Jones, E., & Harmon Jones, C. (2002). Testing the action-based model of cognitive dissonance: The effect of action orientation on postdecisional attitudes. *Personality and Social Psychology Bulletin, 28,* 711–723.

Harris, J. C. (1995). *Developmental neuropsychiatry* (Vol. 1). New York: Oxford University Press.

Harris, J. C. (2003). Pinel orders the chains removed from the insane at Bicetre. *Archives of General Psychiatry, 60,* 442.

Harris, T. (2003). Depression in women and its sequelae. *Journal of Psychosomatic Research, 54,* 103–112.

Hart, F., & Risley, T. (1996). Cited in B. Bower, Talkative parents make kids smarter. *Science News, 150,* 100.

Hartwell, S. (2003). Deviance over the life course: The case of homeless substance abusers. *Substance Use & Misuse, 38,* 475–502.

Harvey, G. A., Bryant, R. A., & Tarrier, N. (2003). Cognitive behaviour therapy for posttraumatic stress disorder. *Clinical Psychology Review, 23,* 501–522.

Hasselt, V. B., & Hersen, M. (Eds.). (1994). *Advanced abnormal psychology.* New York: Plenum Press.

Hatfield, E., & Rapson, R. L. (1995). *A world of passion: Cross-cultural perspective on love and sex.* New York: Allyn & Bacon.

Hauser, M. (2003, July 15). Cited in N. Wade, Early voices: The leap to language. *New York Times,* D1.

Hauser, M. D., Chomsky, N., & Fitch, W. T. (2002). The faculty of language: What is it, who has it, and how did it evolve? *Science, 298,* 1569–1579.

Hayes, K. J., & Hayes, C. H. (1951). The intellectual development of a home-raised chimpanzee. *Proceedings of the American Philosophical Society, 95,* 105–109.

Hazeltine, E., & Ivry, R. B. (2002). Can we teach the cerebellum new tricks? *Science, 296,* 1979–1980.

Healy, M. (2000, November 29). Computer improves mammogram results. *USA Today,* 9D.

Heatherton, T. F., Mahamedi, F., Striepe, M., Gield, A. E., & Keel, P. (1997). A 10-year longitudinal study of body weight, dieting, and eating disorder symptoms. *Journal of Abnormal Psychology, 106,* 117–125.

Heider, F. (1958). *The psychology of interpersonal relations.* New York: Wiley.

Heilman, K. M. (2000). Emotional experience: A neurological model. In R. D. Lane & L. Nadel (Eds.), *Cognitive neuroscience of emotion.* New York: Oxford University Press.

Heiman, J. R. (2002). Sexual dysfunction: Overview of prevalence, etiological factors, and treatments. *The Journal of Sex Research, 39,* 73–78.

Heinrichs, A. M. (2003, July 29). AIDS cases again on rise. *Los Angeles Times,* A1.

Helgeson, V. S. (1994). Prototypes and dimensions of masculinity and femininity. *Sex Roles, 31,* 653–682.

Hellmich, N. (1998, January 14). Study: Olestra chips score well in digestive test, *USA Today,* 1D.

Hellmich, N. (2000, March 29). One way to get to sleep: Get up. *USA Today,* 1A.

Hellmich, N. (2002, June 19). Extra value packs on pounds. *USA Today,* 7D.

Hellstrom, A. (2000). Sensation weighting in comparison and discrimination of heaviness. *Journal of Experimental Psychology, 26,* 6–17.

Helmuth, L. (2002). Redrawing the brain's map of the body. *Science, 296,* 1587–1588.

Helmuth, L. (2003a). Caudate-over-heels in love. *Science, 302,* 1320.

Helmuth, L. (2003b). Fear and trembling in the amygdala. *Science, 300,* 568–569.

Helmuth, L. (2003c). In sickness or in health. *Science, 302,* 808–810.

Helson, R. (1996). In search of the creative personality. *Creativity Research Journal, 9,* 295–306.

Helwig, C. C. (1997). Making moral cognition respectable (again): A retrospective review of Lawrence Kohlberg. *Contemporary Psychology, 42,* 191–195.

Helzer, J. E., & Canino, G. J. (Eds.). (1992). *Alcoholism in North America, Europe, and Asia.* New York: Oxford University Press.

Hemphill, J. F. (2003). Interpreting the magnitudes of correlation coefficients. *American Psychologist, 58,* 78–80.

Henderlong, J., & Lepper, M. R. (2002). The effects of praise on children's intrinsic motivation: A review and synthesis. *Psychological Bulletin, 128,* 774–795.

Henker, B., & Whalen, C. K. (1989). Hyperactivity and attention deficits. *American Psychologist, 44,* 216–233.

Henry, T. (1999, September 15). Sex is No. 1 struggle, teen girls say. *USA Today,* 9D.

Herbert, W. (1999, July 26). Losing your mind. *U.S. News & World Report,* 45–51.

Herkenham, M. (1996, December 16). Cited in D. Ferrell, Scientists unlocking secrets of marijuana's effects. *Los Angeles Times.*

Herman, L. (1999, July 21). Cited in J. Mastro, Dialogue with a dolphin. *San Diego Union-Tribune,* E1.

Herman, W. E. (1990). Fear of failure as a distinctive personality trait measure of test anxiety. *Journal of Research and Development in Education, 23,* 180–185.

Herrnstein, R. J., & Murray, C. (1994). *The bell curve.* New York: Free Press.

Hewstone, M., Rubin, M., & Willis, H. (2002). Intergroup bias. *Annual Review of Psychology, 53,* 575–604.

Hickey, E. W. (1991). *Serial murderers and their victims.* Pacific Grove, CA: Brooks/Cole.

Hickman, G., Bartholomae, S., & McKenry, P. C. (2000). Influence of parenting styles on the adjustment and academic achievement of traditional college freshmen. *Journal of College Student Development, 41,* 41–54.

Hidalgo, R. B., & Davidson, J. R. T. (2000). Posttraumatic stress disorder: Epidemiology and health-related considerations. *Journal of Clinical Psychiatry, 61 (supplement 7),* 5–13.

Higgins, E. T. (2000). Social cognition: Learning about what matters in the social world. *European Journal of Social Psychology, 30,* 3–39.

Higley, D. (2002, July). Cited in M. F. Small, Drunk monkeys. *Discover,* 41–44.

Hill, A. B., Kemp-Wheeler, S. M., & Jones, S. A. (1987). Subclinical and clinical depression: Are analogue studies justifiable? *Personality and Individual Differences, 8,* 113–120.

Hill, A., Niven, C. A., & Knussen, C. (1996). Pain memories in phantom limbs: A case study. *Pain, 66,* 381–384.

Hill, C. E., & Nakayama, E. Y. (2000). Client-centered therapy: Where has it been and where is it going? A comment on Hathaway (1948). *Journal of Clinical Psychology, 56,* 861–875.

Hill, J. O., Wyatt, H. R., Reed, G. W., & Peters, J. C. (2003). Obesity and the environment: Where do we go from here? *Science, 299,* 853–855.

Hill, P. (1995, June). Cited in E. Burnette, Black males retrieve a noble heritage. *APA Monitor.*

Hilts, P. H. (1995). *Memory's ghost: The strange tale of Mr. M and the nature of memory.* New York: Simon & Schuster.

Hiltzik, M. A. (2002, November 17). Nobel Laureate Francis H. C. Crick discovered DNA. Now he's hunting for the very essence of our being—the course of conscious thought. *Los Angeles Times Magazine,* 12–15.

Hirsch, B. J. (1997). Where are the interventions? *Contemporary Psychology, 42,* 1113–1114.

Hirshey, G. (2003, April). Songs from the heart. *Ladies Home Journal,* 122–123.

Hirshkowitz, M., Moore, C. A., & Minhoto, G. (1997). The basics of sleep. In M. R. Pressman & W. C. Orr (Eds.), *Understanding sleep: The evaluation and treatment of sleep disorders.* Washington, DC: American Psychological Association.

Hobson, J. A. (2002). *Making sense of dreaming.* New York: Oxford University Press.

Hoffman, C., Lau, I., & Johnson, D. R. (1986). The linguistic relativity of person cognition: An English-Chinese comparison. *Journal of Personality and Social Psychology, 51,* 1097–1105.

Hofmann, A. (1983). *LSD: My problem child.* Los Angeles: J. P. Tarcher.

Hokanson, J. E., & Butler, A. C. (1992). Cluster analysis of depressed college students' social behaviors. *Journal of Personality and Social Psychology, 62,* 273–280.

Holahan, C. K., & Sears, R. R. (1995). *The gifted group in later maturity.* Stanford, CA: Stanford University Press.

Holden, C. (1995). Sex and the granular layer. *Science, 268,* 807.

Holden, C. (1997). Thumbs up for acupuncture. *Science, 278,* 1231.

Holden, C. (2002). Drug find could give ravers the jitters. *Science, 297,* 2185–2186.

Holden, C. (2003a). Deconstructing schizophrenia, *Science, 299,* 333–335.

Holden, C. (2003b). Future brightening for depression treatment. *Science, 302,* 810–813.

Holden, C. (2003c). Vaccine-autism link dealt blow. *Science, 301,* 1454.

Holden, K. (2000). Researchers pained by effort to define distress precisely. *Science, 290,* 1474–1475.

Hollingworth, L. (2002, March 12). Cited in E. Goode, The uneasy fit of the precocious and the average. *New York Times,* D1.

Hollon, S. D. (2003). Does cognitive therapy have an enduring effect? *Cognitive Therapy and Research, 27,* 71–75.

Hollon, S. D., Haman, K. L., & Brown, L. L. (2002a). Cognitive-behavioral treatment of depression. In I. H. Gotlib & C. L. Hammen (Eds.), *Handbook of depression.* New York: Guilford Press.

Hollon, S. D., Thase, M. E., & Markowitz, J. C. (2002b). Treatment and prevention of depression. *Psychological Science (supplement), 3,* 39–77.

Holloway, J. D. (2003, March). Advances in anger management. *Monitor on Psychology,* 54–55.

Holroyd, C. B., & Coles, M. G. H. (2002). The neural basis of human error processing: Reinforcement learning, dopamine, and the error-related negativity. *Psychological Review, 109,* 679–709.

Honey, R. C. (2000). Associative priming in Pavlovian conditioning. *The Quarterly Journal of Experimental Psychology, 53B,* 1–23.

Hong, Y., Morris, M. W., Chiu, C., & Benet-Martinez, V. (2000). Multicultural minds. *American Psychologist, 55,* 709–720.

Honts, C. R. (1994). Psychophysiological detection of deception. *Current Directions in Psychological Science, 3,* 77–82.

Honts, C. R., Raskin, D. C., & Kircher, J. C. (1994). Mental and physical countermeasures reduce the accuracy of polygraph tests. *Journal of Applied Psychology, 79,* 252–259.

Hoover, N. C., & Pollard, N. J. (2000). Initiation rites in American high schools: A national survey. http://www.alfred.edu/news/html/hazing_study.html

References

Hooyman, N., & Niyak, H. (1999). *Social gerontology* (5th ed.). New York: Allyn & Bacon.

Horgan, J. (1996, December). Why Freud isn't dead. *Scientific American,* 106–111.

Horner, P. J., & Gage, F. H. (2000). Regenerating the damaged central nervous system. *Nature, 407,* 963–970.

Horovitz, B. (2003, July 1). Under fire, food giants switch to healthier fare. *USA Today,* 1A.

Horowitz, J. M. (1999, March 22). Libido letdown. *Time,* 115.

Horowitz, J. M. (2000, August 28). High five for a new hand. *Time,* 44.

Horsburgh, S., Biermann, R., & Howard, C. (2001, December 31). Going strong. *People,* 125–126.

Hotz, R. L. (2000, January 24). A scalpel, a life and language. *Los Angeles Times,* A1.

Howe, M. L. (2003). Memories from the cradle. *Current Directions in Psychological Sciences, 12,* 62–65.

Howieson, D. B., & Lezak, M. D. (1997). The neuropsychological evaluation. In S. C. Yodofsky & R. E. Hales (Eds.), *The American Psychiatric Press textbook of neuropsychiatry* (3rd ed.). Washington, DC: American Psychiatric Press.

Howlett, D. (1997, September 10). Easy-to-concoct drug often makes users turn violent. *USA Today.*

Howlin, P. (1997). Prognosis in autism: Do specialist treatments affect long-term outcome? *European Child & Adolescent Psychiatry, 6,* 55–72.

Hser, Y. I., Hoffman, V., Grella, C. E., & Anglin, D. (2001). A 33-year follow-up of narcotic addicts. *Archives of General Psychiatry, 58,* 503–508.

Hubel, D. H., & Wiesel, T. N. (1979). Brain mechanisms of vision. *Scientific American, 241,* 150–162.

Hughes, J., Smith, T. W., Kosterlitz, H. W., Fothergill, L. A., Morgan, B. A., & Morris, H. R. (1975). Identification of two related pentapeptides from the brain with potent opiate agonist activity. *Nature, 258,* 577–579.

Hui, K. K. S., Liu, J., Makris, N., Gollub, R. L., Chen, A. J. W., Moore, C. I., Kennedy, D. N., Rosen, B. R., & Kwong, K. K. (2000). Acupuncture modulates the limbic system and subcortical gray structures of the human brain: Evidence from fMRI studies in normal subjects. *Human Brain Mapping, 9,* 13–25.

Humphreys, G. W., & Forde, E. M. E. (2001). Category specificity in mind and brain. *Behavioral and Brain Sciences, 243,* 497–509.

Humphreys, G. W., & Muller, H. (2000). A search asymmetry reversed by figure-ground assignment. *Psychological Science, 11,* 196–210.

Hunt, M. (1993). *The story of psychology.* New York: Doubleday.

Hurtley, S. (2000). Showing up emotions. *Science, 290,* 573–674.

Hwang, S. L. (1998, November 13). Threat of impotence aids war on smoking. *San Diego Union-Tribune,* A29.

Ilmberger, J., Rau, S., Noachtar, S., Arnold, S., & Winkler, P. (2002). Naming tools and animals: Asymmetries observed during direct electrical cortical stimulation. *Neuropsychologia, 40,* 695–700.

Irwin, C. E., Burg, S. J., & Cart, C. U. (2002). America's adolescents: Where have we been, where are we going? *Journal of Adolescent Health, 31,* 91–123.

Irwin, M., Mascovich, A., Gillin, J. C., Willoughby, R., Pike, J., & Smith, T. L. (1994). Partial sleep deprivation reduces natural killer cell activity in humans. *Psychosomatic Medicine, 56,* 493–498.

Ito, T. A., Miller, N., & Pollock, V. E. (1996). Alcohol and aggression: A meta-analysis on the moderating effects of inhibitory cues, triggering events, and self-focused attention. *Psychological Bulletin, 120,* 60–82.

Iversen, L. L. (2000). *The science of marijuana.* New York: Oxford University Press.

Izard, C. E. (1993). Four systems for emotion activation: Cognitive and noncognitive processes. *Psychological Review, 100,* 68–90.

Jackendoff, R. (1994). *Patterns in the mind. Language and human nature.* New York: Basic Books.

Jacks, J. Z., & Cameron, K. A. (2003). Strategies for resisting persuasion. *Basic and Applied Social Psychology, 25,* 145–161.

Jacks, J. Z., & Devine, P. G. (2000). Attitude importance, forewarning of message content, and resistance to persuasion. *Basic and Applied Social Psychology, 22,* 19–29.

Jackson, R. L. (1994, May 4). A false sense of sincerity: Some cases belie polygraph results. *Los Angeles Times.*

Jackson, T., Towson, S., & Narduzzi, K. (1997). Predictors of shyness: A test of variables associated with self-presentational models. *Social Behavior and Personality, 25,* 149–154.

Jacobson, J. L., & Jacobson, S. W. (1999). Drinking moderately and pregnancy. *Alcohol Research and Health, 23,* 25–30.

Jacoby, L. L., Debner, J. A., & Hay, J. F. (2001). Proactive interference, accessibility bias, and process dissociation: Valid subjective reports of memory. *Journal of Experimental Psychology: Learning, Memory, and Cognition, 27,* 686–700.

Jaffee, S., & Hyde, J.S. (2000). Gender differences in moral orientation: A meta-analysis. *Psychological Bulletin, 126,* 703–726.

James, W. (1884; reprinted 1969). What is an emotion? In *William James: Collected essays and reviews.* New York: Russell & Russell.

James, W. (1890). *The principles of psychology.* New York: Dover.

Jamison, K. R. (1995). Manic-depressive illness and creativity. *Scientific American, 272,* 62–67.

Janis, I. L. (1989). *Crucial decisions: Leadership in policymaking and crisis management.* New York: Free Press.

Janofsky, M. (2000, September 16). Antidrug program's end stirs up salt Lake City. *New York Times,* A8.

Janus, S. S., & Janus, C. L. (1993). *The Janus report on sexual behavior.* New York: John Wiley & Sons.

Japenga, A. (1994, June 5). Rewriting the dictionary of madness. *Los Angeles Times Magazine.*

Jauhar, S. (2001, May 6). Life out of balance. *New York Times Magazine,* 104–107.

Javitt, D. C., & Coyle, J. T. (2004, January). Decoding schizophrenia. *Scientific American,* 48–55.

Jaycox, L. H., Zoeliner, L., & Foa, E. D. (2002). Cognitive-behavior therapy for PTSD in rape survivors. *Journal of Clinical Psychology/In Session, 58,* 891–906.

Jensen, P. (1999). A 14-month randomized clinical trial of treatment strategies for attention-deficit/hyperactivity disorder. *Archives of General Psychiatry, 56,* 1073–1086.

Jerome, R. (2001, June 4). Disarming the rage. *People,* 56–57.

Jiang, Y., Haxby, J. V., Martin, A., Ungerleider, L. G., & Parasuraman, R. (2000). Complementary neural mechanisms for tracking items in human working memory. *Science, 287,* 643–646.

John, O. P. (1990). The "big five" factor taxonomy: Dimensions of personality in the natural language and in questionnaires. In L. A. Pervin (Ed.), *Handbook of personality.* New York: Guilford.

John, O. P., & Srivastava, S. (1999). The big five trait taxonomy: History, measurement and theoretical perspectives. In L. A. Pervin & O. P. John (Eds.), *Handbook of personality* (2nd ed.). New York: Guilford.

Johnsen, B. H., Thayer, J. F., Laberg, J. C., Wormnes, B., Raadal, M., Skaret, E., Kvale, G., & Berg, E. (2003). Attentional and physiological characteristics of patients with dental anxiety. *Anxiety Disorders, 17,* 75–87.

Johnson, B. E., Kuck, D. L., & Schander, P. R. (1997). Rape myth acceptance and sociodemographic characteristics: A multidimensional analysis. *Sex Roles, 36,* 693–707.

Johnson, C. R., Hunt, F. M., & Siebert, J. J. (1994). Discrimination training in the treatment of pica and food scavenging. *Behavior Modification, 18,* 214–229.

Johnson, J. G., Cohen, P., Smailes, E. M., Kasen, S., & Brook, J. S. (2002). Television viewing and aggressive behavior during adolescence and adulthood. *Science, 295,* 2468–2471.

Johnson, K. (1998, November 28). Survey: Women muscled out by bias, harassment. *USA Today,* A1.

Johnson, K. (1999, April 5). Government agencies see truth in polygraphs. *USA Today,* 11A.

Johnson, L. C., Slye, E. S., & Dement, W. (1965). Electroencephalographic and autonomic activity during and after prolonged sleep deprivation. *Psychosomatic Medicine, 27,* 415–423.

Johnson, S. (2003, March). Brain and emotions: Fear. *Discover,* 32–39.

Johnston, V. (2000, February). Cited in B. Lemley, Isn't she lovely. *Discover,* 43–49.

Jones, D. R., Levy, R. A., Gardner, L., Marsh, R. W., & Patterson, J. C. (1985). Self-control of psychophysiologic response to motion stress: Using biofeedback to treat airsickness. *Aviation, Space and Environmental Medicine, 56,* 1152–1157.

Jones, E. (1953). *The life and work of Sigmund Freud* (3 vols.). New York: Basic Books.

Jones, E., & Berglas, S. (1978). Control of attributions about the self through self-handicapping strategies: The appeal of alcohol and the role of underachievement. *Personality and Social Psychology Bulletin, 4,* 200–206.

Jones, J. W., Gruber, S. A., Barker, J. H., & Breidenbach, W. C. (2000, August 17). Successful hand transplantation. *The New England Journal of Medicine, 343,* 468–473.

Jones, S. M., & Zigler, E. (2002). The Mozart effect: Not learning from history. *Applied Developmental Psychology, 23,* 355–372.

Jones, T. F. (2000). Cited in B. Bower, Mass illness tied to contagious fear. *Science News, 157,* 37.

Jorgensen, R. S., Johnson, B. T., Kolodziej, M. E., & Schreer, G. D. (1996). Elevated blood pressure and personality: A meta-analytic review. *Psychological Bulletin, 120,* 293–320.

Joseph, S., Manafi, E., Iakovaki, A. M., & Cooper, R. (2003). Personality, smoking motivation, and self-efficacy to quit. *Personality and Individual Differences, 34,* 749–758.

Jusczyk, P. W., & Hohne, E. A. (1997). Infants' memory for spoken words. *Science, 277,* 1984–1986.

Kabot, S., Masi, W., & Segal, M. (2003). Advances in the diagnosis and treatment of autism spectrum disorders. *Professional Psychology, Research and Practice, 34,* 26–33.

Kaemingk, K. L., Mulvaney, S., & Halverson, P. T. (2003). Learning following prenatal alcohol exposure: Performance on verbal and visual multitrial tasks. *Archives of Clinical Neuropsychology, 18,* 33–47.

Kagan, J. (1994). *The nature of the child* (10th anniversary edition). New York: Basic Books.

Kagan, J. (1998). Biology and the child. In W. Damon & R. M. Lerner (Eds.), *Handbook of child psychology* (Vol. 1). New York: John Wiley & Sons.

Kagan, J. (2003a). Behavioral inhibition as a temperamental category. In R. J. Davidson, K. R. Scherer & H. H. Goldsmith (Eds.), *Handbook of affective sciences.* New York: Oxford University Press.

Kagan, J. (2003b). Biology, context, and developmental inquiry. *Annual Review of Psychology, 54,* 1–23.

Kagan, J., & Snidman, N. (1991). Temperamental factors in human development. *American Psychologist, 46,* 856–862.

Kagan, J., Reznick, J. S., & Snidman, N. (1988). Biological bases of childhood shyness. *Science, 240,* 167–171.

Kagitcibasi, C., & Poortinga, Y. H. (2000). Cross-cultural psychology. *Journal of Cross-Cultural Psychology, 31,* 129–147.

Kalat, J. W. (2004). *Biological Psychology* (8th ed.). Belmont, CA: Wadsworth.

Kalick, S. M., Zebrowitz, L. A., Langlois, J. H., & Johnson, R. M. (1998). Does human facial attractiveness honestly advertise health? *Psychological Science, 9,* 8–13.

Kalimo, R., Tenkanen, L., Harma, M., Poppius, E., & Heinsalmi, P. (2000). Job stress and sleep disorders: Findings from the Helsinki heart study. *Stress Medicine, 16,* 65–75.

Kandel, E., & Abel, T. (1995). Neuropeptides, adenylyl cyclase, and memory storage. *Science, 268,* 825–826.

Kanner, L. (1943). Autistic disturbances in affective contact. *Nervous Child, 2,* 217–250.

Kantowitz, B. (2002, July 15). In search of sleep. *Newsweek,* 39–47

Kao, G., & Tienda, M. (1995). Optimism and achievement: The educational performance of immigrant youth. *Social Science Quarterly, 76,* 1–19.

Kaplan, D. M. (1972). On shyness. *International Journal of Psycho-Analysis, 53,* 439–453.

Kaplan, R. M., & Saccuzzo, K. P. (2001). *Psychological testing: Principles, applications, and issues* (5th ed.). Belmont, CA: Wadsworth.

Kapur, S., Zipursky, R., Jones, C., Remington, G., & Houle, S. (2000). Relationship between dopamine D2 occupancy, clinical response, and side effects: A double-blind PET study of first-episode schizophrenia. *American Journal of Psychiatry, 157,* 514–520.

Karler, R. (1998). Cited in I. Wickelgren, Teaching the brain to take drugs. *Science, 280,* 2045–2047.

Kassebaum, N. L. (1994). Head start: Only the best for America's children. *American Psychologist, 49,* 123–126.

Katigbak, M. S., Church, A. T., Guanzon-Lapena, M. A., Carlota, A., & del Pilar, G. H. (2002). Are indigenous personality dimensions culture specific? Philippine inventories and the five-factor model. *Journal of Personality and Social Psychology, 82,* 89–101.

Katz, J. (1992). Psychophysiological contributions to phantom limbs. *Canadian Journal of Psychiatry, 37,* 282–298.

Kaufman, A. (2003, February). Cited in E. Benson, Intelligent intelligence testing. *Monitor on Psychology,* 48–51.

Kaufman, A. S. (2000). Tests of intelligence. In R. J. Sternberg (Ed.), *Handbook of intelligence.* New York: Cambridge University Press.

Kaufman, A. S., Reynolds, C. R., & McLean J. E. (1989). Age and WAIS-R intelligence in a national sample of adults in the 20 to 74 age range: A cross-sectional analysis with educational level controlled. *Intelligence, 13,* 235–253.

Kaufman, J., & Zigler, E. (1989). The intergenerational transmission of child abuse. In C. Cicchetti & V. Carlson (Eds.), *Child maltreatment: Theory and research on the causes and consequences of child abuse and neglect.* Cambridge, England: Cambridge University Press.

Kaufman, L. (2000). Cited in B. Bower, The moon also rises—and assumes new sizes. *Science News, 157,* 22.

Kawakami, K., Young, H., & Dovidio, J. F. (2002). Automatic stereotyping: Category, trait, and behavioral activations. *Personality and Social Psychology Bulletin, 28,* 3–15.

Kaye, W. (2002, March). Cited in T. DeAngelis, Further gene studies show promise. *Monitor on Psychology,* 35.

Kazantzis, N., Deane, F. P., & Ronan, K. R. (2000). Homework assignments in cognitive and behavioral therapy: A meta-analysis. *Clinical Psychology: Science and Practice, 7,* 189–202

Kazdin, A. E. (2000). Treatments for aggressive and antisocial children. *Juvenile Violence, 9,* 841–857.

Kazdin, A. E. (2001). *Behavior modification* (6th ed.). Belmont, CA: Wadsworth/Thomson Learning.

Kearins, J. M. (1981). Visual spatial memory in Australian Aboriginal children of desert regions. *Cognitive Psychology, 13,* 434–460.

Kebbell, M. R., Milne, R., & Wagstaff, G. F. (1999). The cognitive interview: A survey of its forensic effectiveness. *Psychology, Crime & Law, 5,* 101–115.

Keck, P. E., & McElroy, S. L. (2003). New approaches in managing bipolar depression. *Journal of Clinical Psychiatry, 64 (supplement 6),* 13–18.

Keefe, F. J., Lumley, M. A., Buffington, A. L. H., Carson, W., Studts, J. L., Edwards, C. L., Macklem, D. J., Aspnes, A. K., Fox, L., & Steffey, D. (2002). Changing face of pain: Evolution of pain research in *Psychosomatic Medicine. Psychosomatic Medicine, 64,* 921–938.

Keenan, K., & Shaw, D. (1997). Developmental and social influences on young girl's early problem behavior. *Psychological Bulletin, 121,* 95–113.

Keiser, R. E., & Prather, E. N. (1990). What is the TAT? A review of ten years of research. *Journal of Personality Assessment, 55,* 800–803.

Keller, H., & Greenfield, P. M. (2000). History and future of development in cross-cultural psychology. *Journal of Cross-Cultural Psychology, 31,* 52–62.

Kelley, H. H. (1967). Attribution theory in social psychology. In D. Levine (Ed.), *Nebraska symposium on motivation* (Vol. 15). Lincoln: University of Nebraska Press.

Kelley, W. M. (2002). Cited in J. Travis, The brain's funny bone. *Science News, 162,* 308–309.

Keltner, D., & Ekman, P. (2000). Facial expression of emotion. Cognitive and social construction in emotions. In M. Lewis & J. M. Haviland-Jones (Eds.), *Handbook of emotions* (2nd ed.). New York: Guilford.

Keltner, D., Ekman, P., Gonzaga, G. C., & Beer, J. (2003). Facial expression of emotion. In R. D. Lane & L. Nadel (Eds.), *Cognitive neuroscience of emotion.* New York: Oxford University Press.

Kemeny, M. C. (2003). The psychobiology of stress. *Current Directions in Psychological Science, 12,* 125–129.

Kendler, K. S., Karkowski, L. M., Neale, M. C., & Prescott, C. A. (2000). Illicit psychoactive substance use, heavy use, abuse, and dependence in a US population-based sample of male twins. *Archives of General Psychiatry, 57,* 261–269.

Kennedy, D. V., & Doepke, K. J. (1999). Multicomponent treatment of a test anxious college student. *Education and Treatment of Children, 22,* 203–217.

Kennedy, J. L., Farrer, L. A., Andreasen, N. C., Mayeaux, R., & Gerog-Hyslop, P. St. (2003). The genetics of adult-onset neuropsychiatric disease: Complexities and conundra? *Science, 302,* 822–826.

Kenworthy, J. B., & Miller, N. (2002). Attributional biases about the origins of attitudes: Externality, emotionality, and rationality. *Journal of Personality and Social Psychology, 82,* 693–707.

Kernberg, O. F. (1999). Psychoanalysis, psychoanalytic psychotherapy and supportive psychotherapy: Contemporary controversies. *International Journal of Psychoanalysis, 80,* 1076–1091.

Kessler, R. C. (1997). The effects of stressful life events on depression. *Annual Review of Psychology, 48,* 191–214.

Kessler, R. C. (2003). Epidemiology of women and depression. *Journal of Affective Disorders, 74,* 25–33.

Kessler, R. C., McGonagle, K. A., Zhao, S., Nelson, C. B., Higher, M., Eshleman, S., Wittchen, H., & Kendler, K. S. (1994). Lifetime and 12-month prevalence of DSM-III-R psychiatric disorders in the United States. *Archives of General Psychiatry, 51,* 8–19.

Khantzian, E. J., & Mack, J. E. (1994). How AA works and why it's important for clinicians to understand. *Journal of Substance Abuse Treatment, 11,* 77–92.

Kiecolt-Glaser, J. K., McGuire, L., Robles, T. F., & Glaser, R. (2002). Emotions, morbidity, and mortality: New perspectives from psychoneuroimmunology. *Annual Review of Psychology, 53,* 83–107.

Kihlstrom, J. F. (1993). The continuum of consciousness. *Consciousness and Cognition, 2,* 334–354.

Kihlstrom, J. F., Glisky, M. L., & Angiulo, M. J. (1994). Dissociative tendencies and dissociative disorders. *Journal of Abnormal Psychology, 103,* 117–124.

Kim, J. H., Auerbach, J. M., Rodriguez-Gomex, J. A., Velasco, I., Gavin, D., Lumelsky, N., Lee, S. H., Nguyen, J., Sanchez-Pernaute, R., Bankiewicz, K., & McKay, R. (2002). Dopamine neurons derived from embryonic stem cells function in an animal model of Parkinson's disease. *Nature, 418,* 50–56.

Kimball, D. R., & Holyoak, K. J. (2000). Transfer and expertise. In E. Tulving & F. M. Craik (Eds.), *The Oxford handbook of memory.* New York: Oxford University Press.

Kimura, D. (1992). Sex differences in the brain. *Scientific American, 267,* 119–125.

King, A. (1992). Comparison of self-questioning, summarizing, and notetaking-review as strategies for learning from lectures. *American Educational Research Journal, 29,* 303–323.

King, F. A., Yarbrough, C. J., Anderson, D. C., Gordon, T. P., & Gould, K. G. (1988). Primates. *Science, 240,* 1475–1482.

King, M. C., & Motulsky, A. G. (2002). Mapping human history. *Science, 298,* 2342–2343.

King, S. (1991, August 25). From hard time to prime time. *Los Angeles Times/Calendar,* 3.

Kinsbourne, M. (1994). Sugar and the hyperactive child. *New England Journal of Medicine, 330,* 355–356.

Kinsey, A. C., Pomeroy, W. B., & Martin, C. E. (1948). *Sexual behavior in the human male.* Philadelphia: Saunders.

Kirk, M. S. (1972, March). Head-hunters in today's world. *National Geographic.*

Kirkcaldy, B. D., Shephard, R. J., & Furnham, A. F. (2002). The influence of type A behaviour and locus of control upon job satisfaction and occupational health. *Personality and Individual Differences, 33,* 1361–1371.

Kirmayer, L. J., Robbins, J. M., & Paris, J. (1994). Somatoform disorders: Personality and social matrix of somatic distress. *Journal of Abnormal Psychology, 103,* 125–136.

Kirsch, I. (1994). Cognitive-behavioral hypnotherapy. In J. W. Rhue, S. J. Lynn & I. Kirsch (Eds.), *Handbook of clinical hypnosis.* Washington, DC: American Psychological Association.

Kirsch, I., & Braffman, W. (2001). Imaginative suggestibility and hypnotizability. *Current Directions in Psychological Sciences, 10,* 57–61.

Kirsch, I., & Lynn, S. J. (1995). The altered state of hypnosis. *American Psychologist, 50,* 846–858.

Kirsch, I., Lynn, S. J., & Rhue, J. W. (1993). Introduction to clinical hypnosis. In J. W. Rhue, S. J. Lynn & I. Kirsch (Eds.), *Handbook of clinical hypnosis.* Washington, DC: American Psychological Association.

Kirsner, D. (1990). Is there a future for American psychoanalysis? *Psychoanalytic Review, 77,* 175–200.

References

Kitayama, S., Duffy, S., Kawamura, T., & Larsen, J. T. (2003). Perceiving an object and its context in different cultures: A cultural look at new look. *Psychological Science, 14*, 201–206.

Kitto, J., Lok, D., & Rudowicz, E. (1994). Measuring creative thinking: An activity-based approach. *Creativity Research Journal, 7*, 59–69.

Kleijn, W. C., van der Ploeg, H. M., & Topman, R. M. (1994). Cognition, study habits, test anxiety, and academic performance. *Psychological Reports, 75*, 1219–1226.

Klein, C. T. F., & Helweg-Larsen, M. (2002). Perceived control and the optimistic bias: A meta-analytic review. *Psychology and Health, 17*, 437–446.

Klein, D. N., Durbin, C. E., Shankman, S. A., & Santiago, N. J. (2002). Depression and personality. In I. H. Gotlib & C. L. Hammen (Eds.), *Handbook of depression*. New York: Guilford Press.

Klein, R. (2002, August 15). Cited in N. Wade, Language gene is traced to emergence of humans. *New York Times*, A18.

Kleinhenz, J., Streitberger, K., Windeler, J., Gubbacher, A., Mavridis, G., & Eiki, M. (1999). Randomised clinical trial comparing the effects of acupuncture and a newly designed placebo needle in rotator cuff tendonitis. *Pain, 83*, 235–241.

Kleinknecht, R. A. (1994). Acquisition of blood, injury, and needle fears and phobias. *Behavior Research and Therapy, 32*, 817–823.

Kleinman, A., & Cohen, A. (1997, March). Psychiatry's global challenge. *Scientific American*, 86–89.

Klich, L. Z., & Davidson, G. R. (1983). A cultural difference in visual memory: On le voit, on ne le voit plus. *International Journal of Psychology, 18*, 189–201.

Klingberg, G., & Hwang, C. P. (1994). Children's dental fear picture test (CDFP): A projective test for the assessment of child dental fear. *Journal of Dentistry for Children, 62*, 89–96.

Klinger, E. (1987, October). The power of daydreams. *Psychology Today*.

Kluft, R. P., & Foote, B. (1999). Dissociate identity disorder: Recent developments. *American Journal of Psychotherapy, 53*, 283–319.

Kluger, J. (2000, June 12). The battle to save your memory. *Time*, 46–57.

Kluger, J. (2002, September 23). Against all the odds. *Time*, 54–56.

Knight, R. A. (1992, July). Cited in N. Youngstrom, Rapist studies reveal complex mental map. *APA Monitor*.

Knutson, J. R. (1995). Psychological characteristics of maltreated children: Putative risk factors and consequences. *Annual Review of Psychology, 46*, 401–431.

Kobasa, S. C. (1982). Commitment and coping in stress resistance among lawyers. *Journal of Personality and Social Psychology, 42*, 707–717.

Kobasa, S. C., Maddi, S. R., & Kahn, S. (1982a). Hardiness and health: A prospective study. *Journal of Personality and Social Psychology, 42*, 168–177.

Kobasa, S. C., Maddi, S. R., & Puccetti, M. C. (1982b). Personality and exercise as buffers in the stress-illness relationship. *Journal of Behavioral Medicine, 5*, 391–404.

Koch, W. (2000, June 16). Big tobacco tells Florida jury it has reformed. *USA Today*, 13A.

Kohlberg, L. (1984). *The psychology of moral development: Essays on moral development* (Vol. 11). San Francisco: Harper & Row.

Kohler, T., & Troester, U. (1991). Changes in the palmar sweat index during mental arithmetic. *Biological Psychology, 32*, 143–154.

Kolata, G. (2000a, May 15). Sharing of profits is debated as the value of tissue rises. *New York Times*, A1.

Kolata, G. (2000b, October 17). How the body knows when to gain or lose. *New York Times*, D1.

Kolata, G. (2001, March 8). Parkinson's research is set back by failure of fetal cell implants. *New York Times*, A1.

Kolata, G. (2003a, February 25). Genetic revolution: How much, how fast. *New York Times*, D7.

Kolata, G. (2003b, May 23). Hormone studies: What went wrong. *New York Times*, F1.

Kolb, B., & Taylor, L. (2000). Facial expression, emotion and hemispheric organization. In R. D. Lane & L. Nadel (Eds.), *Cognitive neuroscience of emotion*. New York: Oxford University Press.

Kolko, D. (1995, April). Cited in T. DeAngelis, Research documents trauma of abuse. *APA Monitor*.

Koopman, J. M. (1995, February 20). Cited in M. Cimons & T. H. Maugh, II, New strategies fuel optimism in AIDS fight. *Los Angeles Times*.

Kopp, C. B., & Neufeld, S. J. (2003). Emotional development during infancy. In R. J. Davidson, K. R. Scherer & H. H. Goldsmith (Eds.), *Handbook of affective sciences*. New York: Oxford University Press.

Koriat, A., Goldsmith, M., & Pansky, A. (2000). Toward a psychology of memory accuracy. *Annual Review of Psychology, 51*, 481–537.

Kornack, D. R., & Rakic, P. (2001). Cell proliferation without neurogenesis in adult primate neocortex. *Science, 29*, 2127–2130.

Kosslyn, S. M. (1995). Introduction. In M. S. Gazzaniga (Ed.), *The cognitive neurosciences*. Cambridge, MA: MIT Press.

Kotulak, R. (2002, March 20). Nicotine digs claws into the brain. *San Diego Union-Tribune*, F1.

Kowalski, R. M. (1996). Complaints and complaining: Functions, antecedents, and consequences. *Psychological Bulletin, 119*, 179–196.

Kraus, S. J. (1995). Attitudes and the prediction of behavior: A meta-analysis of the empirical literature. *Personality and Social Psychology Bulletin, 21*, 58–75.

Kreinin, T. (2003, May 23). Cited in K. S. Peterson, Sexually active teens also are often clueless. *USA Today*, 8D.

Kubovy, M., & Wagemans, J. (1995). Grouping by proximity and multistability in dot lattices: A quantitative Gestalt theory. *Psychological Science, 6*, 225–234.

Kugelmann, R. (1998). The psychology and management of pain: Gate control as theory and symbol. In S. J. Henderikus (Ed.), *The body and psychology*. London: Academy of Hebrew Language.

Kuhl, P. K., Andruski, J. E., Christovich, I. A., Christovich, L. A., Kolzhevnikova, E. V., Ryskina, V. L., Stolyarova, E. I., Sundberg, U., & Lacerda, F. (1997). Cross-language analysis of phonetic units in language addressed to infants. *Science, 277*, 684–687.

Kulman, L. (1999, April 26). What'd you say? *U.S. News & World Report*, 66–74.

Kumpfer, K. L., & Alvarado, R. (2003). Family-strengthening approaches for the prevention of youth problem behaviors. *American Psychologist, 58*, 457–465.

Kurahashi, T., & Menini, A. (1997). Mechanism of odorant adaptation in the olfactory receptor cell. *Nature, 385*, 725–729.

Kurtz, E. (1979). *Not-God: A history of Alcoholics Anonymous*. Center City, MN: Hazelden.

Kurtz, P. (1995, May/June). Is John Beloff an absolute paranormalist? *Skeptical Inquirer*.

Lacey, M. (2002, January 6). In Kenyan family, ritual for girls still divides. *New York Times*, 4.

Lacey, M. (2003, February 6). African women gather to denounce genital cutting. *New York Times*, A3.

LaFee, S. (1996, September 11). Fragile lives. *San Diego Union-Tribune*.

LaFee, S. (1999, October 13). Face value. *San Diego Union-Tribune*, E1.

LaFee, S. (2000, March 29). Sight to behold. *San Diego Union-Tribune*, E12.

LaFee, S. (2001, March 14). Magnum pi. *San Diego Union-Tribune*, F1.

LaFrance, M., Hecht, M. A., & Paluck, E. L. (2003). The contingent smile: A meta-analysis of sex differences in smiling. *Psychological Bulletin, 129*, 305–334.

Lalumiere, M. L., Blanchard, R., & Zucker, K. J. (2000). Sexual orientation and handedness in men and women: A meta-analysis. *Psychological Bulletin, 126*, 575–592.

Lamb, N. (1990). *Guide to teaching strings* (5th ed.). Dubuque, IA: William C. Brown.

Lambert, G. W., Reid, C., Kaye, D. M., Jennings, G. L., & Ester, M. D. (2002). Effect of sunlight and season on serotonin turnover in the brain. *The Lancet, 360*, 1840–1842.

Lambert, M. J., & Bergin, A. E. (1994). The effectiveness of psychotherapy. In A. E. Bergin & S. L. Garfield (Eds.), *Handbook of psychotherapy and behavior change* (4th ed.). New York: Wiley.

Lane, R. D., & Nadel, L. (Eds.). (2000). *Cognitive neuroscience of emotion*. New York: Oxford University Press.

Lange, D. P. (2003, April 7). Fluid approach. *Los Angeles Times*, F2.

Langlois, J. H., Kalakanis, L., Rubenstein, A. J., Larson, A., Hallam, M., & Smoot, M. (2000). Maxims or myths of beauty? A meta-analysis and theoretical review. *Psychological Bulletin, 136*, 390–423.

Langlois, J. H., Roggman, L. A., & Musselman, L. (1994). What is average and what is not average about attractive faces? *Psychological Science, 5*, 214–220.

Lanyado, M., & Horne, A. (Eds.). (1999). *The handbook of child and adolescent psychotherapy*. New York: Routledge.

Lappalainen, J., Kranzler, H. F., Maltson, R., Price, L. H., Van Dyck, C., Rosenheck, R. A., Cramer, J., Southwick, S., Charney, D., Krystal, J., & Gelernter, J. (2002). A functional neuropeptide *Y leu7Pro* polymorphism associated with alcohol dependence in a large population sample from the United States. *Archives of General Psychiatry, 59*, 823–831.

Larabee, M. (1998, April 22). Recent deaths of three children blamed on belief of Oregon church. *Oregonian*.

Larabee, M. (1999, June 28). Balancing rights makes faith-healing bills thorny. *Oregonian*.

Larivee, S., Normandeau, S., & Parent, S. (2000). The French connection: Some contributions of French-language research in the post-Piagetian era. *Child Development, 71*, 823–839.

Latané, B. (1981). The psychology of social impact. *American Psychologist, 36*, 343–356.

Latané, B., & Darley, J. M. (1970). *The unresponsive bystander: Why doesn't he help?* New York: Appleton-Century-Crofts.

Latané, B., & Nida, S. (1981). Ten years of research on group size and helping. *Psychological Bulletin, 89*, 308–324.

Laumann, E., Michael, R. T., Gagnon, J. H., & Kolata, G. (1994). *The social organization of sexuality*. Chicago: University of Chicago Press.

Laurence, R. P. (2003, October 15). Now Limbaugh asks for a rush to change judgment of drug use. *San Diego Union-Tribune*, F7.

Lazarus, R. S. (1999). *Stress and emotion*. New York: Springer.

Lazarus, R. S. (2000). Evolution of a model of stress, coping and discrete emotions. In V. R. Rice (Ed.), *Handbook of stress, coping and health*. Thousand Oaks, CA: Sage.

Leahy, R. L., & Holland, S. J. (2000). *Treatment plans and interventions for depression and anxiety disorders*. New York: Guilford.

Leaper, C. (2000). Gender, affiliation, assertion, and the interactive context of parent-child play. *Developmental Psychology, 36*, 381–393.

Leavy, J. (1996, March 18). With Ritalin, the son also rises. *Newsweek.*

LeBlanc, L. A., Hagopian, L. P., & Maglieri, K. A. (2000). Use of a token economy to eliminate excessive inappropriate social behavior in an adult with developmental disabilities. *Behavioral Interventions, 15*, 135–143.

Ledbetter, D. (2002, July 23). Cited in J. E. Brody, Disorder makes hunger a constant companion. *New York Times*, D5.

LeDoux, J. (2003). Cited in L. Helmuth, Fear and trembling in the amygdala. *Science, 300*, 568–569.

Lee, T. M. C., Liou, H. L., Tan, L. H., Chan, C. C. H., Mahankali, S., Feng, C. M., Hou, J., Fox, P. T., & Gao, J. H. (2002). Lie detection by functional magnetic resonance imaging. *Human Brain Mapping, 15*, 157–164.

Leedham, B., Meyerowitz, B. E., Muirhead, J., & Frist, W. H. (1995). Positive expectations predict health after heart transplantation. *Health Psychology, 14*, 74–79.

LeGrange, D. (2002, March). Cited in T. DeAngelis, Promising treatments for anorexia and bulimia. *Monitor on Psychology*, 38–41.

Leibel, R. (2003). Cited in J. Max, Cellular warriors at the battle of the bulge. *Science, 299*, 846–849.

Leibel, R. L., Rosenbaum, M., & Hirsch, J. (1995). Changes in energy expenditure resulting from altered body weight. *New England Journal of Medicine, 332*, 621–628.

Leinwand, D. (2000, May 9). Heroin's resurgence closes drug's traditional gender gap. *USA Today*, 1A.

Leinwand, D. (2002, February 11). Ecstasy grows as danger to teens. *USA Today*, A1.

Leippe, M. R., & Eisenstadt, D. (1994). Generalization of dissonance reduction: Decreasing prejudice through induced compliance. *Journal of Personality and Social Psychology, 67*, 395–413.

Leland, J. (1994, February 14). Homophobia, *Newsweek.*

Leland, J. (1998, October 26). Not quite Viagra nation. *Newsweek*, 68.

Lemerise, E. A., & Dodge, K. A. (2000). The development of anger and hostile interactions. In M. Lewis & J. M. Haviland-Jones (Eds.), *Handbook of emotions* (2nd ed.). New York: Guilford.

Lemley, B. (2000, February). Isn't she lovely? *Discover*, 42–49.

Lemonick, M. D. (2000, October 30). Teens before their time. *Time*, 66–74.

Lemonick, M. D., & Dorfman, A. (1999, August 23). Up from the apes. *Time*, 50–58.

Lenox, R. H., & Hahn, C. (2000). Overview of the mechanism of action of lithium in the brain: Fifty-year update. *Journal of Clinical Psychiatry, 2000* (supplement 9), 5–15.

Leo, J. (1987, January 12). Exploring the traits of twins. *Time.*

Leonard, W. R. (2002, December). Food for thought. *Scientific American*, 106–115.

Lepore, S. J., Mata Allen, K. A., & Evans, G. W. (1993). Social support lowers cardiovascular reactivity to an acute stressor. *Psychosomatic Medicine, 55*, 518–524.

Lepper, M. R., Henderlong, J., & Gingras, I. (1999). Understanding the effects of extrinsic rewards on intrinsic motivation—Uses and abuses of meta-analysis: Comment on Deci, Koestner, and Ryan (1999). *Psychological Bulletin, 125*, 669–676.

Lerner, A. G., Gelkopf, M., Oyfee, I., Finkel, B., Katz, S., Sigal, M., & Weizman, A. (2000). LSD-induced hallucinogen persisting perception disorder treatment with clonidine: An open pilot study. *International Clinical Psychopharmacology, 115*, 35–37.

Lerner, R. M., & Galambos, N. L. (1998). Adolescent development: Challenges and opportunities for research, programs, and policies. *Annual Review of Psychology, 49*, 413–446.

Leshner, A. I. (2001, June). What does it mean that addiction is a brain disease? *Monitor on Psychology*, 19.

Lester, B. M., LaGasse, L. L., & Seifer, R. (1998). Cocaine exposure and children: The meaning of subtle effects. *Science, 282*, 633–634.

Leucht, S., Barnes, T. R. E., Kissling, W., Engel, R. R. Correl, C., & Kane, J. M. (2003). Relapse prevention in schizophrenia with new-generation antipsychotics: A systematic review and exploratory meta-analysis of randomized, controlled trials. *American Journal of Psychiatry, 160*, 1209–1222.

Leuchter, A. F., Cook, I. A., Witte, E. A., Morgan, M., & Abrams, M. (2002). Changes in brain function of depressed subjects during treatment with placebo. *American Journal of Psychiatry, 159*, 122–129.

Leventhal, H., & Patrick-Miller, L. (2000). Emotions and physical illness: Causes and indicators of vulnerability. In M. Lewis & J. M. Haviland-Jones (Eds.), *Handbook of emotions* (2nd ed.). New York: Guilford.

Levine, R. V., Martinez, T. S., Brase, G., & Sorenson, K. (1994). Helping in 36 U.S. cities. *Journal of Personality and Social Psychology, 67*, 69–82.

Levine, S., & Koenig, J. (Eds.). (1980). *Why men rape: Interviews with convicted rapists.* Toronto: Macmillan.

Levinson, D. F. (2003). Molecular genetics of schizophrenia: A review of the recent literature. *Current Opinion in Psychiatry, 16*, 157–170.

Levitsky, D. (2003, August 11). The "freshman." *U.S. News & World Report*, 54.

Levy, D. (1997). *Tools of critical thinking.* New York: Allyn & Bacon.

Levy, J. (1985, May). Right brain, left brain: Fact and fiction. *Psychology Today.*

Levy, J., & Trevarthen, C. (1976). Metacontrol of hemispheric function in human split-brain patients. *Journal of Experimental Psychology: Human Perception and Performance, 2*, 299–312.

Levy, J., Trevarthen, C., & Sperry, R. W. (1972). Perception of bilateral chimeric figures following hemispheric deconnection. *Brain, 95*, 61–68.

Lewis, A. (2001, March 26). Snakes scarier than public speaking. *USA Today*, A1.

Lewis, C. E. (1991). Neurochemical mechanisms of chronic antisocial behavior (psychopathy). *Journal of Nervous and Mental Disease, 179*, 720–727.

Li, T. K. (2000). Pharmacogenetics of responses to alcohol and genes that influence alcohol drinking. *Journal of Studies on Alcohol, 61*, 5–12.

Lieber, J. (2002, August 12). Swimmer Coughlin may steal show at 2004 Athens Games. *USA Today*, 1C.

Lieberman, D. A. (2000). *Learning: Behavior and cognition* (3rd ed.). Belmont, CA: Wadsworth.

Liebert, R. M., & Spiegler, M. D. (1994). *Personality: Strategies and issues* (7th ed.). Pacific Grove, CA: Brooks/Cole.

Liebowitz, M. R., Heimberg, R. G., Schneier, F. R., Hope, D. A., Davies, S., Holt, C. S., Goetz, D., Juster, H. R., Lin, S. H., Bruch, M. A., Marshall, R. D., & Klein, D. F. (1999). Cognitive-behavioral group therapy versus phenelzine in social phobia: Long-term outcome. *Depression and Anxiety, 10*, 89–98.

Lilienfeld, S. O. (1993). Do "honesty" tests really measure honesty? *Skeptical Inquirer, 18*, 32–41.

Lilienfeld, S. O. (2003). When worlds collide. *American Psychologist, 7*, 176–188.

Lilienfeld, S. O., Kirsch, I., Sarbin, T. R., Lynn, S. J., Chaves, J. F., Ganaway, G. K., & Powell, R. A. (1999). Dissociative identity disorder and the sociocognitive model: Recalling the lessons of the past. *Psychological Bulletin, 125*, 507–523.

Lilly, J. C. (1972). *The center of the cyclone.* New York: Bantam.

Lindsay, J. J., & Anderson, C. A. (2000). From antecedent conditions to violent actions: A general affective aggression model. *Personality and Social Psychological Bulletin, 26*, 533–547.

Lipkin, R. (1995). Additional genes may affect color vision. *Science News, 147*, 100.

Lipton, F. R., Siegel, C., Hannigan, A., Samuels, J., & Baker, S. (2000). Tenure in supportive housing for homeless persons with severe mental illness. *Psychiatric Services, 51*, 479–486.

Lipton, S. D. (1983). A critique of so-called standard psychoanalytic technique. *Contemporary Psychoanalysis, 19*, 35–52.

Lisanby, S. H., Maddox, J. H., Prudic, J., Devanand, D. P., & Sackeim, H. A. (2000). The effects of electroconvulsive therapy of memory of autobiographical and public events. *Archives of General Psychiatry, 57*, 581–590.

Liska, K. (1994). *Drugs & the human body* (4th ed.). New York: Macmillan.

Litt, M. D., Kalinowski, L., & Shafer, D. (1999). A dental fears typology of oral surgery patients: Matching patients to anxiety interventions. *Health Psychology, 18*, 614–624.

Little, B. R. (1999). Personality and motivation: Personal action and the conative evolution. In L. A. Pervin & O. P. John (Eds.), *Handbook of personality* (2nd ed.). New York: Guilford.

Locke, E. A., & Latham, G. P. (2002). Building a practically useful theory of goal setting and task motivation. *American Psychologist, 57*, 705–717.

Loehlin, J. C. (2000). Group differences in intelligence. In R. J. Sternberg (Ed.), *Handbook of intelligence.* New York: Cambridge University Press.

Loehlin, J. C., Neiderhiser, J. M., & Reiss, D. (2003). The behavior genetics of personality and the NEAD study. *Journal of Research in Personality, 37*, 373–387.

Loesch, D. Z., Huggins, F. M., Bui, Q. M., Epstein, J. L., Taylor, A. K., & Hagerman, R. J. (2002). Effect of the deficits of fragile X mental retardation protein on cognitive status of fragile X males and females assessed by robust pedigree analysis. *Developmental and Behavioral Pediatrics, 23*, 416–423.

Loftus, E. (1999). Repressed memories. *Forensic Psychiatry, 22*, 61–69.

Loftus, E. (2000, April 25). Cited in J. E. Brody, Memories of things that never were. *New York Times*, D8.

Loftus, E. (2003, February 17). Cited in J. Gottlieb, Memories made to order at UCI. *Los Angeles Times*, 81.

Loftus, E. F. (1975). Leading questions and the eyewitness report. *Cognitive Psychology, 7*, 560–572.

Loftus, E. F. (1979). The malleability of memory. *American Scientist, 67*, 312–320.

Loftus, E. F. (1993). The reality of repressed memories. *American Psychologist, 48*, 518–537.

Loftus, E. F. (1997a, September). Creating false memories. *Scientific American*, 70–75.

Loftus, E. F. (1997b). Repressed memory accusations: Devastated families and devastated patients. *Applied Cognitive Psychology, 11*, 25–30.

Loftus, E. F., & Hoffman, H. G. (1989). Misinformation and memory: The creation of new memories. *Journal of Experimental Psychology: General, 118*, 409–420.

References

Loftus, E. F., & Loftus, G. R. (1980). On the performance of stored information in the human brain. *American Psychologist, 35,* 409–420.

Loftus, E. F., Miller, D. G., & Burns, H. J. (1978). Semantic integration of verbal information into a visual memory. *Journal of Experimental Psychology: Human Learning and Memory, 4,* 19–31.

Logothetis, N. K. (1999, November). Vision: A window on consciousness. *Scientific American,* 69–75.

Logue, A. W., Ophir, I., & Strauss, K. E. (1981). The acquisition of taste aversions in humans. *Behavior Research and Therapy, 19,* 319–335.

Lohman, D. F. (2000). Complex information processing and intelligence. In R. J. Sternberg (Ed.), *Handbook of intelligence.* New York: Cambridge University Press.

Long, J. D., Gaynor, P., Erwin, A., & Williams, R. L. (1994). The relationship of self-management to academic motivation, study efficiency, academic satisfaction, and grade point average among prospective education majors. *Psychology, A Journal of Human Behavior, 31,* 22–30.

Lonsway, K. A., & Fitzgerald, L. F. (1994). Rape myths: In review. *Psychology of Women Quarterly, 18,* 133–164.

Lopez, S. R., & Guarnaccia, P. J. (2000). Cultural psychopathology: Uncovering the social worlds of mental illness. *Annual Review of Psychology, 51,* 571–598.

Lord, C. (2002, October 22). Cited in L. Tarkan, Autism therapy is called effective, but rare. *New York Times,* D2.

Lorenz, K. (1952). *King Solomon's ring.* New York: Crowell.

Lovaas, I. (1999, September). Cited in H. McIntosh, Two autism studies fuel hope—and skepticism. *Monitor: American Psychological Association, 28.*

Lovaas, O. I. (1987). Behavioral treatment and normal educational and intellectual functioning in young autistic children. *Journal of Consulting and Clinical Psychology, 55,* 3–9.

Lovaas, O. I. (1993). The development of a treatment-research project for developmentally disabled autistic children. *Journal of Applied Behavior Analysis, 26,* 617–630.

Lovaas, O. I., & Buch, G. (1997). Intensive behavioral intervention with young children. In N. N. Singh (Ed.), *Prevention and treatment of severe behavior problems.* Pacific Grove, CA: Brooks/Cole.

Loviglio, J. (2003, June 25). Scientists probing where untruths lie. *San Diego Union-Tribune,* F3.

Low, A., Bentin, S., Rockstroh, B., Silberman, Y., Gomolla, A., Cohen, R., & Elbert, T. (2003). Semantic categorization in the human brain: Spatiotemporal dynamics revealed by magnetoencephalography. *Psychological Science, 14,* 367–373.

Loy, I., & Hall, G. (2002). Taste aversion after ingestion of lithium chloride: An associative analysis. *The Quarterly Journal of Experimental Psychology, 55B,* 365–380.

Luborsky, L., Rosenthal, R., Diguer, L., Andrusyna, T. P., Berman, J. S., Levitt, J. T., Seligman, D. A., & Krause, E. D. (2002). The dodo bird verdict is alive and well—mostly. *Clinical Psychology: Science and Practice, 9,* 2–12.

Ludwig, A. M. (1995). *The price of greatness: Resolving the creative and madness controversy.* New York: Guilford.

Lupart, J. L., & Pyryt, M. C. (1996). "Hidden gifted" students: Underachiever prevalence and profile. *Journal for the Education of the Gifted, 20,* 36–53.

Lykken, D. T. (2003). Cited in D. Watson, Happiness is in your jeans. *Contemporary Psychology, 48,* 242–243.

Lynam, D. R., Milich, R., Zimmerman, R., Novak, S. P., Logan, T. K., Martin, C., Leukefeld, C., & Clayton, R. (1999). Project DARE: No effects at 10-year follow-up. *Journal of Counsulting and Clinical Psychology, 67,* 590–593.

Lynn, S. J., Kirsch, I., Barabasz, A., Cardena, E., & Patterson, D. (2000). Hypnosis as an empirically supported clinical intervention: The state of the evidence and a look to the future. *International Journal of Clinical and Experimental Hypnosis, 48,* 239–259.

Lynn, S. J., Loftus, E. F., Lilienfeld, S. O., & Lock, T. (2003, July/August). Memory recovery techniques in psychotherapy. *Skeptical Inquirer,* 40–46.

Lyon, R. (1999, November 22). Cited in B. Kantrowitz & A. Underwood, Dyslexia and the new science of reading. *Newsweek,* 72–78.

Maccoby, E. E. (1984). Socialization and developmental change. *Child Development, 55,* 317–328.

Macfarlane, A. J. (1975). Olfaction in the development of social preferences in the human neonate. *CIBA Foundation Symposium, 33,* 103–117.

MacGregor, J. N., Ormerod, T. C., & Chronicle, E. P. (2001). Information processing and insight: A process model of performance on the nine-dot and related problems. *Journal of Experimental Psychology: Learning, Memory and Cognition, 27,* 176–201.

Mackenzie, D. (2000, July). Remote heart surgery. *Popular Science,* 65.

Mackie, D. M., & Skelly, J. J. (1994). The social cognition analysis of social influence: Contributions to the understanding of persuasion and conformity. In P. G. Devine, D. L. Hamilton & T. M. Ostrom (Eds.), *Social cognition: Impact on social psychology.* New York: Academic Press.

Macmillan, M. (1997). *Freud evaluated.* Cambridge, MA: MIT Press.

Macnee, C. L., & McCabe, S. (2000). Microstressors and health. In V. R. Rice (Ed.), *Handbook of stress, coping and health.* Thousand Oaks, CA: Sage.

MacQueen, G., Marshall, J., Perdue, M., Siegel, S., & Biennenstock, J. (1989). Pavlovian conditioning of rat mucosal mast cells to secrete rat mast cell protease II. *Science, 243,* 83–85.

Macrae, C. N., & Bodenhausen, G. V. (2000). Social cognition: Thinking categorically about others. *Annual Review of Psychology, 51,* 93–120.

Madianos, M.G., Papgeelis, M., Ioannovich, J., & Dafni, R. (2001). Psychiatric disorders in burn patients: A follow-up study. *Psychotherapy and Psychosomatics, 70,* 30–37.

Magidoff, R. (1973). *Yehudi Menuhin.* London: Robert Hale.

Magnier, M. (2000, March 25). Japanese on a fast track to addiction. *Los Angeles Times,* A2.

Magnusson, A. (2000). An overview of epidemiological studies on seasonal affective disorder. *Acta Psychiatrica Scandinavica, 101,* 176–184.

Magnusson, A., Axelsson, J., Karlsson, M. M., & Oskarsson, H. (2000). Lack of seasonal mood change in the Icelandic population: Results of a cross-sectional study. *American Journal of Psychiatry, 157,* 234–238.

Mahowlad, M. (2003, February 2). Cited in C. Brown, The man who mistook his wife for a deer. *New York Times Magazine,* 34–41.

Maier, S. R., Watkins, L. R., & Fleshner, M. (1994). Psychoneuroimmunology. *American Psychologist, 49,* 1004–1007.

Maldonado, P. E., Godecke, I., Gray, C. M., & Bonhoffer, T. (1997). Orientation selectivity in pinwheel centers in cat striate cortex. *Science, 276,* 1551–1555.

Malle, B. F., Knobe, J., O'Lauglin, M. J., Pearce, G. E., & Nelson, S. E. (2000). Conceptual structure and social functions of behavior explanations: Beyond person-situation attributions. *Journal of Personality and Social Psychology, 79,* 309–326.

Manderscheid, R. W., & Sonnenschein, M. A. (1992). *Mental health, United States, 1992.* Washington, DC: U.S. Department of Health and Human Services.

Mann, K., Hermann, D., & Heinz, A. (2000). One hundred years of alcoholism: The twentieth century. *Alcohol & Alcoholism, 35,* 10–15.

Manning, A. (1996, September 17). Caught dirty-handed: Many fail to wash when they should. *USA Today.*

Manning, A. (1998, February 23). Operating with sexism. *USA Today,* D1.

Manning, A. (2000a, May 2). The changing deaf culture. *USA Today,* D1.

Manning, A. (2000b, June 13). Kid obesity tips scales towards diabetes epidemic. *USA Today,* D8.

Maratsos, M., & Matheny, L. (1994). Language specificity and elasticity: Brain and clinical syndrome studies. *Annual Review of Psychology, 45,* 487–516.

Marcus, D. K., & Miller, R. W. (2003). Sex differences in judgments of physical attractiveness: A social relations analysis. *Personality and Social Psychology Bulletin, 29,* 325–335.

Marcus, M. B. (2000, October 2). Don't let false alarms scare you off prenatal tests, but do get the facts first. *U.S. News & World Report,* 69–70.

Mareschal, D., & Quinn, P. C. (2001). Categorization in infancy. *TRENDS in Cognitive Science, 5,* 443–450.

Marklein, M. D. (2002, January 28). California rewrites college admissions. *USA Today,* D1.

Marmar, C. R., Neylan, T. C., & Schoenfeld, F. B. (2002). New directions in the pharmacotherapy of posttraumatic stress disorders. *Psychiatric Quarterly, 73,* 259–270.

Marquis, C. (2003, March 13). Total of unmarried couples surged in 2000 U.S. census. *New York Times,* A18.

Marsa, L. (2002, March 25). Trauma therapy's new focus. *Los Angeles Times,* S8.

Marsh, A. A., Elfenbein, A., & Ambady, N. (2003). Nonverbal "accents": Cultural differences in facial expressions of emotion. *Psychological Science, 14,* 373–376.

Marta, E. (1997). Parent-adolescent interactions and psychosocial risk in adolescents: An analysis of communication, support, and gender. *Journal of Adolescence, 20,* 471–487.

Marten, K., Shariff, K., Psarakos, S., & White, D. J. (1996, August). Ring of dolphins. *Scientific American,* 83–87.

Martin, A., Wiggs, C. L., Ungerfelder, L. G., & Haxby, J. V. (1996). Neural correlates of category-specific knowledge. *Nature, 379,* 649–652.

Martin, C. L. (2000). Cognitive theories of gender development. In T. Eckes & H. M. Trautner (Eds.), *The developmental social psychology of gender.* Mahwah, NJ: Lawrence Erlbaum.

Martin, C. L., Ruble, D. N., & Szrkrybalo, J. (2002). Cognitive theories of early gender development. *Psychological Bulletin, 128,* 903–933.

Martin, G. L. (1982). Thought-stopping and stimulus control to decrease persistent disturbing thoughts. *Journal of Behavior Therapy and Experimental Psychiatry, 13,* 215–220.

Martin, L. (1986). Eskimo words for snow: A case study in the genesis and decay of an anthropological example. *American Anthropologist, 88,* 418–423.

Martin, S. (2001, June). Substance abuse is nation's No. 1 health problem, but there is hope. *Monitor on Psychology,* 10–11.

Maslach, C. (2003). Job burnout: New directions in research and intervention. *Current Directions in Psychological Science, 12,* 189–192.

Masling, J. M. (1997). On the nature and utility of projective tests and objective tests. *Journal of Personality Assessment, 69,* 357–370.

Maslow, A. H. (1968). *Toward a psychology of being* (2nd ed.). New York: Van Nostrand.

Maslow, A. H. (1970). *Motivation and personality.* New York: Harper & Row.

Maslow, A. H. (1971). *The farther reaches of human nature.* New York: Viking Press.

Mason, D. J., & Kohn, M. L. (2001). *The memory workbook.* New York: Harbinger Publications.

Masters, W. H., & Johnson, V. E. (1966). *Human sexual response.* Boston: Little, Brown.

Masters, W. H., & Johnson, V. E. (1970). *Human sexual inadequacy.* Boston: Little, Brown.

Masters, W. H., & Johnson, V. E. (1981). Sex and the aging process. *Journal of the American Geriatrics Society, 19,* 385–389.

Mastro, J. (1999, July 21). Dialogue with a dolphin. *San Diego Union-Tribune,* E1.

Mathews, T., Reiss, S., & Artholet, J. (1990, February 19). The threat of a white backlash. *Newsweek.*

Matson, J. L., & Ollendick, T. H. (1977). Issues in toilet training normal children. *Behavior Therapy, 8,* 549–553.

Matsuda, L. A., Lolait, S. J., Brownstein, M. J., Young, A. C., & Bonner, T. I. (1990). Structure of a cannabinoid receptor and functional expression of the cloned cDNA. *Nature, 346,* 561–564.

Matsumoto, D., & Ekman, P. (1989). American-Japanese cultural differences in intensity ratings of facial expressions of emotion. *Motivation and Emotion, 13,* 143–157.

Matsumoto, D., Consolacion, T., Yamada, H., Suzuki, R., Franklin, B., Paul, S., Ray, R., & Uchida, H. (2002). American-Japanese cultural differences in judgments of emotional expression of different intensities. *Cognition and Emotion, 16,* 721–747.

Matthews, G., Zeidner, M., & Roberts, R. D. (2003). *Emotional intelligence: Science and myth.* Cambridge, MA.: MIT Press.

Matthews, K. A., & Haynes, S. G. (1986). Type A behavior pattern and coronary disease risk. *American Journal of Epidemiology, 123,* 923–960.

Matthias, R. E., Lubben, J. E., Atchison, K. A., & Schweitzer, S. T. (1997). Sexual activity and satisfaction among very old adults: Results from a community-dwelling medicare population survey. *Gerontologist, 37,* 6–14.

Mattson, S. N., Schoenfeld, A. M., & Riley, E. P. (2001). Teratogenic effects of alcohol on brain and behavior. *Alcohol Research and Health, 25,* 185–191.

Maugh, T. H., II. (2002a, April 21). Use of eye cells in treating Parkinson's shows promise. *Los Angeles Times,* S3.

Maugh, T. H., II. (2002b, July 7). Drug resistance complicates HIV therapy. *Los Angeles Times,* A3.

Maugh, T. H., II. (2003, February 18). AIDS researchers optimistic about new medications. *Los Angeles Times,* A11.

Max, D. T. (2001, May 6). To sleep no more. *New York Times Magazine,* 74–78.

Mayer, J. D., Salovey, P., & Caruso, D. (2000). Models of emotional intelligence. In R. J. Sternberg (Ed.), *Handbook of intelligence.* New York: Cambridge University Press.

Mayes, A. R. (2000). Selective memory disorders. In E. Tulving & F. M. Craik (Eds.), *The Oxford handbook of memory.* New York: Oxford University Press.

Mayhew, J. E. W. (2003). A measured look at neuronal oxygen consumption. *Science, 299,* 1023–1024.

Mayr, E. (2000, July). Darwin's influence on modern thought. *Scientific American,* 79–83.

Mazzoni, G., & Cornoldi, C. (1993). Strategies in study time allocation: Why is study time sometimes not effective? *Journal of Experimental Psychology: General, 122,* 47–60.

Mcallister, H. A., Baker, J. D., Mannes, C., Stewart, H., & Sutherland, A. (2002). The optimal margin of illusion hypothesis: Evidence from self-serving bias and personality disorders. *Journal of Social and Clinical Psychology, 21,* 414–426.

McCall, R. B. (1994). Academic underachievers. *Current Directions in Psychological Science, 3,* 15–19.

McCarry, J. (1996, May). Peru begins again. *National Geographic.*

McClearn, G. E., Johansson, B., Berg, S., Pedersen, N. L., Ahern, F., Petrill, S. A., & Plomin, R. (1997). Substantial genetic influence on cognitive abilities in twins 80 or more years old. *Science, 276,* 1560–1563.

McClelland, D. C. (1985). *Human motivation.* Glenview, IL: Scott, Foresman.

McClelland, D. C., Atkinson, J. W., Clark, R. W., & Lowell, E. L. (1953). *The achievement motive.* New York: Appleton-Century-Crofts.

McClelland, J. L. (2000). Connectionist models of memory. In E. Tulving & F. M. Craik (Eds.), *The Oxford handbook of memory.* New York: Oxford University Press.

McConnell, J. V., Cutler, R. L., & McNeil, E. B. (1958). Subliminal stimulation: An overview. *American Psychologist, 13,* 229–242.

McCrae, R. R., & Costa, P. T., Jr. (1990). *Personality in adulthood.* New York: Guilford.

McCrae, R. R., & Costa, P. T., Jr. (1997). Personality trait structure as a human universal. *American Psychologist, 52,* 509–516.

McCrae, R. R., & Costa, P. T., Jr. (1999). A five-factor theory of personality. In L. A. Pervin & O. P. John (Eds.), *Handbook of personality* (2nd ed.). New York: Guilford.

McCrae, R. R., Costa, P. T., Jr., Hrebickova, M., Osteandorf, F., Angleitner, A., Avia, M., Sanz, J., Sanchez-Bernardos, M. L., Kusdil, M. E., Woodfield, R., Saunders, P. R., & Smith, P. B. (2000). Nature over nurture: Temperament, personality and life-span development. *Journal of Personality and Social Psychology, 78,* 173–186.

McDaniel, M. A., & Einstein, G. O. (1986). Bizarre imagery as an effective memory aid: The importance of distinctiveness. *Journal of Experimental Psychology: Learning, Memory and Cognition, 12,* 54–65.

McDonough, M., & Kennedy, N. (2002). Pharmacological management of obsessive-compulsive disorder: A review for clinicians. *Harvard Review of Psychiatry, 10,* 127–137.

McDougall, W. (1908). *Social psychology.* New York: Putnam.

McDowell, J. (1992, February 17). Are women better cops? *Time.*

McEachin, J. J., Smith, T., & Lovaas, O. I. (1993). Long-term outcome for children with autism who received early intensive behavioral interventions. *American Journal on Mental Retardation, 97,* 359–372.

McElrath, D. (1997). The Minnesota model. *Journal of Psychoactive Drugs, 29,* 141–144.

McEwen, B. S. (2002, December 17). Cited in E. Goode, The heavy cost of stress. *New York Times,* D1.

McGaugh, J. L. (1990). Significance and remembrance: The role of neuromodulatory systems. *Psychological Science, 1,* 15–25.

McGaugh, J. L. (1999, February). Cited in B. Azar, McGaugh blazes on down his own path to keys of memory. *APA Monitor,* 18.

McGehee, D. A. (2002). Cited in R. Kotulak, Nicotine digs claws into brain. *San Diego Union-Tribune,* F1.

McGinnis, J. M., & Foege, W. H. (1993). Actual causes of death in the United States. *Journal of the American Medical Association, 270,* 2207–2212.

McGrath, B. B. (2003). A view from the other side: The place of spirits in the Tongan social field. *Culture, Medicine and Psychiatry, 27,* 29–48.

McIntosh, A. R., & Lobaugh, N. J. (2003). When is a word not a word? *Science, 301,* 322–323.

McKay, R. (2002, June 21). Cited in N. Wade, Stem cell progress reported on Parkinson's. *New York Times,* A18.

McKenna, K. (1994, November 13). He just did it. *Los Angeles Times Calendar.*

McKerracher, L., & Ellezam, B. (2002). Putting the brakes on regeneration. *Science, 296,* 1819–1820.

McKinley, J. C., Jr. (2001, May 9). Court opens door to data on eyewitness fallibility. *New York Times,* A27.

McNally, R. J. (1999). On eye movements and animal magnetism: A reply to Greenwald's defense of EMDR. *Journal of Anxiety Disorders, 13,* 617–620.

McWhorter, J. H. (2000). *Losing the race.* New York: Free Press.

Meck, W. (1996). Cited in V. Morell, Setting a biological stopwatch. *Science, 271,* 905–906.

Megargee, E. I. (1997). Internal inhibitions and controls. In R. Hogan, J. Johnson & S. Briggs (Eds.), *Handbook of personality psychology.* New York: Academic Press.

Melzack, R. (1989). Phantom limbs, the self and the brain. *Canadian Psychology, 30,* 1–16.

Melzack, R. (1997). Phantom limbs. *Scientific American, Special Issue,* 84–91.

Melzack, R., & Wall, P. D. (1983). *The challenge of pain.* New York: Basic Books.

Menaker, M. (2003). Circadian photoreception. *Science, 299,* 213–214.

Merz, C. N. B., Dwyer, J., Nordstrom, C. K., Walton, K. G., Salerno, J. W., & Schneider, R. H. (2002). Psychosocial stress and cardiovascular disease: Pathophysiological links. *Behavioral Medicine, 27,* 141–147.

Messer, S. B., & Warmpold, B. E. (2002). Let's face facts: Common factors are more potent than specific therapy ingredients. *Clinical Psychology: Science and Practice, 9,* 21–25.

Mestel, R. (1999, January). Sexual chemistry. *Discover,* 32.

Mestel, R. (2003a, April 15). Human Genome is completed: Now comes the hard part. *Los Angeles Times,* A18.

Mestel, R. (2003b, May 19). Rorschach tested. *Los Angeles Times,* F1.

Metrebian, N., Shanahan, W., Stimson, G. V., Small, C., Lee, M., Mtutu, V., & Wells, B. (2001). Prescribing drug of choice to opiate dependent drug users: A comparison of clients receiving heroin with those receiving injectable methadone at a West London drug clinic. *Drug and Alcohol Review, 20,* 267–276.

Metz, M. E., & Pryor, J. L. (2000). Premature ejaculation: A psychophysiological approach for assessment and management. *Journal of Sex & Marital Therapy, 26,* 293–320.

Meyer, G. J., Finn, S. E., Eyde, L. D., Kay, G. G., Moreland, K. L., Dies, R. R., Eisman, E. J., Kubiszyn, T. W., & Reed, G. M. (2001). Psychological testing and psychological assessment. *American Psychologist, 56,* 128–165.

Mignot, E. (2000, August 30). Cited in A. Manning, Narcolepsy is caused by loss of particular brain cells. *USA Today,* D10.

Mignot, E. (2002, January 8). Cited in D. Tuller, A quiet revolution for those prone to nodding off. *New York Times,* D7.

Milgram, N. A., Dangour, W., & Raviv, A. (1992). Situational and personal determinants of academic procrastination. *Journal of General Psychology, 119,* 123–133.

References

Milgram, S. (1963). Behavioral study of obedience. *Journal of Abnormal and Social Psychology, 67,* 371–378.

Milgram, S. (1974). *Obedience to authority.* New York: Harper & Row.

Milgrom, P., Mancl, L., Kng, B., & Weinstein, P. (1995). Origins of childhood dental fear. *Behaviour Research and Therapy, 33,* 313–319.

Milgrom, P., Quang, J. Z., & Tay, K. M. (1994). Cross-cultural validity of a parent's version of the Dental Fear Survey Schedule for children in Chinese. *Behavior Research and Therapy, 32,* 131–135.

Milgrom, P., Vigehesa, H., & Weinstein, P. (1992). Adolescent dental fear and control: Prevalence and theoretical implications. *Behavior Research and Therapy, 30,* 367–373.

Milham, M. P., Erickson, K. I., Banich, M. T., Kramer, A. F., Webb, A., Wszalek, T., & Cohen, H. J. (2002). Attentional control in the aging brain: Insights from an fMRI study of the Stroop task. *Brain and Cognition, 49,* 277–296.

Millan, M. J. (1986). Multiple opioid systems and pain. *Pain, 27,* 303–347.

Miller, F. G., Quill, T. E., Brody, H., Fletcher, J. C., Gostin, L. O., & Meier, D. E. (1994). Regulating physician-assisted death. *New England Journal of Medicine, 331,* 119–122.

Miller, G. (1956). The magical number seven, plus or minus two: Some limits on our capacity for information processing. *Psychological Review, 48,* 337–442.

Miller, G. (2003). Singing in the brain. *Science, 299,* 646–648.

Miller, J. (1995, April). Cited in T. DeAngelis, Research documents trauma of abuse. *APA Monitor.*

Miller, L. (2003, April 24). 42,890 U.S. traffic deaths in 2002 are most since 1990. *San Diego Union-Tribune,* A6.

Miller, M. (2003, July 7). When anxiety runs sky-high. *Los Angeles Times,* F1.

Miller, M. A., & Rahe, R. H. (1997). Life changes scaling for the 1990s. *Journal of Psychosomatic Research, 43,* 279–292.

Miller, M., Azrael, D., Hemenway, D., & Solop, F. I. (2002). "Road rage" in Arizona: Armed and dangerous. *Accident Analysis and Prevention, 34,* 807–814.

Miller, R. (2003, November). Cited in K. Wright, Staying alive. *Discover,* 64–70.

Miller, R. W., & C'deBaca, J. (1994). Quantum change: Toward a psychology of transformation. In T. F. Heatherton & J. L. Weinberger (Eds.), *Can personality change?* Washington, DC: American Psychological Association.

Miller, T. Q., Turner, C. W., Tindale, R. S., Posavac, E. J., & Dugoni, B. L. (1991). Reasons for the trend toward null findings in research on Type A behavior. *Psychological Bulletin, 110,* 469–485.

Milstein, M. (1993, October 27). A dizzying dilemma. *San Diego Union-Tribune.*

Milton, J., & Wiseman, R. (1999). Does Psi exist? Lack of replication of an anomalous process of information transfer. *Psychological Bulletin, 125,* 387–391.

Milton, J., & Wiseman, R. (2001). Does Psi exist: Reply to Storm and Ertel (2001). *Psychological Bulletin, 127,* 434–438.

Minda, J. P., & Smith, J. D. (2001). Prototypes in category learning: The effects of category size, category structure, and stimulus complexity. *Journal of Experimental Psychology: Learning, Memory and Cognition, 27,* 775–799.

Mirsky, A. F., & Quinn, O. W. (1988). The Genain quadruplets. *Schizophrenia Bulletin, 14,* 595–612.

Mischel, W. (1968). *Personality and assessment.* New York: Wiley.

Mischel, W., & Peake, P. K. (1982). Beyond deja vu in the search for cross-situational consistency. *Psychological Review, 89,* 730–755.

Mischel, W., & Shoda, Y. (1995). A cognitive-affective system theory of personality: Reconceptualizing situations, dispositions, dynamics, and invariance of personality structure. *Psychological Review, 102,* 246–268.

Mischel, W., Shoda, Y., & Rodriguez, M. L. (1989). Delay of gratification in children. *Science, 244,* 933–937.

Mittleman, M. A. (1999). Cited in S. Carpenter, Cocaine use boosts heart-attack risk. *Science News, 155,* 358.

Miyazaki, T., Ishikawa, T., Iimori, H., Miki, A., Wenner, M., Fukunishi, I., & Kawawura, N. (2003). Relationship between perceived social support and immune function. *Stress and Health, 19,* 3–7.

Moldin, S. O., Reich, T., & Rice, J. P. (1991). Current perspectives on the genetics of unipolar depression. *Behavior Genetics, 21,* 211–242.

Moller, H. J., & Nasrallah, H. A. (2003). Treatment of bipolar disorder. *Journal of Clinical Psychiatry, 64* (supplement 6), 9–17.

Money, J. (1987). Sin, sickness or status? *American Psychologist, 42,* 384–399.

Monk, T. H., Kennedy, K. S., Rose, L. R., & Linenger, J. M. (2001). Decreased human circadian pacemaker influence after 100 days in space. *Psychosomatic Medicine, 63,* 881–885.

Monnot, M. (1999). Function of infant-directed speech. *Human Nature, 10,* 415–443.

Montgomery, G. H., & Bovbjerg, D. H. (1997). The development of anticipatory nausea in patients receiving adjuvant chemotherapy for breast cancer. *Physiology & Behavior, 61,* 737–741.

Montgomery, G. H., DuHamel, K. N., & Redd, W. H. (2000). A meta-analysis of hypnotically induced analgesia: How effective is hypnosis? *International Journal of Clinical and Experimental Hypnosis, 48,* 138–153.

Montoya, A. G., Sorrentino, R., Lukas, S. E., & Price, B. H. (2002). Long-term neuropsychiatric consequences of "ecstasy" (MDMA): A review. *Harvard Review of Psychiatry, 10,* 212–220.

Moore, R. Y. (1997). Circadian rhythms: Basic neurobiology and clinical applications. *Annual Review of Medicine, 48,* 253–266.

Moore, T. M., Scarpa, A., & Raine, A. (2002). A meta-analysis of serotonin metabolite 5-HIAA and antisocial behavior. *Aggressive Behavior, 28,* 299–316.

Morey, L. C. (1997). Personality diagnosis and personality disorders. In R. Hogan, J. Johnson & S. Briggs (Eds.), *Handbook of personality psychology.* New York: Academic Press.

Morgan, A. B., & Lilienfeld, S. O. (2000). A meta-analytic review of the relation between antisocial behavior and neuropsychological measures of executive function. *Clinical Psychology Review, 20,* 113–136.

Morgan, D. (1995, July 11). Cited in C. Sullivan, Mother called fit for trial in sons' deaths. *San Diego Union-Tribune.*

Morral, A. R., McCaffrey, D. F., & Paddock, S. M. (2002). Reassessing the marijuana gateway effect. *Addiction, 97,* 1493–1504.

Morrison, A. (1993). Cited in H. Herzog, Animal rights and wrongs. *Science, 262,* 1906–1908.

Morse, J. (2002, April 1). Women on a binge. *Time,* 56–62.

Moseley, J. B., O'Malley, K., Petersen, N. J., Menke, T. J., Brody, B. A., Kuykendall, D. H., Hollingsworth, J. C., Ashton, C. M., & Wray, N. P. (2002). A controlled trial of arthroscopic surgery for osteoarthritis of the knee. The *New England Journal of Medicine, 347,* 81–88.

Moss, D. (1993, August 3). A painful parting in Michigan. *USA Today.*

Moss, M. (2002a, June 27). Spotting breast cancer: Doctors are weak link. *New York Times,* A1.

Moss, M. (2002b, June 28). Mammogram team learns from its errors. *New York Times,* A1.

Mukerjee, M. (1997, February). Trends in animal research. *Scientific American,* 86–93.

Muller, R. A., Behen, M. E., Rothermel, R. D., Chugani, D. C., Muzik, O., Mangner, T. J., & Chugani, H. T. (1999). Brain mapping of language and auditory perception in high-functioning autistic adults: A PET study. *Journal of Autism and Developmental Disorders, 29,* 19–31.

Mumford, M. D., Connelly, M. S., Helton, W. B., Strange, J. M., & Osburn, H. K. (2001). On the construct validity of integrity tests: Individual and situational factors as predictors of test performance. *International Journal of Selection and Assessment, 9,* 240–257.

Mundy, C. (1994, June 2). The lost boy. *Rolling Stone.*

Munk, M. H. J., Roelfsema, P. R., Konig, P., Engel, A. K., & Singer, W. (1996). Role of reticular activation in the modulation of intracortical synchronization. *Science, 272,* 271–277.

Munoz, H. (2003, May 30). Working to get more female police officers. *Los Angeles Times,* B2.

Murnane, K., Phelps, M. P., & Malmberg, K. (1999). Context-dependent recognition memory: The ICE theory. *Journal of Experimental Psychology–General, 128,* 403–415.

Murphy, C., Schubert, C. R., Cruickshanks, K. J., Klein, B. E., Klein, R., & Nondahl, D. M. (2002). Prevalence of olfactory impairment in older adults. *Journal of the American Medical Association, 288,* 2307–2312.

Murphy, K. R. (1993). *Honesty in the workplace.* Pacific Grove, CA: Brooks/Cole.

Murray, B. (1997, May). Is it a rise in ADHD, or in students' false claims? *APA Monitor.*

Murray, D. J., Kilgout, A. R., & Wasykliw, L. (2000). Conflicts and missed signals in psychoanalysis, behaviorism, and Gestalt psychology. *American Psychologist, 55,* 422–426.

Murray, H. (1943). *Thematic Apperception Test manual.* Cambridge, MA: Harvard University Press.

Musto, D. F. (1996, April). Alcohol in American history. *Scientific American,* 78–83.

Musto, D. F. (1999). The impact of public attitudes on drug abuse research in the twentieth century. In M. D. Glantz & C. R. Hartel (Eds.), *Drug abuse: Origins & interventions.* Washington, DC: American Psychological Association.

Mydans, S. (2003, March 11). Clustering in cities, Asians are becoming obese. *New York Times,* A3.

Myrtek, M. (1995). Type A behavior pattern, personality factors, disease, and physiological reactivity: A meta-analytic update. *Personality and Individual Differences, 18,* 491–502.

Nader, K. (2003). Cited in B. Bower, Restoring recall. *Science News, 164,* 228–229.

Nagarahole, E. L. (1994, March 28). Tigers on the brink. *Time.*

Nagtegaal, J. E., Laurant, M. W., Kerkof, G. A., Smits, M. G., van der Meer, Y. G., & Coenen, A. M. L. (2000). Effects of melatonin on the quality of life in patients with delayed sleep phase syndrome. *Journal of Psychosomatic Research, 48,* 45–50.

Naimi, T. S., Brewer, R. D., Mokdad, A., Denny, C., Serdula, M. K., & Marks, J. S. (2003). Binge drinking among U.S. adults. *Journal of the American Medical Association, 289,* 70–75.

NAMHC (National Advisory Mental Health Council). (1996). Basic behavioral science research for mental health: Perception, attention, learning, and memory. *American Psychologist, 51,* 133–142.

Nangle, D. W., Erdley, C. A., Carpenter, E. M., & Newman, J. E. (2002). Social skills training as a treatment for aggressive children and adolescents: A developmental-clinical integration. *Aggression and Violent Behavior, 7,* 169–199.

Nash, J. M. (2002a, May 6). The secrets of autism. *Time,* 46–56.

Nash, J. M. (2002b, November 11). Inside the womb. *Time,* 68–78.

Nash, M. J. (2002, September 2). Cracking the fat riddle. *Time,* 47–55.

Nash, M. R. (2001, July). The truth and the hype of hypnosis. *Scientific American,* 47–55.

Natale, V., & Cicogna, P. (2002). Morningness-eveningness dimension: Is it really a continuum? *Personality and Individual Differences, 32,* 809–816.

Nathan, P. E., Stuart, S. P., & Dolan, S. L. (2000). Research of psychotherapy efficacy and effectiveness: Between Scylla and Charybdis. *Psychological Bulletin, 126,* 964–981.

NCSDR (National Commission on Sleep Disorders Research). (1993). *Wake up America: A national sleep alert.* Washington, DC: Department of Health and Human Services.

Neath, I. (1998). *Human memory.* Pacific Grove, CA: Brooks/Cole.

Neher, A. (1991). Maslow's theory of motivation: A critique. *Journal of Humanistic Psychology, 31,* 89–112.

Nehlig, A. (1999). Are we dependent upon coffee and caffeine? A review of human and animal data. *Neuroscience and Biobehavioral Reviews, 23,* 563–576.

Neisser, U., & Libby, L. K. (2000). Remembering life experiences. In E. Tulving & F. M. Craik (Eds.), *The Oxford handbook of memory.* New York: Oxford University Press.

Neisser, U., Boodoo, G., Bourchard, T. J., Jr., Boykin, A. W., Brody, N., Ceci, S. J., Halpern, D. R., Loehlin, J. C., Perloff, R., Sternberg, R. J., & Urbina, S. (1996). Intelligence: Knowns and unknowns. *American Psychologist, 51,* 77–101.

Neitz, J., Neitz, M., & Kainz, P. M. (1996). Visual pigment gene structure and the severity of color vision defects. *Science, 274,* 801–803.

Neitz, M., & Neitz, J. (1995). Numbers and ratios of visual pigment genes for normal red-green color vision. *Science, 267,* 1013–1016.

Nelson, K. B., Grether, J. K., Croen, L. A., Dambrosia, J. M., Dickens, B. F., Jelliffe, L. L., Hansen, R. L., & Phillips, T. M. (2001). Neuropeptides and neurotrophins in neonatal blood of children with autism or mental retardation. *Annals of Neurology, 49,* 597–606.

Nelson, R. J., Demas, G. E., Huang, P. L., Fishman, M. C., Dawson, V. L., Dawson, T. M., & Snyder, S. H. (1995). Behavioural abnormalities in male mice lacking neuronal nitric oxide synthase. *Nature, 378,* 383–386.

Netting, J. (2001). Teams find probable gene for sweet sense. *Science News, 159,* 263.

Neugarten, B. (1994, May). Cited in B. Azar, Women are barraged by media on "the change." *APA Monitor.*

Neverlien, P. O., & Johnsen, T. B. (1991). Optimism-pessimism dimension and dental anxiety in children aged 10–12. *Community Dentistry Oral Epidemiology, 19,* 342–346.

New York Times, (2003, April 25). Middle school boy shoots his principal then kills himself. A20.

Newcombe, N. S. (2002). The nativist-empiricist controversy in the context of recent research on spatial and quantitative development. *Psychological Science, 13,* 395–401.

Newman, L. S. (2001). A cornerstone for the science of interpersonal behavior? Person perception and person memory, past, present, and future. In G. B. Moskowitz (Ed.), *Cognitive social psychology.* Mahwah, NJ: Lawrence Erlbaum.

Neziroglu, F., Hsla, C., & Yargura-Tobias, J. A. (2000). Behavioral, cognitive, and family therapy for obsessive-compulsive and related disorders. *The Psychiatric Clinics of North America, 23,* 657–670.

NICHD. (1997). The effects of infant child care on infant-mother attachment security: Results of the NICHD study of early child care. *Child Development, 68,* 860–879.

NICHD. (2001). Nonmaternal care and family factors in early development: An overview of the NICHD study of early child care. *Applied Developmental Psychology, 22,* 457–492.

NICHD. (2003). Does quality of child care affect child outcomes at age $4\frac{1}{2}$? *Developmental Psychology, 39,* 451–469.

Nichelli, P., Grafman, J., Pietrini, P., Alway, D., Carton, J. C., & Miletich. (1994). Brain activity in chess playing. *Nature, 369,* 191.

NIDA (National Institute on Drug Use). (2003). High school and youth trends. http//www.drugabuse.gov/Infofax/HSYouthtrends

Niedenthal, P. M., & Setterlund, M. C. (1994). Emotion congruence in perception. *Personality and Social Psychology Bulletin, 20,* 401–411.

Nisbet, M. (1998, May/June). Psychic telephone networks profit on yearning, gullibility. *Skeptical Inquirer,* 5–6.

Nisbet, R. (2000, August 8). Cited in E. Goode, How culture molds habits of thought. *New York Times,* D1.

Niznikiewicz, M. A., Kubicki, M., & Shenton, M. E. (2003). Recent structural and functional imaging findings in schizophrenia. *Current Opinion in Psychiatry, 16,* 123–147.

Nobler, M. S., & Sackeim, H. A. (1998). Mechanisms of action of electroconvulsive therapy: Functional brain imaging studies. *Psychiatric Annals, 28,* 23–29.

Noonan, D. (2001, June 25). The ultimate remote control. *Newsweek,* 71–75.

Noonan, D., & Cowley, G. (2002, July 15). Prozac vs. placebos. *Newsweek,* 48–49.

Norenzayan, A., & Nisbett, R. E. (2000). Culture and causal cognition. *Current Directions in Psychological Science, 9,* 132–135.

Noriyuki, D. (1996, February). Breaking down the walls. *Los Angeles Times,* E1.

Norman, D. A. (1982). *Learning and memory.* New York: Freeman.

Nosofsky, R. M., & Zaki, S. R. (2002). Exemplar and prototype models revisited: Response strategies, selective attention, and stimulus generalization. *Journal of Experimental Psychology: Learning, Memory and Cognition, 28,* 924–940.

Nour, N. (2000, July 11). Cited in C. Dreifus, A life devoted to stopping the suffering of mutilation. *New York Times,* D7.

Novak, V. (September 10, 2001). New Ritalin ad blitz makes parents jumpy. *Time,* 62–63.

Nowak, R. (1994). Chronobiologists out of sync over light therapy patents. *Science, 263,* 1217–1218.

Nurius, P. S., & Berlin, S. S. (1994). Treatment of negative self-concept and depression. In D. K. Granvold (Ed.), *Cognitive and behavioral treatment: Methods and applications.* Pacific Grove, CA: Brooks/Cole.

Nyberg, L., & Cabeza, R. (2000). Brain imaging of memory. In E. Tulving & F. M. Craik (Eds.), *The Oxford handbook of memory.* New York: Oxford University Press.

Nyberg, L., Marklund, P., Persson, J., Caberza, R., Forkstam, C., Petersson, K. M., & Ingvar, M. (2003). Common prefrontal activations during working memory, episodic memory, and semantic memory. *Neuropsychologia, 41,* 371–377.

Offer, D., Kaiz, M., Howard, K. I., & Bennett, E. S. (2000). The altering of reported experiences. *Journal of the American Academy of Child and Adolescent Psychiatry, 39,* 735–742.

Office of Justice. (2002). Rape and sexual assaults. www.ojp.usdoj.gov/bjs/

Ohayon, M. M., & Shapiro, C. M. (2002). Tenses of insomnia epidemiology. *Journal of Psychosomatic Research, 53,* 525–527.

Ohayon, M. M., Lemine, P., Arnaud-Briant, V., & Dreyfus, M. (2002). Prevalence and consequences of sleep disorders in a shift worker population. *Journal of Psychosomatic Research, 53,* 577–583.

Ohman, A. (2002). Automaticity and the amygdala: Nonconscious responses to emotional faces. *Current Directions in Psychological Science, 11,* 62–66.

Ohman, A., Flykt, A., & Esteves, F. (2001). Emotion drives attention: Detecting the snake in the grass. *Journal of Experimental Psychology: General, 130,* 466–478.

Oldenburg, A. (2002, December 11). Oprah pounds away. *USA Today,* D2.

Olfson, M., Marcus, S. C., Druss, F. B., Elinson, L., Tanielian, T., & Pincus, H. A. (2002)). National trends in the outpatient treatment of depression. *Journal of the American Medical Association, 287,* 203–209.

Olshansky, J. (2003, November). Cited in K. Wright, Staying alive. *Discover,* 64–70.

Olshansky, J., Hayflick, L., & Carnes, B. A. (2002, June). No truth to the fountain of youth. *Scientific American,* 92–95.

Olson, L., & Houlihan, D. (2000). A review of behavioral treatments used for Lesch-Nylan syndrome. *Behavior Modification, 24,* 202–222.

Onishi, N. (2001, February 12). On the scale of beauty, weight weighs heavily. *New York Times,* A4.

Onishi, N. (2002, October 3). Globalization of beauty makes slimness trendy. *New York Times,* A4.

Oostdam, R., & Meijer, J. (2003). Influence of test anxiety on measurement of intelligence. *Psychological Reports, 92,* 3–20.

O'Regan, J. K., Deubel, H., Clark, J. J., & Rensink, R. A. (2000). Picture changes during blinks: Looking without seeing and seeing without looking. *Visual Cognition, 7,* 191–211.

O'Shaughnessy, E. (1999). Relating to the superego. *International Journal of Psychoanalysis, 80,* 861–870.

Osofsky, J. D. (1995). The effects of exposure to violence on young children. *American Psychologist, 50,* 782–788.

Ost, L., Helstrom, K., & Kaver, A. (1992). One versus five sessions of exposure in the treatment of injection phobia. *Behavior Therapy, 23,* 263–282.

O'Sullivan, M. (2003). The fundamental attribution error in detecting deception: The boy-who-cried-wolf effect. *Personality and Social Psychology Bulletin, 29,* 1316–1327.

Owley, T., McMahon, W., Cook, E. H., Laulhere, T., South, M., Mays, L. Z., Shernoff, E. S., Lainart, J., Modahl, C. B., Corsello, C., Ozonof, S., Risi, S., Lord, C., Leventhal, B. L., & Filipek, P. A. (2001). Multisite, double-blind, placebo-controlled trial of porcine secretin in autism. *Journal of the American Academy of Child and Adolescent Psychiatry, 40,* 1293–1299.

References

Ozer, D. J. (1999). Four principles for personality assessment. In L. A. Pervin & O. P. John (Eds.), *Handbook of personality* (2nd ed.), New York: Guilford.

Paabo, S. (2003, July 15). Cited in N. Wade, Early voices: The leap to language. *New York Times*, D1.

Page, A. C. (2002). Nature and treatment of panic disorder. *Current Opinion in Psychiatry, 15*, 149–155.

Page, A. C. (2003). The role of disgust in faintness elicited by blood and injection stimuli. *Anxiety Disorders, 17*, 45–58.

Page, A. C., Bennett, K. S., Carter, O., Smith, M., & Woodmore, K. (1997). The blood-injection symptoms scale (BISS) assessing a structure of phobic symptoms elicited by blood and injections. *Behaviour Research and Therapy, 35*, 457–464.

Painter, K. (1997, August 15–17). Doctors have prenatal test for 450 genetic diseases. *USA Today.*

Palmer, S. E. (2002). Perceptual grouping: It's later than you think. *Current Directions in Psychology, 11*, 101–106.

Palomares, R. (2003, February). Cited in E. Benson, Intelligent intelligence testing. *Monitor on Psychology*, 48–51.

Pandina, R. J., & Johnson, V. L. (1999). In M. D. Glantz & C. R. Hartel (Eds.), *Drug abuse: Origins & interventions*. Washington, DC: American Psychological Association.

Pantelis, C., Velakoulis, D., McGorry, P. D., Wood, S. J., Suckling, J., Phillips, L. J., Yung, A. R., Bullmore, E. T., Brewer, W., Soulsby, B., Desmond, P., & McGuire, P. K. (2003). Neuroanatomical abnormalities before and after onset of psychosis: A cross-sectional and longitudinal MRI comparison. *Lancet, 361*, 281–288.

Pappas, G. D., Lazorthes, Y., Bes, J. C., Tafani, M., & Winnie, A. P. (1997). Relief of intractable cancer pain by human chromaffic cell transplants: Experience at two medical centers. *Neurological Research, 19*, 71–77.

Parker, G. (2000). Personality and personality disorder: Current issues and directions. *Psychological Medicine, 30*, 1–9.

Parks, G. (1997). *Half past autumn.* New York: Bulfinch Press & Little, Brown & Company.

Pascalis, O., de Haan, M., & Nelson, C. A. (2002). Is face processing species-specific during the first year of life? *Science, 296*, 1321–1323.

Patel, M. R., Piazza, C. C., Martinez, C. J., Volkert, V. M., & Santana, C. M. (2002). An evaluation of two differential reinforcement procedures with escape extinction to treat food refusal. *Journal of Applied Behavior Analysis, 35*, 363–374.

Patterson, D. R., Everett, J. J., Bombadier, C. H., Questad, K. A., Lee, V. K., & Marvin, J. A. (1993). Psychological effects of severe burn injuries. *Psychological Bulletin, 113*, 362–378.

Patton, G. C., Harris, R., Carlin, J. B., Hibbert, M. E., Coffey, C., Schwartz, M., & Bowes, G. (1997). Adolescent suicidal behaviours: A population-based study of risk. *Psychological Medicine, 27*, 715–724.

Paul, S. M., Extein, I., Calil, H. M., Potter, W. Z., Chodoff, P., & Goodwin, F. K. (1981). Use of ECT with treatment-resistant depressed patients at the National Institute of Mental Health. *American Journal of Psychiatry, 138*, 486–489.

Paulesu, E., Frith, C. D., & Frackowiak, R. S. J. (1993). The neural correlates of the verbal component of working memory. *Nature, 362*, 342–345.

Pawlow, L. A., & Jones, G. E. (2002). The impact of abbreviated progressive muscle relaxation on salivary cortisol. *Biological Psychology, 60*, 1–16.

Payne, D. G., Toglia, M. P., & Anastasi, J. S. (1994). Recognition performance level and the magnitude of the misinformation effect in eyewitness memory. *Psychonomic Bulletin and Review, 1*, 376–382.

Peake, P. K., Hebl, M., & Mischel, W. (2002). Strategic attention deployment for delay of gratification in working and waiting situations. *Developmental Psychology, 38*, 313–326.

Pear, R. (2000, June 11). Interns' long workdays prompt first crackdown. *New York Times*, D2.

Pearce, J. M., & Bouton, M. E. (2003). Theories of the associative learning in animals. *Annual Review of Psychology, 52*, 111–139.

Peele, S. (1997). Utilizing culture and behaviour in epidemiological models of alcohol consumption and consequences of western nations. *Alcohol & Alcoholism, 32*, 51–64.

Pelham, W. E., Bender, M. E., Caddell, J., Booth, S., & Moorer, S. H. (1985). Methylphenidate and children with attention deficit disorder. *Archives of General Psychiatry, 42*, 948–952.

Penley, J. A., Tomaka, J., & Wiebe, J. S. (2002). The association of coping to physical and psychological health outcomes: A meta-analytic review. *Journal of Behavioral Medicine, 25*, 551–603.

Pennebaker, J. W., Colder, M., & Sharp, L. (1990). Accelerating the coping process. *Journal of Personality and Social Psychology, 58*, 528–537.

Pennisi, E. (2002). Sequence tells mouse, human genome secrets. *Science, 298*, 1863–1864.

People. (2002, October 2). Downsized diva. 91.

Peplau, L. A. (2003). Human sexuality: How do men and women differ? *Current Directions in Psychological Science, 12*, 37–40.

Perez-Pena, R. (2003, March 16). Broad movement is backing embryo stem cell research. *New York Times*, 18.

Perlis, M. L., Smith, M. T., Cacialli, D. O., Nowakowski, S., & Orff, H. (2003). On the comparability of pharmacotherapy and behavior therapy for chronic insomnia: Commentary and implications. *Journal of Psychosomatic Research, 54*, 51–59.

Perry, C. (1997). Admissibility and per se exclusion of hypnotically elicited recall in American courts of law. *International Journal of Clinical and Experimental Hypnosis, 45*, 266–279.

Persons, J. B. (1997). Dissemination of effective methods: Behavior therapy's next challenge. *Behavior Therapy, 28*, 465–471.

Pert, C. B., Snowman, A. M., & Snyder, S. H. (1974). Localization of opiate receptor binding in presynaptic membranes of rat brain. *Brain Research, 70*, 184–188.

Pesonen, A. K., Raikkonen, K., Keskivaara, P., & Keltifkangas-Jarvinen, L. (2003). Difficult temperament in childhood and adulthood: Continuity from maternal perceptions to self-ratings over 17 years. *Personality and Individual Differences, 34*, 19–31.

Peters, T. (2003). *Re-imagine!* New York: DK Publishing.

Peterson, K. S. (2001, May 25). 43% of 1st marriages end in 15 years. *USA Today*, A2.

Peterson, L. R., & Peterson, M. J. (1950). Short-term retention of individual verbal terms. *Journal of Experimental Psychology, 58*, 193–198.

Peterson, L., & Brown, D. (1994). Integrating child injury and abuse-neglect research: Common histories, etiologies, and solutions. *Psychological Bulletin, 116*, 293–315.

Petitto, L. A. (1997, December 11). *Cited in R. L. Hotz, The brain: Designed to speak the mind. Los Angeles Times.*

Petitto, L. A., & Marentette, P. F. (1991). Babbling in the manual mode: Evidence for the ontogeny of language. *Science, 251*, 1493–1496.

Petri, H. L., & Govern, J. M. (2004). *Motivation* (5th ed.). Belmont, CA: Wadsworth.

Petrill, S. A. (2003). The development of intelligence: Behavioral genetic approaches. In R. J. Sternberg, J. Lautrey & T. I. Lubart (Eds.), *Models of intelligence*. Washington, DC: American Psychological Association.

Petrovic, P., Kalso, E., Petersson, K. M., & Ingvar, M. (2002). Placebo and opioid analgesia—imaging a shared neuronal network. *Science, 295*, 1737–1740.

Petty, R. E., & Cacioppo, J. T. (1986). *Attitudes and persuasion: Classic and contemporary approaches.* Dubuque, IA: William C. Brown.

Petty, R. E., Wegener, D. T., & Fabrigar, L. R. (1997). Attitudes and attitude change. *Annual Review of Psychology, 46*, 609–647.

Peyser, M. (2000, July 17). Venus rising. *Newsweek*, 46.

Peyser, M., Biddle, N. A., Brant, M., Wingert, P., Hackworth, D. H., & O'Shea, M. (1995, August 28). Sounding retreat. *Newsweek.*

Pezdek, K. (1995, February 11). Cited in M. Dolan, When the mind's eye blinks. *Los Angeles Times.*

Piaget, J. (1929). *The child's conception of the world.* New York: Harcourt Brace.

Picchioni, D., Goeltzenleucher, B., Green, D. N., Convento, M. J., Crittenden, R., Hallgren, M., & Hicks, R. A. (2002). Nightmares as a coping mechanism for stress. *Dreaming, 12*, 155–169.

Pierce, B. H. (1999). An evolutionary perspective on insight. In D. H. Rosen & M. D. Luebbert (Eds.), *Evolution of the psyche. Human evolution, behavior, and intelligence*. Westport, CT: Praeger/Greenwood Publishing.

Piliavin, J. A., Dovidio, J. F., Gaertner, S. L., & Clark, R. D. (1982). Responsive bystanders: The process of intervention. In V. J. Derlega & J. Grzelak (Eds.), *Cooperation and helping behavior*. Orlando, FL: Academic Press.

Pillard, R. C., & Bailey, M. J. (1995). A biologic perspective on sexual orientation. *The Psychiatric Clinics of North America, 18*, 71–84.

Pillemer, D. B. (1984). Flashbulb memories of the assassination attempt on President Reagan. *Cognition, 16*, 63–80.

Pincus, T., & Morley, S. (2001). Cognitive-processing bias in chronic pain: A review and integration. *Psychological Bulletin, 127*, 599–617.

Pingitore, R., Dugoni, B. L., Tindale, R. S., & Spring, B. (1994). Bias against overweight job applicants in a simulated employment interview. *Journal of Applied Psychology, 79*, 909–917.

Pinker, S. (1994). *The language instinct.* New York: William Morrow.

Pinker, S. (1995). Introduction. In M. S. Gazzaniga (Ed.), *The cognitive neurosciences.* Cambridge, MA: MIT Press.

Pinker, S. (2000, April 10). Will the mind figure out how the brain works? *Time*, 90–91.

Pinker, S. (2002). *The blank slate: The modern denial of human nature.* New York: Viking.

Pinnell, C. M., & Covino, N. A. (2000). Empirical findings on the use of hypnosis in medicine. *International Journal of Clinical and Experimental Hypnosis, 48*, 170–194.

Piomelli, D. (1999). Cited in J. Travis, Marijuana mimic reveals brain role. *Science News, 155*, 215.

Piper, W. E., Joyce, A. S., McCallum, M., Azim, H. F., & Ogrodniczuk, J. S. (2002). *Interpretive and supportive psychotherapies*. Washington, DC: American Psychological Association.

Pi-Sunyer, X. (2003). A clinical view of the obesity problem. *Science, 299*, 859–860.

Ploghaus, A., Becerra, L., Borras, C., & Borsook, D. (2003). Neural circuitry underlying pain modulation: Expectation, hypnosis, placebo. *Trends in Cognitive Science, 7*, 197–200.

Plomin, R., & Caspi, A. (1999). Behavioral genetics and personality. In L. A. Pervin & O. P. John (Eds.), *Handbook of personality* (2nd ed.). New York: Guilford.

Plomin, R., & Crabbe, J. (2000). DNA. *Psychological Bulletin, 126*, 806–828.

Plomin, R., & McGuffin, P. (2003). Psychopathology in the postgenomic era. *Annual Review of Psychology, 54*, 205–228.

Plomin, R., & Petrill, S. A. (1997). Genetics and intelligence: What's new? *Intelligence, 24*, 53–77.

Plummer, W., & Ridenhour, R. (1995, August 28). Saving grace. *People.*

Polaschek, D. L. L., Ward, T., & Hudson, S. M. (1997). Rape and rapists: Theory and treatment. *Clinical Psychology Review, 17*, 117–144.

Poldrack, R. A., & Packard, M. G. (2003). Competition among multiple memory systems: Converging evidence from animal and human brain studies. *Neuropsychologia, 41*, 245–251.

Polivy, J., & Herman, C. P. (2002). Causes of eating disorders. *Annual Review of Psychology, 53*, 187–213.

Pollak, S. D., & Kistler, D. J. (2002). Early experience is associated with the development of categorical representations of facial expressions of emotion. *Proceedings of the National Academy of Sciences, 99*, 9072-9076.

Pomerleau, A., Bolduc, D., Malcuit, G., & Cossette, L. (1990). Pink or blue: Environmental gender stereotypes in the first two years of life. *Sex Roles, 22*, 359–367.

Posner, M. I., & Raichle, M. E. (1994). *Images of mind.* New York: Freeman.

Posner, M. J., & DiGirolamo, G. J. (2000). Cognitive neuroscience: Origins and promise. *Psychological Bulletin, 126*, 873–889.

Post, R. (1994). Creativity and psychopathology: A study of 291 world-famous men. *British Journal of Psychiatry, 165*, 22–34.

Postmes, T., & Spears, R. (1998). Deindividuation and antinormative behavior: A meta-analysis. *Psychological Bulletin, 13*, 238–259.

Poulton, R., Thomson, W. M., Davies, S., Kruger E., Brown, R. H., & Silva, P. (1997). Good teeth, bad teeth, and fear of the dentist. *Behaviour Research and Therapy, 35*, 327–334.

Powell, D. H., & Whitla, D. K. (1994). Normal cognitive aging: Toward empirical perspectives. *Current Directions in Psychological Science, 3*, 27–31.

Pratkanis, A. R. (1992). The cargo cult science of subliminal persuasion. *Skeptical Inquirer, 16*, 260–286.

Prentice, D. A., & Carranza, E. (2002). What women and men should be, shouldn't be, are allowed to be, and don't have to be: The contents of prescriptive gender stereotypes. *Psychology of Women Quarterly, 26*, 269–281.

Pressman, M. R., & Orr, W. C. (Eds.). (1997). *Understanding sleep: The evaluation and treatment of sleep disorders.* Washington, DC: American Psychological Association.

Priester, J. R., & Petty, R. E. (1995). Source attributions and persuasion: Perceived honesty as a determinant of message scrutiny. *Personality and Social Psychology Bulletin, 21*, 637–654.

Prince, S. E., & Jacobson, N. S. (1997). A review and evaluation of marital and family therapies for affective disorders. *Journal of Marital and Family Therapy, 21*, 377–402.

Project Match Research Group. (1997). Matching alcoholism treatments to client heterogeneity: Project MATCH posttreatment drinking outcomes. *Journal of Studies on Alcohol, 58*, 7–29.

Pruitt, D. G. (1971). Choice shifts in group discussion: An introductory review. *Journal of Personality and Social Psychology, 20*, 339–360.

Pullum, G. K. (1991). *The great Eskimo vocabulary hoax.* Chicago: University of Chicago Press.

Pychyl, T. A., Coplan, R. J., & Reid, P. A. M. (2002). Parenting and procrastination: Gender differences in the relations between procrastination, parenting style and self-worth in early adolescence. *Personality and Individual Differences, 33*, 271–285.

Quinn, P. C. (2002). Category representation in young infants. *Current Directions in Psychological Science, 11*, 66–70.

Quinn, P. C., Ramesh, S. B., Brush, D., Grimes, A., & Sharpnack, H. (2002). Development of form similarity as a Gestalt grouping principle in infancy. *Psychological Science, 13*, 320–328.

Rabasca, L. (1999, December). Not enough evidence to support "abstinence-only." *Monitor of American Psychological Association, 39.*

Rabasca, L. (2000a, March). Humanistic psychologists look to revamp their image. *Monitor on Psychology,* 54–55.

Rabasca, L. (2000b, November). In search of equality. *Monitor on Psychology,* 30–31.

Rabkin, S. W., Boyko, E., Shane, F., & Kaufert, J. (1984). A randomized trial comparing smoking cessation programs utilizing behavior modification, health education or hypnosis. *Addictive Behaviors, 9*, 157–173.

Rachman, S. (2002). Fears born and bred: Non-associative fear acquisitions. *Behaviour Research and Therapy, 40*, 121–126.

Rahman, Q., & Wilson, G. D. (2003). Born gay? The psychobiology of human sexual orientation. *Personality and Individual Differences, 34*, 1337–1382.

Raichle, M. E. (1994). Visualizing the mind. *Scientific American, 270*, 58–64.

Raine, A. (2002). Biosocial studies of antisocial and violent behavior in children and adults: A review. *Journal of Abnormal Child Psychology, 30*, 311–326.

Raine, A., Lencz, T., Bihrle, S., LaCasse, L., & Colletti, P. (2000). Reduced prefrontal gray matter volume and reduced autonomic activity in antisocial personality disorder. *Archives of General Psychiatry, 57*, 119–127.

Raine, A., Reynolds, C., Venables, P. H., & Mednick, S. A. (2002). Stimulation seeking and intelligence: A prospective longitudinal study. *Journal of Personality and Social Psychology, 82*, 663–674.

Raine, R. (2002, April 29). Cited in J. Foreman, Roots of violence may lie in damaged brain cells. *Los Angeles Times,* S1.

Rainville, P., Duncan, G. H., Price, D. D., Carrier, B., & Bushnell, M. C. (1997). Pain affect encoded in human anterior cingulated but not somatosensory cortex. *Science, 277*, 968–971.

Ramachandran, V. S., & Anstis, S. M. (1986). The perception of apparent motion. *Scientific American, 254*, 102–109.

Ransdell, E., & Eddings, J. (1994, May 9). The man of the moment. *U.S. News & World Report.*

Rao, S. M. (2002, September). Cited in K. Wright, Times of our lives. *Scientific American,* 59–65.

Rapoport, J. L. (1988). The neurobiology of obsessive-compulsive disorder. *Journal of the American Medical Association, 260*, 2888–2890.

Rapp, B. (Ed.). (2000). *The handbook of cognitive neuropsychology: What deficits reveal about the human mind.* Philadelphia: Psychology Press.

Rasmussen, C., Knapp, T. J., & Garner, L. (2000). Driving-induced stress in urban college students. *Perceptual and Motor Skills, 90*, 437–443.

Rasmussen, K. G. (2003). Clinical applications of recent research on electroconvulsive therapy. *Bulletin of the Menninger Clinic, 67*, 18–31.

Ratcliff, R., & McKoon, G. (2000). Memory models. In E. Tulving & F. M. Craik (Eds.), *The Oxford handbook of memory.* New York: Oxford University Press.

Rauschecker, J. P., & Shannon, R. V. (2002). Sending sound to the brain. *Science, 295*, 1025–1029.

Rechtschaffen, A. (1997, August). Cited in T. Geier, What is sleep for? *U.S. News & World Report.*

Reed, M. K. (1994). Social skills training to reduce depression in adolescents. *Adolescence, 29*, 293–302.

Reed, S., & Breu, G. (1995, June 6). The wild ones. *People.*

Reed, S., & Cook, D. (1993, April 19). Realm of the senses. *People.*

Reed, S., & Esselman, M. (1995, August 28). Catching hell. *People.*

Reed, S., & Free, C. (1995, October 16). The big payoff. *People.*

Reed, S., & Stambler, L. (1992, May 25). The umpire strikes back. *People,* 87–88.

Reeve, C. (2002). *Nothing is impossible: Reflections on a new life.* New York: Random House.

Reid, J. B., Taplin, P. S., & Lorber, R. (1981). A social interactional approach to the treatment of abusive families. In R. B. Stuart (Ed.), *Violent behavior: Social learning approaches to prediction, management and treatment.* New York: Brunner/Mazel.

Reisler, J. (2002, February 24). Technology; improving sound, easing fury. *Newsweek,* 16.

Reitman, V. (1999, February 22). Learning to grin—and bear it. *Los Angeles Times,* A1.

Renfrey, G., & Spates, C. R. (1994). Eye movement desensitization: A partial dismantling study. *Journal of Behavior Therapy and Experimental Psychiatry, 25*, 231–239.

Rescorla, R. A. (1966). Predictability and number of pairings in Pavlovian fear conditioning. *Psychonomic Science, 4*, 383–384.

Rescorla, R. A. (1987). A Pavlovian analysis of goal-directed behavior. *American Psychologist, 42*, 119–129.

Rescorla, R. A. (1988). Pavlovian conditioning. *American Psychologist, 43*, 151–160.

Research Triangle Institute. (1994). *Past and future directions of the D.A.R.E. program: An evaluation review.* Washington, DC: National Institute of Justice.

Resnick, M., Bearman, P. S., Blum, R. W., Bauman, K. E., Harris, K. H., Jones, J., Tabor, J., Beuhring, T., Sieving, R. E., Shew, M., Ireland, M., Bearinger, L. H., & Udry, J. R. (1997). Protecting adolescents from harm. *Journal of the American Medical Association, 278*, 823–832.

Rey, G. (1983). Concepts and stereotypes. *Cognition, 15*, 237–262.

Reyner, L. A., & Horne, J. A. (2000). Early morning driver sleepiness: Effectiveness of 200 mg caffeine. *Psychophysiology, 7*, 251–256.

Reyneri, A. (1984). The nose knows, but science doesn't. *Science.*

Reynolds, A. J., Temple, J. A., Robertson, D. L., & Mann, E. A. (2001). Long-term effects of an early childhood intervention on educational achievement and juvenile arrest. *Journal of the American Medical Association, 285*, 2339–2346.

Rhee, S. H., & Waldman, I. D. (2002). Genetic and environmental influences on antisocial behavior: A meta-analysis of twin and adoption studies. *Psychological Bulletin, 128*, 490–529.

Ricaurte, G. A. (2003, September 6). Cited in D. G. McNeil, Jr., Report of ecstasy drug's risks is retracted. *New York Times,* A8.

References

Ricaurte, G. A., Yuan, J., Hatzidimitrious, G., Cord, B. J., & McCann, U. D. (2002). Severe dopaminergic neurotoxicity in primates after a common recreational dose regime of MDMA ("ecstasy"). *Science, 297,* 2260–2263.

Ricca, V., Mannucci, E., Mezzani, B., Moretti, S., Di Bernardo, M., Bertelli, M., Rotella, C. M., & Faravelli, C. (2001). Fluoxetine and fluvoxamine combined with individual cognitive-behaviour therapy in binge eating disorder: A one-year follow up study. *Psychotherapy and Psychosomatics, 70,* 298–306.

Riccio, D. C., Millin, P. M., & Gisquet-Verier, P. (2003). Retrograde amnesia: Forgetting back. *Current Directions in Psychological Science, 12,* 41–44.

Rice, G., Anderson, C., Risch, N., & Ebers, G. (1999). Male homosexuality: Absence of linkage to microsatellite markers at Xq28. *Science, 284,* 665–667.

Richter, P. (1997, April 17). Pentagon to OK peyote for religious rites. *Los Angeles Times.*

Richters, J. M. A. (1997). Menopause in different cultures. *Journal of Psychosomatic Obstetrics and Gynecology, 18,* 73–80.

Ridderinkhof, K. R., de Vlugt, Y., Bramlage, A., Spaan, M., Elton, M., Snel, J., & Band, G. P. H. (2002). Alcohol consumption impairs detection of performance errors in mediofrontal cortex. *Science, 298,* 2209–2211.

Rieke, M. L., & Guastello, S. J. (1995). Unresolved issues in honesty and integrity testing. *American Psychologist, 50,* 458–459.

Rilling, M. (2000). John Watson's paradoxical struggle to explain Freud. *American Psychologist, 55,* 301–312.

Rimland, B. (1964). *Infantile autism.* New York: Appleton-Century-Crofts.

Ritter, M. (2000, January 17). Camera wired to brain provides some useful vision for blind man. *San Diego Union-Tribune,* A6.

Rivas-Vazquez, R. A. (2003). Benzodiazepines in contemporary clinical practice. *Professional Psychology: Research and Practice, 34,* 324–328.

Rivera, C. (2000, June 9). Helping hands for mentally ill. *Los Angeles Times,* A1.

Roan, S. (1997, March 26). Faint chances. *Los Angeles Times.*

Roan, S. (1998, March 16). A reason for hope. *Los Angeles Times,* S1.

Roan, S. (2002, June 17). A new way to treat alcoholism. *Los Angeles Times,* S1.

Robbins, J. (2000, July 4). Virtual reality finds a real place as a medical aid. *New York Times,* D6.

Roberts, B. W., Helson, R., & Klohnen, E. V. (2002). Personality development and growth in women across 30 years: Three perspectives. *Journal of Personality, 70,* 79–102.

Robichaud, M., Dugas, M. J., & Conway, M. (2003). Gender differences in worry and associated cognitive-behavioral variables. *Anxiety Disorders, 17,* 501–516.

Robins, L. N., & Regier, D. A. (Eds.). (1991). *Psychiatric disorders in America.* New York: Free Press.

Robins, L. N., Tipp, J., & Przybeck, T. (1991). Antisocial personality. In L. N. Robins & D. A. Regier (Eds.), *Psychiatric disorders in America.* New York: Free Press.

Robinson-Riegler, B., & McDaniel, M. A. (1994). Further constraints on the bizarreness effect: Elaboration at encoding. *Memory and Cognition, 22,* 702–712.

Roche, T. (2001, May 28). Voices from the cell. *Time,* 29–38.

Rock, I., & Palmer, S. (1990). The legacy of Gestalt psychology. *Scientific American, 263,* 84–90.

Rodgers, J. E. (1982). The malleable memory of eyewitnesses. *Science.*

Rodriguez-Tome, H., Bariaud, F., Cohen-Zardi, M. F., Delmas, C., Jeanvoine, F., & Szylagyi, P. (1993). The effects of pubertal changes on body image and relations with peers of the opposite sex in adolescence. *Journal of Adolescence, 16,* 421–438.

Roediger, H. L., & McDermott, K. B. (2000). Distortions of memory. In E. Tulving & F. M. Craik (Eds.), *The Oxford handbook of memory.* New York: Oxford University Press.

Roediger, H. L., III, Gallo, D. A., & Geraci, L. (2002). Processing approaches to cognition: The impetus from the levels-of-processing framework. *Memory, 10,* 319–332.

Roese, N. J. (2001). The crossroads of affect and cognition: Counterfactuals as compensatory cognition. In G. B. Moskowitz (Ed.), *Cognitive social psychology.* Mahwah, NJ: Lawrence Erlbaum.

Rogers, C. R. (1951). *Client-centered therapy: Its current practice, implications, and theory.* Boston: Houghton Mifflin.

Rogers, C. R. (1980). *A way of being.* Boston: Houghton Mifflin.

Rogers, C. R. (1986). Client-centered therapy. In I. L. Kutash & A. Wolf (Eds.), *Psychotherapists' casebook.* San Francisco: Jossey-Bass.

Rogers, C. R. (1989). Cited in N. J. Raskin & C. R. Rogers, Person-centered therapy. In R. J. Corsini & D. Wedding (Eds.), *Current psychotherapies* (4th ed.). Itasca, IL: F. E. Peacock.

Rogers, L. (2001). *Sexing the brain.* New York: Columbia University Press.

Rogers, P. (2003, March 3). Say it ain't so, Cleo. *People,* 101–104.

Rogers, P., & Morehouse, W., III. (1999, April 12). She's got it. *People,* 89.

Rolls, E. T. (2000). Memory systems in the brain. *Annual Review of Psychology, 51,* 599–630.

Romney, D. M., & Bynner, J. M. (1997). A re-examination of the relationship between shyness, attributional style, and depression. *Journal of Genetic Psychology, 158,* 261–270.

Root, R. W., II, & Resnick, R. J. (2003). An update on the diagnosis and treatment of attention-deficit/hyperactivity disorders in children. *Professional Psychology: Research Practice, 34,* 34–41.

Rorschach, R. (1921; reprinted 1942). *Psychodiagnostics.* Bern: Hans Huber.

Rortvedt, A. K., & Miltenberger, R. G. (1994). Analysis of a high-probability instructional sequence and time-out in the treatment of child noncompliance. *Journal of Applied Behavior Analysis, 27,* 327–330.

Rosch, E. (1978). Principles of categorization. In E. Rosch & B. B. Lloyd (Eds.), *Cognition and categorization.* Hillsdale, NJ: Lawrence Erlbaum.

Rose, D. A., & Kahan, T. L. (2001). Melatonin and sleep qualities in healthy adults: Pharmacological and expectancy effects. *The Journal of General Psychology, 128,* 401–421.

Rosellini, L. (1998, April 13). When to spank. *U.S. News & World Report,* 52–58.

Rosenberg, K. P. (1994). Notes and comments: Biology and homosexuality. *Journal of Sex and Marital Therapy, 20,* 147–150.

Rosenthal, R. (2002, November). Covert communication in classrooms, clinics, courtrooms, and cubicles. *American Psychologist,* 839–849.

Rosenthal, S. L., Burklow, K. A., Lewis, L. M., Succop, P. A., & Biro, F. M. (1997). Heterosexual romantic relationships and sexual behaviors of young adolescent girls. *Journal of Adolescent Health, 21,* 238–243.

Rosenzweig, M. R. (1992). Psychological science around the world. *American Psychologist, 47,* 718–722.

Ross, B. M., & Millsom, C. (1970). Repeated memory of oral prose in Ghana and New York. *International Journal of Psychology, 5,* 173–181.

Ross, P. E. (1991). Hard words. *Scientific American, 264,* 138–147.

Roth, D., Slone, M., & Dar, R. (2000). Which way cognitive development? *Theory and Psychology, 10,* 353–373.

Rotter, J. B. (1990). Internal versus external control of reinforcement: A case history of a variable. *American Psychologist, 45,* 489–493.

Routh, D. K. (1994). *The founding of clinical psychology (1896) and some important early developments: Introduction.* New York: Plenum Publishing.

Rowan, A. N. (1997, February). The benefits and ethics of animal research. *Scientific American,* 79–94.

Roy-Byrne, P. P., & Fann, J. R. (1997). Psychopharmacologic treatments for patients with neuropsychiatric disorders. In S. C. Yudofsky & R. E. Hales (Eds.), *American Psychiatric Press textbook of neuropsychiatry* (3rd ed.). Washington, DC: American Psychiatric Press.

Rozin, P. (1986). One-trial acquired likes and dislikes in humans: Disgust as a U.S. food predominance, and negative learning predominance. *Learning and Motivation, 17,* 180–189.

Rozin, P. (2003). Introduction: Evolutionary and cultural perspectives on affect. In R. D. Lane & L. Nadel (Eds.), *Cognitive neuroscience of emotion.* New York: Oxford University Press.

Rozin, P., Haidt, J., & McCauley, C. R. (2000). Disgust. In M. Lewis & J. M. Haviland-Jones (Eds.), *Handbook of emotions* (2nd ed., pp. 637–653). New York: Guilford.

Rozin, P., Kabnick, K., Pete, E., Fischler, C., & Shields, C. (2003). The ecology of eating: Smaller portion sizes in France than in the United States help explain the French paradox. *Psychological Science, 14,* 450–454.

Rubin, D. C., & Kozin, M. (1984). Vivid memories. *Cognition, 16,* 81–95.

Ruegg, R., & Frances, A. (1995). New research in personality disorders. *Journal of Personality Disorders, 9,* 1–48.

Rugg, M. (1995). La difference vive. *Nature, 373,* 561–562.

Ruiter, R. A. C., Abraham, C., & Kok, G. (2001). Scary warnings and rational precautions: A review of the psychology of fear appeals. *Psychology and Health, 16,* 613–630.

Ruiz-Bueno, J. B. (2000). Locus of control, perceived control, and learned helplessness. In V. R. Rice (Ed.), *Handbook of stress, coping and health.* Thousand Oaks, CA: Sage.

Rush, A. J. (2003). Toward an understanding of bipolar disorder and its origins. *Journal of Clinical Psychiatry, 64 (supplement 6),* 4–8.

Rutherford, M. (2001, March). What did you say? *Time, Bonus Section Generations,* G8–9.

Rutter, M., & Silberg, J. (2002). Gene-environment interplay in relation to emotional and behavioral disturbance. *Annual Review of Psychology, 53,* 463–490.

Sackeim, H. A., & Stern, Y. (1997). Neuropsychiatric aspects of memory and amnesia. In S. C. Yudofsky & R. E. Hales (Eds.), *The American Psychiatric Press textbook of neuropsychiatry* (3rd ed.). Washington, DC: American Psychiatric Press.

Sackeim, H. A., Prudic, J., Devanand, D. P., Nobler, M. S., Lisanby, S., Peyser, S., Fitzsimons, L., Moody, B. J., & Clark, J. (2000). A prospective, randomized, double blind comparison of bilateral and right unilateral electroconvulsive therapy at different stimulus intensities. *Archives of General Psychiatry, 57,* 425–434.

Sacks, O. (1995). *An anthropologist on Mars.* New York: Alfred A. Knopf.

Sadler, B., Pappelbaum, S., & Murphy, M. W. (2000, April 14). Here's a smoking trend that just isn't improving. *San Diego Union-Tribune,* B9.

Salovey, P., & Mayer, J. D. (1990). Emotional intelligence. *Imagination, Cognition, and Personality, 9,* 185–211.

Salovey, P., & Pizarro, D. A. (2003). In R. J. Sternberg, J. Lautrey & T. I. Lubart (Eds.), *Models of intelligence.* Washington, DC: American Psychological Association.

Salovey, P., Rothman, A. J., Detweiller, J. B., & Steward, W. T. (2000). Emotional states and physical health. *American Psychologist, 55,* 110–121.

Salthouse, T. A., Legg, S., Palmon, R., & Mitchell, D. (1990). Memory factors in age-related differences in simple reasoning. *Psychology and Aging, 5,* 9–15.

Samelson, F. (1980). J. B. Watson's little Albert, Cyril Burt's twins, and the need for a critical science. *American Psychologist, 35,* 619–625.

SAMHSA (Substance Abuse and Mental Health Services Administration). 2001 National Household Survey on Drug Abuse (NHSDA). http://www.samhsa.gov/

Samuel, D. (1996). Cited in N. Williams, How the ancient Egyptians brewed beer. *Science, 273,* 432.

San Diego Union-Tribune. (2003, April 27). "Gothika" a Montreal thriller for Dutton. F8.

Sands, R., Tricker, J., Sherman, C., Armatas, C., & Maschette, W. (1997). Disordered eating patterns, body image, self-esteem, and physical activity in preadolescent school children. *International Journal of Eating Disorders, 21,* 159–166.

Sapienza, B. G., & Bugental, J. F. T. (2000). Keeping our instruments finely tuned: An existential-humanistic perspective. *Professional Psychology: Research and Practice, 31,* 458–460.

Sapolsky, R. M. (2002, December 17). Cited in E. Goode, The heavy cost of stress. *New York Times,* D1.

Sarraj, I. (2002, June 21). Cited in J. Bennet, Rash of new suicide bombers showing no pattern or ties. *New York Times,* A1

Sarwer, D. B., & Durlak, J. A. (1997). A field trial of the effectiveness of behavioral treatment for sexual dysfunctions. *Journal of Sex & Marital Therapy, 23,* 87–97.

Satcher, D. (2000). Mental health: A report of the Surgeon General—executive summary. *Professional Psychology, Research and Practice, 31,* 5–13.

Savage-Rumbaugh, S. (1991). Cited in A. Gibbons, Deja vu all over again: Chimp-language wars. *Science, 251,* 1561–1562.

Savage-Rumbaugh, S. (1998, January 19). Cited in S. Begley, Aping language. *Newsweek.*

Savage-Rumbaugh, S., & Lewin, R. (1994). *Kanzi.* New York: Wiley.

Sax, L. J. (2002, September 11). Cited in M. Duenwald, Students find another staple of campus life: Stress. *New York Times,* D5.

Saxe, L. (1994). Detection of deception: Polygraph and integrity tests. *Current Directions in Psychological Science, 3,* 69–73.

Saywitz, K. J., Mannarino, A. P., Berliner, L., & Cohen, J. A. (2000). Treatment for sexually abused children and adolescents. *American Psychologist, 55,* 1040–1049.

Scanlon, M., & Mauro, J. (1992, November–December). The lowdown on handwriting analysis. *Psychology Today.*

Scarr, S., & Weinberg, R. A. (1976). IQ test performance of black children adopted by white families. *American Psychologist, 31,* 726–739.

Schachter, S., & Singer, J. (1962). Cognitive, social and physiological determinants of emotional state. *Psychological Review, 69,* 379–399.

Schacter, D. L. (1996). *Searching for memory.* New York: Basic Books.

Schacter, D. L. (1997, October). Cited in E. Yoffe, How quickly we forget. *U.S. News & World Report.*

Schacter, D. L. (2001). *The seven sins of memory: How the mind forgets and remembers.* New York: Houghton Mifflin.

Schacter, D. L., Wagner, A. D., & Buckner, R. L. (2000). Memory systems of 1999. In E. Tulving & F. M. Craik (Eds.), *The Oxford handbook of memory.* New York: Oxford University Press.

Schaufeli, W. B., & Peeters, M. C. W. (2000). Job stress and burnout among correctional officers: A literature review. *International Journal of Stress Management, 7,* 19–48.

Schaufeli, W. B., Martinez, I. M., Pinto, A. M., Salanova, M., & Bakker, A. R. (2002). Burnout and engagement in university students. *Journal of Cross-Cultural Psychology, 35,* 464–481.

Schemo, D. J. (2003, June 11). After criticism, House Republicans rewrite Head-Start program. *New York Times,* A24.

Schenck, C. H. (2003, January 7). Cited in E. Goode, When the brain disrupts the night. *New York Times,* D1.

Schiff, M., Duyme, M., Dumaret, A., & Tomkiewicz, S. (1982). How much could we boost scholastic achievement and IQ scores? A direct answer from a French adoption study. *Cognition, 12,* 165–196.

Schlaggar, B. L., Brown, T. T., Lugar, H. M., Visscher, K. M., Miezin, F. M., & Petersen, S. E. (2002). Functional neuroanatomical differences between adults and school-age children in the processing of single words. *Science, 296,* 1476–1479.

Schmid, R. E. (2002, June 1). Normal protein in brain possible cause of Parkinson's. *San Diego Union-Tribune,* A8.

Schmidt, M. (1997). In D. J. Cohen & F. R. Volkmar (Eds.), *Handbook of autism and pervasive developmental disorders* (2nd ed.). New York: John Wiley & Sons.

Schnurr, P. P., Friedman, M. J., & Bernardy, N. C. (2002). Research on posttraumatic stress disorder: Epidemiology, pathophysiology, and assessment. *Journal of Clinical Psychology/In Session: Psychotherapy in Practice, 58,* 877–889.

Schoemer, K. (1996, August 26). Heroin. *Newsweek.*

Schooler, J. W. (1994). Seeking the core: The issues and evidence surrounding recovered accounts of sexual trauma. *Consciousness and Cognition, 3,* 452–469.

Schooler, J. W., & Eich, E. (2000). Memory for emotional events. In E. Tulving & F. M. Craik (Eds.), *The Oxford handbook of memory.* New York: Oxford University Press.

Schroeder, D. A., Penner, L. A., Dovidio, J. F., & Piliavin, J. A. (1995). *The psychology of helping and altruism: Problems and puzzles.* New York: McGraw-Hill.

Schuckit, M. (2002, June 17). Cited in S. Roan, A new way to treat alcoholism. *Los Angeles Times,* S1.

Schuckit, M. A. (2000). *Drug and alcohol abuse* (5th ed.). New York: Kluwer Academic.

Schuh, K. J., & Griffiths, R. R. (1997). Caffeine reinforcement: The role of withdrawal. *Psychopharmacology, 130,* 320–326.

Schulman, K. A., Berlin, J. A., Harless, W., Kerner, J. F., Sistrunk, S., Gersh, B. J., Dube, R., Taleghani, C. K., Burke, J. E., Williams, S., Eisenberg, J. M., & Escarce, J. J. (1999). The effect of race and sex on physicians' recommendations for cardiac catheterization. *The New England Journal of Medicine, 340,* 618–626.

Schultz, R. T., Gauthier, I., Klin, A., Fulbright, R. K., Anderson, A. W., Volkmar, F. R., Schudlarski, P., Lacadie, C., Cohen, D. J., & Gore, J. C. (2000). Abnormal ventral temporal cortical activity during face discrimination among individuals with autism and Asperger syndrome. *Archives of General Psychiatry, 57,* 331–340.

Schulz, R., & Curnow, C. (1988). Peak performance and age among superathletes: Track and field, swimming, baseball, tennis, and golf. *Journal of Gerontology, 43,* 113–120.

Schulz, S. C. (2000). New antipsychotic medications: More than old wine in new bottles. *Bulletin of the Menninger Clinic, 64,* 60–75.

Schwab, J., Kulin, H. E., Susman, E. J., Finkelstein, J. W., Chinchilli, V. M., Kunselman, S. J., Liben, L. S., D'Arangelo, M. R., & Demers, L. M. (2001). The role of sex hormone replacement therapy on self-perceived competence in adolescents with delayed puberty. *Child Development, 72,* 1439–1450.

Schwab, M. E. (2002). Repairing the injured spinal cord. *Science, 295,* 1029–1030.

Schwartz, B. L. (1999). Sparkling at the end of the tongue: The etiology of tip-of-the-tongue phenomenology. *Psychonomic Bulletin & Review, 6,* 379–393.

Schwartz, B., & Reisberg, D. (1991). *Learning and memory.* New York: Norton.

Schwartz, C. E., Wright, C. I., Shin, L. M., Kagan, J., & Rauch, S. L. (2003). Inhibited and uninhibited infants "grown up": Adult amygdalar response to novelty. *Science, 300,* 1952–1953.

Schwartz, N. (1999). Self-reports: How the questions shape the answers. *American Psychologist, 54,* 93–105.

Schweinhart, L. J., & Weikart, D. P. (1980). *Young children grow up: The effects of the Perry Preschool Program on youth through age 15* (Monograph No. 7). Ypsilanti, MI: High/Scope Educational Research Foundation.

Sciutto, M. J., Terjesen, M. D., & Bender Frank, A. S. (2000). Teacher's knowledge and misperceptions of attention-deficit/hyperactivity disorder. *Psychology in the Schools, 37,* 115–122.

Seal, M. (2002). Placebo effect really is all in your mind. *Trends in Cognitive Sciences, 6,* 280.

Searles, J. (1998, September). Write on! Learn to read his handwriting and read his mind. *Cosmopolitan,* 310–311.

Sedikides, C., Campbell, W. K., Reeder, G. D., & Elliot, A. J. (1998). The self-serving bias in relational context. *Journal of Personality and Social Psychology, 74,* 378–386.

Sees, K. L., Delucchi, K. L., Masson, C., Rosen, A., Clark, H. W., Robillard, H., Banys, P., & Hall, S. M. (2000). Methadone maintenance vs 180-day psychosocially enriched detoxification for treatment of opioid dependence. *Journal of the American Medical Association, 283,* 1303–1310.

Seligman, M. E. P. (1970). On the generality of the laws of learning. *Psychological Review, 77,* 406–418.

Seligman, M. E. P. (2002, December 9). Cited in M. Elias, What makes people happy psychologists now know. *USA Today,* A1.

Selye, H. (1993). History of the stress concept. In L. Goldberger & S. Breznitz (Eds.), *Handbook of stress: Theoretical and clinical aspects* (2nd ed.). New York: Free Press.

Senden, M. von. (1960). *Space and sight: The perception of space and shape in the congenitally blind before and after operation* (P. Heath, Trans.). New York: Free Press.

Senécal, C., Koestner, R., & Vallerand, R. J. (1995). Self-regulation and academic procrastination. *Journal of Social Psychology, 135,* 607–619.

References

Seppa, N. (2000). Stem cells repair rat spinal cord damage. *Science News, 157,* 6.

Serpell, R. (2000). Intelligence and culture. In R. J. Sternberg (Ed.), *Handbook of intelligence.* New York: Cambridge University Press.

Serpell, R. (2003, February). Cited in E. Benson, Intelligence across cultures. *Monitor on Psychology,* 56–58.

Shadish, W. R., Navarro, A. M., Matt, G. E., & Phillips, G. (2000). The effects of psychological therapies under clinically representative conditions: A meta-analysis. *Psychological Bulletin, 126,* 512–529.

Shannon, C. (1994). Stress management. In D. K. Granvold (Ed.), *Cognitive and behavioral treatment.* Pacific Grove, CA: Brooks/Cole.

Shapiro, C. M. (1981). Growth hormone sleep interaction: A review. *Research Communications in Psychology, Psychiatry and Behavior, 6,* 115–131.

Shapiro, F. (1991). Eye movement desensitization and reprocessing: From MD to EMD/R—A new treatment model for anxiety and related trauma. *Behavior Therapist, 14,* 133–135.

Shapiro, F. (2002). EMDR 12 years after its introduction: Past and future research. *Journal of Clinical Psychology, 58,* 1–22.

Shapiro, F., & Maxfield, L. (2002). Eye movement desensitization and reprocessing (EMDR): Information processing in the treatment of trauma. *Journal of Clinical Psychology, 58,* 933–948.

Shapiro, J. P., Loeb, P., Bowermaster, D., Wright, A., Headden, S., & Toch, T. (1993, December 13). Special report. *U.S. News & World Report.*

Shapiro, L. (1992, August 31). The lesson of Salem. *Newsweek.*

Shapiro, S. L., Shapiro, D. E., & Schwartz, G. E. R. (2000). Stress management in medical education: A review of the literature. *Academic Medicine, 75,* 748–759.

Sharp, D. (2000, August 10). Family embraces ear implants. *USA Today,* D9.

Sharp, D. (2003, February 20). Senior suicides to increase as U.S. ages. *USA Today,* A3.

Shaywitz, B. A., Shaywitz, S., Pugh, K. R., Constable, R. T., Skudlarski, P., Fulbright, R. K., Bronen, R. A., Fletcher, J. M., Shankweiler, D. P., Katz, L., & Gore, J. C. (1995). Sex differences in the functional organization of the brain for language. *Nature, 373,* 607–609.

Shaywitz, B. A., Sullivan, C. M., Anderson, G. M., Gillespie, S. M., Sullivan, B., & Shaywitz, S. E. (1994). Aspartame, behavior, and cognitive function in children with attention deficit disorder. *Pediatrics, 93,* 70–75.

Shaywitz, S. E. (2003, July 28). Cited in C. Gorman, The new science of dyslexia. *Time,* 52–59.

Shaywitz, S. E., Shaywitz, B. A., Fulbright, R. K., Skudlarski, P., Mencl, W. E. Constable, R. T., Pugh, K. R., Holahan, J. M., Marchione, K. E., Fletcher, J. M., Lyon, G. R., & Gore, J. C. (2003). Neural systems for compensation and persistence: Young adult outcome of childhood reading disability. *Biological Psychiatry, 54,* 25–33.

Shea, M. T., & Zlotnick, C. (2002). Understanding and treating PTSD: Introduction. *Journal of Clinical Psychology/In Session: Psychotherapy in Practice, 58,* 869–875.

Shea, M. T., Elkin, I., Imber, S. D., Sotsky, S. M., Watkins, J. T., Collins, J. F., Pilkonis, P. A., Beckham, E., Glass, D. R., Dolan, R. T., & Parloff, M. B. (1992). Course of depressive symptoms over follow-up: Findings from the National Institute of Mental Health Treatment of Depression Collaborative Research Program. *Archives of General Psychiatry, 49,* 782–787.

Sheaffer, R. (1997, May/June). Psychic departures and a discovery institute. *Skeptical Inquirer,* 21.

Sheehan, D. V. (2002). The management of panic disorder. *Journal of Clinical Psychiatry, 63 (supplement 14),* 17–21.

Shenour, E. A. (1990). Lying about polygraph tests. *Skeptical Inquirer, 14,* 292–297.

Sherman, J. W. (2001). The dynamic relationship between stereotype efficiency and mental representation. In G. B. Moskowitz (Ed.), *Cognitive social psychology.* Mahwah, NJ: Lawrence Erlbaum.

Shermer, M. (2002, December). Mesmerized by magnetism. *Scientific American,* 41.

Shettleworth, S. J. (1993). Where is the comparison in comparative cognition? *Psychological Science, 4,* 179–184.

Shetty, A. K., & Turner, D. A. (1996). Development of fetal hippocampal grafts in intact and lesioned hippocampus. *Progress in Neurobiology, 50,* 597–653.

Shilts, R. (1988). *And the band played on.* New York: Penguin.

Shimaya, A. (1997). Perception of complex line drawings. *Journal of Experimental Psychology: Human Perception and Performance, 23,* 25–50.

Shizgal, P., & Arvanitogiannis, A. (2003). Gambling on dopamine. *Science, 299,* 856–857.

Shoghi-Jadid, K., Small, G. W., Agdeppa, E. D., Kepe, V., Ercoli, L. M., Siddarth, P., Satyamurthy, N., Petric, A., Huang, S., & Barrio, J. R. (2002). Localization of neurofibrillary tangles and beta-amyloid plaques in the brains of living patients with Alzheimer disease. *American Journal of Geriatric Psychiatry, 10,* 24–35.

Shorkey, C. T. (1994). Use of behavioral methods with individuals recovering from substance dependence. In D. V. Granvold (Ed.), *Concepts and methods of cognitive treatment.* Pacific Grove, CA: Brooks/Cole.

Sidtis, J. J., Volpe, B. T., Wilson, D. H., Rayport, M., & Gazzaniga, M. S. (1981). Variability in right hemisphere language function after callosal section: Evidence for a continuum of generative capacity. *Journal of Neuroscience, 1,* 323–331.

Siegel, J. M. (2003, November). Why we sleep. *Scientific American,* 92–97.

Siegel, R. K. (1989). *Intoxication.* New York: Dutton.

Sigelman, C. K., & Shaffer, D. R. (1995). *Life-span human development.* Pacific Grove, CA: Brooks/Cole.

Silke, A. (2003). Deindividuation, anonymity, and violence: Findings from Northern Ireland. *Journal of Social Psychology, 143,* 493–499.

Sillery, B. (2002, June). At what level of the animal hierarchy do we find true sleep? *Popular Science,* 89.

Simcock, G., & Hayne, H. (2002). Breaking the barrier? Children fail to translate their preverbal memories into language. *Psychological Science, 13,* 225–231.

Simon, B., & Sturmer, S. (2003). Respect for group members: Intragroup determinants of collective identification and group-serving behavior. *Personality and Social Psychology Bulletin, 29,* 183–193.

Simonton, D. K. (2000). Creativity: Cognitive, personal, developmental, and social aspects. *American Psychologist, 55,* 151–158.

Singer, M. T., & Lalich, J. (1997). *Crazy therapies: What are they? Do they work?* San Francisco: Jossey-Bass.

Sinha, G. (2001, June). Out of control. *Popular Science,* 47–52.

Skinner, B. F. (1938). *The behavior of organisms.* New York: Appleton-Century-Crofts.

Skinner, B. F. (1953). *Science and human behavior.* New York: Macmillan.

Skinner, B. F. (1989). The origin of cognitive thought. *American Psychologist, 44,* 13–18.

Skinner, N., & Brewer, N. (2002). The dynamics of threat and challenge appraisals prior to stressful achievement events. *Journal of Personality and Social Psychology, 83,* 678–692.

Sloman, S. A. (1996). The empirical case for two systems of reasoning. *Psychological Bulletin, 119,* 3–22.

Slone, K. C. (1985). *They're rarely too young . . . and never too old "to twinkle"!* Ann Arbor, MI: Shar Publications.

Slutske, W. S., Heath, A. C., Madden, P. A. F., Bucholtz, K. K., Statham, D. J., & Martin, N. G. (2002). Personality and the genetic risk for alcohol dependence. *Journal of Abnormal Psychology, 111,* 124–133.

Small, G. W., Propper, M. W., Randolph, E. T., & Spencer, E. (1991). Mass hysteria among student performers: Social relationship as a symptom predictor. *American Journal of Psychiatry, 148,* 1200–1205.

Small, M. F. (2002, July). Drunk monkeys. *Discover,* 41–44.

Smiley, J. (2000, May 7). The good life. *New York Times Magazine,* 58–59.

Smith, D. (2002, June). Where are recent grads getting jobs? *Monitor on Psychology,* 28–32.

Smith, D. (2003, March). Angry thoughts, at-risk hearts. *Monitor on Psychology,* 46–47.

Smith, E. E. (2000). Neural bases of human working memory. *Current Directions in Psychological Science, 9,* 45–49.

Smith, E. R. (1994). Social cognition contributions to attribution theory and research. In P. G. Devine, D. L. Hamilton & T. M. Ostrom (Eds.), *Social cognition: Impact on social psychology.* New York: Academic Press.

Smith, L. (1993, July 13). Men in the making. *Los Angeles Times.*

Smith, M. T., Perlis, M. L., Park, A., Smith, S., Pennington, J., Gils, D. E., & Buysse, D. J. (2002). Comparative meta-analysis of pharmacotherapy and behavior therapy for persistent insomnia. *American Journal of Psychiatry, 159,* 5–11.

Smith, N. T. (2002). A review of the published literature into cannabis withdrawal symptoms in human users. *Addiction, 97,* 621–632.

Smith, P. (2003, February 19). First hand-transplant recipients progressing. *USA Today,* D5.

Smith, S. M., Gleaves, D. H., Pierce, G. H., Williams, T. L., Gilliland, T. R., & Gerkens, D. R. (2003). Eliciting and comparing false and recovered memories: An experimental approach. *Applied Cognitive Psychology, 17,* 251–279.

Snyder, C. R., Shenkel, R. J., & Lowery, C. R. (1977). Acceptance of personality interpretations: The "Barnum effect" and beyond. *Journal of Consulting and Clinical Psychology, 45,* 104–114.

Sohn, E. (2002, June 10). The hunger artists. *U.S. News & World Report,* 45–50.

Solomon, P. R., Adams, F., Silver, A., Zimmer, J., & DeVeaux, R. (2002). Ginkgo for memory enhancement. *Journal of the American Medical Association, 288,* 835–840.

Sosin, M. R. (2003). Explaining adult homeless in the US by stratification or situation. *Journal of Community & Applied Social Psychology, 13,* 91–104.

Sozzi, G., Veronese, M. L., Negrini, M. J., Baffa, R., Cohicelli, M. G., Inoue, H., Tornielli, S., Pilotti, S., DeGregorio, L., & Pastorino, U. (1996). The FHIT gene 3p14.2 is abnormal in lung cancer. *Cell,* 17–26.

Spanos, N. P. (1994). Multiple identity enactments and multiple personality disorder: A sociocognitive perspective. *Psychological Bulletin, 116,* 143–165.

Spanos, N. P. (1996). *Multiple identities and false memories: A sociocognitive perspective.* Washington, DC: American Psychological Association.

Spear, L. P. (2000). Neurobehavioral changes in adolescence. *Current Directions in Psychological Science, 9,* 111–114.

Spearman, C. (1904). "General intelligence" objectively determined and measured. *American Journal of Psychology, 15*, 201–293.

Spector, P. E., Cooper, C. L., Sanchez, J. I., O'Driscoll, M., Sparks, K., Bernin, P., Bussing, A., Dewe, P., Hart, P., Lu, L., Miller, K., de Moraes, R. F., Ostrognay, G. M., Pagon, M., Pitariu, H., Poelmans, S., Radhakrishnan, P., Russinova, V., Salamatov, V., Salgado, J., Shima, S., Siu, O. L., Stora, J. B., Teichmann, M., Theorell, T., Vlerick, P., Westman, M., Widerszal-Bazyl, M., Wong, P., & Yu, A. S. (2001). Do national levels of individualism and internal locus of control relate to well-being: An ecological level international study. *Journal of Organizational Behavior, 22*, 815–832.

Spencer, R. M. C., Zelaznik, H. N., Diedrichsen, J., & Ivry, R. B. (2003). Disrupted timing of discontinuous but not continuous movements by cerebellar lesions. *Science, 300*, 1437–1439.

Sperling, G. A. (1960). The information available in brief visual presentations. *Psychological Monographs, 74 (Whole No. 498).*

Sperry, R. W. (1974). Lateral specialization in the surgically separated hemisphere. In R. O. Schmitt & F. G. Worden (Eds.), *The neurosciences: Third study program.* Cambridge, MA: MIT Press.

Sperry, R. W. (1993, August). Cited in T. Deangelis, Sperry plumbs science for values and solutions. *APA Monitor.*

Spiegler, M. D., & Guevremont, D. C. (2003). *Contemporary behavior therapy* (4th ed.). Belmont, CA: Wadsworth/Thomson Learning.

Spielman, D. A., & Staub, E. (2000). Reducing boys' aggression: Learning to fulfill basic needs constructively. *Journal of Applied Developmental Psychology, 21*, 165–181.

Spillar, K., & Harrington, P. (2000, February, 18). This is what you get when men rule the roost. *Los Angeles Times*, B7.

Spitz, H. H. (1997). Some questions about the results of the Abecedarian early intervention project cited by the APA task force on intelligence. *American Psychologist, 52*, 72.

Spitzer, R. L., Gibbon, M., Skodol, A. E., Williams, J. B. W., & First, M. B. (Eds.). (1994). *DSM-IV casebook.* Washington, DC: American Psychiatric Association.

Spitzer, R. L., Terman, M., Williams, J. B., Terman, J. S., Malt, U. F., Singer, F., & Lewy, A. J. (1999). Jet lag. *American Journal of Psychiatry, 156*, 1392–1396.

Springer, S. P., & Deutsch, G. (1997). *Left brain, right brain* (5th ed.). New York: Freeman.

Squire, L. R. (1994). Declarative and nondeclarative memory: Multiple brain systems supporting learning and memory. In D. L. Schacter & E. Tulving (Eds.), *Memory systems 1994.* Cambridge, MA: MIT Press.

Squire, L. R., & Knowlton, B. J. (1995). Memory, hippocampus, and brain systems. In M. S. Gazzaniga (Ed.), *The cognitive neurosciences.* Cambridge, MA: MIT Press.

Squire, L. R., & Zola-Morgan, S. (1991). The medial temporal lobe memory system. *Science, 253*, 1380–1386.

Stahl, S. M. (2000). *Essential psychopharmacology* (2nd ed.). New York: Cambridge University Press.

Stahl, S. M. (2002). Don't ask, don't tell, but benzodiazepines are still the leading treatments for anxiety disorder. *Journal of Clinical Psychiatry, 63*, 756–757.

Stanford, J. N., & McCabe, M. P. (2002). Body image ideal among males and females: Sociocultural influences and focus on different body parts. *Journal of Health Psychology, 7*, 675–684.

Stanley, M. A., & Novy, D. M. (2000). Cognitive-behavior therapy for generalized anxiety in late life: An evaluative overview. *Journal of Anxiety Disorders, 14*, 191–207.

Steele, C. (1995, December 11). Cited in E. Woo, Can racial stereotypes psych out students? *Los Angeles Times*, A1.

Stein, J. (2003, August 4). Just say Om. *Time*, 50–55.

Stein, M. B., Goldin, P. R., Sareen, J., Zorrilla, L. T. E., & Brown, G. G. (2002). Increased amygdala activation to angry and contemptuous faces in generalized social phobia. *Archives of General Psychiatry, 59*, 1027–1034.

Steinberg, J. (2003, February 11). Flaws seen in campus policies replacing affirmative action. *New York Times*, A23.

Steiner, R. (1989). Live TV special explores, tests psychic powers. *Skeptical Inquirer, 14*, 2–6.

Stephen, M., & Suryani, L. K. (2000). Shamanism, psychosis, and autonomous imagination. *Culture, Medicine and Psychiatry, 24*, 5–40.

Steptoe, A., & Wardle, J. (1988). Emotional fainting and the psychophysiologic response to blood and injury: Autonomic mechanisms and coping strategies. *Psychosomatic Medicine, 50*, 402–417.

Steriade, M. (1966). Arousal: Revisiting the reticular activating system. *Science, 72*, 225–226.

Stern, G. S., McCants, T. R., & Pettine, P. W. (1982). Stress and illness: Controllable and uncontrollable life events' relative contributions. *Personality and Social Psychology Bulletin, 8*, 140–143.

Stern, R. M., & Koch, K. L. (1996). Motion sickness and differential susceptibility. *Current Directions in Psychological Science, 5*, 115–119.

Sternberg, R. J. (1995). For whom the Bell Curve tolls: A review of *The Bell Curve. Psychological Science, 6*, 257–261.

Sternberg, R. J. (1999). *Cupid's arrow: The course of love through time.* New York: Cambridge University Press.

Sternberg, R. J. (2000). The holy grail of general intelligence. *Science, 289*, 399–401.

Sternberg, R. J. (2001). What is the common thread of creativity? *American Psychologist, 56*, 360–362.

Sternberg, R. J. (2003a). Our research program validating the triarchic theory of successful intelligence: Reply to Gottfredson. *Intelligence, 31*, 399–413.

Sternberg, R. J. (2003b, February). Cited in E. Benson, Intelligence across cultures. *Monitor on Psychology*, 56–58.

Sternberg, R. J. (2003c, June). It's time for prescription privileges. *Monitor on Psychology*, 5.

Sternberg, R. J., & O'Hara, L. A. (2000). Intelligence and creativity. In R. J. Sternberg (Ed.), *Handbook of intelligence.* New York: Cambridge University Press.

Sternberg, R. J., & Soriano, L. J. (1984). Styles of conflict resolution. *Journal of Personality and Social Psychology, 47*, 115–126.

Sternberg, R. J., & Yang, S. (2003, February). Cited in E. Benson, Intelligence across cultures. *Monitor on Psychology*, 56–58.

Sternberg, R. J., Lautrey, J., & Lubart, T. I. (2003b). Where are we in the field of intelligence, how did we get here, and where are we going? In R. J. Sternberg, J. Lautrey & T. I. Lubart (Eds.), *Models of intelligence.* Washington, DC: American Psychological Association.

Sternberg, R. J., Lautrey, J., & Lubart, T. I. (Eds.). (2003a). *Models of intelligence.* Washington, DC: American Psychological Association.

Sternberg, S. (1998, November 2). Michael DeBakey's living legacy. *USA Today*, D1.

Sternberg, S. (2002, November 27–28). Women now make up half of AIDS cases, U.N. study finds. *USA Today*, A1.

Stetter, F., & Kupper, S. (2002). Autogenic training: A meta-analysis of clinical outcome studies. *Applied Psychophysiology and Biofeedback, 27*, 45–98.

Stevens, J. E. (1994, February 27). Tribeswomen disfigure themselves in name of tourism. *San Diego Union-Tribune.*

Stice, E. (2002). Risk and maintenance factors for eating pathology: A meta-analytic review. *Psychological Bulletin, 128*, 825–848.

Stich, S. S. (2003, November). Animal attraction. *Time Bonus Section*, 34.

Stickgold, R. (2000, March 7). Cited in S. Blakeslee, For better learning, researchers endorse "sleep on it" adage. *New York Times*, D2.

Stillman, J. A. (2002). Gustation: Intersensory experience par excellence. *Perception, 31*, 1491–1500.

Stokstad, E. (2002). Violent effects of abuse tied to gene. *Science, 297*, 752.

Stolberg, S. G. (2001, April 22). Science, studies and motherhood. *New York Times*, 3.

Stone, B. (2002, June 24). How to recharge the second sense. *Newsweek*, 54.

Strahan, E. J., Spencer, S. J., & Zanna, M. P. (2002). Subliminal priming and persuasion: Striking while the iron is hot. *Journal of Experimental Social Psychology, 38*, 556–568.

Strain, E. C., Mumford, G. K., Silverman, K., & Griffiths, R. R. (1994). Caffeine dependence syndrome. *Journal of the American Medical Association, 272*, 1043–1048.

Straker, G. (1994). Integrating African and Western healing practices in South Africa. *American Journal of Psychotherapy, 48*, 455–467.

Strassman, R. J. (1995). Hallucinogenic drugs in psychiatric research and treatment: Perspectives and prospects. *Journal of Nervous and Mental Diseases, 183*, 127–138.

Straus, M. A., & Stewart, J. H. (1999). Corporal punishment by American parents: National data on prevalence, chronicity, severity, and duration, in relation to child and family characteristics. *Clinical Child and Family Psychology Review, 2*, 55–70.

Strauss, N. (1994, June 2). Kurt Cobain 1967–1994. *Rolling Stone.*

Streissguth, A. P., Barr, H. M., Bookstein, F. L., Sampson, P. D., & Olson, H. C. (1999). The long-term neurocognitive consequences of prenatal alcohol exposure: A 14-year study. *Psychological Science, 10*, 186–190.

Stritzke, W. G. K., Lang, A. R., & Patrick, C. J. (1996). Beyond stress and arousal: A reconceptualization of alcohol—Emotion relations with reference to psychophysiological methods. *Psychological Bulletin, 120*, 376–395.

Stromeyer, C. F., III. (1970, November). Eidetikers. *Psychology Today.*

Stromswold, K. (1995). The cognitive and neural bases of language acquisition. In M. S. Gazzaniga (Ed.), *The cognitive neurosciences.* Cambridge, MA: MIT Press.

Struckman-Johnson, C., Struckman-Johnson, D., & Anderson, P. B. (2003). Tactics of sexual coercion: When men and women won't take no for an answer. *The Journal of Sex Research, 40*, 76–86.

Stumpf, D. A., Cranford, R. E., Elias, S., Fost, N. C., McQuillen, M. P., Myer, E., Poland, R., & Queenam, J. T. (1990). The infant with anencephaly. *New England Journal of Medicine, 322*, 669–674.

Stuss, D. T., & Levine, B. (2002). Adult clinical neuropsychology: Lessons from studies on the frontal lobes. *Annual Review of Psychology, 53*, 401–433.

Stutts, J. C., Wilkins, J. W., Osberg, J. S., & Vaughn, B. V. (2002). Driver risk factors for sleep-related crashes. *Accident Analysis & Prevention, 841*, 1–11.

Suarez, E.C. (2003, March). Cited in D. Smith, Angry thoughts, at-risk hearts. *Monitor on Psychology*, 46–47.

Suddath, R. L., Christison, G. W., Torrey, E. F., Casanova, M. R., & Weinberger, D. R. (1990). Anatomical abnormalities in the brains of monozygotic twins discordant for schizophrenia. *New England Journal of Medicine, 322,* 789–794.

Sullivan, R. M., Taborsky-Barba, S., Mendoza, R., Itano, A., Leon, M., Cotman, C. W., Payne, T. R., & Lott, I. (1991). Olfactory classical conditioning in neonates. *Pediatrics, 87,* 511–518.

Suzuki, S. (1998, January 27). Cited in Shinichi Suzuki: Started music classes for toddlers. *Los Angeles Times,* B8.

Svensen, S., & White, K. (1994). A content analysis of horoscopes. *Genetic, Social and General Psychology Monographs, 12,* 5–38.

Svirsky, M. A., Robbins, A. M., Kirk, K. I., Pisoni, D. B., & Miyamoto, R. T. (2000). Language development in profoundly deaf children with cochlear implants. *Psychological Science, 11,* 153–158.

Swayze, V. W., II. (1995). Frontal leukotomy and related psychosurgical procedures in the era before antipsychotics (1935–1954): A historical overview. *American Journal of Psychiatry, 152,* 505–515.

Sweet, R. A., Mulsant, B. H., Gupta, B., Rifai, A. H., Pasternak, R. E., McEachran, A., & Zubenko, G. S. (1995). Duration of neuroleptic treatment and prevalence of tardive dyskinesia in late life. *Archives of General Psychiatry, 52,* 478–486.

Swerdloff, R. (1998, August 27). Cited in T. H. Maugh II, A genetic enigma. *Los Angeles Times,* B2.

Swets, J. A., Dawes, R. M., & Monahan, J. (2000). Psychological science can improve diagnostic decisions. *Psychological Science in the Public Interest, 1,* 1–26.

Swim, J. K., Aikin, K. J., Hall, W. S., & Hunter, B. A. (1995). Sexism and racism: Old-fashioned and modern principles. *Journal of Personality and Social Psychology, 68,* 199–214.

Sylvester, C. Y. C., Wager, T. D., Lacey, S. C., Hernandez, L., Nichols, T. E., Smith, E. E., & Jonides, J. (2003). Switching attention and resolving interference: fMRI measures of executive functions. *Neuropsychologia, 41,* 357–370.

Synder, S. (2002). Forty years of neurotransmitters. *Archives of General Psychiatry, 59,* 983–995.

Szyfelbein, S. K., Osgood, P. F., & Carr, D. B. (1985). The assessment of pain and plasma B-endorphin immunoactivity in burned children. *Pain, 22,* 173–182.

Taddese, A., Nah, S. Y., & McCleskey, E. W. (1995). Selective opioid inhibition of small nociceptive neurons. *Science, 270,* 1366–1369.

Talarico, J. M., & Rubin, D. C. (2003). Confidence, not consistency, characterizes flashbulb memories. *Psychological Science, 14,* 455–461.

Talbot, M. (1999, October 17). The Rorschach chronicles. *New York Times Magazine,* 28–35.

Talbot, M. (2000, January 9). The placebo prescription. *New York Times Magazine,* 34.

Tallal, P. (1995, August 29). Cited in S. Begley, Why Johnny and Joanie can't read. *Newsweek.*

Tamis-LeMonda, C. S., Bornstein, M. H., Baumwell, L., & Dakmast, A. M. (1996). Responsive parenting in the second year: Specific influences on children's language and play. *Early Development and Parenting, 5,* 173–183.

Tamres, L. K., Janicki, D., & Helgeson, V. S. (2002). Sex differences in coping behavior: A meta-analysis review and an examination of relative coping. *Personality and Social Psychology Review, 6,* 2–30.

Tankova, I., Adan, A., & Buela-Casal, G. (1994). Circadian typology and individual differences. A review. *Personality and Individual Differences, 16,* 671–684.

Tannen, D. (1990). *You just don't understand: Women and men in conversation.* New York: William Morrow.

Tannen, D. (1994). *Talking from 9 to 5.* New York: William Morrow.

Tanner, L. (2000, May). Pediatrician guidelines issued to spot disorder. *San Diego Union-Tribune,* A1.

Tanouye, E. (1997, July 7). Got a big public speaking phobia? *San Diego Union-Tribune.*

Tanzi, R. (2000, January 31). Cited in G. Cowley, Alzheimer's: Unlocking the mystery. *Newsweek,* 46–51.

Tao, K. (1987). Infantile autism in China. *Journal of Autism and Developmental Disorders, 2,* 289.

Tao, K. T., & Yang, X. L. (1997). China. In D. J. Cohen & F. R. Volkmar (Eds.), *Handbook of autism and pervasive developmental disorders* (2nd ed.). New York: John Wiley & Sons.

Tarkan, L. (2002, October 22). Autism therapy is called effective, but rare. *New York Times,* D2.

Tashkin, D. (1996, December 16). Cited in D. Ferrell, Scientists unlocking secrets of marijuana's effects. *Los Angeles Times.*

Tawa, R. (1995, March 12). Shattering the silence. *Los Angeles Times.*

Taylor, J., & Miller, M. (1997). When time-out works some of the time: The importance of treatment integrity and functional assessment. *School Psychology Quarterly, 12,* 4–22.

Taylor, M. (2001, November, 27). Customs seized record drug loads at border in past year. *San Diego Union-Tribune,* A1.

Taylor, S. E. (1981). The interface of cognitive and social psychology. In J. Harvey (Ed.), *Cognition, social behavior, and the environment.* Hillsdale, NJ: Erlbaum.

Taylor, S. E., Kemeny, M. E., Reed, G. M., Bower, J. E., & Gruenewald, T. L. (2000a). Psychological resources, positive illusions, and health. *American Psychologist, 55,* 99–109.

Taylor, S. E., Klein, L. C., Lewis, B. P., Gruenwald, T. L., Gurung, R. A. R., & Updegraff, J. A. (2000b). Biobehavioral responses to stress in females: Tend and befriend, not fight-or-flight. *Psychological Review, 107,* 411–439.

Teicher, M. (2000, April 10). Cited in J. S. Fischer, Taking a picture of a mind gone awhirl. *U.S. News & World Report,* 48.

Teicher, M. H. (2002, March). The neurobiology of child abuse. *Scientific American,* 68–75.

Tekcan, A. I., & Peynircioglu, Z. F. (2002). Effects of age on flashbulb memories. *Psychology and Aging, 17,* 416–422.

Temple, E., Deutsch, G. K., Poldrack, R. A., Miller, S. L., Tallal, P., Merzenich, M. M., & Gabrieli, J. D. E. (2003). Neural deficits in children with dyslexia ameliorated by behavioral remediation: Evidence from functional MRI. *Proceedings of the National Academy of Science, 100,* 2860–2865.

Terman, J. S., Terman, M., Lo, E., & Cooper, T. B. (2001). Circadian time of morning light administration and therapeutic response in winter depression. *Archives of General Psychiatry, 58,* 69–75.

Terman, L. M. (1916). *The measurement of intelligence.* Boston: Houghton Mifflin.

Terman, L. M., & Oden, M. H. (1959). *The gifted group at mid-life* (Vol. 5). Stanford, CA: Stanford University Press.

Terrace, H. S. (1981). A report to an academy, 1980. *Annals of the New York Academy of Sciences, 364,* 94–114.

Thapar, A., & McGuffin, P. (1993). Is personality disorder inherited? An overview of the evidence. *Journal of Psychopathology and Behavioral Assessment, 15,* 325–345.

Thase, M. E., Jindal, R., & Howland, R. H. (2002). Biological aspects of depression. In I. H. Gotlib & C. L. Hammen (Eds.), *Handbook of depression.* New York: Guilford Press.

Thelen, E. (1995). Motor development. *American Psychologist, 50,* 79–95.

Thomas, A., & Chess, S. (1977). *Temperament and development.* New York: Brunner/Mazel.

Thomas, E. (2003, October 20). I am addicted to pain prescription medication. *Newsweek,* 43–47.

Thombs, D. L. (1995). Problem behavior and academic achievement among first-semester college freshmen. *Journal of College Student Development, 36,* 280–288.

Thompson, C., Cowan, T., & Frieman, J. (1993). *Memory search by a memorist.* Hillsdale, NJ: Lawrence Erlbaum.

Thompson, P. M., Cannon, T. D., Narr, K., van Erp, T., Poutamen, V. P., Huttunen, M., Loonqvist, J., Standertskjold-Nordenstam, C. G., Kaprio, J., Khaledy, M., Dail, R., Zoulmalan, C. I., & Toga, A. W. (2001). Genetic influences on brain structure. *Nature Neuroscience, 4,* 1253–1258.

Thompson, R. A. (1998). Early sociopersonality development. In W. Damon & R. M. Lerner (Eds.), *Handbook of child psychology* (Vol. 1). New York: John Wiley & Sons.

Thorndike, E. L. (1898). Animal intelligence: An experimental study of the associative process in animals. *Psychological Review Monograph Supplement, 2*(8).

Tolman, D. L., Striepe, M. I., & Harmon, T. (2003). Gender matters: Constructing a model of adolescent sexual health. *Journal of Sex Research, 40,* 4–12.

Tolman, E. C. (1948). Cognitive maps in rats and men. *Psychological Review, 55,* 189–208.

Tolson, J. (2003, November 10). Faith & freedom. *U.S. News & World Report,* 60–62.

Tomes, H. (2000, July/August). Why did APA take so long? *Monitor on Psychology,* 57.

Tompkins, J. (2003a, June 16). A night owl resets his body clock. *Los Angeles Times,* F1.

Tompkins, J. (2003b, June 16). How light became a therapy. *Los Angeles Times,* F1.

Tonegawa, S., & Wilson, M. (1997). Cited in W. Roush, New knockout mice point to molecular basis of memory. *Science, 275,* 32–33.

Torrey, F. E., Bowler, A. E., Taylor, E. H., & Gottesman, I. I. (1994). *Schizophrenia and manic-depressive disorder.* New York: Basic Books.

Towle, L. H. (1995, July 31). Elegy for lost boys. *Time.*

Townsend, E., Dimigen, G., & Fung, D. (2000). A clinical study of child dental anxiety. *Behaviour Research and Therapy, 38,* 31–46.

Tramer, M. R., Carroll, D., Campbell, F. A., Reynolds, D. J. M., Moore, R. A., & McQuay, H. J. (2001). Cannabinoids for control of chemotherapy induced nausea and vomiting: Quantitative systematic review. *British Medical Journal, 323,* 16–21.

Tranel, D., Benton, A., & Olson, K. (1997). A 10-year longitudinal study of cognitive changes in elderly persons. *Developmental Neuropsychology, 13,* 87–96.

Travis, J. (2002). A tasty discovery about the tongue. *Science News, 161,* 221–222.

Treffert, D.A., & Wallace, G. L. (2002, June). Island of genius. *Scientific American,* 76–85.

Tresniowski, A., & Bell, B. (1996, September 9). Oprah buff. *People,* 81.

Triandis, H. C. & Suh, E. M. (2002). Cultural influences on personality. *Annual Review of Psychology, 53,* 133–160.

Tripathi, H. L., Olson, K. G., & Dewey, W. L. (1993). Borphin response to endurance exercise: Relationship to exercise dependence. *Perceptual and Motor Skills, 77,* 767–770.

Tripician, R. J. (2000, January/February). Confessions of a (former) graphologist. *Skeptical Inquirer, 44–47.*

Troster, A. I. (2000). Introduction to neurobehavioral issues in the neurosurgical treatment of movement disorders: Basic issues, thalamotomy, and nonablative treatments. *Brain and Cognition, 42,* 173–182.

Trzesniewski, K. H., Donnelian, M. B., & Robins, R. W. (2003). Stability of self-esteem across the life span. *Journal of Personality and Social Psychology, 84,* 205–220.

Tsai, G., Gastfriend, D. R., & Coyle, J. T. (1995). The glutamatergic basis of human alcoholism. *American Journal of Psychiatry, 152,* 332–340.

Tsien, J. Z. (2000). Building a brainier mouse. *Scientific American,* 62–68.

Tulving, E. (2002). Episodic memory: From mind to brain. *Annual Review of Psychology, 53,* 1–25.

Tulving, E., & Craik, F. M. (Eds.). (2000). *The Oxford handbook of memory.* New York: Oxford University Press.

Turk, D. J. (2002). Cited in B. Bower, All about me: Left brain may shine spotlight on self. *Science News, 162,* 118.

Turkheimer, E. (2000). Three laws of behavior genetics and what they mean. *Current Directions in Psychological Science, 9,* 160–164.

Turner, M., & Griffin, M. J. (1999). Motion sickness in public road transport: The relative importance of motion, vision and individual differences. *British Journal of Psychology, 90,* 519–530.

Turner, S., & Scherman, A. (1996). Big brothers: Impact on little brothers' self-concepts and behaviors. *Adolescence, 31,* 875–882.

Tuunainen, A., Wahlbeck, K., & Gilbody, S. (2002). Newer atypical antipsychotic medication in comparison to clozapine: A systematic review of randomized trials. *Schizophrenia Research 56,* 1–10.

Twenge, J. M. (1997). Changes in masculine and feminine traits over time: A meta-analysis. *Sex Roles, 36,* 305–325.

Tyack, P. L. (2000). Dolphins whistle a signature tune. *Science, 289,* 1310–1313.

Ulett, G. A. (2003, March/April). Acupuncture, magic and make-believe. *Skeptical Inquirer,* 47–50.

Ullman, S. E. (1997). Review and critique of empirical studies of rape avoidance. *Criminal Justice and Behavior, 24,* 177–204.

Ullman, S. E., Karabatsos, G., & Koss, M. P. (1999). Alcohol and sexual aggression in a national sample of college men. *Psychology of Women Quarterly, 23,* 673–689.

Underwood, P. W. (2000). Social support: The promise and the reality. In V. R. Rice (Ed.), *Handbook of stress, coping and health.* Thousand Oaks, CA: Sage.

UNESCO. (2001, July 3). The tower of Babel is tumbling down—slowly. *U.S. News & World Report,* 9.

Unis, A. S., Muncon, J. A., Rogers, S. J., Goldson, E., Osterling, J., Gabriels, R., Abbott, R. D., & Dawson, G. (2002). A randomized, double-blind, placebo-controlled trial of porcine versus synthetic secretin for reducing symptoms of autism. *Journal of the American Academy of Child and Adolescent Psychiatry, 41,* 1315–1321.

Ursu, S., Stenger, V. A., Shear, M. K., Jones, M. R., & Carter, C. S. (2003). Overactive action monitoring in obsessive-compulsive disorder: Evidence from functional magnetic resonance imaging. *Psychological Science, 14,* 347–353.

Vahtera, J., Kivimaki, M., Uutela, A., & Pentti, J. (2000). Hostility and ill health: Role of psychosocial resources in two contexts of working life. *Journal of Psychosomatic Research, 48,* 89–98.

Valenstein, E. S. (1986). *Great and desperate cures.* New York: Basic Books.

Valtin, H. (2002). "Drink at least eight glasses of water a day." Really? Is there scientific evidence for "8 x 8"? *American Journal of Physiology, 283,* R993–R1004.

Van de Castle, R. L. (1994). *Our dreaming mind.* New York: Ballantine.

van Derbur Atler, D. (1991, June). The darkest secret. *People.*

Van Essen, D. (1997, January 13). Cited in S. Brownlee & T. Watson, The senses. *U.S. News & World Report,* 51–59.

Van Essen, D. C., Anderson, C. H., & Felleman, D. J. (1992). Information processing in the primate visual system: An integrated systems perspective. *Science, 255,* 419–423.

Van Gerwen, L. J., Spinhoven, P., Diekstra, R. F. W., & Van Dyck, F. (1997). People who seek help for fear of flying: Typology of flying phobics. *Behavior Therapy, 28,* 237–251.

Van Manen, K., & Whitbourne, S. K. (1997). Psychosocial development and life experiences in adulthood: A 22-year sequential study. *Psychology and Aging, 12,* 239–246.

van Praag, H., Schinder, A. F., Christie, B. R., Toni, N., Palmer, T. D., & Gage, F. H. (2002). Functional neurogenesis in the adult hippocampus. *Nature, 415,* 1030–1034.

Van Rossum, E. F. C., Koper, J. W., Huizenga, N. A. T. M., Uitterlnden, A. G., Janssen, J. A. J. L., Brinkman, A. O., Grobee, D. E., de Jong, F. H., van Duyn, C. M., Pols, H. A. P., & Lamberts, S. W. J. (2002). A polymorphism in the glucocorticoid receptor gene, which decreases sensitivity to glucocorticoids in vivo, is associated with low insulin and cholesterol levels. *Diabetes, 51,* 3128–3134.

VandenBos, G. R. (1996). Outcome assessment of psychotherapy. *American Psychologist, 51,* 1005–1006.

Vandewater, E. A., Ostrove, J. M., & Stewart, A. J. (1997). Predicting women's well-being in midlife: The importance of personality development and social role involvements. *Journal of Personality and Social Psychology, 72,* 1147–1160.

Vargas, J. S. (1991). B. F. Skinner: The last few days. *Journal of the Experimental Analysis of Behavior, 55,* 1–2.

Vargha-Khadem, F. (2000, November 20). Cited in J. Fischman, Seeds of a sociopath. *U.S. News & World Report,* 82.

Vastag, B. (2003). Addiction poorly understood by clinicians. *Journal of the American Medical Association, 290,* 1299–1303.

Vecera, S. (2002, June). Cited in R. Adelson, Figure this: Deciding what's figure, what's ground. *Monitor on Psychology,* 44–45.

Venter, J. C. (2000, August 22). Cited in N. Angier, Do races differ: not really, genes show. *New York Times,* D1.

Vergano, D. (2001, June 19). As many opinions as treatments in tobacco fight. *USA Today,* D8.

Vergano, D. (2002, September 11). Rehabilitation eases Reeve's paralysis. *USA Today,* D6.

Verhovek, S. H. (2002, February 7). As suicide approvals rise in Oregon, half go unused. *New York Times,* A16.

Verlinden, S., Hersen, M., & Thomas, J. (2000). Risk factors in school shootings. *Clinical Psychology Review, 29,* 3–56.

Videbech, P. (2000). PET measurements of brain glucose metabolism and blood flow in major depressive disorder: A critical review. *Acta Psychiatrica Scandinavica, 101,* 11–20.

Viglione, D. J., & Hilsenroth, M. J. (2001). The Rorschach: Facts, fictions, and future. *Psychological Assessment, 13,* 452–471.

Vogel, S. (1999, April). Why we get fat. *Discover,* 94–99.

Vogele, C., Coles, J., Wardle, J., & Steptoe, A. (2003). Psychophysiologic effects of applied tension on the emotional fainting response to blood and injury. *Behaviour Research and Therapy, 41,* 139–155.

Volkow, N. D., Chang, L., Wang, G. L., Fowler, J. S., Ding, Y. S., Sedler, M., Logan, J., Franceschi, D., Gatley, J., Hitzemann, R., Gifford, A., Wong, C., & Pappas, N. (2001). Low level of brain dopamine D_2 receptors in methamphetamine abusers: Association with metabolism in the orbitofrontal cortex. *American Journal of Psychiatry, 158,* 2015–2021.

Vredenburg, K., Flett, G. L., & Krames, L. (1994). Analogue versus clinical depression: A critical reappraisal. *Psychological Bulletin, 113,* 327–344.

Waddell, C. (1998). Creativity and mental illness: Is there a link? *Canadian Journal of Psychiatry, 43,* 166–172.

Waddington, J. L., Lane, A., Scully, P., Meagher, D., Quinn, J., Larkin, C., & O'Callaghan, E. (2000). Early cerebro-craniofacial dysmorphogenesis in schizophrenia: A lifetime trajectory model from neurodevelopmental basis to "neuroprogressive" process. *Journal of Psychiatric Research, 33,* 477–489.

Wade, N. (2002, June 21). Stem cell progress reported on Parkinson's. *New York Times,* A18.

Wade, N. (2002a, July 4). Schizophrenia may be tied to 2 genes, research finds. *New York Times,* A11.

Wade, N. (2002b, December 13). Gene may play a role in schizophrenia. *New York Times,* A23.

Wade, N. (2003a, February 25). Double helix leaps from lab into real life. *New York Times,* D1.

Wade, N. (2003b, July 15). Early voices: The leap to language. *New York Times,* A18.

Wade, T. (2002, March). Cited in T. DeAngelis, Further gene studies show promise. *Monitor on Psychology,* 35.

Wakefeld, J. (2001, July). A mind for a consciousness. *Scientific American,* 36–37.

Walker, A., & Parmar, P. (1993). *Warrior marks: Female genital mutilation and sexual blinding of women.* New York: Harcourt Brace.

Wallechinsky, D. (1986). *Midterm report.* New York: Viking.

Wallerstein, R. S., & Fonagy, P. (1999). Psychoanalytic research and the IPA: History, present status and future potential. *International Journal of Psychoanalysis, 80,* 91–109.

Walsh, J. K., & Lindblom, S. S. (1997). Psychophysiology of sleep deprivation and disruption. In M. R. Pressman & W. C. Orr (Eds.), *Understanding sleep: The evaluation and treatment of sleep disorders.* Washington, DC: American Psychological Association.

Walton, K. G., Schneider, R. H., Nidlich, S. I., Salerno, J. W., Nordstrom, C. K., & Merz, C. N. B. (2002). Psychosocial stress and cardiovascular disease part 2: Effectiveness of the transcendental meditation program in treatment and prevention. *Behavioral Medicine, 8,* 106–123.

Wanek, J. E. (1999). Integrity and honesty testing: What do we know? How do we use it? *International Journal of Selection and Assessment, 7,* 183–196.

Wang, Q. (2003). Infantile amnesia reconsidered: A cross-cultural analysis. *Memory, 11,* 65–80.

Wang, S. C. (2000). In search of Einstein's genius. *Science, 289,* 1477.

Ward, A., Tiller, J., Treasure, J., & Russell, G. (2000). Eating disorders: Psyche or soma? *International Journal of Eating Disorders, 27,* 279–287.

Warden, C. H. (1997). Cited in J. Travis, Gene heats up obesity research. *Science News, 151,* 142.

Wartik, N. (1994, August 7). The amazingly simple, inexplicable therapy that just might work. *Los Angeles Times.*

References

Watanabe, T. (2000, October 31). Exorcism flourishing once again. *Los Angeles Times*, A1.

Watson, J. B. (1924). *Behaviorism*. Chicago: University of Chicago Press.

Watson, J. B., & Rayner, R. (1920). Conditioned emotional reactions. *Journal of Experimental Psychology, 3,* 1–14.

Webb, W. B. (1983). Theories in modern sleep research. In A. Mayes (Ed.), *Sleep mechanisms and functions*. Wokingham, England: Van Nostrand Reinhold.

Weber, E. H. (1834). *De pulsu, resorptione, auditu et tactu: Annotationes anatomical et physiological*. Liepzig: Koehler.

Weed, W. S. (2000, June). Smart pills. *Discover*, 82.

Weinberg, R. A., Scarr, S., & Waldman, I. D. (1992). The Minnesota transracial adoption study: A follow-up of IQ test performance at adolescence. *Intelligence, 16,* 117–135.

Weinberger, D. R. (2001, March 10). A brain too young for good judgment. *New York Times*, A7.

Weinberger, D. R., Goldberg, T. E., & Tamminga, C. A. (1995). Prefrontal leukotomy. *American Journal of Psychiatry, 152,* 330–331.

Weiner, B. (1991). Metaphors in motivation and attribution. *American Psychologist, 46,* 921–930.

Weiner, B., & Graham, S. (1999). Attribution in personality psychology. In L. A. Pervin & O. P. John (Eds.), *Handbook of personality* (2nd ed.). New York: Guilford.

Weinraub, B. (2000, May 24). Out of "Spin City" and onto a new stage. *New York Times*, B1.

Weisberg, R. W. (1993). *Creativity: Beyond the myth of genius*. New York: Freeman.

Weiss, K. R. (1997, January 13). Survey finds record stress in class of 2000. *Los Angeles Times*.

Weissman, M. M. (1993, Spring). The epidemiology of personality disorders. A 1990 update. *Journal of Personality Disorders, Supplement,* 44–62.

Weitzenhoffer, A. M. (2002). Scales, scales, and more scales. *American Journal of Clinical Hypnosis, 44,* 209–219.

Welch, K. L., & Beere, D. B. (2002). Eye movement desensitization and reprocessing: A treatment efficacy model. *Clinical Psychology and Psychotherapy, 9,* 165–176.

Weller, E. B., Young, K. M., Rohrbaugh, A. H., & Weller, R. A. (2001). Overview and assessment of the suicidal child. *Depression and Anxiety, 14,* 157–163.

Wells, G. L., & Olson, E. A. (2003). Eyewitness testimony. *Annual Review of Psychology, 54,* 277–295.

Wells, G. L., Malpass, R. S., Lindsay, R. C. L., Fisher, R. P., Turtle, J. W., & Fulero, S. M. (2000). From the lab to the police station. *American Psychologist, 55,* 581–598.

Wenzlaff, R. M., & Luxton, D. D. (2003). The role of thought suppression in depressive rumination. *Cognitive Therapy and Research, 27,* 293–308.

Wenzlaff, R. M., & Wegner, D. M. (2000). Thought suppression. *Annual Review of Psychology, 51,* 59–91.

Werle, M. A., Murphy, T. B., & Budd, K. S. (1993). Treating chronic food refusal in young children: Home-based parent training. *Journal of Applied Behavior Analysis, 26,* 421–433.

Werner, E. E. (1989). Children of the garden island. *Scientific American, 260,* 106–111.

Werner, E. E. (1995). Resilience in development. *Current Directions in Psychological Science, 4,* 81–85.

Werner, E. E., & Smith, R. S. (2001). *Journeys from childhood to midlife: Risk, resilience and recovery*. Ithaca, NY: Cornell University Press.

Werner, J. S., & Frost, M. H. (2000). Major life stressors and health outcomes. In V. R. Rice (Ed.), *Handbook of stress, coping and health*. Thousand Oaks, CA: Sage.

Westen, D. (1998a). Unconscious thought, feeling, and motivation: The end of a century-long debate. In R. F. Bornstein & J. M. Masling (Eds.), *Empirical perspectives on the psychoanalytic unconscious*. Washington, DC: American Psychological Association.

Westen, D. (1998b). The scientific legacy of Sigmund Freud: Toward a psychodynamically informed psychological science. *Psychology Bulletin, 124,* 333–371.

Westen, D., & Gabbard, G. O. (1999). Psychoanalytic approaches to personality. In L. A. Pervin & O. P. John (Eds.), *Handbook of personality* (2nd ed.), New York: Guilford.

White, A. (2003, November 28). Cited in G. Bryson, Adult brain gets "wired" during the teen years. *San Diego Union-Tribune*, A19.

White, J. M., & Porth, C. M. (2000). Evolution of a model of stress, coping and discrete emotions. In V. R. Rice (Ed.), *Handbook of stress, coping and health*. Thousand Oaks, CA: Sage.

White, R. (2002). Memory for events after twenty years. *Applied Cognitive Psychology, 16,* 603–612.

Whorf, B. L. (1940). In J. B. Carroll (Ed.), *Language, thought, and reality: Selected writing of Benjamin Lee Whorf*. Cambridge, MA: MIT Press.

Whorf, B. L. (1956). *Language, thought, and reality*. New York: Wiley.

Wickett, J. C., Vernon, P. A., & Lee, D. H. (1994). In vivo brain size, head perimeter, and intelligence in a sample of healthy adult females. *Personality and Individual Differences, 16,* 831–838.

Widiger, T. A., & Clark, L. A. (2000). Toward DSM-V and the classification of psychopathology. *Psychological Bulletin, 126,* 946–963.

Wiebe, D. J. (1991). Hardiness and stress moderation: A test of proposed mechanisms. *Journal of Personality and Social Psychology, 60,* 89–99.

Wierson, M., & Forehand, R. (1994). Parent behavioral training for child noncompliance: Rationale, concepts, and effectiveness. *Current Directions in Psychological Science, 3,* 146–150.

Wigboldus, D. H. J., Dijksterhuis, A., & van Knippenberg, A. (2003). When stereotypes get in the way: Stereotypes obstruct stereotype-inconsistent trait inferences. *Journal of Personality and Social Psychology, 84,* 470–484.

Wiggins, J. S. (1997). In defense of traits. In R. Hogan, J. Johnson & S. Briggs (Eds.), *Handbook of personality psychology*. New York: Academic Press.

Wilcoxon, H. C., Dragoin, W. B., & Kral, P. A. (1971). Illness-induced aversions in rat and quail: Relative salience of visual and gustatory cues. *Science, 171,* 826–828.

Wilens, T. E., Biederman, J., Mick, E., Farone, S., & Spencer, T. (1997). Attention deficit hyperactivity disorder (ADHD) is associated with early onset substance use disorders. *Journal of Nervous and Mental Disease, 185,* 475–482.

Wilhelm, F. H., & Roth, W. T. (1997). Clinical characteristics of flight phobia. *Journal of Anxiety Disorders, 11,* 241–261.

Wilkinson, D., & Murray, J. (2001). Galantamine: A randomized, double-blind, dose comparison in patients with Alzheimer's disease. *International Journal of Geriatric Psychiatry, 16,* 852–857.

Will, G. F. (2001, September 17). About cocaine and bananas. *Time*, 78.

Williams, B. K., & Knight, S. M. (1994). *Healthy for life*. Pacific Grove, CA: Brooks/Cole.

Williams, D. (1992). *Nobody nowhere*. New York: Times Books.

Williams, D. (1994). *Somebody somewhere*. New York: Times Books.

Williams, D. E., Kirkpatrick-Sanchez, S., & Iwata, B. A. (1993). A comparison of shock intensity in the treatment of longstanding and severe self-injurious behavior. *Research in Development Disabilities, 14,* 207–219.

Williams, J. E., & Best, D. L. (1990). *Measuring sex stereotypes* (Vol. 6, rev. ed.). Newbury Park, CA: Sage Publications.

Williams, M. A., & Gross, A. M. (1994). Behavior therapy. In V. B. Hasselt & M. Hersen (Eds.), *Advanced abnormal psychology*. New York: Plenum Press.

Williams, S. P. (2000, April 24). A new smoking peril. *Newsweek*, 78.

Willing, R. (2003, May 23). Attitudes ease toward medical marijuana. *USA Today*, A3.

Wilson, B. (1996, February 7). Cited in G. Braxton, TV violence poses risk to viewers, study says. *Los Angeles Times*, F-1.

Wilson, D., Killen, J. D., Hayward, C., Robinson, T. N., Hammer, L. D., Kraemer, H. C., Varady, A., & Taylor, C. B. (1994). Timing and rate of sexual maturation and the onset of cigarette and alcohol use among teenage girls. *Archives of Pediatric and Adolescent Medicine, 148,* 789–795.

Wilson, G. T., Fairburn, C. C., Agras, W. S., Walsh, B. T., & Kramer, H. (2002). Cognitive-behavioral therapy for bulimia nervosa: Time course and mechanisms of change. *Journal of Consulting and Clinical Psychology, 20,* 267–274.

Wilson, S. R., Levine, K. J., Cruz, M. G., & Rao, N. (1997). Attribution complexity and actor-observer bias. *Journal of Social Behavior and Personality, 12,* 709–726.

Wilson, T. D., & Linville, P. W. (1982). Improving the academic performance of college freshmen: Attribution therapy revisited. *Journal of Personality and Social Psychology, 42,* 367–376.

Wimbush, F. B., & Nelson, M. L. (2000). Stress, psychosomatic illness, and health. In V. R. Rice (Ed.), *Handbook of stress, coping and health*. Thousand Oaks, CA: Sage.

Wincze, J. P., & Carey, M. P. (1991). *Sexual dysfunction: A guide for assessment and treatment*. New York: Guilford.

Wineberg, H., & Werth, J. L., Jr. (2003). Physician-assisted suicide in Oregon: What are the key factors? *Death Studies, 27,* 501–518.

Winner, E. (2000). The origins and ends of giftedness. *American Psychologist, 55,* 159–169.

Winner, E. (2002, March 12). Cited in E. Goode, The uneasy fit of the precocious and the average. *New York Times*, D1.

Winningham, R. G., Hyman, I. E., Jr., & Dinnel, D. L. (2000). Flashbulb memories? The effects of when the initial memory report was obtained. *Memory, 8,* 209–216.

Winograd, E., & Soloway, R. M. (1986). On forgetting the locations of things stored in special places. *Journal of Experimental Psychology: General, 115,* 366–372.

Winters, K. C., Stinchfield, R. D., Opland, E., Weller, C., & Latimer, W. W. (2000). The effectiveness of the Minnesota Model approach in the treatment of adolescent drug abusers. *Addiction, 95,* 601–612.

Wise, T. N., & Birket-Smith, M. (2002). The somatoform disorders for DSM-V: The need for changes in process and content. *Psychosomatics 43,* 437–440.

Witelson, S. F., Glezor, I. I., & Kigar, D. L. (1995). Women have greater density of neurons in posterior temporal cortex. *Journal of Neuroscience, 15,* 3418–3428.

Witelson, S. F., Kigar, D. L., & Harvey, T. (1999). The exceptional brain of Albert Einstein. *Lancet, 353,* 2149–2153.

Witkin, G. (1995, November 13). A new drug gallops through the West. *U.S. News & World Report.*

Witkin, G., Tharp, M., Schrof, J. M., Toch, T., & Scattarella, C. (1998, June 1). Again. *U.S. News & World Report,* 16–18.

Wittman, J. (1994, January 5). Nausea, euphoria alternate marks of chemotherapy. *San Diego Union-Tribune.*

Wiznitzer, M. (2000, Fall/Winter). Cited in J. Raymond, The world of the senses. *Newsweek, Special Edition,* 16–18.

Wolf, T. H. (1973). *Alfred Binet.* Chicago: University of Chicago Press.

Wolitzky, D. L., & Eagle, M. N. (1997). Psychoanalytic theories of psychotherapy. In P. L. Wachtel & S. B. Messer (Eds.), *Theories of psychotherapy: Origins and evolution.* Washington, DC: American Psychological Association.

Wolpe, J. (1958). *Psychotherapy by reciprocal inhibition.* Stanford, CA: Stanford University Press.

Wolpe, J. (1990). *The practice of behavior therapy* (4th ed.). London: Pergamon Press.

Wolpe, J., & Lazarus, A. A. (1966). *Behavior therapy techniques.* London: Pergamon Press.

Wolpe, J., & Plaud, J. J. (1997). Pavlov's contributions to behavior therapy. *American Psychologist, 52,* 966–972.

Wood, J. M., Garb, H. N., Lilienfeld, S. O., & Nezworski, M. T. (2002). Clinical assessment. *Annual Review of Psychology, 53,* 519–543.

Wood, J. M., Nezwoski, M. T., Lilienfeld, S. O., & Garb, H. N. (2003). *What's wrong with the Rorschach?* San Francisco: Jossey-Bass.

Wood, W., & Eagly, A. H. (2002). A cross-cultural analysis of the behavior of women and men: Implications for the origins of sex differences. *Psychological Bulletin, 128,* 699–727.

Wood, W., Christensen, P. N., Hebl, M. R., & Rothgerber, H. (1997). Conformity to sex-typed norms, affect and the self-concept. *Journal of Personality and Social Psychology, 73,* 523–535.

Woods, S. C., Schwartz, M. W., Baskin, D. G., & Seeley, R. J. (2000). Food intake and the regulation of body weight. *Annual Review of Psychology, 51,* 255–277.

World Health Organization. (1993). *International classification of disease and related health problems* (10th rev.). Geneva: Author.

Wride, N. (1989, June 14). Odyssey of a skinhead. *Los Angeles Times.*

Wright, I. C., Rabe-Hesketh, S., Woodruff, P. W. R., David, A. S., Murray, R. M., & Bullmore, E. T. (2000). Meta-analysis of regional brain volumes in schizophrenia. *American Journal of Psychiatry, 157,* 16–25.

Wright, K. (2002, September). Times of our lives. *Scientific American,* 59–65.

Wright, K. (2003, November). Staying alive. *Discover,* 64–70.

WuDunn, S. (1997, May 11). In Japan, use of dead has the living uneasy. *New York Times,* 1.

Yamashita, I. (1993). *Taijin-kyofu or delusional social phobia.* Sapporo, Japan: Hokkaido University Press.

Ybarra, M. J. (1991, September 13). The psychic and the skeptic. *Los Angeles Times.*

Yeargin-Allsop, M., Rice, C., Karapurkar, T., Doernberg, N., Boyle, C., & Murphy, C. (2003). Prevalence of autism in a US metropolitan area. *Journal of the American Medical Association, 289,* 49–55.

Yehuda, R. (2000, August 2). Cited in E. Goode, Childhood abuse and adult stress. *New York Times,* A14.

Yerkes, R. M. (1921). *Psychological examining in the United States Army (Memoir No. 15).* Washington, DC: National Academy of Sciences.

Yoffe, E. (1997, October). How quickly we forget. *U.S. News & World Report.*

Young, M. W. (2000, March). The tick-tock of the biological clock. *Scientific American,* 64–71.

Yule, W., & Fernando, P. (1980). Blood phobia: Beware. *Behavior Research and Therapy, 18,* 587–590.

Yurgelun-Todd, D. (1999, August 9). Cited in S. Brownlee, Inside the teen brain. *U.S. News & World Report,* 44–45.

Zajonc, R. B. (1984). On the primacy of affect. *American Psychologist, 39,* 117–123.

Zakaria, F. (2003, August 25). Suicide bombers can be stopped. *Newsweek,* 57.

Zaragoza, M. S., & Lane, S. M. (1994). Source misattributions and the suggestibility of eyewitness memory. *Journal of Experimental Psychology: Learning Memory, and Cognition, 20,* 934–935.

Zeidner, M. (1998). *Test anxiety: The state of the art.* New York: Plenum Press.

Zeineh, M. M., Engel, S. A., Thompson, P. M., & Bookheimer, S. Y. (2003). Dynamics of the hippocampus during encoding and retrieval of face-name pairs. *Science, 299,* 577–580.

Zeki, S. (1993). *A vision of the brain.* Cambridge, MA: Blackwell Scientific.

Zemore, S. E., Fiske, S. T., & Kim, H. (2000). Gender stereotypes and the dynamics of social interaction. In T. Eckes & H. M. Trautner (Eds.), *The developmental social psychology of gender.* Mahwah, NJ: Lawrence Erlbaum.

Zener, K. (1937). The significance of behavior accompanying conditioned salivary secretion for theories of the conditioned response. *American Journal of Psychology, 50,* 384–403.

Zeng, R. G., & Shannon, R. V. (1994). Loudness-coding mechanisms inferred from electric stimulation of the human auditory system. *Science, 264,* 564–566.

Zernike, K. (2001, February 15). Antidrug program says it will adopt a new strategy. *New York Times,* A1.

Zigler, E. (1995, January). Cited in B. Azar, DNA-environment mix forms intellectual fate. *APA Monitor.*

Zigler, E., & Seitz, V. (1982). Social policy and intelligence. In R. J. Sternberg (Ed.), *Handbook of human intelligence.* Cambridge, England: Cambridge University Press.

Zigler, E., & Styfco, S. J. (1994). Head start: Criticisms in a constructive context. *American Psychologist, 49,* 127–132.

Zigler, E., & Styfco, S. J. (2001). Extended childhood intervention prepares children for school and beyond. *Journal of the American Medical Association, 285,* 2378–2380.

Zimbardo, P. G. (1970). The human choice: Individuation, reason and order versus deindividuation, impulse and chaos. In W. J. Arnold & D. Levine (Eds.), *Nebraska symposium on motivation.* Lincoln: University of Nebraska Press.

Zimmerman, B. J. (2000). Self-efficacy: An essential motive to learn. *Contemporary Educational Psychology, 25,* 82–91.

Zimmerman, M. A., Copeland, L. A., Shope, J. T., & Gielman, T. E. (1997). A longitudinal study of self-esteem: Implications for adolescent development. *Journal of Youth and Adolescence, 26,* 117–141.

Zola, S. M., & Squire, L. R. (2000). The medial temporal lobe and the hippocampus. In E. Tulving & F. M. Craik (Eds.), *The Oxford handbook of memory.* New York: Oxford University Press.

Zucker, K. J. (1990). Gender identity disorders in children: Clinical descriptions and natural history. In R. Blanchard & B. W. Steiner (Eds.), *Clinical management of gender identity disorders in children and adults.* Washington, DC: American Psychiatric Press.

Photo Credits

This page constitutes an extension of the copyright page. We have made every effort to trace the ownership of all copyrighted material and to secure permission from copyright holders. In the event of any question arising as to the use of any material, we will be pleased to make the necessary corrections in future printings. Thanks are due to the following authors, publishers, and agents for permission to use the material indicated.

Front Matter

x: (#A) Craig McClain; **xi:** (#B) © George Frey; **xiii:** (#I) © Michael Nichols/Magnum Photos; **xiv:** (#C,F,G) PhotoDisc, Inc.; **xv:** (#A) PhotoDisc, Inc.; (#G) © Werner Bokerberg/The Image Bank, altered by Doug Stern/*U.S. News & World Report*; **xvi:** (#C,H) PhotoDisc, Inc.; **xix:** (#A) PhotoDisc, Inc.; Pages xxiii through xxxvii—see individual credits for page numbers shown. **xxxviii:** (infant with blocks) PhotoDisc, Inc.

Module Openers

One, p. 2: Copyright © Ian Parnell **Two, p. 26:** © Firefly Productions/Corbis **Three, p. 46:** © Robert Harding Picture Library **Four, p. 66:** © Alamy Images **Five, p. 92:** Erwin Gebhard/Journal Sentinel, Milwaukee **Six, p. 120:** © Digital Vision/Getty Images **Seven, p. 146:** © Fabrik Studios/Aurora Photos **Eight, p. 168:** © John Acurso/Corbis **Nine, p. 194:** © Deb Cram/Portsmouth Herald **Ten, p. 212:** © Lynn Johnson/Aurora Photos **Eleven, p. 238:** © Doug Levere **Twelve, p. 260:** © mediacolor's/Alamy **Thirteen, p. 280:** © Index/Bridgeman Art Library **Fourteen, p. 304:** © butterflyalphabet.com/IndexStock Imagery **Fifteen, p. 328:** © 2003 AP/Wide World Photos **Sixteen, p. 358:** © David Turnley/Corbis **Seventeen, p. 376:** © Oliviero Toscani for BENETTON **Eighteen, p. 406:** © Avis Studio **Nineteen, p. 432:** © Bruce Dale/National Geographic Society Collection **Twenty, p. 456:** Courtesy of Sony Electronics, Inc. **Twenty-one, p. 480:** © 2003 AP/Wide World Photos **Twenty-two, p. 508:** © 2003 AP/Wide World Photos **Twenty-three, p. 530:** © Ethan Hill **Twenty-four, p. 554:** © Mark Wilson/Getty Images **Twenty-five, p. 580:** © Sandy Huffaker/Getty Images

Module 1

4: Courtesy of Doubleday/AB/Times Books/Random House, by permission of Donna Williams **5:** right, (#5) Reprinted with permission of Times Books **5:** (smiling girl) Craig McClain **6:** (smiling girl) Craig McClain **7:** © Dana Fineman/VISTALUX **10:** center, (book cover) Reprinted with permission of Times Books **13:** (blinking light) © Tony Freeman/PhotoEdit **14:** (Calkins) Courtesy, Margaret Clapp Library Archives, Wellesley College, photo by Patridge **14:** (Sanchez) The Institute of Texan Cultures, University of Texas, San Antonio **14:** (Howard) Robert Guthrie Collection **15:** (left #1) Courtesy of Doubleday/AB/Times Books/Random House, by permission of Donna Williams **15:** (left #3 smiling girl) Craig McClain **15:** (left #4) © Dana Fineman/VISTALUX **15:** (right #11) © Tony Freeman/

PhotoEdit **15:** (right #7) Reprinted with permission of Times Books **18:** left, © David Young-Wolff/PhotoEdit **18:** center, © Lori Adamski Peek/Stone/Getty Images **19:** right, © 1988 Joel Gordon **19:** left, © Doug Menuez/Corbis-Saba **20:** bottom, © Hangarter/The Picture Cube/Index Stock **22:** (left #1) Courtesy of Doubleday/AB/Times Books/Random House, by permission of Donna Williams **22:** (left #3 smiling girl) Craig McClain **22:** (right #13) Courtesy, Margaret Clapp Library Archives, Wellesley College, photo by Patridge **23:** (left #16) © Doug Menuez/Corbis-Saba **23:** (right #18) © Hangarter/The Picture Cube/Index Stock

Module 2

27: right, © Joe McDonald/Animals, Animals **27:** top, © Jose Azel/Aurora Quanta Productions **28:** top, © Jose Azel/Aurora Quanta Productions **31:** right, (tiger) © Belinda Wright/DRK Photo **31:** left, © Joe McDonald/Animals, Animals **31:** center, © Peter Weimann/Animals, Animals **32:** top, © Jose Azel/Aurora Quanta Productions **33:** left, © Edward Thomas/eStockPhoto **34:** bottom right, John Sholtis, The Rockefeller University, New York. Copyright © 1995 Amgen, Inc. **34:** bottom left, *People Weekly* © 1995 Alan S. Weiner **34:** top right, © Richard E. Schultz **35:** left, © Michael McLaughlin **36:** top, © Jose Azel/Aurora Quanta Productions **36:** bottom center, © Jose Azel/Aurora Quanta Productions **38:** (left #1) © Jose Azel/Aurora Quanta Productions **38:** (left #2) © Joe McDonald/Animals, Animals **38:** (left #4) © Richard E. Schultz **39:** top, © Michael McLaughlin **40:** center, Craig McClain **40:** bottom, Craig McClain **41:** Courtesy of the Foundation for Biomedical Research **42:** (left #1) © Jose Azel/Aurora Quanta Productions **42:** (left #4) © Joe McDonald/Animals, Animals **43:** (right #14) Craig McClain **44:** PhotoDisc, Inc.

Module 3

47: top, © Melchior Digiacomo **48:** top, © Melchior Digiacomo **49:** Courtesy of Center on Aging and Department of Molecular and Medical Pharmacology, University of California, Los Angeles **50:** © Alfred Pasika-SPL/Photo Researchers, Inc. **51:** left, *People Weekly* © 1992 Taro Yamasaki **51:** right, *People Weekly* © 1998 Photo by Frank Veronsky **55:** bottom right, Courtesy of Johns Hopkins University, Office of Public Affairs **55:** top right, Courtesy of Miles Herkenham, Ph.D., Section of Functional Neuroanatomy, NIMH **55:** left, PhotoDisc, Inc. **58:** top, © AP/Wide World Photos **59:** top right, Adalberto Rios Szal Sol/PhotoDisc **59:** center, © Borys Malkin/Anthro-Photo **59:** bottom, © G.I. Bernard/Animals, Animals/Earth **62:** (right #7) *People Weekly* © 1992 Taro Yamasaki **63:** (right #13) © AP/Wide World Photos

Module 4

67: bottom right, By courtesy and kind permission of Cynthia de Gruchy **67:** bottom left, © Patrick Farrell/*Miami Herald* photo **67:** top right, © Peter A. Simon/Phototake, NYC **68:** bottom, By courtesy and kind

permission of Cynthia de Gruchy **69:** bottom right, Craig McClain **70:** left, Digital Stock Corporation **71:** (center and bottom right) Digital Stock Corporation **71:** top, Courtesy of Dr. Marcus Raichle, University of Washington **71:** top, Courtesy of Dr. Marcus Raichle, University of Washington **72:** bottom right, © David Stewart/Stone/Getty Images **74:** left, Martin Sereno/© 1996 Reprinted with permission of *Discover* Magazine **74:** right, © Patrick Farrell/Miami Herald photo **75:** left, Courtesy of Dr. Hanna Damasio, Human Neuroanatomy & Neuroimaging Laboratory, Dept of Neurology, University of Iowa College of Medicine. Published in 1994 in Science, 264, p 1104. Copyright © 1994 by the American Association for the Advancement in Science. Reprinted with permission of author and publisher **76:** bottom, Courtesy of J.A. Fiez, Dept of Neurology, Washington University School of Medicine **80:** top right, © Paul Berger/Stone/Getty Images **80:** bottom left, © Topham/OB/The Image Works **81:** top right, © David Stewart/Stone/Getty Images **83:** (left #2) Digital Stock Corporation **83:** (right #5) © David Stewart/Stone/Getty Images **85:** right, © PhotoDisc, Inc. **88:** (left #3) Courtesy of Dr. Marcus Raichle, University of Washington **89:** (left #16) © Paul Berger/Stone/Getty Images

Module 5

93: (center #2) PhotoDisc, Inc. **97:** bottom right, Based on Images of the Mind by M. I. Posner & M. E. Raichle, 1994. W. H. Freeman and Company. **98:** center, Digital Stock Corporation **99:** (top & right center) Normal and altered reproduction of Vincent van Gogh self-portrait reprinted by permission of Los Angeles Times Syndicate, originally appearing in *Popular Science*, July 1995 issue, "Color for the Color Blind: Self Portrait of Van Gogh." **99:** bottom, Courtesy of Graham-Field, Inc. **100:** top left, © 2002 AP/Wide World Photos **100:** bottom left, © Tony Freeman/Photo Edit **104:** left, © M.P. Kahl/DRK Photo **104:** bottom right, © Tony Freeman/Photo Edit **107:** bottom, © 1989 Jonathan Levine **108:** top left, © 1986 Steven Green-Armytage/The Stock Market/Corbis **110:** right, Danielle Pellegrini/Photo Researchers, Inc. **110:** top, © Burt Glinn/Magnum Photos **110:** center, © Guy Mary-Rousseliere **110:** left, © Malcolm S. Kirk **110:** bottom, © Malcolm S. Kirk **112:** top, Digital Stock Corporation **113:** top, © 2003 AP/Wide World Photos **113:** bottom, © Leonard Freed/Magnum Photos **114:** right, © AP/Wide World Photos **115:** bottom, © James M. Kubus, Greensburg, PA **117:** (left #17) © Danielle Pellegrini/Photo Researchers, Inc.

Module 6

121: right, © Howard Sochurek/The Stock Market/Corbis **122:** right, © Howard Sochurek/The Stock Market/Corbis **123:** left, © Al Francekevich/The Stock Market/Corbis **123:** bottom, © Pat Bruno/Positive Images **124:** bottom, Custom Medical Stock Photo **126:** Painting by Richard Haas, photo © Bill Horsman **127:** top, Painting by Richard Haas, photo © Bill Horsman **128:** right, © Pat Bruno/Positive Images **129:** center, Random House photo by Charlotte Green **130:** right,

Digital Stock Corporation 130: top, Photo Courtesy of Nikon Inc., photography © Jerry Friedman 130: bottom left, © Bob Daemmrich/Stock, Boston 130: top left, © Peter Turner/The Image Bank/Getty Images 131: top right, © Gamma Press 131: bottom left, © Garry Gay/The Image Bank/Getty Images 131: bottom right, © Robert Holmes/Corbis 131: top left, © Stephen Firsch/Stock, Boston 132: right, © John Elk/Stock, Boston 132: left, © Robert P. Comport/Animals,Animals/Earth Sciences 133: center right, Craig McClain 133: top left, © Baron Wolman/Woodfin Camp & Associates 134: (left #3) Custom Medical Stock Photo 134: (left #4) Painting by Richard Haas, photo © Bill Horsman 134: (right #13) © Garry Gay/The Image Bank/Getty Images 135: top right, PhotoDisc, Inc. 136: (dog) PhotoDisc, Inc. 136: bottom, By courtesy of Takahiko Masuda and Dr. Richard Nisbett, University of Michigan 136: center, Digital Stock Corporation 136: top, © Ric Ergenbright/Corbis 137: left, Digital Stock Corporation 137: center, Digital Stock Corporation 137: right, © 1991 Jim Amentler 138: bottom, © Dana Fineman/VISTALUX 140: (center below) © Globus Brothers/The Stock Market/Corbis 140: (center top) PhotoDisc, Inc. 140: top right, © Gianni Dagli Orti/Corbis 141: center, (Howard Stern) by Allen Tannenbaum/Corbis Sygma. Photo illustration by Doug Stern. *U.S. News & World Report.* Reproduced by permission. 141: center, (Marilyn Monroe) © Doc Alain/Retna, Inc., (Julia Roberts) © Bill Davila/Retna, Inc., Photo illustrations by Doug Stern. *U.S. News & World Report.* Reproduced by permission. 141: bottom right, (Queen Elisabeth) Courtesy of Colors Magazine, Rome 141: center right, (Schwarzenegger) Courtesy of Colors Magazine, Rome 141: left, 2000 Computer Motion Photograph by Bobbi Bennett, John Macneill 141: top right, Ames Research Center/NASA, photo by Walt Sisler 142: (left #1) © Al Francekevich/The Stock Market/Corbis 142: (right #7) © Peter Turner/The Image Bank/Getty Images 143: (right #14) Courtesy of Colors Magazine, Rome 144: © Alyson Aliano

Module 7

147: right, © Alan Hobson/Science Source/Photo Researchers 147: left, © Murrae Haynes/Mercury Pictures 148: (far left) © Michael S. Yamashita/Corbis 148: center right, Craig McClain 148: right, © David Stewart/Stone/Getty Images 148: center left, © Tony Freeman/Photo Edit 149: center, © Cesar Paredes/The Stock Market/Corbis 149: left, © Robert E. Daemmrich/Stone/Getty Images 149: right, © Tim Shaffer/Reuter Newmedia, Inc./Corbis 150: top left, © Murrae Haynes/Mercury Pictures 153: left, © Alan Hobson/Science Source/Photo Researchers 158: (left #1) © Michael S. Yamashita/Corbis 159: top, Digital Stock Corporation 161: bottom, Craig McClain 162: center, © Carol Fords/Stone/Getty Images 162: left, © Paul Buddle 163: right, © Dan McCoy/Rainbow 163: center, © Louis Psihoyos/Matrix 164: (left #1) © Michael S. Yamashita/Corbis 165: (right #17) © Paul Buddle 166: © Fran Heyl & Associates

Module 8

169: left, Craig McClain 170: center, Craig McClain 171: bottom, Craig McClain 172: top center, © Michael Salas/The Image Bank/Getty Images 172: right, © Myrleen Ferguson/Photo Edit 173: center, Courtesy, Rainbow Babies and Children's Hospital, University Hospitals of Cleveland, Dr. Howard Hall. Photo © Joe Glick 174: top, © James Porto 178: top left, Craig McClain 180: (psilocybe) © Joy Spurr/Bruce Coleman Inc. 180: bottom left, © Andy Small/Corbis 180: center left, © Michael and Patricia Fogden/Corbis 180: top, © Robert Pickett/Corbis 181: (left above) © Joseph Sohm/Chromosohm, Inc./Corbis 181: top, © David Muench/Corbis 181: center, © Scott Houston/Corbis Sygma 181: bottom left, © Scott Houston/Corbis Sygma 182: top, Courtesy, Joseph E. Seagram's and Sons, Inc. 182: right, Craig McClain 183: bottom, © Andrew Lichtenstein/Corbis Sygma 184: (left # 1) Craig McClain 184: (left #4) © James Porto 184: (left #2) Craig McClain 184: (right #10) Craig McClain 184: (right #7) © Robert Pickett/Corbis 184: (right #8) Scott Houston/Corbis Sygma 185: top, © Pat Bruno/Positive Images 185: left, © Richard Kalvar/Magnum Photos 186: left, © Brooks Kraft/Corbis Sygma 187: left, Courtesy of D.A.R.E. America 188: left, © Pat Bruno/Positive Images 189: right, © Pat Bruno/Positive Images 190: (left #1) Craig McClain 190: (right #14) © Robert Pickett/Corbis 191: (left #19) © Brooks Kraft/Corbis Sygma 191: (right #20) Courtesy of D.A.R.E. America 192: © Pat Bruno/Positive Images

Module 9

195: bottom, Digital Stock Corporation 196: right, Craig McClain 200: bottom right, Courtesy of Professor Stuart Ellins, California State University, San Bernadino, CA. 200: top, PhotoDisc, Inc. 201: (center left & bottom right) © AP/Wide World Photos 201: top left, Runk/Schoenberger/Grant Heilman Photography 201: bottom left, © Christian Abraham 201: top right, © Michael Stuckey/Comstock 202: top left, PhotoDisc, Inc. 204: bottom right, (rabbit) PhotoDisc, Inc. 204: (rat) PhotoDisc, Inc. 204: (toddler smiling & yelling) Digital Stock Corporation 205: top, © Schmid-Langsfeld/The Image Bank/Getty Images 206: top, Digital Stock Corporation 207: top, Digital Stock Corporation 209: (rat) PhotoDisc, Inc. 209: (toddler) Digital Stock Corporation

Module 10

213: right, © Frederick Charles 213: left, © George Frey 214: right, (rat) PhotoDisc, Inc. 216: top, Courtesy of Wurlitzer Jukebox Company 216: left, © Peter Southwick/Stock, Boston 217: (top and bottom) © George Frey 218: left, © Henley & Savage/Stone/Getty Images 219: left, PhotoDisc, Inc. 220: top, © 1971 *Time*, Inc. TimePix. Reprinted by permission. 221: (Fixed interval) © Vince Cavataio/Allsport Photographic Ltd./USA. 221: (Fixed ratio) © Andy Sacks/Stone/Getty Images 221: (Variable ratio) ©

Michael P. Gadomski/Photo Researchers, Inc. 221: top right, © 2003 AP/Wide World Photos 222: top, © George Frey 222: center, © George Frey 222: left, © Stephen Kraseman/DRK Photo 223: (rat) PhotoDisc, Inc. 223: top, © Frederick Charles 224: (bobo doll) Craig McClain 225: center, © Barry Lewis/Network/Corbis Saba 225: bottom left, © Jon Lowenstein/Aurora Photos 226: left, (Sultan) From *The Mentality of Apes,* by Wolfgang Koehler, Routledge & Kegan Paul. Reproduced by permission of International Thomson Publishing Services, Ltd. 226: center left, (banana) Craig McClain 226: (gun) PhotoDisc, Inc. 226: right, PhotoDisc, Inc. 227: (left # 6) PhotoDisc, Inc. 227: (left #8) © Stephen Kraseman/DRK Photo 227: (right #11) Craig McClain 227: (right #12) © Jon Lowenstein/Aurora Photos 228: right, Photo by Ron Garrison, © Zoological Society of San Diego 228: left, PhotoDisc, Inc. 228: top, © Mitsuaki Iwago/National Geographic Society/Minden Pictures 229: left, © Arthur C. Smith, III/Grant Heilman Photography 229: right, © Kennan Ward Photography/Corbis 231: (top & right) © Hiroji Kubota/Magnum Photos 233: right, © 1998 Danny Gonzalez 233: top, © Dan McCoy/Rainbow 234: (right #11) © Michael P. Gadomski/Photo Researchers, Inc. 234: (right #13) © Stephen Kraseman/DRK Photo 234: (right #8) PhotoDisc, Inc. 235: (left #14) © Jon Lowenstein/Aurora Photos 235: (left #19)Photo by Ron Garrison, © Zoological Society of San Diego 235: (right #23) © Hiroji Kubota/Magnum Photos

Module 11

239: top right, AP/Wide World Photos 239: left, Courtesy of Rajan Mahadevan 239: center right, © John Harding 240: left, PhotoDisc, Inc. 241: center, (eyes) PhotoDisc, Inc. 242: top, (face) PhotoDisc, Inc. 242: (prefrontal cortex) From "A Head for Figures," by Brian Butterworth, *Science,* 284, p. 928. By permission of B. Butterworth. 243: center, Courtesy of Rajan Mahadevan 244: left, PhotoDisc, Inc. 244: bottom, PhotoDisc, Inc. 245: (bear) PhotoDisc, Inc. 245: (frog) PhotoDisc, Inc. 245: (owl) PhotoDisc, Inc. 246: left, Digital Stock Corporation 246: right, PhotoDisc, Inc. 247: top, AP/Wide World Photos 250: top right, AP/Wide World Photos 250: top left, © John Harding 252: (left #5) Courtesy of Rajan Mahadevan 252: (left #7) PhotoDisc, Inc. 252: (right #13) AP/Wide World Photos 253: top, Bob Carey/Los Angeles Times Photo 254: bottom, Courtesy of Prof. Ralph Norman Haber 254: top, © Doug Levere 256: (left #5) PhotoDisc, Inc. 257: (left #13) AP/Wide World Photos 257: (right #18) Bob Carey/*Los Angeles Times* Photo 258: AP/Wide World Photos

Module 12

263: bottom, Digital Stock Corporation 264: bottom left, (faces in graph) PhotoDisc, Inc. 264: bottom right, PhotoDisc, Inc. 264: top, © Laura Dwight 267: (strawberry) PhotoDisc, Inc. 267: bottom, © Topham/OB/The Image Works 268: center left, PhotoDisc, Inc. 268: right, PhotoDisc, Inc. 269: (woman on phone) PhotoDisc, Inc. 269: bottom, © Bill

Photo Credits

Ballenberg **270:** (face: left #4) PhotoDisc, Inc. **270:** (strawberry: right #11) PhotoDisc, Inc. **272:** (meeting) PhotoDisc, Inc. **272:** top, © Tad Janocinski/The Image Bank/Getty Images **274:** bottom right, UPI/Corbis Bettmann **274:** bottom left, UPI/Corbis Bettmann **276:** (right #14) PhotoDisc, Inc. **277:** (left #22) © Tad Janocinski/The Image Bank/Getty Images **277:** (right #24) UPI/Corbis Bettmann **278:** *People Weekly* © 1996 Adolphe Pierre-Louis

Module 13

280: © La Coveta Alta de la Roca del Lladoner en Valltora, Spain/Index/Bridgeman Art Library **281:** (Bill Gates) AP/Wide World Photos **281:** (Gregg Cox) © Stephen Ellison/Corbis Outline **281:** (Midori) Photo by Brigitte Lacombe, courtesy of Cerritos Center for the Performing Arts, California **281:** (Serena Williams) © Thomas COEX/AFP/Corbis **281:** (Steve Lu) *Los Angeles Times* Photo by Bob Chamberlin **282:** (Bill Gates) AP/Wide World Photos **282:** (Gregg Cox) © Stephen Ellison/Corbis Outline **282:** (Midori) Photo by Brigitte Lacombe, courtesy of Cerritos Center for the Performing Arts, California **282:** (Serena Williams) © Thomas COEX/AFP/Corbis **282:** (Steve Lu) *Los Angeles Times* Photo by Bob Chamberlin **283:** (Midori) Photo by Brigitte Lacombe, courtesy of Cerritos Center for the Performing Arts, California **283:** (Serena Williams) © Thomas COEX/AFP/Corbis **283:** (analytical) PhotoDisc, Inc. **283:** (practical) PhotoDisc, Inc. **283:** (problem solving) PhotoDisc, Inc. **285:** top, Corbis-Bettmann **285:** left, PhotoDisc, Inc. **285:** center, PhotoDisc, Inc. **286:** top left, Courtesy, John Fitzgerald Kennedy Library/Museum, #C283-51-63 **286:** top center, Photo by Deborah Feingold, courtesy of *Parade Magazine* and Marilyn vos Savant. **286:** top right, UPI-Bettmann Corbis **288:** top left, Courtesy of Marian Burke. **288:** top right, Photo by Deborah Feingold, courtesy of *Parade Magazine* and Marilyn vos Savant **289:** (classroom) PhotoDisc, Inc. **289:** right, PhotoDisc, Inc. **289:** bottom left, © 2003 AP/Wide World Photos **291:** right, PhotoDisc, Inc. **291:** center, © Natalie Behring-Chisholm/Getty Images **292:** top, Photo by Brigitte Lacombe, courtesy of Cerritos Center for the Performing Arts, California **292:** center, © Myrleen Ferguson/PhotoEdit **293:** left, (boy in graph) PhotoDisc, Inc. **293:** right, (crayons) PhotoDisc, Inc. **293:** top, ©Anne Rippy/The Image Bank/Getty Images **294:** ("decided?") © Anthony Barboza **294:** ("how") © Anthony Barboza **294:** ("is") © Anthony Barboza **294:** ("race") © Anthony Barboza **295:** (left #1) *Los Angeles Times* Photo by Bob Chamberlin **295:** (left #2) Photo by Brigitte Lacombe, courtesy of Cerritos Center for the Performing Arts, California **295:** (left #3) PhotoDisc, Inc. **295:** (left #4) PhotoDisc, Inc. **296:** UPI-Bettmann/Corbis **297:** top, Adapted from S.F. Witelson, D. L. Kigar, & T. Harvey, Fig. 2, *The Lancet*, 353, 1999, with permission of the authors. **297:** bottom, From "A Head for Figures," by Brian Butterworth, Science, 284, p.928. By permission of B. Butterworth. **298:** top, 1991 © Ira Block/The Image Bank/Getty Images **299:** left,

PhotoDisc, Inc. **299:** top, © Jacques Chenet/Woodfin Camp & Associates **300:** (left #1) *Los Angeles Times* Photo by Bob Chamberlin **301:** (left #12) © Natalie Behring-Chisholm/Getty Images **301:** (right #14) UPI-Bettmann/Corbis **301:** (right #15) From "A Head for Figures," by Brian Butterworth, *Science*, 284, p. 928. By permission of B. Butterworth. **302:** © Judy Griesedieck

Module 14

305: top right, *Los Angeles Times* Photo by Paul Morse **305:** left, © Charles Allen/The Image Bank/Getty Images **306:** (Black Puli) © Animals/Animals **306:** (Chihuahau) PhotoDisc, Inc. **306:** (Dalmation) PhotoDisc, Inc. **306:** (bassett hound) PhotoDisc, Inc. **306:** (brown dog) PhotoDisc, Inc. **306:** (rabbit) PhotoDisc, Inc. **306:** (tabby cat) PhotoDisc, Inc. **307:** (apple) PhotoDisc, Inc. **307:** (clown) PhotoDisc, Inc. **307:** (turtle) PhotoDisc, Inc. **307:** top left, PhotoDisc, Inc. **308:** bottom, PhotoDisc, Inc. **308:** top, © Richard Pohle/Sipa Press **309:** center, Craig McClain **310:** left, *Los Angeles Times* Photo by Paul Morse **310:** right, © 1994 Gordon Parks **311:** top, Courtesy of and by permission of John Johnson, Ltd. on behalf of Stephen Wilshire **314:** top, From Conel, J. L. 1939, 1941, 1959. *The Postnatal Development of the Human Cerebral Cortex*, 6 Volumes, Cambridge: Harvard **314:** right, © Al Hamdan/The Image Bank/Getty Images **314:** left, © Romilly Lockyer/The Image Bank/Getty Images **315:** (babbling) © Romilly Lockyer/The Image Bank/Getty Images **315:** (right & sentences) © Frank Bates/The Image Bank/Getty Images **315:** (single word) © Al Hamdan/The Image Bank/Getty Images **315:** (two words) © Laura Dwight **315:** left, © Laura Dwight **316:** center, Courtesy of Robert Zatorre, and Denise Klein, McGill University **316:** bottom, PhotoDisc, Inc. **316:** top, © Jeremy Horner/Corbis **317:** (left #4) Craig McClain **317:** (right #8) © Romilly Lockyer/The Image Bank/Getty Images **317:** (right #9) © Jeremy Horner/Corbis **318:** PhotoDisc, Inc. **319:** right, PhotoDisc, Inc. **319:** left, © P H Cornut/Stone/Getty Images **320:** top, *Los Angeles Times* Photo by Brian Vander Brug **321:** top, By courtesy of Takahiko Masuda and Dr. Richard Nisbett, University of Michigan **321:** bottom, From Shaywitz, et al.,1995, "Sex differences in the functional organization of the brain for language," *Nature*, 373, 607-609. Courtesy of NMR Research/Yale Medical School **322:** center, (dolphins) © 1989 Ed Kashi **322:** bottom, (dolphins) © 1989 Ed Kashi **322:** top, Author's collection **323:** center, Courtesy of Lanugage Research Center, Georgia State University, Dr. Duane Rumbaugh, © 1991 Public Sphere **323:** bottom, © Michael Nichols/Magnum Photos **323:** top, © Ronald H. Cohn/The Gorilla Foundation, Woodside, California 94062 **324:** (left #3) Craig McClain **324:** (right #7) Courtesy of and by permission of John Johnson, Ltd. on behalf of Stephen Wilshire **325:** (left #11) © Jeremy Horner/Corbis **325:** (right #17) Shaywitz, et al., 1995 Courtesy of NMR Research/Yale Medical School **325:** (right #19) © Michael Nichols/Magnum Photos **326:** Digital Stock Corporation

Module 15

329: left, Jay Mather/Corbis Sygma **329:** right, *San Diego Union-Tribune*/John McCutchen **330:** left, © John Dominis/Time Life Pictures/Getty Images **330:** top right, © Michael Melford/The Image Bank/Getty Images **331:** right, © Mike Malyszko/Stock, Boston **331:** left, © Richard Sjoberg **332:** center, PhotoDisc, Inc. **332:** right, PhotoDisc, Inc. **332:** top left, © William Campbell/*Time Magazine* **334:** top, PhotoDisc, Inc. **334:** center, © Les Stone/Corbis Sygma **335:** top, © Kim Newton/Woodfin Camp & Associates **336:** bottom, Courtesy of Jeffrey M. Friedman, Rockefeller University **336:** top, © Bob Sacha **337:** top, © FoodPix **337:** left, © FoodPix **337:** center, © Guang Nu/Reuters Newmedia, Inc./Corbis **338:** top, © George B. Shaller/Bruce Coleman, Inc. **340:** left, Tony Freeman/Photo Edit **340:** bottom, © George Simian/Corbis **341:** top left, PhotoDisc, Inc. **341:** top right, PhotoDisc, Inc. **341:** bottom, © Left Lane Productions/Corbis **342:** top, (graph photos) PhotoDisc, Inc. **343:** top, © Red Morgan/ *Time Magazine* **345:** right, S. Wanke/PhotoLink/PhotoDisc, Inc. **346:** top, *Los Angeles Times* Photo by Gina Ferazzi **346:** bottom, © Mariella Furrer/Saba Press Photos **347:** (left #1) © Michael Melford/The Image Bank/Getty Images **347:** (left #4) © Mike Malyszko/Stock, Boston **347:** (right #15) S. Wanke/PhotoLink/PhotoDisc, Inc. **348:** right, © 2003 AP/Wide World Photos **348:** top, © *San Diego Union-Tribune*/John McCutchen **350:** top, Photo by Dr. Alfred McLaren. Reprinted with permission from *Science News*, the weekly newsmagazine of science, copyright © 1995 by Science Service, Inc. **350:** left, PhotoDisc, Inc. **350:** right, PhotoDisc, Inc. **351:** top, © Jason Goltz **352:** top left, UPI/Bettmann/Corbis **352:** center left, UPI/Bettmann/Corbis **352:** center right, © AP/Wide World Photos **352:** bottom, © L. Schwartzwald/Corbis Sygma **353:** © Scott Goldsmith **354:** (left #1) © Richard Sjoberg **354:** (left #4) Courtesy of Jeffrey M. Friedman, Rockefeller University **355:** (left #13) © Mariella Furrer/Corbis Saba **355:** (left #14) PhotoDisc, Inc. **355:** (right #17) UPI/Bettmann/Corbis

Module 16

359: right, Idaho Statesman/© Tom Shanahan **359:** left, © Warren Bolster/Stone/Getty Images **360:** (center right & center bottom) PhotoDisc, Inc. **361:** (center left & bottom right) PhotoDisc, Inc. **361:** top right, Idaho Statesman/© Tom Shanahan **361:** center right, PhotoDisc, Inc. **362:** left, © Photo24/Brand X Pictures/Getty Images **363:** center, (wolf) © Photo24/Brand X Pictures/Getty Images **364:** center, (2nd down) Digital Stock Corporation **364:** center, (3rd down) Digital Stock Corporation **364:** center, (4th down) Digital Stock Corporation **364:** top, Digital Stock Corporation **365:** top left, Digital Stock Corporation **365:** center, © Topham/OB/The Image Works **366:** top left, *Idaho Statesman*/© Tom Shanahan **366:** bottom left, PhotoDisc, Inc. **366:** bottom right, PhotoDisc, Inc. **367:** bottom right, PhotoDisc, Inc. **367:** center right, © Burt Glinn/Magnum Photos **367:** top, © Kevin Peterson/

Photodisc Green/Getty Images **368:** (left #1) © Warren Bolster/Stone/Getty Images **368:** (left #5) © Photo24/Brand X Pictures/Getty Images **368:** (right #10) *Idaho Statesman*/© Tom Shanahan **368:** (right #11) © Kevin Peterson/Photodisc Green/Getty Images **368:** (right #7) Digital Stock Corporation **368:** (right #8) © Topham/OB/The Image Works **369:** top, © Carlo Allegri/Getty Images **370:** top, © AFP/Getty Images **370:** bottom left, Photograph by Joel Reicherter, reprinted by permission and courtesy of the photographer **371:** bottom, © AFP/Getty Images **372:** (left #5) © Photo24/Brand X Pictures/Getty Images **372:** (right #7) Digital Stock Corporation **373:** (left #11) *Idaho Statesman*/© Tom Shanahan **374:** © Noburo Hashimoto

Module 17

377: left, © AP/Wide World Photos **377:** © Melchoir Digiacomo **378:** top, UPI-Bettmann Corbis **379:** left, © Pascal Goetgheluck/Photo Researchers, Inc. **379:** right, © Petit Format/Science Source/Photo Researchers, Inc. **380:** top, Lennart Nilsson, *The Incredible Machine*, National Geographic Society, by permission of Bokforlaget Bonnier Alba AB. **381:** center, PhotoDisc, Inc. **381:** right, © George Steinmetz **382:** center left, PhotoDisc, Inc. **382:** right, PhotoDisc, Inc. **382:** bottom left, PhotoDisc, Inc. **383:** center right, © Laura Dwight **383:** bottom, © Elyse Lewin/The Image Bank/Getty Images **383:** top, © Laura Dwight **384:** center, (crying) © David M. Grossman/Photo Researchers, Inc. **384:** left, *People Weekly* © 1995 Taro Yamaski **384:** bottom, PhotoDisc, Inc. **385:** top, © AP/Wide World Photos **385:** center, © Melchoir Digiacomo **386:** bottom, © Brad Martin/The Image Bank/Getty Images **386:** right, © Joseph Nettis/Stock, Boston **387:** top right, © Brad Martin/The Image Bank/Getty Images **387:** bottom right, © Joseph Nettis/Stock, Boston **388:** top, PhotoDisc, Inc. **388:** center, PhotoDisc, Inc. **389:** right, (3) Craig McClain **389:** left, © Doug Goodman/Photo Researchers, Inc. **389:** left, © Doug Goodman/Photo Researchers, Inc. **390:** bottom left, PhotoDisc, Inc. **390:** right, PhotoDisc, Inc. **391:** right, *Jean Piaget* © Etienne Delessert **391:** right, © Doug Goodman/Photo Researchers, Inc. **392:** center, PhotoDisc, Inc. **393:** top, PhotoDisc, Inc. **394:** top, PhotoDisc, Inc. **394:** bottom, © Mike Teruya/Free Spirit Photography **395:** left, © Bob Daemmrich/Stock, Boston **395:** right, © Charles Gupton/Stock, Boston **395:** top, © Jon Feingersh/The Stock Market/Corbis **396:** top left, PhotoDisc, Inc. **396:** top left, PhotoDisc, Inc. **396:** bottom left, © Topham/OB/The Image Works **397:** bottom right, Olivero Toscani for BENETTON. **397:** center left, PhotoDisc, Inc. **397:** center, PhotoDisc, Inc. **398:** (right #10) PhotoDisc, Inc. **399:** right, © Lila Abu Lughod/AnthroPhoto **399:** left, © Steven Winn/AnthroPhoto **400:** left, UPI-Bettmann Corbis **400:** right, © Christopher Little/Corbis Outline **401:** Private Collection **402:** (right #7) © Melchoir Digiacomo **403:** (left #17) PhotoDisc,Inc. **403:** (right #22) © Steven Winn/AnthroPhoto **403:** (right #23) Private Collection

Module 18

407: right, H. Armstrong Roberts **407:** left, *Los Angeles Times* Photo by Tammy Lechner **408:** center, © David Michael Kennedy **409:** center, © Lauren Greenfield **410:** top, *Los Angeles Times* Photo by Tammy Lechner **410:** right, PhotoDisc, Inc. **411:** left, PhotoDisc, Inc. **411:** center right, PhotoDisc, Inc. **411:** bottom right, PhotoDisc, Inc. **413:** right, PhotoDisc, Inc. **413:** left, © David Michael Kennedy **414:** left, (top & center) © David Michael Kennedy **414:** bottom left, © Lauren Greenfield **414:** top, © Lawrence Manning/Corbis **415:** top left, PhotoDisc, Inc. **415:** top center, PhotoDisc, Inc. **415:** top right, PhotoDisc, Inc. **415:** bottom left, PhotoDisc, Inc. **415:** right, PhotoDisc, Inc. **416:** center, *Los Angeles Times* Photo by Tammy Lechner **416:** top, PhotoDisc, Inc. **416:** bottom, © David Michael Kennedy **417:** left, H. Armstrong Roberts **417:** bottom right, © Mike Clarke/Getty Images **417:** bottom left, © Bob Grant/Archive Photos/Getty Images **418:** top, *Los Angeles Times* photo by Dave Garley **418:** left, PhotoDisc., Inc. **418:** right, PhotoDisc., Inc. **419:** top, H. Armstrong Roberts **420:** (left, right & bottom) PhotoDisc, Inc. **421:** (right #10) H. Armstrong Roberts **421:** (right #11) PhotoDisc., Inc. **421:** (right #8) PhotoDisc, Inc. **421:** (right #9) PhotoDisc, Inc. **422:** center, © Andrew Brusso/Corbis Outline **423:** top, Bettmann Corbis **424:** top, © David J. Sams/Stock, Boston **424:** center, © Werner Bokeberg/The Image Bank/Getty Images; altered by Doug Stern/*U.S. News & World Report* **425:** left, PhotoDisc, Inc. **425:** right, PhotoDisc., Inc. **426:** PhotoDisc, Inc. **427:** center, PhotoDisc,Inc. **428:** (left #1) © Lawrence Manning/Corbis **428:** (right #7) © David Michael Kennedy **428:** (right #9) PhotoDisc, Inc. **429:** (right #15) © David J. Sams/Stock, Boston **429:** (right #17) PhotoDisc, Inc.

Module 19

433: right, © Fox/Shooting Star **433:** left, © Sin/Doralba Picerno/LGI Photo Agency **434:** © Ian Tilton/Retna Ltd., Inc. **436:** top, © Frank Micelotta/Corbis Outline **438:** bottom right, © Ian Tilton/Retna Ltd., Inc. **438:** top right, © Mike Hashimoto/NGI/LGI Photo Agency **439:** center, © Mike Hashimoto/NGI/LGI Photo Agency **440:** center, Courtesy, Adler School of Professional Psychology. Reproduced by permission of Kurt Adler. **440:** right, Courtesy, Association for the Advancement of Psychoanalysis. **440:** left, National Library of Medicine, Bethesda, MD **442:** top, © Fox/Shooting Star **442:** bottom, ©Photo 3045/by J. O. Alber/Gamma Press **443:** top, J. Howard Miller/National Archives/Bettman Corbis **443:** bottom, © Bob Adelman/Magnum Photos **444:** bottom, © Francois Lochon/Gamma **444:** top, © Laura Dwight/Corbis **444:** center, © Nancy Moran/Corbis Sygma **445:** center, PhotoDisc, Inc. **445:** bottom, © Harry Benson **445:** top, © Jose Azel/Woodfin Camp & Associates **446:** © Robert Durell **447:** (right #10) © Jose Azel/Woodfin Camp & Associates **448:** top, © Jason Goltz **449:** top right, © Walter Wick/Telegraph Colour Library/FPG International/Getty Images **449:** bottom, ©

Walter Wick/Telegraph Colour Library/FPG International/Getty Images **450:** center, © Ian Tilton/Retna Ltd., Inc. **450:** top, © Mike Hashimoto/NGI/LGI Photo Agency **453:** (left #11) © Robert Durell **453:** (left #14) © Jason Goltz **453:** (right #15) © Walter Wick/Telegraph Colour Library/FPG International/Getty Images **454:** *Los Angeles Times* Photo by Rick Meyer

Module 20

457: right, © Alan Weiner **457:** left, © Tomas Muscionico/Contact Press Images **458:** bottom left, IDAF/Sipa Press **458:** bottom right, © David Turnley, *Detroit Free Press*/Corbis **458:** top, © Nils Jorgensen/RDR Productions/Rex Features, London **459:** right, PhotoDisc, Inc. **459:** top, © Peter Turnley/Corbis **460:** left, PhotoDisc, Inc. **461:** *People Weekly* © 1998 Photo by Frank Veronsky **462:** right, (beauty queen) © Joshua-Ets-Hokin/PhotoDisc, Inc. **462:** right, (clown) PhotoDisc. Inc. **462:** right, (criminal) PhotoDisc. Inc. **462:** right, (graduate) PhotoDisc. Inc. **462:** right, (nun) PhotoDisc. Inc. **462:** top left, © Alan Weiner **462:** center left, © *Los Angeles Times* Photo by Lawrence K. Ho **463:** (beauty queen) © Joshua-Ets-Hokin/PhotoDisc, Inc. **463:** (clown) PhotoDisc. Inc. **463:** (criminal) PhotoDisc. Inc. **463:** (graduate) PhotoDisc. Inc. **463:** (nun) PhotoDisc, Inc. **464:** top, © 2003 AP/Wide World Photos **464:** bottom, © Galen Rowell/Corbis **465:** left, (above) © Barbara Penoyar/PhotoDisc, Inc. **465:** left, (below) © Barbara Penoyar/PhotoDisc, Inc. **465:** right, © Werner Bokeberg/The Image Bank/Getty Images; altered by Doug Stern/*U.S. News & World Report* **466:** bottom left, PhotoDisc, Inc. **466:** bottom right, PhotoDisc, inc. **466:** top, © Michael Nichols/Magnum Photos **467:** (left and center) © Michael Nichols/Magnum Photos **467:** bottom right, PhotoDisc, Inc. **468:** center, © 2003 AP/Wide World Photos **469:** right, (#10) PhotoDisc, Inc. **469:** right, (left #11) © Barbara Penoyar/PhotoDisc, Inc. **469:** right, (right #11) © Barbara Penoyar/PhotoDisc, Inc. **469:** left, (#4) PhotoDisc, Inc. **469:** left, (#5) PhotoDisc, Inc. **469:** right, (#9) PhotoDisc, Inc. **471:** top, James Bennet/ *The New York Times* **471:** center, © 2003 AP/Wide World Photos **472:** top right, © Photo 3045 Pool: by J.O. Alber/Gamma **473:** top, (criminal) PhotoDisc, Inc. **473:** top, (nun) PhotoDisc, Inc. **473:** bottom right, (twins w/dogs) © Michael Nichols/Magnum Photos **473:** bottom left, PhotoDisc, Inc. **473:** top left, © Nils Jorgensen/RDR Productions/Rex Features, London **474:** left, PhotoDisc, Inc. **474:** bottom right, PhotoDisc, Inc. **474:** top right, PhotoDisc, Inc. **475:** top, Corel Gallery **475:** center right, PhotoDisc, Inc. **475:** bottom right, PhotoDisc, Inc. **475:** left, Photodisc, Inc. **476:** (right #6) © *Los Angeles Times* Photo by Lawrence K. Ho **477:** (left #14) James Bennet/ *The New York Times* **478:** top, PhotoDisc, Inc.

Module 21

481: right, Arlene Gottfried, *Life Magazine* © Time Inc. **481:** left, Craig McClain **482:** left, PhotoDisc, Inc.

Photo Credits

482: center, PhotoDisc, Inc. **482:** right, PhotoDisc, Inc. **483:** left, PhotoDisc, Inc. **484:** top left, PhotoDisc, Inc. **484:** top right, PhotoDisc, Inc. **484:** right, © Paul Berger/Stone/Getty Images **486:** bottom, PhotoDisc, Inc. **487:** top center, PhotoDisc, Inc. **488:** top, Digital Stock Corporation **488:** bottom left, © Lennart Nilsson, *The Incredible Machine*, National Geographic Society, by permission of Bokforlaget Bonnier Alba AB. **489:** top center, PhotoDisc, Inc. **490:** top, Arlene Gottfried, *Life Magazine* © Time Inc. **490:** left, © L.D. Gordon/The Image Bank/Getty Images **490:** center, © Photo Edit **491:** center, PhotoDisc, Inc. **491:** bottom right, © 1991 David Turnley , Detroit Free Press/Corbis **491:** top left, © David Liam Kyle/Sportslight Photography **493:** left, PhotoDisc, Inc. **493:** right, © Arlene Gottfried, *Life Magazine* © Time Inc. **494:** top, © Chuck Fishman/Contact Press Images **495:** left, PhotoDisc, Inc. **495:** right, PhotoDisc, Inc. **497:** top, PhotoDisc, Inc.; **498:** right, (#10) PhotoDisc, Inc. **498:** right, (#12) Craig McClain **498:** right, (#13) © Chuck Fishman/Contact Press Images **498:** right, (#14) PhotoDisc, Inc. **498:** left, (#9)© L.D. Gordon/The Image Bank/Getty Images **499:** right, PhotoDisc, Inc. **499:** left, © R. W. Jones/Corbis **500:** © Ann States/Corbis Saba **501:** (inset in graph and right) © Black/Toby **502:** top, PhotoDisc, Inc. **502:** right, PhotoDisc, Inc. **502:** left, PhotoDisc, Inc. **503:** right, PhotoDisc, Inc. **503:** left, PhotoDisc, Inc. **505:** left, (#17) PhotoDisc, Inc. **505:** left, (#18) © Ann States/Saba **505:** right, (#20) PhotoDisc, Inc. **506:** top, *Los Angeles Times* Photo by Gina Ferazzi

Module 22

509: right, © Elizabeth Roll **509:** left, © Reuters/Corbis **510:** right, © Henrik Drescher **511:** top right, (and center) *San Diego Union-Tribune*/Rick McCarthy **511:** left, PhotoDisc, Inc. **511:** bottom right, © Henrik Drescher **512:** center, © AP/Wide World Photos **512:** top, © William Cambell/*Time Magazine* **513:** © AP/Wide World Photos **514:** top, © AP/Wide World Photos **514:** right, © Elizabeth Roll **515:** © Reuters/Corbis **518:** center, © Elizabeth Roll **520:** left, © Marvin Mattelson **521:** left, (#2) © Henrik Drescher **521:** left, (#3) *San Diego Union-Tribune*/Rick McCarthy **521:** left, (#4) © AP/Wide World Photos **522:** right, PhotoDisc, Inc. **522:** left, © David Young-Wolff/PhotoEdit **523:** bottom left, *People Weekly* © 2001 Axel Koester **524:** bottom, © Elizabeth Roll **524:** top, © Elizabeth Roll **526:** left, (#1) *San Diego Union-Tribune*/Rick McCarthy **526:** left, (#4)© AP/Wide World Photos **527:** left, (#14) © Marvin Mattelson **528:** top, *Los Angeles Times* Photo by Perry C. Riddle

Module 23

531: left, © Robert Gauthier (originally appeared in *San Diego Union-Tribune*) **531:** right, © Robert Gauthier (originally appeared in *San Diego Union-Tribune*) **532:** left, © Evan Agostini/Getty Images **532:** center, © Robert Gauthier (originally appeared in *San Diego Union-Tribune*) **533:** bottom left, © 1997 Time Inc., Reprinted by permission **533:** top, © Evan Agostini/Getty Images **533:** right, © Matthew Klein/Corbis **534:** left, © Evan Agostini/Getty Images **534:** right, © Robert Gauthier (originally appeared in *San Diego Union-Tribune*) **535:** left, © Photo Researchers, Inc. **536:** right, © Reuters/Corbis **538:** left, © Robert Gauthier (originally appeared in *San Diego Union-Tribune*) **539:** center, Courtesy of Edna Morlok **539:** top left, © Robert Gauthier (originally appeared in *San Diego Union-Tribune*) **540:** left, Courtesy of Drs. E. Fuller Torrey & Daniel R. Weinberger, NIMH, Neuroscience Center, Washington D.C **540:** right, © Robert Gauthier (originally appeared in *San Diego Union-Tribune*) **541:** top, © Robert Gauthier (originally appeared in *San Diego Union-Tribune*) **541:** right, © Robert Gauthier (originally appeared in *San Diego Union-Tribune*) **543:** right, (#10) © Robert Gauthier (originally appeared in *San Diego Union-Tribune*) **545:** center, Craig McClain **547:** (top and left) PhotoLink/PhotoDisc, Inc. **551:** left, (#16) Craig McClain **551:** right, (#19) PhotoLink/PhotoDisc, Inc.

Module 24

555: right, Digital Stock Corporation **555:** left, Mary Evans /Sigmund Freud Copyrights/Sulloway **555:** top center, PhotoDisc, Inc. **556:** bottom left, National Library of Medicine, #A-13394 **556:** center left, National Library of Medicine, neg. 93072 **556:** right, Photo by Ken Smith of painting in Harrisburg State Hospital/LLR Collection **557:** left, © AP/Wide World Photos **557:** right, © Bernard Gotfryd/Woodfin Camp & Associates **558:** right, PhotoDisc, Inc. **559:** bottom, S. Wanke/PhotoLink/PhotoDisc, Inc. **561:** bottom, Mary Evans /Sigmund Freud Copyrights/Sulloway **563:** © Zohar Lazar **566:** center, Digital Stock Corporation **566:** top left, PhotoDisc, Inc. **567:** bottom right, © Elizabeth Roll **572:** center, © Roger Dashow/AnthroPhoto **573:** *Los Angeles Times* Photo by Al Seib **574:** top, PhotoDisc, Inc. **574:** bottom, PhotoDisc, Inc. **575:** right, © Paul Buddle **576:** left, (#1) National Library of Medicine **577:** right, (#22) © Roger Dashow/AnthroPhoto

Module 25

581: left, © Ted Hardin **582:** bottom right, By permission of Dr. Victor Johnston, author of *Why We Feel* **582:** right, © Robin Holland/Corbis Outline **582:** top left, © Ted Hardin **582:** top right, © Ted Hardin **583:** From "The Effect of Race and Sex on Physicians' Recommendations for Cardiac Catheterization" by K. A. Schulman et al., 1999, *The New England Journal of Medicine*, 2/5/99, pp. 621–622. Copyright © 1999, Massachusetts Medical Society. Reprinted by permission. **583:** bottom left, PhotoDisc, Inc. **583:** bottom right, PhotoDisc, Inc. **584:** center left, PhotoDisc, Inc. **584:** bottom, PhotoDisc, Inc. **584:** center right, PhotoDisc, Inc. **584:** top, © James Wilson/Woodfin Camp & Associates **585:** right, PhotoDisc, Inc. **585:** top, © Robert Johnson/Getty Images **586:** top, *Los Angeles Times* Photo by Vince Campagnore **586:** left, PhotoDisc, Inc. **586:** right, PhotoDisc, Inc. **587:** top, PhotoDisc, Inc. **587:** left, PhotoDisc, Inc. **589:** top, © Wade Spees **590:** Photo by A. L. Wendrof, courtesy of the Anti Defamation League of B'nai B'rith, San Francisco and Gregory Withrow **591:** bottom, © 1997 Gregory Pace/Corbis Sygma **591:** top, © Stephen Jaffe/AFP/Getty Images **595:** top, © Alan Weiner **596:** right, Jim LoScalzo/ *U.S. News & World Report* **596:** left, *People Weekly* © 1993 Taro Yamasaki **597:** left, © Bill Ross/Woodfin Camp & Associates **597:** right, © Dan Miller/Woodfin Camp & Associates **597:** center, © Reuters/Corbis **598:** (all) PhotoDisc, Inc. **599:** left, (#1) © Ted Hardin **599:** right, (#10) © Stephen Jaffe/AFP/Getty Images **599:** right, (#13) © Bill Ross/Woodfin Camp & Associates **599:** right, (#15) PhotoDisc, Inc. **599:** left, (#4) PhotoDisc, Inc. **599:** left, (#6) PhotoDisc, Inc. **599:** left, (#8) Photo by A. L. Wendrof, courtesy of the Anti Defamation League of B'nai B'rith, San Francisco and Gregory Withrow; **600:** top left, © Photo24/Brand X Pictures/Getty Images **600:** right, © Topham/OB/The Image Works **600:** center left, © Zig Leszczynski/Animals Animals **601:** top, PhotoDisc, Inc. **601:** left, PhotoDisc, Inc. **601:** right, © 2003 AP/Wide World Photos **602:** center, (left and right) PhotoDisc, Inc. **602:** top, PhotoDisc, Inc. **603:** bottom, © Thomas Hartwell/Corbis Saba **604:** bottom, PhotoDisc, Inc. **604:** bottom, PhotoDisc., Inc. **604:** bottom, PhotoDisc., Inc. **604:** right, © Topham/OB/The Image Works **606:** left, (#1) © James Wilson/Woodfin Camp & Associates **606:** left, (#5) PhotoDisc, Inc. **606:** right, (#9) © Stephen Jaffe/AFP/Getty Images **607:** left, (#13) Jim LoScalzo/ *U.S. News & World Report* **607:** right, (#17) © Topham/OB/The Image Works **607:** right, (#20) PhotoDisc., Inc. **608:** PhotoDisc, Inc.

Figure/Text Credits

Module 1

6: Graph data from "Changes in the Palmar Sweat Index During Mental Arithmetic," by T. Kohler and U. Troester, 1991, *Biological Psychology, 32,* 143–154. **7:** Graph data from "Isolating Gender Differences in Test Anxiety: A Confirmatory Factor Analysis of the Test Anxiety Inventory," by Howard T. Everson, Roger E. Millsap, & Caroline M. Rodriguez, 1991, *Educational and Psychological Measurement, 51,* p. 247. **8:** Bar graph data from "The Relationship of Self-Management to Academic Motivation, Study Efficiency, Academic Satisfaction, and Grade Point Average Among Prospective Education Majors," by J. D. Long, P. Gaynor, A. Erwin and R. L. Williams, 1994, *Psychology: A Journal of Human Behavior, 31,* 22–30. **16:** Graph data from "Comparison of Self-Questioning, Summarizing, and Notetaking-Review as Strategies for Learning from Lectures," by A. King, 1992, *American Educational Research Journal, 29,* 303–23. **17:** Pie graph data from "Psychological Science Around the World," by M. R. Rosenzweig, 1992, *American Psychologist, 47,* 718–22. **21:** Excuses list from "Excuses, Excuses," by D. A. Bernstein, 1993, *APS Observer,* March, 1993 p. 4. Copyright © 1993 by the American Psychological Society. Reprinted by permission of the author. **24:** Based on Thomas H. Maugh II, *Los Angeles Times,* December 9, 1999, p. A1; Owley et al., 2001, *Journal of the American Academy of Child and Adolescence Psychiatry, 40,* 1293–1299; A. S. Unis, et al., 2002, *Journal of the American Academy of Child and Adolescence Psychiatry, 41,* 1315–1321.

Module 2

30: Bar graph data from "Aspartame, Behavior, and Cognitive Function in Children with Attention Deficit Disorder," by B. A. Shaywitz, C. M. Sullivan, G. Anderson, S. M. Gillespie, B. Sullivan & S. E. Shaywitz, *Pediatrics,* 93, 70–5. **33:** Bar graph Long Beach United School District: anti-social behavior decrease in schools where children wear uniforms, data from Long Beach, CA. United School District, 1993–1994 versus 1994–1995. **37:** Bar graph data from W. E. Pelham, M. E. Bender, J. Caddell, S. Booth & S. H. Moorer, 1985, "Methylphenidate and children with attention deficit disorder," *Archives of General Psychiatry, 42,* 948–952. **44:** Adapted from "Frequent Sexual Activity May Help Men Live Longer, Study Finds" by Lawrence K. Altman, 1997, New York Times News Service. Copyright © 1997 by The New York Times Company. Adapted by permission.

Module 3

64: Based on S. Lafee, "At Hand and Ahead." *San Diego Union-Tribune,* March 8, 2000, p. E-1.

Module 4

79: (bottom left) From "Language Specificity and Elasticity: Brain and Clinical Syndrome Studies," by M. Maratsos and L. Matheny, 1994, *Annual Review of Psychology, 45,* 487–516. **79:** (bottom right) Adapted from Left Brain, Right Brain, by S. P. Springer and G. Deutsch,

4/e, 1989. W. H. Freeman. **84:** Figures (left) adapted from "Sex Differences in the Brain," by D. Kimura, 1992, *Scientific American, 267,* 119–125. **90:** Based on Sandra Blakesless, "Brain damage during infancy stunts moral learning, study finds," New York Times News Service in *The Los Angeles Times,* October 9. 1999, A-1.

Module 5

114: (bottom left) John Karapelou/© 1993 The Walt Disney Co. Reprinted with permission of *Discover Magazine.* **114:** (top & left) Illustration by K. Daniel Clark from "Newsfronts-Science & Technology," by Dawn Stover, *Popular Science,* August 1997 p. 29. Reprinted by permission. **117:** (right #20) John Karapelou/© 1993 The Walt Disney Co. Reprinted with permission of *Discover Magazine.* **118:** Based on J. Weiss, "So-called Mozart Effect May Be (yawn) Just a Dream," *San Diego Union-Tribune,* 2/12/2000, p. E-5; The Mozart effect: not learning from history?, by S. M. Jones & E. Zigler, 2002, *Applied Developmental Psychology, 23,* 355–372.

Module 6

135: Bar graph (right) based on data from "Emotion congruence in Perception," by P. M. Niedenthal and M. C. Sutterlund, *Personality and Social Psychology, 20,* 401–411. **144:** Based on M. Abrams, 2002, "Sight/Unseen," *Discover* (June), 54–59.

Module 7

147: Living in a cave text adapted from an article in *Newsweek,* June 5, 1989. **166:** Based on R. Abelson, 2002, "Limits on residents hours worry teaching hospitals," *The New York Times,* June 14, 2002, A16; S. Gupta, 2002, "Is your doctor too drowsy?," *Time,* March 11, 2002, 85; Robert Pear, 2000, "Interns? Long Workdays Prompt First Crackdown," *The New York Times,* June 11, 2000, p. 2D; S. L. Cohen, 2000, "Hi, I'm Your Doctor. I Haven't Sleep in 36 Hours," *USA Today,* March 22, 2000, p. 29A.

Module 8

170: Bar graph data and examples from "Individual Differences in Response to Hypnosis," by B. L. Bates, 1994. In J. W. Rhue, S. J. Lynn & I. Kirsch (Eds.), *Handbook of Clinical Hypnosis.* American Psychological Association. **173:** Bar graph on left Adapted from "Effects of Hypnosis on Regional Cerebral Blood Flow During Ischemic Pain with and without Suggested Hypnotic Analgesia," by H. J. Crawford, R. C. Gur, B. Skolnick, R. E. Gur & D. M. Benson, *International Journal of Psychophysiology, 15,* 181–195. **175:** Data from 2001 NHSDA (National Household Survey on Drug Abuse) U.S. Department of Health and Human Services. **178:** Bar graph data from "Actual Causes of Death in the United States," by J. M. McGinnis and W. H. Foege, 1993, *Journal of the American Medical Association, 270,* 2207–2212. **188:** Adapted from "How AA Works and Why It's Important for Clinicians to Understand," by E. J. Khantzian and J. E. Mack, 1994, *Journal of Substance Abuse Treatment, 11,* 77–92. **192:** Based

on C. Knapp, "An Alcoholic's Private Anguish," *Los Angeles Times,* July 17, 2000, p. E2.

Module 9

195: Adapted from "Cross-cultural Validity of a Parent's Version of the Dental Fear Survey Schedule for Children in Chinese," by P. Milgrom, J. Z. Quang, & K. M. Tay, 1994, *Behavior Research and Therapy, 32,* 131–135. **196:** Bar graph data from "Pitch Discrimination in the Dog," by H. M. Anrep, 1920, *Journal of Physiology, 53,* 367–385. **206:** Adapted from "Emotional Fainting and the Psychophysiologic Response to Blood and Injury: Autonomic Mechanisms and Coping Strategies," by A. Steptoe and J. Wardle, 1988, *Psychosomatic Medicine, 50,* 402–417. **210:** Adapted from "Study: Olestra Chips Score Well in Digestive Test," by Nanci Hellmich, *USA Today,* January 14, 1998. Copyright © 1998 by *USA Today.* Adapted by permission.

Module 10

214: Graph on right Based on *Behavior of Organisms,* by B. F. Skinner, 1938. Appleton-Century-Crofts. **215:** top, Skinner box illustration from *Introduction to Psychology* by E. Bruce Goldstein, 1995. Brooks/Cole. **216:** Adapted from "Treating Chronic Food Refusal in Young Children: Home-Based Parent Training," by M. A. Werle, T. B. Murphy & K. S. Budd, 1993, *Journal of Applied Behavior Analysis, 26,* 421–433. **218:** Graph adapted from "Discrimination Training in the Treatment of Pica and Food Scavenging," by C. R. Johnson, F. M. Hunt & J. J. Siebert, 1994, *Behavior Modification, 18,* 214–229. **219:** Bar graph data from "A Comparison of Shock Intensity in the Treatment of Longstanding and Severe Self-Injurious Behaviors," by D. E. Williams, S. Kirkpatrick-Sanchez & B. A. Iwata, 1993, *Research in Development Disabilities, 14,* 207–219. **220:** Reinforcement diagram from *Psychology: Themes and Variations,* by Wayne Weiten, 2nd ed., figure 6.13. Copyright © 1992 by Wadsworth, Inc. Reproduced by permission. **220:** top, Skinner box illustration from *Introduction to Psychology* by E. Bruce Goldstein, 1995. Brooks/Cole. **221:** Based on data from the U.S. Department of the Navy and an illustration by Suzy Parker, *USA Today,* March 27, 2003, p. 8D. **223:** top, Skinner box illustration from *Introduction to Psychology* by E. Bruce Goldstein, 1995. Brooks/Cole. **224:** Bar graph data from "Influence of Models' Reinforcement Contingenices on the Acquisition of Imitative Responses," by A. Bandura, 1965, *Journal of Personality and Social Psychology, 1,* 589–596. **225:** Bar graph data from "Relative Efficacy of Densensitization and Modeling Approaches for Inducing Behavior, Affective and Attitudinal Changes" by A. Bandura, E. B. Blanchard & B. Ritter, 1969, *Journal of Personality and Social Psychology, 13,* 173–179. **227:** top, Skinner box illustration from *Introduction to Psychology* by E. Bruce Goldstein, 1995. Brooks/Cole. **230:** Graph from "Analysis of a High-Probability Instructional Sequence and Time-Out in the Treatment of Child Noncompliance," by A. K. Rortvedt and R. G. Miltenberger, 1994, *Journal of*

Figure/Text Credits

Applied Behavior Analysis, 27, 327–330, figure 1a. Copyright © 1993 Society for the Experimental Analysis of Behavior. Reprinted by permission of the author. **232:** Bar graph data from "Behavioral Treatment and Normal Educational and Intellectual Functioning in Young Autistic Children," by O. I. Lovaas, 1987, *Journal of Consulting and Clinical Psychology, 55,* 3–9. **236:** Based on M. D. Lemonick, "Spare the Rod? Maybe," *Time,* August 25, 1997, 65; L. Rosellini, "When to Spank," *U.S. News & World Report,* April 15, 1998, 52–58; B. Schulte, "Spanking Backfires, the Latest Study Says," Knight-Ridder; appeared in *San Diego Union-Tribune,* August 15, 1997, A1.

Module 11

241: Bar graph data from "The Information Available in Brief Visual Presentations," by G. A. Sperling, 1960, *Psychological Monographs, 74* (Whole No. 498). **242:** Graph data from "Short-Term Retention of Individual Verbal Items," by L. R. Peterson and M. J. Peterson, 1950, *Journal of Experimental Psychology, 58,* 193–198. **244:** Bar graph data from "Accuracy and Distortion in Memory for High School Girls," by H. P. Bahrick, L. K. Hall & S. A. Berger, 1996, *Psychological Science, 7,* 265–271. **245:** Graph data from "Two Storage Mechanisms in Free Recall," by M. Glanzer and A. R. Cunitz, 1966, *Journal of Verbal Learning and Verbal Behavior, 5,* 351–360. **247:** Bar graph data from "B-Adrenergic Activation and Memory for Emotional Events," by L. Cahill, B. Prins, M. Webert & J. McGaugh, 1994, *Nature, 371,* 702–704. **249:** Bar graph data from "Depth of Processing and the Retention of Words in Episodic Memory," by E. I. M. Craik and E. Tulving, 1975, *Journal of Experimental Psychology, General, 104,* 268–294. **253:** Bar graph data from "Repeated Memory of Oral Prose in Ghana and New York," by B. M. Ross and C. Millson, 1970, *International Journal of Psychology, 5,* 173–181. **253:** Excerpt from *Remembering: A Study in Experimental and Social Psychology,* by F. C. Bartlett, p. 65, 1932. Cambridge University Press. Copyright © 1932. Reprinted with the permission of Cambridge University Press. **255:** Adapted from "Vivid Memories," by D. C. Rubin and M. Kozin, 1984, *Cognition,* 16, 81–95. Copyright © 1984 by Elsevier Science Publishers BV. Adapted by permission from Elsevier Science. **258:** Based on "Decade of Accusations" by M. Sauer, *San Diego Union-Tribune,* August 29, 1993, D1.

Module 12

261: Adapted from "Nearly 2,000 Witnesses Can Be Wrong," by R. Buckout, 1980, *Bulletin of the Psychonomic Society, 16,* 307–310. **262:** Memory figure based on Learning and Memory, by D. A. Norman, 1982. W. H. Freeman & Company. **264:** Graph (bottom) data from "Fifty Years of Memory for Names and Faces," by H. P. Bahrick, P. O. Bahrick & R. P. Wittlinger, 1975, *Journal of Experimental Psychology: General, 104,* 54–75. **272:** Bar graph data from "Visual Spatial Memory in Australian Aboriginal Children of Desert Regions," by J. M. Kearins, 1981, *Cognitive Psychology, 13,* 434–460.

273: Bar graph data from "Repeatedly Thinking About a Non-Event: Source Misattributions Among Pre-Schoolers," by S. J. Ceci , M. L. C. Huffman, E. Smith & E. Loftus, 1994, *Consciousness and Cognition, 3,* 388–407. **278:** Adapted from "Second Time Around," by Michael Haederle, *Los Angeles Times,* May 23, 1996 p.E-1. Copyright © 1996 by *Los Angeles Times.* Adapted by permission of the publisher.

Module 13

287: Graphs Adapted from "Age and WAIS-R: A Cross-Sectional Analysis with Educational Level Controlled, " by A. S. Kaufman, C. R. Reynolds & J. E. McLean, 1989, *Intelligence, 13,* pp. 246, 247. Copyright © 1989 by Ablex Publishing Company. Adapted by permission. **292:** Bar graph data from "Familial Studies of Intelligence: A Review," by T. J. Bouchard and M. McGue, 1981, *Science, 212,* 1055–1059. Additional data from Plomin & Petrill, 1997. **294:** Graph adapted with the permission of The Free Press, a Division of Simon & Schuster Inc. from *The Bell Curve: Intelligence and Class Structure in American Life,* by Richard Hernstein and Charles Murray, 1994, p. 279. Copyright © 1994 Richard J. Hernstein and Charles Murray. **295:** (right #7) Graph adapted from "Age and WAIS-R A Cross-Sectional Analysis with Educational Level Controlled, " by A. S. Kaufman, C. R. Reynolds & J. E. McLean, 1989, *Intelligence, 13,* pp. 246, 247. Copyright © 1989 by Ablex Publishing Company. Adapted by permission. **299:** Graph adapted from "Young Children Grow Up: The Effects of the Perry Preschool Program on Youth Through Age 15," by L. J. Schweinhart and D. P. Weikart, 1980, *Monographs of the High/Scope Educational Research Foundation,* 1980, No. 7. Courtesy of L. J. Schweinhart. **302:** Based on S. Braun, "Max the Bookie Won't Stop and That's a Sure Thing," *Los Angeles Times,* August 7, 1999, A1.

Module 14

309: Top and p. 317: Adapted from *Conceptional Blockbusting: A Guide to Better Ideas,* by James L. Adams, pp. 17–18. Copyright © 1974 by James L. Adams. Used with permission of W. H. Freeman & Co., Publishers. **311:** Bar graph data from "Creativity and Psychopathology: A Study of 291 World-Famous Men," by F. Post, 1994, *British Journal of Psychiatry, 165,* 22–34. **326:** Article adapted from "The Language of Learning," by Robert Lee Hotz, 1997, *Los Angeles Times,* Sept. 18, 1997, p. B2. Copyright © 1997 by the *Los Angeles Times.* Adapted by permission of the publisher.

Module 15

342: Bar graph data from *The Social Organization of Sexuality,* by E. Laumann, R. T. Michael, J. H. Gagnon & G. Kolata, 1994. University of Chicago Press. **345:** Centers for Disease Control and Prevention, 1999. **348:** (left) (TAT) From *Abnormal Psychology* by Barlow/Durand, 2/E, pg 79. Copyright © 1997. Brooks/Cole Publishing. **351:** Math scores data from *National Educational Longitudinal Study of 1988,* National Opinon Research

Center, University of Chicago. **356:** Based on Horowitz, 1999, March 22; Leland, 1998, October 26; Roan, 1998, March 16; Mestel, 1999, January.

Module 16

370: (center) Redrawn from an illustration by John Tom Seetin in "Working Knowlege," *Scientific American, 277*(6), December, 1997, p. 132. Reprinted by permission the illustrator. All rights reserved. **371:** Bar graph data from "Detection of Deception: Polygraph and Integrity Tests," by L. Saxe, 1994, *Current Directions in Psychological Science, 3,* 69–73. Additional data from "Lie-detector tests found too flawed to discover spies," by W. J. Broad, *New York Times,* October 9, 2002, A1. **374:** Based on V. Reitman, "Learning to Grin ? and Bear It," *Los Angeles Times,* February 22, 1999, A1.

Module 17

380: Bar graph adapted from a figure in *The Developing Human: Clinically Oriented Embryology,* 4th ed., by Keith L. Moore. W. B. Saunders Co., Copyright © 1988 by Keith L. Moore. Adapted by permission of the author. **387:** Data from "Temperamental Factors in Human Development," by J. Kagan and N. Snidman, *American Psychologist, 46,* 856–862. **404:** Adapted from "An Angry Child Can Change" by Michael Ryan, *Parade,* April 14, 1996, pp. 20–21. Reprinted by permission of *Parade* and Scovil Chichak Galen Literary Agency on behalf of the author. Copyright © 1996 by Michael Ryan.

Module 18

407: Branndi adapted from the *Los Angeles Times,* December 22, 1991, pp. E-1, E-12. **407:** Prom queen adapted from *Midterm Report,* by D. Wallechinsky, 1986. Viking Press. **410:** Branndi adapted from the *Los Angeles Times,* December 22, 1991, p. E-13. **413:** Ida and Christopher excerpt from *Parade Magazine,* July 14, 1991, pp. 6–7 Reprinted with permission from Parade. Copyright © 1991. **420:** Graph based on data from "Marital Happiness Cross the Family Life Cycle: A Longitudinal Analysis," by M. H. Benin and I. B. Robinson, cited in *Time,* August 25, 1997, p. 24. **420:** List adapted from "Preferences in Human Mate Selection," by D. M. Buss and M. Barnes, 1986, *Journal of Personality and Social Psychology, 7,* 3–15. American Psychological Association. **423:** List [center] adapted from "Mate Preferences in 37 Cultures," by D. M. Buss, 1994. In W. J. Lonner & R. Malpass (Eds.), Psychology and Culture. Allyn and Bacon. **423:** List [bottom] adapted from "International Preferences in Selecting Mates," by D. M. Buss, A. Abbott, A. Angleitner, A. Asherian, A. Biaggio, A. Blanoco-Villasenor, A. Bruchon-Scwietzer, H. Y. Ch'U, J. Czapinski, B. Deraad, B. Ekehammar, N. E. Lohamy, M. Fioravanti, J. Georgas, P. Gjerde, R. Guttmann, E. Hazan, S. Iwawaki, H. Jankiramaiah, F. Khosroshani, D. Kreitler, L. Lachenicht, M. Lee, K. Kiik, B. Little, S. Mika, M. Moadel-Shahid, G. Moane, M. Montero, A. C. Mundy-Castle, T. Niit, E. Nsenduluka, R. Pienkowski, A. M. Pirttila-Backman, J. P. De Leon, J.

Rousseau, M. A. Runco, M. P. Safir, C. Samuels, R. Sanitioso, R. Serpell, N. Smid, C. Spencer, M. Tadinac, E. N. Tordorova, Z. K. Troland, L. Van Den Brande, G. Van Heck, L. Van Langenhove & K. S. Yang, 1990, *Journal of Cross-Cultural Personality, 21,* 5–47, and additional data from "Mate Preferences in 37 Cultures," by D. M. Buss. In W. J. Lonner & R. Malpass (Eds.), Psychology and Culture. Allyn & Bacon. **426:** Center text adapted from *People Magazine,* May 21, 1990, pp. 56–59. **430:** Article based on W. Herbert, "Losing Your Mind," *U.S. News & World Report,* July 26, 1999, 45–51; and J. Kluger, "The Battle to Save Your Memory," *Time,* June 12, 2000, 46–57.

Module 19

450: (TAT) From Abnormal Psychology by Barlow/ Durand, 2/E, p. 79. Copyright © 1997. Brooks/Cole Publishing. **454:** Adapted from "Friends, Others Offer Complex View of Rathbun," by Robert J. Lopez and Eric Slater, *Los Angeles Times,* December 11, 1995, p. B-1. Copyright © 1995 by *Los Angeles Times.* Adapted by permission of the publisher.

Module 20

467: Bar graph data from "Genes, Environment, and Personality," by T. J. Bouchard, 1994, *Science, 264,* 1700–1701. American Association for the Advancement of Science. Add'l data from Bouchard & Loehlin, 2001. **468:** Bar graph data from "Genes, Environment, and Personality," by T. J. Bouchard, 1994, *Science, 264,* 1700–1701. American Association for the Advancement of Science. Add'l data from Bouchard & Loehlin, 2001, Plomin & Crabbe, 2000. **478:** Adapted from "Companies Using Personality Tests for Making Hire That Fit," by Carol Smith, *Los Angeles Times,* February 9, 1997, p. D5.

Module 21

481: Text about Sandra Sullivan, adapted from an article by Sasha Nyary, *Life Magazine,* April, 1992 pp. 62–65. **483:** Bar graph data from "The Use of Cognitive Appraisal to Reduce Stress Reactions: A Replication," by A. C. Dandoy and A. G. Goldstein, 1990, *Journal of Social Behavior and Personality, 5,* 272–285. **483:** Situation list data from *USA Today,* August 19, 1987, p. 4D. **486:** List Adapted from "The Factor Structure of Self-Reported Physical Stress Reactions," by J. C. Smith and J. M. Seidel, 1982, *Biofeedback and Self-Regulation, 7,* 35–47. **488:** Bar graph data from "Psychological Stress and Susceptibility to the Common Cold," by S. Cohen, D. A. J. Tyrrell & A. P. Smith, 1997, *New England Journal of Medicine, 325,* 606–612. **490:** Scale: Reprinted from *Journal of Psychosomatic Research,* 11 by T. H. Holmes and R. H. Rahe in "The Social Readjustment Rating Scale," 213–218, Copyright © 1967, with permission from Elsevier Science. **490:** Text about Sandra Sullivan, adapted from an article by Sasha Nyary, *Life Magazine,* April, 1992 pp. 62–65. **494:** Graph adapted from "Hardiness and Stress Moderation: A Test of Proposed Mechanisms," by D. J. Wiebe, 1991, *Journal of Personality and Social Psychology, 60,* pp. 89–99, p. 94. American Psychological Association. **495:** Bar graph data from "Stress and Illness: Controllable and Uncontrollable Life Events' Relative Contributions," by G. S. Stern, T. R.

McCants & P. W. Pettine, 1982, *Personality and Social Psychology Bulletin, 8,* 140–143. **497:** Change in blood pressure data from "Social Support Lowers Cardiovascular Reactivity to an Acute Stressor," by S. J. Lepore, K. A. Mata Allen & G. W. Evans, 1993, *Psychosomatic Medicine, 55,* 518–524. **497:** Probability graph data from "Social Support, Negative Life Events and Mental Health," by O. S. Dalgard, S. Bjork & K. Tambs, 1995, *British Journal of Psychiatry, 166,* 29–34. **501:** Graph data from "Body Temperature Changes During the Practice of g Tum-mo-Yoga," by H. Benson, J. W. Lehmann, M. S. Malhotra, R. F. Goldman, P. J. Hopkins & M. D. Epstein, 1982, *Nature, 295,* 234–235. **505:** (right #19) Graph data from "Body Temperature Changes During the Practice of g Tum-mo-Yoga," by H. Benson, J. W. Lehmann, M. S. Malhotra, R. F. Goldman, P. J. Hopkins & M. D. Epstein, 1982, *Nature, 295,* 234–235. **506:** Adapted from "The Diagnosis," by Mary Herczog, *Los Angeles Times,* December 8, 1997, p. S-1. Copyright © 1997 by *Los Angeles Times.* Adapted by permission of the publisher.

Module 22

514: Pages 514–515: Syndrome titles from *Diagnostic and Statistical Manual of Mental Disorders,* Fourth Edition. Copyright © 1994 American Psychiatric Association. **516:** Bar graph data from "Lifetime and 12-month Prevalence of DSM-III-R Psychiatric Disorders in the United States," by R. C. Kessler, K. A. McGonagle, S. Zhao, C. B. Nelson, M. Hugher, S. Eshleman, H. Wittchen & K. S. Kendler, 1994, *Archives of General Psychiatry, 51,* 8–19. **518:** Bar graphs data on phobias from "Panic and Phobia" by W. W. Eaton, A. Dryman & M. M. Weissman. 1991. In L. N. Robins & D. A. Regier (Eds.), *Psychiatric Disorders in America: The Epidemiological Catchment Area Study.* Free Press. **519:** Bar graph data from "Current Status of Pharmacological and Behavioral Treatment of Obsessive-Compulsive Disorder," by G. B. Stanley and S. M. Turner, 1995, *Behavior Therapy, 26,* 163–186. **522:** Bar graph data from "The Place of Culture in Psychiatric Nosology: Taijin Kyofusho and DSM-III-R," by L. J. Kirmayer, 1991, *Journal of Nervous and Mental Disease, 179,* 19–28. **525:** Graphs adapted from "International Advances in the Treatment of Social Phobia," by J. R. T. Davidson, 1994, *Journal of Clinical Psychiatry, 55,* 123–129. **528:** Adapted from "Prisoners of Love" by Pamela Warrick, *Los Angeles Times,* January 23, 1997, p. E-1. Copyright © 1997 by *Los Angeles Times.* Adapted by permission of the publisher.

Module 23

531: (Chuck Elliot) Adapted from "Breakdown into the Shadows of Mental Illness, " by C. Brooks, *San Diego Union-Tribune,* February 27, 1994, p. 4. **531:** (Michael McCabe) Adapted from "Shadowland: Three Profiled in Mental Illness Series Are Strving to Improve Their Condition" " by C. Brooks, *San Diego Union-Tribune,* February 27, 1995. **533:** Bar graph data from "Current Perspectives on the Genetics of Unipolar Depression," by S. O. Moldin, T. Reich & J. P. Rice, 1991, *Behavior Genetics, 21,* 211–242. **535:** (left) Bar graph data from "Use of ECT in the United States in 1975, 1980 and 1986," by J. W. Thompson, R. D. Weiner & C. P. Myers, 1994, *American Journal of Psychiatry, 151,* 1657–1661. 1995 data from "Shock Therapy," by D. Cauchon, *USA*

Today, December 6, 1995. Additional data from "Taking the Shock Out of Electroshock," by J. S. Fisher, *U.S. News & World Report,* January 24, 2000. **535:** (left) Excerpt from "Electroboy," by Andy Behrman, *New York Times Magazine,* January 27, 1999, p. 67. Reprinted by permission of *The New York Times.* **535:** (right) ECT treatment graph adapted from "Use of ECT with Treatment-Resistant Depressed Patients at the National Institute of Mental Health," by S. M. Paul, I. Extein, H. M. Calil, W. Z. Potter, P. Chodiff & F. K. Goodwin, 1981, *American Journal of Psychiatry, 138,* 486–489. **537:** Graph data from "An Open Trial of Sertraline in Personality Disordered Patients with Impulsive Aggression," by R. J. Kavoussi, J. Liu & E. F. Caccaro, 1994, *Journal of Clinical Psychiatry, 55,* 137–141. **539:** Bar graph data from *Schizophrenia Genesis: The Origins of Madness,* by I. I. Gottesmann, 1991. W. H. Freeman & Company; with additional data from "The Epidemiology of Schizophrenia in a Finnish Twin Cohort," by T. D. Cannon, J. Kaprio, J. Lonnqvist, M. Huttunen & M. Koskenvuo, 1998, *Archives of General Psychiatry, 55,* 67–74. **542:** Data from "Duration of Neuroleptic Treatment and Prevalence of Tardive Dyskinesia in Late Life," by R. A. Sweet, B. H. Mulsant, B. Gupta, A. H. Rifai, R. E. Pasternak, A. McEachran & G. S. Zubenko, 1995, *Archives of General Psychiatry, 52,* 478–486. **543:** (#5) Bar graph data from "Current Perspectives on the Genetics of Unipolar Depression," by S. O. Moldin, T. Reich & J. P. Rice, 1991, *Behavior Genetics, 21,* 211–242. **543:** (#7) ECT treatment graph adapted from "Use of ECT with Treatment-Resistant Depressed Patients at the National Institute of Mental Health," by S. M. Paul, I. Extein, H. M. Calil, W. Z. Potter, P. Chodiff & F. K. Goodwin, 1981, *American Journal of Psychiatry, 138,* 486–489. **545:** Bar graph data from "The Diagnosis of Multiple Personality Disorder: A Critical Review, by T. A. Fahy, 1988, *British Journal of Psychiatry, 153,* 597–606; and "Multiple Identity Enactments and Multiple Personality Disorder: A Sociocognitive Perspective," by N. P. Spanos, 1994, *Psychological Bulletin, 116,* 1434–1465. **546:** Bar graph data from "Lifetime and 12-month Prevalence of DSM-III-R Psychiatric Disorders in the United States," by R. C. Kessler, K. A. McGonagle, S. Zhao, C. B. Nelson, M. Higher, S. Eshleman, H. Wittchen & K. S. Kendler, 1994, *Archives of General Psychiatry, 51,* 8–19. **547:** Bar graph data from "Exercise treatment for major depression: Maintenance of therapeutic benefits at 10 months," by M. Babyak, et al., 2000, *Psychosomatic Medicine, 62,* 633–638. **552:** Adapted from "Recovered" by Shari Roan, *Los Angeles Times,* January 30, 1996, p. E-1. Copyright © 1996 by *Los Angeles Times.* Adapted by permission of the publisher.

Module 24

560: Therapy Session Adapted from "A Critique of So-Called Standard Psychoanalytic Technique," by S. D. Lipton, 1983, *Contemporary Psychoanalysis, 19,* 35–52. **564:** Therapy Session: Adapted from "Person-Centered Therapy," by N. J. Raskin and C. R. Rogers, 1989. In

Figure/Text Credits

R. J. Corsini and D. Wedding (Eds.), *Current Psychotherapies,* 4th ed. F. E. Peacock. **565:** Therapy Session: Adapted from *Cognitive Therapy of Depression,* by A. T. Beck, A. J. Rush, B. F. Shaw & G. Emery, 1979, pp. 145–146. Guilford Press. **566:** Therapy Session: Adapted from *Clinical Behavior Therapy,* by M. R. Goldfried and G. C. Davison, 1976. Holt, Rinehart & Winston. **573:** Bar graph data from "Eye Movement Desensitation: A Partial Dismantling Study," by G. Renfrey and C. R. Spates, 1994, *Journal of Behavior Therapy and Experimental Psychiatry, 25,* 231–239. **578:** Adapted from "Exorcism Flourishing Once Again," by T. Watanabe, October 31, 2000, *Los Angeles Times,* A1.

Module 25

587: Bar graphs adapted from "Improving the Academic Performance of College Freshman," by T. D. Wilson and P. W. Linville, 1982, *Journal of Personality and Social Psychology, 42,* 367–376, Copyright © 1982 by the American Psychological Association. Adapted by permission of the author. **592:** Asch study based on "Effects of Group Pressure Upon Modification and Distortion of Judgements," by Solomon Asch, 1958. In E. Maccoby, T. M. Newcomb & E. L. Hartley (Eds.), *Readings in Social Psychology* (3rd Ed.). Holt, Rinehart & Winston. **594:** Bar graph adapted from "Behavioral Study of Obedience," by S. Milgram, 1963, *Journal of Abnormal and Social Psychology, 67,* 371–378. **606:** (#8) Bar graph adapted from "Improving the Academic Performance of College Freshman," by T. D. Wilson and P. W. Linville, 1982, *Journal of Personality and Social Psychology, 42,* 367–376, Copyright © 1982 by the American Psychological Association. Adapted by permission of the author. **608:** Adapted from "Teen Pregnancies Force Town to Grow Up" by Sheryl Stolberg, *Los Angeles Times,* November 29, 1996.

Name Index

Name Index

Name Index

Name Index

Subject Index

Subject Index

Subject Index

Subject Index

sensory development, 382
sexual behavior, 338–339, 341, 343
shyness, 449
stress, 486
taste, 106
temperament, 387
weight, 34
See also Nature-nurture question
Genetic markers, 539
Genital cutting, 346, 603
Genital stage of psychosexual development, 392, 439
Genuineness, 564
Germany, 11, 399
Germinal stage, 379
Gerontology, 424
Gestalt approach, 13, 126–127
Gestures, 367
G (general intelligence) factor, 282, 283, 291, 297
Ghana, 253
GH (growth hormone), 152, 156
Ghrelin, 335
Giftedness, 289, 378
Gilbert, Roland, 446
Ginkgo biloba, 415
Glass ceiling, 586
Glial cells, 48
Glucose, 335, 485
Glutamate, 177, 539, 541
Glycogen, 485
Goal-setting, 20, 309
Gonads, 82
Goose bumps (piloerection), 56, 485
Gorillas, 323
Goto, Hiroyuki, 239
Gottman, John, 422
Gould, Stephen Jay, 85, 296
Grades. *See* Academic achievement
Graham, Lawrence, 581, 582
Grammar (syntax), 312, 315, 322
Gratification, delay of, 460
Great Britain, 179
Grojsman, Sophia, 107
Group cohesion, 596
Group dynamics, 596–598
Group norms, 596
Group polarization, 598
Group therapy, 189
Groupthink, 598
Growth hormone (GH), 152, 156
Growth needs, 443
Grubs, 110
Guilt, 436
Guinness Book of Records, 511

H

Hair, 56, 141, 485
Hair cells, 103
Hair receptors, 108
Halcion, 162
Hallucinations, 180, 186, 538
Hallucinogens, 180–181
Haloperidol, 541
Hammer (ear), 102

Handwriting analysis, 287, 451
Hangover, 182
Happiness, 366, 420. *See also* Emotions
Hardiness, 494
Harm/loss appraisals, 482
Harvard, Beverly, 457, 462
Harvey, Thomas, 297
Hassles, 490
Hazing, 581, 592, 594, 596
Head injuries. *See* Brain damage
Head Start, 298–299
Head transplants, 64
Hearing, 100–104
artificial, 115
and brain structure, 78, 103
infancy, 382
and memory, 241
Heart rate, 485
Helping, 595, 597
Hemingway, Ernest, 311
Hemispheres (brain), 7, 73, 76, 86–87, 321
Hereditary factors. *See* Genetic factors
Hering, Ewald, 99
Heritability, 293, 466. *See also* Genetic factors
Herman, Louis, 322
Heroin, 73, 179
Hesse, Herman, 311
Heterosexual orientation, 341
Heuristics, 308
High need for achievement, 348
Hindbrain, 73, 74
Hippocampus
and adolescence, 411
and child abuse, 401
and gender differences, 84
and memory, 47, 80, 186, 268
neuron growth in, 49
and preparedness, 229
Hispanic Americans, 14
Hispanic Journal of Behavioral Science, 14
Historical approaches, 12–13
Histrionic personality disorder, 536
HIV positive status, 345. *See also* AIDS
Hobson, J. Allan, 161
Hofmann, Albert, 169, 180
Holistic thinking, 136, 321
Holistic view, 442
Hollywood love, 419
Homelessness, 557
Homeostasis, 81
Homo erectus, 69
Homo sapiens, 69
Homosexual orientation, 341, 343, 516
Honesty (integrity) tests, 474
Hopeful values, 351
Hormone replacement therapy, 425
Hormones
and adolescence, 411
and aging, 425

and emotion, 361
and endocrine system, 82
and hunger, 335, 336, 352
and memory, 247, 255
and sexual behavior, 339
and stress, 484, 485
Horney, Karen, 440
Horoscopes, 475
Hostility, 496
Howard, Ruth, 14
Human Genome Project, 68
Humanistic theories, 442–446, 461
Maslow's hierarchy of needs, 332–333, 348, 443, 596
overview, 5, 10
Humor, 70
Hunger, 334–337, 352
eating disorders, 332, 337, 353
Hyperactivity. *See* Attention-deficit/hyperactivity disorder
Hyperopia (farsightedness), 95
Hypnosis, 169, 170–173
and repressed memory, 251
student activities, 184, 190–193, 623–624
Hypnotic analgesia, 172, 173
Hypnotic induction, 170
Hypocretin neurons, 163
Hypothalamus
and autonomic nervous system, 81
and biological clocks, 150, 155, 157
and endocrine system, 82
and hunger, 335
overview, 80
and Prader-Willi syndrome, 332
and puberty, 408
and sexual behavior, 339
and stress, 484, 485
Hypotheses, 36

I

Iceland, 159
Iconic memory, 241
Id, 436, 437
Ideal (optimal) weight, 334
Ideal self, 444
Identical twins, 292
Identity, 416
Identity vs. role confusion stage of psychosocial development, 393, 417
Illusions, 132–133, 140
Imagery exercises, 524, 575
Imaginative suggestibility, 171
Imagined exposure, 525, 567
Imagined perception, 172
Imitation, 225, 231, 323
Immigrants
achievement, 351, 448
intelligence, 296
language acquisition, 316
Immune system, 111, 157, 488–489
Implicit (nondeclarative/procedural) memory, 149, 246, 248, 268, 441
Impossible figures, 132, 137

Impotency, 425
Imprinting, 228, 330
Incentive theory of motivation, 331, 350
Independent variables, 36
Individualistic cultures, 592
Individual psychology, 440
Indonesia, 572
Inductive reasoning, 318
Industrial settings, 17
Industry vs. inferiority stage of psychosocial development, 393
Infancy, 382–388
cognitive development, 388, 389
development overview, 397
emotional development, 384–387
facial expressions, 364, 365
language, 314
motor development, 383
and nature-nurture question, 377
sensory development, 382
sleep, 156
social development, 392, 393
Infatuated love, 419
Inferential statistics, 613–616
Inferior frontal gyrus, 320
Inferior parietal lobe, 297
Informational influence theory of the bystander effect, 597
Ingroup, 598
Inhibited/fearful children, 386, 387
Inhibited female orgasm, 344
Inhibitory transmitters, 54
Initiative vs. guilt stage of psychosocial development, 393
Innate language factors, 313, 316
Inner ear, 102–103, 104
Insanity, 509
Insects, as food, 110
Insecure attachment, 385
Insight, 226, 309
Insight therapies, 560–565
client-centered therapy, 564
cognitive therapy, 565
overview, 559
short-term dynamic psychotherapy, 562
Insomnia, 162, 163, 332, 568, 575
Instinct theory of motivation, 330
Insula, 419
Integration, 492
Integrity (honesty) tests, 474
Integrity vs. despair stage of psychosocial development, 417
Intelligence, 281–303
artificial, 308
and brain size, 85, 284, 297, 322, 323
and correlation, 33, 85
and creativity, 311
cross-cultural approach, 282, 291
definitions, 282–283, 292
early measurement of, 284–285, 296
emotional, 369
and intervention programs,

298–299
IQ score distribution, 288–289
IQ tests, 14, 286–287, 290–291, 296
and music, 118
nature-nurture questions, 292–294
new approaches, 297
and race, 290, 294, 296
student activities, 295, 627–628
Intelligence quotient (IQ), 282
and cognitive development, 391
and correlation, 33
and emotional intelligence, 369
and g factor, 282
historical origins, 285
and intervention programs, 298–299
limitations of, 14, 290–291, 296
score distribution, 288–289
tests, 286–287
See also Intelligence
Intensity
of emotions, 360, 367
and perception, 123
Interactive model of sexual orientation, 341
Interference, 242, 265, 266, 267, 271
Internal attributions, 585
Internal locus of control, 459, 495
International Classification of Disease and Related Health Problems (ICD-10), 546
Interneurons, 56
Interpersonal conflicts, 492
Interpersonal therapy, 353
Interposition, 130
The Interpretation of Dreams (Freud), 160
Interpreting function of attitudes, 589
Interval timing clock, 150
Intervention programs, 298–299, 404
Interview research, 34
Intestines, 335, 485
Intimacy vs. isolation stage of psychosocial development, 417
Intrinsic motivation, 331, 350
Introspection, 12, 13
Intrusive thoughts, 574, 575
Inuit people, 110, 161, 319, 367
In vivo (real) exposure, 525, 567
Ions, 52
IQ. *See* Intelligence quotient
Iris, 95
Isolation experiment, 147

J
Jagger, Mick, 417
James, William, 12
James-Lange theory of emotions, 360
Japan
dental fears, 205
drug use, 176

emotions, 367, 374
gender roles, 399
mental disorders, 516, 522
organ transplants, 603
See also Asian people/cultures
Jet lag, 151
JND (just noticeable difference), 123
Job performance, 289
Journal of Black Psychology, 14
Journal of Cross-Cultural Psychology, 11
Journal of Humanistic Psychology, 10
Journal of the American Psychoanalytic Association, 563
Jung, Carl, 440
Justice orientation, 412
Just noticeable difference (JND), 123

K
Kagan, Jerome, 386
Kanzi (bonobo), 323
Kasparov, Gary, 308
Kastak, David, 322
Kearins, Judith, 272
Keller, Helen, 115
Kelley's covariation model of attribution, 585
Kennedy, John F., 286
King, Martin Luther, Jr., 443
Kinkel, Kipland, 523
Klinefelter's syndrome, 339
Koffka, Kurt, 13
Kohlberg, Lawrence, 412
Kohlberg's theory of moral reasoning, 412
Köhler, Wolfgang, 13, 226
Koko (gorilla), 323
Korea, 185. *See also* Asian people/cultures
Kroc, Ray, 310
Kume, Wakana, 603

L
Labeling, 516
Laboratory experiments, 34, 35
Laboratory settings, 34, 35
Laborit, Henri, 557
Lange, Carl, 360
Language, 312–316
acquisition, 314–316
animals, 322–323
and autism, 7
and brain structure, 78
Chomsky's theory of, 313, 315
defined, 305
dyslexia, 320
and evolution, 69
gender differences, 321, 396
naming, 71
oral vs. written, 253
and personality, 459
rules of, 312
and thinking, 319
See also Speech
Language stages, 314

Larynx, 316
LASIK surgery, 95
Latency stage of psychosexual development, 392, 439
Lateral hypothalamus, 335
Lateral prefrontal cortex, 297
Latinos, 14
Law of effect, 196, 214
L-dopa, 60
Lead poisoning, 381
Learned associations, 337
Learning
biological factors, 228–229
cognitive learning, 196, 213, 223–226
and concept formation, 307
defined, 195
and gender differences, 84
observational, 223, 224–225, 459, 493, 600
and phobias, 525
student activities, 203, 208–211, 227, 234–237, 624–625
Suzuki method, 231
types of, 196
See also Classical conditioning; Operant conditioning
Learning-performance distinction, 224
Lens, 95
Leptin, 335, 336
Lesbians. *See* Homosexual orientation
Levels-of-processing theory, 249
Lewis, Jim, 466, 467
Lie detector (polygraph) tests, 370–371
Lief, Harold, 250
Life expectancy, 424
Light and shadow, 131
Light therapy, 151
Light waves, 94, 96, 98
Limbaugh, Rush, 464
Limbic system, 80–81, 112, 161, 186, 362, 411
Limb reattachment, 51
Limitations, 491
Linear perspective, 130
Linguistic relativity, theory of, 319
Links to Learning. *See* Student activities
Lithium, 534
Little Albert case, 204, 224, 555, 566
Liver, 335, 485
Lobotomies, 75
Locus of control, 459, 495
Loftus, Elizabeth, 250
Loneliness, 497
Longitudinal method, 386, 417, 441, 465
Long-term memory, 240, 244–246, 268, 269
Long-term potentiation (LTP), 269
Lottery winners, 366

Loudness, 100, 104
Loukaitis, Barry, 523
Lovaas, Ivar, 232
Love, 419–420, 423, 528
Love Lab, 422
LSD, 148, 169, 180
LTP (long-term potentiation), 269
Lu, Steve, 281
Lucy (*Australopithecus afarensis*), 67, 69
Lung cancer, 33

M
Magic, 138
Magic mushrooms, 180
Magnetic resonance imaging (MRI), 70, 321. *See also* Neuroscience
Magnets, 27, 31
Mahadevan, Rajan, 239
Maintenance programs (weight loss), 352
Maintenance rehearsal, 242, 249
Major depressive disorder, 532, 534, 547
Major life events, 490
Maladaptive behavior approach to mental disorders, 511
Male-female differences. *See* Gender differences
Mammograms, 122
Mandela, Nelson, 457, 458, 459
Mania, 534
Manic-depression. *See* Bipolar I disorder
Marijuana, 186
Marriage, 332, 420, 422, 423
Maslow, Abraham, 10, 332, 443. *See also* Humanistic theories; Maslow's hierarchy of needs
Maslow's hierarchy of needs, 332–333, 348, 443, 596
Mass hysteria, 520
Maturation, 383
McCabe, Michael, 531, 538–541, 558
McCarty, Osceola, 595
McClelland, David, 348
McDougall, William, 330
MDMA (ecstasy), 181
Mean, 611
Measurement, 37, 369. *See also* Diagnosis; Intelligence quotient; Statistics
Measures of central tendency, 611–612
Measures of variability, 612–613
Median, 611–612
Medical marijuana, 186
Medical therapy, 559. *See also* Drug treatments
Medications. *See* Drug treatments
Meditation, 501, 503
Medulla, 73, 74, 182
Melatonin, 151
Melzack, Ronald, 58
Memory, 239–259, 261–279

Subject Index

on emotions, 84, 268, 360, 362–363, 366
and Freudian theory, 441
on gender differences, 84, 85, 321, 396
on hypnosis, 173
on implicit memory, 441
on intelligence, 297
on language, 315, 316, 321
on memory, 77, 80, 242, 245, 246, 263, 268
on mood disorders, 533, 549
on moral reasoning, 412
on motivation, 330
on nervous system control, 501
on operant conditioning, 219
on pain, 112, 113
on perception, 132
on personality disorders, 537
on placebos, 31
on relationships, 419, 420
on schizophrenia, 540, 541
on school shootings, 523
on stress, 484
on temperament, 387
on vision, 97
See also Brain; Nervous system
Neuroses, 513, 561
Neurotransmitters
and aggression, 55, 600
and drug use, 59, 175, 176, 179, 181, 183, 186, 330
and mood disorders, 533, 534
overview, 53, 54–55
and Parkinson's disease, 60
and personality disorders, 537
and schizophrenia, 539, 541, 542, 557
and seasonal affective disorder, 159
and sleep, 157
See also Nervous system; Reward/pleasure center
Neutral stimulus, 197, 198, 217. *See also* Classical conditioning
Newborns. *See* Infancy
New Guinea, 110
Nicotine, 33, 174, 178, 336, 381
Nigeria, 603
Nightmares, 163
Night terrors, 154, 163
Nim (chimpanzee), 323
Nitric oxide, 55
NMDA, 183
Nodes, 263
Noncompliance, 230, 568
Nondeclarative (procedural/implicit) memory, 149, 246, 248, 268, 441
Nonintellectual factors, 291
Non-REM sleep, 152, 154
Nonshared environmental factors, 467, 468
Norepinephrine, 59, 181, 247, 485, 533, 534
Normal aging, 424
Normal curve, 610

Normal distribution, 288, 610, 613
Norman, Donald, 262
Norms, 595, 596
Nose, 107. *See also* Smell
Note-taking strategies, 16, 21
Nothing Is Impossible: Reflections on a New Life (Reeve), 461
Nucleus accumbens, 175, 330, 366
Nutrasweet (aspartame), 30
Nutrition. *See* Food

O
Obedience, 593–594
Obesity, 34, 334, 337
Objective personality tests, 369, 474, 475
Object permanence, 389
Observation, 35
Observational learning, 223, 224–225, 459, 493, 600
Obsessive-compulsive disorder (OCD), 519, 567
Obsessive-compulsive personality disorder, 536
Occipital lobe, 74, 79
Occipito-temporal area, 320
OCD (obsessive-compulsive disorder), 519, 567
OCEAN (Big Five traits), 463, 467, 468
Oedipus complex, 439
Olanzapine, 542
Old age, 424
memory, 415, 430
sexual behavior, 425
sleep, 155, 156
suicide, 427
See also Adulthood
Olestra, 210
Olfaction (smell), 106–107, 382
Olfactory cells, 49, 107
One Flew Over the Cuckoo's Nest, 535
One-sided messages, 591
One-trial learning, 200
Operant conditioning, 213–222
applications of, 216, 230, 232–233
vs. classical conditioning, 217
concepts in, 222
cross-cultural approach, 231
defined, 196, 213
origins of, 214
procedures for, 215
reinforcement, 215, 216, 218–219, 220–221, 604
Operant response, 214, 215
Opiates, 179
Opium, 179
Opponent-process theory of color vision, 99
Optic nerve, 96, 97
Optimal (ideal) weight, 334
Optimal sleep pattern, 162, 575
Optimism, 495
Oral stage of psychosexual development, 392, 439
Oral tradition, 253

Organic factors in sexual problems, 344
Organic mental disorders, 514
Organic retardation, 288
Organ transplants, 603
Orgasm, 344
Origin of Species (Darwin), 69
Ossicles, 102
Outer ear, 102
Outgroup, 598
Overgeneralization, 315, 548, 565
Overlapping, 130
Overweight, 334–335, 337, 352
Ovulation, 379
Own-race bias, 274

P
Pacinian corpuscle, 108
Pagano, Bernard, 274
Pain
and adaptation, 93
and brain structure, 77
and classical conditioning, 205
and hypnosis, 172, 173
overview, 112–113
and placebos, 111, 112
and touch, 108
Palmar sweating, 6
Pancreas, 82
Panic attacks, 517
Panic disorder, 517
Paper-and-pencil tests, 348, 369
Paradoxical sleep, 153. *See also* Rapid eye movement (REM) sleep
Paranoid personality disorder, 536
Paranoid schizophrenia, 538, 546
Paraphilias, 344
Parasympathetic division (nervous system), 72, 81, 484, 501
Parentese (motherese), 314, 316, 326
Parenting
and achievement, 351, 448
and adolescence, 413
and aggression, 404
and attachment, 385
and behavior therapy, 216, 230, 233, 401
and child abuse, 400–401, 568
Freudian theory on, 436
and gender roles, 395
and humanistic theories, 445
and infant development, 382, 383
and language, 314, 315, 316, 326
and nature-nurture question, 377
and procrastination, 9
and temperament, 387
See also Childhood; Environmental factors; Infancy
Parent Management Training (PMT), 604
Parietal lobe, 74, 77, 297, 320
Parieto-temporal area, 320
Parkinson's disease, 60–61
Parks, Gordon, 305, 310
Partial reinforcement, 220–221

Passionate love, 419
Pathological aging, 424
Patterson, Francine, 323
Pavlov, Ivan, 196, 199, 202
Paxil, 519
Peg method, 271
Penis envy, 439, 440
People of color, 329, 348. *See also* Discrimination; Race
Perception, 121–145
constancy, 128
creating, 140–141
cross-cultural approach, 136–137
depth, 129–131, 382
extrasensory, 138–139
illusions, 132–133, 140
imagined, 172
organizational rules, 126–127
person, 582–584
vs. sensation, 93, 124–125
student activities, 134, 142–145, 622
subliminal, 122, 135
thresholds, 122–123
See also Senses
Perceptual constancy, 128
Perceptual sets, 137
Perceptual speed, 415
Perfect negative correlation coefficient, 32
Perfect positive correlation coefficient, 32
Performance goals, 20
Peripheral cues, 335
Peripheral nervous system (PNS), 51, 72
Peripheral route for persuasion, 591
Peripheral theories of emotions, 360
Permissive parents, 413
Personal beliefs, 27, 30, 210, 588, 589
Personal distress, 595
Personal factors, 458, 471
Personal identity (self-identity), 416
Personality, 433–455, 457–479
and academic achievement, 448
adolescence, 416
adulthood, 417
and aggression, 601
assessment, 450–451, 474–475, 478, 512
and creativity, 311
disorders, 515, 536–537
and eating disorders, 353
humanistic theories, 442–446, 472
and hunger, 337
and mood disorders, 533
shyness, 449
social cognitive theory, 449, 458–461
stability of, 465, 470
and stress, 494–496, 499
student activities, 447, 452–455, 469, 476–479, 632–633
study of, 18
theory overview, 472–473

Subject Index

Subject Index

Subject Index